The Law of Social Security

Second edition

A I Ogus BCL MA
Professor of Law in the University of Newcastle

E M Barendt BCL, MA
of Gray's Inn, Barrister;
Fellow of St Catherine's College, Oxford

London
Butterworths
1982

England	Butterworth & Co (Publishers) Ltd 88 Kingsway, London WC2B 6AB
Australia	Butterworths Pty Ltd 271–273 Lane Cove Road, North Ryde, NSW 2113 Also at Melbourne, Brisbane, Adelaide and Perth
Canada	Butterworth & Co (Canada) Ltd 2265 Midland Avenue, Scarborough, Ont M1P 4S1
	Butterworth & Co (Western Canada) Ltd 409 Granville Street, Ste 856, Vancouver, BC V6C 1T2
New Zealand	Butterworths of New Zealand Ltd 33–35 Cumberland Place, Wellington
Singapore	Butterworth & Co (Asia) Pte Ltd Crawford Post Office Box 770 Singapore 9119
South Africa	Butterworth & Co (South Africa) (Pty) Ltd 152–154 Gale Street, Durban 4001
United States of America	Mason Publishing Company Finch Bldg, 366 Wacouta Street, St Paul, Minn 55101
	Butterworth (Legal Publishers) Inc 160 Roy Street, Ste 300, Seattle, Wash 98109
	Butterworth (Legal Publishers) Inc 381 Elliot Street, Newton, Upper Falls, Mass 02164

ISBN Hardcover 0 406 63362 2
Softcover 0 406 63361 4

Typeset by Singapore National Printers Pte Ltd

Printed and bound in Great Britain by
Billing and Sons Limited Worcester

Preface to second edition

Our main task in preparing this second edition has been to take account of the many and substantial legislative changes which have occurred, particularly since the Conservative government took office in 1979. This has resulted in the almost complete rewriting of chapter 12 (on supplementary benefits) and major amendments to other chapters. Nor does the pace of reform seem to be slackening. At the time of writing the Social Security and Housing Benefits Bill is being considered by Parliament. We provide, at relevant places in the text, an account of the general principles of the two schemes — statutory sick pay and housing benefits — which it is anticipated will be introduced in 1983, but the details will not be available until the statutory instruments consequential on the legislation have been drafted. The parliamentary session 1982–83 is also likely to see a radical restructuring of the industrial injuries scheme; its flavour may be gained from the White Paper published late in 1981, to which frequent reference is made in chapter 8.

Quite apart from the revisions made necessary by reform, we have sought to improve the quality of the text by eliminating a number of errors which crept into the first edition (critics and colleagues have been most helpful in drawing our attention to them), and by reformulating discussion in many areas as our views on the subject-matter and the best way of presenting it have changed. Our basic aims have, however, remained unaltered. We are conscious that there are some who would prefer us to concentrate more on the technical detail of the law and others who suggest that our concern with the theoretical and policy issues is not taken far enough. Maintaining the appropriate *via media* between these two positions is not easy, but we are consoled by the fact that now, as never before, there are publications available which attempt to meet all the very diverse needs of those interested in social security law.

We are happy again to record our gratitude to the officials of the Department of Health and Social Security who have kept us liberally — sometimes embarassingly so — supplied with information and materials, and to the staff of Butterworths for the expeditious handling of our manuscript and their constant reassurance when time and the whims of government seemed to be gaining the upper hand. We are no less indebted to Ashley Wilton who commented on several chapters and Christine Markham, Helen Farr and Audrey Hiscock for their uncomplaining ordering of our often untidy efforts.

We have divided the responsibility between us on slightly different lines from the first edition: A.I. Ogus prepared chapters 1–4 and 6–10, and E.M. Barendt chapters 5 and 11–16. We have attempted to state the law as we understand it to be in January 1982, though we have been able to incorporate references to later developments either in the text or in the Appendix. The rates of contribution and benefit which we state for 1982–83 are those in force from the last week of November 1982.

A.I.O.
E.M.B.
January 1982

Foreword to the first edition

by the Rt. Hon. Lord Scarman, OBE, Lord of Appeal in Ordinary

Social security is now the subject of rights and duties. Inevitably, therefore, it is a legal subject. Anthony Ogus and Eric Barendt by this work have committed themselves, without compromise or condition, to this basic proposition: and I commend their work to all who understand the need of a legal approach to a legal subject. But they do not — nor I for that matter — under-rate the value of the contributions other disciplines make to the development of a coherent and well-grounded national system of social security; and, of course, no lawyer can understand, or help forward, the law unless he is capable of an inter-disciplinary approach.

I expect this book to become one of the indispensable textbooks of the law. Certainly an authoritative, and independent, work is needed. At present, tribunals and practitioners have to rely heavily on the material produced, but not invariably published, by the Department of Health and Social Security. The department does a fine job: but it is not, and never has been, the office of a government department to declare or interpret the law. If law is to be administered justly, the independence, as well as the skills, of the lawyer must be mobilised. *Ogus and Barendt* will become, I hope, a name as familiar to the lawyer as Chitty, Salmond, Buckley, and Simon.

Finally, this work gives us an opportunity of measuring the extent to which our social security law satisfies the obligations accepted by the United Kingdom as a signatory of the European Social Charter 1961 and the International Covenant on Economic, Social, and Cultural Rights 1966. If any doubt should continue to be entertained that social security has to be part and parcel of English law, our international obligations are the answer.

I commend this book to lawyers primarily — but also to members of the other disciplines concerned with the behaviour of man in society; to politicians; and to all who are concerned to ensure that humanity and compassion are secured by law as well as by generosity.

Scarman

Extract from preface to the first edition

The growth of interest in social security law, both of teachers and practitioners, has been rapid in the last few years. The process has not been free from controversy: opinions differ both as to the academic merit of the subject and to the preferred method of presentation. Some contend that the social security system has not sufficient intellectual weight for the serious student of law; others view the educational objective more in terms of fostering the arithmetic ability to calculate the entitlement of a given individual to benefit rather than of providing any analysis of the principles of the system as a whole. A third approach stresses the desirability of covering, within one university course, broad and diverse areas of the welfare system including not only social security but also housing, education and legal services. We do not adopt these perspectives. The book has been written from a conviction that social security should take its place alongside other, more traditional, legal subjects as fully worthy of critical study, and its unity and technical character make it, in our view, more suitable for this purpose than the necessarily vague outlines of 'welfare' or 'poverty' law.

Legal education has tended in the past to concentrate on law as a method of determining relationships between individuals. While public law — the relationship between the state and the individual — has not been neglected, attention has been focussed for the most part on the formal or constitutional nature of the relationship rather than on its substance. The emphasis has been on the individual's ability to invoke judicial controls over unlawful executive activity rather than on the content of the rights conferred on the individual by the state within the proper exercise of its powers. While social security law raises problems of the constitutional limits of executive powers, it also lays down in considerable detail rules which materially affect the lives of all members of the community. As a body of law, it consists of a complex network of primary and subordinate legislation and case-law (notably Commissioners' decisions, though in some areas judicial rulings are not unimportant), the scrutiny of which provides an excellent training in the handling of a variety of legal instruments. As a reflection of competing social and economic policies, it reveals the way in which a very important branch of state activity has evolved, and how general objectives and strategies are translated into particular principles and rules of law.

In contrast to their counterparts in most other countries, the British universities have accepted 'social administration' as an intellectual discipline in its own right, though necessarily it has relied on other disciplines such as economics, history and sociology for its tools of analysis. Social security, in the context of general social policy, has featured prominently in its publications. This work does not attempt to compete with such studies. Quite apart from the limits to our own competence, we have not the space here both to expound a complex area of law and to subject the policies on which it is based to rigorous interdisciplinary analysis. At the same time, we have sought to explain the law in terms of its policy background and the insights offered by other disciplines, as we believe that the functioning of a social security system cannot be understood without reference to the objectives and values which it incorporates.

This goal has, with other factors, created the problem of preserving a satisfactory balance between historical and policy background, general principle and technical rules. In writing this book we have had in mind not only law students but also practitioners and other professional groups with an interest in this area. To accomplish these various objectives, we have adopted a compromise solution. We have inset not only, as is customary in legal texts, quotations and case summaries, but also technical rules which do not raise issues of legal principle.

As we explain in the opening chapter, the term 'social security' is open to several interpretations, and the scope of this book proceeds from no precise and unchallengeable definition. We have decided to confine ourselves to an account of those financial benefits which are administered by the Department of Health and Social Security. This means that, on the one hand, we do not treat the National Health Service, the various housing allowances, or redundancy payments, but on the other hand we do include the war pensions and industrial injury schemes.

A.I.O.
E.M.B.

Oxford
April 1978

Contents

2 Contributions

3 Unemployment benefit

Chronological table of statutes

References in this Table to *Statutes* are to Halsbury's Statutes of England (Third Edition) showing the volume and page at which the annotated text of the Act will be found.

Chronological table of statutory instruments

SI—*continued* PAGE

SI—*continued*

List of British cases

Table of EC cases

Note on citation of Social Security Commissioner Decisions

Reported decisions of the Social Security (formerly National Insurance) Commissioners provide a most important source of social security law. There has been a standard method for citing these decisions since 1951. It starts with the prefix 'R', indicating that the case is reported. There then follows in parenthesis the series initial, denoting the particular social security benefit involved in the case. There are now ten series:

(A)	Attendance allowance
(F)	Family allowances and child benefit
(FIS)	Family income supplement
(G)	General — miscellaneous benefits (maternity benefit, widow's benefit, guardian's allowance, child's special allowance, invalid care allowance and death grant)
(I)	Industrial injuries benefits
(M)	Mobility allowance
(P)	Retirement pensions
(S)	Sickness and invalidity benefits
(SB)	Supplementary benefit
(U)	Unemployment benefit

After the series initial, the number and (after an oblique stroke) the year of the case follow. For example, *R(P) 9/55* refers to the ninth reported retirement pensions case in 1955, and *R(I) 12/75* refers to the twelfth reported decision on industrial injuries benefits in 1975. The decisions are published individually by HMSO, and then bound every four years. Industrial injuries cases are bound in separate volumes.

Numbered decisions of the Commissioners are not published, but may be read at the Commissioners' offices (see p. 595, and Appendix). A few of these decisions are discussed in this book. They are identified by reference to two letters ('C' standing for 'Commissioner', and the relevant series letter), followed by the appropriate number and year. Thus, *CG 17/69* refers to the seventeenth numbered case in 1969 concerning one of the miscellaneous benefits, e.g. maternity, widow's benefit.

Before 1951 a reported case was referred to simply by its number and series initial, with the addition of the suffix 'K' or 'KL'. For both numbered decisions, and reported decisions up to the end of 1950, the letter 'S' or 'W' is added after the 'C' to denote a Scottish or a Welsh case. For example, *CS 11/49 (KL)* refers to the eleventh English decision of the Commissioner on sickness benefit during 1949, a case which has been reported; *CSU 14/48 (KL)* refers to the fourteenth Scottish case on unemployment benefit in 1948 — and a decision which has been reported. Now a reported decision merely indicates in the heading whether it is a Scottish or a Welsh case.

Some reference is made in this book to decisions of the Northern Ireland Commissioners. Such decisions are cited in much the same way as British cases, though the number and year precede the series initial. These initials also differ from those used in citing British decisions. They are:

(AA)	Attendance allowance
(DG)	Death grant
(FA)	Family allowances
(ICA)	Invalid care allowance
(II)	Industrial injuries benefits
(IVB)	Invalidity benefits
(MB)	Maternity benefit
(NCIP)	Non-contributory invalidity pension
(P)	Retirement pensions, widow's benefit, guardian's allowance, child's special allowance
(SB)	Sickness benefit
(UB)	Unemployment benefit

Thus, *R 1/71 (FA)* refers to the first reported Northern Ireland decision during 1971 on family allowances. Before 1960 the letter 'R' was omitted. There have not hitherto been any reported decisions on supplementary benefit or family income supplement; the series initials will be (Supp Ben) and (FIS) respectively.

Table of decisions

Decisions of the Social Security Commissioner

Decisions of the Northern Ireland Commissioner

Abbreviations

Statutes

CBA	Child Benefit Act
FAA	Family Allowances Act
FANIA	Family Allowances and National Insurance Act
FISA	Family Income Supplements Act
IIDA	Industrial Injuries and Diseases (Old Cases) Act
NAA	National Assistance Act
NHIA	National Health Insurance Act
NIA	National Insurance Act
NI(II)A	National Insurance (Industrial Injuries) Act
NISBA	National Insurance and Supplement Benefit Act
SBA	Supplementary Benefits Act
SSA	Social Security Act
SSBA	Social Security Benefits Act
SSCA	Social Security (Contributions) Act
SSHBA	Social Security and Housing Benefits Act
SS(MP)A	Social Security (Miscellaneous Provisions) Act
SSPA	Social Security Pensions Act
UIA	Unemployment Insurance Act
WCA	Workmen's Compensation Act

Books

Atiyah	*Accidents, Compensation and the Law* (3rd edn)
Calvert	*Social Security Law* (2nd edn)
Dupeyroux	*Droit de la Sécurité Sociale* (8th edn)
George	*Social Security: Beveridge and After* (1968)
Handbook	DHSS, *Supplementary Benefits Handbook* (1980)
Harris	*William Beveridge* (1977)
Kaim-Caudle	*Comparative Social Policy and Social Security* (1973)
Lynes	*The Penguin Guide to Supplementary Benefits* (4th edn)
Micklethwait	*The National Insurance Commissioners* (1976)
Ogus	(ed) Köhler and Zalher *A Century of Social Insurance* (1982) pp. 150–264
Townsend	*Poverty in the United Kingdom* (1979)
Walley	*Social Security: Another British Failure?* (1972)

Reports and Papers

Beveridge	Social Insurance and Allied Services (1942, Cmd 6404)
Finer	Report of the Committee on One-Parent Families (1974, Cmnd 5629)
Fisher	Report of the Committee on Abuse of Social Security Benefits (1973, Cmnd 5228)
Industrial Injuries Compensation	DHSS Discussion Document, *Industrial Injuries Compensation* (1980)
McCarthy	Report of the Royal Commission of Inquiry: Social Security in New Zealand (1972)
Pearson	Report of the Royal Commission on Civil Liability and Compensation for Personal Injury (1978, Cmnd 7054-I), vol I
Reform of the Industrial Injuries Scheme	White Paper: Social Security Act 1975 — Reform of the Industrial Injuries Scheme (1981, Cmnd 8402)
Social Assistance	DHSS Review of the Supplementary Benefits Scheme (1978)
Social Insurance, Part I	White Paper: Social Insurance, Part I (1944, Cmd 6550)
Social Insurance, Part II	White Paper: Social Insurance, Part II, Workmen's Compensation (1944, Cmd 6551)

Chapter 1

Social security and social policy

Part 1 Objectives of social security

A General

For Beveridge, the aim of social security was the fulfilment of need:

> to abolish want by ensuring that every citizen willing to serve according to his powers has at all times an income sufficient to meet his responsibilities.[1]

Others have laid stress on the redistributive function:

> to decrease inequalities in the distribution of incomes and command-over-resources-over-life set by the economic system.[2]

A third perspective emphasises social integration. The New Zealand Royal Commission on Social Security recognised that an important goal of the system should be to

> ensure . . . that everyone is able to enjoy a standard of living much like that of the rest of the community, and thus is able to feel a sense of participation in and belonging to the community.[3]

It is apparent from these statements that it is impossible to divorce the objectives of social security from political ideologies and values, and the starting point for an account of the policy issues involved in the system must be an outline of such ideologies and values as have had an influence on its development.

B Ideologies

There are, of course, risks inherent in over-simplifying political creeds and inevitably any one current system of social security reflects a multitude of influences. Yet the isolation of three fundamentally different ideologies and the attitude of each to social welfare should help to clarify the choice of objectives in social security as well as the historical and political background of the British system.

1 Para 444.
2 Titmuss *Commitment to Welfare* (2nd edn) p. 65.
3 *McCarthy* p. 65.

i Repressive individualism

In the period of emergent industrialism and capitalism, welfare was to be achieved through personal effort.[4] Each individual was considered free to maximise his own expectations through activities and transactions unfettered by state intervention. There was thought to be work available for anyone who wanted it, and destitution was therefore seen as resulting not from social or economic forces but rather from personal failings, a view bolstered by the Puritan ethic of work.[5] Moreover, poverty constituted not only a deviation from moral discipline, but also a threat to civil order, as it was typically associated with crime and political unrest.[6] In this context relief of the poor was necessarily repressive and punitive: a generous system of welfare would have encouraged more idleness and therefore more social chaos. The poor law perfectly reflected this ideology,[7] and it is nowhere better epitomised than in the workhouse system, established on a widespread basis in the eighteenth century, and administered nationally from 1834.[8] Relief was granted to able-bodied persons only if they were willing to subject themselves to the rigours of the workhouse, where life was intentionally made harsh and repellant. The guiding principle was the so-called doctrine of 'less eligibility'. In the words of the Poor Law Commissioners,

> the first and most essential of all conditions is that the situation of the individual relieved shall not be made really or apparently so eligible as the situation of the independent labourer of the lowest class.[9]

Some mitigation of the doctrine was granted only where it was patent that the individual's plight arose from accident rather than from personal inaptitude, thus for the blind, the crippled and the aged.[10]

ii Liberal individualism

The second ideology may have grown out of a similar industrial system but the political climate had changed. There had arisen new humanitarian ideals, associated first with the philanthropist movement, and subsequently more generally with the middle classes who had benefited most from the industrial and commercial expansion.[11] However, as the economy became more than ever dependent on an efficient labour force, it became appreciated that social welfare conferred on the working population might improve rather than hinder productivity.[12] Both movements inspired the massive welfare measures taken in the nineteenth century to improve health and environmental conditions.[13] Such improvements, however, in no way provided direct financial help to the poorer sections of the community.

4 *Tawney Religion and the Rise of Capitalism* (1921) pp. 253–273.
5 Ibid, at pp. 218–249.
6 Fraser *Evolution of the British Welfare State* (1973) pp. 28–31.
7 The classic study is Webb and Webb *History of English Local Government* (1927) vol 7. See also Marshall *The Old Poor Law 1795–1834* (1968), and Rose *The English Poor Law 1780–1930* (1971).
8 *Webb and Webb*, n.7, above, at pp. 215–264.
9 Report of Royal Commission on Poor Law (1834), para 228.
10 The so-called system of 'out-relief': see Bruce *The Coming of the Welfare State* (4th edn) pp. 117–128.
11 Gilbert *The Evolution of National Insurance in Great Britain* (1966) pp. 22–27; *Ogus* pp. 166–171.
12 Rimlinger *Welfare Policy and Industrialisation in Europe, America and Russia* (1971) pp. 36–38.
13 See generally, *Bruce*, n.10, above, at pp. 128–153.

The advent of the labour movement as a political force stimulated progress in this direction. The trade unions were able to press for higher wages and, more significantly for our purposes, the friendly societies and industrial assurance societies offered some collective insurance protection against hazards to the breadwinner, notably those of premature death and funeral expenses.[14] This system of alleviating need accorded well with the laissez-faire doctrine of welfare through individual initiative: it maintained the traditional virtues of thrift and foresight; and its cost did not impede economic progress.[15] The limitations of this method of social welfare were obvious: it did not cover the large variety of hazards to which the earner was subject, and the lowest wage-earners were unable to afford contributions.[16]

The ideology which emerged of liberal individualism, or welfare capitalism, reaffirmed faith in the competitive market system as the moral and just way to prosperity: it aimed to reward endeavour with material gain and continued to rest primarily on the responsibility of the individual freely to determine his own style and level of living.[17] But at the same time it was recognised that there would be some who would fall victims to the free play of market forces. In the first place, the industrial processes themselves created dangers and thereby imposed costs on workers. For such directly caused losses as injuries or death resulting from employment risks, private law was the suitable instrument for compensation, and though at the time the law of tort was hindered in its remedial capacity by the doctrine of common employment and the need affirmatively to prove fault,[18] the solution was found in the quasi-tortious Workmen's Compensation Act 1897,[19] which based liability on a no-fault principle. To reconcile the scheme with the need for continuous economic expansion and the fact that the employer might be morally innocent, it nevertheless limited compensation to generally no more than one half of the workman's lost earnings.[20] Outside this relatively narrow area the principle according to which the burden was to be assumed by the activity creating the risk was inoperative; other social hazards could not be so directly connected with particular enterprises. Thus for a second group whose state of need could not be attributed to personal failings, typically the unemployed and the sick, another solution had to be found. The natural resort was the insurance principle which would engender the traditional virtue of individual responsibility and investment of personal resources, and would not be far removed from the typical market economy device of the 'exchange' transaction.[1] The notion that such risks were something which the community as a whole should bear received partial recognition by the sharing of insurance costs between the employer (who would pass it on in the form of prices) and the employee; but in order that individual initiative should not be stifled and to discourage idleness, benefit would be paid at only a

14 See generally, Gosden *The Friendly Societies in England 1815–1875* (1961) and *Self Help: Voluntary Associations in the Nineteenth Century* (1973).
15 George *Social Security and Society* (1973) pp. 17–18; Pinker *Social Theory and Social Policy* (1971) pp. 90–91.
16 See Majority Report of the Royal Commission on the Poor Law (1909, Cd 4499), p. 536.
17 The classic modern restatements are Friedman *Capitalism and Freedom* (1962) and Hayek *The Constitution of Liberty* (1960). See generally George and Wilding *Ideology and Social Welfare* (1976) ch 2.
18 *Ogus* pp. 173–175; Hanes *The First British Workmen's Compensation Act* (1968).
19 Pp. 259–261, below.
20 P. 259, below.
1 *Pinker*, n.15, above, at pp. 135–144.

survival level.[2] This was the scheme adopted for unemployment and sickness under the National Insurance Act 1911.[3] It was also applied by analogy in 1925 to those risks against which individuals might be expected to provide – old age or premature death – but which, in the case of low-earners, typically went unprotected.[4] In such cases, the compulsory insurance of manual workers and low-paid non-manual workers could be justified within the liberal philosophy on grounds of paternalism.

There was left a hard core of poverty cases outside these two categories, either because the individual's contribution record was inadequate, or because the duration of the interruption of employment was excessive. The cases might be undeserving and in 1909 the Majority of the Royal Commission on the Poor Law could still argue that it was necessary to treat them as a distinct group of society whose predicament was, in some way, attributable to defects in moral character.[5] But humanitarian sentiments were allowed to prevail. A means-tested financial benefit had already in 1908 been introduced to protect the aged from the poor law,[6] and a similar device, in the form of unemployment assistance, was adopted for the vast numbers of unemployed who during the inter-war period had exhausted their right to insurance benefit.[7]

The pattern established by the end of the 1930s – social insurance covering the major causes of income loss and conferring benefit at a flat-rate survival level, combined with a scheme of residual means-tested assistance for those remaining – was in its essence left unaltered by the programme instituted in 1946–47 and inspired by the Beveridge Report. His primary aims were to make the insurance scheme more comprehensive (it was extended to groups hitherto excluded, and the coverage of work accidents and diseases was transferred from the individual employer's responsibility), to substitute 'subsistence' for 'survival' as the minimum level, to unify its administration, but, most important of all, to rationalise it in terms of the liberal ideology. He was eager to recognise the freedom of the individual to pursue his own welfare above the subsistence level.

> Social security must be achieved by cooperation between the State and the individual. . . . The State in organising security should not stifle incentive, opportunity, responsibility; in establishing a national minimum, it should leave room and encouragement for voluntary action by each individual to provide more than that minimum for himself and his family.[8]

As will be seen, the specific programme sponsored by Beveridge failed, but the ideology inherent in it continues to exert a considerable influence on contemporary social policy. It is evident in the continuing breadth and volume of the occupational coverage of sickness and retirement.[9] It has also received impetus from the reforms and policies of the Thatcher administration, with its concern to reduce public expenditure, engender individual responsibility and preserve work incentives.[10]

2 *Bruce*, n.10, above, at pp. 198–199.
3 See generally, *Ogus* pp. 182–187.
4 Widows', Orphans' and Old Age Contributory Pensions Act 1925.
5 N. 16, above, at p. 643.
6 Old Age Pensions Act 1908: p. 189, below.
7 The major measure was the Unemployment Act 1934. See pp. 76 and 451–452, below. below.
8 Para 9.
9 *Townsend* pp. 809–811.
10 See further, pp. 10, 20 and 410, below.

iii Collectivism

The third ideology takes as its starting point a rejection of the market system as the method of achieving a just distribution of social welfare.[11] The notion that the state should provide merely a minimum amount sufficient for subsistence purposes through some residual institutional machinery is discredited. The social services, and social security in particular, should be concerned to remedy inequities resulting from the market economy; they should therefore incorporate as a primary objective the redistribution of resources from the rich to the poor.[12] While 'need' remains the typical criterion for determining to whom this programme is to be directed, it is given a broader perspective. No longer is it to be confined to describe those who are 'poor' in the sense that their resources are insufficient to maintain themselves according to some objective standard of minimum subsistence. Need is, instead, seen as something which is relative to the general prosperity and level of earnings, and therefore reflects the grosser inequalities in a society at any given time.[13] Welfare is to be 'universalist' in that it is to be conferred on all those within broadly based social categories (the aged, the sick, the disabled, large families) without the socially divisive and stigma-producing means test.[14] Indeed, some exponents of the ideology look beyond the more immediate aim of income support to the remoter and necessarily vaguer goal of social integration, enabling all persons fully to participate in and belong to the community.[15]

While this last aspect has remained at best a tacit element in British social policy since the Second World War, the collectivist objectives as a whole are fully evident in the family allowances scheme[16] introduced in 1945, and, outside the social security field, in the National Health Service and the education programme. Even so, the universalist and redistributional features were to become ambivalent. The real value of family allowances was allowed to decline, and it was only in the late 1960s and 1970s that there was renewed pressure for a significant degree of state family endowment.[17] Within the health and educational fields, there continues to be great scope for privately financed facilities. For the purposes of the present book, the conflict between the individualist and the collectivist approach to welfare has taken its sharpest form over the relative roles of state and occupational schemes in the provision for retirement. The huge growth in group and other forms of private coverage, itself a result of the low level of benefit offered by the flat-rate (and even later the graduated) national insurance scheme, was regarded as socially divisive by many arguing from a collectivist perspective.[18] Many of the occupational schemes did not correspond to Beveridge's model of voluntary and individual initiative based on freedom of choice, since they were often compulsory and offered few alternatives.[19] At the same time, they tended to discriminate against bad risks, who might be unable to obtain appropriate

11 Tawney *The Acquisitive Society* (1931) chs 4–5; Titmuss *Commitment to Welfare* (2nd edn) chs 12–13.
12 *Titmuss*, n.11 above ch 16.
13 See p. 21, below and the references cited there.
14 *Titmuss* ch 10; Townsend *Sociology and Social Policy* (1975) pp. 149–153.
15 E.g. *Townsend*, n.14, above, ch 2; Room *Sociology of Welfare* (1979) ch 16.
16 See generally, Hall, Land, Parker and Webb *Change, Choice and Conflict in Social Policy* (1975).
17 E.g. Bull (ed) *Family Poverty* (2nd edn) and p. 423, below.
18 Titmuss *Social Policy* (1974) ch 7; *Townsend*, n.14; above, ch 19.
19 *Titmuss*, n.18, above, at p. 94.

coverage, and against manual workers who, unlike their clerical and managerial counterparts, would probably achieve their optimal earning level at an early stage in their working life, and who would thereby suffer if, as was typically the case, the basis of the earnings-related pension was the earnings-level immediately before retirement.[20] The Conservative plan of integrating the occupational with the state approach by allowing the latter to play only a residual role[1] was unacceptable to the Wilson government of 1974, and when the new earnings-related scheme was introduced a year later, it offered a more equal form of partnership between the two: the state pension, when fully operative, would include a substantial earnings-related element, but individuals were given the ability to opt instead for an occupational scheme which satisfied certain conditions.[2]

Collectivist influences may be seen at work in the non-contributory and non-means tested benefits for the disabled (introduced in the period 1975–77)[3] but in this field too there is considerable interplay and overlap between public and private provision. The new statutory sick pay scheme, replacing sickness benefit for short periods,[4] and the proposals to deduct the value of social security disability benefits from common law damages,[5] are particularly significant in this connection.

The relative lack of discussion of the social integration objective has been attributed by some to what is regarded as a developing political and ideological consensus.[6] The phenomenon, it is argued, is common to affluent industrial societies and is an inevitable consequence of working class and trade union satisfaction with a capitalist system from which they have derived a proportionately increasing share of its resources. On the other hand, the intellectual left continues to stress that social security does little more than remove the worst excesses of the capitalist system, has no impact on the fundamental inequalities which exist within our society, and, as such, should be regarded primarily as an aid to the coercive control of the labour force.[7]

C Values

i General

Some of the most important social, political and economic values, such as freedom and individual responsibility or equality and community responsibility, are closely associated with the ideologies described above. There are, however, others which are not necessarily identifiable with any particular ideology and yet which exert to a greater or lesser extent an influence on social security legislation.

ii Demographic aims

There are two distinct objectives which may be referred to as demographic and with which a social security system may be concerned. The first relates

20 *Titmuss*, n.18, above, at p. 98.
1 White Paper Strategy for Pensions (1971, Cmnd 4755); p. 192, below.
2 Pp. 220–224, below.
3 Pp. 166–186, below.
4 Pp. 160–162, below.
5 P. 419, below.
6 George *Social Security and Society* (1973) pp. 29–32.
7 E.g. Kincaid *Poverty and Equality in Britain* (1973); Jordan *Poor Parents* (1974); Higgins 9 Jo Soc Pol 1.

to the size of the population. Of course, one of the effects of adequate financial provision for the aged is to increase the longevity of life and thus the population as a whole.[8] The welfare of the aged is so obviously a *sine qua non* of social security, that the problem does not call for discussion. In some countries the level of family endowment is thought to have a significant impact on the birth rate and in this sense social security has been regarded as an instrument of demographic policy.[9] Undeniably it played an important role in the introduction of family allowances in Britain.[10] In the recent discussions of family endowment, however, demographic issues have been relatively neglected.

The second demographic notion, that of the mobility of labour, has featured more prominently in recent British social policy.[11] On the one hand, the legislation has been concerned to encourage persons to acquire new occupational techniques when they become redundant either because of natural labour wastage or because of their own physical disabilities. An individual's contribution record is maintained and his right to benefit preserved during periods of retraining or rehabilitation,[12] and perhaps the chief motivation for the introduction in 1966 of earnings-related supplement to unemployment benefit was the perceived need to soften the blow of unemployment and thus to encourage labour mobility.[13] On the other hand, a recipient of unemployment benefit may be disqualified if after a substantial period, usually six months, he refuses an offer of a suitable position in another district.[14] Much of the international provision in the social security field has been designed to encourage the mobility of labour from one state to another. The prime example is the legislation emanating from the European Economic Communities.[15]

iii The family

On a superficial analysis it may appear as if the social security system serves to undermine the integrity of the family unit. In an historical sense, it is true that originally support by other family members was the first and sometimes the only refuge from destitution,[16] and that this function has to a considerable extent been superseded by state financial provision. But while dependence on remoter family relationships may, to some extent, have diminished in importance,[17] the legal interdependence of the inner family unit has in fact increased and is in no way overridden by the social security system which intervenes to replace maintenance obligations only when they remain unfulfilled.[18] The other argument turns on the extent of support for natural, as opposed to legal, family relationships. It is said that recognition of 'illicit' relationships acts as an incentive to marital

8 *Dupeyroux* pp. 188–198.
9 *Dupeyroux* pp. 207–210; *Kaim-Caudle*, pp. 18–21, Mirinoff [1980] Soc Services Rev 301. For a comparison of family endowment in the EEC countries, see Bradshaw and Piachaud (1980) 47 Poverty 21.
10 Hall, Land, Parker and Webb *Change, Choice and Conflict in Social Policy* (1975) pp. 170–174.
11 See generally Bartholomew (ed) *Manpower Planning* (1976).
12 Pp. 69–70, below.
13 NEDC Report on Conditions Favourable to Faster Growth (1963), paras. 50–52.
14 Pp. 112–117, below.
15 Ch 16, below.
16 Weber *Theory of Social and Economic Organisation* (ed Parsons, 1947) pp. 136–139.
17 Schweinitz *England's Road to Social Security* (1943) pp. 223–225.
18 See generally *Finer* Part 4, and pp. 508–512, below.

breakdown.[19] It must be conceded that for some, but by no means all, purposes, social security has regard to the consequences of such a relationship rather than the legal family as the basic unit. This occurs, for example, in the case of the means-tested benefits,[20] child benefit[1] and dependants' increases to personal benefits,[2] but in other instances *de facto* relationships are ignored: a woman living with a man has no title to widow's benefit should he die, and cannot rely on his contributions to her own retirement pension; she will be the object of a dependant's increase to his benefit only if she is caring for a child.[3]

There is little evidence to suggest that such state support as exists for *de facto* families acts as an incentive to marriage breakdown.[4] Even if it does, the consequent evil has to be weighed against the competing desire to protect the welfare of children by not forcing couples to continue to cohabit when a marriage has already disintegrated, and by recognising new obligations that may arise from alternative, if illicit, relationships.[5] Whether for the purposes of social security, the 'family' is that recognised by the law generally or a broader concept, it is indisputable that its economic welfare constitutes one of the primary objectives of the system. This is evident not only from the attempts to make child benefit and family income supplement underwrite intra-family maintenance, but also from the way in which, in sharp contrast to that of some other countries, British law has traditionally concentrated its income maintenance programme on family needs rather than earnings replacement.[6]

iv Sex equality

There have always been significant differences in social security systems between the treatment of men and women.[7] Although this area of law was deliberately excluded from the sex discrimination legislation, nevertheless in response to pressure from several quarters, in particular the European Commission,[8] recent governments have made steady progress towards greater sex equality. As regards single women, the pre-war discrimination based on the assumption that they were 'poor risks' was abolished in 1945[9] and the only difference remaining is that the retirement age for women is five years earlier than that for men.[10]

The different treatment of married women stemmed in part from the practice of regarding the family as a single financial unity. The model which traditionally dominated social policy thinking was that of the wife doing the housework and rearing the children while the husband was the

19 The argument is stated and repudiated in Friedmann *Law in a Changing Society* (2nd edn) pp. 287–289. See also *Finer* para 2.7.
20 Pp. 461–465, below.
1 P. 432, below.
2 P. 369, below.
3 P. 369, below.
4 Cf. *Finer* pp. 6–18.
5 The issue has been very fully discussed in the context of divorce legislation: see Cretney *Principles of Family Law* (3rd edn) pp. 81–86, and the references there cited.
6 Cf pp. 20 and 364–365, below.
7 See generally Land in Barker and Allen (eds) *Sexual Divisions and Society* (1976) pp. 108–132; Townsend *Sociology and Social Policy* (1975) ch 17; Wilson *Women and the Welfare State* (1977); ISSA Studies and Research no 5, *Women and Social Security* (1973).
8 Lipman-Blumen and Bernard *Sex Roles and Social Policy* (1979); Atkins [1981] JSWL 16.
9 P. 61, below.
10 Pp. 194–196, below.

breadwinner.[11] Thus entitlement to the means-tested benefits, which aggregate the resources and needs of the family or household, was in general restricted to the husband or male partner. In 1980 the position was changed: a couple, married or unmarried, would be able to nominate which partner was the primary breadwinner and hence be entitled to benefit, though this reform will not be brought into effect until 1983.[12] Despite stringent criticism from the National Insurance Advisory Committee,[13] two non-contributory disability benefits introduced in the 1970s continue to adopt the discriminatory model. A husband, but not a wife, may claim the invalid care allowance for the loss of income involved in caring for a disabled person[14] — it is assumed that the role is one which a wife is normally expected to undertake without reward. At first glance, the so-called housewives' non-contributory invalidity pension might seem to be an equalisation measure for it is payable to a woman who is incapable of performing normal household duties.[15] But it is in fact discriminatory for a woman must show that she is incapable both of this unpaid and also of paid employment, while a male claimant need only establish the latter: the possibility that a man might undertake household duties is ignored.

The position of a married woman *earner* within the insurance system was for a long time regarded as subsidiary. Account was taken of the fact that employment was liable to interruption for childbirth and, in the words of Beveridge, her earnings were 'a means not of subsistence but of a standard of living above subsistence', and thus in the case of unemployment or sickness she could fall back on her husband's support.[16] A complex set of rules was formulated to reflect this lower status, including notably the ability to opt out of the insurance scheme. With changing social attitudes, and the increasing participation of married women in the labour market,[17] this option was abolished for those marrying after April 1977.[18] Another anachronism existed in relation to dependency allowances.[19] A husband claimant was paid an allowance for his wife (provided she was not earning more than a stipulated amount), but a wife claimant could receive an allowance for her husband only if he was wholly dependent on her and was incapable of self support. Following an EEC Directive, legislation has removed the anomaly: from 1984 additions will be payable for husband or wife, subject in both cases to an earnings limit imposed on the dependent spouse. However the logic of these reforms has not been pursued in the case of survivor benefits. A widow receives substantial benefit and thus is not expected to maintain herself by earnings if she has dependent children, or is aged over 50.[20] But outside the industrial injury and war pension schemes, a husband receives no benefit on the death of his wife: the assumptions must be that husbands are not financially dependent on wives and that, as regards housework and care, it is easy for them to find a

11 *Walley* pp. 75–76, 156–161, 206–207, 240–241; Clark and Ogus 5 Br Jo Law and Society 7.
12 Pp. 462 and 527, below.
13 1980, Cmnd 7905 and 7955.
14 Pp. 178–180, below.
15 Pp. 168–170, below.
16 Para 108.
17 Beveridge relied on the fact that before the Second World War only about 12½% of married women of working age were gainfully employed (para 108). In 1978 the figure was 62%: General Household Survey 1978, Table 5.1.
18 Pp. 62–63, below.
19 Pp. 368–369, below.
20 Pp. 230–233, below.

replacement spouse.[1] Nor at present does there appear to be any inclination to follow the Swedish example of establishing an allowance payable to fathers who temporarily cease work to care for a new-born child.[2]

v Redistribution and general economic welfare

As we have seen,[3] one important objective of social security is the redistribution of resources from the richer to the poorer members of the community. The extent to which such redistribution actually occurs depends on the criteria adopted for the selection of beneficiaries and the method of financing; these matters will be discussed in subsequent pages.[4] While economists and others have developed theoretical constructs for the level of redistribution which should occur in a 'fair' society,[5] in practice this is generally determined by what proves to be politically acceptable.[6]

An argument which is adduced to limit the degree of redistribution requires some consideration here, if only because it has featured prominently in the Conservative government's social and economic policy. It is to the effect that social welfare transfers necessarily lead to losses in the aggregate wealth of a society and that therefore only a limited amount of such transfers are compatible with sustained economic growth. The losses referred to can be particularised as follows:[7] first, high levels of benefit paid to those unemployed or sick reduce work incentives and hence productivity; secondly, the marginal tax rates necessary to finance progressive redistribution have the same effect, but also reduce the amount available for investment and thus deplete the capital stocks of society; thirdly, the administration of the transfers is costly to administer and thus employs resources which could be put to more productive use.

As regards the effect of high taxation on productivity and investment it ought to be observed that empirical evidence for the proposition is weak.[8] It is not much stronger in the case of beneficiaries[9] but nevertheless the social security legislation assumes the problem to be highly significant because it incorporates powerful controls against voluntary unemployment and other, less direct, work incentives. The former include the medical tests for incapacity for work,[10] the availability condition for unemployment benefit,[11] the disqualification for voluntarily leaving employment[12] and the array of legislative provisions and administrative machinery designed to detect and penalise abuse.[13] The indirect method has been to fix the rate of

1 *Clarke and Ogus*, n.11, above. Statistics, however, show that the remarriage rate of widowers is higher than that of widows.
2 See Baude in *Lipman-Blumen and Bernard*, n.8, above, ch 4.
3 P. 1, above.
4 Pp. 12–19, and 25–31, below.
5 E.g. Rawls *A Theory of Justice* (1971). See generally, Phelps (ed) *Economic Justice* (1973).
6 It has thus been argued that to be viable redistribution must benefit at least half of the electorate: Buchanan and Bush 64 Am Econ Rev Proceedings 153.
7 Cf McClements *The Economics of Social Security* (1978) ch 4.
8 Okun *Equality and Efficiency* (1975) pp. 96–100; cf Kay and King *The British Tax System* (2nd edn) pp. 30–35.
9 *Okun*, n.8, above, at p. 97, where the disincentive effect is reported as having related to the work effort of secondary earners within low-income families. Cf Townsend, who argues that controls over work are more social than economic: Fabian Pamphlet *Social Services for All* (1970) ch 10.
10 Pp. 146–154, below.
11 Pp. 101–106, below.
12 Pp. 110–112, below.
13 Pp. 497–501, 575–580, below.

benefit such that the claimant does not lose financially by returning to work. The poor law, it will be recalled, explicitly adopted the principle that recipients of welfare should be worse off than those in the lowest paid employment.[14] The national assistance and supplementary benefit schemes for many years contained the 'wage stop' rule, according to which claimants were not to receive more by way of benefit than they would have earned in their normal employment, notwithstanding that the amount in question was below the officially recognised subsistence level.[15] Earnings-related supplement, when it existed, fell short of 100 per cent indemnity and the level of flat-rate benefit is generally well below the average wage. In fact, if work incentives are the primary motivations for these rules, the system is remarkably inefficient in ensuring that no claimants are better off with benefit than in employment. The much discussed 'poverty trap' exists for many who lose entitlement to a considerable range of means-tested benefits when their income exceeds a certain point.[16] The Secretary of State for Social Services has conceded that one of the consequences of maintaining the real value of the means-tested benefits while reducing the value of others in accordance with the government's policy on public expenditure has been to narrow the difference between the income of those in work and those out of work and thus to exacerbate the problem, at least in the short term.[17]

Social welfare transfers generate benefits as well as costs to aggregate economic welfare. For example, it produces a healthier and more efficient labour force than would otherwise be the case[18] and it helps to stabilise the economy by reducing the severity of depressions and putting a brake on booms.[19] Whatever the net losses, when these benefits have been taken into account, these must be weighed against the social value of redistribution, even though it may be impossible to quantify this. There is, in short, a trade-off to be made between equity and efficiency.[20]

Part 2 Strategies

A Introduction

In Part 1 we considered the range of objectives that a social security system might adopt. In this part we discuss the different strategies available to meet these objectives. Social security, as we define it for the purpose of this book,[1] is a system of cash benefits conferred on individuals satisfying conditions of entitlement. In section B, we consider how recipients may be selected and classified according to their needs. Section C is concerned with the principles for assessing benefits, and section D with the methods of financing them. Finally, in section E we contrast the cash benefit system with two other types of social welfare: benefits in kind, and fiscal relief.

14 P. 2, above.
15 *Lynes* (2nd edn.) pp. 110–126.
16 Pp. 524–526, below.
17 Third Report of Social Services Committee 1979–80, HC 702, para 95.
18 This was, of course, acknowledged in the 19th century: p. 2 above.
19 Richardson *Economic and Financial Aspects of Social Security* (1961) pp. 215–218.
20 *McClements*, n.7, above, at pp. 88–96; *Okun*, n.8, above.
1 Cf p. 38, below.

B Selection and classification of need

i General

The primary question arising under a system of cash benefits relates to the circumstances in which and the persons to whom benefits are paid. To postulate that a social welfare system must be 'selective' is merely to state the obvious. The same benefits cannot be enjoyed to the same degree by all members of society. Even the most 'universal' of schemes, such as the social dividend proposal (described later in this chapter[2]) which purports to grant benefit to all, nevertheless effectively takes it back from many through the medium of taxation. The debate on 'universality versus selectivity'[3] is thus concerned not with a choice between two extreme alternatives but rather on the nature and extent of the selectivity process. At a very broad level, two fundamentally different approaches should be distinguished. In the first, generally referred to as the means test method, the target is poverty as such, and the primary condition of entitlement is a level of resources below a stipulated amount. The second attempts to focus on presumed needs (often but not exclusively involving income deprivation) arising from certain circumstances, e.g. unemployment, disability, old age, the maintenance of children. The one approach is not necessarily coterminous with the other – it is possible that entitlement to a particular benefit may depend on conditions both of non-financial circumstances and of income[4] – but the relative weight to be given to each strategy raises an important issue of social policy.

ii Means-tested benefits

The primary assumption behind the means test approach is that deprivation of income and other resources constitutes the greatest need on which the social security system should concentrate. It is typically combined with concern that welfare expenditure (which involves a substantial degree of redistribution) should be limited to cases of *demonstrated* need and that the conditions for receipt should be kept within carefully observed limits.[5] The process has, however, been attacked by a battery of arguments.[6] Means tests are regarded as socially divisive not the least because those who are subject to them are conscious of the continuity of a tradition dating back to the poor law.[7] They imply strong control functions by governments and bureaucrats whose attitudes may be coloured by their own moral judgments of poverty.[8] This leads to a conclusion that 'there is a general discouragement to use means-tested services which is built into their operating rules and administration by a society which sets great store by self-help and thrift'.[9] Finally it is claimed that means tests are stigmatising and for that reason result in a lower than desirable take-up rate.[10] The stigma issue is a

2 P. 36, below.
3 See esp. *McCarthy* ch 14; Titmuss *Commitment to Welfare* (2nd edn) ch 10; Townsend *Sociology and Social Policy* (1975) ch 9; Davies *Universality, Selectivity and Effectiveness in Social Policy* (1978) ch 7.
4 See Collard in Bull (ed) *Family Poverty* (2nd edn) ch 2.
5 Cf *Beveridge* para 369; *Townsend*, n.3, above, at pp.136–137; Rejda *Social Insurance and Economic Security* (1976) pp. 405–408.
6 See National Consumer Council Paper *Means-Tested Benefits* (1976) and the references cited in n.3, above.
7 *Townsend*, n.3, above, at pp. 149–153; NCC Paper, n.6, above, at pp. 15–17.
8 See generally Stevenson *Claimant or Client* (1973).
9 *Townsend* p. 880.
10 On stigma generally see Goffman *Stigma: Notes on the Management of Spoiled Identity* (1963); *Stevenson*, n.8, above, ch 1; *Titmuss*, n.3, above, ch 3; Pinker *Social Theory and Social Policy* (1971) ch 4.

complex one and the evidence is less conclusive than impressionistic discussions have assumed.[11] The notion that self-declarations of poverty are of their nature degrading is commonly held, but, as has been observed,[12] the humiliation may result not so much from the process of claiming relief as from the poverty itself which is revealing of personal failure, particularly when it is associated with circumstances of living which are commonly regarded as morally unacceptable, e.g. unemployment or fatherless families.[13] The evidence for the take-up problem is more tangible. The estimates of take-up rates – the proportion of those eligible for a given benefit who actually receive it – are of course unreliable in that there is never a certain way of discovering how many people in fact satisfy eligibility conditions at any one time.[14] Nevertheless, surveys, both governmental and independent, have revealed a situation which few would regard as satisfactory.[15]

The latest official figures, which are thought to overestimate take-up because of the inadequacies of the Family Expenditure Survey on which they are based,[16] reveal the following proportion of those eligible who received benefit: rent allowances 55 per cent, rate rebates 70 per cent, supplementary benefit 74 per cent, free school meals and rent rebates 80 per cent.[17] This resulted, for these benefits alone,[18] in a saving on public expenditure in 1977–78 of some £430 million. Some of the failures to claim are undoubtedly due to ignorance;[19] the means test approach places a high premium on publicity and communication, hence the widespread call for improvements in the methods of distributing information.[20]

The selectivity process involved in means tests by implication aims at locating those in greatest need at lowest cost. However, in practice they emerge as an expensive form of welfare. The administration of supplementary benefits costs some 13 per cent of benefit expenditure,[1] compared with 5 per cent for the contributory benefits.[2] Undoubtedly one reason for this is the complexity of the means-testing process,[3] and the problem is intensified by the proliferation of different tests for different benefits: in Britain today, if local authority grants are included, there are about 45

11 *Davies* n.3, above, ch 3.
12 *Pinker*, n.10, above, at pp. 141–144.
13 *Stevenson*, n.8, above, at pp. 16–17.
14 NCC Paper, n.6, above, at pp. 25–26.
15 See particularly, ibid, at pp. 27–36.
16 Mr S Orme, Minister of State, 910 HC Official Reports (5th series), written answers col *160*.
17 For details of the sources see (1980) 44 Poverty 39.
18 The latest estimate of FIS take-up is (for 1975) 75%, but the government has declared itself unable to speculate on the amount saved: 971 HC Official Reports (5th series), col 480.
19 In a study made in Islington it was found that 72% of non-take up of six benefits examined resulted from ignorance: Lister *Take-Up of Means-Tested Benefits* (1974) p. 17. Cf the doubts expressed in SBC Discussion Paper *Take-Up of Supplementary Benefits* (1978) pp. 8–9.
20 NCC Paper, n.6, above, ch 4. Some such improvements have been made e.g. in the design of leaflets and the form of letters to claimants but their effect is as yet uncertain: cf SBC Discussion Paper, n.19, above, at p. 9; SBC Annual Report 1978, ch 6; SBC Annual Report 1979, ch 12; Briggs and Rees *Supplementary Benefits and the Consumer* (1980). For the consequences of an intensive publicity campaign in Strathclyde, see 10 Jo Soc Pol 552.
1 SBC Annual Report 1979, Cmnd. 8033, p. 130.
2 Social Security Statistics 1981, Table 44.02.
3 Cf Donnison 5 Jo Soc Pol 337, 352–354.

different means-tested benefits, and though entitlement to some will follow automatically from entitlement to others (the 'passport principle') this is not generally the case.[4] Indeed, it has been argued that, at least as presently administered, means tests inequitably shift many of the costs of selection (e.g. those resulting from problems in dealing with bureaucracy, waiting, frustration, travelling) from the public purse to the individual who, *ex hypothesi*, is not in a position to bear them.[5]

General considerations of the merits of means tests leave open the question as to the form such tests might take. The McCarthy Royal Commission in New Zealand was quick to assert what appeared to it to be a fundamental distinction between 'means tests' and 'income tests': the former but not the latter take into account the claimant's capital resources.[6] The income test was less stigmatising as the claimant's total circumstances need not be opened to public scrutiny; it also avoided any incentive to dissipate capital resources to gain entitlement. In Britain, while the level of capital resources disregarded under the present supplementary benefit scheme is reasonably generous,[7] the tradition has always been to take them into account presumably on the ground that to disregard them creates inequities between claimants. This same problem is inherent in the difficult choice between simplicity and comprehensiveness:[8] to do justice to each recipient involves a rigorous scrutiny of all his circumstances which is both expensive and disagreeable. If the objective is to be achieved by rules conferring rights, there is a danger of creating a complex and unwieldy body of law which those directly concerned would be unlikely fully to understand. If the more flexible alternative of a wide discretion is preferred, this creates the risk of bureaucratic power and apparent arbitrariness.

There has been no consistent development in British social policy either towards or against means tests. The early forms of welfare were, of course, almost wholly dependent on this method: it was adopted in the poor law – its 'workhouse test'[9] – and under the Speenhamland system.[10] While the creation of national insurance in the early years of this century was clearly directed towards eliminating reliance on the poor law, it proved to be inadequate to cope with the massive unemployment between the wars, and through unemployment assistance the means test again became a regular feature of the welfare system.[11] Beveridge's aim was to reduce means-tested welfare to a minimum: he foresaw a gradual reduction in the numbers reliant on national assistance as resulting from the more comprehensive national insurance network.[12] His hopes were not to be realised both because national insurance benefits were stubbornly kept below the typical subsistence level and because the scheme failed to cope adequately with two social hazards, marital breakdown and long-term disability.[13] While expressing disquiet at the number of individuals in receipt of

4 See generally NCC Paper, n.6, above, at pp. 53–62.
5 Collard in Bull (ed) *Family Poverty* (2nd edn) p. 42.
6 *McCarthy* p. 139.
7 See pp. 483–484, below.
8 *Stevenson* n.8, above, ch 2; *Social Assistance* ch 3; Wilding in Alder and Bradley (eds) *Justice, Discretion and Poverty* (1976) ch 4; Titmuss 42 Political Q 113; and p. 454, below.
9 See generally Taylor in Martin (ed) *Comparative Development in Social Welfare* (1972) ch 3.
10 See generally, *Neuman*, ibid, ch 4.
11 Bruce *The Coming of the Welfare State* (4th edn) pp. 262–272.
12 Para 23.
13 Pp. 447–448, below.

national assistance, or supplementary benefit as it subsequently became, governments of the period 1960 to 1974 continued to tolerate and even extend the means-tested approach, through, for example, the introduction of family income supplement,[14] exemption from prescription charges,[15] rate and rent rebates.[16] The Labour administration of 1974–75 introduced a number of measures designed to reduce the numbers relying on supplementary benefit, notably earnings-related pensions, more generous family benefits, and non-contributory disability benefits.[17] But in 1978 some five million people were still dependent on supplementary benefit.[18] Faced with the huge cost of making major inroads into this figure (e.g. in 1979 terms it would cost some £2.2 billion a year in increased pensions to reduce it by one-half[19]), the Conservative government instituted a substantial reform of the system on the assumption that for the foreseeable future means-testing would continue to play a primary role in social welfare.[20] It had also to acknowledge that, as a result of increased unemployment as well as reductions made to contributory benefits, the numbers in receipt of supplementary benefits would rise, at least in the short term.[1]

iii Criterion of assumed needs

The alternative strategy of selecting circumstances or individuals whose needs are assumed rather than demonstrated is more widely favoured. Inevitably it raises the fundamental question, to which reference has already been made,[2] of what is comprehended by 'needs' and of whether their satisfaction is properly the subject of state intervention as opposed to individual initiative. If the hypothesis is accepted that the objective of a social security system is to make provision for economic insecurity, then it appears possible to list the typical causes of such insecurity, and to summarise, within an historical perspective, the forms of benefit developed in our system.

I CAUSES OF ECONOMIC INSECURITY

There have been several attempts to categorise the causes of insecurity,[3] perhaps the best known being that of Beveridge.[4] The variety of circumstances causing financial hardship is infinite. While some are regarded uncontroversially as properly the subject of individual initiative, for example, property loss through fire, theft or vandalism,[5] and others are endemic in a society of mixed cultures and values, for example, lack of ambition, idleness, personal extravagance,[6] there is a broad category of

14 Ch 13, below.
15 SI 1971/340, made under Health Services and Public Health Act 1968. See now SI 1981/501.
16 Housing Finance Act 1972 and SI 1974/421. For the revised scheme, to be introduced in 1983, see pp. 470–471, below.
17 White Paper, Better Pensions (1974, Cmnd 5713), paras 3–4; Report on Social Security Provision for Chronically Sick and Disabled People 1973–74, HC 276, para 58.
18 SBC Annual Report 1979, Cmnd. 8033, p. 62.
19 White Paper, Reform of the Supplementary Benefits Scheme (1979, Cmnd 7773), para 6.
20 Pp. 453–455, below.
1 White Paper, The Government's Expenditure Plans 1980–81 to 1983–84 (1980, Cmnd 7841), Table 2.12.
2 P. 5, above.
3 E.g. Turnbull, Williams and Cheit *Economic and Social Security* (4th edn) pp. 3–4; Krause 18 Zeitschrift f₃r Sozialreform 385, 509.
4 Paras 311–312.
5 Ibid, at para 312.
6 Rejda *Social Insurance and Economic Security* (1976) pp. 8–9.

hazards which in most industrially developed societies are regarded as appropriate for state intervention. They may be divided into three groups.

i *Earnings loss* According to Beveridge,[7] about 75 per cent of cases of financial need arose from interruption or loss of earning power: the main instances being personal disability, maternity, old age and unemployment.

ii *Loss of maintenance* Impairment of the breadwinner's income necessarily results in the problems of maintaining those who are dependent on him, but the same need can arise from the wage-earner's death, or the breakdown of the family through separation or divorce.

iii *Special expenses* In addition there are a number of special needs which may arise independently of the individual's employment history: they include the support of children, hospital and other medical needs, funeral expenses, education and housing costs.

2 BRITISH METHODS OF PROVIDING FOR ECONOMIC INSECURITY

It may be found helpful to give at this stage a brief guide to the British development of cash benefits for each of the above causes of economic insecurity. Full treatment is reserved for the chapter devoted to the benefits in question.

a *Earnings loss*

Industrial accidents and diseases[8] The first to benefit from special treatment were those injured or contracting diseases as a result of their employment. The Workmen's Compensation Act 1897 originally imposed responsibility on the employer. In 1946, the state assumed control, and benefits became payable under a national insurance scheme.

War pensions[9] Provision for those injured while active in the armed forces was developed in the nineteenth century by various procedures. During the First World War responsibility was assumed by a new Ministry of Pensions. The benefits available for lost earnings are mostly analogous to those available for industrial injuries, and though Orders in Council rather than legislation govern entitlement the system is now administered by the Department of Health and Social Security.

Unemployment[10] State unemployment insurance was introduced for certain industries in 1911, and was, during the interwar years, extended to other employments. The 1946 Act completed the process.

Sickness and invalidity[11] Compulsory sickness insurance was also introduced in 1911. Sickness benefit was payable for the first six months, and disablement benefit (at a lower rate) thereafter. The scheme was administered by the Approved Societies. These were abolished in 1946, as was the distinction between short-term and long-term benefits. In 1970, however, a new invalidity allowance was created to assist those incapable of work for more than six months, and in 1975 a pension was introduced for those in the same group who were unable to satisfy the contribution requirements.

7 Para 11.
8 Ch 8, below.
9 Ch 9, below.
10 Ch 3, below.
11 Ch 4, below.

From April 1983, employees will receive statutory sick pay instead of sickness benefit for the first eight weeks of incapacity.

Maternity[12] Maternity allowance, to provide compensation for lost earnings during confinement, was introduced in 1946.

Invalid care[13] In 1975 an invalid care allowance was created for relatives and others (though not wives) who would, but for the decision to look after an invalid, have been in paid employment.

Old age[14] A means-tested, non-contributory, pension was introduced in 1908 for those over 70 years. Contributory pensions became payable under the Widows', Orphans' and Old Age Contributory Pensions Act 1925 to insured persons between the ages of 65 and 70 (after which they passed to the non-contributory scheme). Under the 1946 Act, the system was replaced by a contributory retirement pension payable on *retirement* to a man over 65 and a woman over 60, and to a man aged 70 and a woman aged 65 irrespective of whether he/she was still at work. A non-contributory pension for those aged 80 and over was introduced in 1971.

b *Loss of maintenance*

Loss of earnings of breadwinner[15] Increases to the benefits listed above to assist in the maintenance of dependants were introduced unsystematically. They were added as an emergency measure to the unemployment insurance scheme in 1921, but soon thereafter became permanent. For workmen's compensation the principle was admitted as late as 1940, and no provision at all was made in the pre-war sickness and old-age schemes. Under the 1946 Acts dependency increases became payable as an addition to all earnings-replacement benefits.

Death of breadwinner Survivor benefits for widows and children of the deceased existed from the beginning in the war pensions[16] and workmen's compensation[17] schemes. The history of provision for other widows is complicated.[18] The 1925 Act introduced a contributory scheme under which all widows of insured persons received a pension. The scheme was restructured in 1946 so that after the initial widow's allowance, payable to all for six months, benefit continued at a substantial rate only if the woman had dependent children (widowed mother's allowance) or was aged 40 or over (widow's pension). Following further modifications in 1957 and 1970, widows between 40 and 50, without dependent children, received at a reduced rate. Where both parents of a child had died, an orphan's pension became, under the 1925 Act, payable to his guardian, and in 1946 the benefit was renamed guardian's allowance.[19] In 1957 there was introduced the child's special allowance to compensate a divorced woman whose former husband had been contributing to the maintenance of the child.[20]

12 Pp. 246–249, below.
13 Pp. 177–181, below.
14 Ch 5, below.
15 Pp. 364–371, below.
16 Pp. 357–360, below.
17 P. 330, below.
18 Pp. 227–236, below.
19 Pp. 251–258, below.
20 Pp. 236–239, below.

Outside the industrial injuries[1] and war pension[2] schemes there is no provision for widowers or other adult dependants.

Breakdown of marriage Beveridge's tentative suggestion that on the breakdown of a marriage, the woman should receive a temporary separation benefit[3] was not implemented, and apart from the child's special allowance mentioned above, there has never been a benefit specifically directed to cover this need. In 1974 the Finer Committee recommended the creation of a guaranteed maintenance allowance for one parent families[4] but the government has not yet committed itself to the principle, and hitherto the only advantage conferred on this group has been an increased rate of child benefit.[5]

c *Special expenses*

Family support[6] Family allowances were introduced in 1945, but were payable only to families with two or more children. In 1975 they were superseded by the child benefit which became payable to all families with children.

Maternity[7] The maternity grant, a lump sum intended to assist with the expenses incurred from confinement, was payable under the health insurance scheme of 1911; in 1982 it became a non-contributory benefit. The 1946 Act in addition provided for an attendance allowance to cover the costs of domestic help. The two benefits were effectively merged in 1953, and by the same legislation a new home confinement grant was introduced, on the assumption that home births were more expensive. The assumption proved to be unreal and this grant was abolished in 1964.

Funeral expenses[8] The need to avoid the humiliation of a pauper's funeral had for a long time stimulated the private insurance market, but the national insurance death grant was created only in 1946. At first there were complex rules to determine the persons entitled to receive the benefit. Since 1957 it became payable into the estate of the deceased person and in practice is therefore claimed by his personal representatives.

Disabled The need to provide additional resources for the severely disabled over and above the standard benefit was acknowledged first in the area of war pensions[9] and subsequently adopted in the industrial injuries scheme.[10] In both schemes there are allowances payable for constant attendance and for exceptionally severe disablement. Other disabled persons had to wait much longer for analogous provision. The attendance allowance, introduced in 1970, is payable to persons so severely disabled that they require frequent attention or constant supervision.[11] A mobility

1 Pp. 334–335, below.
2 P. 354, below.
3 Para 347.
4 Vol I, pp. 284–314.
5 P. 443, below.
6 Ch 11, below.
7 Pp. 249–251, below.
8 Pp. 239–244, below.
9 Pp. 355–357, below.
10 Pp. 323–326, below.
11 Pp. 171–177, below.

allowance was established in 1975 for those unable, or virtually unable, to walk.[12]

Others There are a large number of other cash benefits, conferred either nationally or locally, and concerned with such diverse needs as health, education and housing. These are not regarded as 'social security benefits' and do not come within the scope of this book.[13]

C Levels of cash benefit

i Flat-rate or earnings-related

Having determined the circumstances in which a cash benefit will be payable, the social security system must then decide on what principle that benefit will be calculated. Where it is intended as some replacement for the interruption or loss of earnings, the fundamental issue arises whether the benefit should be flat-rate or earnings-related. The main theoretical argument in favour of the latter approach is that based on free-enterprise incentives, a predictably popular creed in the United States of America:

> A free-enterprise society which stresses the rewards of individual initiative should also embody incentive principles: that the higher income secured by the higher-paid worker should be reflected in high social security benefits when he cannot work.[14]

Allied to this is the notion, popular with some trade unions, that benefit is merely a 'deferred wage' and therefore should reflect the collective bargaining process which determined the amount of that wage.[15] The argument is a compelling one in a wholly state-controlled economy where the state is both the employer and the provider of benefits, on the assumption that the initial wage level accords with the distributional dictates of its conception of social justice.[16] For this very reason it is opposed by those who argue that an earnings-related scheme reinforces differentials, on the whole dictated by market forces, and which may therefore be inequitable.[17] As the New Zealand Royal Commission has observed, 'differentials in market earnings are based on ability to take advantage of the market rather than on conditions of equity'.[18] This viewpoint is linked to the principle that the social welfare system should operate as a mechanism for redistribution rather than merely as a compensation for losses incurred through social risks.[19]

The debate may involve fundamental issues of social philosophy but typically the matter is decided by more pragmatic, political considerations. Increasing affluence, as manifest in post-war industrial societies, reinforces concern for the preservation of differentials.[20] As recent history on wages

12 Pp. 181–186, below.
13 Reference should be made to e.g. Pollard (ed) *Social Welfare Law* (1977).
14 Burns *Social Security and Public Policy* (1956) p. 40. See also Richardson *Economic and Financial Aspects of Social Security* (1960) p. 42, and *Walley* p. 145.
15 *Burns*, n.14, above, at p. 41; *George* p. 36.
16 *McCarthy* p. 173.
17 George *Social Security and Society* (1973) pp. 32–33, 51; Lister *Social Security: The Case for Reform* (1975), Poverty Pamphlet No 22, pp. 39–40; Kincaid *Poverty and Equality in Britain* (1973) pp. 236–237.
18 *McCarthy* p. 170.
19 Cf pp. 5–6, above.
20 *George* p. 36, and see the Swedish Report *Social Policy and How It Works* (1969).

policy has confirmed, there is no great popular desire for more equality.[1] This goes a long way to explain the gradual movement in British social policy away from Beveridge's flat-rate principle of subsistence to the earnings-related approach. Beveridge regarded protection of resources above the subsistence level as a matter for individual initiative.[2] In fact, national insurance benefits were for a long time regarded as inadequate, and there emerged a glaring disparity between those who were able and willing to augment state provision by occupational schemes, and those who were not. This image of 'two nations' was the inspiration for the Labour party's national superannuation programme of earnings-related provision, an approach which, while arguably ideologically inconsistent with the socialist objective of egalitarianism, nevertheless found a convenient justification in the notion that the privileges of the minority would be passed to the majority.[3]

The Conservative government's answer was the scheme of graduated pensions,[4] a solution which at the time appeared to be attractive but which turned out in practice to be a method more for replenishing the depleted National Insurance Fund than for providing an adequate income for old age.[5] The Labour party, returned to power in 1964 with national superannuation playing a prominent part in its election manifesto, nevertheless postponed full implementation of the programme in order that the matter be subjected to further study. As an interim measure, earnings-related supplements were introduced in 1966 for the short-term unemployment and sickness benefits.[6] In 1969 the full programme emerged as a Bill but was lost at the dissolution of Parliament. The new Conservative administration adopted the principle of earnings-related benefits but with a much more prominent role given to occupational schemes.[7] In 1975, the Labour party, once more in power, instituted its new earnings-related scheme, applicable to retirement, widow's and invalidity pensions.[8] This trend, which brought the British system closer to the Continental tradition of social insurance, dating from Bismarck's pioneering scheme,[9] was halted when the Conservative government abolished, as from 1982, the earnings-related supplements to the short term benefits for unemployment, sickness, maternity and widowhood. The questionable justifications advanced for this, one of the most major reversals of social policy in recent years, were that the supplements had been diminishing in value and effectiveness and that earnings could be more efficiently reflected in redundancy and sick pay schemes.[10] It was also seen as anticipating the taxation of the relevant benefits which the government planned to introduce at a later stage.[11]

1 See generally *George*, n.17, above, at pp. 73–79.
2 Para 302.
3 Labour Party Pamphlet *National Superannuation* (1957).
4 Pp. 218–219, below.
5 It provided a modest return for contributions and offered no protection against inflation: see *George* pp. 52–53; White Paper on National Superannuation and Social Insurance (1969, Cmnd 3883), para 20; Lynes *Pensions Rights and Wrongs* (1963), Fabian Pamphlet.
6 See first edition of this book, pp. 424–426.
7 Pp. 192–193, below.
8 Pp. 163, 193, 233, below.
9 Köhler and Zacher (eds) *The Evolution of Social Insurance 1881–1981* (1982).
10 Mr P Jenkin, Secretary of State, 980 HC Official Report (5th series), col 1660.
11 P. 34, below.

ii Determination of benefits according to need

Despite the initial move towards the earnings-related principle described in the last paragraph, there remains a substantial area of benefits which do not vary according to the previous earnings of the recipients. These include not only the flat-rate components in the standard income-replacement benefits for sickness, unemployment and retirement, but also those designed to accommodate special expenses or needs and those which are means-tested. For all within this category, decisions must be taken on the appropriate level of financial support. There has been a considerable amount of literature devoted to this question, much of it concerned with theoretical problems of assessing need and defining poverty. Less well treated are the political and other pressures which in practice operate on governmental decision-makers in this area.

a *Assessing needs*

The Beveridge objective, it will be recalled, was that of a minimum level of 'subsistence' on the basis of 'normal needs'. How were such needs to be assessed? Already earlier in the century some scientific measurement had been attempted, notably by Rowntree. He drew up a list of 'consumption necessities', e.g. food, clothing and housing expenditure.[12] The method was adopted by Beveridge as a guide;[13] he applied a variable of age and also added a margin for inefficiency in spending. In another respect, however, his criteria were more stringent than those proposed by Rowntree who had allowed a small amount for 'personal sundries', e.g. trade union subscriptions, newspapers, radio, beer, tobacco.[14] Of course, as determinants for individual needs, these models were deficient, in that they had to be based on perceived averages.[15] Any shortfall was therefore to be remedied by supplementary schemes based on detailed means tests. This handicap was only one of a number of aspects which were vigorously criticised by commentators in the 1950s and 1960s. The most comprehensive and widely publicised was that of Townsend.[16] He rejected any absolute objective notion of poverty based on subsistence requirements: he regarded it instead as a relative concept to be measured only by reference to the living standards of a particular society at a particular time. Others have stressed that poverty is a psychological state dependent on an individual's own expectations:[17] this may be conditioned by his own or his neighbour's previous level of earnings or standard of living. Finally there is the perspective which has regard to the effect of deprivation on the lives of individuals within the community – a state of 'virtual non-participation'.[18] In the latest large scale survey of poverty, Townsend sought to incorporate these broader dimensions by focusing not only on objective standards as reflected in data on the distribution of resources but also on individuals'

12 *Poverty – A Study of Town Life* (1901); *Human Needs of Labour* (1937).
13 Paras 217–232; cf *Harris* pp. 396–399.
14 *Human Needs of Labour* (1937) p. 61.
15 Cf *Social Assistance* para 5.5. The problem of variations in rent Beveridge felt to be particularly acute but after some hesitation decided that to make a separate award for household needs would be impracticable: paras 193–216.
16 (1954) Br Jo of Sociology 330 and (1962), ibid, 210. See also the collection of essays, Townsend (ed) *The Concept of Poverty* (1970).
17 E.g. Runciman *Relative Deprivation and Social Justice* (1966).
18 See Economic Council of Canada *The Challenge of Growth and Change* (1968). The definition won the approval of the NZ Royal Commission: *McCarthy* pp. 104–105. See also Goldthorpe in Wedderburn (ed) *Poverty, Inequality and Class Structure* (1974) ch 11.

perceptions of what constitutes poverty, the effect of environmental factors, and the relevance to deprivation of categorisation into one of the social minorities (e.g. single parents, non-whites, unemployed).[19]

b *Fixing scales of benefit*

Undoubtedly the data available on the needs of particular disadvantaged groups influence to a certain extent governmental decisions on the level of benefits, but it is important to appreciate that there are other factors which may play an equal if not primary role. Regard has typically been had not only to the level of prices but also to the general level of earnings: a system in which benefits are significantly above the incomes of the lower paid is likely to be politically unacceptable, if for no other reason than it is thought to have an effect on work incentives.[20] Similarly there are considerations of equity as between different categories of social security beneficiaries: this has led, for example, to differences between the contributory and non-contributory invalidity pensions,[1] even though these benefits may be directed towards identical needs. The level of social security payments is also necessarily dependent on the general economic policy pursued by government. The restraints imposed on public expenditure by the current Conservative administration which have resulted in reductions in the real value of some, particularly short-term, benefits are considered to be crucial to the control of inflation and the revitalisation of the economy.[2] However controversial this policy may be, it is at least consistent with general strategy and in this sense is 'rational'.[3] As such it is to be contrasted with the way in which decisions as to social welfare spending have been reached on purely political grounds: for example, the raising of benefits to a generous level in the year before a general election is by no means unknown. A remarkable feature of the past two decades or so has been the growth of pressure groups identified with particular categories of beneficiaries or disadvantaged people.[4] They have had a significant influence on decision-making, especially in the area of family[5] and disability[6] benefits.

c *The problem of inflation*

Inflation has such an immediate impact on the level of benefits that some special discussion is called for.[7] It would seem to be a cardinal principle of social justice that the real value of social security benefits, at least if directed at income maintenance, should be maintained. The principle has been widely acknowledged and in 1973 was explicitly incorporated in the law in the form of a statutory duty.[8] However the Thatcher government found the principle to be incompatible with its economic policy and

19 *Townsend*.
20 *McCarthy* ch 19; *Fisher* paras 35–36; Burns *Social Security and Public Policy* (1956) ch 4. The argument has been attacked by e.g. Kincaid *Poverty and Equality in Britain* (1973) ch 12 and Jordan *Poor Parents* (1974) ch 4.
1 P. 171, below.
2 White Paper, The Government's Expenditure Plans 1980–81 (1979, Cmnd 7746).
3 Though see the criticisms of the Commons' Social Services Committee, 3rd Report 1979–80, HC 702.
4 Donnison *The Politics of Poverty* (1982) pp. 126–134.
5 Banting *Poverty, Politics and Policy* (1979).
6 Walker in Jones (ed) *Yearbook of Social Policy 1975* pp. 204–207.
7 For general discussions see *Dupeyroux*; Pechman, Aaron, Taussig *Social Security: Perspectives for Reform* (1968) pp. 96–104; Wilson (ed) *Pensions, Inflation and Growth* (1974).
8 P. 410, below.

undertook to preserve the real value only of supplementary benefit. It was argued that other beneficiaries should help to shoulder the burden of the struggle to control inflation and reactivate economic growth.[9] To the extent that the principle is accepted there exists a choice of method for adjusting to inflation. In the first place, there is the question whether the determining criterion should be wage or price rises. To a certain extent this raises the same issues as those already described in relation to flat-rate or earnings-related benefit.[10] In periods of industrial growth, it is arguable that social security recipients should benefit from increased prosperity as reflected in earnings levels;[11] on the other hand, when rising prices outstrip earnings, for example during a wage freeze, there is a danger that those beneficiaries at the very bottom of the income scale will suffer the most.[12] There is considerable diversity of approach to these questions in the various social security systems:[13] in Britain the up-rating duty is imposed only with reference to price rises – the former rule that pensions were to be revised in the light of either prices or earnings, whichever was more advantageous to the beneficiary, was abrogated as being too expensive to implement.[14]

Secondly, it must be decided whether benefits are to be adjusted automatically through the application of some prices- or earnings-index. The main argument for indexing is that of certainty and the reduction of time-lag between the inflationary changes and modifications to the benefits scale.[15] The objection to the method is that it deprives government policy of flexibility – it may be desirable on grounds of social or economic justice to show preference for a particular group of individuals.[16] Opinions will differ as to whether this is an advantage or a disadvantage, but, more tacitly than openly, the ability to adjust to inflation in different proportions has played an enormously important role in British social policy since the Second World War. For political reasons, rights to benefit once created are difficult to remove, but if change is felt to be desirable it may be achieved by the indirect method of allowing the real value of benefits to be eroded through inflation. Two examples should suffice to illustrate the process. The differentials between industrial injury and non-industrial sickness benefit were, after much discussion, accepted in 1946.[17] Today the principle of discrimination is not so easily defended and successive governments have undermined it by maintaining the arithmetic differential rather than the proportional differential between the two schemes. The death grant was formerly regarded as important. Now priorities seem to have changed and the lump sum payable has remained the same since 1967.[18]

Thirdly, if legislation does not provide for the automatic adjustment of benefits, the question remains how frequently should up-rating take place and with reference to what period of time. The problem is not an easy one to solve for, on the one hand, it involves balancing the high administrative costs of frequent adjustments against social costs resulting from delayed

9 See the government's reply to the Social Services Committee Report, n.3, above (1980, Cmnd 8086), para 34.
10 P. 19, above.
11 Trinder in Young (ed) *Poverty Report 1975* p. 58.
12 Trinder in Willmott (ed) *Sharing Inflation?* (1976) chs 2–4.
13 *Wilson*, n.7, above, at pp. 374–378.
14 P. 410, below.
15 *Trinder*, n.11, above, at p. 54.
16 *Pechman, Aaron, Taussig*, n.7, above, at pp. 101–102.
17 P. 262, below.
18 P. 241, below, though see p. 244, below, for reform proposals.

up-rating; and, on the other hand, attempts to base adjustments on predictions of future rates of inflation are notoriously haphazard.[19]

iii Determination of earnings-related benefits

Some of the problems inherent in relating benefits to a claimant's previous earnings are of a practical nature; for example, the type of earnings of which account may be taken and the nature of proof required.[20] Others raise delicate questions of social policy. To achieve equity as between those, typically manual workers, whose optimal earnings are reached at an early age and those, typically white-collar workers, who reach their earnings peak later in life, it may be necessary to have regard to widely divergent periods as the basis for the calculation.[1] In systems where short-term benefits are earnings-related, regard is generally had to the claimant's wages in the period immediately before that of entitlement;[2] but for long-term benefits, it is thought fairer to take account of that period when the earnings were highest in real terms.[3] Neither of these approaches copes adequately with the case where an individual is rendered unemployable. It is rare indeed for a social security system (in contrast to the common law method of awarding damages for future lost earnings[4]) to base the earnings award on future hypothetical income, though the New Zealand Accident Compensation scheme has, to a certain extent, incorporated the principle.[5]

Between what limits of earnings should the base for the calculation be set? Of course, all schemes must set an upper limit: to allow a millionaire to claim as sickness benefit a proportion of all his lost earnings would offend notions of social justice. Typically, where contributions are earnings-related a ceiling is imposed to limit the liability of high salary-earners and at least on analogy with the principles of insurance (though not in accordance with redistributive objectives),[6] there should be a correlation between liability and entitlement. Imposing a lower earnings limit is not an invariable practice, but in terms of administrative costs it makes little sense to have regard to earnings below the subsistence level where the earnings-related benefit constitutes a supplement to a flat-rate benefit designed to provide maintenance at that level.[7]

The question of what proportion of lost earnings should be recoverable is not susceptible to a precise answer as it depends on several factors. First, there is the ubiquitous issue of work incentives: most systems regard 100 per cent indemnities as inadvisable on this ground. Secondly, regard must be had to the circumstances of the typical beneficiary: most people expect to tolerate some drop in living standards when no longer earning. On the other hand, the needs of some, particularly those disabled, may well

19 For an account of the relevant principles under SSA 1975, see pp. 411–413 below.
20 Pp. 404–409, below.
1 Cf White Paper, Better Pensions (1974, Cmnd 5713), p. iii.
2 E.g. in France: *Dupeyroux* p. 397. The rules for calculating the British earnings-related supplement which was abolished in 1982 meant that there was often a substantial gap between the period of reference and the period of benefit: see the first edition of this book, p. 426.
3 Thus the British pensions scheme has regard to the claimant's best 20 years of working life: p. 220, below.
4 Cf Ogus *Law of Damages* (1973) pp. 184–192.
5 Accident Compensation Act 1972, ss. 117–118.
6 Cf p. 26, below.
7 There is, however, a danger of regressive distribution if the threshold is set too high, as may have been the case when in 1966 the supplement became payable on earnings only above £9: Kincaid *Poverty and Equality in Britain* (1973) pp. 99–101.

increase. Thirdly, account has to be taken of tax considerations.[8] Finally, confusion may be created by overlap between components of benefit designed to compensate for lost earnings and those designed to supply needs. Our flat-rate system took account of family needs through the award of dependants' increases.[9] The method remained unaffected by the introduction of earnings-related benefits. The flat-rate system may not have been sufficient to guarantee the level of subsistence for which it was intended; the earnings-related benefits may appear to be ungenerous;[10] but since the family man is entitled to both, the relationship between his previous income, when working, and his financial situation on benefit involves highly complex calculations which will vary greatly between individuals.[11] A generous interpretation of this state of affairs would suggest that this compromise between divergent policy objectives creates a satisfactory redistributive effect in that those with large families stand to gain most and inequitable earnings differentials are corrected. A more cynical interpretation suggests that there is now no rational framework underlying the level of income support offered by our social security system, that different, half-hearted strategies have been instigated to respond to different political demands, and that the end result is an uncoordinated conglomeration of financial handouts.

D Financing of benefits

There are two main methods of financing social security benefits: by a fund the resources of which are earmarked exclusively for the purpose, and by general taxation. The first approach is often, though as will emerge largely misleadingly, referred to as the 'insurance' method. It may itself involve either flat-rate or earnings-related contributions.

i The insurance concept

At the centre of the British system is the contributory scheme. Until 1973 this was referred to as 'national insurance'. Following recodification, the concept has been replaced by the blanket term 'social security' which includes both contributory and non-contributory (but confusingly not means-tested) benefits.[12] Though the change may create ambiguities and will take some time to pass into general public use, it does have the merit of diverting attention from the notion of insurance which has for so long dogged our system. The preoccupation can be explained on historical grounds.[13] Private insurance to cover what are today regarded as social risks, e.g. retirement and premature death, was widespread in the nineteenth century[14] and greatly influenced the German and British developments in social welfare. The notion was consistent with the then prevailing liberal and individualistic philosophy.[15] Under the National Insurance Act 1911 benefit was seen to rest on past economic performance rather than

8 Cf pp. 33–34, below.
9 Pp. 364–371, below.
10 *Kincaid*, n.7, above, at pp. 99–101.
11 Cf *Walley* pp. 205–209.
12 See *Micklethwait* ch 3, and p. 38 below.
13 *Ogus* pp. 232–236; Burns *Social Security and Public Policy* (1956) ch 2; Titmuss *Social Policy* (1974) ch 7.
14 Gosden *Self-Help: Voluntary Associations in the 19th Century* (1973).
15 Cf pp. 2–4, above.

need per se, and bad risks, those employed in certain industries, women and children, were excluded. The scheme was popular with the middle classes for it seemed to encourage thrift and also with the working classes because it created, for the first time, a framework of legal rights to welfare.[16] As was pointed out by Beveridge,[17] and has since been stated by many others,[18] the analogy between the contributory schemes and private insurance is an inappropriate one. In a private insurance scheme premiums are based on the risk attendant on the particular circumstances of the insured person (age, sex, health, occupation, family commitments). Provided that the risk-rating is sufficiently precise, there can properly be no redistribution between insured individuals except in the very limited sense that those for whom the risk does not materialise will support those who become subject to it. The trend in social security legislation has been almost wholly against relating contributions to the degree of risk. Thus at an early stage unemployment insurance and workmen's compensation were extended to industries particularly sensitive to the hazards in question, without varying the rates of contributions.[19] The separate categorisation of married women has been ended by the 1975 legislation, at least for those marrying after 5 April 1977,[20] so that apart from minor exceptions,[1] all that remains is the very broad division between the employed, the self-employed and the non-employed.[2] There is, it should be noted, an argument that, at least as regards certain hazards which might be avoided by more careful management, employers' contributions should be 'experience-rated'.[3] But in Britain, in sharp contrast to some other systems,[4] the incentive or prevention objectives of social welfare have been kept distinct from the financing provisions.

The second important respect in which contributory schemes differ from private insurance relates to the actuarial basis of their administration. The latter must be actuarially sound in the sense that the benefits payable must be closely related to contributions already paid. A social security fund, on the other hand, may adopt the 'pay as you go' approach so that benefits payable at a particular time are related not to previous accumulations of contributions but to the finances made available from current contributions.[5] As a result there may be redistribution as between generations of insured persons. The history of the British scheme is revealing in this respect. Since the 1911 Act contributions have theoretically been 'actuarially related' to benefits;[6] this meant that contributions would be sufficient to meet the expected demand for benefit. But it rested on two assumptions:[7] that all insured persons would enter the scheme at the age of 16; and that there would be no increases in the rate of benefit. Both were,

16 Pinker *Social Theory and Social Policy* (1971) p. 90.
17 Paras 24–25.
18 E.g. *McCarthy* pp. 145–146; Richardson *Economic and Financial Aspects of Social Security* (1960) pp. 145–146; *George* pp. 45–46; McClements *Economics of Social Security* (1978) pp. 32–33; *Pearson* para 271.
19 Pp. 75 and 265, below.
20 Pp. 62–63, below.
1 Pp. 64–65, below.
2 P. 441, below.
3 *Burns*, n.13, above, at pp. 165–171; *Atiyah* pp. 572–576 and pp. 264–265, below.
4 *Kaim-Caudle* pp. 100–101, 231–232, 294–295.
5 See generally *Burns*, n.13, above, ch 10; *Richardson*, n.18, above, ch 5; Wilson *Pensions, Inflation and Growth* (1974) pp. 35–42.
6 See e.g. NIA 1946, s. 19(1)(a).
7 *George* pp. 50–51.

and continued to be, patently false. Beveridge's proposal that payment of the full rate of retirement pension should be gradually reached only after 20 years of contributions[8] was unacceptable to the post-war government,[9] and the need for constant revision of benefit to keep pace with rising prices rendered further inoperative the 'actuarial principle'. This is not to imply that it is devoid of influence on the present social security system. The new earnings-related component in the pensions scheme is closely related to the contributions actually made (as revalued on an annual basis) and will be payable in full only when the requisite number of years' contributions have been accumulated.[10] It is perhaps the single feature in the current system which truly reflects the insurance principle.[11]

ii Types of contribution

The first question arising under a contributory scheme is whether both employers and employees should participate. Some would argue that the problem is an unreal one, for whichever group pays the net effect is, in the long run, the same: an employer paying the contributions will pay less in the form of wages.[12] Most economists, however, regard the problem as a complex one:[13] the proportions in which the cost will be distributed between consumer (through higher prices), investor (through lower profits) and employee (through lower wages) will vary according to such factors as the elasticity of demand for the goods or services in question, the bargaining power of the wage-earners and the level of unemployment. To the extent that the burden falls on consumers, the distributional effect is likely to be regressive since lower-income groups spend proportionately more on consumption. Conversely, Beveridge contended that social security provision was one of the costs of production which should be reflected in the price of the product if competition was not to be distorted.[14] The other arguments he deployed for employers' contributions were of a more amorphous character: it is in the interest of the employer that his employees' health and welfare should be protected; he should feel 'concerned for the lives of those who work under (his) control, should think of them not as instruments in production but as human beings';[15] finally it was desirable that employers should have a basis for participation in the administration and strategies of the scheme. Whatever weight be given to these various factors, there is, it is submitted, one overriding consideration: a tax on employers is an easy source of revenue and one that tends to be politically popular.[16] This is reflected in the fact that since 1976 a surcharge on employers' contributions has been levied, having as its object nothing other than a general increase in government revenue.[17]

Should contributions be flat-rate or related to the ability to pay? The principle of the flat-rate contributions was as central to Beveridge's philosophy as that of flat-rate benefit: taxation according to capacity

8 Paras 240–243.
9 *Social Insurance* Part I, paras 84–86.
10 P. 220, below.
11 Kay and King *The British Tax System* (2nd edn) pp. 22–24.
12 Kincaid *Poverty and Equality in Britain* (1973) pp. 89–90.
13 Eckstein in Bowen, Harbison, Lester, Samuels (eds) *The American System of Social Insurance* (1968) ch 3; Pechman, Aaron, Taussig *Social Security – Perspectives for Reform* (1968) ch 8; *George* pp. 47–48.
14 Para 276.
15 Ibid.
16 *George* p. 48.
17 National Insurance Surcharge Act 1976.

> involves a departure from existing practice, for which there is neither need nor justification and which conflicts with the wishes and feelings of the British democracy. . . . Contribution means that in their capacity as possible recipients of benefits the poorer man and the richer man are treated alike.[18]

The rhetoric in this passage should not be allowed to cloud the real issue: the extent of redistribution to be admitted as a central objective of the system. Beveridge's commitment to the 'insurance' principle led him to forswear a substantial degree of redistribution which would have resulted from financing by progressive taxation methods, but the alleged dichotomy between on the one hand an 'insurance fund' and on the other hand earnings-related contributions is a false one. There is no reason, in principle, why the 'fund' or 'earmarked taxes' approach, even if used to finance flat-rate benefits, should not be combined with earnings-related contributions.[19] Beveridge's dogmatic preference for flat-rate contributions was indeed one of the reasons why his plan eventually failed. The burden on the lower paid of contributions sufficient to support an adequate level of benefits was too great. In the result a shift to a system of earnings-related contributions was inevitable. As has already been suggested,[20] the introduction of the graduated pension scheme in 1959 may be seen less as an attempt to provide a satisfactory degree of income maintenance for beneficiaries than a necessary boosting of the National Insurance Fund through earnings-related contributions. Once, however, the principle of earnings-related benefits had become widely accepted, adoption of an earnings-related method of contribution became mandatory and automatic: continuance of a flat-rate method would, of course, have resulted in redistribution in the wrong direction. The extension of contributions liability to individuals deriving profits from business undertakings, not only to those wholly self-employed but also to those combining salaried employment with self-employment,[1] brought the contribution assessment close to income tax, but several important differences remain: contributions are not payable on income unconnected with earnings or profitable undertakings; liability is imposed only up to a prescribed upper limit and is non-cumulative, in the sense that it is calculated on income for each week, whatever the amounts earned or not earned in other weeks; finally, the rate of contributions is uniform throughout the scale of income, whereas for tax it is progressive.

In determining the principles and level of contributions there is clearly a need to maintain equity as between different sections of the community. It is in this respect that difficulties have arisen in comparing the position of the self-employed with that of other contributors. The liability of the former increased substantially as a result of the changes described in the last paragraph and it was alleged that this was discriminatory when regard was had to the exclusion of this group from entitlement to unemployment and industrial injury benefits and the earnings-related elements in other benefits.[2] The government has sought to repudiate this charge, arguing inter alia that it is appropriate to compare self-employed contributions not with employees' contributions but with the aggregate of contributions for

18 Para 273.
19 Cf Lister *Social Security: The Case for Reform* (1975), Poverty Pamphlet No 22, pp. 39–41.
20 P. 20, above.
1 Pp. 55–56, below.
2 National Federation of Self Employed Policy, Strategy and Tactics Committee Research Paper No 3 (1977), and see pp. 78 and 266, below.

employed persons (i.e. from both employer and employee).[3] Against this it is said that many self-employed persons run small businesses with employees of their own and that therefore they must pay in addition to their own contributions those for their employees, without having the facility to distribute the cost through increased prices to the extent that it is possible for larger enterprises.[4] But this is tantamount to saying that the basis of employers' contributions should be a profits rather than a payroll tax and if this were accepted successful enterprises would be subsidising the less successful, a consequence not easily reconcilable with traditional social insurance objectives.

iii General taxation

Under Beveridge's plan and consistently thereafter, a place in the contributory scheme was alloted to general taxation but it was a small one (between 10 per cent and 20 per cent).[5] It was thought desirable not on redistributional principles but because it was clear that contributions recovered by the flat-rate method would otherwise be insufficient. In contrast, and, by definition, non-contributory benefits were to be financed from general taxation. In the post-war rationalisation, the scope for this approach was intended to be limited. True, family allowances constituted a major device for redistribution but Beveridge at least was equivocal on whether they should be financed from general taxation or from the national insurance fund, and in the end recommended the former on the pragmatic ground that the rate of contributions was already as high as the lower paid could afford.[6] Moreover, the other non-contributory scheme, national assistance, was regarded as a safety net, resort to which would gradually disappear. Paradoxically, while national assistance, and its successor supplementary benefit, increased in importance as more and more became dependent on it, the extent of redistribution through the family allowances scheme declined as the level of benefit did not keep pace with rising prices. The period 1970 to 1975, however, saw a very marked shift towards benefits financed from general taxation: family income supplement, payable to low wage-earners, the attendance allowance and the non-contributory invalidity pension, invalidity care allowance, mobility allowance, and family endowment was revitalised by the new child benefit. This trend was not to continue. Although the maternity grant became a non-contributory benefit, its real value declined; the proposal for a guaranteed maintenance allowance for single parent families was not implemented; and in 1981–82 the government reduced the Treasury supplement to the National Insurance Fund from 18 per cent to 13 per cent.

There has been much discussion, particularly by economists,[7] on the respective merits of contributory schemes and general taxation as methods

3 DHSS Discussion Document *The Self Employed and National Insurance* (1980), esp. para 26.

4 Research Paper, n. 2, above, at paras 36 and 39.

5 *Beveridge* para 282.

6 Para 415. For the background to FAA 1945 generally see the excellent study by Land in Hall, Land, Parker, and Webb *Change, Choice and Conflict in Social Policy* (1975) ch 9. See also *Harris* pp. 343–344.

7 Burns *Social Security and Public Policy* (1956) ch 9; *Eckstein,* n.13, above; *Pechman, Aaron, Taussig*, n.13, above; Culyer *The Economics of Social Policy* (1975) pp. 202–204; Rejda *Social Insurance and Economic Security* (1976) pp. 162–172; *Dupeyroux* pp. 164–180; *McCarthy* ch 16.

for funding social security benefits. The arguments are difficult to unravel because not only do the contributory schemes themselves contain several different strategies (employer or employee, flat-rate or earnings-related), but also because the effect of the methods on industrial growth and level of earnings is still highly controversial. The general consensus of opinion is, however, as one might expect, that the taxation approach is more redistributional, and therefore preferable on grounds of social justice, while the contribution approach tends to greater economic efficiency and therefore increased overall welfare. As important as these theoretical studies are, they do not feature much in the discussions within the political arena. Instead, we tend to be confronted with broad vague sentiments based on what the public allegedly wants. Thus Beveridge felt able to report that

> benefit in return for contributions, rather than free allowances from the State, is what the people of Britain desire,[8]

and the mood was echoed in the government White Paper which followed it.[9] The Crossman Paper on National Superannuation discredited arguments for a move to general taxation methods:

> people do not want to be *given* rights to pensions and benefits; they want to *earn* them by their contributions.[10]

The vacuity of these statements may be self-evident, but their very existence provides the key to understanding why in the British and other systems the contributory approach remains the primary strategy for social security provision: the popularity of the method rests on its psychological appeal.[11] People are prepared to subscribe more by way of contributions, which they see as offering returns in the form of personal and family security, than they would be willing to pay by taxation, which might be diverted to a wide variety of uses.[12] They are led to believe that because of their contributions to the scheme they are participating in its administration and may thus exercise closer political control on its development.[13] As has been observed, however, the same degree of public scrutiny should operate through the parliamentary supervision of public spending generally, if our political system is functioning properly.[14] Indeed, the Royal Commission in New Zealand regarded as an important reason for preferring the taxation approach the flexibility inherent in a system which does not tie funds down to a particular form of social welfare but rather allows different political administrations to take different views on social priorities.[15] One undeniably genuine and important factor is that of stigma. Sociologists have shown that we have been conditioned to bestow greater esteem on systems built on exchanges (benefits in *return* for contributions) than those incorporating unilateral transfers.[16] Nevertheless, one may question whether this is an attitude which our social security system should foster, and whether it is appropriate to perpetuate beliefs in what are, in

8 Para 21.
9 *Social Insurance* Part I, para 6.
10 White Paper, National Superannuation and Social Insurance (1969, Cmnd 3883), para 25.
11 *McCarthy* p. 158; *Eckstein*, n.13, above, at p. 51; Wilson *Pensions, Inflation and Growth* (1974) p. 28.
12 National Superannuation, n.10, above, at para 25.
13 *Beveridge* para 274.
14 *Culyer*, n.7, above, at p. 203.
15 *McCarthy* p. 158.
16 Pinker *Social Theory and Social Policy* (1971) ch 4; Pruger 2 Jo Soc Pol 289.

most respects, unreal differences between general and earmarked taxation. In the words of one commentator, the main effect of our 'contributory system' is 'to create confusion among the contributors/tax payers and fiscal illusion'.[17]

E Other forms of welfare provision

The policy-maker concerned to confer welfare on different groups within society has three broad strategies available to him. He may arrange for cash payments to be made (what we refer to as 'social security'), he may provide for benefits in kind (typically known as 'social services'), or he may exploit possibilities created by the fiscal systems, through e.g. tax reliefs. In this section we explore the relationship between social security and the other forms of welfare, and discuss some of the issues involved in the choice between the various strategies.

i Benefits in cash or in kind

Social welfare, as broadly construed, embraces a wide range of benefits in kind, among many others those for health, education and housing. On a simple view, these services may be regarded as complementary to, and independent from, the cash benefits which form the subject-matter of this book: cash benefits, it might be said, are designed for income maintenance, whereas the services are designed to fulfil other objectives of social policy. However, the relationship between the two is both more complex and yet, paradoxically, relatively neglected in the literature and governmental policy statements.[18] Three different approaches emerge from the three ideologies described in Part 1 of this chapter.

During the first period of public welfare, as represented by the poor law, attention was directed to poverty as a threat to order and stability.[19] As a remedial measure, the transfer of money was regarded as inappropriate since it neither guaranteed the protection of society nor did it constitute a sufficient incentive to avoid poverty. Moreover it was assumed that, almost as a matter of definition, people who were poor could not be trusted to use the money wisely.[20] The result was a combination of setting the poor to work and providing them with the minimum necessities of life in kind, the impotent through the system of 'poorhouses', the able-bodied through the workhouse, and the uncontrollable through penal institutions. Under the second, liberal individualist, approach, welfare is to be achieved through the operation of market forces and free enterprise.[1] Those substantially disadvantaged by poverty from participating fully in the system must be compensated by a degree of financial support. How that money is to be spent remains a matter of individual liberty and responsibility. Benefits in kind are thus reserved for those who are incapable of exercising that responsibility: the senile and the mentally handicapped.[2] This particular

17 *Culyer*, n.7, above at p. 204.

18 Cf International Social Security Association Studies and Research Nσ 6, *The Role of Social Services in Social Security* (1974); DHSS Report on Social Security Provision for Chronically Sick and Disabled People 1973–74, HC 276, paras 26–28.

19 Cf p. 2, above.

20 Report of Royal Commission on Poor Law (1834), pp. 276–277.

1 Cf p. 2, above.

2 Richardson *Economic and Financial Aspects of Social Security* (1960) pp. 51–52; Steiner *The State of Welfare* (1971) pp. 17–20.

philosophy continues to exert a strong influence on our welfare system, and, in particular, may be used to explain why in specified circumstances supplementary benefit is conferred in kind rather than cash.[3] Indeed, if the tenets of individualism are accepted, there is no reason why it should not be extended more widely to cover health services (as in most Western European systems[4]) and even education, through the provision of 'education vouchers'.[5]

The third collectivist approach is characterised by increased attempts at social integration and a very broad provision of social services.[6] While not opposed to income redistribution as such, the protagonists of this view place much greater reliance than the individualists on the extensive use of benefits in kind. The emphasis results from certain criticisms of the individualist philosophy. First, certain types of good, for example, health or education, are not proper subjects for the operation of market forces either because the social costs of mistaken decisions are too great or because, adopting a paternalist stance, it is not to be assumed that in such areas individuals always act as rational maximisers of their own welfare.[7] Secondly, the model ignores the causes of poverty; by the careful use of services to prevent as well as to react to social hazards, the problem of inadequate income may, in some cases, be avoided.[8] Thirdly, the income redistribution technique is less sensitive to specific needs and less personal in its administration – the individual guidance implicit in the social service model may both respond in a humane way to individual circumstances and at the same time encourage greater social activity and participation.[9]

Certain consequences of adopting the benefits in kind approach should, however, be noted: it is generally much more costly to administer than the simple provision of cash benefit; it distorts the price structure in that it induces greater consumption of certain goods;[10] and it creates problems for legal enforcement. An individual deprived of a cash benefit may without undue difficulty appeal to a tribunal, whereas his counterpart inadequately met by the social services may find that either the authority concerned was under no duty to provide the service, or if it was, that a court will not be prepared to enforce it.[11]

ii Social security and taxation

The relationship between the social security and taxation systems constitutes an important feature of the policy issues arising under social legislation.[12] There are three independent but related matters which call for

3 P. 573, below.
4 See Roemer *The Organisation of Medical Care under Social Security* (1969), ILO Studies and Reports No 73, and Martin (ed) *Comparative Developments in Social Welfare* (1972) ch 8.
5 See Culyer *The Political Economy of Social Policy* (1980) pp. 246–248.
6 Cf p. 5, above.
7 Titmuss *Commitment to Welfare* (1968) pp. 147–150; *Culyer*, n.5, above, ch 7.
8 DHSS Report, n.18, above, at para 27; Crosland *The Future of Socialism* (1961) pp. 145–146; Lebel in ISSA Studies and Research No 6, n.18, above, at pp. 126–127.
9 *Lebel*, n.8, above, at p. 125; DHSS Report, n.18, above, at para. 26; *Crosland*, n.8, above, at p. 148; *Titmuss*, n.7, above, at p. 150.
10 *Dupeyroux* pp. 228–231.
11 *Lebel*, n.9, above, at p. 125. Mandamus has been claimed but so far never granted for a breach of the duty to provide accommodation under the Housing (Homeless Persons) Act 1977.
12 See in general Atkinson 1 Jo Soc Pol 135–148, and Kay and King *The British Tax System* (2nd edn) ch 8.

discussion: first, the manner in which the tax system may, through its granting of reliefs, itself operate as a direct instrument of income support; secondly, the extent to which social security benefits are taxable, and the implications which this has on the degree of redistribution; thirdly, the desirability or otherwise of integrating taxation with social security.

a *Tax as an instrument for income support*

Since the introduction of progressive taxation in 1907 there has been what Titmuss has described as 'a remarkable development of social policy operating through the medium of the fiscal system'.[13] Most significantly this has taken the form of family support, through the granting of children's and other dependants' allowances[14] – the amount of income permitted to be accumulated before tax is imposed. If applied consistently throughout the tax structure, the system of reliefs has a retrogressive effect, for the value of the relief increases as the rate of tax increases. This fact added weight to the movement to introduce family allowances[15] – a benefit of equal value to all families. But, in 1945, it was not regarded as a sufficient reason for replacing tax relief by family benefits. It was felt that there was a difference of principle between the two systems. The Chancellor of the Exchequer had argued that while the family allowance was 'intended to reduce financial hardship arising from the maintenance of children . . . tax relief given in respect of children represents a recognition of the fact that the possession of children reduces the capacity to pay'.[16] The difficulty with the argument is that it confuses two different questions of equity: as between those with family commitments and those without, it is of course proper that the burden on the former should be reduced; but as between those with higher incomes and those less well endowed it is wrong that the former should gain a disproportionate advantage. It was this consideration which led in 1968 to a new, compromise, solution: the so-called 'claw-back'.[17] The amount by which family allowances were increased was in effect deducted from the individual's tax relief. This, in turn, was superseded by an arrangement under which the new child benefit, itself tax-free, replaced the relief on children. The implementation of this reform was, however, delayed when it became apparent that it involved a delicate problem of distribution *within* the family: while tax relief had increased the take-home pay of the breadwinner (usually the father), the cash benefit is normally paid to the mother.[18]

b *Tax liability of beneficiaries*

In the last paragraph we saw how the value of tax reliefs increases in proportion to the taxable income of an individual. If a social security benefit is not taxable, there is a similar problem, for its value will also vary according to the tax liabilities of the recipient. The consequent possibility of inequity as between different beneficiaries might be thought to be academic since most social security benefits are payable only when the

13 *Essays on the Welfare State* (2nd edn) p. 45.
14 There are also minor forms of tax relief for the blind and disabled; see Whiteman and Wheatcroft *Income Tax* (2nd edn) pp. 919, 945.
15 See Hall et al *Change, Choice and Conflict in Social Policy* (1975) pp. 199–202, and p. 421, below.
16 White Paper on Family Allowances: Memorandum by the Chancellor of the Exchequer (1942, Cmd 6134), p. 5. See also *Beveridge* para 422.
17 See generally Lynes in Bull (ed) *Family Poverty* (2nd edn) ch 10.
18 P. 437, below.

claimant has no earnings. But income tax liability is cumulative over the tax year and so a beneficiary who has sufficient income during the rest of the tax year to take him above the tax threshold will gain from the fact if the benefit does not form part of his taxable income. Quite apart from this problem of equity, such a situation may also give rise to significant work disincentives. First, with tax thresholds set at their currently low level, a beneficiary with a large number of dependants may be better off out of work than when employed.[19] The anomaly is increased if, as is often the case with white-collar workers who would otherwise be liable for a substantial amount of tax, support is forthcoming also from occupational schemes.[20] Secondly, the existence of the progressive system of taxation collected by the PAYE method means that during spells of unemployment or sickness an employee may be entitled to weekly refunds of tax paid on his anticipated annual earnings, thus creating a kind of 'parallel system of . . . benefits . . . calculated on the mythical basis that the worker, during his unemployment or sickness, had no social security income at all'.[1]

The policy of the post-war government was that all income-maintenance benefits[2] should be taxed. On grounds of impracticability the policy had to be reversed in 1949 with regard to the short-term benefits: beneficiaries could not be incorporated into the PAYE scheme and taxes had thus to be collected retrospectively; the recovery of millions of small debts by the Inland Revenue was uneconomic.[3] Given the circumstances then prevailing, the decision was not unreasonable. Since 1949, however, the situation has changed dramatically. On the one hand, the real value of benefits has increased so that the amounts involved are no longer negligible. On the other hand, the administration of tax and social security is more clearly integrated than it was – indeed, the records of taxpayers are now kept under their national insurance numbers. In 1980 the Conservative government announced its intention of extending taxation to most income-maintenance benefits.[4] Widow's benefits,[5] retirement and invalidity pensions were already taxable.[6] The contributory and supplementary benefits payable to the unemployed were added to the list in 1981,[7] though the measure was not brought into effect until July 1982. Statutory sick pay which, from April 1983, replaces entitlement to sickness benefit for short periods of incapacity will be taxable, but specific proposals have still to be made on other benefits hitherto exempt from tax.

c *Integration of tax and social security*

The perceived need both to rationalise the existing relationship between taxation and social security and to remove anomalies created by untaxed benefits was joined by a third force which saw in an integrated tax-welfare scheme the way to abolish poverty altogether. The movement which attracted considerable attention in the 1970s developed from three different sources. The first was located in the United States of America and

19 *Walley* p. 208; *Kay and King*, n.12, above, at pp. 110–115.
20 Houghton *Paying for the Social Services* (1968), IEA Occasional Paper 16, p. 29.
1 *Walley* p. 207.
2 Though anomalously not industrial injury benefit.
3 *Houghton* n.20, above, at p. 28, and see Report of the Committee on the Taxation of Pensions for Retirement (1954, Cmd 9063), paras 271–294.
4 Sir G Howe, Chancellor of the Exchequer, 980 HC Official Report (5th series), col 1460.
5 But not those payable under the war pensions scheme.
6 See Simon *Taxes* (3rd edn) para C4.122.
7 Finance Act 1981, s. 29.

was inspired by the conviction of some economists, notably Milton Friedman, that welfare is best achieved through competitive capitalism and by a reduction in state intervention.[8] Poverty, as inhibiting freedom or full participation in the economy, is to be eliminated, and the most efficient way of achieving this is to extend the tax system downwards so that those below the poverty level should receive instead of contribute – the negative income tax.[9] The system was more fully worked out by other American writers,[10] and a moderate version was adopted by the Nixon administration, though it failed to pass through Congress.[11] The second source comprised commentators on this side of the Atlantic. Less influenced, perhaps, by the ideological factors than by the methods proposed, they regarded as cumbersome and inefficient the coexistence of various benefit schemes, particularly when the tax system provided in effect a means-tested approach without stigma. The Labour party at one time dallied with the idea of using tax returns for national assistance claims.[12] Others proposed to adopt the American model of negative income tax.[13] A slightly less ambitious, but arguably more practical, plan to cover employed persons and national insurance beneficiaries was advanced by the Conservative government in 1972.[14] The Tax Credit scheme, as it was called, though in general endorsed by a Parliamentary Select Committee[15] never reached the stage of draft legislation and there are no signs of the idea being resurrected.

The third stream of influence extends back to 1943 when, as an alternative to the Beveridge plan, Lady Rhys Williams urged the adoption of a 'social dividend', the payment to all members of society of weekly amounts necessary for the ordinary needs of living.[16] This notion has been elaborated and modified by others,[17] and is associated with less dramatic versions of the same theme which would concentrate on universal and generous child or family endowment.[18] While the Child Benefit Act 1975, with its universal coverage and its replacement of tax allowances, can be seen as a step in this direction, the level of endowment falls far short of that envisaged by the advocates of the social dividend.[19]

There is not the space here to consider the details of the various proposals,[20] but the fundamental ideas are not hard to grasp and they raise difficult policy issues. The negative income tax involves an extension of

8 *Capitalism and Freedom* (1962).
9 Ibid at pp. 190–192.
10 See especially, Green *Negative Taxes and the Poverty Problem* (1967) and Theobald (ed) *The Guaranteed Income* (1967).
11 See generally Moynihan *The Politics of a Guaranteed Income* (1973).
12 Election Manifesto 1964.
13 Notably Lees, Lloyds Bank Rev, Oct 1967, 1–15 and a study group sponsored by the Institute of Economic Affairs, *Policy for Poverty* (1970), Research Monograph 20.
14 Green Paper, Proposals for a Tax-Credit System (Cmnd 5116).
15 1972–73 HC 341.
16 Rhys Williams *Something to Look Forward To* (1943).
17 Notably Brown and Dawson *Personal Taxation, Incentives and Tax Reform* (1969).
18 The most influential have been those of *Walley* pp. 191–202 (see also Bull (ed) *Family Poverty* (2nd edn) ch 9), and of the Child Poverty Action Group: see Field and Townsend *A Social Contract for Families* (1975).
19 See pp. 424–425, below.
20 The literature of the subject is immense. In addition to the works already cited see Atkinson *Poverty in Britain and the Reform of Social Security* (1969) ch 9; Barker in Bull (ed), n.18, above, ch 5; Atkinson *Tax Credit System and the Redistribution of Income* (1973); Meade Committee Report *The Structure and Reform of Direct Taxation* (1978) ch 13; Kay and King *The British Tax System* (2nd edn) ch 8.

existing tax schedules below a certain exemption level. If an individual's income falls above that level, he is taxed in the normal way; if it falls below, he receives a payment representing some proportion of the difference between his income and the exemption level. The level itself would be fixed according to socially acceptable variables, but on most proposals these would be confined to the size of the family and possibly the age of its members. The exclusion of other than economic criteria would mean that the traditional categories of the contributory benefit schemes (e.g. unemployment, sickness, retirement etc.) would be abandoned. The scheme would be administered principally by tax returns. If intended to be fully comprehensive, it would therefore be necessary to extend the system of income statements to those at present outside the tax structure, and would also involve the creation of additional machinery to cope with sudden changes in earnings and family circumstances. The social dividend proposal, on the other hand, would make use of the tax system only for the purpose of 'clawing back' resources from those who have sufficient to take them above the threshold; the dividend itself, assessed according to family needs, would be automatically paid. A universal tax credit system would have a similar effect: an individual would be given a tax credit according to family size and this would be set off against his tax liability if any. Those with insufficient income would be paid the credit in whole or in part. The Conservative proposal, it should be noted, was not universal in this sense as it would cover only those in employment.

The first advantage claimed for universal schemes is that they avoid the problems inherent in means-tested benefits of stigma and low take-up.[1] Secondly, it is argued that by abolishing all the various categories involved in the typical social security schemes the system would become at once more comprehensive and simpler; it would also focus on those in greatest need.[2] Such objectives are obviously appealing but it may be objected that elimination of the categories is neither possible nor desirable. To avoid abuse, it would presumably be necessary for the unemployed to register as available for work or be relieved from this obligation for a specific reason, e.g. sickness, retirement or family responsibilities, and thus for administrative purposes some categorisation is inevitable.[3] Further, it may be appropriate to differentiate between various categories of claimants on the grounds that their needs are not identical: it is not obvious, for example, that a man retired at 55 should be paid the same as someone considerably older, or that a disabled person should receive no more than if he had been made redundant.[4] Finally, no system of computerised assessment would be able to deal adequately with special circumstances which occur suddenly and which require immediate assistance so that some form of discretionary aid would have to complement the general scheme.[5]

The third advantage of the proposals would be the elimination of the work disincentives which arise from the lack of coordination in the present system between the tax threshold and entitlement to untaxed benefits.[6] Of course, those who support existing plans to tax benefits argue that these should go a long way towards solving the problem.[7] But quite apart from

1 *Lees*, n.13, above, at pp. 9–10. These problems are discussed at pp. 12–14, above.
2 *Lees*, n.13, above, at pp. 7–9, IEA Study, n.13, above, at pp. 35–36.
3 Meade Committee, n.20, above, at p. 293.
4 *McCarthy* pp. 162–163.
5 Green Paper, n.14, above, at para 1.
6 Ibid, para 103; cf. p. 34, above.
7 P. 34, above.

this, the proposals would create their own set of disincentives: financing the various schemes would impose a high marginal tax rate (e.g. 55–60 per cent)[8] on those whose income is above the break-even point. It has been concluded that 'both social dividend and negative income tax schemes require either unacceptably low guaranteed levels of social support or unacceptably high marginal rates of tax'.[9]

While the viability of the proposals can be seen thus to depend on a number of complicated financial and administrative questions, it should not be forgotten that attitudes are also coloured by ideological convictions.[10] Most of those arguing for integration between the tax and social security systems tend to see poverty as the difference between those below and those above a certain level of income and they therefore seek to guarantee to all members of society a standard of living at that particular level. Their opponents see poverty as a reflection of economic and social inequalities generally and fear that such a concentrated effort on the income question along would deflect attention from the more important objective of social and economic integration.

Part 3 Scope and structure of book

A Scope

The term 'social security' in legal and non-legal contexts carries a variety of meanings which must be carefully distinguished if ambiguity is to be avoided.[11] First, as one area of social policy it is used both in British and international sources to connote the measures necessary to secure the political and economic objective of freedom from want. It was in this sense that it was adopted by Beveridge,[12] and subsequently, under his influence, passed into international currency[13] within the auspices of such institutions as the International Labour Organisation[14] and the Council of Europe.[15] Secondly, as a legal term of art, it was admitted relatively late into British legislation and as such remains a source of some confusion.[16] In institutional terms, the Ministry of Social Security[17] later superseded by the Department of Health and Social Security,[18] was concerned with the national schemes of income maintenance: national insurance, family allowances, supplementary benefits and war pensions. But as used in the

8 *Kay and King*, n.20, above, at p. 119; cf Meade Committee, n.20, above, at pp. 271–276.
9 *Kay and King*, n.20, above, at p. 119.
10 Cf *Barker*, n.20, above, at pp. 65–69.
11 See, in general, *Micklethwait* ch 3; *George* ch 1; Rejda *Social Insurance and Economic Security* (1976) p. 9; Doublet *Sécurité Sociale* (5th edn) pp. 11–19; Kaufmann *Sicherheit als Soziologisches und Sozialpolitisches Problem* (1970) ch 3.
12 Paras 11–13, and 300.
13 There is, however, little uniformity on whether the expression, as used in international instruments, includes medical care and social assistance.
14 See Declaration of Philadelphia (1944), art 3(f) and Convention No 102 on Minimum Standards of Social Security (1952). See further, p. 624, below.
15 E.g. European Code of Social Security (1964). See further, p. 625, below.
16 *Micklethwait* ch 3.
17 Created by Ministry of Social Security Act 1966. To add to the confusion the Act whose primary purpose was the replacement of national assistance by the supplementary benefit scheme was subsequently renamed the Supplementary Benefit Act 1966 by SSA 1973, s. 99(18).
18 SI 1968/1699. For the history of the administrative changes see ch 14, below.

Social Security Acts of 1973 and 1975, and the subordinate instruments made under those Acts, the term is applied to those benefits which were formerly payable under the national insurance schemes (industrial and non-industrial) and which are now referred to as 'contributory benefits'[19] together with the non-contributory benefits for the aged, the disabled, mothers and guardians.[20] 'Social security' in this narrow legal sense does not include child benefit or the means-tested family income supplement and supplementary benefit. Thirdly, and paradoxically in the light of this development, in popular current usage it is often intended to refer solely to the means-tested supplementary benefit scheme.[1]

For the purpose of determining the scope of this book, we have adopted the institutional meaning. We are concerned to describe the law governing entitlement to such financial benefits as are administered by the Department of Health and Social Security, arising primarily from the following instruments (as amended):

Social Security Act 1975;
Supplementary Benefits Act 1976;
Family Income Supplements Act 1970;
Child Benefit Act 1975;
Naval, Military and Air Forces Service Pensions Order 1978.

B Structure

In the first part of the book (chapters 2 to 10) we deal with those benefits which are governed principally by the Social Security Act 1975. However, because of the close relationship between the industrial injury and war pension schemes, we have inserted our account of the latter within this part, notwithstanding that it is governed by Orders in Council, so that the two chapters (8 and 9 respectively) may be read consecutively. The rest of this part is concerned with the system of contributions (chapter 2) and those benefits entitlement to which depends on the fulfilment of contribution conditions, viz:

unemployment benefit (chapter 3), invalidity and sickness benefits (chapter 4), retirement pensions (chapter 5), widow's benefit, child's special allowance and death grant (chapter 6) and maternity allowance (chapter 7).

It also contains accounts of the non-contributory benefits payable under the Social Security Act 1975 (placed near those contributory benefits to which they most closely relate):

non-contributory invalidity pension, attendance, invalid care and mobility allowances (chapter 4), old age pension (chapter 5), widow's pension (chapter 6), maternity grant and guardian's allowance (chapter 7).

Finally, in chapter 10 there is a discussion of certain concepts which are common to several or most of the above benefits:

increases for dependants; marriage; cohabitation; residence and presence; hospital in-patients; imprisonment and detention in legal custody; public policy; Christmas bonus; the calculation of earnings; the uprating of benefits; overlapping benefits.

19 SSA 1975, Part II, ch I.
20 Ibid, ch II.
1 *Micklethwait* p. 26.

The next part treats the three schemes which are independent of the Social Security Act 1975, viz child benefit (chapter 11) and the means-tested supplementary benefits (chapter 12) and family income supplement (chapter 13).

The book concludes with matters arising in connection with all above-mentioned schemes: the administration of benefits (chapter 14), adjudication (chapter 15), and the impact on the British system of certain international legal obligations, notably those emanating from the European Economic Community (chapter 16).

Chapter 2

Contributions

Part 1 Introduction

In chapter 1 the various methods of financing social security benefits were considered, and it was seen how British policy has continued to favour the contributory approach. In this chapter we describe the liability to pay contributions and the general principles governing the fulfilment of contribution conditions. The basic concepts are derived from the insurance schemes existing before the Second World War but their character has since changed in several fundamental respects.

A Risk-related insurance

As has already been explained,[1] private insurance influenced the development of national insurance, and this is particularly evident in the early efforts of the state schemes to relate liability to the risks attached to particular categories of individuals or employments. The first unemployment insurance of 1911 covered only those trades in which the employment pattern was thought to be reasonably stable.[2] Moreover, employers of men who by the age of 60 had paid more by way of contribution than they had received by way of benefit were entitled to a refund.[3] This right lasted only until 1920, at which time also insurance coverage was extended to all manual workers engaged under a contract of service, and non-manual workers of a similar description whose income was below a certain level.[4] However, the principle of differentiation was not totally abandoned, for industries with particularly low unemployment might adopt their own special scheme and, with the approval of the Minister, opt out of national insurance,[5] an arrangement permitted for the finance and banking industries until 1946.[6] Unemployment insurance was extended to agriculture only in 1936 and then at special rates of benefit and contribution.[7] Other forms of insurance did not call for the same degree of differentiation but the health scheme was administered by Approved

1 P. 25, above.
2 P. 75, below.
3 NIA 1911, s.94.
4 UIA 1920.
5 Ibid, s.18.
6 See SR & O 1938/589 and 656.
7 UI (Agriculture) Act 1936.

Societies, who could offer by way of benefit in return for the nationally determined rate of contributions whatever they wished above the national minimum.[8] Finally, mention should be made of the low rates of contribution paid, and the even lower benefits received, by women on the ground that they were 'poor risks'.[9]

B Comprehensive insurance

One of the primary objectives of the Beveridge plan, and the legislation which implemented it, was to abolish such vestiges of the risk-related approach which remained, and to establish a fully comprehensive system in which all would share in supporting the burden of those subjected to the prescribed social risks:

> The term 'social insurance' . . . implies both that it is compulsory and that men stand together with their fellows.[10]

The policy gave rise to four important modifications of the pre-war schemes. First, compulsory insurance was extended to those previously above the income limits. Secondly, it included those substantially free from one or more of the social risks (e.g. civil servants in relation to unemployment) or with sufficient protection under their terms of employment (e.g. the police in relation to sickness and old age – though members of HM Forces in a somewhat analogous position were allowed to pay a lower rate of contributions[11]). Thirdly, the Approved Societies were no longer to administer health insurance, and the special arrangements for agriculture, banking and finance were also abolished. Finally, the self-employed were covered for all purposes except unemployment and industrial injury. The special status of women as such was also eradicated; instead, the legislation singled out for special treatment those who were married. They could opt out of insurance in their own right, and, if they elected to stay in, would pay lower contributions and receive lower benefits.[12] The comprehensive coverage was completed by the compulsory insurance of all remaining persons over 16 who were not gainfully employed: in return for their weekly contribution, they qualified for all benefits except those for unemployment, sickness and industrial injury.[13] Contributions could not, of course, be extracted from those on very low incomes and the problem was met by, on the one hand, exempting from liability (and also therefore from entitlement to all benefits) those whose income did not exceed £2 a week,[14] and, on the other hand, excusing from the payment of contributions, but nevertheless crediting for certain purposes, those unemployed or incapable of work or undergoing education or training.[15] While Beveridge's assumption was that many would participate in occupational schemes to lift their income above the standard subsistence rate of benefit, there was no question of using this as an argument to justify exemption from the national scheme. Different considerations were, however, to prevail when earnings-related pensions

8 P. 138, below.
9 P. 461, below.
10 *Beveridge* para 26.
11 P. 64, below.
12 P. 61, below.
13 NIA 1946, s.4(2)(c).
14 Ibid, s.5(1)(a)(iii).
15 Ibid, s.5(1)(a)(i)–(ii).

were introduced, first with the limited graduated scheme of 1959,[16] and subsequently with the more comprehensive approach of 1975.[17] In both cases, contributions to the state earnings-related element was voluntary in the sense that those with sufficient coverage elsewhere might opt out.

C Liability according to capacity

The policy issues raised by the nature of the contributions payable have already been discussed in chapter 1.[18] Here it is necessary merely to relate how the insurance system gradually evolved towards a principle of liability according to capacity to pay. Under the early schemes, flat-rate contributions of the worker were matched by those of his employer, generally on an equal basis,[19] and the fund was augmented by a grant from the Exchequer. Certain concessions were, however, made for low-wage earners; they paid a reduced contribution.[20] The principles were maintained under the 1946 reconstruction, except that the liability of the employer was somewhat lower than that of the employee.[1] The flat-rate approach, of which Beveridge was such an enthusiastic advocate, proved insufficient to finance benefits at the desired level and a shift to an earnings-related method became inevitable. Under the graduated pensions scheme, those contributing paid 4½ per cent of their earnings between £9 and £15, the employer being liable for a similar amount.[2] The hybrid system for those in employment of flat-rate and graduated contributions was replaced in 1973–75 by a single system of contributions paid on earnings between a much wider band, but with a reduction for those contracting out of the new earnings-related pensions scheme.[3] The assimilation to an income tax method of financing was taken even further by imposing on the self-employed, in addition to a flat-rate liability, a charge on profits and gains,[4] notwithstanding that the earnings-related supplements for sickness, maternity and widow's benefits continued to be unavailable to this group. In times when pay restraint was an important economic objective, it was politically easier to impose increased contributions not only on the self-employed but also on employers. So, in contrast to the position prevailing after 1946, the liability of the latter was set at a rate higher than that of employees.[5]

D Unity of administration

Before the co-ordinating legislation of 1946 there were in effect three independent insurance schemes: those for unemployment and for health, both dating from 1911,[6] and that for widows', orphans' and old age

16 Pp. 218–219, below.
17 Pp. 222–224, below.
18 Pp. 27–29, below.
19 Though not under the original national health scheme to which the employer paid 3d a week and the male employee 4d: NIA 1911, Sch 2.
20 See e.g. NHIA 1924, Sch 2.
1 The ratio was approximately 55–45: NIA 1946, Sch 1.
2 NIA 1959, s.1(1).
3 P. 52, below.
4 P. 59, below.
5 P. 55, below.
6 NIA 1911.

pensions established in 1925.[7] But the financing of the health and pensions schemes was amalgamated so that in practice each insured person had to maintain two insurance records, in the form of cards to which stamps representing weekly contributions were affixed. In 1946 the three schemes were replaced by a single national insurance system, with the weekly contribution stamp serving for all the contributory benefits. The independent industrial injuries scheme superseded the workmen's compensation legislation, which had imposed liability for compensation on the individual employer, but the contributions to this insurance fund were added automatically to those payable for employed persons under the main scheme. In 1973 the separate industrial injuries fund was abolished and henceforth benefits were financed by the ordinary National Insurance Fund. The introduction of earnings-related contributions necessarily made their calculation and collection more complicated and under the legislation of 1973–75 administration was simplified by combining the process with that of income tax assessment, notably for employed persons through the PAYE system.[8] The affixing of stamps to an insurance card remains only for the flat-rate contributions by the self-employed, and even they can be paid by direct debit from the contributor's bank or by National Giro.[9]

E Outline of system

The monies collected from social security contributions are neither used exclusively for the financing of social security benefits nor do they provide the funds necessary for all such benefits.

i *Social security benefits financed by contributions* All contributory benefits (formerly insurance benefits), viz those for unemployment, sickness, invalidity, widowhood, retirement (Categories A and B), child's special allowance, maternity allowance and death grant, and benefits for industrial injuries (including old workmen's compensation cases) are so derived.

ii *Social security benefits financed by general taxation* All remaining social security benefits are financed from the Exchequer, thus child benefit, family income supplement, supplementary benefits, war pensions and the non-contributory benefits under the Social Security Act 1975, viz attendance allowance, non-contributory invalidity pension, invalid care allowance, mobility allowance, guardian's allowance, maternity grant and Category C or D retirement pensions.

iii *Other purposes financed by contributions* The social security contributions are used partly to finance the National Health Service, the Redundancy Fund and the Maternity Pay Fund.[10]

The funds collected under the Social Security Act 1975 are derived from three sources: insured persons, employers and the Exchequer. The Exchequer contributes currently 13 per cent per year of the amount of all other contributions used for contributory benefits (i.e. excluding the sums payable for the National Health Service, the Redundancy and Maternity

7 Widows', Orphans' and Old Age Contributory Pensions Act 1925.
8 See generally, SI 1979/591, Part V.
9 Ibid, reg 54(3).
10 See SSA 1975, ss.1(1) and 134, as amended by Employment Protection Act 1975, SSCA 1981 and SSCA 1982.

Pay Funds).[11] Contributions from insured persons and employers are divided into four categories:

Class 1 Primary contributions from 'employed earners' and secondary contributions from 'employers and other persons paying earnings', both being earnings-related.
Class 2 Flat-rate contributions from self-employed earners;
Class 3 Voluntary flat-rate contributions from earners and others;
Class 4 Contributions payable on the basis of profits or gains arising from a trade, profession or vocation.

Part 2 describes the principles of categorisation, the methods of assessing liability and also the grounds on which persons may be exempt from contributions. In Part 3 we consider the position of married women, widows and other special categories of contributions. Finally, Part 4 is concerned with the contribution conditions which must be satisfied for entitlement to benefit and the rules to assist those otherwise unable to qualify.

Part 2 Classification of contributions

A General

This Part is devoted to the principles governing liability to pay contributions of Classes 1, 2 and 4 and entitlement to pay those in Classes 2 and 3. Under the pre-1973 legislation insured *persons* were categorised accordingly.[12] Under the new scheme, the classification is of *contributions*. The important reason for this change of terminology is that an insured person may now be liable to pay contributions both as an employed (Class 1), and as a self-employed, person (Classes 2 and 4). The law defining the various categories remains, however, substantially unchanged. In particular, regard must be had to the complex case-law distinguishing between employed and self-employed persons. In this connection, it is worth observing that adjudication of disputes as to classification and the fulfilment of contribution conditions is within the jurisdiction not of the normal statutory authorities, viz insurance officer, local tribunals and Commissioner, but of the Secretary of State.[13] A question of law arising from any such decision may be referred for final determination to the High Court (or in Scotland the Court of Session) either by the Secretary of State if he thinks fit or by a person aggrieved by the decision.[14] Many of the High Court decisions are of course published in the ordinary law reports, and for the period 1950–60, HMSO published selected decisions of the Minister on classification questions.[15]

11 SSA 1975, s.1(5), as amended by SSCA 1982, s.2. The figure can be varied by order by up to 2%: SSCA 1981, s.2(2).
12 NIA 1965, s.1(2).
13 SSA 1975, s.93: cf p. 583, below.
14 SSA 1975, s.94.
15 The 'M' Decisions. It is not clear why publication ceased in 1960.

B Primary Class 1 contributions

Class 1 contributions may confer title to any contributory benefit. The primary contributions of this class are payable by 'employed earners'.[16] An 'employed earner' is defined as

> a person who is gainfully employed in Great Britain either under a contract of service, *or* in an office (including elective office) with emoluments chargeable to income tax under Schedule E.[17]

The second alternative was added in 1973,[18] the intention being to correlate Class 1 contributors with Schedule E tax payers and thus to facilitate the collection of contributions through the PAYE system.

i Gainfully employed

For both alternative formulations, the contributor must be 'gainfully employed'. This replaces the phrase 'gainfully occupied' used in the earlier legislation.[19] The significance of the modification is unclear. A body of case-law had been built around the interpretation of 'gainfully occupied' for the purposes not only of the classification of contributors but also in relation to retirement pensions[20] and increases for dependants.[1] One possible view is that, in the light of different policy considerations, it was thought desirable to keep distinct the interpretation of the phrase in its various contexts. If so, this would justify the authorities approaching the changed statutory formula *de novo*. A more likely explanation is that the notion of 'occupation' was thought to be too restrictive when applied to the new category of 'office with emoluments'.[2] If this is correct, it should follow that the interpretation of the concept has remained substantially unchanged. The basic idea is that the contributor

> receives from his master under the contract of employment something by way of remuneration for the services which he is contractually bound to render to the master under the contract of service.[3]

Under the former legislation, it was important to determine what was to be regarded as 'remuneration'.[4] Under the new system the problem no longer arises because contributions are earnings-related and there is a body of rules, described below,[5] governing the nature and calculation of 'earnings' for this purpose.

ii Contract of service

The classification of individuals into employed and self-employed persons, as characterised by the distinction between a 'contract of service' and a 'contract for services', has been a regular legal conundrum and not only in social security law. The Social Security Act 1975 makes only a marginal

16 SSA 1975, s.1(2).
17 Ibid, s.2(1)(a).
18 SSA 1973, s.1(7).
19 NIA 1965, s.1(2).
20 Ibid, s.30(2), cf pp. 200–201, below.
1 NIA 1965, s.43(1)(b); cf p. 368, below.
2 Cf *R(P) 2/76*, para 22, R J A Temple, Chief Comr.
3 Per Slade J, *Vandyk v Minister of Pensions and National Insurance* [1955] 1 QB 29 at 38.
4 See, by way of analogy, the decisions on retirement pensions and dependants' increases: pp. 200–206, below.
5 P. 53, below.

effort to alleviate the problems by prescribing that 'contract of service' means

> any contract of service or apprenticeship, whether written or oral and whether expressed or implied.[6]

Resort must therefore be had to the case-law.[7] As implied above, decisions on the matter are not limited to social security law: many other legal consequences flow from the existence of a contract of service, for example, the right to a redundancy payment and the imposition of vicarious liability on the employer. The first question thus arises whether decisions on such other areas may legitimately throw light on the problem under discussion. On one view, the different legal consequences give rise to different policy issues, and it is therefore dangerous to cross legal boundaries.[8] It can be argued that a classification which only affects the reciprocal rights and duties of two persons, the employer and employee, does not involve the public interest,[9] which is clearly relevant in determining liability to pay social security contributions. There are also policy considerations which apply only in the social security context; for example, whether the nature of the occupation is such that insurance against unemployment and industrial injuries, exclusive to Class 1 contributors, is regarded as appropriate. But the better view appears to be that there are uniform answers to the problem.[10] When Parliament uses the term 'contract of service', it must be assumed to have in mind the traditional judicial interpretation of the phrase, and it would create great confusion and administrative inconvenience if an individual was an 'employee' for some purposes but not for others.

The principles governing the distinction between a contract of service and one for services are not easy to state for two reasons: first, because there are differing views on the extent to which the issue is one of law rather than of fact (and thus within the jurisdiction of the High Court or Court of Session);[11] secondly, because judicial views on the nature of the distinction have changed substantially over the years and there is currently no uniformly accepted criterion which can be applied to all cases.

The classical nineteenth-century test was one of supervision and control: 'a servant is a person subject to the command of his master as to the manner in which he shall do his work'.[12] The first High Court decisions under the National Insurance Act 1946 placed great reliance on this criterion,[13] but its limitations in the modern technological and commercial world soon provoked a more critical attitude. It was obvious in the first place that there could be little or no direct control over the work of a professional or skilled employee, such as a doctor working in a hospital,[14] a

6 Sch 20.

7 There are particularly valuable descriptions in Atiyah *Vicarious Liability* (1967) pp. 35–69, and Rideout *Principles of Labour Law* (3rd edn) pp. 1–15.

8 *Rideout*, n.7, above, at p. 11.

9 Thus, on such matters the court should not interfere with the parties' own classification: cf p. 49, below.

10 Cf *Atiyah*, n.7, above, at pp. 32–33.

11 See generally p. 585, below.

12 Per Bramwell B, *Yewens v Noakes* (1880) 6 QBD 530 at 532–533.

13 *Gould v Minister of National Insurance* [1951] 1 KB 731, [1951] 1 All ER 368; *Stagecraft v Minister of National Insurance* 1952 SC 288. That the 'control' theory still has considerable influence on the DHSS administration may be inferred from its use in the leaflets which are issued to members of the public. See e.g. NI 39: 'although not conclusive in itself the existence of a right of control is a strong indication that there is a contract of service'.

14 *Cassidy v Minister of Health* [1951] 2 KB 243, [1951] 1 All ER 574, CA.

theatrical or circus artist[15] or a political columnist,[16] nor where the employer was a corporate entity and the employee was of a high status, e.g. a company director.[17] Secondly, it is imprecise. The 'employer' of an independent contractor, for example, may reserve to himself the right to direct not only what is to be done, but in broad outlines how it is to be done.[18]

Dissatisfaction with the control test prompted Denning LJ (as he then was) to formulate a new criterion, whether the alleged employee was 'part and parcel of the organisation',[19] whether he was 'employed as part of the business, and his work is done as an integral part of the business'.[20] This approach, and an analogous test of 'economic reality' emanating from the United States Supreme Court,[1] have attracted some support.[2] They have the advantage of directing attention to the admittedly important issue of whose assets are involved in the undertaking and who stands to profit or lose on its outcome, but it can be objected that, though these are factors to be taken into account, they are no more decisive than was (or is) the control element. It has indeed become obvious, and is readily acknowledged in almost all recent cases on the subject,[3] that it is a question of having regard to a number of factors, any number or combination of which might be relevant in a given case. The mere reference to such factors does not, of course, indicate how they are to be deployed, or what weight is to be given to each. For the most part, judges have refused to be drawn on this issue, contenting themselves with the general proposition that the relative importance of the various factors will vary from case to case.[4]

Some of the more important factors, to which the Secretary of State should attribute such weight as in his discretion seems appropriate, may be described as follows.

a *Supervision of work* Though the control test has rightly been repudiated as the sole or decisive criterion, close and regular supervision of the work process clearly remains an important factor, especially for less skilled occupations.[5]

15 *Whittaker v Minister of Pensions and National Insurance* [1967] 1 QB 156, [1966] 3 All ER 531.
16 *Beloff v Pressdram* [1973] 1 All ER 241.
17 *Lee v Lee's Air Farming* [1961] AC 12, [1960] 3 All ER 420, PC; NB by virtue of his 'office', such a person is now a Class 1 contributor; p. 50, below.
18 E.g. *Construction Industry Training Board v Labour Forces* [1970] 3 All ER 220 (contract construction labourer); *Addison v London Philharmonic Orchestra Ltd* [1981] ICR 261 (orchestral musician); M25 (tailoring outworker); M48 (BBC interviewer).
19 *Bank voor Handel en Scheepvaart v Slatford* [1953] 1 QB 248 at 295.
20 *Stevenson, Jordan and Harrison v Macdonald and Evans* [1952] 1 TLR 101 at 111, CA.
1 *United States v Silk* 331 US 704 (1946). See also a dictum of Lord Wright in *Montreal Locomotive Works v Montreal and A-G* [1947] 1 DLR 161 at 164, PC.
2 Notably in *Market Investigations v Minister of Social Security* [1969] 2 QB 173, [1968] 3 All ER 732, and *Addison v London Philharmonic Orchestra Ltd*, n.18, above.
3 *Ready Mixed Concrete South East Ltd v Minister of Pensions and National Insurance* [1968] 2 QB 497, [1968] 1 All ER 433; *Willy Scheidegger Swiss Typewriting School (London) Ltd v Minister of Social Security* (1968) 5 KIR 65; *Construction Industry Training Board* case, n.18, above; *Rennison & Son v Minister of Social Security* (1970) 10 KIR 65; *Challinor v Taylor* [1972] ICR 129, NIRC; *Ferguson v John Dawson & Partners (Contractors)* [1976] 3 All ER 817, [1976] 1 WLR 346, CA.
4 E.g. Cooke J in *Construction Training Board* case, n.18, above, at 224; Bridge J in *Rennison's* case, n.3, above, at 68.
5 *Amalgamated Engineering Union v Minister of Pensions and National Insurance* [1963] 1 All ER 864, [1963] 1 WLR 441; *Construction Training Board* case, n.18, above; and compare, e.g. two decisions on timber fellers, M34 and M40.

b *Powers of appointment and dismissal* This factor is often mentioned,[6] but if it refers to the appointment and dismissal of the person whose classification is in question it is generally helpful only in indicating to which of two 'employers' he is contractually engaged.[7] More important for the present purpose is whether the 'employee' has the power to employ a substitute to assist him or to whom his duties may be delegated.[8]

c *Form of remuneration* The typical contract of service provides for regular remuneration in the form of a salary or wages, while the typical contract for services prescribes a fixed sum for the job. The distinction accords well with the 'economic reality' theory. In the words of Lord Widgery CJ, 'if a man agrees to perform an operation for a fixed sum and thus stands to lose if the work is delayed, and to profit if it is done quickly, that is the man who on the face of it appears to be an independent contractor working under a contract for services'.[9] While the method of payment may thus provide some guideline,[10] it is not a very reliable criterion. There have been cases where an individual paid on the basis of time has been held to be self-employed.[11] Conversely, the courts have not shown great reluctance to find a contract of service where the employee is paid a fixed rate for the job[12] or where both parties have sought artificially to transform the nature of the contract by converting wages into a different form of payment, e.g. the so-called 'lump'.[13]

d *Duration of contract* Again, there is a tendency for the duration of contracts for services to be determined according to a specific undertaking, or at least a specific (and often short) time period, whereas a contract of service will often be of an indefinite period. The factor has been adverted to in some cases,[14] but it can at best play a subordinate role. There are many occupations where the pattern is reversed.[15]

e *Equipment* The question whether the 'employee' is bound to use his own plant or equipment is perhaps of greater assistance. It too is related to the 'economic reality' idea. A worker who uses his own equipment is investing his own resources in the undertaking and thus there is a strong argument for not categorising him as an employee.[16] But the criterion carries force only where such an investment is on a large scale.[17] In many occupations it is customary for an employee under a contract of service to provide his own tools.[18]

6 E.g. by Lord Thankerton in one of the first judicial attempts to enumerate the relevant factors: *Short v Henderson* (1946) 62 TLR 427 at 429, HL.
7 E.g. *Mersey Docks and Harbour Board v Coggins and Griffith (Liverpool) Ltd* [1947] AC 1, [1946] 2 All ER 345, HL; M5; M14; M35; and see p. 54, below.
8 *Ready Mixed Concrete* case, n.3, above; M23; M25; M34; M48.
9 *Global Plant v Secretary of State for Health and Social Security* [1971] 3 All ER 385 at 391.
10 E.g. *Gould's* case, n.13, above; *Construction Training Board* case, n.18, above; *Challinor v Taylor*, n.3, above.
11 E.g. *Ready Mixed Concrete* case, n.3, above.
12 E.g. *Market Investigations* case, n.2, above.
13 *Ferguson v John Dawson*, n.3, above; and see further p. 50, below.
14 E.g. *Argent v Minister of Social Security* [1968] 3 All ER 208, [1968] 1 WLR 1749; M48.
15 E.g. *Stagecraft v Minister of National Insurance* 1952 SC 288; *Construction Training Board v Labour Forces* [1970] 3 All ER 220; *Ready Mixed Concrete* case, n.3, above; *Willy Scheidegger* case, n.3, above.
16 *Midland Sinfornia Concert Society Ltd v Secretary of State for Social Services* [1981] ICR 454 at 467.
17 E.g. *Inglefield v Macey* (1967) 2 KIR 146; *Ready Mixed Concrete* case, n.3, above.
18 E.g. M14.

f *Place of work* If the work is undertaken at the individual's own premises he is more likely to be regarded as self-employed. If, on the other hand, the occupation is peripatetic (e.g. a sales representative) the question is usually resolved by the degree of supervision exercised by the 'employer'.[19]

g *Obligation to work* Under some contracts, it is left to the person 'employed' to decide how much, if at all, he is to work. If so, it is very persuasive evidence that he is self-employed.[20] The case must be contrasted with that in which the individual is given an option whether or not to work for a specific period (e.g. a day) and in which, if he so agrees, he is under an obligation to perform specific tasks during that period. Such a contract will often be one of service.[1]

h *Discretion on hours of work* A related idea is that the more discretion an individual has as to when he performs his duties, the more likely he is to be classified as self-employed.[2] But the criterion is in no way decisive, and there are instances of contracts of service being held to confer such a broad discretion.[3]

The question remains as to the weight, if any, to be given to any attempts by the parties themselves conclusively to determine the issue by a declaration in the contract. It is a question which has assumed, in recent years, increased importance, in the light of efforts, particularly in the construction industry, to avoid the financial burdens of the employment relationship arising from both fiscal and social security legislation.[4] The approach taken by the judiciary has, with one notable exception,[5] been uniform. While regard must be had to the obligations arising from the explicit terms of the contract to see whether they are more consistent with a contract of service or a contract for services, the exact terminology in fact used may be of no legal significance.[6] Two alternative justifications have been advanced for this approach. Some judges purport to search for the true 'intentions' of the parties which, they argue, are to be found in the obligations arising under the contract rather than from the exact terminology employed. The problem with this argument is that in many cases the terminology will indeed represent the intentions of the parties.[7] To overcome this objection other judges have relied overtly on public policy

19 E.g. *Ready Mixed Concrete* case, n.3, above; *Willy Scheidegger* case, n.3, above; *Market Investigations* case, n.2, above; *Global Plant* case, n.9, above; M22; M33.

20 E.g. *Willy Scheidegger* case, n. 3, above; *Addison v London Philharmonic Orchestra Ltd*, n.2, above; M9; M11; M17; M47; M51; M65.

1 E.g. *Market Investigations* case, n.2, above.

2 E.g. *Willy Scheidegger* case, n.3, above; M9; M11; M13; M17; M25; M44.

3 E.g. *Market Investigations v Minister of Social Security* [1969] 2 QB 173, [1968] 3 All ER 732; *Global Plant* case, n.9, above; M40; M60.

4 See the Report of The Committee of Inquiry under Professor Phelps Brown into Certain Matters Concerning Labour (1968, Cmnd 3714); Davis and Freedland *Labour Law* (1979) pp. 463–470; and de Clark 30 MLR 6. The social security implications of the problem were fully discussed in the House of Commons Standing Committee E Debates on the Social Security Bill 1973, cols 83–122.

5 Lawton LJ in *Ferguson v John Dawson* [1976] 3 All ER 817 at 827–829, CA.

6 *Inglefield v Macey*, n.17, above; *Ready Mixed Concrete v Minister of Pensions and National Insurance* [1968] 2 QB 497, [1968] 1 All ER 433; *Construction Training Board v Labour Forces* [1970] 3 All ER 220; *Rennison v Minister of Social Security* (1970) 10 KIR 65; *Ferguson v John Dawson* (majority judgments), n.5, above; *BSM (1257) Ltd v Secretary of State for Social Services* [1978] ICR 894; *Young and Woods v West* [1980] IRLR 201.

7 See Lawton LJ in *Ferguson v John Dawson*, n.5, above, at 828.

considerations. 'I think that it would be contrary to the public interest if . . . the parties, by their own whim, by the use of a verbal formula, unrelated to the reality of the relationship, could influence the decision . . . .'[8] If there is such a principle of public policy, it is one which is both obscure in its origins[9] and vague in its scope. The efforts of the judiciary to distinguish between genuine and bogus self-employment have been matched by a variety of responses from the legislature. On the one hand, the increased burden of contributions under Classes 2 and 4 resulting from the 1973–75 legislation has made the status of self-employment less attractive.[10] On the other hand, the Secretary of State has been given power to make regulations for securing that the liability to pay Class 1 contributions is not avoided by 'abnormal practice' in relation to the payment of earnings.[11]

iii Office with emoluments

The second category of primary Class 1 contributions was introduced to ensure that Class 1 was co-extensive with tax liability under Schedule E. The term 'office' has never been rigourously defined but it has been employed in tax legislation for well over a century and has acquired there a special meaning, to distinguish it from 'employment', 'profession' or 'vocation'.[12] In the leading case of *Edwards (Inspector of Taxes) v Clinch*,[13] a majority of the House of Lords recently reaffirmed that it involves 'a degree of continuance (not necessarily continuity) and of independent existence: it must connote a post to which a person can be appointed, which he can vacate and to which a successor can be appointed'.[14] So, someone appointed to conduct a public inquiry on a temporary, ad hoc and personal basis was not an 'office-holder'. There are, of course, many honorary office-holders, but if emoluments – statutorily defined as including 'salaries, fees, wages, perquisites and profit'[15] – are payable, they are chargeable to income tax under Schedule E and thus give rise to liability for Class 1 contributions. Examples of those who have been so classified are: company directors (where there is no contract of service),[16] trustees and executors,[17] consultants under the National Health Service,[18] accountants acting as company auditors,[19] solicitors acting as company registrars.[20]

iv Classification by the Secretary of State

As has already been indicated, decisions on the classification of individual cases are in the first instance made by the Secretary of State. Quite independently of this jurisdiction, he has reserved to him two further powers, the exercise of which affects the classification of an individual or

8 Per Megaw LJ in *Ferguson v John Dawson*, n.5, above, at 825.
9 Some authority may be found in the landlord/tenant case of *Addiscombe Garden Estates v Crabbe* [1958] 1 QB 513, [1957] 3 All ER 563, CA.
10 See pp. 59–60, below.
11 SSA 1975, Sch 1, para 4(c)–(d).
12 See e.g. Simon *Taxes* (3rd edn) para C4.113.
13 [1981] 3 All ER 543 (Lords Edmund-Davies and Bridge dissenting).
14 Per Lord Wilberforce, ibid, at 546.
15 Income and Corporation Taxes Act 1970, s.183(1).
16 *McMillan v Guest* [1942] AC 561, [1942] 1 All ER 606.
17 *Dale v IRC* [1954] AC 11, [1953] 2 All ER 671, HL.
18 *Mitchell and Edon v Ross* [1962] AC 814, [1961] 3 All ER 49, HL.
19 *Ellis v Lucas* [1967] Ch 856, [1966] 2 All ER 935.
20 *IRC v Brander and Cruickshank* [1971] 1 All ER 36, [1971] 1 WLR 212, HL.

an occupation. Under the first, intended to counter the practice of 'lump' payments by means of which employers and employees collaborate in an attempt to avoid Class 1 contributions, he may

> where he is satisfied as to the existence of any practice in respect of the payment of earnings whereby the incidence of earnings-related contributions is avoided or reduced by means of irregular or unequal payments, give directions for securing that such contributions are payable as if that practice were not followed.[1]

A rather unhappy feature of this provision is that it appears to confer an absolute discretion, there being no right of appeal to the High Court or other authorities. The second, of a more traditional nature, confers on him the power to shift earners in prescribed occupations from one class to another.[2] In some cases, the power will be exercised where there is genuine doubt as to the appropriate classification of a given occupation. In others, it will be a conscious act of policy to extend or reduce insurance cover where this is deemed appropriate in the light of the social needs and circumstances of the occupation in question.[3] Perhaps the most important issue is whether an occupation, otherwise to be categorised as Class 1, should be excluded from unemployment benefit, and, conversely, an occupation, otherwise characterised as Class 2, should be so included. One advantage accruing from the 1973 alignment of Class 1 with Schedule E tax liability is that the number of occupations transferred from one class to another has been substantially reduced.[4] The prevailing Categorisation of Earners Regulations fall into two groups.

a *Employments treated as Class 1*[5] These contain four occupations: (a) office cleaners, (b) certain part-time lecturers, teachers and instructors,[6] (c) ministers of religion receiving a stipend or salary, (d) employment by a spouse for the purposes of that spouse's employment, — and the general group of those working under an agreement with an agency where the agency is paid by the 'employer' (excluding cases where the employee works at the employer's house or on other premises supervised by him and and where he works as an entertainer or as a model).

b *Employments disregarded*[7] The second group comprises employments which are excluded from both Classes 1 and 2, viz employment by a member of the family in a private home occupied by both the employer and employee which is not employment for the purposes of the trade or business of that employer; self-employment, where this is not the individual's ordinary employment; employment as a returning or counting officer in an election or referendum; and employment in this country in connection with the Visiting Forces Act 1952.

There is another set of Regulations which extend and restrict the concept of employed earner's employment for the purposes of the industrial injury scheme.[8] This is considered below in chapter 8.[9]

1 SI 1979/591, reg 22.
2 SSA 1975, s.2(2).
3 The principle has been made explicit by the National Insurance Advisory Committee in its various pronouncements on classification issues: see e.g. its Report of Share Fishermen 1947–48 HC 137, and on Actors, Artistes and Entertainers (1952, Cmd 8549).
4 For the pre-1973 Regulations, see SI 1972/555.
5 SI 1978/1689, Sch I, Part I.
6 For details see ibid, para 4.
7 Ibid, Part III, as amended by SI 1980/1713.
8 SI 1975/467.
9 P. 266, below.

v Residence or presence

The Act refers to gainful employment in Great Britain.[10] The more detailed conditions as to residence and presence are contained in the Contributions Regulations.[11] In a subsequent chapter, the meaning of such concepts as 'resident' and 'ordinarily resident' which are common to other areas of the law is considered.[12] Here it will be sufficient to state the rules for primary Class 1 contributions.[13]

(1) The major condition is that at the time of employment the earner is resident or present in GB – temporary absences being disregarded – or is then ordinarily resident in GB.

(2) If, however, he is not normally resident or employed in the UK, but, in pursuance of employment which is mainly abroad for an employer whose place of business is also outside the UK, he works for a time in GB, contributions are payable only when he has been continuously resident in GB for 52 contribution weeks. The same proviso applies also to other non-residents who, on vacation from full-time studies abroad, are in GB on temporary employment in some way connected with their studies and to those working in GB as apprentices for foreign masters.

(3) Even if an employee is working abroad, he may still be liable to contribute if he is ordinarily resident in GB, was resident there before the commencement of the employment and (most important of all) his employer has a place of business in GB. The liability exists only for the first 52 contribution weeks of the foreign employment.

vi Age

To be liable, the earner must be over 16[14] and under pensionable age (65 for men, 60 for women).[15]

vii Calculation of contributions

Those with very low earnings are exempt from liability to contribute. The threshold is supplied by the statutory lower earnings limit,[16] a figure fixed annually by the Secretary of State and roughly equal to the basic state pension[17] (in 1982–83, £29.50 per week). Persons with earnings above the threshold pay a specified percentage of all earnings up to an upper earnings limit,[18] which is about seven times the lower limit (in 1982–83, £220 per week). The percentage (in 1982–83, 8.75 per cent) is determined by the Secretary of State, having regard to the current liabilities of the National Insurance Fund, but legislation is required if he wishes to increase a previous year's rate by more than ¼ per cent.[19] Those opting out of the state

10 SSA 1975, s.2(1).
11 SI 1979/591.
12 Pp. 391–393, below.
13 SI 1979/591, regs 119–120.
14 SSA 1975, s.4(2)(a).
15 SSPA 1975, s.4(1), though secondary contributions are payable in respect of employment above the relevant ages.
16 SSA 1975, s.4(1)(a).
17 DHSS Discussion Document, *The Self-Employed and National Insurance* (1980), para 15. Originally it was intended that it should approximate to one-quarter of average earnings: White Paper, Strategy for Pensions (1971, Cmnd 4755), para 40.
18 SSA 1975, s.4(1)(b).
19 Ibid, s.122(6), as amended by SSA 1980, Sch 1, para 13.

earnings-related pension scheme pay $2\frac{1}{2}$[20] per cent less on earnings between the lower and upper earnings limits[21] (they pay the normal rate on earnings below the lower limit) and, as will be seen,[1] there are reductions for certain women and some other categories of contributors.

The earnings on which the calculation is based are the individual's gross remuneration from his employment or employments.[2] This is deemed by legislation to include sick pay,[3] maternity pay and certain other payments made by employers under the Employment Protection (Consolidation) Act 1978.[4] Without specific authority, it is regarded by the DHSS as also including payments to cover travel between home and work.[5] However, the following items are disregarded.[6]

(1) payments on account of a person's earnings, comprising sums on which contributions have already been made;
(2) holiday payments where a number of employers contribute to a central holiday fund (as in the construction industry);
(3) gratuities not paid directly or indirectly by the employer;[7]
(4) payments in kind;
(5) payments to or from trustees;
(6) pension payments;
(7) VAT payable on earnings;
(8) fees received by ministers of religion not forming part of the stipend or salary;
(9) travelling expenses paid to disabled persons;[8]
(10) payments under profit-sharing schemes;
(11) redundancy payments;
(12) reimbursement of expenses incurred in the employment.

If husband and wife are jointly engaged in employment and the earnings therefrom are paid jointly, the amounts of earnings upon which the calculation of contributions is based are the same as those assessed by the Inland Revenue for the purposes of income tax.[9]

C Secondary Class 1 contributions

i Designation of contributors

Secondary Class 1 contributions are payable by 'employers and other persons paying earnings'.[10] The statutory definition of the contributor

20 2.15 per cent after 6 April 1983: SI 1982/493.
21 SSPA 1975, s.27(2).
1 Pp. 63–65, below.
2 SSA 1975, s.3(1), and Sch 1, para 1; SI 1979/591, reg 18. Where a person is engaged in both contracted-out and non-contracted-out employment, he pays the contracted-out rate on so much of his earnings in the contracted-out employment as do not exceed the upper earnings limit, and the non-contracted-out rate on any remainder of the aggregated earnings up to that limit: SSA 1975, Sch 1, para 1A, added by SSA 1980, Sch 1, para 16.
3 SSHBA 1982, ss.23 and 37.
4 SS(MP)A 1977, s.18, as amended by Employment Protection (Consolidation) Act 1978, Sch 16, para 29, and SI 1977/622, reg 2. The other payments covered are: arrears paid under an order for reinstatement; pay under an order of continuation of employment; and remuneration paid under a protective award.
5 See Leaflet NP 15, para 21.
6 SI 1979/591, reg 19.
7 See for discussion NIAC Report on Draft Contribution Amendment Regulations (1980, Cmnd 8117).
8 Under Disabled Persons (Employment) Act 1944, s.15.
9 SI 1975/591 and see Tiley *Revenue Law* (3rd edn) paras 9.20–9.37.
10 SSA 1975, s.1(2).

depends on the status of the earner: if he works under a contract of service, the secondary contributor is his employer;[11] if he is engaged in an office with emoluments, it is either 'such person as may be prescribed in relation to that office', or if no such person is prescribed 'the government department, public authority or body of persons responsible for paying the emoluments of the office'.[12] There is little to add to the provisions concerning an office-holder. As regards employment under a contract of service, the principles elaborated under that head should assist in determining not only the existence of such a contract, but also the parties to it. Where it is clear that an earner is employed under a contract of service, but unclear with which of two parties the contract was made, the issue should be resolved by answering such questions as: who supervised the work? who paid the employee? who had the right to appoint and dismiss him?[13] Cases of doubt, and cases where the party legally categorised as an employer under a contract of service is regarded as an inappropriate secondary contributor, may be regulated by the Secretary of State's power to transfer liability to another prescribed person.[14] Under current regulations:[15]

(1) An office cleaner is employed by the person for whom the work is done, unless he/she is supplied and paid by an agency, in which case the agency is the employer.
(2) In other cases, where an employee renders personal services under an agreement with an agency, the agency is treated as the employer.
(3) Where the earner is employed in a company which has gone into voluntary liquidation but which carries on business under a liquidator, the person holding the office of liquidator at the time of the employment is treated as the employer.
(4) A barrister's clerk is treated as being employed by the head of his chambers.
(5) In respect of Anglican ministers of religion, the secondary contributions are payable by the Church Commissioners; for other ministers, by the administrators of the fund from which the minister's remuneration is paid.

Where an earner is employed under two or more independent contracts of service, and is paid by each employer an amount equal to or exceeding the lower earnings limit, both will be liable to contribute. However, if the earnings in one or more of the employments are lower than that limit, and the relevant employer carries on business in association with another employer, the earnings may be aggregated to achieve the necessary liability and the contributions are then payable by each of those employers on a proportionate basis.[16]

ii Residence

Liability for secondary contributions arises only where the party otherwise liable is resident or present in Great Britain or has a place of business there.[17] The same regulation optimistically adds that even if these

11 Ibid, s.4(4)(a).
12 Ibid, s.4(4)(b).
13 Atiyah *Vicarious Liability* (1966) pp. 160–161; and see Lord Porter in *Mersey Docks and Harbour Board v Coggins and Griffith (Liverpool) Ltd* [1974] AC 1 at 17. Two reported decisions of the Minister, M14 and M35, by implication, apply these criteria.
14 SSA 1975, s.4(5)(b).
15 SI 1978/1689, Sch 3.
16 SI 1979/591, reg 13.
17 Ibid, reg 119(1)(b).

conditions are not met an employer may pay the contributions 'if he so wishes'.

iii Amount

The employer remains liable for secondary contributions even after the employee has reached pensionable age and for this reason is himself not liable.[18] In other respects, the secondary contributor's liability is contingent on that of the primary contributor, who must thus have earnings above the lower limit, and the basis of calculation is similar: a specified percentage (in 1982–83, 12.7 per cent) of earnings — calculated according to rules already described[19] – up to the upper limit, with a reduction of 4½ per cent on earnings between the lower and upper limits for contracted-out employments.[20] Reductions are also made for special categories,[1] including registered dock workers, who are excluded from the state redundancy scheme.[2] It should be noted that the secondary contributor's liability includes the so-called National Insurance Surcharge (in 1982–83, 2.5 per cent). This has nothing to do with social security: it was introduced in 1976 as a simple method of levying extra revenue for general government purposes, and the amounts so derived are paid into the Consolidated Fund.[3]

D Class 2 contributions

Contributions under Class 2 may confer title to any contributory benefit except unemployment benefit, and the earnings-related additional components in pensions.[4] They are payable by self-employed earners[5] and differ from Class 1 contributions in three important respects: since *ex hypothesi* there is no contract of service, there is for each employment only one contributor; the contribution is payable on a flat-rate basis; a self-employed person who is not liable to contribute because, for example, his earnings are too small or he does not satisfy the residence conditions may pay voluntarily.

i Persons liable

A self-employed person is defined as

> a person who is gainfully employed in Great Britain otherwise than in employed earner's employment (whether or not he is also employed in such employment).[6]

a *Combinations of employments*

The negative and rather confusing formulation means that if a person is in a gainful employment for which Class 1 contributions are not payable[7] he is

18 SSPA 1975, s.4(1).
19 P. 53, above.
20 SSPA 1975, s.27(2). From 6 April 1983, the reduction is 4.1%: SI 1982/493.
1 Pp. 64–65, below.
2 SI 1979/591, reg 133 (reduction by 0.2%).
3 National Insurance Surcharge Act 1976, s.2(1).
4 SSA 1975, s.13(1), (3).
5 Ibid, s.1(2).
6 Ibid, s.2(1)(b).
7 This includes the single case where the Secretary of State has prescribed that someone employed under a contract of service shall nevertheless be treated as a self-employed earner: SI 1978/1689, Sch 1, Part II.

necessarily self-employed[8] even though he may concurrently and independently be employed in a Class 1 employment. The liability to pay under the two classes (and as we shall see also under Class 4) was a major innovation of the Social Security Act 1973. The justification for the new approach is not immediately apparent but may readily be inferred from general policy considerations. The acceptance of an earnings-related principle for contributions naturally led to the conclusion that a proportionate part of a self-employed person's profits should be payable whether or not he was also employed under a contract of service: hence Class 4. But as will be seen, it was thought too expensive administratively to impose such a charge on profits below a certain figure.[9] The flat-rate contribution under Class 2 is therefore fixed so that it roughly represents the same percentage of that figure as the Class 4 contribution does of liable income above it.[10]

b *Gainful employment*

The shift in terminology from 'gainfully occupied in employment' to 'gainfully employed' has already been the subject of comment in relation to Class 1 contributions.[11] As was suggested there, the authorities on the interpretation of the earlier formulation should be used as guidelines for the term currently employed. In the present context, the matter is of more than academic interest, for while there is no liability to pay where earnings are below a certain level, the self-employed earner if 'gainfully employed' may in such circumstances voluntarily contribute. Thus an individual undertaking a new enterprise will be *entitled* to pay Class 2 contributions as soon as he is 'gainfully employed', notwithstanding that his current failure to make substantial profits exempts him from *liability* to pay. 'Gainfully occupied' under the former legislation was held not necessarily to imply the making of a net profit on an enterprise.[12] Thus in relation to self-employment, it was said that

> the question is not to be posed at any particular time, has he in fact received some net profit from his activities . . . but does he hold himself out as being anxious to become employed for purpose of gain?[13]

The answer to this latter question is a matter of fact for the determining authority. But assistance may be derived from decisions on analogous issues within other areas of social security law, notably in relation to retirement pensions.[14]

c *Continuing employment*

The boundaries of self-employment are not always easy to determine. To a certain extent, the answer will be supplied by the 'gainfully employed' criterion discussed in the last paragraph. To reinforce the notion that regard should be had to an individual's endeavours over a substantial period rather than to short-term and spasmodic profit/loss accounting, the Regulations prescribe that where a person is a self-employed earner (or is treated as such)

8 Unless disregarded, p. 51, above.
9 DHSS Discussion Document, *The Self-Employed and National Insurance* (1980), paras 8, 39.
10 Ibid, para 18.
11 P. 45, above.
12 *Vandyk v Minister of Pensions and National Insurance* [1955] 1 QB 29.
13 Per Slade J, ibid at 38.
14 Pp. 200–201, below.

the employment shall . . . be treated as continuing unless and until he is no longer ordinarily employed in that employment.[15]

d *Residence*

A self-employed earner is liable to pay contributions only if he is either ordinarily resident in Great Britain or was resident there for a period of at least 26 of the immediately preceding 52 contribution weeks.[16] Where he is not liable under these rules an earner may nevertheless voluntarily contribute.[17]

e *Age*

The contributor must be over 16 years[18] and under pensionable age (men 65, women 60).[19]

ii Exceptions

There are two grounds on which a self-employed person may be excepted from liability to pay contributions: inability to earn, and low earnings. As regards the first, he must show that throughout the week for which the exception is claimed (excluding Sunday or an equivalent rest day), he received sickness, invalidity, industrial injury benefit, unemployability supplement, invalid care or maternity allowance, or was in prison or detained in legal custody.[20] An exception for low earnings has existed ever since self-employed persons were compulsorily insured in 1946,[1] the justifications being to exclude occasional profit makers and to reduce administrative expenditure. The minimum earnings figure (for 1982–83) is £1,600 a year. Earnings, for this purpose, means 'net earnings' from the employment,[2] and is effectively such income as is chargeable to income tax under Schedule D:[3] thus from gross earnings may be deducted expenses necessarily incurred in connection with the employment.[4] In furtherance of this policy of integrating contributions and tax liability, the regulations adopt the Inland Revenue rule of allowing assessments to be based on earnings from a preceding tax year.[5] Earnings for a particular year are treated as less than the threshold if, in the preceding year, the individual's earnings were less than that amount and there had since been no material change of circumstances, or if in the year for which exception is claimed the earnings are expected to be less than that amount.[6] The onus is on the self-employed earner to claim exception, and if he is successful he will be granted a certificate of exception. When an exception is granted on either of the two grounds specified in this paragraph, the self-employed person may voluntarily pay contributions (either of Class 2 or of Class 3).[7]

15 SI 1978/1689, Sch 2.
16 SI 1979/591, reg 119(1)(d). For 'resident' and 'ordinarily resident' see pp. 391–393, below.
17 But only if he is either present in GB, in the week in question, or if abroad, had been resident there and had paid Class 1 or 2 contributions for three years immediately preceding his departure: SI 1979/591, regs 119(1)(c) and 121.
18 SSA 1975, s.7(1), as amended by Education (School-leaving Dates) Act 1976, s.2(4).
19 SSPA 1975, s.4(2).
20 SI 1979/591, reg 23.
1 See in general, NIAC Report on Liability for Contributions of Pensions with Small Incomes (1955, Cmd 9432).
2 SI 1979/591, reg 25(2).
3 See Tiley *Revenue Law* (3rd edn) chs 13–16.
4 *Tiley*, n.3, above, ch 13.
5 *Tiley*, n.3, above, paras 13.70–13.96.
6 SI 1979/591, reg 25(1)(b).
7 Ibid, regs 23(3) and 26(b).

iii Amount

Whether contributions are mandatory or voluntary, the amount is the same: the flat-rate payment in 1982–83 of £3.75 per week. There may, however, be introduced under regulations a special, higher, rate to cover exceptional cases where individuals are treated as self-employed earners but are not liable to pay Class 4 contributions.[8] At the time of writing, no such regulation has been introduced.

E Class 3 contributions

Beveridge's conception of social insurance was a comprehensive one – all of working age were to be included. Under his scheme, as implemented in the 1946 legislation, there was to be a third class of *compulsory* contributions, for those who would need provision for medical treatment, retirement and funeral expenses, and who were not in a gainful occupation but were of working age.[9] Typically included were students, unmarried women engaged in unremunerated domestic work, those retiring early under an occupational pension scheme, and persons in receipt of private income. Of course they must have had resources to pay contributions, and so there were exemptions for those below a minimum income level.[10] This class of contributions, so defined, was abolished by the 1973 Act. The new Class 3 allows only for *voluntary* contributions, and these may be paid either by non-employed persons or those contributing in Classes 1 or 2, but with deficiencies in their contribution record. They may enable a person to qualify only for widow's benefit, retirement pensions (Categories A and B), child's special allowance and death grant.[11] The amount of such contribution is the flat-rate sum, in 1982–83, of £3.65.

i Persons entitled to contribute

The contributor must be over 16[12] and under pensionable age (65 for men, 60 for women),[13] and with some exceptions resident in Great Britain during the year for which he makes his contribution.[14]

ii Making up a reckonable year

The 1975 Act prescribes that:

> payment of Class 3 contributions shall be allowed only with a view to enabling the contributor to satisfy contribution conditions of entitlement to benefit.[15]

As will be seen, for those benefits for which Class 3 payments may count, a year of contributions will only qualify towards entitlement if a minimum number of contributions has been made. At the end of each contribution year a Class 1 contributor is sent a statement of his account indicating any shortage, and how many Class 3 contributions will be necessary to make up

8 SSA 1975, s.7(4).
9 Paras 310 and 317.
10 See NIA 1946, s.5(1)(a)(iii).
11 SSA 1975, s.13(1).
12 Ibid, s.8(1).
13 SI 1979/591, reg 28(1)(e).
14 Ibid, reg 119(1)(e). Those abroad can contribute on the same conditions as are prescribed in relation to Class 2 voluntary contributions: n.17, p. 57, above. For 'residence' see pp. 391–393, below.
15 SSA 1975, s.8(2).

a reckonable year. Class 2 contributors with an incomplete record may, as already indicated, voluntarily pay additional contributions of that class, but if they wish to secure entitlement only to the more limited benefits available to Class 3 contributors, they may in the alternative make up the number with additional payments of the latter class. There are rules to prevent an individual making unnecessary contributions, e.g. where his record is complete for a given year, or where he will be credited with contributions for that year.[16] If such payments have nevertheless been made, the contributor is entitled to a refund,[17] though he may, if he prefers, have the extra contributions appropriated to satisfy conditions for another tax year.[18]

F Class 4 contributions

It was evident that if the self-employed were to make earnings-related contributions to the National Insurance Fund, this in practice could be achieved only by integrating assessment and administration with the fiscal system.[19] A fourth category of contributions was therefore created which would effectively coincide with tax liability under Schedule D of the Income Tax Acts. Entitlement to benefit, however, is established by reference only to contributions of Classes 1, 2 or 3; Class 4 is simply the most convenient means of securing earnings-related contributions from those paying Class 2 contributions. The principle of coincidence with tax liability is stated in the Social Security Act thus:

> Class 4 contributions shall be payable in respect of all annual profits or gains immediately derived from the carrying on or exercise of one or more trades, professions or vocations, being profits or gains chargeable to income tax under Case I or Case II of Schedule D . . . and the contributions shall be payable (a) in the same manner as any income tax . . . and (b) by the person on whom the income tax is (or would be) charged, in accordance with assessments made from time to time under the Income Tax Acts.[20]

For the nature and extent of this liability, then, reference should be made to the standard texts on taxation.[1] What follows is an account of those aspects of the assessment which are peculiar to Class 4 contributions.

i Persons liable

The condition of residence in the United Kingdom is that applied under the Income Tax Acts,[2] but in contrast to that legislation, liability for contributions does not extend to earners who are under 16 or over pensionable age.[3] As with income tax, a husband and wife may either aggregate their income or be assessed separately. In the case of the latter, the wife's separate assessment will be treated as the base for her contributions.[4] If income is, however, aggregated, as under tax law, the

16 SSPA 1975, s.5(1) and SI 1979/591, reg 28.
17 Ibid, regs 32–33.
18 SSA 1975, s.8(2)(a) and SI 1979/591, reg 30.
19 For the policy considerations relevant to the liability of the self-employed, see pp. 28–29, above.
20 SSA 1975, s.9(1).
1 E.g. Tiley *Revenue Law* (3rd edn) chs 13–16.
2 *Tiley*, n.1, above, ch 38.
3 SSA 1975, s.9(8) as amended by SSPA 1975, Sch 5.
4 SSA 1975, Sch 2, para 4(1).

husband will be liable to pay contributions on his wife's profits and gains, though they will nevertheless be regarded as her contributions.[5] In the case of partnerships, as under tax law, each partner is liable according to his share of the profits,[6] but contributions are not payable by those liable to tax as trustees, administrators, executors and other nominal holders of property.[7]

A person charged for income tax under both Schedule E and Schedule D, because he is both employed under a contract of service and derives profits from a trade or business, for that reason will also be liable to pay contributions of both Classes 1 and 4, provided that in either case his earnings or profits exceed the relevant lower limit. Some difficulty is caused where tax and social security liability do not correspond in this way. Thus, while actors, musicians and those working for agencies pay Class 1 contributions, their earnings or profits are nevertheless chargeable to tax under Schedule D. The solution provided by the regulations is to deduct from the profits and gains chargeable to Schedule D, the amount of earnings on the basis of which the Class 1 contributions were assessed, so that liability for Class 4 will be attracted only if the remainder exceeds the threshold.[8] Conversely, a person paying Class 2 contributions but whose earnings are chargeable to tax under Schedule E, will be liable for Class 4 at the same rate as other self-employed persons, though in his case liability is deferred until the end of the relevant tax year and any payments will thereafter be recovered by the DHSS and not the Inland Revenue.[9]

ii Amount of liability

In 1982–83, the amount payable is 6.00 per cent of profits and gains between £3,450 and £11,000 per year chargeable under Schedule D. Account must therefore be taken of such deductions and reliefs as are there provided,[10] but the following tax reliefs do not apply for the purposes of Class 4 contributions:[11] personal allowances;[12] payments under annuity contracts and trust schemes;[13] the carrying forward of losses;[14] the payment of interest.[15] Someone liable for both Class 1 and Class 4 contributions will not have to pay, in aggregate, more than the maximum which would have been payable on contributions of a single class.[16]

Part 3 Special categories

A Married women and widows

i General

The policy issues relevant to social security discrimination between men and women were described in chapter 1.[17] Here we trace the history of the

5 Ibid, para 4(3).
6 Ibid, para 5.
7 Ibid, para 6.
8 SI 1979/591, reg 61.
9 SSA 1975, s.10 and SI 1979/591, regs 71 and 78.
10 See *Tiley*, n.1, above, ch 13.
11 SSA 1975, Sch 2, para 3(2).
12 Under Income and Corporation Taxes Act 1970, Part 1, ch II.
13 Ibid, ss.226–227.
14 Ibid, s.173.
15 Ibid, s.175 and Finance Act 1972, s.75.
16 SI 1979/591, reg 71.
17 Pp. 8–10, above.

role of women within the contributory scheme, and describe such special rules as currently exist governing their liability (or entitlement) to contribute. Treatment of the special rules on the fulfilment of contribution conditions is reserved until the general discussion of that subject in Part 4.

Before the Second World War, women insured under the unemployment and health schemes, whether married or single, both paid less by way of contributions and received less by way of benefit. But the amount paid was disproportionately large in comparison with the amount received, apparently because women were regarded as poor risks.[18] Why a similar approach was not taken to poor-risk male workers is not clear. As regards single women, Beveridge recommended removal of the anomaly: in terms of risk, it was no longer appropriate to treat them as a separate category, and, in terms of subsistence needs, the average cost of feeding them was only 1s a week less than that of men.[19] Indeed, to achieve the same level of benefit, they were to pay less,[20] it being assumed that many would marry and would eventually claim retirement pensions on the basis of the husband's contributions.

The position of a married woman was, however, very different: 'all women by marriage acquire a new economic and social status, with risks and rights different from those of the unmarried'.[1] They gain a legal right to maintenance, at the same time agreeing to perform a vital, but unpaid, service. The underlying notion is that of the family as a single economic unit, the wife doing the housework for the husband, who in return maintains her. According to the figures then available,[2] over 80 per cent of married women of working age regarded marriage as their sole occupation. Even if a wife was an earner, she was different from a single woman in that employment was liable to interruption for childbirth, and, more significantly, her earnings were 'a means, not of subsistence but of a standard of living above subsistence'.[3] It followed that in sickness or unemployment she did not need compensation on the same scale as the primary breadwinner; she could fall back on her husband's income, or his benefit if his earnings were interrupted. It was therefore proposed that a married woman who was an earner could choose either to opt out of the scheme, and thus become wholly dependent on her husband's contributions for retirement pension and maternity grant, or else to contribute in her own right.[4] In the case of the latter she would receive only two-thirds of the standard rate for unemployment and sickness benefit. To meet any criticisms of equity, and to provide a substantial benefit for a need which was particularly applicable to married women contributors, it was also proposed that maternity allowance would be 50 per cent higher than the standard short-term benefit.[5] These proposals were implemented in full by the 1946 legislation,[6] and remained in force until 1975. The only two significant modifications occurring between those dates both curtailed

18 Land in Barker and Allen (eds) *Sexual Divisions and Society* (1976) p. 109.
19 Para 123; cf *Harris* pp. 403–405.
20 Under NIA 1946, Sch 1, the standard weekly rate of contributions by employed persons was 4s 9d (males) and 3s 9d (females).
1 *Beveridge* para 108.
2 Beveridge relied on the 1931 census. He regarded the much higher figures for wartime work (see Thomas *Women at Work: Wartime Social Survey* (1944)) as a temporary phenomenon.
3 *Beveridge* para 108.
4 As a non-earner, she might similarly opt between contributions under Class IV and relying on her husband's contributions.
5 *Beveridge* para 113, and see p. 246, below.
6 NIA 1946, s.59 and SI 1948/1470.

some of the advantages of the married woman's special status: in 1953, the level of maternity allowance was reduced to that of the other short-term benefits,[7] and in 1959 contributions to and benefits from the graduated retirement benefit scheme were to be paid in full.[8]

The status thus attributed to married women had other implications for the contributory scheme. In the first place, it meant that any contributions paid before marriage by a woman who subsequently decided to opt out were ignored. Secondly, it meant that there was a problem in maintaining a contribution record, particularly for retirement pension purposes, should the marriage end by death or dissolution before pensionable age was reached. To meet this problem certain concessions were made: the contribution conditions for the various benefits were eased, special credits were available, and (after 1970[9]) the woman might rely on her former husband's insurance record, both before and during the marriage, even if he had since remarried.

By the 1970s, the social and economic climate had changed considerably. In 1978 some 62 per cent of married women of working age were in paid employment.[10] The movement against sex discrimination had intensified, and the social security position of married women was a prime target.[11] The main criticisms were that in contemporary economic conditions her earnings had become an essential element in the family's income, no longer the subordinate accessory which Beveridge had assumed, and that full reliance on the husband's insurance record rendered the wife's position vulnerable, not only on termination of the marriage but also during its currency – she had no means of ensuring that contributions were being paid.[12] The shift to a universal earnings-related contribution scheme in the Social Security Act 1973 provided an obvious opportunity to make fundamental changes to the married woman's option, but the Conservative government resisted pressure from the opposition for such action, chiefly on the ground that since under the existing arrangements only one quarter of married women earners had chosen to contribute independently, they must be assumed to have known what was best for them and that compulsory insurance would impose on them an inequitable burden, for they would not receive a sufficient return for their contributions.[13]

The new Labour government proposed to abolish the married woman's option as part of its new approach to retirement pensions. The ability, for the purpose of the woman's pension entitlement, to take into consideration such years during which she was 'precluded from regular employment by responsibilities at home'[14] was regarded as the key provision which would ensure a fair return for her contributions, and it was complemented by other measures. The new scheme would dispense with the rule hitherto in force that a married woman was entitled to a pension on her own

7 NIA 1953, s.6.
8 NIA 1959, s.1; the argument was that the 'graduated' element, being designed to provide a level of benefit above subsistence, was appropriate for contributors without discrimination according to sex or marital status: White Paper, Pensions for Old Age (1958, Cmnd 538), para 37.
9 NIA 1970, s.3.
10 General Household Survey 1978, Table 5.7.
11 See e.g. Report of Labour Party Study Group, *Towards Equality: Women and Social Security* (1969).
12 See in particular the contributions of Mr M Meacher in the Standing Committee E Debates on the Social Security Bill 1973, cols 228–231.
13 Ibid, at cols 217–224 (Mr P Dean, Under-Secretary of State).
14 SSPA 1975, s.19(3): see p. 209, below.

contributions only if she had paid contributions or received credits for at least a half of the weeks between marriage and her reaching pensionable age.[15] Most widows would inherit the whole of the earnings-related component which their husbands had earned. Finally, a retired widow would be able to base her entitlement to such a component on her own earnings as well as those of her husband.

In order that existing family arrangements should not be unduly prejudiced by the decision to abolish the option, those already married or widowed when the new provisions came into force were allowed to choose between 'full' and 'reduced' liability.

ii Entitlement to reduced liability

Only the following categories of women are entitled to reduced liability.

(1) Those married on 5 April 1977 who have elected[16] for reduced liability or who had opted out of liability under the previous scheme and have not elected for full liability.[17]

(2) Those widowed before 6 April 1977 and who are currently entitled to widow's benefit under the industrial, non-industrial or war pension schemes.[18] They must have elected for reduced liability or have opted out of liability under the previous scheme.[19]

(3) Those widowed after 5 April 1977 who had reduced liability immediately prior to the husband's death.[20] The reduced liability continues until the end of the tax year in which the death occurred, if that was before 1 October, or until the end of the following tax year, if the death occurred subsequent to that date. It may continue thereafter only if the widow is currently entitled to widow's benefit under the industrial, non-industrial or war pension schemes.

iii Duration of reduced liability

Provided that the conditions for one of the above categories are satisfied, the period of reduced liability will run until the woman reaches pensionable age (60), but it terminates earlier:

(1) on the date of a dissolution of marriage by divorce or annulment; or

(2) at the end of the tax year in which she ceases to be qualified to the relevant widow's benefit; or

(3) at the end of the tax year in which she revokes her election for reduced liability; or

(4) at the end of any two consecutive tax years subsequent to 5 April 1978 during which she is neither a self-employed earner nor is engaged in employment which attracts Class 1 contributions liability.[1]

iv Nature and consequences of reduced liability

For those who satisfy these rules, the effect is not, as before the 1975 Pensions Act, to relieve them from liability for all contributions. Reduced

15 Cf p. 210, below.

16 Election must have been made in the prescribed form and within the prescribed time-limits: see SI 1979/591, reg 100(3)–(7).

17 Ibid, regs 100(1) and 108. For the meaning of marriage, see pp. 377–382, below.

18 SI 1979/591, reg 100(1), (8). See generally pp. 230–233, 333–334 and 358–359, below.

19 Remarriage does not affect a reduced liability already validly established: SI 1979/591, reg 101(2).

20 Ibid, reg 103.

1 Ibid, reg 101(1).

liability gives them exemption from paying Class 2 contributions[2] and disentitles them from paying Class 3 contributions.[3] But the obligation to pay those of Class 4 remains unaffected and, as regards Class 1, the liability is reduced to 3.2 per cent rather than excluded altogether.[4] These payments are more akin to taxes than to contributions for they cannot assist in gaining title to any benefits or to the crediting of contributions during periods of sickness, unemployment or domestic responsibilities.[5]

B Other special cases

Certain categories of occupation are selected for special treatment either because provision is not necessary for some hazards (e.g. unemployment) or because there are difficulties in fulfilling the normal conditions for contributions.

i HM forces

One of the consequences of the Beveridge principle of universality was to extend insurance to Crown employees, who had previously been excluded from the national schemes. The principle, affirmed in the Social Security Act 1975, is that the provisions apply 'to persons employed by or under the Crown in like manner as if they were employed by a private person'.[6] However, members of HM forces are in a special position:

- During the currency of their service, they do not lose earnings for reasons of sickness, invalidity or unemployment and benefit is not payable for these contingencies.[7] In their case, the aim is merely to ensure that they will be sufficiently covered, in terms of contributions, for needs arising after they have returned to civilian life. Class 1 contributions are therefore payable, but the rate is reduced by 1.05 per cent (primary) and 1.3 per cent (secondary).[8] For the purposes of satisfying the residence conditions for contributions, a serving member of the forces[9] is treated as 'present in Great Britain'.[10]

ii Employment on the Continental Shelf

The problem here is simply that of satisfying the residence requirements. Regulations therefore prescribe that

- an employment in an area designated under the Continental Shelf Act 1964 in connection with the exploitation of resources, or the exploration, of the sea bed and subsoil, is deemed to be employment within GB.[11]

2 Ibid, reg 100(1)(b).
3 Ibid, reg 105.
4 Ibid, reg 104, as amended by SSCA 1982, s.1(3). The liability of the employer for secondary Class 1 contributions remains unaffected.
5 SSPA 1975, s.3(4), does enable regulations to be made so that earnings factors (which are necessary to satisfy the contribution conditions for benefits – see p. 65, below) may be derived from reduced liability contributions, but hitherto the power has not been exercised.
6 SSA 1975, s.127(1).
7 SI 1975/493, reg 2, as amended by SI 1975/1058, reg 15. This does not apply to certain members of the territorial or reserve forces or of the Ulster Defence Regiment. Maternity allowance is payable to members of HM forces.
8 SI 1979/591, reg 115(1), as amended by SSCA 1982, Sch 1.
9 For the definition of 'serving member of the forces' see SI 1979/591 reg 1(2) and Sch 3.
10 Ibid, reg 114.
11 Ibid, reg 85.

iii Airmen

Similar considerations apply to airmen:

– Provided that the employer has a place of business in GB, if the aircraft is British, or the principal place of business is in GB, in the case of other aircraft, the airman is treated as present in GB,[12] though if he is neither domiciled nor has a place of residence there, no contributions are payable.[13]

iv Mariners and registered dock workers

– For a person employed as a mariner,[14] the normal residence requirements for contributions are replaced by the simple condition that he is domiciled or resident in GB.[15] Certain mariners and registered dock workers are excluded from the operation of the Redundancy Payments scheme, and the primary and secondary Class 1 contributions for such persons are reduced by 0.35 per cent and 0.15 per cent respectively.[16] If the mariner's employment is wholly or partly on a 'foreign-going ship',[17] the secondary liability is reduced by a further 0.6 per cent.[18] There are also special methods of calculating earnings for the purpose of earnings-related contributions.[19]

Part 4 Contribution conditions

Under the system in force before 1975, contributions were predominantly flat-rate. It was therefore convenient to express the conditions of contributions for the various benefits in terms of the number of weekly contributions paid (or credited) during a specified period (often a 'contribution year'). With the adoption of the earnings-related system and the interdependence with tax liability, such concepts were no longer feasible, and so they have been replaced by 'earnings factors' (representing the amount of earnings on which liability to contribute is based) and the 'tax year' (6 April–5 April) as the usual contributory period. Apart from the provision necessary for the new earnings-related additional component to long-term benefits, the principles governing the contribution conditions and the modes of satisfying them remain substantially unaltered.

A Earnings factors

Contributions to Class 1 are earnings-related, those of Class 2 and Class 3 are flat-rate. In any one tax year, an individual might combine contributions of one class with those of either or both of the other classes. It was therefore necessary to create some common denominator whereby equivalent conditions could be exacted from those paying different types of contributions. The device chosen was the 'earnings factor': this is a sum

12 Ibid, reg 82(1). For the definition of 'airmen' and 'British aircraft' see ibid, reg 81.
13 Ibid, reg 82(2).
14 For definition, see ibid, reg 86.
15 Ibid, reg 87.
16 Ibid, regs 89(1) and 113(1), as amended by SSCA 1982, Sch 1.
17 For definition see SI 1979/591, reg 86.
18 Ibid, reg 89(1)(b).
19 Ibid, regs 90–97, as amended by SI 1982/206.

expressed in pounds representing the aggregate of contributions made by an individual in each tax year in each class.[20] For Class 1 contributions, the factor approximates to the earnings between the lower and upper earnings limit on which the contributions are calculated.[1] For Class 2 or 3 contributions (which are flat-rate) it is the lower earnings limit for Class 1 contributions multiplied by the number of contributions made in the relevant tax year.[2] Similar principles govern the calculation of the earnings factors derived from credited and contracted-out contributions,[3] though these are calculated separately from factors derived from contributions actually paid in non-contracted-out employment.

One important function of the earnings factors is to determine the amount of the earnings-related component in the new pensions scheme.[4] Because of what is often a substantial gap in time between the payment of the contributions and the receipt of the benefit, it is necessary to 'revalue' the earnings factors to keep pace with inflation. Under the Pensions Act, therefore, the Secretary of State is directed to review in each tax year the general level of earnings obtaining in Great Britain, and if he concludes that the earnings factors for any previous tax year have not maintained their value in relation to the general level of earnings, he must lay before Parliament an order directing that the earnings factors shall be increased by such percentages as he thinks necessary to restore their values.[5]

B Conditions for benefit

In the section of the book devoted to the individual contributory benefits, the contribution conditions of each will be specified. At this stage, it will be convenient to review the general pattern of rules. The aim of these rules has been to preserve a fair balance between the average contributor and the average beneficiary.[6] This objective of equity has given rise to two fundamental principles. The first is that the claimant's record of contributions should be sufficient in terms both of initial establishment in the scheme and of consistency over a period of time. The second is that there should be a difference according to whether he is claiming a short-term or a long-term benefit. In the case of the latter, where he will draw heavily on the fund's resources, it is appropriate that the tests should be more stringent. There is, in fact, also a third category of benefits where for political and other reasons it is thought sufficient that a minimal degree of contributions has taken place (e.g. death grant and child's special allowance). The latter benefits excepted, the contribution rules conform to a general pattern; these are expressed in terms of earnings factors, but it should be noted that claimants to long-term benefits may satisfy an alternative set of conditions formulated in terms of pre-1975 contributions.[7]

20 SSA 1975, s.13(5).
1 Ibid, s.13(5)(a). For the technically precise mode of calculation, see SI 1979/676, Sch 1, Part I. No earnings factors are derived from secondary Class 1 contributions or from reduced liability contributions: SSA 1975, s.13(3), cf p. 64, n.5, above.
2 SSA 1975, s.13(5)(b) and SI 1975/468, Sch 1, Part II.
3 Ibid, Part I, paras 4–7.
4 Pp. 220–221, below.
5 SSPA 1975, s.21(2), (3), as amended by SSA 1979, s.10(2), and SSA 1980, s.3(1). For the prescribed increases to the earnings factors since 1978, see SI 1982/607.
6 See NIAC Report on the Question of Contribution Conditions and Credits Provisions (1956, Cmd 9854), para 36.
7 See SI 1979/643.

i Initial condition

The first test, based on the idea of initial establishment in the scheme, can be satisfied only by contributions actually paid, i.e. credits do not qualify. In the case of short-term benefits (unemployment and sickness benefit, maternity and widow's allowance) it is that during any one tax year since the age of 16 the claimant has paid contributions, the earnings factor from which is at least 25 times the lower earnings limit for that year.[8] For those contributors at the lower end of the income scale (or making flat-rate Class 2 contributions) this will mean approximately six months' contributions. For the long-term benefits (retirement pensions, Categories A and B, and the remaining widow's benefits – but not invalidity benefit, entitlement to which depends on fulfilling the conditions for sickness benefit) the qualifying earnings factor is 52 times the lower earnings limit (equivalent to one year's contributions at the lowest end of the scale).[9]

ii Continuing condition

For the second qualifying condition, credits are equivalent to paid contributions, but the difference between the short-term and long-term benefits becomes considerable. For the former, the earnings factor derived from contributions paid or credited during the tax year immediately preceding the year during which the entitlement to benefit falls must have been at least 50 times the lower earnings limit.[10] For the latter, the position is more complicated as the contributions determine entitlement not merely to the basic component in the benefit, but also to the earnings-related additional component. To qualify for the basic component, for each of not less than 90 per cent of the tax years of his working life (viz between 16 and pensionable age) the claimant must have paid, or been credited with, contributions the earnings factor of which was 52 times the lower earnings limit.[11] Alternatively, that earnings factor must be achieved for one half of 90 per cent of the working life (or 20 years, if that is less) and during each of the remaining years of working life the contributor was 'precluded from regular employment by responsibilities at home'.[12] The additional component is based on the surplus of earnings factors above the minimum qualifying factor for each tax year.[13] It should be observed, however, that entitlement to the additional component is not conditional on satisfying the contribution requirements for the basic component; thus someone without title to the basic component because, for example, his contribution record was not sufficient over the relevant proportion of the working life will still receive the additional component based on those years when he did achieve a surplus of earnings factors.

C Credits

The system of crediting contributions is designed to assist those who are already established in the scheme but, for reasons beyond their control, have been unable to continue to make the requisite payments, sufficient to

8 SSA 1975, Sch 3, paras 1–4.
9 Ibid, para 5, as amended by SSPA 1975, s.19(2).
10 SSA 1975, Sch 3, paras 1–3.
11 Ibid, para 5, as amended by SSPA 1975, s.19(2).
12 SSA 1975, Sch 3, para 5(6), inserted by SSA 1979, Sch 1, para 3. See further, p. 209, below.
13 SSPA 1975, s.6(4), and see generally pp. 220–222, below.

satisfy the second condition.[14] To the extent that crediting is permitted, the beneficiaries are being subsidised by other contributors and for this reason it has been said both that there must be 'real and substantial justification' for the granting of the facility,[15] and that the beneficiary must show a significant degree of participation in the scheme during non-credited periods.[16] It is for the latter reason that married women who have elected for reduced liability[17] generally cannot be credited with Class 1 contributions.[18] With this exception, there are five main categories of contributors entitled to credits: those unemployed or otherwise incapable of work; those caring full-time for invalids; those engaged in full-time education or training; new entrants; and women whose marriage has been terminated.

i Unemployed or incapable of work

A Class 1 credit is available in respect of each week of unemployment or incapacity.[19] In effect, the period must be one which counted for unemployment, sickness, maternity or invalidity benefit, or a non-contributory invalidity pension, or would have so counted if an appropriate claim had been made.[20]

Shortly after these provisions came into force, it transpired that they were more generous to claimants than had been intended, in particular because the introduction of the non-contributory invalidity pension[1] enabled those with only the remotest connection with the contributory scheme to gain credits. Therefore, to preserve the notion of significant participation in the scheme, rules were promulgated in 1977 restricting the circumstances in which claimants to unemployment and sickness benefit and maternity allowance could avail themselves of credited contributions.[2] Such a claimant has to satisfy *one* of the following conditions:

(1) at some time during the tax year of the credits in question he actually paid contributions amounting to an earnings factor of at least 13 times the lower earnings limit;
(2) at some time during that year he made a claim, and satisfied the contribution conditions, for unemployment benefit, sickness benefit or maternity allowance;
(3) at some time during that year he was in receipt of invalidity pension, invalid care allowance, injury benefit, unemployability supplement, or a training allowance;
(4) the credits in question related to a period when his entitlement to unemployment or sickness benefit had expired.[3]

14 SI 1975/556, reg 3. A credited Class 1 contribution is equivalent to a payment at the lower earnings limit then current.
15 NIAC Report in Credits for Approved Training Courses (1953, Cmd 8860), paras. 17–18. See also Report on Contribution Conditions and Credits, n.6, above.
16 Mr S Orme, Minister for Social Security, 928 HC Official Report (5th series), cols 1475–1476.
17 See pp. 62–63, above.
18 SI 1978/409, reg 2(2).
19 SI 1975/556, reg 9(1).
20 Ibid, reg 9(2)–(5), as amended by SI 1981/1501, and SI 1982/96. Very short periods of work during the week are disregarded, but credits are not granted during periods of entitlement to statutory sick pay: p. 160, below.
1 Cf pp. 166–171, below.
2 SI 1977/778, reg 2, inserting reg 9(9) in SI 1975/556.
3 Cf pp. 134–135, below.

ii Full-time care of invalid

As will be seen,[4] the invalid care allowance is intended for those who care for an invalid but who otherwise would be in full-time employment. Their position is therefore similar to that of the unemployed or incapable and they are granted Class 1 credits for each week for which they are paid the allowance.[5]

iii Starting credits

Individuals begin contributing to the scheme at different ages, according to their circumstances. Many will commence employment on reaching the school-leaving age of 16; others will remain in full-time education for several more years. At whatever time the entry is made, it will rarely coincide with the tax year (the base period for contribution conditions) and unless concessions are made a substantial number of payments will have no insurance significance. The system of credits goes some way to maintaining equity between these various categories of entrant. The rules may be classified according to the type of benefit for which credit is claimed.

(1) For retirement pensions and widow's benefits, only a small concession is made. A person is entitled to the number of Class 3 credits necessary to bring the relevant earnings factor up to a reckonable year for the first three years of possible employment, viz the tax year during which he reached the age of 16 and the two following tax years.[6]

(2) For unemployment and sickness benefits and maternity allowance, Class 1 credits are granted for the 'relevant past year' (the base of the contribution conditions for these benefits) if it was a year in which the contributor reached 17, or any previous years.[7]

iv Education and training

The third set of rules makes concessions for those who start contributing late, or interrupt their contribution record, because they are engaged in education or training. It is not, however, thought appropriate that all persons engaged in education or training courses at whatever age and for whatever purpose should be subsidised by the fund.[8]

a *Course begun before age twenty-one*

In this case, the policy is an ungenerous one: it is simply to grant credits for the year in which full-time education, apprenticeship or a training course approved by the Secretary of State ended, so that the year may be constituted a reckonable year for the purposes of entitlement to unemployment benefit, sickness benefit or maternity allowance.[9]

b *Interruptions for approved training courses*

Clearly it is felt desirable to encourage individuals to improve their capacity for a job or equip themselves with the necessary skills for a new one. This form of vocational training, it may be argued, is in the national interest, and therefore justifies some form of subsidisation by the National

4 Pp. 177–181, below.
5 SI 1975/556, reg 7A, added by SI 1976/409. Widows who would have been paid the allowance but for the Overlapping Regulations are also entitled to the credit.
6 SI 1975/556, reg 4(1).
7 Ibid, reg 5(1).
8 See NIAC Report on Credits for Approved Training Courses, n.15, above.
9 SI 1975/556, reg 8.

Insurance Fund.[10] Thus the Regulations prescribe that[11] a contributor shall be granted credits for each week during any part of which he was engaged in a course of full-time training approved by the Secretary of State, provided that all of the following conditions are satisfied:

(1) the course was not in pursuance of his employment;
(2) he had reached 18 before the beginning of the tax year during which the week in question began;
(3) the course was not intended to last more than one year;[12] and
(4) for at least one of the last three tax years before the course began, he had paid or had been credited with contributions amounting to at least 50 times the lower earnings limit for that year.[13]

v Termination of marriage

A woman may obtain employment for the first time where a marriage has been terminated by death or dissolution or when children cease to require full-time attention. The position of such a woman is analogous to that of new entrants and similar credit facilities are available.

(1) For the purpose of satisfying the 'continuing' condition of unemployment benefit, sickness benefit, and maternity allowance, a woman whose marriage has been terminated may be credited with the necessary number of Class 1 contributions for any year during the whole or any part of which the marriage was subsisting. During one year which was either the last year before the marriage terminated or any subsequent year, she must, however, have paid Class 1 or Class 2 contributions, the earnings factor derived from which was at least 25 times the lower earnings limit for that year.[14]
(2) For the same purpose, a widow who ceases to be entitled to widow's allowance or widowed mother's allowance (in the latter case because she has no longer dependent children of the relevant age to care for[15]) will be credited with the requisite number of Class 1 contributions for every year up to and including that in which she ceased to be entitled to the widow's benefit referred to.[16]
(3) For the purposes of entitlement to death grant and retirement pension, a widow is credited with such Class 3 contributions as are necessary to enable her to acquire the requisite earnings factor for periods before 5 April 1978 during which she was entitled to a widow's benefit (other than the age-related widow's pension, or, if she was widowed before 6 April 1975, the widow's basic pension).[17]

D Other assistance in satisfying contribution conditions

i Aggregate of contributions by new entrants

The credit facilities available to new entrants serve to assist them only in satisfying the second of the two contribution conditions. The fortuitous

10 NIAC Report, n.15, above, at paras 20–21.
11 SI 1975/556, reg 7.
12 Though if it was training of a disabled person under the Employment and Training Act 1973, it may be permitted for 'such longer period as is reasonable in the circumstances': SI 1975/556, reg 7(2)(b).
13 This condition may be waived if 'in the circumstances of the case there is reasonable ground': ibid, reg 7(2)(a).
14 SI 1974/2010, reg 2.
15 See pp. 230–232, below.
16 SI 1974/2010, reg 3(1)(b).
17 Ibid, reg 6, as amended by inter alia SI 1977/1484, reg 2.

timing of their entry in relation to the relevant tax years may constitute an obstacle to the fulfilment of the first condition. The legislation, therefore, makes a further concession for entitlement to the short-term benefits (viz unemployment and sickness benefits, and maternity and widow's allowance).

- Where the last complete tax year, before the beginning of the year in which occurred the event for which benefit is claimed, was either the year in which the claimant first became liable for contributions of Classes 1 or 2, or the year preceding that year, he may for the purposes of satisfying the first contribution condition for the short-term benefits, aggregate the contributions which he has actually paid, and that aggregate is then treated as having been paid in the last complete year.[18]

ii Widows deemed to satisfy first condition

Widows joining, or rejoining, the scheme once their entitlement to widow's allowance or widowed mother's allowance has expired are faced with a similar problem, and for the purposes of entitlement to unemployment and sickness benefit or maternity allowance, they are deemed to have satisfied the first contribution condition.[19]

iii Invalidity pensioners

The first condition for a widowed mother's allowance, a widow's pension, or a retirement pension (Categories A and B) is deemed to be satisfied if the relevant contributor was entitled to an invalidity pension at any time during the year in which he reached pensionable age or died, or the year preceding that year.[20]

iv Employment abroad

For the purpose of claims for unemployment and sickness benefit and maternity allowance, a person who is employed abroad but who is ordinarily resident in Great Britain is, subject to certain conditions, treated as if he paid Class 1 contributions at the lower earnings limit for the period of absence.[1]

v Spouse's contributions and retirement pensions

As will be revealed in chapter 5, a woman who is, or has been, married may rely on her husband's contributions for the purposes of a Category B retirement pension and, if the marriage has been terminated, also for a Category A pension: from 6 April 1979 an equivalent facility was granted to widowers.[2]

18 SSA 1975, Sch 3, para 8, as amended by SSA 1979, Sch 3, para 10. He is deemed to satisfy this condition if he has been able successfully to apply the aggregation principle to a previous claim for another short-term benefit (except widow's allowance) and the contributions in question were of the appropriate class: SSA 1975, Sch 3, paras 9–13.

19 SI 1974/2010, reg 3(1)(a), as amended by SI 1978/508.

20 SSA 1975, Sch 3, para 5(5).

1 SI 1975/564, reg 18, and SI 1975/553, reg 11, both as amended by SI 1977/1509, reg 3. Of course, this facility only applies to periods during which he is not liable to pay contributions under the rules stated above, p. 52.

2 P. 212, below. For assistance granted to widows and widowers in relation to invalidity pension, see p. 164–165, below.

E Partial satisfaction of contribution conditions

To avoid an 'all or nothing' solution, the legislation has always provided for a reduced benefit where the second contribution condition has been only partially satisfied. For short-term benefits (unemployment and sickness benefits and maternity allowance) 75 per cent of the standard rate is payable if the earnings factor derived from the claimant's contributions is between 25 and 37½ times that limit.[3] The same percentages are applied to increases for adult dependants, but increases for child dependants are payable in full even though the second condition is not fully satisfied.[4] For retirement pensions (Categories A and B), widowed mother's allowance and widow's pension, entitlement to any additional, earnings-related component is unaffected but the basic component is calculated according to the proportion of reckonable years (i.e. years in which the qualifying earnings factor has been achieved) to the number of years of working life prescribed for the benefit in question.[5] As with the short-term benefits, increases for adult dependants are subject to the same reduction and increases for child dependants are payable in full. However, if the percentage is less than 25 per cent, neither the basic component nor the increase for the dependant (adult or child) is payable.

3 SI 1975/564, reg 14; SI 1975/553, reg 8.
4 SI 1977/343, reg 14, as substituted by SI 1977/1509, reg 5(2).
5 SI 1979/642, reg 6.

Chapter 3

Unemployment benefit

Part 1 Introduction

A General

Unemployment, as a major cause of earnings loss and financial hardship, has from the beginning been an object for protection under social security legislation. Yet it differs from other social hazards similarly so protected in one important respect: unlike the natural phenomena of sickness, old age, birth and death, it results in a large degree from the interplay of economic forces. As such, the level of unemployment to be tolerated, the means of combating it and the extent of financial support granted to victims, can be influenced by a government as part of its overall economic policy.[1] By its control of investment, rates of interest, taxation, pay and prices, it may stimulate demand for goods and services which will induce a high level of employment.[2] More directly, it may pay subsidies to employers to retain or engage persons who would otherwise be unemployed.[3] According to neo-classical economic theory, 'full employment' can typically be achieved by such interventionist measures only at the cost of inflation and reduced productivity and hence has been largely forsworn by the current Conservative administration. In contrast, measures aimed at so-called frictional unemployment, where there is an excessive supply of labour in the wrong location or with inappropriate skills, are generally uncontroversial politically: the encouragement of mobility of industry and workers through regional policies, the adaptation of the labour force to new industrial processes and technology through training schemes and allowances; the provision of information and guidance on vacant situations.[4]

1 The literature on the subject is immense. Lawyers should find particularly helpful e.g. Hauser and Burrows *The Economics of Unemployment Insurance* (1969); Creedy *The Economics of Unemployment in Britain* (1981); Sinfield *What Unemployment Means* (1981).

2 The policy originated in Keynes *The General Theory of Employment, Interest and Money* (1936).

3 Employment Subsidies Act 1978.

4 On the unemployment benefit offices and employment offices which, following the Employment and Training Act 1973, replaced employment exchanges, see Hill in Showler and Sinfield (eds) *The Workless State* (1980) ch 5. On the broader services and schemes administered by the Manpower Services Commission, see its booklet *Review of Services for the Unemployed* (1981). For a comparative survey, see OECD *Unemployment Compensation and Related Employment Measures* (1979).

The extent to which the form and level of financial benefits payable to the unemployed affect their willingness to accept redundancies, to remain unemployed, or to seek employment elsewhere, is a much disputed question.[5] But it seems clear that high levels of unemployment, as are currently being experienced, will be tolerated politically only where those rendered unemployed as a result can sustain a reasonable standard of living. Of course, the main instrument for financially assisting the workless is unemployment benefit, which forms part of the contributory social security system and with which we are concerned in this chapter. But there are several other schemes, outside the scope of this book, directed towards analogous, if not identical, purposes. A worker made redundant may receive payments from his employer and, under the statutory scheme introduced in 1965, those who have worked for the same employer for at least two years prior to the redundancy are entitled to lump sum compensation.[6] The rationale of the scheme is not primarily welfare or income-maintenance but more the recognition that the employee has some form of 'proprietary interest' in his job for the deprivation of which he should be compensated. In recent years the Department of Employment has instituted a number of measures to deal with specific aspects of unemployment; two of these are still operative at the time of writing.[7] Under the Job Release Scheme, those close to, but who have not yet attained, pensionable age are entitled to a special allowance if they retire and the vacancy is filled by an unemployed person. The Temporary Short Time Working Compensation Scheme is concerned to encourage work-sharing: if an employer withdraws an impending redundancy and instead puts employees on short time, they receive about 75 per cent of their normal pay for each day spent without work.[8]

B History[9]

Prior to the twentieth century, relief from the consequences of unemployment took one of two forms: private schemes of insurance administered by trade unions and friendly societies, or resort to the antiquated and degrading poor law. Once it became widely recognised that unemployment was not, in the great majority of cases, the result of personal moral failing but rather the product of economic forces, there was an obvious case for some form of state protection outside the poor law. The Royal Commission on the Poor Law, reporting in 1909,[10] placed great reliance on the system of labour exchanges (established on a national basis some four years previously[11]), and the redeployment of labour and industry. The Majority recommended the extension of unemployment insurance but felt

5 The introduction of statutory redundancy payments and the earnings-related supplement to unemployment benefit in 1965–66 was followed by a rapid rise in unemployment. See the arguments and studies considered in Hawkins *Unemployment* (1979) pp. 33–35.
6 Now governed by Employment Protection (Consolidation) Act 1978: see generally Grunfield *Law of Redundancy* (2nd edn).
7 Cf *Review of Services for the Unemployed*, n.4, above.
8 See also p. 91, below.
9 Tillyard *Unemployment Insurance in Great Britain 1911–1948* (1949); Cohen *Unemployment Insurance and Assistance in Britain* (1938) ch 1–3; Harris *Unemployment and Politics, 1886–1914* (1972); *Ogus* pp. 179–186 and 202–205.
10 Cd 4499.
11 Unemployed Workmen Act 1905.

that it should continue to exist on a voluntary basis and should be administered independently for each trade group.[12]

The most penetrating analysis of unemployment in the early years of this century came from Beveridge.[13] For him, the creation of labour exchanges was only part of a broader approach to unemployment which though influenced by economic policy required residual support in an insurance scheme: the unemployed must be able 'to subsist without demoralisation till they can be reabsorbed again after industrial transformations'.[14] The philosophy was reflected in Part II of the National Insurance Act 1911 which established the first compulsory system of unemployment insurance in a major industrialised country, with the employee, the employer and the state contributing in equal proportion. However, its experimental nature should not be overlooked. It was restricted to certain industries (notably engineering and shipbuilding) which were liable mainly to seasonal fluctuations and fell midway between those which had a relatively stable employment record, and for which the need was therefore less pressing, and those liable to chronic unemployment and which were therefore difficult to handle. It covered only 2¼ million of a 10 million working population. Moreover, the benefits payable were not generous: for each of five contributions paid, an insured person during unemployment might receive a weekly benefit of 7s but only for a maximum of 15 weeks a year.[15] The scheme was not regarded as providing a substitute for wages but rather a supplement to personal savings to avoid resort to charity or the poor law. In short, it was conceived of as a temporary lifebelt.[16]

The First World War was responsible for certain important changes. On the one hand, an Act of 1916 extended the scheme to all persons working on munitions.[17] On the other hand, soldiers returning to civilian life but unable to find employment were not insured, and were granted a donation or 'dole'.[18] This led to the feeling that those unemployed through no fault of their own were entitled to relief as of right, which, in turn, induced the government to promise a universal insurance scheme. A reform of 1920 went a long way in fulfilling the promise.[19] The scheme now covered all workers except those in agriculture, domestic service and the civil service, the numbers insured rising from 4 to 11 millions. The ex-serviceman's donation had also made special provision for dependants. There was a growing awareness that unemployment was a family rather than an individual problem, and it had become manifestly clear that an unemployed married man with children was often unable to maintain the family without resort to the poor law. The result was the introduction of dependants' allowances.[20] The reform was a fundamental one: it meant that the insurance fund was now the primary source for maintaining the majority of the unemployed.[1]

12 N.10, above, at para 604. The Minority Report reached similar conclusions (p. 1200) but concluded that compulsory insurance in some industries was practicable.
13 *Unemployment: A Problem of Industry* (1909). See also *Harris* ch 6.
14 *Beveridge*, n.13, above, at p. 236.
15 NIA 1911, Sch 7.
16 Royal Commission on Unemployment Insurance, Final Report (1932, Cmd 4185), para 198.
17 NI (Part II) (Munition Workers) Act 1916.
18 Paid under powers conferred on the Board of Trade by ibid, s.3(1).
19 UIA 1920.
20 Under the Unemployed Workers' Dependants (Temporary Provisions) Act 1921, made permanent by UIA 1922, s.1.
1 *Tillyard*, n.9, above, at p. 69.

Unfortunately the burden placed on the scheme became, in times of great economic depression, too heavy to bear. The actuaries in computing the level of contributions and benefits had assumed an unemployment level of 5.32 per cent. Between 1920 and 1940 the figure never fell below 10 per cent, and during some periods was much higher. The result was a debt of £59 million in the insurance fund, and as a concession to extreme political and economic pressure both at home and abroad, in 1932 the government made its notorious cut in benefit of 10 per cent.[2] But there was a second problem, even graver. In the 1920s it became evident that a large proportion of unemployment in Britain was confined to certain industries which were situated in narrow geographical areas. In consequence, in these areas there was chronic and long-term unemployment, against which the scheme gave no protection, for benefit was given only for a limited period. The only method of saving the persons affected from the poor law was to establish an uncovenanted benefit scheme which would run alongside standard insurance. Throughout the interwar years some such system continued to operate, though under different guises. Under the 1920 Act, for example, benefit might be paid in advance of contributions on the assumption that in the long run such contributions would be made.[3] An 'uncovenanted benefit' was introduced in 1921[4] (later known as 'extended' or 'transitional' benefit). This was payable at the discretion of the Minister[5] in the exercise of which he might investigate the personal and financial circumstances of the claimant, a practice of course impossible under the standard insurance scheme. The Blanesburgh Committee, reporting in 1927,[6] found this dual system to be unsatisfactory and recommended that all benefits should be paid as of right. The proposal was enacted[7] but the onset of extreme economic difficulties meant that the aim of abolishing uncovenanted benefit was never realised. The 'transitional arrangements' which were intended to be superseded were several times extended. Indeed in 1933 the number of claimants in receipt of transitional benefit exceeded those on insurance benefit.

A major review of the system was undertaken by the Royal Commission on Unemployment Insurance in 1930–32.[8] As implemented by the Unemployment Act of 1934, its recommendations established a pattern which, subject to certain modifications, has remained in force ever since. The basis was a distinction, hitherto only partially recognised, between insurance and relief. The former should continue (and indeed be extended to certain industries as yet excluded, notably agriculture) along traditional lines of covenanted benefit, limited in duration. When the right to benefit had been exhausted special assistance, based on a means test, would be provided and administered by the Unemployment Assistance Board. The latter was, of course, the precursor of the Supplementary Benefits Commission, and details of its subsequent history will be found in a later chapter.[9]

Under Beveridge's plan and the subsequent legislation, unemployment was integrated into the general scheme of social insurance and was made

2 SR & O 1932/814. See Gilbert *British Social Policy 1914–39* (1972) pp. 162–175.
3 UIA 1920, s.8(4).
4 UIA 1921, s.3.
5 For a short period in 1924–25 the claimant had a right to such benefit (UIA (No 2) 1924, s.1(1)) but this was soon repealed by UIA 1925, s.1.
6 Published by Ministry of Labour.
7 UIA 1927.
8 Interim Report (1931, Cmd 3872); Final Report (1932, Cmd 4185).
9 Pp. 451–452, below.

compulsory for all employed earners. It was, in fact, Beveridge's intention that the benefit should be of unlimited duration.[10] But the recommendation was not found acceptable: there were fears that it would be an inducement to abuse, and his suggested safeguard – a requirement that an individual undergo training after six months' unemployment – was regarded as impracticable.[11] The only major modification to the scheme subsequent to 1946 was the introduction of the earnings-related supplement in 1966.[12] This was however abolished by the Conservative government in 1982, as part of its programme of economies in the public sector. Ironically, the latter reform took place at a time when unemployment had attained a level not experienced since the 1930s. The consequence both of reduced benefit[13] and of increased long-term unemployment – unemployment benefit is payable for a maximum of a year – has been an ever-growing reliance on supplementary benefit.[14] So far, however, the government has revealed no intention of altering the principles of entitlement, or of raising the amount payable.

C Scope and structure

The law governing entitlement to unemployment benefit is complex. The difficulties result partly from the need to adapt the system to changing industrial practices (particularly the shift from six-day to five-day working) and partly from the relationship between social security and labour law. The problems have been exacerbated by a reluctance in the DHSS to reformulate traditional concepts, some of which are outmoded, and a tendency instead to prefer patchwork solutions, occasionally implemented by poorly drafted regulations.[15]

Viewed from a very broad level of generality, however, the structure of the system is not difficult to comprehend. Apart from the contribution conditions (Part 2), entitlement rests on two fundamental notions. The first is that the claimant should be unemployed (Part 3). The complexities in this area of the law arise primarily from the fact that benefit may be payable notwithstanding that the contract of employment between the claimant and his employer is still subsisting, viz for periods of lay-off or short-time. The second idea is that the unemployment should be involuntary, that is, must result from external economic factors rather than from the claimant's own conduct or physical condition. If he is physically or psychologically incapable of work he must satisfy the relevant criteria for the disability benefits. The involuntary nature of the unemployment is judged first by the requirement (Part 4) that he is 'available' for work and subsequently by the sanctions of disqualification imposed where the claimant voluntarily leaves his employment, is dismissed for misconduct, or refuses a suitable offer of employment (Part 5). On one view, the notion may also account for the disqualification of those involved in a trade dispute (Part 6). The remainder of the chapter is largely devoted to an account of the rules governing special categories of employment, notably seasonal workers (Part 7), and the duration and amount of benefit (Part 8).

10 Paras 129–130.
11 *Social Insurance* Part I, para 67.
12 For details, see 1st edn of this book, pp. 424–426.
13 In 1980–81, it was raised by 5% less than the increase in prices: p. 413, below.
14 In 1975–76, it was responsible for 46% of social security spending on the unemployed; it was predicted that this figure would rise to 61% in 1982–83: White Paper on Public Expenditure (1981, Cmnd 8175), Table 2.12.1.
15 Cf Ogus, 4 ILJ 12.

Part 2 Contribution conditions

Only persons who have paid Class 1 contributions can qualify for unemployment benefit.[16] The exclusion of the self-employed has not been controversial:[17] it has generally been regarded as too difficult to ascertain when they are not gainfully occupied. In the words of Beveridge, 'the income of a farmer, a shopkeeper or a business manager may come at any time; how busy or how active he is on a particular day is largely within his own control. It is not practicable to have a general system of maintaining earnings of persons gainfully occupied otherwise than by way of employment, by benefits conditional upon not working or appearing to work on a particular day.'[18]

The contribution conditions for Class 1 contributors are:

(1) the claimant must have paid contributions of that class for any one year before the date of claim, and the earnings factor derived from such contributions must be not less than that year's lower earnings limit multiplied by 25; and

(2) in the last complete year before the year in which falls the beginning of the period of interruption of employment, the claimant must have paid, or been credited with, contributions of that class, the earnings factor from which must be not less than that year's lower earnings limit multiplied by 50.[19]

In recent years, governments have expressed concern about the growing number of students who apply for unemployment benefit: it has been argued that they can take advantage of the starting credit facility[20] without showing any real attachment to the insurance scheme and that, with employment prospects being poor, particularly in the short vacations, they are not in a genuine sense 'available for work' during those periods.[1] This view was not endorsed by a majority of the National Insurance Advisory Committee, who found that the government's proposals to impose special contribution conditions on students were unduly discriminatory.[2] Notwithstanding the Committee's view, the government has since implemented its proposals. Under the new rules[3] an additional contribution condition must be satisfied by students (defined as 'following a course of full-time education at an establishment recognised by the Secretary of State as being, or comparable to, a university, college or school') who claim unemployment benefit during the academic year, that is from the beginning of the first term to the end of the last term, but not the summer vacation. The condition is that for each of the last two tax years before the benefit year in which the claim is made they should have paid contributions, the earnings factor from which is at least 50 times the lower earnings limit for the year in question. Once the condition has been satisfied, it is not imposed in relation to any subsequent claim for unemployment benefit.

16 SSA 1975, s.13(1): the one exception is share fishermen, p. 130, below.
17 Though see Lister and Field *Wasted Labour* (1978) pp. 18, 62–63.
18 Para 122. See also DHSS Discussion Document *The Self-Employed and National Insurance* (1980) paras 44–45.
19 SSA 1975, Sch 3, para 1. For the concepts involved see ch 2, above.
20 See p. 69, above.
1 See NIAC Report on draft regulations (1977, Cmnd 6976) and NIAC Report on Unemployment Benefit for Students (1979, Cmnd 7613).
2 Ibid, para 17. Hence any such amendment, it was argued, should be enacted by Parliament.
3 SI 1975/564, reg 20, inserted by SI 1979/934, reg 2.

Part 3 Unemployment

A General

Benefit is payable in respect of 'any day of unemployment which forms part of a period of interruption of employment'.[4] This proposition contains a number of diverse elements. For the purposes of exposition they will be classified as follows. The first question is whether the claimant is 'unemployed' in the sense that he is not engaged in a profitable activity (section B). It is then necessary to show that the day of unemployment in respect of which the claim is made is one recognised by the law as forming part of a period of interruption of employment (section C). In cases where the contract with the employer is still subsisting but the employee has been laid-off or put on short-time working, there are additional requirements to be satisfied (section D).

B Whether unemployed

Benefit is not payable for any day in which the claimant 'is engaged in any employment'.[5] 'Employment', as used here, is not limited to the notion of a contract of service, for it includes 'any trade, business, profession, office or vocation'.[6] The general principle is that a claimant is unemployed if he is not engaged in an activity from which he intends to derive remuneration or profit. Such activity can conveniently be considered under four heads.

i Contracts of service

In general, a person engaged to work for remuneration under a contract of service cannot be unemployed. Payments in kind rather than money may constitute remuneration,[7] but not the mere reimbursement of expenses.[8] On the other hand, subject to the special regulations on subsidiary employment,[9] it does not generally assist the claimant to show that the amount of remuneration was small. In *R(U) 4/64*

> C attended an occupational centre where disabled persons were employed on light simple work for what the local tribunal described as a 'nominal wage'. He was held to be following a gainful occupation: 'he attended during normal working hours to do certain set industrial work for a prescribed payment'.[10]

But the amount may be so small as to indicate that it was intended as a gratuitous payment rather than contractual remuneration.[11] To be contrasted with the above decision is *R(U) 2/67*.

> C attended a training centre for mentally disabled persons. Light work was undertaken by patients and the products were sold. But the object

4 SSA 1975, s.14(1)(a).

5 SI 1975/564, reg 7(1)(h). Older regulations (e.g. SI 1967/330, reg 7(1)) used the term 'occupation', but the change is not thought to be significant: *R(U) 4/77*, para 5; *R(U) 5/81*, para 9 (Tribunal decision).

6 SSA 1975, Sch 20, and see *R(U) 3/77*, para 7, J G Monroe, Comr.

7 *CU 236/50*; *CWU 42/50*. This may constitute an infringement of the Truck Acts but the claimant cannot rely on the illegality of the contract as the basis for the claim that he was unemployed: *UD 1404/27* (Umpire's decision under the old Unemployment Insurance legislation).

8 Cf *R(U) 6/77*, para 7.

9 P. 83, below.

10 *R(U) 4/64*, para 7.

11 *R(U) 4/63*.

> was therapeutic not commercial and the weekly payments of £1 were not regarded as remuneration but 'more in the nature of pocket money given as an incident of rehabilitation treatment'.[12]

The remuneration need not have been actually paid to the claimant on the day or days for which the claim is made.[13] So a person working according to an unexpired contract is employed, notwithstanding that his employer defaults on payment.[14] The same is true of someone who, following a change of jobs, has to work for a certain period before receiving wages.[15] Prima facie, for the purposes of unemployment benefit, a person is 'employed' from the date on which his obligation to work under the contract begins to the date when it is discharged.[16] But there are several important qualifications to this principle.

a *Contract suspended*

The contract may subsist but be suspended where, for example, the employee has been laid-off or put on short-time working. During such periods of inactivity he may claim unemployment benefit, though, as will be seen,[17] he must satisfy certain special rules.

b *No work available*

The fact that on a particular day or period of days an employee is given no work by his employer does not, of course, necessarily mean that he is unemployed. Most importantly, he cannot claim benefit for any period during which, under the terms of the contract, he is bound to make his services available to the employer; when, in short, he is 'on call'.[18] That this principle may lead to harsh consequences is evident from cases concerning part-time professional footballers. The contracts contained a clause whereby, in return for the payment of a small weekly sum, the player was to attend for training whenever the club so required. The statutory authorities were compelled to hold that he was employed for the whole of the week[19] unless it could be found that the attendance clause had been modified or waived in practice.[20] Where, on the other hand, the employment is for a specific job of work and it does not oblige the employee to make himself available to the employer throughout the period of the contract, he may be unemployed when he is not actually engaged on the job in question.[1] In *R(U) 1/73*:

> A census enumerator was appointed in March 1971. He was paid a lump sum for the execution of certain specific duties which were to begin on 1 April 1971. R S Lazarus, Commissioner, held that he was gainfully employed only from this latter date.

The decision contrasts with several in which it was held that a census *officer* was employed throughout the period of appointment.[2] In the 1973 case, the

12 *R(U) 2/67*, para 11.
13 *R(U) 16/64*; *R(U) 6/77*; *CSU 1/81*.
14 *R(U) 5/75*.
15 He may nevertheless be entitled to supplementary benefit: p. 458, below.
16 *R(U) 3/72*, R J A Temple, Comr.
17 Pp. 90–101, below.
18 *R(U) 5/58*; *R(U) 10/80*; and see the decisions on guarantee agreements, p. 100, below.
19 *R(U) 24/53*; *R(U) 10/57*; *R(U) 23/57*; *R(U) 10/72*.
20 *R(U) 8/59*.
1 *R(U) 20/51*.
2 Those reported are *R(U) 16/61* and *R(U) 3/72*. They were confirmed in *R(U) 5/81* (Tribunal decision).

Commissioner, though critical of these earlier decisions, felt able to distinguish them on the ground that census officers were given different instructions: they had to attend a training session before the duties commenced.[3] This fact was not regarded as significant in the earlier decisions and *R(U) 1/73* seems to depart from the view apparently held previously that the duration of the occupation is conclusively established by the contract of employment. But the departure does seem to be a proper one. In the words of the Commissioner, 'I find it hard to see the logic of holding that a person follows the occupation of census enumerator on a day on which his employer does not require him to, and he does not, do any part of the specified job for which he is employed'.[4]

The situation in which the employee is instructed to do particular jobs at particular times must be distinguished from that in which the employee is effectively given discretion as to how he allocates the work over time, for example, a commercial salesman[5] or a research consultant.[6] In both cases it was held that the claimant was not unemployed during periods when he decided not to work.

c *Contract terminated*

Although the period of employment will end when the employee's contractual obligation to work or be available for work is discharged, it may be difficult to determine when this has taken place. For example, both parties may anticipate and intend that the employment relationship will be resumed after the expiration of a short period. Is the employee unemployed during that period? The decisions of the Commissioner reveal two different approaches.

(1) Under the first, it was held that if the employee received some payment[7] in consideration of which he agreed to return to the employment, there was a contract of employment subsisting throughout the period, and he was not unemployed.[8]

(2) A new approach was taken by the Commissioner in 1968.[9] Regard was had to the extent of the claimant's obligations during the interim period. If he agreed to be at the disposal of the employer when required, he was properly to be regarded as gainfully employed.[10] But if he was free to do whatever he liked throughout the period, he was not gainfully employed.[11]

There might be thought to be strong arguments for the general adoption of approach (2). It is more consistent with the decisions which hold that benefit is payable during the currency of a contract when no work is available to the employee.[12] Moreover, approach (1) was popular at a time when the concept of 'termination' was given a special meaning. The doctrine (originating in the Umpires' decisions under the old Unemployment Insurance Acts) was that a contract was not 'terminated' if it was intended that the relationship of employment should be resumed at the

3 *R(U) 1/73*, para 10, R S Lazarus, Comr.
4 Ibid, at para 14.
5 *R(U) 11/60*.
6 *CSU 1/81*.
7 Though not so small that it could be regarded as a gratuity: *R(U) 20/51*.
8 *CU 28/48*; *CU 62/48*; *R(U) 8/54*. In *R(U) 38/52*, the claimant was not bound to return but because of past practice was 'expected' to return. It is difficult, on any ground, to support the decision that she was gainfully occupied.
9 *R(U) 6/68*, H Magnus, Comr. See also *R(U) 7/68* (Tribunal decision).
10 *R(U) 10/80*.
11 *R(U) 6/68*.
12 P. 80, above.

next available opportunity. As will be seen,[13] the doctrine no longer applies. Nevertheless, in recent years the Commissioner has had to grapple with contracts of employment, typically those involving work on oil-rigs, in which the employee is engaged on a rota system, for example two weeks on duty, followed by two weeks off duty. He has invariably held that the employee is not unemployed during the off-duty period.[14] In one such case, the employer had the right to recall the claimant during that period, and so the decision was compatible with approach (2).[15] In another, one of the terms of the contract referred to 26 weeks of 'continuous employment', which was held to imply that the claimant had been engaged on an indefinite basis.[16] In two further cases, the Commissioner was content to have regard to 'the consistent pattern of employment' which, he said, rendered the employment more compatible with a 'continuing or running contract'.[17] As has been suggested,[18] there seems to be a strong case for making special provision for this form of employment, where high rates of remuneration are paid for intensive periods of work alternating with substantial periods of rest. This would then not prejudice the general application of approach (2).

ii Other profitable activity

Other forms of profitable activity will also defeat a claim. But difficulties arise as to determining what is so to be regarded. It seems clear, on the case-law, that it is the expectation of profits rather than their actual receipt which is decisive.[19] According to the Commissioner, 'a gainful occupation is one in which a person is engaged with the desire, hope and intention of obtaining for himself, directly and personally, remuneration or profit in return for his services and efforts'.[20] So, the claimant may show a net loss during the period in question and still be gainfully employed.[1] As regards the activity, the authorities must assess, on the evidence available, the period of time during which it might reasonably be concluded that the claimant was *personally* active in the enterprise.[2] Regard is had to such factors as the number of hours in which he was so engaged, relative to the amount of work which might reasonably be done.[3] The mere fact that the claimant is the proprietor of, or a partner in, a business is not sufficient by itself to render him gainfully employed,[4] though in practice to succeed in his claim he will have to show that his assumption of responsibilities and management involved only a negligible amount of time.[5]

iii Periods of training

A person may engage on a training course for the purpose of equipping himself or re-equipping himself for a trade or profession. Where he

13 P. 95, below.
14 *R(U) 10/80*; *R(U) 14/80*; *R(U) 4/81*; *R(U) 5/81*.
15 *R(U) 10/80*, I O Griffiths, Comr.
16 *R(U) 5/81*.
17 *R(U) 4/81*, para 8, D Reith, Comr; *R(U) 14/80*, I Edward-Jones, Comr.
18 Ibid, para 2.
19 See also in relation to retirement, pp. 200–201, below, and the nature of earnings, p. 404, below.
20 *CU 30/49*, para 5.
1 *R(U) 12/55*.
2 *R(U) 11/57*.
3 *CU 235/50*; *R(U) 8/55*. See also *R(U) 1/67*.
4 *R(U) 11/57*.
5 *R(U) 22/64*.

receives a training allowance from public funds (e.g. from the Manpower Services Commission), the Overlapping Regulations provide that its value shall be deducted from any unemployment benefit payable.[6] But the law on whether he is disentitled to that benefit on the ground that he is gainfully employed is strangely uncertain. Where, during the currency of the contract of service, an employer requires an employee to undergo training, he is surely not to be regarded as unemployed.[7] But the case where the training takes place before the contract begins is more problematic. The standard approach taken by the Umpire under the Unemployment Insurance Acts was to determine on the evidence available whether, explicitly or implicitly, an employer had undertaken to employ the claimant on his successful completion of the course. If so, whether or not he received remuneration, the claimant was gainfully employed.[8] For several years, this principle was applied to the modern legislation,[9] but in *R(U) 3/67* the Commissioner adopted a quite different perspective. He argued that under the National Insurance legislation then in force a person was employed if he was gainfully occupied in employment, and not employed if he was not so gainfully occupied. Attendance at a training course was neither an 'occupation' nor was it 'gainful'. The wording of the relevant regulation has since been changed[10] – 'occupation' has been replaced by 'employment' – and so the authority of the decision is to that extent reduced. The solution adopted has the merit of simplicity and also avoids the weakness in the old approach, whereby a trainee without income and not yet engaged under a contract was disentitled. If applied literally, it seems to suggest that a trainee receiving remuneration from a prospective employer might nevertheless qualify for benefit. However, it is very unlikely that the statutory authorities would be drawn to this conclusion, and in any event the trainee would probably fail to satisfy the 'availability' test.[11]

iv Subsidiary employment

It is regarded as inappropriate to disentitle a claimant on the ground that he is engaged in subsidiary employment if it is only marginally profitable and it is consistent with him being available for full-time employment. For the employment to be disregarded, the onus is on the claimant[12] to satisfy four conditions.[13] These were substantially amended in 1982: see the Appendix.

a *Earnings not to exceed £2 per day*

The policy of exempting part-time work from consideration is subject to the important qualification that it must not be too profitable. The current limit[14] represents a welcome increase on the previous sum which had remained unchanged for ten years. The method of calculating the earnings for the purpose of the rule is described in chapter 10.[15]

6 SI 1979/597, reg 6, on which see p. 415, below.
7 There is no direct authority for this but it appears to be a necessary implication of *R(U) 3/67*, para 9, H Magnus, Comr.
8 *UD 4903*. The undertaking was inferred where the training was made a condition precedent of the employment: *UD 2605/28*.
9 *CU 162/50*; *R(U) 30/51*; *R(U) 4/59*.
10 Cf p. 79, n.5, above.
11 P. 102, below.
12 *R(U) 16/64*; *R(U) 2/67*.
13 SI 1975/564, reg 7(1)(h).
14 Ibid, as amended by SI 1982/96.
15 Pp. 404–409, below.

b *Available for full-time employment*
The claimant must be available for full-time employment in an employed earner's employment. This repeats a condition which must in any event be satisfied by anyone claiming unemployment benefit and which is fully considered below.[16]

c *Subsidiary employment consistent with full-time employment*
The Commissioner has discredited the view that 'consistency' is tautologous with 'availability'. While availability is partially dependent on the claimant's attitude – whether he is willing to take on full-time employment compatible with the subsidiary employment – 'consistency' involves looking at the circumstances of the employment at the time of the claim and assessing the prospects of obtaining full-time employment consistent with it.[17] Thus in *R(U) 12/59*

> C, who was unemployed, found part-time work as a relief park keeper. His duties began at 4 p.m. Although he was *available* for full-time employment as a factory machinist, he had no reasonable prospects of finding such employment ending before 4 p.m. He could not rearrange his hours of work in the park, and the subsidiary employment was thus inconsistent with the full-time employment for which he was available.

It follows, of course, that where the contract for the subsidiary employment prescribes that the employee be at the disposal of the employer whenever required it cannot be consistent with full-time employment.[18] On the other hand, if the working hours can be rearranged or fewer demands are made on the claimant's time, 'consistency' may be established.[19]

d *Subsidiary employment not usual main occupation*
A fourth condition was added in 1955: the subsidiary employment had to be 'different in nature from' the full-time occupation.[20] The object of the provision was clearly to prevent collusion: an employer dismissing the claimant and then re-engaging him at a nominal wage. But by concentrating on the *nature* of the occupation, the regulation cast its net too wide. In one instance it was applied to disentitle a man who was registered for employment as a general farmworker but who, outside his normal working hours, cultivated his own small holding.[1] A 1960 amendment narrowed the fourth condition, so that it was only to apply where the subsidiary employment was of a type giving rise to Class 1 contribution liability.[2] The present position is, therefore, that if the subsidiary employment is employed earner's employment, that must not be of the same nature as the claimant's usual main occupation.[3]

C Periods of unemployment

It will be recalled that title to benefit rests on proof of a 'day of unemployment which forms part of a period of interruption of employment.'[4] It is now necessary to consider the meaning of 'day' and 'period'.

16 Pp. 102–105, below.
17 *R(U) 4/64*; *R(U) 2/67*.
18 *R(U) 24/53*.
19 *R(U) 31/53*; *R(U) 4/64*; *R(U) 4/77*.
20 SI 1955/143, reg 2.
1 *R(U) 26/58*. See also *R(U) 12/57*.
2 SI 1960/781, reg 2.
3 SI 1975/564, reg 7(1)(h). For 'employed earner's employment' see pp. 45–50, above.
4 SSA 1975, s.14(1)(a).

i Day of unemployment

The minimum unit of time recognised for benefit purposes is a day: a claimant cannot be unemployed on part only of a day. If he is employed for more than a token amount[5] on a particular day, it will not constitute a day of unemployment. If this principle were employed universally it would cause hardship to night-workers who might lose a shift but still work for more than a token amount on each calendar day.[6] The Regulations, therefore, allow for an exception to the general rule: where a person works through midnight he is deemed to be employed on that day on which the greater part of his shift falls.[7] For the exception to apply, however, the shift must begin within 24 hours of one calendar day and end within 24 hours of the following day; the general principle applies to longer periods of unemployment. Thus in *R(U) 18/56*

> C was employed as a deckhand on a trawler from 18.00 hours on Monday to 02.00 hours on Wednesday. He claimed benefit for Monday on the ground that the greater part of his shift fell on Tuesday and Wednesday. But it was held that the Night Regulations did not apply.[8]

ii Days of rest

Benefit is payable on the basis of a six-day week. Thus the daily rate is one-sixth of the appropriate weekly rate.[9] It follows that the seventh and rest day of the week is not a day of unemployment.[10] Six-day workers who normally[11] work on Sunday but not on another day may, if unemployed, claim for Sunday but not for that other day.[12] Even if a claimant does not normally work on Sunday, nevertheless if he is available for work on that day and objects on religious grounds to working on another day, that other day is substituted for Sunday.[13]

iii Compensated days

If a person receives money in substitution of wages for a period after the termination of the contract, it is sound policy that for such a period he should not be entitled to unemployment benefit. The principle that compensated days should not rank as days of unemployment has been recognised since 1924,[14] but in modern times its formulation and application have caused considerable difficulties. Today there is a wide variety of severance payments which an employer may, and under legislation must, make. The problem is to what extent these should be covered by the principle and, if so, for what period they should disentitle the recipient. Prior to 1966 a claimant was ineligible for benefit if he continued to receive wages or received compensation which was substantially equivalent to the

5 In *CS 37/53* 15 minutes was disregarded, but in the Northern Ireland decision *2/56 (UB)* 20 minutes was sufficient to defeat the claim. See also *CI 263/49*.
6 See *CS 363/49*, decided when the anomaly existed for sickness benefit.
7 SI 1975/564, reg 5(2): where the shifts are of equal duration he is deemed to be employed the second day. Where he works through Saturday/Sunday midnight the same rules apply to determine the week in which the shift falls: *R(U) 37/56*.
8 But see *Calvert* p. 120, who argues that the decision, though consistent with the policy of the regulation, is not justified by its wording.
9 SSA 1975, s.14(8).
10 Ibid, s.17(1)(e).
11 For the meaning of 'normally' see pp. 92 and 95, below.
12 SI 1975/564, reg 4(1).
13 Ibid, reg 4(3).
14 See UIA (No 2) 1924, s.1(4).

wages lost.[15] This proved to be too restrictive an approach and in 1966 was replaced by the concept of payment in lieu either of notice to terminate or, if the contract was for a term certain, of the remuneration which would have been paid if the contract had not been terminated.[16] This too was thought to be insufficiently broad – in particular it could not apply to employees (e.g. civil servants) whose contract was not for a term certain and who were legally not entitled to notice. The current regulation 7(1)(d), introduced in 1971,[17] provides that

> a day shall not be treated as a day of unemployment if it is a day in respect of which a person receives a payment (whether or not a payment made in pursuance of a legally enforceable obligation) in lieu either of notice or of the remuneration which he would have received for that day had his employment not been terminated. . . .[18]

Finally, in 1976, special provision was made to disentitle the claimant for days for which certain types of compensation (notably for unfair dismissal) were payable under the Employment Protection legislation.[19]

a *Payments covered*

For the claimant to be caught under the general regulation, the payments in question must have been made in lieu either of notice or of the remuneration which he would have received if the contract had not been terminated. In other words, some nexus must exist between the payment and the period of notice required or the claimant's prospective remuneration for the unexpired portion of the term for which he was engaged.[20] The fact that an employee voluntarily accepts redundancy does not by itself imply the absence of such a nexus,[1] though if the payment which induces the agreement is not calculated by reference to the period of notice or remuneration which would otherwise have been paid the regulation does not apply.[2] The period of notice referred to is that required by the contract or the general law of employment.[3] Cases such as those of Crown servants in which there is no legally enforceable right to notice but where it is customarily given are also covered: that is the import of the passage in parentheses introduced by the 1971 reform.[4] However ambiguous they may appear, these words were not intended, and should not be construed, to cover payments of a purely gratuitous nature: 'a payment which is made truly *ex gratia* (i.e. out of kindness) by an employer, and not having the characteristic of either a payment in lieu of notice or in lieu of remuneration, would be outside the ambit' of the regulation.[5] Payments

15 SI 1948/1277, reg 6(1)(d). For the meaning attributed to 'substantially equivalent' compensation, see SI 1954/117, reg 3(2).
16 SI 1966/1049, reg 7(1).
17 SI 1971/807, reg 2.
18 SI 1975/564, reg 7(1)(d).
19 SI 1976/328 and SI 1976/677, adding reg 7(1)(l) to SI 1975/564. See also p. 100, below.
20 *R(U) 2/80*, para 16, V G H Hallett, Comr.
1 *R(U) 9/73*, paras 13–14 (Tribunal majority opinions).
2 *R(U) 2/80*.
3 See on this the standard labour law texts (e.g. Davies and Freedland *Labour Law* (1979) pp. 229–234). In *R(U) 7/80*, D G Rice, Comr, had regard to the period of 90 days consultation before redundancy required by the Employment Protection Act 1975, s.99, for the waiver of which the payment was made, even though the right to the consultation was vested in the employee's union and not in himself.
4 *R v National Insurance Comr, ex parte Stratton* [1979] QB 361 at 371, per Lord Denning MR. See also *R(U) 8/73*, para 19 (Tribunal majority).
5 *R(U) 7/73*, para 45 (Tribunal majority), and see *R v National Insurance Comr, ex parte Stratton*, n.4, above, per Lord Denning MR at 372.

representing a reward for past services or simple compensation for the loss of a job are similarly treated; they are not intended to reflect prospective remuneration.[6]

The real difficulty arises where, as in most cases, the payment includes elements both of reward for past service and of the lost prospective earnings. To sever the payment into its constituent elements would be too difficult and is not encouraged.[7] In two Commissioners' decisions of 1968, it was held that a payment was caught by the regulation if it contained *any* element representing future remuneration.[8] As has been pointed out, where the element is insignificant this can lead to the grotesque result that the employee is disentitled to unemployment benefit for what may be a substantial period of notice.[9] The view taken of these decisions by the Court of Appeal in the leading case of *R v National Insurance Comr, ex parte Stratton* was ambivalent.[10] In a subsequent decision, the Commissioner purported to find in the *Stratton* case authority for a different approach, that regard was to be had to 'the true nature of the terminal payment'.[11] Though this is a doubtful interpretation of the judgments in *Stratton*,[12] it provides a fairer and less artificial solution. On this basis, a statutory redundancy payment escapes the regulation as its *main* purpose is to provide compensation for the loss of the proprietary interest in the job,[13] and this is true of analogous payments made to members of the armed forces on redundancy, under the special government scheme.[14] The character of the payment will naturally depend on the intention of the parties to the agreement or scheme under which it is made: the description given to it by them may be some evidence of its character but is by no means conclusive.[15] Payments calculated by reference to future remuneration are normally regarded as payments in lieu, and this is generally true even if the payment exceeds[16] or falls short of [17] the amount that would have been earned in the period of notice.[18] An award of damages for wrongful dismissal is necessarily so treated,[9] and this extends to a settlement made in pursuance of such a claim.[20]

6 Ibid at 370. See also Templeman LJ at 376.
7 Ibid at 371, per Lord Denning MR, approving *R(U) 3/68*, para 8. See also *R(U) 7/73*, paras 35–37, and *R(U) 4/80*, para 6.
8 *R(U) 2/68*; *R(U) 3/68*.
9 Per Cantley J in *R v National Insurance Comr, ex parte Stratton* [1978] 1 WLR 1041 at 1045, Div Ct, echoed by Bridge LJ on appeal [1979] QB 361 at 373.
10 Lord Denning MR thought that the ruling in *R(U) 3/68* was correct (ibid at 370–371) but this seems to be inconsistent with his ruling that a redundancy payment, which includes elements both of compensation for past services and future remuneration, escaped the regulation. Bridge LJ clearly disliked the principle in *R(U) 3/68*; he conceded that his conclusion might not be reconcilable with that decision, but thought it inappropriate to overrule it (ibid at 374). The attitude of Templeman LJ was obscure.
11 *R(U) 4/80*, para 6, H A Shewan, Comr. But contrast this with *R(U) 1/80*, J G Monroe, Comr, which is consistent with the 1968 decisions.
12 Mesher [1980] JSWL 117, 119.
13 *R(U) 6/73*, para 10a, H Magnus, Comr, approved in *R v National Insurance Comr, ex parte Stratton* [1979] QB 361 at 370, per Lord Denning MR, at 376, per Templeman LJ. Bridge LJ thought that the regulation did not apply for the different reason that such payments are made after employment has been terminated by notice or effluxion of time: ibid at 373.
14 *Ex parte Stratton*, ibid; and see *R(U) 1/80*.
15 *R(U) 7/73*, para 45, and see *R(U) 29/55*; *R(U) 4/56*; *R(U) 10/58*; *R(U) 8/73*; *R(U) 1/80*; *R(U) 7/80*.
16 *R(U) 7/73*.
17 *R(U) 2/68*; *R(U) 3/68*.
18 *R(U) 1/80*.
19 *R(U) 4/56*, para 10; *R(U) 3/68*, para 6.
20 Ibid.

The position of unfair dismissal compensation is mainly governed by special provision. A claimant's right to unemployment benefit for the period between the termination of employment and the date of a tribunal award is unaffected, but the National Insurance Fund may recoup money from the employer.[1] Where a so-called 'compensatory award' for unfair dismissal or for non-compliance with an order of reinstatement or re-engagement includes a sum representing remuneration which the tribunal considers would reasonably have been paid to the employee for future days, those days cannot rank as days of unemployment.[2] An award calculated without reference to future remuneration (including the so-called 'basic award') does not fall within this provision and *ex hypothesi* there is no ground for treating it as a payment in lieu under regulation 7(1)(d).[3] Settlements of unfair dismissal claims are also not covered by the special provision. Prior to the introduction of the latter in 1976, they were generally treated as payments in lieu[4] and this would seem to be the appropriate characterisation, provided it can be reasonably inferred that the payment included a significant element based on future remuneration.[5] Finally, the claimant is disentitled for days in respect of which there is payable to him remuneration under a protective award, in accordance with the Employment Protection legislation.[6]

b *Duration of disentitlement*

The Regulations referred to above cannot operate to disentitle a claimant for a period exceeding a year after the termination of the contract. Subject to this maximum, the general rules for determining the duration of the disentitlement, as laid down by the Commissioner,[7] are as follows. Where the contract is for a fixed term (i.e. there is no requirement as to notice), the claimant in receipt of a relevant payment will be disentitled for the rest of that term. Where he is entitled to notice, he is barred for the period of notice, as determined by the contract (or the general law of employment), whether or not the sum was intended to be limited to that period. As a rule of thumb this has the merit of avoiding detailed investigation into daily rates of pay to ascertain the number of days of remuneration the payment was intended to represent,[8] but as was pointed out by Bridge LJ in the *Stratton* case, it can lead to 'absurd and extravagant results', for example, when a small payment is received in lieu of a substantial period of notice.[9] In a more recent decision the Commissioner has stressed that it is only a general rule.[10] There is authority for treating the payment as being made for less than the full period of notice where it was made without prejudice

1 SI 1977/674, Part III.
2 SI 1975/564, reg 7(1)(l), inserted by SI 1976/328, reg 2, and SI 1976/677, reg 2. See now Employment Protection (Consolidation) Act 1978, ss.71, 74. The same principle applies to interim relief payable under s.79 of that Act.
3 *R v National Insurance Comr, ex parte Stratton*, n.13, above, per Templeman LJ at 376. Lord Denning MR in the same case (at 370–371) suggests that unfair dismissal awards should be treated as payments in lieu, but he seems to have in mind cases which include both the basic and compensatory awards. Curiously both judges overlooked the special provisions in reg 7(1)(l).
4 *R(U) 5/74*.
5 *CU 2/78*.
6 Employment Protection Act 1975, ss.101, 103, and SI 1975/564, reg 7(1)(l)(v), inserted by SI 1976/328, reg 2.
7 *R(U) 37/53*; *R(U) 6/73*; *R(U) 7/73* (Tribunal majority).
8 Ibid, paras 38–40.
9 [1979] QB 361 at 373.
10 *R(U) 1/80*, paras 8–9, J G Monroe, Comr.

to any later claim for more;[11] and in one unreported case, the Commissioner held that settlement of an unfair dismissal claim was intended to cover a longer period than that of the notice to which the claimant was entitled.[12] Where, as in the case of Crown servants, the employee is not legally entitled to a period of notice, the authorities may have regard to the period of notice which was in practice given.[13] Failing that, they will have to ascertain as best they can from the circumstances the number of days intended to be covered by the compensatory payment.[14]

iv Waiting-days

In some systems of unemployment insurance, the claimant is eligible for benefit on the first day of unemployment,[15] but the British scheme in common with the majority, has always insisted that a waiting-period be served. During the time of greatest unemployment between the wars the period was a week,[16] but in 1937[17] the current rule was adopted that benefit is not available for the first three days of a period of interruption of employment.[18] All the evidence shows that the administrative costs of paying benefit for one or two days is disproportionately large.[19] There is a widespread assumption that an individual is generally able to absorb a few days of earnings loss, and if he is not he may be entitled to supplementary benefit.[20] Further, in many cases the employer, through a guarantee agreement or otherwise, indemnifies his employees against short spells of unemployment and, under the Employment Protection legislation, he is bound to provide a limited form of such coverage.[1] These factors were also used to justify the decision in 1971 to abolish the right hitherto enjoyed by those unemployed for two weeks or more retrospectively to claim for the three days.[2]

v Periods of interruption of employment

Where a claimant is subject to intermittent periods of unemployment (e.g., where he is on short-time) it would clearly be impossibly severe to impose the three waiting-days for each such period. By means of the so-called 'continuity' and 'linking' rules, the legislation therefore enables him to aggregate spells of unemployment, so that he will be disentitled for only the first three days of the aggregate 'period of interruption of employment'. The 'continuity' rule prescribes that a 'period of interruption of

11 *R(U) 5/72*.
12 *CU 2/78*.
13 *R(U) 8/73* (Tribunal majority).
14 *R(U) 1/79*, R J A Temple, Chief Comr. The point was not considered in the judgments of the Divisional Court [1978] 1 WLR 1041 and Court of Appeal [1979] QB 361 as in both courts it was held that the payment did not disentitle the claimant.
15 E.g. in W. Germany and France.
16 UIA (No 2) 1921, s.3(3).
17 SR & O 1937/194, reg 2(b).
18 SSA 1975, s.14(3). The days in question must be those which rank as days of unemployment or incapacity for the purposes of unemployment and sickness benefit: ibid, s.17(1)(c). It follows that e.g. days of rest, p. 85, above, compensated days, pp. 85–86, above, and (if the claimant is on short-time) 'normal idle days', pp. 94–97, below, cannot count as waiting days.
19 See NIAC Report on Very Short Spells of Unemployment (1955, Cmd 9609).
20 Ch 12, below.
1 See p. 91, below.
2 SSA 1971, s.7(1) and see Sir K Joseph, Secretary of State, introducing the Second Reading of the Bill, 816 HC Official Report (5th series) cols 61–63.

employment' exists where he is unemployed for any two days (consecutive or not)[3] within six consecutive days, for example:[4]

> C is unemployed on Monday and Friday within the same week. These two days constitute a single period of interruption of unemployment.

The 'linking' rule then provides that any two such periods not separated by more than eight weeks are treated as one period of interruption of employment.[5]

> If, in the above example, C is unemployed again on the Monday and Friday of the following week, the two periods of interruption of employment are linked so that he will be entitled to benefit for the Friday of week 2 (the waiting-days being the Monday and Friday of week 1 and the Monday of week 2). Subject to the rules to be described in the next section, he will continue to be entitled for each subsequent day of unemployment forming part of a period of interruption of employment (i.e. satisfying the two-in-six continuity rule) which is not separated from the previous such period by more than eight weeks.

D Benefit during suspension, lay-off or short-time

i General

Notwithstanding that the contract of employment is subsisting, an employee may be 'unemployed' in the sense that the employer is unable to provide him with work.[6] He may be 'laid-off' (i.e. the contract of employment is suspended until work is once more available[7]) or he may be put on 'short-time' (i.e. his regular hours of work and therefore generally also his wages are reduced by a certain amount every week). The decision to suspend, rather than terminate, the employment may be based on an expectation that the economic difficulties being experienced by the employer are only temporary and on a consequent desire to keep the workforce intact. But reducing the work available to, and therefore the earnings of, many, instead of dismissing a few may also constitute a more equitable distribution of the effects of recession and in that social policy sense be more desirable.[8] However justifiable the decision, there is unquestionably a need to compensate those losing earnings as a result, and in Britain this has traditionally been done by means of the conventional unemployment insurance scheme.[9] Nevertheless, there are powerful objections to this method of solving the problem.[10] The administrative costs of paying benefits for short and often irregular periods are high, and the employment

3 For this purpose, a 'day of unemployment' includes a day when the claimant attends a training course or (if aged over 60) for which he receives a supplementary allowance without having to register for work: SI 1975/564, reg 10, as substituted by SI 1981/1501; and see p. 461, below.
4 SSA 1975, s.17(1)(d).
5 Ibid, as amended by SSA (No 2) 1980, s.3. Prior to this reform the periods could be separated by 13 weeks.
6 See generally Income Data Services Handbook *Lay-offs and Short-time* (1976).
7 For a statutory definition see Redundancy Payments Act 1965, s.5(1).
8 Sorrentino in Showler and Sinfield (ed) *The Workless State* (1981) p.196.
9 Other countries have generally developed special schemes for so-called 'partial unemployment': *Showler and Sinfield*, n.8, above at pp. 194–196 and OECD *Unemployment Compensation and Related Employment Policy Measures* (1979) pp. 39–40.
10 Dept of Employment Consultative Document on Compensation for Short-Time Working (1978); Ogus 4 ILJ 12, 13–15.

services are not suited to dealing with persons who already have an employer but who in theory must make themselves available for other work. There is also the economic argument that contributors to the National Insurance Fund should not have to subsidise those industries which regularly have to lay off workers,[11] particularly when, as the evidence reveals,[12] patterns of work are commonly fixed to attract the maximum amount of benefit.

The force of these arguments has been increasingly recognised in recent years and attempts have been made to devise other methods of compensating employees. The most favoured of such methods is for the employer to assume responsibility by agreements guaranteeing a minimum amount of wages or work. In the hope that guarantee agreements would become universal, the Labour government in 1966 sought to discharge the National Insurance Fund from liability for benefit for periods of unemployment of less than a week. The policy was put into effect immediately as regards earnings-related supplement,[13] but for the flat-rate benefit was postponed[14] while employers and unions made the appropriate arrangements. Although ten years later it was estimated that about 80 per cent of workers liable to be put on short-time were covered by some such agreement, the guarantee was usually for considerably less than a week's pay and subject to stringent conditions.[15] Moreover, the guarantee could often be suspended so that employees could still claim unemployment benefit. Rather than remove entitlement to the flat-rate benefit in all cases, the government introduced, in the Employment Protection Act 1975, compulsory guarantee payments, though these too were unambitious: only for a maximum of five 'workless' days within a period of three months, and subject to an overall limit of £30 (now £40[16]) for that period.[17] This solution, in turn, was hardly satisfactory, not only because of the low level of guaranteed payments but also because its interaction with entitlement to unemployment benefit generated some anomalies.[18] In 1978 the government issued far-reaching proposals under which employers would be obliged to guarantee 75 per cent of normal pay to employees put on short-time which did not involve more than one week's continuous lay-off.[19] A substantial proportion of the payments would be refunded to employers from a new fund, to which employers and the Exchequer would contribute. There would also be special, though temporary, arrangements during periods of high unemployment, when employers would be entitled to a 100 per cent refund provided they could show that short-time was the alternative to redundancy and that there was a good chance that normal working would eventually be resumed. Something akin to these special arrangements was in fact introduced under the Employment Subsidies Act 1978, and assumed considerable importance in the years 1979–81, covering about one-quarter of a million workers placed on short time.[20] But the

11 First Report of the Royal Commission on Unemployment Insurance (1931, Cmd 3872), para 777.
12 Consultative Document, n.10, above.
13 NIA 1966, s.2.
14 Originally only for three years (ibid, s.3(1) but then indefinitely: NIA 1969, s.12(3).
15 Consultative Document, n.10, above.
16 SI 1980/2019.
17 Employment Protection Act 1975, ss.22–28; now Employment Protection (Consolidation) Act 1978, ss.12–18.
18 See p. 101, below.
19 Consultative Document, n.10, above, on which see Partington 7 ILJ 187.
20 See Freedland 9 ILJ 254.

permanent proposals have not yet been implemented and so the unwieldy and complex law governing entitlement to unemployment benefit for those laid-off or on short-time and which now calls for examination continues in force. Those claiming benefit where the contract of employment has not been terminated are subject to four special rules. The subject is divided accordingly.

ii 'Full extent normal' rule

Clearly to justify the payment of benefit to a man on short-time, his work during the week in question must be less than that which is normal for him in his current employment. Two rules, both unfortunately highly complex, have been devised to meet this objective. The first disentitles those who, notwithstanding the short-time, have been engaged for their normal amount of work.[1] The regulation provides that:

> [A] day shall not be treated as a day of unemployment if on that day a person does no work and is a person who does not ordinarily work on every day in a week (exclusive of Sunday or the day substituted [therefor], but who is, in the week in which the said day occurs, employed to the full extent normal in his case. . . .[2]

It is not entirely clear what must be proved or by whom.[3] The Commissioner has treated it as imposing on the insurance officer the onus to prove both (1) that the claimant does not ordinarily work six days a week, *and* (2) that in the week in question he was employed to the full extent normal.[4] The policy justification for condition (1), the exclusion of six-day workers, is obscure.[5] Condition (2), whether he is employed to the full extent normal, is determined according to the number of hours (not days) he works in the week in question,[6] so that a six-day worker may work the same number of hours as before but over fewer days and yet not be disentitled under the rule. It is irrelevant to the operation of the rule whether or not the employee has lost earnings; this gives rise to the further anomalies that a claimant may work fewer hours for the same amount of pay and still be entitled to benefit, while a person working the same hours but for reduced pay is disentitled under the rule. An objective standard is applied to the two conditions in the regulation: in determining whether the claimant ordinarily worked six days a week (for(1)) or what was normal for him (for (2)), the authorities are not concerned with his intentions or desires. It is always a question of fact to be ascertained on the basis of his employment record.[7] Further, his actual record prevails over his duties and expectations under the contract of employment.[8] Thus, if he is obliged to work five days a week but there is not enough work to keep him occupied for more than four days, four days is his 'normal' week.[9] The evidence to which reference may be made has caused some difficulty. In the years following the introduction of the regulation the Commissioner tended to look at the

1 Under the former unemployment insurance scheme, the rule was evolved through the Umpire's decisions. See e.g. *UD 4149/38*.
2 SI 1975/564, reg 7(1)(e).
3 *Ogus*, n.10, above, at p. 16.
4 *R(U) 13/59*.
5 *Calvert* p. 78.
6 *R(U) 13/62*.
7 *CU 518/49*; *R(U) 2/52*; *R(U) 13/60*; *R(U) 3/74*.
8 *R(U) 19/58*.
9 *R(U) 13/56*.

claimant's record during the period of 12 months immediately previous to the date of claim.[10] The adoption of this period soon crystallised into a rule of law. But this proved to be too rigid an approach, and it became necessary to create exceptions to the rule so that the authorities could look beyond the 12 months period when in the circumstances it was not the appropriate test for 'normality'.

The first and most important such circumstance is when the claimant's record of employment has been affected by adverse industrial conditions. In applying the 'full extent normal' rule

> no account shall be taken, in determining either the number of days in a week on which he ordinarily works or the full extent of employment in a week which is normal in his case, of any period of short-time working due to adverse industrial conditions.[11]

But the phrase 'adverse industrial conditions' has not been broadly interpreted: to justify looking beyond the 12-months period the conditions must have been temporary or sporadic.[12] There must be a reduction below the standard level of employment: for the purposes of the regulation a dropping of overtime is not 'short-time'.[13]

The second express exception to the 12-months reference period arises where the claimant's pattern of employment was irregular or casual. Indeed in these circumstances, the 'full extent normal' rule cannot function at all[14] and the regulations provide that the rule shall not apply to a person unless

> (a) there is a recognised or customary working week in connection with his employment; or
> (b) he regularly works for the same number of days in a week for the same employer or group of employers.[15]

Even with such exceptions, the 12-months reference period cannot be universally applied. If the claimant's pattern of work has changed significantly within the last year (e.g. he may have changed his job or the terms of his employment), it is obvious that regard must be had to the newly established pattern even though it has not existed for a year.[16] Indeed, more recently, the Commissioner, influenced by decisions on analogous points arising under the 'normal idle day' rule[17], has begun to favour a generally more flexible approach. The 12-months approach is but one method of determining on the facts what, at the time of the claim, was normal for the claimant.[18]

The existence of a holiday[19] within the week of the claim will reduce what is normal for that week[20] but the fact that there is a holiday on a day on which the claimant does not normally work will not affect his claim.[1]

10 *CU 518/49*.
11 SI 1975/564, reg 7(1)(e).
12 *R(U) 13/60*.
13 *R(U) 2/73*, H A Shewan, Comr.
14 *R(U) 32/51*; *R(U) 37/56*.
15 SI 1975/564, reg 7(2).
16 *R(U) 1/72*, H A Shewan, Comr.
17 Pp. 95–96, below.
18 *R(U) 1/72*.
19 For the general provisions on holidays see pp. 97–100, below.
20 *R(U) 16/55*.
1 *R(U) 5/57*, Tribunal decision, overruling *R(U) 9/54*.

iii 'Normal idle day' rule

The second rule, designed to test that there has been a genuine reduction in the work available to the claimant, was rendered necessary by the fact that, while unemployment benefit is payable on the basis of a six-day working week,[2] many (now most) employees are engaged for less than that amount per week. Quite apart from Sunday, there is for such workers at least one other 'normal idle day'. It would clearly be anomalous if a four-day worker losing one day a week could claim both for that day and the two other days when he would not normally work – thus entitling him to 3/6 of weekly benefit – while a five-day worker losing one day could claim for two days – entitling him to 2/6 of weekly benefit. Worse still, a six-day worker losing a single day might not be able to claim even for that day, as he would typically not satisfy the two-in-six continuity rule.[3] Following consideration of the matter by the National Insurance Advisory Committee,[4] the government introduced in 1957 a rule disentitling the claimant from benefit for any day on which he would not normally work, unless he were unemployed on all the other days (excluding Sunday or its substitute) of the week.[5] However, like the 'full extent normal' rule, this solution while eliminating some anomalies created others. If, as part of the short-time arrangements, an employee now works a 'normal idle day' instead of a normal working day, he is not prevented from claiming benefit for the latter day and thus will be more favourably treated than an employee who does not switch his working pattern in this way. For example:

> C and D normally work on four days, Monday to Thursday inclusive. During a recession, C works on Monday and Friday. He can claim for three days (Tuesday, Wednesday and Thursday, none of which are 'normal idle days'). But if D works on Monday and Tuesday he can only claim for two days (Wednesday and Thursday – but not Friday which is a 'normal idle day').

Quite apart from this weakness, the indigestible statutory provision which enshrines the rule has given rise to considerable difficulties and necessary modifications. As reenacted in 1975 it prescribes that

> where a person is an employed earner and his employment as such has not been terminated, then in any week a day on which in the normal course that person would not work in that employment or in any other employed earner's employment shall not be treated as a day of unemployment unless each other day in that week [other than Sunday or a substitute therefor] on which in the normal course he would so work is a day of interruption of employment.[6]

a *Employment terminated or treated as terminated*

The rule only applies where the claimant's employment has not been terminated. Clearly if his engagement with the employer has ceased he should receive a full week's benefit even though that week includes days when he would not normally work. But difficulties have been encountered in deciding when, for this purpose, a contract has been terminated. The

2 P. 85, above.
3 See p. 90, above. He would however satisfy the rule if his 'lost' day were altered from week to week.
4 Report on Very Short Spells of Unemployment (1955, Cmd 9609), and see Ogus 4 ILJ 12, 16–17.
5 NIA 1957, s.4(1).
6 SSA 1975, s.17(1)(b).

Commissioner has been faced with a choice between applying the ordinary contractual meaning of termination (viz that the rights and obligations of the parties have ceased[7]) and adopting the special meaning attributed to 'termination' by the Umpire under the old Unemployment Insurance Acts. On the latter view, the contract was not to be regarded as terminated unless the claimant had been 'finally' discharged without any intention of resuming the relationship of employer and employee on the next available opportunity.[8] For a long time, the special meaning prevailed,[9] notwithstanding a 'stream of indignant appellants who could not understand how their employment could be said not to have terminated when their contract of employment no longer subsisted'.[10] The line of decisions upholding this second approach was questioned by a single Commissioner in 1967[11] and effectively overruled by a Tribunal of Commissioners in 1968.[12] Hence the general law of contract now applies, though, as we have seen,[13] the construction of the contract is sometimes highly problematical.

There are a number of cases in which the regulations treat the employment as having been terminated, even though in accordance with the general law of contract it has been only suspended. Most of these deal with situations for which the 'normal idle day' rule is inappropriate because the claimant has not established a 'normal' pattern of work – for that reason they are considered below.[14] The single case calling for mention here is that where the claimant's employment has been 'indefinitely suspended'. *Ex hypothesi*, he has not been put on short-time but has been laid-off for an indefinite period and there is therefore every justification for paying him a full week's benefit, even for days when he would not normally work. To invoke this exception to the 'normal idle day' rule, the claimant must show not only that the employment has been 'indefinitely suspended' but also that it has lasted for at least six continuous days.[15]

b *What is normal*

Where the rule does apply, the onus is on the insurance officer to prove that a day for which benefit is claimed is one on which the claimant would not normally work.[16] If that is satisfied, the claimant can only escape disentitlement if he is able to show that his normal days of work in the week in question[17] are also days of interruption of employment, in other

7 Cf p. 81, above.

8 *UD 16930/31*. For an interesting parallel in the law of redundancy, see Grunfeld *Law of Redundancy* (2nd edn) pp. 344–354.

9 E.g. *R(U) 16/59*; *R(U) 11/61*. In N. Ireland one decision went so far as to hold that where in one week C was regularly employed by different employers, (i) the 'employment' was the totality of all employments, and therefore (ii) the termination of contract with one employer did not terminate the 'employment' as a whole: *16/59 (UB)*.

10 *R(U) 7/68*, para 26 (Tribunal decision).

11 *R(U) 4/67*, J S Watson, Comr. It was not necessary to decide which approach was right, as on either view the claimant succeeded.

12 *R(U) 7/68*. It was said that the Umpire had employed the doctrine not to interpret the word 'termination' but rather to decide whether or not the claimant had been 'continuously unemployed', a concept not relevant to modern legislation: ibid, para 20.

13 Pp. 81–82, above.

14 Pp. 96–97, below.

15 SI 1975/564, reg 16(2). The period is determined in accordance with SSA 1975, s.17(3)(a) and SI 1975/564, reg 6: Sundays and days of customary or recognised holiday do not count, but days of incapacity which would otherwise have been days of suspension do count.

16 *R(U) 14/59*, para 11.

17 The work must be in 'employed earner's employment', on which see pp. 45–50, above.

words, that he has been 'laid-off' for the whole of the week in question.[18] In deciding what is 'normal' for both parts of the rule, the authorities have by and large followed the pattern established for the 'full extent normal' rule. They have experienced similar difficulties and have sought to apply similar solutions. The contract of employment may provide evidence as to what is 'normal' – for example, where it envisages a rota system of working[19] – but regard is typically had more to the claimant's actual record of work.[20] The 12-months reference period was adapted to meet the requirements of the new condition: during the period of 12 months immediately preceding the claim, but ignoring holidays and sickness, had the claimant worked on the day in question more often than he had not?[1]

But this practice was no more successful at coping with the varying situations to which it was applied. It was clearly inappropriate where an employee had moved to a new situation or was governed by a new agreement, and whether working on a particular day is 'normal' for him must be judged in the light of the changed circumstances rather than on his record during the last year.[2] Short-time work due to adverse industrial conditions was to be excluded, a principle later recognised in an extraordinarily complex form by the regulations,[3] though given the same interpretation as the parallel provision governing the 'full extent normal' rule.[4]

In cases where the claimant's work pattern has been irregular or not relevant to his current employment, it is impossible to apply any test of 'normality' and so the regulations exclude the 'normal idle day' rule altogether by treating the employment as having been terminated. The cases so governed are as follows.

(a) There is not a recognised or customary week in connection with the employment.[5]

(b) The claimant does not regularly work for the same number of days in a week for the same employer or group of employers.[6]

(c) The claimant works in casual employment.[7] This provision predates[8] and has probably been superseded by cases (a) and (b). When clearly operative, it was given a restrictive interpretation by the Commissioner.[9]

18 A person employed on a rota basis, two weeks of work followed by two weeks of rest, is not assisted by this when claiming for days during a week of rest: he cannot show that one other day in the week is normally a day of work: *R(U) 10/80*; *R(U) 6/81*.
19 *R(U) 10/80*; *R(U) 14/80*; *R(U) 6/81*.
20 *R(U) 19/58*; *R(U) 22/58*.
1 *R(U) 14/59*.
2 *R(U) 18/62*; *R(U) 14/60*; *R(U) 1/72*.
3 SI 1975/564, reg 16(3)(d) provides that in any week of short-time due to adverse industrial conditions, the employment is to be treated as if 'terminated' immediately after its commencement, thus excluding from operation the 'normal idle day' rule. But reg 16(5) then stipulates by an equally circumlocutory formula that it shall nevertheless not be treated as a day of unemployment if, quite apart from the short-time, it would still have been a normal idle day. See in general *R(U) 17/60*.
4 The conditions must involve some temporary reductions in the working hours general in the relevant industry (*R(U) 13/60*), thus excluding conditions peculiar to the claimant (*R(U) 14/60*) and general recessions in trade (*R(U) 1/64*).
5 SI 1975/564, reg 16(6)(a). 'Week' can be read as 'weeks': *R(U) 6/81*.
6 SI 1975/564, reg 16(6)(b).
7 Ibid, reg 16(3)(a).
8 It was introduced by SI 1957/1319. Cases (a) and (b) were introduced by SI 1966/1049.
9 See especially, *R(U) 16/59* and *R(U) 11/61*. In both decisions, 'casual' was given a special meaning. The question was whether at the end of each spell of employment the claimant might reasonably expect to be re-employed almost immediately. This interpretation was intended to render the test consistent with the special meaning at the time attributed to 'termination' but since overruled (p. 95, above).

(d) The employer for whom he is working in the week in question is not his usual employer.[10]

iv The 'holiday' rule

a *General*

The questions whether, and to what extent, a holiday should affect entitlement to benefit may be viewed from two different perspectives. On the *broader* perspective, payment during a holiday should in principle be excluded. A holiday is in its nature relief provided by the employer so that the employee may 'enjoy rest, recreation or amusement'.[11] The employee is thus estopped from claiming that circumstances have prevented him from pursuing his gainful occupation. But this view cannot be maintained without substantial qualifications. On the one hand, it can hardly be applied to someone whose contract of employment has been terminated. It would be speculative and impracticable for the authorities to make inquiries whether, if he had been employed in his normal occupation, the claimant would have been on holiday on a certain day or week. At the most, then, the principle can only apply where the contract of employment has been merely suspended. On the other hand, the principle draws no distinction between holidays with pay and holidays without pay, and yet the distinction must be crucial. It is only the employee on holiday *without* pay that has any legitimate claim, and yet on the general principle he is bracketed with another who continues to receive his ordinary wage. This last consideration lies at the heart of the *narrower* perspective. On this view, there is no need for a general principle governing holidays. The legislation should simply be concerned to protect those who are *involuntarily* on holiday *without pay*. Such persons may be ascertained by applying the ordinary rules which refuse to characterise as days of unemployment days for which remuneration is received[12] and disqualify from benefit where employment is left voluntarily.[13] On either view, there is the independent question whether a claimant, who is admittedly unemployed, but who is absent on holiday from his normal place of residence, nevertheless satisfies the ordinary requirement of being 'available' for suitable employment.[14]

On the general question of entitlement during periods of holiday, the history of the British system has been far from consistent. Originally, there were no special provisions,[15] but the Umpire of his own initiative decided that a claimant on holiday was not 'continuously unemployed'.[16] This then hardened into a rule of law[17] and was applied irrespective of whether or not the claimant had received any holiday pay. The modern law has in general maintained this position: if the employment has not been terminated or indefinitely suspended, a day of 'recognised or customary holiday in connection with that employment' is not to be treated as a day of unemployment.[18] The broader perspective was thus explicitly admitted into the system, and with it came all its attendant difficulties: problems in deciding what are customary holidays, distinctions between termination

10 SI 1975/564, reg 16(3)(b).
11 Per H Magnus, Dep Comr, *R(U) 1/66*, para 22.
12 Pp. 85–89, above.
13 Pp. 110–112, below.
14 P. 104, below.
15 UIA 1939, s.1 made statutory provision for the exclusion of holidays from unemployment benefit but owing to the outbreak of war the section never came into force.
16 *UD 228/12*.
17 *UD 7712* and see the 'codifying decision' *UD 18284/32*.
18 SI 1975/564, reg 7(1)(i).

and suspension, and still the need to provide for the man who is forced to take a holiday without pay – a need which was only partially met by a typically complex measure in 1966. By adopting the narrower perspective many systems[19] not only find a more complete solution to this problem, but at the same time avoid the subtle and complex difficulties to which the British approach so unnecessarily gives rise.[20]

b *Recognised and customary holidays*

The first question to be decided is whether the day in question is 'a recognised or customary holiday in connection with that employment'. There must be an agreement, express or implied, between the employer and the employee that on the day in question the employee is relieved from his working duties for the purposes of rest, recreation or amusement.[1] A mere agreement not to work is insufficient. If it is envisaged that the employee will take a break from his ordinary employment and take work elsewhere he is not 'on holiday'.[2] The existence of an agreement is to be determined according to the facts, regard being had in particular to the length of time during which the alleged holiday was habitually observed,[3] and whether extra payments are made for such work.[4] Although the holiday must be recognised or customary 'in connection with that employment', it need not, it seems, refer to the claimant's individual employment as distinct from the general conditions applying at his factory or place of work. This somewhat surprising proposition results from *R(U) 3/53*.

> For the purposes of their trade cycle, C's employers wished to change the dates of the factory's annual holiday. The large majority of employees agreed and the employers allowed those who wished to abide by the original agreement to take their holiday at the earlier date. It was held, however, that they were not entitled to benefit during the period when the majority took their holiday (and when the factory consequently closed). The minority were subject to the wishes of the majority. A claimant may be on holiday even if he does not wish to be so.

A similar principle operates to disentitle those on casual employment. If a man habitually works in a certain place and that place closes for an agreed holiday, the casual employee is prima facie bound by that agreement unless he can show that it does not apply to him because, for example, he had another source of employment outside the place of work in question.[5] But the existence of an alternative occupation or source of employment creates problems which are not easy to solve. In *R(U) 7/63*

> a professional musician worked partly as a school-teacher and partly as a performer. In his former capacity he generally worked four days a week.

19 Including most of those in the USA. Thus, e.g. the Illinois Unemployment Compensation Act does not in principle exclude holidays from the ambit of the fund. A simple provision (§ 440) assimilates 'vacation pay' to 'wages', and a claimant entitled to such 'wages' is ineligible for benefits for any week in which the sums equal or exceed the weekly benefit amount.

20 As *Calvert* points out (pp. 103–104), it is, however, sometimes difficult to determine whether or not an employee receives holiday pay.

1 *R(U) 1/66* (Tribunal decision).

2 *R(U) 8/64*.

3 *R(U) 39/53*; *R(U) 27/58*. Cp. *R(U) 11/53* which is hard to reconcile with these decisions. *Semble*, it places too much weight on the requirement of an agreement.

4 *R(U) 11/53*.

5 *R(U) 18/54*; *R(U) 31/56*.

During the school's Easter vacation he did not work on these four days and received no holiday pay. It was held that he was entitled to benefit. He was not 'on holiday' from his employment as a whole which included his other occupation as a performing musician.

The same approach was taken by a Tribunal of Commissioners in a later decision.[6] They concluded that it would have been too artificial and impracticable to hold that a person could be on holiday for part only of a week. It is submitted, with respect, that this is only because the holiday rule is itself artificial and impracticable. The same result in *R(U) 7/63* could have been reached by the simpler route: (i) was the claimant unemployed on the day in question? (ii) did he receive remuneration for that day?

The existence of a special holiday rule is also responsible for another difficulty. Some 'agreed holidays' have their origin in a slack period of trade. It is established law that if there is an agreement that there should be a holiday, the actual reasons for its institution are irrelevant.[7] This means that there will be an awkward transitional stage between 'short-time working' when benefit will be payable, and an implied 'holiday' when it will not. But the crucial question should surely be not whether there was a 'holiday' but whether the employees were paid when they were not working.

c *Suspension of contract*

If the contract has been either 'terminated' or 'indefinitely suspended', the holiday rule will not apply. As elsewhere,[8] the special meaning attributed to 'termination' by the Umpire under the old Unemployment Insurance Acts was for a long time applied.[9] Following a similar change to the 'normal idle day' rule, a Tribunal of Commissioners in 1968 departed from a long line of authority and held that the ordinary contractual meaning of 'termination' should henceforth prevail.[10] For the purposes of this rule, 'indefinite suspension' is equated with termination and this is construed in accordance with the 1966 provisions on short-time unemployment.[11]

d *Holidays without pay*

It has been seen that one of the defects of the British system is that it draws no general distinction between holidays with and without pay. With this handicap it was faced with an anomaly:[12] a man who changed his employment may not have qualified for holiday pay, and yet he may be unable to work because at the place of employment there is a general holiday shutdown. A simple solution would have been to exclude from the operation of the holiday rule holidays involuntarily taken without pay,[13] but as will have emerged from earlier remarks, such a step would effectively have robbed the holiday rule of any function. A compromise but complex solution was therefore adopted. The regulations effectively provide that if in the same period of 12 months (beginning for this purpose on 1 March) as the holiday in question, the claimant has already been on holiday (under a

6 *R(U) 18/64*.
7 *UD 18284/32*; *R(U) 4/52*.
8 Pp. 81 and 95, above.
9 E.g. *R(U) 12/54*; *R(U) 19/54*; *R(U) 1/62*; *R(U) 18/64*; *R(U) 1/66*.
10 *R(U) 8/68*.
11 P. 95, above.
12 See NIAC Report on Very Short Spells of Unemployment (1955, Cmd 9609), paras 63–65.
13 For a summary of the US law on this point see Anno. 30 ALR 2d 366. See also 64 Mich L Rev 1100.

contract of employment) equalling or exceeding the period of the present holiday in question, the holiday rule shall not apply to disentitle the claimant from benefit for this latter period.[14]

v Compensated days

The final question arising under this section is how entitlement to benefit for short-term unemployment may be affected by guarantee and other payments. Under the Employment Protection (Consolidation) Act 1978 the employer is *bound* to pay the employee for five 'workless days' within a period of three months, but only to a current maximum of £40 for that period.[15] Regulations then provide that a day on which a sum is payable under the Act is not to be treated as a day of unemployment.[16] The same applies to payments under agreements which have been made the subject of an exemption order by an appropriate Minister,[17] and also to payments arising from a scheme made under the Employment Subsidies Act 1978,[18] for example, the Temporary Short Time Working Compensation Scheme.[19] For payments which do not come within any of these categories, the general principles as developed by the Commissioner apply. One crucial question is whether the agreement is construed to confer remuneration on the employee on the day or days when he does not work. The earlier decisions tended to draw a distinction between two classes of agreement: those in which the employer guaranteed a weekly *wage*; and those in which he guaranteed a certain amount of *work*. In the former case it was inferred that the intention was to pay the sum for the *whole* of the week, and that therefore the employee could not be 'unemployed' for any part of that week.[20] The same inference could not be drawn for the 'work' guarantees[1] and not unnaturally, in order that short-time workers should have access to the fund, many employment contracts were modified so that they might be characterised as belonging to this latter type.

In *R(U) 21/56*, however, a Tribunal of Commissioners held that a mere change of wording of an agreement made solely for the purposes of unemployment benefit, and which had no effect industrially, and which did not modify the rights and obligations of the parties could not by itself confer a title to benefit. The emphasis was shifted from the question of what the employer guaranteed to what the employee undertook in consideration of the guarantee. The new approach focused on whether or not, under the agreement, the employee was bound to make himself available to the employer on the days of the alleged unemployment.[2] This involves examining the *legal* consequences of the agreement: the fact that the employer is in practice prepared to regard the employee as available for other employment is irrelevant.[3]

14 SI 1975/564, reg 7(1)(i).
15 Ss. 12–15; and see Hepple, Partington and Simpson 6 ILJ 54.
16 SI 1975/564, reg 7(1)(l), inserted by SI 1976/328. For criticisms of these provisions, see Hepple et al, n.15, above, and Dept of Employment Consultative Document *Compensation for Short-Time Working* (1978).
17 Under Employment Protection (Consolidation) Act 1978, s.18.
18 SI 1975/564, reg 7(m), inserted by SI 1978/608.
19 P. 91, above. See generally, Freedland 9 ILJ 254.
20 *R(U) 27/51*.
1 *CWU 49/50*; *R(U) 13/51*; *R(U) 23/55*.
2 See further *R(U) 2/58* and *R(U) 15/61*.
3 *R(U) 1/76*, H A Shewan, Comr.

That entitlement to benefit may confer advantages not only on the short-time worker (the benefit may be more valuable than the guaranteed sum[4]) but also on the employer (who may be relieved from paying anything above the limit imposed by the Employment Protection Act) has led to joint efforts to undermine the validity of the guarantee agreement. While an agreement can, subject to the Employment Protection Act, be varied or abrogated, this must be done by mutual agreement: a unilateral decision to this effect or the mere rearrangement of the work timetable will be ineffective.[5] The Commissioner has also held that an agreement cannot be revoked retrospectively.[6]

Part 4 Availability

A General

The unemployment must be involuntary. The notion is incorporated in various areas of the law. First, there are the administrative requirements that a claim be made in person at an unemployment benefit office,[7] and that the claimant then register for work at an Employment Office, Jobcentre or, in the case of young persons, Careers Office.[8] Curiously, the requirement to register is not supported by statutory authority, and, at the time of writing, the government is actively considering a proposal that it should be abandoned.[9] Secondly, there is a condition for unemployment benefit that the claimant be 'available' for suitable employment – the subject matter of this Part. Thirdly, there are various grounds for disqualification where effectively the unemployment results from his own conduct or attitude.[10]

As regards availability, the difficulty has been to formulate a test which provides sufficiently precise guidelines for those administering it and yet is flexible enough to allow for consideration of all the relevant factors, including the claimant's age, qualifications, working capacity and intentions, as well as the general level of unemployment and characteristics of the labour market particular to the locality.[11] Under the National Insurance Act 1911, the claimant had to prove that he was 'capable of work but unable to obtain suitable employment'.[12] Faced with a sudden and dangerous rise in unemployment in the 1920s, the government decided that the conditions of eligibility had to be strengthened and introduced the notorious requirement that the claimant must prove that he was 'genuinely

4 See Hepple et al, n.15, above, who comment on the substantial gap between the level of unemployment benefit and the guaranteed amounts under the Employment Protection legislation.
5 *R(U) 10/73* (Tribunal decision); *R(U) 1/75*.
6 *R(U) 1/76*.
7 SI 1979/628, reg 4, and p. 558, below.
8 Report of Joint DE/DHSS Rayner Scrutiny, Payment of Benefits to Unemployed People (1980), para 2.02.
9 Ibid, paras 4.03–4.37. The main grounds for the proposal were that compulsory registration does not provide a test of willingness to work and that the control function could more effectively be performed by unemployment review officers (on which see p. 498, below).
10 Pp. 106–118, below.
11 *Fisher* para 237, and for economic considerations see Worswick (ed) *The Concept and Measurement of Involuntary Unemployment* (1976).
12 S.86(3).

seeking whole-time employment but unable to obtain such employment'.[13] Although regarded by employers as an essential feature of unemployment insurance,[14] it had a serious impact on the workings of the scheme,[15] and was bitterly attacked by the trade union movement.[16] As it was interpreted, the new condition seemed to require that a claimant look around for work where there might be none available. An adverse decision left a stigma which was difficult to remove. On the recommendations of a committee,[17] the condition was repealed in 1930.[18]

Under the 1946 Act, the question was simply whether the claimant was 'available for employment,[19]' and this was construed to mean whether there was a reasonable prospect of his obtaining the work for which he *held* himself available.[20] This resulted in the anomaly that some claimants might place such restrictions on their availability that for all practical purposes they were not available. On the recommendations of the National Insurance Advisory Committee,[21] a regulation was therefore introduced which limited the restrictions which an unemployed person might place on his availability.[1] In 1980 the working of this area of law was critically examined by a joint Department of Employment and DHSS team.[2] In its view, the 'availability' condition, as then administered, was inefficient and too imprecise. Its recommendations, which the government hopes to implement in 1982, will be considered after the account of the current law.

B Statutory test

The Social Security Act 1975 provides that a day shall not be treated as a day of unemployment unless on that day the claimant

> is capable of work and he is, or is deemed in accordance with regulations to be, available to be employed in employed earner's employment.[3]

The onus is on the claimant to satisfy the condition.[4] The requirement of capacity excludes cases where sickness or invalidity benefit is appropriate.[5] The limitation to 'employed earner's employment' means that availability for self-employed or other uninsured work is irrelevant.[6] The regulations referred to treat the condition as satisfied while the claimant is engaged in manning a lifeboat or serving part-time in a fire brigade,[7] and proposals are currently being considered to add various forms part-time voluntary or charitable work.[8] Subject to these qualifications, the Commissioner has

13 It was applied to claims for uncovenanted benefit by UIA 1921, s.3(3)(b), and extended to covenanted benefit by UIA (No 2) 1924, s.3(1).
14 Report of the Committee on the Procedure and Evidence for the Determination of Claims for Unemployment Insurance Benefit (1929, Cmd 3415) (the Morris Report), para 37.
15 In 1928–29 of approx. 10 million claims, 340,000 were denied benefit for not genuinely seeking work: ibid, at para 36.
16 Ibid, at para 38.
17 Ibid, at para 43.
18 UIA 1930, s.6.
19 S.11(2)(a)(i).
20 See esp. *R(U) 12/52* (Tribunal decision).
21 Report on the Availability Question (1953, Cmd 8894).
1 SI 1955/143.
2 Report, n.8, above.
3 S.17(1)(a).
4 *R(U) 12/52*; *R(U) 34/53*.
5 See *R(U) 24/51*, and ch 4, below.
6 *R(U) 14/51*. For the meaning of 'employed earner's employment' see pp. 45–50, above.
7 SI 1975/564, reg 9.
8 See now SI 1982/96, summarised in the Appendix.

traditionally ruled that he must prove both (i) that there is a reasonable prospect of his obtaining the relevant employment; and (ii) that he is willing and able at once to accept a suitable offer.

i Reasonable prospect

In determining whether there are reasonable prospects of employing the claimant on his stated terms of availability, the authorities have regard to such factors as his employment history (in particular, whether in the past he has succeeded in obtaining employment on these terms),[9] and the attitude of employers.[10] The requirement is not a difficult one to satisfy, for it is not limited to the locality in which the claimant is registered, and even in times of recession, there is likely to be a reasonable prospect of his finding work somewhere.[11]

ii Willingness and ability to accept

The general rule is that claimants must be 'prepared to accept at once any offers of suitable employment brought to their notice'.[12] The authorities will normally assume that the claimant is prepared to accept such offers,[13] but the rule may be invoked to disentitle him where his 'statements or actings' suggest the contrary,[14] most obviously where he actually refuses a suitable offer.[15] In some cases, the question turns on whether he is *able* to accept. He cannot be available if, during the relevant period, he is contractually bound to be at the disposal of another employer.[16] On the other hand, participation in training courses has been generously construed, so that if the claimant can be readily contacted and can take up an offer immediately he will be regarded as available.[17] If he is absent from the locality this will not generally be possible. This is a ground on which the claimant in *R(U) 5/80* could have been disentitled.

> He had been employed abroad for several years, but on losing his job there came to England to set up home. During the period for which he claimed benefit, he was however in England only a few days, mainly for the purpose of arranging his personal affairs.

In holding that he did not satisfy the 'availability' condition, the Commissioner nevertheless stated a general principle which seems to recall the 'genuinely seeking' work test applied in the inter-war years. He said that

> availability implies some active step by the person concerned to draw attention to his availability: it is not a passive state in which a person may be said to be available provided he is sought out and his location is ascertained.[18]

It is not clear what the Commissioner meant by 'active step'. There is no authority for such a requirement to be satisfied by the generality of claimants, but it may have been intended to apply only to those who are itinerant. As such it would be in accord with the approach traditionally

9 *CU 10/49*; *R(U) 44/53*.
10 *R(U) 6/72*, D Neligan, Comr.
11 *Calvert* pp. 109–110.
12 *R(U) 1/53*, para 7, adopting *UD 6986/30*.
13 *R(U) 2/57*.
14 *R(U) 3/65*, para 11, H A Shewan, Dep Comr.
15 *R(U) 4/53*; *R(U) 15/58*.
16 *R(U) 11/51*; *R(U) 1/53*; *R(U) 1/69*, and see p. 80, above.
17 *CWU 47/49; CU 162/50*.
18 *R(U) 5/80*, para 14, J S Watson, Comr.

taken to absences for holidays. Under the former legislation, the Umpire laid down three conditions which in such circumstances are to be satisfied,[19] and these were subsequently adopted by the Commissioner:[20]

(1) the claimant must be ready and willing immediately to return and accept an offer of suitable employment; and
(2) he must have taken reasonable and satisfactory steps to ensure that any such offer would be brought to his notice without delay;[1] and
(3) there was nothing connected with his absence which would have prevented him accepting at once any such offer.

Though this approach may be sound in theory, in practice, as the joint Department of Employment and DHSS team found, it is a 'fiction'.[2] Jobs are not offered to claimants while on holiday. The team recommended that considerable savings on the administrative costs of applying these holiday rules could be made if claimants were given an entitlement to two weeks holiday in any one year during which they would not be required to be available for work.[3] The government hopes to implement this recommendation in 1982.

C Reasonable restrictions test

The additional test imposed by the regulations applies where

> a person places restrictions on the nature, hours, rate of remuneration or locality or other conditions of employment which he is prepared to accept and as a consequence of those restrictions has no reasonable prospects of securing employment. . . .[4]

The essence of the matter is that the lack of reasonable prospects should result from restrictions which the claimant himself *places* on his availability. If the restrictions result from such natural characteristics as age or sex, the regulation does not apply.[5]

If it does apply, the claim for benefit will fail unless one of three conditions is satisfied.

i Adverse but temporary industrial conditions

Under the first the claimant must prove that

> he is prevented from having reasonable prospects of securing employment consistent with those restrictions only as a result of adverse industrial conditions in the locality or localities concerned which may reasonably be regarded as temporary, and having regard to all the circumstances, personal and other, the restrictions which he imposes are reasonable.[6]

19 *UD 7550/35*.
20 *R(U) 3/65* and *R(U) 4/66*, though in the latter case O George, Dep Comr, thought that the conditions might be regarded as more appropriate for the exceptional employment circumstances prevailing at the time they were devised.
1 If he moves from place to place there is a presumption that he cannot satisfy this condition: *R(U) 2/57*.
2 Report of Joint DE/DHSS Rayner Scrutiny, Payment of Benefits to Unemployed People (1980), para 5.36.
3 Ibid, paras 5.39–5.41.
4 SI 1975/564, reg 7(1)(a).
5 *CU 3/71*, cited in Mesher *Compensation for Unemployment* (1976) p. 45. This was considered to be unduly advantageous to men aged 60–65 who retired from their normal employment and were in receipt of an occupational pension, but for whom there was rarely suitable employment available. After much debate, it was decided to reduce the benefit payable to such persons, rather than alter the rules of availability: p. 129, below.
6 SI 1975/564, reg 7(1)(a)(i).

The concept of 'adverse industrial conditions' has already been the subject of discussion.[7] The limitation to such conditions as are 'temporary' has been interpreted to connote the idea of abnormality: ordinary seasonal fluctuations, such as those typically prevailing in seaside resorts, are not included.[8] The second limb contains a requirement analogous to that applicable under condition (iii), and may be conveniently considered under that head.

ii Physical condition

Alternatively, the claimant may show that 'the restrictions are nevertheless reasonable in view of his physical condition'.[9] The provision is illustrated by *R(U) 6/72:*

> A technical manager, suffering from a heart condition, on medical advice retired at the age of 62. He claimed benefit but restricted his availability to offers of employment at a minimum salary of £5,500 a year in his home town or its close environs. There was no reasonable prospect of finding such employment and it was held that in the light of his physical condition, the restriction to the locality (but not that as to remuneration) was reasonable.

iii Generally reasonable

The third alternative is the broadest and confers a necessary degree of flexibility on the authorities. The claimant must prove that

> the restrictions are nevertheless reasonable having regard both to the nature of his usual occupation and also to the time which has elapsed since he became unemployed.[10]

The consideration of 'usual occupation' is designed to protect job skills, and the general standard of remuneration to which the claimant is accustomed. On the other hand, the protection cannot last indefinitely, so that after a reasonable time has expired he must be prepared to accept an offer of a less appropriate kind.[11] The restrictions may, in any event, only be 'reasonable' if they relate to the nature of the claimant's occupation. Thus an actor who held himself available only on certain days when he was not required by the BBC was disentitled: the restrictions arose not from his occupation as an actor but from the particular arrangement with the BBC.[12] In other respects, the authorities have a broad discretion in determining reasonableness so that account may be taken of the claimant's general intentions,[13] the way he defines his 'occupation',[14] his domestic circumstances[15] and the state of the labour market in the locality.[16]

D Reform

The 1980 Review Team carefully examined the functioning of the 'availability' rules and found it to be unsatisfactory.[17] The availability of the

7 P. 93, above.
8 *R(U) 3/59*.
9 SI 1975/564, reg 7(1)(a)(ii).
10 Ibid, reg 7(1)(a)(iii).
11 *R(U) 3/59* and see the analogous principle in the disqualification provisions, p. 114, below.
12 *R(U) 1/69*, E R Bowen, Comr.
13 *R(U) 33/58*.
14 *R(U) 3/59*; *R(U) 1/69*.
15 *R(U) 14/57*; *R(U) 17/57*; *R(U) 6/59*.
16 *R(U) 17/57*; *R(U) 6/72*.
17 N.2, above, paras 4.38–4.59.

claimant is questioned only rarely, and generally only when a doubt is raised by some particular event, such as the refusal of an apparently suitable job. This is mainly because availability is in practice tested by the staff at the Jobcentre, and they give this task very low priority compared with their other functions. It is therefore proposed that responsibility for initiating availability tests should be transferred to Unemployment Review Officers,[18] operating in conjunction with the Unemployment Benefit Offices. The latter would apply a formal test of availability when the claim for benefit is first made. If the claimant is prepared to accept a job on similar terms to his last employment, this would be regarded as sufficient to satisfy the availability test, at least for a period of three months. If, on the other hand, he is unwilling to return to his last job or similar work, the test would be whether in the district where the claimant is prepared to work, any vacancies of the kind sought are available. After three months of unemployment, claimants who are manual workers would be expected to accept any manual work within their abilities; and non-manual workers would be expected to accept any non-manual work within their abilities. The government hopes to implement these recommendations in 1982.

Part 5 Disqualification for voluntary unemployment

The idea that unemployment must be involuntary may be seen as justifying not only the condition that a claimant be 'available' for employment, but also the circumstances in which he may be disqualified from benefit for a maximum period of six weeks. These may be conveniently grouped under three headings:

(a) losing employment through misconduct;
(b) voluntarily leaving employment without just cause;
(c) without good cause, refusing or failing to take, a reasonable opportunity to secure employment.

Part 5 concludes with an account of the principles determining the period of disqualification.

A Misconduct

The first ground for disqualification arises where the claimant has 'lost his employment as an employed earner through his misconduct'.[19] The rule was to be found in the National Insurance Act of 1911,[20] and has existed effectively in the same form ever since. However, the exact policy considerations on which it is based have never been made entirely explicit,[1] and as a result its interpretation and evolution have not been wholly consistent. Three alternative theories may be invoked to support the disqualification.

a *Punishment* From a moral or social point of view, a worker who has been dismissed for misconduct is unworthy of the support of the fund: he has transgressed the ethical standards of the community.

18 These would have greater powers than are currently exercised under the supplementary benefit scheme: pp.497–498, below.
19 SSA 1975, s.20(1)(a).
20 NIA 1911, s.87(2).
1 For an economic appraisal, see Fenn in Burrows and Veljanovski (eds) *The Economic Approach to Law* (1981) ch 13.

b *Suitability* The claimant should be disqualified where his own actions reveal him as unsuitable for the job. The fund is intended to cover only those who lose employment through external circumstances, and not those whose lack of skill results in dismissal.

c *Voluntary unemployment* The purpose of the disqualification is to protect the fund against voluntary unemployment. Benefit is therefore to be denied to a claimant who knew or should have known that his conduct was reasonably likely to incur dismissal.

The first theory has been most explicitly rejected in the United Kingdom.[2] The third theory is more consistent with the general purpose of the legislation, and its influence can be seen in certain decisions,[3] but like most doctrines dependent on mental states, it creates grave problems of proof.[4] The suitability theory, though less attractive on policy grounds, can account for most of the law on this subject. The authorities seek to apply an objective standard of conduct to each worker. In general, they seem not to be concerned whether he appreciated, or might reasonably have appreciated, that his conduct was likely to lead to dismissal.

i Dismissal caused by misconduct

In principle, the insurance officer must prove that the claimant was dismissed for an act or omission which constituted 'misconduct'.[5] But the requirement of 'dismissal' and its causal relationship with the alleged misconduct have been broadly construed. The contract of employment need not have been terminated by the employer: it will suffice if, as a result of the misconduct, both parties regard the employment as ended.[6] Nor need the 'dismissal' follow as an immediate consequence of the misconduct. In one case, a bus driver was convicted of a driving offence. He was disqualified even though the immediate cause of his dismissal was the loss of his licence rather than the commission of the offence.[7]

ii Misconduct connected with employment

If a man were to be disqualified for misconduct committed in any circumstance, in effect the system would be regarding the employer's attitude to the misconduct as conclusive, and would be adopting a punitive approach to the claimant's entitlement. If, however, it requires that the misconduct be related to the employment, it may still question whether the dismissal warrants disqualification, as viewed from the policy dictate of protecting the insurance fund. The Commissioner has adopted this latter stance and ruled that the conduct must be 'causally but not necessarily directly connected with the employment'.[8] The test is whether the misconduct, whenever and wherever it occurred, was such that it would induce a reasonable employer to dispense with the services of the claimant

2 *CU 190/50*; *R(U) 27/52*; *R(U) 8/74* (Tribunal decision). Some American jurisdictions prescribe a *further* period of disqualification for those convicted of a criminal offence connected with the employment, while some impose special disqualifications for 'gross misconduct': Packard 17 Villa L Rev 635.

3 *CU 190/50*; *R(U) 35/53*; *R(U) 24/55*.

4 In the US jurisdictions where this theory is favoured, the courts allow a presumption of knowledge in many situations: Packard, n.2, above.

5 *R(U) 2/77*, R J A Temple, Chief Comr, and see *R(U) 2/81*, para 9.

6 *R(U) 17/64*; *R(U) 2/76*.

7 *R(U) 7/57*.

8 *R(U) 2/77*, para 15, R J A Temple, Chief Comr. See also *R(U) 1/71*.

on the ground that he was not fit to hold the particular situation.[9] Of course, this will generally depend on the nature both of the misconduct and of the employment. What a man does outside his working hours may be totally irrelevant to his work or his employer's interests. A railway fireman who was dismissed for fighting in a railway carriage on his return from work was not disqualified.[10] But the misconduct may so closely affect his suitability for the job that it will justify disqualification no matter where and when it occurs. Such was the case where a park keeper was convicted of gross indecency with another man.[11]

iii Types of conduct

The use of the unqualified term 'misconduct' is unhelpful in determining the standard of conduct which is to be applied. Indeed, in the early years of the scheme it caused some embarrassment as it had to be explained to many women claimants that it was not intended to refer to their moral behaviour.[12] A Royal Commission, reporting in 1932, felt that the choice of language was unfortunate but was unable to suggest any positive improvement.[13] According to the Commissioner, the conduct must be such that it renders the claimant an unfit person to hold the job[14] and will include

> industrial shortcomings, disobedience, faulty workmanship, idleness, unauthorised absence, some types of carelessness, and conduct . . . connected with the employment adversely affecting the claimant's proper discharge of his duties.[15]

But the refusal to leave[16] or to join a trade union[17] does not constitute misconduct.

iv Blameworthiness

It is generally said that there must be blameworthiness,[18] but exactly what must be proved in terms of mental attitude is far from clear. On occasions, the Commissioner has tended towards a test appropriate to the 'voluntary unemployment' theory and spoken of the necessity of showing 'deliberate' or 'wilful negligence'.[19] The view most popularly held, however, is that a wilful or reckless breach of the appropriate standard is not required. A valuable illustration is provided by *R(U) 8/57*.

> C, the manager of a branch pharmacy, was dismissed when cash was found to be missing in the shop. He was prosecuted for, but acquitted of, embezzlement.[20] It was held that this was not sufficient to bar disqualification. 'Serious carelessness' only was required, and this might legitimately be inferred from the evidence.

9 *R(U) 2/77*.
10 *UD 4120*.
11 *R(U) 1/71*, R G Micklethwait, Chief Comr.
12 Tillyard *Unemployment Insurance in Great Britain 1911–48* (1949) pp. 24–25.
13 Final Report (1932, Cmd 4185), para 443. To meet the objection, the ground for disqualification has in practice frequently been called 'industrial misconduct': see esp. *R(U) 24/55* and *R(U) 1/71*.
14 *R(U) 24/55*; *R(U) 7/57*.
15 *R(U) 2/77*, para 15, R J A Temple, Chief Comr.
16 *UD 1528/26*.
17 *R(U) 2/77*.
18 E.g. ibid, at para 15.
19 *R(U) 34/52*, cp 'culpable negligence' (*R(U) 35/53*). Some schemes have attempted to introduce such language into the statutory definition: e.g. the West German Arbeitsförderungsgesetz ξ 119(1)(i) and the Massachusetts Employment Law, ξ 25(3)(2).
20 On the significance of other proceedings generally see p. 109, below.

The Commissioner observed, more generally,

> Misconduct . . . may be constituted by mere carelessness; but in considering whether a person has been guilty of misconduct it is necessary to discriminate between that type and degree of carelessness which may have to be put up with in human affairs, and the more deliberate or more serious type of carelessness which justifies withholding unemployment benefit because the employee has lost his employment through his own avoidable fault.[1]

v Relevance of other legal proceedings

The situation in which an employee is dismissed for misconduct may have important repercussions in other areas of law. The conduct may constitute a criminal offence. The employee may allege that he was wrongfully dismissed (i.e. his employer acted in breach of contract), or that he was entitled to the statutory remedy for unfair dismissal. The dispute may have been the subject of a court hearing or of an adjudication by an industrial or disciplinary tribunal. In all such situations, the question arises as to the significance for the disqualification issue of the findings of such court or tribunal.

It is evident that in many instances the concept of 'misconduct' will be wider than a criminal offence with which the claimant was charged. In such a case an acquittal by a criminal court will in no sense be conclusive of the disqualification point. The authorities must make up their own mind.[2] Where the claimant has been *convicted*, there is no question of double jeopardy since the object of the disqualification is not to punish him,[3] but there is nevertheless some difficulty as to the weight to be given to the conviction. It clearly has evidentiary value,[4] but despite an earlier Commissioner's decision to the contrary,[5] it now seems clear that it will not be regarded as conclusive proof that the facts which were the basis of the criminal charge and also constituted the alleged misconduct actually occurred. In a recent sickness benefit case,[6] the Commissioner adopted a compromise position whereby the initial onus lies on the insurance officer to show that a conviction relates to the benefit issue involved. The onus then passes to the claimant to show that, notwithstanding the conviction, he is nevertheless entitled to the benefit in question.

The position is far from clear as regards the decisions of disciplinary bodies. It would seem to depend on how 'judicial' in character is the tribunal and the nature of the information emanating from its findings. It is on these two grounds that one may reconcile two apparently conflicting decisions of the Commissioner.

> In *R(U) 7/61*, the dismissal of a nurse for sleeping on duty and for failing to do her rounds was confirmed by a Hospital Management Committee. But 'misconduct' was not proved as the insurance officer had no details of the incidents on the basis of which the claimant had been dismissed, and he gained no assistance from the decision of the Committee.

1 *R(U) 8/57*, para 6.
2 *R(U) 10/54*; *R(U) 8/57*.
3 *CU 190/50*; *R(U) 27/52*; *R(U) 7/75*.
4 *R(U) 10/54*.
5 *R(U) 24/55*.
6 *R(S) 2/80*, J S Watson, Comr. He applied the principle of the Civil Evidence Act 1968, s.11(2)(a) (on which see *Stupple v Royal Insurance Co Ltd* [1971] 1 QB 50, [1970] 3 All ER 230) even though that Act does not apply to social security tribunals.

In *R(U) 10/67*, a police disciplinary committee had found a police constable guilty of a drinking offence. Here the disciplinary proceedings were more formal (a 'quasi-judicial' trial) and though not regarded as 'absolutely conclusive' for social security purposes they were nevertheless treated as 'very cogent evidence'. The claimant was disqualified.

One would have thought that a finding by an industrial tribunal that an employee was entitled to compensation for an unfair dismissal would be almost conclusive that the same employee was not guilty of such misconduct as to be disqualified from unemployment benefit. Certainly it is appropriate for the authorities to take full cognisance of any *evidence* given to the industrial tribunal,[7] but its finding as to whether or not an employee has been unfairly dismissed is in no sense conclusive of the social security issue whether the claimant has been guilty of misconduct.[8] There are different questions of law involved: whether a person has been unfairly dismissed in the main depends on the conduct of the *employer*, whereas for unemployment benefit the main emphasis is on the behaviour of the *employee.*[9] The onus and standard of proof applicable may also differ between the two tribunals.[10]

B Voluntarily leaving without just cause

The second ground for disqualification is that the claimant

> has voluntarily left such employment [as an employed earner] without just cause.[11]

Such a provision is a typical feature of all unemployment insurance schemes, and has remained in a virtually unchanged form since the creation of the British system in 1911.[12] On the traditional theory, it may be justified on the ground that here unemployment is caused not by external circumstances but by the claimant himself.[13] For disqualification to be imposed, three conditions must be satisfied:
(a) the claimant *left* the employment;
(b) the leaving was *voluntary*;
(c) it was *without just cause*.

i Leaving

The onus is on the insurance officer to show that the claimant left his employment.[14] 'Leaving' is not confined to terminating the contract of employment, but includes any temporary severing of the employment relationship, including absenteeism.[15]

7 *R(U) 2/74*, para 15, R G Micklethwait, Chief Comr, and see *R(U) 4/78*, para 6, H A Shewan, Comr.
8 *R(U) 2/74*; *R(U) 4/78*; *R(U) 3/79*.
9 *R(U) 2/74*, para 14.
10 *R(U) 4/78*, para 6.
11 SSA 1975, s.20(1)(a).
12 NIA 1911, s.87(2).
13 Cf *R(U) 20/64*, para 8 (Tribunal decision).
14 Ibid, and see Kempfer 55 Yale LJ 147.
15 *R(U) 20/64*, para 7.

ii Voluntary

The onus is also on the insurance officer to show that such leaving was voluntary.[16] It is this condition which distinguishes the case from dismissal for misconduct,[17] but in some cases it will be of no great significance which of the two is adopted,[18] and the word 'voluntarily' has been broadly construed so that it might extend to cases of termination by the employer which are instigated by the employee but which do not amount to misconduct.[19] In *R(U) 16/52*

> C was engaged as a canteen assistant subject to passing a medical examination. She refused to undergo an X-ray test and was dismissed. She was disqualified for leaving her employment voluntarily without just cause. 'It is an established principle of unemployment insurance', said the Commissioner, 'that, if a person deliberately and knowingly acts in a way which makes it necessary for the employer to dismiss him, he may be regarded as leaving his employment voluntarily'.[20]

But if the dismissal is not the 'natural consequence' of his actions, the leaving will not be voluntary. Thus in *R(U) 9/59*,

> C was dismissed when he refused to join the employer's superannuation scheme. He did not know at the time he entered the contract that he would be expected to join, and therefore his conduct did not 'invite' dismissal.[1]

The increasing prevalence of early retirement schemes has caused some difficulties, for here the leaving of the employment may be not only permitted but actually encouraged by an employer who may, for example, provide financial incentives for this course of action. Nevertheless, the Commissioner has consistently held that, provided the employee has some real choice in the matter, the leaving is still voluntary.[2]

iii Without just cause

Once it has been established that the claimant voluntarily left his employment, the onus passes to him to show that he did so for 'just cause'.[3] The phrase is broad and flexible. Legislation provides no guidance on how it is to be interpreted and the Commissioner has warned against laying down any hard and fast rules.[4] It seems, however, that the alleged 'just cause' must relate to the claimant's own circumstances: in a recent case, in which a school teacher had been encouraged to take an early retirement, the Commissioner was not prepared to regard the 'public interest' of savings in the education budget or of making way for younger members of the profession as constituting 'just cause'.[5] Ironically it seems that self-

16 *UD 10841/30*.
17 *R(U) 9/59*.
18 Cf p. 107, above.
19 *R(U) 5/71*, but see *R(U) 2/77*, para 26, where R J A Temple, Chief Comr, suggests that as the principle is not to be found in the Act itself it should be applied with restraint.
20 *R(U) 16/52*, para 8.
1 See also *R(U) 2/77* (refusal to join trade union).
2 *R(U) 20/64*; *R(U) 4/70*; *R(U) 3/81*.
3 *R(U) 20/64*, para 7.
4 *R(U) 14/52*, para 5, cited with approval by a Tribunal of Commissioners in *R(U) 20/64*, para 9.
5 *R(U) 2/81*, para 10, E R Bowen, Comr; affirmed by the Court of Appeal in *Crewe v Anderson (National Insurance Officer)* (1982) Times, 3 May.

interest, rather than altruism, is necessary. Examples of the wide variety of such situations which have been allowed are:

– reduction in wages,[6] non-compliance by the employer with the contract of employment,[7] lack of confidence in mental or physical ability to perform duties,[8] pressing domestic or personal circumstances,[9] difficulty of travel to work,[10] reluctance to join a trade union,[11] general grievances about working conditions.[12]

But though such circumstances may constitute a good reason for leaving the employment, they may not be sufficient in themselves to avoid disqualification. It is a general principle that a dissatisfied employee should look for an alternative situation before leaving his present job.[13] He need not actually have secured a vacant post,[14] but the prospects of his finding one must be good.[15] The principle has not been rigidly applied. For example, it was not invoked where a wife left her job to join her husband who had been posted elsewhere,[16] nor to a spouse who was not the principal breadwinner and who was left to look after a child who would otherwise have remained unattended.[17] Nor was it applied where the current employment did not provide any opportunities for looking for another job,[18] or where the relations between the claimant and his employer or his fellow employees had become so strained that it was in the interest of all that he should quit immediately.[19] As regards grievances about working conditions and other disputes with an employer, there is another general principle, which is again subject to the undue friction exception, that before tendering his notice, a claimant should seek to redress the grievances by making representations to the employer through the proper channels, usually with the assistance of his trade union.[20]

C Unreasonable refusal of suitable offer

The third ground for disqualification directed against voluntary unemployment comprises a number of variations on the same theme: the claimant unreasonably refuses an offer or fails to take the appropriate steps to obtain employment which is suitable for him. Originally, there was no

6 *R(U) 15/53*.
7 *CU 248/49*.
8 *R(U) 3/73*.
9 *R(U) 31/59*.
10 *R(U) 20/69*.
11 *R(U) 38/53*.
12 *R(U) 33/51*. There may be an overlap here with the criteria applied in deciding whether the claimant had unreasonably refused an offer of suitable employment, pp. 113–116, below.
13 *CU 96/48*; *R(U) 14/55*; *R(U) 20/64*.
14 *R(U) 4/73*.
15 *R(U) 20/64*; *R(U) 4/70*.
16 *R(U) 19/52*: the decision must be read in the light of SI 1974/2010, reg 8, which provides that for the purposes of the disqualification provisions the test for married women 'shall be determined on the same basis as that applicable to a single woman, but not so as to exclude such consideration of the responsibilities arising from her marriage as is reasonable in the circumstances of the case'.
17 *R(U) 6/59*.
18 *R(U) 25/52*.
19 *UD 5287*.
20 *R(U) 33/51*; *R 3/65 (UB)*. Contrast *R(U) 18/57*: the Commissioner held that such steps were not necessary where the *employer* issued an ultimatum to do additional work, or withdraw.

explicit legislative provision to cover these contingencies: they were treated merely as conclusive evidence of the claimant's failure to satisfy the condition that he be available for suitable work. This led to an anomaly. A man who was held to be unavailable for work would never qualify for benefit whereas one who voluntarily left or who was dismissed for misconduct would be disqualified only for a maximum of six weeks. Sensibly the insurance officer in such circumstances exercised his discretion[1] to review entitlement to benefit after six weeks of unemployment.[2] In 1930, refusal of, or failure to apply for, suitable employment became an independent ground for disqualification,[3] and with minor amendments has remained unchanged since. Of course, the claimant must continue to show that he is available for suitable employment,[4] and there is inevitably some overlap between the two areas of law[5] – most obviously on the question whether the restrictions the claimant places on his availability are reasonable.[6] But there is an important difference. The availability test is a *general* one: it is concerned with the claimant's attitude to the labour market. The grounds for disqualification to be considered in this section are concerned with the claimant's refusal or failure to follow a *particular* course of conduct, or to accept a *particular* offer of employment.

There are, in fact, four different grounds of disqualification which fall under the general heading of refusal of suitable employment:

(a) refusal or failure to apply for a suitable situation, or refusal to accept that situation when offered;
(b) neglect to take advantage of a reasonable opportunity of suitable employment;
(c) refusal or failure to carry out official recommendations;
(d) refusal or failure to take advantage of a reasonable opportunity of training approved by the Secretary of State.

i Refusal of suitable employment

The most widely used, and most frequently contested, of the four grounds arises where

> after a situation in any suitable employment has been properly notified to him as vacant or about to become vacant, he has without good cause refused or failed to apply for that situation or refused to accept that situation when offered to him.[7]

a *Onus of proof*

The burden is first on the insurance officer to show that a situation, which is prima facie suitable, has been offered or notified to the claimant. It is then for the latter to prove either that employment was not suitable or that he had good cause for refusing it, or failing to apply for it.[8]

1 Under UIA (No 2) 1921, s.10, the insurance officer was bound to review every six weeks if the claimant renewed his application.
2 See e.g. Emerson and Lascelles *Guide to the Unemployment Insurance Acts* (1928) p. 101.
3 UIA 1930, s.4, implementing a recommendation of the Committee on Procedure and Evidence for Determination of Claims for Unemployment Insurance Benefit (1929, Cmd 3415) paras 43–44.
4 Pp. 102–105, above.
5 See e.g. *R(U) 2/59*.
6 P. 105, above.
7 SSA 1975, s.20(1)(b).
8 *R(U) 26/52*.

b *Notification and refusal*

'Properly notified' in the subsection includes communications not only from offices administered by the Employment Service Agency, but also from a local education authority, any other recognised agency, or indeed from an employer seeking to fill a vacancy.[9] The claimant cannot complain that the information provided was insufficiently detailed. So long as the broad nature of the situation is clear, it is his duty to find out further particulars.[10] 'Refusal', too, has been widely construed. An explicit rejection of the offer is unnecessary: it is sufficient if the claimant's conduct was such as positively to discourage the employer from offering him the situation.[11]

c *Suitability of employment*

The real problem in this area is to decide what employment is 'suitable'. The Act does not define the concept, but some guidance is supplied by section 20(4), which provides that

> employment shall not be deemed to be employment suitable in the case of any person if it is either —
> (a) employment in a situation vacant in consequence of a stoppage of work due to a trade dispute; or
> (b) employment in his usual occupation in the district where he was last ordinarily employed at a rate of remuneration lower, or on conditions less favourable, than those which he might reasonably have expected to obtain having regard to those which he habitually obtained in his usual occupation in that district, or would have obtained had he continued to be so employed; or
> (c) employment in his usual occupation in any other district at a rate of remuneration lower, or on conditions less favourable, than those generally observed in that district by agreement between associations of employers and of employees or, failing any such agreement, than those generally recognised in that district by good employers;
>
> but, after the lapse of such an interval from the date on which he becomes unemployed as in the circumstances of the case is reasonable, employment shall not be deemed to be unsuitable by reason only that it is employment of a kind other than employment in his usual occupation if it is employment at a rate of remuneration not lower, and on conditions not less favourable, than those generally observed by agreement between associations of employers and of employees or, failing any such agreement, than those generally recognised by good employers.

The provision in section 20(4)(a) was designed to prevent employers from using the threat of disqualification to force individuals to be employed as 'blacking labour'. It has not caused any difficulty, and consistently with its purpose it has been held not to extend to a situation in which a man, himself laid off as a result of a trade dispute, is offered work by another employer.[12] As regards the remainder of the subsection, the intention of the draftsman seems to have been to prescribe two different standards of 'suitability'. During the first period of unemployment, the claimant should be entitled to refuse employment which was not in his usual occupation, and on terms less favourable than he would have enjoyed if he had continued in his former job, or, if in another district, than were generally recognised in the trade. But after the lapse of a reasonable time, he should be less optimistic in his search for work and be prepared to accept work in a

9 SSA 1975, s.20(5)(a).
10 *R(U) 32/52*.
11 *R(U) 28/55* (claimant presented himself for interview with the prospective employer in a dirty and unshaven state).
12 *R(U) 1/52*.

different occupation, though on conditions generally prevailing in that trade.

If the parliamentary spokesmen are to be believed,[13] this was indeed the general intention, but the specific provisions are more cautiously worded. Conditions (b) and (c) only apply if the claimant is offered employment in his *usual* occupation, and the import of the subsection is that if the terms offered are less favourable than he might reasonably expect, the situation is not necessarily to be regarded as suitable. This falls short of the apparent intention of the provision in two major respects: first, it has no bearing on the suitability of an offer of employment in a different occupation; secondly, offers on terms less favourable may still, if regard is had to concomitant circumstances, be regarded as suitable. Because the subsection involves a *negative* proposition, that the 'employment shall not be deemed to be . . . suitable' if conditions (a), (b) or (c) are satisfied, it leaves open the possibility that notwithstanding the fulfilment of any one of those conditions, an employment *may* be found to be suitable if regard is had to other circumstances. However, the Chief Commissioner has construed the subsection as if it commenced 'employment *shall* be deemed to be *unsuitable* . . .'.[14] He has thus concluded that if the claimant succeeds in bringing his case within (b) or (c) the authorities cannot (whatever the concomitant circumstances) characterise the employment as suitable. This interpretation is consistent both with common sense and with the apparent object of the provision, but is not justified by its wording.

The proviso for the subsection (beginning 'but after the lapse of such an interval . . .') does accord with the stated intention of prescribing a less exacting standard of suitability than that enshrined in the first half of section 20(4). Literally construed, it provides that after a reasonable lapse of time, an employment will not necessarily be unsuitable merely because it involves a different occupation, though it may be so treated on consideration of other circumstances. This would seem to be both workable and just, but the Chief Commissioner, to achieve consistency with his unorthodox interpretation of the first part of section 20(4), has been forced to give it a strange and restricted meaning. Notwithstanding the disjunctive 'but', he construes it as providing a solution for a different factual hypothesis, rather than qualifying the first half of section 20(4).[15] If the *only* reason for holding the employment to be unsuitable is that it is different from the claimant's usual occupation, the authorities, if the other conditions are satisfied, are precluded from finding that it is unsuitable. Such a hypothetical situation would be rare indeed, and on the Chief Commissioner's own admission practically robs the provision of any effect. Again his reading involves a misconstruction of the words actually used. This time he has read 'shall not be deemed to be unsuitable' as being 'shall be deemed to be suitable'. There is an obvious need for statutory clarification of the ambiguities raised by section 20(4).

It remains to consider the practical questions arising from the subsection. What is a man's 'usual occupation' is of course, a question of fact. On the one hand, he must have followed it for some substantial time.[16] On the other hand, what was his usual occupation may have lapsed through

13 Mr S Buxton, Pres. Bd. of Trade, introducing the Amendment to NI Bill 1911, cl 62, on which the current provision is based: 31 HC Official Report (5th series) cols 1074–1077.

14 *R(U) 5/68*, R G Micklethwait.

15 Ibid, at para 13.

16 *UD 7678* suggests that this should normally be three years, but there is no reported decision on the point under modern legislation, and apparently the DHSS have regard to periods of shorter duration: cf the cases on equivalent points under the industrial injury scheme: p. 311, below.

continuous unemployment, disability or a change of locality.[17] To determine whether the rate of remuneration or the conditions of employment are 'habitually observed' or 'generally observed in that district' regard is to be had to such collective agreements as have been made. These may however be inconclusive. So in one case, it was held that the claimant was not entitled to refuse an offer on the ground that no tea-break was provided, when some employers in the area permitted a tea-break and others did not.[18] However, in Northern Ireland, a Tribunal of Commissioners faced with an analogous dichotomy (two rates of pay) focused on the reference in the subsection to 'good' employers, and held that the claimant was entitled to hold out for the higher rate.[19]

Subject to the Chief Commissioner's doubtful ruling that in some circumstances the authorities are *bound* to hold an offer suitable or unsuitable, the statutory provisions are not conclusive on the suitability question and regard must be had to other factors. For example, it would be unfair to regard as conclusive the fact that the terms on which the claimant was offered employment in his usual occupation were as favourable as those he enjoyed in his former employment, if the long-term prospects in the situation offered were particularly dim.[20] Further, a claimant may sometimes legitimately claim that to accept an offer of employment of a lower status than that to which he was accustomed would prejudice his future chances of returning to his former occupation.[1] Of course, it will always be sufficient for him to show that the employment offered was beyond his abilities.[2] A typical ground for refusal is that the situation offered was incompatible with the claimant's domestic responsibilities.[3] Mere inconvenience for the family is not sufficient: a claimant must be prepared to make reasonable adjustments to his or her personal circumstances.[4] But the case is different where there are children or other dependent relatives whose needs must be catered for.[5]

d *Without good cause*

The claimant may escape disqualification if the refusal or failure was with 'good cause'. In fact, this adds little to the substantive requirements of the subsection, for if there is good cause to refuse an offer of employment, it will not be an offer of 'suitable employment'. 'Suitability' and 'without good cause' are alternative formulations of the same principle, and the Commissioner has not distinguished between them.[6]

ii Neglect to avail himself of reasonable opportunity of suitable employment

The ground for disqualification considered above arises only when the

17 *R(U) 15/62*.
18 *R(U) 9/64*.
19 *R 16/60 (UB)*.
20 Thus a claimant on short-time is justified in refusing an offer of full-time work in a similar occupation with another firm, if the long-term prospects in that other firm are no better: *R(U) 34/56*. See also *R(U) 10/61*.
1 Accepted in *R 21/60 (UB)*, but not in *R(U) 35/52* where the offer was only for two weeks employment.
2 *R(U) 26/52*; *R(U) 32/52*.
3 For married women, see the rule cited at n.16, p. 112, above.
4 *12/52 (UB)*.
5 E.g. *R(U) 20/60*. NB the existence of such circumstances may render the claimant's prospects of finding employment remote and therefore exclude him from benefit on the ground of unavailability: p. 105, above.
6 See e.g. *R(U) 20/60*.

claimant has failed to apply for a situation, or has refused an offer which was made to him. Of the remaining grounds, the first two are also based on the concept of 'suitable employment' but are not limited to any specific vacancy and therefore are broader in scope. A person may be disqualified if

> he has neglected to avail himself of a reasonable opportunity of suitable employment.[7]

Notwithstanding (or perhaps because of) the breadth of this provision, it is apparently seldom invoked by the authorities[8] and as a result there is little by way of guidance on its meaning.[9] It has been employed in the exceptional situation when a claimant so behaves at or before an interview that he effectively deters a prospective employer from offering him a vacancy.[10] Unlike the other grounds for disqualification under section 20(1) there is here no defence of just (or good) cause. But this is not significant. As seen above, there is, in principle, no distinction between a defence based on just cause, and another claiming that the employment in question was 'unsuitable'. So here the factors which would have been relevant to the finding of good cause are the same as those considered in determining whether the employment was 'suitable' or the opportunity not taken was 'reasonable'.[11]

iii Failure to carry out official recommendations

The claimant will be disqualified if

> he has without good cause refused or failed to carry out any official recommendations given to him with a view to assisting him to find suitable employment, being recommendations which were reasonable having regard to his circumstances and to the means of obtaining that employment usually adopted in the district in which he resides.[12]

'Official recommendations' for this purpose are defined as 'recommendations in writing made by an officer of the Employment Service Agency, a local education authority, or the Secretary of State'.[13]

iv Failure to avail himself of reasonable opportunity of training

Finally, the Act disqualifies a claimant who

> has without good cause refused or failed to avail himself of a reasonable opportunity of receiving training approved by the Secretary of State in his case for the purpose of becoming or keeping fit for entry into, or return to, regular employment.[14]

This used to be treated as merely one instance of a failure to carry out written directions[15] but since 1946 has constituted a separate provision. The reason for the change of emphasis is the increasing interest in retraining and rehabilitative schemes.[16] The training scheme in question does not have

7 SSA 1975, s.20(1)(c).
8 Private communication from DHSS.
9 For its use under the UIAs, see esp. *UD 11734/34*.
10 *R(U) 28/55*.
11 *R(U) 5/71*, H A Shewan, Comr.
12 SSA 1975, s.20(1)(d).
13 Ibid, s.20(5)(b).
14 Ibid, s.20(1)(e).
15 E.g. *UD 6424/36*.
16 Cf p. 73, above.

to be administered by the Department of Employment, but it has to be approved by the Secretary of State for the particular claimant. His determination that the training is suitable is conclusive and cannot be reviewed by the statutory authorities.[17] But it is still open to the claimant to contend that he had good cause for the refusal or failure;[18] or that the opportunity given to him was not, in the circumstances, 'reasonable'.

D Period of disqualification

Under the 1911 Act there was a mandatory period of disqualification of six weeks.[19] Since 1920,[20] a shorter period may be imposed, the matter being determined by the statutory authorities, viz the insurance officer, insurance tribunal or Commissioner.[1] This involves a discretion but it is one which must be exercised judicially, taking into account all the relevant circumstances.[2] In 1954 a Commissioner ruled that normally the maximum period should be imposed, and that there was a 'heavy burden' on the claimant to show that this would not be justifiable because of the special circumstances of his case.[3] The principle was not universally followed, and in 1974 was repudiated by a Tribunal of Commissioners.[4] The discretion conferred by the legislation was not to be fettered in this way:

> the correct approach is to adhere firmly to the statutory language, regarding each case as one in which a sensible discretion has to be exercised in such manner as the justice of the case requires.[5]

The implication is that previous decisions of the Commissioner under the 1954 principle are no longer authoritative, but it might be useful to list some of the circumstances which in the past have been used to justify a period of less than the maximum:

(1) where the maximum will cause hardship, because of the claimant's domestic circumstances[6] or because he has already been subject to a serious sanction;[7]
(2) where he has come close to justifying his loss of employment (through just or good cause) but has just failed;[8]
(3) where the insurance fund is already sufficiently protected (e.g. because the claimant is no longer unemployed).[9]

Where the ground for disqualification was misconduct or leaving voluntarily the period will run, in general, from the date of discharge:[10] in other cases it will commence on the date when the claimant refused an offer, or failed to take an appropriate step.

17 *2/57 (UB)*.
18 See e.g. *R 10/60 (UB)*.
19 NIA 1911, s.87(2).
20 UIA 1920, s.8(2); and see UIA 1935, s.8(2).
1 SSA 1975, s.20(1).
2 *R(U) 27/52*; *R(U) 8/74*.
3 *R(U) 17/54*.
4 *R(U) 8/74*.
5 Ibid, at para 20. See also *R(U) 3/79*, para 5, where H A Shewan, Comr, stresses the importance of tribunals indicating on the face of their decision that they have actively exercised the discretion.
6 *R(U) 27/52*.
7 *R(U) 1/71*.
8 *R(U) 35/52*; *R(U) 20/64*.
9 E.g. *R(U) 20/64*.
10 *CU 155/50*. If, however, the claimant continues to receive remuneration (e.g. by payment in lieu of notice) it will run from the date when it is no longer payable: *R(U) 35/52*.

Part 6 Trade disputes disqualification

A Introduction

With the remaining ground for disqualification, we enter into a highly controversial area. The scheme must here grapple with problems of industrial relations,[11] and, needless to say, political opinions are well to the fore in discussions of the substantive law. The general position is that unemployment resulting directly from trade disputes in which the claimant was 'involved' should not give him a title to benefit. There is a widespread assumption that such a limitation must exist, and the principle finds a place in almost every system of unemployment insurance.[12] But the theoretical or policy justifications of the principle are not so obvious as may appear and require some consideration.[13]

In the first place, it is said that this is but another instance of *voluntary* unemployment (like misconduct, leaving, refusal, etc.), and, as such, does not come within the risk of unemployment for which the insurance fund was established. However, at least by itself, this is not a complete justification, for if applied consistently, it would compel the law to distinguish between *strikes* and *lockouts*, and this it fails to do. Moreover, the other grounds of disqualification based on voluntary unemployment recognise that in certain circumstances the leaving or refusal of employment may be excused on grounds of 'just' or 'good cause'. Here there are no such qualifications. There is, indeed, a fundamental rule that the authorities should not enter into the merits of the dispute.

Secondly, resort is had to the idea of industrial neutrality:

> the National Insurance Fund, to which both employers and employees contribute, should not become involved in industrial disputes . . . the scheme should not be open to the criticism that it is supporting one side or the other.[14]

While this is, on the face of it, an appealing argument, it leaves open the question as to what constitutes 'neutrality'. It may not be neutral for payments to be made to strikers (and, as will be seen, the same may be said of supplementary benefits which are paid to the families of strikers[15]), but it is arguable that it is equally not neutral if workers with a legitimate grievance are deterred from taking industrial action because of the refusal to pay benefit.

The neutrality argument appears often to be a gloss on the less compromising stance taken by others, that on economic and political grounds, contributors to the fund should not financially support those who withdraw their labour.[16] There are some who would find unattractive a further alteration in the balance of power between employers and trade unions; there are others whose concern would be not to encourage industrial stoppages, and therefore losses in productivity. Finally, removal of the disqualification would arouse the hostility of those contributors who

11 This was the one area of unemployment insurance law to be considered in detail by the Royal Commission on Trade Unions and Employers Associations (the Donovan Commission). See its Report (1968, Cmnd 3623), paras 953–993.

12 Schindler 38 Col LR 858; Hickling *Labour Disputes and Unemployment Insurance in Canada and England* (1975).

13 Cf Lesser 55 Yale LJ 167; Shamir 17 U of Chi LR 294; 2nd Memo of Ministry of Social Security to Royal Commission, Minutes of Evidence, pp. 2310–2318; Gennard *Financing Strikers* (1977). See also on supplementary benefit, pp. 501–507, below.

14 Memo n.13, above at p. 2310.

15 P. 504, below.

16 Conservative Political Centre *Financing Strikers* (1974).

are not able effectively to express their grievances by withdrawing their labour. Whether or not such arguments are found acceptable depends, in the last resort, on political attitudes.

B General rule

The Social Security Act 1975, section 19(1), provides that a

> person who has lost employment as an employed earner by reason of a stoppage of work which was due to a trade dispute at his place of employment shall be disqualified for receiving unemployment benefit so long as the stoppage continues.

The onus is on the insurance officer[17] to prove that (i) there was a trade dispute; (ii) it was at the claimant's place of employment; (iii) it resulted in a stoppage; (iv) the claimant lost employment as a result of that stoppage.

i Trade dispute

This is statutorily defined as

> any dispute between employers and employees, or between employees and employees, which is connected with the employment or non-employment or the terms of employment or the conditions of employment of any persons, whether employees in the employment of the employer with whom the dispute arises, or not.[18]

This is an interesting example of a statutory definition being lifted from another context in which it served a completely different purpose. It was based on that in the Trade Disputes Act 1906[19] whose object was to create an *immunity* from certain actions in tort.[20] It is not surprising, therefore, that the definition has given rise to some strange decisions. No one would question the application of the term 'trade dispute' to strikes (official or unofficial),[1] lockouts,[2] and demarcation disputes,[3] at least where the dispute arose between a group of employees and their employer or another group of employees.[4] But in *R(U) 1/74*

> in pursuance of a national pay claim, building labourers withdrew their labour on a number of building sites. The site on which C worked was unaffected until pickets from a nearby site came and persuaded C and his fellow employees not to work. R S Lazarus, Commissioner, relying on certain decisions concerned with common law immunities,[5] held that there was a trade dispute between C's employer and the pickets who arrived from other sites, notwithstanding that he was not *their* employer.

Even more doubtful was the decision in *R(U) 2/53*.

> C was prevented from working by the unlawful acts of pickets who threatened him with violence. It was held that C lost his employment as a result of the trade dispute between himself and the pickets!

17 *R(U) 17/52*.
18 SSA 1975, s.19(2)(b).
19 S.5(3).
20 See the historical survey in *R(U) 1/74*, paras 12–15, R S Lazarus, Comr.
1 *R(U) 5/59*.
2 *R(U) 17/52*.
3 *R(U) 14/64*.
4 The claimant need not himself be a party to the dispute: *R(U) 3/69*.
5 E.g. *Huntley v Thornton* [1957] 1 All ER 234, [1957] 1 WLR 321.

The necessary connection between the dispute and 'the employment or non-employment or the terms of employment or the conditions of employment' has caused some difficulty. In *R(U) 26/59* it was held that a dispute as to whether an employee was entitled to an income tax rebate under his contract of employment was not a trade dispute, since it was concerned with the existence of a term, not with whether there *should* be such a term. The distinction is an elusive one and was ignored by the Commissioner in a later case.[6]

Apart from a short period during the 1920s when the claimant could escape disqualification if he could show that the stoppage was due to the employer contravening an agreement,[7] the tradition has been that the authorities should not attempt to adjudicate on the merits of the dispute,[8] and so it is of no avail to claim that there was 'just cause' for the withdrawal of labour. There are persuasive arguments for this approach: it would be very difficult for insurance officers to reach an objective decision on the merits of a particular dispute, and it would be very costly in terms of time and money.[9] But as a consequence it may penalise employees who have undisputedly legitimate grounds for grievance. So, in one case, a disqualification was imposed on those who had been dismissed by an employer when they had objected to a reduction in wages.[10] The Donovan Commission assumed that the same result would ensue where the substance of the dispute was that the employer had been in breach of contract,[11] and most recently the Divisional Court has held that complaints that the employer was in contravention of the health and safety legislation may quite properly be characterised as a 'trade dispute'.[12]

It is not entirely clear when a difference of opinion becomes a dispute but 'a question . . . must reach a certain stage of contention before it may properly be termed a dispute'.[13] While it will usually end by some form of agreement, it will no longer operate to disqualify from benefit if it results in one party totally severing relations with the other.[14]

ii Place of employment

The general rule does not require that the claimant himself be involved in the trade dispute. Subject to the exceptions on non-participation and lack of direct interest considered below,[15] it is sufficient if the dispute was located at his place of employment. The traditional justification for what is effectively a presumption of participation or interest in the dispute is that there is 'a common bond of mutual interest and loyalty . . . between workers at one place of employment which enables them to be distin-

6 *R(U) 3/71*, J S Watson, Comr, and see *Calvert* p. 157.
7 UIA (No 2) 1924, s.4(1). It was repealed by UIA 1927, s.6. See generally *Gennard* n.13, above, pp. 16–19.
8 Sir J Simon Sol. Gen., introducing the trade disputes clause in the 1911 Bill, 31 HC Official Report (5th series), col 1729; Report of the Committee on Unemployment Insurance (Blanesborough Committee) (1927); Donovan Commission Report, n.11, above, para 994.
9 Ibid.
10 *R(U) 27/56*.
11 (1968, Cmnd 3623), para 994.
12 *R v National Insurance Comr, ex parte Thompson* (1977), published as Appendix to *R(U) 5/77*. A contrary view had been taken by the Umpire (see esp. *UD 306/29*) and the N. Ireland Commissioner (*R 20/60 (UB)*). The British Chief Commissioner, whose decision was upheld by the Divisional Court, was more cautious in his disinclination to follow the Umpire: see *R(U) 5/77*, paras 26–29.
13 *R(U) 21/59*, para 6.
14 *R(U) 17/52*.
15 Pp. 126–128, below.

guished from other workers.'[16] In the days of the small family firm this rationalisation may have been attractive, but in the industrial conditions prevailing today, its appeal is less obvious.

If, in theory, the identification of the dispute with the place of employment is not easy to justify, in practice the application of the test is even more elusive. Section 19(2)(a) of the Social Security Act 1975 defines a claimant's place of employment as 'the factory, workshop, farm or other premises or place at which he was employed . . .'. This still leaves open what is to be considered as 'other premises or place'. It is clear that each case must be decided on its facts, and that some fairly arbitrary lines must be drawn. In one case, it was held that 'the place of employment' of someone loading ships was the whole of the docks,[17] while in another the place of employment of a man working in an engineering shop attached to a group of collieries, but physically separated from them, was not the colliery.[18] To cope with this section 19(2)(a) continues:

> where separate branches of work which are commonly carried on as separate businesses in separate premises or at separate places are in any case carried on in separate departments on the same premises or at the same place, each of these departments shall . . . be deemed to be a separate factory or workshop or farm or separate premises or a separate place, as the case may be.

The onus of proving certain premises are the claimant's place of employment (the first part of section 19(2)(a)) is on the insurance officer. The onus of proving that they constitute a separate business (the second part of section 19(2)(a)) is on the claimant.[19] It is a formidable obstacle, for he must satisfy the authorities (i) that there are 'separate branches' of work at his place of employment; and (ii) that typically elsewhere such branches are carried on as 'separate businesses in separate premises or at a separate place', and (iii) that at his place of employment the branches are carried on 'in separate departments'. He will not succeed on (i) if the branch of work in question is 'a step in an integrated process of production'.[20] As regards (ii), much will depend on evidence of the practices of other firms that the claimant is able to adduce.[1] The concepts of 'branches', 'businesses' and 'departments' are none of them terms of art, and all involve questions of degree. Determination by the authorities may be based on somewhat arbitrary classifications of industrial processes, totally unrelated to the policy behind the rule which is based on the alleged material interest and loyalty of those working on the same enterprise. Suggestions to modify the provision have, however, as yet gone unheeded.[2]

iii Stoppage due to trade dispute

There may be disqualification only where there has been a cessation of work by a significant number of employees[3] arising from an unwillingness

16 Memo of Ministry of Social Security, to Royal Commission, Minutes of Evidence, p. 2312.
17 *R(U) 4/58*; cf *UD 5568* where it was held that a person employed on a barge was not employed in the same place as the dockers at the dock where the barge happened to be.
18 *UD 5145/26*.
19 *R(U) 1/70*, R.G Micklethwait, Chief Comr.
20 *R(U) 4/62*, para 7.
1 Ibid, and see: *R(U) 6/51*; *R(U) 24/57*; *R(U) 1/70*.
2 The Donovan Commission rejected, on the 'community of interest' argument, the proposal of the CBI that the definition of 'place of employment' should be extended; and, on the grounds that it would encourage selective strikes, that of the TUC that it should be narrowed: n.11, above, at paras 970–972.
3 *R(U) 7/58*.

on their part to work or from a refusal by the employer to provide work until the dispute is settled.[4] The stoppage must constitute a move, by either side, in the contest, the intention of both parties being eventually to resume normal working.[5] If an employer or the whole group of employees decide categorically that they do not wish the employment relationship to continue on *any* terms, the cessation of work no longer forms part of the trade dispute.[6] The question is then whether persons unemployed as a result should be disqualified on the grounds either of voluntarily leaving or of misconduct. To determine whether an allegedly absolute discharge or withdrawal was intended to be taken seriously may obviously create an acute problem of interpretation for the authorities. A series of Commissioner's decisions shows that many such statements, though formulated in the most categorical terms, are not to be taken at their face value.[7]

The stoppage of work must be 'due to' the trade dispute, but the nature of the causal link involved has given rise to some difficulty where it has been impracticable or impossible to restart work immediately after the settlement of the dispute. For example, in *R v Chief National Insurance Comr, ex parte Dawber*,[8]

> the stoppage had created a risk of damage to the industrial plant. Notwithstanding attempts by the employer to forestall damage, it did in fact occur, and he laid off all employees while repairs were carried out. Both the Chief Commissioner and the Divisional Court held that the employees were disqualified from benefit during the lay-off, as the continued stoppage was due to the original dispute.

For the requisite causal connection to exist, it did not have to be shown that the continuance of the stoppage was an 'inevitable' consequence of the dispute; it is sufficient if it was 'reasonably foreseeable'.[9] Moreover, the fact that the employer might not have adopted the most appropriate method of forestalling damage to the plant did not break the chain of causation. It may have been an error of judgment but it was

> something done not unreasonable or otherwise objectionable. And . . . it does not lie in the mouth of those who put the employers in a position of emergency where they had to take a decision to say that, because that was the wrong decision, it breaks the chain of causation.[10]

iv Loss of employment by reason of stoppage

The claimant must have lost his employment 'by reason of the stoppage' which was itself due to the trade dispute. If the loss of employment results from a fresh, supervening cause, such as the closure of the employer's business when that closure is attributable not to the trade dispute but to other financial pressures, there is no disqualification from benefit.[11] The principles determining this causal relationship should, *mutatis mutandis*, be those described in the previous paragraph, but, presumably out of a fear

4 *R(U) 19/51*.
5 *R(U) 17/52*; *R(U) 11/63*.
6 *R(U) 1/65*.
7 *R(U) 17/52*; *R(U) 19/53*; *R(U) 36/53*; *R(U) 27/56*; *R(U) 11/63*; *R(U) 1/65*.
8 (1980), published as Appendix to *R(U) 9/80*.
9 Ibid, at para 10, J G Monroe, Comr; per Forbes J, Appendix, p. 10. See also *R(U) 19/51*, para 11.
10 Per Forbes J, Appendix to *R(U) 9/80*, p. 8.
11 *R(U) 15/80*, R J A Temple, Chief Comr. The question whether, and when, a particular business has closed down is not easy to determine. For guidance, see ibid, at para 17.

that certain unworthy claimants might otherwise succeed, the authorities have taken a special approach in three situations.

In the first, the claimant loses his employment before the stoppage begins. The temporal factor is not regarded as an insuperable obstacle to disqualification. In *R(U) 30/55*,

> C left his employment without giving any reasons. A trade dispute was then in progress but a stoppage which would have affected C and his fellow employees did not start until four days later. C was disqualified for the duration of the stoppage. The Commissioner was prepared to assume that C anticipated what was going to happen and was not prepared to run the risk of being implicated in the stoppage, thus losing his benefit.

This may seem to be a harsh decision – the claimant could in any event have been disqualified for six weeks for voluntarily leaving without just cause – but it is not atypical. Indeed, in dealing with cases where the employer discharges or suspends the claimant immediately before the stoppage the authorities have traditionally invoked the so-called '12-day rule'. If the discharge occurred within 12 working days of the stoppage there was a presumption that the employment was lost by reason of the stoppage[12] and that if there had been no stoppage the claimant would have resumed the employment.[13] While the presumption was rebuttable, the rule might nevertheless operate harshly and, with the insistence on 12 days, was certainly rigid and artificial.[14] In one recent decision, the Commissioner has reserved his opinion as to the validity and applicability of the rule in present-day circumstances,[15] and in practice the rule is now very rarely invoked.[16]

Secondly, it has been consistently held that the disqualification cannot be avoided by an allegation that a claimant, losing his employment during a trade dispute, would *in any event* have been unemployed for part or all of that period for reasons of redundancy or short-time,[17] or because he was a casual worker.[18] These rulings seem contrary to principle, but they have been justified on the ground that any other view would lead to extreme administrative difficulties, it being necessary to prophesy, for example, the identity of workers who would have been made redundant or the days when they would have been laid off.[19]

Thirdly, the authorities do not take the reference to 'loss' of employment entirely literally. The claimant need not have been employed on the day immediately prior to the date of unemployment in question.[20] The effect of the stoppage may have been to obstruct an employer's intention to re-engage a workman who had been off work for a period.[1]

12 *R(U) 20/57*. The rule was originally formulated by the Umpire (*UD 18901/31*). A Tribunal of Commissioners reasoned that because the wording of the disqualification provision remained the same under the National Insurance Acts, the legislature intended that the rule should be retained.

13 *R(U) 31/57*.

14 Per H A Shewan, Comr, R(U) 6/71, para 8.

15 Ibid.

16 Private communication from DHSS.

17 *R(U) 11/52*; *R(U) 32/55*; *R(U) 17/56*; *R(U) 29/59*; *R(U) 12/61* all affirmed in *R(U) 12/72* (Tribunal decision, which overruled the single inconsistent decision in *CSU 3/68*).

18 *R(U) 12/80*.

19 *R(U) 12/72*, para 12.

20 Ibid, at para 12 and *R(U) 13/72*.

1 E.g. *R(U) 19/56*.

v Other employment

The disqualification does not apply to a claimant who

> during the stoppage . . . has become bona fide employed elsewhere in the occupation which he usually follows or has become regularly engaged in some other occupation.[2]

The grounds for disqualification, whatever they may be, cannot apply where the claimant has genuinely removed himself from the ambit of the dispute. But this will not be the case if he takes a temporary job for a very short time solely to requalify for benefit. The onus, then, is on the claimant to show that the new employment was 'bona fide'.[3] This means both that the employment was a genuine one and that it was taken up for an honest motive.[4] The mere fact that the employment was of short duration does not, by itself, justify an inference that the employment was not bona fide.[5] But such an inference may be drawn where it is clear from the evidence that the claimant did not intend permanently to sever relations with his original employer.[6]

C The proviso

The breadth of the general rule is evident. There may be a stoppage at the claimant's place of employment with which his connection is remote and yet his benefit is lost. Such a situation in fact occurred in the moulders' strike of 1920 and the unfairness of the general rule, standing alone, was fully revealed.[7] After much discussion, hesitation and amendment,[8] the Unemployment Insurance (No 2) Act of 1924 was introduced to provide relief for those who could prove that they were neither participating in, financing, or directly interested in the dispute, nor belonged to a grade or class the members of which were participating in, financing or directly interested in the dispute. Doubts were still felt as to the equity of this amendment. In the general strike of 1926 members of a class of colliery workers throughout the country were disqualified because other members of the same class in one *particular* district belonged to a union which was financing the dispute. The Blanesborough Committee reporting in 1927 doubted whether an entirely satisfactory form of wording could ever be found but recommended that the 'grade or class' should be specifically linked to the claimant's place of employment.[9] This was implemented in 1927,[10] but for many years thereafter the TUC continued to express dissatisfaction, and eventually in 1965 the matter was specifically referred to the Royal Commission on Trade Unions and Employers' Associations.[11] The Commission was highly critical of the law then prevailing. In the first place, it rejected the principle that an individual should be 'involved' in a

2 SSA 1975, s.19(1).
3 *R(U) 39/56*.
4 *R(U) 6/74*, H A Shewan, Comr.
5 Ibid, at para 10.
6 Ibid.
7 See 131 HC Official Report (5th series) cols 935–936.
8 For the history see 1st Memo of Ministry of Social Security to Donovan Royal Commission: n.11, p. 119, above, Minutes of Evidence, pp. 2298–2304.
9 Committee on Unemployment Insurance (1927), para 137.
10 UIA 1927, s.6.
11 1968, Cmnd 3623.

dispute merely because he was 'financing' it, which had consistently been held to include membership of a union or association which was financially supporting those involved in the dispute.[12] Apart from common membership, the individual might have no other interest in the dispute.[13] Secondly, it recommended abolition of the rule which served to disqualify a claimant belonging to 'a grade or class of workers of which . . . there were members employed at his place of employment any of whom are participating in or financing or directly interested in the dispute'.[14] It regarded as unreliable the traditional justification that there was a 'community of interest' between such workers.[15] The proposals of the Commission lay dormant until 1975 when they were implemented by the Employment Protection Act.[16] The present position is, then, that to escape disqualification the onus is on the claimant[17] to prove

> that he is not participating in or directly interested in the trade dispute which caused the stoppage of work.[18]

i Participating

The Commissioner has regarded it as both 'dangerous and unnecessary to seek to define' the meaning of 'participating'[19] but it connotes the idea of knowingly doing something or refraining from doing something which contributes to the continuance of the dispute.[20] It should involve active support of one of the parties: a man who merely abstains from *voting* against strike action has been held not to 'participate'.[1] On the other hand, it does not seem to require very positive action. In one case, attendance at a meeting called to find a solution to the dispute was regarded as exemplifying 'participation'.[2]

ii Directly interested

This is intended to catch those who are not *actively* connected with the dispute (and who are therefore not 'participating in' it)[3] but whose interests are directly affected by it. The difficulty is, of course, to determine who comes within this category. 'Directly interested' is not defined in the legislation and it has been left to the Commissioners and judges to offer guidelines on how the phrase is to be interpreted. It is clear, in the first place, that the interest of the employees in question in the dispute is not necessarily confined to remuneration but may include anything relating to the terms and conditions of employment.[4] Typically, the 'direct interest' will be evident from the fact that the resolution of the dispute will lead to changes in the claimant's own terms of employment; but the Commissioner has stressed that ' "directly interested" relates to the trade dispute and not to the outcome of the dispute . . . and a "direct interest" may arise even

12 See e.g., *R(U) 15/55*; *R(U) 1/70*; *R(U) 12/71*.
13 N.11, above, at para 985.
14 NIA 1965, s.22(1) proviso (b).
15 N.11, above, at paras 975–976.
16 S.111(1).
17 Per Lord Avonside, *Watt v Lord Advocate* 1979 SLT 137, at 144.
18 SSA 1975, s.19(1)(a), as amended.
19 Per H Magnus, Comr, *R(U) 5/66*, para 9.
20 *Calvert* p. 165.
1 *R(U) 5/66*. See also *R 3/68 (UB)*.
2 *R(U) 6/61*.
3 Per Lord President Emslie, *Watt v Lord Advocate* 1979 SLT 137, at 140.
4 *R(U) 5/79*, para 12, J S Watson, Comr. Thus e.g. safety equipment: *R(U) 3/71*; *R(U) 5/77*.

when there has been no resultant change'.[5] *A fortiori* it does not have to be shown that the claimant benefited from the settlement of the dispute. On the other hand, he will not be disqualified merely because his chances of resuming work and of negotiating future wages were affected or blocked by the continued existence of the dispute.[6]

The essence of the matter is the nature of the causal link between the dispute and the claimant's own terms of employment. For a long time, the Commissioner applied the provision as if the word 'directly' did not appear,[7] that is, he was prepared to impose disqualification where the dispute concerned the pay or working conditions of another grade or class of employees but the settlement of which was thought likely to lead to changes in the claimant's pay or working conditions.[8] Such an approach might obviously lead to absurd results. In days when relativity of remuneration and pay differentials are highly prized, and when the terms of collective bargains are given wide publicity, it is obvious that the resolution of a single dispute can affect a very large number of workers who may have only the remotest connection with those involved in the dispute. In recent years, therefore, the authorities have sought to restrain the broad interpretation previously placed on the 'directly interested' criterion. They have attempted to express the notion of 'directness' in two sets of explanations. The first alludes to the *closeness* of the relationship between those involved in the dispute and those who stand to be affected by it, so that, according to Lord President Emslie, in the leading case of *Watt v Lord Advocate*,[9]

> the issues in the dispute should embrace not only the interests of those taking part in it but the interests of others including the claimant as well with the result that its outcome is likely to have consequences, virtually immediate and automatic, for workers other than those engaged in it.

The second explanation is quite consistent with this but concentrates instead on what is necessary to break the chain of causation. Thus, in the words of R S Lazarus, Commissioner,

> [The] interest will not be direct if some act or event must be interposed between the outcome of the dispute and the occurrence of the change in the claimant's terms of employment.[10]

The application of these dicta is necessarily a question of degree and judgment, but it may be helpful to consider illustrations falling either side of the dividing line. In *R(U) 5/79*.

> a bonus scheme was introduced for one category of employees at a plant. Another category excluded from the scheme withdrew their labour. It was held that the first group were not directly interested in the dispute since they would not be directly affected by any settlement reached with the other group; any change affecting the first group would not be

5 *R(U) 5/59*, para 13, J S Watson, Comr.
6 *Watt v Lord Advocate*, n.17, above.
7 Cf Hepple and O'Higgins *Individual Employment Law* (2nd edn) para 1–476.
8 *R(U) 3/56*; *R(U) 25/56*; *R(U) 1/60*; *R(U) 4/65*. See also *Punton v Ministry of Pensions and National Insurance (No 2)* [1963] 2 All ER 693, [1963] 1 WLR 1176; affd [1964] 1 All ER 448, [1964] 1 WLR 226.
9 N.17, above, at 141, elaborating on *R(U) 13/71*, para 8, H A Shewan, Comr. See also *R(U) 8/80*, para 17, I O Griffiths, Comr.
10 *R(U) 8/72*, para 16. See also *R(U) 8/80*, para 16.

automatic but would have to result from further negotiations and agreement.

In *R(U) 8/80*,

> the subject of the dispute was the wage rate for employees represented by five different trade unions. The employers' offer was accepted by three unions, including that of which the claimant was a member. The employers were not prepared to pay different increases to different unions and the whole work force was laid off when members of the dissenting unions organised a 'go slow' action. The claimant had a direct interest since any improved offer consequent on the dispute would be paid to him.

D Period of disqualification

Unlike the disqualifications for voluntary unemployment, no maximum period is stipulated for trade disputes. It is to last 'so long as the stoppage continues'[11] though, as we have seen,[12] it may cease earlier if the stoppage is no longer the result of the trade dispute. The question arises whether the period of disqualification will come to an end if the claimant can subsequently satisfy the conditions of the proviso, that he is no longer participating in or directly interested in the dispute, even though he was unable to satisfy these conditions when the claim for benefit first arose. During the currency of the dispute he may, for example, have left the employment. On a liberal interpretation of section 19(1) it would seem that this course of argument is open to him, for the proviso uses the present tense: 'he *is* not participating in or directly interested in the trade dispute . . .'. This approach was validated by the Umpire,[13] and also proved acceptable to a Commissioner in 1978.[14] However, it has since been rejected by a Tribunal of Commissioners.[15] They ruled that to escape disqualification by means of the proviso, the claimant must show that he *has never* been participating in or directly interested in the dispute. To justify this apparent gloss on the statutory language, they refer to the exception to the general rule of disqualification, where the claimant has become employed elsewhere,[16] and argue that this exception would be otiose if the proviso were to be given the alternative interpretation: a man employed elsewhere cannot be 'participating in . . .' the dispute.[17] The reasoning is somewhat unhistorical because the employment exception dates from 1911,[18] while the proviso was introduced in 1924.[19] It also gives rise to a seemingly unfair asymmetry for the Tribunal also ruled that while once disqualified a claimant cannot subsequently invoke the proviso, nevertheless if he initially satisfied the conditions of the proviso, he must still continue to satisfy them for each subsequent day of the stoppage.[20] Although the point is not disclosed on the face of the Tribunal decision, it

11 SSA 1975, s.19(1).
12 P. 123, above.
13 *UD 2156/37*; *UD 15/46*.
14 *CU 6/78*.
15 *R(U) 4/79*, endorsing *CSU 1/79*.
16 P. 125, above.
17 *CSU 1/79*, para 9, approved in *R(U) 4/79*, para 11.
18 NIA 1911, s.87.
19 UIA (No 2) 1924, s.4.
20 *R(U) 4/79*, para 10(2).

is likely that the Commissioners were conscious of the danger of encouraging claimants to terminate their employment in the expectation that the employer would reinstate them when the dispute had been resolved.[1]

Part 7 Special provisions

A General

The nature of certain occupations makes it difficult to accommodate them within the framework of the ordinary law of unemployment benefit. For such cases, specific provision has been made.

i Students

Students claiming benefit during the academic year are subject to a special contribution condition. The rule and the reasons for its introduction have already been considered.[2]

ii Armed Forces

A member of the forces may not receive benefit while serving.[3] He does become entitled on leaving, and will not be disqualified under the 'voluntary leaving' rule[4] if he does so at his own request,[5] though a six-week disqualification will be incurred if he is dismissed for disciplinary reasons.[6]

iii Occupational pensioners

For some years, successive governments have been concerned about the growing practice whereby men aged between 60 and 65 retire from their normal employment, become entitled to an occupational pension and then claim unemployment benefit, often with the expectation that no suitable employment will be available for them. The National Insurance Advisory Committee considered that to impose a special availability rule on such persons would be neither acceptable nor workable, but recommended that the benefit payable should, to a certain extent, take account of the receipt of the occupational pension.[7] Two legislative proposals to implement these recommendations failed to pass through Parliament, but eventually the principle of abatement of unemployment benefit was introduced by the Social Security (No 2) Act 1980.

Section 5 of this Act provides for a weekly reduction from unemployment benefit of 10p for each 10p of occupational pension[8] above a prescribed amount (in 1982–83 £35 per week).[9] Sums paid solely as compensation for redundancy and not provided for in the occupational

1 Cf *CSU 1/79*, and Mesher [1980] JSWL 122.
2 P. 78, above.
3 SI 1975/493, reg 2.
4 Pp. 110–112, above.
5 SI 1975/493, reg 3(2).
6 Ibid, reg 3(1).
7 Report on the Question of Conditions for Unemployment Benefit and Contribution Conditions for Occupational Pensioners (1968, Cmnd 3545). See also the report on Draft Regulations, 1969–70 HC 211.
8 For definition, see SSA (No 2) 1980, s.5(3).
9 Reduction should be made first from the personal element of the benefit: ibid, s. 5(1A), inserted by SSHBA 1982, Sch 4, para 34.

pension scheme are disregarded.[10] There are rules for calculating the weekly value of a pension when it is not paid on a weekly basis.[11] It should also be noted that where as a consequence of these rules the occupational pensioner receives nothing by way of unemployment benefit, nevertheless the period in which, but for the reduction, he would have been entitled to unemployment benefit still counts as days of unemployment for the purpose of the provision which limits the duration of unemployment benefit to 312 days.[12]

iv Mariners

Mariners pose problems both because they enjoy substantial periods of paid leave (as do those working on oil-rigs, though as yet there are no special rules governing their entitlement[13]) and because when not employed they are sometimes absent from Great Britain. Regulations thus provide:

(1) that days in a period of paid leave are not to be treated as days of unemployment;[14] and

(2) that they are deemed to be available during days of absence from Great Britain.[15]

v Share fishermen

A share fisherman holds a somewhat anomalous position under the social security system. His remuneration takes the form of a share in the profits of the fishing boat and he is not employed under a contract of service.[16] As such he pays Class 2 contributions and yet for the purposes of entitlement to unemployment benefit they are treated as Class 1 contributions.[17] These circumstances necessitate two special conditions.

- A condition is added to the ordinary rule of availability[18] requiring the *claimant* to prove that on the alleged day of unemployment he did no work as a share fisherman,[19] and had not neglected to avail himself of a reasonable opportunity of employment as a fisherman.[20]
- Secondly, if the claimant is the master or member of the crew of a fishing boat, and either the master or member of the crew of that boat (though not necessarily the claimant himself)[1] is owner or part-owner, he must show that the failure to fish on that day resulted from either (1) the state of the weather;[2] or (2) repairs or maintenance of the boat; or (3) absence of fish in the normal fishing grounds; or (4) 'any other good cause'.[3]

10 SI 1981/73, reg 3.

11 Ibid, reg 5. Where payment starts later than the beginning of the first week, the payment for that week is disregarded: ibid, reg 4.

12 Ibid, reg 6, and see p. 134, below.

13 Cf p. 82, above.

14 SI 1975/529, reg 2, but payment of establishment benefit under the Merchant Navy Scheme does not prevent a day being treated as a day of unemployment: ibid, reg 6(3).

15 Ibid, reg 6(3).

16 See the definition in SI 1975/529, reg 1(2).

17 Ibid, reg 8(1).

18 P. 102, above.

19 On which, see *R(U) 9/52*; *R(U) 9/53*; *R(U) 1/81*.

20 SI 1975/529, reg 8(5).

1 *R(U) 6/63*.

2 See *R(U) 1/81*.

3 SI 1975/529, reg 8(6). For the interpretation of 'good cause' see e.g. *R(U) 7/55*; *R(U) 17/55*; *R(U) 3/64*.

B Seasonal workers: policy

The most important of the special rules apply to seasonal workers. This is a form of labour which is inefficient in that it gives rise to high overhead costs and low productivity, and creates shortages and surpluses of labour at different periods of the year.[4] Better organisation of the labour market and the advance of technology has reduced the amount of seasonal work in industries which are not, in their essence, seasonal. But there are still some occupations which are almost wholly seasonal (e.g. working in holiday resorts), and there is evidence that there may be as many as one million people who engage, or intend to engage, in seasonal work.[5] The problem arises how such special circumstances are to be accommodated within the framework of unemployment benefit law. There would seem to be three main solutions. One might simply apply the ordinary principles of eligibility, and impose such restraint on the granting of benefit as might seem desirable by means of the requirement that the claimant must be 'available' for employment. This is the general position in the United States,[6] and prevailed in Britain until 1931.[7] The objection was that workers whose occupation was only seasonal were only nominally 'available': they were not really attached to the labour market during their off-season. A second view was that a special insurance fund should be established, but this was rejected on the grounds of administrative inconvenience, and that the fund would not have sufficient income to pay benefits at an acceptable level.[8] The third method was that favoured by the Royal Commission on Unemployment Insurance[9] and implemented by regulations made in 1931.[10] These were found to accomplish their object only imperfectly, and were refashioned several times. In 1975–77 the National Insurance Advisory Committee re-examined this area of law.[11] With one dissentient, it found that there was a continued need for special conditions. It was conceded that the current law was cumbersome, might sometimes operate harshly, and was difficult to operate, but it was doubted whether a more satisfactory way of dealing with the problem could be found. The recommendations were therefore confined to minor improvements to the detailed rules.[12] As yet, these proposals have not been implemented.[13]

The current Regulations prescribe that a seasonal worker claiming benefit during his off-season should satisfy two special conditions. For the purposes of exposition it is first necessary to explain the meaning of 'seasonal worker' and 'off-season'.

C Definition of seasonal worker

In terms of policy there seems to be a choice between a narrow and a broad concept of a seasonal worker. On the narrow view the rules should only

4 Smith in Ross (ed) *Employment Policy and the Labour Market* (1965) ch 6.
5 NIAC Report on Seasonal Workers (1977, Cmnd 6991), para 30.
6 Corp. Juris. Secundum, vol 81, pp. 411–412.
7 See e.g. *UD 4720*.
8 See Report of the National Insurance Advisory Committee on Seasonal Workers, 1948–49 HC 202, paras 18–21.
9 First Report (1931, Cmd 3872), para 125.
10 SR & O 1931/818.
11 N.5, above.
12 See pp. 132 and 133, below.
13 They were, apparently, accepted by the Labour government before it lost office: NIAC Report on Draft Regulations (1979, Cmnd 7622).

apply to those persons whose employment is truly 'seasonal', that is their work (e.g. in agriculture or tourism) varies according to climatic conditions. This is the definition preferred by the National Insurance Advisory Committee,[14] and seems to have been the original view taken. Under an amendment in 1935 a seasonal worker must have been employed 'in an occupation or occupations of a seasonal nature'.[15] On a broader view, it extends more generally to persons who are regularly employed for certain portions of the year (e.g. a school-meals attendant). This seems to be the position under the Regulations now in force. A 'seasonal' worker is defined as:

> a person whose normal employment is for a part or parts only of a year in an occupation or occupations of which the availability or extent varies at approximately the same time or times in successive years; or any other person who normally restricts his employment to the same, or substantially the same, part or parts only of the year.[16]

The onus of proving that the claimant is a seasonal worker is on the insurance officer,[17] though once this has been established it shifts to the claimant to show that the pattern of seasonal work has come to an end.[18] The seasonal nature of the work need not be voluntary: a disabled man may be forced by his handicap to take on only this kind of work.[19] Several more specific points under the statutory definition now arise for discussion.

i Part(s) of a year

The shift of emphasis from the narrower to the broader meaning of seasonal workers can be seen most clearly in the pattern of employment which must be established. The Commissioners originally construed 'part or parts of the year' in accordance with the climatic theory of 'seasonal' to include only those who were substantially unemployed for a period of three months.[20] This was felt to be too lax and, following an amendment to the Regulations in 1952,[1] 'part or parts of a year' may now be of any duration, and may be aggregated, so that, however, the total period of unemployment during the year is not less than seven weeks.[2] There is no *lower* limit to the amount of *employment* necessary to qualify as seasonal, so that a man whose only work during the year was to assist the GPO over Christmas was properly to be regarded as coming within the regulation.[3] The minimum of seven weeks of unemployment may be spread over the whole year.[4] The only concession to the more traditional concept of 'seasonal' is that the periods of employment must recur at approximately the same times of the year; and this has been given a flexible interpretation. In one case, a variation in the starting dates of employment of ten weeks and in the finishing dates of nine weeks was not regarded as too great.[5]

14 N.5, above, paras 61–66.
15 SR & O 1935/804, reg 2.
16 SI 1975/564, reg 19(2).
17 *R(U) 23/53*.
18 *R(U) 14/53*; *R(U) 19/54*.
19 *R(U) 43/52*; *R(U) 4/64*. Also, where no other employment is available: *R(U) 8/81*.
20 *R(U) 5/51*; *R(U) 7/51* (Tribunal decision).
1 SI 1952/1466, reg 2(3).
2 SI 1975/564, reg 19(1), as modified by SI 1979/940. NIAC proposed that the period be extended to 13 weeks: n.5, above, para 67.
3 *R(U) 3/61*.
4 *R(U) 5/64*.
5 *R(U) 8/62*.

ii Normal employment

In establishing the pattern, regard is to be had only to the claimant's 'normal employment'. This is a question of fact and is determined in a way similar to that of the analogous issue of a claimant's normal working week.[6] To decide whether or not the normal employment is for part or parts only of the year, the authorities are instructed to concentrate on 'factors inherent in the nature or conditions of the occupation' rather than 'factors abnormal to that occupation . . . notwithstanding that those factors persist for a prolonged period'.[7] There is a well established convention that three years of work governed by this provision raise a presumption that the claimant is a seasonal worker.[8] But it is 'a yardstick and not a magic wand. It does not solve all cases'.[9] It may be rebutted where sickness renders it difficult to discern a pattern,[10] or where the claimant has moved to a new district.[11]

D Duration of off-season

Once it has been established that the claimant is a seasonal worker it is necessary to calculate the duration of his off-season, for the special conditions only apply to a claim during that period. The regulation, not surprisingly, defines the 'off-season' as the part of the year (or aggregate of parts) when the claimant is normally not employed, but then excludes from consideration any period shorter than seven days.[12] The prevailing practice is to take the average periods of non-employment over the last three years, discounting abnormally short periods of work which were irrelevant to the claimant's usual occupation.[13]

E Special conditions for seasonal workers

Claims for benefit during the seasonal worker's off-season are subject to two special conditions.

i Registration

He must have been registered for employment with the Manpower Services Commission or local authority for the last two years or from the time he became a seasonal worker whichever is the later.[14] The object is to demonstrate that the claimant remains in 'the field of employment' during the off-season.[15] But it can only show his attitude to the labour market in the past and, as the National Insurance Advisory Committee found, has little practical effect.[16] They therefore recommended its abolition. In any event three types of period are exempted from this requirement:

(1) 'Any period during which he was employed or was incapable of work.'[17]

6 Pp. 92–93, above.
7 SI 1975/564, reg 19(1), as modified by SI 1979/594. See also *R(U) 8/81*.
8 *R(U) 3/51*, and see *R(U) 4/75* (Tribunal decision).
9 Ibid, at para 16.
10 *R(U) 36/51*.
11 *R(U) 14/53*.
12 SI 1975/564, reg 19(1), as modified by SI 1979/594.
13 *R(U) 29/51*.
14 SI 1975/564, reg 19(2)(a), as modified by SI 1979/594.
15 NIAC Report on Seasonal Workers (1977, Cmnd 6991), para 68.
16 Ibid.
17 On which see pp. 79–84, above and pp. 148–154, below.

(2) 'Any inconsiderable period'.[18]

(3) 'Any temporary period throughout which he was not available to be employed by reason only of domestic necessity or compulsion of law, or by reason of any other circumstances of an exceptional character'.[19]

ii Substantial employment

In addition he must prove *either*

(1) that 'in his current off-season he has had a substantial amount of employment' before the date of claim; or

(2) that '(having regard to all the circumstances of his case, including the nature and extent of his employment (if any) in any past off-seasons and the industrial or other relevant conditions normally obtaining in the district or districts in which he is available to be employed) he can or could reasonably expect to obtain, after that day in his current off-season, employment which, together with his employment (if any) before that day in that off-season, constitutes a substantial amount of employment'.[20]

'Substantial amount of employment' is defined in the Regulations as

> employment which is equal in duration to not less than one-fourth (or such other fractional part as may, in the circumstances of the particular case, be reasonable) of the current off-season.[1]

The primary calculation, therefore, involves ascertaining the duration of the off-season and seeing whether the amount of employment actually obtained or likely in all the circumstances to be obtained exceeds one-fourth. Under (2), there is inevitably an element of speculation. But resort may be had to the claimant's past employment record, and for this purpose the authorities will adopt much the same approach as was appropriate to determine whether or not the claimant was a 'seasonal worker'.[2]

Even if the claimant fails the one-fourth test, he may yet persuade the authorities to exercise their discretion to accept a smaller amount of employment, though the reported decisions reveal a noticeable reluctance to do this.[3]

Part 8 Duration and amount of benefit

A Duration

Unemployment benefit is not payable after 312 days (not counting Sunday or a substitute rest day) of one period of interruption of employment.[4] This includes days for which the claimant was entitled to, but did not claim, benefit,[5] unless he is able to show that by failing to claim 'he did not intend

18 E.g. 9 days in 2 years (*R(U) 13/56*) but not 22 days in 2 years (*R(U) 26/55*).

19 'Circumstances of an exceptional nature' have been held to include a full-time educational course (*R(U) 19/64*) but not mere distance to the employment exchange or other inconvenience (*R(U) 7/52*).

20 SI 1975/564, reg 19(2)(b), as modified.

1 Ibid, reg 19(1).

2 P. 132, above, and see *R(U) 21/55*; *R(U) 14/61*; *R(U) 2/63*.

3 *R(U) 14/61*; cp *R(U) 5/55*.

4 SSA 1975, s.18(1). For 'period of interruption of employment' see pp. 89–90, above.

5 See also n.3, p. 90, above.

. . . to avoid the necessity of requalifying for benefit'.[6] To re-establish title after the 312 days the claimant must be in employment as an employed earner[7] for 13 weeks, and in each of those weeks must be so employed for at least 16 hours.[8]

B Amount

The weekly standard rate of unemployment benefit is in 1982–83, £25.00, to which may be added increases for dependants.[9] The earnings-related supplement, introduced in 1966,[10] was abolished as from 3 January 1982.[11] Men aged 65–70, and women aged 60–65, who have not retired, but who would have been entitled to a Category A or B retirement pension if they had retired, are paid at the current rate of the relevant pension.[12]

6 SI 1975/564, reg 11(1). The same applies where, as a result of abatement, an occupational pensioner receives nothing by way of unemployment benefit: p. 130, above.
7 SSA 1975, s.79(4).
8 Ibid, s.18(2), as amended by SS(MP)A 1977, s.17(1).
9 Pp. 364–376, below.
10 NIA 1966, s.2.
11 SSA (No 2) 1980, s.4.
12 SSA 1975, s.14(6). For details, see ch 5, below.

Chapter 4

Benefits for sickness and disability

Part 1 General

A Scope of chapter

An independent study carried out in 1976–77 concluded that 'the present UK system of benefits for handicapped people is a ragbag of provisions based on differing, sometimes conflicting and anachronistic principles'.[1] Not all these benefits are properly to be described as 'social security', and some which are appropriately so termed are dealt with elsewhere in the book. Excluded from the present chapter are the following.

i *Benefits in kind* There is a wide variety of facilities provided for sick and disabled people under the National Health Service and by such legislative measures as the Chronically Sick and Disabled Persons Act 1970 and the Disabled Persons Act 1981.[2]

ii *Schemes for disability resulting from specific causes* For historical and policy reasons, there are special social security schemes for those disabled as the result of industrial accident or diseases or of service in the armed forces. These will be described in chapters 8 and 9 respectively. In 1979 two new schemes were introduced to remedy deficiencies in the private law. Both are administered by the DHSS but are not primarily seen as social security measures. The Vaccine Damage Payments Act provides for compensation where severe disablement results from vaccination against certain diseases or contact from persons so vaccinated;[3] the Pneumoconiosis etc. (Workers Compensation) Act confers lump sum benefits on those who have suffered from specific lung diseases as a result of their employment but who received no tort compensation because their employer ceased business before the manifestation of the symptoms.[4] Since 1964 there has existed a criminal injury compensation scheme: ex gratia payments, analogous to tort damages, are made to those sustaining personal injury directly attributable to a crime of violence. The scheme is financed from general taxation, but is not administered by the DHSS.[5]

1 Simkins and Tickner *Whose Benefit*? (1978) p. 17.
2 See generally Topliss *Provision for the Disabled* (2nd edn).
3 See Dworkin [1978–9] JSWL 330.
4 See Carson, ibid, pp. 350–351.
5 *Atiyah* ch. 13.

iii *Family fund*[6] This was set up in 1973 as an immediate response to the thalidomide disaster. It originally conferred benefits in cash and kind for families having the care of a child with a severe congenital disability, but subsequently all severely handicapped children became eligible. It is financed by government but is administered by the Joseph Rowntree Memorial Trust.

This chapter is concerned with the general disability benefits payable under the Social Security Acts. In Part 2 we consider the contributory benefit for sickness which is payable for the first six months of incapacity – though from April 1983 for short periods of sickness employees will receive instead statutory sick pay – and in Part 3 the invalidity benefit for periods of incapacity longer than six months. Parts 4 to 7 cover the non-contributory benefits introduced in the 1970s: non-contributory invalidity pension, attendance allowance, invalid care allowance and mobility allowance.

B History[7]

The origins of the provisions for sickness benefit in the National Insurance Act 1911 may be found in two different sources. Support for the sick had been one of the chief preoccupations of the friendly societies. These had existed for several centuries, but with industrialism had come into their own in the nineteenth century[8] as providing assistance, both economic and social, for the more prosperous workman or artisan who wished to protect himself and his family from the squalor of the poor law. In 1905, their total membership amounted to no less than 6 million.[9] It was not, therefore, surprising that when the inadequacies of the poor law to cope with the sick and disabled were most clearly manifested[10] – and when the need for a compulsory insurance scheme had become fully evident[11] (in fact over one-half of the working population had no form of sickness insurance[12]) – it was thought appropriate to build on the foundations of the friendly societies. The other main influence was the system of sickness insurance already operating in Germany which had come to the attention of Lloyd George during his researches into old age pensions.[13] The political battles fought on the exact nature of the scheme to be introduced were fierce. The friendly societies, the insurance companies and particularly the medical profession all campaigned vigorously to preserve their vested interests.[14] The result was a compromise. The provision of medical services was administered by specially created bodies, the Insurance Committees, on which insured persons, medical practitioners, local authorities and central government were represented. But the administration of cash benefits was in the hands of 'Approved Societies', such friendly societies, trade unions, insurance

6 Bradshaw *The Family Fund* (1980).
7 Harris *National Health Insurance 1911–1946* (1946); Levy *National Health Insurance, a Critical Study* (1944).
8 Gosden *The Friendly Societies in England, 1815–1875* (1961), and *Self-Help: Voluntary Associations in the 19th Century* (1973).
9 Bruce *The Coming of the Welfare State* (4th edn) p. 112.
10 Report of Royal Commission on Poor Laws and Relief of Distress (1909, Cd 4499).
11 Ibid, at pp. 107–110.
12 Mr D Lloyd-George, 25 HC Official Report (5th series) col 610.
13 In 1911 the government issued a Memorandum on Sickness and Invalidity Insurance in Germany, Cd 5678.
14 See esp. Gilbert *The Evolution of National Insurance in Great Britain* (1966) chs 6–7.

and collecting societies as satisfied two conditions: they were not carried on for profit and they were subject to the absolute control of their members.[15] The individual would enrol with the society of his choice but, within certain statutory limits, the society had power to make rules and regulations governing the payment of benefit,[16] and might decline to accept a person as member (except on the ground of age).[17] The scheme covered initially all manual workers, and non-manual workers earning less than £160 per annum.[18] In return for weekly contributions (4d for men, 3d for women[19]) the insured person would, on proof of incapacity for work, be entitled to 10s per week (7s 6d for women) from the fourth day of incapacity for a maximum of twenty-six weeks.[20] After that period had elapsed, 'disablement benefit' was payable so long as he remained incapable of work, though the amounts in question were half those for sickness benefit.[1] Further, to qualify the claimant must have been insured and paid contributions for twenty-six weeks in the case of sickness benefit, and 104 weeks in the case of disablement benefit.[2] The individual society could, however, pay additional benefits at its discretion and in the manner it thought fit from any surplus in its funds. The result was that benefits varied widely according to the membership and geographical location of the society. No doubt the intention was to preserve the 'private' nature of friendly society insurance, but it seemed hardly to be compatible with a compulsory scheme.[3]

In contrast to unemployment insurance which underwent many changes between 1911 and 1946, the structure of health insurance, at least as regards sickness and disablement benefits, remained more or less intact until the wholesale revision at the end of the Second World War. The number of persons insured was gradually increased.[4] Contribution and benefit rates were increased in 1920[5] and, in the light of the economic conditions of the time, contribution requirements were relaxed[6] and Treasury subsidies reduced.[7] The Royal Commission on Health Insurance, reporting in 1926,[8] recommended certain minor changes in contribution requirements and these were effected two years later.[9] Its most substantial criticisms, however, went largely unheeded until Beveridge's Report in 1942. The scheme, it was said, was too little concerned with health improvement — 'sickness insurance' would have been a more appropriate title than 'health insurance'. The intended democratic nature of the Approved Societies had become a fiction — they were ordinary commercial undertakings in a different guise.[10] Perhaps most important of all,

15 NIA 1911, s.23.
16 Ibid, s.27.
17 Ibid, s.13.
18 NIA 1911, ss.1, 2.
19 Ibid, s.30 (to which were added 3d from the employer and 2d from the Treasury).
20 Ibid, s.8(1)(c).
1 Ibid, s.8(1)(d).
2 Ibid, s.8(8).
3 *Harris,* n.7, above, pp. 88–93.
4 By NHIA 1928 compulsory insurance was extended to e.g. sub-contractors in the building and other trades.
5 E.g. sickness benefit of 15s per week for men: NHIA 1920, s.2.
6 By the Prolongation of Insurance Act 1926, and similar subsequent measures.
7 Notably the Economy (Miscellaneous Provisions) Act 1926 reduced the state contribution from 2s 9d to 1s 7d.
8 Cmd 2591.
9 NHIA 1928.
10 The minority recommended the abolition of the Approved Societies and the transfer of their functions to local authorities.

benefit was inadequate in that, unlike unemployment benefit, it did not provide for dependants' allowances. The 1926 Report, then, in some ways looked forward to the substantial reforms proposed by Beveridge and implemented by the government after the Second World War.

The fundamental achievement of this period was, of course, the establishment of the National Health Service.[11] The provision of medical services and of medicaments was extricated from the insurance scheme and they were made freely available to all. Sickness benefit was brought more into line with unemployment benefit: the rates were assimilated and for the first time sick claimants were paid an allowance for dependants. At the same time, though remaining ineligible for unemployment benefit, the self-employed became entitled to sickness benefit. This was, however, a controversial measure. At first it was thought to be too impracticable to administer and in the original 1946 Bill there was a waiting-period of 24 days for such persons. This was eventually removed,[12] but the price to be paid was an increase of 3d in the contributions demanded of the self-employed. The Approved Societies were abolished and their functions transferred to the newly created Ministry of National Insurance. Disablement benefit also disappeared and sickness benefit became payable for an unlimited duration provided that the contribution requirements had been satisfied. But the distinction between short-term and long-term incapacity was not entirely eradicated: the contribution conditions became much more stringent after a year's entitlement to benefit.[13] Indeed, the distinction was broadened in 1966 when earnings-related supplement was introduced only for the first 26 weeks of incapacity.[14] This important advance left unaffected those who had been incapable of work for a longer period. The Labour administration of the late 1960s proposed, as part of its National Superannuation scheme, an earnings-related pension for such persons,[15] but the Bill lapsed. The succeeding Conservative government adopted an alternative strategy: the invalidity benefit introduced in 1971[16] was in effect the standard flat-rate sickness benefit plus a small allowance which varied according to the claimant's age at the onset of incapacity and which was based on the assumed greater loss of those giving up work at an earlier stage in their working life. The emphasis on satisfying needs rather than providing earnings replacements was taken further by certain complementary measures which rendered the conditions of invalidity benefit more favourable to the claimant than those of sickness benefit: there was no reduction for contribution deficiencies; higher increases were paid for dependent children;[17] and there was an easier criterion of dependency for a working wife.[18]

During the 1960s the political background to provision for the disabled had altered significantly. On the one hand, there had emerged some powerful pressure groups,[19] concerned to bring to public attention the

11 National Health Service Act 1946, implementing proposals in the White Paper (1944, Cmd 6502).
12 See esp. 423 HC Official Report (5th series) cols 350–364.
13 NIA 1946, s.12(2).
14 NIA 1966, s.2.
15 See White Paper, National Superannuation and Social Insurance (1969, Cmd 3883), para 88, and the Bill of the same name, cl 12.
16 NIA 1971, s.3: pp. 162–165, below.
17 P. 365, below.
18 P. 368, below.
19 The most influential has probably been the Disablement Income Group formed in 1965. There is now a co-ordinating organisation, the Disability Alliance, which lists about 30 associations concerned with the welfare of the disabled. See, generally, on these movements Walker in (ed) Jones *Yearbook of Social Policy in Britain 1975* pp. 204–207.

plight of the disabled, to conduct inquiries and publish their findings, and to campaign actively for reform. On the other hand, the 'rediscovery' of poverty in the 1960s had brought to light that disability featured prominently among the causes of deprivation and financial hardship.[20] Under the influence of these movements, the government sponsored in 1968–69 a massive survey of handicapped and impaired persons in Great Britain (OPCS Survey).[1] The findings largely confirmed the conjectures of those campaigning for more generous financial support. It was estimated that there were about three million 'impaired' persons, that is those lacking part or all of a limb, or having a defective organ or mechanism of the body, and that about 1,100,000 were 'handicapped' in the sense that they had difficulty in carrying out the normal functions of daily living.[2] A disturbingly high proportion (35–40 per cent) of the 'handicapped' were in receipt of supplementary benefit, including 225,000 under pensionable age but incapable of work for more than six months, of whom 135,000 were not entitled to a contributory benefit.[3] Indeed it was estimated that a further 50,000 were entitled to, but did not, claim supplementary benefit.[4]

The first priority was to make better provision for the severely disabled.[5] Successive governments have so far remained unimpressed by the arguments[6] for a comprehensive income maintenance scheme according to the degree of disablement. Quite apart from economic considerations it is said that such a broad approach is oversimplified.

> No clear picture emerges of the 'problem of disablement'. There are, in fact, a number of different interlocking problems rather than one single problem. No simple analysis can be made and no single simple solution is appropriate. . . . There must be priorities. The greatest needs must be identified and met first on the basis of a sound programme of cash benefits and services which takes account both of the practical limitations of detailed assessments of need and of the choices expressed by disabled people themselves.[7]

Efforts have therefore been directed at isolating specific needs and attempting to satisfy them with non-contributory benefits. One of the most significant findings of the OPCS Survey was the large number of persons 'handicapped' in the sense that they required assistance to cope with the normal functions of living.[8] The Labour administration had proposed to compensate the more severe cases within this group with their 'attendance allowance', included in the National Superannuation Bill of 1969,[9] and the succeeding Conservative government adopted this part of the programme. An allowance was introduced in 1970[10] for those requiring attention or

20 See particularly Abel-Smith and Townsend *The Poor and the Poorest* (1965) p. 62.
1 The Report of the Survey by the Office of Population Censuses and Surveys was published in 3 volumes: Part One, Harris *Handicapped and Impaired in Great Britain* (1971); Part Two, Buckle *Work and Housing of Impaired Persons in Great Britain* (1971); Part Three, Harris, Smith and Head *Income and Entitlement to Supplementary Benefit of Impaired People in Great Britain* (1972).
2 *Harris*, n.1, above, at p. 18.
3 Report on Social Security Provision for Chronically Sick and Disabled People, 1973–74, HC 276, at paras 8 and 41.
4 *Harris, Smith and Head*, n.1, above, at pp. 42–43.
5 Report on Social Security Provision, n.3, above, at para 54.
6 See particularly Disablement Income Group *Realising a Comprehensive Disability Income* (1975) and Disability Alliance *Poverty and Disability* (1975); and Walker and Townsend (eds) *Disability in Britain* (1981), pp. 49–51, 200–204.
7 Report on Social Security Provision, n.3, above, at paras 52–53.
8 *Harris*, n.1, above, at pp. 16–20.
9 National Superannuation and Social Insurance Bill 1969, cl 17.
10 NI (Old persons' and widows' pensions and attendance allowance) Act 1970, renamed NIA 1970 by NIA 1972, s.8(4).

supervision both during the day and at night, and two years later a lower-rate allowance was added to cover cases where the requisite attendance was required either during the day or at night.[11] In 1975 this was complemented by a measure designed to assist those who sacrificed their own work opportunities to care for persons in receipt of attendance allowance: the non-contributory invalid care allowance.[12] Quite apart from the justice of compensating a group who performed an unattractive and unpaid task, there was the economic consideration that by so doing they relieved the social services of additional burdens.

The dependence on supplementary benefit of many disabled persons resulted, of course, from their inability to satisfy the conditions for the contributory benefits: the majority of these had been disabled from birth, but there was also a substantial number who had not worked sufficiently to pay the requisite number of contributions.[13] In 1975 the non-contributory invalidity pension was introduced to cater for this group.[14] It became payable in circumstances similar to those of the contributory invalidity pension but without contribution conditions and (to achieve equity as compared with those who had contributed to the National Insurance Fund) at a lower rate.[15] At this level, it is not clear that the pension has fully achieved the desired objective of obviating recourse to the means-tested supplementary benefit, and there is evidence that those who had not been dependent on the latter profited most from the additional resources made available.[16]

There were three other categories of disabled persons which attracted attention: the immobile, housewives, and children. Those unable to walk but able to drive had for some time been entitled to invalid carriages or, if they owned a car, to a private car allowance; but the disabled passenger was not assisted and the safety and reliability of the carriage had been subjected to considerable doubt.[17] Rather than switch entitlement to a small car, which would have involved a considerable increase in expenditure, the government decided to introduce, as an alternative to the invalid carriage, a cash allowance payable to adults of working age and children aged five and above who were unable, or virtually unable, to walk.[18] In 1976 the doubts regarding the safety of the carriage were confirmed and it was decided to phase it out of production.[19] The mobility allowance thus remains as the main form of assistance conferred on immobile persons.

Consideration of the disabled housewife featured prominently in the campaign conducted by the pressure groups.[20] The OPCS Survey revealed that there were some 225,000 housewives prevented by their disability from doing the household chores,[1] though of these only about one fifth were under pensionable age without entitlement to any personal benefit.[2] Those not engaged in remunerative employment were not, of course,

11 NIA 1970, s.2. See generally pp. 171–177, below.
12 It was introduced by SSBA 1975, s.7. See generally pp. 177–181, below.
13 Report on Social Security Provision, n.3, above, at para 24.
14 SSBA 1975, s.6.
15 Pp. 166–171, below.
16 Simkins and Tickner *Whose Benefit* (1978) p. 60.
17 See the government-sponsored Report by Lady Sharp, Mobility of Physically Disabled People (1974).
18 Introduced by SSPA 1975, s.22. See generally pp. 181–186, below.
19 P. 182, below.
20 E.g. Disablement Income Group *Creating a National Disability Income* (1972) pp. 19–20.
1 *Harris,* see n.1 on p. 140, above, at pp. 63–91.
2 Report on Social Security Provision for Chronically Sick and Disabled People, 1973–74, HC 276, at para 43.

entitled to sickness or invalidity benefit. The solution adopted in 1977 was to extend to this group entitlement to the non-contributory invalidity pension if they were able to show that they were 'incapable of performing normal household duties'.[3] While on the face of it this innovatory measure had much to commend it, it suffered from the serious objection that it was discriminatory:[4] it assumed that only married women were primarily responsible for housework, and to receive benefit they had to satisfy not only the 'household duties' test but also the condition applied to all claimants, that they were incapable of paid work

The chief difficulty posed by disabled children was that the extent of the problem was largely unknown. The OPCS Survey did not cover persons under sixteen, and such estimates as have been made of the number handicapped range from 80,000 to 350,000.[5] Moreover, as with the immobile, it was not clear whether the main effort should be directed at improving facilities or granting cash allowances.[6] Attendance allowances had been payable for children aged two or more,[7] and those aged five and over were to become entitled to the mobility allowance. But it was the plight of the thalidomide children which prompted immediate government action. Since 1973 a Family Fund established on a non-statutory basis and administered by the Rowntree Memorial Trust has conferred benefits on severely disabled children. The government, which initially contributed £3 million, and has since continued to finance the scheme, indicated however that this was not intended as compensation for disablement, but rather to complement services already provided by statutory and voluntary bodies.[8]

The trend in government policy since the publication of the OPCS Survey has clearly been to improve financial provision for the long-term disabled, as opposed to those incapable of work for only short periods. The trend has been reinforced by the latest series of reforms. First, from April 1979, recipients of the contributory invalidity pension became entitled to an earnings-related component, though only on the basis of contributions made to the new pensions scheme.[9] In contrast, the earnings-related supplement to the short-term sickness benefit was abolished in 1982.[10] One reason for the disparity in treatment was the fact that an increasing proportion of employees received substantial sick pay from their employers during short spells off work — almost 90 per cent according to the latest estimate.[11] In an effort partly to rationalise this overlap and partly to reduce public expenditure, the government has introduced a radical reform as a result of which, as from April 1983, an employer will be bound to pay a prescribed amount of sick pay for the first eight weeks of incapacity for work and during this period entitlement to sickness benefit is abolished.[12] Consequential reductions are made to the employer's contributions liability and there will be an estimated £30 million savings in the administrative expenses of the National Insurance Fund, since the DHSS

3 SSBA 1975, s.6.
4 See the NIAC Report (1980, Cmd 7955).
5 See Disability Alliance *Poverty and Disability* (1975) pp. 4–5; *Pearson* paras 1514–1520, and *Townsend* ch 21.
6 Report on Social Security Provision, n.2, above, at para 45.
7 Pp. 176–177, below.
8 848 HC Official Report (5th series) written answer cols 241–242. See generally Bradshaw *The Family Fund* (1980).
9 SSPA 1975, s.14, and p. 164, below.
10 SSA (No 2) 1980, s.4.
11 13 HC Official Report (6th series) cols 642–643.
12 SSHBA 1982, Part I.

will be relieved from processing about 90 per cent of sickness benefit claims.[13] There are three rates of statutory sick pay, depending on the earnings of the employee, but no dependency allowances are payable; in some cases, this will mean that those with large families will be disadvantaged by the new scheme.[14]

Whatever the merits of this last, controversial measure, it is to be acknowledged that in the last decade there has been a considerable improvement in social security provision, particularly for the long-term disabled.[15] Nevertheless there remain three fundamental features which should not escape criticism. First, the piecemeal nature of reform has given rise to a vast and complex array of benefits, with different criteria of entitlement and varied according to whether the claimant has been a social security contributor or to whether his disability resulted from a specific cause, for example an industrial accident or military service.[16] In her 1974 Report, the Secretary of State declared that it was necessary 'to develop a comprehensive long-term strategy and coherent philosophy for meeting the needs of disabled people',[17] and it may be argued that this is exactly what is lacking in the present approach. In this regard, the proposals made by the Disability Alliance for a comprehensive disability income appear to be attractive.[18] This would distribute resources so that people with equally severe disabilities would be entitled to similar amounts, irrespective of the cause of their disablement. Some two million people would be eligible and the government has stated that it would cost some £2–3 billion to implement.[19] Its proponents, however, argue that this fails to take account of savings of expenditure (including administrative costs) of the present system and suggest that the figure is closer to £1½ billion (in 1981 terms).[20] Such a comprehensive approach would also meet the second general criticism which is that the present system concentrates almost entirely on total incapacity for work as the criterion for income. There is a large group of disabled individuals who manage to work full-time or part-time but who, as a result of their condition, suffer substantial losses to their earning capacity. Britain is one of the few member states of the EEC offering no assistance for permanent partial incapacity which does not result from an industrial accident or disease.[1] The third criticism is directed against the sex discrimination incorporated in the rules governing entitlement to two of the non-contributory benefits. Both assume the stereotype of a married woman staying at home to perform household duties and care for the family. The first, the non-contributory invalidity pension, has already been mentioned;[2] the second, the invalid care allowance, is payable to all persons caring for a severely disabled person *except* married women living with their husbands (or other women living with a man as his wife). These

13 Green Paper, Income During Initial Sickness (1980, Cmd 7864), para 3, and Memorandum to the 1982 Bill.
14 Cf Second Report of Committee on Social Services, 1980–81, HC 113, paras 21–24.
15 Report on Social Security Provision, n.2, above, para 6.
16 *Pearson* paras 264–269; Simkins and Tickner *Whose Benefit* (1978), esp. ch 2.
17 N.2, above, para 3.
18 See n.6 on p. 146, above.
19 Mr R Prentice, Minister for Social Security, 981 HC Official Report (5th series) col 507.
20 Walker and Townsend (eds) *Disability in Britain* (1981) Appendix. An interim measure would be the payment of the new benefit to the 80,000 most severely disabled persons, at a net increase in cost of £120 million: ibid, p. 204.
1 *Kaim-Caudle* pp. 192–193; Commission of the European Communities *Comparative Tables of the Social Security Systems* (11th edn), Table VI; *Pearson* paras 814–821.
2 P. 142, above.

provisions have not been affected by the EEC Directive on Equality of Treatment in Social Security,[3] and though they have been trenchantly criticised by the National Insurance Advisory Committee[4] and the Equal Opportunities Commission,[5] the government has not yet revealed an intention to reform them.

C Definitions of disability

Broadly speaking, the legislation adopts five different criteria of disability:

(1) 'Incapacity for work'[6] – used for the purposes of sickness, invalidity (contributory or non-contributory) and industrial injury benefits.
(2) 'Incapable of performing normal household duties'[7] – applied to married women claiming the non-contributory invalidity pension.
(3) Requiring 'attention' and 'supervision' from another person[8] – a test devised for attendance allowance.
(4) 'Inability or virtual inability to walk'[9] – for the purposes of mobility allowance.
(5) 'Degree of disablement'[10] – the extent of impairment, typically based on prescribed physical conditions, for the purposes of the industrial disablement pension.

The problem of finding appropriate criteria for disability is one that has, in recent years, been of great concern to sociologists and others attempting to establish the extent of need within the community, and the appropriate methods of coping with it.[11] A glance at the criteria listed above reveals that, with the exception of the anatomical/clinical test used for the purposes of the industrial disablement pension, they are primarily *functional*, that is, they are concerned not with the physical degree of disablement but rather its effect on the life (particularly working life) of the person in question. This is, indeed, in line with much of the current theory on this subject. Any attempt to define disability by a clinical comparison to the ideal healthy man, or the reasonably healthy man on the Clapham omnibus, is doomed to failure.[12] Nevertheless attention may be drawn to some limitations inherent in the criteria as adopted by our social security system. First, (and this is only to repeat a point made in the last section) there is very great emphasis on the incapacity to undertake remunerative employment. This is because inability to earn remains the most substantial and most typical form of financial loss. But in terms of social costs it might not always be the most decisive or appropriate criterion. It is argued that regard should be had not only to such activities as self-care, mobility, and performing household duties (to a lesser or greater extent recently adopted within the system) but also to establishing and maintaining relationships

3 Cf p. 9, above, and p. 366, below.
4 Report on the Household Duties Test for Married Women (1980, Cmnd 7955); and Report on Extension of Title to Invalid Care Allowance to Non-Relatives (1980, Cmnd 7905).
5 *Behind Closed Doors* (1981).
6 Pp. 148–154, below.
7 Pp. 168–170, below.
8 Pp. 174–175, below.
9 Pp. 182–184, below.
10 Pp. 302–307, below.
11 See particularly: Townsend *The Disabled in Society* (1967); Blaxter *The Meaning of Disability* (1967); Sainsbury *Registered as Disabled* (1970); Nagi *Disability and the Severely Disabled: Concepts and Prevalence* (1975).
12 Forder *Concepts in Social Administration* (1974) pp. 42–43.

both within and outside the family.[13] Secondly, there is the degree of functional disability. Most of the definitions adopted assume an either/or dichotomy – the claimant is either able to perform the function in question, or he is not. It is important to recognise that generally there is a scale of difficulty with which the function can be undertaken – from being able to perform it only with very great difficulty through to performance with only moderate difficulty – and the condition may be progressive or fluctuating.[14] This point assumes some significance once it is appreciated that pain, as such, is not a quantifiable matter, and its existence must to a certain extent depend on self perception.[15] This has implications both for the method of establishing incapacity,[16] and for the delicate question of avoiding disincentives to work.[17] Thirdly, there is the problem of assessment and adjudication. Though the precise impact of medical evidence and opinions varies according to the benefit in question,[18] it is clear that in practice and for most purposes the views of the medical profession, either in the form of medical statements by general practitioners, or of examination by specialist medical tribunals, are regarded as decisive, if not conclusive. The difficulty with this is that it assumes that medical practitioners are in a better qualified position to decide not only clinical questions relating to the degree of impairment, but also on the effects which that impairment has on the life of the individual. This has prompted some to argue for a more flexible method of determining incapacity, for example, by the participation of social workers.[19] The present position doubtless reflects existing opinions about the 'reliability' and 'status' of the medical as opposed to the social work professions. A move from the objective 'medical' to the subjective 'social' definition of disability would clearly require a major readjustment not only of the legislation itself but also of the method of adjudication. It would also necessarily confer a much wider degree of discretion than exists at present (with a consequent increase of administrative costs), and this might, in turn, provoke feelings of injustice and resentment which those arguing for reform are keen to eliminate.

Part 2 Sickness benefit

A General

The income maintenance of those who are unable to work because they are sick remains one of the cardinal purposes of social welfare. Its importance may be gauged from the fact that in 1980 there were over 300 million recorded days of incapacity in connection with claims to benefit.[20]

It might have been assumed that the improvement in medical facilities and techniques over past decades, in particular that resulting from the introduction of the National Health Service, would have led to an overall

13 *Blaxter,* n.11, above, ch 8; *Townsend* pp. 686–693.
14 *Sainsbury,* n.11, above, at pp. 37–41.
15 Nagi 38 Ind Medicine and Surgery 27; *Blaxter,* n.11, above, at pp. 11–13.
16 Pp. 149–152, below.
17 P. 146, below, and see Nagi and Hadley, 25 Ind Lab Rel Rev 223.
18 See generally pp. 150–151 and 170–171, below.
19 *Townsend,* n.11, above, at pp. 5–6 and *Blaxter*, n.11, above, at pp. 6–7.
20 Social Security Statistics 1981, Table 3.70; and the number of total days lost must be considerably higher since the statistics do not record the sickness of those uninsured, nor periods of absence of less than 4 days.

improvement in the health of the community and consequently to a diminishing reliance on sickness benefit.[1] In fact, the contrary has occurred. Absence for sickness has shown a steady increase over a number of years. The inference has been drawn that payment of sickness benefit has encouraged 'absenteeism'.[2] But this is an over-simplification. Correlation between the value of benefit and the level of incapacity is at best very imprecise. Of course, it is to some extent natural that when the rate of sickness benefit is increased the rate of absence should also rise, because a person who on grounds of health *should* have stayed at home, but could not afford to, may now do so.[3] It has been suggested that recent increases in the sickness rate may be accounted for by growing problems of job dissatisfaction,[4] but some small part might be attributable to changing attitudes in the medical profession.[5] Minor ill-health, including psychological disorder, may no longer be ignored in the way it was.[6]

To qualify for benefit, the claimant must show that he has satisfied the contribution requirements (section B), that the days for which the claim was made were days of 'incapacity for work' (section C). Conversely, there are grounds on which he may be disqualified from benefit (section D). From April 1983, sickness benefit will not be payable for periods (generally the first eight weeks of incapacity) during which the claimant is entitled to statutory sick pay (section E).

B Amount and contribution conditions

The law governing contribution conditions and the amount payable is exactly the same as that for unemployment benefit,[7] with one major exception: the self-employed qualify for this benefit and therefore title may be based on Class 2 contributions.[8]

C Incapable for work

Sickness benefit is payable in respect of 'a day of incapacity for work'.[9] A day is not so regarded unless

> on that day [the claimant] is, or is deemed . . . to be, incapable of work by reason of some specific disease or bodily or mental disablement.[10]

This definition of incapacity is a long-standing one in social security law.[11] It places the onus of proof on the claimant.[12]

1 This formed the basis of one of the arguments used for a National Health Service: Ross *The National Health Service in Great Britain* (1952) p. 15.
2 CBI *Absenteeism* (1970).
3 *Kaim-Caudle* p. 105; Reid and Robertson (eds) *Fringe Benefits, Labour Costs and Social Security* (1965) pp. 224–226.
4 Taylor 25 Brit Jo of Ind Medicine 106; cp Martin and Morgan *Prolonged Sickness and the Return to Work* (1975) pp. 157–163.
5 This had been foreseen by the Government Actuary in 1946: Report on the Financial Provisions of the NI Bill 1946 (Cmd 6730), Appendix, para 15.
6 Office of Health Economics *Work Lost Through Sickness* (1975) p. 27.
7 Pp. 78 and 135, above. But from April 1983 the contribution conditions will be waived for those incapable of work as the result of an industrial accident or disease: p. 293, below.
8 SSA 1975, s.13(1).
9 Ibid, s.14(i)(b). For the rules determining which days qualify, see pp. 154–155, below.
10 SSA 1975, s.17(1)(a)(ii).
11 See e.g. NIA 1911, s.8(1)(c).
12 *R(S) 13/52*.

i Some specific disease or bodily or mental disablement

Whether the claimant comes within the statutory definition of incapacity is a question of fact[13] for which resort must be had to expert medical opinion. While it is impossible to state a general scientific criterion which will resolve the problem in all cases, certain fundamental guidelines do emerge from the reported decisions. A disease has been defined as 'a departure from health capable of identification by its signs and symptoms, an abnormality of some sort'.[14] Pregnancy does not come within this definition, and the legislation makes provision for this condition through maternity benefit.[15] Under earlier legislation, a woman entitled to the latter could not draw sickness benefit for the first four weeks following her confinement.[16] This rule was repealed in 1966,[17] but without indicating under what conditions a woman in such circumstances might qualify. Certainly she should be entitled on proof of a physical or mental disablement resulting from, but going beyond, the ordinary incidents of pregnancy.[18] There is no reported decision on the question whether damage to a prosthesis, such as an artificial limb, can constitute 'bodily disablement', but for analogous purposes under the industrial injuries scheme it has been held that such damage is to be treated as 'personal injury' where the prosthesis concerned is so intimately linked with the claimant's body as to form part of that body.[19]

As medical science has shown greater awareness of different types of psychological disorder, so there has been a natural tendency to extend the certification for 'mental disablement'.[20] Any condition which incapacitates a claimant from work and which is accepted as such in a doctor's statement should be sufficient.[1] But the legislation must necessarily assume some principle of moral responsibility, or 'work-shy' persons might claim to be mentally disabled. Of course, the distinction between a 'disease' and a 'defect of character' is sometimes very difficult to draw. In *R(S) 6/59*

> C manifested the symptoms of Munchausen's syndrome, a condition under which a person habitually presents himself at hospital for the treatment of an apparently acute illness, giving particulars of a physical disability, which does not in fact exist. The Commissioner decided that he was not incapable on the grounds, first that the condition did not itself affect his capacity to work – a surprising view to take – and, secondly, that it was in any case a defect of character rather than a disease – a plausible view but one necessarily involving some value judgment as to responsibility.[2]

The disability must be the substantial cause of the incapacity for work. Factors extraneous to the physical or mental condition, such as the personal or domestic circumstances of the claimant, are thus irrelevant.[3] A person with limited mobility who, as a result of the weather, cannot get to his normal place of work may not draw benefit.[4]

13 *R(S) 7/53.*
14 *CS 221/49,* para 3.
15 Ch 7, below.
16 NIA 1965, s.19(7).
17 NIA 1966, s.3(3).
18 *CS 221/49.*
19 *R(I) 8/81,* p. 267, below.
20 Cf p. 146, above.
1 *R(S) 4/56.*
2 See also *CS 1/81,* noted at [1982] JSWL 48.
3 *R(S) 13/54.*
4 *R(S) 8/53; 2/58 (SB).*

ii Incapable of work

The disease or disablement must render the claimant incapable of work. If taken absolutely literally this would exclude a large proportion of claims, for there are many conditions of disablement in which a person is nevertheless capable of doing *some* kind of remunerative work. The difficulty was appreciated as long ago as 1914[5] and it was, presumably, only that the relevant authorities did not construe the provision literally that delayed amendment until 1973. In that year, the type of work of which the claimant must be incapable was limited to 'work which (he) can reasonably be expected to do',[6] though this was intended only to restate the traditional interpretation of the statutory test.[7]

Whether it is reasonable for the claimant to take on work of which he is admittedly capable but which is different from his normal occupation is, of course, a delicate issue. It involves, as the Commissioner has indicated, striking a balance 'between the interests of the claimant on the one hand and the interests of the National Insurance Fund and other contributors on the other'.[8] For some time, an administrative practice has existed within the DHSS: during the first six months of indisposition[9] a claimant need generally only show that he is incapable of following his usual occupation,[10] unless it is obvious that he will never become fit for that type of work but is able to perform some other work.[11] When called upon to consider this practice, the Commissioner in *R(S) 2/78* was reluctant to admit the validity of a 'hard and fast' rule:

> Reasonableness, rather than any specific measure of time, is the crucial matter. It is not normally reasonable, in the case of a short-term incapacity, to expect a claimant to change his occupation. If incapacity is continued, it may become reasonable to do so. Just at what stage must depend on the circumstances of the particular case: not merely age, education, experience and state of health, but other possible factors such as the nature of the claimant's normal occupation, how long he has been engaged in it, whether his incapacity for it is likely to be permanent or long-continued, whether he is likely to be adaptable to a new form of employment, and possibly whether he is due to retire at no distant date.[12]

So, in the instant case, he concluded that a salesman suffering from osteoarthritis of spine and hypertension could, after five months of benefit, reasonably attempt other kinds of work.[13] Whether the Commissioner's approach will prove to be too imprecise for expediting the large number of cases in which the problem arises[14] is a matter for conjecture.

5 Report of the Departmental Committee on Sickness Benefit Claims under the National Insurance Act (1914, Cd 7687), paras 110–113.
6 NISBA 1973, s.5(1), (3), now incorporated in SSA 1975, s.17(1)(a).
7 *R(S) 2/78,* para 6. It was felt to be necessary as a result of the confusion created by a more liberal interpretation given by Bean J in *Chesterfield Football Club v Secretary of State for Social Services* [1973] QB 583, [1973] 1 All ER 679 to an analogous question arising under the contribution provisions.
8 *R(S) 3/81*, para 11, D G Rice, Comr.
9 Not necessarily the current period of interruption of employment: *CS 17/79*, noted at [1981] JSWL 59.
10 Or all such occupations, where he follows more than one: *CS 8/79*, noted at [1978–9] JSWL 443.
11 *Fisher* Appendix 7, paras 6–7.
12 *R(S) 2/78*, para 8, H A Shewan, Comr.
13 See also *R(S) 3/81:* unreasonable to hold to an occupation after 18 months merely because pursuit of another occupation would involve the loss of valuable pension rights.
14 Cf Ogus in Burrows and Veljanovski (eds) *The Economic Approach to Law* (1981) 210 at 221.

The 'alternative' work, to which reference is made, may be only part-time, provided always that it is 'remunerative work . . . for which an employer would be willing to pay, or work as a self-employed person in some gainful occupation'.[15] The principle has been applied to two factual situations which have provoked some difficulties. A housewife may have given up her normal job as a result of illness but she may have continued to do the housework at home. In 1951 a Tribunal of Commissioners held that if she does the work of a normal household this is prima facie evidence that she is capable of doing the same work for remuneration and thus is excluded from benefit.[16] However, it may be rebutted if the only duties she performs are 'light', e.g. the purchase and preparation of food.[17] More problematic are the cases of self-employed persons who are capable of doing some form of management or supervision of their own business. A large number of reported decisions have been concerned with this issue,[18] and it is obviously difficult to draw the line between an active manager and a mere onlooker. Perhaps the greatest assistance is to be had from the approach suggested by a Northern Ireland Commissioner.[19] According to him, the question is whether the work which the claimant is capable of doing is of such substance or extent as either (1) would be likely to command remuneration if it was carried out for an outside employer, or (2) materially affected the day-to-day carrying on of the business. To determine these points regard may be had to e.g. the size and ownership of the business, the nature of accounting and drawing of profits, and whether there was a change of personnel consequent on the claimant's disability.

It is in principle irrelevant that there is available in the locality no work for which the claimant is admittedly capable or that the prospects of finding such work are poor.[20] In such circumstances he is expected to register for such work and claim unemployment benefit.[1] But as a qualification to this, it has been suggested that if *no* prospect for the work in question exists this may itself render that type of work unreasonable for the claimant.[2] Nor, apparently, will the rule be applied strictly to someone rendered virtually unemployable by an intermittent disablement, so that he is able to work only irregularly.[3]

iii Evidence of incapacity

The Medical Evidence Regulations provide that evidence of incapacity shall be furnished by the claimant either 'by means of a certificate in the form of a statement in writing given by a doctor' in the manner prescribed by the Regulations, or 'by such other means as may be sufficient in the circumstances of any particular case'.[4] The alternative, unprescribed method is designed to cater for those, particularly Christian Scientists, who

15 *R(S) 11/51*, para 5 (Tribunal decision).
16 *R(S) 11/51*.
17 *R 3/60 (SB)*.
18 See, inter alia, *R(S) 5/51*; *R(S) 22/51*; *R(S) 2/61*; *R(S) 4/79*; *R(S) 10/79*. See also the cases considered pp. 201–206, below.
19 *5/57 (SB)*, para 3.
20 *R(S) 21/51*; *R(S) 24/51*; *R(S) 1/79*.
1 For the difficulties arising where claimants for unemployment benefit are subject to periods of sickness, see Dept of Employment and DHSS *Payment of Benefit to Unemployed People* (1981) paras 5.69–5.83.
2 *R(S) 17/51*; *R(S) 10/54*.
3 *R(S) 9/79*, para 8, J N B Penny, Comr, contrasting the position with that of housewives' non-contributory invalidity pension, p. 169, below. *Quaere* whether the dictum survives the change in linking rules effected by SSA (No. 2) 1980, s.3, p. 154, below.
4 SI 1976/615, reg 2(1).

on grounds of conscience prefer not to attend for medical treatment,[5] but it is far from clear what sort of evidence will in such circumstances satisfy the authorities. In one case an acknowledgement by an employer of the claimant's incapacity was regarded as insufficient.[6] On the other hand, the fact of hospitalisation will raise a presumption of incapacity and this remains true even where after investigation the claimant is found not to be suffering from the suspected disease.[7]

The normal method, the prescribed form of certification by the claimant's general practitioner, has undergone several changes since its formulation in 1948,[8] the most important being in 1976 as a result of representations made by the British Medical Association and recommendations of the Fisher Committee on Abuse of Social Security.[9] The previous practice according to which the doctor 'certified' that in his opinion the patient was incapable of work at the time of examination[10] was replaced by a statement that he advises the patient to refrain from work.[11] The new formulation was intended as a more accurate reflection of the clinical responsibility towards the patient.[12] The other rules may be summarised briefly.[13]

- The statement must contain a diagnosis of the claimant's disorder justifying the advice to refrain from work. Where the doctor is of the opinion that work may be resumed within a period of two weeks, he is to issue a 'closed' statement, that is, one specifying the date when the claimant should be fit to resume. In other cases it will be an 'open' statement, the doctor merely indicating the minimum period during which the patient should abstain from work. This should not be a period greater than six months, unless (for the purposes of invalidity benefit) the claimant has already, on the advice of the doctor, refrained from work for six months.[14] In such a case, if it is his opinion that work should not be resumed for the foreseeable future, the doctor will simply enter 'until further notice'. Where a claimant has been the subject of an 'open' statement but nevertheless becomes fit to resume work, the doctor should issue a 'closed' statement to that effect. In such cases, where there are no longer any clinical signs of the previously disabling disorder, the doctor need not specify a diagnosis.

Normally medical statements in the above form will be regarded by the insurance officer as sufficient proof of incapacity. But in certain situations, for example, where the period of incapacity has been longer than originally anticipated, or where repeated short-term claims have been received, and where the claimant has been on holiday or on strike,[15] the insurance officer is likely to take steps to verify the claimant's condition, either by a reference to the Regional Medical Officer, or by an officer visiting the

5 See Report of the National Insurance Advisory Committee on the draft regulations 1975–76, HC 349, para 32.
6 *R(S) 13/51*.
7 *R(S) 1/58*.
8 See SI 1948/1175.
9 *Fisher* paras 201, 213–216.
10 See SI 1967/520 as amended by SI 1974/416.
11 SI 1976/615, Sch 1, Part III.
12 N.5, above, at para 6 and see *Fisher* para 187.
13 SI 1976/615, Sch 1, and see DHSS *Medical Evidence for Social Security Purposes* (2nd edn).
14 Extending the previous maximum period of 13 weeks: see NIAC Report, n.5, above, at paras 22–26.
15 *Fisher* Appendix 7.

claimant in his home.[16] The usual practice[17] in the former case is to advise the claimant to see his own doctor for an examination, and then to present himself for a further examination by the Medical Officer. The latter's opinion is then communicated to the claimant's doctor who thus has an opportunity to disagree, stating his own views. Should a conflict of opinion remain unresolved, it is the duty of the determining authorities to examine all the evidence and form their own view.[18] They are in no sense bound to prefer the Medical Officer's opinion. Indeed, in several cases, the Commissioner has rejected his evidence.[19] Conversely, the medical statement by the claimant's own doctor is in no sense conclusive, and it may be overridden even where the conflicting evidence is of a non-medical character, such as the cases where a claimant allegedly disabled by influenza could not be found at home[20] or another supposed to be suffering from a sprained ligament was seen cycling.[1] If the authorities are dissatisfied as to the evidence produced by either side they may, if they think it advisable, order a further examination, perhaps by a specialist.[2]

In adverting to all relevant information available, the authorities may take into account the claimant's past medical and employment record. This may reveal a pattern which gives rise to a suspicion of malingering. In several cases, for example, the claimant's record has shown a number of claims for short periods near public holidays.[3] This by itself is not necessarily prejudicial to his case, but if it is supported by other factors which cast doubt on his doctor's statement, it may serve to disentitle him from benefit.[4] Of course, it would be quite wrong to use a long-term record of bad health as evidence *against* the claimant. Unless, therefore, there are additional facts which render the evidence suspect, it may help him to prove that he is incapable of work, especially if there is a seasonal cycle in his record of illness.[5]

The processes involved in validating incapacity for work are complex and have inevitably given rise to criticisms.[6] It is evident that notwithstanding the recent reforms to accommodate its objections, the medical profession is unenthusiastic about its role as supervisor of claims.[7] It is regarded as a time-wasting activity, and one that interferes with the doctor-patient relationship, particularly where the alleged illness is not accompanied by physical manifestations and where the medical statement is little more that 'the written expression of the doctor's opinion on his patient's veracity'.[8] These factors were undoubtedly an influence on the government's decision in 1982 to institute a system of self-certification for short spells of sickness.[9] For 'a spell of incapacity' lasting seven days or less, or for the first seven

16 *Fisher* Appendix 7. There is a power to disqualify the claimant should he fail to co-operate: p. 156, below.
17 See *R(S) 7/53.*
18 The insurance officer may decide on this evidence not to renew entitlement to benefit, but he cannot rely on medical evidence alone to review an award already made on the ground that there has been a relevant change of circumstances: *R(S) 6/78,* and see p. 605, below.
19 E.g. *R(S) 15/54*; *30/58 (SB).*
20 *R(S) 16/54.*
1 *3/59 (SB).*
2 This is particularly true of psychiatric illnesses: e.g. *R(S) 4/56.*
3 *R(S) 16/54*; *R(S) 5/60*; *R(S) 1/67*; *R(S) 15/55.*
4 *R(S) 4/60.*
5 *4/59 (SB)*; *R(S) 1/67.*
6 Sainsbury *Measuring Disability* (1973) pp. 14–15, *Fisher* paras 185–194.
7 Ibid, at paras 186–188.
8 Ibid, at para 187.
9 See SSAC Report on Draft Regulations (1982, Cmnd 8560).

days of a longer spell, the claimant now signs a declaration, stating that he has been unfit for work for the relevant period.[10] It should be noted, however, that the period in question must immediately follow one in which the claimant worked or was not incapable of working;[11] if it is linked with another period of incapacity he must obtain a doctor's certificate in the normal way. Of course, these new rules create possibilities for abuse, but they should be seen in the light of the statutory sick pay scheme which, from April 1983, will replace sickness benefit for most employees for the relevant period and which contains no compulsory procedure for medical certification.[12]

iv Deemed incapable

The Regulations allow for a claimant to succeed in three situations where he is not 'incapable of work' within the principles described above.

a *Precautionary or convalescent reasons for not working*

The first has its origin in the way the approved societies administered benefits under the old national health insurance scheme.[13] The idea was that persons who were capable of working but whose doctor advised them on health grounds not to, should be encouraged to follow that advice, without losing benefit. In fact, there has never been a special form of medical certification for this purpose, and in the past doctors and administrators have not been too concerned to distinguish cases of genuine incapacity for work from those where absence of work is regarded as medically desirable.[14] Nevertheless, in strict law, there is a special set of conditions which must be satisfied if the claimant is to be paid benefit in the latter situation. He must prove that

> (i) he is under medical care in respect of a disease or disablement . . .
> *and*
> (ii) it is certified by a registered medical practitioner that for precautionary or convalescent reasons consequential on such disease or disablement he should abstain from work,
> *and*
> (iii) he does no work.[15]

For the purposes of (i), 'medical care' is to be broadly construed: it covers all cases where the claimant receives advice from the doctor in relation to the disease or disablement.[16] As regards (ii), it is not necessary for the doctor to use any particular form or language: 'a letter or other informal document would suffice, provided that the advice can be taken to be a certificate and includes reasons that can be recognised as precautionary or convalescent'.[17] Such advice is a necessary, but not a sufficient, condition for entitlement:[18] the insurance officer is to take account of all the circum-

10 SI 1976/615, reg 5(1), inserted by SI 1982/699.
11 Ibid, reg 5(2).
12 See pp. 160–162, below.
13 See *R(S) 1/79*, para 11.
14 *R(S) 2/79*, para 15.
15 SI 1975/564, reg 3(1)(a), as amended by SI 1978/394.
16 *R(S) 8/61*; *R(S) 1/72*; *R(S) 1/79*. Cp the narrow interpretation in *R(S) 24/54*.
17 *R(S) 2/79*, para 19 (Tribunal decision).
18 *R v National Insurance Comr, ex parte Department of Health and Social Security,* Smith J dissenting, quashing *R(S) 1/79*, reported as Appendix to that decision. See also *R(S) 2/79*, paras 9–11.

stances, including the medical evidence, to determine whether there is some medical reason why the claimant should have abstained from work.[19]

b *Carrier of infectious disease*

This covers the case where the claimant though capable of work represents a risk to others at his place of employment. But here the mere advice of a doctor is insufficient; he must show that

> he is excluded from work on the certificate of a Medical Officer for Environmental Health and is under medical observation by reason of his being a carrier, or having been in contact with a case, of infectious disease.[20]

c *Therapeutic work*

The fact that a claimant does some work is, of course, prima facie evidence that he is capable of such work, and thus not entitled to benefit. But the work in question must be of a type for which he would be remunerated as an employed person or would constitute the gainful occupation of a self-employed person.[1] Work carried out primarily for therapeutic purposes for little reward would not typically come within this definition, but there is a special regulation to resolve any doubt on the matter. A claimant who is found not to be incapable of work 'by reason only of the fact that he has done some work . . . may be deemed to be so incapable if that work is' either

> work which is undertaken under medical supervision as part of his treatment while he is a patient in or of a hospital or similar institution

or

> work which is not so undertaken and which he has good cause for doing

and

> from which, in any case of work of either description, his earnings, if any, are ordinarily not more than £20.00 a week.[2]

The first category of excepted work is not broad. The claimant must be a patient of the institution in question, though he need not be a resident. Thus in *R(S) 3/52*,

> C, suffering from tuberculosis, was engaged for two-and-a-half days a week in a factory specially operated for the rehabilitation of tuberculosis victims. He attended hospital as an out-patient once every two months. It was held that he was a patient 'of' (though not 'in') a hospital.

The rule on hospitalisation, at least as interpreted, is a very artificial one. If, in the last case, the claimant had been under the supervision of a specialist without attending a hospital he would not have succeeded.[3]

The second and alternative category of excusable work is much vaguer. It used to apply only to work undertaken as a 'non-employed' person,[4] but

19 Per Wien J, *R v National Insurance Comr, ex parte Department of Health and Social Security*, n.18, above.

20 SI 1975/564, reg 3(1)(b) and see *R(S) 1/72*, para 14, D Neligan, Comr.

1 P. 82, above.

2 SI 1975/564, reg 3(3), inserted by SI 1979/1299. This regulation was originally an exception to the rule that a day on which the claimant worked was not to be treated as a day of incapacity (see 1st edn of this book, pp. 157–158). It is assumed that its transfer to the regulation deeming incapacity for work has not involved any change in meaning.

3 See *R(S) 5/52*.

4 Cf SI 1967/330, reg 7(h).

this limitation no longer obtains. Nor need the claimant show that the work was undertaken under medical supervision, but 'good cause' for doing the work must be proved. The meaning of the phrase in this context has received little attention from the Commissioner, but it seems clear that medical (i.e. therapeutic) reasons will suffice.[5]

v Exclusion of certain days of incapacity

Benefit is payable for any day of incapacity[6] which forms part of a period of interruption of employment[7] but this is subject to certain exceptions. For the most part, they correspond to the equivalent provisions on unemployment benefit to which reference should be made.[8] Here it is intended to concentrate on those rules which are peculiar to sickness benefit.

a *Not first three days*

As with unemployment, benefit is not payable for the first three days of a period of interruption of employment.[9] Until 1980, the period of interruption of employment was defined by reference to the 'continuity' and 'linking' rules. The former allowed any two days (consecutive or not) within a period of six consecutive days to count as a period of interruption of employment and the latter treated any two such periods not separated by more than thirteen weeks as a single period. In relation to sickness (and invalidity) benefit, the 'continuity' rule was considered by the Conservative government to be largely unnecessary, given the typical coverage of sick pay scheme, and in some cases to give rise to abuse.[10] Following an amendment by the Social Security Act (No. 2) 1980, the claimant must now establish four or more consecutive days of incapacity for work to constitute a period of interruption of employment, and the 'linking' rule has been altered so that now a new period of interruption of employment commences (and hence the need to serve three waiting days arises again) when there has been a gap of eight weeks.[11] It has, however, been recognised that the new 'continuity' rule may cause hardship for kidney dialysis patients, and under the Social Security Act 1981 the Secretary of State has issued regulations to modify the requirement for such persons.[12]

b *Not compensated days*

Sickness benefit is not payable to a person currently in receipt of a training allowance from the Manpower Services Commission, the Minister of Agriculture, Fisheries and Food or the Secretary of State.[13] More importantly, as from April 1983, it will not be payable during a 'period of entitlement' to statutory sick pay.[14] As will be seen,[15] this is, in general, the

5 *R(S) 4/79,* para 11, V G H Hallett, Comr. An intention merely to earn some money is insufficient: *CS 8/79,* noted [1978–9] JSWL 443.
6 Incapacity for part only of a day is deemed to be for the whole of that day: SI 1975/564, reg 3(2).
7 SSA 1975, s.14(1)(b).
8 Pp. 85–90, above.
9 P. 89, above.
10 Mr P Jenkin, Secretary of State, 980 HC Official Report (5th series) cols 1660–1611.
11 S.3, though not if the period of interruption of employment follows immediately on a period of entitlement to statutory sick pay: n.16, below.
12 S.5, and SI 1982/642.
13 SI 1975/564, reg 7(1)(f).
14 SSHBA 1982, s.10 and Sch 2, para 1.
15 Pp. 160–161, below.

first eight weeks of incapacity within one tax year. Once that period has elapsed, however, the claimant is entitled to sickness benefit without serving the three waiting days.[16] Moreover, the receipt of sick pay from the employer beyond the statutory period does not affect entitlement to sickness benefit. This contrasts with unemployment benefit which is not available for days for which the claimant has received payment in lieu of wages.[17] But the employer, or sick pay fund, can – and often does – have an arrangement whereby the sick pay is reduced by the amount of benefit received.[18]

c *Not Sunday (or its substitute)*
Benefit cannot be claimed for Sunday, or a rest day normally substituted for Sunday.[19]

d *Not when entitled to invalidity benefit*
The claimant cannot, of course, claim sickness benefit when he becomes entitled to the more generous invalidity benefit. Under the law current at the time of writing, this takes place when he has been entitled to sickness benefit[20] for 168 days in respect of *one* period of interruption of employment.[1] From April 1983, this will be modified for those benefiting under the new sick pay scheme: the equivalent period of sickness benefit is reduced to 120 days (the initial 48 days being the period of entitlement to statutory sick pay).[2]

D Disqualification

As with unemployment, there are certain grounds on which the claimant may be disqualified from benefit for a maximum period of six weeks. The underlying purposes of these provisions are threefold: to protect the fund against fraudulent claims; to exclude from benefit those who are incapacitated or remain incapacitated as a result of their own deliberate conduct; and to reinforce the machinery for the control and administration of the system.

i Misconduct

The first ground is where the claimant has 'become incapable of work through his own misconduct'.[3] Under the old National Health Insurance Acts,[4] an approved society might, in accordance with its own rules and subject to the approval of the Minister, suspend an insured person from benefit for misconduct.[5] The principle was derived from and analogous to[6] the defence of 'serious and wilful misconduct' under the Workmen's Com-

16 SSHBA 1982, Sch 2, para 3. But there must not be a gap of more than 57 days between the periods of sick pay and sickness benefit entitlement: ibid, para. 4.
17 Pp. 85–89, above.
18 Alternatively, the employee may receive the sick pay unabated and the employer receives a refund from the National Insurance Fund: SSA 1975, s.92.
19 SSA 1975, s.17(1)(e).
20 Including any period of entitlement to maternity allowance.
1 SSA 1975, s.15(1).
2 SSHBA 1982, Sch 1, para 5.
3 SSA 1975, s.20(2)(a): SI 1975/564, reg 12(1)(a).
4 E.g. NHIA 1936, s.64(1).
5 See the Model Rules issued by the Ministry, esp. No 13(1)
6 See Reported Decision on Appeals and Applications under NHIA 1936, s.163, No CIII.

pensation Act.[7] The rules of some societies spelt out in greater detail the types of misconduct which would entitle them to disqualify the sick person. Thus, according to one,[8] benefit might be refused if the condition was 'wilfully incurred' by 'fighting, wrestling, using weapons (except in self-defence), drunkenness, indecent or disorderly conduct, venereal disease'. The modern provision does not limit the misconduct to 'serious' or 'wilful', and it is possible to argue that it extends to reckless disregard of precautions ordered or recommended by, for example, an employer or a doctor.[9] The only reported decision, however, carries the implication that the conduct must be wilful.[10] The incapacity was due to alcoholism and it was held that the claimant could only rebut the inference of misconduct if he could show that his will-power had been so impaired that he was unable to moderate his drinking. There are two explicit situations in which disqualification is not to be imposed: where the incapacity is due to venereal disease or to pregnancy.[11]

ii Examination

Disqualification may be incurred if the claimant

> fails without good cause to comply with a notice in writing given by or on behalf of the Secretary of State requiring him to attend for and submit himself to medical or other examination on a date not earlier than the third day after the day on which the notice was sent and at a time and place specified in that notice. . . .'[12]

It will be recalled that the insurance officer may wish to verify a claimant's alleged disability by requiring him to submit to an examination by the Regional Medical Officer. Not surprisingly, the requirement is reinforced by a sanction, hence the above regulation. Of course illness or physical disability preventing the claimant attending for examination will constitute good cause.[13] What of those who on grounds of religious conviction or otherwise object to medical examination? The question was considered in *R(S) 9/51*. It was held that a Christian Scientist who satisfied the authorities on the conviction of her beliefs should not be disqualified. The onus of proof was on her, and it was not sufficient to show that she was a member of a church whose tenets forbade her submission to treatment or examination. The crux of the matter was her *personal* attitude, and this must be based on a firm conviction that her religious beliefs required her to refuse.

iii Treatment

The third ground of disqualification arises where the claimant

> fails without good cause to attend for, or to submit himself to, medical or other treatment.[14]

The rationale here is similar to that justifying the misconduct rule. The incapacity must not be voluntarily incurred. Consequently the claimant

7 WCA 1897, s.1(2)(c). The same notion of 'wilful misconduct' is incorporated in art 648(4) of the International Labour Code, 1951.
8 N.6, above, Decision XIII.
9 Potter and Stansfield *National Insurance* (2nd edn) p. 111.
10 *R(S) 2/53*.
11 SI 1975/564, reg 12(1)(a).
12 Ibid, reg 12(1)(b).
13 But the test is an objective one: it will be insufficient if the claimant merely 'thinks' that he is not well enough to attend: n.6, above, Decision XXXVIII.
14 SI 1975/564, reg 12(1)(c).

must take reasonable steps to regain his capacity to work. As regards 'good cause', there is little to add to what was said under 'examination'. But difficult questions arise as to the steps in recovery which might reasonably be required of an individual. Should he be compelled to undergo an operation for which he has a morbid fear? The matter was very fully discussed at the Committee stage of the 1911 Bill.[15] On the one hand, it was argued that to compel a person to be vaccinated or to undergo an operation interfered with a fundamental liberty, and in many cases would involve a risk greater than that inherent in avoiding the treatment.[16] The opposing view was that the contributors to the fund ought not to support for a number of years a man who refused to undergo on wholly inadequate grounds an operation which was necessary for his health and which could not possibly endanger his life.[17] A compromise solution was reached, and the amendment so formulated has been incorporated in the legislation ever since. In its present from it provides that the

> disqualification shall not apply to any failure to attend for or to submit to vaccination or inoculation of any kind or to a surgical operation, unless the failure is a failure to attend for or submit to a surgical operation of a minor character, and is unreasonable.[18]

As with the other grounds of disqualification, little guidance is to be found in the Commissioners' decisions on what might be regarded as 'unreasonable' failure, and how a distinction is to be drawn between 'major' and 'minor' operations. On the latter point, however, both the policy inherent in the provision, and the currency of medical usage,[19] suggest that a 'minor' operation is one which, in ordinary circumstances, does not involve a risk to life.

iv Rules of behaviour

Under the old National Health Insurance Acts an approved society might, subject to the approval of the Minister, make rules governing the behaviour of the insured person during sickness or disability.[20] The Model Rules prepared by the Minister, and in practice adopted by most societies,[1] prescribed certain standards of conduct. After 1946 these were incorporated in the draft Unemployment and Sickness Benefit Regulations, but, following recommendations of the National Insurance Advisory Committee,[2] were significantly amended before they were brought into effect. The requirements that the claimant should 'obey the instructions' of his doctor and answer 'any reasonable enquiries . . . as to the instructions given by the doctor' were regarded as otiose. As conditions of benefit, they were considered to be oppressive, and in so far as they were thought necessary to ensure that the claimant was taking sufficient steps to facilitate his recovery this objective was met by the independent requirement that he should refrain from conduct calculated to retard his recovery. Under the

15 29 HC Official Report (5th series) cols 330–342.
16 See e.g. Mr D Lloyd-George ibid, at col 333.
17 See e.g. Mr A Chamberlain, ibid, at cols 334–335.
18 SI 1975/564, reg 12(1)(c).
19 See Dorland *Medical Dictionary* (26th edn) at p.927.
20 NHIA 1936, s.64.
1 The 1938 version of the Rules are set out in Lesser *The Law of National Health Insurance* (1939) pp. 1108–1109.
2 1947–48, HC 162, para 26.

Regulations now in force, disqualification may be imposed if the claimant fails without good cause to observe any one of three rules.

> (1) 'to refrain from behaviour calculated to retard his recovery, and to answer any reasonable enquiries. . . by the Secretary of State or his officers directed to ascertaining whether he is doing so'.[3]

This, together with the 'misconduct' provision, constitute the statutory safeguards against voluntary disability. The latter ground governs cases where the voluntary conduct causes the incapacity; the behaviour provision applies throughout the period of disability. The word 'calculated' is not to be taken too literally. The test is an objective one: was the behaviour likely to retard recovery?[4] On the other hand, there has been a limited interpretation of the 'recovery' which has been retarded. It must be from a disease or disablement: it cannot be invoked against a claimant who declines to continue rehabilitative treatment which was having no effect on his physical condition.[5] There are few reported instances of this ground for disqualification. In *R(S) 21/52* it was held to have been rightly imposed on a claimant who, suffering from influenzal bronchitis, nevertheless undertook a motoring expedition 60 miles away and was there taken ill.

The requirement as to the answering of enquiries is regarded as an essential part of the control mechanism of sickness benefit, but the provision expressly excludes 'enquiries relating to medical examination, treatment or advice'.[6] This resulted from the National Insurance Advisory Committee's dislike of the approved society rules of which it was one.[7] It was thought to be too much of an intrusion into the privacy of the relationship between the medical practitioner and his patient.

> (2) 'Not to be absent from his place of residence without leaving word where he may be found.'[8]

The purpose of this rule is to provide a safeguard against deliberate and persistent avoidance of the DHSS visiting officers. The pre-war rules tended to be more rigorous, not only stipulating certain times when the claimant must be at home, but also restraining him from leaving his locality at any time without either just cause or the consent of the Society. The present form of the rule has been considered unnecessarily restrictive by some,[9] but in practice it will not be invoked by the Department unless visits by officers have already proved to be ineffective[10] and it is, in any case, subject to the defence of good cause.[11]

> (3) 'To do no work for which remuneration is, or would ordinarily be, payable. . . .'[12]

A person who works may be disentitled from benefit on the ground that it is prima facie evidence that he is not incapable of such work.[13] The provision quoted above is different in two respects. First, it gives rise to disqual-

3 SI 1975/564, reg 12(1)(d)(i).
4 *R(S) 21/52.*
5 *R(S) 3/57.*
6 SI 1975/564, reg 12(1)(d)(i).
7 N.2, above.
8 SI 1975/564, reg 12(1)(d)(ii).
9 See the Report of the National Insurance Advisory Committee, n.2, above.
10 *Fisher* para 181.
11 *R(S) 6/55.*
12 SI 1975/564, reg 12(1)(d)(iii).
13 Cf p. 153, above.

ification for a maximum period of six weeks; it does not disentitle the claimant altogether. Secondly, unlike the ground for disentitlement, it is not confined to 'work which the person can reasonably be expected to do'.[14] In other words, a claimant may be disqualified, but not disentitled, if during a period when he is incapable of work which is regarded as suitable for him (for the first six months, generally his normal occupation[15]), he does another kind of work 'for which remuneration is, or would ordinarily be, payable'.[16] However, it is provided that this should not include work of a therapeutic nature.[17] The conditions which the claimant must satisfy to obtain relief from disqualification on this ground have been described in a previous section.[18]

v Good cause

The claimant may avoid disqualification if he is able to show 'good cause'. Mere ignorance of rules of conduct will not suffice.[19] The following of medical advice, if unambiguous and specific, that the claimant should do a little work,[20] or should absent himself from his residence for a few days, has been held to constitute good cause.[1]

vi Relevance of other legal proceedings

The circumstances relied on to justify disqualification may also have been the subject of other legal proceedings, for example a criminal prosecution for making false representations to obtain benefit. A finding of fact made in such proceedings is not regarded as conclusive for social security purposes, but may nevertheless be used as evidence by the statutory authorities.[2] In his latest reported decision on the point, the Commissioner held that a conviction for an offence relating to the same benefit for the same period as is in issue should shift the onus of proof onto the claimant to show that, notwithstanding the conviction, he is entitled to benefit.[3]

vii Period of disqualification

The maximum period of disqualification under the Act is six weeks. As with unemployment benefit,[4] the authorities have an unfettered discretion and the factors considered in that context apply equally here.[5]

14 Cf SSA 1975, s.17(1)(a), and p. 148, above.
15 P. 148, above.
16 On which see p. 82, above.
17 SI 1975/564, reg 12(1)(d)(iii), as amended by SI 1979/1299.
18 P. 153, above.
19 *R(S) 21/52.*
20 *R(S) 10/60.*
1 *R(S) 6/55.*
2 See also, on unemployment benefit, pp. 109–110, above.
3 *R(S) 2/80*, J S Watson, Comr, applying by analogy the principle contained in the Civil Evidence Act 1968, s.11(2)(a) – on which see *Stupple v Royal Insurance Co Ltd* [1971] 1 QB 50 – even though that Act does not apply to social security determinations. Cp *R(S) 10/79* where it was held that when the evidence on which the convictions was based is not made available to the statutory authorities and the evidence that is available is plainly inconsistent with any grounds upon which the conviction could have been based, the fact of criminal conviction should be ignored.
4 P. 118, above.
5 See esp. *R(U) 8/74.*

E Statutory sick pay

Since the Second World War there has been a considerable growth in occupation sick pay; in 1981 it was estimated that some 90 per cent of employees participated in some such scheme.[6] Notwithstanding the major overlap with sickness benefit, entitlement to the latter remained unaffected. Of course, the employer might, and usually did, take account of the social security provision in calculating the amount of sick pay;[7] but there was still a duplication of administrative effort, since two claims for payment would typically have to be processed. It was, therefore, mainly to reduce administrative expenditure that the Government Green Paper of 1980 proposed that the employer should be bound to confer sick pay, at a minimum level, for the first eight weeks of incapacity, during which period sickness benefit would not be payable.[8] This would, moreover, facilitate a further aspect of government social policy, the taxation of short-term benefits.[9] The proposals provoked considerable opposition,[10] not only from trade unions and poverty pressure groups who argued that they would involve a radical departure from the notion of comprehensive state welfare established since Beveridge and less rhetorically that the suggested flat-rate payment, without dependency additions, would disadvantage families in comparison with sickness benefit, but also from the CBI who felt that the additional burden on the employer would not be sufficiently compensated by the simple reduction of 0.5–0.6 per cent in social security contributions proposed by government. This latter point was eventually conceded by the government and the Social Security and Housing Benefits Act 1982 which implemented the scheme made provision for a 100 per cent reimbursement by the National Insurance Fund of statutory sick pay. The government did, however, resist a further concession sought by the CBI, that social security contributions should be credited for periods of statutory sick pay. Under such an arrangement an employer would have had no financial incentive to verify the validity of his employees' claims. On the other hand, the scheme as enacted, in contrast to the sickness benefit provisions,[11] still leaves it to the employer to decide what medical evidence will be required. There is, then, the risk of a dishonest employer in times of bad business 'laying off' 'sick' employees substantially at the cost to other contributors to the National Insurance Fund.

The provisions of the 1982 Act governing statutory sick pay (hereafter SSP) are expected to be brought into force in April 1983.

i Persons covered

The scheme broadly covers all those employed under a contract of service.[12] Married women with reduced contributions liability are included but not persons over pensionable age or earning less than the lower

6 See the debate on the Second Reading of the Social Security and Housing Benefits Bill, 13 HC Official Report (6th series) cols 642–643.
7 Cf p. 155, above.
8 Income During Initial Sickness: A New Strategy (Cmnd 7864).
9 Cf p. 34, above.
10 See Appendix 2 to the Second Report of the Committee on Social Services, 1980–81, HC 113, for a summary of the published responses to the Green Paper.
11 Cf pp. 149–152, above.
12 SSHBA 1982, s.1(1). On 'contract of service', see pp. 45–50, above.

earnings limit then in force;[13] nor if the contract is for a specific period of less than 12 weeks.[14]

ii Period of incapacity for work

The first condition of entitlement is that the day for which SSP is claimed forms part of a period of incapacity for work.[15] This is almost identical to the equivalent requirement for sickness benefit;[16] in particular, there must be four or more consecutive days of incapacity – i.e. three waiting days have to be served. But a period so constituted cannot be linked with another such period if it is separated by more than two weeks, compared with the eight weeks allowed for sickness benefit.

iii Period of entitlement

Secondly, the employee must show that the day in question also falls within a 'period of entitlement'.[17] This will typically limit the employer's liability to the first eight weeks of a period of incapacity within one tax year.[18] But SSP is superseded by the maternity allowance when the conditions for that benefit are satisfied,[19] and title to sickness benefit, invalidity benefit or maternity allowance is preserved (and SSP is not payable) if the day of incapacity is separated from a prior period of entitlement to one of these benefits by less than eight weeks.[20] Further, the employee is not entitled to SSP if he has done no work for his employer under the contract of service, or if that contract has expired;[1] nor for days when a trade dispute has stopped work at the place of employment.[2]

iv Qualifying days

The final condition is that the day of claim is a 'qualifying day'.[3] This is, effectively, a day on which he is required by the employer to be available for work. So, an employee working a four-day week may only be paid SSP for absences on the specified days, though for each such day he will be entitled to one-fourth of the weekly rate.

13 SSHBA 1982, Sch 1, para 2.
14 Except where the contract has become one for a longer period, or it was preceded by another contract with the same employer and the period between the two contracts was less than eight weeks: ibid, para 3.
15 Ibid, s.2.
16 Pp. 148–154, above, except that here the work of which the employee must be incapable is 'of a kind which he might reasonably be expected to do under the contract': SSHBA 1982, s.1(3).
17 Ibid, s.3 and Sch 1.
18 Ibid, s.5.
19 Ibid, ss. 3(2)(d) and 3(8)–(9).
20 Ibid, Sch 1, paras 2(d)–(e) and 5.
1 Ibid, s.3(2)(c), though a period of entitlement in relation to one contract of service may form part of a period of entitlement in relation to another such contract: ibid, s.3(4). Further, regulations may provide that an employer's liability should continue where the contract of service has been brought to an end solely, or mainly, for the purpose of avoiding liability for SSP: ibid, s.3(7).
2 Ibid, Sch 1, para 2(g), but not if the employee can show that he did not participate in, or have a direct interest in, the trade dispute: ibid, para 7. The law governing the equivalent disqualification from unemployment benefit applies here: pp. 119–128, above.
3 SSHBA 1982, s.4.

v Amount

There are three rates of SSP according to the normal weekly earnings of the employee.[4] From April 1983, weekly payments of £37.00, £31.00 and £25.00 will be made to those earning, respectively, £60.00 or over, between £45.00 and £60.00, and less than £45.00. There are no increases for dependants.

vi Adjudication

While this scheme should properly be regarded as part of employment law, the analogy with social security is so strong that the authorities responsible for adjudication in that system have a similar jurisdiction here. Thus the Secretary of State determines questions on the scope of the scheme, e.g. whether there is a contract of service – with an appeal on issues of law to the High Court (Court of Session in Scotland) – and the statutory authorities (insurance officer, local tribunals, Commissioner) determine questions of entitlement.[5] Decisions of the latter, entitling an employee to SSP, are enforceable by order of the county court (Sheriff Court in Scotland).[6]

Part 3 Invalidity benefit

A General

The level of benefit payable to the long-term sick or disabled under the contributory scheme has been the subject of conflicting policy and legislative changes. The Government White Paper of 1944 proposed that the full flat-rate benefit should be payable only for a maximum of three years, the disabled person being entitled thereafter to 'invalidity pension' equivalent to the lower rate of retirement pension.[7] It was recognised that there was a need for more generous provision, but it was felt that 'sickness benefit of unlimited duration would be psychologically unwise and would tend to encourage those subject to recurrent periods of sickness to lapse into chronic invalidity'.[8] This position was politically unacceptable and the 1946 Act reverted to what had substantially been Beveridge's recommendation:[9] a benefit payable until retirement age, but subject to a more stringent contribution condition after receipt of the benefit for 52 weeks – the claimant had to have paid contributions for three years since entering the scheme.[10] The introduction in 1966 of earnings-related supplements for the first six months of sickness benefit[11] added further emphasis to the view that the long-term disabled were being unduly neglected.[12] It was not surprising, therefore, that a long-term earnings-related pension

4 Ibid, s.7(1). There is a duty to review the rate annually and to up-rate, identical to that applied to income maintenance benefits under the Social Security Acts: ibid, s.7(3)–(10), and pp. 411–413, below.
5 SSHBA 1982, ss.11–12, cf pp. 585–596, below.
6 SSHBA 1982, s.16.
7 *Social Insurance,* Part I, para 65.
8 Ibid, at para 67.
9 Para 330.
10 NIA 1946, s.12(2).
11 NIA 1966, s.2(2).
12 See the parliamentary debates on the NI Bill 1959, 606 HC Official Report (5th series) col 836 and the NI Bill 1966, 724, ibid, cols 75–77.

was included as part of the Labour government's National Superannuation scheme of 1969.[13] The Bill lapsed at the 1970 election, and the proposal was not adopted by the incoming Conservative government. Its continued adherence to the principle of flat-rate benefit led to the introduction of a compromise solution described by one commentator as 'a complete novelty and a marked departure from previous thinking about social insurance in this or (so far as I know) any other country'.[14] The new idea was that after six months the standard flat-rate benefit (which would then be called 'invalidity pension') would be supplemented by an allowance graded according to the age at which the claimant became incapable of work; the younger he was at the time of disablement, the higher rate he would receive.[15] The explanation for this differential was not only that the younger disabled person would typically have greater financial commitments but also, according to the government of the day,[16] that during his normal working life an earner should be able to put something aside for his days of retirement and that a disabled person should be compensated for his inability to do this. The emphasis on family need was reinforced by conferring on pensioners a higher increase for dependent children than those paid with sickness benefit[17] and a more generous test of dependency for a working wife.[18] All these elements were retained by the Labour administration and, under its programme for 'Better Pensions',[19] were combined with an earnings-related invalidity pension, to be calculated in the same way as the Category A retirement pension and to come into effect in 1979.[20] While on the face of it this appears to constitute a substantial improvement in the financial provision for invalidity pensioners, it should be noted that the earnings-related component is based only on contributions made to the new pensions scheme since 1977, that this scheme does not mature until 1998, and finally, and in contrast to retirement pensioners, it cannot be assumed that invalidity pensioners will have been able to maintain substantial contributions throughout their working life.

The 1975 Pensions Act dealt with one other alleged weakness of the traditional scheme. As a minor step in the direction of sex equality, it enabled a widower, incapable of work when his wife dies, to base his pension on her earnings record if it is better than his own.[1] It remains to state the principles governing entitlement to invalidity benefit. It will be noted that the requirements are so closely linked to those of sickness benefit, that most of the relevant concepts will have already been the subject of discussion.

13 See the White Papers on National Superannuation and Social Insurance (1969, Cmnd 3883), para 88 and Social Insurance: Proposals for Earnings-Related Short-Term and Invalidity Benefits (1969, Cmnd 4125), paras 25–27. The proposal to introduce an invalidity pension at 60% of the claimant's earnings to a maximum of one and a half times the national average was incorporated in the National Superannuation and Social Insurance Bill as cl. 12.
14 *Walley* p. 238.
15 The proposal was implemented by NIA 1971, s.3.
16 Sir K Joseph, Secretary of State, introducing the NI Bill 1971: 816 HC Official Report (5th series) col 1015. The assumption has been challenged. See *Walley* p. 234, Sainsbury *Registered as Disabled* (1970) ch 4 and Mrs S Williams in the debate on the 1971 Bill: 816 HC Official Report (5th series) cols 1035–1036.
17 P. 365, below.
18 P. 368, below.
19 (1974, Cmnd 5713), paras 30–32.
20 SSPA 1975, s.14.
1 Ibid, s.16.

B The pension

The pension is payable for any day of incapacity for work[2] in a period of interruption of employment during which the claimant has been entitled to sickness benefit for 168 days.[3] From April 1983, this figure is reduced to 120 days if the claimant has qualified for the maximum period of eight weeks statutory sick pay and that period is not separated from the current period of interruption of employment by more than two weeks.[4] The existence and length of a period of interruption of employment for invalidity pension purposes is determined by the rules already mentioned in relation to sickness benefit:[5] in particular any four or more consecutive days of incapacity for work may be linked with any other such period if the gap between them is no more than eight weeks. The 168 (or 120) days include days for which a maternity allowance was payable and any 'waiting days'.[6] The pension is payable until a man is 70, or a woman is 65. If the claimant is over pensionable age (65 for men, 60 for women) he must not have retired from regular employment[7] but must have satisfied the contribution requirements for a Category A or B retirement pension.[8] Apart from this special rule there are no contribution conditions as such for the basic component in the invalidity pension, though of course the claimant must have satisfied the appropriate conditions for the 168 (or 120) days receipt of sickness benefit. The amount payable is in 1982–83 £31–45 per week, together with any increase for dependants,[9] but in the case of a person over pensionable age is at the same rate as the retirement pension to which he would otherwise have been entitled.[10]

Broadly speaking, the additional, earnings-related, component to the pension is calculated in the same ways as the category A retirement pension, as described in the next chapter.[11] But there are three differences which should be mentioned: first, those contracted-out of the pension scheme, and who have thus paid reduced contributions, will nevertheless receive the full amount of additional component, unabated by the receipt of an occupational pension;[12] secondly, the earnings on which the component is calculated will be those up to and including the last tax year before the invalidity pension becomes payable (instead of the year in which the claimant reaches pensionable age);[13] thirdly, the invalidity pension (at the time of writing) is not taxable.

There are special provisions governing widows and widowers. The former qualifies for invalidity pension when her entitlement to widow's allowance or widowed mother's allowance ceases (provided this occurs after 5 April 1979)[14] if she has been incapable of work for 168 (from April 1983, 120 if she has qualified for statutory sick pay) days of a period of

2 For the meaning of this, see pp. 147–155, above.
3 SSA 1975, s.15(2).
4 SSHBA 1982, Sch 2, para 5.
5 P. 154, above.
6 SSA 1975, s.15(1).
7 Ibid, s.15(1)(b)(ii), and see pp. 197–207, below.
8 SSA 1975, s.15(2), as amended by SSPA 1975, Sch 4, para 4.
9 Pp. 364–376, below.
10 SSA 1975, s.15(4).
11 Pp. 364–376, below.
12 Cp p. 223, below, for retirement pensions.
13 SSPA 1975, s.14.
14 SSA 1979, Sch 1, para 17.

interruption of employment and she is able to satisfy the contribution conditions for *widow's* pension.[15] She is then paid at the rate either of invalidity pension or of widow's pension whichever is more favourable to her.[16] Outside the industrial injury and war pension schemes[17] there are no benefits for widowers as such, but the Social Security Pensions Act 1975 made some special provision for those who are invalids. A man who, after 6 April 1979, becomes a widower and who was at the death of his wife, or within 13 weeks thereafter,[18] incapable of work, and remains so incapable for the standard period of 168 (or 120) days of a period of interruption of employment, is entitled to an invalidity pension, which is based on either his own contributions or those of his deceased wife, whichever gives him the higher rate.[19]

C The allowance

The allowance is payable to invalidity pensioners who were under 60 (men) or 55 (women) on the first day of incapacity within the period of interruption of employment in question.[20] Regulations provide that for this purpose a day may be treated as one of incapacity for work even though the claimant was not, because of special rules applicable to him, eligible for sickness or invalidity benefit on that day.[1] Thus the age of a member of the forces, or of an employee not drawing benefit because of the provision of sick pay under his contract of employment,[2] or of a recipient of widow's allowance will be taken as at the first date on which, but for the special rules, he or she would have been entitled to sickness benefit.[3] For reasons which have already been indicated,[4] there are three rates at which the allowance is paid: the highest rate (in 1982–83, £6.90 per week) for those under 40 on the date when the period of incapacity began (or where the latter was before 5 July 1948); the middle rate (in 1982–83, £4.40 per week) for those aged 40 to 49 on the relevant date; the lowest rate (in 1982–83), £2.20 per week) for men aged 50 to 59 or women aged 50 to 54 on the relevant date.[5] Once title to the allowance has been established before pensionable age (65 for men, 60 for women), it is paid indefinitely thereafter, and so may be added to a retirement pension. However, the age-groups for the two higher rates of allowance are somewhat less generous for those who reached pensionable age before 6 April 1979: viz highest rate, under 35 on the relevant date; middle rate, 35 to 44 on the relevant date.[6]

15 SSPA 1975, s.15(1)–(2). For the contribution conditions, see pp. 231–232, below.
16 SSPA 1975, s.15(3), qualified by SI 1978/529, reg 2.
17 Pp. 334 and 359, below.
18 SI 1978/529, reg 4.
19 SSPA 1975, s.16 and SSA 1979, Sch 1, para 18.
20 SSA 1975, s.16(1).
1 SI 1975/564, reg 8(1).
2 In accordance with the arrangements authorised by SSA 1975, s.92: see n.18 on p. 155, above.
3 SI 1975/564, reg 8(2).
4 P. 163, above.
5 SSA 1975, s.16(2), as amended by SSA 1979, Sch 1, para 10.
6 Ibid.

D Disqualification and other rules governing claims

In all other respects the rules governing invalidity benefit are identical to those of sickness benefit. This applies to the method of proving incapacity,[7] the rules of behaviour and disqualifications,[8] and the effect of residence in hospital or abroad.[9] Reference should therefore be made to the relevant discussions elsewhere in this work.

Part 4 Non-contributory invalidity pension

A General

The OPCS survey of 1968–69 revealed that 40 per cent of the 'very seriously handicapped', 37 per cent of the 'severely handicapped' and 35 per cent of the 'appreciably handicapped' were in receipt of supplementary benefit.[10] This was an embarrassment to a system of social insurance which had purported to provide adequate coverage for the sick and disabled. One of the problems was, of course, that the congenitally disabled were unable to satisfy the then existing contribution conditions for long-term sickness benefit. In 1975, as the first step in its four-stage plan to help those unable to benefit from the contributory scheme, the Labour government introduced the non-contributory invalidity pension (NCIP), similar in scope to the contributory pension, but payable at approximately two-thirds of the rate and with no entitlement to the additional allowance.[11] The basic criterion of entitlement was that employed for sickness and invalidity benefit, incapacity for work, which means remunerated employment. This was not obviously appropriate for those primarily engaged in unremunerated work, such as caring for a home and family. On the assumption that NCIP should be paid to those incapable of this kind of work, two problems presented themselves: how was this group to be legally defined? And what test of incapacity should be applied to them? The answers which were eventually forthcoming and which were brought into force in 1977 may be seen, in retrospect, as being both crude and discriminatory. The group was defined as comprising married women living with husbands, and other women cohabiting with men. For the NCIP to be payable, *any* such woman had to satisfy a dual criterion: that she was incapable of work (the standard condition) and that she was incapable of performing normal household duties. The innovatory character of the latter itself engendered difficulties and the sex discriminatory aspects intensified the criticisms.[12] Figures culled from DHSS sources revealed that 65 per cent of all women applying for NCIP during one week in 1979 had been in paid employment during the last five years, and 75 per cent had given up work for reasons connected with disability.[13] The National Insurance Advisory Committee made a

7 Pp. 149–151, above.
8 Pp. 155–159, above.
9 Pp. 387–389, 394–395, below.
10 Harris, Smith and Head *Income and Entitlement to Supplementary Benefit of Impaired People in Great Britain* (1972).
11 SSBA 1975, s.6, re-enacted as SSA 1975, s.36.
12 Cf Richards [1978–9] JSWL 66; Loach and Lister *Second Class Disabled* (1978); Equal Opportunities Commission *Behind Closed Doors* (1981); Glendenning (1981) 48 Poverty 13–18.
13 (1981) 48 Poverty at 15.

thorough investigation of the matter and in its report, published in 1980, urged the government to reformulate the law in non-discriminatory terms.[14] This could be done by introducing alternative tests for NCIP not according to sex or married status but according to whether the claimant (male or female) had been in regular employment in the labour market or else regularly engaged in housework. Should this approach prove not to be feasible, they suggested that the special condition for housewives should gradually be phased out. As yet, the government has responded to neither suggestion.

B Entitlement

With the exception of the 'normal household duties' test imposed on married women, the principles of entitlement to NCIP to a large extent coincide with those of the contributory invalidity pension (IP).

i Incapacity for 196 days

The benefit is payable for any day on which the claimant is 'incapable of work',[15] provided that

> he has been so incapable for a period of not less than 196 consecutive days ending immediately before that day.[16]

The period of 196 days is in effect the same as the 168 days required for the IP – the latter, being based on entitlement to sickness benefit, necessarily excludes Sundays (or their substitutes)[17] – but there is an important difference. For IP purposes, the claimant may aggregate spells of incapacity within one period of interruption of employment when they are not separated by more than eight weeks.[18] For NCIP, on the other hand, the test is 196 *consecutive* days of incapacity. However, once this initial requirement has been fulfilled, continuous entitlement is based on a less strict criterion. The condition of 196 days is deemed to have been met for those persons already entitled to NCIP as regards any subsequent days of incapacity within the same period of interruption of employment.[19] The 'period of interruption of employment' is construed according to the rules already described for sickness benefit,[20] so it means that the 196 consecutive waiting days will have to be served again only if the claimant is regarded as capable of work for a period of eight weeks or more.

ii Exclusions

Those under 16 or receiving full-time education are excluded from the scheme.[1] However, under the relevant regulations, a claimant is not to be treated as receiving full-time education if he is over 19, or, (if 16 to 19) unless the Secretary of State certifies that he is receiving such education at

14 Cmnd 7955.
15 Cf pp. 146–155, above.
16 SSA 1975, s.36(1)5.
17 P. 155, above.
18 P. 164, above.
19 SI 1975/1058, reg 6.
20 P. 154, above.
1 SSA 1975, s.36(2).

an establishment recognised by the Secretary as being, or comparable to, a university, college or school.[2]

iii Housewives

What is generally referred to as 'housewives' non-contributory invalidity pension' or HNCIP[3] is not a different benefit but simply NCIP payable to a woman who has to satisfy the additional household duties test. The definition of those so affected involves the somewhat simplistic assumption that a woman living with a man, or substantially dependent on him, is invariably responsible for the housework. So, if

(a) she is married and either
  (i) she is residing with her husband, or
  (ii) he is contributing to her maintenance at a weekly rate not less than the weekly rate of such a pension; or
(b) she and a man to whom she is not married are living together as husband and wife,[4]

she must show not only that she is incapable of work, the condition applied to all NCIP claimants, but also that 'she is incapable of performing normal household duties'.[5] A regulation defines the circumstances in which a woman is or is not conclusively[6] to be treated as satisfying the latter condition. The incapacity must result from 'some specific disease or bodily or mental disablement'.[7] This requirement is shared by most disability benefits and has already been discussed.[8] More importantly, regulation 13A(2) provides that

> a woman shall be treated as incapable of performing normal household duties if without substantial assistance from or supervision by another person, she cannot or cannot reasonably be expected to perform such duties to any substantial extent, but she shall not be treated as so incapable if, without such assistance or supervision, she can or can reasonably be expected to perform such duties to any substantial extent.[9]

This raises a number of issues for interpretation and determination.

a *Normal household duties*

What are regarded as *normal* household duties will vary according to the circumstances of the particular claimant.[10] This is reinforced by another regulation which provides (i) that a woman satisfying regulation 13A(2) is not disentitled by the fact that she would not have been regarded as incapable 'in substantially different household circumstances' and (ii) that if she is not incapable of normal household duties in her actual circum-

2 SI 1975/1058, reg 5(1). In determining the duration of the education, temporary interruptions are to be disregarded: ibid, reg 5(2).
3 See DHSS Leaflet NI 214.
4 SSA 1975, s.36(2). For the meaning of 'married' see pp. 377–382, below, of 'residing with', pp. 371–373, below, of 'contributing to. . . maintenance', pp. 373–376, below, and of 'living with a man as his wife', pp. 384–386, below.
5 SSA 1975, s.36(2).
6 See *R(S) 6/79*, para 9, R J A Temple, Chief Comr, interpreting SI 1975/1058, reg 13A, as amended by SI 1978/1340. In *R(S) 7/78*, a Tribunal of Commissioners had held that the regulations previously in force were not so conclusive and that a claimant could succeed under the independent operation of SSA 1975, s.36(2).
7 SI 1975/1058, reg 13A(1), inserted by SI 1977/1312.
8 P. 147, above.
9 SI 1975/1058, reg 13A(2), inserted by SI 1978/1340.
10 *R(S) 5/78*.

stances, she cannot qualify on the basis that she would have been incapable in different circumstances.[11] So regard must be had to the size and composition of the family and the physical environment in which the duties have to be performed, including the facilities available.[12] However, the relevant circumstances do not include the claimant's physical condition. In *R(S) 5/78*, the Chief Commissioner rejected the insurance officer's 'disgraceful'[13] argument that what was 'normal' for the claimant was what she had become accustomed to in the light of her disability: 'normal household duties' are those 'appropriate to her own circumstances, all of which, if she were capable, she would be expected to do'.[14] There are a number of duties which typically arise in most households and these are set out on the application form which the claimant must complete.[15] They include: shopping, the preparation of meals and washing-up, washing and ironing, cleaning and making beds. Regard may be had to 'other household duties which, as a matter of common knowledge, normally arise in any household',[16] but they should not simply regard the aggregate of *ancillary* activities as amounting to substantial household duties.[17]

b *Incapable to a substantial extent*

The rather cumbersome way in which regulation 13A(2) refers to what the woman both can and cannot do was designed to reverse the decision by a Tribunal of Commissioners on a previous version of the regulation, that the ability to perform normal household duties to a substantial extent did not necessarily imply that the claimant was not unable to perform the duties to a substantial extent.[18] As a result, a finding that she is able to perform the duties to a substantial extent is sufficient to disentitle her.[19] 'Substantial' is to be given its ordinary meaning: 'weighty, ample, or considerable'[20] – it is a question of fact and degree.[21] In *R(S) 5/81*, the Commissioner came to the important conclusion that this 'should be determined by considering the household duties as a whole and not by deciding whether or not she is incapable of performing each particular task on its own'.[1] Regard should also be had to temporal factors; if the disablement is only intermittent and the claimant is able satisfactorily to perform her duties at other times, she may not succeed in establishing that she has been substantially incapable for the requisite period of 196 consecutive days.[2]

c *Without substantial assistance*

Entitlement depends on the claimant's inability to perform the duties 'without substantial assistance from or supervision by another person'. The fact that she has a home help provided by the local social services department is not by itself sufficient for entitlement.[3] It is, of course, evidence

11 SI 1975/1058, reg 13A(3), inserted by SI 1977/1312.
12 Cf NIAC Report on Draft Regulations (1977, Cmnd 6900), para. 22.
13 Mesher [1978–9] JSWL 55.
14 *R(S) 5/78,* paras 11–12.
15 DHSS Leaflet NI 214.
16 *R(S) 7/79*, para 11, R J A Temple, Chief Comr.
17 *R(S) 11/81*, para. 14, J. Mitchell, Comr.
18 *R(S) 7/78*. This was not followed by the N. Ireland Commissioner: *34/78 (NCIP)*.
19 *R(S) 6/79*.
20 *R(S) 5/78*, para 15, R J A Temple, Chief Comr.
21 *R(S) 5/81*, para 5, J S Watson, Comr.
1 Ibid. See also *R(S) 11/81*.
2 *R(S) 9/79*, J N B Penny, Comr, contrasting the position with that where incapacity for paid work needs to be shown: p. 149, above.
3 *R(S) 7/79*, R J A Temple, Chief Comr.

that some household help is considered to be required; but the authorities must examine the extent to which the home help (or other person) provides a necessary relief from the household duties.

d *Determination*

Evidence of incapacity is supplied by the claimant completing a comprehensive claim form which sets out questions relating to the household circumstances, and her ability to cope with various tasks. It is normally supplemented by a full medical report, based on an examination by her doctor at the claimant's home. The insurance officer then decides the question of incapacity by reference both to the form and the medical report.[4] This process and the rigour of the criteria to be satisfied have caused much distress and resentment.[5] No doubt, the very novelty of the legal provisions is partly responsible, but it is to be hoped that if, and when, the discriminatory aspects of HNCIP are removed, consideration will also be given to improving the administration of the benefit.

iv Residence and presence

NCIP (and HNCIP) being non-contributory, it is necessary to establish a sufficient connection with this country to justify entitlement. The claimant must have been present in Great Britain for at least 168 of the 196 qualifying days of incapacity.[6] Moreover, unless he is an airman, a merchant seaman, a member of the armed forces, or employed on the continental shelf (or a member of a family of such a person),[7] he must satisfy three further conditions:[8]

(a) he must be present in GB on the day for which the claim is made;
(b) he must have been so present for an aggregate of 26 weeks in the 12 months immediately preceding that day; and
(c) he must have been resident in GB for an aggregate of 10 years in the 20 years immediately preceding that date, or, if he is under 20 years of age, for an aggregate of 10 years since birth.

Once these conditions have been satisfied, they are deemed to have been satisfied for all subsequent days of incapacity during the same period of interruption of employment.[9]

v Persons of pensionable and retiring age

The pension is payable to a person who has reached pensionable age (i.e. 65 for men, 60 for women) only if he was entitled to it (or would have been entitled to it if not barred by the rules on overlapping benefits[10]) immediately before reaching that age.[11] He must, of course, continue to satisfy the condition as to incapacity for work. Once, however, he has reached 'retiring' age (i.e. 70 for men, 65 for women) this no longer applies and he may continue to receive the pension provided that he was receiving it immediately before attaining the retiring age in question.[12]

4 NIAL Report, n.12, above, at para 11.
5 See Equal Opportunities Commission *Behind Closed Doors* (1981) pp. 7–14.
6 SI 1975/1058, reg 4(2), as substituted by SI 1978/1845. The amendment was a response to criticism of the previous rule which required presence in GB for all 196 days and the rigours of which were highlighted in *R v National Insurance Comr, ex parte Fleetwood* (1978) 122 Sol Jo 146, reported as Appendix to *R(S) 3/78*.
7 SI 1975/1058, reg 3(2), substituted by SI 1977/342.
8 SI 1975/1058, reg 3(1). For the meaning of 'present' and 'resident' see pp. 391–393, below.
9 SI 1975/1058, reg 3(3).
10 Ibid, reg 7.
11 SSA 1975, s.36(4).
12 Ibid, s.36(5) and SI 1975/1058, reg 8.

C Disqualification and other rules governing claims

The remaining rules all follow the pattern established for the contributory sickness and invalidity benefits. This includes the issue of medical statements,[13] the disqualifications for misconduct, failure to attend for examination or treatment, or working,[14] and the special rules governing hospital in-patients, and persons detained in lawful custody.[15]

D Amount

The weekly rate of NCIP (and HNCIP) is (in 1982–83) £19.70, which is approximately two-thirds of the standard rate for IP. A similar proportion governs the amount of increases for adult dependants, but those for child dependants are payable at the full IP rate.[16]

Part 5 Attendance allowance

A General

The new concern for the disabled manifested in the 1960s was directed in particular to a major group insufficiently protected under existing schemes, comprising those who needed substantial personal assistance from another in matters of self-care. The attendance allowance was proposed in 1969 as part of the Labour government's National Superannuation plan,[17] and was adopted by the Conservative government immediately on assuming power in 1970.[18] Provision was made for a single flat-rate benefit payable to a person requiring either 'frequent attention throughout the day and prolonged or repeated attention during the night; or. . . continual supervision from another person in order to avoid substantial danger to himself or others'.[19] The joint test on the first of the alternative conditions excluded many potential claimants, and in 1973 a lower rate of allowance became payable to those who required the necessary attendance either during the day or during the night.[20] To adjudicate on the medical requirements an Attendance Allowance Board was created, but in practice claims are determined by one or more medical practitioners, to whom the Board's powers are delegated.[1] An appeal lies to the Commissioner, but only on questions of law.[2] The first years of the scheme were by no means troublefree,[3] and in 1973, 267 out of 287 such appeals were successful.[4] As will emerge, many of the Commissioners' rulings clarified the legal principles, but they have

13 Pp. 149–151, above.
14 SI 1975/1058, reg 12: see pp. 155–160, above.
15 Pp. 394–401, below.
16 Pp. 364–376, below.
17 See White Paper, National Superannuation and Social Insurance (1969, Cmnd 3883), paras 90–91 and the 1969 Bill, cl 17.
18 NI (Old persons', and widows' pension and attendance allowance) Act 1970, s.4, renamed as NIA 1970 by NIA 1972, s.8(4).
19 NIA 1970, s.4(2).
20 NIA 1972, s.2(1).
1 See generally, pp. 601–603, below.
2 P. 602, below.
3 Carson 26 NILQ 291.
4 Though in the same year leave to appeal was refused in another 187 cases: DHSS Annual Report 1973 (Cmnd 5700), para 11.8.

regarded some of the disablement criteria as giving rise to questions of medical fact, rather than of law, which therefore come within the exclusive jurisdiction of the Attendance Allowance Board, in practice the delegated medical practitioners. The difficulties that this has posed for claimants are reflected in the large numbers who seek a review, effectively a second determination, of the initial medical decision. In 1979, 12,536 claimants were awarded the allowance following such a review after their original application had been rejected.[5]

B Degree of disability

The OPCS Survey used very detailed criteria to determine the number of persons who required substantial personal assistance from others in matters of self-care.[6] For the purposes of the attendance allowance it was decided not to adopt such precise tools, but rather to allow the decision-making authority (in this case the Attendance Allowance Board) considerable discretion. The Social Security Act 1975 lays down two conditions both of which must be satisfied for the higher rate of allowance (in 1982–83 £26.25 per week), but the fulfilment of either is sufficient for the lower rate (in 1982–83 £17.50 per week). The 'day' condition is that the claimant

> is so severely disabled physically or mentally that, by day, he requires from another person either —
> (i) frequent attention throughout the day in connection with his bodily functions, or
> (ii) continual supervision throughout the day in order to avoid substantial danger to himself or others.[7]

The 'night' condition is that:

> he is so severely disabled physically or mentally that, at night, he requires from another person either —
> (i) prolonged or repeated attention during the night in connection with his bodily functions, or
> (ii) continual supervision throughout the night in order to avoid substantial danger to himself or others.[8]

i Nature of tests

The first issue that arises under this provision is whether the two tests raise questions of law, and thereby come within the jurisdiction of the Commissioners (and eventually the ordinary courts), or are rather questions of fact on which the medical decisions are final. The issue is part of the general nature of decision-making and is treated as such in another chapter.[9] It is necessary here to see what implications the general principles have for entitlement to this specific benefit. On the one hand, the tendency has been for the courts to treat the question as to whether 'the words of the statute do or do not as a matter of ordinary usage of the English language cover or apply to the facts which have been proved' as a question not of law

5 Smith (1981) 48 Poverty 9 at 11. He suggests that the system of determination should be radically restructured.
6 These are set out in Appendix D of Harris *Handicapped and Impaired in Great Britain* (1971).
7 SSA 1975, s.35(1)(a).
8 Ibid, s.35(1)(b).
9 Pp. 602–603, below.

but of fact.[10] It follows that the fulfilment of the above conditions is regarded primarily as a medical question to be decided by the Board.[11] On the other hand, where a word is capable of different shades of meaning, decisions as to the correct shade of meaning in a given statute are a matter of construction and therefore of law.[12] This is the relevant principle in determining whether the Board's decision contains a false proposition of law ex facie, one of the grounds on which the Commissioner may entertain an appeal against such a decision.[13]

ii Severely disabled

The invalid must be 'severely disabled physically or mentally'. There is no reported decision in which a claimant has failed to satisfy this criterion, and it would seem to be no obstacle that the disability is attributable solely to age.[14]

iii Requires

It is important to observe that the attention or supervision referred to in the statutory conditions must be 'required' rather than 'provided'. In other words, the test is based on the objective existence of the need rather than on the actual provision of a service.[15]

iv Night and day

The first condition applies to day time attention; the second to night time. The distinction is crucial, since the claimant seeking a higher rate of benefit must satisfy both conditions, but 'night' is not defined in the Act. To resolve a conflict of different interpretations of this word,[16] the Divisional Court in 1974 ruled that it meant

> that period of inactivity, or that principal period of inactivity through which each household goes in the dark hours, and the . . . beginning of the night (could be measured) from the time at which the household, as it were, closed down for the night.[17]

This definition was adopted because it had clearly been the intention of Parliament to treat as more onerous on members of the household attention provided during the night as opposed to during the day: this will occur if the attendant has to interrupt his normal period of repose to deal with the invalid. It follows that the definition applies equally where the latter is a child, even though its sleeping hours are more prolonged.[18]

10 Per Lord Reid, *Brutus v Cozens* [1973] AC 854 at 861: applied by the Divisional Court in *R v National Insurance Comr, ex parte Secretary of State for Social Services* [1974] 3 All ER 522 at 526 and by R G Micklethwait, Chief Comr, in *R(A) 3/74*.

11 Per R G Micklethwait, Chief Comr, *R(A) 1/73*, para 13.

12 Per Lord Widgery CJ, *R v National Insurance Comr*, n.10, above, at 526.

13 For this and other grounds, see pp. 602–603, below.

14 See e.g. *R(A) 2/80*, where the claimant was senile, (the Court of Appeal in *R v National Insurance Comr, ex parte Secretary of State for Social Services* [1981] 2 All ER 738, [1981] 1 WLR 1017 quashed the decision allowing her claim, but on other grounds).

15 *R(A) 1/72*; *R(A) 1/73*; *R(A) 3/74*; *R(A) 1/75*.

16 See e.g. *CA 9/72*, which adopted the traditional (but inappropriate) common law definition of 'sunset to sunrise' and *R(A) 1/73*.

17 *R v National Comr, ex parte Secretary of State for Social Services* [1974] 3 All ER 522 at 527.

18 *R(A) 1/78*.

v Attention in connection with bodily functions

This is relevant for the purposes of both the day and night conditions, though in relation to the former the attention must be 'frequent', which means 'several times, not once or twice',[19] while for the latter it must be 'prolonged', that is, lasting for 'some little time',[20] or 'repeated', which means at least twice.[1] The common condition of 'attention in connection with bodily functions' has caused some difficulty. The notion of 'attention' is not controversial. It is broader than the notion of dealing with a specific health risk.[2] According to Dunn LJ in *R v National Insurance Comr, ex parte Secretary of State for Social Services* (the *Parker* case),[3] attention

> indicates something more than personal service, something involving care, consideration and vigilance for the person being attended . . . a service of a close and intimate nature.[4]

But what of 'bodily functions'? This might literally include, as Forbes J in the *Parker* case suggested, 'every mode of action of which the fit body is capable at the dictate of the normal brain'.[5] As such, it would cover functions of which the invalid is capable, and those quite irrelevant to his circumstances and needs — which would surely be inconsistent with the purpose of the provision. The narrower interpretation of Lord Denning MR therefore seems to be preferable. According to him 'bodily functions'

> include breathing, hearing, seeing, eating, drinking, walking, sitting, sleeping, getting in and out of bed, dressing, undressing, eliminating waste products, and the like, all of which an ordinary person, who is not suffering from any disability, does for himself. But they do not include cooking, shopping or any of the other things which a wife or daughter does as part of her domestic duties, or generally which one of the household normally does for the rest of the family.[6]

Finally, the attention must be 'in connection with' the bodily functions. This involves a test of remoteness or proximity, as to which there has again been a diversity of opinion.[7] The Court of Appeal held in the *Parker* case that ordinary domestic duties such as shopping and cooking (including the preparation of a special diet) are too remote.[8] These were to be distinguished from

> duties that are out of the ordinary, doing for the disabled person what a normal person would do for himself, such as cutting up food, lifting the cup to the mouth, helping to dress and undress or at the toilet.[9]

vi Continual supervision to avoid substantial danger to himself or others

This is the alternative requirement for both day and night conditions. In comparison with 'attention', 'supervision' is a more passive concept: ready

19 Per Lord Denning MR, *R v National Insurance Comr, ex parte Secretary of State for Social Services* (the *Parker* case) [1981] 2 All ER 738 at 741.
20 Ibid. See also *R 1/72 (AA)*, para 22.
1 Per Lord Denning MR, *Parker* case, n.19, above, at 741.
2 *R(A) 3/78,* R J A Temple, Chief Comr.
3 N.19, above, at 742.
4 See to similar effect: Lord Denning MR, ibid, at 741; *R(A) 3/74*, para 11; *R(A) 3/80*, para 8.
5 Quoted at [1981] 2 All ER 738 at 740. See also Dunn LJ, ibid, at 742.
6 Ibid, at 741. *R(A) 3/78*, para 12.
7 See the authorities reviewed in *R(A) 2/80,* paras 9–17. The latter confirmed a new trend which commenced in *CA 2/79*, and included *R(A) 1/80*, that cooking for the invalid was a relevant factor. But the decision in *R(A) 2/80* was quashed by the Court of Appeal, n.19, above.
8 Ibid, per Lord Denning MR at 741, per Dunn LJ at 744, per O'Connor LJ at 745.
9 Per Lord Denning MR, ibid, at 741–742.

to intervene if necessary and thus precautionary and anticipatory rather than active.[10] During the day, '*continual* supervision' will usually involve overseeing or watching,[11] as would be expected of a childminder in care of young children. At night, it is generally considered sufficient if the assistant is sleeping in the same, or perhaps an adjacent, room and can respond to any summons for help.[12] What constitutes 'substantial danger to himself or others' is less certain. It has been suggested that the phrase, though incapable of precise definition, should not be narrowly construed — the risk of harm could result not only from a fall but also from exposure, neglect 'and a good many other things'.[13] In any event, the question for the medical authorities is not whether those suffering from the claimant's disorder are typically prone to a particular risk, but whether the claimant himself was, as a result of his condition, exposed to a risk which was not too remote.[14]

vii Intermittent needs

The phrases 'by day . . . throughout the day . . . at night . . . during the night' do not indicate on how many days (or nights) during the week the need must occur. It is clear that the conditions do not have to be satisfied on each and every day (or night),[15] but apart from this ruling the Commissioners have generally left it to the discretion of the medical authorities to reach a decision on the frequency and pattern of the need.[16] In 1977 the Attendance Allowance Board advised its delegated medical practitioners that, subject to each case being considered individually, a person suffering from renal failure should require at least three sessions a week on a kidney machine if he is to qualify. The Chief Commissioner held in *R(A) 4/78* that this did not amount to an error of law. Following that decision, the government made special provision for this group of claimants. A person receiving dialysis treatment for two or more sessions a week is deemed to satisfy either the day or the night condition, and thus is entitled to the allowance at the lower rate, provided that he does not receive the treatment as an NHS out-patient.[17]

C Period

The Attendance Allowance Board must be satisfied that the conditions of entitlement have been fulfilled for a period of six months,[18] though a claim may be made before that period has elapsed.[19] The allowance is then payable for such period as the Board considers that the invalid is likely to continue to fulfil the conditions.[20] The period of six months need not be served again if he recovers but subsequently suffers a relapse and again satisfies the requirement within two years from the beginning of the last six months period.[1]

10 *CA 6/72*, para 10; *R(A) 2/75* para 9.
11 Ibid.
12 Ibid, and *R(A) 3/74*; cp *R(A) 4/74*.
13 *R(A) 1/73*, para 17, R G Micklethwait, Chief Comr.
14 *R(A) 1/81*. See also *R(A) 5/81*, discussed in the Appendix.
15 See esp. *R(A) 3/74* and *R(A) 4/78*.
16 Ibid, para 28.
17 SSA 1975, s.35(2A), inserted by SSA 1979, s.2(3) and SI 1975/598, regs 5B and 5C, inserted by SI 1979/375.
18 SSA 1975, s.35(2)(b).
19 Ibid, s.35(4)(a).
20 Ibid, s.35(2)(a).
1 SI 1975/598, reg 5A, inserted by SI 1979/375.

D Residence

– The invalid must be ordinarily resident in GB, present in GB on every day for which the attendance allowance is claimed, and have been present in GB for an aggregate of not less that 26 weeks in the year immediately preceding the date of the claim.[2] For the purpose of the latter two conditions, however, he is deemed to be present in GB (i) if an absence is for a temporary purpose and has not lasted for more than six months; or (ii) where the absence is temporary and for the specific purpose of being treated for an incapacity from which he suffered before he left GB, and the Secretary of State certifies that it is consistent with the proper administration of the Act that he should be treated as though he were present in GB.[3] There is also relief for airmen, mariners, persons employed on the continental shelf and members of the armed forcés and their families.[4]

E Exclusions

The Act stipulates that 'a person' is entitled to attendance allowance.[5] In *R(A) 3/75*, Dr Barnardo's, the well known charity, a body corporate, sought to argue that the phrase incuded legal as well as natural persons. The claim was rightly rejected. The conditions to be satisfied for the benefit can hardly be applied to someone other than the individual himself, let alone an institution. Explicit exclusions apply to those who are already in receipt of state subsidy for their accommodation.[6]

– More precisely the Regulations provide that it shall be a condition for receipt of the allowance that a person aged 16 or over is not maintained free of charge while undergoing medical treatment as an in-patient in either an NHS hospital or another hospital or similar institution in pursuance of arrangements made with the Secretary of State.[7] The exclusion also applies: where such a person is living in accommodation provided for him, or in which the cost of accommodation is borne wholly or partly out of public funds, in pursuance of a number of enactments listed in the Schedule to the Regulations, but not to a person under 18 so accommodated in a private house.[8] Moreover, a claimant already in receipt of the allowance remains entitled to it for the first four weeks of the treatment or accommodation referred to.[9]

There are also special rules for children (i.e. those under 16 years). Allowances are not paid to those under two years,[10] and in other cases the attention or supervision required must be 'substantially in excess of that

2 SI 1975/598, reg 2(1)(a)–(c). For the meaning of the terms 'resident' and 'present' see pp. 391–393, below.
3 SI 1975/598, reg 2(2)(d)–(e), as substituted by SI 1977/342, and amended by SI 1977/1679.
4 SI 1975/598, reg 2(2)(a)–(c), as substituted by SI 1977/342.
5 SSA 1975, s.35(1).
6 Ibid, s.35(6).
7 SI 1975/598, reg 3, as amended by SI 1980/1136. A person is only to be regarded as 'not being maintained' free of charge if he pays charges which are intended to cover the whole cost of accommodation and services (excluding the cost of treatment): ibid, and see *R(A) 3/75*.
8 SI 1975/598, reg 4, as amended by SI 1979/1684. Where accommodation is provided in pursuance of one of the scheduled enactments, it is irrelevant that the claimant himself contributes to the cost: *R(A) 2/79*.
9 SI 1975/598, reg 5.
10 Ibid, reg 6(2)(a).

normally required by a child of the same age and sex'.[11] The person entitled to receive the allowance on behalf of the child is determined according to rules of priority:

- First, the allowance is not payable in any case where the child is not child; failing that any other person living with the child, or a mother, father, grandparent, brother or sister not living with the child but contributing to the cost of providing for him.[12] Of course, only one person is entitled to an allowance in respect of one child for any one period of time, and if more than one person satisfies the rules it is payable to the individual nominated under the discretion conferred on the Secretary of State.[13]

There are exclusions analogous to those regarding adults in hospital and analogous accommodation, but in this instance the Regulations are broader in impact.

- First, the allowance is not payable in any case where the child is not accommodated in a private household unless the person who would otherwise be entitled to receive it is contributing to the cost of providing for the child[14] at a weekly rate of at least the amount of the attendance allowance (over and above any contribution required for entitlement to child benefit or increases to a contributory benefit).[15] Secondly, it is excluded where the child is undergoing medical treatment or other treatment as an in-patient in a hospital or similar institution,[16] except where the maintenance is not free of charge, and the person claiming benefit is contributing to the cost of providing for the child at the rate stated above.[17] The 'four weeks' rule governing the entitlement of adults in such institutions also applies to children.[18] Finally, the exclusion also applies where the child is living in accommodation provided for him or financed wholly or partly from public or local funds in pursuance of the scheduled enactments,[19] but not where he is living in a private dwelling house with a parent or foster-parent.[20]

Part 6 Invalid care allowance

A General

A household in which a severely disabled person requires attendance may suffer from financial hardship not only directly through the needs of the invalid, but also from the sacrifices made by other members of the household in looking after him. In a study carried out by Sainsbury,[1] it emerged that about two-thirds of disabled persons requiring care received it from

11 SI 1975/598, reg 6(2)(c)–(d).
12 Ibid, reg 6(4), and see SI 1977/1361, reg 4.
13 SI 1975/598, reg 6(5) as amended by SI 1977/1361, reg 4. If according to these rules a woman is entitled, payment may nevertheless be made to her husband living with her.
14 For general problems arising under this notion of maintenance, see pp. 373–376, below.
15 SI 1975/598, reg 7(1)(a), as amended by SI 1977/342, reg 15(3) and SI 1977/417, reg 2(6). On entitlement to child benefit and dependants' increases see pp. 428–444 and pp. 366–367, below, respectively.
16 SI 1975/598, reg 7(1)(c).
17 Ibid, reg 7(3), and n.15, above.
18 SI 1975/598, reg 7(2) and above at n.9.
19 SI 1975/598, reg 7(1)(b), and at n.8, above.
20 SI 1975/598, reg s.7(1)(b), and 7(5) as amended by SI 1977/1341 and SI 1979/1684.
1 *Registered as Disabled* (1970) p. 135.

relatives, and frequently this would involve a complete or partial interference with the relative's own earnings potential. Quite apart from the social justice of compensating such persons, the granting of state financial support also makes economic sense. In many cases, the care supplied voluntarily by the individual involves a saving on public facilities which would otherwise have been necessary. In addition, an estimated 11,500 persons were in receipt of supplementary benefit substantially because they had forsaken gainful employment to care for an elderly or disabled relative,[2] and, as with NCIP, there was pressure to transfer such persons to a non-means tested benefit. The arguments apply not only to the care of severely disabled persons but also to that of small children, those temporarily sick and elderly persons. The government was not, however, prepared to introduce a general 'home care' allowance.[3] The non-contributory invalid care allowance (ICA) was introduced by legislation in 1975.[4] Initially entitlement was limited to a prescribed category of relatives of the invalid.[5] This had no obvious justification apart from saving on public expenditure and it led to some arbitrary distinctions. The limitation was abolished in 1981,[6] but the opportunity was not taken at that time to amend another, and perhaps more important, exclusion, that of married or cohabiting women. As with HNCIP,[7] this was based on the crude assumption that such persons are not normally active in the labour market. Although the matter was outside its terms of reference, the National Insurance Advisory Committee felt impelled to criticise the discrimination implicit in the law,[8] but as yet there has been no response from government.

B Persons for the care of whom ICA is payable

As indicated above, the category of persons for the care of whom the allowance was made payable was not intended to be wide. The Act limits it to 'a severely disabled person',[9] and this is defined[10] as a person in receipt of attendance allowance[11] or the industrial injuries constant attendance allowance[12] (or its equivalent under the war pensions scheme[13]). This definition has the merit of avoiding the addition of yet another concept of disability to those already existing in the law. But it does mean that where the conditions of entitlement to the attendance allowance are satisfied, perhaps only marginally, the household will effectively benefit from the two allowances, while a marginal decision that the conditions have not been satisfied results in neither being payable.

2 Report on Security Provision for Chronically Sick and Disabled Persons 1973–74, HC 276, para 61.
3 Ibid, at para 60.
4 SSBA 1975, s.7, reenacted as SSA 1975, s.37.
5 See the first edition of this book, pp. 181–182.
6 SI 1981/655.
7 P. 168, above.
8 Report on Extension of Title to Invalid Care Allowance to Non-Relatives (1980, Cmnd 7905). See also Equal Opportunities Commission *Behind Closed Doors* (1981) pp. 14–23.
9 SSA 1975, s.37(1).
10 SI 1976/409, reg 3.
11 SSA 1975, s.37(2), and see pp. 172–177, above.
12 Pp. 324–325, below.
13 P. 355, below.

C Persons entitled to ICA

There are two substantive conditions which the claimant must satisfy:

(a) he is regularly and substantially engaged in caring for that person; and
(b) he is not gainfully employed.[14]

i Nature of care

The linking of the ICA with attendance allowance is sufficient in itself to establish that the severely disabled person is in substantial need of care, but it was still necessary to provide more guidelines for the requirement of 'regularly and substantially engaged in caring. . .'. It was decided that the best approach was to set a minimum number of hours' care which was consistent with the notion of it being a full-time occupation for the claimant, but yet which was not 'so high as to cause the claimant to have to examine in detail what among her activities constituted "caring" and whether the minimum had been met'.[15] The result was the creation of the '35 hours' rule formulated in the following regulation:

> a person shall be treated as engaged and as regularly and substantially engaged in caring for a severely disabled person on every day in a week if, and shall not be treated as engaged or regularly and substantially engaged in caring for a severely disabled person on any day in a week unless, as at that week he is, or is likely to be, engaged and regularly engaged for at least 35 hours a week in caring for that severely disabled person.[16]

The reason for the rather circuitous form of this provision is that the base period of the claim is for 'any day' of care, but the 35 hour criterion of course applies to a calendar week. It is not, however, clear that the rule as formulated has achieved the stated objective of relieving the authorities of deciding what constitutes 'caring', or how 'regular' it is to be. Is it to be assumed that the mere presence of the claimant in the premises of the disabled person will be sufficient, or is some more active role required? As yet, there is no reported decision which provides guidance on these matters.

The care provided by the relative may be temporarily interrupted by, for example, his own absence or the invalid's need to enter hospital. To achieve flexibility, and to reduce the administrative expenses of frequent investigation, the '35 hours' rule is relaxed in certain circumstances. The Regulations provide that the rule is deemed to have been satisfied if

– (1) the claimant has only temporarily ceased to satisfy the conditions; and (2) he has satisfied them for an aggregate period of 14 or more weeks in the immediately preceding six months; and (3) he would have satisfied them for at least 22 weeks in such a period but for the fact that he or the disabled person was undergoing treatment as an in-patient in a hospital or similar institution.[17]

ii Gainful employment

The intention being to confer benefit only on those engaged full-time in the care of the invalid, it was thought appropriate to have some form of earnings rule. Indeed, the Department appears at one stage to have con-

14 SSA 1975, s.37(1).
15 NIAC Report on Draft Regulations, 1975–76, HC 271, para 12.
16 SI 1976/409, reg 4(1).
17 Ibid, reg 4(2).

sidered the argument that in principle all earnings should be taken into account.[18] However, the fact that the majority of persons benefiting from the new allowance would already have been in receipt of supplementary benefit, to which the earnings disregard of £4 (£6 in the case of single parents) applied, induced the proposal that a similar disregard of £4 should apply to the ICA. The recommendation of the National Insurance Advisory Committee that this should be raised to £6[19] was accepted, and in 1982 the amount was doubled to £12.00. This limit must not be exceeded in the week immediately preceding that in which ICA is claimed, and all subsequent weeks of entitlement.[20] The ordinary rules for the computation of earnings apply to this provision,[1] but the claimant is entitled to have disregarded any earnings during a week in which he temporarily ceases to satisfy the 'caring' provisions, or during a week in which he was, with the authority of his employer, absent from employment.[2]

D Exclusions

As has been indicated, a woman, residing with her husband or being maintained by him, or living with a man as his wife is excluded; so also are persons under 16 or receiving full-time education.[3]

E Persons of pensionable and retiring age

Mutatis mutandis the NCIP rules governing the entitlement of persons above pensionable and retiring age[4] apply. The claimant may accumulate ICA with a retirement pension, but only if he was entitled to the former immediately before attaining pensionable age.[5] After retiring age, he will continue to be entitled even if he no longer satisfies the conditions provided that he was entitled immediately before reaching that age.[6]

F Residence and presence

There are three requirements to be satisfied.

- On the date for which the allowance is claimed, the claimant must be (i) ordinarily resident in GB and (ii) present in GB; and (iii) must have been present in GB for an aggregate of 26 weeks in the 12 months immediately preceding that date.[7] For the purposes of (ii) and (iii) a temporary absence is disregarded if it did not exceed a continuous period of four weeks or if it was specifically for the purpose of caring for the invalid who was also absent from GB (provided that at the time the latter did not lose his entitlement to attendance allowance or its equivalent).[8] The usual disregards of absence for those employed on the continental shelf, members of the forces and their families, also apply.[9]

18 See NIAC Report, n.15, above, at para 18.
19 Ibid, at paras 20–23.
20 SI 1976/409, reg 8(1).
1 Pp. 404–409, below.
2 SI 1976/409, reg 8(2).
3 SSA 1975, s.37(3).
4 P. 170, above.
5 SSA 1975, s.37(5).
6 Ibid, s.37(6).
7 SI 1976/409, reg 9(1).
8 Ibid, reg 9(2).
9 Ibid, reg 9(3).

G Amount

ICA is a flat-rate benefit equivalent in amount to the NCIP (in 1982–83 £19.70 per week), and the increases for dependants also follow that benefit.[10] Of course, not more than one person can claim the allowance for the same period,[11] and two or more who satisfy the conditions may elect, by sending an appropriate notice to the Secretary of State, which is to benefit; in default of such election, entitlement is determined at the discretion of the Secretary of State.[12]

Part 7 Mobility allowance

A General

The new policy towards the disabled of isolating particular needs and providing income on a flat-rate, non-contributory basis, inevitably became directed to the question of mobility. This was not an easy subject to treat, because help in this area had existed for a considerable period of time primarily in the form of kind rather than money.[13] Since 1921 invalid vehicles, generally a single-seat three-wheeler, were supplied to war pensioners. After the Second World War, however, those receiving a war pension at 20 per cent or more might opt instead for a small car, which might be driven by a 'nominated' driver if the pensioner so preferred.[14] The provision for other disabled persons was not so generous. In exercise of his powers under the National Health Service[15] the Minister of Health (now the Secretary of State for Social Services) made the three-wheeler available to a severely disabled person who came within one of the following categories:[16] (i) loss of both legs, one being amputated above or through the knee; (ii) defects in the locomotor system, or a severe chronic lung or heart condition so that, to all intents and purposes, he was unable to walk; (iii) a slightly less severe disability but which still seriously limited walking ability, and as a result he needed personal transport to get to and from work. The three-wheeler had of course to be driven by the invalid himself. In 1964 the government decided to extend to a small category of persons the facility of a small car, as already granted to war pensioners. The category of benefit was selected according to social rather than physical circumstances: the claimant had either to be living with a relative, who was himself eligible for a three-wheeler or was blind, or to be for a substantial part of the day in sole charge of a young child.[17] In 1972 haemophiliacs were added to this group, but in all cases the claimant had to be capable of driving himself, and no one else was allowed to drive the car. Alongside

10 SI 1976/409, regs 12, 13. See pp. 364–371, below.
11 SSA 1975, s.37(7).
12 SI 1976/409, reg 7.
13 See the government-sponsored report by Lady Sharp, Mobility of Physically Disabled People (1974).
14 Ibid, para 11.
15 The National Health Service Act 1946, s.3(1) conferred a general power to provide 'medical, nursing and other services required at or for the purposes of hospitals'. Under the Health Services and Public Health Act 1968, s.33, it became more specific: to 'provide invalid carriages for persons appearing to him to be suffering from severe physical defect or disability. . .'; see now National Health Service Act 1977, s.5(2) (a).
16 The criteria were set out in a DHSS circular. See Sharp, n.13, above. Appendix D, para 1.
17 Ibid, para 5.

these provisions, certain cash allowances were made available. Those entitled to the three-wheeler or car were exempt from road vehicle excise duty; and, in response to the mounting pressure for the issue of cars rather than three-wheelers, from 1972 those qualifying for a three-wheeler might be allowed, as an alternative, a tax free sum of £100 per annum to help them run and maintain their own car.[18] The latter was seen as a temporary holding measure, while the whole structure of mobility benefits was examined. The appropriate report, on a study undertaken by Lady Sharp, was published in 1974,[19] and its findings were critical of the prevailing system. First, existing facilities were distributed inequitably – in particular, they were limited to invalids who themselves were able to drive. Secondly, the three-wheeler itself was unsatisfactory — it was dangerous, noisy, uncomfortable, liable to break down, and could not carry a passenger. The recommendation was that it should be replaced by a small car as soon as this became economically feasible, but with a narrower range of individuals retaining the right to elect instead for a cash allowance to help maintain and run the car.

The provision of cars would indeed have been too expensive, and the new Labour government resisted Lady Sharp's proposal as it would have reduced the range of disabled persons entitled to assistance. Instead it was decided to provide as an alternative to the three-wheeler a flat-rate, non-contributory mobility allowance. This solution, implemented by the Social Security Pensions Act 1975,[20] did not, however, prove to be entirely satisfactory. On the one hand, there was continuing concern for the safety of the three-wheeler; on the other hand, the allowance was insufficient for many of those without a vehicle of any kind to finance the necessary means of locomotion.[1] As regards the first of these problems, the government decided to phase out production of the vehicle and to allow those already in possession of one to qualify automatically for the mobility allowance, as and when they gave up use of it.[2] Secondly, the 'Motability' scheme was established to help immobile persons to get maximum value for their resources, and in particular to enable them to lease or obtain on hire-purchase a car on favourable terms.[3] A number of other measures had also been taken to reduce the costs of motoring, including exemption from hire-purchase restrictions on standard cars,[4] and rate relief on garages.[5]

B Entitlement

i Inability to walk

The basic statutory test of entitlement is that the claimant is 'suffering from physical disablement such that he is either unable to walk or virtually unable to walk'.[6] The Regulations then prescribe more specifically the conditions which must be satisfied.

> A person shall only be treated . . . as suffering from physical disablement such that he is either unable to walk or virtually unable to do so, if his physical

18 Ibid, para 7.
19 N. 13, above.
20 S.22, inserting s.37A in SSA 1975.
1 Cf DHSS Research Report No 7, *The Impact of Mobility Allowance* (1981).
2 SS(MP)A 1977, s.13.
3 Carson [1978–9] JSWL 38, and see SI 1978/1131, authorising the payment of the allowance directly to Motability.
4 SI 1976/1135, art 2(2).
5 General Rate Act 1967, s.45(1).
6 SSA 1975, s.37A(1).

condition as a whole is such that, without having regard to circumstances peculiar to that person as to place of residence or as to place of, or nature of, employment, —

(a) he is unable to walk; or
(b) his ability to walk out of doors is so limited, as regards the distance over which or the speed at which or the length of time for which or the manner in which he can make progress on foot without severe discomfort, that he is virtually unable to walk; or
(c) the exertion required to walk would constitute a danger to his life or would be likely to lead to a serious deterioration in his health.[7]

The claimant must, therefore, fulfil one of the three conditions (a), (b) or (c). Before these are examined, it is necessary to consider factors which are common to all three.

ii Factors common to alternative conditions

a *Physical disablement*

A controversial feature of the mobility allowance,[8] and one which distinguishes it from other disability benefits, is its restriction to physical disablement, thus excluding cases such as agoraphobia where the inability to walk results solely from mental disablement.[9] Nevertheless, the distinction between the two types of disablement is not always easy to draw. Down's syndrome, or mongolism, provides a good example, and in a case decided on a version of the Regulations previously in force, the Chief Commissioner indicated that the weight to be attached to physical and mental disablement where both factors were present was for the medical adjudicating authorities to determine.[10] In amending the Regulations, it was hoped to clarify the issue by concentrating on the effect of a disabling condition, rather than its causation.[11] It is to be observed that under the new version regard is to be had to the claimant's 'physical condition as a whole'. It may have been the intention, by employing this wording, to admit cases, such as mongolism, where a mental blockage, itself the result of the physical condition, inhibits walking,[12] but the matter must remain in doubt until an authoritative ruling is received from the Commissioner.

b *Personal circumstances*

Circumstances relating to the physical condition of the claimant are, of course, crucial, but the Regulations provide that the authorities should ignore where he lives and the place and nature of his employment. In other words, the extent of mobility is to be determined by a mechanical test, not by reference to the purpose of the locomotion.[13] No doubt, in social policy terms it might be desirable to link the criterion to what was reasonably necessary for the claimant to participate in the minimal essential activities of life, or to reach, for example, his place of employment,[14] but in legal and administrative terms this would be difficult to formulate and might lead to inequitable treatment between different claimants.

7 SI 1975/1573, reg 3(1), as amended by SI 1979/172.
8 Cf *Pearson* para 534.
9 *R(M) 1/80*.
10 *R(M) 2/78*.
11 See NIAC Report on Draft Amendment Regulations (1979, Cmnd 7491), para 6.
12 Douglas (1980) 48 Poverty 6–7.
13 *R(M) 3/78*, paras 9–12, J S Watson, Comr.
14 Douglas, n.12, above, at 7.

c *Use of prostheses etc.*
Ability to walk is to be judged having regard to a prosthesis or artificial aid which the claimant habitually wears or uses.[15] So if such an appliance enables him to walk, when he might otherwise not do so, he is not entitled. Of course, a claimant still unable (or virtually unable) to walk with the appliance will succeed.[16]

d *Ability to benefit from locomotion*
The allowance is not available to all severely disabled persons. Legislation provides that it is payable only where the invalid's condition is 'such as permits him from time to time to benefit from enhanced facilities for locomotion'.[17] This obviously excludes human vegetables and those whom it is unsafe to move,[18] but it is arguable that of the remainder there will be few who will not receive some benefit from the occasional sortie, and it is not easy to draw a line between the deserving and the undeserving except on some arbitrary basis.

iii The alternative conditions
Subject to these general considerations, the claimant must satisfy one of the following conditions.

a *Total inability to walk*
This condition almost speaks for itself. 'Walk' means 'to move by means of a person's legs and feet or a combination of them'.[19]

b *Virtual inability to walk*
The present wording of the second, crucial, condition results from amendments made in 1979.[20] It requires the medical authorities to ascertain qualitatively and quantitatively the limits of the claimant's ability to walk outdoors without severe discomfort, having regard to distance, speed, length of time or manner; they are to ignore 'any extended outdoor walking accomplishment which the claimant could or might attain only with severe discomfort'.[1]

c *Exertion constituting risk to life or health*
It is important, for this condition, to establish a connection or a relationship between the 'exertion required to walk' and the danger to life or a risk of serious deterioration in health. So, for example, a person advised medically not to walk because he might, in the process, be subject to an epileptic fit is not entitled on this ground alone, for there is no causal relationship between the exertion of walking and the risk of a fit.[2]

iv Determination of medical questions
On submission of a claim, the insurance officer normally arranges for an examination by a medical practitioner and/or the medical board.[3] He then

15 SI 1975/1573, reg 3(2), as amended by SI 1979/172.
16 NIAC Report, n.11, above, para 13.
17 SSA 1975, s.27A(2)(d), inserted by SSPA 1975, s.22.
18 *CM 1/77*, noted at [1978–9] JSWL 56.
19 *R(M) 3/78*, para 10, J S Watson, Comr; but also an intended direction; *R(M) 2/81*.
20 On which see NIAC Report, n.11, above.
1 *R(M) 1/81*, para 9, I Edwards-Jones, Comr.
2 *R(M) 3/78*.
3 SI 1975/1573, regs 13–15.

makes a decision in the light of all the medical evidence. If denied the allowance on medical grounds, the claimant may appeal to the medical board, or, if already examined by that body, to the medical appeal tribunal.[4] From the decision of the latter, there is an appeal on matters of law only to the Commissioner.[5]

v Prior entitlement to mobility assistance

As indicated above, the government has decided to phase out the supply of invalid vehicles. A person entitled to such a vehicle may not in addition receive mobility allowance, but if he elects no longer to use it, the allowance becomes payable. For this purpose, he is deemed to satisfy the medical criteria, provided that his physical condition has not improved.[6]

vi Exclusions

We have seen in the last paragraph that a person granted an invalid carriage is excluded from the mobility allowance until he elects no longer to use it.[7] In addition, in exercise of a power conferred under the overlapping benefits provisions,[8] the Secretary of State has excluded wholly or partly those receiving a grant, or receiving any payment by way of grant under the National Health Service Act 1977 towards the cost of running a private car, or any payment out of public funds which he regards as analogous thereto.[9] The regulation apportions the payments over the various weeks of entitlement, and the weekly amounts so apportioned are deducted from the claimant's mobility allowance.

vii Period

The allowance is payable for any period throughout which the claimant satisfies the criteria stated above, but it must also be established that the 'inability or virtual inability to walk is likely to persist for at least 12 months from the time when a claim for the allowance is received by the Secretary of State'.[10]

C Age

Under the 1975 Act, the allowance was not payable to persons over pensionable age.[11] The Social Security Act 1979 extended entitlement to those under 75. Persons between 65 and 75 must, however, have been entitled on reaching the age of 65 or, in certain circumstances, 66.[12] The provision marks another, if minor, step in the equal treatment of men and women: by adopting 65 rather than pensionable age as the date by which title must have been established, Parliament has allowed women another five years in which to qualify.

4 Ibid, regs 16–18, and see pp. 596–600, below.
5 SI 1975/1573, reg 19 and pp. 600–601, below.
6 SS(MP)A 1977, s.13(1) and SI 1977/1229.
7 SSA 1975, s.37A(6) and SI 1975/1573, reg 8. But see now Appendix.
8 SSA 1975, s.85(2).
9 SI 1975/1573, reg 8, as amended by SI 1981/1817.
10 SSA, s.37A(2)(a).
11 Ibid, s.37A(5)(a).
12 S.3, amending SSA 1975, s.37A(5)(a).

The allowance is not payable for children under five.[13] In the case of other children (aged 5 to 15 inclusive) the benefit is payable to an adult, appointed according to typical rules of priority to receive the allowance.[14] This is an interesting provision, for it appears to be the first time that a benefit intended to assist a child 'follows' that child wherever he may be living, whether, for example, with a foster parent, in hospital, or in residential care. It is to this end that the Regulation insists that the recipient of the allowance must give an undertaking to use it for the child's benefit.[15]

D Residence and presence

In the ordinary case three conditions must be satisfied.[16]

- During the period for which benefit is claimed the invalid must be (i) ordinarily resident in GB; (ii) present in GB; and (iii) he must have been present there for an aggregate of 52 weeks in the 18 months immediately preceding that period. Temporary absences not lasting for more than a continuous period of 26 weeks, and those for the special purposes of treating the incapacity, are disregarded.[17] There are the usual special provisions for airmen, mariners, those employed on the continental shelf, and members of the forces and their families.[18]

E Disqualifications and other rules relating to claims

Broadly speaking, the benefit is administered in the same way as the sickness and invalidity benefits, so that the 'rules of behaviour' and the disqualifications for misconduct, failing to attend for examination or treatment formulated for those benefits, apply also here.[19]

F Amount

The allowance is a flat-rate sum (in 1982–83 £18.30 per week[20]). As with attendance allowance, it is not deductible from supplementary benefit.[1]

13 Ibid. The Pearson Commission recommended that entitlement be extended to children aged two or more: para 1533.
14 Viz mother or father living with the child, or failing that, such person as the Secretary of State may determine: SI 1975/1573, reg 21.
15 Ibid, reg 21(3).
16 Ibid, reg 2. For the meaning of 'ordinarily resident' and 'present', see pp. 391–393, below.
17 SI 1975/1573, reg 2(3)(b)–(c).
18 Ibid, reg 2(3)(a).
19 Ibid, reg 7: see pp. 155–160, above.
20 For up-rating, see p. 412, below.
1 SSA 1975, s.37A(8), and p. 486, below. For tax liability, see Appendix, note to pp. 33–34.

Chapter 5

Retirement pensions

Part 1 Introduction

A General

In terms both of the number of recipients and of total expenditure, retirement pensions are undoubtedly the most important benefit provided by the British social security system. In 1981 about 9 million people were in receipt of them. The expenditure on pensions was over £10,000 million, about a half the total budget for social security payments.[1] This proportion is typical of developed countries.[2] With continuing increases in the number of old people, both absolutely and in proportion to the rest of the population, the significance of retirement pensions is likely to increase.[3] In a democratic country the old are an element of the electorate which governments cannot easily ignore; both for this political reason and out of considerations of social justice, it is likely that expenditure on pensions will continue to rise.

Nevertheless the state does not have a monopoly in making provision for the aged. Many of them regard it as their own business to provide for themselves and their families in old age through savings and insurance policies. The years since the last war have seen a rapid growth in occupational pensions, which are generally earnings-related, often affording their recipients an appreciable addition to the state retirement pension.[4] By 1971 it seems that about half the working population was covered by such schemes.[5] However, often the benefits afforded by occupational pensions are relatively meagre, and there are sometimes other drawbacks, in particular the absence of inflation-proofing. For these reasons, quite apart from the fact that many people are still not covered by

1 First report of the Social Security Advisory Committee, (1982), Table 1.2.

2 *Kaim-Caudle* p. 131. For a comparative overall survey, see the OECD paper, *Old Age Pension Schemes* (1977).

3 The proportion of people in Great Britain of pensionable age (65 for men, 60 for women) in 1851 was 4.0%, in 1948 it was 13.2% and in 1971 16.1%. By 1975 it had risen to 23.0%: DHSS Memorandum *Pension Age* (1976) para 2. Also see *Growing Older* (1981, Cmnd 8173), ch 1.

4 Among the leading works on occupational pension schemes are: Hosking *Pension Schemes and Retirement Pensions* (4th edn); Ellison *Private Occupational Pension Schemes* (1979). Recent information may now be found in the reports of the Occupational Pensions Board.

5 See the White Paper, Better Pensions (1974, Cmnd 5713).

a scheme, it has not been possible for governments simply to rely on occupational pensions to remedy the deficiencies of state provision.

When the present system of flat-rate retirement pensions was introduced in 1946, subsequent to the Beveridge Report,[6] it was envisaged that the pension would eventually be adequate for subsistence needs without supplementation from other sources. However, despite the fact that pensions have generally more than kept pace with the rises in prices and average earnings,[7] it is clear that the level at which they have been paid has not been high enough to remove the dependence of large numbers of pensioners on means-tested assistance.[8] In 1979, just under 2 million (including pensioner wives) were dependent on supplementary benefit.[9] The fact is that the state pension by itself has not been enough to ensure a standard of living above the official poverty line – measured by the scale rates for supplementary benefit plus the rent addition.[10]

The apparent inadequacy of the flat-rate insurance benefit, together with the problems posed by the relationship between state and private occupational schemes, were the two issues which dominated discussion about retirement pensions in the 1960s and early 1970s. Moreover, the differing approaches which Labour and Conservative governments used to adopt to the right balance between state and private provision made the subject of pensions reform highly controversial. Now that the Conservatives have accepted the Social Security Pensions Act 1975, with its structure of state earnings-related pensions and contracting-out for approved occupational schemes, the debate has subsided. In fact, neither the abortive Conservative scheme embodied in the Social Security Act 1973,[11] nor the structure which came into effect in April 1978, has affected the principal conditions of eligibility for a retirement pension. The questions which have given rise to most legal difficulty, in particular the meaning of 'retirement' and the assessment of earnings for the purposes of the 'earnings rule', are the same now as they were after the passing of the National Insurance Act 1946.

The main part of this chapter involves a critical analysis of the rules and policies concerning the standard *contributory* retirement pensions, now known as Category A and Category B retirement pensions.[12] There is then a short discussion of graduated benefit, followed by an exposition of the scheme for earnings-related components to retirement pensions established by the 1975 legislation. The chapter concludes with an account of the two non-contributory pensions, Category C and Category D retirement pensions.[13]

6 Paras 233 ff.
7 See the figures in Social Security Statistics 1980, Table 46.09.
8 See ch 12, below.
9 See the Annual Report of SBC 1979, (Cmnd 8033), para 8.12.
10 An additional payment for rent is payable as part of the means-tested benefit. The Beveridge Report rejected the suggestion that a rent payment should be added to the insurance benefits, including retirement pensions.
11 The proposed scheme, which never took effect because of its immediate repeal by the Social Security (Consequential Provisions) Act 1975, is briefly discussed below, p. 192.
12 The categorisation was introduced by SSA 1973 and has been retained by the legislation now in force, SSA 1975, ss. 28, 29: see pp. 208–212, below.
13 Category C retirement pensions were introduced by the NI (Old persons' and widows' pensions and attendance allowance) Act 1970, renamed as NIA 1970 by NIA 1972, s.8(4): see p. 224, below. Category D retirement pensions were introduced by NIA 1971: see p. 225, below.

B History

i The Old Age Pensions Act 1908[14]

Pressure for the introduction of state old age pensions began in the 1870s. The pamphlets of an Anglican clergyman, the Rev William Blackley, and of Charles Booth first drew attention to the acute poverty of many old people and the inadequacy of the poor law to deal with it. The call for the introduction of some state provision was taken up by the trades union movement and the new Labour party. It also attracted a few Liberals, prominent among them being Joseph Chamberlain.[15] It was resisted, however, by the Charity Organisation Society, which constantly emphasised the unique virtues of self-help, and by the friendly societies, worried that any contributory scheme, such as that introduced in Bismarck's Germany in 1889, would hamper their own recruitment of funds.

The introduction in 1899 of a non-contributory pensions scheme in New Zealand increased interest in proposals for a state pension. The following year a Parliamentary Select Committee recommended the introduction of a means-tested scheme. Even the friendly societies were gradually won over to support non-contributory pensions to be financed by taxation; and in 1906 Asquith, then Chancellor of the Exchequer, promised to introduce old age pensions on this basis as soon as there was a budget surplus. The Old Age Pensions Act 1908 provided for a means-tested pension at a maximum of five shillings a week.[16] This was payable to anyone aged seventy on an annual income of less than £21, with a reduced pension on a sliding scale to persons with less than £31 a year. Persons who had been in receipt of poor relief for the previous two years were not entitled, nor were those who had recently been in prison or who had failed to maintain themselves and their dependants. At a time when it was more common than it is now to draw a distinction between the deserving and undeserving poor, these qualifications did not seem surprising. Payment was made, as it still is, through local post offices, but the administration was in the hands of local authority committees, assisted, where investigation of facts was necessary, by the Board of Customs and Excise.[17] Although many aspects of the scheme now appear quaint, at least the principle was established that in certain circumstances anyone over seventy was entitled to support from the state.

ii The establishment of contributory pensions[18]

The Old Age Pensions Act 1919 relaxed the means test a little and, more importantly, enabled a person on poor law relief to receive a pension.[19] But it was not long before there was more radical reform. The increasing number of pensioners imposed a large burden on the Treasury at a time

14 See in particular, the very full account in Gilbert *The Evolution of National Insurance in Great Britain* (1966) ch IV. Also see Bruce *The Coming of the Welfare State* (4th edn) pp. 173–181; Fraser *The Evolution of the British Welfare State* (1975) pp. 139–143.

15 In 1895, Chamberlain joined the Conservative government; his interest in pensions waned over the years, but he continued to support a voluntary, contributory scheme.

16 Ss.1–3, and Schedule. See *Harris* pp. 99–103.

17 The Board retained their functions with regard to the administration of non-contributory pensions until 1947: see *Bruce,* n.14, above, at p. 181. For administration of benefits, see ch 14, below, p. 539.

18 *Bruce*, n.14, above, at pp. 246–254; Gilbert *British Social Policy 1914–1939* (1970) pp. 235–254; *Fraser*, n.14, above, at pp. 189–190.

19 S.3(1).

when the government wished to reduce taxation.[20] Another factor which induced change was the more widespread acceptance of the contributory principle after its successful use in the health and unemployment insurance schemes.

The Widows', Orphans' and Old Age Contributory Pensions Act 1925,[1] for which Neville Chamberlain, then Minister of Health, was largely responsible, introduced contributory pensions for those between 65 and 70 who were covered by the health insurance scheme.[2] The additional contributions were shared equally between employer and employee. The old age pension was payable irrespective of means and the other restrictive conditions existing under the 1908 Act. At the age of seventy the pensioner received his pension under the old non-contributory scheme, without the application of a means test, which, therefore, only applied to those already in receipt of the non-contributory pension. Criticism from the Labour benches focused on the low level of the Exchequer contribution to the insurance fund.[3] But, generally, the reform was welcomed as completing the structure of insurance benefits which had been started by the pre-war Liberal government.

iii Pensions reform and the Beveridge Report

Under the 1925 Act pensions were only payable at the married couple rate when *both* spouses were over 65. Husbands with dependent wives under 65 only received a single person's pension. This created an anomaly if, immediately before he reached 65, the husband had been in receipt of unemployment benefit, because then he would also have received an additional payment for his dependent wife. The couple would thus become worse off when the husband reached pensionable age unless his wife was also 65. In response, therefore, to considerable pressure, particularly from women's organisations, the Old Age and Widows' Pensions Act 1940 reduced the pensionable age for women from 65 to 60.[4] This applied whether the claim was brought by an insured woman in her own right or for the wife of an insured pensioner. The change was in accordance with the position in a number of the Dominions, such as Australia and New Zealand,[5] and it increased from 28 per cent to 63 per cent the proportion of cases in which the married couple pension rate was payable on the husband attaining pensionable age.[6] The only criticism of the measure was that it did not go far enough. Some MPs argued with the National Spinsters' Association that the pensionable age for women should be reduced to 55.[7] However, the discrepancy between the relevant ages for men and women has recently given rise to considerable controversy; it is arguable that in a laudable attempt to remove one anomaly, the 1940 Act created more serious problems than it solved.

The other change during the Second World War which should be mentioned here is the availability from 1940 of supplementary pensions administered by the Assistance Board.[8] Pensioners whose means did not equal their basic requirements could supplement their pensions from the

20 See *Bruce,* n.14, above, at p. 246.
1 Ss.1(1)(c) and 7–8.
2 This had been introduced by NIA 1911: see ch 4, above, p. 137.
3 See *Bruce,* n.14, above, at pp. 252–253.
4 S.1(1).
5 357 HC Official Report (5th series) col 2148.
6 357 HC Official Report (5th series) col 1198.
7 Ibid, cols 1269 and 2142.
8 See ch 12, p. 452, below, for a discussion of this aspect of the history of supplementary benefits.

Board's funds rather than have recourse as previously to the poor law authorities. The numbers of people who applied for the new form of assistance showed how inadequate their pensions were.[9]

But the most important aspect of this period was the discussion in the Beveridge Report and the adoption (for the most part) of its recommendations in the National Insurance Act 1946. The Report drew attention to the reasons why old age pensions present particular difficulties: first, old age far exceeds in importance all other causes of inability to earn and to maintain a reasonable standard of living; secondly, the economic and social consequences of old age vary considerably from person to person.[10] Thus, although the frequent recourse to supplementary pensions showed that for many the pension was inadequate, the fact that, at the start of the war, about one-third of all persons over 65 did not receive either a state pension or any form of public assistance revealed that some were able to manage on their own resources.

Beveridge argued that it would be prohibitively expensive for the state to pay everyone on reaching 65 (or 60) a subsistence income sufficient to remove the necessity to apply for assistance.[11] For this reason, he recommended that the payment of pensions should be made conditional on the claimant's retirement from regular employment. The Report made it clear that the purpose of this condition was not to encourage early retirement from work, but to reduce the cost of the state pensions scheme. Those able to remain at work were to be encouraged to do so by the promise of an increment to the pension to be paid on their eventual retirement. It was envisaged that more people over 65 would remain at work, though this expectation has not been fulfilled.[12] Beveridge also proposed that full pensions should not be payable immediately, but should be phased in gradually over a 20-year period to allow the National Insurance Fund to accumulate.[13] For obvious political reasons, the new Labour government decided to introduce the full rate immediately, a step which dramatically increased the cost and led to the reforms of the late 1950s.[14]

The National Insurance Act 1946 adopted the Beveridge scheme of retirement pensions and increments for postponed retirement, supported by an earnings rule designed to prevent evasion of the retirement condition.[15] There were two respects in which the Act was more generous than both the previous law and Beveridge's proposals. First, a pensioner with a wife under 60 was now entitled to claim a dependant's allowance for her; this had the effect of equating his pension to that payable to a married couple, both of whom were of pensionable age. This change, however, removed one of the arguments put forward for the lowering of the pensionable age for women in 1940.[16] Secondly, the Beveridge retirement condition was not to be applied to men over 70 or women over 65, who were thus entitled to full pension no matter to what extent they worked, a modification urged by a number of small traders.[17]

9 *Bruce*, n.14, above, at p. 294.

10 Paras 233–235.

11 Para 244. *Harris* pp. 394, 412.

12 Para 255; see p. 216, below.

13 Para 241. *Harris* pp. 411–412.

14 Shenfield *Social Policies for Old Age* (1957) p. 98.

15 The reasons for these particular rules are considered in more detail at the relevant parts of the chapter: see pp. 197 and 212, below.

16 P. 190, above.

17 Mr J Griffiths, Minister of Pensions and NI., 418 HC Official Report (5th series) cols 1733 ff.

iv The move towards earnings-related pensions

Under the Beveridge proposals, retirement pensions, like the other contributory benefits, were to be flat-rate. This principle was maintained rigorously until the late 1950s. In 1958 the government proposed a graduated pensions scheme, under which earnings-related contributions and benefits would be paid in addition to the flat-rate provisions.[18] The principal purpose of the scheme was to supplement through graduated contributions the National Insurance Fund which was seriously in deficit and, for this reason, the additional benefits were not generous.[19] Contracting-out was permitted on condition that the contracted-out employee enjoyed rights under his occupational scheme at least as good as those available under the state graduated scheme. In practice only higher paid earners, who were members of the better endowed occupational schemes, contracted out.[20] A major disadvantage of the new scheme was that the earnings-related addition was not inflation-proof; any attempt at this would have had serious repercussions on the occupational schemes because the contracting-out provisions would in effect have required them also to protect their members against inflation.

The Labour party has often disliked contracting-out on the ground that it may permit the higher-paid to bear a disproportionately small burden of the costs of national insurance. In any case, when earnings-related supplements to short-term benefits were introduced in 1966, no contracting-out was allowed. Everyone had to pay the supplementary graduated contributions used to finance *both* the short-term benefits *and* the addition to the existing graduated pension.[1] Three years later, the Labour government published proposals for radical reform, in particular the introduction of earnings-related pensions at 42½ per cent of male average earnings.[2] Lower paid employees' pensions would be more generous, so the proposals involved a substantial element of redistribution. Most importantly, the scheme based pensions on average lifetime earnings, revalued in line with changes in national earnings, so that the pension was in effect not only inflation-proof but geared to rising living standards. Contracting-out from part of the superannuation scheme was to be permitted. However, before the Bill became law, the government was defeated at the 1970 election, and it became the Conservatives' turn to attempt reform of retirement pensions.

Their proposals at least reached the statute book, but were never implemented. The distinctive characteristic of this scheme, embodied in the Social Security Act 1973, was the emphasis on the role of occupational pension schemes in supplementing the basic state pension.[3] The basic pension was to be financed by earnings-related contributions from employee (collected through PAYE) and employer, the latter being required to pay more than the former.[4] The Exchequer contribution was to remain at about 18 per cent of the total employee and emloyer contribu-

18 Provision for Old Age: The Future Development of the National Insurance Scheme (1958, Cmnd 638): see pp. 40–43, above, for the history of contributions.
19 For a discussion of graduated pensions, see pp. 218–219, below.
20 For a criticism of the graduated pensions scheme, see *Walley* ch XI, *passim*.
1 NIA 1966, ss.1–4.
2 White Paper, National Superannuation and Social Insurance: Proposals for Earnings-Related Social Security (1969, Cmnd 3883). The proposals are summarised in *Kaim-Caudle* p. 171.
3 See the White Paper, Strategy for Pensions (1971, Cmnd 4755), esp. paras 23–28.
4 The employer's contribution was 7.25% of the employee's PAYE earnings, the employee's contribution being 5.25%.

tions. In most other respects, the provision for a basic retirement pension did not differ from that which has been made since 1946. Occupational pension schemes had to satisfy a new administrative body, the Occupational Pensions Board, on various matters. The main conditions related to the level of benefits – a weekly pension of not less than 1 per cent of total earnings in each year of pensionable employment and some protection of its value against inflation.[5] Employees who did not belong to a recognised occupational scheme were to be required, with their employers, to contribute to the state reserve scheme, which was to be organised by an independent Board of Management. Pensions under this scheme were not to be made conditional on retirement nor subject to an earnings rule. These two interdependent features are not generally to be found in occupational schemes, and were, therefore, thought inappropriate for a state reserve scheme modelled on such arrangements.[6]

The Conservative government's preference for occupational schemes was shown by the fact that, while tax relief for contributions to occupational schemes continued, those to the state reserve scheme were not to be tax deductible.[7] To a large extent it was envisaged that eventually the reserve scheme would cater only for those who worked in lower paid employment, (where the employers could not satisfy the conditions laid down by the Pensions Board), and for those temporarily waiting to become members of an occupational scheme.[8] Some critics, however, thought the reserve scheme might be sufficiently attractive to discourage younger people from joining occupational schemes.[9] On the other hand, older contributors would have fared poorly in the state reserve scheme, as there was, unusually for British schemes, no element of subsidy from the younger to the older generations. It was partly for this reason and partly because of the absence of guaranteed inflation-proofing that the Labour government, which took office in 1974, decided not to use the Conservatives' state reserve scheme as the basis for its own plans for an earnings-related pension.

The Labour scheme, which replaced the provisions embodied in the Social Security Act 1973,[10] was introduced in the White Paper, 'Better Pensions'.[11] This reversed the relationship between the state and occupational schemes in the previous government's legislation. Now occupational schemes must follow for the most part the standards set by the state scheme for contracting-out to be allowed. Indeed, the government considered an arrangement, common in European countries, under which private pensions merely 'topped up' the state provisions, instead of permitting contracting-out.[12] But recent improvements in private pension schemes made this drastic step unnecessary. The details of the new state scheme are considered later in this chapter.[13]

5 See Cmnd 4755, paras 57–62, for the conditions of recognitions by the Occupational Pensions Board.
6 Ibid, at para 73.
7 Ibid, at paras 70 and 72.
8 Ibid, at para 77.
9 *Walley* pp. 168–176; for a more critical view of the Conservative proposals, see Titmuss *Social Policy* (1974) pp. 102–120.
10 The relevant provisions of the 1973 Act were repealed by the Social Security (Consequential Provisions) Act 1975, s.3
11 (1974), Cmnd 5713.
12 Ibid, para 56. See *Kaim-Caudle* ch VI, for a survey of some European systems.
13 Pp. 219–224, below.

Part 2 Entitlement to a retirement pension

In this Part of the chapter the conditions of entitlement to a retirement pension, as laid down now in the Social Security Act 1975, are set out. Generally, they have not been altered by the reform of the pensions system except for the contribution requirements where major changes have been made, in particular in their application to married women.[14] Most of these conditions, therefore, apply to eligibility for both the flat-rate basic component of the contributory pension and the newer earnings-related component introduced by the 1975 reforms; the special rules relating to the latter are set out in Part 5 of the chapter.

A Pensionable age

i Policy

The first condition of eligibility for a retirement pension (Category A or Category B)[15] is that the claimant has attained pensionable age.[16] 'Pensionable age' is 65 for men and 60 for women.[17] The lower age for women dates from 1940, when the war-time government made the change under pressure from women's organisations. The principal object was to enable the typical married couple, where the husband was 65 and the wife a few years younger, to draw the full married couple's pension.[18] However, this reason can no longer support the distinction, since a dependant's allowance for a wife of any age has been paid to a retired husband over 65 since the National Insurance Act 1946. The allowance raises the husband's total pension to the sum payable to a married couple both of whom are over pensionable age.[19]

In the last 20 years the difference between the pensionable ages for men and women has become increasingly controversial. Even if they were the same, women would draw pensions on average for considerably longer than men, because of their greater life expectancy.[20] The moves towards sexual equality as expressed in the Equal Pay Act 1970 and the Sex Discrimination Act 1975 reinforce dissatisfaction with the difference. The question was first considered by the Committee on the Economic and Financial Problems of the Provision for Old Age in 1954.[1] It concluded that though in principle there was much to be said for the restoration of the age parity which had existed before 1940, the savings achieved by a raising of the pensionable age for women would be small. Moreover, because of the introduction of the dependant's allowance by the 1946 legislation, any increase would for the most part only affect unmarried women.[2] A dissent from this view was expressed by Dr (now Dame) Janet Vaughan – the sole woman member of the Committee – who thought the change should be made for reasons of principle. More recently, the various courses by which equality of pensionable age might be achieved were considered by the Equal Opportunities Commission (EOC), the body set up under the Sex

14 See pp. 208–211, below.
15 The categories of retirement pensions are discussed below, pp. 208–212.
16 SSA 1975, ss. 28, 29.
17 Ibid, s.27(1).
18 See p. 190, above.
19 The amounts payable for Category A and B retirement pensions are set out below, p. 212.
20 See the figures given in the DHSS Memorandum *Pension Age* (1976) para 1.
1 Cmd 9333 (the 'Phillips Committee').
2 Ibid, at para 193.

Discrimination Act 1975.[3] Although it did not come to any firm conclusions on any of the alternative approaches, it thought that, with suitable transitional arrangements to protect the expectations of existing women contributors, it would not be politically impossible to raise the female pensionable age to 65.[4]

Other proposals to equalise the pensionable ages have included the suggestion that that for men should be reduced to 60; a Private Member's Bill to this effect was introduced in 1976.[5] It was strongly resisted by the government on the ground of the extra costs it would entail – about £1,700 million a year.[6] Against this it could be contended that the withdrawal of men between 60 and 65 from the labour market would ease unemployment, and that there would be consequent savings in sickness and unemployment benefit. It was estimated in 1976 that this might reduce the cost of the reform by about a third to £1,000 million.[7] A third approach, also considered by the EOC in its discussion paper, would be to reduce the pensionable age for men to 64½ and raise that for women to 60½ and then gradually work to the position where everyone would draw a retirement pension at 62½.[8] In its recent White Paper, Growing Older, the government thought this change might be acceptable, provided a considerable period of notice were given.[9]

It does seem hard to defend the distinction in pensionable ages on other than political grounds. Many countries do not draw it, e.g. France, Germany, the Netherlands, Ireland, Canada and the United States, though some do, e.g. Austria, Belgium and Australia.[10] Sometimes the special position of single women is recognised: in Denmark, a pension is payable in this case at 62, as compared with a pensionable age of 67 for men and married women,[11] while in New Zealand, the age pension may be payable to a single woman of 55 who is unable to work because of her ill-health.[12] A comparison with other countries, therefore, shows that there is no insuperable objection in principle to the payment of pensions at a common pensionable age, but it may, of course, be more difficult to make the change to this position when women have been accustomed to more favourable treatment. Nevertheless, it is hoped that parity will gradually be achieved, even though the economic arguments make immediate reform unlikely.

Connected with this issue is the question whether there should continue to be a fixed retirement age, beneath which no pension at all is payable, or whether there should be a system of flexible retirement. Under this alternative, the full pension would be payable at a 'normal' retirement age, say, 63 for both men and women if parity is achieved, but a reduced

3 *Sex Equality and the Pension Age* (1976).
4 Ibid, at pp. 18–20. Jersey has done this successfully.
5 The Bill was introduced by Mr G Janner, 906 HC Official Report (5th series) col 1321.
6 See the Memorandum submitted by the DHSS to the EOC, n.20, above, at para 22.
7 Ibid, at para 26. Also see *Growing Older* (1981, Cmnd 8173), para 3.9.
8 N.3, above, at pp. 20–21. The DHSS Memorandum, n.20, above, at paras 36–37 pointed out in 1976 that the cost of an immediate common pensionable age of 62½ would be about £700 million – this is because there are relatively few women who receive pensions on their own contributions record, and consequently there would be little saving in raising their pensionable age to 62½.
9 N.7, above, at para 3.11.
10 *Kaim-Caudle* pp. 191–192. *Growing Older*, n.7, above, at para 3.8. For France, see Lynes *French Pensions*, Occasional Papers on Social Administration (1967) and *Dupeyroux* pp. 473–475.
11 *Kaim-Caudle* p. 148.
12 New Zealand Social Security Act, 1964, s.16.

pension would be paid to anyone who left, or substantially reduced, his work at a lower age, say 60.[13] This idea has clear attractions. Quite apart from the choice it gives individuals, it takes account of the undoubted fact that working ability remains unimpaired in certain occupations longer than in others, particularly industrial and manual work. Largely for these reasons, the Conservative and Liberal parties and the CBI supported the proposal in their evidence to the EOC. And such schemes have been introduced in other countries, notably France, West Germany and Sweden.[14] But there are considerable disadvantages which led the EOC to conclude that a flexible retirement scheme was not 'as attractive as at first appears'.[15] In particular, such a system would be expensive: the state would lose social security contributions and have to pay out pensions earlier. Consequently the rate at which pensions were paid to those who opted for early retirement would be very low, and the choice would therefore be attractive only to those with substantial occupational pensions. Alternatively, if as in Sweden a reduced pension was payable only to a claimant who continued to work 17 hours a week, much would depend on the willingness of employers to engage older employees on a part-time basis. And there would have to be an earnings rule to prevent persons with substantial earnings receiving a partial pension as a supplement to their salary.[16]

At a time of high unemployment it is hardly surprising that the TUC and the Labour party prefer to support the proposal that the pensionable age for men should be reduced to 60.[17] Not only is there the argument from parity with women; it can also be contended that pensions are not now seen, as perhaps they used to be, as primarily compensation for a total inability to earn, but are regarded as income earned by the retired to enable them to enjoy the last 20 years or so of their life in comfort. But such a step seems ruled out, at least for the moment, by its considerable expense. The present Conservative government seems anxious to keep a common pensionable age and a flexible retirement system as long-term aims; these objectives may become more feasible if the economic situation improves and also as the level of earnings-related pensions rises during the next 15 years.[18] Further proposals may be made by the Commons Select Committee on Social Services which studied all aspects of the retirement age during the 1981–82 session.

ii The law

In two recent cases the issue has arisen whether the claimant is a 'man' or a 'woman' for the purpose of determining pensionable age under section 27 of the Social Security Act 1975. In the first,[19] the applicant argued that, although born a male, she had been issued with a woman's national insurance card in her adopted female name after she had received medical therapy, and, therefore, had been led to believe she would be treated as a woman for pension purposes. The Chief Commissioner, however, concluded that as the claimant remained biologically male, no pension could

13 See the EOC paper, n.3, above, at pp. 9–13, and 21–2.
14 See *Growing Older*, n.7, above, at para 3.6. For France, see *Dupeyroux* pp. 473–474.
15 N.3, above, at p. 22.
16 *Growing Older* n.7, above, at para 3.12.
17 EOC paper, n.3, above, at p. 8.
18 Growing Older, n.7, above, at para 3.13.
19 *R(P) 1/80*.

be paid until the age of 65 was reached; the extra-statutory issue of a woman's national insurance card could not raise an estoppel binding the statutory authorities.[1] The same result was reached in *R(P) 2/80*, where the Commissioner was faced with a more powerful argument for treating the claimant as a woman: she contended that under section 27 what was important was the applicant's social rather than biological role, since as a woman she would be expected to retire at 60 and therefore the award of a pension would then be appropriate. This ingenious contention was rightly rejected, first, on the ground that the relevant sections of the 1975 Act indicate that a 'woman' is someone capable of forming a valid marriage with a husband,[2] and secondly, there was no evidence that Parliament ever intended to make more favourable provision for women because in practice they retired earlier than men.[3]

There are few other legal difficulties concerning the age condition. Generally the claimant will prove his age by reference to his birth certificate, though a population census has been accepted as providing satisfactory evidence.[4] In an important case in which the applicant was a Pakistani immigrant from a district where there had been at the relevant time no register of births, it was held that documentary evidence is not the only method of proof to establish the claimant's age; medical evidence is admissible.[5] The Commissioner pointed out that sometimes in this situation unsatisfactory documentary evidence is tendered out of a desire to improve the case or to please the authorities, and that this should not prejudice the applicant's argument where there is other evidence that it is well-founded.

It might seem that a retirement pension should be payable from the exact date the claimant reaches 65 (or 60), (assuming the retirement condition is satisfied), and the Social Security Act 1975 certainly states that a claimant is entitled to retirement pension on reaching pensionable age.[6] But the Claims and Payments Regulations provide that benefit is only to commence from a Thursday.[7] The result is that entitlement to pension starts on the Thursday following the claimant's birthday, rather than on the day when the claimant reaches pensionable age. In *R(P) 2/73* it was regarded as far-fetched to argue that the regulation was unreasonable and, therefore, ultra vires in that it 'discriminated' against certain claimants in respect of the date of their birth.[8]

B The retirement condition

i Policy

The second condition for entitlement to a pension is the feature which is the most characteristic of the British pensions system — the retirement condition, introduced by the 1946 legislation after the recommendation in the Beveridge Report.[9] In order for a man to obtain a pension between 65

1 The Chief Comr, R J A Temple, doubted the use of the estoppel doctrine in *Robertson v Minister of Pensions* [1949] 1 KB 227, [1949] 2 All ER 767: see p. 564, below.
2 SSA 1975, ss.28–9.
3 For the origins of the lower pensionable age for women, see p. 190, above.
4 *CP 11/49*.
5 *R(P) 1/75*, R J A Temple, Comr.
6 SSA 1975, ss. 28, 29.
7 SI 1979/628, reg 16(6). This point is more fully discussed in the chapter on Administration of benefits, p. 571, below.
8 Per H A Shewan, Comr. See also *R(P) 16/52*.
9 P. 191, above.

and 70, or for a woman to obtain one between 60 and 65, he (or she) must show that he (or she) has retired from regular employment. As has been explained earlier, the object of the requirement is to reduce pensions expenditure by making provision only for those who are not working. Those who are able to carry on working are encouraged to do so by the prospect of an increment to their pension when it is eventually payable – in any case not later than 70 (or 65 in the case of a woman), when the retirement condition is no longer applicable.[10] It must, therefore, be seen in conjunction with the provision for increments to pensions for deferred retirement and also together with the earnings rule. This latter rule is designed to prevent the evasion of the retirement condition which would otherwise be possible if the claimant left employment on attaining pensionable age, and then resumed full-time work shortly after obtaining his pension.

Britain is almost alone in imposing a retirement condition on claimants below a certain age. None of the continental European countries does so, nor does Australia or New Zealand.[11] The earnings-related scheme in Canada, introduced in 1965, does impose a retirement condition, but the basic provision under the earlier Old Age Security Acts does not.[12] In the United States, the principal scheme under the Social Security Acts assumes a retirement condition,[13] and it does this indirectly by the imposition of a very low earnings limit, which makes retirement in fact, if not in law, a necessary condition for making a claim.

Rather surprisingly the retirement condition has attracted comparatively little criticism, though, as will be seen, the earnings rule which complements it has often been challenged.[14] The Phillips Committee in 1954 did not find support for the abolition of the retirement condition.[15] The reasons for this general acceptance of the change from old-age pensions to retirement pensions are hard to state accurately. It may be suggested, however, that one explanation lies in the general move towards earlier retirement; fewer and fewer people remain at work after reaching the age of 65 (or 60, in the case of women).[16] This, of course, may itself be influenced by the retirement condition, but the trend is probably partly attributable to cultural and social factors, and partly to the expansion of occupational schemes providing benefits on the person's retirement. Moreover many employers, particularly during times of high unemployment, automatically retire their employees when they reach pensionable age. A second explanation for the absence of strong criticism may be that the condition has been very liberally interpreted by the Commissioners, so that it is possible to do a substantial amount of part-time work without losing entitlement to the state pension. This has been particularly true since the addition in 1960 of the alternative rule that an applicant may be treated as retired if his earnings are not expected to exceed those stated in the earnings rule.[17]

10 SSA 1975, s.27(5).
11 *Kaim-Caudle* ch VI *passim*.
12 Ibid, at pp. 175–183.
13 See Appendix VI to the Phillips Committee Report (Cmd 9333), and the discussion by Shenfield, *Social Policies for Old Age* (1957), pp. 111–113.
14 See pp. 212–214, below.
15 N.13, above, at para 195.
16 George *Social Security and Society* (1973) pp. 109–114. Figures supporting this observation are given in the DHSS Memorandum to the EOC, *Pension Age* (1976) at para 16. Also see The Earnings Rule for Retirement Pensioners, 1978, HC 697, App 3.
17 The change was made by the NIA 1960, s.3: see pp. 206–207, below.

Nevertheless it may still be argued that to some extent the retirement condition does discourage people able and willing to do so from working. The alternative of part-time work, particularly in industry, may be virtually impossible to secure. It can also be added that occupational and civil service pensions do not generally impose a condition of retirement from all work, and in this way the rule discriminates against those wholly reliant on their state pension.[18] In the last few years both Labour and Conservative governments have indicated their willingness to consider abolition of the retirement condition, together with the earnings rule which is necessary to support it, when financial circumstances permit.[19] But the review of the earnings rule undertaken in 1978 did not envisage this step as a high priority in view of the additional expenditure it would involve,[20] and in the present economic climate reform is very unlikely. The Conservative government is probably more willing to contemplate abolition as a long-term goal, perhaps as one aspect of a change to a flexible retirement scheme: under this, men and women would probably be able to receive a full pension at the 'normal' pensionable age without giving up work, but of course if they wished to claim a reduced pension earlier, they would probably be required to retire from full-time work – and this would need to be supported by an earnings rule.[1]

ii The law: general provision

The legal requirement of 'retirement' is exacted by sections 28(1) and 29 of the Social Security Act 1975; it is that the person concerned 'has retired from regular employment'.[2] The term 'retirement' is not defined as such in the legislation, but section 27(3) sets out certain circumstances in which a person is to be *treated* as retired from regular employment; in practice it is the construction and interpretation of this subsection (and its predecessors) which have occupied the attention of the Commissioners. It is worth setting out its principal terms:

> . . . a person may . . . be treated as having retired from regular employment at any time after he has attained pensionable age —
> (a) whether or not he has previously been an earner;
> (b) notwithstanding that he is, or intends to be, an earner, if —
> (i) he is or intends to be so only occasionally or to an inconsiderable extent, or otherwise in circumstances not inconsistent with retirement, or
> (ii) his earnings can be expected not to exceed, or only occasionally to exceed, the amount any excess over which would, under section 30(1) below (earnings rule), involve a reduction of the weekly rate of his pension;. . . .

It will be seen that a person may be treated as retired, despite the fact that he is earning or intends to be earning in employment, if one of four conditions is satisfied.[3] Most of the reported decisions on retirement pensions have concerned the satisfaction of these requirements. However,

18 See Shenfield, n.13, above.
19 Mr D Ennals, Secretary of State, 921 HC Official Report (5th series) col 1175; for the present government's position, see *Growing Older* (1981, Cmnd. 8173), at para 3.4.
20 The Earnings Rule for Retirement Pensioners, n.16, above, at p. 25.
1 *Growing Older*, n.19, above, at para 3.12. For the connection of the retirement condition and the earnings rule, see pp. 212–214, below.
2 SSA 1975, ss.28(1) and 29. See *Micklethwait* p. 116, where it is argued that the formulation should be: 'is retired'. The point is discussed p. 202, below.
3 See *Micklethwait* p. 116, where it is contended that it would be a drafting improvement to enumerate the four conditions, instead of dealing with them in just two subparagraphs.

before they are considered, some general remarks should be made about the meaning of 'retirement'.

a *There is no necessity that the person has been employed at some time*
The notion of 'retirement' strongly suggests that the claimant must have been employed and then have given up his work. This will almost always be the case. But section 27(3)(a) makes it clear that this need not be so, although, of course, a person who has not been working may not have paid contributions for entitlement to a Category A retirement pension.[4] But a woman may be eligible for a Category B pension on the basis of her husband's contributions, and she may well not have worked before her 'retirement'.

b *There is no necessity for the person to have retired in consequence of reaching pensionable age*
In order to claim a retirement pension (Categories A and B) the claimant must show that he or she has retired and has reached pensionable age. But the two events need not be connected. Thus, in *CP 70/50* the claimant, the owner of a ladies hairdressers, gave up regular work in this business when she was 52; since then she had only worked a few hours a week. When she reached 60, she claimed a pension, and it was held that she was entitled to it, although she had not retired in consequence of attaining pensionable age.

c *The meaning of 'employment'*
The claimant must show that he has retired from 'regular employment'. In Schedule 20 to the 1975 Act, 'employment' is defined to include 'any trade, business, profession, office or vocation'.[5] This confirms the wide meaning given to the notion of 'employment' by the Commissioner. In *CP 7/49*

> A convent Sister was compelled by persistent arthritis to give up full-time work, and did only very light work such as writing letters and arranging flowers for one or two hours a day.

It was held that the Sister was in 'employment', as this concept covered a vocation, including a religious vocation.[6] The fact that the claimant was not rewarded in cash, but by way of free board and lodging did not matter, since payment in kind constitutes remuneration for work and, therefore, an indication that the claimant is 'engaged in a gainful occupation' (the term used in the 1946 Act), or as the present Act formulates it in section 27(3)(b), 'is, or intends to be, an earner'. Further, in *R(P) 2/76*, R J A Temple, the Chief Commissioner, held that a city councillor in receipt of attendance allowances was pursuing a gainful occupation and, therefore, had not retired. It did not matter that he was not 'employed' in the narrow sense of being under a contract of service or for services.

'Employment' includes employment under a contract for services, so that a claimant who continued after pensionable age to live with an old friend as a paid companion was held not to have retired.[7] It was said in this case that it might have been different if the claimant were living with a near

4 For contribution conditions for Category A and B retirement pensions, see pp. 208–209, below.
5 See on this pp. 45–51, above.
6 Cp *R(P) 7/54*, where it was held that membership of a purely devotional religious community did not constitute 'employment'.
7 *CP 21/49*.

relative, and the money was paid as a gratuity out of affection. However in *R(P) 3/52*, the claimant gave up full-time work in order to look after her brother-in-law and his mentally deficient daughter in return for free board and lodging. The Commissioner awarded her a pension, but only on the ground that her employment was 'in circumstances not inconsistent with retirement'. It would appear, therefore, that the suggestion in the earlier case that work for a close relative would not constitute 'employment' is wrong.

It is not exactly clear how relevant the fact that the claimant continues to earn is to the question whether he has retired from regular employment. The provision (section 27(3)(b)) that a person may be treated as retired in certain circumstances, notwithstanding that he continues to earn, implies that normally the receipt of such earnings is incompatible with retirement. In some cases, the Commissioner appears to have drawn this inference: thus, in *R(P) 7/52*, the claimant who continued to work his farm, albeit on a reduced scale, for the purposes of making a living (rather than as a pure hobby) was held not to have retired.[8] Moreover, the fact that the earnings or profits are very low does not mean that the claimant is not continuing in employment.[9]

But in a few cases the Commissioner does not appear to have put so much weight on the fact of continued earnings, and has looked more at the nature and amount of the work done by the claimant after the alleged retirement in order to determine whether he has in fact retired. This was the approach adopted in a case where a former coal-dealer let out four properties at a substantial rent; as he performed no work in connection with this, his income did not preclude a holding that he had retired.[10] This is surely correct in that it could not be said that the claimant was 'engaged in a gainful occupation', though his income from letting out his property was much the same as it would have been had he been engaged in running a property business. However, in *R(P) 19/56*, where the claimant was a partner with his son in a dairy business, but performed only very light duties after reaching pensionable age, it was held that he could not be treated as retired. The Commissioner said:

> In determining whether the claimant was at the relevant time retired, I therefore take into account not only the evidence as to his activities, but also the circumstance that he was a partner, and the circumstance that his financial return from the venture in which he was a partner was a substantial one.[11]

It appears that the extent of the financial return and the nature of the work done by the claimant are both relevant in determining whether or not he has retired.[12]

d *The claimant's intentions for the future*

The mere fact that the claimant is not working at the time of his alleged retirement is not by itself enough to show that he has retired from regular

8 It was, moreover, held that his work was inconsistent with retirement, so he could not take advantage of the third condition in s.27(3)(b)(i); cp *R(P) 6/53*.
9 Though it may mean that the 'earnings' condition is applicable: see p. 206, below.
10 *CP 129/50*, and see *R(P) 16/56* for the same approach, though with a different result.
11 It was said that the result would have been different if the claimant had been merely a shareholder in a farming enterprise. (See also *R(P) 9/56*.)
12 'Earnings' are defined by SSA 1975, s.3, as including any remuneration or profit derived from an employment. This is perfectly compatible with the submission in the text. Similar questions arise with regard to the computation of earnings: pp. 404–408, below.

employment. The retirement must be final and intended to be permanent.[13] From the Act itself it would appear that the absence of any intention to earn in the future is enough;[14] but it may be that the insurance officer requires the claimant to show a positive intention not to work,[15] and the cases are not inconsistent with this view. An illusory intention to resume work will not, however, preclude a finding of retirement: thus, when a miner entertained hopes of working again, though this was impossible because of his injuries, it was held that he had retired from employment.[16] The opposite decision was reached when a claimant had a reasonable expectation of resuming work.[17] It is quite irrelevant for this purpose that at the time concerned the claimant is actually doing little or no work.[18]

It is arguable that the requirement that the applicant does not intend to earn in the future (however interpreted) is virtually impossible to apply, and that the only relevant criterion should be whether he is working at the time when he claims a retirement pension. This might be the appropriate test if the law required only that the person *is* retired.[19] But the legislation demands that the claimant *has* retired. The requirement would be too easy to evade – by a temporary cessation of work at 65 (or 60) – if the claimant's future intentions were ignored altogether. The present position, however, does lead to the odd result that a person who has abandoned work at 65 and subsequently changes his mind and resumes work is entitled to receive a retirement pension,[20] while a person out of work at 65, but open-minded about the possibility of taking on work later, is not so entitled.[1] It seems unfortunate that this anomaly has not been corrected in any of the many pensions reforms since the war.

iii The law – 'Treated as retired'

The most frequent source of legal difficulty has been whether to *treat* a claimant who is working, and intends to continue to work, part-time as retired. Section 27(3)(b) of the 1975 Act (set out on page 199) provides that a claimant may be treated as retired if one of four alternative conditions is satisfied. The first three of these have existed unamended since the 1946 legislation. The fourth – the 'earnings' condition, as it is generally known – was added by the National Insurance Act 1960. In practice it is this fourth condition which is the most easily satisfied by claimants: provided it can be shown that his earnings from part-time work are not expected generally to exceed the amount permitted by the earnings rule (now £57), the person concerned will be treated as retired.[2] The other three conditions will, therefore, only be relevant if the applicant cannot satisfy this requirement, because his earnings are unusually high. They are

13 See *141/49 (P)* where there is a full treatment of this point by the Northern Ireland Commissioner.
14 S.27(3)(b).
15 *Calvert* p. 271.
16 *CP 49/49.*
17 *R(P) 8/51* and see *R(P) 8/52.*
18 *R(P) 10/53.*
19 This has been suggested as more desirable by *Micklethwait* p. 116
20 His pension may, of course, be reduced or extinguished by the earnings rule: pp. 212–215, below
1 The anomaly is substantially lessened by the introduction of the earnings proviso, now SSA 1975, s.27(3)(b)(ii): see p. 206, below. Moreover, if he is genuinely available for work, he may be entitled to unemployment benefit at the retirement pension rate: SSA 1975, s.14(6); see p. 135, above.
2 For the earnings rule, see pp. 212–215, below.

as a result relatively unimportant, as is evidenced by the fact that the number of reported decisions on these provisions has sharply declined since 1960. However, the case-law on the interpretation of the three conditions in section 27(3)(b)(i) is extremely interesting and, as it may still occasionally be significant,[3] it merits some treatment before the 'earnings' condition is discussed.

It might have been thought that these three conditions – earning 'only occasionally or to an inconsiderable extent, or otherwise in circumstances not inconsistent with retirement' – would bear distinct meanings. But in fact they have been so construed that there is considerable overlap between them.

a *An earner 'only occasionally'*

There does not appear to be any recent reported case in which this condition has been applied. Indeed, it is arguable that it is otiose in that occasional work is merely the opposite of 'regular employment'; someone who works 'only occasionally' has, it might be submitted, left regular employment and, therefore, satisfied the retirement condition. The Commissioner's approach seems consistent with this. In *CP 33/49* it was held that a school meals attendant, employed for 12½ hours a week during term-time, was not working 'only occasionally'; her employment was regular. Similarly, someone employed as a chair collector in the holiday months was not considered to be working only occasionally.[4] The seasonal nature of the work was discounted. Perhaps the most marginal case was *R(P) 16/55*. There a shop assistant working two full days (and a total of 16 hours) a week did not satisfy this condition.[5] The Commissioner said that a claimant is not working 'only occasionally' when he 'works regularly at fixed recurring weekly periods, and not merely now and then or as occasion requires'. In the most recent case, the Commissioner decided that an author was not engaged in his occupation only occasionally, as he proposed to rely on his writing as one source of income.[6]

b *An earner 'to an inconsiderable extent'*

This exception also is now of very little importance. The leading modern authority is *CP 33/49*, where a school meals attendant worked 12½ hours a week after reaching pensionable age. The Commissioner upheld the '12 hour rule', formulated by the Umpire in construing the identical provision in the earlier Contributory Pensions Regulations of 1946.[7] This stated that the claimant was engaged in a gainful occupation to an inconsiderable extent if he was working for not more than 12 hours a week, or (if more) less than one quarter of the normal working hours of a week for the relevant occupation. It was further decided that the hours have to be considered in relation to the normal working months of the trade in question: it was, therefore, wrong for the claimant to contend that, averaged out over the whole year, her working week was less then twelve hours. She was accordingly not treated as retired. The application of the rule can be illustrated by reference to two cases in the same year: in the first,[8] a convent Sister whose light duties came to no more than one or two hours a

3 As in *R(P) 2/76*: p. 205, below.
4 *R(P) 8/52*.
5 But the third condition was applied, so the applicant was treated as retired.
6 *R(P) 1/60*; also see *R(P) 2/53*.
7 Reported Decision UP 4/47, construing SR & O 1946/1508, reg 10(1).
8 *CP 7/49*.

day was treated as retired under this condition, while in the second,[9] a paid companion whose duties took up at least 24 hours a week was held not to be in a gainful occupation to an inconsiderable extent.

It might be thought that the Commissioner would take account of the actual work done by the claimant, rather than his attendance at the place of work in determining whether he is engaged in a gainful occupation to an inconsiderable extent.[10] But in *CP 126/49*, where a woman was put on 3½ hours a day light work after straining her heart, it was decided that the fact that she was not required to work for all these hours was irrelevant. Nor are low earnings indicative of employment to an inconsiderable extent.[11] Now that the earnings condition has been introduced, the point is an academic one, but it is suggested that as the second condition has been drafted since 1965 in terms of an *earner* to an inconsiderable extent, the amount of the claimant's earnings might well be considered relevant.

c *An earner 'otherwise in circumstances not inconsistent with retirement'*

This third condition produced a large number of cases until the early 1960s when the earnings condition was introduced. It is arguable that the use of the word '*otherwise*', following the first and second conditions, suggests that the frequency of, and the hours worked in, the claimant's part-time employment are irrelevant to the third condition.[12] But the Commissioners' view is that the frequency and regularity of the work are material, though not conclusive, factors in determining whether this condition is satisfied. The result is that in many cases claimants working for well over the number of hours, which would entitle them to be treated as retired under the first or second condition, have been treated as retired under the third. It is, in fact, often difficult to see exactly what factors have persuaded Commissioners to come to the conclusion that the person is working 'in circumstances not inconsistent with retirement'.

The leading case is the Tribunal decision in *R(P) 8/54*:

> The claimant who had been employed in the school meals service since 1943, gave notice of retirement, but stated that she intended to continue in the same employment, working 12½ hours a week. The Tribunal held that this would not be inconsistent with retirement, as it was the type of work which someone who had retired from regular employment might well perform.

There are two points which may be emphasised. First, although the hours of work and level of earnings were not conclusive, they were both relevant factors in determining whether the third condition was satisfied. In this case it was satisfied, though the hours exceeded the number (12) relevant to the second condition. Secondly, it was decided that a claimant need not show some specific circumstance causing a change of occupation, or an alteration in the terms of his employment, for the work to be consistent with retirement.[13]

Although it is unnecessary to show a change of circumstances to satisfy the condition, such a change may influence the Commissioner in treating the claimant as retired.

9 *CP 21/49*.
10 The formulation, 'engaged in a gainful occupation to an inconsiderable extent', was employed in the legislation until NIA 1965, when the present requirement in terms of 'an earner' was introduced.
11 *R(P) 1/52*.
12 See *Calvert* p. 276.
13 On this point the Tribunal overruled *R(P) 15/52*.

In *R(P) 6/54*, a railway station porter intended to retire from his regular employment and immediately to start part-time work for 20 hours a week as an outside porter. He was to work for tips, and not regular wages. The Commissioner ruled that the change in the nature of his employment enabled him to be treated as retired; it was unlikely that he would in fact work for the full 20 hours, though he would be in attendance for that time.

It, therefore, seems that for this condition, unlike the second one, actual work may be more relevant than the hours of attendance. But, in another case, it was emphasised that it is the present scale of the claimant's activity, rather than whether there has been a reduction in his working hours, which is important.[14]

Although the number of hours worked may be low enough to enable the claimant to succeed on this third condition (though more than the upper limit of 12 imposed for the second one), it seems that the Commissioners will also draw an upper limit on the hours worked beyond which it is virtually impossible to contend that the work is not inconsistent with retirement. (It could be argued that this too is an incorrect view of the scope of the third condition and that, in principle, there should be no upper limit.) Apart from *R(P) 6/54* (the railway station porter case), there have been very few cases where more than 18 hours' work a week has been held not inconsistent with retirement.[15]

In a number of cases it has been emphasised that there must be some aspect of the part-time work which is particularly characteristic of occupations followed by elderly people who have given up their regular employment. The nature of the work, the freedom which the claimant has to choose his hours, the pressure under which he works (or lack of it), and whether it is done as a hobby or is still pursued as a substantial source of livelihood are all relevant factors in determining whether it presents such features.[16] In an interesting recent case, the Chief Commissioner, R J A Temple, rejected the argument that the work of a city councillor presented special features which were characteristic of the occupations followed by retired people; in view of the number of hours (generally 30) which the claimant spent weekly on council business, it could not be said that his work was not inconsistent with retirement.[17]

In *R(P) 11/55*, it was suggested that the claimant must point to a special feature characteristic of post-retirement occupation. However, in *R(P) 13/55* where a Methodist minister had retired from full-time work and later took up duties as a part-time supernumerary minister, the test was formulated in a slightly different way:[18]

> Having regard to the rather inconclusive nature of the inferences falling to be drawn, in this case, from the size of congregation, hours of work involved, and amount of remuneration, I am not prepared to say that there is any feature in the

14 *R(P) 8/56*. Also see *R(P) 1/54* (reduction from 45 to 20 hours a week was not enough for the claimant to be treated as retired).

15 *R(P) 10/55* and *R(P) 2/59* are two such cases. In rather more cases 18 hours' work has been held inconsistent with retirement: *R(P) 4/57*; *R(P) 5/57*; *R(P) 6/55*; *R(P) 11/55*; *R 1/60 (P)*; *R(P) 2/76*.

16 See *R(P) 6/55* and *R(P) 11/55*.

17 *R(P) 2/76*. The case incidentally shows that the third condition may still be important despite the introduction of the earnings condition. The attendance allowances claimed by the applicant precluded any reliance on that condition.

18 The Commissioner followed *R(P) 9/54* (Baptist minister with similar duties) and did not follow *R(P) 11/52*, where the Methodist minister's duties seem to have been lighter than those in *R(P) 13/55*; *R(P) 11/52* may now be regarded as wrongly decided.

occupation which would render it unreasonable to speak of a person engaged in it as having retired from regular employment.[19]

This formulation would appear more favourable to the claimant, but it seems from the cases to make comparatively little difference, and the Commissioner does not appear to be wedded to one version of the test rather than the other.[20]

The position of self-employed persons may present particular difficulties.

In *R(P) 12/55*, the woman gave up employment as a school meals attendant on reaching pensionable age, and then kept a small sweet shop in her house, open for 13 hours a day. Although this occupation was found to be characteristic of those pursued by retired people, it was held that she could not be treated as retired because the number of hours for which the shop was open made the manner of its pursuit inconsistent with retirement.[1]

A claimant, however, who worked 20 hours a week in his own off-licence business, where trade was light, was held to have retired.[2] The freedom which he enjoyed to organise his own hours was emphasised as a crucial factor. But it was not decisive in *R(P) 1/60* where a writer was not treated as retired under this condition because he set no specific limit to the number of hours devoted to his writing.

In summary, the Commissioners appear concerned in applying this condition to see whether there is some feature of the work undertaken by the claimant which is characteristic of the work generally done by elderly people, and in determining this the hours of work are extremely relevant. But the level of the claimant's earnings is not generally of much significance.[3] Some of the decisions are hard to reconcile, as is perhaps inevitable where the Commissioners are asked to interpret such a vague and imprecise requirement.

d *The earnings condition*

It has already been pointed out that the retirement condition creates the apparent anomaly that a person is not entitled to claim a pension if he intends to work after pensionable age (subject to the qualifications as to part-time work, etc. just discussed), while if he has retired, he may then resume work and keep his pension, subject to the earnings rule.[4] This anomaly was mitigated to some extent by the relatively liberal interpretation of the first three conditions for being treated as retired. But, as has been said, for the most part the level of the claimant's earnings was not relevant in determining whether they were satisfied. This was particularly hard on lower-paid workers such as women in textile factories,[5] who worked long hours and were, therefore, unable to satisfy the three conditions. For this reason, the earnings condition was introduced by the National Insurance Act 1960. The effect of the change was well summa-

19 *R(P) 13/55*, para 9.
20 E.g. in *R(P) 4/57*, the test in *R(P) 11/55* was applied, while in *R(P) 5/57*, the test in *R(P) 13/55* was followed, but in both cases the result was that the claimant was not treated as retired.
1 The Commissioner followed *R(P) 12/53* (sub-postmistress keeping office open for 44 hours a week was not treated as retired, even though the business was very slight).
2 *R(P) 2/59*.
3 *R(P) 16/56*.
4 See p. 202, above.
5 630 HC Official Report (5th series) col 220.

rised by Mr Douglas Houghton, the opposition spokesman, during the uncontentious committee stage:[6]

> It will mean that they can go to the limit of the earnings rule irrespective of the number of hours worked without finding themselves questioned as to whether what they are doing is inconsistent with retirement.

Under the earnings condition, the claimant will be treated as retired if his earnings are expected not to exceed, or only occasionally to exceed, the amount above which a deduction from the pension would be made under the earnings rule. For 1982–83 this amount is £57. Thus, if the claimant's anticipated weekly earnings from part-time work are only £50, he will be treated as retired under this fourth condition, while if his earnings are likely to be £65, he must satisfy one of the first three conditions already discussed. Under a recent technical amendment,[7] the earnings condition will apply when the claimant's earnings are not generally expected to exceed the amount above which a deduction would be made from his pension, *including* any additional component and graduated retirement benefit; this extends the scope of the condition and enables more persons to be treated as retired under it. The calculation of earnings for this purpose raises general problems common to many social security benefits, and is therefore dealt with in chapter 10.[8]

iv Notice of retirement

Under the Act, the claimant must give notice of retirement in order to be treated as retired.[9] This requirement must be distinguished from that of a claim for a pension, which is discussed in chapter 14.[10] The Claims and Payments Regulations require that the notice be given in writing to the Secretary of State, specifying the date of retirement. This date must, of course, not be earlier than that of the relevant pensionable age, and not later than four months after the giving of the notice.[11] The date of retirement specified may antedate that of the notice for up to three months; this period may be extended up to 12 months, if there was good cause for the delay in giving the retirement notice.[12] The requirement does not apply to a man over 70 or woman over 65, as they are deemed to retire on reaching that age.[13]

There is some case-law on what constitutes a valid notice of retirement. A recorded note of a conversation with a claimant taken by an insurance officer may amount to such notice,[14] as may a notice of appeal.[15] In one case, a British subject gave notice of his retirement to the Sécurité Sociale in Paris on his 65th birthday.[16] The Commissioner held that the Sécurité Sociale, under the reciprocal arrangements in force between the United Kingdom and France for the payment of pensions, could be regarded as agents of the Ministry of Pensions and, therefore, the notice was valid.

6 Ibid, col 1096.
7 SSA 1980, s.3(2), amending SSPA 1975, s.11.
8 See pp. 404–408, below.
9 SSA 1975, s.27(4).
10 *R(P) 3/59*; see pp. 552–561, below.
11 SI 1979/628, Sch 2, para 4(2).
12 Ibid, Sch 2, para 4(3). For the meaning of 'good cause for delay', see pp. 565–569, below.
13 SSA 1975, s.27(5).
14 *R(P) 4/53*.
15 *R(P) 8/51*.
16 *R(P) 14/55*.

Granted that the retirement condition must be met to the satisfaction of the authorities, there does not appear to be any reason why this requires special notice, and cannot be treated like any other disputed matter when a claim is made. But it does not seem, on the other hand, that the requirement gives rise to any difficulty, particularly since notice may be given in normal circumstances up to three months after the date of retirement.

C Contributions

The third requirement of entitlement to a Category A or B retirement pension is that the claimant has satisfied the contribution conditions. This is in practice much more important than the retirement condition, since failure to satisfy that will only prevent the award of a pension for the five years until the person is deemed to have retired,[17] while the omission to pay contributions may render him ineligible for these categories of pension.[18] A person may claim a Category A pension on the basis of his (or her) *own* contributions, or a Category B pension on the basis of a husband's (or under the Social Security Pensions Act 1975[19] a deceased wife's) contributions. Naturally a person is not entitled to both a Category A and a Category B pension, even though the contribution conditions for entitlement to each may be met; he is, however, entitled to the pension which is more favourable to him.[20] Now under the Social Security Pensions Act 1975 (hereinafter referred to as 'the Pensions Act'), if because of deficient contributions he (or she) is not entitled to the whole of a Category A pension, part of the Category B pension to which he would otherwise not be entitled may be used where the claimant's spouse has died to supplement the deficiency in the former benefit.[1] This is one of the ways in which a claimant may now benefit from a spouse's contributions.[2] Exposition of the contributions requirements is particularly difficult, first, because of the special rules applying to married women and widows, and secondly, because of the changes made by the Pensions Act 1975. The position of married women and the contribution requirements for the earnings-related component are discussed later in this chapter. In this section we are concerned with the general contribution requirements for the basic component in Category A and Category B retirement pensions.

These are set out in paragraph 5 of Schedule 3 to the Social Security Act 1975, as amended by section 19 of the Pensions Act 1975. The amended conditions are:

(a) the claimant must have paid in at least one year contributions of the relevant class equal to a sum 52 times the lower earnings limit;[3] and
(b) the claimant must have paid or been credited with contributions equivalent to that sum for nine-tenths of his working life.[4]

17 SSA 1975, s.27(5); p. 198, above.
18 The claimant may be eligible for a non-contributory retirement pension: pp. 224–225, below.
19 S.8: p. 212, below.
20 The rates of basic Category A and B pensions are set out below, p. 212.
1 SSA 1975, s.27(6).
2 SSPA 1975, s.9: this provision does not apply where the death of the husband or wife occurred, and the surviving spouse attained pensionable age, before 6 April 1979.
3 Before 6 April 1979, the requirement was the payment of contributions equal to a sum 50 times the lower earnings limit.
4 For details, see SSA 1975, Sch 3, para 5(4).

The effect of this second contribution condition is that where the claimant's working life has been more than 40 years, up to five years' payment of contributions may be missed.

The continuing contributions condition is, however, modified to enable persons who have been out of the employment field for considerable periods (generally, though not necessarily, married women) to be eligible for a retirement pension. It is enough for a claimant to comply with the second, continuing condition for half the number of the required years (i.e. half of nine-tenths of his working life), or at least 20 years if that is less, provided he (or she) can establish that for all the other years, he was 'precluded from regular employment by responsibilities at home'.[5] Regulations define the meaning of this phrase. The claimant will be regarded as satisfying the requirement if for any year after April 1978, (a) he receives child benefit for any child under 16, (b) he is regularly engaged in caring for a person in receipt of the attendance allowance or of a constant attendance allowance under either the war pensions or industrial injuries scheme, or (c) he is in receipt of supplementary benefit, as a person exempted from the requirement to be available for work because he is looking after an elderly or incapacitated person.[6]

Under the Regulations it is provided that a retirement pension (either Category A or B) may be paid at a reduced rate to a person who does not fully satisfy the second contributions requirement.[7] This rate is the proportion of those years of contributions liability (that is nine-tenths of the years of the claimant's working life), in which contributions amounting to the sums prescribed have in fact been paid or credited. But no benefit is payable at all unless this proportion is at least 25 per cent.

Before the Pensions Act there were provisions enabling a widow, or a divorced woman, to substitute her former husband's contributions for her own where the latter were themselves insufficient to meet the continuing contributions condition.[8] Under the Pensions Act a claimant may in certain circumstances make use of his or her former spouse's contributions for the purpose of securing a Category A retirement pension where in the year in which the marriage ended (through death or divorce) or any previous year his (or her) own contributions were inadequate.[9] In the case of divorce it does not matter whether the claimant's marriage ended before or after he reached pensionable age, but a widow or widower can generally only take advantage of the regulations when the marriage terminated before he attained the relevant age.[10] Under these rules the claimant may take the benefit of his former spouse's contributions for both the first and second contributions conditions.[11] He may not, however, use *both* these provisions to secure a full Category A pension *and* supplement that pension by the Category B pension to which he may be entitled on the death of his former spouse.[12]

5 SSA 1975, Sch 3, para 5(6), inserted in the Act by SSA 1979, Sch 1, para 3: see p. 67, above. Also see Atkins [1980] JSWL 33.
6 SI 1978/508, reg 2, amended by SI 1981/330.
7 SI 1979/642, reg 6.
8 SSA 1975, s.28(3).
9 SSPA 1975, s.20. This provision does not apply to a person attaining pensionable age before 6 April 1979 if the marriage also ended before that date: SSA 1979, Sch 1, para 20.
10 SI 1979/642, reg 8(1).
11 Ibid, reg 8(3)(4), and see Sch 1.
12 Ibid, reg 8(5), and see p. 208, above for this provision by which Category A and B pensions may be accumulated.

D Married women

The pensions position of a woman who is, or has been, married is sufficiently complex to justify separate treatment. It has become even more complex as a result of the Pensions Act. She may be entitled to claim a Category A pension on the basis of her own contributions. Alternatively she may be entitled to a Category B pension on the basis of her husband's, or former husband's, contributions.

i Claim by married women on their own contributions (Category A pension)

The Social Security Act 1975[13] provided that a married woman was not entitled to a Category A pension unless (in addition to the usual requirements) she showed either that her marriage occurred after she was 55, or alternatively, she satisfied the second contributions requirement for at least half the number of tax years between the date of her marriage and the date when she reached 60. However, the law was changed by the Pensions Act 1975, which repealed this provision of the consolidation Act, and, therefore, removed these additional requirements for those women who reached pensionable age on or after 6 April 1979. The position of married women has been further improved by the provision enabling the second contributions condition to be satisfied if they are paid for half the working life (or 20 years) where the contributor in other years was not at work because of domestic responsibilities.[14]

ii Claim on a husband's contributions (Category B pension)

A woman who is, or *has been*, married may in certain circumstances be entitled to a Category B retirement pension by virtue of her husband's contributions. These are set out in section 29 of the Social Security Act 1975. They are unaffected by the Pensions Act 1975, though this legislation has extended Category B pensions to widowers.[15] Two preliminary points should be mentioned before the conditions of entitlement are examined in detail.

First, where the woman's husband is still alive (and has himself reached pensionable age and retired), it does not generally make any difference that his wife is entitled to a Category B pension, since in most circumstances (whether she is under or over pensionable age) a dependant's allowance will be paid to her husband in respect of her.[16] This allowance is the same as the lower rate of Category B retirement pension paid to a woman whose husband is still alive.[17] A Category B pension is, however, payable at a higher rate (and now with an earnings-related component) when the wife becomes a widow, and largely for this reason entitlement to the pension may be important. Moreover, the dependency allowance is an

13 S.28(2).

14 SSPA 1975, s.20: p. 209, above.

15 P. 212, below.

16 For dependants' allowances, see pp. 367–368, below. They are only payable in certain circumstances set out by SSA 1975, ss. 45–46, so there may be cases where a husband is not entitled to an increase for his wife, though she is entitled to a Category B pension on the basis of his contributions.

17 For the two rates at which a Category B retirement pension is payable, see p. 212, below.

increase to the *husband's* pension, and, therefore, may be reduced because of his earnings as well as hers. The Category B pension, paid directly to the wife, is only subject to a reduction if *her* earnings exceed the prescribed limit under the earnings rule.[18]

Secondly, the United Kingdom system, under which a pension may be payable to a wife on the basis of her husband's contributions, or a dependant's allowance may be paid in respect of her whatever her age, is generous compared with most other systems. In some countries, e.g. Austria, Germany and the USA, a pension is only payable to a woman either if she is a widow, or alternatively she has paid contributions for her own pension.[19]

The circumstances in which a married woman or widow may claim a Category B retirement pension when she has attained pensionable age (60) are as follows:

(1) Where a woman is married at the time she reaches pensionable age, she may claim such a pension at the lower rate if both she and her husband have retired, and he is 65 and has satisfied the contribution conditions for a Category A retirement pension.[20]

(2) She may also claim a Category B pension at the lower rate if she marries her husband after she is 60, subject otherwise to the same conditions as in (1).[1]

(3) A widow may claim a Category B pension at the higher rate if her husband died after she reached pensionable age, provided that before his death he had satisfied the contributions conditions. In this case there is no need for the woman to have retired. The reason is that if the woman were under pensionable age, she would be entitled under the same conditions to a widow's pension, eligibility for which is not dependent on retirement.[2]

(4) Where the woman's husband has died before she reaches 60, she may claim a Category B pension, *if she has retired* and was entitled, immediately before she became 60, to a widow's pension in consequence of his death. In this case there is no separate contributions requirement for entitlement to the retirement pension; but she would only have been entitled to the widow's pension if the contributions conditions for that benefit had been satisfied. The Category B pension is paid at the same rate as the widow's benefit.[3] The effect here of the imposition of the retirement condition is that the claimant may opt either to receive the retirement pension (retirement condition exacted before she is 65) or to continue with her widow's pension (no retirement condition exacted): it does not generally seem to matter which benefit is chosen, though, of course, the former benefit may be reduced because of the earnings rule.[4]

18 For the earnings rule, see pp. 212–215, below.
19 *Kaim-Caudle* p. 192.
20 SSA 1975, s.29(2). The contribution conditions are discussed p. 208, above.
1 Ibid, s.29(3).
2 Ibid, s.29(4). For widow's pension, see ch 6, below, pp. 232–233.
3 SSA 1975, s.29(5) and see SI 1979/642, reg 7: for the rates of widow's pensions, see p. 233, below.
4 Pp. 212–215, below, for the earnings rule. In certain circumstances it will be advantageous for the widow to claim retirement pension, e.g. if her husband was over 65 when he died and had deferred his retirement, thereby earning an increment to his pension (p. 217, below).

E Widowers

The Pensions Act 1975 has extended entitlement to a Category B pension to widowers. Section 8 provides that a retired man may claim it if his wife died when they were both over pensionable age, and she had satisfied the second contributions condition for a Category A pension.[5] This Category B pension is paid at the same rate as the Category A pension to which the wife was, or would have been, entitled: it consists of the basic and (where appropriate) the additional earnings-related component.[6] This reform would appear to cover the relatively rare case where a wife's contribution record is superior to her husband's, and goes some way to achieving a degree of sex equality in the pensions area. But the conditions are much harder to satisfy than those which apply to a woman's Category B pension, and the law may still be considered to discriminate irrationally against men: it seems the legal position will not be affected by the EEC Sex Equality Directive.[7]

F Amounts of contributory retirement pensions

The basic rates of the two contributory retirement pensions are for 1982–83 as follows: Category A retirement pension, £32.85; Category B pension, £32.85 (the higher rate) and £19.70 (the lower rate). Since 6 April 1979 these retirement pensions have consisted in most circumstances of the flat-rate basic component, and an additional earnings-rated component. The circumstances in which this second component is paid and the method by which it is calculated are discussed in Part 5;[8] a graduated retirement benefit may also be paid in addition to these components, the details of which are outlined in Part 4.[9]

Part 3 Consequences of the retirement condition

We have emphasised already the importance of the retirement condition. In this Part of the chapter a number of aspects of the pensions system dependent on it are considered. Foremost among these is the controversial earnings rule. The other topics discussed here are the increments to the pension which may be earned if retirement is postponed beyond pensionable age, and the process of deretirement – when a retired person chooses to end his retirement and resume full-time work.

A The earnings rule

i Policy

The Beveridge Report advocated an earnings rule to support the retirement condition.[10] The government accepted this, and the National Insurance Act 1946 contained the rule. An amendment was moved during the

5 SSPA 1975, s.8, as amended by SSA 1979, Sch 1, para 4.
6 For earnings-related pensions, see pp. 219–222, above.
7 See pp. 9–10, above.
8 Pp. 220–222, below.
9 P. 218, below.
10 Para 248.

Committee stage of the Bill to delete it, but it was successfully resisted.[11] If the rule did not exist, it would be too easy for a person of pensionable age to obtain a pension on cessation of work, and then resume full-time employment afterwards without loss of income. The earnings rule prevents this by providing for a reduction or extinction of the pension if a certain earnings limit is exceeded. It applies to persons less than five years over pensionable age, i.e. men under 70 and women under 65.[12] Although frequently criticised, both in principle and on its detail, the rule has consistently been defended (at least until recently) by governments and expert committees.[13]

The arguments against the earnings rule are first, that it is unfair to people who have paid contributions all their working life for a pension, part or all of which may be forfeited if they choose to continue working after reaching pensionable age; and secondly, it provides a disincentive to those who are able to work and might thereby make a useful contribution to the economy. There is a misconception that the rule prohibits the earning of more than a certain wage. It does not do so; it merely provides for a reduction or extinction of the pension if earnings exceed the amount prescribed by the legislation. The first argument may be countered by the contention that people are not contributing towards an *old-age* pension, but to a *retirement* pension with an earnings limit. If this were understood, it could not be contended that the earnings rule disappoints reasonable expectations. There is more in the second argument: the earnings rule may well deter some people from working, or from working as much as they might like to. But the number of pensioners affected is much smaller than is popularly believed. A 'Retirement Survey' conducted in 1977 for the DHSS showed that only about 5,000 pensioners, about 4 per cent of those pensioners actually earning, were having their pension reduced because of the rule. Of course, many more were limiting their earnings owing to its existence, but it was found that half of these pensioners did so under a misconception as to the amount of 'permitted' earnings.[14] It is in fact very difficult to make reliable assessments of the effect of the earnings rule on retirement pensioners; for example, it is possible that if it were abolished, the numbers of those who now choose to defer retirement altogether because they wish to continue in more or less full-time work would drop, so it could be that its continued existence actually keeps some people in full-time work.[15] In the most recent review of the earnings rule conducted by the Secretary of State, it was thought likely on the basis of the Retirement Survey that about 40 per cent of those at present deferring retirement would continue to do so if the earnings rule and retirement condition were abolished. The others would be entitled to a pension on reaching the relevant age, and this would entail a substantial increase to the total expenditure on retirement pensions.[16]

It is indeed largely for these reasons of cost that neither the 1974–79 Labour government nor the present Conservative administration has felt

11 423 HC Official Report (5th series) cols 677–692.

12 SSA 1975, s.30(1).

13 The Phillips Committee Report (Cmd 9333) para 194; Report of the National Insurance Advisory Committee on the Earnings Limit for Retirement Pensions (1966, Cmnd 3197), para 13. But see now the more critical treatment of the rule in the Secretary of State's report, The Earnings Rule for Retirement Pensioners and the Wives of Retirement and Invalidity Pensioners, 1977–78, HC 697.

14 1977–78 HC 697, paras 2.5–2.9.

15 Ibid, ch 4. Also see NIAC Report, n.13, above, at paras 19–28.

16 1977–78, HC 697, paras 4.6–4.13.

able to propose abolition of the earnings rule, though both parties are committed to its eventual disappearance. The 1978 review estimated the net cost (increased expenditure on pensions less tax revenue) would be about £64 million, and this figure would be twice as high if all persons currently deferring pensions took them immediately.[17] It was therefore concluded that additional expenditure on those persons presently affected by the earnings rule could not be justified as a priority, and this seems clearly right. Nor did the report think there was any real case for abolishing the rule in the case of dependent wives' earnings: in this context it provided a useful test of dependency, and there would be much to be said for its retention here, even if it were eventually abolished for retirement pensioners themselves.[18]

The difficulty of reform in the present economic climate is shown by the present government's general reluctance to increase the earnings limit in the last few years. During the late 1970s the limit had been increased on a number of occasions (from £9.50 in 1974/5 to £40 in 1977), and in 1979 the new Conservative government raised it to £52.[19] It was then not increased until 1982, when it became £57.[20] Moreover, the limit need now no longer be reviewed and increased annually to keep pace with inflation,[1] and the government has not used the power created by the Social Security Act 1979 to phase out the rule gradually by substituting shorter periods for the present five-year period (65–69 for men, 60–64 for women).[2] For the moment financial prudence prevails over long-term aspirations; in any case those retirement pensioners with a capacity to work and earn reasonable sums may not be thought to have the highest claims for increased expenditure and it seems odd for the present administration to pretend otherwise.

When it was introduced in 1946, the earnings rule provided only for extinguishment of that part of the retirement pension equivalent to the excess earned over the stipulated limit – thus, for each £1 earned over the limit, £1 would be deducted from the pension. The National Insurance Advisory Committee Report of 1956 recommended that there should be a band within which only half the excess earnings should be deducted (the 'proportionate band'), and this was implemented by the National Insurance Act 1956.[3] The effect of this reform is to some extent to reduce the deterrent effect of the earnings rule, and to encourage more pensioners to work. At the moment the proportionate band is £4.[4] It is arguable that this is too narrow, in view of the increase in average earnings and the substantial raising of the earnings limit in the late 1970s.

There has been left to the end what is perhaps the most difficult and fundamental question of all, though it is one which has been surprisingly little debated. The law provides for a reduction of pension if the pensioner is in receipt of 'earnings'. It is often hard to decide what this term means for the purposes of the rule;[5] in particular, narrow lines have to be drawn between profits from a business on the one hand, and shares or gratuitous payments on the other. However, in the context of the pensioner's needs,

17 Ibid, ch 6.
18 Ibid, ch 5. And see p. 368, below.
19 SI 1979/993.
20 See 19 HC Official Report (6th series) col 852.
1 SSA (No 2) 1980, s.2, and see pp. 410–413, below, for up-rating generally.
2 SSA 1979, s.4.
3 NIA 1956, s.1, implementing the proposals in the NIAC Report (Cmd 9752).
4 SSA 1975, s.30(1)(a).
5 Pp. 404–408, below.

it is not obvious why he should suffer a deduction from his pension in the former case and not in the latter. In other words, what is the justification for the present *earnings* rule as opposed to a rule which provides for a reduction of pension in the light of the pensioner's means? The answer, of course, lies in the history of provision for old age, and the close connection of the earnings rule with the retirement condition. In defence of the present position, it may be said that it is right for the state not to pay a pension (or to pay a reduced one) to someone who is willing to support himself by regular employment; on the other hand it would be wrong not to allow someone to supplement his state pension by an occupational pension or the proceeds of insurance policies, annuities, and shares, probably provided for out of his income when he was in regular employment. Although the distinction between earnings and other income may sometimes be a fine one, its erosion would lead to the replacement of the present system by a means-tested retirement pension, presumably financed by general taxation. This would be a complete departure from the Beveridge structure and the fundamental principles of the welfare state. Compared with this, change in the opposite direction through the abolition of the earnings rule itself would be relatively minor.

ii Application of the rule

Section 30 of the Social Security Act 1975 provides that:

- where the earnings of a person (less than five years over pensionable age) exceed the earnings limit for the week before that for which he is entitled to the pension, it is to be reduced by half the excess up to £4 (the proportionate band) and for the whole of the excess after this £4.

The earnings rule applies separately to a wife's earnings, so that the dependant's increase for her (but not his pension) may be reduced by her earnings.[6] It may also be reduced by his earnings, as the increase of benefit forms part of his pension.[7] The 'week' for the purposes of estimating the claimant's earnings is the calendar week, ending on the Saturday before the week for which he is entitled to his pension.[8] A proviso to section 30(1) makes it clear that the subsection does not affect the pension payable for the first week of retirement – in other words, the fact that his earnings for his last week of employment exceed the earnings limit will not affect the first pension payment.[9]

There is a considerable amount of case-law, in addition to the Computation of Earnings Regulations,[10] concerning what income is to be regarded as 'earnings' and how it is to be assessed. The rules are relevant to a number of benefits, apart from retirement pensions, and are, therefore, discussed in chapter 10 (General Provisions).[11]

iii The rule under the Social Security Pensions Act 1975

Section 11 of the Pensions Act, as amended by section 5(2) of the Social Security (Miscellaneous Provisions) Act 1977, provides that the earnings rule is only to apply to the basic component (for 1982–83, £32.85). It will

6 SSA 1975, s.48.

7 In this respect a married couple will be more favourably placed if the wife is entitled to a Category B retirement pension: this is her pension and is unaffected by her husband's earnings: see p. 210, above.

8 SSA 1975, Sch 20: see p. 571, below, for payment of retirement pensions.

9 See *R(P) 2/56*.

10 SI 1978/1698.

11 Pp. 404–409, below.

not apply to the earnings-related part of the pension (the 'additional component'), nor any increase of pension for deferred retirement which is attributable to this additional component, nor any graduated retirement benefit.[12]

B Increments for deferred retirement

Although the retirement condition inevitably encouraged people to give up work on reaching pensionable age, Beveridge hoped and expected that those able to continue work beyond the age of 65 (or 60) would do so.[13] They were to be induced by the prospect of increments to their pensions, either on retirement, or on reaching 70 (or 65 in the case of women) when the retirement condition would no longer be applicable. The increments to the standard rate would give the persons concerned some, if not all, of the savings consequent on their postponed retirement.

In fact it has been doubted whether this aspect of the Beveridge scheme has worked. The Phillips Committee in 1953 found there was no evidence that the prospect of increments encouraged people to stay on at work after reaching pensionable age: 'a small prospective increase in the pension later on, though welcome when it comes, can seldom affect the decision'.[14] On balance, however, it thought there would be unfavourable public reaction to the abolition of increments, and no change was recommended. The increments themselves have been too low and the social forces inducing early retirement too strong to allow the success of this feature of the retirement pensions scheme.[15] During the 1970s the numbers deferring retirement declined, particularly from 1974 to 1977 when there were frequent increases in the earnings limit and it became consequently more attractive to retire and work part-time. This decline has now been halted as the limit has remained static.[16] While rather under 10 per cent of persons who reach pensionable age now exercise their option to defer, the Social Security Statistics show that overall 23 per cent of all pensioners have some increment to their pension for a deferred retirement, though the average increment is only £1.42 a week.[17]

Entitlement to an increment is now governed by Schedule 1 to the Pensions Act which made a number of changes to the previous law in this area. A pensioner can claim an increment for each period of six consecutive 'days of increment', assessed as one-seventh per cent of the weekly rate of the relevant pension (Category A or B, as the case may be).[18] But the minimum increment under the Schedule is 1 per cent of that rate, so in effect there must be at least 42 days of deferred retirement to earn any increment (42 days at one-seventh per cent equals 1 per cent). Regulations define 'days of increment', providing inter alia that days for which the claimant has received certain other social security benefits (e.g. unemployment, sickness and invalidity benefit) do not count for this purpose.[19] An increment may now be assessed by reference to

12 See p. 206, above, for the earnings' retirement condition.
13 Paras 244 ff.
14 The Phillips Committee Report (Cmd 9333) at paras 200–201.
15 See *George* p. 159.
16 HC 697 (1978), para 2.13 and App 3.
17 Social Security Statistics 1980, Table 13.43.
18 SSPA 1975, Sch 1, paras 1–2.
19 SI 1979/642, reg 4.

both the basic and additional earnings-related components of the pension (whether Category A or B). Moreover, increments are increased by the same percentage as the basic pension under an up-rating order, whether they are earned before or after the order came into force: thus, if shortly before the end of the period of deferment the pension rate is increased by a certain percentage, all increments earned before that date in the previous five years are similarly increased.[20]

The Pensions Act also made a number of improvements to the rules under which a spouse may benefit from increments earned by his or her partner. Where a married woman is entitled to a Category B pension, and her husband has deferred his retirement, she will earn the same percentage increments to her pension as he does to his Category A pension.[1] On her husband's death, a widow may now receive the whole increments to which he had been entitled (or would have been entitled had he retired immediately before his death), and similarly a widower, provided he was over pensionable age on his wife's death, may inherit her increments.[2] These will be paid in addition to any increments the survivor may have earned himself through postponing his retirement. Regulations, however, provide that a woman is not to derive an increment from her deceased husband if she remarries before she reaches pensionable age and becomes entitled to her pension: in that eventuality, she should look to the second husband for pension rights based on a spouse's contributions.[3]

C Deretirement

The National Insurance Act 1957, section 1, introduced the procedure by which a retirement pensioner under 70 (or 65) might elect to deretire. The former pensioner may accordingly resume full-time work, thus earning increments to his pension when he eventually retires or becomes 70 (or 65). The option does not appear to have been often used. The National Insurance Advisory Committee in 1966 found that only about 2,500 pensioners a year had elected to deretire.[4] It adduced two reasons for this. First, the decision entailed at that time payment of contributions and loss of pension with any addition for dependants, so that the pensioner must be confident of a relatively good income to afford the election; secondly, deretirement results in a loss of flexibility, in that the person concerned must give up his work to regain his pension, while if he has not deretired, all he needs do to obtain a full pension is to reduce his earnings. The latter reason does not appear very convincing since, as we have seen, retirement need not involve a total cessation of work. Largely because there did not seem to be any widespread demand for it, the Committee did not recommend that it should be possible for those over pensionable age to move frequently into and out of retirement. The position is still that a person may elect *only once* to deretire.[5]

20 SSPA 1975, Sch 1, para 2(5).
1 Ibid, Sch 1, para 5.
2 Ibid, Sch 1, para 4 (and see amendment made by SSA 1979, Sch 1, para 6, which provides that a survivor's inherited increments may be up-rated during the period between his or her former spouse's death and the date the former becomes entitled to a retirement pension).
3 SI 1980/1168, reg 2, and see NIAC Report (Cmnd 7970).
4 Report of the National Insurance Advisory Committee on the Earnings Limit for Retirement Pensions (1966, Cmnd 3197), at paras 57–62.
5 SI 1979/642, reg 2(2)(a).

The Regulations provide that a husband who is entitled to a Category A pension may not so elect unless his wife, if entitled to a Category B pension on his contributions, consents to his election or unless 'that consent is unreasonably withheld'.[6] The only reported case on this provision comes from Northern Ireland. In *R 6/60 (P)*,

> A man, whose wife refused her consent to his deretirement, contended that she had a substantial private income and, therefore, her withholding of consent was unreasonable. The Commissioner held that in fact her resources were slighter than the husband thought, and that to refuse consent because of the substantial financial detriment which would be occasioned by the loss of her pension was not to withhold it unreasonably.

The Commissioner said that it was for the husband to show that the wife had acted unreasonably, and that examples of such unreasonable behaviour would be pique, spite or a desire just to stand in his way.[7]

Because of its consequences – loss of entitlement to pension and any dependants' increases – deretirement is regarded as a serious step. For this reason, notice of an election to deretire must be made in writing, and a document should not be construed as good notice, unless it is clearly intended to be one.[8] Unlike a retirement notice, it may not take effect before the date on which it is given.[9]

Though there is no evidence that the present position with regard to deretirement creates substantial problems, it is difficult to conclude that it is wholly satisfactory. With a liberally construed retirement condition and a generous earnings limit, there seems comparatively little scope for the deretirement procedure. And if there is a case for it, it appears odd that the election can only be made once. The real difficulty is perhaps attributable to the nature of the retirement condition itself, that it focuses on a past state ('has retired'), rather than imposes, as has been suggested,[10] a continuing condition ('is retired'). Of course, there would be practical difficulties in the latter alternative, but its adoption would avoid the artificialities of the deretirement procedure.

Part 4 Graduated retirement benefit

Graduated retirement benefit[11] was introduced by the National Insurance Act 1959, this legislation marking the first departure from the principle of flat-rate contributions and benefits laid down in the Beveridge Report.[12] Under the National Insurance Act 1965[13] (the relevant provision of which is

6 Ibid, reg 2(2)(b).

7 The Commissioner followed with approval the approach taken in cases where consent is refused to the assignment of a lease: *Shanly v Ward* (1913) 29 TLR 714, CA. Compare the objective approach now taken in the consent to adoption cases: Cretney *Principles of Family Law* (3rd edn) pp. 548–551.

8 *R(P) 1/61*.

9 SI 1979/642 reg 2(4).

10 See p. 202, above.

11 The legislation uses the term 'benefit', though the DHSS leaflets refer to graduated pension, and the two words are used interchangeably here.

12 See p. 42, above, for graduated contributions.

13 Ss.36, 37 (the sections are now kept in force by SI 1978/393, made under the Social Security (Consequential Provisions) Act 1975).

still in force) the benefit is an addition to the weekly rate of retirement pension payable to a person over pensionable age who has retired from regular employment: the supplement is calculated as 2½p for each unit of graduated contributions paid by the claimant.[14] A unit is £7.50 in the case of a man, and £9.00 for a woman; any contributions totalling a half or more of a unit are treated as a complete unit.[15] So, for example, a man who paid £177 in graduated contributions is entitled to 60p a week graduated pension, and a woman who paid £135 will receive 38p a week.[16]

This additional benefit can be paid to a person who is not entitled to a standard retirement pension because he does not satisfy the contributions conditions for the latter.[17] But the requirements that the claimant has attained pensionable age and has retired are exacted.[18] A married woman may be entitled to this benefit on the basis of her own graduated contributions, and may draw it even if she is not able to claim her Category B pension because her husband has not yet retired. A widow is entitled to the graduated pension earned on her own contributions *and* half that earned by her husband.[19] If a person entitled to graduated benefit does not retire on reaching pensionable age, half the sum to which he was entitled at that time counts as additional graduated contributions; an extra graduated pension is then payable when he eventually retires or reaches 70 (or 65).[20]

The graduated pensions scheme was widely thought inadequate as an attempt at an earnings-related provision.[1] One weakness in particular was that the benefit was not proof against inflation. With the introduction of fully earnings-related pensions under the Pensions Act 1975, there is no place for the older scheme. Graduated contributions have not been payable since April 1975, though the additional benefit will continue to be paid to those who had acquired a right (actual or prospective) to it at that time.[2] In 1979, 52 per cent of all pensioners were in receipt of graduated pensions, though these averaged only 58p a week.[3] However, under the Pensions Act the amount of the graduated pension may be increased under the up-rating provisions of the Social Security Act.[4]

Part 5 The Social Security Pensions Act 1975[5]

In this Part an outline is given of the scheme established by the Pensions Act 1975. Some aspects have already been mentioned: the alterations in contributions requirements,[6] the changes effected in the position of married women, widows and widowers,[7] and the scope of the

14 NIA 1965, s.36(1).
15 Ibid, s.36(2), (3).
16 DHSS Leaflet NI 15, para 12.
17 Pp. 208–209, above.
18 NIA 1965, s.36(1). The earnings rule has not applied since April 1979.
19 Ibid, s.37.
20 SI 1978/393, Sch 2. This applies even if the deferred retirement occurs after April 1975, when payment of graduated contributions ended.
1 P. 192, above.
2 SI 1978/393, reg 3.
3 Social Security Statistics 1980, Table 13.45.
4 SSPA 1975, s.24(1) implemented by SI 1978/393: for up-rating of benefits generally, see pp. 410–413, below.
5 See Mesher 39 MLR 321 for an admirable summary of the Act.
6 See p. 208, above.
7 P. 210, above.

earnings rule under the new regime.[8] Here attention is concentrated first, on the state earnings-related pension and secondly, on its relationship with occupational schemes.

A General

The Labour government which took office in 1974 was dissatisfied with the Conservatives' Social Security Act 1973 on the grounds of the priority it gave to occupational pensions and the inadequate provision in the state reserve scheme for those who were shortly to retire.[9] The Labour plan as originally outlined in the White Paper 'Better Pensions'[10] provides for a state earnings-related element in the weekly pension ('the additional component') which is paid to anyone whose employer has not contracted-out and made satisfactory arrangements for occupational pensions for his employees. The scheme enables some earnings-related pension to be paid to those who were near retirement when it was introduced in 1978 – though maximum benefits will not be paid until after the pensioner has contributed for twenty years. The earnings-related pension is inflation proof and, as will be seen,[11] the state has taken over responsibility for the inflation proofing of that part of the contracted-out occupational pensions which is equivalent to the additional component, once it is in payment.

B Earnings-related pensions

The fundamental rules for assessing the earnings-related additional component, which together with the basic component and any graduated benefit now constitute the rate of a retirement pension, are set out in section 6 of the Pensions Act.[12] For an additional component to be payable there must be surpluses in the pensioner's earnings factors, that is amounts in excess of the lower, qualifying earnings limit for the last relevant year (that is, the last tax year before the pensioner reaches pensionable age), this limit being necessary to establish entitlement to the basic pension.[13] Surpluses are taken into account for 20 years, or if there are more than that number of surpluses, the 'best' 20 years.[14] (This formula is more satisfactory for manual workers than the assessment of pensions with regard to the final year's earnings or the average of the last few years, which is a common feature of occupational pension schemes.) As the additional component is paid at the weekly equivalent of $1\frac{1}{4}$ per cent of the amount of the surpluses, it follows that the earnings-related component after 20 years will be 25 per cent of the claimant's earnings above the lower earnings limit. It is a popular misconception that the scheme does not come into effect until 1998: this of course is not true, though the maximum earnings-related component will not be paid until then. Additional components are already

8 P. 216, above.
9 The Conservative scheme embodied in the 1973 Act is briefly discussed above, p. 192.
10 (1974) Cmnd 5713.
11 P. 223, below.
12 This section determines the rate of a Category A retirement pension; see p. 221, below, for Category B pensions.
13 SSPA 1975, ss.6(1) and 6(6). And see p. 65–66, above, for the concepts 'earnings factors' and 'earnings limit'.
14 SSPA 1975, s.6(2).

in payment, though for 1979 the average amount was understandably small – only £0.70p in that year.[15]

Two further points should be made at this stage. First, a person's earnings factors are subject to a ceiling, about seven times the lower earnings limit, and this means that the surpluses which may be taken into account for the additional component are similarly subject to a ceiling.[16] This feature which is not necessarily present in private occupational schemes, ensures some measure of a redistributive element in the state scheme.[17] Secondly, it was said in the previous paragraph that the surpluses in the claimant's earnings factors are determined by reference to the qualifying or lower earnings limit for the last relevant year. This formula necessitates the provision for revaluation of earnings factors in the light of inflation: the Secretary of State is required to review the general level of earnings annually and any changes which have taken place since the end of the period taken into account in the previous review, and then to increase the earnings factors in order to make up any fall in value which has occurred.[18] These complex rules may be illustrated by an example adapted from one given in the relevant DHSS leaflet:[19]

> C has contributed to the earnings-related scheme for five years before his retirement, during which period his earnings increased from £3,000 to £4,400 and earnings generally rose by 10 per cent annually. The qualifying, lower limit for entitlement to the basic pension is £1,014. For the final year his surplus is £3,386 (£4,400 minus £1,014) and to this figure must be added the surpluses for the previous four years. These are assessed by deducting for each year £1,014 from the *revalued* earnings factor. The total surpluses come to £16,870. The weekly additional component is 1¼ per cent of this, divided by 52, i.e. £4.06 a week.

Naturally entitlement to the earnings-related pension (whether as an additional component to a Category A or B retirement pension) depends on the satisfaction of the age and retirement conditions, but the same is not true for the contributions conditions. All that is necessary for the additional component is that contributions have been paid on earnings between the lower and upper earnings limits, and the maximum component will be payable when this has been done for 20 years; the second contributions condition for the basic pension, payment of contributions for nine-tenths of the claimant's working life, need not be met, though in practice it will be unusual for someone to be eligible for the additional and not the basic component.[20]

Under the Pensions Act there are also provisions enabling a widow to be paid an earnings-related additional component to her Category B pension on the basis of her former husband's contributions, and a widower to be paid this component on the basis of his wife's contributions if they were both over pensionable age when she died.[1] But the pensioner is not entitled to an earnings-related pension on the basis of both his own and his former

15 Social Security Statistics 1980, Table 13.47.
16 SSPA 1975, s.1(3) and see p. 52, above.
17 See the OECD paper, *Old Age Pension Schemes* (1977) pp. 56–7.
18 SSPA 1975, s.21, as amended by SSA 1979, s.10.
19 DHSS leaflet, NP 32, p. 11.
20 See pp. 208–209, above, for the contributions conditions for entitlement to a basic pension.
1 SSPA 1975, ss.7–8.

spouse's contributions,[2] so regulations made under section 9 of the Pensions Act provide that the maximum additional component to which a person may be entitled is the amount he would have been entitled to, if (a) he had reached pensionable age and retired on the day when (but for section 27(6) of the Social Security Act 1975) he would have become entitled to both a Category A and a Category B pension (or would have become so entitled had he retired), and (b) in each relevant year he had an earnings factor equal to 53 times that year's upper earnings limit.[3] In effect, this means that the maximum pension a widow will be entitled to is that she would have earned had she paid contributions up to her husband's death on earnings up to the upper earnings limit.

The new earnings-related scheme does not, from an international perspective, break new ground: indeed, the OECD paper, *Old Age Pension Schemes*, shows that Britain was rather late in providing such pensions under the state scheme.[4] The reason for this is probably the widespread existence of occupational schemes and the failure of the two political parties to agree on the right balance between state and private provisions.[5] In the event the 1975 Act provoked comparatively little opposition during its passage and it has now been fully accepted by the Conservatives. It is anticipated that when in 1998 the scheme is fully mature, it will provide a married man with a pension of about half average national earnings,[6] and it may be hoped with some, though not entire, confidence that this will remove the level of provision for retirement pensioners from party politics. On the other hand, two inevitable aspects of the scheme are troublesome. First, it will be very difficult for a prospective pensioner to calculate his future pension: he will have to estimate his best 20 years' earnings, keep a note of the revisions of his earnings factors, and then calculate his pension with regard to these figures and the basic component. The scheme itself is complicated to explain, though the DHSS leaflets will prove helpful to persevering readers. The second point is that it will become more and more expensive, as the earnings-related components increase,[7] and this will be particularly worrying as more pensioners are supported by a relatively smaller working population.

C Occupational pensions and contracting-out[8]

Much the most complicated part of the 1975 Pensions Act is that regulating occupational pension schemes and their relationship with the state earnings-related provision. There can be no contracting-out, of course, from the basic component. But sections 26–29 permit partial contracting-out from the full earnings-related contributions and benefits, where the occupational scheme provides the pensions required by the Act, and where the appropriate consents have been given by the Occupational Pensions

2 The principle that there can be no double entitlement, discussed above, p. 208, applies to the earnings-related component as it does to the basic pension.
3 SI 1979/1428, made under SSPA 1975, s.9(3).
4 Pp. 55–63.
5 See pp. 192–193, above, for the recent history of pensions reform.
6 *Growing Older* (1981, Cmnd 8173), para 2.6.
7 Ibid, para 2.7. The cost of the scheme will *increase* expenditure by £1,300m by the end of the century.
8 See Ellison *Private Occupational Schemes* (1977) ch 13; Jackson *Occupational Pensions – The New Law* (1977) chs 11–14.

Board.[9] When these conditions are met, the employee pays 2.5 per cent less in contributions above the lower earnings limit, and the employer's contribution is reduced by 4.5 per cent.[10] The claimant then receives his earnings-related state pension (calculated according to the formula described in the preceding section) minus the additional component or 'the guaranteed minimum pension' (GMP), whichever is less.[11]

The GMP is calculated in much the same way as the state additional component. In effect it is a weekly amount calculated as a percentage of the person's total earnings for the years (since the Pensions Act) of his working life.[12] If the person concerned (in 1975) is less than 20 years under pensionable age, then the percentage is 1¼ per cent of earnings over the remaining years of his working life; otherwise it is 25 per cent of his earnings for the years in his working life after the provisions come into force.[13] However, there is no provision for taking into account the 'best' twenty years of the person's working life, as there is for the calculation of the state earnings-related component. The earnings on the basis of which GMP is calculated are revised to allow for earnings increases in line with the statutory procedure.[14] Every approved occupational scheme must at the least provide this minimum pension,[15] and must also provide a widow's pension of not less than half the earner's GMP.[16] In determining the amount of state pension to which the pensioner in a contracted-out scheme is entitled, the GMP (if less than the additional component) is deducted. It follows from this that the government is in effect providing the *subsequent* inflation-proofing when a pensioner is in receipt of an approved occupational pension, by continuing to pay the difference between the full state pension (basic plus additional component, revised annually to allow for inflation) and the guaranteed minimum pension (calculated at the pensioner's retirement) which must be provided by the occupational scheme.

Although the state guarantees the equivalent of the additional component against inflation, occupational pensions schemes must provide security against changes in the value of earnings *during the person's working life*. They must grant a pension of not less than 1¼ per cent of either his average annual salary throughout his service in contracted-out employment or his final salary, in either case multiplied by his years of service up to forty.[17] Moreover, where they assess pension by reference to average salary, this must be revalued as with earnings factors for the state additional component.[18] Occupational schemes are left a certain amount of freedom with regard to the assessment of the salary by reference to which the person's pension is calculated;[19] they may also provide for a minimum period of service before the person qualifies for benefits in excess of the GMP.[20]

9 SSPA 1975, s.30. The Board was set up by the SSA 1973 to regulate occupational schemes and is one of the few survivals of that legislation.
10 SSPA 1975, s.27(2).
11 Ibid, s.29(1).
12 Ibid, s.35: see DHSS leaflet, NP 32, p. 12.
13 The exact formula in the second case is 25/*N*% of the total earnings factors for the tax years in the person's working life from 1978–79, *N* being the number of years of working life since section 36 came into effect, viz November 1975: SI 1975/1689.
14 SSPA 1975, s.35(5). For the statutory procedure, see SSPA 1975, s.21 as amended by SSA 1979, s.10, and p. 221, above.
15 SSPA 1975, s.33(1)(b).
16 Ibid, s.36.
17 Ibid, s.34(2).
18 Ibid, s.34(2). These schemes are comparatively rare.
19 Ibid, s.34(5).
20 Ibid, s.34(3).

Generally, occupational benefits will be more generous than the GMP, and in some cases a pension up to half the annual average salary, or much more typically, the final salary will be provided. But this will not be the case where the minimum period of service is not completed, or the person leaves his employment well before he reaches pensionable age. Here, the pensioner may only receive the GMP. There are special provisions when an earner's employment is terminated before he reaches the scheme's normal pension age, involving in some cases the payment of a 'limited revaluation premium' by the employer to the state to cover the cost of annual revision in the light of inflation.[1] The protection of 'early leavers', they are called, and the transfer of occupational pension rights have also entailed some very complicated provisions in the 1975 Act, but an exposition of these would be outside the scope of this book.

Part 6 Non-contributory pensions

A Category C retirement pensions

This pension was introduced by the National Insurance (Old persons' and widows' pensions and attendance allowance) Act 1970,[2] primarily to provide for those who were uninsured under the pre-1948 schemes and who were over pensionable age when the 1946 Act came into effect. They never had the chance to establish eligibility to a pension under this legislation. For a number of years backbenchers of both parties had attempted to help this group, but the Labour government had consistently rejected moves to provide them with pensions on the grounds that such a step would violate the contributory principle and not necessarily assist those most in need.[3] The 1970 Act was the first measure of the new Conservative government. However, it was pointed out that it did not provide any assistance for people who had been able to qualify for a pension under the 1946 Act, but for some reason – probably deficient contributions – had failed to do so. Moreover, the rate of this new pension was lower than the equivalents at that time of the full Category A or higher rate Category B retirement pension; it was considered inappropriate to pay the same amount as that receivable by persons who had contributed fully to the National Insurance Fund.[4]

The Category C pension is payable to a person who was over pensionable age on 5 July 1948, has been resident in Great Britain for a period of at least ten years between that date and 1 November 1970 and was ordinarily resident there on 2 November 1970 or on the date of the claim.[5] A woman, married to a man in receipt of this pension, is also entitled to it, provided she is over pensionable age and has retired.[6] Further, the Regulations provide for its payment in certain conditions to the widow of a man who was over pensionable age on 5 July 1948.[7] These requirements are broadly as follows:

1 Ibid, ss.35(7) and 45.
2 S.1. The Act was renamed NIA 1970, by NIA 1972, s.8(4).
3 Mr D Houghton, 803 HC Official Report (5th series) col 1017.
4 Mr P Dean, Under-Secretary of State, ibid, at col 1551.
5 SSA 1975, s.39(1), and SI 1979/642 reg 9. For the concepts of 'residence' and 'ordinary residence', see pp. 391–393, below.
6 SSA 1975, s.39(1)(b).
7 SI 1979/642, reg 11.

– she is over pensionable age, has retired, and was over 40 when her husband died; and *either*
(a) her husband was entitled to a Category C pension, *or*
(b) he died before 2 November 1970 and she satisfied specified residence conditions.

Analogous conditions are imposed for the payment of a Category C pension to a woman whose marriage to a husband (over pensionable age on 5 July 1948) was terminated by divorce.[8] It will be noted that in some circumstances the pension is conditional on the claimant's retirement, though this is generally not required. However, rather oddly, both Category C and D pensions are known in the legislation as retirement pensions.

The Category C pension is paid at two rates: a lower rate (for 1982–83, £11.80), where the claimant is, and has been since she became entitled, a married woman, and a higher rate in all other cases (for 1982–83, £19.70).

B Category D retirement pensions

A year after Category C pensions were introduced, the same government provided for non-contributory pensions to all persons over 80.[9] Any person over 80, not entitled to any other category of pension and who satisfies the residence conditions, is entitled to a Category D retirement pension.[10] It is not entirely clear why this measure so closely followed the introduction of Category C pensions; probably the government became convinced that the needs of all those over 80 should be met, irrespective of the circumstance whether they had ever had the chance to join the 1946 Act scheme.[11] In any case, the numbers of people covered by this new pension were estimated then to be only about 50,000. The amount of the Category D pension is £19.70 except where the pensioner is, and has been since she became entitled to it, a married woman, when it is paid at the lower rate of £11.80.

It appears that virtually everyone entitled to a Category C retirement pension would be entitled to a Category D pension if he were not able to claim the former. The major exceptions are wives (or widows) of husbands who were over pensionable age on 5 July 1948; they are entitled to a Category C pension, but will not (if under 80) be entitled to a Category D retirement pension. This group will decline in numbers over the next few years and it will then be appropriate to consider whether it is necessary to retain the separate Category C retirement pension.[12] The number of recipients of Category D pensions may also be expected to decline, as there will be fewer claimants still alive who did not exercise the option to pay contributions afforded them by the 1946 legislation. But there will always be some people whose contribution record is deficient, in particular those immigrants and British citizens returning from abroad who have not been obliged to pay contributions for their working life; it will be necessary to keep the Category D retirement pension as a residual provision for them.

8 Ibid, reg 12.
9 NIA 1971, s.5.
10 SSA 1975, s.39(1)(c): the residence conditions are set out in SI1979/642, reg 10. These conditions are discussed in *Re an Italian Widow* [1982] 2 CMLR 93.
11 Sir K Joseph, Secretary of State, 816 HC Official Report (5th series) cols 1013–1014.
12 The Social Security Statistics for 1980 show that about 2,000 women under 80 benefit from the Category C pension: Table 13.35.

C The age addition

The National Insurance Act 1971 also introduced an additional payment of 25p (known as the 'age addition') for pensioners of all categories over 80.[13] As Sir Keith Joseph said during the Second Reading in the House of Commons, 'this age addition recognises, albeit in a small way, the special claims of very elderly people, who on the whole need help rather more than others'.[14] In fact the measure now appears as an insignificant gesture since its value has not been increased since its introduction. A person in receipt of certain other prescribed benefits, and who would be entitled to a retirement pension if he were to claim it rather than continue in receipt of the alternative benefit, is also entitled to the addition.[15] It need not be claimed, and is therefore paid automatically.[16]

13 The provision is now in SSA 1975, s.40(1).
14 816 HC Official Report (5th series) col 1019.
15 SSA 1975, s.40(2): see SI 1979/642, reg 17, which prescribes these other benefits. For the age addition to supplementary benefit, see p. 469, below.
16 SI 1979/628, reg 3(c): see p. 552, below (claims and payments).

Chapter 6

Benefits on death

It is convenient to consider together, in one chapter, three benefits payable on the death of a contributor. These are widow's benefits (Part 1), child's special allowance, payable when the deceased was maintaining a child of a former marriage (Part 2), and death grant, a sum paid for partial indemnity of funeral expenses (Part 3).

Part 1 Widow's benefits

A General

It has been written of the history of British provision for widowhood that 'no part of our social security has shown such a consistent pattern of political failure as this'.[1] The problems have arisen for a variety of reasons: there have been differing views concerning the extent to which widows should be regarded as part of the potential labour force, and the extent to which benefit should be regarded as an unqualified return on the husband's contributions or rather a limited entitlement based on need. At the same time, it has been necessary to take account of the public sympathy aroused by widowhood and the tendency to distinguish it from other circumstances where a family is deprived of a breadwinner (e.g. divorce).

Lloyd George had planned to extend his programme of national insurance to cover widowed mothers and orphans. His failure to do so resulted not from any unwillingness on the part of the Liberal government but from a massive political lobby organised by the industrial assurance companies, which saw in the proposal a threat to their business and to the livelihood of their employees.[2] After the First World War, political pressure, particularly from women's associations, for some form of mother's pension had grown,[3] and the hostility of the industrial assurance companies had abated. The notion of a comprehensive scheme for all unsupported mothers was firmly resisted – it would be inappropriate and impracticable to make provision for deserted or divorced wives on a

1 *Walley* p. 249.
2 Gilbert *The Evolution of National Insurance in Great Britain* (1966) pp. 326–343.
3 *Finer* App 2, paras 77–88.

contributory insurance basis[4] – but there was an acknowledged powerful case for a widowed mother's pension. Yet what emerged in the Baldwin government's proposal was the surprising notion of a pension of ten shillings per week payable for life or until remarriage to *all* widows, regardless of means or family commitments. Payment to childless widows was by no means a popular move[5] but Churchill, influenced by the administrative difficulties of providing a more selective scheme and by the naive assumption that if the husband had paid his contributions, the insurance principle would require that benefit could not be refused to the widow,[6] steered the measure through Parliament as part of the Widows', Orphans' and Old Age Contributory Pensions Act 1925.

The rashness of this decision had long-term harmful effects on the future of widows' benefits. The flat-rate universal scheme meant that widows with families suffered economic hardship while childless recipients were relatively well off. The hostility of Beveridge to the scheme is evident from the incisive terms in which he criticised it:

> there is no reason why a childless widow should get a pension for life; if she is able to work, she should work.[7]

Under his plan, the abolition of long-term entitlement of childless widows or those able to work was to be accompanied by more generous treatment of widows with children. He proposed a short-term benefit payable to all widows for 13 weeks, to allow them to adjust to the new circumstances, and a pension payable only for so long as there were dependent children.[8] The government, while accepting these two basic principles, was also impressed by an argument which he had rejected, that a pension equal to a retirement pension should be paid to a widow who, at her husband's death or when her youngest child ceased to be dependent upon her, had reached an age at which she would find it hard to take up paid work.[9] It also considered it unfair to deprive childless widows of rights already conferred on them by their husband's contributions, so the 'ten shillings pension' would still be paid when the husband had died before 1948.

The embodiment of these proposals in the National Insurance Act 1946 may have implemented this new policy,[10] but the formulation of particular rules consistent with that policy exercised the minds of successive governments and necessitated some important changes in the period after 1950. These included the abolition of an earnings rule, the provision of earnings-related additions, and the revising of the methods of determining when it would be unreasonable to expect the widow to work. These will be described at relevant stages in the discussion of the various benefits available, and Part 1 will conclude with a critique of the present law.

4 Second Interim Report of the Committee on Insurance and Other Social Services (Anderson Committee) (1923), available at the Public Record Office. See *Finer* n.3, above, and Gilbert *British Social Policy 1914–1939* (1970) pp. 242–244.
5 Opposition was expressed by the trade unions and indeed by some members of the government itself: *Walley* pp. 63–64.
6 Ibid, p. 64.
7 Para 153.
8 Para 346.
9 *Social Insurance*, Part I, para 121.
10 It was reiterated by the National Insurance Advisory Committee in its Report on the Question of Widow's Benefits (1956, Cmd 9684), para 27.

B Widowhood

A claimant must, of course, prove that she 'has been widowed'. This involves two elements: she was lawfully married to a man, and while so married he died. The first will be considered in detail in chapter 10;[11] the second calls for treatment here. The primary method of proof is by a certificate issued by the Registrar General,[12] but other less formal means will suffice, it being necessary to satisfy the statutory authorities on the balance of probabilities that the husband is dead.[13] The real problem arises where he has been absent for some years and nothing has been heard of him. In Scotland since 1977 legislation has provided that if, on a balance of probabilities, it is determined that a missing person has not been known to be alive for a period of at least seven years, a decree may be granted declaring that that person died seven years after the date on which he was last known to be alive.[14] It has been decided that the social security statutory authorities are competent to apply this criterion for benefit purposes.[15] In England, on the other hand, while a similar presumption has been created for several specific areas of law,[16] social security is not one of them, and efforts have consequently been made to find something equivalent in the common law. The reported decisions of the Commissioner on the point suggest that no such general presumption exists. In *R(G) 1/62* it was held that at common law a man is presumed to live his normal span, and that the onus is on the claimant to rebut the presumption by evidence that, for example, he was last seen setting out on a dangerous mission, or was known to be at the site of a calamity. Such evidence had been available in an earlier case when a claim succeeded ten months after the hat and jacket of the missing spouse had been found at the landing stage of a port.[17] In the 1962 case no equivalent circumstances could be invoked and, despite the fact that nothing had been heard of the husband for 25 years, the claim failed. It may be, however, that the latter decision is not conclusive on the point. It purported only to apply pre-1977 Scots law and the English decision of *Chard v Chard*[18] was not cited. In that case Sachs J, having carefully reviewed the relevant authorities, advanced a proposition to cover the situation where legislation had not intervened, and where there was no acceptable affirmative evidence that the missing person was alive at some time during a continuous period of seven years or more. It was to the effect that,

> if it can be proved first, that there are persons who would be likely to have heard of him over that period, secondly that those persons have not heard of him, and thirdly that all due inquiries have been made appropriate to the circumstances,

the missing person will be presumed to have died at some time within that period.[19] Whether this dictum should be applied to social security law

11 Pp. 377–392, below.
12 Under a special arrangement with the DHSS. See SSA 1975, s.160. The certificate, formerly issued free of charge, now costs £1.25: SI 1981/265.
13 *R(G) 4/57*.
14 Presumption of Death (Scotland) Act 1977, s. 2(1)(b).
15 *R(G) 1/80*, J G Mitchell, Comr, holding that a 'statutory tribunal' which, under s.2(3) of this Act, has jurisdiction to grant such a decree includes an insurance officer, the local tribunal and the Commissioner.
16 See e.g. Offences against the Person Act 1861, s.57 (as a defence to bigamy); Matrimonial Causes Act 1973, s.19(3) (dissolution of marriage); and generally Treitel 17 MLR 530.
17 *R(G) 4/57*.
18 [1956] P. 259.
19 Ibid, at 272.

remains an open question. *Chard v Chard* was concerned with the validity of a subsequent marriage. The policy considerations relevant to a benefit intended as a replacement for the husband's maintenance which, *ex hypothesi*, is not paid in cases of prolonged absence, may point to a different conclusion. But it does seem undesirable that English and Scots law should differ, a situation which is hardly compatible with the British basis of social security law.

C Remarriage and cohabitation

All widow's benefits cease on remarriage and payment is suspended during a period in which she is living with a man as his wife[20] (the latter concept is discussed in chapter 10[1]). Under the industrial scheme,[2] and in some foreign systems,[3] a lump-sum is payable to a widow on remarriage, presumably as an incentive to her to relieve the public fund of her support. Whether it has such an effect is highly speculative, but in any event, there is no obvious reason for the different treatment of industrial and non-industrial widows.

D Widow's allowance

The initial benefit is paid to enable the widow to readjust to her new circumstances of life, and is the most generous flat-rate personal benefit available under our social security system (in 1982–83, £45.95 per week). To this may be added an increase for dependent children,[4] but the addition based on the average earnings of the deceased husband which had been payable since 1966 has now been abolished.[5] Irrespective of her family circumstances, the allowance is payable to a widow under pensionable age at the death of the husband, (or over if he was not then entitled to a Category A retirement pension) provided that the husband had satisfied the contribution conditions,[6] viz

- in any one year ending before the date on which he attained pensionable age or died, he must have actually paid Class 1, 2 or 3 contributions, and the earnings factor derived from such contributions must be not less than that year's lower earnings limit multiplied by 25.[7]

Under the 1946 Act, the allowance was payable only for 13 weeks,[8] but in 1966 the period was extended to 26 weeks.[9] Entitlement begins on the date of death.[10]

E Widowed mother's allowance

For Beveridge, care of a family constituted the principal reason for making long-term provision for widows.[11] To determine the circumstances in which

20 SSA 1975, ss.24(2), 25(3) and 26(3).
1 Pp. 384–386, below.
2 P. 334, below.
3 *Finer* App 3, para 70.
4 SSA 1975, s.41, pp. 366–367, below.
5 SSA (No 2) 1980, s.4.
6 SSA 1975, s.24(1).
7 Ibid, Sch 3, para 4; for earnings factors etc. see ch 2, above.
8 NIA 1946, s.17(2)(a).
9 NIA 1966, s.4(3), re-enacted as SSA 1975, s.24(2).
10 *R(G) 3/52*.
11 Para 153, where he used the term 'guardian's allowance'.

such care might be presumed, the legislation imposes conditions similar to those employed where an increase to a personal benefit for child dependants is claimed.[12] It may, however, be questioned whether the two situations are truly analogous: the widowed mother's allowance (WMA) is based on the idea that family responsibilities prevent a widow working, which implies that the child or children should be living with the widow; the increases to personal benefit are meant to assist the claimant with *financial* obligations.[13]

The necessary relationship between the widow and child or children is, for the most part, governed by the principles of child benefit.[14] The claimant must prove either that she is pregnant by her late husband or that she is entitled to child benefit in respect of a child who is either

(a) a son or daughter of the woman and her late husband; *or*
(b) a child in respect of whom her late husband was immediately before his death entitled to child benefit;[15] *or*
(c) if the woman and her late husband were residing together immediately before his death, a child in respect of whom she was then entitled to child benefit.[16]

As will be seen, child benefit is generally not payable for children aged 16 to 19 or those absent from Great Britain.[17] The traditional test of dependency for WMA was not so limited and so to preserve the broader base for the allowance, those 'entitled to child benefit' in the rules cited above are 'deemed' to include those who would have been entitled to child benefit if the child in question had been under 16 or present in Great Britain.[18]

The contribution conditions are different from those applicable to the widow's allowance, resembling instead those imposed for retirement pensions. They are:[19]

(1) in any year ending before that in which the husband died or reached pensionable age, he must actually have paid contributions of Classes 1, 2 or 3 and the earnings factor derived therefrom must be not less than the qualifying earnings factor for that year. The condition is deemed to be satisfied if he was entitled to invalidity pension at any time during the year in which he attained pensionable age or died, or the year immediately preceding that year.
(2) for each year of his working life, less one year for each ten years' working life, he must have paid or been credited with contributions of Classes 1, 2 or 3, and the earnings factor derived therefrom must be not less than the qualifying earnings factor for the year in question. This condition is deemed to have been fulfilled if the husband had satisfied the criterion for at least half the number of years (or 20 of

12 Cf pp. 366–367, below.
13 In 1956 NIAC had drawn attention to the anomaly (Report on the Question of Widow's Benefits (1956, Cmd 9684, paras 76–78) but its recommendation to exclude benefit in cases of non-residence has not been implemented.
14 Ch 11, below.
15 This is deemed to include a child of the widow's previous marriage if the husband of *that* marriage was immediately before *his* death entitled to child benefit for that child and the woman was entitled to child benefit at the time of the death giving rise to the present entitlement to WMA: SI 1979/642, reg 16(2).
16 SSA 1975, s.25(1), (2), as amended by CBA 1975, Sch 4, para 9.
17 Pp. 428 and 441, below.
18 SI 1979/642, reg 16(1).
19 SSA 1975, Sch 3, para 5 as amended by SSPA 1975, s.19(1), (2). On the concepts involved see ch 2, above.

them, if that is less than half) and in the remaining years he was precluded from regular employment by responsibilities at home.

The emphasis placed by Beveridge and post-war governments on the WMA, as fulfilling the needs of widows with family commitments, was not always fully reflected in the amounts payable. Under the 1946 Act[20] the widow was paid a flat-rate weekly sum less than that of the widow's allowance, and equal to that of the widow's pension, and in addition received for each of the qualifying children the standard rates of increase to personal benefit for dependent children. In 1956 the inadequacy of this provision was revealed by the fact that about 30 per cent of WMA recipients were also in receipt of a national assistance grant, a proportion higher than that for any other category of national insurance beneficiary.[1] Since that date a number of steps have been taken to improve the financial provision, generally by assimilating the allowance to the long-term benefits available on retirement and invalidity. Thus the additions for child dependants were raised to an amount substantially higher than those paid with the short-term benefits.[2] Secondly, the widowed mother became entitled to an additional component calculated on the earnings-related contributions made by her deceased husband under the new pensions scheme.[3] Originally, as with retirement pensions, the allowance was reduced for earnings above a prescribed level.[4] This was an extremely unpopular rule and there was continuous pressure for its removal.[5] After a number of concessions had been made, the rule was finally abolished in 1964.[6] The allowance itself is equivalent to the basic component in the retirement pension (in 1982–83, £32.85 per week).

F Widow's pension

The continuance of provision for a widow after her last child reaches an age of non-dependency has been the subject of greatest dispute and the most important changes since the 1946 Act. Beveridge saw no reason to distinguish between widows and single women and concluded that, apart from a 'training' allowance, nothing beyond the ordinary benefits for unemployment and sickness should be conferred on the childless widow until pensionable age.[7] The post-war government felt that this would create hardships for elderly widows who had little or no working experience, and quite independently of its decision to maintain the 'ten shillings pension' for those childless widows already qualified under the old scheme, introduced a new, long-term pension payable to those aged 50 or over when the husband died, or 40 or over when entitlement to WMA ceased.[8] In both cases, it was felt necessary to establish evidence of prolonged absence from the labour market by requiring proof that the claimant had

20 NIA 1946, Sch 2, Part I.
1 NIAC Report, n.13, above, at para 38.
2 FANIA 1956, s.2(1). See pp. 365–366, below.
3 Pp. 233–234, below.
4 Cf pp. 212–216, above.
5 The NIAC, while remaining committed to the principle underlying the earnings rule, had found great difficulties in its application: see Report on the Earnings Rule (1955, Cmd 9752). A proposal for its abolition for several years played a leading role in the Labour Party Manifesto. See the parliamentary debate on the National Insurance Bill 1964, 702 HC Official Report (5th series) col 1297 ff.
6 NIA 1964, s.1(5).
7 Para 156.
8 NIA 1946, ss.17(1)(c) and 18(1)(a).

been married for a period of at least ten years,[9] though if the widow was incapable of self-support, the pension was payable irrespective of the duration of the marriage or her age at her husband's death or when WMA ceased.[10] In 1956 this concession was revoked,[11] but at the same time the duration of marriage test for all widows was reduced to three years[12] and subsequently, in 1970, abolished altogether.[13]

As regards the age condition, the distinction between those who had, and those who had not, been entitled to WMA was an eleventh hour political concession made before the 1946 Bill was passed, and was difficult to justify except on sentimental grounds. In 1956, following the National Insurance Advisory Committee's recommendations,[14] the preferential treatment for widowed mothers was removed and henceforth the '50 year' age test was to apply to all, except, of course, those already benefiting from the earlier concession.[15] This second instance of the rare practice of actually narrowing entitlement to social welfare was not to remain effective for long. The main objection was the all-or-nothing distinction which depended on the widow's exact age when her husband died or when her entitlement to WMA ceased. Accordingly, as part of its National Superannuation plan, the Labour government proposed to introduce a sliding scale of pensions for those aged between 40 and 50 at the relevant date. The proposal was resurrected by the succeeding Conservative government and was implemented in 1970.[16]

As a result of these various modifications, the present rule for entitlement is that the widow must have been over 40 years of age[17] at the date of the husband's death or when she ceased to be entitled to WMA.[18] If at that date, she was under 50, the weekly rate of pension (in 1982–83, £32.85) is reduced by 7 per cent for each year of age less than 50 (any fractions of a year counting as one whole year).[19]

– Thus a benefit payable to a widow aged 47 at her husband's death is reduced by 21 per cent, and if aged 41 by 63 per cent.

The contribution conditions are the same as those for WMA,[20] and as with that benefit, no earnings rule applies.

G Earnings-related additions

The new pensions scheme, introduced in 1975, and described in detail in a previous chapter,[1] may have been primarily directed at providing an adequate income during old age but it was also designed to have a

9 Ibid, ss.17(1)(c) and 18(1)(b).
10 Ibid, s.18(3).
11 Except for those already entitled to it: FANIA 1956 s.2(6).
12 Ibid, s.2(2), following a NIAC recommendation: n.13, above.
13 NIA 1970, s.3, which, however conferred a power by regulations to exclude or reduce pension where the husband had attained pensionable age before marriage and had died within a year. The power was never exercised and was itself abolished by SSA 1973, Sch 28.
14 NIAC Report on the Question of Widow's Benefits (1956, Cmd 9684), para 45.
15 FANIA 1956, s.2(5).
16 NI (Old persons' and widows' pensions and attendance allowance) Act 1970, s.2, (renamed NIA 1970 by NIA 1972).
17 For guidance on how age is to be determined see p. 197, above.
18 SSA 1975, s.26(1).
19 Ibid, s.26(2).
20 Ibid, Sch 3, para 5; p. 231, above.
1 Pp. 219–224, above.

considerable impact on widows' rights.[2] Her ability to inherit her husband's pension entitlement means that not only will the level of financial support available to her be increased (though substantially only when the scheme matures[3]) but also that there is a significant return on the husband's contributions should he die prematurely.

Under the Social Security Pensions Act 1975, a woman whose husband died after 5 April 1979 and who is entitled to a widowed mother's allowance or a widow's pension may augment those benefits with an additional component calculated, as with a Category A retirement pension,[4] on contributions made by the husband above the qualifying earnings factor for a particular year.[5] This component is payable even if because of deficiencies in the contribution record the widow is not in receipt of the full basic rate of the allowance or the pension, or the husband, at the time of his death, was not paid the full basic rate of retirement pension.[6] On the other hand, and perhaps inconsistently, the rule which provides for a reduction in a widow's pension where entitlement to this commences between the age of 40 and 50[7] operates also to reduce the amount of additional component payable: by 7 per cent for each year of age less than 50.[8]

H Old cases

In order to protect those with vested interests under pre-war legislation, equivalents to WMA and the flat-rate pension are payable to widows of persons over pensionable age on 5 June 1948.[9]

I Other benefits

The special circumstances affecting a widow, particularly that she might be thrown onto the labour market, having previously been entirely dependent on her husband's support, or with an incomplete contributions record, have been used to justify provisions facilitating her entitlement to other benefits. The most important of these relate to retirement pension and have already been described.[10] It remains to mention here some special rules governing entitlement to benefits which may be claimed before the retirement.

(1) As regards the short-term benefits for sickness, unemployment and maternity, once entitlement to WMA has ceased, she is deemed to satisfy the first contribution condition, and is granted credits sufficient to satisfy the second condition.[11]

(2) Where during a period of entitlement to WMA or the pension, the widow claims for sickness benefit, unemployment benefit or maternity allowance, she is not allowed to accumulate the proceeds with her

2 See White Paper, Better Pensions (1974, Cmnd 5713), pp. iii–iv.
3 Cf p. 220, above.
4 P. 220, above.
5 SSPA 1975, s.13. Widows whose husbands contracted-out may, like retirement pensioners, benefit from the arrangement whereby the state scheme effectively provides inflation-proofing support for an occupational pension: ibid, s.28, and pp. 222–223, above.
6 SI 1979/642, reg 6(1).
7 P. 233, above.
8 SSPA 1975, s.13(3).
9 SI 1979/642, regs 13–15.
10 Pp. 210–211, above.
11 SI 1974/2010, reg 3(1).

widow's benefit, but is paid at the rate of whichever of the relevant benefits is more favourable to her.[12]

(3) The widow may claim invalidity benefit after 168 days of incapacity, even though (as required in the normal case) she has not been drawing sickness benefit for this period.[13] The invalidity pension is calculated on the basis either of her own contributions or of those of her deceased husband, whichever is more favourable to her.[14] The same applies *mutatis mutandis* to a widower,[15] one of the few concessions made to this category of social security claimant.

J Critique

The history of widows' pensions has been a struggle between two conflicting principles: that of providing universal income maintenance for a widow irrespective of age and family circumstances, and that of guaranteeing an income to a widow only when she is deemed to be unlikely to obtain the necessary income support for herself. The result of the struggle has been a compromise solution conditioned as much by political sentiment as by any clear objective and sociological perspective.[16] The phenomenon has not been peculiar to Britain. The writer of a comparative survey has observed that,

> the variety of responses [to the problems of widowhood] is due to historical circumstances and the unequal strength of the pressure groups influencing public opinion and the public authorities. It seldom follows any logical pattern.[17]

There are, perhaps, four major criticisms that can be made of the existing provisions. First, the system divides widows into certain categories which are based on assumptions of their needs as individuals in certain situations of life,[18] whereas it is arguable that the need for security belongs to the family rather than the widow, who may not herself suffer any financial loss. Secondly, it does not take sufficient heed of the changing pattern of women's participation in industry. The rules on widow's benefits, particularly following the abolition of the earnings rule, are based on the stereotype of the woman looking after the family, with paid employment being regarded as an exceptional activity. This no longer reflects social reality: in 1978 70 per cent of married women aged 34–44 were employed in full-time or part-time work.[19] Thirdly, the relatively generous treatment of widows contrasts starkly with the position of widowers, and, as such, is a blatant example of sex discrimination.[20] While the Social Security Pensions Act 1975 has made a modest attempt to mitigate the inequality by allowing a husband to rely, in certain circumstances, on his deceased wife's

12 Ibid, reg 3(10). The inability to accumulate the benefits seems to be inconsistent with the policy which allows the widow to supplement her allowance or pension with earnings of whatever amount.

13 SSPA 1975, s.15(2).

14 Ibid, s.15(3).

15 Ibid, s.16(3).

16 Cf Marris *Widows and their Families* (1958) ch 7.

17 Laroque 106 Int Lab Rev 1, 7. See also Tamburi in (1973) 5 ISSA Studies and Research, *Women and Social Security* 128 ff.

18 *Marris*, n.16, above, at p. 91.

19 HMSO General Household Survey 1978, Table 5.1.

20 There is provision for a widower's pension under the industrial injury and war pension schemes, but in both cases the conditions of entitlement are highly restrictive: pp. 334 and 359, below.

contributions for the purposes of his invalidity or retirement pension, it leaves unaffected the basic principle. The lack of provision to cover lost household services may rest on the questionable assumption that it is easier for the widower than for the widow to find a replacement spouse.[21] Quite apart from this, it fails to take account of the working wife's contributions to the family income. In both the United States of America[1] and the Federal Republic of Germany[2] there have been important judicial decisions declaring unconstitutional social security legislation which confers death benefits only on the widow.

Part 2 Child's special allowance

A General

There was one group of women with dependent children who might suffer hardship on the death of the children's father because they would not be eligible for widowed mother's allowance. These were women whose marriage had been terminated by divorce and who since then had received some provision from the former husband for the children of the marriage (or other children). Although this provision might cease, they would not then become entitled to any benefit on the husband's death for the simple reason that they were not widows. The Royal Commission on Marriage and Divorce drew attention to the gap and recommended that such a woman should be entitled to draw an allowance under the national insurance system for children living with her if the death of her former husband resulted in the loss of the money he had been contributing towards their maintenance.[3] The National Insurance Advisory Committee adopted this recommendation, subject to the modification that the benefit should be payable to a divorced woman, whether she had been the 'guilty' party or not.[4] The proposal was implemented by section 5 of the National Insurance Act 1957.

Four years later, some changes were made to the structure of the benefit, the most important of which was that the value of the child's special allowance (CSA), was no longer to be limited by reference to the amount contributed for the maintenance of the child (or children) by the former husband before his death.[5] In 1982–83, £7.95 is payable for each child, the same amount as is paid by way of increase to a widow's benefit for dependent children. Nothing is paid for the ex-wife herself; in this respect her position is still worse than that of a widow. The number of recipients of a child's special allowance has been relatively small though it has been slowly rising. In 1980, 878 women received it (as against 198 in 1960).[6]

21 Cf Clarke and Ogus 5 Br Jo Law and Society 1.
1 *Weinberger v Wiesenfeld* 95 S Ct 1225 (1975), noted in 44 Ford L Rev 170.
2 Decision of Federal Constitutional Court 12 March 1975, BVerfGE 39, 169.
3 1956, Cmd 9678, paras 714–716. The former husband might, of course, have made some financial provision for the children after his death, but this does not affect the entitlement to the allowance. In this respect the current provision goes beyond the Royal Commission's proposal.
4 Report on Question of Dependency Provisions (1956, Cmd 9855), paras 72–73.
5 FANIA 1961, s.7(2)(b).
6 DHSS Social Security Statistics 1981, Table 9.35.

B Entitlement

Section 31 of the Social Security Act 1975 (as amended by the Child Benefit Act)[7] sets out the conditions for entitlement to CSA. There are broadly three requirements, in addition to the rule which limits the benefit to a woman whose marriage has been terminated by divorce, or, under the Regulations, whose voidable marriage has been annulled.[8] A woman who entered into a bigamous marriage in all good faith is not entitled to a CSA on the death of her former 'husband', because a bigamous marriage is void.[9] The distinction in this context between a void and voidable marriage seems difficult to defend, as the financial loss to the woman's children on the man's death may not differ.[10] The allowance is not payable if the woman remarries or lives with a man as his wife.[11]

i Death and contribution conditions

The first requirement is that the woman's former husband must have died[12] and must have satisfied the contribution conditions.[13] These are that:

– in any one year ending before the date on which the husband attained pensionable age or died, he must have actually paid Class 1, 2 or 3 contributors, and the earnings factor derived from such contributions must be not less than that year's lower earnings limit multiplied by 50.[14]

ii The relationship between woman and child

As with WMA the necessary relationship between the woman and the child falls into line with the child benefit scheme. She must be entitled to child benefit in respect of the child at the time of the claim and, *either* she *or* her former husband must have been so entitled immediately before his death.[15] The alternative condition based on the husband's entitlement is treated as satisfied if the child in question is a child of the marriage terminated by divorce, and for that purpose also any absence of the child from Great Britain is ignored.[16] The child need not be a son or daughter of the marriage which has ended in the divorce.

iii Support of child by husband

It is the third requirement which has raised the only points of difficulty for the Commissioner. Section 31(c) of the 1975 Act requires

> either:
>
> (i) that the husband had before his death been contributing at not less than the prescribed weekly rate to the cost of providing for that child, or

7 Sch 4, para 10.
8 SI 1975/497, reg 3.
9 *R(G) 3/59*.
10 In family law, the financial provisions on the termination of a void marriage are the same as those which obtain at the end of a voidable one. On the other hand, social security law generally does not accord any significance to a void marriage: p. 379, below.
11 SSA 1975, s.31 proviso, as amended by SS(MP)A 1977, s.22(2). See generally on this pp. 384–386, below.
12 Cf p. 229, above.
13 SSA 1975, Sch 3, Part I, para 6.
14 For pre-1975 contributions; see SI 1979/643, reg 8.
15 SSA 1945, s.31(b), as amended by CBA 1975, Sch 4, para 10. For entitlement to child benefit, see ch 11, below. There is a minor category of persons so entitled who are treated as not so entitled: see SI 1977/342, reg 3.
16 SI 1975/497, reg 4, inserted by SI 1977/342, reg 6(3).

(ii) at the date of that husband's death she was entitled, under an order of a court, trust or agreement which she has taken reasonable steps to enforce, to receive (whether from that husband or from another person) payments in respect of that child at not less than that rate provided or procured by that husband.

Limb (ii) of this provision was introduced in 1967 as an alternative to the requirement of the actual providing of money by the former husband.[17] It enables CSA to be claimed where the woman has unsuccessfully attempted to enforce a maintenance or financial provision order against him. The case-law interpreting the first limb of section 31(c) must, therefore, now be read in the light of the possibility that the claimant might succeed under this alternative head. The prescribed rate under the regulation is 25p a week;[18] and has not been increased since the allowance was introduced in 1957. The combination of this and the fact that the allowance has not since 1961 been limited to the amount actually paid by the former husband,[19] underlines the lack of real significance of the former husband's contributions as a qualifying requirement. The allowance cannot now, as it was originally, be justified as providing 'compensation' for the loss of the husband's support, but may rather be seen simply as a substitute for the widowed mother's additional allowance for her children. It is arguable that the requirement that the husband has been contributing to the cost of providing for the child now serves so little purpose that it could be abolished.

The notion of 'contributing . . . to the cost of providing for the child' in the first limb of section 31(c) is common to other areas of social security law, notably that governing entitlement to increases to personal benefit for child dependants. Guidance on its interpretation may therefore be had from discussions in that context.[20] There are, however, points of special interest to the CSA which must be considered here. The first arises from the fact that, for the purposes of the allowance, the husband must have been contributing 'before his death', even though the payments need not be *received* by that time.[1]

In *R(G) 5/59*, where the husband had made only three or four payments under a court order in the four years before his death, the Commissioner ruled that the phrase, 'had before his death been contributing', meant 'had *immediately* before his death been contributing'. Otherwise the words 'before death' would have no significance at all. A second reason for this interpretation was that the purpose of the allowance was to confer a benefit on a woman who suffered financial loss on her former husband's death, and this would only be the case if he had been contributing immediately before that time. For the reasons given in a previous paragraph this second argument is perhaps now of less weight, but the Commissioner's interpretation of the provision and his disallowance of the claim on the facts were obviously correct.[2]

On the other hand, the fact that payments were irregular will not be a decisive obstacle to entitlement. As with the analogous test governing

17 NIA 1967, s.1(2) and Sch 4, para 4.
18 SI 1975/497, reg 2.
19 P. 236, above.
20 Pp. 373–376, below.
1 See *R(G) 17/59*, where the husband died before the sale of a house, half the proceeds of which were to be paid to the former wife, could be completed and a deed of covenant signed.
2 See also *R(G) 6/59*, In *R(G) 5/59*, the claimant had tried to enforce the maintenance order, and therefore her claim would now probably succeed on the basis of limb (ii).

entitlement to dependants' increases, the Commissioner has been prepared to average payments over a substantial period (e.g. a year),[3] and because the prescribed rate of contributions is so low (25p a week) even infrequent payments made during such a period will probably satisfy the requirement.

Involuntary and temporary cessations in the payment of contributions are also generously treated. For the purposes of the CSA, this is important because of the proximity of the husband's death. Thus the Commissioner has held that a period in hospital when the husband was suffering from a terminal illness might be ignored,[4] but such an illness does not cover 'a long period of incapacity which ultimately terminates in death': it means a period when the person is dying.[5] In other circumstances, entitlement turns on whether an interruption was temporary or permanent. In deciding this issue, regard will be had to the reason for the interruption, the husband's general contributions record and his attitude to the children during the period. In *R(G) 15/59*

> the claimant's former husband contributed regularly to the maintenance of her two children until he became unemployed just over four months before he died. Although he was a sick man for this period, he did secure employment for about eight weeks, and then he entered hospital for the six weeks before his death.,The Commissioner ruled (1) that the period in hospital when the husband was suffering from a terminal illness should be ignored, and (2) that the earlier cessation of payments when he became unemployed was temporary and involuntary. An allowance was therefore awarded.

It was not until the husband entered hospital that it became clear he would not recover, so that before that time there was every prospect that payments would be resumed, and throughout he had taken an interest in the children. These factors were not present in *R(G) 3/60*, where the husband stopped paying maintenance shortly after he had left his work because of infirmity, and there was never any chance that he would be able to resume payments in the 18 months before his death. The Commissioner held that the cessation of payments, though involuntary, was not temporary.

Part 3 Death grant

A General

Although the payment of a state lump sum benefit on death dates only from 1946, the need to provide for a decent burial has played an important part in the history of social policy. The desire to avoid imposing on relatives the humiliation of a pauper's funeral was an important cultural phenomenon of the industrial revolution and accounts in part for the rapid expansion of friendly and burial societies, but particularly industrial assurance companies, in the nineteenth century.[6] Indeed, by 1874, one company alone, the Prudential, had over one million policy holders.[7] The

3 *R(G) 15/59* and p. 373, below.
4 *R(G) 15/59*.
5 *R(G) 3/60*.
6 An extensive history of the matter is to be found in Wilson and Levy *Industrial Assurance* (1937).
7 Bruce *The Coming of the Welfare State* (4th edn) p. 112.

large commercial interest in the funeral expenses insurance resulted in stalwart opposition to any attempt to transfer the insurance to state management.[8] Fierce competition between the companies resulted in allegations of sharp practice and exploitation. A series of committees investigated the matter,[9] and their recommendations as implemented by legislation,[10] did much to strengthen the law. But when Beveridge again surveyed the problem during the Second World War, he found that there was a very strong case for further drastic reform.[11] First, the administrative costs of insurance were very high, averaging over 37 per cent of premiums paid. Secondly, there was a high proportion of abortive insurance, i.e. policies which lapsed before they could mature.[12] Thirdly, the cost of insurance constituted a substantial drain on the resources of the lower-income groups: 'hundreds of thousands of families with less than enough to live on contribute substantial proportions of their incomes to industrial assurance'.[13]

Beveridge therefore proposed to incorporate 'funeral grants' into his social insurance scheme. A lump sum, varying according to age, would be payable on the death of a contributor, or a member of his family.[14] The proposal was adopted by the government,[15] and was included in the 1946 Act. However, the method of conferring payment proved to be almost wholly misconceived. The grant could be claimed by any person who had 'reasonably incurred or reasonably intends to incur . . . any expenses of an appreciable amount, in connection with the funeral of the deceased',[16] but this was not to include a body corporate or an unincorporated association.[17] The rule created very substantial difficulties in the administration of the grant.[18] More than one person might come within the statutory provision, and though the Minister had power to determine priority as between claimants, and to suspend payment, this did not wholly solve the problem.[19] The fact that the grant was not payable to legal, as opposed to natural, persons proved to be inconvenient where, for example, a firm had paid for the funeral expenses.[20] Entitlement on mere proof of intention to incur the expenditure meant that individuals could benefit without paying out some or all of the money received. Finally, delicate questions of fact arose from the interpretation of what was 'reasonably' incurred, what was an 'appreciable' amount, and what were expenses 'in connection with the

8 See Gilbert *Evolution of National Insurance in Great Britain* (1966) pp. 328–332.
9 Royal Commission to inquire into Friendly and Building Societies (Northcote Commission) (1872–74), First Report, C 452, Second Report C 514, Third Report C 842, Fourth Report C 961; Report of Departmental Committee on the Business of Industrial Assurance Companies and Collecting Societies (Parmoor Committee) (1920, Cmd 614); Committee on Industrial Assurance and Assurance on the Lives of Children under Ten Years of Age (Cohen Committee) (1933, Cmd 4376).
10 Notably the Assurance Companies Acts 1909 and 1923.
11 Paras 157–160 and Appendix D.
12 The evidence revealed that the number of policies so failing in any one year was about two-thirds of the number issued: ibid, Appendix D, para 79.
13 The estimated figure was 3–5% of income: ibid, at para 80.
14 Paras 159–160 and 350.
15 *Social Insurance*, Part I, paras 132–138.
16 NIA 1946, s.22(1), (2). The expenses were deemed to include those incurred by the attendance of the claimant or other persons at the funeral, the purchase of mourning, and any loss of remuneration: ibid, s.22(2).
17 Ibid, s.22(4).
18 See the NIAC Report on the Death Grant Question (1956, Cmnd 33).
19 See e.g. *CG 115/50*, and *R(G) 6/55*.
20 See e.g. *R(G) 2/52*; *CG 192/50*; *R(G) 8/52*.

funeral.'[1] To meet the difficulties, the National Insurance Advisory Committee proposed a radical revision of the rules of entitlement:[2] the grant would constitute an asset of the deceased which would form part of his estate on death (as with arrears of other national insurance benefits). It would therefore be for his personal representatives to claim, and the sum payable would be fixed, irrespective of the amount actually spent on the funeral and concomitant purposes. The new principle was introduced in 1957,[3] and with some modifications, has been in force ever since.

The most remarkable feature of the subsequent history of the grant is that the amounts payable have remained unchanged since 1967 and are only 50 per cent higher than the rate in 1948. The standard sum is £30.00, but is reduced for young persons (under three, £9.00; three to six, £15.00; six to nineteen, £22.00), and for men who had reached 55 and women who had reached 50 on 5 July 1948, £15.00,[4] on the basis that their contributions to the scheme had not bèen substantial. The grant now covers about 10 per cent of the cost of a simple funeral,[5] and is considerably lower than the amounts paid out for this contingency under the supplementary benefits scheme. The situation has attracted much criticism and during the passage of the Social Security Bill 1979, the Conservative opposition successfully introduced an amendment to impose a duty on the Secretary of State to 'review' the amount of death grant to determine whether it has declined in value.[6] But in contrast to the up-rating provisions in relation to other benefits,[7] this does not contain a complementary duty to revise the amount in the light of the review.

One explanation for the failure of successive governments to maintain the value of the grant might lie in their perception that cultural attitudes to local authority funerals (the modern equivalent of paupers' funerals) have changed, but this is hard to reconcile with the fact that the supplementary benefit system reimburses expenditure on *private* funerals. A second possibility is that, following the 1957 shift in entitlement from those incurring expenditure to the deceased person's estate, the benefit has lost such connection as it once had with actual funeral expenses, and has become no more than a subsidy by social security contributors to the estates of deceased persons, thus undermining the original objective of the scheme.[8] Thirdly, it may simply reflect the fact that today the contributory scheme is seen as being concerned exclusively with income maintenance and that the reimbursement of special expenditure has no proper place within it.

There is, finally, the question of administrative costs; they consume about one-half of the amount paid out to beneficiaries.[9] Given that the grant is now of only marginal value to most families, the present government has recognised the need for radical reform. Its proposals, published in March 1982, are summarised at the end of this chapter.

1 E.g. CG 65/50; *CG 66/50*; *CG 145/50*; *R(G) 21/52*.
2 N.18, above.
3 NIA 1957, s.7.
4 SSA 1975, Sch 4, Part II, para 2.
5 DHSS Consultative Document *The Death Grant* (1982), para 5.
6 SSA 1979 s.13.
7 Pp. 411–413, below.
8 *Calvert* p. 248.
9 *The Death Grant*, n.5, above, at para 6.

B Persons whose death is covered

The deceased must be within one of the statutory categories.[10] They are as follows.

(a) The deceased was himself a contributor.[11]

(b) The deceased was at death the husband, wife, widow or widower of the contributor or a child in respect of whom the contributor was entitled to child benefit.[12]

(c) The deceased was under 16 years and either (i) was predeceased by a contributor who at his death was entitled in respect of him to child benefit, or (ii) was the posthumous son or daughter of the contributor.[13] Alternatively, it will be sufficient if one of the child's parents is or was a contributor, or a contributor was immediately before the child's death entitled to a dependant's increase for that child.[14]

The remaining two categories were designed to assist those who for some legitimate reason might not have made any or sufficient contributions before their death.

(d) The deceased (1) was a child during the tax year in which he died or the preceding tax year, or at his death was aged 16 to 19 and was at that time incapacitated for regular employment, *and* (2) would have satisfied the conditions of category (c) if he had still been a child at his death.[15]

(e) The deceased (1) was over 19 at his death; (2) continuously since reaching that age had been incapacitated for regular employment; and (3) was at death residing (or would, if not living in an institution,[16] have been residing) with a near relative,[17] who was either a contributor or the wife or widow of a contributor.[18]

C Persons excluded

It has been held, both in Britain[19] and in Northern Ireland,[20] that a still-born child is not a 'person' for the purpose of this benefit, a view which has been criticised as not necessarily following from the language of the Act, and as flouting the intention of the legislature.[1] The child must, therefore, be living at the time of birth, and this means breathing.[2] Persons who had reached pensionable age on 5 July 1948 are excluded,[3] on the ground that they had not contributed to the scheme. Persons who die abroad are also

10 SSA 1975, s.32(1).
11 Ibid, s.32(2)(a).
12 Ibid, s.32(2)(b), as amended by CBA 1975, Sch 4, para 11. For entitlement to child benefit, see ch 11, below.
13 SSA 1975, s.32(2)(c), as amended by CBA 1975, Sch 4, para 11.
14 SI 1975/565, reg 2(1), as amended by SI 1977/342. For increases for child dependants see pp. 366–367, below.
15 SI 1975/565, reg 3.
16 'A school, hospital or establishment accepted by the Secretary of State as providing residential accommodation for disabled persons': SSA 1975, s.32(3)(b).
17 For the prescribed list of near relatives see: ibid, s.32(3)(c).
18 Ibid, s.32(2)(d).
19 *R(G) 3/51*.
20 *R 1/68 (DG)*.
1 Calvert 20 NILQ 52.
2 *R(G) 3/51*, in which the Commissioner preferred the evidence of a post-mortem examination to that of the midwife who had contended that the child had lived for five minutes.
3 SSA 1975, s.32(5).

excluded[4] unless the case comes within the prescribed exceptions established by the Regulations:

- viz members of the forces, airmen, mariners, workers on the Continental Shelf, persons entitled (or who would have been entitled if the relevant conditions had been satisfied) to other contributory benefits, and, most important of all, persons normally resident in GB who die within 13 weeks of leaving GB.[5]

D Contributions

It was always the intention of the creators of the scheme that the contribution requirements for the death grant should be easily met[6] and this is certainly the case.

- The 'contributor' referred to in paragraph B must in any one year before that in which the deceased died, or in which the contributor reached pensionable age or himself died, have actually paid contributions of Classes 1, 2 or 3, the earnings factor derived from which is not less than 25 times that year's lower earnings limit.[7]

E Payment

As indicated above, the primary feature of the 1957 reform was to transfer entitlement from individuals incurring expenditure to the estate of the deceased person himself, on analogy with arrears of personal benefit which are payable after the beneficiary's death. The Claims and Payments Regulations provide that, as regards any benefit payable on death, the Secretary of State may 'appoint such person as he may think fit to proceed with or to make a claim for the benefit',[8] but also, in case of death grant, prescribe that claims may be made by persons aged 16 or more who are the personal representatives, legatees, next of kin or creditors of the deceased.[9] It is not inconceivable that in a given case either no such person exists or no such claim is made. Consequently the Secretary of State has power to pay the grant to 'any person who gives an undertaking in writing to pay the whole or part of the deceased's funeral expenses', on condition, however, that if the person fails to carry out the undertaking the grant is repayable.[10] It is presumably under this Regulation that a local authority, exercising its duty to dispose of the body of a deceased person when no other suitable arrangements have been made,[11] and also probably any other legal entity, may be paid the death grant. The Secretary of State is given power to distribute benefit among the possible beneficiaries, but in the normal case it will be paid to the executors or administrators. If none has been appointed then the sum will be paid to the next of kin, if he or she has

4 Ibid.
5 SI 1975/563, reg 7.
6 *Social Insurance*, Part I, para 135, and see *The Death Grant*, n.5, p. 241, above, at para 1.
8 SI 1979/628, reg 29(1).
7 SSA 1975, Sch 3, para 7. For 'earnings factor' and 'earnings limit' see ch 2, above.
8 SI 1979/628, reg 29(1).
9 Ibid, reg 29(2). 'Personal representatives' are confined to executors and administrators. See *R(G) 3/65* where it was held that the grant was not payable to a hospital almoner who intended to transfer it to a charity nominated by the deceased.
10 SI 1979/628, reg 29(4).
11 NAA 1948, s.50(1). The authority may recover from the deceased's estate the expenses incurred, less what has been received by way of death grant: ibid, s.50(4), as amended by Social Security (Consequential Provisions) Act 1975, Sch 2, para 5.

incurred the expenditure.[12] But to meet exceptional circumstances, the discretion is drawn in even wider terms. First, 'the Secretary of State may dispense with strict proof of the title of any person' claiming under the Regulations;[13] secondly, 'under arrangements made by the Secretary of State with the consent of the Treasury' in cases of emergency (probably local or national disasters), the grant may be paid pending the determination of a claim, without proof of satisfaction of the relevant conditions.[14] Payment is suspended where a person qualified to receive death grant is imprisoned or detained in legal custody,[15] but in this case payment may be made to a person appointed by the Secretary of State to receive and deal with it on behalf of the beneficiary.[16]

F Reform

The Consultative Document published by the government in March 1982[17] recognised that the death grant, at its present value, can make only a modest contribution to the cost of funerals. It would have to be raised to £195 to match its value in 1949, but 'it is far from clear whether most families need anything like this sum from the state in order to meet funeral costs'.[18] The solution proposed is, therefore, to focus on cases where the estate is small and the person meeting the funeral costs has a low income. The implication is that the contributory grant should be replaced by a non-contributory benefit, payable at a higher level but on a selective basis. However, to avoid the undesirability of imposing a means-test at the time of bereavement, the government proposes that entitlement should follow automatically (the 'passport principle') for those already in receipt of a means-tested benefit. The options considered are: (i) recipients of supplementary benefit and family income supplement; (ii) those in (i) plus all recipients of rent rebates or rent allowances; (iii) those in (i) plus recipients of rent rebates or allowances with income below the 'housing needs allowance' level.[19] The claimant within the appropriate category would then sign a declaration that, to the best of his knowledge, the deceased's estate did not exceed (say) £1,500 (excluding the value of an owner-occupied house). A special dispensation would be granted to war pensioners.

12 DHSS Leaflet, NI 49, para 4.
13 SI 1979/628, reg 29(7).
14 SI 1975/565, reg 6.
15 Ibid, reg 5(1), and pp. 398–401, below.
16 SI 1975/565, reg 5(2).
17 *The Death Grant*.
18 Ibid, at para 7.
19 As currently payable under Housing Finance Act 1972, Sch 3, para 8.

Chapter 7

Miscellaneous benefits

Part 1 Maternity benefits

A General

Childbirth has for long been recognised as a social risk justifying protection under a social insurance scheme,[1] even if, as with retirement, it is in most cases an event voluntarily induced by the insured person. Traditionally, the payment of benefit was seen as fulfilling two objectives: protecting the health of the mother and her child and alleviating part of the financial hardship caused by childbirth.[2] To these ends the National Insurance Act 1911 conferred a lump sum grant on the mother, whether she was insured herself or the wife of an insured person. The provision in the post-Beveridge scheme of a maternity allowance for the income maintenance of the mother during periods before and after confinement was to reflect other and broader social purposes. Initially this was reconcilable with traditional concerns for the health of the mother – it encouraged her to give up work well before childbirth.[3] But in time it was to be rationalised as one of a series of measures designed to advance the social and economic status of women, and in particular to consolidate their participation in the labour market.[4] These measures included: the right to resume work with a particular employer; the right to maternity pay from that employer; and equally important, if less assured legally, the provision of child care facilities.[5] No doubt the logical consequence of a sex equalisation policy would be, as in Sweden, the introduction of a 'parental' benefit, payable to either a mother or father who temporarily gives up work to care for young children.[6]

The coexistence of financial provision from three different sources, the contributory allowance, the (now) non-contributory grant, and maternity pay from the employer which is however retrievable from the state Maternity Pay Fund and against which is set off the amount of the allowance, appears to give rise to a clumsy and wasteful overlapping of

1 Cf NIAC Report on Maternity Benefits (1952, Cmd 8446), paras 6–13; *George* pp. 128–129.
2 Ibid, p. 128.
3 *Beveridge* para 341; *Walley* pp. 223–224.
4 See generally Creighton *Working Women and the Law* (1979) esp. pp. 37–51; Winch [1981] JSWL 321; Upex and Morris 10 ILJ 218.
5 See generally Terry [1978–79] JSWL 389.
6 Agell in Samuels (ed) *Social Security and Family Law* (1979) pp. 173–174.

resources. In 1980 the arrangements were reviewed by the DHSS and, with the aim not only of simplification and administrative savings but also of a more equitable redistribution of the resources currently available, it made suggestions for three alternative but radical reforms.[7] Under the first, which presumably could not be sustained politically, the moneys now used for both income-maintenance schemes would be transferred to the lump sum grant which is payable to all mothers. The second would retain the grant in its existing form but place all responsibility for income maintenance on the employer,[8] on analogy with the government's new sick pay scheme.[9] Under the third, the employer would be relieved of the administrative burden and the resources of the Maternity Pay Fund would be used to increase either the grant or the allowance, according to whether the financial needs of non-earners or those of working mothers were considered to be the more pressing. Rather surprisingly in the light of its commitment to the sick pay scheme, the government announced in January 1981 that it did not intend to proceed with any of these proposals, apparently on the ground that there had been no general agreement on which was the most desirable.[10] A more likely explanation is that the programme for reform in other areas of social security was thought to give rise to sufficient complexities and controversy.

B Maternity allowance

i General

The maternity allowance, introduced by the National Insurance Act 1946, compensates the mother for the loss of income resulting from her confinement. It was originally paid at a higher rate than unemployment and sickness benefit.[11] Unlike the grant, entitlement to the allowance could not be based on the husband's contributions, but it was nevertheless payable to a married woman who had exercised the option not to pay contributions – she received an appropriate number of credits for this purpose.[12] Furthermore, those not entitled to the maternity allowance were paid instead a so-called 'attendance allowance' for four weeks after the confinement.[13] Major changes were made to these arrangements in 1953: the attendance allowance was abolished; the maternity allowance became payable at the level of the other short-term benefits; and the married woman's entitlement became dependent on her having paid the requisite number of contributions.[14]

ii Entitlement

a *Maternity allowance in respect of expectation of confinement*

In the normal circumstances an allowance will be claimed before confinement when the woman gives up work. She is entitled if she is pregnant and

7 DHSS Discussion Document *A Fresh Look at Maternity Benefits* (1980), on which see Dalley [1981] JSWL 329.

8 A form of the allowance would have to be retained for those not entitled to maternity pay, notably the self-employed.

9 Pp. 160–162, above.

10 997 HC Official Report (5th series) col 519 (Written Answer).

11 Cf p. 61, above.

12 She was credited with the appropriate number of contributions: SI 1948/1470, reg 9.

13 NIA 1946, s.14(1).

14 NIA 1953, ss.1–6.

'has reached a stage in her pregnancy which is not more than' 14 weeks before the expected week of confinement.[15] The period for which it is awarded ('the maternity allowance period') is 18 weeks, starting with the 11th week before the expected week of confinement.[16] A woman ceases to be entitled if her pregnancy is terminated, otherwise than by confinement, before the start of the maternity allowance period.[17]

Where an allowance is awarded on this basis, it is generally the 'expected week of confinement' which is relevant for determining the maternity allowance period, and not the actual date of confinement. This is the case even if after the original award it becomes clear that the birth took place outside the expected week. Thus in *R(G) 8/55*,

> the midwife, who completed the certificate of expected confinement, wrongly stated that the birth was expected on 2 August, when the doctor expected it a month later. The confinement had taken place before the insurance officer became aware of this clerical mistake. The Commissioner held that, 'the review of the decision should be based on what the "expected week of confinement" really was'. The actual date of the confinement was wholly irrelevant for determining the maternity allowance period.[18]

Two qualifications must be made. First, if the woman is confined before the usual maternity allowance period, i.e. more than 11 weeks before the expected week of confinement, then the period for which the allowance is payable becomes the 18 weeks from the week in which the confinement takes place.[19] Secondly, if the woman has not been confined by the end of the expected week of confinement, the maternity allowance period may be extended.[20]

b *Maternity allowance by virtue of fact of confinement*

A woman may alternatively claim a maternity allowance when she has actually been confined. In that case it is generally payable for a seven-week maternity allowance period, beginning with the week of confinement.[1] In some cases it may be paid for more than this period. Where the woman was in fact confined more than 11 weeks before her expected date of confinement, then she may receive the allowance for the 18 weeks beginning with the week of confinement.[2] Secondly, where she shows that she did not work for the period up to 11 weeks before the week of confinement *and* had good cause throughout this time for her failure to make a claim on the basis of her expectation, then she will be entitled to an allowance from the start of this period until six weeks after the week of confinement.[3]

c *Meaning of 'confinement'*

'Confinement' means 'labour resulting in the issue of a living child, or labour after 28 weeks of pregnancy resulting in the issue of a child whether

15 SSA 1975, s.22(1)(a), and SI 1975/553, reg 4(1).
16 SSA 1975, s.22(2).
17 SI 1975/553, reg 4(2): see *R(G) 4/56*.
18 See also *R(G) 2/61*.
19 SI 1975/553, reg 5(1).
20 Ibid, reg 5(2), (3).
1 Ibid, reg 6(1).
2 Ibid, reg 6(2).
3 Ibid, reg 6(3): see pp. 565–569, below, for the meaning of 'good cause'.

alive or dead'.[4] Thus, a woman whose 6 months' pregnancy terminated without the issue of a live child is not entitled,[5] nor is a woman who delivers a 'hydatidiform mole'.[6] Where labour begins on one day and the birth takes place the following day, the latter is the day of confinement.[7]

The only difficulties appear to arise in cases where the woman has a miscarriage after a number of weeks' pregnancy, and it has to be calculated whether that period has amounted to 28 weeks in order to establish entitlement. In *R(G) 4/56*, the Commissioner estimated the period by counting back from the expected date of confinement – on the assumption that the gestation period was the 273 days stated in a medical dictionary. In another case, the Commissioner accepted the evidence of a gynaecological registrar, who had examined the foetus, in reaching the conclusion that the woman had not been pregnant for more than 23 to 25 weeks.[8]

The term 'pregnancy' is not defined in the legislation. This omission enabled a Commissioner in Northern Ireland to hold that a woman was 'confined', when she produced, only two months before the expected date of confinement, a foetus which had ceased developing three months after conception.[9]

iii Contribution conditions

These are that the claimant must

(1) in any one year before the beginning of the maternity allowance period have paid Class 1 or 2 contributions, and the earnings factor derived from those contributions must be not less than that year's lower earnings limit multiplied by 25;

(2) in respect of the last complete year before the year containing the period of the interruption of employment which includes the beginning of the maternity allowance period have paid or been credited with Class 1 or 2 contributions, and the earnings factor derived from those contributions must be not less than that year's lower earnings limit multiplied by 50.[10]

iv Disqualification

A woman who has been awarded the allowance may become disqualified from receiving it in certain circumstances.[11]

(1) A woman doing any work in employment, whether as employee or self-employed, during the maternity allowance period is to be disqualified for such part of that period (not less than the number of days worked) as is reasonable.

The force of the phrase, 'does any work in employment', is to make it clear that a woman who does housework cannot be disqualified. In contrast to sickness benefit, the claimant cannot contend here that she has failed to observe the requirement for 'good cause', and the disqualification is for a reasonable period, rather than a maximum of six weeks.[12]

4 SSA 1975, s.23(1)(a).
5 *CWG 1/49*.
6 *CG 3/49*.
7 SAA 1975, s.23(1)(b).
8 *R(G) 12/59*.
9 *R 1/64 (MB)*.
10 SSA 1975, Sch 2, para 3. For the term 'period of interruption of employment', see SSA 1975, s.17(1)(d), pp. 89–90, above.
11 SI 1975/553, reg 9.
12 For sickness benefit disqualifications, see pp. 155–159, above.

(2) If during the maternity allowance period, the claimant fails without good cause to take due care of her health and answer reasonable inquiries concerning it, she may similarly be disqualified for a reasonable period.

(3) If she fails without good cause to attend a medical examination, she will be disqualified for a reasonable period.[13] But if the confinement occurs after the failure to attend, she is not disqualified from the allowance for the days of, and after, the confinement.

v Amount

For 1982–83 the weekly amount of the flat-rate maternity allowance is £25.00. Increases for child dependants, and in some cases for the claimant's husband, may also be payable;[14] an allowance may be increased in respect of the child for whose birth the claimant is confined.[15] The earnings-related supplement previously paid with the allowance[16] was abolished in 1982.[17]

vi Maternity pay

The statutory right to maternity pay from the employer has to a large extent superseded in importance the social security allowance as an instrument of income maintenance.[18] The mother receives nine-tenths of her gross weekly pay less the allowance, whether or not this is actually paid.[19] But the period of entitlement is limited to six weeks after the 11th week before the expected confinement[20] – though this may of course be extended under the individual contract of employment. To qualify under the employment protection legislation, the woman must have been continuously employed for two years and must continue in employment up to 11 weeks before the expected week of confinement.[1] The employer is entitled to claim a rebate from the state Maternity Pay Fund of the statutory amount of maternity pay.[2]

C Maternity grant

Under the National Health Insurance scheme of 1911 a lump-sum grant was payable to the mother if she was either insured herself or the wife or widow of an insured person,[3] the first social insurance benefit to be paid to someone other than the contributor. According to Beveridge, it was not 'intended to cover the whole cost of maternity, which has a reasonable and natural claim upon the husband's earnings'.[4] Nevertheless, when the National Insurance Advisory Committee came to review the grant as provided for in the 1946 legislation, it concluded that it was 'by far the least

13 See p. 156, above, for the similar disqualification from receipt of sickness benefit.
14 See pp. 364–369, below.
15 SSA 1975, s.41(3).
16 Although this supplement was itself introduced by SSA 1973, s.17(4), since 1966 a recipient of the allowance could receive the supplement payable with sickness benefit.
17 SSA (No 2) 1980, s.4.
18 For a critical account, see Creighton *Working Women and the Law* (1979) pp. 42–46.
19 Employment Protection (Consolidation) Act 1978, s.35.
20 Ibid, s.34.
1 Ibid, s.33(3).
2 Ibid, s.39.
3 NIA 1911, s.8(1)(e).
4 Para 341.

adequate, in relation to the contingency for which it was designed, of all the National Insurance Benefits'.[5] There was the additional criticism that it failed to differentiate between the expenses incurred on home and hospital confinement respectively. The Committee consequently recommended that a new home confinement grant should supplement the existing grant.[6] This was implemented in 1953 but was abolished 11 years later,[7] on the ground that mothers were now discharged from hospital more rapidly than had previously been the case and so the difference in costs of a hospital and home birth was not substantial.[8] This reversal, while not in itself dramatic, may be seen retrospectively as the start of a general decline in the importance of the maternity grant. As with death grant,[9] successive governments have allowed its real value to decline, and the sum currently paid, £25, has remained unchanged since 1969.[10] In recent years there has been increasing criticism of this trend.[11] The government response has not been to uprate the grant but instead to reclassify it as a non-contributory benefit, financed by general taxation rather than the National Insurance Fund.[12] It was estimated that some 60,000 more mothers would qualify for this benefit.[13] Under the new provisions, which came into force on 4 July 1982, the claimant has to satisfy in addition to the principal condition of confinement certain requirements as to presence in Great Britain.

i Confinement

The claimant must establish either (a) that she 'has been confined'[14] or (b) that at the date of claim she is pregnant at a stage not more than 11 weeks before the expected week of confinement.[15] Under condition (a), title to the grant only arises after the confinement.[16] But, of course, substantial expenditure may be incurred before the birth, e.g. on buying a cot or clothes. For this reason, the alternative condition (b) was introduced. The National Insurance Advisory Committee thought there was some danger that a woman receiving the grant 11 weeks before an anticipated birth might not spend it wisely, and recommended that the period should be reduced to eight weeks.[17] It was reduced in 1954 to nine weeks, but it has since returned to 11 weeks.

ii Conditions as to presence

The decision to recharacterise the grant as a non-contributory benefit made it necessary for the government to stipulate some alternative

5 Report on Maternity Benefits (1952, Cmd 8446), para 39.
6 Ibid, paras 22–35.
7 NIA 1964, s.1(4).
8 Miss M Herbison, Minister of Pensions and NI, 702 HC Official Report (5th series) cols 1305–1306.
9 P. 241, above.
10 The Secretary of State is under a duty each year to review the amount payable to see whether it has retained its value (SSA 1979, s.13) but he is under no consequential duty to uprate; cf p. 412, below.
11 See e.g. SSAC Report on Draft Maternity Grant Regulations (1981, Cmd 8336), para 10.
12 SSA 1980, s. 5.
13 Standing Committee E Debates on the 1980 Bill, col 740.
14 SSA 1975, s.21(1).
15 SI 1975/553, reg 3.
16 For the meaning of 'confinement', see pp. 247–248, above.
17 N.5, above, at paras 98–99.

connection with Britain. This has been achieved through conditions as to presence in this country, prescribed by regulations.[18]

(a) The claimant must have been present in Great Britain for at least 182 days in the 52 weeks immediately preceding the week of confinement.[19] But the 182 days are deemed to include periods of temporary absence during which she was either in receipt of child benefit or abroad for the purposes of her own or her husband's employment, in respect of which contributions are payable.[20]

(b) If the woman claims *before* confinement, she must in addition be present in Great Britain on the date of claim.[1] If she claims *after* confinement, she is not disentitled by reason that the confinement took place abroad if either she was entitled to child benefit in the following week or her absence was not intended to last for more than four weeks or she (or her husband) had for the last tax year an earnings factor derived from paid or credited contributions of not less than 50 times the lower earnings limit.[2]

(c) Serving members of the forces and the wives of such persons are generally exempt from these conditions.

iii Multiple births

More than one maternity grant may be paid in the event of a multiple birth.[3] There is, of course, a risk that one or more of a number of twins, triplets, etc. will not long survive child birth and, therefore, an excessive amount could be paid by way of maternity grants. This contingency led to a change in the Regulations in 1954; since then a mother is only to be entitled 'for each child who has lived for at least 12 hours after being born'.[4] The reform was accepted by the majority of the National Insurance Advisory Committee, but Titmuss dissented on the ground that the necessity to prove survival caused embarrassment for the mother and difficult administrative work for the hospital staff.[5] It is submitted that if both twins die within the 12 hours, one grant would be payable under the general rules, but it is possible that a literal construction of the regulation dictates that no grant is payable in this circumstance! That would be a wholly unjustifiable result of what is in any case arguably a harsh rule.

Part 2 Guardian's allowance

A General

Guardian's allowance (GA) is a non-contributory benefit, which is broadly payable to a person looking after a child, both of whose parents are dead. The allowance was introduced in 1946, replacing the orphan's pension which had been payable since the Widows', Orphans' and Old Age Contributory Pensions Act 1925. This had provided a weekly pension

18 SI 1981/1157, amending inter alia SI 1975/553. For the meaning of 'present in Great Britain', see p. 391, below.
19 SI 1975/553, regs 3(b) and 3A(1), as substituted by SI 1981/1157.
20 SI 1975/553, reg 3B, inserted by SI 1981/1157.
1 SI 1975/553, reg 3(b)(ii), as substituted by SI 1981/1157.
2 SI 1975/563, reg 3(4), inserted by SI 1981/1157.
3 SSA 1975, s.21(4).
4 SI 1975/553, reg 2.
5 Report on Draft Regulations 1953–54, HC 97.

payable to 'the guardian or the other person having the charge of the child', in respect of any orphan, defined as a child both of whose parents were dead.[6] The National Insurance Act 1946, unlike the 1925 legislation, enabled an allowance to be paid where one of the child's parents was dead and the other could not be traced.[7]

The fact that in certain circumstances GA may be paid in respect of a child, whose parents are not both dead, raises the difficult question: what is the rationale or principle justifying the payment of this benefit? Is it primarily designed to 'compensate' the child for the loss of his parents or, on the other hand, to provide some state assistance to encourage a person to look after a child who for some reason lacks parental support? The rationale for the pension paid under the 1925 Act would appear to have been the former, since entitlement was dependent on the child having the status of an orphan.[8] Now that the requirements for entitlement have been relaxed, the question is less easy to answer. The policy seems to be to pay an allowance where one parent is dead and the other can for practical purposes be treated as non-existent so that the child is virtually an orphan, but not to pay an allowance merely because the surviving parent neglects his responsibilities to the child.[9] Whatever the merits of this distinction, the formulation of the policy in the legal requirements for entitlement has produced difficulties for the Commissioners. Thus, in *R(G) 10/52*, a Tribunal ventured the opinion that GA is payable either when the child concerned has the status of an orphan or 'the relationship normally uniting parents with each other or with their child no longer obtains'. But the Northern Ireland Commissioners have adopted an even broader approach, and have suggested in effect that it is the absence of a parent (or parents) able to assume financial responsibilities for the child, which now justifies the award of the allowance.[10] This uncertainty about the principle underlying the GA is largely responsible for the complex law discussed in the next section.

There would appear to be two alternative paths of reform, both of which would be in a sense more logical than the present complicated position. First, entitlement to GA could be extended to cover anyone looking after a child who is without financial support from a parent, whether this is because both parents are dead, or the surviving parent cannot be found or, if found, cannot be induced to contribute towards his maintenance. Indeed, on this basis, there would be no justification for insisting on the present requirement that at least one parent is dead. Alternatively it may be questioned whether there is any justification for paying guardians a special allowance. The second course, therefore, would be to abolish it altogether. It can be argued to this end that the former orphan's pension was introduced before family allowances were payable, and that its successor, the guardian's allowance, should now be reconsidered in the light of the introduction of the more generous child benefit scheme.[11] It is not clear that a guardian should receive assistance in respect of a child

6 S.4. NB: orphan's pension was not, and the guardian's allowance is not, restricted to the 'guardians' of a child in the sense in which that term is used in family law: see Cretney *Principles of Family Law* (3rd edn) pp. 429–430.

7 NIA 1946, s.19(1), proviso (ii); see now the comparable provision in SSA 1975, s.38(2)(b).

8 Widows', Orphans' and Old Age Contributory Pensions Act 1925, s.44; and see the views of the Commissioners in *R(G) 10/52*.

9 See NIAC Report 1948, HC 165, paras 8–13.

10 *R 3/74 (P)*; *R 3/75 (P)* (Tribunal decision), paras 9–10: see p. 255, below. This is clearly opposed to the view of NIAC in 1948: n.9, above.

11 Cf *R(G) 2/80*, para 20, M J Goodman, Comr.

living with him beyond the provision afforded anyone else (including a parent) discharging the same responsibilities. But until child benefit rates approach that of the allowance, GA is unlikely to be abolished. The legislation lays down three alternative conditions to determine whether the child is without parental support and further rules governing who are parents for this purpose. There are additional requirements on the connection with Great Britain and entitlement to child benefit. The discussion is divided accordingly.

B Child without parental support

i Both parents dead

The first of the alternative conditions relates to the conventional meaning of orphanhood: both parents must be dead.[12] The principles governing proof of death have been considered in chapter 6.[13]

ii One parent dead and the other missing

The second alternative is

> that one of the child's parents is dead and the person claiming a guardian's allowance shows that he was at the date of the death unaware of, and has failed after all reasonable efforts to discover, the whereabouts of the other parent.[14]

The claimant must show that *one* of the child's parents is dead by the normal means of proof.[15] He will not succeed if he can merely show that he is unaware of, (or has failed after all reasonable efforts to discover), the whereabouts of both parents. To allow a claim to succeed on these facts would be finally to abandon the principle that the child must be an orphan, or be in a position very similar to this. But it can be argued that the normal parent-child relationship is as much absent if both parents are 'missing', as it is if one is dead and the other's whereabouts cannot be discovered.[16]

Under the 1946 Act the rule was that an allowance could be paid if one parent was dead, and the other 'cannot be traced'.[17] A Tribunal of Commissioners interpreted this as requiring the claimant to demonstrate that there was no evidence indicating whether the second parent was alive or dead.[18] On this objective test it was not enough for him to show that he was unable himself by reasonable efforts to discover the parent; his claim would be defeated if there was *any* evidence to suggest that the other parent was still alive. On the recommendation of the National Insurance Advisory Committee,[19] the rule was changed to the present formulation, now contained in section 38(2)(b). The meaning of this is not, however, entirely plain. In particular, it is not clear if the requirement is satisfied when there is evidence that the second parent is still alive, but the claimant cannot find out after reasonable efforts where he is living. The views of the

12 SSA 1975, s.38(2)(a).
13 Pp. 229–230, above. In *R(G) 11/52* a Tribunal of Commissioners indicated that the presumption of death after seven years' absence could be relied on in guardian's allowance cases.
14 SSA 1975, s.38(2)(b).
15 Cf n.13, above.
16 See the statement of principle in *R(G) 10/52,* set out on p. 252, above.
17 NIA 1946, s.19(1).
18 *R(G) 11/52.*
19 NIAC Report on Question of Dependency Provisions (1956, Cmd 9855), para 88.

British and the Northern Ireland Commissioners would appear to differ on this question.

The principles relevant to a determination whether a claimant 'has failed after all reasonable efforts to discover the whereabouts' of the second parent were stated in *R 2/61 (P)* by the Northern Ireland Commissioner. The test is subjective in the sense that the claimant must have made those inquiries of the parent's 'whereabouts' which could reasonably have been expected of him: '. . . the onus lies upon the person claiming the allowance to show that he has made such efforts to the best of his particular ability'.[20] Where there are no profitable lines of inquiry, only very slight efforts will be expected; but a claimant who made no attempt to find the father, because she did not think it would be in the child's best interests to do so, was refused an allowance.[1] Efforts made before the death of the other parent may be taken into account, but in general it seems that the claimant must make an attempt to discover the whereabouts of the missing parent *after* the other's death.[2]

A claim will fail if the whereabouts of the missing parent are discovered otherwise than by the efforts of the claimant. This was decided in *R(G) 3/68*:

> In April 1967 an allowance was claimed in respect of a child whose father had died in February, and the whereabouts of whose mother were unknown. Later that month, and again in May and June, the child received letters from his mother from an address in the Soviet Union; but she did not reply to letters sent to her concerning wardship proceedings taken by the claimant. The Commissioner, R S Lazarus, held that the mother's whereabouts had been discovered, and that GA was not payable.

The decision is important on four points, on the last two of which the Northern Ireland Commissioners have taken a different attitude.

(a) The Commissioner ruled that the insurance officer and local tribunal should not disregard facts which have come to light since the date of the claim. In the case it became clear that the mother was still alive only after it was made, but this was enough to defeat it. In the converse case where the claimant was aware of the parents's whereabouts at the date of the other's death, but since then the parent has disappeared and the claimant has not discovered his whereabouts, both the British and the Northern Ireland Commissioners take the view that an allowance is not payable.[3]

(b) In *R(G) 3/68* the mother's whereabouts were not discovered *by reason of* the claimant's efforts. The Commissioner ruled that this did not matter; an allowance could not be paid if the whereabouts were discovered by an means by the time the case was decided. This has met with the approval of F A Reid, a Northern Ireland Commissioner,[4] and seems clearly right.

(c) The address given by the mother in *R(G) 3/68* indicated a town, from which it could at most be inferred that the letters were written. But

20 *R 2/61 (P)*, para 15. There is no reason to think that the British Commissioner would not agree with this statement of principle.
1 *R(G) 4/59*.
2 *R 1/73 (P)*, T A Blair, Comr, on this point, *R(G) 10/55*, decided on the pre- 1957 formulation, still appears relevant.
3 See *R 3/75 (P)*, where the British Commissioner's views in *CG 1/75* are discussed.
4 *R 3/74 (P)*.

the Commissioner ruled that 'whereabouts' and 'residence' were not synonymous, and that, therefore, the fact that the claimant did not know exactly where the mother lived was irrelevant: he did know the mother's *whereabouts*. But the Northern Ireland Commissioners in *R 3/74 (P)* took a stricter view. In an urban environment. ' "whereabouts" must be taken to mean a place identifiable with some particularity'.[5] Knowledge of a village where the parent lived would be adequate, but usually the name of a city or large town would be too imprecise. This point is integrally connected with the fourth one.

(d) The Commissioner in *R(G) 3/68* supported his interpretation with some observations on the principles underlying the availability of a guardian's allowance. He said that entitlement did not merely depend on the absence of a person under an enforceable legal duty to maintain the child, but on the entire non-existence of the parent-child relationship.[6] In effect, he concluded that the claimant could not take advantage of the relaxation of the rule that both parents were dead, if it was clear that the second parent was alive. As the letters from the Soviet Union indicated here that the mother was alive, the claim failed.

This view of the meaning of section 38(2)(b) has been rejected by the Northern Ireland Commissioner in *R 3/74 (P)* and by a Tribunal in *R 3/75 (P)*. In both cases, it was said that the section might enable a claimant to succeed if he could not discover the whereabouts of the second parent, i.e. precisely where he is living, even though there is good evidence that he (or she) is alive. The continued existence of the parent-child relationship did not preclude the award of GA. In the later case, the Tribunal said that if the British Commissioner were right, the provision would have been drafted: '. . . to discover whether he is still alive'.

The difference between the two approaches may be illustrated simply by reference to an example given in *R 3/75 (P)*:[7]

> C claims an allowance in respect of a child, one of whose parents is dead and the other is missing. About the time of the claim, C receives a letter from the second parent without an address or legible postmark. It seems that the British Commissioner would refuse to award GA in this case – he certainly would if it was clear which town the letter came from – while in Northern Ireland, the Commissioners would award GA, unless the claimant was able to discover where the parent lived.

It is submitted that the interpretation placed upon the provision by the Northern Ireland Commissioners is to be preferred. The other view seems to reduce the significance of the legislative change referred to earlier to a mere reformulation of the requirement.[8] On the other hand, the Report of the National Insurance Advisory Committee which recommended that change does seem to bear out the more restrictive view taken in *R(G) 3/68*.

iii One parent dead, and the other in prison

The third situation giving rise to entitlement is where 'one of the child's parents is dead and the other is in prison',[9] and a parent is to be treated as being in prison if

5 Ibid, at para 7, per F A Reid, Comr.
6 He quoted with approval the Commissioners in *R(G) 10/52*: see p. 252, above.
7 At para 9.
8 P. 253, above.
9 SSA 1975, s.38(2)(c).

> he is serving a sentence of imprisonment of not less than five years or of imprisonment for life, or is in legal custody as a person sentenced or ordered to be kept in custody during Her Majesty's pleasure or until the directions of Her Majesty are known.[10]

In assessing the five years for this purpose, no account is taken, inter alia, of any period of the sentence served before the first parent's death.[11] The alternative to a prison sentence, that of detention in legal custody, covers orders for an accused to be detained following a finding that he is unfit to plead or not guilty of a criminal charge on the ground of insanity,[12] but perhaps surprisingly has been held not to apply where the parent was detained in Broadmoor following a conviction of manslaughter by reason of diminished responsibility.[13] The relevant provision of the Mental Health Act which allowed for release by the Secretary of State was regarded as being inconsistent with the notion of 'custody during Her Majesty's pleasure or until the directions of Her Majesty are known'.

Where the condition is satisfied the amount of GA is reduced by any contribution made by the parent in prison or custody to the cost of providing for the child.[14] This suggests that, in this case at least, the rationale for payment of the allowance is not 'compensation' for loss of the normal parent-child relationship, but for loss of the financial support usually provided by parents.

C Meaning of 'parents'

i Step-parents

Following a legislative change in 1957,[15] the term 'parent' as used in the provisions considered above does not include a step-parent, so the fact that one step-parent is alive does not disentitle the person looking after the child from the allowance. A step-parent himself may be entitled, since the disqualification in section 38(6) (a parent is not to be entitled to a guardian's allowance in respect of his child), does not apply to him.

ii Adopting parents

Where a valid adoption order has been made in favour of two spouses jointly, they (and not the natural parents) are to be treated as the child's parents for the purposes of section 38(2).[16] Therefore for GA to be awarded, either both adopting parents must be dead, or one of them must be dead and the other's whereabouts cannot be discovered, etc. Where a child has been adopted by one person, GA may be payable on his death.

iii Parents of illegitimate children

In the case of an illegitimate child, where

> (a) a person has been found by a court of competent jurisdiction to be the father of the child, or
>
> (b) . . . in the opinion of the determining authority the paternity of the child has been admitted or established,

10 SI 1975/515, reg 5.
11 Ibid, reg 5(2)(a).
12 *R(G) 4/65* and *R(G) 2/80*, para 12.
13 Ibid, paras 13–19.
14 SI 1975/515, reg 5(6).
15 NIA 1957, s.6.
16 SI 1975/515, reg 2.

the mother and father (so determined) of the child are regarded as its parents for GA purposes.[17] For the allowance to be payable, therefore, *either* both the natural father and mother must have died, *or* one of them must be dead and the other must be missing, or in prison. This does not apply, however, if the child in question has previously been adopted, for then it is the death of the adoptive parents which is necessary as a precondition for the availability of GA. Moreover, for the provision to be invoked there must be determinations as to both the illegitimacy of the child and its paternity. As regards the first of these conditions, there is a common law presumption that a child born during the subsistence of a marriage is legitimate.[18] The Commissioner has held that the Family Reform Act 1969, section 26, applies to determinations under social security legislation,[19] so that the presumption may be rebutted 'by evidence which shows that it is more probable than not' that the child is illegitimate. As regards paternity, this is deemed to be 'admitted' by the entry of the father's name on the birth certificate.[20] But an order by a district registrar of the High Court under section 41 of the Matrimonial Causes Act 1973 is not regarded as a finding of paternity by 'a court of competent jurisdiction' and is therefore not conclusive of the issue.[1]

A difficult question is whether the term 'parent' in the relevant provision of the legislation includes the *natural* father of the child. This is important because section 38(6) provides that the allowance is not payable to a parent of the child. 'Parent' is not now, and never has been, defined in the social security legislation, but a Tribunal of Commissioners in *R(G) 12/55* ruled that a natural father is a 'parent' for the purposes of entitlement to guardian's allowance. Therefore, he was not entitled when he looked after the child subsequent to the death of its adoptive parents.[2] This ruling has been criticised as a matter of interpretation, as generally the word 'parent' in a statute does not include the natural father.[3] Moreover, it is arguable that the specific provision that, for the purposes of section 38(2) of the Act, the natural father is to be treated as a parent in certain circumstances implies that generally he should not be so treated. On the other hand, if the natural father were eligible to receive GA in the rare circumstances which obtained in this case, it seems that in theory the natural mother should similarly be entitled if she looked after her child on the death of its adoptive parents, though it would be odd to hold that she was not a 'parent'. On balance, therefore, the ruling by the Tribunal seems correct.

iv Divorced parents

If the child's parents have been divorced and on the death of one of those parents, 'the child was not in the custody of, or being maintained by, the other parent *and* there was no order of a court granting custody of the child to that other parent or imposing any liability on him for the child's

17 Ibid, reg 3(1).
18 *Banbury Peerage Case* (1811) 1 Sim & St 153.
19 *R(G) 2/81,* paras 16–17, M J Goodman, Comr.
20 See *R(G) 15/52*; *R(G) 4/59*.
1 *R(G) 2/81*.
2 This appears to be the only situation where a natural father could claim GA with any plausibility; in other cases he would have to be dead before the payment of the allowance could arise!
3 See *Calvert* p. 250. He criticises the Tribunal for not giving enough weight to the decision of the Court of Appeal in *Re M* [1955] 2 QB 479, [1955] 2 All ER 911.

maintenance', then entitlement arises on the death of the first parent.[4] In this case the parent-child relationship has already been severed with the other parent, so there is every justification for modifying the usual requirement for both parents to have died before GA is awarded. However, the mere fact that a court order has been made against the surviving spouse means that the parent-child relationship has not been destroyed and the allowance is not payable; it does not matter that no money has been paid under the order.[5]

D Connection with Great Britain

A feature common to the non-contributory benefits is the need to establish a sufficient connection with Great Britain, typically by prescribing conditions as to residence or presence. As regards the claimant for a guardian's allowance, and the child for whom it is claimed, these are contained in the rules governing child benefit, for, as will be seen in the next paragraph, entitlement to this benefit is a pre-condition for receipt of the allowance. In addition the claimant must show that one of the child's *parents* had a sufficient connection with this country.

– One such parent must either have been born in the United Kingdom or by the date of the death of the parent whose death gives rise to the claim for GA must have been present in Great Britain for at least 52 weeks in any period of two years after attaining the age of 16.[6]

E Entitlement to child benefit and amount of allowance

The claimant must be entitled to child benefit (or treated under regulations as so entitled) for the child for whom GA is claimed.[7] Where a husband and a wife are residing together,[8] and both satisfy this and all other conditions of the allowance, it is the wife who is entitled.[9] But payment may be made to either, unless she elects that it is not to be made to her husband.[10]

The weekly amount of the allowance in 1982–83 is £7.95, for each child.

4 SI 1975/515, reg 4. This applies also to the annulment of a voidable marriage: ibid, reg 4(3).
5 See *R(G) 10/52*.
6 SI 1975/515, reg 6, as substituted by SI 1977/342. For the meaning of 'present', see p. 391, below.
7 SSA 1975, s.38(1), as amended by CBA 1975, Sch 4, para 12(a). For cases where entitlement is deemed, see p. 367, below.
8 On which see pp. 371–373, below.
9 SSA 1975, s.38(5), as amended by CBA 1975, Sch 4, para 12(c).
10 SI 1975/515, reg 6A, inserted by SI 1977/342.

Chapter 8

Industrial injury

Part 1 Introduction

A History

Provision for the consequences of industrial accidents and diseases has always taken a prominent position among social welfare systems. Typically it manifests four characteristics:

> It is the oldest branch of social security, it provides the most generous benefits, it is a pace-setter for other social security provisions and it is administered as a separate entity.[1]

The surge of legislation at the end of the nineteenth century in the industrialised countries was quite remarkable in its coincidence.[2] The movement may be attributed to a number of causes:[3] the increasing power of the trades unions; the inadequacies of the tort system as a means of compensation; social concern at the high accident rate in industry; the need for an incentive to industrial safety and the rehabilitation of disabled members of the labour force.

The British Workmen's Compensation Act 1897, in certain respects, bore traces of the traditional common law liability, but in more important respects foreshadowed a system of social insurance. Liability was imposed on the employer himself, but compensation was payable for all accidents 'arising out of and in the course of employment', irrespective of proof of negligence.[4] Loss was effectively shared between employer and the employee, for the latter might claim at most only one half of his average earnings,[5] and that subject to a statutory maximum.[6] Short-term claims were excluded by a waiting period of three weeks.[7] The principle of individual employer's liability led naturally to an adversarial method of adjudicating claims, and, though provision might be made for less formal

1 *Kaim-Caudle* p. 65.

2 1883, Italy; 1884, Germany; 1894, Norway; 1897, UK; 1898, France and Denmark.

3 Cf *Atiyah* pp. 360–363; *Dupeyroux* pp. 38–44; Wilson and Levy *Workmen's Compensation* (1939) vol 1, ch 1; *Ogus* pp. 166–175.

4 In 1897 £1.00 per week (WCA 1897, Sch 1, para 1(b)). The WCA 1923, s.4(1) raised the maximum to £1.50.

5 WCA 1897, s.1(1).

6 Ibid, Sch 1, para 1(b). Under WCA 1923, s.4(2), for workmen earning less than £2.50 per week, the proportion was fixed on a scale varying from 50%–75%.

7 WCA 1897, s.1(2)(a), reduced to one week by WCA 1906, s.1(2)(a) and three days by WCA 1923, s.5.

arbitration, proceedings would typically be taken in the county courts and often, on appeal, to the higher courts.[8] Apart from cases of death, for which a lump sum of three years' annual earnings, to a maximum of £300, was payable to dependants,[9] compensation would normally take the form of weekly payments. However, the concept of a 'private right' was used to support the idea that an individual might compromise his claim for a lump sum settlement. Indeed, after six months of payments, an employer had the *right* to redeem the continuing obligation by a lump sum, provided only that it was registered with, and obtained the approval of, a county court judge.[10]

Originally the Act was confined in its scope to certain dangerous trades.[11] In 1906, it was extended to cover all manual occupations, and those non-manual workers earning less than £250 a year.[12] Employment-related illnesses had been a major source of hardship, and in the same year, compensation became payable to those suffering from certain specified diseases which were attributable to the nature of the employment.[13] The only other substantial reform before the scheme was abolished in 1946 was the introduction of increases for dependants. It was regularly urged that payment according to earnings (and only partial compensation at that) did not provide sufficient security for those with large family responsibilities. As regards death cases, the point was conceded in 1923, after which child dependants' allowances might supplement the lump sum to the widow,[14] but despite a firm recommendation for similar provision for living claimants,[15] it was not until 1940 that the proposal was implemented.[16]

The brevity of this account should not be allowed to disguise the complexity of the scheme's operation, the frequency of government reviews and legislative changes, and the general contention and dissatisfaction which it engendered. The criticism reached its height in the late 1930s with the publication by Wilson and Levy of their massive sociological and comparative treatise on the subject.[17] A Royal Commission established in 1938 curtailed its inquiries on the outbreak of war and its task was assumed by Beveridge as part of his overall survey of social security. His own dislike of the scheme is immediately apparent: 'the pioneer system of social security in Britain was based on a wrong principle and has been dominated by a wrong outlook'.[18] From his exposition of the weaknesses of workmen's compensation the following may be highlighted: the adversarial nature of adjudication which was disruptive of good industrial relations and which created problems of adequate representation for the workman;[19] the lack of any obligation on employers to insure against liability with the consequent

8 See *Wilson and Levy* n.3, above, vol 2, at pp. 255–262; Young *Industrial Injuries Insurance* (1964) pp. 79–81.
9 WCA 1897, Sch 1, para 1(a)(i), p. 330, below.
10 WCA 1897, s.1(3)–(4).
11 These are listed ibid, s.7.
12 WCA 1906, s.13.
13 Ibid, s.8.
14 WCA 1923, s.2.
15 Report of Committee on Workmen's Compensation (Holman Gregory Report) (1920, Cmd 816), para 62.
16 WC (Supplementary Allowances) Act 1940, s.1(1).
17 Wilson and Levy *Workmen's Compensation* (1939).
18 Para 80.
19 Para 79(i)–(ii); *Wilson and Levy*, n.17, above, vol 2, ch 15. The point was also stressed in *Social Insurance* Part II, para 23.

lack of security for accident victims;[20] the ability to compromise a claim for a lump sum settlement, which presupposed equality of bargaining power and under which a claimant was tempted to accept less than his due;[1] the high administrative costs of the scheme, resulting in part from the inefficiencies of the private insurance market[2] and in part from the excessive resort to litigation.[3]

Beveridge's plan to unify responsibility and administration of industrial injuries compensation under a national insurance scheme, and at the same time to afford more generous benefits than those available for unemployment and sickness,[4] and without contribution requirements, was accepted. The exact form and level of benefits remained, however, a matter for considerable dispute. The proposal to pay a rate of benefit which would, only after a period of thirteen weeks' incapacity, be higher than that for sickness,[5] was rejected: preferential treatment was to be provided throughout.[6] Conversely, the government was not prepared to depart from the general principle of flat-rate benefits in favour of an earnings-related pension,[7] as Beveridge had recommended.[8] It proposed, for long-term cases, the tariff method of compensation, derived from the war pensions scheme and based on the degree of disablement.[9] This idea of basing benefits on need rather than earnings-potential proved to be unacceptable politically, and there ensued an unsatisfactory compromise combining the tariff benefit with the so-called 'special hardship allowance' which compensated for impaired earning capacity.

Apart from the introduction in 1966 of a new allowance for the very seriously disabled,[10] the substance of the law governing industrial injury benefits remained during the period until 1982 largely unaltered. Administratively, however, there was a gradual process of integrating the scheme within the general structure of social security. In 1973–75 the high point of this process was reached by the abolition of the separate Industrial Injuries Fund,[11] and by the inclusion of both the general national insurance and the industrial injury schemes in the Social Security Acts. These developments took place against the background of a marked improvement in the general social security provision for the disabled,[12] and of a decline in the real value of the preferential treatment offered under the industrial injury scheme.[13] Not surprisingly, therefore, the structure of the scheme and its very existence have been subjected to critical scrutiny within the last decade or so. The Pearson Royal Commission on Civil Liability and Compensation

20 Para 79(iii). If the defendant was insured, the worker's position was more secure. The Employers' Liability Insurance Companies Act 1907 (later incorporated into the Assurance Companies Act 1909) required a deposit of £20,000 with the Board of Trade.
1 Para 79(iv); *Wilson and Levy*, n.17, above, vol 2, ch 7.
2 Para 79(vii). Appendix E of the Report revealed that the proportion of administrative costs to premiums paid was, for some insurance companies, 46%.
3 In 1938 alone 75 appeals had gone to the Court of Appeal: Potter and Stansfield *National Insurance (Industrial Injuries)* (2nd edn) p. 8.
4 Paras 97–105.
5 Para 332.
6 *Social Insurance* Part II, paras 26–27.
7 Ibid, at paras 28–29.
8 Para 332.
9 *Social Insurance* Part II, para 29; and see pp. 303–304 and 353, below.
10 P. 325, below.
11 SSA 1973, s.94. It may not have been irrelevant that, at the time, the Industrial Injuries Fund, unlike the non-industrial fund, was showing a healthy surplus.
12 Pp. 139–142, above.
13 P. 263, below.

for Personal Injury concluded that the scheme 'had stood the test of time'[14] and argued for its extension,[15] though it also found several respects in which it could be improved.[16] A more radical stance was taken by a DHSS team in a study consequential on the Pearson Report and published as a discussion document in 1980.[17] They focused, in particular, on the high cost of administering a system which in practice offered to most of its beneficiaries a relatively small material advantage over the general social security provisions. The government accepted the force of this criticism and in its White Paper, published in 1981,[18] indicated a general commitment to restructure the scheme so as to concentrate resources on the more seriously disabled. The first step was taken in the Social Security and Housing Benefits Act 1982, which abolished the short-term injury benefit, leaving it to sick pay and sickness benefit to provide for those off work during this period, as the result of an industrial injury or disease. The reforms proposed for the second stage – at the time of writing they have not yet been presented to Parliament – include, on the one hand, abolition of industrial death benefit and a reduction in the level of pensions paid to the less seriously disabled and, on the other, an increase in the pension payable to the more seriously disabled and an improvement in the method of compensating impaired earning capacity. Details of the proposals are given at appropriate places in the ensuing discussion.

B Industrial preference

Fundamental to the recent debate on the future of the industrial injuries scheme has been the question whether the industrial preference, that is, the more favourable treatment given to the victims of industrial accidents and diseases over those disabled by other causes, can still be justified.[19] The classic arguments for the preference are to be found in a famous passage in the Beveridge Report.[20] Having conceded that, 'a complete solution is to be found only in a completely unified scheme for disability without demarcation by the cause of disability', he nevertheless submitted three grounds for maintaining a differential.

> First, many industries vital to the community are also specially dangerous. It is essential that men should enter them and desirable, therefore, that they should be able to do so with the assurance of special provision against their risks. . . . Second, a man disabled during the course of his employment has been disabled while working under orders. This is not true generally of other accidents or of sickness. Third, only if special provision is made for the results of industrial accident and disease, irrespective of negligence, would it appear possible . . . to limit the employer's liability at Common Law to the results of actions for which

14 Para 283.

15 To cover e.g. the self-employed, commuting accidents and a wider range of industrially-caused diseases: see ch 17. The proposed scheme for road accidents would be modelled on industrial injuries: ch 18.

16 E.g. increases short-term benefit and an advanced entitlement to full payment of the earnings-related element in the invalidity pension.

17 *Industrial Injuries Compensation*.

18 *Reform of the Industrial Injuries Scheme* (Cmnd 8402).

19 There is a wealth of literature on the subject. See, especially: *Atiyah* pp. 366–370; Report of the Royal Commission of Inquiry on Compensation for Personal Injury in New Zealand (1967), paras 52–54; Higucha 102 Int Lab Rev 109; *Industrial Injuries Compensation* pp. 1–12; Walker 15 Soc Pol and Admin 54.

20 Paras 80–86.

he is responsible morally and in fact, not simply by virtue of some principle of legal liability.

The main difficulty with the first argument is that it confuses the source of the injury – the environmental condition of working – with its consequences. The fact that an individual may be subjected to a greater hazard at work than elsewhere does not mean that his need will be greater if the risks materialise. If there is a case for discrimination between various groups of disabled persons it must surely be made according to the gravity of the consequences to the individual and his family rather than to the cause of the injury. The loss of a breadwinner's income may create the greatest potential hardship and it will arise whether an employee is injured at work or elsewhere. The argument based on the need to pay more compensation to those encountering higher risks in special occupations also logically leads to the probably unacceptable proposition that workers in low-risk industries should receive less than steeplejacks or bricklayers. Beveridge himself conceded that the second and third arguments were less convincing than the first, and the notion of working 'under orders' is certainly an artificial and arbitrary one. Can it be said that an individual crossing the street, or using a dangerous product at home, is incurring a risk any more 'voluntarily' than an employee at work? The third argument has been superseded, somewhat ironically, by later events. Notwithstanding the more generous social security provision, common law liability for industrial injuries has been extended rather than, as Beveridge had hoped, reduced.[1] What remains is the political fact that those initially privileged have been unwilling to sacrifice their more generous treatment in favour of a broader based scheme.[2] This was hinted at in the Pearson Report: the Commission acknowledged that Beveridge's arguments 'carry a good deal less weight now' and it declined to endorse the principle of differentiation.[3] But paradoxically its own proposals would, if implemented, significantly increase the value of the industrial preference.[4] The explanation for this apparent inconsistency must be found in the desire to make the Report's proposals attractive to the trade union movement.[5]

Independent of justice considerations is an economic argument against the industrial preference, and it clearly had a decisive influence on the government's reform proposals of 1981. The industrial injury scheme is costly to administer, absorbing 13.3 per cent of benefit expenditure, compared with 4.2 per cent for the general contributory scheme,[6] and yet the advantage accruing to most industrial injury beneficiaries had become quite small. Successive governments had allowed the value of the preference to erode through the process of inflation. So, in terms of 1982–83 rates, injury benefit is only 12 per cent higher than sickness benefit, compared with 75 per cent in 1946, and the current advantage enjoyed by 'industrial' widows is only 55p per week.[7]

1 P. 419, below.
2 In Australia the National Compensation Bill encountered strong opposition from the trade unions on the ground that it would abolish advantages hitherto enjoyed under the workmen's compensation scheme: *Pearson* vol 3, para 812.
3 Para 290.
4 N.16, above.
5 Para 284.
6 *Industrial Injuries Compensation* para 1.1.
7 Though there is also a widower's pension, not payable under the general scheme: p. 334, below.

C Financing

When workmen's compensation, with its notion of individual employer liability, was replaced by social insurance the question arose whether all risks should be pooled, as for unemployment and sickness, or whether each industry should continue to bear at least a part of its own accident costs, by, for example, varying the contribution on the basis of the industry's accident record.[8] There are two main arguments for relating the financial responsibility of the industry or firm to the risks created by its activities. The first is that it acts as an incentive to safety and the prevention of injuries.[9] Secondly, it avoids the price distortion which results from a low-risk industry subsidising a high-risk industry: for example, the accident record of the mining industry is high, and it has been calculated that if the industrial injury scheme were risk-related, the 'fair' price of coal (in 1969) would have been higher by 15p per ton.[10] Such distortion, it is argued, leads to over-employment in dangerous industries and insufficient expenditure on accident prevention.[11] Opponents of the differential approach doubt the force of the incentive argument. A system of risk-rating, or premium-loading, can hardly be based on culpability; it discriminates unfairly between large and small enterprises; and such evidence as is available suggests that it has no significant effects on safety.[12] The price-distortion argument is countered by the principle of social interdependence. No industry works in isolation from others. Coal, for example, is used in the production of many other goods.[13] Further, price distortion may indeed be appropriate. In 1944 the government noted that hazardous employments included certain important industries like mining and shipping which have to face foreign competition.[14] Finally, even if the differential approach may be more equitable it is certainly much more expensive to administer.[15] In the light of such considerations, Beveridge formulated a compromise solution: a general pooling of responsibility with a special charge on certain high-risk industries.[16] The proposal did not win the approval of the government[17] and the National Insurance (Industrial Injuries) Act 1946 created a fund based on flat-rate contributions (five-twelfths each from the employer and employee, the remaining one-sixth being paid by the Exchequer). In 1975 the Industrial Injuries Fund was abolished,[18] and since then the scheme has been financed by the general National Insurance Fund. Despite a recommendation of the Robens Committee on Safety and Health at Work to reopen the issue of risk-rating,[19] and a greater readiness in foreign systems to apply this method,[20] the principle of uniform contributions has

8 Report of the Royal Commission of Inquiry on Compensation for Personal Injury in New Zealand (The Woodhouse Report) (1967), at paras 328–336; Report of the Committee on Safety and Health at Work (1972, Cmnd 5034) (Robens Report), paras 428–430; Atiyah 4 ILJ 1, 89; Phillips 5 ILJ 148; *Pearson* paras 898–904.
9 Calabresi *The Cost of Accidents* (1970); Ison *The Forensic Lottery* (1967) ch 5.
10 *Kaim-Caudle* p. 71.
11 Phillips, n.8, above, at pp. 150–151.
12 Woodhouse Report, n.8, above, at para 336; Atiyah, n.8, above, at pp. 90–102; cp Phillips, n.8, above, at pp. 157–160.
13 Woodhouse, n.8, above, at para 335.
14 *Social Insurance* Part II, para 23(iii).
15 See e.g. the very complex French system of differentials: *Dupeyroux* pp. 787–796.
16 Paras 88–92.
17 *Social Insurance* Part II, para 31.
18 P. 261, above.
19 N.8, above, at para 447.
20 *Kaim-Caudle* pp. 69–75.

remained unchanged. The Pearson Commission, with one dissenter (significantly an economist),[1] reaffirmed the principle, mainly on the ground that risk-relating contributions for each employer, or industry, would involve substantial administrative costs which would outweigh any benefits in terms of increased safety.[2]

D Plan of chapter

Claims for all categories of benefit under the industrial injuries scheme must satisfy two conditions:

(a) that the person injured or killed was an employed earner (Part 2); *and*

(b) that the injury or death was caused by 'accident arising out of and in the course of his employment' and in Great Britain (Part 3) or resulted from a disease prescribed in relation to that employment (Part 4).

Injury benefit (Part 5) is paid for the first six months of incapacity for work. After that period disablement benefit (Part 6) is paid for loss of physical or mental faculty and may be supplemented by certain increases and additions (Part 7). The chapter concludes with a discussion of certain miscellaneous matters (Part 8) and death benefit (Part 9).

Part 2 Persons covered

The Workmen's Compensation Act 1897 covered only specified dangerous employments,[3] but in 1906 was extended to all persons working under a contract of service or apprenticeship, with a few exceptions, the most important of which were non-manual workers earning more than £250 (subsequently £420) a year.[4] The 1946 state scheme covered the same categories, but included also all non-manual employees irrespective of income, and did not permit contracting-out which had been possible under workmen's compensation. In general, the categories of insured persons were the same as those regarded as 'employed persons' for the purposes of the non-industrial national insurance schemes. However, there were reasons for creating distinctions between the scope of the two schemes: first, 'employment' in the non-industrial scheme was confined to those working a minimum number of hours a week, a limitation which had not existed under the Workmen's Compensation Act and which was therefore considered inappropriate for the industrial scheme; secondly, the non-industrial benefits were, in general, payable only on the fulfilment of certain contribution conditions, whereas under the industrial scheme, as with its predecessor, the employee was covered as from the first day of employment, irrespective of contributions. For these reasons the scope of the two schemes had to be distinguished precisely and this was achieved in the Schedules to the 1946 Acts.

The amalgamation of the two schemes in 1975 resulted in a change of terminology from 'insured persons' to 'employed earners', the expression used to denote Class 1 contributors to the non-industrial scheme.[5] The

1 Paras 940–948.
2 Paras 898–904.
3 WCA 1897, s.7.
4 WCA 1906, ss.1, 13.
5 SSA 1973, s.94(2), as amended by NIA 1974, s.6(5) and Sch 4, para 27(b).

effect has been to extend industrial injuries benefits to some who had been self-employed before 1975, notably 'office-holders' (e.g. directors of limited companies).[6] The present position is, then, that the scheme covers those who are 'employed earners', as the term is interpreted for the contribution provisions of the Social Security Act 1975.[7] But the claimant for industrial injury benefit need not have paid, or be liable for, Class 1 contributions; he may, for example, be exempt from such contributions on the ground of low earnings,[8] and still be covered by the scheme.[9] Moreover, the Secretary of State has power to extend or exclude, by regulation, categories of employed earners for the purposes of the scheme.[10] The more important categories so regulated may be summarised as follows.

(1) Included are apprentices, members of fire brigades and other rescue services, mine inspectors, special constables.[11]
(2) Excluded is employment (i) by a relative or spouse where not for the purpose of trade or business,[12] and (ii) as a military or civilian member of a visiting force or as a member of an international headquarters or defence organisation unless, in either case, the civilian is ordinarily resident in the United Kingdom.[13]
(3) The employment must be in Great Britain,[14] but workers on the Continental Shelf,[15] and mariners and airmen employed on, respectively, a British ship or aircraft[16] are included.

As with analogous questions arising under the non-industrial schemes, disputes as to classification are determined not by the statutory authorities but by the Secretary of State.[17] He is also given power to direct that where a contract of service is rendered void or unlawful as a result of non-compliance with any statutory requirement passed for the protection of employed persons, the employment is nevertheless, for the purposes of industrial injury benefits, to be treated as an employed earner's employment.[18] In the recent White Paper,[19] the government has declared that it does not intend to implement the recommendation of the Pearson Commission that the scheme be extended to cover the self-employed.[20] There did not seem to be a demand from the self-employed themselves for this protection and in any event it would give rise to serious practical difficulties, for example, determining whether there has been an accident 'in the course of employment'.[21]

6 See p. 50, above.
7 SSA 1975, ss.2(1)(a) and 50(1). See generally, pp. 45–50, above.
8 P. 52, above.
9 Married women with reduced liability (p. 63, above) are also covered.
10 SSA 1975, s.51(1)–(2) and SI 1975/467, as amended.
11 Ibid, Sch 1, Part I.
12 Where employed by a spouse for the purposes of business, the claimant must also be a Class I contributor: ibid, Part II.
13 Ibid, inserted by SI 1980/1714.
14 SSA 1975, s.2(1)(a).
15 SI 1975/467, Sch 1, Part I, para 7.
16 Ibid, Sch 2; cf p. 65, above.
17 SSA 1975, s.93(1)(d) and *R(I) 2/75*. See generally, pp. 583–585, below.
18 SSA 1975, s.156.
19 *Reform of the Industrial Injuries Scheme,* paras 63–65.
20 Paras 851–857.
21 See also *Industrial Injuries Compensation* paras 6.16–6.31.

Part 3 Industrial injury

Entitlement to the various industrial benefits is fundamentally based on proof that the 'employed earner suffers personal injury caused . . . by accident arising out of and in the course of his employment'.[1] This contains three different elements:[2]
(a) a personal injury,
(b) caused by an accident (in Great Britain),
(c) arising out of and in the course of employment.
The discussion will be divided accordingly.

A Personal injury

This means a 'hurt to body or mind'.[3] Thus it includes a nervous disorder or nervous shock.[4] Even a trivial hurt which is ephemeral, like the watering of an eye,[5] will qualify, though, as will be seen,[6] to recover injury or disablement benefit, the claimant must proceed to establish incapacity for work or loss of faculty respectively. Real difficulty arises where there is damage to a prosthesis, such as an artificial limb. In *R(I) 7/56* it was ruled that there had to be an injury to the living body of a human being. This was decided at a time when replacement surgery was in its infancy and in *R(I) 8/81* the Commissioner was prepared to give 'personal injury' a broader interpretation. On his view, the test was 'whether or not the prosthesis has become so intimately linked with the body that on any realistic assessment of the situation it can be said to have become part of that body'.[7] On this definition, there is no doubt that where the prosthesis damaged is a living tissue or synthetic material inserted into the body, the claimant has sustained a 'personal injury'. In cases of external appliances it is a question of fact and degree. The Commissioner suggested that the 'intimate link with the body' might be regarded as broken by the detachability of the appliance. A claimant would succeed where damage is inflicted on an artificial limb permanently attached to the body but not, for example, where the appliance in question is a pair of spectacles[8], a hearing-aid or a crutch.

B Accident

The personal injury must be caused 'by accident' and this must have happened within Great Britain.[9] There are exceptions to the geographical limitation. Apart from reciprocal arrangements under bilateral treaties,[10] there is special provision to cover accidents:
(a) on the territory of an EEC Member State;[11]
(b) in continental shelf areas of Norway or an EEC Member State;[12]

1 SSA 1975, s.50(1).
2 Cf Lord Denning MR in *Re Dowling* [1967] 1 QB 202 at 217.
3 Per Lord Simon, *Jones v Secretary of State for Social Services* [1972] AC 944 at 1020.
4 *R(I) 49/52*; *R(I) 22/59*.
5 *R 5/60 (II)*.
6 Pp. 294 and 299, below.
7 Para 14, D G Rice, Comr.
8 *R(I) 1/82*.
9 SSA 1975, s.50(5).
10 Cf pp. 625–626, below.
11 SI 1975/563, reg 10C, inserted by SI 1979/463, and modified by SI 1982/388.
12 Ibid.

(c) to mariners and apprentice pilots;[13]
(d) to airmen, and to others on a flight starting within Britain.[14]
The exclusion of other accidents abroad suffered by persons otherwise covered by the scheme has led to criticism both from the TUC and the CBI.[15] The government has now decided that such accidents should be covered, provided that the employment in question is one which gives rise to contributions liability in this country.[16]

The requirement of an 'accident' has a twofold object: to exclude sickness,[17] and to facilitate proof that the injury was work-caused.[18] But it has given rise to considerable difficulty and has been removed in several jurisdictions.[19] In Britain, judicial interpretation and legislative intervention have greatly reduced the rigours of the original test and it remains to be seen whether it succeeds in fulfilling the declared objectives.

i Meaning of 'accident'

The starting point must be Lord Macnaghten's famous dictum in 1903:[20]

> The expression 'accident' is used in the popular and ordinary sense of the word as denoting an unlooked-for mishap or an untoward event which is not expected or designed.

But 'popular' meanings are notoriously unreliable and, as critics have pointed out,[1] nowhere more so than in this context. It soon became clear that Lord Macnaghten's definition was neither accurate nor sufficient. In the first place, while it was construed to exclude deliberate acts by the injured party himself, it has been held to include a deliberate, even unlawful, act of a third party. The point was decided in *Trim Joint District School v Kelly*,[2] in which pupils assaulted and killed a schoolmaster responsible for discipline. Secondly, the phrase 'not expected' could not be taken seriously. An event need not be unforeseeable or exceptional to constitute an 'accident'.[3] To take a frequently encountered example, a man incapacitating himself by heavy exertions does not have to prove that the strain was violent or exceptional for his job.[4]

There has been considerable debate on the question whether, by its very nature, the accident must be 'external' to the claimant: that is, whether the accident is always independent of the 'injury' or whether what constitutes the 'injury' may also constitute the 'accident'. A situation may arise where

13 SI 1975/470, reg 2.
14 SI 1975/469, reg 2.
15 *Industrial Injuries Compensation*, paras 6.2–6.15.
16 *Reform of the Industrial Injuries Scheme*, paras 61–62.
17 Report of Departmental Committee on Workmen's Compensation (1904, Cd 2208), para 103; Canadian Commission of Inquiry into Workmen's Compensation (1966) (Tysoe Commission), p. 178.
18 Report of Departmental Committee on Disease Provisions of National Insurance (Industrial Injuries) Act (Beney Committee) (1955, Cmd 9548), para 55.
19 In the USA: California, Iowa and Massachusetts (Horovitz 12 Law Soc Jo 465, 493). See also the Model Workmen's Compensation Act prepared by the Council of State Legislation in 1963. In Australia: New South Wales and Victoria (Luntz 40 ALJ 179).
20 *Fenton v J Thorley & Co Ltd* [1903] AC 443 at 448.
1 See *Trim Joint District School Board of Management v Kelly* [1914] AC 667 at 681, per Lord Loreburn; *Re Dowling* [1967] 1 AC 725 at 759, per Lord Wilberforce; *Jones v Secretary of State for Social Services* [1972] AC 944 at 1009, per Lord Diplock. See also Bohlen 25 Harv L Rev 378.
2 N.1, above. See also *CI 51/49* and *R(I) 30/58*.
3 *Clover Clayton v Hughes* [1910] AC 242; *CWI 6/49*; but the 'abnormality' of an event may be relevant in proving the causal link between the injury and the accident: p. 270, below.
4 *CI 5/49*.

due to a strain, an internal physiological change occurs, resulting in eventual disability to the claimant. On one view (now, it seems, the prevailing view), in such a case 'accident' and 'injury' are interchangeable terms: they cannot be independently defined.[5] On another view,[6] the distinction is between a 'causative incident' (the accident), something external which has a physiological effect on part of the claimant's anatomy, or a psychological effect on his mind, *and* the adverse physical or medical consequences of that condition (the injury). In the case of incapacity caused by heavy exertion, the distinction is difficult to draw but nevertheless must exist: the 'accident' is the physical exertion and the 'injury' is the consequent physiological change. Within the context of the present discussion, the matter is entirely linguistic. No practical consequences flow from the difference of views. In either case, there is a 'personal injury by accident'. The debate is relevant only to the issue, arising under claims for disablement benefit, of the relative competence of the statutory and medical authorities in determining the aetiology of the disability.[7]

The essence of the 'accident' requirement, and the focal point of much of the case-law, is the difficult question whether the claimant's condition was caused by an 'event' as opposed to a 'process'. It is, of course, a method of distinguishing between an accident insurance scheme and a health insurance scheme. This is not to say that industrial illness or diseases are excluded from the scheme but, as will be seen, there is separate provision for them.[8] The notion of 'accident' in the words of Lord Porter,[9] and subsequently adopted by a Tribunal of Commissioners,[10] does not include the growth of incapacity by a continuous process. The claimant must be able to point to 'an incident or series of incidents . . . which caused or contributed to the origin or progress of the disease'.[11] Inevitably the inquiry is an elusive one, and many decisions are difficult to reconcile. A few will illustrate the difficulty and give some indication of the present tendency of Commissioners' decisions.

> Strain to chest muscles caused by the daily lifting of heavy weights is not covered,[12] but a claimant, who, when lifting heavy equipment on a particular day, felt severe pains in the chest and subsequently suffered from coronary thrombosis, was entitled to succeed. He had experienced a physiological change at that particular time.[13]
>
> A worker who developed a psychoneurotic condition having worked near a machine which produced explosive reports at irregular intervals recovered. Each explosion was 'an accident' and thus the condition was the result of a 'series of accidents'. The interval between each such explosion was not so short that the series was to be regarded as a single continuous process.[14] On the other hand, a claimant who became sick on inhaling gas which leaked from the vehicle he used from time to time did not succeed: the illness was caused by the taking of breath on an infinite number of occasions, and these did not constitute separate incidents.[15]

5 *Re Dowling*, n.1, above, *Jones*'s case, n.1, above.
6 *Jones*'s case, n.1, above; per Viscount Dilhorne at 987, per Lord Diplock at 1009–1010.
7 Pp. 300–302, below.
8 Pp. 288–292, below.
9 *Roberts v Dorothea Slate Quarries* [1948] 2 All ER 201 at 205–206, HL.
10 *CI 257/49*.
11 Ibid, at para 11.
12 *R(I) 42/51*.
13 *R(I) 54/53*.
14 *R(I) 43/55*.
15 *R(I) 32/60*.

Apart from the somewhat arbitrary nature of some of these distinctions, it is apparent from other decisions that certain illogicalities may ensue. A claimant will be fortunate if the condition, though developing gradually, manifests itself on a particular occasion. Thus in *R(I) 18/54* the claimant had been using a pad for three months, the buckle of which rubbed against a nerve. One day, he felt a numbness in his leg, and he was allowed to recover on the basis that this constituted a particular incident.[16] Even more anomalously, a person who encounters an employment risk only once will be in a better position than one who is exposed to it regularly. Hence, a nurse who had come into contact with, and was infected by, a child with poliomyelitis succeeded,[17] but a doctor who was attending a large number of patients infected with tuberculosis and subsequently contracted the disease was refused benefit. It was assumed that he must have been infected by the regular penetration of bacteria into his system.[18] It must be noted, however, that once the claimant has succeeded in establishing, on the balance of probabilities, that the injury resulted from an event or a series of events,[19] his claim will not be jeopardised by his failure to identify the specific occasion when the condition began or was aggravated: for procedural purposes the earliest probable date will be taken.[20]

ii Causal link between accident and injury

The claimant must also prove, on the balance of probabilities, that the accident 'caused' the injury.[1] This does not mean that it has to be the sole cause of the injury; it is sufficient if it is a contributory cause, in combination with, for example, a condition from which the claimant already suffered.[2] It is irrelevant that the previous condition rendered the claimant more susceptible to the later event.[3] But, at the same time, the accident must have been 'an efficient cause (*causa causans*) and not a mere condition (*causa sine qua non*)' in which the earlier cause operated.[4] Thus in *R(I) 4/58*,

> The claimant suffered from burns when his clothing, which had been soaked in inflammable liquid in a work accident, caught fire when coming into contact with a cigarette which he was lighting at home. It was held that the *causa causans* of the injury was the lighting of the cigarette, and not the accidental soaking.

iii Critique

It will be apparent from the analysis above that the requirement of an 'accident' has produced severe difficulties and it may be seriously questioned whether there are not preferable alternatives. The traditional justification for the requirement is that it preserves the distinction between a scheme concerned to compensate injuries and one providing relief for

16 The case should be compared with *R(I) 11/74* in which the claimant was unable to advert to a specific date.
17 *CI 159/50.*
18 *CI 83/50*
19 See *R(I) 8/66.*
20 *CI 49/49*; *CI 196/50.*
1 In contrast to the war pension scheme, where the burden of proof of the causal link between service and the disability generally favours the claimant; p. 348, below.
2 *R(I) 19/63.*
3 *CI 147/50.*
4 *R(I) 14/51*, para 6. See also *R(I) 12/58*, para 5.

sickness. In the usual case it does indeed have this effect, but the distinction itself is not wholly conclusive in determining the scope of the British scheme. On the one hand, a claimant will succeed if he can show that an illness (not an injury) was attributable to an event rather than to a process. On the other hand, as will be seen, he is entitled to benefit if he suffers from a prescribed disease, provided that it was contracted in the appropriate prescribed employment. One alternative, then, would be to link the two concepts and allow recovery for any injury or disease which was work-caused. The possibility is considered later in connection with prescribed diseases.[5] An alternative, less radical, is that proposed by Sir Owen Woodhouse as part of his recommendations for new schemes in both New Zealand[6] and Australia.[7] The idea is to incorporate in legislation a list of all possible forms of accident to be made the subject of compensation, and for such a purpose it might be possible to adopt a classification of injuries and external causes of injury prepared by the World Health Organisation.[8] Of course, like all attempts at exhaustive listing, this could not be a perfect solution and would have to be supplemented by some residual general clause. But it might serve to remove some of the doubt and uncertainty which the case-law on the more traditional approach reveals.

C Employment risk

i General

It is of the essence of an industrial injuries insurance scheme that the accident must be connected with the employment. In 1897, the Workmen's Compensation Act contained a test which was adopted by English speaking jurisdictions throughout the world, and remains the basis of the current scheme: personal injury by accident 'arising out of and in the course of employment'.[9] This classic formulation, perhaps the most notorious in the whole of social security law, has been responsible for vast amounts of disputed claims and complex litigation. In 1920, a judge in the House of Lords was moved to remark that:

> The language of the Act and the decisions upon it are such that I have long since abandoned the hope of deciding any case upon the words 'out of and in the course of' upon grounds satisfactory to myself or convincing to others;[10]

and two years later a Departmental Committee reported that:

> No other form of words has ever given rise to such a body of litigation.[11]

The original Act sought to delimit the connection with the employment more precisely by requiring that the accident should occur, 'on, in or

5 P. 288, below.
6 Report of Royal Commission of Inquiry into Compensation for Personal Injuries in New Zealand (1967), para 289(c).
7 Report of National Committee of Inquiry into Compensation and Rehabilitation in Australia (1974), para 350.
8 The relevant parts are conveniently published in a Schedule to the draft Bill at the end of the Australian report.
9 WCA 1897, s.1.
10 Per Lord Wrenbury, *Armstrong, Whitworth & Co v Redford* [1920] AC 757 at 780, HL.
11 Departmental Committee Report on Workmen's Compensation (Holman Gregory Report) (1920, Cmd 816), para 29.

about' the employer's premises,[12] but this condition was soon abandoned.[13] Most obviously it discriminated against employees whose work took them away from the employer's premises. Other common law jurisdictions have attempted to mitigate the rigours of the statutory test by amending the formula. Thus, in some systems, the workman need only show that the accident arose '*in* the course of employment',[14] while in others he is given the alternative of proving that it happened 'out of *or* in the course of employment'.[15] But no formula adopted (and this includes non-English speaking jurisdictions[16]) has managed to alleviate problems involved in establishing the connection between the work and the accident.[17] As Atiyah has observed:

> The difficulty is inherent in the system; it has nothing to do with the 'meaning' of . . . words. . . . The difficulty is inherent in the concept of insurance against special 'employment' risks.[18]

The most significant reforms, therefore, both in Britain and elsewhere, have not been through a modification of the basic formula, but rather by specific extensions of the scheme to cover contingencies which might not otherwise have been regarded as employment risks. As will be seen, the most important developments in this respect have been the coverage of certain accidents occurring on a journey to or from work,[19] or caused by a natural event or the conduct of a third party.[20]

ii The statutory test

It has long been a subject of debate whether the formula 'out of and in the course of employment'[1] involves two different principles or only a single test. It has sometimes been said that the authorities should treat the phrase as a combined whole.[2] The more generally accepted view is that the 'in the course of' criterion delimits the time, place and activity of the work, while the 'out of' criterion concerns itself with the cause or connection between the accident and the work.[3] In the simple case, the distinction is obvious. A man working at his bench inadvertently spikes himself with a pin which he had earlier put in his trouser pocket. The accident arises 'in the course of' his employment but not 'out of' it. But there are other situations where there is an inevitable overlap between the two tests. If, for example, an employee injures himself through horseplay on his employer's premises and during the normal hours of duty, it might be said either that the accident did not arise out of the employment because the risk was not caused by his work, or that it did not arise in the course of employment,

12 WCA 1897, s.7(1).
13 WCA 1906, s.1(1).
14 E.g. in the USA: N. Dakota, Pennsylvania, Texas and Washington.
15 E.g. in Australia, New South Wales.
16 See e.g. *Dupeyroux* pp. 506–518.
17 Cf *Pearson* para 896.
18 *Atiyah* pp. 374–375.
19 Pp. 278–279, below.
20 Pp. 284–285, below.
1 It should be noted that since the scheme now covers 'office-holders' as well as 'employed earners' (p. 266, above), the appropriate test for those in the former category would seem to be whether the accident arose out of and in the course of the office: see *CI 6/78* and Partington 7 ILJ 251, 8 ILJ 64. It is not, however, yet clear whether this test will require any modification to the principles expounded in this section.
2 See e.g. *CSI 63/49*; *R(I) 62/51*.
3 E.g. per Lord Wright, *Dover Navigation v Craig* [1940] AC 190 at 199, HL; *R(I) 10/52*; *R(I) 2/63*.

because the claimant's activity at the time interfered with and diverged from his ordinary working duties. For the sake of clarity of exposition, the traditional distinction has been followed in this work, and the overlap recognised at appropriate points in the discussion.

iii In the course of employment

a *General principles*

According to the classic formulation of Lord Loreburn,

> An accident befalls a man 'in the course of' his employment if it occurs while he is doing what a man so employed may reasonably do within a time during which he is employed, and at a place where he may reasonably be during that time to do that thing.[4]

From this, it will be seen that the limits to the course of employment are determined by three different criteria: place, time and activity. A claimant will set up a prima facie case if he is able to show that the accident occurred at his normal *place* of work during his normal *hours* of work. His *activity* at the time of the accident may be relevant in two different respects. It may serve to defeat a prima facie case by showing that the claimant interrupted the time element in the work or deviated from the spatial element for reasons unconnected with his employment. Or it may serve to extend the 'course of employment' to cover hours or places not normally considered as within its ambit. The discussion will proceed accordingly.

It must also be observed that the notion of employment covers functions and objectives which are regarded as reasonably incidental to the actual work process. The contract of employment is rarely relevant or helpful in determining what is to be so regarded. Obviously this varies enormously according to the nature of the work and the status of the claimant, and the courts and the Commissioner have been reluctant to lay down general principles. But during the course of the analysis which follows it will be seen that resort is usually had to two different but related notions. Under the first (supervision test) the adjudicating authority considers whether the accident happened while the claimant was under the authority, supervision or control of his employer.[5] The alternative and complementary criterion (public zone test) is concerned to ascertain whether the activities of the claimant at the time of the accident were such as to distinguish him from an ordinary member of the public.[6]

b *Fixed place and hours of work*

Most employees have fixed places and hours of work. The task, here, is to determine what, for the purposes of benefit, are to be regarded as the limits of the employment, though this is not always easy. The mere fact that during a period when not actually working an employee must remain available to be summoned by his employer – in other words, when he is 'on call' – is not sufficient by itself to bring that period within the course of employment.[7] But if his freedom of movement is limited or his activities

4 *Moore v Manchester Liners Ltd* [1910] AC 498 at 500–501.

5 See particularly *R(I) 84/51*. The test is traditionally used to establish circumstances in which an employer is vicariously liable for the acts of his employee: Atiyah *Vicarious Liability* (1967) ch 5, and is also favoured by the French industrial injuries scheme (*Dupeyroux* pp. 510–515).

6 See particularly *R(I) 61/51*.

7 *R(I) 10/52*, para 8; *R(I) 11/55*, para 6; *R(I) 5/81*.

controlled by the employer, then, in accordance with the 'supervision test', he may be covered.[8] This seems to be the best explanation of the perhaps surprising decision in *R v National Insurance Comr, ex parte Reed.*[9]

> A police sergeant was permitted to take lunch at home during his period on duty, but throughout he remained on call. He was injured while travelling back to the police station and the Divisional Court held that he was entitled to benefit. Woolf J stressed that his choice as to where refreshment could be taken was limited and while at home he was still responsible for performing his duties.[10]

The limits of work, as defined by the contract, are not rigidly applied. The law allows the claimant a certain amount of time and space to 'prepare himself for, or to disengage himself from', his employment.[11] As regards time, the course of employment includes a reasonable period at either end of his official hours of duty.[12] What this amounts to may depend on the nature of the job and the character of the claimant. Thus, a 62 year old worker who preferred to take a leisurely bath rather than be involved in the crush for buses home was covered.[13] Arriving early the more properly to equip oneself for work will be generously treated,[14] but not if the intention is instead to fit in a game of billiards.[15]

As regards place, the exact area is difficult to locate. It generally includes the premises in which the claimant is about to work, or has just worked, and the access to them.[16] The 'public zone' test will usually be conclusive in determining the necessary limits. The claimant must be within an area excluded from public access,[17] but this is to be decided according to existing practice rather than legal rights.[18] The question is whether the members of the public make substantial use of that part of the land.[19] Equally, the mere fact that the land on which the accident occurs is owned by the employer is rarely conclusive.[20] British Railways and the National Coal Board own vast areas of land, and the claimant may be on a part of it miles from his place of work.[1] Conversely, a social worker injured while descending a staircase common to several households may recover, though her business took her to only one.[2] The authorities must determine the part of the land on which the claimant normally works, and this may be particularly difficult in agricultural cases.[3] It is not possible to reconcile all the decisions.[4] In some cases the authorities are apparently prepared to

8 *R(I) 49/51*; *R(I) 11/55*.
9 (1980) reported as Appendix to *R(I) 7/80*, and see *R(I) 5/81*, paras 11–14.
10 Cp J G Monroe, Comr, who drew a distinction between being employed to stand by, and being given leave of absence on condition that the employee stands by: *R(I) 7/80*, para 8.
11 *Gane v Norton Hill Colliery* [1909] 2 KB 539, CA; *R(I) 61/51*; *R(I) 3/72*.
12 *R v National Insurance Comr, ex parte East* [1976] ICR 206.
13 *R(I) 22/51*.
14 *R v National Insurance Comr, ex parte East*, n.12, above.
15 *R(I) 1/59*.
16 *R(I) 7/52*; *R(I) 5/67*.
17 Even if the claimant's duties sometimes take him into the 'public zone': *R(I) 72/51*; *R(I) 7/62*. See also *R(I) 7/52*; *R(I) 23/55*; *R(I) 70/57*. 'Access' here means qua member of the public – not, of course, for business purposes: *R(I) 41/57*.
18 *R(I) 43/51*; *R(I) 1/68*.
19 Per Lord Macmillan, *Northumbrian Shipping Co Ltd v McCullum* (1932) 25 BWCC 284, HL.
20 *CI 65/49*; *R(I) 67/52*; *R(I) 43/51*.
1 *CI 69/49*; *R(I) 67/52*.
2 *R(I) 3/72*.
3 See *R(I) 7/52* and *R(I) 42/56*.
4 Cf *R(I) 42/56*, para 11.

show some indulgence, and avoid nice distinctions which would have the effect of depriving the claimant of benefit. They may then admit a claim on the vague basis that the claimant had 'so nearly approached the means of access as to make it reasonable to hold that he had returned to the sphere in which his employment operated'.[5]

c *Extensions for authorised or incidental purposes*

The spatial and temporal boundaries may be extended for purposes which are reasonably necessary for, or incidental to, the employment.[6] In *R v National Insurance Comr, ex parte Michael*, the Court of Appeal stressed that the 'reasonably incidental' test is not part of the statutory formula and should not be applied without careful consideration: 'if the injury is not suffered in the actual course of the work which the employee is engaged to do, it must have at least been suffered by reason of some event incidental to *that work*'.[7] Obviously this covers, primarily, situations where the employer directly or indirectly authorises the employee to perform his duties outside normal hours, or his usual locality, e.g. where a bus conductor was required by her employer to make a cup of tea for herself and the driver at the end of each journey.[8] But it seems that 'employer' in this context must be strictly construed. An unauthorised request from an immediate superior will not bring the resulting activity within the scheme.[9] This may operate harshly, for the employee may find it difficult to refuse the request and feel that his prospects of promotion will otherwise suffer. But the test should be a subjective one: if *he* has reasonable grounds to think that the request has the implied authority of the employer, he should succeed.[10] Where the claimant is under no obligation to carry out the activity, but is merely permitted to, the case is more difficult. Clearly mere knowledge of, or acquiescence by, the employer is insufficient. The issue becomes whether or not the activity in question is sufficiently connected with the employment. There are obvious cases like working overtime,[11] collecting equipment or clothing necessary for work,[12] or taking a bath after duty in a mine.[13] The receipt of wages comes within the scope of employment but not the cashing of a money order representing them: the processes of employment are complete when the money order is received by the employee.[14] Participants in a trade union meeting are also covered, provided that it is directly concerned with the terms and conditions of employment with the particular employer.[15]

The status of recreational activities is problematic. In the leading case of *R v Industrial Injuries Comr, ex parte Michael*, the Court of Appeal held

5 *R(I) 3/53*, para 4; cp *R(I) 10/81*.
6 *Armstrong, Whitworth & Co v Redford* [1920] AC 757 at 777, 779, 780; *R v Industrial Injuries Comr, ex parte Amalgamated Engineering Union (No 2)* [1966] 2 QB 31 at 48, 50, 51.
7 Per Roskill J, [1977] 2 All ER 420 at 427. See also Lord Denning MR at 423–424.
8 *R(I) 21/53*; cf *R(I) 5/77*. See also the cases where the employee is obliged to participate in physical education, competition or other 'outside' activities e.g. *CI 228/50*; *R(I) 4/51*; *R(I) 80/52*; *R(I) 66/53*; *R(I) 39/56*.
9 *R(I) 36/55*; *R(I) 8/61*.
10 In *R(I) 36/55*, paras 7, 8, the Commissioner speaks of acting under the 'ostensible' authority of the employer.
11 *R(I) 52/52*.
12 *R(I) 72/54*; *R(I) 20/58*.
13 *CI 22/49*.
14 *R(I) 34/53*. In W. Germany the legislation expressly extends the protection to cover such activity: Reichsversicherungsordnung § 548(1).
15 *R(I) 63/55*; *R(I) 9/57*; *R(I) 46/59*. See also *CI 526/75* noted at 6 ILJ 123.

that a police constable injured when playing football for his force was not covered by the statutory formula.[16] The court was not impressed by the argument, which had been regarded as sufficient by some Commissioners,[17] that such activity improved the fitness and morale of the force and therefore was in pursuance of the employment. At the same time, the view held by one Commissioner,[18] that recreation can never come within the course of employment, was rejected.[19] Clearly, a claimant will succeed if he can show that he was required by his employer to participate in the activity,[20] and it is doubtful whether the *Michael* ruling has affected the authority of previous decisions entitling a claimant injured while engaged in physical exercises as part of a training course authorised by the employer,[1] or in games which were regarded as therapeutically valuable to patients at the hospital where he was employed.[2]

Injuries incurred while meeting an emergency may be covered even if the incident occurred away from the employee's place of work or outside his normal working hours.[3] It is, however, necessary that the action can be construed as being in some way in the employer's interests (e.g. the protection of his property[4]) and was reasonable in the circumstances.[5]

d *Accidents while travelling*

Accidents to the claimant while travelling have always posed special problems for industrial injury schemes, and they have been the subject of much dispute both general and specific. For the purposes of discussion it is necessary to distinguish between three types of case.[6]

(1) The employee is required to make a journey for purposes necessary or incidental to his employment.

(2) The employee's work is peripatetic: that is, the employment consists of travelling from place to place.

(3) The employee merely travels to and from his work.

(1) This is merely an instance of the situation discussed in the preceding section. The employee's place and hours of work are defined but he is required by his employer, expressly or impliedly, to make a journey for purposes connected with the employment.[7] Thus, an employee instructed to proceed at a specified time from one working place to another is protected.[8] Travel from home to work does not, in general, come within this category even if the claimant is paid for travelling time or for expenses incurred.[9] The distinction is between a journey *to* duty and a journey *on* duty.[10] But there are exceptions all of which may be justified on the

16 N.7, above. See also *R(I) 2/80* and *R(I) 4/81*.
17 *R(I) 13/66*; *CI 7/73*.
18 *R(I) 5/75*, para 21, J S Watson, Comr.
19 N.7, above, per Roskill LJ at 426, per Lawton LJ at 431.
20 See e.g. *R(I) 3/81*.
1 *R(I) 31/53*; *R(I) 66/53*; *R(I) 2/68*, and see *Ex parte Michael*, n.7, above, per Lawton LJ at 430–431.
2 *R(I) 3/57*.
3 *R(I) 63/54* (Tribunal decision). See also p. 287, below.
4 *R(I) 63/54*; cp *R(I) 6/63*.
5 *R(I) 32/54*.
6 Cf Ogus 4 ILJ 188.
7 See generally, *R v National Industrial Injury Benefits Tribunal, ex parte Fieldhouse* (1974) 17 KIR 63, DC, *Vandyke v Fender* [1970] 2 QB 292, [1970] 2 All ER 335, CA, *R(I) 5/77*, and *R(I) 14/81*.
8 *R(I) 11/57*; *R(I) 4/59*; *R(I) 39/59*.
9 *R(I) 9/51*; *R(I) 34/57*; *R(I) 3/71*.
10 *R(I) 45/52*, para 3; *R(I) 14/81* para 7.

supervision principle: an employee obliged by his employer to travel to work by a specific mode of transport;[11] an employee called out from home by his employer for a specific purpose (e.g. an emergency) and under a duty, expressly or impliedly, to arrive by the shortest practical route and as quickly as possible.[12] The suggestion has also been made that the exclusion of journeys to and from work should be confined to cases involving 'reasonable daily travelling distance or commuter distance', and that different considerations apply where the journey involves longer distances.[13] But the suggestion was rejected by a Commissioner who decided that a civil servant injured during the journey from his home to a temporary place of employment some 100 miles away was not entitled.[14] Nor does it make any difference if the employee is carrying with him tools or essential equipment for his work:[15] to succeed he must show that he had to make some special and required journey to deliver or collect such equipment.[16] The question whether an employee injured while staying away from home during the course of his travels may succeed is resolved along similar lines. If the employee is required by his employer to stay at a particular place,[17] or is in some way supervised by his employer there,[18] benefit is payable. If he is free to stay where he likes, he is not covered during the passage to, or while at, the chosen accommodation.[19]

(2) Certain types of employment are peripatetic: they necessarily involve frequent journeys. Obvious examples of such situations are sales representatives,[20] insurance agents,[1] journalists[2] and home helps.[3] In such cases, benefit is payable for accidents occurring during travel for the purposes of the work. But in defining the limits of the course of the employment, an important distinction has to be drawn.[4] A person who has no fixed hours and no precisely definable place of work may be protected against injuries occurring on his way home.[5] Conversely, a person whose work requires him to be at particular places at particular times is treated no differently from other employees who have fixed places of work. His employment does not begin until he arrives at his first call, unless his employer specifies a particular route or mode of transport.[6] To decide into which of the two categories a particular case falls involves consideration of the circumstances of the job. But there has been a noticeable tendency in recent Commissioners' decisions to take a more restricted view of peripatetic occupations. A decision of 1967[7] in which a home help unsuccessfully claimed benefit for an injury inflicted while travelling from her home to her first call – she worked on her own and was not required to

11 *R(I) 8/51*; *R(I) 17/51*; *R(I) 3/81*.
12 *R(I) 21/51*; *R(I) 27/56*: the mere fact that the employee is required to report for duty earlier than normal is not sufficient – his employer is not concerned with the mode or speed of his journey.
13 *CI 21/68*.
14 *R(I) 3/71*, J S Watson, Comr.
15 *R(I) 48/52*; *R(I) 78/53*; *R(I) 16/58*.
16 *R(I) 34/59*.
17 *R(I) 30/57*.
18 *CI 347/50*.
19 *R(I) 22/54*; *R(I) 4/81*.
20 *R(I) 38/53*.
1 *CSI 63/49*.
2 *R(I) 55/53*.
3 *R(I) 2/67*.
4 Ibid, at para 10, and see *R(I) 14/81* (Tribunal decision).
5 E.g. *R(I) 4/70*.
6 *R(I) 19/57*; *R(I) 2/67*; *R(I) 12/75*.
7 *R(I) 2/67*. See also *R(I) 12/75*.

report for information at any office – may be contrasted with one of 1954[8] in which a chief fire officer succeeded when injured travelling from his home to the annual dinner of the local fire brigade.

(3) If the journey comes within neither category described above, it is difficult to regard it as creating an 'employment risk'. In terms of the 'public zone' principle, the commuting employee is in a position no different from other members of the public, and, as regards the 'supervision' principle, the employer generally exercises no control over the journey. Yet there has been considerable political pressure to extend industrial injury schemes to cover commuting accidents and in several foreign jurisdictions special provision has been made for them,[9] notwithstanding the blurring of the concept of employment risk which is involved, and the practical problems of definition and administration to which it gives rise.[10] The Pearson Commission found the arguments to be very finely balanced but by a bare majority of one recommended that accidents to and from work should be covered.[11] The government, on the other hand, considers the objections, both of principle and of practice, to be significantly greater and has therefore rejected the proposal.[12]

The current legislation in Britain offers only very limited coverage for commuting accidents, such as would be justifiable on the 'supervision' principle. Section 53(1) of the Social Security Act 1975 provides that:

> An accident happening while an employed earner is, with the express or implied permission of his employer, travelling as a passenger by any vehicle to or from his place of work shall, notwithstanding that he is under no obligation to his employer to travel by that vehicle, be deemed to arise out of and in the course of his employment if —
> (a) the accident would have been deemed so to have arisen had he been under such an obligation; and
> (b) at the time of the accident, the vehicle —
> (i) is being operated by or on behalf of his employer or some other person by whom it is provided in pursuance of arrangements made with his employer; and
> (ii) is not being operated in the ordinary course of a public transport service.

The requirement in the opening paragraph that travel in the vehicle be permitted by the employer might seem to be otiose when regard is had to the condition in (b) that the vehicle be operated by him or by another under an arrangement with him. But the Commissioner has held that they are independent conditions, both of which must be satisfied.[13] The first envisages permission given prior to the event, though exceptionally subsequent permission may be acceptable provided that it is express.[14] As regards the second condition, the employer need not initiate the arrangement, and need not himself own or provide the vehicle,[15] but there must be something more than a mere undertaking by a third party to provide a vehicle for the use of the employees. The employer must be involved in

8 *R(I) 64/54*.
9 E.g. Australia, France, W. Germany and Sweden: *Pearson* vol 3, paras 384, 471, 600, 717. See also International Labour Organisation's Recommendation 121 (1964).
10 Cf *Industrial Injuries Compensation* paras 6.38–6.43. For the difficulties arising in France, see *Dupeyroux* pp. 523–535.
11 Paras 858–867.
12 *Reform of the Industrial Injuries Scheme*, paras 66–67.
13 *R(I) 5/80*, R S Lazarus, Comr.
14 Ibid, para 7.
15 *R(I) 49/53*.

some way in the running of the service:[16] an unauthorised conveyance of the employee, even for the employer's purposes, will not suffice.[17] The 'public zone' principle features in the exclusion of vehicles 'operating in the ordinary course of a public transport service'. But the words do not imply that the vehicle must be provided by a private company. The question is whether members of the public may and do habitually use the service.[18] On this point, the authorities have regard to such factors as whether the service is advertised in the ordinary timetable, whether it connects directly with the employer's premises, whether it ceases during closure of the factory.[19] A claimant cannot be a 'passenger' if he is also driving the vehicle.[20] A 'vehicle' includes 'a ship, vessel, hovercraft, aircraft'[1] and, perhaps surprisingly, need not be designed to carry a passenger (e.g. a tractor).[2] The accident must happen while the claimant is 'travelling as a passenger', so that walking to meet the vehicle, or between two vehicles, is not included.[3]

e *Interruptions and deviations*

The 'course of employment' includes not only the objective elements of time and space but also the subjective one of the claimant's activity.[4] The traditional criterion is that of performing a duty for the employer,[5] but the tendency has been to mitigate the rigours of this notion and to concentrate instead on what is 'reasonably incidental to' the employment: 'if the man is doing something for his own purposes which is reasonably incidental to his employment, he is still acting in the course of his employment'.[6] Only *material* interruptions of the working pattern destroy the connection with the employment:[7] trifling or inadvertent departures are disregarded.[8] Of course, what is reasonably incidental to a man's employment is a question very much for individual judgment, but the case-law has established a pattern of activities and events which are normally to be regarded as coming within or outside the course of employment.

i *Deviation from journey* Most obviously, an employee who deviates from a journey for purposes unconnected with his work, e.g. to visit a public house, will not succeed.[9] But stopping to take a meal en route is covered.[10] The position of an employee whose duties are peripatetic will, of course, be more flexible, as, *ex hypothesi*, he has no fixed hours or places of work. Thus a salesman returning home after entertaining a business associate

16 *R(I) 5/60*.
17 *R(I) 5/80*.
18 *R(I) 67/51*: a claim does not fail merely because the public is entitled to use the service (though ordinarily this will be the case) if there is evidence that it rarely does so.
19 *R(I) 15/57*.
20 *CI 49/49*; *R(I) 9/59*.
1 SSA 1975, s.53(2).
2 *R(I) 42/56*.
3 *R(I) 67/52*; *R(I) 48/54*.
4 See especially Lord Finley LC in *Davidson & Co v M'Robb* [1918] AC 304 at 314–315.
5 See e.g. *St Helens Colliery Co Ltd v Hewitson* [1924] AC 59, HL.
6 Per Salmon LJ, *R v Industrial Injuries Comr, ex parte Amalgamated Engineering Union (No 2)* [1966] 2 QB 31 at 51, CA. See also *R(I) 1/77* (putting up Xmas decorations).
7 *R(I) 4/73*, per H A Shewan, Comr, at para 5.
8 Per Salmon LJ, *R v Industrial Injuries Comr, ex parte Amalgamated Engineering Union, (No 2)* n.6, above; per O'Connor J, *R v National Insurance Comr, ex parte East* [1976] ICR 206 at 208.
9 *R(I) 40/55*.
10 *CI 148/49*.

succeeded.[11] But a point may be reached in his travels where he steps beyond the boundaries of his employment. Generally the employee will have discretion where he stays overnight so the course of employment will be broken from the point at which his journey ends.[12] An apparent deviation may, however, be covered where the employee had no reasonable alternative. Thus in one case,[13] the widow of an employee succeeded when her husband, a passenger in his employer's van, had departed from the prescribed route to enable a fellow employee to visit a doctor: it would have been unreasonable to expect the deceased to have left the van during the deviation.

ii *Breaks between spells of duty* There is a large number of cases involving accidents to employees in breaks between spells of duty, and it is impossible to reconcile all of them. Certainly, as one Commissioner remarked,[14] some fine distinctions are necessary (though undesirable) if decisions are to be based on logical principles. But the 'logical principle' involved is a vague one of the supervision and control of the employer, which does not make the prediction of decisions easy. Lunch and tea breaks, if spent on the employer's premises, are usually protected,[15] but not if the employee is off the premises and free to do what he likes,[16] nor, or course, if he exceeds the time allocated.[17] Quite apart from formal breaks, many occupations involve lulls in the working effort. A distinction is drawn between voluntary idleness which will interrupt the course of employment,[18] and a lull imposed by the pattern of work. If, in the latter case, an employee, to fill in time, does something not unreasonable, not prohibited by his employer, and which does not interrupt someone else's work, he will succeed.[19] But this will not be so if he removes himself completely from his sphere of operations so that he is no longer under the supervision of his employer.[20]

iii *Non-working activities* Even though a claimant may have been at his place of work during his normal working hours, what he was doing at the time of the accident may have been so far removed from his duties that he is regarded as having been outside the course of employment. The widow of an employee killed while taking a nap during night duty could not recover.[1] The interruption of work to achieve something entirely for personal purposes is similarly treated: a level-crossing keeper fetching milk from the garden;[2] a factory worker leaving work without permission to

11 *R(I) 38/53*.
12 *R(I) 22/51*; *R(I) 51/61*; *R(I) 22/54*; cp where the employee is bound, in practice if not by the terms of his employment, to stay at a particular place: *CI 374/50*; *R(I) 30/57*.
13 *R(I) 40/56*.
14 *R(I) 11/55*, para 5.
15 *R(I) 11/53*, but not at the beginning or end of a day's work *(CI 120/49*; *R(I) 11/54)* unless the meal or refreshment is regarded as part of the employee's remuneration (*R(I) 15/55*).
16 *R(I) 84/52*; *R(I) 24/53*; *R(I) 4/79*; *R(I) 10/81*. See also *R(I) 6/76* where the employee was forced to vacate the premises as the result of a bomb scare. If, however, the claimant continues to perform an employment duty during the break he is covered: *R(I) 20/61*; *R v National Insurance Comr, ex parte Reed* (1980) reported as Appendix to *R(I) 7/80*, p. 274, above.
17 *R(I) 49/57*; *Ex parte AEU*, n.6, above.
18 *Ex parte AUE*, ibid.
19 *R(I) 46/53*; *R(I) 13/66*; *R(I) 13/68*.
20 *R(I) 1/58*.
1 *R(I) 68/54*; cp where sleeping is involuntary: *R(I) 36/59*.
2 *R(I) 9/59*.

accompany a fellow employee to the work stores.[3] As regards physical activities not reasonably incidental to work, e.g. smoking, retrieving a lost object, or saying something to a fellow employee, there has been a significant change of attitude within recent years. The former approach was to refuse benefit if the claimant was voluntarily so engaged,[4] but to allow it where he was responding in a natural or instinctive way to a situation initiated by another.[5] Such an approach led to invidious inquiries into mental attitudes and was hardly practicable. The new attitude was led by the Court of Appeal in *R v Industrial Injuries Comr, ex parte Amalgamated Engineering Union (No. 2)*,[6] Lord Denning MR said:

> In the ordinary way, if a man while at his place of work, during his hours of work, is injured by a risk incidental to his employment, then the right conclusion usually is that it is an injury which arises out of and in the course of the employment, even though he may not be doing his actual work but chatting to a friend or smoking or doing something of that kind.[7]

Although these remarks were obiter, they have been taken as affecting the authority of prior decisions. The course of employment is not broken merely because, at the time, the employee was doing something for his own purposes. The question is, first, whether the interruption was a natural one and, secondly, whether it was a reasonable use of the employee's time. A decision of 1973 reveals the impact of the new approach.

> C, a factory worker, was acting as agent for a football pools firm. While being handed a coupon by a fellow employee he was injured. It was held that though strictly speaking he was not, at the time, doing something he was employed to do, nevertheless it did not involve a *material* interruption of his employment.

iv Out of the employment

a *General causal test*

The second element in the statutory test requires that the accident arises 'out of (the) . . . employment'.[8] It is not sufficient that the accident happens within the temporal and spatial limits of the employment: it must be causally linked to it.[9] For example, a man may suffer from a heart attack while he is working, but benefit is not payable unless, in some way, the condition resulted from his work. The courts and tribunals have been wary of precise formulations on this point.[10] Some have generalised in terms of employment being the 'proximate' cause of the accident;[11] others have stipulated that it be the *causa causans*, rather than the *causa sine qua non*, of the accident.[12] In a decision of 1963, a Tribunal of Commissioners

3 *R(I) 1/58.*
4 *R(I) 68/52*; *R(I) 78/52*; *R(I) 32/55*; *R(I) 41/56.*
5 *R(I) 57/54*; *R(I) 21/60.*
6 [1966] 2 QB 31.
7 Ibid, at 49.
8 SSA, 1975, s.50(1).
9 *Dover Navigation Co Ltd v Craig* [1940] AC 190, [1939] 4 All ER 558; *R(I) 16/61*; *R(I) 2/63.*
10 See e.g. *Dover Navigation* case, n.9, above, per Viscount Maugham at 193 and Lord Wright at 199; *R(I) 2/63*, para 20.
11 E.g. *R(I) 8/54*; *R(I) 75/54*; *R(I) 27/60.*
12 E.g. *R(I) 13/65*; *R(I) 26/59.*

attempted to be more specific.[13] Basing their view on some prominent House of Lords decisions under the Workmen's Compensation Acts,[14] the Commissioners argued that the crucial question is whether the claimant's own act (or by implication an 'external cause') creates a risk which is different from that created by the employment. Once the *sine qua non* test is satisfied, i.e. it is established that the accident would not have happened but for the employment, then it will generally be held to have arisen out of that employment, unless the claimant (or another) added or created 'a different risk . . . and this different risk was the real cause of the accident'.[15] But like all similar tests of causation, it is of limited utility. The authorities will always have to form their own decision on the facts of a given case,[16] guided only by the general orientation of the test, which in this instance implies that the requirement of a causal link should be liberally construed.

b *Statutory presumption*

Under the Workmen's Compensation Acts, the onus of proving that the accident arose both out of and in the course of employment lay on the claimant. In 1946, it was felt that some of the difficulties of establishing the causal link might be mitigated if the burden was on the authorities to prove that the accident did *not* arise out of the employment. The statutory presumption in its present form provides that:

> an accident arising in the course of an employed earner's employment shall be deemed, in the absence of evidence to the contrary, also to have arisen out of that employment.

Its introduction was greeted by some as a revolutionary measure which would lead to a great improvement in the claimant's position.[18] They were to be disappointed. No major change did result and it is not difficult to see why. For the presumption to apply, not only must the claimant prove that the accident occurred in the course of the employment,[19] but also there must be no 'evidence to the contrary'. In fact, in almost every disputed case, there is *some* evidence to the contrary. The approach taken by the Commissioners is that the presumption applies only if there is *nothing* in the known circumstances from which it might reasonably be inferred that the accident did not arise out of the employment.[20] Thus an epileptic found injured at the foot of a staircase could not invoke the principle: the fact of his epilepsy was 'evidence to the contrary'.[1] The first sign of a more generous interpretation of the provision came in 1964.[2]

> C, a post office engineer, was repairing a fault in a phone booth when a young man opened the door apparently to make a call. C remembered

13 *R(I) 2/63*.
14 Notably *Thom v Sinclair* [1917] AC 127; *Upton v Great Central Rly Co* [1924] AC 302; *Harris v Associated Portland Cement Manufacturers Ltd* [1939] AC 71; and *Cadzow Coal Co Ltd v Price* [1934] 1 All ER 54.
15 *R(I) 2/63*, para 26.
16 Ibid, at para 16.
17 SSA 1975, s.50(3).
18 See Mr R Prentice, Standing Committee B Debates on the Family Allowances and National Insurance Bill 1961, cols 51–52.
19 *CI 47/49*.
20 *CI 3/49*, approved in *R v National Insurance (Industrial Injuries) Comr, ex parte Richardson* [1958] 2 All ER 689, [1958] 1 WLR 851, DC. See also *R(I) 41/55* and *R(I) 30/60*.
1 *CI 68/49*.
2 *R(I) 1/64*.

nothing more until he arrived home bleeding from a head wound. The Commissioner discounted the possibility that C might have provoked an assault as being too 'speculative' and thus not constituting contrary evidence. The presumption therefore applied and C was awarded benefit.

c *Pre-existing conditions*

A major problem that arises in applying the general causation principles concerns the effect of pre-existing conditions. An employee may have a latent physical disability (e.g. a heart condition) unconnected with his work. Should the disability manifest itself during the course of the employment, the authorities must decide whether the accident arose 'out of' that employment. The problem is resolved on principles analogous to those already described concerning the causal link between the 'accident' and the 'injury'.[3] If the employment provides merely the background or setting for the event, the claimant will not succeed.[4] The work must contribute in a material degree to the risk.[5] Once that is established, the fact that the prior condition rendered him more liable to sustain an accident will be irrelevant. So in *R(I) 11/80*

> C, who suffered from postural hypotension, fell during his course of work at a factory, and was rendered unconscious when his head struck the floor. The Commissioner, J G Monroe, held that he could succeed on the alternative grounds: (i) that he fainted as a result of changing his posture, which he did for the purpose of his employment; or (ii) that, in any event, the fact that he came into physical contact with the employer's premises was sufficient to associate the accident with the employment.[6]

d *Common risks*

The causation test implicit in the requirement that the accident arise out of the employment carries with it the assumption that the employment creates a risk for the claimant which is greater than, or at least different from, that to which he would have been subject as a member of the public. Should the assumption not be justified, the employment may not be the substantial cause of the accident. In principle, then, an employee struck by lightning,[7] or bitten by an animal,[8] while working should not succeed. The employment has not exposed him to a risk greater than that to which an ordinary member of the public is subject. On the other hand, if the 'accident has occurred to the workman by reason of the employment bringing about his presence at the particular spot and so exposing him to a danger . . .', he will be entitled.[9] So a seaman suffering from heat exhaustion while working aboard a vessel in the Arabian sea was clearly covered, and it was irrelevant that other persons living in tropical climates are exposed to the same risk.[10] Here the employment took the claimant to a locality to which he would otherwise not have gone. While the theoretical distinction

3 P. 270, above. Cf the rules governing war pension claims: pp. 343–345, below.
4 *R(I) 12/52*.
5 *R(I) 73/51*.
6 Applying a dictum of Lord Atkin in *Brooker v Thomas Borthwick & Sons (Australia) Ltd* [1933] AC 669 at 677. See also *CI 82/49*
7 *R(I) 7/60*.
8 *CI 101/50*; *R(I) 89/52*.
9 Per Russell LJ, *Lawrence v George Matthews (1924) Ltd* [1929] 1 KB 1 at 20, CA.
10 *R(I) 4/61*, following *Dover Navigation Co Ltd v Craig* [1940] AC 190, [1939] 4 All ER 558.

between these cases may be clearly recognised, there is a large shady area between them which cannot easily be divided according to any precise criterion. As a consequence, the authorities tended to approach the problem casuistically, declining to justify their decisions in terms of principle. The resulting unpredictability may be gauged from comparing two, unhappily typical, cases:

> A foreign body struck the eye of a lorry driver while on the road. He was not entitled: 'I do not think that a person driving a lorry is thereby exposed to any greater risk of getting something in his eye than anyone else'.[11]

> A piece of grit entered the eye of a police motorcyclist when on patrol duty. He succeeded: 'a man who is employed to drive a motor-bicycle about the streets of a city is exposed by his employment to a greater risk of getting something in his eye than a person not so employed'.[12]

The confusion created by such decisions led to dissatisfaction with the statutory formula. The reaction of some Commissioners was to aid the injured person by broadening the category of 'locality risks'. They were prepared to hold, more often than was perhaps justifiable, that the employment had taken the claimant to the particular spot where he encountered the hazard. It was so decided in the case of a bus driver stung by a wasp[13] and that of an agricultural worker struck by lightning.[14] Another device was to find an intermediate agent which intervened between the original hazard and the injury and so to regard it, rather than the original hazard, as the 'proximate cause' of the injury. Thus when an employee, riding a bicycle on her employer's business, was blown off by a freak gust of wind, the Commissioner felt able to decide in her favour on the somewhat artificial ground that 'the proximate cause was that she fell from her bicycle while travelling on duty, and it does not seem to me to be necessary to consider any remoter cause'.[15]

Such generous approaches were by no means universal. In 1958, the Divisional Court held that a bus conductor, attacked while on duty by a gang of youths, could not succeed because his position was no different from that of any other person on the bus.[16] The decision created consternation among the trade unions, and there was immediate pressure for legislative reform.[17] It was forthcoming in 1961, the method chosen being to extend the coverage of the scheme to certain specified risks.[18] The provision, as re-enacted in 1975, is that:

> an accident shall be treated . . . as arising out of an employed earner's employment if —
> (a) the accident arises in the course of the employment; and
> (b) the accident either is caused by another person's misconduct, skylarking or negligence, or by steps taken in consequence of any such misconduct, skylarking or negligence, or by the behaviour or presence of an animal (including a bird, fish or insect), or is caused by or consists in the employed earner being struck by any object or by lightning; and

11 *R(I) 62/53*, para 3.
12 *R(I) 67/53*, para 5. See also *R(I) 71/53*.
13 *R(I) 5/56*.
14 *R(I) 23/58*.
15 *R(I) 27/60*, following a similar idea in *R(I) 46/54*.
16 *Ex parte Richardson*, n.20, above.
17 See General Council Report of the TUC (1960).
18 FANIA 1961, s.2.

(c) the employed earner did not directly or indirectly induce or contribute to the happening of the accident by his conduct outside the employment or by any act not incidental to the employment.[19]

The risks selected for special protection manifestly reflect particular situations in which claimants had previously encountered difficulty in recovering benefit, and there is no obvious common principle to which they all relate.[20] The cumulative effect of this provision, and the Commissioners' decisions previously referred to, reduces the significance of the 'out' requirement, provoking one commentator to the conclusion that

> we appear to have got very close to the stage when an accident arising in the course of employment will almost inevitably fall within the system.[1]

But, so far at least, successive governments have refused to abandon the 'out' requirement. To do so, it is argued, would make nonsense of the existence of the special scheme for work-caused accidents.[2] The argument is obviously sound, but it seems hard to reconcile with the policy behind the 1961 reform.

e *Claimant's conduct*

The third condition of the 1961 provision quoted above, that the claimant should not contribute to the accident by conduct outside the employment, restates a principle existing in the case-law prior to the enactment and falls now for consideration. It is clear, in the first place, that the mere negligence or carelessness of the claimant is not by itself sufficient to bar entitlement to benefit:[3] the legislation has not incorporated the common law doctrine of contributory negligence. For some time, under the Workmen's Compensation Acts, the courts did flirt with the notion of so-called 'added risk'. According to this doctrine, 'a peril voluntarily superinduced on what arose out of the employment, to which the workman was neither required nor had authority to expose himself',[4] would deprive him of a remedy. The doctrine has been discredited,[5] and held not to apply to the social security scheme.[6] It has been supplanted by another principle of causation more favourable to the claimant: the conduct of an employee will defeat his claim only if (1) he 'added or created a different risk' to or from that arising from the employment and (2) 'this different risk was the real cause of the accident'.[7] In the case in which this test was propounded,

> C, attempting to light a cigarette, as permitted by his employer, ignited gas which was escaping from an unlit blow-pipe. He was awarded benefit. C's act converted a potential risk into an actual explosion. 'It did not make it a different danger or create a fresh one'.[8]

19 SSA 1975, s.55(1).
20 See the Standing Committee B Debates on the 1961 Bill.
1 *Atiyah* p. 376, and see *Micklethwait* pp. 82–83.
2 Mr J Boyd Carpenter, Minister of Pensions and NI, in the Standing Committee B Debates on the 1961 Bill, cols 59–60.
3 *Harris v Associated Portland Cement Manufacturers Ltd* [1939] AC 71; *R(I) 36/59*.
4 Per Viscount Haldane, *Lancashire and Yorkshire Rly Co v Highley* [1917] AC 352 at 361. See also *Barnes v Nunnery Colliery Co Ltd* [1912] AC 44 and *Plumb v Cobden Flour Mills Co Ltd* [1914] AC 62.
5 *Thomas v Ocean Coal* [1933] AC 100; *Noble v Southern Rly Co* [1940] AC 583, [1940] 2 All ER 383.
6 *R(I) 2/63*; *R 4/70 (II)*.
7 *R(I) 2/63*; *R(I) 3/63*.
8 *R(I) 2/63*, para 29.

In contrast in another case,

> In an effort to warm himself, C poured petrol onto a fire and was burned by the conflagration. Fires were prohibited on the site, but in terms of causation C's act had added or created a different risk from that inherent in the circumstances of the employment.[9]

It is convenient here to consider the relevance of the fact that the claimant's conduct was prohibited by his employer or by the law generally. In the early years of the Workmen's Compensation Act, employers were frequently able to rely on the existence of such a prohibition as a defence.[10] The position was altered in 1923,[11] when the legislature provided that an act would be

> deemed to have arisen out of and in the course of employment, notwithstanding that the workman was . . . acting in contravention of any statutory or other regulation . . . or of any orders given by or on behalf of his employer, or that he was acting without instructions from his employer, if such act was done by the workman for the purposes of and in connection with his employer's trade or business.

It was optimistically argued by some that this effectively overruled the 'out' requirement. Such an interpretation, though perhaps feasible on a literal view of the phrase 'acting without instructions', was obviously unintended: it would place disobedient employees in a better position than obedient ones. The argument was quickly denounced by the House of Lords.[12] 'Acting without instructions' was equated with an implied prohibition. More importantly, the provision left open the possibility that the employee was, in any event, acting outside the scope of his employment. If so, he failed. The effect of the 1923 reform was merely to prevent a certain class of evidence being sufficient of itself to oust the right to compensation.[13] It did not operate to extend the scope of the employment. The point was confirmed by legislative amendment when the provision was incorporated into the national insurance scheme.[14] A new condition was added. For the fiction to apply, the claimant must now show that:

(a) the accident would have been deemed so to have arisen had the act not been done in contravention of any such regulations or orders, or without such instructions as the case may be; and
(b) the act is done for the purposes of and in connection with the employer's trade or business.[15]

On condition (a), the claimant must show that apart from the contravention the accident arose out of and in the course of employment. Thus, if he is doing something quite different from that which he was employed to do, he cannot benefit from the provision.[16] For example, in *R v D'Albuquerque, ex parte Bresnahan*[17]

> D, a dock labourer engaged in loading a ship, attempted to move an obstacle with a fork lift truck which had been left unattended by its

9 *R(I) 24/51*.
10 See e.g. *Lowe v Pearson* [1899] 1 QB 261, CA.
11 WCA 1923, s.7.
12 *Kerr v James Dunlop & Co*[1926] AC 377.
13 Per Viscount Dunedin, ibid, at 386.
14 NI(II)A 1946, s.8.
15 SSA 1975, s.52.
16 *CI 11/49*; *R(I) 77/54*; *R(I) 7/55*; *R(I) 41/56*; *R(I) 12/61*.
17 [1966] 1 Lloyds Rep 69, DC.

driver. He fell into the dock with it and was drowned. His widow failed. It was not within the scope of his employment to use a fork lift truck and therefore condition (a) was not satisfied.

Whether the act is 'done for the purposes of and in connection with the employer's trade or business' has been given a generous interpretation in the recent cases. Thus, it was held to be in the interests of both the employer and the employee (though prohibited by the former) that a locomotive driver should take a short cut on his way from the railway shed to a station.[18]

f *Emergencies*

It is an obvious principle that the causal link with the employment is not broken if the accident occurs through the employee responding to an emergency. To this end, section 54 of the Social Security Act 1975 provides that

> An accident happening to an employed earner in or about any premises at which he is for the time being employed for the purposes of his employer's trade or business shall be deemed to arise out of and in the course of his employment if it happens while he is taking steps, on an actual or supposed emergency at those premises, to rescue, succour or protect persons who are, or are thought to be or possibly to be, injured or imperilled, or to avert or minimise serious damage to property.

The provision does not cover all possible emergencies; in particular, the emergency must have occurred 'in or about' premises where the employee is working.[19] But it is complemented by a case-law doctrine which holds that the act of meeting an emergency arises out of the employment if it can be construed as being in some way in the interests of the employer and was reasonable in the circumstances.[20]

v Special cases

Finally, mention should be made of rules which deem that accidents occurring to special categories of employee arise out of and in the course of employment.

(a) Airmen and mariners are covered if the accident occurs when returning from work abroad at the employer's expense.[1]

(b) An airman travelling to his work in an aircraft is deemed to have the permission of his employer, for the purpose of section 53(1),[2] and to like effect a mariner travelling to his work in a vessel need not show that this was under an arrangement with his employer.[3]

(c) A mariner employed on a vessel as a pilot is covered for accidents while on board, while embarking or disembarking, or while returning (without undue delay) to a port other than that from which he normally plies his trade.[4]

18 *R(I) 5/67*.
19 On which, see *R(I) 6/63*.
20 *CI 280/49*; *R(I) 63/54*; *R(I) 46/60*.
1 SI 1975/469, reg 3(a); SI 1975/470, reg 3(a).
2 SI 1975/469, reg 3(c).
3 SI 1975/470, reg 3(c).
4 Ibid, reg 4.

Part 4 Industrial diseases

A General

Soon after the passing of the first Workmen's Compensation Act, it became clear that the 'personal injury by accident' formula was inadequate to cope with sickness or disease resulting from employment. It has already been seen[5] that in principle an incapacity resulting from a 'process' as opposed to an 'event' is not caught by the general provisions. Granted that protection should be afforded in these cases, there would appear to be two basic possibilities:[6] (1) to provide a general definition of occupational disease as an alternative to the 'accident' formula, the claimant having to satisfy the authorities (with or without the aid of a presumption) that the disease was contracted as a result of his employment; (2) to create a list of specified diseases which experience and medical expertise have shown to be typical risks for certain specified categories of employment. Generally with the aid of a presumption, the claimant would then have to show that he contracted a prescribed disease as a result of working in the prescribed occupation. Persuasive arguments can be made out for either approach.[7] (1) has the great advantage that its scope is wider (those suffering from non-prescribed diseases in (2) are without remedy) and it is more flexible: legislatures, it is claimed, cannot keep pace with new and changing industrial risks. The advantages claimed for (2) tend to be more incidental to the policy of providing compensation for those suffering from industrial diseases. Thus it is said that the requirement of prescription encourages more detailed and intensive study of the problems, which in turn contributes to safety and rehabilitation systems. The more general coverage in (1) creates difficulties of proof (particularly of causation) and thereby greater uncertainty and, it is claimed, is thereby more costly and more conducive to false claims and abuse. Most countries including Britain have adopted the more restrictive approach in (2).[8] But recommendations have been made both by the EEC[9] and the International Labour Organisation[10] for a so-called 'mixed system' which effectively combines the two approaches: the claimant benefits from a presumption that he incurred a scheduled disease from employment in a relevant occupation; but if he is suffering from a non-scheduled disease, the onus is on him to establish the causal link with the employment. Such a system operates in Denmark and the Federal Republic of Germany and was urged on the British government by the Pearson Commission.[11] The matter was fully considered by the Industrial Injuries Advisory Council in a report published in 1981.[12] While acknowledging the merits of the individual proof method, it felt unable to recommend that a claimant suffering from *any* non-prescribed disease should be allowed to assert that it was causally linked with his employment. A number of diseases which are common in the general population and which are often thought to be connected in some way with certain types of employment would give rise to considerable

5 Pp. 269–270, above.
6 Cf Riesenfeld 52 Calif L Rev 531, 542–543.
7 Sears and Groves 31 Rocky Mountain L Rev 462; Angerstein 18, ibid, 240.
8 See generally IIAC Report on Industrial Diseases (1981, Cmnd 8393), paras 6–32.
9 Recommendation 2188/62.
10 Recommendation No 121 (1964).
11 Paras 880–887.
12 N.8, above.

difficulty. Medical opinion would differ as to their aetiology, thus leading to a lack of uniformity in decisions on entitlement, and claimants might have inappropriately high expectations of success.[13] The preferred solution was to allow a system of individual proof for all diseases except those thought likely to lead to such problems; these would include lung cancer, strokes, coronary diseases and mental diseases.[14]

While the reaction of the government to this proposal is awaited, the British scheme remains limited to protection against prescribed diseases. The principle was introduced by the Workmen's Compensation Act of 1906.[15] A Departmental Committee set up shortly after the passing of the Act felt that a new disease should be included only if it were so specific to the prescribed employment that in individual cases the causal link with the employment could be established without difficulty, or, in other words, that the claimant would be unlikely to contract it outside his work.[16] Thus bronchitis was not added since 'it would attract endless litigation, as no one knows whether the sufferer has contracted it from dust irritation, or would have contracted it anyway, as hundreds of other people in the locality do'.[17] The approach was subjected to severe criticism from trade unionists who argued that it was too restrictive, but two committees reviewing the law between the wars resisted change.[18] The principle of inclusion was reiterated in the National Insurance (Industrial Injuries) Act 1946,[19] and is still law, section 76(2) of the Social Security Act 1975 providing that:

(a) [the disease] ought to be treated, having regard to its causes and incidence and any other relevant considerations, as a risk of their occupations and not as a risk common to all persons; and
(b) it is such that, in the absence of special circumstances, the attribution of particular cases to the nature of the employment can be established or presumed with reasonable certainty.

Although the principle has remained unaltered, it is clear that the practice has shifted significantly.[20] In the early days, the emphasis was on showing that the disease was peculiar to the specified employment, and not to others. Later, the crux became whether the employment created a vulnerability to the disease greater than that of the general public, even though other employments were equally susceptible. While proviso (b) remains a serious obstacle to the admission of some diseases, there is apparent a tendency to attach less importance to it. So in 1974 occupational deafness was added,[1] notwithstanding the finding of the Industrial Injuries Advisory Council that loss of hearing is a common affliction and has 'a number of different causes'.[2]

13 IIAC Report, n.8, above, at paras 144–149.
14 Ibid, para 159.
15 S.8, following proposals of a Departmental Committee (1904, Cd 2208).
16 Report of the Departmental Committee on Compensation for Industrial Diseases (Gladstone Committee) (1907, Cd 3495).
17 Ibid, at para 25.
18 Report of the Departmental Committee on Compensation for Industrial Diseases (Holman Gregory Committee) (1920, Cmd 816); Report of the Departmental Committee on Compensation for Industrial Diseases (1932).
19 S.55(2).
20 Young *Industrial Injuries Insurance* (1964) p. 26.
1 SI 1974/1414.
2 Report on Occupational Deafness (1973, Cmnd 5461), para 45.

B Proof of prescribed disease

Proof that the claimant is suffering from a prescribed disease or injury 'due to the nature of (his) employment' is an alternative basis of entitlement to that provided by 'a personal injury caused by accident arising out of and in the course of employment'.[3] Inconvenient overlaps between the two criteria are prevented by the provision that

> a person shall not be entitled to benefit in respect of a disease as being an injury by accident arising out of and in the course of any employment if at the time of the accident the disease is in relation to him a prescribed disease by virtue of . . . that employment.[4]

To establish entitlement on the basis of a prescribed disease the claimant must satisfy three conditions:
(a) he suffers from a prescribed disease;
(b) that disease is prescribed in relation to his occupation;
(c) the disease developed as a result of employment in that occupation.

i Suffering from prescribed disease

A Schedule to the Prescribed Diseases Regulations lists descriptions of conditions covered by the scheme.[5] The claimant must prove that he is suffering from or has suffered from one such condition which resulted in the incapacity for work or loss of faculty, on which title to injury and disablement benefits are respectively based.[6] Evidence is normally supplied through doctors specialising in the relevant diseases.[7] A decision is then made by the insurance officer in the light of that evidence. He may refer the question, or an appeal may be brought against his decision, to a medical board, and from that body to a medical appeal tribunal.[8] Because of the expertise required for pneumoconiosis and byssinosis claims, there are special boards constituted to diagnose these diseases,[9] and the right of appeal to a medical appeal tribunal is more limited.[10]

ii Disease prescribed for claimant's occupation

Against the description of each disease, there is listed in the Schedule the occupation or occupations for which the disease is prescribed. The claimant's task is to prove that he has been employed in the relevant occupation on or after 5 July 1948.[11] It is important to appreciate that the scheduled description is not a legal categorisation of the type of occupation but a factual account of work actually undertaken.[12] It follows that though a

3 SSA 1975, s.76(1).
4 Ibid, s.76(5).
5 SI 1980/377, Sch 1, Part I. For proposals to restructure the Schedule, see IIAC Report, n.8, above, paras 70–75.
6 Though NB: those suffering from pneumoconiosis, diffuse mesothelioma or occupational deafness are not entitled to injury benefit: SI 1980/377, reg 34.
7 DHSS Leaflet NI2. Details of likely symptoms and after effects of prescribed diseases are given in the DHSS Booklet, *Notes on the Diagnosis of Occupational Disease* (2nd edn).
8 SI 1980/377, Part V. On these bodies see generally pp. 596–601, below.
9 SI 1980/377, regs 49–51.
10 Ibid, reg 49(5), as amended by SI 1982/566.
11 SI 1980/377, reg 2(a). For older cases see p. 329, below. In the cases of pneumoconiosis, byssinosis and occupational deafness, there are further conditions to be satisfied: see SI 1980/377, reg 2(b)–(d).
12 Therefore it is not sufficient for the claimant to establish that he was contractually bound to undertake such work. The question is whether he actually *did* the work: *CI 59/49*; *R(I) 3/78*.

claimant's employment may in theory include work in the prescribed activity, in practice he may not be engaged at all on it, or only for a trivial amount of time. In such circumstances he will not be entitled to benefit.[13] The scheduled descriptions of the occupation vary from the very vague[14] to the highly specific.[15] Many have been the subject of Commissioners' case-law, but consideration of it lies beyond the scope of this work.[16]

iii Causal link between occupation and disease

Finally the claimant must establish the causal link between employment in the prescribed occupation and the prescribed disease. In the ordinary case, there is a presumption that the disease was due to the nature of the relevant occupation if he was employed in it at any time within one month preceding the date of the development of the disease.[17] But there are cases where the rule does not apply or is varied.

(1) Inflammation or ulceration of the throat or mouth and non-infective dermatitis – there is no presumption for these diseases and the onus is on the claimant to establish the causal link.[18]
(2) Tuberculosis – for the presumption to apply, he must have been first employed in the relevant occupation at least six weeks before the date of development, and have been last so employed not more than two years before that date.[19]
(3) Occupational deafness – for the presumption to apply, he must have been employed for an aggregate of at least 20 years in a relevant occupation.[20]
(4) Pneumoconiosis – the presumption applies if, on aggregate, he has been employed for two years in a relevant occupation.[1]
(5) Byssinosis – the presumption applies if he has been employed in the relevant occupation for any period since 5 July 1948.[2]

The 'date of development' varies according to the benefit claimed. For injury benefit, it is the first day on which the claimant was incapable of work as a result of the disease, or if later, the date from which benefit is payable; for disablement benefit, the day on which he first suffered the relevant loss of faculty or the date from which benefit is payable; for death benefit, the date of death.[3]

To rebut the presumption, where it exists, the insurance officer must prove on the balance of probabilities that the disease was not due to the nature of the relevant occupation.[4] In some cases, he will seek to show that it was caused by employment in an occupation not prescribed.[5] In others, the disease may allegedly arise from activities or contacts outside his employment[6] or from a condition pre-existing in the claimant before the

13 E.g. *CI 265/49*; *R(I) 40/57*.
14 E.g. Prescribed Diseases Nos 22 and 35: 'work in or about a mine'.
15 E.g. Prescribed Disease No 39.
16 Reference should be made to Neligan *Social Security Case-Law – Digest of Commissioners' Decisions* (1980) ch 9.
17 SI 1980/377, reg 4(1).
18 Ibid.
19 Ibid, reg 4(2).
20 Ibid, regs 2(d) and 4(5).
1 Ibid, reg 4(3).
2 Ibid, reg 4(4).
3 Ibid, reg 6.
4 *R(I) 37/52*.
5 E.g. *R(I) 9/53*.
6 E.g. *R(I) 20/52*.

commencement of the occupation.[7] In all cases, the question is not whether the employment was the sole cause of the disease: it is sufficient if it was the real and substantial cause.[8]

C Recrudescence and fresh attacks

If a claimant has already been awarded benefit for a particular disease and has recovered wholly or partly, but then suffers a further attack, the consequences will vary according to the time when the attack occurs and whether it is regarded as a recrudescence or rather a fresh attack. If it occurs during an injury benefit period or during a period taken into account by an assessment of disablement relating to the earlier attack, there are two possibilities. If it is treated as a recrudescence of the earlier attack it cannot give rise to a new claim but may be taken into account as a basis for reviewing the previous assessment of disablement.[9] If it is found to be a fresh attack, the normal rules apply and the claimant is treated as if no previous claim had been made.[10] If the further attack occurs outside the periods mentioned, it is treated as being contracted afresh and the claim is unaffected by the earlier receipt of benefit.[11] Decisions as between recrudescence and fresh attack are made by those bodies which determine diagnosis questions.[12]

Part 5 Injury benefit

A General

Most state systems of compensation distinguish between temporary and permanent disablement. For non-industrial cases, as has been seen, different provision is available for sickness benefit, payable for the first six months, and invalidity benefit, payable thereafter.[13] For industrial disablement, the historical arguments for such a distinction were less compelling. Under the Workmen's Compensation Acts compensation was payable for a proportion of the employee's lost wages, whatever the duration of the disability, though after six months, the employer liable could insist on the commutation of the weekly payment into a lump sum.[14] Beveridge's recognition, based on both theoretical and political grounds, of the need to maintain a differential between industrial and non-industrial cases,[15] prompted the recommendation that for the first thirteen weeks the injured employee should rely on sickness benefit; thereafter he might be awarded a pension based on two-thirds of his lost earnings (to a statutory maximum).[16] The need for the distinction was felt to be acute only for those industrial accidents which resulted in prolonged disability. The post-war govern-

7 E.g. *R(I) 37/52*; *R(I) 38/52*.
8 *R(I) 10/53*.
9 SI 1980/377, reg 7(4).
10 Ibid, reg 7(3) and see *R(I) 10/53*.
11 SI 1980/377, reg 7(1)(b).
12 P. 290, above.
13 Ch 4, above.
14 See generally Willis *Workmen's Compensation* (37th edn) pp. 406–414.
15 Para 85.
16 Para 100.

ment, in its White Paper, rejected the proposal.[17] It recognised the need for a differential but felt justified in extending it to short-term as well as long-term cases. For the initial period, then, the claimant was to be paid a flat-rate benefit, but on a scale higher than that to be awarded for sickness or unemployment. Thirteen weeks was also thought to be an inappropriately short and inflexible period. The transfer from the flat-rate benefit to the disablement pension should take place 'at a date appropriate to the circumstances of the individual case' when the consequences of the accident had 'settled'.[18] Entitlement to short-term benefit, like sickness benefit, would require proof of *total* incapacity for work, whereas the long-term benefit would be based not on lost earning capacity but on the degree of disablement, which might be partial or total. This latter concept underwent significant modifications in implementation; in particular, as will be seen,[19] Parliament resiled from a system of compensation wholly unrelated to earning capacity.

The relationship between the short-term injury benefit and the long-term disablement benefit, and indeed the very existence of the former, came to be reconsidered in 1980–81. As we have seen, the industrial preference (the difference between industrial injury benefits and the general benefits for sickness and invalidity) has become increasingly subject to criticism,[20] and this is reinforced by the fact that the real value of the preference for short-term beneficiaries has not been maintained in line with inflation. 'Considerable administrative cost is therefore incurred to deal with hundreds of thousands of cases in most of which little extra benefit is at stake'.[1] A study carried out by DHSS officials mooted the possibility of abolishing injury benefit.[2] The government accepted the idea,[3] and proceeded forthwith to implement the reform by the Social Security and Housing Benefits Act 1982, notwithstanding the view that the matter could be postponed until decisions had been made on other changes proposed in the 1981 White Paper. As a result, entitlement to injury benefit will lapse from April 1983.[4] For most employees who would have been so entitled the loss will be marginal since they will receive statutory sick pay for the first eight weeks off work and sickness benefit thereafter. A claimant unable to satisfy the contribution conditions stipulated for the latter will nevertheless be entitled to that benefit, provided that his incapacity is attributable to an industrial accident or prescribed disease.[5] The abolition of injury benefit will necessarily create some administrative problems, for the need to investigate the circumstances of an accident will arise only when the long-term disablement benefit is claimed.[6] To reduce the difficulties, from April 1983, entitlement to the latter benefit will begin 13 weeks after the accident, instead of six months, as is typically the case under current law.[7]

17 *Social Insurance* Part II, para 26.
18 Ibid, at para 27.
19 P. 298, below.
20 Pp. 262–263, above.
1 *Industrial Injuries Compensation* para 2.7. The difference between injury and sickness benefit is currently £2.73 per week.
2 Ibid, paras 2.19–2.32.
3 *Reform of the Industrial Injuries Scheme*, ch 2.
4 SSHBA 1982, s.39(1).
5 Ibid, s.39(4), inserting s.50A in SSA 1975.
6 N.1, above, at paras 2.29–2.36; n.3, above, at para 17.
7 SSHBA 1982, s.39(2).

Under the law which will remain in force until April 1983, the claimant is

entitled to injury benefit in respect of any day during the injury benefit period on which, as the result of the relevant injury, he is incapable of work.[8]

B Incapacity for work

The claimant must first prove incapacity for work on the days for which benefit is claimed. The requirement is exactly the same as that for the sickness and invalidity benefits, and the authorities have applied identical principles. These have been discussed in some detail in chapter 4.[9]

C Causal link between injury and incapacity

Secondly, the claimant must establish that the incapacity resulted from the 'personal injury caused by . . . accident arising out of and in the course of his employment' or the 'personal disease or injury due to the nature' of the employment.[10] In general, it can be said that the employment injury must be the 'effective cause' (*causa causans*) of the incapacity but need not be its sole cause.[11] This means that though the incapacity would not have occurred but for a condition afflicting the claimant prior to the accident, he may still recover,[12] provided he can show that the accident rendered him more prone to the consequences of the earlier condition, or, to put it another way, aggravated that condition.[13] In other cases, the employment injury occurs first and the question is whether a subsequent incapacity is still linked to it. Courts interpreting the workmen's compensation legislation tended to use the common law test of whether a *novus actus interveniens* broke the chain of causation.[14] In *R(I) 3/56*, a Tribunal of Commissioners attempted to reformulate the guiding principles: if the immediate cause of the incapacity is injury by a non-industrial accident, the claimant may still succeed if he can prove that an injury previously arising from an industrial accident was the 'effective cause' of the non-industrial accident;[15] if, as a result of a non-industrial accident, the condition arising from an industrial accident is aggravated, or the period of incapacity prolonged, he will be entitled so long as the industrial injury condition continues to be the 'effective cause' of the incapacity, even though the industrial accident was not in any other way linked to the non-industrial accident.[16] Though the wording of these rules may be difficult, the principles emerging are typical of those applied to causal questions throughout the law, and the question is always one of fact, the authorities, with the aid of medical evidence, judging

8 SSA 1975, s.56(1).
9 Pp. 148–155, above.
10 Though those suffering from pneumoconiosis or byssinosis are not entitled to injury benefit: SI 1980/377, reg 34.
11 *Dunham v Clare* [1902] 2 KB 292, CA (a case on the analogous provision under the WCA, and rejecting the view that the incapacity must be the 'natural and probable consequence' of the injury – the test then prevailing in the law of tort). See also *R(I) 3/56*.
12 *Laverick v W Gray & Co Ltd* (1919) 12 BWCC 176, CA; *CI 50/50*; *R(I) 3/56*.
13 *CI 4/49*; *CI 147/50*; cp *CI 168/49*; *CI 413/50*; *R(I) 33/51*.
14 *Dunham v Clare*, n.11, above, *Hogan v Bentick West Hartley Collieries (Owners) Ltd* [1949] 1 All ER 588, CA.
15 See *R(I) 9/52*; cp *CI 114/49*.
16 *Brown v George Kent Ltd* [1913] 3 KB 624, CA.

the matter from a common sense point of view.[17] Cases where the causal link has been allegedly broken by the negligence of a third party (e.g. a doctor) gave rise to some difficulty under the Workmen's Compensation Acts. Though the point has not been the subject of a reported decision under social security legislation, the principle must hold good that if the incapacity resulted substantially from the third party's act and the employment injury was only the condition of, or setting for, the act, resort must be had to a remedy against the third party rather than to the insurance fund.[18] Alternatively, it may be argued that the incapacity resulted from the claimant's own reluctance to undergo an operation rather than from the original employment injury. In theory, no doubt, such a finding is possible,[19] but the unreasonableness of the claimant's decision must be certain beyond any doubt for the authorities to refuse benefit on this basis,[20] and, as will be seen, there are statutory grounds to disentitle a claimant for behaving 'in a manner calculated to retard his recovery' or for wilful obstruction of medical treatment.[1]

D Benefit period

i Days of incapacity

The basis of entitlement to injury benefit being incapacity for work, it naturally falls into line with the other social security benefits which are payable where employment ceases. Thus the day for which benefit is claimed must, consistently with the rules on unemployment and sickness benefits, form part of a 'period of interruption of employment'.[2] Three waiting-days must be served, though, as for sickness benefit, the linking rule provides that any two periods of four consecutive days of incapacity not separated by more than eight weeks are treated as one period of interruption of employment.[4] The other rules governing the days for which benefit is payable apply equally here, so that:

(1) Sunday (or its substitute) is not treated as a day of incapacity;[5]

(2) Where the claimant is a night worker, the night-shift is attributed to the second of the two days unless the greater portion falls in the first day.[6]

ii Duration of benefit

Injury benefit is payable for a maximum of 156 days (excluding Sundays) beginning with the day of the accident giving rise to the employment injury.[7] After the expiration of that period, the claimant may, of course, be entitled to disablement benefit.

17 The reports of the Commissioners' decisions contain a number of cases to guide the authorities on the aetiology of certain regularly occurring types of incapacity.

18 *Rocca v Stanley Jones & Co Ltd* (1914) 7 BWCC 101, CA; *Hogan v Bentick West Hartley Collieries (Owners) Ltd*, n.14, above; and see the cases on criminal law: *R v Jordan* (1956) 40 Cr App Rep 152 (CCA); *R v Smith* [1959] 2 QB 35 [1959] 2 All ER 193 (Cts Martial App Ct).

19 *Warncken v Moreland* [1909] 1 KB 184, CA; cf on special hardship allowance p. 318, below; on the criminal law, *R v Blaue* [1975] 3 All ER 466, [1975] 1 WLR 144, CA; and on the law of damages, Ogus *Law of Damages* (1973) pp. 181–182.

20 *Tutton v Owner of the Majestic* [1909] 2 KB 54, CA.

1 P. 328, below.

2 SSA 1975, s.56(5)(a): cf p. 89, above.

3 SSA 1975, s.56(5)(b).

4 Ibid, s.56(6), incorporating s.17(1)(d), as amended by SSA (No 2) 1980, s.3.

5 SSA 1975, s.17(1)(e), p. 85, above.

6 SI 1975/564, reg 5, p. 85, above and see *R(I) 31/55*.

7 SSA 1975, s.56(4).

iii Unavailability of disablement benefit

The transition from injury to disablement benefit may take place before the period of 156 days has expired, if the claimant is no longer incapable of work,[8] and so, in the alternative, the injury benefit period is defined as the part of the 156 days for which 'disablement benefit in respect of the accident is not available'.[9] Clearly, double recovery is to be avoided, but the position becomes complicated where during the period of 156 days the injured person claims for disablement benefit, because he is capable of returning to work, but then is subjected to a further period of incapacity resulting from the original accident. In such circumstances, the legislation impliedly confers on him a right to elect between the two benefits. It does so in a circumlocutory way by providing that:

> where he makes a claim for disablement benefit in respect of the accident before the end of that period and does not withdraw it before it is finally determined, then if on any day of that period not earlier than the making of the claim he is not so incapable of work, the fact that he is or may be so incapable on a subsequent day of the period shall be disregarded. . . .[10]

Disablement benefit is not 'available' if the claimant withdraws his claim 'before it is finally determined' and hence injury benefit will be payable.[11] The subsection gives no clue as to when this condition will be satisfied. On one extreme view, the claim might be regarded as finally determined when the insurance officer makes his initial decision on the disablement benefit application. The other extreme interpretation is that withdrawal is possible until the time has elapsed for all possible appeals to the medical authorities, to the statutory authorities and perhaps even to the ordinary courts. Neither view is plausible. The latter interpretation is obviously highly impracticable, and the former would considerably undermine the policy of election which obviously inspired the provision. After lengthy consideration of the matter the Commissioner in 1963[12] reached a sensible compromise solution:[13] the *normal* time for appeal to the medical authorities on the assessment of disability must have expired.[14] The possibility of the claimant being given leave to appeal out of time is ignored.[15] The course of action most favourable to a claimant will depend on whether the aggregate of entitlement to disablement benefit and the various additions will exceed the amount payable for injury benefit.

E Amount

Injury benefit is a flat-rate weekly sum (in 1982–83, £27.75), to which may be added increases for dependants.[16] There is a lower rate (in 1982–83,

8 Ibid, s.57(4).
9 Ibid, s.56(4).
10 Ibid, s.57(4).
11 *R(I) 15/63*.
12 *R(I) 14/63*.
13 Following a Northern Ireland decision to the same effect: *R 59/61 (II)*.
14 On this see p. 598, below. Where the assessment is a provisional one, the appeal procedure referred to relates to that award rather than the final determination: *R(I) 14/63*, para 30.
15 The Commissioner left open the question whether a right of appeal to the Commissioner himself from the medical appeal tribunal falls within the appropriate concept of proceedings.
16 Pp.364–376, below.

£25.00) for beneficiaries under 18 without dependants,[17] and only one-third of the latter sum is paid to the parent or guardian of those under 16 not engaged in full-time, or substantially full-time, employment.[18]

Part 6 Disablement benefit

A General

Once the need to distinguish between short-term and long-term accident victims had been recognised,[19] the question arose as to the method of awarding compensation for the latter. In the first place, it was clear that in contrast to injury benefit, provision should be made for those who were only partially disabled, that is, whose earning capacity had been reduced rather than eliminated altogether. Such persons had been covered by the workmen's compensation legislation, and the principle of compensation applicable there, both to totally and to partially disabled, had been that of 50 per cent (and for lower paid workers 75 per cent) of lost earnings, though subject to a statutory maximum.[20] Beveridge preferred to retain this mode of compensation, but on the level of two-thirds of lost earnings, to bring the scheme in line with the more generous protection offered by European and American systems.[1] The post-war government was not, however, prepared to accept this recommendation. It was seen as conflicting with the then generally held dogma of social insurance that any differential in benefit should be based on need, typically according to the extent of family responsibility, rather than on earnings.[2] Further, it was felt that one of the main weaknesses of the workmen's compensation scheme had been the difficulty of calculating the earnings-based award: predictions had to be made not only on the future earnings of the claimant in the light of his reduced capacity, but also on those which he would have received if he had not been injured. The government proposed what was described as 'an entirely new approach' (though it had formed the basis of the war pensions scheme for some time[3]): benefit payable according to the degree of disablement, irrespective of actual earnings loss. The rates would be assessed on the claimant's assumed needs, and therefore might include increases for family responsibilities and for any additional care and attention necessary. The refusal to take account of earnings would act as a general incentive to rehabilitation and work generally. The philosophy at first gained considerable support; even Beveridge appeared to have been convinced by it.[4] But when its implications were gradually digested, it became increasingly clear that the total disregard of the earnings factor was not viable, and in the face of growing opposition (particularly from the trade unions), the government was forced to make compromise after

17 SSA 1975, Sch 4, Part V, para 1(b).
18 SI 1975/559, reg 3(2), as amended by SI 1976/1736 and SI 1980/1631.
19 P. 293, above.
20 WCA 1925, s.9(2). In 1940 child allowances, analogous to those payable with unemployment benefit, were introduced: WC (Supplementary Allowances) Act 1940.
1 Paras 99–100.
2 *Social Insurance* Part II, paras 28–29.
3 Cf p. 339, below.
4 See his contributions to the Commons debate on *Social Insurance* Part II: 404 HC Official Report (5th series) col 1436.

compromise, so that what eventually emerged was very different in both substance and form from the original proposals.

First, at an early stage, it was realised that provision had to be made for those who were rendered totally unemployable as a result of the accident. The work incentive argument could not be applied to them, and they would naturally feel aggrieved if they were to receive the same benefit as others who were still able to earn: hence the unemployability supplement.[5] There was a second category of injured persons who would also have fared better under the workmen's compensation scheme. The courts there had developed a special doctrine to cover so-called 'odd-lot' cases, where the injury had rendered the worker incapable of work normally available on the market, but not of special employment which in practice, because of his lack of training or geographical or social circumstances, might not have been available.[6] On the Second Reading of the 1946 Bill, the government introduced an amendment which would enable the authorities to add 25 per cent to the assessment of disablement (though not so as to exceed 100 per cent) if the claimant were able to show that he was no longer capable of following his previous occupation, and could not be so retrained as to enable him to follow one of an equivalent standard.[7] At the Committee stage this was felt to be an unattractive rule as it would have operated unfairly for those assessed at between 75 per cent and 100 per cent, and a flat-rate addition of 11s 3d was substituted.[8] Between the passing of the 1946 Act and its coming into effect, however, even this solution was found to be wanting. It was too inflexible a method of treating those whose earnings had been only partially affected: it was considered too low for some workers, and yet inappropriate for those, e.g. juveniles, who had not yet established a clear employment pattern. At the eleventh hour, the government therefore introduced a new Bill which would enable the authorities to award a sum for lost earnings up to a limit of 15s 0d – a special hardship allowance.[9]

Though there have been amendments to the rate of benefit and the introduction of an allowance for the exceptionally severely disabled,[10] the structure of disablement benefit has remained unaltered. What emerges is a jumble of benefit and allowance, some parts directed towards need, others towards income replacement. Yet the system as a whole is consistent with neither objective and seems to have no overall rational structure. As will be seen, the White Paper of 1981 made radical proposals to deal with specific anomalies arising under the present law, but it failed to confront the fundamental issues of the level and purposes of compensation in this context. It is much to be regretted that so little heed seems to have been paid to foreign systems, some of which adopt a more rational, and less cumbersome, approach to these questions.

The typical European scheme combines a scale of disablement with the claimant's earning potential, so that for 100 per cent disablement there is an effective indemnity of his full earning capacity, and for lesser degrees of incapacity the figure is reduced on a proportionate basis (e.g. for 30 per cent disablement, he will receive a pension based on 30 per cent of his pre-accident earnings),[11] though in all cases there is a maximum above which

5 P. 309, below.
6 See Willis *Workmen's Compensation* (37th edn) pp. 308–313.
7 414 HC Official Report (5th series) col 276.
8 See Standing Committee A Debates on the Bill, cols 514–528.
9 NI(II)A 1948, s.1 and see pp. 310–323, below.
10 Pp. 325–326, below.
11 See *Kaim-Caudle* pp. 91–93 and *Dupeyroux* pp. 551–555.

earnings will not be taken into account. The typical American scheme (still based on the workmen's compensation model) continues to compensate for a proportion (two-thirds to three-quarters) of actual lost earnings, generally combined with a small family allowance,[12] and this approach, based on actual earnings loss, is also incorporated in the New Zealand accident compensation scheme (which is not confined to employment injuries).[13] The interesting proposals for accident compensation in Australia combined this traditional method for the totally incapacitated, with the scale method of assessment applied to 60 per cent of the *national average earnings* for those only partially disabled.[14]

For the analysis of the prevailing principles under the British industrial injuries scheme it is proposed to deal in this Part with the basic disablement benefit and in Part 7, with increases and allowances which might be added.

B Loss of faculty

Under the original 1946 Act, title to disablement benefit was based on proof that the claimant had, as a result of the industrial accident, sustained a loss of faculty which was likely to be permanent or substantial.[15] The requirement posed a severe obstacle for a large range of employees who sustained only minor injuries – in 1953 it was estimated that 10 per cent of all claimants had been refused benefit on this ground.[16] In that year, Parliament replaced the formula by the simple requirement that the employee

> suffers as a result of the relevant accident from loss of physical or mental faculty such that the assessed extent of the resulting disablement amounts to not less than 1 per cent.[17]

The government now considers that this reform went too far, in the sense that it admitted too many minor claims for compensation.[18] It therefore proposes that where the loss of faculty is only temporary the lower limit of entitlement should be 10 per cent.

Current legislation does not define 'loss of faculty', as used in the provision quoted above. It is one link in the statutory chain of causation: accident – injury – loss of faculty – disablement, and its meaning, therefore, must be understood in the light of those other elements.[19] Whereas 'injury' covers all the adverse physical or mental consequences of the accident,[20] 'loss of faculty' connotes 'impairment of the proper functioning of part of the body or mind',[1] and this is 'a cause of disabilities

12 See the Report of the National Commission on State Workmen's Compensation Laws (1972), pp. 63–70.
13 Accident Compensation Act 1972, s.113, and see *Pearson* vol III, paras 871–876.
14 See Report of the Australian Commission of Inquiry into Compensation and Rehabilitation (1974), paras 389–401.
15 NI(II)A 1946, s.12(1)(a). 'Substantial' meant a disablement of 20% or more: ibid, s.12(1)(a)(ii).
16 Mr O Peake, Minister of NI, introducing the second reading of the NI(II) Bill (No 2) 1953; 516 HC Official Report (5th series) col 2109.
17 NI(II)A 1953, s.3, now SSA 1975, s.57(1).
18 *Reform of the Industrial Injuries Scheme*, para 21.
19 *Jones v Secretary of State for Social Services* [1972] AC 944, per Lord Diplock at 1009–1010 and Lord Simon at 1019.
20 Per Lord Diplock, ibid, at 1010; 'hurt to body or mind': Lord Simon, ibid, at 1020.
1 Per Lord Simon, ibid, cf 'loss of power or function of an organ of the body': Lord Diplock, ibid, at 1010.

to do things which in sum constitute the disablement' which is the subject of the assessment.[2] If this seems to be very complicated, its practical importance is small. In some cases, the medical authorities have mistaken their proper function by failing to recognise a loss of faculty where the existence of such loss was patent (e.g. a condition which rendered a hand sensitive) but which did not entail a significant degree of disablement. As the Commissioner pointed out,[3] the proper ground for refusing benefit in such a case was that the extent of disablement was less than 1 per cent rather than that there was no loss of faculty at all.[4] However, it seems in a case like this that the medical authorities are not bound to make an assessment; for the Act provides that 'there shall be deemed not to be any relevant loss of faculty where the extent of the resulting disablement, if so assessed, would not amount to 1 per cent'.[5]

What amounts to an 'impairment of the proper functioning' may sometimes cause difficulties. In one case, the malfunctioning of one kidney was regarded as a loss of faculty, even though the claimant could survive by using the other kidney.[6] For some time there was doubt as to whether disfigurement constituted a loss of faculty, on the ground that a person does not put his appearance to any use. The traditional view that it was covered is confirmed by the Social Security Act 1975 which provides that 'references to loss of physical faculty include disfigurement, whether or not accompanied by any actual loss of faculty'.[7] This oddly-worded subsection does imply, however, by using the contradistinction of '*actual*' loss of faculty, that were it not for the Act, disfigurement would not be regarded as a loss of faculty.[8]

C Causal link with relevant accident

The next task is to establish that the loss of faculty resulted from the industrial accident or prescribed disease. The onus of proof is on the claimant and the standard is the balance of probabilities.[9] The ordinary principles of causation apply,[10] so the claimant need not show that the accident was the sole or even *the* effective cause – it is sufficient if it was *a* real and effective cause.[11] The major problem here has been the question of competence to make a binding decision on the point. One of the disablement questions to be resolved by the medical authorities is 'whether the relevant accident has resulted in a loss of faculty'.[12] But disablement benefit generally follows an award of injury benefit, and for this purpose the *statutory* authorities (viz insurance officer, local insurance tribunal, and Commissioner) will have made a decision that the claimant had sustained an injury by accident arising out of and in the course of employment. Section 38(3) of the National Insurance (Industrial Injuries) Act 1965

2 Per Lord Diplock, ibid.
3 *R(I) 6/61*.
4 The same point emerges in *R(I) 7/63* and *R(I) 14/66*.
5 SSA 1975, s.57(3). The government has rejected the suggestion that compensation should be available for those sustaining a loss of earnings unaccompanied by a loss of faculty: n.18, above, at para 68.
6 *R(I) 14/66*.
7 SSA 1975, s.57(2).
8 But see *R(I) 39/60*.
9 *R(I) 12/62*.
10 Cf pp. 294–295, above.
11 *R(I) 3/66* (Tribunal decision).
12 SSA 1975, s.108(1)(a).

provided that such a decision should be 'final'. The Act was ambiguous on what aspects of that decision were to be regarded as 'final', and 'final' for what purposes. It was, of course, clear that the medical authorities could not challenge a decision that an accident had arisen out of and in the course of employment[13] but could they reopen the question whether the physical condition of the claimant *resulted from* the accident? For a long time it was assumed that they could. On the one hand, it was argued that there were two different statutory chains of entitlement: for an injury benefit (accident – injury) and for a disablement benefit (accident – loss of faculty – disablement); and on the other hand, the policy arguments seemed strongly to favour this interpretation. Injury benefit was for a short-term disability and it was desirable to make a speedy decision. Conversely, where benefit was payable for a substantial number of years, it was necessary to examine the nature of the claimant's condition and its aetiology more carefully by referring the question to the medical authorities, and the latter should be able to depart from the earlier, less expert decision taken by the statutory authorities.[14] The view was challenged in 1966 and for the next six years there was a prolonged and complex debate on the matter which was twice taken to the House of Lords.

In *Re Dowling*,[15] the House of Lords held, with Lord Wilberforce dissenting, that the demarcation of jurisdiction hitherto accepted was wrong. A finding in that case by the insurance officer that the claimant had suffered an injury by accident was held to be binding on the medical authorities. Such determination was regarded as the starting point of their jurisdiction (or as Lord Hodson put it, 'a ticket of admission'[16]). In the case in question, the 'injury', a cardiac condition caused by exertion at work, was, in a sense, also 'the accident' (the problem has already been discussed[17]), and the speech of at least one judge[18] could be read as limiting the decision to such a case. The argument was that the medical authorities had no jurisdiction to decide whether there had been an 'accident' and in this type of case such a finding necessarily meant that there had also been an 'injury'. It was on this ground that the Commissioner sought in several subsequent cases to distinguish the *Dowling* decision, holding that it did not apply where the 'accident' was clearly external to, and separate from, the 'injury'.[19] The matter was taken again to the House of Lords in 1971, when two cases were heard *en banc*.[20] Their Lordships, by a majority,[1] again decided that the statutory authorities' finding that there had been an 'injury by accident' was binding on the medical tribunal, and that *Dowling* should not be overruled. Nor were they prepared to distinguish the former decision on the ground that it was an 'accident/injury' case.[2]

The government of the day sought to reverse the effect of the ruling as soon as possible, but the matter provoked a bitterly fought debate in a Standing Committee of the House of Commons. The opposition viewed the measure as a deliberate and direct attack on workers' rights. Mrs

13 NI(II)A 1965, s.49(4), re-enacted as SSA 1975, s.107(4).
14 See esp. the speech of Lord Diplock in *Jones'* case, n.19, above, at 1007.
15 *Minister of Social Security v Amalgamated Engineering Union* [1967] 1 AC 725.
16 Ibid, at 749.
17 Pp. 268–269, above.
18 Lord Hodson, n.19, above, at 751.
19 See e.g. *R(I) 10/68*.
20 *Jones v Secretary of State for Social Services; Hudson v same* [1972] AC 944.
1 Viscount Dilhorne, Lords Wilberforce and Diplock dissenting.
2 See especially Lord Simon, n.20, above, at 1022–1023. On this point, the views of the other members of the majority are, however, less explicit.

Barbara Castle, for example, concluded that it was 'designed to establish the victory of unimaginative bureaucracy'.[3] But it was passed[4] and, in its re-enacted form, prescribes that a decision by the statutory authorities that a claimant sustained an injury by an industrial accident is to be regarded as determining only that the accident arose out of and in the course of employment, that it was an insured employment,[5] and that benefit was not precluded because the accident happened outside Great Britain, but

> neither any such decision nor the reference to a medical board or medical appeal tribunal . . . in connection with any claim to or award of disablement benefit is to be taken as importing a decision as to the origin of any injury or disability suffered by the claimant, whether or not there is an event identifiable as an accident apart from any injury that may have been received.[6]

Tremendous!

It is now clear beyond doubt that the pre-1966 position has been restored, and that the medical authorities have an unfettered power to decide that the loss of faculty did not result from the relevant accident.[7]

D Assessment of disablement

i General

The final link in the chain is the degree of disablement on which the award of benefit is based. It will be recalled that entitlement to injury benefit depends on incapacity for work. The aim of the long-term benefit is very different. Although the unemployability supplement and special hardship allowance are based on loss of earning capacity, disablement benefit itself is assessed solely by reference to the physical or mental capacities of the claimant, whether or not these result in any loss of earnings.[8] The benefit is payable for the hardships caused by the injuries per se, and the ability to earn, or indeed to claim unemployment or sickness benefit on the grounds appropriate to them, does not affect entitlement. The general principle of assessment is to take into account all disabilities incurred as a result of the loss of faculty

> to which the claimant may be expected, having regard to his physical and mental condition at the date of the assessment, to be subject during the period taken into account by the assessment as compared with a person of the same age and sex whose physical and mental condition is normal.[9]

With the exception of the factors mentioned in this provision, measurement is objective: 'the assessment shall be made without reference to the particular circumstances of the claimant other than age, sex and physical and mental condition'.[10] It follows that not only is the effect of the disability on the claimant's earning capacity irrelevant,[11] but personal and social

3 Standing Committee D Debates on the National Insurance Bill 1972, col 373.
4 NIA 1972, s.5.
5 Though this is determined by the Secretary of State, p. 266, above.
6 SSA 1975, s.117(3).
7 The statutory authorities have an indirect power to review a decision on the point if satisfied that it was given in ignorance of, or was based on a mistake as to, some material fact; or that there has been a relevant change of circumstances since the decision was given; SSA 1975, s.104(1). This applies to all decisions under the Social Security Act and is dealt with at pp. 603–605, below.
8 See the Report of the Inter-Departmental Committee on Assessment of Disablement due to Specified Injuries (1947, Cmd 7076), paras 5–7.
9 SSA 1975, Sch 8, para 1(a).
10 Ibid, para 1(c).
11 *R(I) 3/61*.

circumstances are also ignored.[12] On its review of the principles of assessment in 1965, a Departmental Committee found no good reason for departing from this objective approach.[13] The finding has been criticised by many, particularly sociologists,[14] who feel that insufficient regard has been paid to the considerable amount of research which has taken place in the last twenty years on the functional, social and psychological effects of disability.[15] Resentment and conflict, it has been argued, are bound to result from a method of assessment in which the criteria used are so particularistic about the disability itself and so vague about its actual social consequences for the patient, and empirical work has shown that claimants of industrial injury benefit feel the system of compensation to be unjust and incomprehensible.[16] The problem of definition is common to all disabilities and, as such, it has already been considered in chapter 4.[17]

ii Assessment for prescribed conditions

Schedule 2 of the Industrial Injuries (Benefit) Regulations[18] contains a tariff of the prescribed degrees of disablement. The first column sets out descriptions of the injury and the second column the degree of disablement, expressed as a percentage of total disablement (e.g. loss of a hand and a foot, 100 per cent; loss of thumb, 30 per cent etc.). For each specified condition, then, the prima facie assessment is the prescribed degree of disablement, but the medical authorities are not tied to this figure: it is subject

> to such increase or reduction . . . as may be reasonable in the circumstances of the case where, having regard to the [statutory provisions and regulations] . . . that degree of disablement does not provide a reasonable assessment of the extent of disablement resulting from the relevant loss of faculty.[19]

The conditions specified in the tariff must, it seems, be construed literally. Thus, for example, reference to the loss of the phalanx of a finger does not cover loss of *part* of the phalanx of a finger.[20] Although the Act specifically entitles the Secretary of State to make special provision for the difference between injuries to the hand and arm of right- and left-handed persons,[1] he has not yet done so. But it may be a suitable case for the medical authorities to increase or reduce assessment in the exercise of their discretion referred to above.

Clearly, the fact that a specific disablement results from two or more industrial accidents or diseases can give rise to no more benefit than if it had resulted from a single accident or disease;[2] but suppose that the claimant, following a single accident, suffers from two of the conditions

12 In *R(I) 6/75* C sought to have his assessment of disability reduced from 20% to 19% on the ground that the consequent award of a lump sum gratuity instead of a pension would enable him to purchase a small business. The reduction was quashed by the Commissioner.
13 Report of the Committee on the Assessment of Disablement (McCorquodale Committee) (Cmnd 2847).
14 See esp. Townsend *The Disabled in Society* (1967).
15 See the references cited in *Townsend* and Blaxter *The Meaning of Disability* (1976).
16 *Blaxter* pp. 187–189.
17 Pp. 144–145, above.
18 SI 1975/559.
19 Ibid, reg 2(6).
20 *R(I) 22/63*.
1 SSA 1975, Sch 8, para 2.
2 SI 1975/559, reg 2(5) (regard is had to the latest accident or disease). See also pp. 326–327, below.

specified in the tariff, may the prescribed degrees of disablement be aggregated? For a long time the problem created a great deal of uncertainty.[3] The position has been clarified by legislative changes.[4] The prima facie application of the prescribed degree occurs only where the condition in question is 'the sole injury which a claimant suffers as a result of the relevant accident . . . whether or not such injury incorporates one or more other injuries' as specified.[5] In other words, if one injury is incorporated into another, the assessment should be made according to the prescribed degree of the more serious disability. Where the accident results in two separate injuries, there is no automatic assessment under the tariff, and the principles next to be described apply.

iii Assessment for non-prescribed conditions

For conditions not specified in the Schedule, assessment is at large. It is a question of fact, and the decision of the medical authorities will generally be regarded as conclusive, though they 'may have such regard as may be appropriate to the prescribed degrees of disablement' of the injuries specified in the Schedule.[6] The prescribed degrees of disablement, then, provide a guideline for the appropriate assessment, but no more. In one case,[7] the claimant suffering from a condition of the finger which was more severe than one prescribed finger condition but less severe than another prescribed finger condition sought to argue that as a matter of *law* medical authorities were bound to assess at a figure between the two prescribed degrees of disablement. The argument was rejected. The discretion of the medical authorities was not to be fettered by thus enlarging the Schedule. In cases where the claimant has sustained multiple (and separate) injuries, and there is no composite disability for which the Schedule prescribes an assessment, the medical authorities must form their own judgment on the total disablement resulting from the various injuries.[8] They may compare this total condition with those giving rise to the prescribed degrees of disablement and select an appropriate figure.

iv Reductions for disability resulting from extraneous causes[9]

The fact that the claimant's condition results in part from an extraneous cause, that is, one not arising from an industrial accident, in principle justifies a reduction in the assessment of the disability. It is felt that the Fund should not be charged with the burden of such disabilities as the claimant would have suffered if he had not been injured in the industrial accident. The policy is a simple one to understand, but the provisions implementing it have caused great difficulties. The chief concern has been to see that generous treatment should be given to an employee who sustains two disabilities, only one of which is caused by an industrial accident, but which are in some way connected, so that the total disability resulting is greater than the sum of the two disabilities taken separately. A simple example will illustrate the point.

3 See *CSI 74/50*; *R(I) 39/61*; *R v Industrial Injuries Comr, ex parte Cable* [1968] 1 QB 729.
4 NIA 1969, s.7(1)(a) and SI 1970/1551.
5 SI 1975/559, reg 2(6).
6 Ibid, reg 2(7).
7 *R(I) 23/63*.
8 *R v Industrial Injuries Comr, ex parte Cable*, n.3, above.
9 Lewis 43 MLR 514.

Under the tariff, the loss of vision in one eye, the other being normal, is 30 per cent, but the loss of sight 'to such an extent as to render the claimant unable to perform any work for which eyesight is essential' is assessed at 100 per cent.[10] Thus a claimant, already blind in one eye, who loses the sight of the other eye in an industrial accident under the ordinary principle unmodified would be entitled to only 30 per cent but the effect of the accident has been to increase disablement from 30 per cent to 100 per cent.[11]

The solution originally adopted was the so-called 'paired-organs' rule. Where the claimant sustained an injury to one of a pair of similar organs, whose functions were interchangeable or complementary, and the other had already been incapacitated – in an industrial accident or otherwise – the total disablement was treated as resulting from an industrial injury.[12] Application of the doctrine, however, produced difficulties and anomalies,[13] and in 1969–70 it was replaced by a new set of rules.[14]

IMP — to ESSAY —

a *Total disablement*

The medical authorities should first assess the total disablement resulting from the relevant loss of faculty, whether or not it was derived in part from another cause.[15] In so doing, they should not merely arbitrate between two opposing views (those of the claimant and those of the Department) but rather obtain all the information which they regard as relevant, and assess the disablement resulting from the relevant loss of faculty on the balance of probabilities.[16] They may then, for the purpose of making a reduction from the first assessment, only take account of causes other than the relevant accident to the extent allowed by the Industrial Injuries (Benefit) Regulations 2(3) and 2(4).[17] These apply to disabilities from other causes suffered, respectively, before and after the industrial accident. But for there to be a 'disability' for this purpose, there must have been some inability to perform a bodily or mental process which manifested itself; a constitutional or latent condition which simply renders the sufferer more prone to such an inability cannot be invoked as a ground for reducing benefit.[18]

b *Other disability preceding industrial accident*

Regulation 2(3) provides that where the disability, defined as above, preceded the industrial accident, the medical authorities must assess what degree of disablement would have resulted from that disability if the industrial accident had not occurred and deduct it from the total disablement.

E.g. C has suffered an amputation to one foot. In the industrial accident he suffers an amputation to the other foot. Total disablement is 90 per

10 SI 1975/559, Sch 2, items 32 and 4 respectively.
11 Cf *R(I) 1/79*.
12 SI 1964/504, reg 2(4).
13 See *R v Medical Appeal Tribunal, ex parte Burpitt* [1957] 2 QB 584; see also Report of the Industrial Injuries Advisory Council on the Rules Governing the Assessment of Disablement (1956, Cmd 9827); and Micklethwait 37 Medico-Legal Jo 172, 185.
14 NIA 1969 s.7(1)(a); SI 1970/1551.
15 SI 1975/559, reg 2(2).
16 *R v Industrial Injuries Comr, ex parte Cable*, n.3, above; *R v National Insurance Comr, ex parte Viscusi* [1974] 2 All ER 724, [1974] 1 WLR 646, CA.
17 SI 1975/559.
18 *R(I) 13/75*; *R(I) 3/76*; *R(I) 1/81*.

cent. If there had been no industrial accident he would have been disabled to the extent of 30 per cent. Benefit is then payable on an assessment of 90 per cent – 30 per cent = 60 per cent.

c *Industrial accident preceding other disability*

In the converse case where the industrial accident precedes the other disability, the solution is not so simple. On the ordinary principles of causation, it is arguable that no account should be taken of the fact that the subsequent event has exacerbated the claimant's condition, since it has superseded the effect of the industrial accident. This was indeed the position prevailing before the 1970 reform, and yet it created an apparent inequality of treatment according to the sequence of events.[19] The Committee which reviewed the issue in 1956[20] was divided on the issue. The minority opinion was that the assessment should take account of the greater incapacity caused by the non-industrial accident (as in regulation 2(3)), but the majority found no justification for such a 'radical' departure from the ordinary rules of causation. Aware, presumably, of the political repercussions of strict adherence to the ordinary rules, however, they suggested the compromise solution of taking into account 50 per cent of the increase in disability. A compromise solution was in fact adopted by the Department in 1970, but not that proposed by the Committee. It was decided to take into account the *whole* of the increase for those more seriously injured, but to ignore it altogether for those less seriously injured.[21] The dividing line was arbitrarily made at an 11 per cent disablement. Regulation 2(4), which now incorporates the solution, lays down two rules.

(1) The authorities should only take into account the disablement which would have resulted if the non-industrial accident had not occurred.

E.g. C loses the whole of a ring finger in an industrial accident. As a result of a later non-industrial accident, the hand containing that finger is rendered useless. Benefit is payable only for the disability of the ring finger = 7 per cent.

(2) Where the assessment made under the first rule is 11 per cent or more, a solution analogous to that in regulation 2(3) is adopted. From the assessment of total disablement is deducted the degree of disablement resulting solely from the non-industrial accident (i.e. if the industrial accident had not occurred).

E.g. in an industrial accident, C is amputated through the left foot. He is subsequently amputated through the right foot. Amputation of a foot is 30 per cent, thus the second rule applies. Total disablement is 90 per cent from which is deducted 30 per cent for the right foot. Benefit is payable for 60 per cent.

d *Where 100 per cent disablement*

A special rule operates where the total assessment of disablement is 100 per cent. In such circumstances the medical authorities are given power *not* to reduce for the fact that some of the disablement has been caused by a non-industrial event, if they are satisfied that, 'in the circumstances of the

19 Cf at common law *Baker v Willoughby* [1970] AC 467, [1969] 3 All ER 1528; *Jobling v Associated Dairies Ltd* [1980] 3 All ER 769.
20 N.13, above.
21 SI 1970/46.

case, 100 per cent is a reasonable assessment of the extent of disablement resulting from the loss of faculty'.[1] This is designed to cover cases where the disability caused by the industrial accident itself, without the addition of disability arising from an extraneous event, would amount to 100 per cent. It would obviously be unjust to make a deduction merely because the non-industrial event has made the claimant's condition even worse. The anomaly arises because the tariff knows no degree of assessment higher than 100 per cent.

e *Period of assessment*

The assessment is made for the period 'during which the claimant has suffered and may be expected to continue to suffer from the relevant loss of faculty', but beginning not earlier than the end of the injury benefit period[2] (from April 1983, 13 weeks after the accident[3]). It will in any event terminate on the claimant's death,[4] but it may be limited to an earlier day, on the ground either that the disability is expected to end by that date or because the assessment is a provisional one. A provisional assessment is to be made where 'the condition of the claimant is not such, having regard to the possibility of changes therein (whether predictable or not) as to allow of a final assessment'.[5] If the assessment is final, it may be modified only by a review – to be considered in the next paragraph. If it is provisional the claimant's condition must be examined again at the end of the period for which the assessment was made, and the new assessment (either provisional or final) will apply from that time.[6] A provisional assessment is in no sense binding on a subsequent assessment, and the medical authorities determining the latter may come to a different view on whether a condition which was also the subject of the previous assessment resulted from the relevant accident.[7] On the other hand, a subsequent assessment cannot modify the benefit for the earlier period.[8]

E Review

The statutory and medical authorities have a general power to review a decision where satisfied that it was given in ignorance of, or was based on a mistake as to, some material fact.[9] This is considered in chapter 15.[10] But what of changes taking place in the claimant's condition *since* the time of the original hearing? The principle has always been that once a final (not a provisional) decision has been made, the receipt of benefit should not be affected by an amelioration in the claimant's condition: the assumption is that the prospect of a reduction in benefit might inhibit recovery.[11] Even though the result is asymmetrical, the assessment of disablement may be

1 SI 1975/559, reg 2(6).
2 SSA 1975, Sch 8, para 4; see p. 295, above.
3 P. 293, above.
4 SSA 1975, Sch 8, para 4.
5 Ibid.
6 Ibid.
7 *R v Industrial Injuries Comr, ex parte Howarth* (1968) 4 KIR 621, CA; *R v National Insurance Comr, ex parte Viscusi*, n.16, above.
8 *R(I) 8/69*.
9 SSA 1975, ss.104, 110(1), as amended by SSA 1979, Sch 3, para 9. As regards the Commissioner and the medical authorities, there must be 'fresh evidence' to this effect.
10 Pp. 603–605, below.
11 Cf Luntz *Compensation and Rehabilitation* (1975) pp. 75–76.

increased for subsequent deterioration. Under the 1946 legislation the claimant had to show an unforeseen aggravation to his condition which was *substantial*, and even then the medical authorities would have power to review only if to refuse him a revision would create 'substantial injustice'.[12] These harsh limitations provoked strong criticism, and they were revised in 1953.[13] Since that date, it has been sufficient if the medical board is satisfied

> that since the making of the assessment there has been an unforeseen aggravation of the results of the relevant injury,[14]

though if the original assessment was made, confirmed or varied by a medical appeal tribunal, then the leave of that body must be obtained.[15] The aggravation must be 'unforeseen' in the sense that it was not taken into account in the earlier assessment, and, of course, it must have been substantially caused by the relevant injury – the principles of causation applied are the same as those governing the injury/loss of faculty connection.[16] The power of revision is in no way inhibited by the earlier assessment, and as *R(I) 7/65* shows the final assessment might not favour the claimant.

> Following an operation to his injured elbow, C sought a review, on the ground of unforeseen aggravation, of a 5 per cent life assessment previously made. On review, the medical board made a provisional reassessment of 10 per cent for six months, followed by subsequent assessments at 7 per cent, 3 per cent and finally 2 per cent for life. The Commissioner held that the final assessment of 2 per cent did not constitute an error of law, notwithstanding that it was less than the 5 per cent life assessment originally made.

The 1953 reform also plugged another gap. Where unforeseen aggravation is shown, the medical authorities may now alter a previous finding that no loss of faculty had resulted from the relevant accident.[17]

F Benefit

Where the extent of disablement is assessed at less than 20 per cent, benefit is payable in the form of a gratuity.[18] A maximum amount is prescribed for a 19 per cent disability (in 1982–83, £3,560) and for each lesser degree of disablement there is a corresponding figure proportional to that amount.[19] If the award is for life,[20] or for seven years or more, that sum is payable.[1] If the period is less, the claimant receives such a proportion of the sum as the

12 NI(II)A 1946, s.40(2).
13 NI(II)A 1953, Sch 1.
14 SSA 1975, s.110(2).
15 Ibid, s.110(5). The granting of leave is discretionary and the statutory authorities have no jurisdiction to overturn it: *R(I) 15/68*.
16 *R(I) 18/62* and p. 300, above.
17 Now SSA 1975, s.110(3).
18 Ibid, s.57(5).
19 SI 1975/559, Sch 2. See *Industrial Injuries Compensation* para 3.30–3.32, on the question whether 19% is the appropriate figure.
20 If the award is for 'life', and the claimant dies before the commencement of the period for which it is payable, his personal representative is not entitled: *R(I) 23/52* (cp. *R(I) 59/54* where C died before examination of the medical board which subsequently – and perhaps surprisingly – assessed at 14% 'for life'. It was held that the gratuity was payable to his estate).
1 SI 1975/559, reg 6(a).

period in question bears to seven years (e.g. for one year, one-seventh of the stipulated amount).[2] The award of a gratuity is non-recurring – it is a once-for-all entitlement – and in general is payable in a lump sum,[3] but regulations empower the authorities to pay it by way of instalments 'at such times as appear reasonable in the circumstances of the case' if (1) the claimant is under 18 or (2) the amount exceeds £52 and the claimant requests that the payment be made by way of instalment.[4] For amounts of 20 per cent or over, a pension of a legislatively prescribed amount (proportional to the degree of disablement) is payable on a weekly basis for the period stipulated in the award.[5] For example, in 1982–83, the relevant rates for 100 per cent and 50 per cent are £53.60 and £26.80 respectively.[6] As part of its policy to confer preferential treatment on more seriously disabled beneficiaries, the government has proposed some revision of the amounts payable so that, for example, a 30 per cent assessment would give rise to payment of 25 per cent of the maximum pension, and an 80 per cent assessment would lead to an 85 per cent pension.[7]

Part 7 Increases and additions

A Unemployability supplement

The original disinclination to take account of earnings losses led quite logically to the notion that a claimant might accumulate his disablement benefit with sickness or invalidity benefit should he remain incapable of work. He might, however, fail to satisfy the contribution conditions for these benefits and, to provide for this situation, the unemployability supplement was introduced. Following the change effected by the Social Security and Housing Benefits Act 1982, whereby the contribution conditions will be waived for the victims of industrial accidents and prescribed diseases,[8] the need for the supplement will no longer arise, and legislation abolishing it may be anticipated in the near future.[9]

Pending this reform, the Social Security Act provides for an increase to disablement pension (but not gratuity) if

> as the result of the relevant loss of faculty the beneficiary is incapable of work and likely to remain so permanently.[10]

The criterion of incapacity is that used elsewhere in social security law (notably for the sickness and invalidity benefits[11]). In the words of the Commissioner, the claimant must prove that:

2 Ibid, reg 6(b).
3 SI 1979/628, reg 20(2).
4 Ibid, reg 20(3). The decision on the form of assessment is not susceptible of appeal: ibid, reg 20(4).
5 SSA 1975, s.57(6).
6 There are lower rates for beneficiaries under 18 not entitled to a dependant's increase.
7 *Reform of the Industrial Injuries Scheme*, para 22. For the heavier 'weighting' in favour of more serious cases in France, see *Dupeyroux* p. 553.
8 P. 293, above.
9 *Reform of the Industrial Injuries Scheme*, para 43.
10 SSA 1975, s.58(1).
11 Pp. 148–154, above.

> Having regard to his age, education, experience, state of health and other personal factors, there is no work or type of work which he can reasonably be expected to do.[12]

The difficulty of obtaining such employment because of the labour market conditions generally, or those pertaining in the claimant's locality, is regarded as irrelevant.[13] The criterion, so elaborated, is one of fact for the statutory authorities to decide, and though the opinion of the medical authorities will be taken into account, along with other relevant evidence, it is not conclusive.[14] The fact that the claimant has been able to work will, of course, in general disentitle him. To encourage some activity, and rehabilitation, the Act provides that for the purpose of entitlement to unemployability supplement such work is to be ignored if the earnings therefrom do not exceed a prescribed amount,[15] in 1982–83, £1,040 a year.

The incapacity must 'result from' the relevant loss of faculty. The ordinary principles of causation apply,[16] so that the loss need be only a material or substantial, not the sole, cause of the disability. Further, the authorities have been prepared to extend the so-called 'last straw' doctrine to unemployability supplement. In deciding the causation issue, they are entitled to look at the claimant's aggregate disablement, even though part of his condition results from extraneous causes or constitutional conditions. If he can prove that a small degree of disablement resulting from the loss of faculty, when added to his constitutional condition, changed him from a person 'capable' of work to a person 'incapable', he will succeed.[17]

Consistent with the purpose of the supplement, the amount payable is the same as that for the contributory invalidity benefit,[18] including increases for dependants and the allowance, which varies according to the claimant's age on the first day of incapacity, but excluding the earnings-related component.[19]

B Special hardship allowance

i General

The history of how the allowance for partial, as opposed to total, loss of earnings was belatedly introduced into the industrial injuries scheme has already been related.[20] The essence of the matter is a comparison between the claimant's position before the accident and that consequent on his physical disabilities. For the purposes of exposition, however, a distinction is drawn between the conditions for entitlement and the methods of quantifying the allowance payable. Title to the allowance requires proof that 'as the result of the relevant loss of faculty', the claimant *either*

> (a) is incapable, and likely to remain permanently incapable, of following his regular occupation; *and*

12 *CI 99/49*, para 10.
13 Ibid and *R(I) 43/54*.
14 *CI 44/49*; *R(I) 10/61*.
15 SSA 1975, s.58(3).
16 Cf pp. 294–295, above.
17 *R(I) 10/61*.
18 Pp. 164–165, above.
19 SSA 1975, s.58(4).
20 P. 298, above.

(b) is incapable of following employment of an equivalent standard which is suitable in his case . . .

or

is, and has at all times since the end of the injury benefit period[21] been, incapable of following that occupation or any such employment.[1]

ii Regular occupation

The first element in the comparison between the claimant's pre-accident and post-accident situation is his 'regular occupation' at the time of the accident. One might have expected that the term would be endowed with a highly specific and technical meaning. Happily this has not been the case. It will be recalled[2] that for the purpose of the prescribed diseases provisions the authorities, in attributing a 'prescribed occupation' to the claimant, are concerned less with the name given to his category of employment than with its nature. So here, the Commissioner has shown on a number of occasions that the claimant's 'regular occupation' is to be regarded as a question of fact, determinable on consideration of all the relevant evidence: the label given to the employment by the employer, or employees and employers generally, or trade union rules and agreements, is not thought to be particularly helpful.[3] Consistently with this, though surprisingly given the overall policy of the legislation, a Tribunal of Commissioners has held that the regular occupation need not be in an 'employed earner's employment' (i.e. one covered by the industrial scheme).[4] There is thus no magic in the finding of a specific category of work. The object is rather to establish a pattern of earnings on the basis of which the subsequent comparison can be made. If the claimant fails to establish such a pattern, the increases will not be payable;[5] but the authorities have shown great readiness to find a regularity although the duration of the employment is very limited. In one case,[6]

> C had been employed for ten weeks as a trainee impressioner. The normal period of training was four to eight weeks, and it appeared most unlikely that C would eventually have qualified. It was held that C's 'regular occupation' was 'trainee impressioner', notwithstanding the fact that the training period, *in any event*, would have come to an end in another four weeks.

The date when the regular occupation must be considered is that of the accident, or, in the case of a prescribed disease, the formally attributed date of development.[7] A rigid application of the latter rule may cause hardship. The date of development selected by the medical authorities may be arbitrary, and frequently is later than that of the appearance of the first

21 From April 1983, this will be the period of 90 days since the accident: SSHBA 1982, Sch 4, para 13.
1 SSA 1975, s.60(1).
2 P. 290, above.
3 *R(I) 28/51*; *R(I) 66/51*; *R(I) 11/65*; *R(I) 6/75*.
4 *R(I) 15/56* (Tribunal decision). The Act expressly requires that 'employment of an equivalent standard' for the purposes of the post-accident occupation shall include only employed earners' employment but makes no corresponding limitation as regards the pre-accident regular occupation. The Commissioners inferred that the omission was deliberate: the number who would be insured for the purpose of disablement benefit but whose *regular* occupation was not in an insurable employment would necessarily be small, and it was not thought fair or worthwhile to exclude them from the SHA.
5 *R(I) 3/60*; *R(I) 18/60*.
6 *R(I) 1/63*.
7 *CI 440/50*.

symptoms.[8] Should the claimant, as a result of these symptoms, have abandoned or retired from his employment before the selected date he will have no 'regular occupation' on which to ground his claim. To meet the problem, the regulations provide that if the claimant has, as a consequence of a prescribed disease, abandoned an occupation before the date of development of that disease, for the purposes of entitlement to special hardship allowance

> Any occupation he has so abandoned may be treated as his regular occupation . . . if it would have been so treated had the date of development . . . fallen immediately before he so abandoned it.[9]

Other difficulties may be encountered where, though in regular employment in the period before the accident, the claimant has moved from one type of employment to another, with consequent changes in his pattern of earnings. The general principle applied is that the authorities should have regard to the whole employment history rather than to an isolated period before, or at the time of, the accident (or date of development).[10] They will be primarily concerned with the claimant's own intentions. If he voluntarily transfers from one type of employment to another he may rapidly establish the new 'regular occupation'.[11] But if the change was necessitated by his state of health, and he hoped eventually to return to his former occupation, the latter may still be treated as his 'regular occupation'.[12] If, at the time of the accident, he has been engaged in an occupation for a substantial period of time, there is a presumption that that has now become the relevant occupation,[13] though this may still be rebutted, as in *R(I) 44/52*.

> C changed from bus-driving to store-keeping to earn more money. At the time of the accident he was not yet earning more. It was held that bus-driving was still his regular occupation, as he would have returned to it if he were unable to secure the hoped-for increase of earnings.

The non-technical interpretation of 'regular occupation' has also led to the conclusion that more than one occupation can be included, so that the earnings therefrom can be aggregated.[14] However, the Act explicitly provides that 'reference to a person's regular occupation is to be taken as not including any subsidiary occupation of his'.[15] It seems evident that the draftsman of the original provision had not contemplated the varieties of activities and earnings which claimants would argue came within their 'regular occupation'. The efforts of the Commissioner to exclude casual work and yet include normal overtime pay, to exclude subsidiary occupations, and yet include co-equal occupations, has challenged his ingenuity and created some nice and perhaps arbitrary distinctions. Voluntary work done for the employer outside the normal activities (e.g. the work's fire brigade[16]) is 'subsidiary', but work which is, in some way, contemplated by the contract of employment, without being obligatory under it, may be included (e.g. a colliery repairer working regular weekends on overtime as

8 Cf p. 291, above.
9 SI 1975/1537, reg 19. The causal connection between the abandonment and the relevant disease may, however, be difficult to prove. See *R(I) 8/58*; *R(I) 13/58*; and *R(I) 31/58*.
10 *CI 80/49*; *R(I) 5/52*.
11 *R(I) 65/54*.
12 *CI 80/49*; *R(I) 5/52*.
13 *R(I) 22/52*: three years.
14 *R(I) 43/52*; *R(I) 33/58*; *R(I) 6/75*.
15 SSA 1975, s.60(2)(a).
16 *R(I) 58/54* and see *R(I) 13/62*.

a shaftsman[17]). A combination of two or more activities, with the same employer or for different employers will be covered,[18] but not if one of those activities is clearly subordinate to the other(s), typically where a full-time employee engages in private contract or other work in his spare time.[19] The dividing line between these various distinctions is obscure and some of the decisions are impossible to reconcile.[20] In principle it is difficult to see why regular overtime payments should be included but regular subsidiary work for an external source excluded.

Is account to be taken of promotion or the prospect of advancing to a different, better-paid, occupation? The original legislation drew a sharp distinction between the prospects of advancement, and therefore of a higher standard of remuneration, *within* a particular occupation, and the prospects of promotion to a different occupation or grade. Only the former were to be considered by the authorities.[1] This was subject to the obvious objection that decisions would turn on verbal distinctions – between 'grades' and 'occupations' – which fell harshly on trainees and others who had every reason to expect that qualification or promotion would normally ensue.[2] After consultations with the TUC, the government in 1961[3] extended the concept of regular occupation to include

> employment in the capacities to which the persons in that occupation (or a class or description of them to which he belonged at the time of the relevant accident) are in the normal course advanced, and to which, if he had continued to follow that occupation without having suffered the relevant loss of faculty, he would have had at least the normal prospects of advancement.[4]

To invoke this provision, the claimant must first show that the position which he would have obtained would have constituted an 'advancement'.[5] Typically this will arise through promotion, though it also covers cases where greater earnings are payable as a result of seniority, as with many appointments in the public sector which provide for annual salary increments. But 'the mere transfer from a lower paid to a higher paid job does not necessarily constitute advancement', since the higher pay may be intended to compensate for certain less attractive features of the new situation.[6] Once 'advancement' in the sense described has been established, the onus is on the claimant to satisfy two further conditions:[7] first, objectively, he must show that advancement to the alleged occupation or grade was normal for persons in his occupation; and secondly, subjectively, that he possessed the personal qualities and employment record to justify advancement according to this normal pattern. The existence of the first, objective, test will debar the abnormally gifted or industrious worker from reaping the benefits of these qualities,[8] and to that extent still leaves room for improvement.

17 *R(I) 24/55* and see *R(I) 10/65*.
18 *R(I) 43/52*; *R(I) 16/54*; *R(I) 11/65*; *R(I) 6/75* (same employer); *R(I) 33/58* (different employers).
19 *CWI 30/50*; *R(I) 54/54*; *R(I) 9/61*. The fact that C receives payment from an external source for work carried out primarily for his employer will not disentitle him: *R(I) 60/52*.
20 E.g. *R(I) 24/55* and *R(I) 2/70*.
1 NI(II)A 1946, s.14(2), now SSA 1975, s.60(2).
2 See *CI 442/50*; *R(I) 44/51*; *R(I) 53/52*; *R(I) 29/55*; *R(I) 3/60*.
3 FANIA 1961, s.3(1).
4 Now SSA 1975, s.60(3).
5 *R(I) 12/81*.
6 Ibid, para 9, D G Rice, Comr.
7 *R(I) 8/67*.
8 See *R(I) 8/73* and *R(I) 8/80*.

iii The 'permanent' condition

The first of the two alternative conditions requires the claimant to prove that he '(a) is incapable, and likely to remain permanently incapable, of following his regular occupation; and (b) is incapable of following employment of an equivalent standard which is suitable in his case'.[9]

a *Whether post-accident work is regular occupation*

After the accident the claimant may have returned to his pre-accident employment, and yet his capacity for the work may have been adversely affected. The question thus arises whether for the purpose of limb (a) of the first condition he is thereby rendered incapable of following his regular occupation. According to a Tribunal of Commissioners, the test is whether 'he is unable to fulfil all the ordinary requirements of employers in that field of labour'.[10] The mere fact that the claimant has been unable to earn as much as before is (as will be seen) a necessary condition, but taken by itself is not sufficient. However, 'if a person obtains employment in his old job only through charity or because he has an exceptional employer, he should be regarded as incapable of following his regular occupation'.[11] As for the analogous purpose of determining what was his regular occupation, not much significance is to be attributed to labels attached to the work: regard must be had to the nature of the activity.[12] An employee unable to perform the normal incidents of his regular occupation (e.g. a miner compelled to work in dust-free conditions[13] or a stevedore incapable of lifting heavy cargo[14]) will satisfy the condition. Traditionally, the view has been taken that a mere reduction in productivity (e.g. the loss of overtime) is not sufficient,[15] though a claimant has succeeded where he could work only part-time, instead of full-time,[16] and where he had to rely substantially on his workmates to maintain the previous output.[17] In 1977, the Commissioner, J G Monroe, considered that the traditional approach was unsatisfactory and refused to apply it to a pieceworker whose speed of work had been reduced.[18] In relation to such a worker he held that the test should be whether the claimant is 'incapable of attaining the standard of remuneration . . . of his regular occupation'.[19] It remains to be seen whether this more generous approach will be followed in relation to other types of employment.

b *Whether post-accident work is equivalent*

Section 60(1)(b) requires the claimant to prove that he is incapable of following a suitable employment of an equivalent standard to his regular occupation. For some time, the Commissioners in interpreting this condition applied the same test as they used for the purpose of assessing the amount of the allowance, as prescribed by s.60(6),[20] viz the difference

9 SSA 1975, s.60(1).
10 *CI 443/50*, para 11.
11 Ibid para 12.
12 *R(I) 28/51*.
13 *R v Industrial Injuries Comr, ex parte Langley* [1976] ICR 36, DC; *R v National Insurance Comr, ex parte Steel* [1978] 3 All ER 78, DC.
14 *R(I) 28/51*. See also *CI 201/50* and *R(I) 39/55*.
15 *CI 443/50*; *CI 447/50*; *CI 448/50* (all Tribunal decisions).
16 *CI 444/50* (Tribunal decision).
17 *R(I) 39/52*; *R(I) 5/55*; cp *R(I) 29/52*.
18 *R(I) 4/77*.
19 Ibid, para 10, applying the principle propounded in *R v National Insurance Comr, ex parte Mellors* [1971] 2 QB 401, [1971] 1 All ER 740, p. 321, below.
20 Pp. 319–320, below.

between the claimant's probable standard of remuneration in his regular occupation and that of the employment which he is capable of following after the accident.[1] Subsequently, they recognised that there were important differences between section 60(1)(b) which determined *entitlement* and section 60(6) which was a matter of *quantification*.[2] For the former, it was necessary to take a longer view: whether, in general, over a period of say twelve months, the level of earnings[3] had become equivalent to that available in the regular occupation – short-term differences were relevant only to section 60(6).[4] Further, in *Ex parte Humphreys*, the Court of Appeal stressed that the 'standard of remuneration' was for the purposes of section 60(1)(b), to be determined by an objective, impersonal, test, the normal earnings of persons employed in the suitable post-accident occupation which the claimant was capable of following.[5] This, then was to be compared with the normal earnings of persons employed in the claimant's regular occupation.[6]

The employment which is of an 'equivalent standard' must be one covered by the industrial scheme, i.e. 'an employed earner's employment'.[7] In addition it must be 'suitable in his case'. This is judged according to the claimant's 'personal qualifications, including his mental and physical capacity'.[8] In general, family and domestic circumstances are irrelevant;[9] the question is, given his physical and psychological condition, his training, experience and general aptitude, was he capable of that kind of employment?[10]

It is unnecessary that the claimant should have worked, continually or otherwise, in the employment which is held to be both suitable and of an equivalent standard.[11] The fact that he has done so, for even a short period, will be persuasive evidence that he is capable of following that employment. If he loses the job for reasons unconnected with the disability resulting from the employment injury (e.g. redundancy as a result of trade recession) his capacity for the employment remains unaffected.[12] The same may apply where he has not yet been able to secure such employment, because, for example, there is no vacancy in his area.[13] On the other hand, care must be taken to avoid attributing to the claimant an earnings potential which he has, in practice, little chance of realising. Thus the employment in question must be a recognised occupation, not having an 'exceptional' character, such as sheltered employment, since the latter is

1 See e.g. *CI 89/50*; *R(I) 40/51*; *R(I) 78/51*.
2 *R(I) 31/59*.
3 'Earnings' here means 'the amount of money (or its equivalent) which a person receives in return for his services' *(R(I) 60/52)*, thus will not include payments to indemnify expenses *(R(I) 1/54)*. See further, pp. 404–409, below.
4 *R(I) 31/59*; *R(I) 5/62*.
5 *R v Deputy Industrial Injuries Comr, ex parte Humphreys* [1966] 2 QB 1, [1966] 3 All ER 885.
6 *R(I) 6/68*; *R(I) 7/68* (Tribunal decisions). In *R v National Insurance Comr, ex parte Mellors* [1971] 2 QB 401, [1971] 1 All ER 740, the Court of Appeal interpreted s.60(6) in such a way as to bring it closer to the objective test required under s.60(1)(b) – see p. 321, below – but the meaning of s.60(1)(b) is unaffected: *R(I) 4/72*; *R(I) 6/77*.
7 SSA 1975, s.60(2)(b), in contrast to 'regular occupation', p. 311, above. For the meaning of 'employed earner's employment' see pp. 45–50, above.
8 *Ex parte Humphreys*, n.5, above, at 18–19.
9 Ibid, at 15–16, 18.
10 Cf *R(I) 4/76*, para 22 (Tribunal decision which was confirmed by the Divisional Court on a certiorari application, without discussion of the point: *Ex parte Steel*, n.13, above).
11 *R(I) 48/53*; *Ex parte Humphreys*, n.5, above.
12 *R(I) 27/57*; *R(I) 42/61*.
13 *R(I) 29/53*.

not indicative of the claimant's earnings capacity in the open labour market.[14]

c *Permanent incapacity*

The incapacity to follow the regular occupation (first limb) but not the incapacity to follow employment of an equivalent standard (second limb) must be shown to be permanent. This poses a severe obstacle for a claimant who, though at present unable to work in his regular occupation, nevertheless cannot prove that this is likely to continue for the indefinite future. The onus of proof is on him[15] and it is not sufficient to show that the loss of faculty, as opposed to incapacity for work, is likely to be permanent.[16] Even more critically, the rule penalises a claimant who, in an effort to rehabilitate himself, returns to his regular occupation and tries to cope, perhaps only for a trial period. Prior to 1953 the difficulty was alleviated only for victims of pneumoconiosis. A regulation creates a rebuttable presumption that such a person satisfies the 'permanent' condition if he has received advice from the Pneumoconiosis Medical Board that he should not follow his regular occupation except under special conditions (e.g. that the environment is dust-free).[17] It also provides that, for the purposes of the condition, any work in the regular occupation or in a suitable employment of equivalent standard which he carried out 'between the date of development of the disease and the date of the current assessment of his disablement, or for a reasonable period of trial thereafter, shall be disregarded'.[18]

iv 'The continuing condition'

The limited assistance given to pneumoconiosis victims did little to help the large number of other industrially disabled persons who, having courageously gone back to their regular occupations after the accident, found that they were for ever barred from the special hardship allowance. In 1953 Parliament was prompted to remedy the defect by providing an alternative test which the claimant might satisfy:[19] that he 'is, and has at all times since the end of the injury benefit period been, incapable' of following his regular occupation or suitable employment of an equivalent standard.[20] The new provision considerably eased the claimant's burden. If, since the time of the accident or development of the disease, he has continuously been incapable of the relevant occupation or suitable employment, there is no longer a need to make predictions as to whether the condition will persist indefinitely. He must, of course, show that throughout the period in question he was in receipt of a disablement pension. If the pension had been limited in duration to a specific date and payment had ceased, the 'continuing' condition is not satisfied even if

14 *R(I) 6/77*, following earlier decisions in *R(I) 42/52*; *R(I) 73/52*; *R(I) 7/58*.
15 *R(I) 7/53* where C had agreed to undergo an operation which if successful (though this was far from certain) would have enabled him to return to his regular occupation.
16 *R(I) 86/52*.
17 Now SI 1975/1537, reg 38(a) and see *R(I) 34/60*; *R(I) 35/60*; *R v National Insurance Comr, ex parte Steel*, [1978] 3 All ER 78. The fact that at the time the 'advice' was received the claimant was already working under the approved conditions does not prevent his relying on the regulation. The provision is based on his 'receiving' the advice, not following it: *R(I) 69/54*.
18 SI 1980/377, reg 38(b). For the 'date of development' see p. 291, above; for the 'date of current assessment' see esp. *R(I) 74/54*; and for 'reasonable period of trial' see *R(I) 44/54* and *R(I) 74/54*.
19 NI(II)A 1953, s.4.
20 SSA 1975, s.60(1), and for amendment operative from April 1983, see n.21, p. 311, above.

subsequently the claimant renewed his claim, or on review his entitlement to disablement benefit was reinstated: the gap in entitlement is decisive.[1] More significantly, taken by itself, the 'continuing' condition is not able to remedy the plight of a claimant who, unwisely or otherwise, returns to work in the hope that he is fit to carry out his duties but eventually succumbs to the effects of his indisposition. The Act therefore supplements the provision by empowering the Secretary of State to make regulations that working in the relevant occupation or employment 'during a period of trial or for purposes of rehabilitation or training or in other prescribed circumstances' shall not prevent the claimant satisfying the condition.[2] In the exercise of this power, the Secretary of State has provided for the disregard of work in the regular occupation or suitable employment of equivalent standard in two different circumstances.

(1) The first arises where he has worked in the relevant occupation or employment 'for the purpose of rehabilitation or training or of ascertaining whether he had recovered from the effects of the relevant injury'.[3] There has been some disagreement as to how broadly this regulation is to be construed. Obviously it covers cases where there is some uncertainty as to the effect of the disability on the claimant's capacity and he returns to the employment to see whether he has in fact recovered sufficiently to enable him successfully to carry out the normal working activities.[4] But it frequently happens that, with or without medical advice, the injured employee returns to work under the belief that he is fit to do so, though perhaps subject to certain restrictions (e.g. avoiding the heavier aspects of his normal duties). After a period of such working, it then transpires that he cannot cope, and he withdraws. In an early case, the Commissioner decided that on such facts, the claimant should not succeed.[5] The work in question was not *for the purpose* of rehabilitation, training or ascertaining whether he had recovered. This approach has been disavowed in later cases.[6] The very object of the regulation was to encourage injured persons to return to work without prejudicing their chance of obtaining special hardship allowance, should the attempt prove to be unsuccessful. A narrow construction would exclude a large number of persons whom it was clearly intended to benefit.[7] Although, therefore, in theory the authorities should consider what was in the mind of the claimant and his doctor during the period of work, there is no dogmatic insistence that the *primary* objective must have been rehabilitation. The period to be disregarded under this regulation is *any* period during which he so works with the approval of the Secretary of State or on the advice of a medical practitioner, and any other period up to six months without such approval or advice.[8]

(2) Secondly, the authorities should disregard work in the relevant occupation or employment 'before obtaining surgical treatment for the effects' of the injury,[9] that is

1 *R(I) 25/57*; *R(I) 29/58*; *R(I) 33/59*. But not where the only reason for the gap is the inability of the medical authorities (under the Determination of Claims and Questions Regulations, SI 1975/558, reg 35) to antedate a revised assessment for more than three months: *R(I) 9/66*, D Neligan, Dep. Comr.
2 SSA 1975, s.60(4).
3 SI 1975/559, reg 9(1)(a).
4 *R(I) 1/69*, R G Micklethwait, Chief Comr.
5 *R(I) 81/53*.
6 *R(I) 13/61*; *R(I) 1/69*.
7 Ibid, at para 11, per R G Micklethwait, Chief Comr.
8 SI 1975/559, reg 9(2)(a).
9 Ibid, reg 9(1)(b).

> any period during which he worked thereat and throughout which it is shown that having obtained the advice of a medical practitioner to submit himself to such surgical treatment he was waiting to undergo the said treatment in accordance therewith, *and* any other period during which he worked thereat and throughout which it is shown that he was in process of obtaining such advice.[10]

'Surgical treatment' in this context does not necessarily involve the use of the surgeon's knife – 'manipulative' treatment will suffice[11] – but it is important that throughout the period for which the disregard is claimed, he should be waiting to obtain the treatment. A doctor should have given a definite opinion that surgical treatment was desirable and that it should be carried out as soon as could conveniently be arranged. The claimant must have accepted the advice and intended to give up work as soon as the arrangement has been made.[12] A substantial period of waiting will raise the presumption that the claimant did not use reasonable zeal and expedition in trying to secure the necessary surgical treatment, and will disentitle him.[13]

v Incapacity

Both of the conditions in section 60(1) are based on proof of an incapacity which results from the relevant loss of faculty. The onus of proving this causal connection is on the claimant,[14] though, in certain circumstances pneumoconiosis victims benefit from a presumption to that effect.[15] On the general causation issue there is little to add to the now familiar principle that the loss of faculty need not be the sole or even primary cause of the incapacity: it is sufficient if it is a substantial cause.[16] The test has been applied typically where the claimant has left the relevant occupation or employment and it is alleged that the incapacity was caused by his age,[17] or by a pre-existing disability,[18] rather than by the loss of faculty resulting from the industrial accident.

Greater difficulties have arisen where objectively the claimant is regarded as fit for his work, but his apprehensions for the consequences of another accident have led to a refusal to continue. Initially the authorities adopted a strict approach: this was not to be regarded as a disability.[19] In one case, a Tribunal of Commissioners was prepared to make special concessions for a worker who had lost the sight of one eye and who feared that another accident would result in total blindness.[20] 'No form of disablement', it was said, 'is more generally dreaded than total blindness, and few are more disastrous in their effect on earning power'.[1] This exception is of very limited application and its legal basis is obscure.[2]

10 Ibid, reg 9(2)(b).
11 *R(I) 13/56.*
12 *R(I) 81/53.*
13 *R(I) 35/57*, where the period was 4½ years.
14 *R(I) 56/51.*
15 The same circumstances in which the presumption described above, p. 316, operates: SI 1980/377, reg 38(a). For the effect of the presumption, see e.g. *R(I) 35/50*, *R v Industrial Injuries Comr, ex parte Langley* [1976] ICR 36, DC and *R v National Insurance Comr, ex parte Steel* [1978] 3 All ER 78, DC.
16 *R(I) 17/59.*
17 *R(I) 29/51*; *R(I) 37/51*; *R(I) 67/53.*
18 *R(I) 64/52*; *R(I) 49/54.*
19 *R(I) 61/52*; *R(I) 44/54.*
20 *R(I) 85/52*, and see *R(I) 8/56*, *R(I) 6/59.*
1 *R(I) 85/52*, para 5.
2 It has been followed in only one reported case *(R(I) 32/59)* and there was an alternative ground for the decision. For criticism, see *R(I) 12/80*, para 14, R S Lazarus, Comr.

Fortunately, a more fruitful line of reasoning has been found. In *R(I) 15/74* it was held that if by reason of his physical condition the claimant could not work in his regular occupation without danger to himself or others he should be regarded as incapable of following that occupation.[2] In other words, the accident has placed him or others at greater risk than would otherwise be the case. But this does not cover the situation where the accident renders the employee unwilling to continue out of fear that the accident will be repeated, when objectively there is no increase in the risk. To succeed here, he must show that his apprehensions themselves constituted a medical condition which was part of his loss of faculty. While recognising this possibility the Commissioner in *R(I) 12/80* decided against the claimant on the ground that the medical authorities in the case had not found that the relevant loss of faculty included any mental condition. It is not, however, clear that the findings of the medical authorities are conclusive on this matter. In *R v Industrial Injuries Comr, ex parte Ward*, Lord Parker CJ expressed the view that for entitlement to the special hardship allowance it is for the statutory authorities to determine the effects on the beneficiary of the relevant loss of faculty and they are not bound by the view taken by the medical authorities, though the latter is obviously of evidentiary value.[4]

vi Duration of allowance

The special hardship allowance is 'payable for such period as may be determined at the time it is granted, but may be renewed from time to time'.[5] Although the authorities have, in consequence, a discretion as to the duration of the allowance, it has been suggested that it should generally be for a substantial period (e.g. 12 months) unless there are special circumstances, most importantly where changes are anticipated in the standard of remuneration either in the claimant's regular occupation or in his post-accident occupation.[6] In the latter case, however, it is undesirable to select a period of less than three months.[7] When the stipulated period comes to an end, the claimant must reapply. A Tribunal of Commissioners, by a majority, has decided that the provision that it 'may be renewed from time to time' is not sufficient to impose a duty on the insurance officer of his own initiative to renew the award.[8]

The allowance is payable even though the claimant has reached pensionable age. This is an odd feature for it is intended to replace lost earnings and at pensionable age the claimant would normally have retired from the regular occupation.[9] It also makes for difficulties of administration: what earnings are to be assumed of man aged (say) 80 in his regular occupation, which might have been heavy work?

vii Amount

Section 60(6) prescribes that the amount of the allowance is to be determined,

3 See also *R(I) 2/81*.
4 [1965] 2 QB 112 128–129, adopting a passage from *R(I) 2/65*, O George, Dep. Comr. Admittedly the passage refers to 'actual physical effects', but there seems to be no reason why psychological effects should not be covered.
5 SSA 1975, s.60(6).
6 *CI 81/49*.
7 *CI 330/50*.
8 *R(I) 6/62*. See also pp. 552–553, below.
9 *Industrial Injuries Compensation* paras 3.62–3.67. See also *Pearson* Annex 6, para 27.

> by reference to the beneficiary's probable standard of remuneration during the period for which it is granted in the employed earner's employments, if any, which are suitable in his case and which he is likely to be capable of following as compared with that in his regular occupation.[10]

The wording of this subsection is very similar to that of section 60(1)(b), in particular the reference to 'standard of remuneration'. As we have seen,[11] the question of entitlement is determined by an objective comparison of the normal earnings of persons employed in the claimant's regular occupation and in the employment of which he is now capable. Section 60(6), on the other hand, which only comes into play when section 60(1) has been satisfied, bases the amount of the allowance on a comparison of the *personal* standard of earnings of the claimant in his regular occupation and in the relevant post-accident employment.[12] Thus in calculating the difference for the latter purpose, the authorities should have regard to the claimant's ability (as evidenced by regular practice[13]) to earn overtime[14] or bonus payments,[15] to any history of absenteeism[16] or to the fact that he was a seasonal worker[17] – whether these incidents of work attached to his pre-accident or to his post-accident employment. At the same time, it must be remembered that the comparison is not based on actual earnings either before or after the accident. It is concerned with probable standards of remuneration and thus may be entirely hypothetical.[18] So, as regards the regular occupation, the authorities must speculate on what would have been the claimant's standard of earnings if he had not been injured and had continued to follow that employment.[19] This means that they must obtain the relevant information on any increases in the basic earnings of persons in that type of employment.[20] No doubt, for the purposes of this probable and hypothetical standard, the authorities may turn at the outset to the claimant's actual earnings,[1] but there is an underlying principle that they should compare 'like with like'. In *Ex parte Humphreys*[2]

> C, unable to continue his regular occupation as a collier at Wrexham, moved to Doncaster where he secured employment as a welder-burner. For domestic and other reasons, he was forced to return to Wrexham. The standard of earnings of a welder-burner was inferior to that of a collier both in Wrexham and in Doncaster. But a welder-burner in Doncaster earned as much as a collier in Wrexham. The Court of Appeal quashed a decision disentitling him to special hardship allowance.

For the purposes of section 60(1), he had succeeded in showing that the standard of remuneration for a welder-burner was not equivalent to that of

10 SSA 1975, s.60(6).
11 P. 315, above.
12 *CWI 17/49*; *R(I) 10/55*; *R(I) 6/68*.
13 Thus not where earned only spasmodically: *CI 81/49*; *R(I) 54/54*.
14 *CI 81/49*; *R(I) 27/57*.
15 *R(I) 66/51*; *R(I) 47/54*.
16 *R(I) 23/51*; *R(I) 61/52*.
17 *R(I) 76/52*; *R(I) 5/53*; *R(I) 56/53*.
18 *R(I) 11/65*; *R(I) 1/68*.
19 *R(I) 14/57*; *R(I) 1/63*.
20 *R(I) 43/52*; *R(I) 88/52*; *R(I) 11/65*. In theory the onus of proving these increases is on the claimant but it would seem from the general sentiments expressed by the Commissioner in *R(I) 8/67* that the analogy with civil law suits will not be pushed very far: the insurance officer is under an obligation (moral?) to assist in collecting and presenting the relevant facts.
1 See e.g. *R(I) 2/70*, and pp. 404–409, below.
2 [1966] 2 QB 1.

a collier, whether in Wrexham or in Doncaster. To calculate the amounts of his increase while in Wrexham, it was necessary to compare what he would earn as a welder-burner *there* as compared with what he would have earned if he had continued as a collier.[3]

Hitherto we have used the expression 'standard of remuneration' as though it were self-explanatory. But in fact it raises serious problems of interpretation. We have seen that for the purposes of section 60(1), it was construed to mean the *amount* rather than the *rate* of earnings, so that if the claimant had to work longer hours for the same amount of money, he would fail to establish a title to the increase.[4] In 1971, for the purpose of calculating the amount of increase under section 60(6), the same issue was taken to the Court of Appeal.[5]

> In his regular occupation as a coal miner, C would have earned £28 1s 9d for working 36¼ hours, no overtime being available. In his post-accident employment as a lorry driver, for a considerably longer period of working (which included overtime), his average earnings were £27 6s 2d.

On the traditional approach he would only have been entitled to the difference between these amounts viz 15s 7d per week. The approach had been challenged by the Chief Commissioner in two unreported decisions.[6] He had taken one hour's working as the basis for the comparison. The difference between the average earning value of each hour's work was multiplied by the number of hours worked in the regular occupation. This more refined approach won the support of only a dissenting judgment in the Divisional Court[7] and was repudiated by the Court of Appeal. If taken to its logical conclusion this form of calculation would involve comparing not only the duration of work in the two relevant occupations but also the domestic advantages or disadvantages, the amount of leisure within the working period, and the relative hazards, strains and inconveniences of the work. Not only were such matters outside the competence of the determining authorities and highly impracticable, but they were also irrelevant to the purpose of the special hardship allowance which was concerned to compensate *financial* losses resulting from the reduced working capacity. The right approach was to compare the level of remuneration which would have probably been received in a normal working week in the regular occupation with the level of remuneration which the *claimant* was capable of receiving in a normal week's work, even though he now works longer hours than in the pre-accident occupation.[8] The approach of the Court of Appeal has the practical advantage of avoiding too detailed an inquiry into the claimant's pre-accident earnings, but it also undermines what had emerged as a clear distinction between the objective and subjective standards applied to the entitlement and quantum issues respectively. That the failure to take account of the claimant's own working pattern prior to the accident will cause problems was impliedly recognised by the judges in the Court of Appeal, for they thought that some special exception would have to be made for part-time workers.[9] If special consideration is to be given to such workers, what of seasonal

3 See also *R(I) 7/68*, overruling *R(I) 10/66*.
4 P. 315, above.
5 *R v National Insurance Comr, ex parte Mellors* [1971] 2 QB 401, [1971] 1 All ER 740.
6 *CI 18/68* and *CI 29/68*, R G Micklethwait, Chief Comr.
7 Donaldson J, [1971] 2 QB 401, 413–415.
8 *R(I) 9/80*.
9 N.5, above, per Lord Denning MR at 421, per Sachs LJ at 424, per Buckley LJ at 426.

workers, those regularly earning bonus payments, or those absenting themselves for private contract work outside? It is respectfully submitted that the approach prevailing before 1971, whereby the post-accident earning capacity was assessed on a subjective basis, is to be preferred.[10]

There is a statutory maximum to the amount payable by way of special hardship allowance. This is, in 1982–83, £21.44, or the amount by which the rate of the claimant's disablement pension (excluding any allowances for dependants, constant attendance or exceptionally severe disablement) falls short of that payable for a 100 per cent assessment, whichever is the less.[11]

viii Critique and reform

As a compromise to cope with the demand for some form of compensation for lost earnings, the allowance, with its rather inappropriate reference to 'special hardship', and its formulation in terms of different *standards* of remuneration in categories of occupation or employment, has proved to be far from ideal. The very complexity of the law, with its attendant uncertainties, as revealed by the length of analysis in this book, is unsatisfactory. More serious, perhaps, are the practical problems involved in its administration. Unusually in social security law, the type of evidence on which title to the allowance and its computation are decided can rarely be secured by the claimant unassisted. Indeed, high administrative costs are incurred by ascertaining on a regular basis not only the claimant's current standards of earnings but what he would have earned if still employed in his regular occupation, and in some cases that occupation might have ceased to exist.[12] The inappropriateness of this form of inquiry is reinforced by the fact that 90 per cent of the beneficiaries of the special hardship allowance are paid at the maximum rate,[13] so that in practice this has become mainly a flat-rate benefit.

In its White Paper of 1981 the government has proposed some major reforms.[14] SHA would be replaced by a new benefit, more appropriately entitled 'reduced earnings allowance'. Most importantly, the maximum award would be raised to the amount payable for a 100 per cent disablement pension. Payment would, however, cease at the deemed age of retirement (70 for men, 65 for women).[15] To solve the problems raised by continual reassessment, it is proposed that the pre-accident earnings on the basis of which the award is first made should in subsequent years simply be up-rated in line with general increases in earnings. Less obviously justifiable is the complementary suggestion that the amount attributed to post-accident earnings should be increased in the same way.[16] The problem with this is that the amount so determined may not, in time, reflect the claimant's actual earning capacity, particularly if his physical condition undergoes some change. If the concern is to reduce the administrative costs incurred in establishing the claimant's actual earnings loss, then it might be

10 Cf *Micklethwait* p. 108.

11 SSA 1975, Sch 4, Part V, para 6.

12 *Pearson* Annex 6, paras 29–38; *Industrial Injuries Compensation* paras 3.44–3.50.

13 Ibid, para 3.43.

14 *Reform of the Industrial Injuries Scheme*, ch 4.

15 The entitlement of those over pensionable age already receiving it would not be affected; it is also proposed that a beneficiary's record for pension purposes should take some account of SHA entitlement: ibid, paras 37–38.

16 Where, for reasons unconnected with the relevant disablement, the claimant becomes unemployable, sickness or invalidity benefit would be treated as earnings for SHA purposes: ibid, para 34.

wiser to imitate some foreign systems[17] and base compensation on an entirely hypothetical impairment of earning capacity: the claimant's pre-accident earnings multiplied by his degree of disablement.

C Hospital treatment allowance

If the basic disablement benefit can be rationalised in terms of compensation for the non-material consequences of disability, expressed broadly as the loss of enjoyment of life, the in-patient at a hospital or analogous institution suffers that loss whether his disablement is assessed at 5 per cent or at 100 per cent. The hospital treatment allowance, which treats such persons as if their disablement had been assessed at 100 per cent, can be justified on this basis. On the other hand, it was originally intended to encourage pensioners to obtain hospital treatment by providing additional financial support.[18] Elsewhere in the social security system, the fact that a beneficiary is obliged to stay in hospital is a ground for reducing, rather than increasing, benefit, to reflect the assumed savings on living expenses.[19] The allowance is thus considered to be anachronistic, and the government has proposed its abolition.[20]

Until this proposal is implemented, the allowance remains payable. The Social Security Act 1975 provides that:

> where a person is awarded disablement benefit but the extent of his disablement is assessed for the period taken into account by the assessment at less than 100 per cent, it shall be treated as assessed at 100 per cent for any part of that period, whether before or after the making of the assessment for the award of benefit, during which he receives, as an in-patient in a hospital or similar institution, medical treatment for the relevant injury or loss of faculty.[1]

Originally the hospital treatment had to be of a kind approved by the Minister.[2] This requirement has since been removed, and the limitation to a 'hospital or similar institution' has been broadly construed so that, for example, rehabilitation centres are included.[3] Since the purpose of the allowance is to benefit those who are forced by their condition to remain within the institution, any degree of attendance which falls short of total residence will disqualify the claimant from being an 'in-patient'.[4] 'Medical treatment' is defined in the Act as 'medical, surgical or rehabilitative treatment (including any course of diet or other regimen)'.[5] It must be 'for the relevant injury or loss of faculty'. If the claimant is in hospital for a completely unconnected purpose he is not entitled unless in addition he receives treatment for the industrially-caused condition which is more than incidental. Thus, a claimant who was in receipt of disablement benefit for head injuries received in an industrial accident, but who was being treated in hospital for tuberculosis, could not succeed merely because he was given

17 E.g. France: see *Dupeyroux* pp. 552–553.
18 *Industrial Injuries Compensation* para 4.16.
19 Pp. 394–398, below.
20 *Reform of the Industrial Injuries Scheme*, para 45.
1 SSA 1975, s.62(1).
2 NI(II)A 1946, s.16.
3 *R(I) 14/56*.
4 So where C stayed the night at home, but was in all other respects treated as an in-patient, he failed: *R(I) 27/54*.
5 SSA 1975, Sch 20.

the occasional aspirin to relieve headaches resulting from the earlier injuries.[6]

The allowance is payable for any period of treatment as an in-patient which coincides with any part of the period taken into account by the assessment of disablement.[7] Short gaps between periods of treatment can be disregarded under a 'linking rule' which provides that 'a person who receives medical treatment as an in-patient for two or more distinct periods separated by an interval of less than a week in each case shall be treated as receiving such treatment continuously from the beginning of the first period until the end of the last'.[8] The effect of an award of the allowance will be to entitle the claimant to a 100 per cent disablement pension for the relevant period. If the assessment was less than 20 per cent and as a result he has been awarded a disablement gratuity wholly or partly for the period for which the allowance is payable, the weekly value of the gratuity so paid will be deducted from the pension.[9]

D Constant attendance allowance

The constant attendance allowance, as part of the 1946 industrial injuries scheme, was introduced before the non-contributory attendance allowance became available to the general population in 1971.[10] The Pearson Commission considered that the maintenance of separate provision was not justified: it felt that 'at these extremes of disablement, cause is less important than effect, and that on grounds of both principle and administrative expediency the two types of attendance allowance should be rationalised'.[11] The government accepts this view and has proposed to abolish constant attendance allowance, leaving industrial injury victims to rely on the allowance payable under the main scheme.[12]

Under the existing legislative structure questions of entitlement, duration and quantum are determined not by the statutory authorities, viz insurance officer, local insurance tribunal, Commissioner, but by the Secretary of State.[13] The result is that in terms of legal principle much concerning this area of the social security system is shrouded in secrecy.[14] Apparently, internal guidelines for interpretation are circulated within the Department, but their contents have been jealously guarded.[15]

The Act provides that where disablement pension is payable at 100 per cent, and as a result of the relevant loss of faculty the claimant 'requires constant attendance', the pension is to be increased by an amount determinable in accordance with regulations and not exceeding the legislatively prescribed amount.[16] The regulations effectively lay down four

6 *R(I) 68/53*.
7 SSA 1975, s.62(1) re-enacting NI(II)A 1953, s.3(3) which had replaced the earlier unsatisfactory requirement that he should have been entitled to disablement benefit when he entered the hospital: NI(II)A 1946, s.16.
8 SI 1975/559, reg 14.
9 SSA 1975, s.62(2).
10 Cf pp. 171–177, above.
11 Para 831.
12 *Reform of the Industrial Injuries Scheme*, paras 46–47. See also *Industrial Injuries Compensation* paras 4.7–4.14.
13 SSA 1975, s.95(1)(b).
14 See the pertinent criticism of Carson 126 NLJ 59.
15 Carson, n. 14, above, at 60.
16 SSA 1975, s.61.

different standards by which the need for attendance is to be judged and for which different rates of increase are to be payable.[17]

(1) Where the claimant is 'to a substantial extent dependent on [constant] attendance for the necessities of life and is likely to remain so dependent for a prolonged period', the lower of the two fixed rates is payable (in 1982–83, £21.50).
(2) If, however, the attendance required for (1) is 'part-time only' then 'such sum as may be reasonable in the circumstances' is payable.[18]
(3) Alternatively, when 'the extent of such attendance is greater by reason of the beneficiary's exceptionally severe disablement', a sum up to 150 per cent of the fixed rate in (1) is payable.
(4) The higher of the two fixed rates (in 1982–83, £43.00 per week) is payable where the claimant is 'so exceptionally severely disabled as to be entirely, or almost entirely, dependent on such attendance for the necessities of life, and is likely to remain so dependent for a prolonged period and the attendance so required is whole-time'.

It is obvious that the vagueness of these principles confers great scope on the decision-maker who, as has been seen, in this case is not challengeable. How are such phrases as 'substantial extent', 'entirely or almost entirely dependent', 'prolonged', 'exceptionally severely disabled', to be construed? No answers can be given. All that can be offered by way of commentary is based on what emerged during the parliamentary debates and on what follows logically from the language of the Act, and the small number of regulations operating in this field. The attendance in question may be provided by anyone; it is not necessary to prove that he came in from outside.[19] But if the claimant is a hospital in-patient, he is entitled only if the treatment he receives there is not provided free.[20] It is unnecessary to show that the claimant actually *receives* the attendance; the statutory criterion is based on need.[1] The highest standard ((4) above) was introduced at the Report stage of the Bill to bring the scheme into line with war pensions,[2] and in the words of the Minister 'will take a considerable amount of attendance and nursing to qualify'.[3]

E Exceptionally severe disablement allowance

The exceptionally severe disablement allowance was introduced in 1966[4] following the recommendations of the McCorquodale Committee on the Assessment of Disablement.[5] It felt that the system then prevailing gave insufficient assistance to some of those in receipt of 100 per cent disablement pension. The 100 per cent assessment contained a wide range of physical conditions, and recipients differed considerably, from those

17 SI 1975/559, reg 11.
18 In 1981–82 it was typically £9.70 per week: *Reform of the Industrial Injuries Scheme*, para 46.
19 Mr J Griffiths, Minister of NI, introducing the 2nd Reading of the 1946 Bill in the House of Commons, 414 HC Official Report (5th series) col 278.
20 SI 1975/559, reg 13(1), though if he was entitled to disablement pension in the period immediately before the date he entered the hospital for treatment, the requirement does not apply for the first four weeks: ibid, reg 13(2).
1 Potter and Stansfield *National Insurance (Industrial Injuries)* (2nd edn) p. 95.
2 On war pensions, see p. 355, below.
3 419 HC Official Report (5th series) col 870. The word 'exceptionally' was added to the regulation by SI 1966/338.
4 NIA 1966, s.6.
5 1965, Cmnd 2847.

who were completely helpless to others substantially short of that condition. The Committee was disinclined to modify the tariff, either by creating differentials between 90 per cent and 100 per cent, or by extending it to 200 per cent – 300 per cent, as had been suggested. Nor did it find appealing the proposal that in cases of severe multiple injuries, the authorities should be allowed to aggregate separate conditions instead of assessing the total disablement. It fell back upon what was the simplest solution: adding yet one more flat-rate addition to the existing pension and allowances. Notwithstanding a recommendation of the Pearson Commission to the contrary,[6] the government does not propose to abolish it.[7]

Under the Social Security Act 1975, the flat-rate increase (in 1982–83, £21.50 per week) is payable to a claimant who is in receipt of 100 per cent disablement pension together with a constant attendance allowance under categories (3) or (4) above, and 'his need for constant attendance of an extent and nature qualifying him for such an increase' of those standards 'is likely to be permanent'.[8] As with the constant attendance allowance, this condition is determined by the Secretary of State, from whose decision there is no appeal.

Part 8 Miscellaneous provisions

It is appropriate now to consider three miscellaneous matters related to claims for industrial injury and disablement benefits. The first concerns persons whose disablement results from successive accidents; the second involves rules governing the behaviour of claimants; and the third describes the position of those whose claim originally arose under the workmen's compensation legislation.

A Successive accidents

Where a claimant's disablement results from two conditions (injury or disease), and both are covered by the industrial injury scheme, benefit is assessed for the total disablement resulting from both. Problems will arise where a separate assessment has been made for the disability resulting from the first accident, and benefit on that basis is already payable. The fundamental principle applied to this situation is that no claimant should receive, in aggregate, more than is payable on a 100 per cent disablement pension.[9] The principle provoked some criticisms during the Committee stage of the 1946 Bill in that it compared unfavourably with the workmen's compensation legislation under which an injured employee was not barred from successive actions.[10] The criticism, however, failed to recognise the difference between the old scheme, based on loss of earnings, and the new scheme (derived from the war pension model) based primarily on loss of faculty.[11] A disablement of more than 100 per cent is a contradiction in terms. The principle is not to be circumvented by entitlement to a lump

6 Para 833.
7 *Reform of the Industrial Injuries Scheme*, para 48.
8 SSA 1975, s.63(1).
9 Ibid, s.91(1)(a).
10 Standing Committee A Debates, cols 350–364.
11 Ibid, at cols 353–354.

sum gratuity. Where, then, a claimant is in receipt of disablement pension for life and he suffers a further loss of faculty for which a disablement gratuity would otherwise be payable, the regulations provide that:

– if the aggregate disablement exceeds that resulting from the first accident, the claimant may elect for a pension in lieu of the gratuity at a rate representing the difference between the aggregate disablement and the rate of his existing pension.[12] The aggregate pension must not, however, exceed 100 per cent,[13] and if a maximum 100 per cent pension is already payable for the first accident, no further gratuity or pension is payable for the consequences of the second accident.[14]

Of course, the principle so formulated takes no account of the possibility that as a result of either accident, the claimant may be entitled to increases for loss of earnings or constant attendance. The regulations, accordingly, modify the principle.

(1) C is in receipt of disablement pension. As a result of a second accident he suffers a further loss of faculty for which a gratuity would normally be payable and he is rendered permanently incapable of work. He may add the unemployability supplement to his disablement pension, as if the permanent incapacity had resulted from the first accident.[15]

(2) If the aggregate disablement resulting from the two accidents is 100 per cent, he is entitled to a constant attendance allowance, notwithstanding that neither loss of faculty, taken by itself, would have so entitled him.[16]

(3) He will not, of course, be entitled to more than one increase for unemployability, constant attendance allowance or for dependants.[17]

B Conduct of the claimant

The legislation lays down rules governing the conduct of a claimant for two independent purposes. First, as a direct instrument of social policy, it attempts to encourage greater personal safety by refusing benefit should the disability have been incurred in certain circumstances, e.g. through the exclusive fault of the injured person. Secondly, to prevent fraud and abuse, it requires the claimant to satisfy certain standards of conduct after the disability has been incurred.

i Conduct at time of accident

Compensation systems have varied considerably in their willingness to treat certain forms of conduct as a ground for disentitling a claimant from benefit. Under the Workmen's Compensation Acts, the employer would escape liability if the injury was caused by the employee's 'serious and wilful default'.[18] After 1906, however, the doctrine was excluded in cases of serious and permanent disablement.[19] In France, benefit may be reduced for the 'inexcusable fault' of the accident victim.[20] In Germany, it may be

12 SI 1975/559, reg 34(1).
13 Ibid, reg 34(2)(b).
14 Ibid, reg 34(2)(a).
15 Ibid, reg 35(1).
16 Ibid, reg 35(3).
17 Ibid, reg 35(4).
18 WCA 1897, s.1(2)(c).
19 WCA 1906, s.1(2)(c).
20 *Dupeyroux* pp. 562–565.

reduced or withheld altogether for injuries caused by criminal acts.[1] In most systems there are exclusions for intentional self-injuries.[2] In Britain, there is no explicit rule comparable to these provisions, but, as has been seen, an intentionally inflicted injury will generally not be regarded as an 'accident'.[3] The lack of sanction for other degrees of faulty conduct has not been controversial. The general opinion is that the prospect of a reduced benefit is unlikely to operate as an effective deterrent.[4]

ii Post-accident conduct

The forms of abuse to which the industrial injuries scheme is susceptible were enumerated by the DHSS in its memorandum to the Fisher Committee:[5] the attribution of non-work accidents to the course of employment; the attribution of unrelated physical conditions to the effect of an industrial accident or disease; the prolongation of incapacity (malingering); the misrepresentation of potential earning capacity (to establish title to special hardship allowance). Most of these risks of abuse are met by the system of medical certification and, in the case of disablement benefit, determination by the medical authorities. These procedures are described elsewhere.[6] In addition, the Social Security Act and regulations made under it impose certain obligations, coupled with sanctions in the event of non-compliance.

(1) 'It shall be the duty of any person claiming or entitled to injury benefit in respect of any injury not to behave in any manner calculated to retard his recovery'.[7] It has been held that in this context 'calculated' does not connote a subjective intention but rather the objective likelihood of the behaviour retarding recovery.[8] However, if the claimant is unsure whether his conduct may have this effect he may plead in defence that he failed to comply with the duty 'for reasonable cause'.

(2) He must, on receipt of the appropriate notice,[9] subject himself to medical examination or treatment[10] (though the disqualification cannot be imposed for a refusal to undergo a 'non-minor' surgical operation.[11]

(3) The victim of an industrial accident must give notice of the accident 'as soon as is practicable after the happening thereof' to his employer.[12]

In the event of non-compliance without reasonable cause with any of these obligations, or if there has been 'wilful obstruction of, or misconduct in connection with' medical examination or treatment, the statutory authority may disqualify the claimant from benefit for a period up to a maximum of six weeks.[13]

1 Reichsversicherungsordnung, ξ 554(1).
2 E.g. New Zealand Accident Compensation Act 1972, s.137; France, Codes des Sécurités Sociales, art 467; Germany, n.10, above, ξ 503. Cp Report of the National Committee of Inquiry into Compensation and Rehabilitation in Australia (1974), which regarded deliberate self-injury as manifesting mental illness and should not therefore lead to disqualification from benefit (para 351(b)).
3 P. 268, above, cf suicide, p. 332, below.
4 *Atiyah* pp. 566–568.
5 Para 222.
6 Pp. 149–152, above, and 303–308.
7 SSA 1975, s.90(1).
8 *R(I) 26/51*.
9 For the requirements as to what constitutes valid notice see SI 1979/628, reg 26(2).
10 SSA 1975, s.89 and SI 1979/628, reg 26(1).
11 SI 1975/559, reg 40(6); cf p. 157, above.
12 SSA 1975, s.88(a) and SI 1979/628, reg 24(1).
13 SSA 1975, s.90; SI 1975/559, reg 40; and see *CI 242/50*.

C Workmen's compensation cases

The industrial injuries scheme applies only to accidents occurring or diseases developing on or after 5 July 1948.[14] Earlier cases were governed by the Workmen's Compensation Acts. In order, however, to maintain approximate equality between beneficiaries under the two schemes, state benefits are available to those with rights of compensation under the old legislation. The numbers involved are small, and, of course, are declining.[15] It is proposed therefore to give a simplified outline of the law now governed principally by the Industrial Injuries and Diseases (Old Cases) Act 1975.[16]

i *Basic allowance* Under the workmen's compensation legislation, those injured after 1923 were more favourably treated.[17] It was therefore felt desirable to provide a more generous supplement for earlier invalids. For such persons, a basic allowance is payable if on or after 21 March 1951 a claimant is entitled to weekly payments of compensation under the WCAs;[18] and he is totally or partially incapacitated for work.[19] In cases of total incapacity the sum payable is such as to bring the compensation up to £2.00 per week.[20] In cases of partial incapacity it is such amount as will bring the compensation up to two-thirds of the estimated loss of earnings resulting from the accident, to a maximum of £2.00 per week.[1]

ii *Major incapacity allowance* To qualify for this allowance the claimant must be entitled, at any time since 5 July 1956, to the basic allowance or to weekly payments of compensation under WCAs for accidents or diseases occurring after 1923. In addition, as a result of the accident or disease, the claimant must be totally incapable of work and likely to remain so for at least 13 weeks.[2] The amount payable is equivalent to the weekly industrial disablement pension for those assessed at 100 per cent less the weekly amount of any WCA compensation and the basic allowance (if any).[3]

iii *Lesser incapacity allowance* This is payable to those who are not entitled to a major incapacity allowance but who are partially or totally incapacitated and who, since 1 March 1966, have been entitled to weekly payments of compensation under WCA for lost earnings.[4] The amount payable is a proportionate part of the lost earnings to a maximum of in 1982–83 of £19.70 on a scale prescribed in regulations.

iv *Additional payments* The major incapacity allowance only brings WCA recipients up to the level of disablement pensions. Additional measures were therefore necessary to confer on them the highly important additions and allowances available under the industrial

14 SSA 1975, ss.50(1) and 76(1).
15 In 1980, supplementary allowances were being paid to 4,039 persons for accidents occurring since 1924 and to 252 persons entitled to compensation before that date: DHSS Social Security Statistics 1981, Table 23.30.
16 For the relevant regulations see (as amended) SI 1966/165.
17 In particular, the Act raised the maximum weekly payment from £1 to £1.50: WCA 1923, s.4(1).
18 So those who settled for a lump sum after that date may also benefit.
19 IIDA 1975, ss.2(1), 2(3)(a) and 2(3), (7).
20 Ibid, s.2(6)(a).
1 Ibid.
2 Ibid, ss.2(1), 2(3)(b), 2(7), 14(4)(a).
3 Ibid, s.2(6)(b).
4 Ibid, s.2(4).

injuries scheme. The Social Security Act 1975, section 159, combined with the appropriate regulations[5], treats those entitled to WCA payments on or after 5 July 1948, and who are, as a result of the relevant injury or disease, incapable of work and likely to remain permanently so incapable as if they came within the general scheme for the purposes of entitlement to unemployability supplement, and the allowances for dependants, constant attendance and exceptionally severe disablement.

v *Diseases resulting from pre-1948 employment* Special provision is also made for those who subsequently became disabled through an industrial disease, but were employed in the prescribed occupation only before 1948.[6] However, the provisions do not extend to all prescribed diseases, but are restricted to those which generally take some considerable time to manifest themselves.[7] The benefits payable are similar to the major and lesser incapacity allowances,[8] to which may be added, in appropriate cases, the supplements and allowances referred to in the previous paragraph.[9]

Part 9 Death

A Introduction

The Workmen's Compensation Act 1897 made provision for those wholly or partly dependent on someone who died as the result of an industrial accident. In the former case, the dependant received a lump sum representing the deceased's earnings over the last three years before his death or £150, whichever was the larger, but not exceeding a maximum of £300.[10] If there was no one wholly dependent on him, those partially dependent would receive a proportionate part of the stipulated amount.[11] The notion that compensation should be based wholly on the deceased's earnings record without regard to the number of dependants came under sharp criticism in the ensuing years.[12] The Holman Gregory Committee, reporting in 1920,[13] was divided on the question as to whether compensation should be based on lost earnings or on need. The former was found to have created hardship in cases of large families, and yet the latter would depart from a fundamental tenet of the workmen's compensation legislation. The 1923 Act adopted a compromise solution. The lump sum payment, based on the earnings record, was retained, but this might be supplemented by a new children's allowance. Where the widow and the children were, at the death, wholly dependent on the deceased, there might be payable for each child a sum representing 15 per cent of the average weekly earnings.[14] For those only partially dependent, a prop-

5 SI 1975/559, regs 43, 44.
6 IIDA 1975, s.5.
7 Ibid, s.5(2), (3).
8 Ibid, s.7(2).
9 Ibid, s.7(3).
10 WCA 1897, Sch 1, para 1(a)(i).
11 Ibid, para 1(a)(ii).
12 E.g. Departmental Committee Report on Workmen's Compensation (1904, Cd 2208).
13 Departmental Committee Report on Workmen's Compensation (Cmd 816).
14 WCA 1923, s.2(a).

ortiónate part might be claimed.[15] The total paid by way of death benefit was not to exceed £600.[16]

The replacement of workmen's compensation by the industrial injury scheme which was not, at least as originally conceived, based on earnings, meant that the method had to be abolished. Beveridge proposed to replace it by a lump sum 'industrial grant' which would supplement a widow's ordinary, non-industrial, benefit (thus maintaining the differential between the industrial and non-industrial schemes) and which would extend to other dependants.[17] The government accepted that special provision should be made for fatal cases resulting from industrial accidents or diseases but was not attracted by the idea of a lump sum.[18] It therefore proposed, and subsequently introduced, a pension, analogous to that payable to non-industrial widows:[19] an initial high flat-rate benefit for the first six months, which would then fall to one level if the widow had children to care for or was otherwise deemed incapable of joining the labour market, and another if she did not come within either of these categories. In this area, the industrial preference (the difference between the industrial and non-industrial schemes) has given rise to a number of advantages:[20] the standard widow's pension is paid at a higher rate; a small pension is payable to a childless widow under 40; benefit is paid for children independently of the widow's entitlement (and thus can continue after she has remarried) and also to widowers and other dependants; a widow can accumulate her pension with other income maintenance benefits (e.g. sickness or unemployment benefit). On the other hand, successive governments have allowed the real value of many of these advantages to be eroded by inflation so that, for example, the standard industrial widow's pension is only 55p higher than that available under the general scheme. The Pearson Commission felt that financial provision for dependants should not vary according to the cause of death and recommended that industrial death benefit be abolished.[21] In the 1981 White Paper, the government declared its intention of implementing this proposal: it doubted whether the marginal value of the industrial preference in this context could justify the administrative expenditure which was substantially higher than that involved in the general scheme, because of the need to establish that the death resulted from an industrial accident or disease.[1]

B Death caused by industrial accident or disease

Industrial death benefit is payable if 'the earner dies as a result of the injury'[2] which of course must have been caused 'by accident arising out of and in the course of his employment' or a prescribed disease. The claimant

15 Ibid, s.2(b).
16 Ibid, s.2, proviso.
17 Para 334.
18 *Social Insurance* Part II, para 30.
19 Pp. 227–233, above.
20 Though the non-industrial scheme is more generous in its 'scaling' of benefit rates of those widowed between 40 and 50: p. 233, above.
21 Paras 835–844. However, somewhat inconsistently, it also suggested that entitlement to the full earnings-related component in the new pensions scheme (p. 234, above) should be accelerated for industrial widows: paras, 840–841. For criticism, see Ogus, Corfield and Harris 7 ILJ 143, 150–151.
1 *Reform of the Industrial Injuries Scheme*, ch 6. See also *Industrial Injuries Compensation* ch 5.
2 SSA 1975, s.50(2)(c).

must first satisfy the ordinary test of an employment accident (or prescribed disease) on principles already described. The problem arising for particular attention here is that of causation.

i Instantaneous death

Although the Act envisages a chain of causation, accident – injury – death, the death may be instantaneous. In other words, the accident will be constituted by the death. In such circumstances, it must be established that it was the condition of the employment which substantially caused the death rather than a pre-existing condition.[3] If the deceased committed suicide, that will be sufficient to take the death outside the employment risk,[4] but, adopting a principle from workmen's compensation law,[5] the Commissioners apply a presumption against suicide. The onus is on the insurance officer to rebut the presumption by 'convincing evidence' that the circumstances of death could be satisfactorily explained only by suicide.[6]

ii Non-instantaneous death

Where the death is not coincidental in time with the accident, the problem becomes solely one of causation. The onus is on the claimant to show, on the balance of probabilities, that the industrial injury 'plays a material part in bringing about death; it may cause death or contribute to or precipitate death or materially accelerate it'.[7] The injury must be the *causa causans* rather than a *causa sine qua non* of death,[8] but need not be the direct cause. In *CI 142/49*,

> D, suffering from dermatitis, a prescribed disease, attended a hospital for treatment of the condition. He subsequently died, inter alia, from pneumonia. It was held that the dermatitis had caused a general lowering of D's resistance to pneumonia which may have been attributable to stripping for examination as part of the treatment for dermatitis in the hospital.

Of course, the chain of causation will be broken if some new cause intervenes and supersedes the effects of the industrial accident or disease.[9] One unfortunate instance of this may be suicide. The 'voluntary' quality of this act will be sufficient to constitute a *novus actus interveniens*, but the dependant may nevertheless succeed if he is able to establish that the state of mind conducive to the suicidal act was itself the result of the industrial accident.[10] This may occur, for example, where the accident causes brain damage, changes the mental disposition of the deceased, intensifies a pre-existing nervous condition or brings about an immediate change in the employee's psychological state which develops into insanity.[11]

The question whether the death resulted from the injury is one of fact. In deciding the issue, the statutory authorities are not bound to follow the

3 See e.g. *R(I) 13/54* and *R(I) 16/56*.
4 *R(I) 42/59*.
5 E.g. *Southall v Cheshire County News* (1912) 5 BWCC 251, CA.
6 *CSI 23/50* and *CI 113/50*.
7 Per J S Watson, Comr, *R(I) 9/67*, para 13, and see *R(I) 54/52*.
8 *R(I) 14/51*.
9 *R(I) 54/52*.
10 *CI 172/50*; *R(I) 2/57*.
11 See the WCA cases cited in *R(I) 38/51*.

opinions of medical boards or any independent witness but must form their own independent judgment on all the evidence available. For guidance, there exists a large number of reported Commissioner's decisions which analyse the relationship between death and certain industrially caused conditions (especially pneumoconiosis);[12] but these, unlike decisions on law, are not treated as binding on the statutory authorities, as medical opinion may change in the course of time.[13]

The difficulties of proof are not to be underestimated, and in two sets of circumstances Parliament has intervened to alleviate the problem.

a *Seriously disabled* If a person dies at a time when he was receiving constant attendance allowance, he is treated as if he died as a result of the injury for which the disablement pension was payable.[14]

b *Victims of pulmonary disease* If a person dies as a result of a pulmonary disease and this occurred during a period of entitlement to disablement pension (assessed at not less than 50 per cent) in respect of pneumoconiosis or byssinosis, the death is treated as if it were caused by the disease in question.[15]

C Widow's benefits

i Entitlement

A widow must first establish that she was, at the time of death, lawfully married to the deceased. This requirement is shared by the non-industrial scheme, and will be discussed in chapter 10.[16] To claim industrial benefit she must in addition establish the necessary degree of dependency on the deceased, that on the death

either
(a) she was residing with him, or
(b) she was receiving or entitled to receive, or would but for the relevant accident have been receiving or entitled to receive from him periodical payments for her maintenance of not less than the prescribed amount.[17]

Why these conditions are thought necessary for the industrial scheme but not for the non-industrial scheme is not obvious. It may be that for the purposes of the latter satisfying the contribution conditions is considered sufficiently onerous. Whatever the reasons for the difference, a widow will not find it difficult to prove maintenance, since the prescribed amount is an average weekly rate of 25p or more.[18] This, and the alternative residence condition, follow the pattern established where an increase to personal benefit is claimed for a dependant. This will be considered fully in chapter 10.[19] Such differences as exist are verbal rather than substantive.[20]

12 See Neligan *Social Security Case Law* (1979) ch 12.
13 *R(I) 9/67*; *R v Deputy Industrial Injuries Comr, ex parte Moore* [1965] 1 QB 465, [1965] 1 All ER 81, CA, and see *Micklethwait* pp. 74–75.
14 SSA 1975, s.75(1), re-enacting NIA 1971, s.8(2).
15 SS(MP)A 1977, s.9(1).
16 Pp. 377–382, below.
17 SSA 1975, s.67(1).
18 SI 1975/559, reg 15. The amount has remained unchanged since 1946.
19 Pp. 371–376, below.
20 The reference to maintenance by 'periodical payments' is peculiar to industrial death benefit but the words import nothing which is not already implied in the general maintenance provisions: see e.g. *R(I) 37/54*. The same applies to the explanatory s.67(3) which provides that '(a) references to a widow receiving or being entitled to receive

ii Form and duration of benefit

The form of the various benefits and their duration also follow the non-industrial model, though with some significant differences. The initial rate of widow's pension for the first 26 weeks[1] after death is equivalent to the (non-industrial) widow's allowance (in 1982–83, £45.95 per week). The two rates for the permanent pension payable at the end of the six months period again parallel those payable under the non-industrial scheme. The higher rate (£33.40 per week) is paid where the widow is either:[2]

(1) entitled to receive allowance for a child of the deceased's family;[3] *or*
(2) is residing with a child under 19 for whom the deceased was entitled to child benefit at his death (or would have been if the child had not left school);[4] *or*
(3) was over 40 when she no longer satisfied the conditions in (1) or (2); *or*
(4) was over 50 at the deceased's death; *or*
(5) was permanently incapable of self-support at that death;[5] *or*
(6) is pregnant by the deceased.

However, unlike the non-industrial scheme: there are no scaled benefit rates for those widowed between the ages of 40 and 50;[6] and in cases not covered by the higher rate, a small pension is payable (in 1982–83, £9.86 per week).[7] At whichever rate, it terminates on death, or remarriage,[8] but in the event of the latter a lump-sum gratuity is paid of 52 times the weekly rate of pension to which the widow was then entitled.[9] It may be doubted whether this special feature of the industrial scheme – a form of state dowry – can be justified today.[10] Payment of the pension is suspended during any period in which the beneficiary is 'living as husband and wife with a man not her husband',[11] though if she remarries following any such period she remains entitled to the gratuity.[12]

D Widower's benefit

The benefit payable to a widower has no parallel in the non-industrial scheme, and even in the case of industrial death it is not widely available, for the claimant must prove that at the time of the wife's death he was both

> being wholly or mainly maintained by her or would but for the relevant accident have been so maintained

and

> was permanently incapable of self-support.[13]

---

payments from the deceased are only to her receiving or being entitled to receive (whether from him or from another) payments provided or procured by the deceased; and (b) "entitled" means, in relation to such payments, entitled under any order of a court, trust or agreement which the widow has taken reasonable steps to enforce'.

1 SSA 1975, s.68(1).
2 Ibid, s.68(2).
3 See p. 335, below.
4 SI 1975/559, reg 16, as substituted by SI 1977/349.
5 See p. 377, below.
6 P. 233, above. The Pearson Commission, para 839, proposed that this should be incorporated in the industrial scheme.
7 SSA 1975, s.68(3).
8 Ibid, s.67(2).
9 Ibid, s.67(2)(b).
10 *Industrial Injuries Compensation* para 5.19; cp *Pearson* para 843.
11 SSA 1975, s.67(2) proviso, as amended by SS(MP)A 1977, s.22(4).
12 SI 1975/559, reg 17.
13 SSA 1975, s.69(1).

For the meaning of 'wholly or mainly maintained' and 'permanently incapable of self-support' reference should be made to discussions elsewhere.[14] The stringency of these conditions is, no doubt, responsible for the fact that in 1980 only *one* widower's pension was being paid.[15] The sex discrimination implicit in the different provisions for widows and widowers has been the subject of comment elsewhere,[16] and this is an area not covered by the EEC Directive on Equal Treatment for Men and Women in Social Security.[17] The Pearson Commission, however, considered that under the industrial injury scheme widowers should be treated no differently from widows,[18] though why this should happen only in relation to an industrial death is by no means clear.[19] Under existing provisions the rate of widower's pension is the same as that of a widow who is not expected to work (in 1982–83, £33.40 a week), but it is not terminable on remarriage or suspended on cohabitation, thus producing further evidence of discrimination.

E Children

Two conditions must be satisfied for claims made on behalf of children of the deceased. The first relates to the relationship between the child and the deceased: at the time of his death, the deceased must have been entitled to child benefit in respect of the child,[20] or be treated by regulations as having been so entitled.[1] The deeming regulations cover, for example, children of another family who were being wholly or mainly maintained by the deceased and posthumous children of the deceased himself. Secondly, the person claiming the allowance in respect of the child must now be entitled (or treated as entitled) to child benefit for that child,[2] and must be residing with the child or contributing to its maintenance.[3] Where there is more than one such person, priority is given to the surviving spouse.[4] A higher rate (in 1982–83, £7.90 per week per child) is paid to the widow,[5] and in some circumstances to a person caring for the child instead of the widow.[6] In other cases, the lower rate is payable (in 1982–83, £0.30 per week, per child). Entitlement to the child's allowance, unlike the widow's pension, does not terminate on the widow's remarriage, though on that event the lower rate becomes payable.[7] This is a unique instance in the social security system of a benefit derived from one marriage continuing through the subsistence of another; as such it has been the subject of criticism.[8]

14 Pp. 373–376 and 377, below, respectively.
15 *Industrial Injuries Compensation* para 5.26.
16 Pp. 235–236, above.
17 P. 366, below.
18 Paras 845–847.
19 Cf *Industrial Injuries Compensation* para 5.27.
20 See ch 11, below.
1 SSA 1975, s.70(1), as amended by CBA 1975, Sch 4, para 25, and SI 1975/559, regs 23B–23E, inserted by SI 1977/342.
2 SSA 1975, s.70(1), as amended by CBA 1975, Sch 4, para 25, and SI 1975/559, reg 23D, inserted by SI 1977/342.
3 SSA 1975, s.70(4), incorporating s.65(1), on which see pp. 371–376, below.
4 SSA 1975, Sch 9, para 1(c). Priority as between others so entitled is determined in accordance with SI 1975/559, Sch 7, as amended by SI 1976/1736 and SI 1977/342.
5 SSA 1975, s.70(2).
6 Ibid, and SI 1975/559, reg 23A, inserted by SI 1977/342.
7 SSA 1975, s.70(2).
8 *Industrial Injuries Compensation* para 5.20.

F Parents and other relatives

There is in theory, a wide range of adult dependants who may claim some benefit in the event of an industrial death. Such provision was made in the 1946 legislation to maintain continuity of an equivalent entitlement under the workmen's compensation scheme. Subsequent governments have found little to justify this aspect of the industrial preference and in consequence the value of the benefits has remained unchanged since 1946. This, combined with the fact that the conditions of entitlement are not easy to satisfy, has meant that few awards are currently in payment (in 1980 only 209).[9] Faced with this anachronism, the Pearson Commission recommended that the entitlement of relatives other than widows and children should be abolished.[10] The law is unhappily also extremely complex, but in the circumstances it does not seem appropriate to provide a detailed analysis.

- A pension is payable to a parent who was wholly or mainly maintained by the deceased: £1.00 a week, or if two qualifying parents are living together £0.75 each.[11] For lesser degrees of maintenance there is a gratuity, to a maximum of £52 (£78 for two parents living together). There is a prescribed list of relatives[12] who may claim in similar circumstances.[13] If he was wholly or mainly maintained by the deceased and (a) he is permanently incapable of self-support, and (b) no other pension is payable in respect of the same death, the £1.00 pension is payable to one such relative. If (a) but not (b) is satisfied a gratuity of £104, may be paid if neither (a) nor (b) is satisfied, a temporary allowance of £1.80 for 13 weeks is payable. For lesser degrees of maintenance a prescribed relative, permanently incapable of self-support, is paid a gratuity to a maximum of £52.

G Women having care of children

A woman having care of a child or children in respect of whom the deceased was entitled (or treated as entitled) to child benefit may also claim.[14] She must prove that at the date of death she was both residing with and was being wholly or mainly maintained by him.[15] Benefit is in the form of a weekly allowance payable as long as the care of the children continues, but ceasing on marriage or remarriage and suspended during a period of cohabitation.[16] As with parents' and relatives' benefits, the sum payable (£1.00 per week) has remained constant since 1946.

9 DHSS Social Security Statistics 1981, Table 22.30.
10 Paras 849–850.
11 SSA 1975, s.71. For the rules on calculating maintenance, see pp. 373–376, below.
12 SI 1975/559, reg 18 and Sch 4.
13 SSA 1975, s.72, and Sch 9.
14 On the position of such a woman under social security law generally, see pp. 369–370, below.
15 SSA 1975, s73(1). For 'residence' and 'maintenance' see pp. 371–376, below.
16 SSA 1975, s.73(3).

Chapter 9

War pensions

Part 1 Introduction

A General

War pensions are almost certainly the most ancient type of state benefit. It is said that they existed in classical Greek times,[1] and in Britain their history has been traced back to the days of King Alfred.[2] The first statutory provisions, for payment of benefit to soldiers and sailors from the local rates, can be found in measures at the end of the sixteenth century.[3] Even if attention is confined to the origins of the present system of disability pensions, the story must be started during the nineteenth rather than the twentieth century. The explanation for this rich heritage is not hard to discover: it has generally been thought right to make special provision for those injured, and also for the relatives of those killed, in the service of their country. War pensions are as old as patriotism itself.

In terms of critical analysis and policy discussion, the war pension scheme is the most neglected area of social security law.[4] This may be due in part to the comparative absence of armed conflict since 1945,[5] and the consequent reduction in the number of claimants. But there are still more pensions currently being paid under this scheme than under the much debated industrial injuries scheme.[6] A second explanation may lie in the peculiarly emotive character of the subject – until recently the special position and privileges of those maimed or killed in the service of their country has not been questioned.[7] Thirdly, it was only in 1978 that the scheme was regulated by statutory instrument and thus became subject to parliamentary scrutiny; traditionally, as part of the Royal Prerogative, it was legally exclusively within the control of the Crown and thus in practice a matter for executive or administrative decision.

1 See the reference to Solon's observation in Plutarch's *Lives* made by Mr J Manders, 401 HC Official Report (5th series) col 1519.
2 39 Halsbury's Laws of England (3rd edn), p. 153, n.(d).
3 E.g. 35 Eliz 1 c. 4 (1592–93); 39 Eliz 1 c. 21 (1597–98); 43 Eliz 1 c. 3 (1601).
4 It was ignored in both *Pearson* and the Report on Social Security Provision for Chronically Sick and Disabled People, 1973–74, HC 276.
5 The scheme does, of course, cover members of the armed forces injured or killed in the Ulster 'troubles', but this compensation issue has not been widely debated and is not mentioned in, for example, the Annual Reports on War Pensioners.
6 DHSS Social Security Statistics 1981, Tables 21.36 and 36.35.
7 Cf Standing Committee B Debates on the Social Security Benefits Bill 1975, col 145. Cp the extensive literature on the 'industrial preference': n.19, p. 262, above.

In this introductory part of the chapter, there is an outline of the modern history of war pensions and an examination of the reasons for their special position in the social security system. Parts 2 and 3 are respectively concerned with the rules regarding entitlement to, and the assessment of, war pensions. Part 4 deals with those payable on the death of a member of the forces, and Part 5 with some miscellaneous rules. Part 6 discusses very shortly other comparable schemes providing pensions for persons outside the regular forces. Administrative and adjudicatory aspects are dealt with in chapters 14 and 15 respectively.

B History

During the early nineteenth century, the Commissioners of the Chelsea Hospital were responsible for the award of disability pensions to soldiers wounded in combat. From 1846 payment of pensions was made by the Secretary of State for War. There was no provision at this time for widows and children; the first move in this direction was the institution of the Patriotic Fund by voluntary subscription in 1854, under which small pensions might be paid to them.[8] During the later part of the century entitlement to pensions was regulated by the terms of the Royal Warrants in the case of soldiers, and by Orders in Council in the case of navy personnel and marines.[9] The Boer War was responsible for a further development: for the first time, disease attributable to war service was compensated in the same way as physical injury.[10]

War pensions became a crucial problem in the course of the First World War. They were frequently debated in Parliament; the political parties vied with each other to initiate measures to improve the lot of the war wounded and bereaved, so much so that alarm was expressed that the subject might be dominated by party considerations, and so lend itself to corruption.[11] Many changes were made in the rules concerning entitlement to pensions, and also, and perhaps more importantly, with regard to their administration. In this latter respect these changes have for the most part survived the last 50 years, so that despite the improvements to the system during the Second World War, the years 1914–18 were perhaps the most influential in the development of war pensions.

In 1914, pensions were administered by four authorities: the Chelsea Commissioners, the War Office, the Admiralty Commissioners (for navy pensions) and the Royal Patriotic Fund Corporation.[12] Considerable disquiet was expressed at this dispersal of authority; in particular, the Chelsea Commissioners, who were responsible for the award of army pensions under the terms of the Royal Warrants, were subjected to criticism.[13] It was irksome to MPs that decisions on entitlement were not

8 The Patriotic Fund was put on a statutory basis by the Patriotic Fund Reorganisation Act 1903.

9 Orders in Council regulating navy personnel disability pensions are passed under the Naval and Marine Pay and Pensions Act 1865; for army soldiers, pensions are paid under the Pensions Pay and Yeomanry Act 1884. Air force disability pensions are paid by orders made under the Air Force (Constitution) Act 1917, s.2.

10 Compare the more cautious treatment of disease in the industrial injuries system, pp. 288–292, above.

11 See the motion introduced by Sir M Barlow, 108 HC Official Report (5th series) col 333.

12 At this time the Patriotic Fund enjoyed Royal patronage and title, a fact which emphasised the importance of war pensions in popular feeling.

13 They were even termed, 'some kind of mystery board or secret society', 80 HC Official Report (5th series) col 1989.

subject to any appeal and that no Minister was answerable for them. The mischief suggested its own remedy. Responsibility was transferred to a new Ministry of Pensions.[14] From that time, decisions were taken in the name of the Minister, and shortly afterwards an appeal tribunal was formally constituted.[15] The latter development did much to dispel anxiety concerning the concentration of power in the hands of the Minister. Legislation passed at the end of the First World War established a legal right to receive a war pension, once it had been awarded by the Minister.[16] Before this payments had been discretionary. (It has, however, never been clear whether there is a legal right to the pension, prior to the Minister's decision.) With regard to the conditions of entitlement, the major changes were: a disability aggravated by war service (as distinct from one attributable to service) attracted a full pension instead of the previous four-fifths award; a claim could be made by a widow in respect of the death of her husband which was not in itself attributable to war service, provided that he was then in receipt of a pension.[17] The principal alteration in the rules of assessment made during the same period was that pensions were from then on to be assessed with regard to the degree of *physical disability itself* rather than the loss of earning capacity. This remains the basis of their assessment.[18] Alternative pensions, as they were then known, could be awarded to compensate for the claimant's loss of earning capacity.

Claims for a disability pension in respect of service after 30 September 1921, were transferred back to the Chelsea Commissioners and the other authorities which had administered them in 1914.[19] Now all claims with regard to service between that date and 3 September 1939 (the outbreak of the Second World War) are handled by the Ministry of Defence.[20] The inter-war years saw, not surprisingly, a decline in the importance of these pensions. The appeal tribunals set up in 1919 did not have jurisdiction over claims brought after September 1921 and, in an attempt to achieve finality, it was provided that awards under the 1919 Royal Warrant were final and unreviewable.[1]

The outbreak of the Second World War, and the consequent increase in claims, necessitated the retransfer of administration to the Ministry of Pensions, which with its departmental successors (now the DHSS) has ever since then remained responsible for war pensions.[2] From 1939 criticism of the entitlement rules mounted and several changes were made in response. By far the most important was the imposition in some cases of the burden of proof on the Ministry to show that the disablement was neither attributable to, nor aggravated by, service.[3] The claimant was given the

14 Ministry of Pensions Act 1916, s.2; further powers were given to the new Ministry by the Naval and Military War Pensions, etc. (Transfer of Powers) Act 1917. See pp. 539–540, below, on the history of the Ministry.

15 War Pensions (Administrative Provisions) Act 1919, s.8.

16 War Pensions (Administrative Provisions) Act 1919, s.7; War Pensions Act 1920, s.8. See also Pensions Appeal Tribunals Act 1943, s.11.

17 The changes were introduced by the Royal Warrant 1917. See the 1st Annual Report of the Minister of Pensions (1918, Cmd 14).

18 P. 353, below.

19 War Pensions Act 1920, s.1.

20 One odd consequence of this is that the Parliamentary Commissioner for Administration has no jurisdiction to investigate complaints of maladministration with regard to the award of pensions for this period: see Parliamentary Commissioner Act 1967, Sch 3, para 10(a), and 1st Report of the PCA for 1967–68, HC 6, para 28.

1 War Pensions Act 1921. However, the Commissioners could, and the DHSS still can, make a discretionary award under the terms of the Dispensing Warrant of 1884.

2 Pp. 539–540, below.

3 Pp. 348–351, below.

benefit of any doubt on this question. It is interesting that a similar relaxation of the law occurred at much the same time in the United States of America.[4] This strong presumption in favour of the claimant is without parallel in the British social security system.[5] Another change enabled claims to be made more than seven years after the termination of the service, though here the claimant has to satisfy an initial evidential burden.[6]

The Royal Warrants issued during this war limited entitlement to injuries due to *war* service. By the Warrant of 1949 pensions could be awarded for disablement occasioned in peace-time service, and, with some qualifications, service in the Territorial and Reserve Forces.[7] Another major development has been the provision of additional benefits for seriously injured servicemen and their dependants, often to cover loss of earning capacity. These have generally been the same as the increases to disablement benefit for industrial injuries.

In 1978 two important reforms took place.[8] The scheme regulating the benefits for the three services was consolidated in a single Order in Council;[9] and this (together with any amendment) is now issued as a statutory instrument, which must be laid before Parliament. The structure of pensions and allowances has remained substantially unchanged since the reforms after the Second World War. The critical scrutiny undertaken of, and the major reforms proposed for, the industrial injury scheme[10] did not directly affect war pensions, but the policy considerations are clearly comparable. In the 1981 White Paper the government announced that it intended to review the war pensions scheme to consider whether it would be appropriate to redistribute resources currently devoted to it.[11]

C Policy

Mention has been made of the privileged position of war pensioners. Not only is there the strong presumption in certain cases that a serviceman suffering from a disability is entitled to a pension, but the level and range of awards is wider than that afforded by other benefits for people suffering from similar disabilities. The most obvious analogy is industrial disablement benefit, which also compensates for a mere disability, not necessarily related to loss of earning capacity.[12] War pensions compare favourably with this benefit, however, in the matters of burden of proof, the absence of any requirement that the injury be attributable to an 'accident' as distinct from a continuous process of events,[13] the concept of 'war' or 'service risk' which is wider than that of 'course of employment',[14] and the range of allowances which supplement the basic disablement benefit in the two cases. It is only relatively recently that the popular appeal of this privileged position has been doubted; in a poll it was found that 82 per cent of those interviewed

4 See Fitzgibbons 31 Iowa L Rev 1 at 13–16.
5 For the weaker presumptions in the claimant's favour in industrial injuries cases, see pp. 282 and 291, above.
6 Royal Warrant (RW) 1964 (Cmnd 2467), art 5: see p. 351, below.
7 RW 1949 (Cmd 6499).
8 Following SS(MP)A 1977, s.12.
9 SI 1978/1525.
10 Pp. 261–262, above.
11 *Reform of the Industrial Injuries Scheme*, para 8.
12 Pp. 297–309, above.
13 Cp for industrial injuries, pp. 268–270, above.
14 Cp pp. 271–287, above.

thought that all disabled people should be given the same benefits irrespective of the cause of their handicap.[15]

Two explanations may be adduced for the traditional preferences given to war pensioners. In the first place, the force of popular sentiment cannot be overestimated. It is this which was responsible for the frequency of parliamentary debates and questions in both wars. In the First World War the facts that the numbers involved were so large, and that frequently the wounded or killed would be conscripts, reinforced the general feeling that those disabled and their families should be generously treated.[16] This political factor has been reinforced by the pressure exerted by the British Legion (now the Royal British Legion) and other ex-servicemen's organisations.

Secondly, it is argued[17] that many of those who are injured in, for example, an industrial accident will have a right of action in tort against the person responsible for the injuries. This certainly accounts for many of those injured in factory and traffic accidents. But a serviceman has generally no right of action in respect of injuries suffered while in combat or in training. Section 10 of the Crown Proceedings Act 1947 provides that neither a member of the armed forces on duty nor the Crown shall be liable for injuries suffered by another member of the forces, if the latter is on duty and the Crown certifies that the injury (or death) will be treated as attributable to service for entitlement to a pension.[18] This argument is analogous to those which were used to justify the special provision for those injured in industrial accidents. The introduction of workmen's compensation in 1897 was partly justified because of the contemporary limitations on common law claims, in particular the defences of volenti non fit injuria and common employment.[19]

Although this second argument cannot be entirely ignored, it does not seem convincing. First, it is not obvious why greater state provision should be made for those whose common law rights of action are excluded by special defences, whether statutory or common law, than for those who never have any right at all. If the emphasis is placed on the criterion of need, as it arguably should be, there seems little reason for putting those injured in service in any special position with regard to state benefits. Moreover, this second argument is wholly irrelevant to the justification for another legal privilege of some war pensioners, the exemption of widow's pension from income tax,[20] and the estates of those who have died from wounds inflicted during active service from capital transfer tax.[1] This suggests that the matter is really one of the popular sentiment that those who have been wounded or die in the service of their country are entitled to some special measure of compensation from the state.

15 See Mr D Price, in Standing Committee B Debates on the Social Security Benefits Bill 1975, col 149.

16 Nothing else would have been compatible with Lloyd George's pledge in 1918 to make 'a fit country for heroes to live in'.

17 See the letter by the National Chairman of the Royal British Legion to *The Times*, 4 February 1975.

18 This does not mean, however, that an injured soldier, or the family of a dead soldier, is assured of a pension or tort damages. In *Adams v War Office* [1955] 3 All ER 245, [1955] 1 WLR 1116, it was held by Glyn-Jones J that the issue of a certificate only enabled a claim to be made on the basis of attributability; it did not entitle the claimant to a pension, and he would fail if the other conditions imposed by the Royal Warrant were not satisfied.

19 See *Atiyah* pp. 360–361.

20 Finance (No 2) Act 1979, s.9.

1 Fiance Act 1975, Sch 7, para 7. For the history of this exemption (previously from estate duty) see Dymond *Death Duties* (15th edn) pp. 1172–1185.

Part 2 Entitlement

A General

The fundamental principle is that a war pension may only be awarded when the disablement or death of the member of the forces is due to service.[2] There must, therefore, be some causal connection between the service and the injury or death; it is not enough that either occurred *during* service.[3] Although, as will be seen, this principle has been applied liberally for the benefit of the serviceman and his dependants, it has often been attacked as unnecessarily restrictive, particularly during the Second World War. It was contended that a war pension should be awarded in respect of any serviceman who died or suffered injury or disease while serving in the forces, irrespective of the cause of the disablement. The need to show some causal connection between service and the disability was arguably productive of too many difficult border line decisions. Manpower and time were wasted in arriving at these, and, it was said, inevitably some deserving claims were rejected.[4] The maxim, 'fit for service, fit for pension', however, never attracted the government. The White Paper of July 1943[5] rejected it partly on the ground that a disablement entirely unrelated to service should be covered by general social security provisions. Another reason was that to treat indiscriminately all disablement arising during service would be to do less than justice to those whose injury or illness was genuinely due to the dangers and risks of service. Since 1945 the fundamental entitlement principle has rarely been criticised; this is perhaps largely attributable to the more generous criteria of eligibility which were introduced towards the end of the war by the relevant Warrant and statutory orders,[6] and their subsequent treatment by the authorities responsible for the adjudication of claims: the Secretary of State; the Pensions Appeal Tribunal and (on questions of law only) the nominated High Court judge.[7]

Article 4 of the Service Pensions Order sets out the basic conditions for entitlement to a pension on a claim in respect of disablement brought within seven years of the end of the member's service; or when the death of a member occurs within that period, whenever the claim is brought:

> Where, not later than 7 years after the termination of the service of a member of the military forces, a claim is made in respect of a disablement of that member, or the death occurs of that member and a claim is made (at any time) in respect of that death, such disablement or death, as the case may be, shall be accepted as due to service . . . provided it is certified that —
> (a) the disablement is due to an injury which —
> (i) is attributable to service; or
> (ii) existed before or arose during service and has been and remains aggravated thereby; or
> (b) the death was due to or hastened by —
> (i) an injury which was attributable to service; or
> (ii) the aggravation by service of an injury which existed before or arose during service.

2 SI 1978/1525, art 3.
3 This principle is similar to that prevailing in the industrial injuries scheme: see p. 281, above.
4 See 391 HC Official Report (5th series) cols 716 ff, esp. col 827.
5 Changes in War Pensions (Cmd 6459).
6 RW 1943 (Cmd 6489) (army); SR & O 1944/99 (navy); HM Order 1943–44, HC 7 (air force).
7 See pp. 617–620, below, for discussion of adjudication.

Article 5 is concerned with entitlement when the claim for disablement is brought, or the death occurs, more than seven years after termination of service. The principles governing the issue of a certificate are the same as those in article 4 except in three important respects. The first relates to the burden of proof: for claims under article 5, the onus of proving that the disablement or death was due to service is initially on the serviceman, while under article 4 it is for the Secretary of State to rebut the presumption of this causal link.[8] Secondly, for the purposes of article 5 it must be certified that 'the death was due to or *substantially* hastened by' an injury attributable to or aggravated by service.[9] Thirdly, while both articles cover only cases of disablement attributable to, or aggravated by, service since 2 September 1939,[10] article 5 provides that an award may be made in respect of death more than seven years after the end of service, irrespective of the date of that service.

B Disablement

'Disablement' means physical or mental injury or damage, or the loss of physical or mental capacity.[11] A successful claim may, therefore, be made for acute hysteria or neurosis, provided, of course, that it is attributable to, or aggravated by, service.[12] 'Injury' is defined as including 'wound or disease'.[13] There is virtually no limit, therefore, to the quality or type of impairment which may entitle the claimant to a war pension, though many difficult cases naturally concern claims in respect of illness and disease where the causation issue is complex. As a consequence of the alternative definition of 'disablement', it has been held that a claimant may be entitled in respect of his injury, even though he has not suffered any loss of capacity for work or the ènjoyment of life.[14] In this case, however, a nil assessment will be made until the time when the injury causes a loss of flexibility or movement in the injured limb, or some other handicap.

Occasionally the question arises whether a particular disease is a separate phenomenon from another injury or illness for which a claim has already been made.[15] If an acute anxiety state is brought about by worry over a disease, in respect of which a pension is already being paid, the appropriate course is to apply for an increase in the assessment for the first disease, not to make an entirely new claim.[16] The test would appear to be whether the further condition is a separate disease rather than part of the accepted illness or injury.

8 Pp. 345–351, below.
9 P. 351, below.
10 Claims for disablement in the 1914–1918 war, of which there are very few, are brought under the Royal Warrants of 1919 (Cmd 457), and 1920 (Cmd 811).
11 SI 1978/1525, Sch 3, Item 22.
12 Cp the more restrictive position under the civilians' scheme, where recovery is limited to personal injuries, p. 363, below.
13 SI 1978/1525, Sch 3, Item 27.
14 *Harris v Minister of Pensions* [1948] 1 KB 222, [1948] 1 All ER 191.
15 E.g. *Secretary of State for Social Services v Yates* (1969) 5 WPAR 765. (The War Pensions Appeal Reports (WPAR) are available for consultation at the DHSS, though they are not published.)
16 *Goodman JA v Minister of Pensions* (1951) 5 WPAR 13. See 5th Report of the PCA, 1972–73 HC 406, Case No C33/T.

C 'Attributable to service'

i General principles

A war pension will be awarded if it is certified that the disablement or death is due to an injury attributable to service. Before the changes introduced by the Royal Warrant of December 1943, the injury had to be '*directly* attributable to service'; the removal of the qualifying adverb was one of the relaxations introduced by the coalition government to ease the conditions for entitlement under the war pensions schemes.[17] The question whether the injury is attributable to service is one of fact, but the nominated judge will allow an appeal by either the claimant or the Secretary of State if the appeal tribunal has applied the wrong principles of law in arriving at its decision.[18] A tribunal makes a mistake of law if it holds that a particular injury or type of disease cannot be attributable to war service merely because a previous decision of the judge in another case was to the effect that that injury or disease was not then attributable to service.[19] In each case the Secretary of State (or medical board) and, on appeal the tribunal, must consider all the circumstances, and must not be bound by previous decisions regarding the same type of injury.

The court's attitude on questions of attributability has been shown clearly in the 'pre-existing disposition' cases. The particular issue there was whether it should be held that a disease or neurosis was attributable to service when the soldier's pre-existing temperament or disposition made him especially vulnerable to it. The court has consistently held that where service brought on a disease, which did not exist before, it was attributable to the service; only if the soldier's condition before service actually amounted to the illness in question, albeit a latent illness, could it be held that the service merely aggravated the injury.[20] Denning J stated the principle to be as follows:

> The task of the Minister and of the tribunal is to ascertain what are the causes of the arising of the disease, not to assess their relative potency. If one of the causes is war service the disease is attributable to war service, even though there may be other causes and, it may be, more powerful causes, operating, and to which it is also attributable.[1]

The court's refusal to evaluate the relative weight of service and other factors in bringing about the disablement, coupled with the fact that the onus of proof is on the Secretary of State in those cases where the claim is brought, or the death occurs, within seven years of the end of service, has meant that in practice the criteria for entitlement are generous. On the other hand, the court has been aware that the law does not embody the maxim, 'fit for service, fit for pension', so that in a number of circumstances a pension has been refused although the disability arose during the

17 See the White Paper, n. 5, above, and the Debate in the House of Commons introduced by Sir J Anderson, Lord President of the Council, 391 HC Official Report (5th series) cols 716–722.

18 *Horsfall v Minister of Pensions* (1944) 1 WPAR 7. Cf pp. 619–620, below.

19 See *Freeman v Minister of Pensions and National Insurance* [1966] 2 All ER 40, [1966] 1 WLR 456 (suicide); *Kincaid v Minister of Pensions* (1948) 2 WPAR 1423 (leukaemia).

20 E.g. *Baird v Minister of Pensions* (1946) 1 WPAR 169; *O'Neill v Minister of Pensions* (1947) 1 WPAR 839. Similar principles have been employed in industrial injuries cases in determining whether an accident caused an injury, to which the claimant's previous condition rendered him more susceptible, p. 270, above.

1 *Marshall v Minister of Pensions* [1948] 1 KB 106 at 109.

claimant's period of service. Three types of cases have proved particularly difficult.

ii Anxiety states

In the first, the question has been whether an acute anxiety state was attributable to service. In one decision it was held that the strain of hard training, followed by the worry induced by orders for foreign service, might well be the precipitating cause of the claimant's acute neurosis, although there was medical evidence to the effect that he had an unstable personality.[2] On the other hand, in two cases, the nominated judge, Denning J, held that the claimant's worry about his wife's relations with other men while he was in the army, leading in both cases to acute neurosis, could not be held attributable on the facts to service.[3] The husband's enforced separation from his wife was not the cause, but only the circumstance in which the real cause of the illness, the wife's conduct, operated. It is not easy to reconcile these cases, and the latter two decisions may be thought wrongly decided in the light of Denning J's principle set out earlier.

iii Suicide etc.

The second difficult question is whether suicide can ever be said to be caused by service in the forces. In *XY v Minister of Pensions*,[4]

> the deceased's fiancée attempted to persuade him to marry her while he was on embarkation leave. He refused, and shortly after his return to service, she wrote calling off the engagement; he then shot himself. Denning J held that the tribunal was right not to attribute the death to service.

However, in a more recent decision,[5] it was held that the suicide was so attributable; the deceased took his life because of the pain and anxiety resulting from a disability which was itself due to service. Edmund Davies J emphasised that each case should be decided on its own facts, and that there is no rule of law prohibiting a suicide's dependants claiming a war pension. A similar problem arises when the deceased accidentally takes his own life through the administration of an overdose.

> A surgeon lieutenant, who suffered from sleeplessness, took an overdose of chloral hydrate, thus straining a weak heart and thereby killing himself. Denning J held that his death was the result of an act exclusively in the deceased's personal sphere, and was not attributable to service.[6]

2 *Hollorn v Minister of Pensions* [1947] 1 All ER 124.

3 *W v Minister of Pensions* [1946] 2 All ER 501; *R J v Minister of Pensions* (1947) 1 WPAR 351.

4 [1947] 1 All ER 38. The decision was followed by *Miers v Minister of Pensions* (1964) 5 WPAR 673, where the deceased shot himself after worries about his army career and promotion prospects. See p. 332, above, for the problem in industrial death benefit cases.

5 *Freeman v Minister of Pensions* [1966] 2 All ER 40, [1966] 1 WLR 456.

6 *Wedderspoon v Minister of Pensions* [1947] KB 662, followed by *Monaghan v Minister of Pensions* (1947) 1 WPAR 971 (where the deceased choked after drinking a bottle of raw spirit found during the Allied advance into Belgium). But cp *Jones v Minister of Pensions* [1946] 1 All ER 312, where it was held that the mere fact that the claimant adopted a course of action within his own control – failure to report sick – did not mean that service was not a cause of his illness.

iv Claimant on leave, etc.

The third line of cases where causation presents particular problems occurs when the serviceman is injured or killed when on leave, or temporarily away from camp.[7] This has been the topic of political debate as well as legal argument. The 1943 White Paper[8] stated that the Ministry of Pensions would relax its attitude to claims in respect of accidents occasioned outside the serviceman's place of duty; it would in future treat accidents sustained in the soldier's spare time, or while he was travelling to and from home on short leave, or when he was travelling between his place of duty and privately arranged accommodation (if he were allowed to live out) as attributable to war service. But an injury or illness arising during a period of full leave would not be treated as so attributable. The nominated judge, however, has pointed out that question of attributability must be decided solely on the facts in the light of the legal provisions. Thus, a bicycling accident suffered on the claimant's day-off,[9] and an accident at the claimant's home where, owing to a lack of room in the barracks, he was billetted,[10] have both been held not to be attributable to service. On the other hand, in two cases the judge held that an injury while on full leave was so attributable. In the first,[11] Denning J held that the injury suffered by a soldier who shot himself in the left foot while cleaning his rifle on embarkation leave was attributable to war service; in the second,[12] Ormerod J decided that the appellant shot in the back with a blank cartridge by some cadets on shooting practice was entitled to a pension, although the incident occurred while he was on leave; the decisive fact was that he was required to wear uniform which may have created the impression in the cadets' minds that he was involved in their exercise!

v Miscellaneous cases

The court has had less difficulty in other situations. Injuries occasioned by playing a game for the serviceman's own amusement are not attributable to service,[13] nor are injuries resulting from private fights between soldiers[14] or from assaults by third parties entirely unrelated to the military character of the victim.[15] But even if the initial injury is not attributable to service, negligent treatment in hospital will enable the claimant to be considered for a pension, if he went to that particular hospital because he was a serviceman, rather than merely because it was the nearest available.[16]

vi Critique

It is difficult to detect any clear principle or policy running through these decisions, despite the attempt by the nominated judges, particularly Denning J, to formulate one. On the one hand, they have been concerned to award a pension when the service has any real causal connection with

7 There are analogous problems in the industrial injuries scheme, when the accident occurs while the employee is travelling, pp. 276–279, above.
8 Changes in War Pensions (Cmd 6459).
9 *Standen v Minister of Pensions* (1947) 1 WPAR 905.
10 *Ridley v Minister of Pensions* [1947] 2 All ER 437.
11 *Williams v Minister of Pensions* [1947] 2 All ER 564.
12 *Giles v Minister of Pensions* (1955) 5 WPAR 445.
13 *Horsfall v Minister of Pensions,* n. 18 above; cf, on industrial injuries, p. 275, above.
14 *Richards v Minister of Pensions* (1956) 5 WPAR 631.
15 *Gaffney v Minister of Pensions* (1952) 5 WPAR 97.
16 *Minister of Pensions v Horsey* [1949] 2 KB 526, [1949] 2 All ER 314. See also *Buxton v Minister of Pensions* (1948) 1 WPAR 1121.

the injury or disease, but on the other hand, they have carefully refrained from holding a claimant entitled merely because the service was a cause (*causa sine qua non*) of the disablement. The case-law sometimes resembles in its apparent inconsistency the decisions of the Commissioners interpreting the 'out of and in the course of employment' test for entitlement to industrial injuries benefit.[17] The absence of such a two-limbed test in the war pensions provisions makes the reasoning less complex than in the Commissioner's rulings, but the results are often as hard to understand. For example, it is difficult to see why a claimant cleaning his rifle on leave should succeed,[18] while a claimant suffering neurosis about his absent wife when he was actually in service failed.[19] In the last resort the decision will depend on the court's judgment how closely related the injury is to the incidents of service life.

D Aggravated by service

The issue whether the claimant is entitled to a pension because service has aggravated an injury, which is primarily attributable to other causes, only arises if it is first found that his injury was not attributable to service conditions.[20] The difference between an award on the basis of attributability and an award on the basis of aggravation is that in the former case the pension is paid as long as the disability continues, while in the latter, it is payable only so long as the disability remains aggravated by the service conditions.[1]

It must be certified that the disablement is due to an injury which 'has been *and remains aggravated*' by service.[2] The construction of this part of Article 4 was considered in the leading case, *Shipp v Minister of Pensions*.[3] Denning J held that it did not mean that the disablement must be found to be aggravated by service at the time the claim was made, or at the date of the Minister's decision. Such a construction would penalise those who made late claims or whose claims were handled slowly by the Ministry; the words must be read as meaning, 'and remains aggravated or remained aggravated during the period of disablement'.[4] A claim may, therefore, be made in respect of a past disablement. However, where a claim in respect of a disablement is brought under article 5 more than seven years after the end of service, the aggravation must remain at the time the claim is made, though it need not subsist after that date.[5] In this case it is reasonable to require the aggravation to remain at this time in view of the long period which has passed since discharge from service. In all cases the tribunal is entitled to consider whether the aggravation remains at the date of the hearing before it, provided the claimant has been told that the question will be raised.[6]

The judge has held that the Secretary of State and tribunal should be reluctant to conclude that the injury is no longer aggravated by service

17 See pp. 271–287, above.
18 *Williams v Minister of Pensions*, n.11, above.
19 *W v Minister of Pensions*, n.3, above.
20 E.g. *Baird v Minister of Pensions* (1946) 1 WPAR 1121.
1 See Denning J in *Marshall v Minister of Pensions*, n.1, above, at 108.
2 SI 1978/1525, art 4(1)(a)(ii).
3 [1946] 1 KB 386.
4 Ibid, at 390.
5 SI 1978/1525, art 5(3).
6 *Ansell v Minister of Pensions* (1948) 3 WPAR 2237.

unless the evidence is quite clear.[7] The reason is that once an award on this basis has been terminated, it cannot be revived. The award should only be terminated if the claimant is in no worse a condition than he was in before the service, or if the disease has progressed to the same extent as it would have done if the man had not been in service.[8] The tribunal may take into account the fact that the claimant is working full-time in coming to its conclusion whether the injury remains aggravated by service.[9]

Rather oddly, aggravation by service may occur before the onset of a disease. Thus, where the serving-man was so weakened by his period of service that he was unable to resist typhoid contracted on leave, his widow was awarded a pension.[10] The reasoning is that the disease, though not attributable to service, was more acute because of his weakened condition. A difficult question arose in *Sullivan v Secretary of State for Social Services*:[11]

> C was discharged in 1962 on the ground of a gastric ulcer attributable to service in respect of which he was awarded a pension. Six years later he claimed a further award on the ground of his anxiety state which arose when he gave up the French horn because of the ulcer. The Secretary of State and tribunal rejected this claim. Willis J concluded it could reasonably be held that C's anxiety state was not attributable to service; but on the alternative argument based on aggravation, the tribunal was wrong to hold that the service factors must cause a deterioration of a condition *before discharge* for an aggravation claim to be made. The aggravation, as in this case, could arise subsequently to the discharge.

As in attributability cases, the problem sometimes arises whether the serviceman's own responsibility for the course of action which leads to the disablement or death precludes a finding that service aggravated the injury.[12] In *Jones v Minister of Pensions*,[13] a hardworking officer with a strong sense of duty refused to report sick. About eighteen months later he died from cancer. Denning J held that the officer's conduct was a reasonable response to the pressures of war service, which was, therefore, responsible for aggravating the disease and so hastening his death.

E Burden of proof

Before 1943 the burden of proof was on the serviceman. The imposition of the burden on the Minister in those cases governed by article 4, where the claim is brought within seven years of the end of service, so that it is for him to show the absence of any connection between service and the injury, was the most important of the reforms made in that year.[14] However, under article 5 an initial burden of proof is on the applicant, so this provision must be considered separately. One point, however, is common to both articles: it is for the applicant to prove that there is a disablement.[15] It is only after this is shown that the cause of the disablement must be considered.

7 *Sanders v Minister of Pensions* (1948) 4 WPAR 31.
8 *Whitt v Minister of Pensions* (1947) 1 WPAR 343.
9 *Collicott v Minister of Pensions* (1948) 3 WPAR 1715.
10 *Bridge v Minister of Pensions* (1946) 1 WPAR 139.
11 (1971) 5 WPAR 799.
12 P. 345, above.
13 [1946] 1 All ER 312.
14 See p. 339, above, for the reforms made in the Second World War.
15 *Royston v Minister of Pensions* [1948] 1 All ER 778.

i Claims under article 4

The relevant provisions of article 4 are:

> (2) . . . in no case shall there be an onus on any claimant under this Article to prove the fulfilment of the conditions set out in paragraph (1)[16] of this Article and the benefit of any reasonable doubt shall be given to the claimant.
>
> (3) . . . where an injury which has led to a member's discharge or death during service was not noted in a medical report made on that member on the commencement of his service, a certificate under paragraph (1) of this Article shall be given unless the evidence shows that the conditions set out in that paragraph are not fulfilled.

a *Article 4(2)*

The judical interpretation of this article has undergone several vicissitudes. The question is whether it imposes on the Secretary of State the general civil burden of proof – to make out his case on the balance of probabilities – or whether it imposes the stricter criminal burden of proof – to show beyond reasonable doubt that the injury was not attributable to, nor aggravated by, service. On a literal construction the latter seems the correct answer, but, as the court has observed,[17] the problem has been complicated by the connected question of the relationship between article 4(2) and article 4(3).

At first both the High Court in England[18] and the Court of Session in Scotland[19] took the view that the burden of proof under article 4(2) was the criminal one. The one difference between article 4(2) and 4(3) was said to be that under the former the issue was to be decided by weighing the evidence adduced by the Minister and the applicant, while under the latter the applicant could rely merely on the presumption.[20] But in *Miller v Minister of Pensions*[1] Denning J held that the burden imposed by article 4(2) was only the ordinary civil one, that is, the Minister had to show on a balance of probabilities that injury was not caused by service conditions. So, although there was medical evidence in the case that it was impossible to show beyond reasonable doubt that war conditions could play no part in causing cancer of the gullet, it was ruled that the relative incidence of the disease in servicemen (approximately seven cases a year out of an average annual total of 1,700) made it clear on a balance of probabilities that the cancer was not attributable to service. In contrast, the judge said that article 4(3) imposed the criminal burden of proof.

The previous position, however, was restored by Edmund Davies J in *Judd v Minister of Pensions*.[2]

> During an exercise in the course of army service, the claimant fell from a strong rope and sustained back injuries. He continued to complain of lumbar pains which were assessed at 30 per cent of a full disability pension. Twenty years later cervical spondylosis was diagnosed, but the Minister and the tribunal rejected any connection between this and the claimant's service, the tribunal stating that it was shown on the balance of probabilities that service had not caused or worsened the disability.

16 See p. 342, above.
17 See Edmund Davies J in *Judd v Minister of Pensions* [1966] 2 QB 580 at 591.
18 *Starr v Minister of Pensions* [1946] 1 KB 345, [1946] 1 All ER 400; *Rowing v Minister of Pensions* [1946] 1 All ER 664.
19 *Irving v Minister of Pensions* 1945 SC 21.
20 Denning J, in *Starr v Minister of Pensions,* n.18, above, at 350.
1 [1947] 2 All ER 372.
2 N.17, above.

Edmund Davies J decided this was the wrong test and, on the facts, made an award.[3]

The judge stated that the opening words of article 4(2) imposed at least the ordinary civil burden on the Minister, and that the concluding words of the paragraph would be redundant if the burden were no higher than that.

A perennial problem has been the application of the principles of proof where the aetiology of the disease concerned is unknown, and surmises about the part played by service conditions are necessarily conjectural. During the Second World War the Ministry had a list of diseases which, according to the weight of medical opinion, could not be held attributable to war service.[4] It was revised from time to time, and was used as a guide rather than as a determinant of particular applications.[5] Nevertheless, its use was criticised in Parliament, and certainly its employment was outside the legal provisions. The nominated judge has consistently ruled that the evidence must show that it is improbable that the service played any part.[6] The leading authority now is *Coe v Minister of Pensions and National Insurance*.[7]

C claimed a pension when symptoms of Behcet's syndrome (a disease causing blindness) appeared 14 months after he had left the navy. The claim was rejected by the Minister as the aetiology of the disease was not known, and it seemed improbable that any service factors could have been responsible. The appeal tribunal dismissed C's appeal, but Edmund Davies J allowed it on the ground that the approach adopted by the Ministry and tribunal imposed an onus on the applicant.

Three rules were laid down to assist the Minister and tribunals in determining such claims.

(1) If the medical evidence is that nothing at all is known about the aetiology of the disease, then neither the presumption in article 4(2), nor that in article 4(3), is rebutted.
(2) If there is evidence before the tribunal to the effect that the disease is one which arises and progresses independently of service factors, then the presumption is rebuttable even if the precise origins are not known.
(3) It is not enough for the Ministry to argue that there is no evidence suggesting any connection between the onset of the disease and service conditions.

As attributability is a question of fact,[8] there is nothing to prevent tribunals coming to different conclusions on the attributability to service of a particular disease of unknown origin; but they must apply the correct test with regard to the onus of proof.[9]

3 The usual course is for the nominated judge to remit the case to the tribunal to reconsider, but in some cases the judge himself is prepared to make an award: See *Moxon v Minister of Pensions* [1945] KB 490, [1945] 2 All ER 124. See p. 620, below, for the nominated judge's powers.
4 Sir W Wormersley, Minister of Pensions, 391 HC Official Report (5th series) cols 796–798.
5 Sir W Wormersley, Minister of Pensions, 402 HC Official Report (5th series) col 1644.
6 *Smith AS v Minister of Pensions* (1947) 1 WPAR 495; *Donovan v Minister of Pensions* (1947) 1 WPAR 609.
7 [1967] 1 QB 238, [1966] 3 All ER 172.
8 P. 344, above.
9 Edmund Davies J in *Coe v Minister of Pensions*, n.7, above, at 243.

b *'The compelling presumption' under article 4(3)*
The presumption applies whenever the serviceman is discharged, or dies, because of an injury not noted in the medical report which was made on him at the start of his service. Its effect is that the pension will be awarded, unless it is shown beyond reasonable doubt that the injury was not attributable to, or aggravated by, service.[10] The serviceman who is invalided has the advantage that his case is automatically considered by the Department.[11] There is no need for him (or his dependants if he is killed) formally to apply for a pension. In cases under article 4(3) the nominated judge has held that the tribunal should look at all the facts[12] and it is not bound to accept that the diagnosis which led to the man's discharge was correct.[13]

ii Claims under article 5
Paragraph (2) of this article provides that where a claim is brought, or the death occurs, more than seven years after the end of service, the disablement or death shall only be certified as due to, or substantially hastened by, service if 'it is shown that the conditions' set out in the article are fulfilled. Paragraph (4) states that where on reliable evidence a reasonable doubt exists whether they are fulfilled, the benefit of that doubt should be given to the claimant. The leading case is *Dickinson v Minister of Pensions*[14] construing the identical provisions in the 1949 Royal Warrant.[15]

> A widow claimed that her husband's death from a coronary was substantially hastened by worry brought on by neurasthenia which in its turn had been aggravated by war service. The Ministry and tribunal dismissed her claim as she had not produced sufficient reliable evidence in its support. Ormerod J upheld the tribunal's approach.

The clear words of article 5(2) supported the general principle that it is for an applicant to make out his claim. Only when a tribunal has found that enough reliable evidence has been adduced in support of the application, is it bound under article 5(4) to give the benefit of any reasonable doubt to the claimant. This decision has been followed in England by the nominated judge in a case[16] arising under the equivalent provisions in the Personal Injuries (Civilians) Scheme 1964,[17] and in a Scottish case on the services' scheme.[18] The *Dickinson* case seems correct as a matter of interpretation of the provisions in the Pensions Order. It is also, it is submitted, right that where a claim is brought (or the death occurs) as long as seven years after the termination of the service, the claimant should be required to adduce some evidence that the disablement or death was connected with service in the forces.

10 *Birchenough v Minister of Pensions* (1949) 4 WPAR 635.
11 See Ministerial Statement, 401 HC Official Report (5th series) col 970.
12 *Troughear v Minister of Pensions* (1947) 1 WPAR 569.
13 *Hayden v Minister of Pensions* (1947) 1 WPAR 775.
14 *Dickinson v Minister of Pensions* [1953] 1 QB 228, [1952] 2 All ER 1031.
15 RW 1949 (Cmd 7699).
16 *Cadney v Minister of Pensions and National Insurance* [1965] 3 All ER 809, [1966] 1 WLR 80.
17 See p. 363, below.
18 *Minister of Social Security v Connolly* 1967 SLT 121.

F Serious negligence or misconduct

Article 6 provides that the Secretary of State may withhold, cancel or reduce an award on the ground that the injury or death 'was caused or contributed to, by the serious negligence or misconduct' of the serviceman. There is surprisingly little case-law on this provision, nor is there any indication how the responsible minister has applied his discretionary power. The two leading cases are both decisions of Ormerod J. In the first,[19] 'serious negligence' was defined 'as negligence of a quality that would certainly call for some criminal action if it were done in civil life'. However, shortly afterwards the judge said this remark was only obiter, and should be related to the particular facts of this case, in which the alleged 'serious negligence or misconduct' consisted in the careless riding of a motor-cycle. In the second case,[20] he, therefore, allowed the Minister's appeal and ruled that the applicant was guilty of serious negligence or misconduct in disobeying an order not to handle enemy ammunition.

It is possible to infer from the comparative dearth of reported decisions that article 6 has rarely been invoked; this may be because the view is taken that it should only apply in extreme circumstances. As in the industrial injuries system,[1] it is clear that the common law test of contributory negligence has no place in the war pensions scheme. But the latter differs from industrial injuries in providing that 'serious negligence or misconduct' may as such debar recovery.[2] In both systems wrongful conduct may lead to a ruling that the injury was not due to the employment or service.[3] Outside the situation where there is deliberate disobedience to orders it is hard to think of circumstances where the application of article 6 is necessary or appropriate.

Part 3 Awards for disablement

War pensions for disablement are payable only after the termination of service.[4] They consist of a basic award, assessed according to the degree of disablement, and a variety of allowances covering dependants, losses to earning capacity of, and the needs of, the more seriously disabled. Without parallel in the social security system, there are differences of treatment according to the rank of the serviceman.[5] Some of these are purely formal: pensions payable to officers are described as 'retired pay'; and this and other allowances for officers are expressed in annual sums and paid either monthly or quarterly, while those for other ranks are expressed and paid weekly. However, more substantially, a component in the basic award is also varied according to rank and this is not intended to reflect earning differentials for which, as has been mentioned, there is separate provision.

19 *Robertson v Minister of Pensions* (1952) 5 WPAR 245, 266.
20 *Minister of Pensions v Griscti* (1955) 5 WPAR 457. This approach is consonant with that of Denning J in *Williams v Minister of Pensions* [1947] 2 All ER 564, where the case was sent back to the tribunal to consider whether the applicant, in shooting himself in the foot, had been guilty of serious negligence or misconduct.
1 P. 285, above.
2 Pp. 327–328, above.
3 Pp. 268, 345, above.
4 SI 1978/1525, art 8(2). In the case of an officer it is payable when he ceases to be on the Active List.
5 The complex rules for determining the relevant rank of a member of the forces for war pension purposes are set out ibid, art 7.

In the light of current social values, these aspects of the scheme must appear to be anachronistic and it is no doubt for this reason that successive governments have not increased the component since 1964.

A The basic award

The principles for assessing the basic award are in almost all material respects identical to those adopted by the industrial scheme; these have been fully analysed in chapter 8.[6] The degree of disablement is determined by comparing the condition of the disabled person with 'the condition of a normal healthy person of the same age and sex, without taking into account the earning capacity of the member in his disabled condition in his own or any other specific trade or occupation, and without taking into account the effect of any individual factors or extraneous circumstances'.[7] This is then expressed as a percentage, total disablement being represented by 100 per cent. A schedule to the Pensions Order sets out assessments for some particular injuries in the same form as is adopted for the industrial injuries scheme;[8] in other cases, the appropriate percentage is determined by the Secretary of State (in practice a medical officer or board of officers appointed by him) or on appeal by a pensions appeal tribunal.[9] Where the serviceman's condition has not stabilised, the assessment is made on an interim basis, and may be subsequently changed.[10] But apart from cases where the decision was reached on a mistaken basis, a final assessment may be revised only if there has been a substantial increase in the degree of disablement.[11]

A pension is payable for degrees of disablement between 100 per cent and 20 per cent inclusive.[12] For 1982–83, the maximum (for 100 per cent) expressed in terms of a weekly payment is £53.60. Awards for disablement of less than 20 per cent are paid as lump sum gratuities.[13] All these sums are supplemented by the rank additions: e.g. for a 100 per cent pension, a Rear-Admiral receives an additional annual sum of £270 and a corporal the weekly sum of £0.17.[14]

B Increases and additions

As under the industrial injuries scheme, there is a variety of supplementary allowances which may be paid to a war pensioner.[15] Although the usual formulation of eligibility is that 'a member of the military forces . . . *may be* awarded' the further allowance, it is not entirely clear that they should be regarded as discretionary. When it is clearly intended to confer a

6 Pp. 302–307, above.
7 SI 1978/1525, art 9(2)(a).
8 Ibid, Sch 1, Part V. Cf p. 303, above.
9 Pension Appeal Tribunals Act 1943, Sch, para 3, and see pp. 617–619, below.
10 SI 1978/1525, art 67(1)(b).
11 Ibid, art 67(1)(a). Cf the different ground for review in industrial injury cases, pp. 307–308, above.
12 SI 1978/1525, art 10.
13 Ibid, art 11.
14 Ibid.
15 Pp. 309–326, above.

discretion on the Secretary of State, this is expressly spelt out in the Pensions Order.[16]

i Allowances for member of the claimant's family

a *General allowance for dependants*

Under the industrial injuries scheme, dependency allowances are paid with disablement benefit only if the claimant is permanently incapable of work.[17] This condition has never been applied to war pensioners and presumably because governments have regarded this distinction as anomalous, the allowances have been allowed to dwindle to a token amount and in the case of a second or subsequent child abolished altogether.[18] There are three categories of adult dependants for whom an increase may be paid: a wife; an unmarried dependant living with the claimant as his wife and caring for a child of his; and a husband, if he was being substantially maintained by the claimant and is incapable of self-support.[19] As regards children, the allowance may be claimed only for the eldest who is under 16 (or under 19 and undergoing full-time education) and then only if no adult dependency allowance is payable.[20] In all cases, the allowance is a proportionate part of £0.60 per week, according to the degree of the claimant's disablement.[1]

b *Education allowance*

This may be paid subject to certain prescribed conditions, most importantly, that the child must be at least five, that the circumstances of the family must be such as to require the extra payment, and that the Secretary of State is satisfied that the type of education concerned is suitable.[2] The amount of the supplement is determined by him, subject to a maximum (for 1982–83, £120 per annum). There is no equivalent allowance in the industrial injuries scheme.

ii Reduced earning capacity allowances

This second group of supplementary payments is designed to compensate the war pensioner for the reduced opportunities for earning which he suffers owing to his disabilities. To some extent, they counterbalance the inflexibility of the basic award, which, as has been said,[3] does not take into account loss of, or reduced, earning capacity.[4]

a *Unemployability allowance*

This is equivalent to the unemployability supplement payable under the industrial injuries scheme,[5] but unlike that benefit it does not require the claimant to prove that he is likely to remain *permanently* incapable of

16 E.g. SI 1978/1525, art 12(3): 'The award, continuance and amount of any allowance in respect of a wife, husband or child who is living apart from the member shall be at the discretion. . .'.
17 P. 310, above.
18 SI 1978/1404.
19 SI 1978/1525, art 12, as amended by SI 1978/1902.
20 SI 1978/1525, art 12(6)–(7), as amended by SI 1980/1955.
1 SI 1978/1525, art 12(2).
2 Ibid, art 13.
3 P. 353, above.
4 For a further discussion of this point, see pp. 297–299, above, in the context of industrial injuries.
5 Pp. 309–310, above.

work.[6] The serviceman may be deemed unemployable even though he has annual earnings up to a prescribed amount,[7] for 1982–83, £1,040. Awards may not, however, be accumulated with retirement pensions.[8] In addition to the personal allowance (in 1982–83, £34.85 per week), increases may also be payable for an adult (in 1982–83, £19.70 per week) and child dependants (in 1982–83, £7.95 per week).[9]

b *Invalidity allowance*

This further payment was introduced in 1971 to match the new form of provision available under the general contributory[10] and industrial injury schemes.[11] It is payable to a recipient of the unemployability allowance if that became payable five or more years before he (or she) reached pensionable age (65 or 60 for women) and that age had not been reached on 20 September 1971.[12] The amounts vary according to the date of onset of unemployability or any incapacity which immediately preceded it: the highest rate (in 1982–83, £6.90 per week) is paid if it fell before 5 July 1948 or when the claimant was under 40; the middle rate (in 1982–83, £4.40) if he was then under 50; and the lowest rate (in 1982–83, £2.20) in other cases.[13]

c *Allowance for lowered standard of occupation*

This allowance, which is payable for reduced earning capacity, is equivalent to the special hardship allowance available under the industrial injuries scheme.[14] The grounds of entitlement are virtually identical,[15] though in the case of a war pensioner his present earning capacity is generally compared with his regular occupation before he entered military service.[16] The allowance, when combined with the pension, may not exceed that payable for 100 per cent disablement,[17] and is in any event subject to a maximum (in 1982–83, £21.44 weekly).

iii Serious disablement allowances

This third group comprises a variety of further allowances which may be conferred in cases of serious disablement.

a *Constant attendance allowance*

This may be awarded in respect of a pensioned disablement, the degree of which is not less than 80 per cent, if it is shown to the Secretary of State's satisfaction that constant attendance is necessary because of the disablement.[18] In an exceptional case of severe disablement, the usual maximum amount payable (in 1982–83, £21.50 weekly) may be increased subject to a

6 SI 1978/1525, art 18(1).
7 Ibid, art 18(2).
8 Ibid, art 18(3), as substituted by SI 1979/113.
9 SI 1978/1525, art 18(4).
10 P. 165, above.
11 P. 310, above.
12 SI 1978/1525, art 19(1).
13 Ibid, Sch 1, Part IV, para 7, as substituted by SI 1979/113.
14 Pp. 310–323, above.
15 SI 1978/1525, art 21, which does not, however, provide for the alternative 'continuing condition' described at pp. 316–318, above.
16 SI 1978/1525, art 21(2).
17 Ibid, art 21(1).
18 SI 1978/1525, art 14.

limit (in 1982–83, £43.00 weekly) There are thus two maxima at which the allowance may be paid, compared with four in the similar provision in the industrial injuries scheme.[19]

b *Severe disablement occupational allowance*

Article 15 provides that a pensioner in receipt of a constant attendance allowance, which has been increased because of his severe disablement, may also receive this further allowance, 'for any period during which he is . . . ordinarily employed in a gainful occupation'. The object of this provision appears to be to compensate the exceptionally severely disabled pensioner who nevertheless is able to pursue an occupation. There is no parallel benefit in the industrial injuries system. It is paid at a flat-rate, in 1982–83, £10.75 weekly.

c *Exceptionally severe disablement allowance*

This was introduced, as was the equivalent provision in the industrial injuries system,[20] following the recommendations of the McCorquodale Committee on Assessment of Disablement.[1] It will be paid when the disablement is, and is in the Secretary of State's view likely to remain, one for which the higher rate of constant attendance allowance is payable, or would be if the serviceman were not in a hospital or other institution.[2] As with the industrial injuries supplement, entitlement is, therefore, geared to eligibility for the constant attendance allowance; however, it does not appear to depend on the pensioner's receipt of a 100 per cent disablement benefit.[3] The amount is (for 1982–83) £21.50 per week.

d *Treatment allowances*

A pensioner receiving medical treatment may claim an allowance equal to the 100 per cent disablement pension, but in lieu of the pension (at whatever rate) payable to him.[4] Unlike the equivalent provision in the industrial injuries scheme, this covers treatment at home as well as in hospital.[5] 'Treatment' is defined as 'a course of medical, surgical or rehabilitative treatment', which the Secretary of State is satisfied the pensioner should receive.[6] It excludes treatment which involves only an occasional interruption in the pensioner's normal work. In this situation, a part-time treatment allowance is payable,[7] subject to a maximum (in 1982–83) of £18.90 per day. In certain cases, increases may be paid for an adult dependant,[8] or where the pensioner has reached 65.[9] The allowance itself may be paid for a discretionary period when treatment as an in-patient at a hospital has been completed but the pensioner is still incapable of work.[10] Finally, the Secretary of State has a broad discretion to indemnify the claimant for 'any necessary expenses in respect of the

19 Pp. 324–325, above.
20 P. 325, above.
1 Committee on the Assessment of Disablement (1965, Cmnd 2647), para 9.
2 SI 1978/1525, art 15.
3 Cp p. 326, above.
4 SI 1978/1525, art 23(1)–(4).
5 Cp p. 323, above.
6 SI 1978/1525, art 23(13).
7 Ibid, art 25.
8 Ibid, art 23(5).
9 Ibid, art 23(2).
10 Ibid, art 24, provided he is not in receipt of an unemployability supplement.

medical, surgical or rehabilitative treatment . . . and of appropriate aids and adaptations for disabled living' where these are not provided under any other legislative scheme.[11]

e *Comforts allowance*
This supplement, like the following two, is without any equivalent in the industrial injuries scheme. It may be awarded where the claimant is in receipt of a constant attendance allowance, and *either* an employability allowance *or* a 100 per cent basic award from multiple injuries which, in the Secretary of State's view, are so serious as to justify the award of a comforts allowances.[12] The rate for 1982–83 is £9.30 weekly. A lower rate of comforts allowance (for 1982–83, £4.65 weekly) is payable to a pensioner who is in receipt of either the constant attendance allowance or the unemployability allowance.[13]

f *Allowance for wear and tear of clothing*
This is generally awarded to a pensioner who regularly wears an artificial limb.[14] Where one artificial limb is worn, the allowance is paid at a lower rate, in 1982–83, £46.00 per annum. A higher rate, £72.00 per annum, is payable where more than one such limb is worn, or the Secretary of State is satisfied that the wear and tear on the pensioner's clothing as a result of the disablement is exceptional.

g *Age allowance*
A supplement is paid to pensioners over 65 with a disablement assessed at 40 per cent or over.[15] This is paid at four different rates depending on whether the degree of pensioned disablement is 40 per cent – 50 per cent (£3.70 weekly), 50 per cent – 70 per cent (£5.85), 70 per cent – 90 per cent (£8.35), or over 90 per cent (£11.70).

Part 4 Awards in respect of death

A General

Awards may be made in respect of a death of a member of the forces which is due to service.[16] As with claims by disabled members of the forces, the conditions of entitlement depend on the date of the material event; in this case, however, they vary according to whether the *death* (rather than the claim in respect of that death) occurs less or more than seven years after the termination of service. If the death occurs not later than seven years after this, the death is to be accepted as due to service, provided it is certified that it was 'due to or hastened by *either* an injury attributable to service, *or* the aggravation by service of an injury which existed before or arose during service'.[17] Where the death occurs more than seven years after

11 Ibid, art 26.
12 Ibid, art 20(1)(a).
13 Ibid, art 20(1)(b).
14 Ibid, art 17(1)(a).
15 Ibid, art 22.
16 Ibid, art 27(1).
17 Ibid, art 4(1)(b). See pp. 344–348, above, for 'attributable to' and 'aggravated by' service.

service, it must be certified that it was due to, or *substantially* hastened by, an injury attributable to, or aggravated by, service.[18]

The general condition that death must be due to service is more restrictive than the approach which obtained in the First World War. Then a widow might receive what was termed a 'modified pension' (half the husband's pension) if he was in receipt of a war pension at the date of his death, even though the death itself was not caused by his war service. This provision seems to have been unique to the British war pensions scheme.[19] Awards of this type were not made after 1921. But there have been two modifications to the general position, though in the first case only for the benefit of widows, and not for all dependants. Since 1966 a temporary allowance has been payable for 26 weeks to the widow, or unmarried dependant who has lived as the wife of a severely disabled pensioner, whatever the cause of his death.[20] It is payable whenever the member of the forces was in receipt of a constant attendance or an unemployability allowance, or in a case where though eligible for the latter, he was in fact in receipt of the lowered standard of occupation allowance.[1] Additional allowances may be paid for this period for the serviceman's children. The second change provides that the death of a member of the forces in receipt of a constant attendance allowance (or one who would have been in receipt of this allowance if he had not been in hospital) is to be treated as due to service for the purposes of awards on his death.[2]

B Widows

As under the industrial injuries scheme,[3] there are two basic rates for widows' pensions. The higher rate (in 1982–83, £42.70 a week) is paid where the widow is not expected to join or rejoin the labour market: where she is over 40, or is in receipt of an allowance for the child of the deceased, or is incapable of self-support.[4] In other cases, the lower rate (in 1982–83, £9.86 a week) is paid.[5] As with disablement pensions, there are additions based on the deceased's rank,[6] but here the status differentials are taken even further, for the widows of the highest ranking officers (in the army, Lieutenant-Colonel and above) are always paid at the higher rate, whatever their age and family commitments. Clearly it is regarded as socially inappropriate for such widows to earn their livelihood!

A widow was formerly only entitled if she was living with the deceased at the date of his death or if the Secretary of State took the view that the separation was attributable to the soldier's mental instability. But this restriction was removed by the Royal Warrant of 1974.[7] A frequent source of controversy during the Second World War was the question whether

18 SI 1978/1525, art 5(1)(b).
19 See Comparative Tables of War Pension Rates in Allied Countries and Germany during Great War (1920, Cmd 474).
20 SI 1978/1525, art 33.
1 A person in receipt of the allowance for lowered standard of occupation may prefer not to apply for the unemployability allowance because of the loss of concurrent social security benefits.
2 SI 1978/1525, art 27(3).
3 Pp. 333–334, above.
4 SI 1978/1525, art 29(1)(a).
5 Ibid, art 29(1)(b).
6 Ibid, Sch 2, Part II, Tables 2 and 4, as amended.
7 Cmnd 5670, art 4.

pensions should only be paid to widows who had married the deceased before his disability arose. It was not until 1946 that the present position was reached that the date of marriage is irrelevant.[8]

An unmarried dependant who has been living as a wife of the member of the forces[9] may be awarded a pension on his death, as long as she has in her charge his child and is in receipt of a child allowance.[16] The amount of this pension is at the discretion of the Secretary of State, subject to a maximum, for 1982–83, £40.25 per week. A supplementary rent allowance may be paid to a widow, or an unmarried dependant, who has lived as a wife, provided the household includes a child. It is not, for 1982–83, to exceed £16.25 but is otherwise subject to the Secretary of State's discretion.[11] Although this provision may not appear generous, it is yet another respect in which the war pensions scheme is unusual. There is no other social security benefit (apart from supplementary benefits) where an allowance is paid for rent. A further allowance is paid to some widows of 65, and then at a higher level when they reach 70.[12]

These benefits cease on the remarriage or cohabitation of the widow (or other recipient).[13] Another feature of the status differential between officers and other ranks emerges at this point. On remarriage, the Secretary of State may award to widows of the latter a gratuity equal to one year's pension.[14] There is no such provision for officers' widows, but they may be more favourably placed in that on the death of the husband of the remarriage, the Secretary may at his discretion restore the lost pension. The Secretary of State has discretion to restore the widow's pension on termination of a period of cohabitation.[15]

C Widowers

A widower may be awarded a pension, where he was dependent on a female member of the armed forces, and is in pecuniary need and incapable of self-support.[16] The rate is at the discretion of the Secretary of State, subject to a maximum payment, for 1982–83, of £42.70 per week.

D Children

An allowance is payable for a child of the deceased if he is under 16, or an apprentice, or in full-time education, or incapable of self-support by reason of an infirmity which arose before he attained 16.[17] The rates (in 1982–83)

8 RW 1946 (Cmd 6799).
9 See SI 1978/1525, Sch 3, Item 51.
10 Ibid, art 30.
11 Ibid, art 31.
12 Ibid, art 32.
13 Ibid, art 42.
14 Ibid, art 42(4).
15 Ibid, art 42(3). Widows' benefits under the Social Security Act 1975 are automatically paid on the termination of cohabitation, for they are only suspended when this begins: p. 334, above.
16 SI 1978/1525, art 34: see p. 334, above, for the similar conditions for a widower's death benefit in industrial injuries.
17 SI 1978/1525, arts 35, 37.

are: for each child £11.25 a week. The amount is increased if the child is under 16 and is not under the control of the surviving parent.[18] Further, an education allowance may be payable in the same circumstances, and subject to the same maximum (£120 per annum), as those which obtain when a disabled serviceman claims this benefit.[19]

E Parents and other relatives

Despite constant pressure in the House of Commons for its reintroduction, the automatic allowance for the parents of a deceased serving-man, which had been payable in the First World War, was not provided in the Warrants issued during the Second World War and afterwards.[20] Article 40 provides that a parent may be awarded a pension only 'if he is in pecuniary need by reason of having reached the age of not less than sixty-five years in the case of a man, or sixty years in the case of a woman, or infirmity or other adverse condition which is not merely or a temporary character'.[1] The Secretary of State must take into account in determining need, the extent to which the deceased member before and during his service supported the parent, and the extent to which he was likely to continue doing so if he had not died. A pension cannot be awarded at all if a widow is in receipt of a pension in respect of the deceased serviceman, unless the parent was actually dependent on him. There is a considerable discretion as to the rate of benefit awarded to parents. There is a maximum and minimum rate (£1.00 and £0.25 a week), and these have not been increased since 1949.[2] Where both parents claim, it is for the Secretary of State to select which parent may receive the award.[3]

Any other person may be awarded a pension if he was dependent on the deceased and is in pecuniary need and incapable of self-support.[4] Not more than one such person may claim, except in the case of juvenile dependants, i.e. a brother, sister, grandchild of less than 16. The Secretary of State's decision as to which of two or more eligible dependants is to benefit is final. The maximum amount payable to an adult dependant, £1.00 a week, and for juvenile dependants £0.30 a week has also been allowed to dwindle in value. The total sum awarded to one parent and another dependant is not to exceed the maximum which may be awarded in exceptional circumstances where there are two eligible parents.[5]

18 Ibid, arts 35(3), 36.
19 Ibid, art 38; see p. 354, above.
20 387 HC Official Report (5th series) col 1511; 391, ibid, col 764; 433 ibid, col 159. See 1st Report of the PCA for 1975–76, HC 37, Case No C 291/V.
1 See p. 336, above, for the equivalent provision in industrial injuries, which employs a similar test for eligibility.
2 See the comparable failure to increase parent's death benefit in the industrial injuries scheme: ibid.
3 SI 1978/1525, art 40(8).
4 Ibid, art 41.
5 Ibid, art 41(4).

Part 5 General miscellaneous provisions

A Overlap provisions

The object of these provisions is to prevent overcompensation from public funds or from a combination of these funds and a damages award. Article 56 provides that the Secretary of State may take into account any other compensation which is, or may be, awarded a claimant and may withhold or reduce the pension or gratuity accordingly. Compensation which might have been obtained but for the unreasonable act or omission of the claimant may also be taken into account for this purpose. 'Compensation' means any periodical or lump sum payment in respect of death or disability for which provision is made under any statute, ordinance, regulation or scheme,[6] or any sum recoverable as damages at common law.[7] A similar rule applies to children who are provided for from public funds.[8] Another overlap measure enables a deduction to be made from a pension or gratuity where the claimant is being cared for in an institution which is supported by public funds, though this does not apply where he has entered it for the purpose of receiving medical or surgical treatment.[9] The pensions of servicemen entering Chelsea Hospital are terminated, but may be restored on departure from it.[10]

B Forfeiture provisions

The Secretary of State may withhold, or direct the forfeiture of, a pension on the ground that the person to, or in respect of whom, it has been awarded is serving a term of imprisonment or detention after a court order, or is deported from or required to leave the United Kingdom.[11] A forfeited pension may be restored upon terms imposed by the Secretary of State. The rule discussed in Part 4 under which a widow's pension may be terminated on remarriage or cohabitation is, of course, tantamount to a forfeiture provision.[12]

There are two other provisions analogous to forfeiture rules. Under the first, the Secretary of State may reduce a pension by not more than half, if the claimant refuses unreasonably to undergo medical, surgical or rehabilitative treatment.[13] Secondly, an award may be cancelled if a pension is not drawn for a continuous period of a year or more.[14]

C Commencing date of awards

Unlike other areas of the social security system,[15] there is no time limit on war pension claims. To avoid administrative difficulties, the general rule

6 This might include the Criminal Injuries Compensation schemes under which awards have been made to soldiers and their families in respect of the Northern Ireland troubles.
7 SI 1978/1525, art 55(3).
8 Ibid, art 58.
9 For the position where the pensioner is receiving medical treatment, see p. 356, above.
10 SI 1978/1525, art 57.
11 Ibid, art 62; cf under SSA 1975, pp. 398–401, below.
12 See p. 359, below.
13 SI 1978/1525, art 63: cf p. 328, above.
14 SI 1978/1525, art 64.
15 Cf pp. 557–564, below.

has traditionally been that awards are payable only from the date of claim. Since 1978, however, back payments can be made to the day after the termination of service if this was due to invaliding and it occurred not more than six months before the claim; where the termination does not result from invaliding, this earlier date applies only if the claim is brought within three months.[16] Even so, the Secretary of State has power to direct an earlier payment 'to any particular case or class of case'. His policy has generally been to do this only where there is substantial evidence that the serviceman was prevented from claiming earlier because of mental or physical disability, or it is clear that there has been some error in processing the claim.[17] In one situation, consequent upon a special report by the Parliamentary Commissioner, the DHSS made a direction back-dating awards in a class of cases not covered by the general rule. After the *Judd* decision,[18] the Department decided it would review any claim which had previously been rejected on the basis of the earlier rules with regard to the burden of proof. The DHSS accepted the Parliamentary Commissioner's recommendation that where a claim was accepted, payments should be made from 4 October 1965 (the date of the *Judd* judgment) rather than from the date when the revision was made.[19] Otherwise, the date of payment would have depended arbitrarily on the order in which the DHSS reviewed the claims.

Part 6 Other war pension and civilian schemes

There are a number of schemes similar to the war pensions scheme providing pensions for those outside the regular armed forces who are injured in war service. The conditions of entitlement are on the whole more restrictive in these schemes, due to the fact that for members of the forces pensionable disablement can be due to any aspect of service, whereas for civilians the disablement must be related specifically to the effects of war. They have been less liberally construed by the nominated judge than the equivalent requirements in the Service Pensions Order. One reason for this was that often the effect of allowing a claim by a merchant mariner or civilian for a pension was to debar him from pursuing his remedy under the workmen's compensation legislation or at common law.[20] In other respects, for example, on the questions of causation and burden of proof, authorities on the construction of these schemes have followed cases on the armed forces provisions[1] and in their turn they have been cited in war pensions cases.[2] There are two principal types of scheme, neither of which is of much practical importance now.

16 SI 1978/1525, art 65. There are equivalent provisions where the award follows a decision on appeal or review.

17 See Parliamentary Commissioner Case No C5 36/L, Annual Report for 1970, 1970–71 HC 261. See also his 4th Report for 1977–78, HC 312, where he is highly critical of the DHSS 'deceitfully withholding' arrears of an element in the pension which through error had not been paid.

18 P. 349, above.

19 2nd Report of the PCA for 1970, 1970–71 HC, 507 (Report on Captain Horsley's Claim).

20 See Tucker J in *Re Kemp* [1945] 1 All ER 571, discussing Personal Injuries (Emergency Provisions) Act 1939, s.3.

1 E.g. *Cadney v Minister of Pensions and National Insurance* [1965] 3 All ER 809, [1966] 1 WLR 80; see p. 351, above.

2 *Minister of Pensions v Chennell* [1947] KB 250 has been an influential authority on problems of causation in the war pensions area.

i Schemes for mariners and other seafaring persons

Under the Pensions (Navy, Army, Air Force and Mercantile Marine) Act 1939, as amended by the Pensions (Mercantile Marine) Act 1942, the Secretary of State may make schemes for the benefit of merchant marines and other seafaring persons who have suffered war injuries, war risk injuries, or have incurred disabilities from certain other specified causes. There are a number of such schemes,[3] administered in much the same way as war pensions; there is a right of appeal from the initial decision in the DHSS to a pensions appeal tribunal.[4] The concepts of 'war injury' and 'war risk injury' have been more narrowly developed than the notion of 'injury attributable to service' in the Pensions Order: for example, a merchant mariner injured by equipment which was not normally kept on board ship during peace-time was held not to have incurred a 'war risk injury'.[5]

ii Civilian Injuries' Scheme

Under the Personal Injuries (Civilians) Scheme 1976,[6] made under the Personal Injuries (Emergency Provisions) Act 1939, a civilian may receive a pension for disablement or incapacity due to a 'war injury', or in the case of a civil defence volunteer a 'war service injury', in both cases sustained between 3 September 1939 and 19 March 1946. 'War service injury' and 'war injury' are both defined in the 1939 Act, the latter being accorded the same definition as in the Pensions (Navy, Army, Air Force and Mercantile Marine) Act of 1939. An appeal lies from the Secretary of State's decision to a pensions appeal tribunal.[7] The nominated judge seems to have adopted a restrictive approach when the claimant has suffered mental shock or hysteria at the sight of war damage. The definitions in the 1939 Act of both 'war injury' and 'war service injury' refer to '*physical* injury', and Tucker J has held that this excludes mental shock, in contradistinction to the position under the armed forces' scheme where 'disablement' is defined to mean 'physical or mental injury or damage'.[8]

A 'war service injury' must have arisen out of and in the course of the performance by the volunteer of his civil defence duties and, therefore, an injury sustained while bicycling to his place of duty did not entitle a defence worker to recover a pension.[9] In an important ruling, often followed in cases under the services' scheme, it was held that a 'war injury' was caused by the discharge of a missile, even though it was a few days before it was carelessly picked up and tampered with by a small boy, resulting in injury to the claimant.[10] The discharge of the missile was not too remote for it to be regarded as the cause of the injury and so a pension was awarded.

3 E.g. the War Pensions (Naval Auxiliary Personnel) Scheme 1946 (SI 1964/1985); the War Pensions (Mercantile Marine) Scheme 1964 (SI 1964/2058).
4 See Pensions Appeal Tribunals Act 1943, s.2.
5 *Douglass v Minister of Pensions* (1952) 5 WPAR 85; also see *Cook v Minister of Pensions* (1948) 1 WPAR 1223.
6 SI 1976/585, as amended.
7 Pensions Appeal Tribunals Act 1943, s.3.
8 *Young v Minister of Pensions* [1944] 2 All ER 308 ('war injury'); *Ex parte Haines* [1945] KB 183, [1945] 1 All ER 349, and *Re Drake* [1945] 1 All ER 576 ('war service injury'): see p. 343, above.
9 *Davis v Minister of Pensions* [1951] 2 All ER 318. For the similar position with regard to such accidents in industrial injuries, see p. 278, above.
10 *Minister of Pensions v Chennell*, n.20, above.

Chapter 10

General provisions

In this chapter we consider a number of issues and concepts which are common to several or all of the benefits payable under the Social Security Act 1975 (viz those discussed in chapters 3 to 8). The principles to be described are themselves primarily drawn from that Act and, as a matter of law, do not govern war pensions, child benefit, family income supplements or supplementary benefits unless, and to the extent that, they are specifically adopted in the legislation concerned with the latter schemes. In practice, however, where there is no reason to adopt a different interpretation, the provisions of the Social Security Act, as developed by the Commissioners' decisions, may properly act as guidelines for the administration of those areas of social security law which are not governed by that Act. This applies particularly to the meaning attributed to such concepts as 'marriage', 'living as man and wife', 'residence', 'presence', 'imprisonment' and 'detention in legal custody'.

Part 1 Increases for dependants

A General

The principle that special allowance should be made for persons dependent on the claimant was, of course, recognised from the beginning as regards benefits which were means-tested. Family support is without doubt the most significant differential in assessing an individual's need. For those benefits governed wholly or partly by the contributory principle such provision is not so obvious but is readily acceptable. If the benefit is intended to provide a minimum standard of living for the claimant, then regard should be had to his family needs, even though, in the absence of a family-weighted contribution, this will mean that those without family obligations will be subsidising those with them. Such a policy occupies a central position in the British tradition of social security because of its reluctance to be committed to an earnings-related principle of income maintenance.[1] As some foreign systems clearly show, a fully effective programme of earnings indemnity is incompatible with the payment of

1 Cf pp. 19–20, above.

dependants' allowances.[2] So long as a 'needs' approach to social welfare predominates we may, therefore, expect a continuing important role for these increases.

In the light of these considerations, the case for broadly based dependency provision might appear to be self-evident but its recognition has been far from consistent. Before the Second World War, it was incorporated in various benefit schemes only gradually and somewhat haphazardly. It was added to the unemployment insurance scheme in 1921 on a temporary basis to relieve 'winter hardships',[3] but in the next year was made permanent.[4] Remarkably, additions for dependants were never included in the national health insurance scheme, and the reasons for the distinction remain far from obvious. They were belatedly added to workmen's compensation in 1940,[5] as a result of continuous complaints that the ceiling to earnings-related compensation was too low for those with heavy family responsibilities. Beveridge in his restatement of the social insurance principle, based as it was on a system of flat-rate benefit, was content to see the increase payable to all recipients of insurance benefit.[6] The contemporaneous introduction of family allowances necessitated a technical modification of the rules, though in no fundamental way interfered with them. By the time earnings-related supplements were introduced for short-term benefits in 1966, the principle of increase for dependants was already firmly entrenched, and there was no serious attempt to argue that it should be discontinued.[7] But the reform prompted the decision to pay the increases on a higher scale to long-term beneficiaries who were not entitled to the supplement.[8] Paradoxically, this more favourable treatment of pensioners was not affected by the introduction of the earnings-related component under the 1975 scheme, nor by the more recent abolition of the earnings-related supplements for short-term beneficiaries. Indeed, quite anachronistically, the position of the latter has been allowed to worsen as a result of two other reforms. First, under the new arrangements for short periods of sickness, the sick pay which will replace sickness benefit will not have to include any allowance for dependants.[9] Secondly, the replacement in 1975 of family allowances by child benefit, payable for the first or only child,[10] was accompanied by consequential changes in the law governing child dependency increases. Some of these were of a technical character, notably the harnessing of entitlement to the increase on entitlement to child benefit. But less commendably, the consolidation of child endowment generally has been used to justify a continuing reduction in the value of child dependency increases payable with the short-term benefits.[11]

The traditional rules on dependency allowances have assumed stereotyped family relationships in which the husband/father is the primary

2 E.g. in W. Germany, Denmark and Netherlands the benefit payable for short-term employment injury bears such a high proportion to lost earnings that no dependants' allowances are payable: *Kaim-Caudle* p. 88. See also *Dupeyroux* pp. 128–132 and *McCarthy* pp. 169–171.
3 Unemployed Workers Dependants' (Temporary Provisions) Act 1921.
4 UIA 1922.
5 WC (Supplementary Allowances) Act 1940.
6 Paras 311 and 325.
7 Cf *Walley* p. 206.
8 P. 366, below.
9 P. 162, above.
10 Ch 11, below.
11 See Lynes *New Society*, 3 April 1980, for criticism.

or only breadwinner, while the wife/mother assumes domestic responsibilities and her earnings, if any, are inessential additions to the family income.[12] The EEC Directive on Equal Treatment for Men and Women in Social Security[13] has prompted the government to make fundamental changes so that, for example, the rules governing a husband's entitlement to claim for a wife and a wife's entitlement to claim for a husband will be harmonised.[14] The relevant provisions will not, however, be brought into force until 1983.

The Social Security Act 1975 makes, with certain exceptions, common provision for all the non-industrial benefits payable under it, but deals with the industrial benefits separately. However, the principles are so similar that they will be considered together, the differences being treated as and when they emerge. There are, moreover, certain key concepts, such as 'maintenance', 'residence' and 'incapacity for self-support' which are common to two or more of the increases which may be claimed. These will be discussed after the rules for each category of dependency have been described.

B Persons for whom increase payable

i Children

Increases for child dependants may be added to those benefits payable under the Act which, broadly speaking, are intended to compensate for loss of full-time earnings. These benefits may be divided into two groups.

(1) Unemployment or sickness benefit (where the beneficiary is under pensionable age), maternity allowance and industrial injury benefit.[15]

(2) Unemployment or sickness benefit (where the beneficiary is over pensionable age); invalidity and Category A, B or C retirement pensions; widow's, widowed mother's, child's special and invalid care allowances; non-contributory invalidity pension; and industrial disablement pension (if accompanied by unemployability supplement).[16]

For reasons which have already been considered,[17] a substantially higher rate of weekly increase (in 1982–83, £7.95 per child) is paid with benefits within group 2. For those within group 1 the corresponding amount is £0.30 per week. To qualify for the increase the beneficiary must satisfy two conditions, the first referring to his relationship with the child and the second to the state of the latter's dependence on him. Where more than one person satisfies these conditions in relation to the same child, priority is given to the person who has been awarded child benefit for that child for the relevant period.[18]

a *Sufficient relationship*

Until 1977 there were complex provisions for determining the children for whom the addition might be claimed. The introduction in that year of child benefit payable to all families with children meant that the rules specifying the nature of the relationship with the child could be largely integrated.

12 Pp. 367–369, below.
13 Dir 79/7, OJ 1979, L6/24.
14 SSA 1980, Sch 1, Part I, on which see Atkins [1980] JSWL 16.
15 SSA 1975, ss.41(2) and 64(1).
16 Ibid, and SI 1977/343, reg 1(3).
17 P. 365, above.
18 SI 1979/597, reg 15(3).

The general rule for the increase simply incorporates the law on child benefit: it is payable where the beneficiary is 'entitled to child benefit in respect of a child or children'.[19] On this test, therefore, reference should be made to the discussion in chapter 11.

In certain respects, however, the pre-1977 rules on increases covered a wider range of relationships than those acknowledged under the new child benefit scheme. To ensure that the entitlement of this broader group is preserved, a regulation enumerates situations in which for the purpose of the increase a person is treated as if he were entitled to child benefit.[20]

(1) The beneficiary is *either* a parent of the child *or* is wholly or mainly maintaining him, *and* is residing with a parent of the child, *and* that parent is living with the child and receives child benefit for him.

(2) The beneficiary is a parent of the child and is contributing to the cost of providing for him at a rate of not less than the amount of increase payable to group 1 beneficiaries, *and* the child benefit is payable to the beneficiary's wife or former wife who is also a parent of the child.

(3) The beneficiary is entitled to a family benefit in respect of that child payable by the government of a country outside the UK.

Conversely, there is a situation where child benefit is payable but the increase is excluded.[1]

- The claimant of the increase (who is entitled to child benefit) is not a parent of the child and someone who is his parent is treated, under section 3(1)(a) of the Child Benefit Act 1975,[2] as responsible for the child. Nevertheless, the claimant remains entitled to the increase if, under the same provision, he is also treated as responsible for the child and he is wholly or mainly maintaining him.

b *Dependence*

The second condition is that the beneficiary must prove *either* that the child in question is living with him *or* that he is contributing to the cost of providing for the child at a weekly rate of not less than the amount of the increase, over and above the amount (if any) received by way of child benefit.[3] If the beneficiary is a married woman residing with her husband, she must in addition prove that he is incapable of self-support.[4] The Social Security Act 1980 provides for both amendment to, and eventual revocation of, this discriminatory condition.[5] As from a yet unprescribed date in 1983, the condition will be that the husband does not earn more than the amount of the increase claimed, rather than that he is incapable of self-support. The condition will be abolished altogether a year later.

ii Wife

An increase for a wife may be claimed to supplement those benefits mentioned in the last section to which a man may be entitled:

- Unemployment and sickness benefits, invalidity and category A or C retirement pensions, non-contributory invalidity pension and invalid

19 SSA 1975, ss.41 and 64(1), as amended by CBA 1975, Sch 4, para 13(a) and 21(a). It is sufficient if a claim for child benefit has been made for the relevant period: *R(S) 3/80*.
20 SI 1977/343, reg 4 A, inserted by SI 1980/585. For the meaning of 'parent' in these rules, see CBA 1975, s.24(a), *R(F) 1/79* and *R(S) 4/81*.
1 SI 1977/343, reg 4 B, inserted by SI 1980/585.
2 See p. 432, below.
3 SSA 1975, ss.43(1), (2) and 65(1), (2), as amended by CBA 1975, Sch 4, paras 15 and 22.
4 SSA 1975, ss.41(6) and 65(4).
5 Sch 1, para 1.

care allowance, industrial injury and disablement pension (if accompanied by an unemployability supplement).[6]

The marriage must be one recognised by law and sufficiently proved.[7] The usual test of dependancy applies: the beneficiary must either be residing with this wife[8] or contributing to her maintenance at not less than the amount of the increase.[9]

An interesting policy question is raised if the wife is herself an earner. If the object of the increase is to satisfy the need for support, a self-supporting wife should be excluded. If, on the other hand, it is to provide compensation for the loss of actual support, then at least up to certain limits it should continue to be payable. Quite apart from this, there is the question of incentive, whether the wife, assuming she is capable of doing so, should be encouraged to work. While the government appears unequivocally to adopt the 'needs' approach,[10] the various statutory provisions are not uniformly consistent with it. Certainly it is adopted in the case of short-term benefits (viz those for unemployment, sickness and industrial injury); the increase is not payable if the wife's weekly earnings exceed the amount of that increase.[11] The same also applies for long-term benefits (retirement, invalidity and disablement pensions) where the wife is not residing with the husband, i.e. where she has to satisfy the alternative maintenance test.[12] In the case of a wife residing with a long-term beneficiary, a different, more liberal, approach was introduced in 1971 to encourage her to supplement the household income.[13] Entitlement to the increase is not affected by earnings up to £45 per week, but beyond that there is a reduction in the increase of 50 per cent for any excess up to £4.00, and of 100 per cent for any greater excess.[14] The figure of £45 has not been changed since 1979 and this may reflect the government's view that the earnings limit is overgenerous when regard is had to the original objective of the rule, which was to provide a test of dependency or need.[15]

Just as the earnings rule differs according to the nature of the benefit, so also does the amount of increase which is payable for adult dependants. The rates (for 1982–83) are: for retirement pensions (Category A or B) £19.70; for invalidity pensions, and unemployment or sickness benefit where the beneficiary is over pensionable age, £18.85; for short-term benefits £15.45; and for non-contributory benefits £11.80.

iii Husbands

Traditional social security law, still in force at the time of writing, assumes that wives are dependent on husbands and not vice versa.[16] In consequence

6 SSA 1975, ss.44(1), 45 and 66(1); SI 1977/343, reg 12 and Sch 2, Part II.
7 Pp. 377–382, below.
8 Pp. 371–373, below.
9 SSA 1975, ss.44(1)(a), 45(2) and 66(1)(A). But NB for the invalid care allowance the claimant *must* prove residence – there is no maintenance alternative: SI 1977/343, Sch 2, para 7(b).
10 Report of Secretary of State on the Earnings Rule for Retirement Pensioners and the Wives of Retirement and Invalidity Pensioners 1977–78, HC 697, para 5.6. The same policy does not apply to earnings of the retirement pensioner himself: p. 213, above.
11 SSA 1975, s.44(1)(b); SI 1977/343, reg 8(1).
12 SSA 1975, s.45(2)(b).
13 NIA 1971, s.4.
14 SSA 1975, ss.45(3)–(4), and 66(4)–(5); SI 1979/1429.
15 Report of Secretary of State, n.10, above, para 5.7. Unlike the earnings rule which applies to retirement pensions (pp. 212–216, above), it is therefore not to be envisaged that this condition will eventually be abolished.
16 For an illustration of the injustice caused by this discriminatory approach, see *R(S) 11/79*.

a married woman may claim for her husband an increase to unemployment, sickness and industrial injury benefits, maternity allowance, invalidity and disablement pension only if she proves, in addition to the standard residence or maintenance alternative requirements for wives' and childrens' increases,[17] that her husband is incapable of self-support.[18] Where payable, the increase is of the same amount as that paid to a husband for a wife.[19]

When the relevant provisions of the Social Security Act 1980 are brought into force (some time in 1983), the wife will no longer have to show that the husband is incapable of self-support, but only that he does not earn more than the amount of the increase claimed.[20] It should be noted, however, that the higher earnings limits imposed on dependent wives of male pensioners[1] will not apply to dependent husbands.

iv Child carers

Another fundamental characteristic of the social security system has been its realistic view of so-called 'common-law' marriages. The relationship is treated as if the parties were married for the purposes of the means-tested benefits,[2] but their position with regard to those benefits payable under the Social Security Act is less favourable.[3] Except for a short period of 'entitlement' under the Unemployment Insurance Acts,[4] dependency increases have not been payable for cohabitees as such. They have, however, been paid for women caring for a child of the beneficiary, and when effect is given to the 1980 reform,[5] they will cover men performing this task.

The claimant must be entitled to both child benefit[6] – or treated as so entitled[7] – and a child's increase to personal benefit[8] in relation to the child who is the subject of the care. As regards the latter, the Commissioner has held that the necessary care will be shown if the person, traditionally referred to as a 'housekeeper', 'to a substantial extent performs those duties for a child, with which a child needs assistance because he or she is a child, or exercises that supervision over a child which is one of the needs of childhood'.[9] It does not connote exclusive care[10] or even a greater amount of care than that provided by the claimant himself.[11] But the mere distant supervision of a child's needs while he is at boarding school does not qualify.[12]

This firm emphasis on the care of a child carries no necessary implication of a sexual relationship with the beneficiary. The child carer need not be

17 Pp. 367 and 368, above.
18 SSA 1975, ss.44(3)(a), 47(1)(a) and 66(1)(b). See p. 377, below.
19 P. 368, above.
20 SSA 1980, Sch 1, paras 2 and 6.
1 P. 368, above.
2 Chs 12 and 13, below.
3 Cf pp. 7–8, above.
4 UIA 1922, s.1(1), repealed by UIA 1927, s.4(2).
5 SSA 1980, Sch 1, para 4.
6 SSA 1975, ss.44(3)(c), 46(2) and 66(1)(d) as amended by CBA 1975, Sch 4, paras 16, 18 and 23.
7 SI 1977/343, reg 4 A, inserted by SI 1980/585. See p. 367, above.
8 SI 1977/343, reg 10(2)(a) (or would have been so entitled but for overlapping provisions).
9 *CS 726/49*, para 11.
10 *UD 10914/31*.
11 *CS 726/49*, paras 9, 10.
12 *R(S) 17/54*.

residing with the beneficiary;[13] indeed, in such a case the increase may be paid even where he is residing with his wife, provided that the latter is in full-time work and does not herself primarily care for the children.[14] It follows too that a female beneficiary in full-time work may claim an increase under this head. The short-term benefits for which the increase may be claimed thus include maternity allowance as well as those for sickness, unemployment and industrial injury.[15] The long-term benefits are Category A and C retirement and invalidity pensions, the non-contributory invalidity pension and invalid care allowance, and the industrial disablement pension (with unemployability supplement).[16]

To qualify for any of these increases the child carer must either be residing with the beneficiary or being maintained by him at not less than the standard rate of the increase, or employed by him for consideration of not less than that amount.[17] The earnings rules applicable to wives[18] operate also with regard to child carers, but with some necessary modifications. The exclusion of those earning more than the amount of the increase is effective for the short-term benefits, but the amounts (if any) which the beneficiary pays the child carer are, of course, ignored, and the exclusion does not apply at all to those employed by the beneficiary and not residing with him.[19] As regards the long-term benefits, the standard earning deduction rules apply to child carers who are residing with the beneficiary, though here also earnings payable by the latter are ignored.[20] There are, moreover, some further limitations which do not apply to wives.

- The child carer must not be imprisoned or detained in legal custody[1] (though it is a little difficult to see how he may be so and yet still caring for the children), or absent from GB.[2] Finally, an increase to disablement or invalidity pension is not payable if the beneficiary has a wife who is entitled to a Category B or C retirement pension.[3]

v Relatives

Until recently, a recipient of a short-term benefit or a long-term disability benefit (but not a retirement pension) could claim an increase for a prescribed relative residing with, and being wholly or mainly maintained by, him.[4] In 1956, the National Insurance Advisory Committee considered that these provisions were based more on the historical antecedents of the scheme than on any logical development of a principle of social insurance,[5] and they were abolished by the Social Security Act 1980.[6] This reform came

13 *CS 726/49*, unless an increase is claimed for an invalid care allowance: p. 368, n.9, above. A non-residing child carer must, however, be maintained by the beneficiary, p. 373, below.
14 *R(S) 20/54*.
15 SSA 1975, ss.44(2), (3) and 66(1)(d).
16 Ibid, ss.46(1) and 66(1)(d); SI 1977/343, reg 1(3).
17 Ibid, reg 10(2)(b). For the invalid care allowance, residence must be proved, p. 368, n.9, above.
18 P. 368, above.
19 SI 1977/343, reg 10(2)(e).
20 Ibid, reg 10(4).
1 Ibid, reg 10(2)(d).
2 Unless he is residing with the beneficiary who himself is not disqualified: ibid, reg 10(2)(c) and (3).
3 SSA 1975, s.46(3), presumably because this is analogous to an increase for a wife, and a beneficiary may not claim increases for both a wife and a resident child carer.
4 For details, see the first edition of this book, pp. 389–390.
5 Cmd 9855.
6 Sch 1, para 3.

into effect on 23 November 1981, but a beneficiary entitled to an increase for a dependent relative immediately before this date would continue to receive it for a maximum of two years, if he satisfied the conditions previously in force.[7]

C 'Residing with' or 'living with' the beneficiary

The principle that a beneficiary should be either maintaining the dependant or residing (or living) with him is not difficult to rationalise. If the beneficiary shares a home with another, and is an earner, it is a reasonable assumption that he is contributing to that other's maintenance. The different formulation for adult dependants ('residing with') and children ('living with') is deliberate. The latter concept was that used in the family allowances, and subsequently the child benefit, legislation and was explicitly incorporated into the national insurance scheme in 1957.[8] As the Commissioner has consistently held, 'living with' does not carry the same meaning as 'residing with'.[9] It seems clear, therefore, that the intention of Parliament was to apply to child dependency increases the interpretation given to the phrase in child benefit law; this is fully discussed in chapter 11.[10] It thus remains to consider the concept of 'residing with' which qualifies the relationship with adult dependants.

The term is not defined in the Social Security Act and guidance is to be had only from the case-law.[11] The basic idea is that the two people concerned should be living under the same roof.[12] This does not mean either that one of them should be the owner or tenant of the property[13] or that, in the case of spouses, they are sleeping in the same bed or otherwise maintaining the normal relationship of husband and wife.[14] But there must be an element of continuity and permanence in the co-residence.[15] In some cases, it will be necessary for the claimant to prove that he has acquired a new 'co-resident'. It will be more difficult to establish that living in a hotel, lodgings or the home of relatives constitutes co-residence than the entering into a tenancy agreement or setting up home with a woman as his wife.[16] More often, the question is whether an admitted co-residence has in fact ceased. On this the legislation is more helpful. Regulations made under the Social Security (Miscellaneous Provisions) Act 1977 lay down three rules.

i Temporary absence

Under the first rule

> two persons shall not be treated as having ceased to reside together by reason of any temporary absence the one from the other.[17]

7 Ibid.
8 NIA 1957, s.6(4).
9 *R(I) 10/51*; *R(U) 11/62*; *R(F) 2/79*.
10 Pp. 433–434, below.
11 The expression also has been used in the Rent Acts (see e.g. *Morgan v Murch* [1970] 2 All ER 100, [1970] 1 WLR 778, CA) and in the law of family maintenance (see e.g. *Curtin v Curtin* [1952] 2 QB 552, DC).
12 Per Lord Goddard CJ, ibid, at 556; *R(P) 15/56*.
13 *CU 201/50*.
14 *Curtin v Curtin*, n.11, above; *R(S) 14/52*: though cp *Hopes v Hopes* [1949] P. 227, [1948] 2 All ER 920, CA, and the child benefit decision *R(F) 3/81*.
15 *CS 3/48*. See also SI 1977/956, reg 2(3), p. 372, below.
16 *R(P) 4/54*; *R(F) 1/62*.
17 SI 1977/956, reg 2(4).

This reinforces the notion that 'residing with' implies a permanent rather than a temporary condition, but it is naturally difficult to draw the line between the two. Some authorities, applying an equivalent rule under regulations previously in force, held that the test depends primarily on the parties' state of mind: did they intend to resume co-residence when the period of separation had ceased? Or has the separation been so long that, on reasonable inference, it was likely to be permanent?[18] On this view, the purpose of the absence becomes important. Thus the acquisition of accommodation removed from the family but near the claimant's employment will not generally be regarded as indicative of 'temporary' absence,[19] but it may be so categorised if the claimant is merely looking for work and intends that the family should join him when he finds it,[20] or lodges near the work but returns home at weekends and for holidays.[1] Other authorities have regarded the intention of the claimant as too elusive a criterion and have concentrated more on the duration of the absence. In the early 1950s the Commissioner devised a rule of thumb that:

> a period of absence which has lasted for more than a year, and of which there is no reasonable prospect of its coming to an end, cannot . . . be spoken of as 'temporary'.[2]

This was then combined with another rule of thumb that the 'reasonable prospect of its coming to an end' should be judged within a period of six months from the date of application.[3] The two tests were regularly applied[4] but they were not regarded as hard and fast rules, and might be ousted by special circumstances.[5] In 1962, a Tribunal of Commissioners reported on a tendency to take a 'much shorter term view of residence', and implied that it would be better to regard the matter as one of degree in each case, rather than argue it in terms of legal presumption.[6]

ii Widows

In relation to widow's benefit the position of persons under 19 who may be engaged in full-time education or training away from home has caused some difficulties.[7] The regulations thus prescribe that

> in the case of a woman who has been widowed, she shall not be treated as having ceased to reside with a child or person under the age of nineteen by reason of any absence the one from the other which is not likely to be permanent.[8]

iii Hospital in-patients

The application of the 'residing with' criterion to cases where the beneficiary or the dependant is in hospital has been equally problematical. The National Insurance Advisory Committee reviewed the matter in 1955

18 See e.g. *CS 3/48*; *CS 6/48*; *R(S) 1/51*.
19 *UD 4053/28*; *UD 5131/29*; *R(S) 1/51*; *R(S) 10/55*; *R(I) 37/55*.
20 *R(S) 14/58*.
1 *UD 6702/29*; *UD 15405/32*.
2 *CP 84/50* unreported, but cited in *R(P) 7/53*, para 8.
3 *R(P) 7/53*.
4 See e.g. *R(U) 15/54*; *R(S) 7/55*; *R(U) 14/58*.
5 See e.g. *R(S) 14/55*.
6 *R(U) 11/62*.
7 Cf *Fox v Stirk and Bristol Electoral Registration Officer* [1970] 2 QB 467, [1970] 3 All ER 7, CA (on franchise qualifications).
8 SI 1977/956, reg 2(3).

and concluded that special provision should be made for spouses.[9] Under the current rule,

> two spouses shall not be treated as having ceased to reside together by reason only of the fact that either of them is, or they both are, undergoing medical or other treatment as an in-patient in a hospital or similar institution, whether such absence is temporary or not.[10]

Where the treatment of a dependant is free under the National Health Service, the need of the beneficiary to support him or her is obviously reduced. For this reason, as will be seen later in this chapter, there are rules for adjusting the rates of the increases.[11] In that context, too, the meaning of 'medical or other treatment as an in-patient in a hospital or similar institution' will be considered.

D Maintenance by beneficiary

In some cases, the beneficiary may prove as an alternative to 'residence' that he was 'maintaining' the dependant. In others, he must prove both 'residence' and 'maintenance'. To establish the required degree of maintenance, the beneficiary must contribute to the cost of providing for the dependant at a weekly rate of not less than the amount of the increase claimed.[12]

i Mode and time of payments

The maintenance question is one of fact and not of legal liability. The mere existence of an obligation to maintain, even if the result of a court order, will not be sufficient to establish title to the increase.[13] The claimant must therefore prove that he has actually been making the appropriate payments during the relevant period, though in the case of an increase for a child the condition is satisfied if the beneficiary gives an undertaking in writing to make such payment and he makes the payment when he receives the increase.[14] In no case does he have to show that the maintenance payments were actually received or consumed by the dependant; for example, the money might be held by the clerk of a court[15] or diverted to the DHSS.[16] The fact that the prescribed amount of maintenance is expressed in terms of weekly payments does not, of course, mean that the actual payments must be made weekly. On the other hand, they must be regular payments which on average equal or exceed the prescribed rate. Thus a payment of an occasional lump sum cannot be treated as regular maintenance and apportioned to weekly payments.[17] Interruptions in payments cannot be

9 Report on the Question of Dependency Provisions (Cmd 9855).
10 SI 1977/956, reg 2(2)(b).
11 Pp. 394–398, below.
12 E.g. SSA 1975, ss.43(2)(a) and 44(1)(a).
13 *R(U) 25/59*; *R(U) 1/77*.
14 SI 1977/343, reg 5(1). For the origins of this regulation, see NIAC Report (1966, Cmnd 2959). It cannot be invoked to support entitlement for a period longer than a week before the undertaking was made: *R(U) 3/78*; cp *R(U) 6/79*, where the undertaking confirmed one that had been made earlier.
15 *CS 638/49*.
16 Cf p. 511, below. There is no reported case on the point but the proposition in the text should be accepted as a matter of principle.
17 *R(U) 14/62*.

ignored,[18] so that if the claimant falls in arrears, he may not count against current payments any payments made to clear arrears.[19] Thus in *R(U) 25/58*

> C was bound, under a court order, to pay his separated wife £1.15 per week. For about 40 weeks prior to his claim for the increase, he was paying her on average £1.30, but of this 15p was arrears. He was therefore unable to show that he was currently contributing at the then prescribed rate of £1.25 per week. As the Commissioner observed, any other ruling would unduly benefit husbands who accumulated arrears.[20]

ii Payment in kind

It has long been recognised that maintenance need not necessarily take the form of a monetary payment. Account may be taken of the regular provision of food, clothing, fuel and other items necessary for sustenance and welfare.[1] So also if the claimant conveys to the dependant his beneficial interest in the matrimonial home.[2] The calculation of maintenance will then proceed on the basis of the rateable value, or interest on the capital value, of the property transferred.[3] In another case, the same principle was applied to the transfer of a business share: the interest obtained on the purchase-money of the share sold was deemed to be a regular contribution to maintenance.[4]

iii Joint maintenors

A regulation deals with the situation, presumably not of frequent occurrence, where a dependant is being maintained by two or more beneficiaries. If the aggregate amount of such maintenance equals or exceeds the rate necessary for any one of them to claim the increase, such increase is payable notwithstanding that no one individual himself is able to satisfy the criterion.[5] The recipient will be the person who makes the largest contributions, or, if there is no such person, then either the eldest member of the group or one designated by the majority in a written notice sent to the Secretary of State.[6]

iv Allocation principle

Sometimes maintenance payments are explicitly allocated as between wife (or ex-wife) and children; sometimes they are not. It would be invidious if the exact classification of the payments were to be decisive in determining whether one or other dependant would qualify for the increase. So long as a marriage is subsisting,[7] the system assumes a principle of non-discrimination between a beneficiary's wife and his children. Where a payment is

18 Compare child benefit, p. 435, below, where the rule is perhaps more generous.
19 *R(U) 11/62*.
20 *R(U) 25/58*, para 7. In *R(S) 3/74* R G Micklethwait, Chief Comr, refused to apply the 'allocation' regulation (p. 375, below) to assist in cases of regular but inadequate payments.
1 *CI 111/50*; *R(I) 10/51*.
2 *R(U) 3/66*, though J S Watson, Dep. Comr, reserved his opinion on whether the position would have been the same if the dependant had sold or let the property in question. In *R(S) 6/52* it was held that such a sale would not affect the claimant's rights.
3 *R(U) 3/66*.
4 *R(I) 37/54*.
5 SI 1977/343, reg 2(2).
6 Ibid, reg 2(2)(b).
7 Cf *R(S) 9/61*.

made to a wife or children or both, the authorities are given discretion to apportion the maintenance in such a way as will entitle the claimant to the largest payment by way of increase.[8] A typical exercise of this power would be as follows.

> C, in receipt of invalidity benefit, is paying by way of maintenance every week £18.00 for his wife and £7.00 for each of two children. If the apparent apportionment were to be binding, C could claim no increase since the currently prescribed amount of maintenance is for an adult dependant £18.85, and for a child £7.95. By notionally apportioning the aggregate of £32.00 into £19.00 for the wife, £8.00 for the first child and £5.00 for the second child, the authorities will be able to confer on C title to an increase for the wife and for the first child.

v Family fund[9]

The technique used for calculating individual dependency in the typical situation where money from various sources is used to support a number of individuals is a judicial creation and owes nothing to legislative prescription. It was originally conceived by judges deciding dependency issues under the Workmen's Compensation Acts,[10] and subsequently adopted by the Umpire adjudicating unemployment insurance claims.[11] There being nothing in the post-war legislation to discourage its continued application, it was in 1949 accepted as part of national insurance law,[12] a decision reaffirmed by Tribunals of Commissioners in later cases.[13]

The fundamental principle is that the authorities should have regard to the normal phenomena of family support rather than to strict legal obligations to maintain.[14] Thus if a woman is in fact supported by her brother, a cousin or a son, it is irrelevant that she is in law wholly dependent on her husband. The modification of the intra-family maintenance obligations resulting from the abolition of the poor law in 1948[15] did not therefore affect the matter.[16] The technique proceeds by calculating the 'unit cost' of each family member. For this, the total family income is divided by the number of individuals (counting two children as one adult).

> In a family group of three adults (H, the husband, W, his wife and B, his brother) and two children (K and L) there will be 4 units. If the total family income is £120.00 (H contributing £70.00, W £10.00 and B £40.00) per week, the unit cost of one adult is £$\frac{120}{4}$ = £30.00 and of one child £15.00.

Each individual then has a surplus or deficit of contribution over cost.

> H has a surplus of £40.00, B a surplus of £10.00, W a deficit of £20.00, and K and L each a deficit of £15.00.

8 SI 1977/343, reg 3.
9 See generally, Kahn-Freund 16 MLR 148, 164–173.
10 See esp. *Main Colliery Co v Davies* [1900] AC 358, HL, and *Hodgson v West Stanley Colliery* [1910] AC 229, HL.
11 See esp. *UD 1838/31*.
12 *CSI 59/49*.
13 *R(I) 1/57* and *R(I) 20/60*.
14 See particularly the speech of Lord Loreburn LC in *Hodgson v West Stanley Colliery*, n.10, above at 232.
15 NAA 1948, ss.1 and 42.
16 *CSI 50/49*.

To assess the degree of dependency of an individual with a deficit on an individual with a surplus, one divides the amount of the deficit proportionally between those providing a surplus.

H is providing $\frac{4}{5}$ of the total surplus and B$\frac{1}{5}$. Thus the extent of W's dependency on H is $\frac{4}{5} \times 20 =$ £16.00, and the extent of K's (or L's) dependency on H is $\frac{4}{5} \times 15 =$ £12.00.

The calculation is to be applied to the family circumstances existing at the time immediately prior to the event (e.g. sickness, unemployment, retirement) for which the benefit is payable: subsequent changes in the composition of the group or financial contributions are to be ignored,[17] and the average or normal contributions of individuals are to be assessed as at that date.[18]

If the method is one of simple arithmetic, it nevertheless raises some delicate issues when applied to actual family situations. It is sometimes argued that the method does not accord with the reality of how a particular family organises its household budget. The answer to this is that it is a convenient and less expensive method of calculating typical expenditure. Complete accuracy is neither obtainable nor (presumably) desirable. The method should be departed from only where there is clear evidence that it substantially conflicts with the actual circumstances.[19] It may be that an individual member consumes more or less than the attributed 'unit cost', e.g. because he is aged or disabled, but it has always been held that no account is to be taken of the actual way in which money is spent.[20] Contributions raise greater difficulties: doubt may be cast on whether a particular sum should constitute a contribution to the household budget, or whether it should be attributed to one person rather than another. It has been held that sums required for personal liabilities or for special needs should be excluded from the calculations.[1] Such needs are, of course, not easy to define but the cases provide some useful examples: life insurance premiums,[2] special clothing for an invalid,[3] a scholarship grant for a child.[4] On the other hand, social security benefits are normally integrated into the household fund.[5] A contributory benefit is regarded as a resource provided by the person on whose contributions the benefit is payable.[6] Non-contributory benefits are attributed to the individual or individuals for whom they are paid. Thus in the case of supplementary benefit, the sum will be apportioned between the claimant and the dependants whose requirements are aggregated with his.[7] A Tribunal of Commissioners has suggested that if a constant attendance allowance were used to pay an outsider to come in and provide the requisite service, the benefit might be excluded from the fund.[8] If that is right the same would apply where a non-industrial attendance allowance is used for the same purpose.

17 *CS 52/50*.
18 *R(I) 10/51*.
19 *R(I) 46/52*; *R(U) 37/52*; *R(I) 20/60*.
20 *CS 52/50*; *R(I) 1/57*; *R(I) 20/60*.
1 *R(I) 1/57*.
2 *CI 111/50*; *CI 266/50*.
3 *CS 221/50* (unreported).
4 *UD 16621/32*.
5 *CP 96/50*; *CI 266/50*; *R(S) 6/53*; *R(I) 8/65*.
6 *CP 96/50*.
7 *R(I) 8/65*.
8 *R(I) 1/57*, para 19, declining to evaluate the merits of *UD 17142/31*.

E Incapable of self-support

Until the relevant provisions of the Social Security Act 1980 are brought into force,[9] claims for a husband require proof that he is 'incapable of self-support'.[10] Even when this condition has been abrogated, a widower claiming death benefit under the industrial injuries scheme will still have to show that, at the death of his wife, he was '*permanently* incapable of self-support'.[11] The government envisages that this benefit will, in its turn, soon be abolished,[12] so that a lengthy analysis of the law does not seem justified.[13]

'Permanently' in this context means 'likely to remain so . . . for the remainder of his life', while 'incapable of self-support' is defined as

> incapable of supporting himself by reason of physical or mental infirmity and is likely to remain so incapable for a prolonged period.[14]

'A prolonged period' has been interpreted by the Commissioner as being not less than six months,[15] but the estimate is taken not at the time of the claim but from when the period of incapacity began.[16] The test is not the same as that of 'incapacity for work',[17] the requirement generally employed to establish title to the disability benefits.[18] First, regard is had to the dependant's capacity over the whole of the relevant period, rather than on specific days;[19] so short periods of self-support may be ignored.[20] Secondly, he may be able to do some work but the remuneration ordinarily payable for that work is insufficient for his self-support. The question is, whether it enables him to maintain 'a reasonable standard of living',[1] and this has been interpreted in practice as being a level of income slightly above that which he would, in his circumstances, have received by way of supplementary benefit, if he had been so entitled.[2]

Part 2 Marriage

A General

While it may be the case that a significant proportion of social welfare provision is concerned with remedying the lack of the traditional family structure, nevertheless much of the social security legislation, particularly that part concerned with contributory benefits, focuses on the unit of the family as defined by the general law.[3] References in the legislation to 'marriage', 'wife', 'husband', 'widow' and 'widower' have all been con-

9 Sch 1, paras 1–2.
10 P. 369, above.
11 P. 334, above.
12 P. 331, above.
13 See the first edition of this book, pp. 397–398, for a fuller account.
14 SSA 1975, Sch 20.
15 *CS 288/50*.
16 *CS 343/49*; *CS 288/50*; *R(S) 2/56*.
17 *CG 4/48*; *CG 5/48*; *R(G) 3/56*.
18 Pp. 146–154, above.
19 *R(G) 3/56*, para 6.
20 *CG 30/49*; *R(G) 3/57*.
1 *CG 3/48*.
2 Ibid, para 10, referring to the National Assistance rates, and see *R(G) 2/57* and *R(G) 2/58*.
3 See generally, pp. 7–8, above.

structed to require the existence of a marriage which is recognised in the United Kingdom,[4] and which was subsisting at the time of the claim or the event which gave rise to entitlement.[5] What is legally recognised as a valid marriage is determined according to the general law of England (or Scotland), including as it does the principles of private international law when, for example, the validity of foreign marriages, or divorces, is in question. There is no space here to describe such rules in detail.[6] Instead a brief outline will be provided, together with such principles as have been developed within the framework of the social security legislation.

B Marriages celebrated in the United Kingdom

A marriage celebrated in England and Wales must have satisfied the rules regarding formalities, which include the necessary preliminaries as well as due solemnisation, whether by civil or religious proceedings.[7] Production of the marriage certificate[8] will constitute prima facie evidence that the marriage has been duly celebrated,[9] but the absence of such a certificate will not be fatal. Provided that the parties can establish with sufficient reliability that a ceremony in due form took place[10] and that it was followed by prolonged cohabitation as husband and wife, a valid marriage will be presumed.[11] The presumption will be rebutted by proof as to the invalidity of the marriage[12] but the standard of proof required is uncertain. One authority suggests that 'clear proof' will be sufficient,[13] but perhaps the better view is that the invalidity must be proved beyond reasonable doubt.[14] Scottish law, in contrast to English law, recognises a marriage 'by habit and repute', but the doctrine is narrowly confined:[15] there must have been a substantial period of cohabitation,[16] the bulk of which was in Scotland,[17] and the parties must have been free to marry[18] and consented, as between themselves, to a state of marriage.[19]

4 *CG 3/49*; *R(S) 4/59*. Thus under Scots law if the claim is made in Scotland.
5 *R(G) 1/52*; *R(P) 14/56*; *R(G) 2/73*.
6 For the English family law see Bromley *Family Law* (6th edn) ch 2, and Cretney *Principles of Family Law* (3rd edn) chs 2–3; for Scots family law see Clive and Wilson *Law of Husband and Wife in Scotland* (1974) chs 3–4 and for the relevant principles of private international law, Dicey and Morris *The Conflict of Laws* (10th edn) ch 15.
7 *Bromley*, n.6, above, at pp. 35–53; *Cretney*, n.6, above, at pp. 4–25.
8 SSA 1975, s.160 makes provision for the obtaining of copies of the certificate for this purpose.
9 *CG 203/49*.
10 See *38/49 (P)*; *R(P) 4/60*; *R(G) 2/70*.
11 *CG 53/50*.
12 *R(G) 1/51*.
13 Per Harman LJ, *Re Taylor* [1961] 1 All ER 55 at 63.
14 Per Sir Jocelyn Simon P, *Mahadervan v Mahadervan* [1964] P 233 at 244–246, adopted (obiter) by R J A Temple, Comr, in *R(G) 2/70*, para 17.
15 See *Low v Gorman* 1970 SLT 356, and generally *Clive and Wilson*, n.6, above, at pp. 116–122. The law appears not to have been affected by the Marriage (Scotland) Act 1977.
16 'Years' rather than 'months': *R(G) 8/56*, para 11.
17 *R(G) 1/71*.
18 *R(P) 1/51*; *R(I) 37/61*; *R(G) 2/82*; cp *R(G) 7/56* which regarded an impediment to marry as fatal only if known to the parties.
19 *R(G) 8/56*; *R(P) 1/58*; *R(G) 1/71*; *R(G) 2/82*.

C Marriages celebrated abroad

In general a foreign marriage will be recognised as valid by English and Scots law if it satisfied the formalities of the law of that jurisdiction where the marriage took place,[20] and if each party had capacity according to his domicile at the time of the alleged marriage.[1] The large number of immigrants, particularly from India and Pakistan, has caused considerable difficulties here. The problem is that sometimes expert evidence on the foreign law in question is required but it will not always be readily available to an insurance officer or local tribunal.[2] Decisions on the domicile of an individual at different stages of his life are also fraught with difficulties, depending as they do on a considerable amount of background information on family circumstances at some remote time or place.[3]

D Effects of marriages void or voidable or terminated by divorce

A marriage which is void[4] because, for example, it is bigamous[5] or within the prohibited degrees[6] has no effect at law and cannot be relied on for the purposes of entitlement to benefit. On the other hand, the fact that a marriage is void may revive an entitlement to widow's benefit from a 'previous' marriage if it had ceased to be payable on the alleged remarriage.[7] The widow may not, of course, claim for any period during which she was cohabiting with the second 'husband' and she will in any event be subject to the rules on time-limits.[8] A marriage which is terminated by divorce is treated as valid until the decree is made absolute, but from that date it is no longer effective to ground entitlement. Though there is no direct decision on the point, it is assumed that a previous entitlement to widow's benefit is not revived by dissolution of a subsequent marriage[9] – in this respect it is different from a marriage held to be void. The problems to which divorced marriages give rise are concerned mainly with whether a foreign decree should be recognised; this is determined by the rules of private international law.[10]

20 *R(U) 1/68* and see *Dicey and Morris*, n.6, above, at pp. 261–285.
1 *R(G) 3/75* and see *Dicey and Morris*, n.6, above, at pp. 285–304.
2 See the remarks of R S Lazarus, Comr, in *R(G) 2/71*, paras 4 and 8.
3 See e.g. *R(P) 1/57*; *R(G) 2/71* and *R(G) 3/75*.
4 See generally *Bromley*, n.6, above, at pp. 71–82.
5 *R(G) 2/63*.
6 *R(G) 10/53*.
7 *CG 28/53*, cited in *R(G) 1/73*.
8 P. 561, below.
9 See *R(G) 1/73*, para 14 (Tribunal majority).
10 Much of the law on recognition of foreign divorces is governed by the Recognition of Judicial Divorces and Legal Separations Act 1971, as modified by the Domicile and Matrimonial Proceedings Act 1973. See, in general, Dicey and Morris *The Conflict of Laws* (10th edn) pp. 341–356. The Commissioner has in several instances been faced with the problem of customary divorces by 'talaq'. In *R(G) 2/71* and *R(G) 4/74* such a divorce was recognised because, on the expert evidence available, it was found that on the balance of probabilities the divorce would have been recognised by the law of domicile even though there was no direct judicial authority in the particular jurisdiction (cp *R(G) 1/70*), though it was important to ascertain whether the correct procedure had been adopted (see *R(G) 5/74*. The Domicile and Matrimonial Proceedings Act 1973, s.16, provides that from 1 January 1974 and subject to certain exceptions, such divorces will no longer be recognised. Divorces obtained before that date are unaffected by the new provision.

Between void marriages and those terminated by divorce comes the third and problematic category of voidable marriages[11] (e.g. those which have not been consummated). Prior to 1971, for most legal purposes, such a marriage was regarded as valid and subsisting until the time of the decree of nullity, but the securing of such a decree would operate to invalidate the marriage retrospectively.[12] Under a legislative reform of 1956,[13] power was given to the Minister to provide by regulations that, for specified purposes, a voidable marriage was to be treated as a marriage terminated by divorce. This power was exercised as regards questions of entitlement arising under guardian's and child's special allowances.[14] The principles governing other benefits under social security legislation were unclear. In particular, there were conflicting decisions on whether a widow who lost benefit on entering a voidable marriage was entitled to claim for all periods except those during which she was cohabiting with the second 'husband'.[15] The process of retrospectively invalidating a marriage caused grave problems in other areas of the law and in 1971, following the recommendations of the Law Commission,[16] the Nullity of Marriage Act was passed, section 5 of which provides that

> a decree of nullity granted . . . on the ground that a marriage is voidable shall operate to annul the marriage only as respects any time after the decree had been made absolute, and the marriage shall, notwithstanding the decree, be treated as if it had existed up to that time.

Some consequences of this provision are undisputed. For the purpose of claiming benefit based on the marriage, it is, during its subsistence to the time of the decree of nullity, to be regarded as valid. It is also clear that a widow cannot claim benefit on a previous marriage for any period before the decree.[17] The problem is, however, whether such a claim is valid for the period *after* the decree: in other words, is the woman's status as a widow revived by the annulment of the second marriage? The arguments are evenly balanced. If attention is focused on the first part of section 5 (down) to the words 'after the decree had been made absolute'), it might be said that, for the period after the decree, the marriage is annulled and therefore to be regarded as if it had never existed. If, conversely, attention is focused on the last limb of section 5 ('and the marriage shall, notwithstanding the decree, be treated as if it had existed up to that time'), it might be said that even for purposes subsequent to the decree the marriage is to be treated as having existed at some time, and thus the woman's status as a widow is forever lost. A Tribunal of Commissioners, having taken into account the Law Commission's report on which proposals the measure was passed, preferred the second interpretation.[18]

11 See generally Bromley *Family Law* (6th edn) pp. 83–99.
12 Ibid, at p. 97.
13 NIA 1957, s.9(1)(c).
14 SI 1957/1392. See now SI 1975/497, reg 3 and SI 1975/515, reg 4(3).
15 In *R(G) 3/72*, following unreported decisions in *CG 2/70*, *CG 1/71* and *CG 2/71*, J S Watson, Comr, held that a widow was not so entitled. In *R(G) 1/53* it had been held that she was entitled.
16 Report No 33, 1970–71 HC 164.
17 *R(G) 1/73*, para 14.
18 *R(G) 1/73*, paras 18–20 and 25. *R(G) 2/73*. Cf the discussions in *Bromley*, n.11, above, at pp. 97–98 and Cretney *Principles of Family Law* (3rd edn) pp. 73–74.

E Polygamous marriages

The extent to which the courts should recognise as valid a polygamous marriage has always been a delicate issue,[19] and entitlement to social security benefits features not least among the problems to which it has given rise. In simple terms, is it to be regarded as fair that contributors with one wife should subsidise those with two? When the matter first arose for decision by the Commissioner, a harsh stance was adopted. It was held that the use of the terms 'wife', 'husband', and 'widow' in the National Insurance Act was intended to incorporate the notion familiar to English law of 'the voluntary union for life of one man and one woman to the exclusion of all others'.[20] The approach had the effect of treating as invalid for social security purposes not only actual polygamous marriages[1] but also any marriage celebrated under a law which permitted polygamy, whether or not it had at all times been in fact monogamous.[2] The only recourse of a person married under such circumstances was to show that the law of the place where the marriage was celebrated had converted it into a monogamous marriage,[3] or that the same result had been achieved by the parties changing their domicile to a jurisdiction which recognised only monogamous marriages.[4] These two avenues were not always open and statutory reform was obviously called for.

Following the National Insurance Advisory Committee's proposals,[5] it was forthcoming in 1956. Henceforth, a marriage which had in fact at all times been monogamous was to be recognised as valid, even where it had been entered into under a law which permitted polygamy.[6] Though this was certainly an improvement on the previously existing law, it was by no means a totally satisfactory solution:[7] it did not cover marriages which were at one time polygamous but which were no longer so; and it did not apply where at the time benefit was claimed the marriage was polygamous but only one wife was resident in Great Britain. The policy argument for extending benefit may be stronger for the first group than for the second, but in either case refusal would seem unfair to a husband who has duly been paying his contributions. Moreover, supplementary benefit is certainly payable[8] and in *Iman Din v National Assistance Board*,[9] it was held that a polygamously married man could be compelled to reimburse the Board for national assistance (the precursor of supplementary benefit) paid to one of his wives. The gaps were partly filled by reform in 1971.[10] In its present version the measure provides that

> a polygamous marriage shall . . . be treated as having the same consequences as a monogamous marriage for any day, but only for any day, throughout which the polygamous marriage is in fact monogamous.[11]

19 See Law Commission Report No 42, 1970–71, HC 227; *Dicey and Morris*, n.10, above, at pp. 308–327, and Pearl [1978–9] JSWL 24.
20 Per Lord Penzance, *Hyde v Hyde and Woodmansee* (1866) LR 1 P & D 130, 133, quoted in *R(G) 18/52*, para 19.
1 *R(G) 6/51*.
2 *R(G) 18/52* (Tribunal decision). See also *R(G) 11/53*, *R(G) 3/55*, *R(G) 7/55* and the critical survey of the case law by Webb 19 MLR 687.
3 As by the Indian Hindu Marriage Act 1955: see *R(G) 12/56*.
4 Under the doctrine of *Ali v Ali* [1968] P. 564, [1966] 1 All ER 664; see *R(G) 5/75*.
5 Report on the Question of Widows' Benefit (1955, Cmd 9684).
6 FANIA 1956, s.3.
7 See Law Commission Report, n.19, above, at paras 125–134.
8 Cf n.20, p. 462, below.
9 [1967] 2 QB 213, [1967] 1 All ER 750, DC.
10 NIA 1971, s.16(3) and SI 1972/1150.
11 SI 1975/561, reg 2(1). For equivalent provisions under CBA 1975, see SI 1976/965, reg 12.

There are also special rules governing entitlement to retirement pensions of women who are parties to a polygamous marriage.[12] The broad effect is that such a woman may claim retirement pension on her husband's contributions as from any date on which the marriage was in fact monogamous, and in such cases the rate of pension payable is that which would have been payable in the case of a monogamous marriage whether or not, prior to the date in question, the marriage had been polygamous.

It should be noted, however, that these provisions only apply to a polygamous marriage which 'was celebrated under a law which, as it applies to the particular ceremony and to the parties thereto, permits polygamy'.[13] As regards English law, marriages celebrated after 31 July 1971[14] in a polygamous form are void if at the time either party was domiciled in England.[15] There seems to be no obvious reason why contributory benefits should be denied to a party of such a marriage when it in fact remains monogamous.[16]

The position of persons who at the time of the claim (or in the case of widow's benefit at the time of the contributor's death) are actually polygamously married is no doubt more delicate. The Law Commission has studied the problem in depth but felt unable to recommend on grounds of administrative feasibility or acceptability by the general public a number of proposed solutions.[17] These included: full entitlement for each wife (with or without increased contributions); a sharing of normal benefit by the wives; nomination by the husband (or the Secretary of State) of one wife for full benefit; full benefit for a wife living in Britain. This last suggestion would seem to be the most attractive and the objection raised to it, that it would be inequitable to the wife (or wives) living abroad, does not seem very persuasive.[18]

Part 3 Living together as husband and wife

A General

For certain purposes social security legislation treats a woman living with a man (not her husband) in the same way as a married woman. Thus a woman loses entitlement to widow's benefit[19] (and its equivalent in the industrial injuries and war pension schemes[20]), child's special allowance,[1] non-contributory invalidity pension[2] and invalid care allowance[3]

12 SI 1975/561, reg 3.
13 Ibid, reg 1(2).
14 For marriages before this date see the controversial decision in *Radwan v Radwan (No 2)* [1973] Fam 35, [1972] 3 All ER 1026, where it was held that the common law permitted a person presently domiciled in England to contract a valid potentially polygamous marriage if the intention of the parties at the time of celebration was to set up a home in a country permitting polygamy.
15 Matrimonial Causes Act 1973, s.11(d).
16 Pearl, n.19, above, at 28.
17 Law Commission Published Working Paper No 21, paras 61–66. The Report which followed (No 42) took the matter no further: n.19, above.
18 See also Pearl, n.19, above, at 29.
19 SSA 1975, ss.24(2), 25(3) and 26(3).
20 Ibid, ss.67(2), 71(3)(b), 72(4)(a) and 73(3) and SI 1978/1525, art 42.
1 SSA 1975, s.31.
2 Ibid, s.36(2)(b).
3 Ibid, s.37(3)(b).

for any period during which she and a man to whom she is not married are living together as husband and wife.[4]

Such a woman is treated in the same way as a married woman in both the supplementary benefits[5] and family income supplements[6] schemes, and her requirements and resources are aggregated with the man's if he claims benefits.

The 'cohabitation rule', as it is often referred to, was included in the national insurance widow's scheme introduced in 1925[7] but, perhaps surprisingly, was not expressly contained in the National Assistance Act 1948. If a woman cohabiting with a man claimed assistance, the National Assistance Board was compelled to use its discretionary powers to refuse an award.[8] In 1966, when supplementary benefits replaced national assistance, the rule was embodied in the legislation,[9] and, subject to a recent change in its formulation, has remained a constant, if controversial, feature of both the contributory and the means-tested schemes.

Though the arguments are equally applicable to both schemes, criticisms of the rule, which became particularly forthright in the late 1960s and 1970s,[10] tended to focus on its effect on supplementary benefit entitlement, and the Supplementary Benefits Commission produced two special reports defending the rule, though instituting changes in its administration.[11]

The main justification advanced by the Commission, and accepted by the Finer Committee on One-Parent Families,[12] is that

> . . . it would be wrong in principle to treat the women who have the support of a partner both as if they had not such support and better than if they were married. It would not be right, and we believe public opinion would not accept, that the unmarried 'wife' should be able to claim benefit denied to a married woman.[13]

Although the rule's existence is regretted, it is, therefore, thought necessary to ensure equity between married and unmarried women. Two main arguments against the rule may be identified. The first is that an unmarried woman is not legally entitled to support for herself or her children (if not his own) from the man with whom she is living.[14] The distinction as regards rights to maintenance between married and unmarried women was regarded as crucial by the Supreme Court of the United States when it held invalid an Alabama regulation disqualifying a family from receiving assistance if, inter alia, a man lived in or visited the mother's house for the purposes of cohabitation.[15] The Commission's answer to this argument was that in general the men concerned do support the woman (and her children) with whom they are living, and that only a small minority refuse to accept responsibility.[16] The risk of hardship for some women did not justify, in its view, abrogation of the rule and the consequent unfairness to those who are married. This argument would

4 SS(MP)A 1977, ss.14(7) and 22(2) and (4), amending the relevant provisions of SSA 1975.
5 SBA 1976, s.34(1) and Sch 1, para 3(1): pp. 403–404, below.
6 FISA 1970, s.1(1)(b).
7 Widows', Orphans' and Old Age Contributory Pensions Act 1925, s.21(1).
8 SBC Report, *Living Together as Husband and Wife* (1976) para 8.
9 SBA 1966, Sch 2, para 3(1).
10 See esp. Lister *As Man and Wife* (1970), Poverty Pamphlet.
11 *Cohabitation* (1971) and *Living Together as Husband and Wife,* n.8, above.
12 Para 5.269.
13 *Cohabitation* para 7.
14 *Living Together as Husband and Wife* para 22.
15 *Smith v King* 88 S Ct 2128 (1968). See also *Van Lare v Hurley* 95 S Ct 1741 (1975).
16 N.8, above, at para 22.

appear to be acceptable, provided the Commission was right in its assessment that relatively few cases of hardship result from the rule's application. The Commission's own evidence suggested that some relationships between the claimant and the man concerned terminate soon after the cessation of benefit payments, and this often leads to a further application for assistance.[17] To some extent this might be thought to cast doubt on the argument for the rule.

The second principal argument is that, whatever the rule's merits in theory, its application leads to such intrusion into privacy and consequent anxiety on the part of claimants that its maintenance cannot on balance be justified.[18] There is no obvious answer to this contention, and it is interesting that in its second report the Commission did not even attempt one. To some extent the solution lies in a more sensitive administration of the rule, and the DHSS has made a number of changes in its practice which should go some way to meeting the criticism.[19]

B The meaning of 'living together'

The term 'cohabiting' was never defined in the social security legislation. This was criticised by the Fisher Committee Report on Abuse of Social Security Benefits,[20] arguing that individuals should not be left in such uncertainty as to what will lead to forfeiture of benefit. But the view has always been taken that precise statutory definition is impossible.[1] Indeed, in one case Lord Widgery CJ said that the phrase 'cohabiting as man and wife', then in force, was 'so well known that nothing I could say about it could possibly assist in its interpretation'.[2] In 1977, the term 'cohabiting' was replaced by 'living together',[3] largely on the ground that the former had acquired a pejorative meaning,[4] but it is clear that no different interpretation was intended.[5]

'Living together as husband and wife' is a ground for forfeiture from both means-tested benefits and those payable under the Social Security Act. The intention is clearly that a uniform interpretation should govern these various provisions.[6] It is therefore proposed to consider together such guidelines on the meaning as emerge from Commissioners' and court decisions, and also the statements of Departmental policy contained in the Supplementary Benefits Handbook[7] which were recently described by Woolf J as 'admirable signposts'.[8] Most of these authorities point to a number of factors whose absence or presence may assist in deciding the issue; but none is to be regarded as conclusive.[9]

17 N.8, above, at paras 30, 34 and 35–48.
18 Ibid, at para 18.
19 For a short discussion of these reforms, see p. 464, below.
20 Para 330(b).
1 N.8, above, at paras 49–51.
2 *R v South West London Supplementary Benefits Appeals Tribunal, ex parte Barnett* (1973) SB Dec 28 (Decision SB4).
3 SS(MP)A 1977, ss.14(7) and 22(2)–(4).
4 N.8, above, at para 52.
5 *R(SB) 17/81*, para 9, D G Rice, Comr.
6 Ibid, para 4; and *R(G) 3/81*.
7 Para 2.12. When a claimant suspected of cohabitation is in receipt of both types of benefit, it seems that in general a decision on a contributory benefit will be followed in administering the means-tested benefit.
8 *Crake v Supplementary Benefits Commission* [1982] 1 All ER 498 at 505. See also *R(SB) 17/81* para 10.
9 *Crake's* case, n.8, above. See also: *R(G) 3/71*, para 5; *R(G) 1/79*, para 8; *R(SB) 17/81* para 11.

i Members of same household

It is a necessary condition for the application of the rule to the means-tested benefits,[10] and an obvious assumption for its application to the contributory benefits,[11] that the man and woman should be members of the same household, i.e., residing together under the same roof.[12] If, for example, he spends much of his time at another house, it will be difficult to infer that the two parties are living together.[13] A finding that they live in the same household is not by itself sufficient. In *Butterworth v Supplementary Benefits Commission*,[14] Woolf J said that the crucial issue was *why* they did so. It was thus a question of their intentions and since in that case the man moved in to help a woman who was in a poor state of health, they did not intend to establish a marriage-like relationship[15] and she remained entitled to benefit. This subjective approach is somewhat novel and though it provided an excellent basis for the decision on the particular facts in *Butterworth*, it will often be an elusive test to apply, and is in any event difficult to reconcile with several other decisions.[16] More recently, the Commissioner has doubted whether 'a person's intention can be ascertained otherwise than by what he or she does and says at the relevant time. It is the conduct of the person concerned to which regard has to be paid'.[17]

ii Duration

The duration and stability of the cohabitation is clearly an important factor.[18] Where there is no evidence as to continuity of co-residence or where its existence remains uncertain, benefit should not be refused, though once it has been established that the required relationship exists, it is much easier to show that it continues.[19] The suggestion that a couple should be allowed to live together for a number of months without entitlement being affected has, however, been rejected.[20]

iii Financial support

The argument that a man can only be held to be living with a woman if he is supporting her financially has been rejected.[1] Apart from anything else, the financial contributions might reflect a commercial relationship (e.g. landlady and lodger) rather than a personal relationship.[2] The Supplementary Benefits Commission thought it unrealistic to place primary emphasis on the level and consistency of financial contributions: this would encourage the man not to support the claimant in order to improve her chance of receiving benefit.[3] Moreover, the assessment of the contributions

10 FISA 1970, s.1; SBA 1976, Sch 1, para 3(1).
11 See e.g. *R(G) 11/55*.
12 On 'residing together', see pp. 371–373, above.
13 Handbook, para 2.12a.
14 [1982] 1 All ER 498 at 502.
15 An intention to *marry* need not be shown: *R(SB) 17/81*.
16 E.g. *Amarjit Kaur Dhanjal v Secretary of State for Social Services* (1981) unreported: see Lyon [1981] JSWL 372, 375.
17 *R(G) 3/81*, para 8, D.G. Rice, Comr.
18 Handbook, para 2.12b; cf *R(P) 6/52*.
19 *Crake*'s case, n.8, above, at 502.
20 SBC Report, *Living Together as Husband and Wife* (1976) para 55(2).
1 *R(G) 2/64*, para 7.
2 Cf *R(G) 3/71*, para 7.
3 N.20, above, at para 55(3). Cp Lister *As Man and Wife* (1970, Poverty Pamphlet) pp. 41–42 where it is suggested that more weight should be given to the financial aspects of the relationship.

would present practical difficulties.[4] Where, however, there *is* evidence that the man and woman do pool their resources, this will be taken into account in determiing whether they live together.[5]

iv Sexual relationship

The existence or absence of a sexual relationship is never conclusive of the relationship of the persons concerned.[6] In some cases, however, it may be of great weight, particularly when it is also established that they have children and intend to marry.[7] This is naturally a sensitive area, and the DHSS has been anxious to emphasise that it is not concerned with the sexual morals of the claimant. Its staff is instructed not to question claimants about their sexual relationship and not to inspect the sleeping arrangements.[8]

v Children

There will be a strong presumption that a man and woman are living together as husband and wife if they are looking after their own children.[9]

vi Public acknowledgement

A public acknowledgement by a woman that she is living with someone as his wife by taking his surname is compelling evidence of cohabitation.[10] On the other hand, little significance is to be attached to a refusal to acknowledge the relationship in public.[11]

Part 4 Residence and presence

A General

The geographical boundaries of the social security system may not seem to raise policy issues of the dimension encountered elsewhere but it has long been an area the difficulties of which have provided a fruitful supply of problems for lawyers. Under the poor law perhaps the question giving rise to most litigation was that concerned with the 'settlement' of paupers, the condition of residence on which the responsibility of parishes was based.[12] Happily, the centralisation of social security obviated the need to distinguish between parts of the country, but the increased facilities for foreign travel, the growth of multinational enterprises and the emergence of the 'migrant worker' underline the continued importance and difficulty of the topic. To some extent the problems have been solved by reciprocal agreements with other national systems and by the 'co-ordinating' Regulations of the European Economic Community. These instruments are

4 *Cohabitation* para 8; *Living Together as Husband and Wife* para 55(3).
5 *R(G) 2/72*; *R(G) 1/79*; *Amarjit Kaur Dhanjal* case, n.16, above; Handbook, para 2.12c.
6 See *Thomas v Thomas* [1948] 2 KB 294, DC, discussing the meaning of 'cohabitation' in the context of matrimonial legislation.
7 *R(G) 2/64*; *R(G) 3/71*.
8 Handbook, para 2.12d.
9 *CG 214/50*; *R(G) 3/64*; *R(G) 3/71*; *R(G) 2/72*.
10 *R(G) 5/68*; *R(G) 1/79*.
11 *CP 97/49*; *R(P) 6/52*.
12 Blackstone *Commentaries* vol 1, p. 362, refers to the 'infinity of expensive law-suits between contending neighbourhoods'. See, generally, Holdsworth *History of English Law* (1938) vol X, pp. 257–269. See also p. 450, below.

described in chapter 16. The discussion in the present chapter is concerned with the limits imposed by the British social security legislation independently of the facilities available under the instruments. The rules emerging will thus indicate the circumstances in which an individual must resort to the additional facilities described in chapter 16.

B The framework

In general, the relationship with Great Britain, as expressed in such concepts as 'residence', 'presence', or (in a very few instances) 'nationality', is relevant for four different purposes.

i Participation in the contributory scheme

There are rules to determine who is compelled (or in the case of non-employed persons and certain self-employed persons who is entitled) to contribute to the scheme. These have been set out in chapter 2.[13]

ii Alternatives to contribution conditions

For those benefits the entitlement to which depends on the fulfilment of contribution conditions there is no *positive* requirement as to residence. Participation in the scheme for the requisite number of years is prima facie sufficient to justify the conferring of benefit. Indeed, to a limited extent, the system is prepared to make concessions to those whose work abroad has prevented them from making the requisite contributions. The rules designed to implement this policy were also mentioned in chapter 2.[14]

iii Disqualifications for absence

The Social Security Act 1975 lays down as a general ground for disqualification for contributory benefits absence (whether of the claimant himself or a dependant for whom an increase is claimed) from Great Britain.[15] This principle, as elaborated and modified in the Regulations, is described in this Part.

iv Requirements for non-contributory benefits

For benefits entitlement to which does not depend on fulfilment of contribution conditions, the need to impose limits on the scheme, according to an individual's connection with Great Britain, is more obvious and important. For each such benefit there is, therefore, a combination of rules generally requiring 'residence', 'ordinary residence', or at least 'presence' in Great Britain. The rules are stated in the appropriate chapters; here it will be necessary only to given an account of the interpretation of the general concepts employed.

C Absence as a ground of disqualification from contributory benefits

The principles applicable proceed according to consistent but sometimes controversial policy dictates. There is no relief for absent persons claiming

13 Pp. 52, 54, 57 and 58, above.
14 P. 71, above.
15 SSA 1975, s.82(5)(a).

unemployment benefit, it being felt desirable to maintain unequivocally the claimant's attachment to the labour market in this country. Those entitled by reason of their incapacity or confinement are given some concessions, notably for temporary absences. The most generous provision is for those whose entitlement in no way rests on their inability to work, because, for example, they have reached pensionable age or are caring for dependent children. Here the disqualification is often removed altogether. The general rule is then that a person is disqualified from receiving benefit (or an increase in benefit for a dependant) during a period during which the person (or the dependant) is absent from Great Britain.[16] The modifications to the rule are as follows.

i Benefits for incapacity

For the purposes of sickness benefit, invalidity benefit, unemployability supplement, and maternity allowance a temporary absence is disregarded if

(a) the Secretary of State has certified that it is consistent with the proper administration of the Act that the disqualification should not apply *and either*

(b) the absence is for the specific purpose of being treated for incapacity which commenced before he left Great Britain *or*

(c) when the absence began he was, and had for six months continuously been, incapable of work and when benefit is claimed he has remained continuously so incapable since the absence began.[17]

The claimant must first establish that the absence is only temporary. No guidance is given for the interpretation of this, but the Commissioner has held that a seasonal worker, absent for the period of his off-season, cannot escape disqualification.[18] In other cases, it depends on the specificity of the intent to return. If there is only a vague hope to return sometime in the future, or when the claimant's health improves, the absence will not be temporary.[19] If there is an unequivocal intention to return when the claimant is fit to do so, the issue turns on the duration of the absence. A practical test, enunciated by the Commissioner, is that at the end of a twelve-month period there should be a reasonable prospect of the residence abroad coming to an end within the next six months.[20]

Condition (a) was originally introduced in 1975 to solve some of the difficulties, described below, arising from the other two conditions. It conferred a discretion on the Secretary of State to determine what was 'reasonable in all the circumstances of the case, having regard in particular . . . to the nature of the person's incapacity and to his location'.[1] In 1976 the Commissioner held that the Regulation was ultra vires.[2] An amendment of 1977 therefore introduced the concept of consistency with the proper administration of the Act.[3] It is to be anticipated, however, that the Secretary of State will continue to have regard to the considerations mentioned under the 1975 Regulation.

16 Ibid. Absence means not physically present (*R(U) 18/60*; *R(S) 16/62*). For the meaning of 'Great Britain' and for other points arising under the rule, see pp. 391–393, below.

17 SI 1975/563, reg 2(1), as amended by SI 1977/1679. For the analogous but not completely identical rule for industrial injury benefit see SI 1975/563, reg 9(1).

18 *R(I) 14/51*; *R(I) 73/54*.

19 *R(S) 3/58*; *R(S) 5/59*; *R(S) 9/59*.

20 *R(S) 9/55*.

1 SI 1975/563, reg 2(1).

2 *CS 5/75*, and see NIAC Report (Cmnd 6967).

3 SI 1977/1679.

Under condition (b), it is necessary to show, first, that the claimant was suffering from the incapacity which commenced before his departure from Great Britain.[4] 'Incapacity' has been given the meaning attributed to it for the purpose of entitlement to benefit:[5] viz an incapacity for work[6] constituted by a specific disease or bodily or mental disablement.[7] The ordinary condition of pregnancy is not sufficient,[8] and the incapacity must have been diagnosed (or capable of being diagnosed) before the absence began.[9] The requirement that the absence must be for the *specific purpose* of being treated has been generously (perhaps too generously) construed. The treatment need not be the sole objective of the absence – it may rank alongside other social or pleasurable purposes.[10] It need not be unavailable in Britain;[11] nor, apparently, need it be actually received by the claimant – it is sufficient if the purpose of the visit was to obtain it.[12] More surprisingly, and arguably wrongly, the specific purpose need not be formulated before the claimant leaves the country.[13] Greater difficulty has arisen from the meaning of 'being treated'. There is general agreement that some activity by a person other than the claimant must be involved,[14] but there is little uniformity on what form is envisaged. Some decisions imply that medical supervision or care is required;[15] others do not regard this as necessary.[16] In cases of mental illness, the authorities scrutinise the nature of the 'treatment' with particular care,[17] but in one case a claimant with psychological problems avoided disqualification when he was assisted in the solving of his spiritual problems by a Doctor of Divinity.[18] On one major issue there is, however, no disagreement: it has repeatedly been held that to go abroad merely to convalesce, for a change of environment, air or food, or to obtain freedom from anxiety, even if undertaken according to medical advice, does not amount to 'being treated'.[19] Indeed, in the only case which has been taken to the Divisional Court in this area the decision was limited to this simple proposition.[20] It is to be regretted that no further guidance was offered on what is a most confusing area of case-law.

The alternative condition (c) was introduced in 1967[1] to assist the long-term incapacitated. In these cases, proximity to the labour market is obviously of less importance. On the other hand, the absence must still be temporary, and therefore the number likely to succeed on this ground must be relatively small.

4 See e.g. *R(S) 35/52*, *R(S) 19/54* and *R(S) 8/59*. In *R(S) 1/77*, para 10, it was said that the incapacity does not have to be subsisting at the time of departure.
5 Cf pp. 147–154, above.
6 *R(S) 9/59*.
7 *R(S) 1/75*.
8 *R(G) 5/53*; *R(S) 1/75*.
9 *R(S) 1/75*.
10 *CSS 71/49*; *R(S) 6/61*.
11 *R(S) 3/54*.
12 *R(S) 6/61*.
13 *CS 317/49*; *R(S) 1/57*; *R(S) 1/75*; *R(S) 1/77*.
14 *CSS 71/49*; *CS 474/50*; *R(S) 10/51*.
15 *R(S) 16/51*; *R(S) 5/61*; *R(S) 2/69*.
16 *R(S) 10/51*; *R(S) 2/51*.
17 See *R(S) 5/61*.
18 *R(S) 1/65*.
19 *R(S) 16/51*; *R(S) 10/52*; *R(S) 25/52*; *R(S) 5/61*; *R(S) 3/68*; *R(S) 1/69*; *R(S) 2/69*; *R(S) 4/80*; *R(S) 6/81*.
20 *R v National Insurance Comr, ex parte McMenemey* (1966), reported as Appendix to *R(S) 2/69*.
1 SI 1967/828.

ii Long-term benefits immune from disqualification

When the benefit in question is paid irrespective of the working capacity of the claimant, supervision of the claim is less important and, arguably, he should receive the return on the contributions paid irrespective of where he chooses to live. The disqualification does not, therefore, apply to retirement pensions, child's special allowance, widow's benefit,[2] industrial disablement and death benefit.[3] On the other hand, those claiming widow's benefit, child's special allowance or retirement pension[4] may not be entitled to an increase resulting from an up-rating of benefit unless they satisfy certain residence conditions.[5] The disqualification is not, however, automatic and it is for the Secretary of State to determine, when issuing the up-rating order, whether or not these special conditions are to apply.[6] The policy is a traditional one: in the 1950s and 1960s when increases were made to the standard rate of pension those resident abroad were not allowed to benefit.[7] In insurance terms it was argued that the contributions on which the pension was based were not actuarially related to the increases and that it would be inequitable for the other contributors to the fund, effectively paying for the increases, to assist those living abroad.[8] In practice, however, relatively few beneficiaries are disadvantaged as they are entitled to the increases under EEC law and reciprocal arrangements with other countries.[9]

iii Death grant

A person, e.g. the administrator of the deceased's estate, may be paid the death grant notwithstanding his absence from Great Britain.[10]

iv Dependants

It is part of the general rule that a claimant may not receive an increase for an absent dependant. In some cases, this caused hardship, for a person resident in Great Britain might, while abroad, have married a person who had never set foot in this country. The foreign spouse would not, as a result of the marriage, 'acquire' the residence of the claimant (as for example under the old rules whereby a woman on marriage acquired the domicile of her husband) and the increase would not be payable.[11] The general rule is therefore modified so that

> a husband or wife shall not be disqualified for receiving any increase (where payable) of benefit in respect of his or her spouse by reason of the spouse's being

2 In the case of widow's allowance, however, the woman or her late husband must have been in GB at the time of the death or the contribution conditions for widowed mother's allowance or widow's pension must have been satisfied: SI 1975/563, reg 4(2).
3 Ibid, regs 4(1), 9(3) and 9(6).
4 This includes the guaranteed minimum pension, payable as part of an occupational pension (on which see p. 223, above).
5 Normally 'ordinary residence' in GB: SI 1975/563, reg 5. See p. 393, below, and *R(P) 1/78*.
6 SI 1975/563, reg 5(1). Disqualifications have been imposed for increases since 1979: SI 1979/1278; SI 1980/1505; SI 1981/1510.
7 See e.g. FANIA 1952, s.5 and SI 1952/2144; NIA 1960, s.2 and SI 1960/2422; NIA 1963, s.1, and SI 1963/394.
8 See the remarks of Mr P Dean, Under-Secretary of State, in Standing Committee E Debates on Social Security Bill 1973, col 783.
9 Cf ch 16, below.
10 SI 1975/563, reg 7(2). For the rules governing the absence of the deceased himself see pp. 242–243, above.
11 See e.g. *CG 32/49* and *55/50 (MB)*.

absent from Great Britain, provided that the spouse is residing with the husband or wife, as the case may be.[12]

As regards increases for child dependants, as has been seen,[13] since 1975 these are generally linked to entitlement to child benefit. The residence and presence requirements of the latter are generally stricter than those applied previously to child dependency increases and so regulations exist to preserve the broader base of entitlement: in general, the increase is payable if the beneficiary or the child is only temporarily absent from Great Britain.[14]

D Some common concepts

It remains to provide an account of the meaning of concepts which are common to the various rules on residence and absence.

i 'United Kingdom' and 'Great Britain'

For some purposes the geographical unit is the 'United Kingdom', but for the majority it is 'Great Britain'. The former means 'Great Britain and Northern Ireland',[15] the latter, England, Wales and Scotland.[16] Notwithstanding the fact that British courts may exercise criminal jurisdiction over British ships, aircraft and embassies, they are not regarded as part of the territory for purposes of the residence requirements.[17] The same is true of the Continental Shelf but special provisions render persons employed there immune from disqualification.[18]

ii Presence and absence

The two concepts are mutually exclusive.[19] To be 'absent' from Great Britain does not necessarily imply that the person concerned must have been present at some time in the past – it simply means not present.[20] Both presence and absence are questions of fact dependent on physical circumstances and concerned in no way with intention, or external events. Thus in a case where a claimant would have arrived in England but for technical problems in the mode of transport, it was to no avail for her to argue that she would but for another's fault have been present in Great Britain.[1]

iii 'Residence'

This is the term most widely used to represent the necessary connection with Great Britain. Its use has not of course been confined to social

12 SI 1975/563, reg 13.
13 P. 367, above.
14 SI 1975/563, reg 13A, inserted by SI 1977/342.
15 Royal and Parliamentary Titles Act 1927, s.2(2).
16 Union with Scotland Act 1706, preamble, art 1; and Wales and Berwick Act 1746, s.3. Northern Ireland, the Isle of Man and the Channel Islands are thus excluded. However, as a result of the relevant reciprocal agreements, the various schemes are almost wholly integrated.
17 *CSG 2/48*; *CP 93/49*; *R(S) 8/59*; *R(I) 44/61*; *R(P) 8/61*.
18 SI 1975/563, reg 11.
19 *R(U) 18/60*.
20 *R(U) 16/62*.
1 *R(S) 8/59*. See also *R(S) 6/81*.

security legislation. There are many other areas, notably taxation,[2] bankruptcy[3] and matrimonial causes,[4] where it features prominently. Although the Commissioner has pointed out the danger of relying on decisions made in quite a different context,[5] nevertheless he has drawn freely from them for ideas in elucidating the term.[6]

The burden of proof is normally on the claimant to show that he is 'resident' in Great Britain at the relevant time.[7] The question is one of fact and degree[8] and does not lend itself easily to definition but reference has been made to the word's ordinary meaning, formulated in the Oxford English Dictionary as 'to dwell permanently or for a considerable time, to have one's settled or usual abode'.[9] Though the claimant need not be physically present at any one particular time, there must be a sufficient amount of physical presence in the place on which the residence may be grounded: a theory of 'constructive residence' is not recognised.[10] Conversely, the degree of permanence necessary need not be such as to render the place in question the claimant's domicile;[11] he may, consequently, be resident in more than one place or country at any one time.[12] But a person who has his matrimonial home in one country is not normally to be treated as resident in another while he is residing at the matrimonial home.[13]

Within these broad outlines there are a number of factors to be taken into account. Perhaps the most important is the intention of the claimant himself. If he intends to settle in one place, he is likely to reside there.[14] In *R(P) 6/58*,

> C returned from Rhodesia where he had been living for nine years in the hope that he would benefit under the will of a relative. Eleven months later, when his expectations were not fully realised, he went back to Rhodesia. It was held that during these eleven months he was 'resident' in GB, as it had been, at the time, his intention permanently to stay there.

Conversely, a person taking a job abroad may still be resident in Britain if he intends to return immediately on its completion.[15] But in this situation the authorities are likely to have regard to the nature of the employment: if

2 E.g. Income and Corporation Taxes Act 1970, ss.49–51; and see *Simon's Taxes* (3rd edn) E5–104.
3 E.g. Bankruptcy Act 1914, s.1(2)(b) and see Williams *Bankruptcy* (19th edn) pp. 51–52.
4 E.g. Matrimonial Causes Act 1973, s.35(1), and see Bromley *Family Law* (6th edn) pp. 8–9.
5 E.g. *R(G) 2/51*; *R(P) 4/54*; *R(P) 1/72*; *R(P) 1/78*.
6 A prime example is the Tribunal decision of *R(F) 1/62*.
7 *R(G) 2/51* (Tribunal decision).
8 *R 5/62 (UB)*; *R(P) 2/67*. See also *Levene v IRC* [1928] AC 217 at 222, HL and *IRC v Lysaght* [1928] AC 234 at 241, 243, HL.
9 Quoted in *Levene v IRC*, n.8, above, at 222, *Fox v Stirk and Bristol Electoral Registration Officer* [1970] 2 QB 463 at 475, 477, CA, and *CG 32/49*.
10 *CG 32/49*; *55/50 (MB)*; *R 5/62 (UB)*; *R(P) 1/72*. For the theory as applied to the poor law see *R v Glossop* (1866) LR 1 QB 227 and *West Ham Union v Cardiff Union* [1895] 1 QB 766.
11 *R(F) 1/62*; *R 1/71 (P)*. For the concept of domicile generally, see Dicey and Morris *Conflict of Laws* (10th edn) ch 7.
12 *R(G) 2/51*; *R(P) 2/67*. See also *Re Norris, ex parte Reynolds* (1888) 4 TLR 452, *Levene v IRC*, n. 8, above, *IRC v Lysaght*, n.8, above, and *Fox v Stirk and Bristol Electoral Registration Officer*, n.9, above.
13 *R(P) 1/78*, para 7, H Magnus, Comr.
14 See esp. the dictum of Somervell LJ in *Macrae v Macrae* [1949] P 397 at 403.
15 *CG 204/49*.

it is of a finite nature, e.g. a fixed term contract, the intention to return will prevail;[16] if, however, it is of indeterminate length, the mere expression of hope to return at sometime in the future will generally be insufficient.[17] Of course, the amount of time actually spent in Britain (or abroad) may be significant – in *Fox v Stirk*[18], Lord Denning MR spoke of a stay amounting to residence when it involves 'a considerable degree of permanence' – but if the intention is unequivocal, even a short time may be sufficient.[19] Another very important factor in practice is the nature of arrangements made for living while the individual is in Britain. It is not necessary that he should own or rent his own accommodation, but if he stays throughout in a hotel or with relatives, he must be able to show that he made his 'home' there.[20] If he leaves furniture and other personal effects in one place, this will help to show that he is still resident there even if he has lived for a considerable period elsewhere.[1] In any event, it is easier to prove a continued residence in one place than a change to another country.[2]

iv 'Ordinarily resident'

Social security law employs the term 'ordinarily resident' less frequently than 'resident'. Where it is used it connotes the idea of residence with 'some degree of continuity'.[3] Its object is to exclude from entitlement persons who live mostly abroad but who come to reside in Great Britain intermittently without wishing to settle here.[4] So in *R(P) 1/78* the Commissioner, H Magnus, held that the claimant who returned to Britain from her matrimonial home in Rhodesia intermittently for family and business reasons was 'resident' but not 'ordinarily resident' here during such periods.

v Days of residence and absence

Where part of a day is spent in this country and part abroad, the question arises whether it will count as a day of residence or of absence.

– The policy has always been not to have regard to fractions of a day. A decision in 1948 held that it was convenient to assume that the state of things which first occurred on a day prevailed throughout that day, so that if a claimant is absent at the beginning of a day he will remain absent until midnight.[5] This view no longer pertains. The current interpretation is that a person bearing the burden of proving that he was resident, or absent, on a day or period, must establish that he was resident or absent *throughout* that day or period.[6]

16 *R(G) 2/51*.
17 *CG 165/50*; *R(G) 5/52*. See also *Lewis v Lewis* [1956] 1 All ER 375. [1956] 1 WLR 200.
18 [1970] 2 QB 463, 475.
19 *R(F) 1/62* and see *Macrae v Macrae*, n.14, above.
20 *R(P) 4/54*; *R(F) 1/62*; *R(P) 1/72*; and see: *Re Norris, ex parte Reynolds*, n.12, above; *Re Erskine, ex parte Erskine* (1893) 10 TLR 32; *Levene v IRC*, n.8, above and *Re Brauch, ex parte Brittanic Securities and Investments Ltd* [1978] Ch 316, [1978] 1 All ER 1004.
1 *R(G) 2/51*; *R(F) 1/62*; *R(P) 2/67*. See also *Hopkins v Hopkins* [1951] P 116, [1950] 2 All ER 1035; *Stransky v Stransky* [1954] P 428 and *Lewis v Lewis*, n.17, above.
2 *R(F) 1/62*; *Macrae v Macrae*, n.14, above.
3 *R(P) 1/78*, paras 7–8, adopting a dictum of Viscount Cave LC in *Levene v IRC*, n.8, above. at 225. See also *Stransky v Stransky*, n.1, above, at 437, per Karminski J.
4 *R(P) 1/78*, para 9, and see *R v London Borough of Barnet, ex parte Shah* [1980] 3 All ER 679.
5 *CU 54/48*.
6 *R(S) 1/66*; *Re a Farm Manager* [1979] 1 CMLR 445 at 446.

Part 5 Hospital in-patients

A General

Where the claimant, or a dependant for whom he is entitled to an increase, is a long-term hospital in-patient, enjoying free maintenance there under the National Health Service, the amount payable is reduced. The policy is an obvious one, and may be seen as part of the provisions for overlapping benefits:[7] to the extent that a person's primary living needs are being supplied by services financed by public funds full benefit is inappropriate.[8] The rules governing personal benefit and dependant's increase are classified according to the length of stay in hospital.

B Adjustments to personal benefit

No adjustment is made for the first eight weeks of free in-patient treatment. It is assumed that expenditure will continue to be incurred during short stays: in particular, it is unlikely that a person will discontinue his occupation of premises, and thus he will remain liable for rent or mortgage repayments. Once, however, this period has elapsed, it is assumed that his living expenses will be significantly reduced, though if he has dependants the family home will still have to be maintained. The rules are classified, therefore, according to the length of stay in hospital, and the existence or non-existence of dependants; they incorporate references to the current rate of the basic component in a Category A retirement pension.[9]

i *From 9–52 weeks* If the claimant has a dependant for whom an increase is, or would but for the rules to be described in the next paragraph be, payable, benefit is reduced by 20 per cent of the basic component; if he has no such dependant it is reduced by 40 per cent; but the reduction in any case is not to leave him with less than 20 per cent of the basic component.[10]

ii *From 53–104 weeks* After a year, the principle is modified so that the claimant himself, while in receipt of treatment, never receives more than 20 per cent of the basic component – often referred to as 'pocket-money' benefit.[11] The next 20 per cent is not payable, but if he has a dependant, and has made an appropriate application to the Secretary of State, any excess remaining is paid to that dependant.[12] A spouse who has also received free in-patient treatment for a year or more is not regarded as a dependant for this purpose. If the claimant has no dependant or the appropriate application has not been made, the next 40 per cent is not payable, and any excess will be paid to him by way of 'resettlement' benefit only when he is discharged from hospital.[13]

7 Cf pp. 413–419, below.
8 See NIAC Reports on Draft Hospital In-Patient Regulations 1948–49, HC 241 and on the Question of Long-Term Hospital Patients (1960, Cmnd 464).
9 SI 1975/555, Part II, as amended by SI 1977/1693 and SI 1979/223. For the amount of basic component, see p. 212, above.
10 For the meaning of 'dependant' see SI 1975/555, reg 2(3).
11 See NIAC Reports, n.8, above.
12 The excess may, alternatively, be paid to another person who satisfies the Secretary of State that he will apply the sum for the benefit of the dependant.
13 On the 'resettlement' benefit, see further pp. 395–396, below.

iii *After 104 weeks* After the two year period has elapsed, a claimant without dependants, is entitled to nothing beyond the 20 per cent 'pocket-money'. If he has dependants (and has made the appropriate application) the adjustment in (ii) is made, except that the following may not count as dependants: (a) a husband, where the wife claimant is in receipt of retirement pension (Categories A or B), contributory or non-contributory invalidity pension or unemployability supplement (unless she is receiving an increase of one of these benefits other than retirement pension for him); (b) a wife entitled to Category A retirement pension where the husband claimant is in receipt of sickness benefit, contributory or non-contributory invalidity pension, retirement pension or unemployability supplement;[14] (c) a spouse in receipt of free in-patient treatment for more than 52 weeks.

C Adjustment to increases for dependants

There are analogous rules governing the adjustment of increases for dependants.[15]

i *Dependent spouse in-patient* Where a dependent spouse has been an in-patient for a period of eight weeks, the rate of increase payable for that person is reduced by 20 per cent of the basic component, though not so as to reduce it to less than 20 per cent of that component. After 104 weeks, if the dependent in-patient is a wife and is still regarded as 'residing with' the beneficiary husband,[16] the reduced increase is not payable at all unless he is regularly incurring expenditure, or causing some payments to be made, on her behalf.

ii *Both beneficiary and dependent spouse in-patients* Where for a period of 52 weeks both have been in-patients, the rate of increase is reduced by 20 per cent of the basic component (though not so as to reduce it to less than 20 per cent of that component), the next 20 per cent is not payable, and any part of the remaining increase exceeding 40 per cent of the basic component is payable for the benefit of a child of the beneficiary's family to some other person undertaking to use it for that purpose or to the dependant (if he/she leaves hospital). If no arrangements to this effect have been authorised, no dependency increase is payable.

iii *Child dependant in-patient* Where a child dependant has been an in-patient for a period of 12 weeks the increase is payable only if the beneficiary is regularly incurring expenditure on his behalf, or causing some such payment to be made for his benefit.

D Resettlement bneefit

As indicated above,[17] money payable during the second year of the treatment may be accumulated and paid to the beneficiary if and when he

14 Though in this case a different rate is payable: SI 1975/555, reg 7(4), as amended by SI 1977/1693.
15 SI 1975/555, Part III, as amended by SI 1977/1693 and SI 1979/233.
16 Cf pp. 371–373, above.
17 P. 394, above.

is discharged. The arrangement is, however, subject to further regulation.[18]

– It is not payable unless the discharge is effected with the approval of the relevant (usually medical) authority – the policy being to discourage persons leaving hospital before they are ready to do so, thereby avoiding further financial burden on the National Health Service[19] – or if he is continuing to receive free in-patient treatment in another NHS institution, or is residing in any prescribed accommodation.[20] Resettlement benefit is payable in weekly instalments during the beneficiary's lifetime but not normally exceeding 160 per cent of the basic component.[1] If the patient resumes the treatment or residence, it is suspended until his next discharge; if the resumption occurs after an interval of more than 28 days, any amount still outstanding is deducted from any future resettlement benefit.

E Incapacity to enjoy proceeds

The condition of some long-term patients is such that there is little use to which the money can be put, and their chances of discharge, and therefore of resettlement benefit, are remote. Prior to 1960 the practice was to accumulate the 'pocket-money' benefit and pay it to the beneficiary's estate on his death. The National Insurance Advisory Committee regarded this as a waste of resources,[2] and as a result a new regulation was introduced.[3] Where a single claimant has been an in-patient for over a year and a medical officer treating him issues a certificate to the effect that no sum, or only a specified weekly sum (less than that to which he would otherwise be entitled) can be applied for the 'personal comfort or enjoyment' of the patient, his weekly entitlement is reduced to that sum (if any). However, this procedure will only be permitted if the beneficiary is himself unable to act, and should he eventually be discharged he will be entitled to additional resettlement benefit equal to the further reduction made during the first 52 weeks.

F Free in-patient treatment

Adjustments are made only for periods of 'free in-patient treatment'. The regulations provide that

– 'a person shall be regarded as receiving or having received free in-patient treatment for any period for which he is or has been maintained free of charge while undergoing medical or other treatment as an in-patient' in a 'hospital or similar institution' maintained or administered under the National Health Service or by the Secretary of State (or Defence Council) or in such an institution 'pursuant to arrangements made by the Secretary of State or by anybody in exercise of functions' on his behalf.[4]

It is clear, in the first place, that the word 'treatment' is a misnomer. The object of these regulations is to avoid overpayments to persons being maintained free of charge in hospitals and similar state-financed institu-

18 SI 1975/555, reg 15.
19 *R(S) 1/54*, para 7.
20 On which, see p. 397, below.
1 The Secretary of State has a discretion to modify this regulation in particular cases.
2 Report on the Question of Long-Term Hospital Patients (1960, Cmnd 964), paras 48–51.
3 SI 1975/555, reg 16.
4 Ibid, reg 2(2). For the institutions covered, see *R(S) 4/53* and *R(S) 2/54*.

tions, and the nature of the treatment offered there is not crucial. Hence the Chief Commissioner has ruled that the phrase should not be the subject of refined distinctions: the mere fact that a person is an in-patient in a hospital is strong prima facie evidence that he is undergoing 'medical or other treatment'.[5] In any event, the receipt of nursing services will be sufficient.[6] In the light of these policy objectives, the finding that he is an 'in-patient' is obviously very important; and the phrase has been consistently interpreted to mean 'housed overnight' at the relevant institution.[7] Thus a person living at home because there are not sufficient beds available at the hospital, even though in all other respects he is treated as an in-patient, is not an 'in-patient' for the purposes of these regulations.[8] The patient must be maintained free of charge and the regulations provide that he shall not be so regarded

> if he is paying or has paid, in respect of his maintenance, charges which are designed to cover the whole cost of the accommodation or services (other than services by way of treatment) provided for him in the hospital or similar institution.[9]

The onus is on the patient to satisfy this condition,[10] and, if necessary, the authorities will inspect the hospital's accounts to verify the proportion of costs paid by him.[11] The 'board and lodging' costs may be borne by the patient himself or by a third party, but none must be financed from public funds.[12]

G Calculation of periods

The periods of in-patient treatment referred to must in principle be continuous, but this is modified by the regulations to take account of the possibilities both of time spent in other accommodation maintained at public expense, and of short interruptions to the free treatment.

i Residence in other accommodation

The period of in-patient treatment is deemed to include any period of prior residence in 'prescribed accommodation'.[13] This is defined as

> any hospital accommodation or similar accommodation in which that person is residing or has resided either as a patient or inmate or as a person in need of care and attention and wholly or partly at the cost of a local authority, the Secretary of State or, . . . (under the National Health Service Acts) anybody in exercise of functions on behalf of the Secretary of State

or

5 *R(P) 1/67*, para 14 (R G Micklethwait).
6 Ibid, at para 13, and see *Minister of Health v General Committee of Royal Midland Countries Home for Incurables at Leamington Spa* [1954] Ch 530 at 541, 547, 549–550, CA.
7 *CS 65/49*; *R(S) 8/51*; R(I) 14/56.
8 *R(I) 27/59*.
9 SI 1975/555, reg 2(2).
10 *CS 59/49*.
11 *R(P) 13/52*. See also *R(S) 2/52*, which took into account the fact that the claimant was an NHS employee from whose salary a deduction was made.
12 *R(S) 4/53*.
13 SI 1975/555, reg 17(2), as amended by SI 1977/1693.

any residential accommodation provided for that person under Part III of the National Assistance Act.[14]

In deciding whether an individual is caught by this provision regard is to be had to the nature of the services made available to him at the institution, rather than to the objective characterisation of the institution itself.[15] If it has been decided by the appropriate authority that the residence is not temporary, it is deemed, for purposes of the rules on adjustment, to have lasted for 52 weeks.[16]

ii Linking of periods

Any two or more periods of free in-patient treatment (or residence in prescribed accommodation) separated by intervals not exceeding 28 days may be linked,[17] though the aggregate period thus taken into account does not include the intervals themselves.[18]

H Benefit to be adjusted

The benefit to be reduced is, with one exception,[19] that which is payable after the Overlapping Regulations have taken effect.[20] The age addition[1] is not affected, however, unless the beneficiary has been an in-patient for more than 52 weeks and he has no wife or child 'residing' with him.[2]

Part 6 Imprisonment and detention in legal custody

A General

The disqualification from benefit (or a dependant's increase) during periods when a person is 'undergoing imprisonment or detention in legal custody'[3] has always existed in social security law,[4] and yet its policy basis remains ambiguous. It may be seen simply as a penal provision to apply to persons who have forfeited their natural rights as citizens.[5] If this were so, it would be appropriate to confine the disqualification to those imprisoned or detained in connection with a criminal offence. As will appear, this is in practice how the provision has been interpreted, though its wording is not so limited. The alternative policy basis is identical to that encountered in relation to hospital in-patients: the detainee is being maintained at public

14 SI 1975/555, reg 15(4). But if the accommodation is maintained by a voluntary organisation or is a registered disabled persons' home or old persons' home under the National Assistance Act 1948, the rule is not to apply unless he has received free in-patient treatment there for at least 8 weeks: ibid, reg 17(3).
15 Compare *R(S) 15/55* with *R(S) 26/54* and *R(S) 6/58*.
16 SI 1975/555, reg 17(2). For the meaning of 'residence' see *R(P) 17/55*; *R(P) 1/67* and pp. 391–393, above.
17 SI 1975/555, reg 17(4).
18 See *R(S) 8/51*. On parts of a day see *CS 131/49*; *R(S) 8/51* and *R(S) 9/52*.
19 See SI 1975/555, reg 18(2).
20 Ibid, reg 18.
1 P. 226, above.
2 SI 1975/555, reg 19. For the meaning of 'residing with', see pp. 371–373, above.
3 SSA 1975, s.82(5).
4 Cf NIA 1911, s.87(3).
5 Per Widgery, arguendo, *R v National Insurance Comr, ex parte Timmis* [1955] 1 QB 139 at 145, DC.

expense and thus has no need of income support.[6] This may indeed be the case but it is to be observed that in comparison with the hospital in-patients rules, those on detention are much stricter: there is no period of eight weeks to adapt to new circumstances; and there is no provision for either 'pocket-money' or 'resettlement' benefit.

B Scope of disqualification

A person shall be disqualified for receiving any benefit, and an increase of benefit shall not be payable in respect of any person as the beneficiary's wife or husband, for any period during which that person is undergoing imprisonment or detention in legal custody.[7]

i Benefits affected

Except for guardian's allowance[8] and industrial disablement benefit,[9] this disqualification applies to all benefits, including the additions and increases to the disablement benefit.

ii Connection with criminal offence

A literal reading of the regulation quoted above indicates that it should cover all cases where the claimant is lawfully detained in custody, in other words, where a court would legitimately refuse an order of habeas corpus. This was, indeed, the interpretation suggested by the Divisional Court in 1955,[10] notwithstanding a stream of earlier Commissioners' decisions which held that the detention must be connected with criminal proceedings or a criminal act.[11] The National Insurance Advisory Committee, when it examined the matter in 1960, manifestly preferred the narrower interpretation.[12] But the amending regulations, consequential on its Report, failed fully to implement this view.[13] They provided that there will be no disqualification for a period of imprisonment or detention in legal custody which arises from criminal proceedings unless a penalty is imposed at the conclusion of the proceedings.[14] This does not make criminal proceedings a condition of the disqualification; it only adds a further condition – that of a penalty – where the detention is connected with criminal proceedings. Thus in strict law the position is that someone, for example, remanded in custody in respect of a criminal charge from which he is later acquitted, does not lose benefit, but those detained for civil contempt are disqualified. However, the adjudicating authorities are not, it seems, prepared to tolerate such a result. In 1974 the High Court of Northern Ireland reiterated the traditional view that the detention had to be connected with

6 Cf p. 394, above.
7 SI 1974/2079, reg 11(1) and SI 1975/559, reg 36.
8 SI 1974/2079, reg 11(2). The allowance is payable to a person appointed by the Secretary of State to receive and deal with it on behalf of the beneficiary: ibid, reg 12(3).
9 SI 1975/559, reg 37(2). Payment of the disablement benefit is, however, suspended: p. 401, below.
10 Per Lord Goddard CJ, *R v National Insurance Comr, ex parte Timmis*, n.5, above, at 149.
11 *R(S) 20/53*; *R(S) 21/52*; *R(P) 10/54*; *R(S) 3/55*; *R(S) 4/55*; *1/55 (SB)*.
12 Report on the Question of Long-Term Hospital Patients (1960, Cmnd 964).
13 SI 1960/1283, now SI 1974/2079, reg 11(3).
14 'Penalty' here means 'a sentence of imprisonment, borstal training, or detention [under the Children and Young Persons legislation] or under s.1(4) of the Criminal Justice (Scotland) Act 1963 or an order for detention in a detention centre': ibid, reg 11(6)(c). It includes a suspended sentence: *R(S) 1/71*.

a criminal offence,[15] and in *R(S) 8/79* the British Commissioner held that a beneficiary who was committed to prison for failing to carry out a maintenance order was not to be disqualified. He admitted that if the point had been raised for the first time, he would have preferred the literal interpretation suggested by the Divisional Court, but he considered himself bound by the authorities adopting the narrower view.[16]

iii Mentally abnormal offenders

If this narrower view be maintained, those detained under the Mental Health legislation but who have not been the subject of criminal proceedings escape disqualification. Understandably, the National Insurance Advisory Committee considered that it was, however, appropriate to disqualify an individual who was transferred from a prison (or analogous institution) to a mental hospital during the currency of a penal sentence.[17] The regulations thus provide[18] that a person shall not be disqualified for a period of

> detention in legal custody after the conclusion of criminal proceedings[19] if it is a period during which he is liable to be detained in a hospital or a similar institution[20] in Great Britain as a person suffering from mental disorder[1] unless
> (a) pursuant to any sentence or order for detention made by the court at the conclusion of those proceedings, he has undergone detention by way of penalty in a prison, a detention centre, a borstal institution or a young offenders' institution; *and*
> (b) he was removed to the hospital or similar institution while liable to be detained as a result of that sentence or order, and, in the case of a person who is liable to be detained (under the Mental Health Act 1959) . . . a direction restricting his discharge has been given.

Thus, a person transferred from a prison, detention centre, borstal or young offenders' institution may be disqualified but only for the period of his original sentence,[2] and for this purpose the Home Secretary, or Secretary of State for Scotland, will issue a certificate stating the earliest date on which the person would have been expected to be discharged.[3] Of course, any other period of detention may well be subject to the rule on hospital in-patients.[4]

15 *R(O'Neill) v National Insurance Comrs* [1974] NI 76, approving *R 1/76 (P)* (Tribunal decision).
16 See also *R(S) 1/81*, para 4. In considering an application to quash this decision, the Divisional Court refers without comment to the fact that the narrower view has been 'accepted by all concerned': *R v National Insurance Comr, ex parte Warry* [1981] 1 All ER 229 at 231.
17 N.12, above, at para 19.
18 SI 1974/2079, reg 11(4).
19 'Criminal proceedings against any person shall be deemed to be concluded upon his being found insane in those proceedings so that he cannot be tried or his trial cannot proceed': ibid, reg 11(6)(g).
20 This means any place (other than prison or analogous institution) in which 'persons suffering from mental disorder are or may be received for care or treatment': ibid, reg 11(6)(b). For 'mental disorder' see n.1, below.
1 The reference to 'mental disorder' is to be construed as including references to any mental disorder within the meaning of the Mental Health Act 1959: SI 1974/2079, reg 11(6)(f).
2 See e.g. *R(P) 2/57*.
3 SI 1974/2079, Reg 11(5).
4 Pp. 394–398, above.

iv Detention abroad

As a matter of construction, it has been held, after protracted litigation, that the provisions apply to periods of detention abroad.[5] To meet the objection that they are in consequence discriminatory under EEC law, because the exceptions considered in the previous paragraphs have reference only to British legislation,[6] the regulations have been amended, so that a claimant is not disqualified if he is detained in circumstances similar to those which if they had existed in Britain would have excepted him from the disqualification.[7] A final problem, as yet unresolved, is whether a criminal conviction abroad is to be treated as conclusive for British social security purposes. A conviction in Britain is certainly conclusive; but the Commissioner and the courts have left it open whether they might go behind a foreign conviction on the ground that it offends British notions of justice.[8]

C Suspension of benefit

It follows from the previous discussion that there are circumstances in which persons undergoing imprisonment or detention in legal custody are not disqualified from benefit. Those transferred to mental hospitals are entitled to receive the benefit themselves;[9] in other cases payment is suspended until their release.[10]

Part 7 Public policy

The social security legislation contains a number of provisions which deny benefit to a claimant on grounds which to a greater or lesser extent include considerations of public policy: for example, he is disqualified from sickness and unemployment benefit if the contigency occured through his own misconduct.[11] In *R v National Insurance Comr, ex parte Connor*,[12] the question arose, apparently for the first time in this context, whether there are general principles of public policy not incorporated in the legislation but which might be invoked by the authorities to deny benefit in appropriate circumstances. In the instant case a woman had been convicted of the manslaughter of her husband. The Chief Commissioner decided that since her status as a widow directly resulted from the unlawful act of manslaughter she had properly been denied benefit; and the Divisional Court upheld this decision.[13]

5 *R(S) 2/81*, following *Ex parte Warry*, n.16, above, and *Kenny v Insurance Officer* [1978] ECR 1489. See further p. 633, below.
6 *Ex parte Warry*, n.16, above, and p. 633, below.
7 SI 1980/1621, inserting reg 11(7)–(8) in SI 1974/2079.
8 *R(S) 1/81*, para 5, J G Monroe, Comr, referring to *R v Brixton Prison Governor, ex parte Caborn-Waterfield* [1960] 2 QB 498, [1960] 2 All ER 178. The Divisional Court in *Ex parte Warry*, n.16, above, did not consider this suggestion.
9 SI 1974/2079, reg 12(2).
10 Ibid, reg 12(1); for guardian's allowance, however, see n.8, p. 399, above.
11 Pp. 106–118 and 115, above.
12 [1981] 1 All ER 769, upholding *R(G) 2/79*, R J A Temple, Chief Comr.
13 Applying by analogy the principles developed in the law of succession (e.g. *Re Giles, Giles v Giles* [1972] Ch 544, [1971] 3 All ER 1141) and private insurance (e.g. *Beresford v Royal Insurance Co Ltd* [1938] AC 586, [1938] 2 All ER 602; *Gray v Barr* [1970] 2 QB 626, [1970] 2 All ER 702).

The argument that the social security legislation constituted a self-contained code, exhaustive of the principles to be applied, was summarily rejected:[14] it was to be assumed that the draftsman formulated the law against the background of the general law.[15] But the question of what conduct has the character to justify disentitlement admits of a less certain answer. According to Lord Lane CJ, 'it is not the label which the law applies to the crime which has been committed but the nature of the crime itself which in the end will dictate whether public policy demands the court to drive the applicant from the seat of justice'.[16] This is clearly a matter of some difficulty, but he found helpful some judicial dicta which, in another context, required that the person's act was wilful and culpable, or deliberate and international.[17] On the evidence of the criminal conviction, Mrs Connor's acts came within this description.

Clearly, more decisions are necessary before the principle can be given a more precise content. It may be, too, that Commissioners and judges will have to devote more attention than they did in *Connor* to the nature of the public policy considerations[18]: should they add disentitlement to the criminal law penalty? What is the public interest in denying benefit to a wrongdoer?

Part 8 Christmas bonus

A General

The origin of this curious, and far from commendable, feature of British social security is to be located in the political and economic circumstances of 1972. The Conservative government was, at the time, planning a major offensive against inflation, mainly through centralised controls on wages and prices. It was acknowledged that certain groups within the community, notably pensioners, were particularly in need of protection against rising prices and while the possibility of introducing statutory obligations for up-rating benefits[19] was being considered, the government decided to make a single lump-sum payment of £10 at Christmas time to long-term social security beneficiaries,[20] as an 'earnest of their good intentions'.[1] Apart from one minor hitch – under the original Act it was not paid to those deprived of a pension by the earnings rule and a new Act had to be swiftly passed to remedy this defect[2] – the measure proved to be politically popular. It was therefore repeated in 1973 and 1974. The Labour government was not initially enthusiastic, preferring to concentrate attention on the major reforms of 1975 but the practice was renewed in 1977 and 1978. The Conservative Party Manifesto for the General Election of 1979 included a

14 On the jurisprudential aspects of this, see Hutchinson and Wakefield 2 Oxf JLS 86, esp. at 95–99.
15 [1981] 1 All ER 769 at 774. See also per Donaldson LJ, *R v Secretary of State, ex parte Puttick* [1981] 1 All ER 776 at 779.
16 [1981] 1 All ER 769 at 774. For a different view, see *Re Hall's Estate, Hall v Knight and Baxter* [1914] P 1.
17 *Hardy v Motor Insurers Bureau* [1964] 2 QB 745 at 760, 762, 766–767; *Gray v Barr* [1970] 2 QB 626 at 640, affd [1971] 2 QB 554 at 568.
18 Cf Robilliard 44 MLR 718 at 720.
19 Cf p. 410, below.
20 Pensioners and Family Income Supplement Payments Act 1972.
1 Sir K Joseph, Secretary of State, 846 HC Official Report (5th series) col 971.
2 Pensioners' Payments and National Insurance Contributions Act 1972.

commitment that the Christmas bonus would continue. Consequently the Pensioners' Payments and Social Security Act of that year established the payment as a permanent feature of the social security system. In social policy terms, it serves little obvious purpose except that of courting political popularity,[3] but its importance is no doubt sufficient to justify a short description of the principles of entitlement.

B Persons entitled

To receive payment, an individual must be entitled (or treated as entitled) to one of the following benefits for a period which includes a day in a prescribed week in December:[4]

- widow's benefit, contributory or non-contributory invalidity or retirement pension, attendance or invalid care allowance; unemployability supplement or allowance or widow's or widower's pension under the industrial injuries scheme; disablement or widow's pension under the war pensions scheme; supplementary pension under the supplementary benefits scheme.

The claimant is treated as being so entitled if the non-receipt is the result of some other payment from public funds or from an employer, or the operation of the earnings rule; so also if his earnings or those of his spouse render him ineligible for supplementary pension.[5]

C Residence

The claimant must be present or ordinarily resident in the United Kingdom or any other EEC member state at any time during the prescribed week.[6]

D Amount

The amount payable for Christmas 1982 is £10. The sum has thus remained unchanged since 1972, though under the 1979 Act it may in future be raised if 'it appears to the Secretary of State that having regard to the economic situation in the United Kingdom, the standard of living in the United Kingdom and such other matters as he considers relevant, the sums . . . should be larger'.[7] A beneficiary may receive a second payment for his spouse if they are both over pensionable age and he is entitled (or treated as entitled) to an increase to the qualifying benefit for that person.[8] The same applies in relation to an unmarried couple, living together as husband and wife, whose resources and requirements are aggregated for the purposes of the supplementary pension.[9] These payments are tax free, and are disregarded for the purposes of any means-tested benefit.[10]

3 Cf Slack 7 Jo Soc Pol 201.
4 Pensioners' Payments and Social Security Act 1979, ss. 1(1)(b) and 2(1).
5 Ibid, s.2(4).
6 Ibid, s.1(1)(a).
7 Ibid, s.4(3).
8 Ibid, s.1(2). Entitlement is deemed in circumstances analogous to those of the personal benefit, n.5, above.
9 Pensioners' Payments and Social Security Act 1979, s.1(2)(c).
10 Ibid, s.1(5).

E Adjudication

Questions of entitlement are determined by the Secretary of State, from whose decision no appeal lies.[11]

Part 9 Earnings

A General

There are a number of rules arising under the Social Security Act 1975 in connection with entitlement to, or assessment of, benefit which refer to the weekly earnings of a person either before benefit was payable or during a period of entitlement. They are for the following purposes:

(1) to calculate the special hardship allowance added to industrial disablement benefit;[12]

(2) to disregard casual or subsidiary work, the earnings from which are below a specified level, where entitlement to benefit is based on incapacity for work, unemployment or retirement – such rules apply to sickness and invalidity benefits,[13] industrial injury benefit,[14] non-contributory invalidity pension[15] and invalid care allowance,[16] unemployment benefit[17] and retirement pension;[18]

(3) to determine whether the earnings of a spouse or child carer disentitle a claimant to a dependant's increase for such a person;[19]

(4) to assess the amount to be deducted from retirement pension for earnings received during the period of entitlement.[20]

The law governing the calculation of earnings for these purposes is primarily to be found in the Computation of Earnings Regulations[1] and the Commissioners' decisions. As such it is significantly different from the methods used to assess and classify contribution liabilities which bear striking resemblances to income tax law.[2]

B What are 'earnings'?

The Social Security Act 1975 provides that ' "earnings" includes any remuneration or profit derived from any employment', the latter term being defined to include 'any trade, business, profession, office or vocation'.[3] These definitions show that a line is to be drawn between earnings, including profits, which are derived from an occupation, and payments which vest in the recipient in some other capacity, e.g. shareholder. The Regulations state more narrowly that ' "earnings" means

11 Ibid, s.3(2).
12 Pp. 310–323, above.
13 P. 153, above.
14 P. 295, above.
15 P. 171, above.
16 P. 180, above.
17 P. 83, above.
18 P. 206, above.
19 Pp. 368–370, above.
20 Pp. 212–216, above.
1 SI 1978/1698.
2 Pp. 53, and 59–60, above.
3 SSA 1975, s.3(1), and Sch 20.

earnings derived from a gainful employment'.[4] It is clear, however, that the term is not confined to the salary or profits drawn from employment or business, and may include, for example, an allowance paid to the holder of an office.[5]

The leading decision is that of the Tribunal of Commissioners in *R(P) 7/61*:

> C claimed an increase of pension for his wife for a period during which she was absent from work through sickness and was in receipt of payments from her employer under a sick pay scheme. This provided that the payments could be withdrawn at any time and the scheme wound up. C contended that for the period in question his wife was not engaged in a gainful occupation, and that the payments did not constitute earnings. Both contentions were rejected.

It was held first, that the wife was still gainfully occupied,[6] as the contract of employment subsisted; it did not matter that she was not actually working during the relevant period.[7] Secondly, the payments were earnings since she received them *as an employee*. Again, the fact that they were described as ex gratia payments was immaterial. A similar broad approach is evidenced by *R(P) 1/65*, where a member of the City Livery Company (a pensioner) was paid a fee each time he attended a meeting of the Company's court. Attendance was voluntary, and it was clear that the claimant would have attended whether a fee was payable or not. It was held that the fees constituted earnings from employment; it was important that the claimant actually received money for his work, and immaterial that his motive was not one of financial gain.[8]

A difficult case on the other side of the line is *R(P) 4/67*:

> C, a former partner in a firm of accountants, was paid £1,000 at the end of his first year of retirement for advisory services rendered to the firm. At no time during this year when the claimant gave advice was it suggested that a payment would be made.

The Commissioner, H Magnus, held that the payment did not constitute earnings, as there was no contractual obligation on either party, and the claimant never expected or even hoped to be paid. It was suggested, however, that any further payment for advisory services would be so construed. The suggestion was borne out by the later case *R(P) 1/69*, where a similar payment made the following year to this claimant was held to constitute 'earnings'.[9] The Commissioner, D Neligan, laid particular emphasis on the fact that the claimant had been awarded earned income tax relief on the £1,000.[10] Other situations where it may be difficult to

4 SI 1978/1698, reg 1(2).

5 See *R(P) 2/76* (a city councillor in receipt of an allowance for attendance held to be gainfully occupied: p. 200, above).

6 This was the term used in NIA 1965, s.30: it does not appear that the change in wording made by the SSA 1975 has any significance; see *R(P) 2/76*, paras 22–23, per R J A Temple, Chief Comr.

7 See *R(U) 4/60* (C's wife gainfully occupied for the whole of the week even though she only worked for three days); cp *R(U) 8/60*, where the wife was not working at all.

8 The Dep. Comr, G Glover, followed Salmon J in *Benjamin v Minister of Pensions and National Insurance* [1960] 2 QB 519, [1960] 2 All ER 851, and not the narrower approach of the Comr in *CP 7/49*; see also *R(P) 2/76*.

9 See also *R(G) 1/60*.

10 The attitude of the tax authorities is relevant, but not decisive: see *R(P) 1/65*, para 10, (G Glover, Dep. Comr).

determine whether payments constitute 'earnings' can now conveniently be discussed under a number of specific headings.

i Director's fees and partnership profits

A director's fees will constitute earnings from employment, even though the duties – attendance at an annual general meeting – are very slight.[11] The fact that he has considerable financial power is enough to make a directorship a gainful employment. In a Northern Ireland case, it was held that a woman who owned a farm (worked by her son) and enjoyed the profits from it was in an analogous position to a director; therefore, the income was treated as earnings, and not as interest on an investment.[12] Partnership profits are clearly earnings for social security purposes, while dividends from a limited liability company are not.[13] Nor is trust income.[14]

ii Payments for assisting in spouse's business

Some nice questions arise when one spouse assists in a business, typically a retail shop, owned and conducted by the other. The approach taken by the Commissioner is that if, say, the wife does appreciable work and brings money into the business, she is to be treated as gainfully employed, and a proportion of the profits will be regarded as her earnings.[15] This principle will not be applied if the amount of work is trivial, or if the wife organises her husband's business while he is temporarily unable to work.[16] On the other hand, the fact that no money passes between the spouses does not preclude a finding that one spouse draws 'earnings' from the other's business.[17]

iii Payments in kind and other miscellaneous payments

The law with regard to payments in kind and other miscellaneous payments is considerably clarified by the Computation of Earnings Regulations.[18] Under regulation 3, the following do not count as earnings:

(a) the value of luncheon vouchers (up to 15p a day);
(b) the value of meals provided at the place of work;
(c) the value of accommodation in which the employee is required to live as a condition of his employment;[19]
(d) the value of food or produce provided for his needs and those of his household;
(e) sums (or remuneration in kind) provided by the employer in December as a Christmas bonus, up to £10.

The implication of this last rule is that other bonuses are to be taken into account.[20] Other remuneration in kind, e.g. board and lodging (not disregarded under the regulations), is to be included and its value is the actual worth of the services, not the amount the claimant has saved by receiving them.[1]

11 *R(P) 9/55*; *R(G) 14/56*.
12 *2/57 (P)* Compare the cases on the 'retirement condition', where there appears to be more emphasis on the work done by the claimant: pp. 200–201, above.
13 *R(P) 9/56*; *R(U) 22/64*.
14 *R(G) 9/55*.
15 *R(P) 7/51*; *R(S) 17/52*.
16 *R(S) 8/56*; *R(U) 11/57*.
17 *R(P) 6/57*, para 3.
18 SI 1978/1698.
19 See *R 2/72 (P)*.
20 See *R(G) 7/59*.
1 *CP 1/48*; *R 5/61 (P)*.

iv Payments assigned or not received by the claimant

The fact that the claimant immediately assigns his or her salary to a third party has been held by a Northern Ireland Commissioner to be irrelevant.[2] So also is the fact that the earnings are not actually received in the week in question.[3] This ruling has been followed with striking effect:

> C claimed an increase of pension for his wife, thinking that the profits from her business in Italy did not amount to earnings, because they were not transmitted to this country. But the earnings rule was applied and the increase refused.[4]

The Commissioner, H A Shewan, held that a man earns what he is entitled to receive in return for his work or services, irrespective of whether he is actually paid.

v Other payments to employees

There is a statutory power for regulations to be made providing that certain payments governed by the Employment Protection (Consolidation) Act 1978, notably maternity pay and protective awards, are to be treated as earnings.[5] At the time of writing, the power has not been exercised. Under the Social Security and Housing Benefits Act 1982, sick pay is to be treated as earnings, though regulations may be made for disregarding any part of the payment attributable to contributions made by the employee.[6]

C Earnings which cannot be immediately ascertained

Special problems are posed by earners whose employment, generally self-employment, produces earnings which 'are not immediately ascertainable'.[7] The various rules on earnings normally refer to a weekly or daily amount and the problems arise, typically in connection with self-employment, where money is not received on this basis. For the purpose of dealing with such cases, the regulations distinguish between two categories of claim.

The first arises where the earner is a retirement pensioner or an adult dependant of a retirement or invalidity pensioner. If a statement of the earner's profits or gains has been or will be delivered to the Inland Revenue, the earnings are to be calculated by dividing the profits or gains by the number of weeks in the relevant assessment period during which he was employed.[8] This is the current income tax year,[9] or, in the case of self-employed claimants, the accounting period, whether or not this is a full year.[10] Pending the delivery of such a statement, the Secretary of State may suspend payment of the pension or dependant's increase and make an interim award instead. When the assessment is finally determined, any

2 *2/59 (P)*.
3 *R(P) 5/53*.
4 *R(P) 1/70*.
5 SS(MP)A 1977, s.18, as amended by Employment Protection (Consolidation) Act 1978, Sch 16, para 29.
6 Ss. 23 and 37.
7 The phrase is used in SI 1978/1698, regs 2(3) and 5(1)(b). Similar problems arise where a claimant for unemployment benefit is pursuing a subsidiary occupation, the earnings from which must not exceed £2 a day, if he is to remain eligible for benefit: these are discussed, pp. 83–84, above.
8 SI 1978/1698, reg 5, on which, see *R(S) 1/82*, discussed in the Appendix.
9 *R(P) 1/73*, para 33, per R G Micklethwait, Chief Comr.
10 *R 2/75 (P)*.

excessive interim payments may be recovered from the beneficiary.[11] In this case, unlike the normal rule governing recovery for overpayment of benefit,[12] the claimant cannot argue that recovery should not be made because he used due care and diligence.[13] Here the overpayment is attributable not to a mistake which has subsequently been reviewed but to a deliberate decision regarding the level of an interim payment.

In all other cases, regulations direct the authorities to calculate the earnings 'as best they may', taking into account available information and 'the probabilities of the case'.[14] By implication this vindicates the practice, previously authorised by the Commissioner,[15] of averaging the claimant's receipts over the period of employment. But the problem of deciding when the claimant was employed is not easy to solve.[16] Unless there is clear evidence of the occupation being seasonal, it should be averaged over a period of twelve months.[17]

D Deductions from earnings

The question next arises as to what deduction may be made from gross profits, wages or salary. The frequency with which retirement pensioners (or the adult dependants of retirement or invalidity pensioners) take in boarders or lodgers made it convenient to formulate a special rule for these cases. Where full board and lodgings is provided, half the amount paid in excess of £6.00 per week is treated as earnings;[18] where less is provided, the authorities should have regard to half the amount of such smaller sum as they consider to be reasonable in the circumstances.[19] In all other cases, the regulations provide an exhaustive list of such deductions as may be made:[20]

(a) social security contributions;
(b) 'expenses reasonably incurred . . . without reimbursement in respect of —'
  (i) travel between home and work, and in connection with and for the purpose of work;
  (ii) premises, tools and equipment for the claimant's work;
  (iii) protective clothing;
  (iv) trade union or professional association subscriptions;
  (v) reasonable provision for the care of another member of the claimant's household, because of his necessary absence from home;
  (vi) the cost (up to 15p) of a meal during hours of work, for which no voucher is given.
(c) 'any other expenses (not being sums the deduction of which from wages or salary is authorised by or under any enactment) reasonably incurred by him without reimbursement in connection with and for the purposes of that employment.'

11 SI 1978/1698, reg 6(3).
12 For this, see pp. 575–577, below.
13 *R(P) 1/73*, cp *R(P) 2/74*.
14 SI 1978/1698 reg 2(3).
15 *R(P) 2/51*.
16 *R(U) 1/67*, and NIAC Report, (1966, Cmnd 3170), paras 52–56.
17 See e.g. *R(P) 4/56* and *R(P) 1/62*.
18 SI 1978/1698, reg 7(a).
19 Ibid, reg 7(b).
20 Ibid, reg 4.

Income tax, whether paid through PAYE or after assessment, is not deductible;[1] nor are contributions payable to occupational pension schemes.[2]

The major legal difficulty arises from the inconsistent interpretation by the Commissioners of the phrase 'in connection with that employment'. In some older cases, this was construed to mean 'in consequence of' the employment; on that approach the expense would be deducted if it was incurred as a result of the work done by the claimant.[3] In at least three more recent reported decisions, the Commissioner has taken the view that this is a gloss on the ordinary meaning of the phrase, and that the expenses must be reasonably connected with the employment.[4] It does not appear, however, that this change in approach would affect previous rulings disallowing deductions for insurance premiums,[5] household rent,[6] subscriptions to a sick fund,[7] and the costs of sending a child to boarding-school when this was the very reason why the claimant went to work.[8]

Whether an expense is reasonable for the purpose of the deduction provisions is to be determined by reference to the level of the claimant's earnings and the particular facts of the case.[9] Among the miscellaneous expenses held to have been reasonably incurred in connection with the claimant's employment have been: the costs of domestic assistance in the home;[10] commission paid to an employment agency;[11] and 15 per cent of the cost of new fixtures and installations for a business, and of the legal expenses incurred in acquiring them.[12] In a Northern Ireland case, the Commissioner ruled that the expenses (in the case, travelling expenses to a holiday camp) should be averaged over the whole of the earning period during which they were incurred.[13]

In conclusion, it is interesting to observe that the allowable expenses for determining earnings compare favourably with those allowed for income tax purposes.[14] Tax legislation, for example, does not authorise deduction of the cost of meals, expenses of looking after a relative, and the Inland Revenue is reluctant to allow for travelling expenses.[15] On the other hand, the allowances are comparable with those under the Supplementary Benefit (Resources) Regulations in assessing a claimant's net earnings, though there income tax and occupational pension contributions may also be deducted.[16]

1 Ibid, reg 4(c), abrogating the previous position whereby PAYE payments were deducted: *R(P) 3/56*; *R(P) 3/62*. The change followed a recommendation of NIAC (1966, Cmnd 3170), paras 41–47. For the different approach to supplementary benefits see p. 485, below.
2 *R(P) 2/75*.
3 *CG 114/49*; *R(P) 2/54*.
4 *R(P) 2/56*; *R(P) 1/64*; *R(P) 1/66*.
5 *R(G) 7/52*.
6 *CP 2/48*.
7 *R(G) 7/52* and see SSA 1975, s.3(1B), inserted by SSHBA 1982, s.37.
8 *R(G) 7/53*; cp *R(G) 9/51*.
9 *R(G) 1/56*; *R(G) 7/62*.
10 *R(G) 7/62*.
11 *R(G) 6/54*.
12 *R(P) 3/57* (but no sum could be deducted for 'depreciated' goodwill).
13 *R 2/72 (P)*.
14 See the remarks to this effect by NIAC, n.16, above, at para 81.
15 See Pinson *Revenue Law* (13th edn) para 3.38.
16 P. 485, below.

Part 10 Up-rating of benefits

A General

The problem of maintaining the value of benefits in relation to rising prices and wages and the various solutions available were considered in chapter 1.[17] It remains here to describe the methods currently adopted under the social security legislation. Prior to 1973, for all benefits except those awarded under the national assistance (subsequently supplementary benefits), war pensions, and family income supplement schemes[18] modifications to the amount payable could be made only by Act of Parliament. Moreover, the government was in no instance bound to ensure that benefits kept pace with inflation, and the real value of some, notably family allowances, declined considerably.[19] The sharp increase in the rates of inflation in the early 1970s and the desire to confer on contributors the security that benefits would retain their value prompted the Conservative government to introduce in 1973 for the most important contributory benefits a mechanism for annual 'up-rating'[20] – a word which one judge has described as 'a recruit to the English language which does not notably enrich it'.[1] This both imposed on the Secretary of State a duty to ensure that such benefits retained their value in relation to the general level of prices and enabled him to adjust the amounts payable by order laid before Parliament. As a result of subsequent amendments, the annual review of long-term benefits was to take account of rises in prices *or* earnings whichever would be more advantageous to beneficiaries.[2]

In retrospect, 1975 may be regarded as the year in which the legal obligations to maintain the value of social security benefits were at their most powerful. In the period since, there has been an almost continual tendency to impair their efficacy, a consequence predominantly of the Conservative government's aim to reduce public expenditure. The relevant measures included: the linking of long-term benefits to increases in prices (rather than prices *or* earnings, whichever was more favourable to beneficiaries);[3] an up-rating of short-term benefits for 1980–81 at 5 per cent *less* than the increase in prices;[4] postponement by two weeks of the coming into force of the up-rating order;[5] release from the obligation to maintain the value of the earnings limits placed on retirement pensioners and the dependants of beneficiaries.[6]

To analyse the current principles, it is necessary to distinguish between the Secretary of State's power to up-rate, his duty to review the value of certain benefits, and a consequential duty, in some cases, to revise the rates in the light of that review.

17 Pp. 22–24, above.
18 War Pensions Act 1921, s.4; NAA 1948, s.5(2); SBA 1966, s.5(2); FISA 1970, s.3(4).
19 Cf p. 422, below.
20 SSA 1973, ss.7–8.
1 Per Megarry VC, *Metzger v Department of Health and Social Security* [1977] 3 All ER 444 at 445.
2 NIA 1974, s.5; SSBA 1975, ss.3–4.
3 SSA 1980, s.1(1).
4 SSA (No 2) 1980, s.1.
5 SSA 1980, s.1(3).
6 Pensioners' Payments and Social Security Act 1979, s.5; SSA (No 2) 1980, s.2.

B Power to up-rate

Under section 124 of the Social Security Act 1975, the Secretary of State has power by order to increase any of the following:

- Benefits, grants and increases for dependants payable under the Act; limits for the earnings rules; and certain allowances payable under the Old Cases Act.

Any such order must be laid in draft before Parliament, together with a report of the Government Actuary giving his opinion on the likely effect on the National Insurance Fund of making the order, and that draft must then be approved by a resolution of each House.[7] Apart from the procedural requirement, the power is without conditions or restrictions:

> for whatever reason he thinks fit, and at whatever time he thinks fit, the Secretary of State may make whatever increase he thinks fit.[8]

There are equivalent provisions conferring power to alter the rates of supplementary benefit,[9] family income supplement[10] and child benefit.[11] In relation to the latter, it cannot be exercised to reduce the amount payable.[12]

C Duty to review value of benefits

The Secretary of State is under a legislative duty to review annually almost all benefits, with the exception of family income supplement and supplementary benefit,[13] to ascertain the extent to which their real value has declined. It is important to distinguish between two groups of benefit which are subject to this duty: as regards the first, which may be broadly described as 'income maintenance' benefits, the Secretary of State is under a complementary duty to up-rate to maintain the real value; no such consequential duty arises in relation to the second group, those concerned to meet particular needs.

i Income maintenance benefits

In each tax year, the Secretary of State is under an obligation to review the amounts payable under the Social Security Act[14] for all contributory, non-contributory and industrial benefits, including increases for dependants, but excluding mobility allowance, the death and maternity grants and the age addition, 'for the purpose of determining whether those sums have retained their value in relation to the general level of prices obtaining in Great Britain'.[15] He is not bound to review at yearly intervals; he is only required to do so in each tax year. Thus, in theory there may be a gap

7 SSA 1975, s.124(2)–(3).
8 Per Megarry VC, *Metzger* case, n.1, above, at 446.
9 SBA 1976, Sch 1, as amended by SSA 1980.
10 FISA 1970, s.2(1), as amended ibid.
11 CBA 1975, s.5(3).
12 Ibid, s.5(4).
13 For discussion of this omission, see SBC Annual Report 1976 (Cmnd 6910), para 9.10 f and *Social Assistance* para 5.48 f.
14 Also: the less incapacity allowances payable under IIDA 1975, ss.2(6)(c) and 7(2)(b); graduated retirement benefits (SI 1978/393); increments in guaranteed minimum pension where retirement is deferred (SSA 1975, s.126A, inserted by SSA 1979, s.12); and statutory sick pay (SSHBA 1982, s.7).
15 SSA 1975, s.125(1), as amended by SSPA 1975, SSA 1980 and SSA (No 2) 1980.

between reviews of anything between a month and nearly two years,[16] but the practice hitherto has been to review every April.[17] The Secretary of State may 'estimate the general level of prices in such manner as he thinks fit',[18] but, as will be seen,[19] he must have regard not only to the past but also to the predicted future rate of inflation, for he must estimate by how much the value of benefits will have declined by the date of the next up-rating order, in practice the November following the April review.

ii Benefits for specific needs

We have already seen how successive governments have allowed the value of the death and maternity grants to be eroded by inflation.[20] During the passage of the Social Security Bill 1979, the Conservative opposition successfully introduced an amendment imposing on the Secretary of State a duty to review the amounts specified for these benefits to see whether they had 'retained their value in relation to the general level of earnings or prices',[1] but without any obligation to revise the amounts in the light of the review. As regards child benefit, the annual duty is to

> consider whether the rate or any of the rates then in force . . . should be increased having regard to the national economic situation as a whole, the general standard of living and such other matters as he thinks relevant,[2]

and there are similar provisions governing the Christmas bonus[3] and the mobility allowance.[4]

D Duty to up-rate

This statutory duty is consequential on the review of the income maintenance benefits, described in the last section. 'If on any such review the Secretary of State concludes that any of the sums in question will not have retained their value' on the date selected for the next up-rating order, he must take the following action.[5] A statement must be made to Parliament specifying: (i) the proposed date of the up-rating order; (ii) 'the percentage by which those sums would, in his opinion, have to be increased in order to restore their value as at that date'; and (iii) the proposed rate of increase, which must not be less than that in (ii). In due course, he must then lay before Parliament a draft of the up-rating order. The latter need not come into force exactly twelve months after the date when the last revision was made: it is sufficient if it comes into force by the end of the month in which the first anniversary of that date falls.[6] This legislative provision enabled the government in 1980 to postpone the date of up-rating by two weeks, at an estimated saving of £100 million.[7] The increase

16 *Metzger* case, n.1, above, at 448.
17 Ibid, at 447; and see Lustgarten and Elliott 126 NLJ 756, 757.
18 SSA 1975, s.125(2), as amended.
19 N. 5, below.
20 Pp. 241 and 250, above.
1 SSA 1979, s.13.
2 CBA 1975, s.5(5).
3 Pensioners' Payments and Social Security Act 1979, s.4(3).
4 SSA 1975, s.37A(4), inserted by SSPA 1975. Since 1979, he is to have regard to any changes in taxation which affect the cost of motoring: SSA 1979, s.3.
5 SSA 1975, s.125(3), as substituted by SSA 1981, s.1(1).
6 SSA 1975, s.126(5), as amended by SSA 1980, s.1(3).
7 See Third Report of Committee on Social Services 1980–81 HC 324.

specified in the order is 'deemed to be a restoration of value',[8] thus presumably excluding the possibility of any judicial review.[9]

The duty to restore the value of the benefits in question is subject to two qualifications. First, it does not apply where it appears to the Secretary of State 'that the amount of the increase would be inconsiderable'.[10] Secondly, he is permitted to

> adjust the amount of the increase so as to secure that the sums specified for any particular benefits continue to differ from each other by the same amount . . . .[11]

This is clear legislative authority for the practice whereby the real value of differentials (e.g. between sickness and industrial injury benefit) which were once regarded as important but which are no longer so easy to justify may be allowed to erode through the process of inflation.[12] The effect of the provision is that where the Secretary of State is concerned to maintain the same amount between two particular benefits, he will increase one of them (e.g. sickness benefit) by the percentage regarded as appropriate for benefits generally, but limit the increase of the other (e.g. injury benefit) so that the monetary difference between the amounts payable remains what it was before the up-rating order.

E Derogations

Of course, a government so minded may always attempt to derogate from these statutory duties by persuading Parliament to enact a measure exempting the Secretary of State from them for a particular purpose or a particular period. A first example occurred in 1980 when the second Social Security Act of that year enabled him to up-rate short-term benefits by 5 per cent less than the increase which would otherwise have been necessary.[13] Further, under the Social Security Act 1981 the Secretary of State was allowed to up-rate in 1981–82 on the basis of a review which assumed that the increase provided for in the 1980–81 order had been 1 per cent more than had actually been the case.[14] This was to take account of the fact that the rate of inflation estimated in April 1980 for the following November had been slightly too high.[15]

Part 11 Overlapping benefits

A General

Any broadly based system of social welfare encounters the problem arising from the availability of two or more benefits to cover the same, or an essentially similar, risk. The problem has two dimensions. The first is concerned with those overlaps in the social welfare system itself; an

8 SSA 1980, s.1(2).
9 Of the type attempted in *Metzger v Department of Health and Social Security* [1978] 3 All ER 753, on the basis of the legislative provisions then in force.
10 SSA 1975, s.126(3).
11 Ibid, s.126(4).
12 See the discussion at p. 23, above.
13 S.1. The Secretary of State was empowered to extend the 5% shortfall to the next two annual revisions.
14 S.1(3).
15 Conversely, the 11% up-rating in November 1982 allows for a 2% shortfall in the 1981 revision.

obvious example is sickness benefit and industrial injury benefit. The general principle to be applied has never been in doubt: 'double provision should not be made for the same contingency'.[16] The principle may be stated thus easily but its implementation is more difficult as it begs the question of what benefits are intended to cover the same contingency: for example, does a war pension deal with the same risk as sickness benefit? Moreover, even where it is conceded that two benefits are concerned with the same risk, the intention may be to allow the beneficiary to accumulate them: one obvious example is child benefit and increases to a personal benefit for dependent children. Finally there is the problem of deciding what are the limits of the social welfare system for the purpose of applying the principle: are local authority benefits included? Most of these questions receive a solution, explicit or implicit, within the social security legislation itself. An account of these rules forms the subject matter of sections B to E. The second dimension poses even greater difficulties. In many cases there is an overlap between public welfare benefits and private provision, e.g. occupational schemes. There is no consistent policy on this issue, partly because there has never been an overall view of the relationship between the public and private sector, partly because the policy issues themselves are so difficult. They include deciding whether benefits are payable 'as of right' as under a private insurance contract, or are payable rather 'according to need'. In section F a brief summary will be given of the various measures taken, most of them discussed in detail in other parts of the book.

B Recipients of benefits payable under SSA 1975

i Income-maintenance benefits

The principle that double payments should not be made for the same contingency finds its first and most obvious application with regard to benefit intended as basic income maintenance. Thus adjustment is made to those in receipt of two or more of the following non-industrial, personal benefits:[17] unemployment and sickness benefit, retirement and invalidity pensions,[18] maternity allowance, widow's benefit, non-contributory invalidity pension, invalid care allowance. Entitlement to benefits not intended as income-maintenance, viz death grant, maternity grant, attendance and mobility allowance, isnot affected;[19] nor, of course, is entitlement to the earnings-related additional component in pensions, or the graduated retirement benefit.[20] The latter are treated as part of the principal benefit which they supplement.[21]

Any adjustment is made according to the following rules:[1]

(1) A non-contributory benefit is deducted from a contributory benefit.

16 NIAC Report on Draft Overlapping Regulations 1948–49, HC 36, para 9. The principle had been stated both by *Beveridge* para 321 and in *Social Insurance* Part I, para 147.
17 SI 1979/597, reg 4(1).
18 An invalidity pension may be paid with widowed mother's allowance or widow's pension, but the sum of the two basic components should not exceed the standard rate for the invalidity pension: ibid, reg 3. Invalidity allowance may be accumulated with retirement pension.
19 SI 1975/554, reg 3(2).
20 Ibid, reg 4(2)(f).
21 Ibid, reg 4(4).
1 Ibid, reg 4(5).

(2) Unless an alternative arrangement has been made, a proportionate part of a benefit paid weekly is deducted from one paid on a daily basis.
(3) In all other cases, the claimant receives the higher or highest of the benefits to which he is entitled.

The relationship between non-industrial benefits and industrial injury benefits or war pensions is necessarily more complicated, and perhaps more controversial. For the purposes of these rules, the original plan was to equate war pensions with industrial injury benefits.[2] However, at the end of the Second World War there was a strong feeling that war pensions should be regarded as 'compensation' for injuries suffered during service in the national cause and were thus different from other benefits intended to 'relieve hardship'.[3] In the result, there may be an accumulation of unemployment, sickness, invalidity benefit or maternity allowance with a war disablement pension. As regards industrial injury benefits, there was an obvious case for adjusting an overlap of a personal benefit for income-maintenance with injury benefit or the unemployability supplement to a disablement pension,[4] but not with the disablement pension itself, as this was compensation for the injury. Widow's benefit is in a category of its own, since by its nature it is more akin to a dependant's benefit than to a personal benefit, so adjustment is made to prevent overlap, not only with the industrial injury benefit and unemployability supplement, but also with the industrial death benefit and (in the light of the policy discussed below) the war pension death benefit.[5] Finally there is a provision to deduct from personal benefit anything received by way of 'training allowance', (i.e. an allowance payable out of public funds[6] by a government department or by or on behalf of the Manpower Services Commission for maintenance during a period of training).[7]

ii Benefits for special needs

The case for adjusting benefits intended to remedy specific needs arises only as regards overlap between the different schemes for disability. Thus the attendance allowance, invalidity allowance, the mobility allowance and the hospital treatment increase may not be accumulated with their equivalents in other schemes.[8]

iii Dependency benefits

Dependency benefits (meaning not only increases to personal benefits for children or adults, but also child's special allowance, and child's allowance under the war pension scheme[9]), for the same dependant for the same period may not be accumulated.[10] Unlike the rule for personal benefits, the

2 See *Social Insurance* Part I, paras 148–149.
3 See statement of Mr H A Marquand, Minister of Pensions, to House of Commons, 454 HC Official Report (5th series) col 1660 and NIAC Report, n.15, above, at para 20.
4 SI 1979/597, Sch paras 1–5: in general the industrial benefit is deductible from the non-industrial benefit.
5 Ibid, para 3.
6 The fund must be a British fund (*R(P) 5/56*) and controlled by the Government (*R(P) 13/56*).
7 SI 1979/597, Sch. Grants for full-time education and teacher training are, however, excluded: ibid, reg 2(1) and see *R(U) 38/56* and *R 1/68 (P)*.
8 SI 1979/597, Sch, paras 6, 7, 10.
9 Ibid, reg 2(1).
10 Ibid, regs 7, 9–10.

regulations on dependants include the war pension scheme: payment to members of a serviceman's family is not regarded as 'compensation' for the injury sustained.[11] There are two exceptions to this: both a war pension allowance for a child's education and a dependency benefit which is part of a war disablement pension (not being payable as an increase to unemployability supplement) are disregarded.[12] The former may be rationalised on the ground that it covers a special need, and the latter in that it is really part of the 'compensation' for the injury.

C Child benefit

The traditional view has been that child benefit, which is payable to all families as a general redistributive device, is distinguishable from child dependency increases which are primarily intended to cope with the additional financial problems arising when the main source of income is lost. The legal position remains that in general they may be aggregated but this principle has now been undermined, first, by the fact that the amount of the increase payable with short-term benefits has diminished as that of child benefit has been raised,[13] and, secondly, by the rule that the dependency increases may not be aggregated with the increase to child benefit paid to single parents.[14]

D Means-tested benefits

Both of the means-tested benefits are concerned to raise income and other resources to a specified level, but there is a difference of emphasis between the two. With a few exceptions, the family income supplement takes into account the receipt of all social security benefits, though since the amount payable is not modified for a period of a year, entitlement to short-term benefits during that period will effectively be disregarded.[15] While it is a general principle of the supplementary benefit scheme to have regard to all forms of income, it also aims at differentiating between claimants according to their special needs. Insofar as social security benefits are directed towards such needs, the legislation allows them to be partly or wholly disregarded in the calculation of resources. The detailed rules are fully discussed below.[16]

Where, under either scheme, a social security benefit is treated (in whole or in part) as a resource, it nevertheless remains payable in full but the amount paid by way of family income supplement or supplementary benefit is reduced. However, in the case of the latter there is a special rule to cover the contingency where the supplementary benefit was not reduced on account of entitlement to another social security benefit payable for the same period. This situation frequently arises because the other benefit is often paid later than the supplementary benefit. Where this occurs, the authority administering the other benefit is given power to deduct from it the amount overpaid by way of supplementary benefit.[17]

11 Cf NIAC Report, n.16, above, at para 23.
12 SI 1979/597, reg 7(3).
13 P. 365, above.
14 SI 1979/597, reg 8.
15 P. 534, below.
16 Pp. 486–487, below.
17 SBA 1976, s.12.

E Recipients of National Health Service facilities

To the extent that a social security beneficiary is being maintained free of charge at a hospital or other institution his need for financial support is reduced, and if the maintenance is financed from public funds, there is a strong argument for reducing the amount of benefit. There are special rules governing this subject which have been fully discussed in Part 5 of this chapter.

F Social security benefits and private rights

In many situations, a person subject to a hazard covered by the contributory or non-contributory schemes will be entitled to benefit from another source directed towards the same hazard but arising by way of private law, for example through an occupational scheme. Indeed, in the Beveridge scheme such arrangements were to form an important part of the general welfare system: while the state was to provide the minimum security for each kind of hazard, 'it should leave room and encouragement for voluntary action by each individual to provide more than that minimum for himself and his family'.[18] The argument logically leads to a principle that a person prudent enough to avail himself of facilities elsewhere should be entitled to reap the reward of his prescience and aggregate the public with the private benefit. Unfortunately, the matter is much more complex. In the first place, it is no longer the policy that the state benefit should provide merely the minimum. The unreality of the Beveridge laissez-faire thesis has emerged through the huge reliance on national assistance and supplementary benefit, and the introduction of earnings-related pensions. Secondly, the insurance basis of the social security scheme has become increasingly undermined as is evident in the shift to earnings-related contributions and the introduction of non-contributory benefits.[19] Thirdly, in those fields where occupational schemes are widespread, e.g. sick pay and retirement, it is illusory to regard them as resulting from the 'voluntary' action of individuals. Most frequently they result from collective bargains between trade unions and employers. Indeed, sick pay and maternity pay to certain limits and for certain periods are compulsory under legislation and have superseded in importance the equivalent social security benefits.[20]

In the light of these considerations, we may briefly survey the position reached in the most important areas of overlap between public and private provision. Because no general principle exists, different rules prevail in different areas, and these have generally been described in the sections of the book devoted to the specific benefits in question. The purpose here is to provide, by way of summary, an outline of the various approaches adopted.

i Private insurance

Life insurance is very common; accident or sickness insurance is comparatively rare and, for practical purposes, private insurance against unemployment (as opposed to redundancy schemes) is non-existent. Where private insurance does exist, it fits neatly into Beveridge's prototype and it has

18 Para 9.
19 P. 26–27, above.
20 Cf pp. 160 and 249, above.

never been doubted that the income so obtained might be fully accumulated with the non-means tested benefits.

ii Redundancy payments

The state redundancy payments scheme is intended to provide compensation for the loss of a job, the employee having been deprived of his proprietary interest in the employment;[21] the social security benefit is intended as a partial replacement of income lost as the result of the redundancy. Entitlement to one benefit is not affected by receipt of another. Other categories of redundancy payments are similarly treated to the extent that they are regarded as compensation for the loss of a job; but if intended as a substitute for the wages which would otherwise be paid, their receipt disentitles the claimant from unemployment benefit.[1]

iii Guarantee payments

Insofar as an employer agrees, or is bound, to maintain a certain degree of remuneration for periods when an employee is laid-off or put on short-time, the employee is to that extent not regarded as unemployed. The guarantee payments are treated as wages and will disentitle him from benefit.[2]

iv Sick pay

The current position is that receipt of sick pay does not affect entitlement to sickness, invalidity, industrial injury or disablement benefit: it is left to the employer or occupational scheme to deal with the overlap, either by reducing the amount of sick pay or by claiming a reimbursement of the amounts received from the public source.[3] From April 1983, statutory sick pay will replace sickness benefit for the first eight weeks of incapacity.[4] Once this period has elapsed, however, the relevant social security benefit may be accumulated with any sick pay still made available.

v Maternity pay

An employer who confers maternity pay in fulfilment of his obligations under the Employment Protection legislation is entitled to make a deduction for maternity allowance.[5] Any payments which exceed the statutory obligations are treated in the same way as non-statutory sick pay.

vi Occupational retirement pension schemes

The desire to maintain an appropriate standard of living in old age, has inevitably been responsible for a degree of private provision which has had the greatest impact on the public sector. It is clearly not feasible to raise revenue in the public sector to such extent that the retirement pension will be fixed at a level regarded as reasonable for all members of society. The effort has been directed more at integrating the private with the public sector, so that under the new pensions arrangements those unlikely to invest in private schemes, or unable to do so, will be able to rely on a genuinely adequate pension, related to their pre-retirement income, while

21 Cf p. 74, above.
1 P. 86, above.
2 Pp. 100–101, above.
3 P. 155, above.
4 P. 160, above.
5 P. 249, above.

those sufficiently covered by a private scheme are able to opt out of the earnings-related component in the public scheme.[6] The complicated arrangements governing the relationship between state and occupational pensions have been fully described in chapter 5.[7]

As has also been seen,[8] a controversial measure enacted in 1980 provided for a pound for pound reduction of unemployment benefit for the proceeds of an occupational pension in excess of a maximum sum. This was to deal with an alleged anomaly whereby men aged 60 to 65 in receipt of such a pension had claimed unemployment benefit without any real expectation that suitable work would be available for them.

vii Tort claims

The overlap between tort claims for personal injury or death and social security provision has been an area of great difficulty and much discussion.[9] Beveridge had assumed that some adjustment was necessary.[10] The Monckton Committee, examining the question in 1946, agreed but sensibly concluded that it would be wrong to disturb full entitlement to the social security benefit.[11] The latter was payable almost immediately and was not subject to problems of proof of fault, or quantum of damages. It recommended instead that the damages award should take account of the benefit paid or payable,[12] a proposal which in its entirety proved to be politically unacceptable, and resulted in an unsatisfactory compromise: a deduction of one half of any sums paid or payable within five years from the time when the cause of action accrued for sickness or invalidity, industrial injury and disablement benefit and non-contributory invalidity pension.[13] No deduction is made from a damages award under the Fatal Accidents Act for any social security benefit.[14] Legislation is silent on the effect of other social security benefits on personal injury claims, and it has been left to judges to apply general common law principles, not however with much consistency. Current decisions seem to favour deduction for unemployment benefit,[15] supplementary benefit[16] and family income supplement[17] but curiously not for attendance or mobility allowance.[18]

The Pearson Royal Commission on Civil Liability and Compensation for Personal Injuries made proposals for substantial reform of these matters; they argued that the full value of social security benefits payable to an injured person or the dependants of a deceased person should be deducted.[19] In 1981, the government declared its intention of implementing these recommendations.[20]

6 P. 222, above.
7 Pp. 222–224, above.
8 P. 129, above.
9 See esp. *Pearson* ch 13; *Atiyah* ch 18.
10 Para 260.
11 Final Report of Departmental Committee on Alternative Remedies (1946, Cmd 6860), paras 41–43.
12 Ibid, at paras 48, 92, 96, 98.
13 Law Reform (Personal Injuries) Act 1948 s.2(1), as amended by NIA 1971, Sch 5, para 1 and Social Security (Consequential Provisions) Act 1975, Sch 2, para 8. For details and the case-law see McGregor *Damages* (14th edn) pp. 815–817.
14 Fatal Accidents Act 1976, s.4(1).
15 *Nabi v British Leyland (UK) Ltd* [1980] 1 All ER 667, [1980] 1 WLR 529.
16 *Plummer v P W Wilkins & Son Ltd* [1981] 1 All ER 91, [1981] 1 WLR 831; *Lincoln v Hayman* [1982] 1 WLR 488.
17 *Gaskill v Preston* [1981] 3 All ER 427.
18 *Bowker v Rose* (1978) 122 Sol Jo 147; *Gohery v Durham County Council* (1978) unreported, Kemp and Kemp *The Quantum of Damages* (4th edn) para 5–323.
19 Paras 467–498.
20 *Reform of the Industrial Injuries Scheme*, ch 8.

Chapter 11

Child benefit

Part 1 Introduction

A General

Until recently, family provision has been treated as the poor relation (or Cinderella[1]) of the social security system. Family allowances were not introduced until 1945, and then in the 1950s and 1960s were neglected: they were rarely up-rated in line with rising living standards, and did not appear to be regarded as significant benefits. The result was that Britain's provision for children has been less generous than that of most other European and some Commonwealth countries.[2] In particular, the allowances were not payable for the first child of the family, though in this respect the British system was not unique.[3] While in the mid 1970s more people were in receipt of them than any other social security benefit (with the exception of retirement pensions), the total amount spent on family allowances was rather less than that on unemployment and on supplementary benefit.[4] In contrast, income tax allowances for children were rather more valuable, and were often increased by the annual Finance Act.[5] They did not, however, benefit families who had a low income and therefore did not pay tax at all. The primary object of the change to child benefit made by the Child Benefit Act 1975 was to integrate the two allowances: this was to be done by paying more to all persons looking after children than was afforded under the family allowances scheme and by gradually withdrawing the tax allowances which had disproportionately benefited higher income groups. It will be seen that there are now doubts whether the aim has been satisfactorily achieved.[6]

In this Part of the chapter, there is first a short outline of the history of family allowances, and then an examination of the reasons which led to their replacement by child benefit. The third section contains a discussion of some of the policy questions arising under the scheme – in particular, the question whether the rate of benefit should be varied according to the child's age or other factors. In Part 2 of the chapter, the legal conditions for

1 The term is used by *Kaim-Caudle* p. 264.

2 See the figures given in (1966) 1 Proverty 15, and Wynn *Family Policy* (1970) Appendix 3.

3 See *Kaim-Caudle* p. 271 (Netherlands) and p. 273 (West Germany). Germany introduced family allowances for the first child in 1975: see (1974) 30 Poverty 27 (M and A Wynn).

4 See the figures in the Annual Report of the DHSS 1975 (Cmnd 6565), para 7.9.

5 In the early 1970s, however, the value of the children's allowances fell relative to the personal tax allowance: see the discussion in (1978) 41 Poverty 5.

6 P. 425, below.

entitlement to child benefit are analysed. Part 3 contains a short discussion of the rules regarding claims to, and payment of, benefit.

B The history of family allowances[7]

The first proposal to introduce a special allowance for the benefit of children was made in 1796 by William Pitt, then Chancellor of the Exchequer. His enlightened attitude is exemplified by his peroration, often quoted in modern debates: 'Let us make relief, in cases where there are a number of children, a matter of right and an honour, instead of a ground for opprobrium and contempt.'[8] But the Bill never became law, because of the pressure of other business; Pitt was more successful, as will be seen,[9] when he introduced income tax allowances for children. It seems that the issue was not discussed widely again until after the First World War, when Eleanor Rathbone founded the Family Endowment Society, an important pressure group in the inter-war years. In her book, *The Disinherited Family*, published in 1924, she argued that it was in the interest of society as a whole to ensure that children were well clothed and fed, and that a state allowance should be paid to make this possible. The case for such a payment took on additional strength from the fact that in 1921 and 1922 dependants' allowances were introduced for the unemployed.[10] The absence of any comparable provision when the man was in work might have been viewed as a disincentive to employment. But, unlike other European countries, there was no move at this time to introduce family allowances in Britain.[11]

The introduction of the Family Allowances Bill in 1945, during the last months of the war-time Coalition government, was largely influenced by the Beveridge Report. This adduced three principal arguments for the payment of family allowances. First, the only way of guaranteeing a reasonable subsistence income for all families, whether the head of the family was in work or not, was to pay an allowance for children: this object could not be secured by wages, as they did not take account of the size of a man's family.[12] Secondly, 'it is dangerous to allow benefit during unemployment or disability to equal or exceed earnings during work. But, without allowances for children, during earning and not earning alike, this danger cannot be avoided.'[13] The third argument seems surprising these days: the provision of family allowances was thought conducive to a higher birth rate.[14] The Beveridge Report further argued that payments should be financed by general taxation, so that the whole community should share in the task of maintaining children. But parents were not to be relieved of their entire responsibility, and for this reason it was recommended that

7 See *Walley* pp. 16–20, 54–55, 70–73; Land in (1966) 2 Poverty 13; Hall, Land, Parker and Webb *Change, Choice and Conflict in Social Policy* (1975) ch 9; *Harris* pp. 341–346; Macnicol *The Movement for Family Allowances 1918–45* (1980).

8 Quoted by Sir W Jowitt, introducing the debate on *Social Insurance*, Part I 404 HC Official Report (5th series) col 988.

9 See p. 423, below.

10 See p. 365, above.

11 In the inter-war years family allowances were introduced in France, Germany and the Netherlands. New Zealand had been the first country to introduce such a scheme – in 1926.

12 Para 411.

13 Para 412.

14 Paras 15 and 413. Churchill gave particular emphasis to this point when he announced the Coalition government's acceptance of Beveridge's proposals in a broadcast in 1943.

nothing should be paid for the first child in a family.[15] Lastly, the Report rejected the argument that the allowance for each child should be reduced as the size of the family increased; there were no real economies of scale when this occurred. A flat rate payment of 8s (40p) was proposed, though Beveridge indicated that at some future time consideration should be given to grading allowances according to the children's age.[16]

The government modified the scheme proposed by Beveridge in some minor respects. The most important change was that a substantial part of the allowance was to be paid in kind through the provision of free school meals and milk. This reduced the cash payment to 5s (25p) a week, which the government proposed should belong to the father. But on a free vote Miss Rathbone's amendment to make allowances the property of the mother was passed.[17] As the title of the Act and the name of the benefit suggested, the allowance was to be paid to families 'for the benefit of the family as a whole'.[18] The claimant was required to show that the family contained at least two children. The legislative provisions defining a 'family' for the purposes of the allowance were complex and gave rise to a number of cases before the Commissioners in which the question was whether a particular child was a member of one or other of two families.[19] (Under the Child Benefit Act these difficulties have largely disappeared.)[20]

The rate of payment was not increased until 1952, and was then raised again for third and subsequent children in 1956. After that there was no change until 1968. The introduction by legislation in 1956 of an extra 2s (10p) for third and subsequent children meant that relatively older children attracted larger allowances, though it is difficult to see this development as fulfilling Beveridge's suggestion that they might be graduated according to age.[1] The 1956 Act also made the allowance payable in respect of children receiving full-time education, or in an apprenticeship, until they reached the age of 18; previously the general age limit had been 16.[2] The 1964 Act further raised the limit for these groups of children to 19.[3]

There is no obvious reason why family allowances were so neglected throughout this period. It has been suggested that to some extent they suffered because they were the first benefit introduced after the Beveridge Report: the 1945 Act was passed before the Attlee Labour government assumed office and, therefore, the role of family allowances in combating poverty was not discussed during the late 1940s.[4] A second reason is perhaps that the demographic argument for their payment was no longer taken seriously; indeed, there was some anxiety that the country might be overpopulated by the end of the century.[5] In fact, there seems very little

15 Para 417. See *Harris* p. 412.
16 Para 421. The argument on the appropriate rates for paying benefit still continues: see pp. 426–427, below.
17 For the similar controversy concerning the allocation of tax credits and child benefit, see p. 424, below.
18 FAA 1945, s.1, repeated in FAA 1965, s.1.
19 See e.g. *R(F) 3/63*; *R(F) 8/64*; *R(F) 1/74*, interpreting FAA 1945, s.3, or the same section of the FAA 1965. The Commissioners assumed jurisdiction to determine these issues in 1959; p. 582, below.
20 Pp. 433–434, below.
1 Cp *George* p. 191.
2 FAA 1945, s.2.
3 FANIA 1964, s.1. The 1945 Act, the 1964 Act and other statutes were consolidated in the FAA 1965.
4 The point is made by *Walley* p. 182.
5 Ibid, at pp. 186–187, and see the same author in Bull (ed) *Family Poverty* (1972) p. 109.

evidence that the availability of family provision affects population trends.[6] But the belief that it does may have been partly responsible for government reluctance to increase the level of payments. Thirdly, it appears that the allowances were among the least 'popular' of the welfare benefits.[7] Certainly, there has until recently not been the same widespread demand for more generous provision for families as there has for pensioners, and it may be for this political reason that governments decided to economise on family allowances.

The last major development before the change to the new system occurred in 1968. There were two increases, the first of 7s (35p) and the second of 3s (15p) within twelve months. The Labour government's intention was that these should benefit the poorer families who did not earn enough to pay income tax. In order to prevent taxpayers benefiting from the increases, an equivalent sum was 'clawed back' from them by a reduction in the value of the children's income tax allowance. The 'claw back' remained a feature of the family allowances system until it was replaced by child benefit under the 1975 Act.[8] The device had first been suggested in the Beveridge Report. The rule was that the amount of the child tax allowance available was to be reduced by the increase in the annual value of the family allowances since 1968 (in 1976, £52), when the person concerned was entitled to and did actually claim the latter.[9] This was the first time family and tax allowances had been considered together; it signalled the advent of the approach which led to the Child Benefit Act 1975.

C The change to child benefit

Before the 1975 legislation is discussed, something should be said about child income tax allowances, because their abolition is a crucial aspect of the new scheme. They were first introduced by William Pitt two years after his unsuccessful attempt to provide a family benefit. But they were abolished in 1806, and were not reintroduced until 1909. From 1957 their value was graduated according to the child's age, a significant difference from family allowances. Thus in 1976–77 before the change to the new system the value of the child tax allowance (CTA) was as follows: for a child under 11, £300; for a child from 11 to 16, £335; and for a child over 16, £365.[10] If he was receiving full-time instruction at any school, university or other educational establishment,[11] there was no age limit.[12] Unlike family allowances, CTA may be claimed in respect of the first child. Although it is only recently that it has become common to look at tax allowances as a type of family endowment, their value to the taxpayer with children has obviously been considerable. Two further points may be made. First, CTA may benefit high earners proportionately more than those on an average income, because it reduces taxable income, and so

6 See Schorr in (1967) 2 Poverty 8.
7 See Bull, n.5, above, at pp. 167–168.
8 There are discussions of the 'claw back' by Kincaid *Poverty and Equality in Great Britain* (1973) pp. 69–73, and by Lynes, n.5, above, at p. 118.
9 Income and Corporation Taxes Act (ICTA) 1970, s.24(1).
10 Finance Act 1976, s.29(2).
11 This included training for a trade, profession or vocation in circumstances where the child was expected to devote all his time to it for at least two years: ICTA 1970, s.10(4).
12 In both family allowances and child benefit (see p. 429, below) there is an upper age limit of 19.

enables the former group to pay tax at a lower rate. Secondly, since tax is normally deducted by PAYE at source, CTA typically benefits the male wage-earner rather than the child's mother.

Towards the end of the 1960s a number of schemes were suggested for integrating family allowances and tax allowances.[13] The Labour party put forward proposals in 1969; then the Conservative government, which took office the following year, recommended their integration as part of a tax credit system.[14] Although the 1974 Labour government was not in favour of this radical reform, it did support a child endowment scheme which had much in common with the tax credit proposal so far as it applied to children. Thus the Child Benefit Bill, introduced in May 1975, enjoyed all party support, and the opposition was only concerned to amend the measure in detail. Its purpose was well summarised by Mrs Castle, the Secretary of State for Social Services:

> It achieves a long overdue merger between child tax allowances and family allowances into a new universal, non-means tested, tax-free cash benefit for all children, including the first, payable to the mother. In this way it ensures that the nation's provision for family support is concentrated first and foremost where it is needed most – on the poorest families; and that it goes to the person responsible for caring for the children and managing the budget for their food, clothing and other necessities.[15]

The scheme has two major advantages over family allowances. First, the benefit of tax allowances is extended to those poorer families who had not been able to take advantage of CTA because their income was too low to pay tax – this was achieved through the more generous level of child benefits. Secondly, the new benefit is payable for the first child. In these respects the measure followed the tax credit proposals.

However, child benefit differs from the original tax credit scheme outlined in the Conservative government's Green Paper.[16] First, the benefit is tax-free, while the tax credit (equivalent to the child benefit) would have been treated as part of the recipient's income for the purposes of tax, as were family allowances. Secondly, it is paid to the mother, while the original proposal was that credits should be payable to the father. But the Select Committee on Tax Credits had recommended that child credit should be paid to the mother, and this approach was followed in the Child Benefit Bill. Mrs Castle referred warmly to the support given by the TUC for this proposal, even though its implementation entailed a reduction in the take-home pay of union members.

The government made it clear that it did not intend to bring the Act into effect until April 1977, though it was pressed by the Conservatives in both Committee and at the Report stage[17] to pay the benefit from April 1976. Instead, an interim child benefit for all children of unmarried or separated parents was paid from that date to deal with the special problems faced by single-parent families.[18] For a short period in 1976 it was suggested that the implementation of the new scheme for other families should be further postponed. The official reason was that the government did not want take-

13 See *George* pp. 196–197; *Walley* pp. 193–194.
14 P. 35, above.
15 892 HC Official Report (5th series) col 330.
16 (1971), Cmnd 5116.
17 Standing Committee A Debates on the Child Benefit Bill 1975, cols 266 ff; 896 HC Official Report (5th series) col 179.
18 CBA 1975, s.16. The interim benefit ceased when child benefit became payable in April 1977.

home pay to be reduced, as it would be on the lowering of the child tax allowances, at a time when it was naturally anxious for its pay policy not to be jeopardised.[19] In fact, there is some suspicion that it was more concerned about the possible public expenditure implications of the change to child benefit when the time came to fix its rates.[20] Eventually in September 1976 it accepted the recommendation of a joint Labour party-TUC working group to introduce child benefit in phases.[21]

The compromise initially was that from April 1977, CTA for children under 11 would be phased out over three years, and the higher tax allowances for older children gradually reduced, but in fact under the Finance Act 1979 with two exceptions all tax allowances were abolished for 1979–80 and subsequent years.[1] Child benefit is tax-free, as originally proposed for the tax credit scheme; this emphasises the non-selectivity of the scheme, but on the other hand means that it is no more beneficial to lower income groups than the better-off. This is important, now that it seems clear that the value of child benefit has not kept pace with inflation, or indeed for some parents, the combined value of the old family allowances and CTA.[2] There has been much criticism of the failure, particularly by the present government, adequately to increase the benefit rate, though in 1980 it did commit itself to maintaining the level of benefit at its present value by annual up-rating.[3] As will be seen at the end of Part 2, the treatment of single parent families has been much more generous.[4] For 1982–83, benefit is £5.85 a week for each child, though a single parent receives an additional £3.65 for his (or her) first child.

It is interesting that even the CPAG which pressed particularly hard for the 1975 reform, has apparently reconsidered whether the new system has really been successful.[5] Two major policy issues which would affect the level of benefit are discussed in the next section. Other alternatives, which may be briefly mentioned here, would be the introduction of income-related child benefit, as in the United States Aid to Families with Dependent Children programme, and the payment of considerably higher benefits with some 'claw-back' through income tax.[6] The first would inevitably arouse the anger of those who oppose means-tests, and the second policy – though attractive on egalitarian grounds – would lead to considerable administrative costs. It may be that the best hope is that when economic circumstances permit, the government will see an increase in child benefit as a top priority in social security provision.

D Two policy questions

For the reasons already given the child benefit scheme represents some advance over the previous system of family and tax allowances. But there remain difficulties, and until these are resolved, it will be hard to come to a

19 The immediate abolition of CTA for children under 11 would have reduced take-home pay by over £3 a week for a two child family.

20 See *New Society*, 17 June and 24 June 1976, containing reports of the Cabinet discussions on the introduction of the child benefit scheme.

21 918 HC Official Report (5th Series) cols 112–114.

1 Finance Act 1979, s.1(4); for the two exceptions, see p. 429 and p. 440, below.

2 See (1979) 43 Proverty 8–9, and (1981) 48, ibid, 31.

3 989 HC Official Report (5th series) col 1063.

4 Pp. 443–444, below.

5 See the article by J Bradshaw (1980) 45 Poverty 15–20.

6 For 'claw-back', see p. 423, above.

final verdict on the success of the change.[7] In particular, there are two questions of policy on which final attitudes have yet to be determined. The first is whether the benefit should be paid at a flat rate or varied according to the child's age and any other relevant factor; the second concerns the approach to up-rating it in the light of inflation.

i Should the benefit be flat-rate or graduated according to age/other factors?

There is a considerable body of evidence which suggests that the expense of providing for a child varies with its age.[8] An adolescent child attending school may cost more than an adult to feed and clothe, while younger children will require much less expenditure. This was recognised by the Beveridge Report.[9] Family allowances had, however, been flat-rate, though after 1956 a higher payment was made for third and subsequent children in one family.[10] The Child Benefit Act 1975 does contemplate that benefit may be paid eventually at different rates. Section 5(2) and (3) provide as follows:

> (2) Different rates may be prescribed in relation to different cases, whether by reference to the age of the child in respect of whom the benefit is payable or otherwise.
> (3) The power to prescribe different rates under subsection (2) above shall be exercised so as to bring different rates into force on such day as the Secretary of State may by order specify.

It does not seem at all clear on a literal construction of these provisions whether the government is under a duty to prescribe different rates or has a discretion whether to do so: the latter would appear to be indicated by subsection (2), but subsection (3) could be interpreted as imposing a duty. The debates in Parliament, even if admissible in a court of law,[11] do not provide any guidance on this point. At all events the power has so far only been exercised to prescribe a different rate for single parent families.

During the debates on the 1975 Bill the opposition proposed the payment of benefit at three different rates, depending on whether the child fell into the age groups, up to 5, 6 to 15, 16 and over.[12] Quite apart from the evidence of the higher costs of providing for adolescents, it was pointed out that the supplementary benefit scales then provided for payment at five different rates for children under 18 depending on their age,[13] and that the child tax allowances which were replaced by child benefit were also graduated.[14] But, although approving of differential rates in principle, the government took the view that more research should be done before this could be implemented. In particular, not enough was known, it was said, about the economic costs of the first child (when the family has to buy clothes, a pram, etc., which may be used for subsequent children) and whether marginal costs are affected by the total number of children in a

7 For a general critique of the scheme, see Trinder *Poverty Report 1976* p. 71. Also see Field, Meacher and Pond *To Him Who Hath* (1977) pp. 222–224, and (1980) 45 Poverty 15.
8 Wynn *Family Policy* (1970) Appendix 3; M & A Wynn (1975–76) 33 Poverty 4.
9 Para 421. Also see *Social Assistance* para 5.29.
10 See p. 422, above.
11 See Cross *Statutory Interpretation* (1976) pp. 134–136.
12 Standing Committee A Debates, cols 73 ff; 895 HC Official Report (5th series) col 223.
13 See pp. 466–467, below.
14 See p. 423, above.

family.[15] Moreover, the payment of a higher child benefit for older children would either have entailed awarding less for younger ones, which would have been politically difficult, or spending more on the total scheme at a time when public expenditure was being reduced.

Although there is a reasonable case for paying higher rates for older children, there is a contrary argument that the poorest families are those with young children (where the mother is unable to go out to work) and therefore a more generous benefit should be paid for children below school age.[16] And it seems that the practice in other countries is more often to pay higher allowances according to the child's rank (i.e. more for the second or third child, etc.) and not according to his age.[17] It is, of course, possible to vary payments according to both factors: for example, an increase could be paid for a child when it became, say, 11, if it were the second or third child, but not if it were the first, though this type of scheme would be expensive to administer.[18]

ii How often should benefit be up-rated?[19]

It has been mentioned how rarely family allowances were increased, and how as a result their contribution to the average family budget became virtually negligible.[20] There was, therefore, some anxiety during the debates on the 1975 Bill that child benefit would similarly lag behind rises in the cost of living. But amendments during the Committee stage to link the benefit with price movements (and in a Labour back-bench amendment to link it with prices or earnings, whichever were the more favourable) were rejected.[1] The government did not regard child benefit as similar to other social security benefits for this purpose and, therefore, rejected automatic annual review. The reason given by Mrs Castle was that it was not a subsistence benefit, but a supplement to what is normally a full wage and, therefore, the considerations relevant to other benefits, such as retirement pensions, did not apply.[2]

However, at the Report stage a government amendment was moved to insert what is now section 5(5):

> In the year beginning with the appointed day[3] and in each subsequent year beginning with the anniversary of that day, the Secretary of State shall consider whether the rate or any of the rates then in force under this section should be increased having regard to the national economic situation as a whole, the general standard of living and such other matters as he thinks relevant.

It should be noted that this does not impose more than a duty to *consider* whether there should be an increase in benefit in the light of all the relevant factors, which might, of course, include the desirability of reducing (or at least, not increasing) public expenditure. And the duty to consider does not arise every twelve months; it may be discharged at any

15 Standiang Committee A Debates, cols 99–100. The Beveridge Report (para 417) and a DHSS report by McClements (unpublished) both suggest that there is no evidence for economies of scale as the family size increases: Standing Committee A Debates, col 81.
16 See Bradshaw (1980) 45 Poverty 15.
17 See *Kaim-Caudle* p. 285, and see p. 253 for the reasons given by the Royal Commission on Social Security (1972) in New Zealand for rejecting age-related benefits.
18 The French system has this complicated structure: see (1975) 31 Poverty 40.
19 For up-rating of social security benefits, see pp. 410–413, above.
20 See p. 422, above.
1 Standing Committee A Debates, col 146.
2 Ibid, at col 161.
3 SI 1976/961, art 2 provided that the appointed day was 4 April 1977.

time during the year in question, which may be nearly two years after the previous review.[4] Although Mrs Castle was right to point out that there was no obligation even to consider an increase in family allowances or tax allowances,[5] the significance of this new legal requirement is even now hard to determine. As already mentioned, there has been much criticism of the failure of governments during the last few years adequately to up-rate the level of child benefit, and it has been pointed out that for some families its value is lower than the combined worth of the family and tax allowances it replaced.[6] In 1980 the government did commit itself to maintaining the value of the benefit in line with inflation and this commitment was honoured the following year.[7] So the relatively vague legal obligation to *consider* an increase in benefit levels is now supported by a more political duty.

Part 2 Entitlement to child benefit

Under section 1 of the Child Benefit Act 1975,

> a person who is responsible for one or more children in any week . . . shall be entitled to a benefit . . . for that week in respect of the child or each of the children for whom he is responsible.

There are two major issues in the determination of entitlement to child benefit: first, whether the child is one in respect of whom benefit is payable, and secondly, whether the claimant is to be treated 'as responsible for a child'. Since two or more persons may concurrently be responsible for the same child, difficult questions as to priority of title to the benefit may arise if there is more than one claim; these are discussed at the end of the second section. The third section is concerned with the residence qualifications which have to be satisfied by both the child and the person responsible for him, and the fourth with the benefit paid to one-parent families.

A The child

Section 2(1) of the Act provides that:

> a person shall be treated as a child for any week in which —
> (a) he is under the age of 16; or
> (b) he is under the age of 19 and receiving full-time education by attendance at a recognised educational establishment.

There is, therefore, a normal age limit under the 1975 Act of 16, with an upper age limit in some circumstances of 19.

i The normal age limit

The normal age limit of 16 provoked comparatively little discussion during the passage of the Bill. It seems that the government chose this age,

4 In this respect the obligation does not appear to differ from that imposed with regard to social security benefits by SSA 1975, s.125(1): p. 411, above.
5 895 HC Official Report (5th series) col 233.
6 P. 425, above.
7 This of course does not mean that the benefit has kept pace with inflation since it was introduced in 1975: see (1981) 48 Poverty 31.

because after a person is 16, he may be entitled to supplementary benefit.[8] Under the previous family allowances scheme, the normal limit was defined by reference to the school leaving age;[9] but as that has now been raised to 16, it is practicable to frame the general rule in terms of that age. This normal age limit is quite common in other countries: it is 16 in New Zealand, Australia, Canada, Belgium, Holland and France. But in some countries, it is higher: 18 in Germany, Italy and Denmark, and 19 in Luxembourg.[10]

In practice the normal age limit has now been modified by regulations made under the Social Security Act 1980.[11] The government was anxious to reduce supplementary benefits expenditure on recent school-leavers,[12] so it is now provided that a school-leaver, 16 or over, may continue to be treated as a child for benefit purposes for a period expiring roughly at the end of the holidays following the date when he left school, though not beyond his 19th birthday.[13] Benefit may be paid during this period even though the child is in receipt of financial support under the Employment and Training Act 1973 or is receiving education by virtue of his work, circumstances in which child benefit is not normally payable for a person between 16 and 19 years old.[14] But an overlap provision makes it clear that no child benefit is payable when the child concerned is eligible to claim a supplementary allowance in his own right.[15]

ii The further age limit of 19

Under the legislation benefit may be paid for a child under 19 only if he is receiving full-time education at a recognised educational establishment. There was some criticism of the failure to extend benefit to children over 16 suffering from a physical handicap. This is a common provision in other European countries,[16] but, as was mentioned in the Committee proceedings,[17] in Britain a handicapped child over 16 is eligible for the non-contributory invalidity pension, and to award child benefit would create an unnecessary overlap.[18]

The upper limit of 19 is low in comparison with other European countries; in France it is 20, while in Germany, Belgium and Luxembourg it is 25, and in the Netherlands, 27.[19] Tax allowances, generally phased out under the scheme, were without an upper age limit at all for dependent children, and there was, therefore, some anxiety on the opposition benches that parents with children at college or university would suffer financial hardship as a result of the change to child benefit. Their position was therefore safeguarded by the temporary preservation of tax allowances: they continued to be payable for a child following at the end of 1976, a full-time course at a university, college, or other educational

8 Standing Committee A Debates, col 10. See ch 12 for entitlement to supplementary benefits.
9 FAA 1965, s.2(1) and (2)(a).
10 See *Kaim-Caudle* ch 8, and the figures given in Standing Committee A Debates, col 39.
11 SSA 1980, s.4(5).
12 See pp. 458–459, below, for the change in supplementary benefits law.
13 SI 1980/1045, reg 2, amending SI 1976/965, reg 7.
14 See p. 431, below, see Appendix.
15 SI 1980/1045, reg 5: see p. 459, below.
16 *Kaim-Caudle* ch 8.
17 Standing Committee A Debates, cols 39–40.
18 For non-contributory invalidity pension, see ch 4, pp. 166–171, above.
19 *Kaim-Caudle* p. 284; Standing Committe A Debates, cols 13–14. Comparisons may be misleading unless account is also taken of the various systems of educational grants.

establishment where no student grant is received or there is no parental contribution on the basis of which a deduction is made from the grant.[20] For students after that date, appropriate adjustments were made to the student grant.[1] There does not appear to be any particular justification for 19 being chosen as the upper age limit, apart from the rather weak argument that this was the rule in the family allowances system.[2] On the other hand, it might be thought odd that child benefit may be paid at all in respect of someone who is legally an adult at the age of 18![3] It would appear that the divergent rules of child benefit and tax allowances with regard to age limits afford yet another example of the inconsistency of approach which British law often adopts to young people who have just become legally adult.[4]

iii 'Receiving full-time education . . . at a recognised educational establishment'

The Act provides that an educational establishment is one 'recognised by the Secretary of State'.[5] Under the Regulations a person may be treated as receiving full-time education if he is in receipt of primary or secondary education, otherwise than at a school by special arrangements made under the Education Act;[6] moreover, in determining whether this condition is satisfied, no account is to be taken of a reasonable interruption of up to six months, or even longer where it is attributable to illness or disability.[7] From the decisions of the Commissioner, interpreting the equivalent provision in the family allowances regulations,[8] it would seem that school holidays, and leaving one school for the purpose of removal to another, would both be treated as reasonable interruptions in full-time education.[9] It was also decided that a child, unable to find a school for several months because of his mental disability, was to be treated as undergoing full-time instruction for that period;[10] but in another case it was held that if education was continued beyond the child's sixteenth birthday *because of* his disability, any delay in finding a suitable school could not be treated as a resonable period of interruption.[11] This distinction would appear applicable in interpreting the child benefit Regulation. Another decision of the Commissioner which may afford guidance in determining whether the child is receiving full-time education is *R(F) 4/62*: there it was held that a person attending a secretarial college for thirteen and a half hours a week, with no homework outside this period, was not in receipt of *full-time* instruction.

Regulations in 1977 provide that benefit is not to be payable in respect of a child under 19 who is receiving 'advanced education'.[12] This term is defined as courses in preparation for a degree, diploma or a teaching qualification, and any other courses certified by the Secretary of State as

20 Finance Act 1977, s.26: see Tiley *Revenue Law* (3rd edn) para 9.47.
1 895 HC Official Report (5th series) cols 202–208.
2 B O'Malley, Minister of State, ibid, col 208.
3 Family Law Reform Act 1969, s.1.
4 See the age limits governing maintenance of children in family proceedings: Cretney *Principles of Family Law* (3rd edn) pp. 481–482.
5 CBA 1975, s.24(1).
6 SI 1976/965, reg 5: there is a comparable provision in reg 5(6) for Scotland. For the meaning of 'education', see *R 1/78 (CB)*.
7 SI 1976/965, reg 6(1). But see SI 1980/1045, reg 2.
8 SI 1969/212, reg 15.
9 *R(F) 4/60*; *R(F) 1/68*.
10 *R(F) 3/60*; cp *R(F) 4/61*.
11 *R(F) 1/68*.
12 SI 1977/543, reg 2(3), inserting new reg 7A to the CB (General) Regulations, SI 1976/965.

above GCE 'A' level standard.[13] But, as mentioned earlier, a parent might still have been temporarily eligible for a CTA in respect of such a child, and for later years an adjustment was made to the student grant.[14]

Under the family allowances rules it was sometimes difficult to determine whether a person receiving instruction at a technical college in connection with his work was to be regarded as receiving full-time instruction at an institution comparable to a school, or was alternatively to be treated as an apprentice.[15] Now that there is no entitlement in respect of apprentices, it is obviously crucial to know when vocational training will satisfy the requirements of section 2(1)(b) of the Act. The Act provides that education received by a child 'by virtue of his employment or of any office held by him' is not to qualify for this purpose[16] unless it is part of a course for at least six months and during that period he receives no financial support from his employment.[17] Amendment regulations now provide that benefit is not to be paid for any child while he is receiving financial support under the Employment and Training Act 1973, or during a period of interruption of employment or full-time education which occurs immediately before the receipt of such support.[18] Nor is it to be paid while he is financially supported by his employers for his education.[19] But reimbursement of the cost of books, equipment, tuition and other fees, and travelling expenses are not to be regarded as financial support for these provisions.[20]

iv Married children

There has been some discussion whether child benefit could ever be obtained in respect of a married child:[1] this would, of course, generally be applicable to a child over 16 with regard to whom it is payable under section 2(1)(b).[2] The government's intention was that benefit should be awarded in respect of a married child if he has left the other spouse and is in receipt of full-time education. This is covered by the General Regulations:[3]

- A person may be entitled to benefit in respect of a married child, provided that person is not the child's spouse, *and* that either the child is not residing with his spouse or that, if he is, the latter is receiving full-time education.[4]

Interesting possibilities occur if the married child is a mother. She will herself be entitled to benefit in respect of her infant merely on the ground

13 Ibid, reg 2(1): the definition is inserted in reg 1(2) of SI 1976/965.
14 See p. 429, above. For the similar overlap provisions for supplementary benefits, see p. 517, below.
15 See the conflicting approaches in *R(F) 4/64* and *R(F) 1/70*. The difference could be important because an apprentice was only eligible for benefit if his earnings did not exceed a specified limit: FAA 1965, s.19.
16 CBA 1975, Sch 1, para 2.
17 SI 1976/965, reg 8(1).
18 SI 1980/1045, regs 2(b) and 4, amending SI 1976/965, regs 6 and 7B.
19 SI 1978/1275, amending SI 1976/965, regs 7 and 8.
20 SI 1976/965, reg 8(2).
1 Standing Committee A Debates, cols 19–22.
2 In a few cases a child under 16 will lawfully be married under a foreign legal system and the marriage will be recognised in England if neither spouse is domiciled there: Morris *The Conflict of Laws* (2nd edn) p. 113.
3 SI 1976/965, reg 10.
4 Ibid, reg 11 as redrafted by SI 1978/540, reg 4, prescribes the circumstances in which persons are not to be treated as having ceased to reside together: p. 439, below.

that it is living with her.[5] Further, her own mother (or other person with whom she is living) will also be entitled to benefit in respect of her. This odd situation could have occurred under the family allowances scheme, though the young mother under nineteen would have to have had two children in order to receive family allowances![6] It does seem, however, that one local tribunal was persuaded that a schoolgirl could not be both a mother and child for family allowances purposes.[7]

v Disqualified children

Benefit is not payable in respect of certain children under Schedule 1 to the Act. Broadly the disqualifications apply if the child in the particular week is 'undergoing imprisonment or detention in legal custody', or is in the care of a local authority in various prescribed circumstances. These are set out in the General Regulations,[8] and are not discussed further here, though it is important to point out that the disqualification only applies if the child has been in detention, care, etc., for more than eight weeks.[9]

B 'Person responsible for the child'

Under section 1, it is the person responsible for a child who is entitled to the benefit in respect of him. This term is primarily defined in section 3(1):

> a person shall be treated as responsible for a child in any week if —
> (a) he has the child living with him in that week; *or*
> (b) he is contributing to the cost of providing for the child at a weekly rate which is not less than the weekly rate of child benefit payable in respect of the child for that week.

The claimant must, therefore, comply with one of these two conditions in order to establish entitlement. In many cases more than one person will satisfy them, and there are, therefore, rules in the Second Schedule to the Act determining which claimant has priority of title to the benefit. These rules are discussed in detail later, but it is perhaps useful to indicate at the outset that generally a person claiming it as 'responsible for a child' under section 3(1)(a) will have priority over a person claiming under section 3(1)(b); in other words, normally the person with whom the child is actually living will be entitled to benefit.[10]

These rules contrast sharply with the equivalent conditions for entitlement to family allowances.[11] As has been mentioned previously, they were paid for every family with two or more children, 'and for the benefit of the family as a whole'.[12] In the typical case eligibility was dependent on proof that the child was 'issue'[13] of the claimant and, therefore, a member of his family. Another person might apply in respect of a child whom he was maintaining, but that claim would always rank lower in priority to one

5 CBA 1975, s.3(1)(a).
6 This, of course, was because family allowances were not payable in respect of the first child of a family.
7 (1975) 31 Poverty 50.
8 SI 1976/965, reg 16. See *R(F) 1/81*.
9 SI 1976/965, reg 16(6): for the similar disqualifications for contributory benefits, see pp. 398–401, above.
10 CBA 1975, Sch 2, para 2: pp. 436–440, below, for discussion of the priority rules.
11 See Calvert *Social Security Law* (1st edn) pp. 259–270.
12 FAA 1965, s.1 (see p. 422, above).
13 Under FAA 1965, s.19, 'issue' meant issue of the first generation, and also see s.17 of that Act for other relevant rules.

made by the parent(s). It was difficult to defend these rules, as their effect was that the person primarily responsible in fact for keeping the child might not receive the allowance.[14] The provisions in the Child Benefit Act are in contrast designed to secure that benefit is paid to the person who prima facie most needs it.[15] No special privileges are conferred on a parent as such, though, of course, in normal circumstances it will be he who will receive it.

i 'Child living with him in that week'

a *General*

The Act does not define 'living with', but it would seem generally to mean living in the same place, under the same roof or in the same residence. The term was used in the family allowances legislation,[16] where it was construed by the Commissioner to mean no more than that the claimant and the child must be living together; it did not necessarily imply a requirement of financial support.[17] On the other hand in an earlier case it had been ruled that the relationship between a parent and a child might be so tenuous that the former could not be said to be 'living with' the latter, even though they both resided in the same premises.[18]

It seems that the Commissioner in construing the term in the Child Benefit legislation will adopt a similar, pragmatic approach. The issue arose in *R(F) 2/79*, where the children of divorced parents spent part of their school holidays with each parent. Both claimed child benefit, and an important question was whether the sons were 'living with' their father when they stayed with him.[19] V G H Hallett ruled that the phrase was not synonymous with 'residing together', nor did it necessarily require the exercise of de facto care and control, though where this did exist it would be an important factor in the argument that the child was living with the person concerned. The issue must be decided on all the relevant evidence. In the circumstances, where the facts were that the father looked after the children while they were with him, paid for their education and was generally responsible for them, they were to be regarded as 'living with' him.[20] In another case it has been emphasised that it is not enough for the child only to spend a small part of the week with his parent.[1]

b *Temporary absence*[2]

Entirely different problems occur when a child and the person responsible for him (usually his mother) are temporarily apart, perhaps because the former is away at school or is in hospital, or because for some reason he is staying with other relatives. An absence of 56 days or less during the 16 weeks preceding the claim is to be disregarded.[3] Thus, where a mother

14 See *Calvert*, n.11, above, at pp. 269–270.
15 Mrs B Castle, Secretary of State, 892 HC Official Report (5th series) col 337.
16 FAA 1965, s.3: it was also used in the National Insurance legislation for the purposes of dependants' allowances: p. 371, above.
17 *R(F) 1/74*. J S Watson, Comr, pointed out that there was a separate provision enabling a person providing for a child to claim benefit, as is the case under the 1975 Act.
18 *R(F) 1/71*. This decision has been mentioned with approval in *R(F) 2/81*, para 12.
19 It was agreed that the children were 'living with' their mother.
20 Where, as in this case, two parents are living with the child, entitlement is determined under the priority rules: see pp. 436–440, below.
1 *R(F) 2/81*.
2 See pp. 371–372, above, for equivalent rules for the contributory benefits.
3 CBA 1975, s.3(2).

boards her child out with a relative for up to eight weeks, she continues to be entitled to benefit as she is to be treated as having her child living with her for that time. Only then (or after cumulative periods totalling 56 days within 16 weeks) would she lose her entitlement on the basis of section 3(1)(a), so that the relative with whom the child is physically living would, if he made a claim, become entitled to benefit in priority to the mother.[4]

In some cases, a longer absence is disregarded in determining whether a person is to be treated as having a child living with him in the particular week. A separation which is attributable solely to the child's 'receiving full-time education by attendance at a recognised educational establishment' is wholly disregarded.[5] If, however, the child is away from the claimant's home for reasons additional to attendance at a school, the latter will not be entitled on a 'living with' basis.[6] Secondly, absence attributable to the child's 'undergoing medical or other treatment as an in-patient in a hospital or similar institution', or being in residential accommodation under the National Health Service Act 1977 (or the National Health Service (Scotland) Act 1978) is to be disregarded for up to 84 consecutive days.[7] In these circumstances an unlimited period of absence (beyond the 84 days) may be ignored if 'the person claiming to be responsible for the child regularly incurs expenditure in respect of the child'.[8] Regulations may be made prescribing the circumstances in which this condition is satisfied[9] but at the moment of writing, none has been issued.

The purpose of these provisions is clearly to enable a person (generally, though not necessarily, a parent) to receive benefit for a child *normally* living with him. This is reasonable as a parent will often spend money on clothes and other articles for a child, even when the latter is away at school or in hospital. In the second situation there may also be the expense of paying frequent hospital visits. But where the child is in hospital for longer than 84 days, it is justifiable to require the claimant to show that he is regularly incurring expenditure.

c *The right to benefit of a voluntary organisation*

A voluntary organisation may be regarded as a person with whom the child is living for any week he is residing in premises managed by that body or is boarded out by it.[10] Very similar provisions to those described in the previous section cover the temporary absence of the child from the voluntary organisation, so that the latter may continue to be entitled to receive benefit, even though the child is not in fact living in its premises.[11] The eligibility of an organisation for benefit here seems to be unique in the social security system;[12] there is no clear reason why it was decided to depart from the general rule that only natural persons are entitled. It

4 Before this period, the relative might claim under s.3(1)(a), but the parent would have the prior entitlement: Sch 2, para 4: p. 438, below.
5 CBA 1975, s.3(3)(a): see p. 430, above, for a discussion of 'full time education at a recognised educational establishment'.
6 See *Hill v Minister of Pensions and National Insurance* [1955] 2 All ER 890, [1955] 1 WLR 899, DC, where a mother was refused family allowances in respect of children taken into care under the Children Act 1948, s.1 and put by the authority into a residential school.
7 CBA 1975, ss.3(3)(b)–(c), and 3(4); SI 1975/965, reg 4.
8 CBA 1975, s.3(4).
9 Ibid, s.3(5).
10 SI 1976/965, reg 17(1).
11 Ibid, reg 17(2).
12 Cp the refusal by the Commissioner to allow Dr Barnardo's to claim attendance allowance: *R(A) 3/75*, p. 176, above.

should be noted, however, that an organisation is not entitled to child benefit on the alternative basis that it is contributing to the cost of providing for him.

ii 'Contributing to the cost of providing for the child'

The second way in which a person may be treated as 'responsible for a child' is when

> he is contributing to the cost of providing for the child at a weekly rate which is not less than the weekly rate of child benefit payable in respect of the child for that week.[13]

An application on this alternative basis will not succeed, because of the priority rules, if a claim has also been made by a person who has the child living with him. The main purpose, therefore, of this second head of eligibility is to cover the case where the parent of a child arranges for it to be boarded with a relative or friend, and it is agreed that the parent should receive the benefit to cover the costs of the child's maintenance to which he is contributing.[14] If, however, the relative or friend himself claims in this situation, then he, and not the parent, would be entitled to the benefit.

Neither the Child Benefit Act nor the Regulations made under it define 'providing for' the child. This might seem odd because the family allowances legislation had defined this phrase.[15] It is, however, also used in the Social Security Act 1975 for the purposes of entitlement to an increase of benefit for a dependent child,[16] and there are a number of Commissioners' decisions interpreting it in this context. In some respects it seems that this legislation was the model for the concepts used in the Child Benefit Act and, therefore, the discussion in chapter 10 would appear to be relevant here.[17]

A problem which occurred under the family allowances legislation, and which may be of importance under the Child Benefit Act, is how periodic, but not weekly, payments made by the claimant to the person actually maintaining the child are to be treated for the purpose of determining the former's entitlement. The point is important because the claimant must contribute at a weekly rate not less than the weekly rate of benefit payable in respect of the child. The principles of 'spreading', as it is known, were set out in *R(F) 8/61*.[18] The period the payments relate to is a question of fact, the determination of which should take into account the payer's intentions. Regular periodic payments may be intended to cover a future period, and then they will be averaged over the number of weeks in this period. But if he has fallen behind with his payments, and then makes a large payment, this may be attributed to arrears.

The only regulations made under the Child Benefit Act in this context provide that where two or more persons make weekly contributions, which individually do not, but together do, equal the amount of the benefit, the aggregate amount is to be treated as paid by one of them or, if they cannot agree on this, by that person nominated by the Secretary of State.[19] But after the week in which benefit is first paid under this arrangement, the

13 CBA 1975, s.3(1)(b).
14 Standing Committee A Debates, cols 44–45.
15 FAA 1965, s.18.
16 SSA 1975, s.43(1)(b).
17 Pp. 373–376, above.
18 See also *R(F) 1/73*.
19 SI 1976/965, reg 2(1), (2).

recipient must contribute the full amount to retain his entitlement. It is further provided that where two spouses are residing together, a contribution made by one of them shall by their agreement, or (in default of that) at the discretion of the Secretary of State, be treated as contributed by the other.[20] It is not entirely clear what is the purpose of this provision, which applies whether the spouses concerned are parents of the child or not. Their ability to 'transfer' benefit to the non-contributing spouse may give a sensible measure of flexibility in some cases. But it is less easy to see the justification for the power of the Secretary of State to treat the non-contributing spouse as the contributor.[1] It appears to enable him in this situation to vary the provision which gives priority, as between a husband and a wife residing together, to the latter.[2] Fortunately, the situation will rarely arise, as the claim of either spouse will have lower priority than a claim by the person with whom the child is living.

iii Priority between persons entitled

It has already been mentioned that one of the principal changes effected by the scheme is the priority given to a claimant with whom the child is living, over other claimants, who might include the child's parents.[3] The Child Benefit Act sets out the relevant rules in Schedule 2. The exposition in this section follows the order of priority laid down there – with some examples to make it clearer. Two important preliminary points should be made. First, entitlement to child benefit is dependent on the making of a claim in the prescribed manner,[4] so if a person with a prior right under these rules has not in fact made a valid claim, they do not come into operation. Secondly, the right conferred by any of the priority rules (except, of course, the first one) only vests if nobody is entitled under one of the previous provisions.

a *Person with prior award*

A person with an existing award of child benefit for a certain week is entitled to priority over anyone else who claims benefit in respect of the same child for that period. But this rule does not apply where the claim is made *for* a week later than the third week after that *in* which it is made.[5] The effect of these provisions is that, whatever the circumstances, a person with an existing award is entitled to priority over all other claimants for up to four weeks.[6] Thus,

> A is paying contributions to the cost of providing for the child and has been awarded benefit in respect of him. B, with whom the child is living,

20 Ibid, reg 2(3).
1 Under the family allowances legislation (FAA 1965, Sch, para 3) the Secretary of State had power to determine whether a child was to be included in his father's or his mother's family, in the absence of agreement between them. But this conflict could only arise if the child was provided for by *both* parents, was living with *both* of them, or was living with one and provided for by the other (see Calvert *Social Security Law* (1st edn) p. 267). The power under the 1975 Act seems wider in that the Secretary of State is able to award benefit in effect to a spouse who does not live with the child or even provide for him.
2 CBA 1975, Sch 2, para 3 (see p. 437, below).
3 See p. 432, above.
4 CBA 1975, s.6(1): p. 444, below (claims and payments).
5 Ibid, Sch 2, para 1. Claims may be made 56 days before the claimant is entitled to benefit: SI 1976/964, reg 4.
6 If it is subsequently decided that the person with the existing award was not entitled to benefit and he has been required to repay it, then the second claimant may be awarded it for that week: SI 1976/964, reg 9, modifying CBA 1975, s.6(3).

claims benefit. A is entitled under the prior award rule for at least the week in which B claims, and may be entitled for the next three weeks.

This rule allows payments to continue, while the authorities investigate the facts to determine whether the new claimant should be awarded benefit.

b *Person having the child living with him*

Any person entitled to benefit by virtue of having the child living with him is entitled to priority over anyone entitled on the alternative basis that he is contributing to the cost of maintenance.[7] This important departure from the rules applicable under the family allowances system represents one of the main advantages of the child benefit scheme. The reason for the change is that generally it is the person with whom the child is living who is primarily responsible for its care, and he should be entitled to priority.

c *Husband and wife*

Subject to the application of the previous rules, if a husband and wife, who are residing together, both claim child benefit, the wife is entitled in priority to her husband.[8] Thus,

> where A and Mrs A live with their children (and nobody has a prior award under the first rule), Mrs A is entitled to the benefit; on the other hand, where they live together, but the child lives with B, it is B who has the prior entitlement and Mrs A will only secure payment if B does not claim or waives his priority.

Family allowances had 'belonged to' the wife, where she and her husband were living together.[9] This was regarded as important, and the government was clear that she should also be entitled to the new benefit. An amendment was moved during the Committee stage of the Bill to provide that where the spouses agree, both should be equally entitled.[10] It was pointed out that there was little evidence that payment of allowances to the mother had alleviated family poverty and that in a number of other countries, e.g. France, the Netherlands, Italy, West Germany and Ireland, they are paid to the father. The government resisted the amendment, contending that in principle it was right for the mother to receive the benefit as she was primarily responsible for feeding and clothing the children. This conclusion had also been reached by the Select Committee of the House of Commons which had investigated the proposals for a tax-credit scheme.[11] There seems little doubt that it is right for the mother to have priority: the benefit may well be her only source of income. In this context it may be pointed out that a wife living with her husband cannot enforce a maintenance order against her husband, at least in the magistrates' courts.[12]

However, if the husband does claim he may be awarded the benefit, provided he submits a written statement signed by his wife that she does not wish to claim it.[13] As with family allowances, the husband may receive

7 CBA 1975, Sch 2, para 2.
8 Ibid, para 3.
9 FAA 1965, s.4.
10 Sir G Young, Standing Committee A Debates, cols 57 ff.
11 P. 424, above.
12 Cretney *Principles of Family Law* (3rd edn) p. 357.
13 SI 1976/964, reg 6(2).

payment of the benefit on behalf of his wife;[14] this will often be appropriate where, for example, the wife is too ill or handicapped to visit the post office to collect the weekly benefit.[15]

These provisions only apply when the husband and wife are residing together. If they are residing apart, the spouse with whom the child is living has priority under the rule described above.[16] Under the General Regulations, the spouses are treated as residing together for any period of absence from each other until either there is a formal separation or they have been apart for 91 consecutive days, and even after those dates they are to be regarded as residing together where the absence is not likely to be permanent.[17] (And they are to be regarded as residing together if one, or both, of them is receiving treatment in hospital, whether this is temporary or not.)[18] The consequence of these provisions may be illustrated by the following example:

> Mrs A leaves her husband and her child, in respect of whom she is in receipt of benefit. Unless there has been a formal separation, the spouses are to be treated under the Regulations as residing together until they have been apart for at least 91 days and, therefore (subject to the other priority rules), Mrs A retains her prior entitlement to benefit. It does not seem that A can claim priority over his wife under the previous priority rule for 56 days. This is because under section 3(2) of the Act, Mrs A is still to be treated as living with her child, despite their absence from one another for 56 days. Until that period is over, A cannot claim to be entitled on the ground that he is living with the child, and his wife is not.[19]

This result seems difficult to defend, as for a considerable period Mrs A has 'abandoned' her child, and Mr A has been looking after it without any support. Under the family allowances legislation,[20] spouses were treated as living apart if one had deserted the other, so this result could not have occurred. It is submitted that the regulation concerning 'residing together' needs reconsideration in the light of this difficulty.

d *Parents*

The fourth priority rule is that, as between a parent and someone who is not a parent, the former is to have priority.[1] 'Parent' for this purpose includes natural parents, step-parents and adoptive parents.[2] The priority is, of course, subject to the previous rules: this can be illustrated by the following two examples.

> Miss A lives with her young child and B, not his father. Each is equally entitled as a person who has the child living with him. Miss A is awarded the benefit because she is a parent, and B is not.

14 Ibid, reg 13(2): see Mr B O'Malley, Minister of State, Standing Committee A Debates, col 71.
15 For the payment of child benefit, see p. 445, below.
16 P. 437, above.
17 SI 1978/540, reg 4, redrafting SI 1976/965, reg 11. Spouses can be treated as separated if they are living under the same roof, but not living as one household: *R(F) 3/81*.
18 SI 1976/965 ibid, reg 11(2), as redrafted.
19 It is possible that before then payment could be made to the husband on the wife's behalf under the power to divert payments conferred on the Secretary of State by SI 1976/964, reg 13(1): p. 445, below.
20 FAA 1965, s.17(1).
1 CBA 1975, Sch 1, para 4(1).
2 Ibid, s.24(3). The status of step-parent continues after the termination of the relevant marriage by death (*R(F) 1/79*) or by divorce (*R(S) 4/81*).

Miss A does not live with her young child; he lives with her brother, B, though Miss A sends B a weekly sum towards the cost of providing for her child. Miss A does not have priority as a parent because B has priority under the earlier rule, which accords entitlement to the person with whom the child is living.[3]

Where two unmarried parents are residing together, the mother enjoys priority;[4] this is comparable to the priority a wife has under the previous rule. The General Regulations provide that two unmarried parents are to be treated as residing together during a period of 'temporary absence',[5] but there is no specific rule (as there is for husband and wife) explaining the meaning of this phrase. The consequences of the Regulations may be illustrated by the following example, similar to that discussed on p. 438, above, concerning a married couple.

Miss A who has been residing with B and is in receipt of benefit in respect of their illegitimate child, leaves that child with B. Under section 3(2) she is to be treated as having the child living with her for 56 days of absence. During this period, she will continue to have priority over B, provided it is held that she is still residing with B, notwithstanding her departure. But if it is decided that the absence is permanent, the rule conferring priority on her as the mother does not apply. It seems in that event that for the period of 56 days priority is to be determined under the rule discussed below, covering priority in other cases, where no previous rule applies. Under this *either* Miss A and B elect which of them is to be entitled *or* priority is decided by the Secretary of State. After 56 days B enjoys priority because he has the child living with him, and Miss A does not.

e *Other cases*

Finally, if none of the other priority rules determines entitlement, benefit is awarded to the person elected jointly by those eligible to claim it, or in default of election, the person chosen by the Secretary of State.[6] Under the General Regulations an election must be made in writing on the appropriate form; it is not permanently binding, and may subsequently be changed.[7] An example of the possible application of this provision was given in the case discussed in the previous paragraph, but a more typical case might be the following:

A and Miss B (a brother and sister living together) look after the young child of Mrs C (their deceased sister). Neither has priority under any of the earlier rules, so they may elect which of them is to receive child benefit. If it subsequently becomes more appropriate for the other to receive it (Miss B who has been in receipt of it may become infirm), another election may be made and entitlement varied.

In *R(F) 2/79*, where the two claimants were parents of the child, but were not married and were not residing together, the Commissioner ruled (as already mentioned)[8] that the child was 'living with' them both. In this

3 Under the family allowances rules (FAA 1965, Sch, para 2) Miss A would have been entitled in this example, as the child would have been her 'issue', and the issue link took priority over the maintenance link: see Calvert *Social Security Law* (1st edn) p. 268.
4 CBA 1975, Sch 2, para 4(2).
5 SI 1976/965, reg 11(3) as redrafted by SI 1978/540, reg 4.
6 CBA 1975, Sch 2, para 5.
7 SI 1976/965, reg 13.
8 P. 433, above.

circumstance, none of the previous priority rules applied and, as they were unwilling to make a joint election, the issue was referred to the Secretary of State. He decided the child's mother was entitled for the relevant weeks, and this was binding on the Commissioner.[9]

f *Waiver of prior entitlement*

A person with a prior entitlement under these provisions may waive it.[10] The procedure for this step is set out in the General Regulations.[11]

– Thus, when a claim is made by A, a person (B) with prior entitlement, who is in receipt of the benefit,[12] may give the Secretary of State notice in writing at a Department office that he does not wish to have priority. In that case the provisions are ousted, and the claimant A is awarded the benefit (provided, of course, that he is otherwise entitled to it).

But the person who has waived his prior entitlement may subsequently make a further claim, and then the priority provisions in the Schedule take effect to give him title to the benefit.[13]

C Residence qualifications

The Child Benefit Act 1975, as modified by regulations made under it,[14] sets out a number of detailed provisions concerning residence qualifications. They concern both the residence, or more accurately, the presence in Great Britain of the child, in respect of whom benefit is claimed and the presence there of the claimant.[15] The law is extremely complex, largely because the government attempted to formulate rules which would combine the presence requirements for family allowances with the more generous conditions for tax allowances. Modifications applying to certain classes of persons were introduced by regulations,[16] but they do not cover immigrants to Britain who are supporting children overseas.[17] (However, the Finance Act 1977 provides that tax allowances will continue to be available for parents unable to claim benefit because their children do not satisfy the residence conditions.)[18]

This section first discusses the general requirements concerning the presence of the child, secondly, those concerning the presence of the claimant and thirdly, the special relaxing provisions, applicable to certain categories of persons, in the Residence and Persons Abroad Regulations 1976.

9 SI 1976/962, reg 8.
10 CBA 1975, Sch 2, para 6.
11 SI 1976/965, reg 14.
12 The problem only arises when the person with the prior entitlement is actually in receipt of the benefit, since under s.6(1) of the Act, no person is entitled to the benefit unless he has claimed it.
13 SI 1976/965, reg 14(2).
14 SI 1976/963.
15 The usual requirements in social security law of 'residence' and/or 'ordinary residence' for which, see pp. 391–393, above, are not exacted in this area.
16 SI 1976/963, Part II.
17 See the criticism of the law in *Divide and Deprive*, a report by the Joint Council for the Welfare of Immigrants and the Child Poverty Action Group.
18 S.25. The provision is kept in force by the Finance Act 1979, s.1(4).

i Requirements with regard to the presence in Great Britain of the child
Section 13(2) provides that:

> Subject to any regulations . . . no child benefit shall be payable in respect of a child for any week unless —
> (a) he is in Great Britain in that week; *and*
> (b) either he or at least one of his parents has been in Great Britain for more than one hundred and eighty-two days in the fifty-two weeks preceding that week.

Both these requirements have been modified by regulations made under section 13(1).

(a) The absence of a child from Great Britain for a particular week will not be material if three conditions are satisfied.[19]

(1) A person must be entitled to benefit for the week immediately before the first week of the child's absence from GB.
(2) The child's absence is both initially and throughout intended to be temporary.[20]
(3) The child must not be absent from GB for more than 26 weeks, *or* more than 156 weeks if the absence is solely attributable to receiving full-time education, *or* for more than such extended period as the Secretary of State allows if the absence is for the purpose of treatment for an illness, etc. which began before the period of absence.

(b) The purpose of the general requirement that either the child or one of his parents must have been present for more than half the year preceding the week for which benefit is claimed is to ensure that it is payable only for those children who have more than a transitory connection with Great Britain. This requirement is modified in certain ways by the Residence and Persons Abroad Regulations,[1] the principal relaxation being that benefit may be payable if the child is in Britain and (though not residing with his parent(s)) is living with another person with whom he is likely to continue to live permanently, and that person satisfies the requirements exacted by section 13(3)(b) of the Act, i.e. has been in Britain for more than 182 days in the year preceding the relevant week. The result is that benefit is payable for a child who has recently been left in Britain with a person who has been resident there for at least half the year preceding the week for which he claims.

ii Requirements with regard to the presence in Great Britain of the person claiming benefit
As under the family allowances legislation,[2] there is a general requirement that the claimant is present in Britain, and has been present there for some time. Subject to regulations, the claimant must be in Great Britain for the week for which he claims benefit, and must have been there for more than 182 days in the 52 preceding weeks.[3] Both these requirements have been modified to cover the cases where the claimant is, or has been, temporarily absent from the country, but still has sufficient connection with it to justify entitlement to benefit.

19 SI 1976/963, reg 2(2).
20 For the meaning of 'temporary absence', see p. 371, above.
1 SI 1976/963, reg 3.
2 FAA 1965, s.20.
3 CBA 1975, s.13(3).

(a) The absence of the claimant from Britain for the relevant week is not material if three conditions are satisfied.[4]

(1) That person must have been entitled to benefit for the week immediately before the first week of his absence from GB.
(2) The claimant's absence is both initially and throughout intended to be temporary.[5]
(3) The absence must not be longer than 26 weeks.

A person's absence for a week is also immaterial with regard to a child born to a mother within 26 weeks of her departure for a temporary absence – so that the claimant (not necessarily the mother) may be entitled to benefit for the 26 weeks following the *mother's* departure from Britain.[6] This enables a claimant to be entitled in respect of a child born abroad, perhaps because its mother wished to join her husband for the birth, even though he has been outside Great Britain for more than 26 weeks, so that he could not take advantage of the modifications in the Regulations.

(b) The general requirement that the claimant must have been present for the six months preceding the week for which benefit is claimed has been modified substantially.[7] In particular, the general condition is not to apply if the person is in fact in Great Britain and is responsible for a child who satisfies the presence requirements of section 13(2). This appreciably reduces the significance of the six months' presence requirement.

iii Special relaxing provisions applicable to certain categories of persons

The general requirements, together with these modifications in the Regulations, may be further relaxed with regard to certain categories of persons by the rules in Part II of the Residence and Persons Abroad Regulations. These additional provisions were a response to the opposition anxiety that the presence requirements for child benefit appeared from the draft Bill to be more onerous than those applicable to the child tax allowances.[8]

– Part II applies to civil servants (other than those recruited outside the United Kingdom for service abroad), serving members of the forces,[9] and people temporarily absent from Britain, by reason only of employment abroad, for an income tax year in which at least half the earnings are liable to United Kingdom income tax.[10] It also applies to spouses of such people.[11]

Any week in which a person to whom Part II applies is away from Britain in connection with his employment is to be treated for the purposes of the presence requirements as one in which he is present there; moreover, a child's absence is to be disregarded entirely if he is living with a person to whom Part II applies, and that person is either a parent or someone who before the week in question was entitled to benefit in respect of him.[12] Days of separation of a child and such a person, which are attributable to the latter being abroad, are to be wholly disregarded under the 1975 Act for

4 SI 1976/963, reg 4(2).
5 P. 371, above.
6 SI 1976/963, reg 4(3).
7 Ibid, reg 5, as amended by SI 1976/1758, reg 4(2).
8 For the residence requirements for tax see Pinson *Revenue Law* (14th edn) paras, 7.17–7.24; see now Finance Act 1977, s.25.
9 Defined by SI 1975/492, reg 1(2).
10 SI 1976/963, reg 6(1)(a)–(c).
11 Ibid, reg 6(1)(d).
12 Ibid, reg 7(1), (2).

the purposes of determining whether he has the child living with him. Thus, a civil servant serving in a foreign embassy may be entitled to child benefit in respect of a child for whom he is responsible, even if the child spends the whole year in Britain, both school-terms and holidays. It seems that he would also be entitled if the child is being educated in and spends his holidays in another country, not the one in which the civil servant is working.[13]

D One-parent benefit

From the scheme's inception there has been more generous treatment of single parent families. Even before the full introduction of child benefit in 1977, an interim benefit was paid in the preceding year for the children of an unmarried or separated parent, not living with another person as his (or her) spouse.[14] When the benefit became payable to all persons responsible for a child, a single parent received an extra 50p a week for his only, or eldest, child, and this differential became £1 in the following year, 1978.[15] The reason for this preferential treatment is almost certainly to be found in the conclusion of the Finer Committee on One-Parent Families that this group, particularly lone mothers with young children, is especially vulnerable and needs more generous social security protection.[16] No government has felt able to implement the Committee's principal recommendation for a new guaranteed maintenance allowance, but the more generous child benefit, together with the modification of the normal earnings disregard for single parents claiming supplementary benefit, have afforded some extra assistance.[17]

Recently the differential has been further widened to £3.00 in 1980 and £3.30 in 1981. In 1982–83 it is £3.65. Further in an attempt to increase the take-up of the benefit, the government in 1980 decided to change its name from the unhelpful 'child benefit increase' to the more graphic 'one-parent benefit'. In effect there is, therefore, a hybrid benefit, which shares the rules for entitlement to the principal benefit described in this chapter and yet also has further legal requirements of its own. It is obviously an important question whether this solution is the most satisfactory method for handling the special needs of one-parent families, and it can also be asked whether the differential is not now too great, even in view of the government's limited resources.[18]

There has been one interesting legal development in the special conditions for entitlement to the increase, now one-parent benefit. Initially the claimant had to be a *parent* of the child in question,[19] but this condition has now been removed: any person may qualify, provided he is not residing

13 Ibid, reg 7(3). The Secretary of State, however, may refuse in his discretion to apply this disregard of days of absence in any case.
14 CBA 1975, s.16: see p. 424, above.
15 See SI 1976/1267, reg 2 and SI 1977/1328, reg 2.
16 The Finer Committee's principal recommendations are briefly discussed in ch 12, pp. 513–514, below.
17 See p. 485, below, for the supplementary benefits disregard, and also p. 531, below, for the different definitions of 'full-time work' for FIS.
18 See (1980) 45 Poverty 15. There is some evidence that now one-parent families are relatively not so deprived as they used to be: see SBC Annual Report 1979 (Cmnd 8033), para 8.22, though of course the availability of one-parent benefit may have brought this about.
19 SI 1976/1267, reg 2(2)(a).

with a parent of the child.[20] This amendment to the regulations followed a decision of the Chief Commissioner, R J A Temple, holding that a step-father was eligible for the increase after the child's mother's death.[1] The other conditions are that the claimant must be living with the child (i.e. he cannot claim under section 3(1)(b) of the Act), must either be unmarried or not residing with his spouse, and must not be living with anyone else as his spouse.[2] The benefit is only paid for an only, or eldest, child; ordinary child benefit is paid for the others in the family. Moreover, one-parent benefit is not paid if the claimant is in receipt of a variety of allowances set out in the regulations, e.g. guardian's or child's special allowance, or a dependant's increase for a child paid with a widow's benefit or retirement pension.[3] In these cases the claimant is in a less vulnerable position.

Part 3 Claims and payments

A Claims

It is provided by section 6(1) that no person is entitled to child benefit unless he makes a claim in the prescribed manner. Thus, as with almost all other benefits, the making of a claim is a necessary condition for entitlement.[4] The particular significance of this point with regard to the priority rules has already been mentioned:[5] these provisions will only operate to defeat a claim if a person with prior entitlement has in fact claimed benefit.

There are one or two special rules concerning the making of claims to child benefit which should be mentioned here.[6] First, a husband who resides with his wife and applies for benefit, may be required to provide a statement by her that she does not wish to make a claim.[7] This ensures that the wife's prior entitlement is protected. There is, however, no similar requirement when the father of a child living with its mother (though not a married couple) applies for benefit. Secondly, a claim may be made in advance by a person who does not at that time satisfy the requirements for entitlement, but expects to do so within 56 days.[8] Benefit may then be awarded, subject to the condition that the claimant does satisfy them when the award takes effect. It may be reviewed if the requirements are not met.[9] Finally, a claim may be made for up to one year after the week in respect of which it is made – an exceptionally generous time-limit.[10]

20 SI 1980/110, reg 2, amending SI 1976/1267, reg 2(2).
1 *R(F) 1/79*.
2 SI 1976/1267, reg 2(2): for the meaning of 'living with' and 'residing with', see p. 433 and p. 438, above.
3 Ibid, reg 2(4)–(5).
4 For the cases when a claim is not required, see p. 552, below.
5 P. 436, above.
6 For the general requirements of a valid claim, see pp. 525–557, below.
7 SI 1976/964, reg 3(2).
8 Ibid, reg 4(1).
9 Ibid, reg 4(2).
10 CBA 1975, s.6(2): for time limits generally, see pp. 557–564, below.

B Payments

The procedure for making payments used closely to follow that established for family allowances. The Department sent the claimant notice that benefit could be collected weekly at a post office by means of an order book obtainable there. During the Committee debates some opposition members argued that there should be power to pay benefit quarterly or monthly in arrears, or on request to provide lump sum payments periodically instead of regular weekly payments,[11] but these suggestions were resisted on the ground that most people were used to, and liked, the latter. Now the Conservative government has made major changes in the payment rules as one part of its attempt to reduce the administrative costs of social security benefits.[12]

Regulations introduced at the end of 1981 provide that from March 1982 child benefit is ordinarily to be paid monthly in arrears.[13] But recipients of benefit before that time may elect to continue with weekly payments; and if they choose to try monthly payments, they may revert to weekly receipt of benefit within six months. Beneficiaries may move to weekly payment at any time if they become lone parents, or receive supplementary benefit or family income supplement. And the regulations give the Secretary of State discretion to pay benefit weekly if the new arrangement gives rise to hardship.[14] These new rules were widely criticised, and the Social Security Advisory Committee unsuccessfully suggested that all families with two or more children should have the option to receive weekly benefit.[15] Although the change might cause initial difficulties for some households, the government could point to some evidence that the majority of mothers would be able to manage with less frequent payments; moreover, it is hard to see why Britain should differ from other West European countries where monthly payment is usual.[16] It is interesting to note also that in New Zealand up to a year's benefit may be paid in advance as a lump sum on the occasion of the birth of a first child or when any child starts secondary education, and parents may apply to have benefits capitalised to enable them to purchase or improve a house.[17]

A provision of some potential importance enables payment to be made to a third party on behalf of the person entitled to it, where this is necessary to protect the child's interests.[18] This in effect permits the DHSS to vary the priority rules by diverting the payment to someone other than the person who is strictly entitled under them.[19]

11 Standing Committee A Debates, cols 181–192.
12 See the Reply to the First Report from the Social Services Committee on Arrangements for Paying Social Security Benefits (1980, Cmnd 8106). For a general discussion, see ch 14, pp. 570–574.
13 SI 1981/1772, amending SI 1976/964.
14 Ibid, regs 6–6E.
15 Cmnd 8453, para 5.
16 N.12, above, at paras 19–20, and Annex II (Rayner review team report), para 3.7.
17 New Zealand Social Security Act 1964, s.36, and see *Kaim-Caudle* pp. 251–252.
18 SI 1976/964, reg 13(1)(a).
19 P. 438, n.19, above.

Chapter 12

Supplementary benefits

Part 1 Introduction

A General

i The role of supplementary benefits

Most social security systems provide some form of public assistance for people in need who are not for one reason or another able to maintain themselves out of other resources. In the British system supplementary benefits now provide this 'safety-net'. With some exceptions, in principle anyone in need is entitled to have it met by an award of supplementary benefit. (The main proviso, fully discussed in Part 2 of this chapter,[1] is that normally benefit is not payable to someone with low earnings; he may instead be eligible for family income supplement.[2]) This general principle has been reflected in the law since the National Assistance Act 1948, the last of the measures which implemented the Beveridge proposals. National assistance was replaced by the present system of supplementary benefits in 1966, though the changes made then were relatively minor.[3] Much more significant reforms were made in 1980 after a review of the scheme, which had been initiated by the Supplementary Benefits Commission (SBC),[4] but was undertaken by a team of DHSS officials.[5] However, the changes were more concerned with the legal structure of the scheme than its substance, and it remains true, therefore, that the place of public assistance in the context of the whole social security system has not been the subject of any searching inquiry since the war.[6]

Certainly, supplementary benefit has always played a more significant role than that envisaged for national assistance by Beveridge. His Report argued that this would decline in importance. It added:

> Assistance will be available to meet all needs which are not covered by insurance. It must meet those needs adequately up to subsistence level, but it must be felt to

1 Pp. 457–458, below.
2 Ch 13, below.
3 Pp. 452–453, below, for a short discussion of the principal changes made by the Ministry of Social Security Act 1966, later renamed the Supplementary Benefit Act 1966, and now consolidated with other legislation in the Supplementary Benefits Act 1976.
4 See pp. 543–544, below, for a short discussion of the Commission. For the initiation of the review, see Annual Report of the SBC 1975 (Cmnd 6615), ch 2, and Annual Report 1976 (Cmnd 6910), ch 1. Also see Donnison *The Politics of Poverty* (1982) pp. 53–60.
5 *Social Assistance* (DHSS, July 1978). See p. 453, below.
6 But see the discussion in *Response of the Supplementary Benefits Commission to Social Assistance* (1979), SBA Paper No 9, esp. chs 2–3.

be something less desirable than insurance benefit; otherwise the insured persons get nothing for their contributions.[7]

However, from the beginning of the post-Beveridge regime, the level of flat-rate insurance benefits has never amounted to more than the standard weekly rate of assistance, and indeed has been less generous than the assistance receivable by a claimant also awarded the further rent allowance.[8] The predictable result has been that those unable to supplement contributory benefits, e.g. unemployment benefit or retirement pensions, with other income have come to rely on public assistance.[9] In practice, therefore, it is the means-tested benefit, rather than (as Beveridge had hoped) the contributory benefits, which now provides the minimum level of income for the poorest section of the community.

This is shown by the number of people in receipt of supplementary benefit. In 1948 there were 1 million recipients; at the end of 1979 benefit was paid to nearly 3 million people,[10] and since then the number has continued to rise, so that in 1982 it is likely it will be paid to 4 million people. Over half the number are over retirement age, the overwhelming majority of whom (95 per cent) are also in receipt of a retirement pension.[11] The next largest group is the unemployed, whose dependence on this benefit has risen dramatically in the last few years;[12] it is followed by single-parent families.[13] Governments have extended non-means tested provisions for certain groups, particularly the disabled,[14] which may have diminished their reliance on assistance. On the other hand, there has been no move to implement the Finer Committee's proposals to confer a benefit as of right on single-parent families,[15] and the number of unemployed claimants has been rising.

The role of supplementary benefits has now to be seen in the context of the recent changes to the level of contributory benefits and other reforms, such as the abolition of the earnings-related supplement.[16] The government has itself recognised that the rise in unemployment, together with the 5 per cent cut in the value of short-term benefits[17] and abolition of the supplement, will mean that more unemployed people will rely on means-tested assistance.[18] The Supplementary Benefits Commission found this growing dependence so alarming that it suggested the introduction of a non-contributory unemployment benefit to reduce the administrative costs and difficulties involved in processing claims to supplementary benefit.[19] At the same time the Commission also expressed concern at the increasing number of lone parents receiving benefit.[20] This group of claimants, and families generally, would be less reliant on public assistance if child benefits were more generous. The higher child benefit paid to one-parent

7 Para 369.
8 Atkinson *Poverty in Britain and the Reform of Social Security* (1969) p. 24; Fiegehen, Lansley and Smith *Poverty and Progress in Britain 1953–1973* (1977) p. 134.
9 *George*, p. 210; *Response of SBC to Social Assistance*, n.6, above, at ch 3.
10 SBC Annual Report 1979, (Cmnd 8033), paras 8.1–8.3.
11 Ibid, para 8.12.
12 Ibid, paras 8.13–8.16.
13 Ibid, paras 8.22–8.23.
14 See ch 4. Also see *Response of SBC to Social Assistance*, n.6, above, at paras 3.17–3.18.
15 P. 513, below.
16 P. 77, above.
17 P. 413, above.
18 3rd Report of Social Services Committee 1979–80, HC 702–II, p. 5, R Prentice, Min. for Social Security.
19 *Response of SBC to Social Assistance*, n.6, above, at para 3.13.
20 Ibid, paras 2.3 and 3.14–3.16.

families may to some extent have reduced their problems,[1] but it is arguable that further steps should be taken, e.g. the introduction of a non-contributory allowance equivalent to the widowed mother's allowance.[2] All these changes would, of course, require increased public expenditure, and for this reason are unlikely to be made in the foreseeable future. But the Commission was right to conclude that supplementary benefit was not performing its intended role as a small safety-net, and further that worthwhile reform is difficult to achieve without consideration of other benefits.[3]

ii Benefits and poverty

In view of the benefit's significance, there has been relatively little official discussion concerning the principles on which the amount of weekly payments is assessed. To some extent this silence has now been broken in the recent *Social Assistance* review.[4] It seems that in 1948 the assistance rates were fixed at a level just above the subsistence standard set by Beveridge for single adults and married couples, but a little below it for a family with children.[5] This standard itself was lower than that arrived at by Rowntree in his studies shortly before the Second World War.[6] Both calculations had proceeded on the assumption that it was possible to measure 'poverty' by reference to absolute standards: a certain amount of money is needed for food, housing and clothing, and then a margin may be added for other expenditure and to allow for inefficiency.[7] There is no reason why weekly payments of public assistance could not be calculated in this way; it is very likely that initially such assessments played some part in the determination of the weekly benefit rates, and it will be seen that now regulations itemise the needs these rates are designed to cover.[8] But on this 'absolute standards' approach, it would be plausible to expect poverty to disappear over the years with continuing economic growth, and that correspondingly the numbers of people relying on assistance would decline.[9] In fact, as has just been mentioned, the opposite has occurred.

It is now more common to measure poverty, not by the absolute approach of a minimum standard of living, but as relative to the general or average quality of life in the country.[10] In his major study, Townsend defined the 'poverty line' as the point at which a person's or family's withdrawal from participation in social activities increases disproportionately in relation to declining resources.[11] The Commission supported this subjective approach.[12] Under it those with an income below, say, 40 per cent of the average industrial wage may be characterised as poor, even though they may have adequate resources to feed and house themselves,

1 Pp. 443–444, above.
2 *Dear SSAC. . .*, CPAG Pamphlet (1980), ch 2.
3 *Response of SBC to Social Assistance*, n.6, above, at paras 3.19–3.27. Also see Donnison *The Politics of Poverty* (1982) pp. 148–151.
4 Para 5.9.
5 *Fiegehen et al*, n.8, above, at p. 13; *Townsend* pp. 242–243.
6 Pp. 21–22, above.
7 It is this further margin which identified people living in what Rowntree described as 'secondary poverty': 'primary poverty' refers to the situation where the people, however carefully they marshal their resources, cannot afford the necessities of life. See *Harris* pp. 393–394.
8 P. 466, below. See *Social Assistance* ch 5.
9 Fiegehen pp. 13–14, Lansley and Smith *Poverty and Progress in Britain 1953–1973* (1977).
10 Ibid, pp. 14–15. See also pp. 21–22, above.
11 *Townsend* pp. 57, 248–262.
12 SBC Annual Report 1978 (Cmnd 7725), paras 1.4 and 3.13. Also see *Donnison*, n.3, above, at pp. 7–8.

and so would not fall beneath the poverty line on the more traditional 'subsistence' approach. The difficulty with the concept of 'relative poverty' is arguably that it confuses poverty with inequality.[13] Whatever the merits of this contention, governments since 1959 have generally acknowledged that those on assistance should have 'a share in increasing national prosperity', thereby abandoning rigid adherence to the subsistence approach.[14] Thus, the scale rates have risen more than the increases in the Retail Prices Index, and until recently have improved relative to the average net earnings of manual workers.[15]

Supplementary benefit rates may be said, therefore, to reflect an uncertain compromise between the old absolute and the relative concepts of poverty.[16] The standards of eligibility for benefit are also now sometimes used to measure the extent of poverty in British society.[17] It is obviously outside the scope of this book to pursue these questions in detail, but some reservations to this test should be stated. First, as supplementary benefit rates are increased, so more people are defined as having a standard of living below the official 'poverty line'. This odd consequence – the more the government attempts to help the poor, the more 'poor' there are – is perhaps inevitable if this relative (and perhaps also tautologous) concept of poverty is adopted. Secondly, the number of recipients of benefit is an unreliable guide to the extent of poverty insofar as otherwise eligible people are disqualified from receiving assistance by the legislation. Persons in full-time work, however low their earnings, are not entitled to benefit, though if living in a family with at least one child, they may be entitled to FIS.[18] Claimants may also be disqualified because of their participation in a trade dispute, or because they are not genuinely looking for work.[19] Finally, an important group, living below the official poverty line but not receiving benefit, are those who for one reason or another do not claim it. The Commission estimated in 1978 that only three-quarters of eligible pensioners, and a slightly higher proportion of persons under pensionable age, claim the benefit to which they were entitled.[20] This meant that a large number of poor people, perhaps 900,000, did not receive any financial assistance. Moreover, an unknown number may not claim the additional single payments which may be made to supplement the weekly scale rate benefit.

B The history of public assistance

Public assistance in Britain has a long history stretching back to the sixteenth century. To some extent the poor law provisions, and the modern reaction to them, have influenced the content of the supplementary benefits scheme.

13 Robson *Welfare State and Welfare Society* (1976) pp. 142–3. But see *Townsend* p. 57.
14 White Paper, Improvements in National Assistance (1959, Cmnd 782), para 3.
15 See for example, SBC Annual Report 1976 (Cmnd 6910), paras 9.14–9.20. Now both short-term and long-term rates are raised in line with prices, rather than earnings (see pp. 467–468, below), and have, therefore, not kept pace with increases in earnings.
16 *Fiegehen et al*, n.9, above, at pp. 15–17.
17 See Atkinson, *Poverty in Britain and the Reform of Social Security* (1969), and in Wedderburn (ed) *Poverty, Inequality and Class Structure* (1974) p. 48. *Townsend* pp. 241–247, is very critical of this approach.
18 The problems of low wage-earners were first raised by Abel-Smith and Townsend *The Poor and the Poorest* (1965). Also see *Fiegehen et al*, n.9, above, at p. 67.
19 Pp. 459, 501, below.
20 Annual Report 1978 (Cmnd 7725), ch 12. For the problem of low take-up generally, see p. 13, above.

i The early history of the poor laws[1]

The first statutes encouraging parishes to assist the deserving poor (the old, sick and infirm) were passed in 1531 and 1536. These Acts, and other subsequent legislation, were consolidated in the famous Poor Relief Act of 1601. Under this overseers, to be appointed in each parish to act under the general supervision of the Justices of the Peace, were to give relief to the deserving poor and to raise local taxes for this purpose. The able-bodied were to be given work. Section 6 imposed a duty on a person's father, grandfather, mother, grandmother and child to maintain him. This assertion of family responsibility was not repealed until the 1948 Act.[2] Until then the primary obligation to maintain rested on the family, and though the parish might give relief to someone neglected by his relatives, it could recover this from the defaulters. Thus, two important features of the poor law regime were established from the outset: first, its local administration which led to inconsistent provision in different areas of the country, and secondly, the emphasis on family responsibility.

Inevitably the administration of the poor law went through many changes in the two centuries before the reforms of 1834. The most important development was the 1662 Act of Settlement. Its object was to prevent poor people wandering round the country, imposing themselves as charges on other parishes. Any person, without property or other means of support, could be removed to his parish of 'settlement', that is generally, where he was born. In effect a pauper had to look to this parish for relief, a restriction which naturally hindered freedom of movement.[3]

The eighteenth century saw the first workhouses, which the able-bodied were required to enter as a condition of securing relief.[4] But the experiment was halted towards the end of the century. The poverty of agricultural workers at this time led to the use of poor law relief to supplement wages in the famous 'Speenhamland system'.[5] This in its turn became one of the reasons for the disquiet responsible for the institution of the Poor Law Commission in 1832. Many felt that relief for the employed merely subsidised low wages, an argument now deployed against the family income supplement.[6]

ii Poor law reform: 1834–1930[7]

The Poor Law Commission found that provision for those able to work was corrupting for the recipients; in future they were only to be given relief in the workhouses. Under the notorious principle of 'less eligibility', conditions there were to be less attractive than those of the poorest worker outside.[8] Thus, the familiar distinction was drawn between the deserving poor, who might benefit from allowances paid outside the workhouse

1 There are many useful accounts of the early history of the poor laws: see de Schweinitz *England's Road to Social Security* (1949) ch 1; Bruce *The Coming of the Welfare State* (4th edn) ch 2; the editors' introduction to *The Poor Law Report of 1834* (ed by S G & E O A Checkland, 1974). A more legal analysis is provided by Jennings *The Poor Law Code* (2nd edn, 1936).

2 See p. 452, below.

3 A reaction to this harsh law may be the present liberal 'residence' qualifications for public assistance: p. 456, below.

4 *Bruce*, n.1, above, at pp. 54–55.

5 Ibid, pp. 55–56; *The Poor Law Report of 1834*, n.1, above, at pp. 18–20.

6 P. 523, below.

7 See the collection of materials in ed. Rose *The English Poor Law 1780–1930* (1971); Rose *The Relief of Poverty 1834–1914* (1972); *Bruce*, n.1, above, at chs 4 and 5.

8 Ibid, at pp. 96–97.

('outdoor relief') and the less deserving who would only in practice be able to secure relief in conditions of extreme destitution. The objective of more efficient administration was achieved first, by the merging of parishes for poor law purposes into unions, with elected Boards of Guardians, and secondly, by the institution of a central Board of three Commissioners, responsible for the making of regulations and the national administration of the poor laws.

Though well intentioned the remedy was perhaps worse than the disease. The horrors of the workhouses, with their degrading treatment of the inmates and the enforced separation of husband and wife, are well-known from the novels of Dickens. The sick and the old were often for reasons of economy housed together with the unemployed. Eventually a Royal Commission was appointed in 1905. All its members were agreed that the 1834 reforms were misconceived, that the workhouses should be abolished and the administrative structure changed. But it was divided in its proposals for specific solutions; partly because of this and partly because other events dominated political discussion, there was no immediate attempt at reform.[9]

During the 1920s unemployment increased, exposing the weaknesses of the poor laws. Many unions, with the workhouses quite inadequate to cope, used their power to afford outdoor relief for the able-bodied in cases of 'urgent necessity'.[10] But they were not all so generous, with the result that provision varied widely from area to area. Naturally those with the heaviest unemployment were the least able to afford the costs of relief. The inherent weakness of local administration and financing became widely recognised. But even then, the solution of national administration was not immediately adopted. Instead by the Local Government Act 1929, the functions of the poor law guardians and unions were transferred to the local authorities to be discharged largely by their public assistance committees.[11] In the following year the last Poor Law Act, a consolidation measure, was passed.[12] A more significant event was the repeal of the Regulation which had made entry into the workhouse a condition of relief to the able-bodied.[13]

iii Unemployment assistance and the end of the poor law 1930–1948

Governments in this period were troubled by the problems of those unemployed who were unable to claim the contributory benefit.[14] In October 1931 the National Government replaced the costly transitional benefits with means-tested transitional allowances for people out of work for more than 26 weeks.[15] These were funded nationally, but administered by the local authority public assistance committees. When it became clear that they were inconsistent in their administration of the allowances, the demand for a national scheme could no longer be resisted. The Unemployment Assistance Act 1934 instituted a Board to administer public

9 The Minority Report, largely the work of Beatrice Webb, was influential in that it proposed the transfer of administering assistance to local authorities.
10 *Bruce*, n.1, above, at p. 255.
11 Ibid, at pp. 258–259.
12 The Act is exhaustively analysed by *Jennings*, n.1, above.
13 SR & O 1930/186, art 6.
14 For unemployment benefit, see ch 3, above.
15 *Bruce*, n.1, above, at p. 269.

assistance for the unemployed.[16] Thus an important group was taken out of the poor law system, and a precedent set for the 1948 reform.

In a number of respects the 1934 scheme is interesting as a forerunner of the modern law of supplementary benefits. Assistance was calculated by reference to the applicant's requirements, based on weekly scale rates, with a deduction for his resources. Extra lump sum payments could be made for exceptional needs, and the regular weekly payments could be increased in special circumstances. An adjustment could be made for particularly high or low rents.[17] An important feature of the scheme was the 'household means' test: the resources of all members of the claimant's household were taken into account before determining that he was in need of assistance.[18] This imposition, in effect, of primary responsibility for maintenance on members of an applicant's household has been a feature of some social security systems,[19] but it nevertheless attracted strong criticism and did not survive long.

During the war years, the Unemployment Assistance Board's functions were increased to embrace the administration of the pensions payable under the Old Age and Widows' Pensions Act 1940,[20] and it was consequently renamed the Assistance Board. Another important group of people was thus taken out of the poor law. A further significant development was the virtual abolition of the 'household means' test by the Determination of Needs Act 1941. In future where the applicant was a householder, only his own resources and those of his wife and dependants were to be taken into account in assessing his need.[1]

It was the Beveridge Report which heralded the final demise of the poor law. It pointed out the anomalies necessarily entailed by the existence of a number of tests, administered by separate authorities, for giving assistance to different groups.[2] Section 1 of the National Assistance Act 1948 repealed the 'existing poor law' – without any trace of Parliamentary regret.[3] The provision of financial assistance became exclusively the function of central government acting through the National Assistance Board (NAB), as it was now called. Many features of the old poor law went: there was no law of settlement, so that it no longer mattered where the applicant was resident when he claimed assistance;[4] the requirement that applicants for assistance be set to work was replaced by a discretionary requirement to register for employment;[5] relief by way of loan, a common provision under the poor law, was abolished as a normal form of assistance.

iv The reform of 1966[6]

In 1948, it was thought right to keep the administration of means-tested assistance entirely separate from that of the insurance benefits, as an

16 For a further discussion of the Board, see ch 14, p. 543, below.
17 See further, p. 470, below.
18 Unemployment Assistance Act 1934, s.38.
19 For the position in the USA, see La France, Schroeder, Bennett and Boyd *Law of the Poor* (1973) pp. 299 ff. For Germany, see Donnison *The Politics of Poverty* (1982) p. 109.
20 For the history of pensions, see ch 5, above, pp. 189–191.
1 The 'household means' test survived in vestigial form for non-householders until 1948: see Determination of Needs Act 1941, Sch 1, para 3(a).
2 Para 372.
3 See 444 HC Official Report (5th series) col 1667, where Miss A Bacon said: 'Today we are burying the Poor Law, and I do not think that many tears will be shed at its passing'.
4 See p. 450, above, for the law of settlement, and p. 456, below, for the modern 'presence' requirement.
5 Pp. 459–461, below.
6 See the discussion in SBC Annual Report 1976 (Cmnd 6910), Appendix A.

aspect of their distinct functions in the social security system.[7] The NAB was, therefore, an independent government department.[8] However, it gradually became apparent that national assistance was playing a more important role than had been foreseen at the end of the war,[9] and that potential applicants were discouraged from applying for it, partly because of the wide area of discretion accorded to officials under the 1948 legislation.

The Labour government decided, therefore, in 1966 to make some changes in the rules for awarding assistance, from that time to be known as supplementary benefit.[10] The major alteration was that the 1966 Act provided for a *right* to benefit in the circumstances set out in the legislation – a change designed to reduce the amount of discretion in the system. This was further reduced by the automatic provision of higher benefit rates for pensioners and for recipients who had been on benefit for two years. Under the 1948 legislation the special needs of these groups had been met by discretionary allowances. The principal administrative change was that the NAB was dissolved, and its functions transferred to the Ministry of Social Security[11] and to the Supplementary Benefits Commission, though the latter was not a separate department.[12] The primary object of these changes was to merge the administration of contributory and means-tested benefits, and thereby remove the stigma associated with claiming the latter.[13] It is arguable, however, that the reforms were relatively minor, and did not justify the claims made for them.[14]

C The reforms of 1980

The Conservative government has recently in the Social Security Act 1980 made the most significant reforms to public assistance since 1948. Change in the structure of the supplementary benefits scheme had been urged by the Supplementary Benefits Commission in its Annual Reports, and in 1976 a team of DHSS officials was formed to take a thorough look at it. Their report was produced two years later.[15] Broadly it found that the system had become too complicated for claimants to understand and for officers to administer. Simplification of the scheme should be effected to make it more intelligible and less costly. In particular awards of discretionary additions to benefit had radically increased in the 1970s, and these were making the scheme both expensive to administer and unfair in its application, since it was difficult to ensure equal and uniform allocation of such payments throughout the country.

The DHSS review was concerned only to look at the supplementary benefits scheme in its present context in the social security system, and it,

7 See Titmuss *Social Security in International Perspective*; *Essays in honor of Eveline M. Burns* (1969) p. 151.
8 See ch 14, pp. 539–543, below.
9 P. 446, above.
10 The change was made by the Ministry of Social Security Act 1966, later renamed the Supplementary Benefit Act 1966 by SSA 1973, s.99(18).
11 Its functions were later transferred to the Secretary of State for Social Services: p. 540, below.
12 Pp. 543–544, below.
13 Miss M Herbison, Minister of Pensions and National Insurance, 729 HC Official Report (5th series) cols 335 ff.
14 Miss M Pike, ibid, at cols 352 ff.
15 *Social Assistance* (DHSS, 1978). For the background to, and comments on, this report, see Donnison *The Politics of Poverty* (1982) chs 5 and 6.

therefore, did not consider whether it was right for public assistance to play the much larger role than Beveridge had envisaged. Another assumption, naturally not shared by some of the review's critics (including the SBC itself), was that worthwhile changes could be made without increasing the costs of the scheme.[16] The result is that the substantive reforms proposed in the *Social Assistance* report, though important in terms of details, were necessarily far from radical. On the other hand, it did recommend a revised legal structure, in which many more of the rules concerning entitlement to benefit would be set out in regulations, or preferably a Code of Practice, which would be published and debated in Parliament. Within six months of assuming office, Mrs Thatcher's administration decided to proceed on the basis of the DHSS team's report. In a White Paper, the principal (or sole) merit of which was brevity, it announced its intention to introduce reform which 'simplifies the scheme as much as possible for claimants and staff'.[17] The result a year later was a major amendment of the 1976 legislation (to be found in Schedule 2 to the Social Security Act 1980) and about a dozen sets of regulations, some of which are difficult for lawyers to understand and almost all of which are wholly incomprehensible to laymen.

As will be seen throughout this chapter, regulations now lay down precise and detailed rules for determining a claimant's requirements and resources (and hence, entitlement to weekly benefit), eligibility for a further lump sum payment to meet an exceptional need, the circumstances in which payment may be withheld or reduced, or made over to a third party, and so on. Indeed statutory instruments are now the primary source of supplementary benefits law, whereas they had played a relatively small part in the system established in 1948 and 1966. Not only do they contain provisions previously set out in the primary Act, but they also regulate areas which were subject to the discretion of the SBC. A claimant and his adviser, therefore, need not rely so extensively as they used to on the Supplementary Benefits Handbook for information about entitlement to benefit, though a revised version of this guide was published at the end of 1980; it constitutes a useful summary of the legal provisions.

Thus the main effect of the reform is increased legalisation and consequent reduction in the role of discretion. This is most true of the supplementary payments which may be made in addition to the standard weekly benefit; these used only to be awarded when the Commission's officer found there were 'exceptional circumstances' or there was an 'exceptional need'. Now entitlement to these further payments is set out in regulations, and discretion is residual only. Indeed, the primary merit of the reform is that it does at least make it absolutely plain what payments claimants may be entitled to, without perhaps entirely eliminating all discretion for the genuinely exceptional case. These changes are reflected in the administrative and adjudicative institutions. There is no longer any need for informal rules and policies to be formulated by the Commission for the guidance of officers exercising broad discretionary powers. The advisory role of the SBC on means-tested benefits has, therefore, been transferred to the new Social Security Advisory Committee, which is concerned to give advice on almost all social security benefits.[18] In those

16 See the criticisms in *Response of SBC to Social Assistance* (1979), SBA Paper No 9, and by Lister [1978–9] JSWL 133.

17 Reform of the Supplementary Benefits Scheme (1979, Cmnd 7773), at para 7. A critical view of the proposals and subsequent legislation is to be found in *Donnison*, n.15, above, at pp. 160–183.

18 See pp. 546–548, below.

areas of supplementary benefits law where there is still room for the exercise of judgment by officers, guidance is issued by a Chief Supplementary Benefits Officer, and some of this has now been published.

Decisions on entitlement to benefit are now taken by benefit officers, and there is then an appeal to a supplementary benefits appeal tribunal, as used to be the case before the reform. What is new is that since November 1980 (when the scheme took effect) there has been a further appeal on a point of law to the Social Security Commissioner (formerly National Insurance Commissioner). It is already clear that their decisions will add to the volume of supplementary benefits law, and in view of the legal complexity of the regulations, it will be surprising if the Commissioners do not play an important part in its future development.[19]

Part 2 Entitlement to supplementary benefit

A General conditions

Section 1 of the amended Supplementary Benefits Act 1976 provides that 'every person in Great Britain of or over the age of 16 whose resources are insufficient to meet his requirements' is entitled to benefit. Depending on the claimant's age, he (or she) will be entitled either to a *pension* or to an *allowance*; entitlement to the latter, but not the former, may be conditional on the claimant being available for employment. Another point which should be made at this stage is that in many cases, principally where a husband and wife are living together, the requirements and resources of one person are aggregated with and treated as those of another, so that only the latter (under the present law, the husband) may be entitled to claim benefit. It should be pointed out too that in some circumstances, a person who satisfies these general conditions will be disqualified from eligibility for benefit: see pp. 457–459 below.

i Age

The claimant must be at least 16. The needs of a child under this age may be met by his requirements being included in those of the person in the household who has to provide for him; the availability of benefit will depend on that person's entitlement.[20] The *Social Assistance* report considered, but rejected, the suggestion that young mothers under 16 should be entitled to claim benefit, particularly if they are disowned by their parents; these cases are better looked after in the context of general welfare help.[1]

The other respect in which the claimant's age is material concerns the difference between an allowance and a pension. The rule is still that it is the claimant's age which is relevant; if he has reached pensionable age (65 for a man, 60 for a woman), he will be entitled to a pension, which automatically is payable at the higher long-term rate. Under the aggregation rule mentioned earlier, it is the husband's age which is decisive, since only he may claim benefit under the present law. Thus, if a husband is 64 and his wife 63, an allowance is payable, while if he is 66 and she is only 40,

19 For the adjudication system, see pp. 605–614, below. (In 1981 there were 38 numbered decisions, of which 21 were reported.)
20 See p. 464, below.
1 Para 4.19. (Also see paras 4.2–4.5.)

a pension can be paid. But after a date in 1983 (not yet announced) a pension will be payable if either member of a couple, married or unmarried, is over pensionable age.[2] This is one of the reforms mandated by the EEC Directive on Equal Treatment for Men and Women.[3]

ii Presence in Great Britain

There is no condition that only a British national or resident may be entitled to benefit.[4] Mere presence in Britain is in principle enough. This is a generous provision, in marked contrast to the poor law which made the pauper look to his native parish for assistance.[5] A claimant may be awarded benefit either at his usual place of residence or at any place where he is staying temporarily. A foreign visitor (who is not an EEC national looking for work) is however generally not entitled to ordinary weekly benefit: this may either be because he cannot satisfy the requirement to be available for work without violating his entry conditions, or because (if not subject to that requirement) he may have only been admitted subject to the understanding that he does not become a charge on public funds.[6] (But in some circumstances such a visitor may be eligible for an urgent needs payment, at least to enable him to return home.)[7] It is interesting to note that unlike the British legislation, the Northern Ireland provisions impose a requirement of five years' residence in the United Kingdom before benefit can be awarded, presumably to discourage people from crossing the border from the Republic to make claims.[8]

Difficulties may occur where a claimant wishes to take a holiday abroad. Generally entitlement will not continue when the recipient is outside the country, but under the regulations this does not apply where the claimant is not required to be available for work, though if this requirement is not exacted owing to his illness, the absence abroad must be for treatment or he must have been incapable of work for the six months prior to his travel. In these circumstances, benefit may be paid for up to four weeks,[9] and on his return (even after the period has elapsed) a single payment may be made to cover a debt owed for a 'continuing commitment', e.g. rent, incurred while he was away.[10]

iii Resources insufficient to meet requirements

This condition of financial need is clearly the one that is generally crucial. The claimant's resources are calculated according to the rules described in Part 4 of this chapter, and then deducted from his requirements which are assessed in various ways set out in Part 3. The short-fall is the amount of weekly benefit. Section 1(3) of the Act provides that no account may

2 SBA 1976, s.1(1)(a).
3 Pp. 8–10, above.
4 For 'residence' and 'presence' requirements under the Social Security Act 1975, see ch 10, pp. 391–393, above.
5 P. 450, above.
6 See SI 1980/1299, Sch 2, para 9A, inserted by SI 1980/1774, Sch, para 16, and see *Lynes* pp. 250–251.
7 P. 496, below.
8 SI 1977/2156, art 8. *Shapiro v Thompson* 89 SCt 1322 (1969) and *Graham v Richardson* 91 SCt 1848 (1971) held that provisions imposing residence and national origin qualifications for entitlement to welfare benefits are prima facie unconstitutional in the United States. These cases are discussed in La France, Schroeder, Bennett and Boyd *Law of the Poor* (1973) pp. 343 ff: also see Harvich 54 Calif L Rev 567.
9 SI 1981/1526, reg 3, made under SBA 1976, s.1A.
10 SI 1981/1528, reg 24.

generally be taken of 'medical, surgical, optical, aural or dental requirements'. This is presumably an overlap provision designed to prevent payment for needs which are already met by the National Health Service.[11] However, under modifying regulations, benefit may be paid for certain heating, attendance, and dietary requirements, or for persons who on medical grounds need more than one bath a week.[12]

Nice questions can arise whether the overlap provision precludes payment for medical expenses incurred outside the NHS. In view of its probable purpose there seems no reason why benefit should not be paid, but in two cases the courts refused to award payment to a claimant who had incurred such costs.[13] In another decision where the claimant applied for benefit to assist him to meet the running costs of medical equipment, the Divisional Court emphasised that consideration should be given to the nature of the equipment and by whom it was provided before deciding whether or not to give benefit:[14] it is suggested that this approach better fulfils the purpose of the overlap section.

B Exclusions from benefit

There are three principal categories of case where a claimant, otherwise eligible for benefit, is not entitled to claim. One of these, persons affected by trade disputes, is fully discussed later in this chapter (Part 7), while the other two are treated here.

i Persons in full-time employment

A person 'engaged in remunerative full-time work' is not generally entitled. With the major exception of the Speenhamland system introduced in 1795,[15] public assistance was not used to supplement low earnings until the introduction of family income supplement (FIS) in 1970.[16] The result is that supplementary benefit is of no assistance to one major group of people living below the official poverty line.[17]

Regulations made under the amended Act now define when a claimant is to be treated as in 'remunerative full-time work'.[18] It must first be work 'for which payment is made, or which is done in expectation of payment'.[19] This formulation follows a ruling of the Court of Appeal which had held, in construing the earlier unamended legislation, that 'remunerative' work meant paid work, rather than work which is done at a profit.[20] When an applicant is running a business at a loss, FIS is the appropriate benefit. Secondly, the applicant is in 'full-time' work if he is engaged in it for 30 hours a week, or 35 hours if he is disabled and his earning capacity is

11 For overlapping benefits generally, see ch 10, pp. 413–419, above.
12 SI. 1980/1299, reg 11(3).
13 *R v Peterborough Supplementary Benefits Appeal Tribunal, ex parte Supplementary Benefits Commission* [1978] 3 All ER 887, DC (osteopathic treatment); *Supplementary Benefits Commission v Lamb* (reported in the Stationery Office publication, (1979) SB Dec 185 (Decision SB 24) (chiropody treatment). See *Donnison* n.15, above, at p. 95.
14 *R v West London Supplementary Benefits Appeal Tribunal, ex parte Wyatt* [1978] 2 All ER 315, [1978] 1 WLR 240, DC.
15 P. 450, above.
16 See ch 13, above.
17 See p. 448, above, for this concept.
18 SI 1981/1526, reg 9, made under SBA 1976, s.6(1).
19 SI 1981/1526 reg 9(1)(a).
20 *Perrot v Supplementary Benefits Commission* [1980] 3 All ER 110, [1980] 1 WLR 1153.

consequently reduced by 25 per cent.[1] This means that generally 'full-time' work has the same meaning for both supplementary benefit and FIS, so the possibility that a person could claim both benefits has been removed; this used to exist because he might have been in full-time work for FIS, but not working enough hours to be disqualified from supplementary benefit. (On the other hand, it is still possible for someone to be in receipt of both benefits: a FIS award subsists for a full year, and during that period he may become unemployed and eligible for benefit.)[2]

It is common practice for employees to be paid in arrears for their work, and this phenomenon explains some of the complications in these regulations. So a claimant will be treated as if he were still in full-time work for a period following the start of a spell of unemployment equivalent to the period of time for which the last wages were paid (assuming they were paid in arrears at the end of his employment).[3] For example, an employee who at the end of his employment receives a week's wages will not be entitled to claim benefit for the first week of his unemployment; or, if he receives then a month's wages in arrears, he will be disentitled to benefit for the month following the start of the period of unemployment. A self-employed person who has not altogether left employment is automatically treated as still in remunerative work for the 14 days after he has ceased to be engaged in it.[4]

The corollary of these rules is that a claimant is not to be treated as engaged in full-time work for the first 15 days of his employment in that work. But obviously he will not qualify for benefit under this provision if there is no gap between this employment and a previous one, or for any period still covered by earnings from his earlier employment and for which he was disqualified for benefit under the provisions discussed in the previous paragraph.[5] The object of the exception to the general work-disqualification rule is to provide benefit for employees who will often not receive wages during the first two weeks at work, and clearly this does not apply if the applicant is still treated as covered by his last salary from a previous employment. When an employee is entitled to benefit under this provision, any wages actually received in these two weeks must be totally or partially deducted under the rules regarding assessment of resources.

There are a few other exceptions to the general rule disqualifying persons in full-time employment. A claimant is not to be so disqualified if he is self-employed but his earning power is substantially impaired through disability, or if he is engaged in child-minding and performs normal household duties, or if he is engaged in a training scheme for which an allowance is paid.[6] However, although a person in full-time work is generally ineligible for weekly benefit (and as will be seen, a single payment), it may be open to him to apply for an urgent cases payment. These awards are now governed by regulations made under the amended legislation, and are discussed in Part 6 of this chapter.

ii Persons in receipt of education

The amended Act provides that a claimant under 19 and in receipt of 'relevant education' is not generally entitled to receive benefit.[7] The term

1 SI 1981/1526, reg 9(1)(a).
2 P. 536, below, for the duration of FIS payments.
3 SI 1981/1526, reg 9(1)(b).
4 Ibid, reg 9(1)(c).
5 Ibid, reg 9(2)(a).
6 Ibid, regs 9(2)(b)–(d).
7 SBA 1976, s.6(2).

means full-time education at a college, school or comparable institution.[8] In these circumstances, child benefit is payable. It should be noted that this disqualification only applies to persons receiving non-advanced education, e.g. GCE 'A' level or below, and does not apply to students attending university or teacher training courses.[9] In this way either the parent is eligible to claim child benefit or the child may (if over 16) be able to claim supplementary benefits: the former, for example, is payable for a child at a sixth form college, but if he goes on to university, he may (subject to special rules discussed in Part 9 of this chapter) be eligible for supplementary benefit.

Regulations now provide that child benefit may be paid for a period up to the end (approximately) of the holiday following the date the person left school, and consequently supplementary benefit is not paid to these school-leavers.[10] This was an economy in the scheme, which had been strongly recommended in *Social Assistance*; there was evidence that claims by school-leavers put a strain on local officers and sometimes were an abuse of the system.[11]

In certain circumstances this category of claimant will not be ineligible: the exclusion does not apply if he is a parent of, and responsible for, a child, if he is unlikely to be able to obtain work because of a handicap, or if he is an orphan or living away from and estranged from his parents or guardians.[12] Moreover, a person attending a course of education or training for up to 21 hours a week will not be disqualified if he is prepared immediately to end that course once suitable employment becomes available.[13]

C The condition of availability for employment

The entitlement of any person to an *allowance* (but not a pension) is now subject to the condition that he is available for employment.[14] Before a very recent change made by the Social Security and Housing Benefits Act 1982,[15] such a person was also usually required to register for work by 'signing on' at a local Jobcentre or the careers office of a local education authority, though in many cases this further condition was waived under the regulations.[16] In 1981 the joint Department of Employment and DHSS scrutiny team, reviewing the arrangements for the payment of benefits to the unemployed, questioned whether compulsory registration with a local Jobcentre really served any useful purpose. It found no evidence that it led to the speedy filling of employment vacancies or discouraged the work-shy from avoiding work: 'registration for such claimants has thus become a fairly meaningless ritual which satisfies the requirements for receiving benefits but which does not usually lead to any subsequent contact with the Jobcentre'. The net result is that someone claiming benefit who is not in

8 Ibid, s.6(3).
9 Handbook, para 1.14.
10 SI 1981/1526, reg 10, and see p. 429 above, for the child benefit rules.
11 *Social Assistance* paras 4.6–4.9.
12 SI 1981/1526, reg 11.
13 Ibid, reg 11(e). There has been controversy concerning the calculation of the 21 hour limit: the Chief Supplementary Benefits Officer has directed that home study periods should be included.
14 SBA 1976, s.5.
15 S.38, amending SBA 1976, s.5.
16 Before the 1980 reforms the Commission had discretion to waive the registration condition, and this power was then incorporated in detailed regulations: SI 1981/1526, reg 6, p. 461, below.

fact trying to find work is most unlikely to be disturbed in this pursuit by the intervention of the Jobcentre.'[17] Under the 1982 Act, which implements the recommendation that registration should generally be voluntary, a requirement to 'sign on' will only be exacted in cases prescribed by regulations, which at the time of writing have not yet been issued.[18]

An applicant must show he is available for employment, that is, work which he can be expected to do and for which he would normally be engaged for not less than 30 hours a week, or if he is disabled, those hours he is capable of working.[19] Generally he will be regarded as available if he satisfies the availability test for unemployment benefit,[20] though he may be treated as available for the purposes of supplementary (but not unemployment) benefit if he is attending a course of education or training for up to 21 hours a week and is prepared to terminate that course immediately a suitable vacancy occurs.[1] But the regulations then go on to provide that in certain circumstances a claimant is not to be treated as available for work; the result is that he is then ineligible for supplementary benefit, whatever his entitlement may be to the contributory benefit. These rules, together with the 40 per cent deduction rule (discussed in Part 7 of this chapter), now form the principal method by which supposedly 'work-shy' claimants are induced to find employment; they replace the discretionary powers to withhold benefit previously exercised by the Supplementary Benefits Commission.[2] It is, to say the least, unfortunate that owing to their incorporation in regulations rather than the principal Act, these important rules were never debated in Parliament. In outline it can be said that a claimant will be treated as unavailable[3] —

(a) if he has without good cause refused to apply for, or accept an offer of, suitable employment when he has been properly notified of the vacancy;[4]

(b) if after two notices he fails to report to an officer of the Department of Employment to make a written declaration of unemployment and availability;

(c) if he is between 18 and 45, with no dependants and not living with a woman over 45 or pregnant, and he lives in an area where there is a reasonable chance of obtaining short-term work, and the benefit officer considers that refusal or withdrawal of the allowance would not be inappropriate.

In the first and third cases the determination of non-availability is not to apply for more than six weeks, and in the latter it may only take effect after the claimant has been given 14 days' written notice; in the second, it may apply until the applicant does report to the Department's officer.

Finally, two other groups are treated as unavailable for employment: share fishermen and students. The rule, however, only covers a student who is actually attending a course or is engaged on a programme of studies,[5] and it does not apply in those circumstances when he is not

17 DE/DHSS Rayner Scrutiny team, *Payment of Benefits to Unemployed People*(1981) para 4.07.
18 SSHBA 1982, s.38.
19 SI 1981/1526, reg 4.
20 See ch 3, pp. 101–106, above.
1 SI 1981/1526, reg 7(2).
2 See the first edition of this book, pp. 536–538.
3 SI 1981/1526, reg 8.
4 This does reproduce a disqualification for the contributory benefit: p. 112, above.
5 SI 1981/1526, reg 2, which defines a 'student' for the purposes of these regulations.

required to be available for employment.[6] In effect this means that in most cases a student will only be eligible for benefit during the long vacation (see Part 9). Here the regulations put into legal form rules previously applied by the SBC in its discretion.

In certain circumstances, set out in great detail in regulations, a claimant is not required to be available for employment. However, these provisions are only relevant when the rules set out in the preceding paragraphs (stipulating when a claimant is not treated as available) do not apply.[7] In other words, provided the claimant does not fall under the special rules for controlling claims by the 'work-shy', he is not required in these circumstances to show his general availability for work. The Supplementary Benefits Commission used to have discretion to waive the requirement to register; now typically the groups exempt from the requirement to be available are listed in a long and complex regulation. They include:

(a) a single person with a dependent child or with a child boarded out to him by a local authority;
(b) a person regularly and substantially engaged in caring for a severely disabled person;
(c) a person incapable of work through disease, disablement or blindness, or a person without prospects of work because of disability;
(d) in various circumstances a pregnant woman;
(e) a student who because of disability would be unlikely, relative to other students, to obtain work within a reasonable time;
(f) a person caring for the child of a close relative;
(g) a person in receipt of a training allowance or an allowance under the Job Release Act 1977;
(h) in various circumstances a person discharged recently from prison.

Perhaps the most important rule, particularly during periods of high unemployment, is that a person who is within ten years of pensionable age, and who has not been in work or required to register for the previous decade, will not be required to show his availability for work if he now has no employment prospects.[8] Even if none of these particular rules applies, a benefit officer has a residual discretion not to require an applicant to show availability where it would be unreasonable in the circumstances.[9]

A claimant who is available for work is then fully entitled to benefit. The imposition of the requirement to be available affects entitlement to the higher long-term rate of supplementary allowance.[10] However, there is now no distinction between the treatment of the earnings of those required to register and be available for work, and the earnings of those not so obliged.[11]

D The 'family unit' for supplementary benefits

The supplementary benefits scheme recognises that it is generally realistic to treat a couple living together (whether married or not) and their children as one unit for benefit purposes.[12] This group is often referred to as 'the assessment unit' in the various regulations, and this term is frequently

6 Ibid, reg 8(1)(a) which refers to ibid, reg 6.
7 Ibid.
8 Ibid, reg 6(f).
9 Ibid, reg 6(u).
10 P. 468, below.
11 P. 485, below.
12 SBC Annual Report 1976 (Cmnd 6910), paras 6.12–6.15.

used in the rest of this chapter. The breadwinner, usually, though of course not necessarily these days, the man, will need assistance for his partner and their children, though correspondingly his financial position will improve if other members of the family can contribute to the family fund. There are also considerable economies of scale where a couple live together, and it is right that the scheme should recognise this. The amended Supplementary Benefits Act 1976, therefore, provides that in some cases the requirements and resources of one person will be aggregated with, and treated as, those of another, and then only the latter will be entitled to benefit.[13] The aggregation provision itself is now considerably complicated by the amendments made in 1980 which are designed partly to achieve greater sex equality, and partly to make the law more precise. The basic rule is that there is to be aggregation of the requirements and resources of a married or unmarried couple, provided they are members of the same household, and also of the requirements and resources of a claimant and a child or other dependant, if the same proviso is satisfied.[14] This formula is in a sense a relic of the notorious 'household means' test which was not finally abolished until 1948.[15] Under this, primary responsibility for the relief of poverty was placed on all other persons living in the household, but now resources of such persons, apart from those covered by the aggregation provision, are entirely irrelevant.[16]

The present legal position is that the wife's, or woman's, requirements and resources are aggregated with those of the man, and only he may claim benefit. This has been heavily criticised as resting on outdated assumptions about the roles of the sexes; it may well be inconvenient when the woman is the sole breadwinner: if she becomes unemployed, benefit will not be awarded, unless the husband (or man) shows he is available, for work. The Supplementary Benefits Commission and *Social Assistance* both recommended reform to bring about sex equality,[17] and this will soon be achieved. After a date (as yet not prescribed) in 1983, the couple's requirements and resources are to be treated as those of that member who satisfies various conditions, which will be set out in regulations.[18] If both, or neither, satisfy these requirements, they may jointly nominate which of them is to be the claimant, and in default of nomination, the Secretary of State may determine this. Until this date, only the male member of a couple living together may claim supplementary benefit.[19] The terms of the aggregation provisions can now be examined.

i Husband and wife who are members of the same household

The aggregation provisions apply only if the husband and wife are members of the same household, and not generally if they are living apart.[20] The wife's requirements and resources are only relevant if the spouses

13 SBA 1976, s.1(2).
14 Ibid, Sch 1, para 3.
15 P. 452, above.
16 See p. 480, below, for the discussion of resources.
17 SBC Annual Report 1976, n.12, above, at ch 6; *Social Assistance* ch 11.
18 The possible ways of achieving sex equality are discussed in *Social Assistance* paras 11.7–11.23.
19 SBA 1976, Sch 1, para 3(1).
20 A wife here may be a wife in a polygamous marriage: see *Imam Din v NAB* [1967] 2 QB 213, [1967] 1 All ER 750, DC. In any case it is provided that the aggregation rules apply to *all* members of a polygamous relationship whether they are regarded by English (or Scottish) law as validly married or not: see SI 1981/1524, reg 8.

form a distinct 'family'. The phrase, 'members of the same household', is not defined in the legislation,[1] so recourse must be had to general principles. In divorce law, where it is commonly an issue whether spouses are living separately, the test seems to be whether cohabitation and all forms of common life have ceased. If they have not, the courts will generally rule, at least if the parties are under the same roof, that they are still living in the same household.[2] This seems to be the appropriate approach here. The fact that a husband is not giving his wife any financial support does not in itself prevent them from being regarded as 'members of the same household'.

Regulations now provide that a temporary absence from each other, because one spouse, for example, is working away from home or on holiday, does not prevent a married couple from being treated as members of the same household. But this relaxation of the general rule does not apply if one spouse goes into prison, has been in hospital for longer than two years or (in some circumstances) has been abroad for more than four weeks.[3] In these situations, they are treated as if they were no longer sharing the same household, and the wife is entitled to be treated separately for benefit purposes. The position of separated and divorced women is treated separately in Part 8 of this chapter.

ii Unmarried couples

The circumstances in which two persons, not married to each other, are regarded as 'living together as husband and wife' have already been discussed in chapter 10.[4] The Commission used to have discretion not to apply the 'living together' rule in exceptional circumstances; now these situations may be prescribed by regulation. There is one such complicated provision which is broadly similar to what used to be Commission policy.[5] Under this benefit may be paid for a *child's* requirements for a period of adjustment, which will normally be four weeks, but which may be extended to ten in some circumstances. The conditions for this payment are first, that one person (A) has been entitled to benefit for a family unit which did not include B (with whom A is now living), but did include a child dependant (C), of whom B is not a parent; secondly that B is not himself entitled to benefit; and thirdly that the loss of income to the unit from withdrawal of A's benefit would be in the officer's view 'disproportionate'. The temporary continuation of A's allowance is intended to permit the new family unit to adjust to circumstances, but if it becomes clear after this that B's wages, together with any other income, will be insufficient to bring the family up to the supplementary benefits level, A may claim an urgent cases payment.[6] This will normally be assessed as the difference between the total income of B's family unit (his resources less any maintenance payments he makes to any former spouse or child not living with him) and the appropriate sum which would be paid under the Requirements Regulations; this urgent payment may be made indefinitely.

1 Nor is it in the Family Income Supplements Act 1970: p. 529, below.
2 E.g. *Hopes v Hopes* [1949] P. 227, [1948] 2 All ER 920, CA: See Cretney *Principles of Family Law* (3rd edn) p. 123. For 'residing together' under the SSA 1975, see pp. 371–373, above.
3 SI 1981/1524, reg 2.
4 Pp. 382–386, above.
5 SI 1981/1524, reg 7.
6 For urgent cases payments generally, see pp. 493–497, below.

When it reconsidered the cohabitation rule (as it was then known) in 1976, the SBC also reviewed some aspects of its administration.[7] The procedure introduced then was that where a visiting officer thinks a claimant is living together with a man, he refers the case to a special interviewing officer, who has been given special training for this delicate work. He explains the rules to her, gives her a leaflet which supplements this explanation, and then submits a report together with her statement to a senior officer. This officer then makes the decision, and if adverse, informs the woman of her right of appeal.[8] A special investigation, which may entail asking questions of neighbours and watching the claimant's house, will only be ordered at a Regional Office when the facts cannot be ascertained by interviewing the woman; the Commission regretted the need for these inquiries, but saw no alternative in view of the number of cases where abuse is detected.[9] It also rejected the Finer Committee's recommendation[10] that where the facts are disputed, every cohabitation case should be referred to an appeal tribunal and in the meantime benefit should be paid. This proposal would encourage frivolous appeals.[11] It does seem that generally the rule and its administration in this area of social security law are less controversial than they used to be.

iii Children and other members of the household

Under the amended legislation there is mandatory aggregation where a person 'is responsible for, and is a member of the same household as', another person if the latter is a child, or is under 19 and receiving 'relevant' (i.e. non-advanced) education,[12] or under the regulations is between 19 and 20 and is attending a course of such education.[13] The result of this in the normal case is simply that a claimant will receive benefit for his child's needs, assessed in accordance with the Requirements Regulations.

Difficulties occurred under the 1976 Act before the recent reforms where the child unusually had resources of his own. It was not clear until a decision of the House of Lords in 1980 whether in these circumstances the claimant had to 'provide for the requirements of' his child and, therefore, whether the aggregation rule applied.[14] The ruling that it did has been confirmed in the new regulations, which make it plain beyond doubt that aggregation of a claimant's and child's requirements and resources is mandatory.[15] This is surely the correct approach; any other solution would undermine the whole object of the family unit rule.

As under the previous law, it seems the requirements of a grandchild may be aggregated. This can still be the case, even if the child's parent (C) is living in the same household as the claimant (A) and the child (B). A regulation, rather unhelpfully, provides that whether A or C is to be regarded as responsible for B is to be decided by reference to the closeness

7 SBC Report, *Living together as Husband and Wife* (1976).
8 Ibid, paras 81–87. Also see now Handbook, para 2.13.
9 *Living together as Husband and Wife*, n.7, above, at paras 88–96.
10 Paras 5.271–5.275.
11 N.7, above, at paras 75–77.
12 SBA 1976, Sch 1, para 3(2).
13 SI 1981/1524, reg 3(5).
14 See the discussion in the first edition, p. 488. The uncertainties were clarified in two cases decided together: *Supplementary Benefits Commission v Jull, Y v Supplementary Benefits Commission* [1981] AC 1025, [1980] 3 All ER 65. Also see SBC Annual Report 1979 (Cmnd 8033), paras 10.12–10.22.
15 SI 1981/1524, reg 3(2).

to, and nature of the relationship with, B.[16] In some circumstances a claimant and dependant are not to be treated as members of the same household, e.g. where the latter had been abroad for more than four weeks, is in prison, or is boarded with the claimant by a local authority or is staying with him in the prospect of adoption.[17]

Part 3 The assessment of requirements

A General

A claimant's requirements might be met in three alternative ways. He might be provided with assistance in kind, at least where this was practicable. If he needed a new suit or toilet articles, he would be provided with them (or voucher for their purchase) on proof that he was unable to afford them. This used to be the general practice in the United States, and does still exist in some states there.[18] It is relatively uncommon in this country.[19] Secondly, cash payments might be awarded for the purposes of purchasing the specific goods or services required by the applicant. This is a common method of meeting requirements in the United States, and is used here to meet an exceptional need (see Part 5 of this chapter). The third means is the one generally used in Britain: a cash payment is made to cover the applicant's assumed needs, which are calculated according to formulae set out in the legislation (or regulations made under it).

The advantage of paying benefit according to a standard scale rate is that it gives the recipient some discretion how to spend it. Thus, in one week he may pay a little more for food than he usually does, while in the next he may spend some money on the cinema or other recreation. Alternatively he may save it for a television licence. Different claimants have varying needs, particularly with regard to clothes and amenities, and the scale rates are fixed so as to enable them to exercise choice. Since the late 1950s it has been generally agreed that those in receipt of assistance should share in increasing national prosperity,[20] and the consequence of this 'commitment' is that weekly payments are designed to be high enough to cover some amenities as well as the goods necessary to carry on a subsistence existence.[1]

In some cases, however, it will be clear that the standard weekly rate is inadequate to meet the claimant's needs. This is particularly likely to be so where he is ill or infirm, and requires additional money to pay for special diets or extra heating. Under the 1976 Act before the recent reform, the Commission had discretion to award weekly increases for such needs in 'exceptional circumstances',[2] but now this discretion has been reduced to detailed rules. An obvious circumstance which varies substantially from one claimant to another is his housing requirements: one will stay virtually free in a friend's house, while another will be paying a high rent. So housing needs are covered separately. The result is that a person's requirements consist of normal requirements, and then the housing and

16 Ibid, reg 3(3).
17 Ibid, reg 4.
18 See La France et al *Law of the Poor* (1973) pp. 258–261, 266.
19 See ch 14, p. 573, below.
20 P. 449, above.
1 Handbook, paras 4.1 and 4.15.
2 See the first edition, pp. 511–519.

additional requirements 'as are applicable in his case'.[3] The rules are set out in great detail in a statutory instrument, and are discussed in this Part of the chapter. The benefit actually paid to the claimant is then calculated by subtracting his resources from the requirements assessed under these rules. The assessment of resources is discussed in Part 4.

B Normal requirements

There are now two scale rates: the ordinary and long-term rates. Exposition of this topic is complicated by the fact that the level of payment under these rates varies for *single* persons (that is, a person not a member of a married or unmarried couple) according to whether he is a householder or not. Boarders are also treated differently.[4] Moreover, the distinction between a householder and non-householder is drawn somewhat differently for normal and housing requirements: treatment of this will be postponed till the latter requirements are discussed.[5]

i Ordinary rate

Regulations now spell out what the scale rates for normal requirements are expected to cover: 'all items of normal expenditure on day-to-day living' (other than housing expenditure), including in particular food, household fuel, the purchase, repair and replacement of clothing and footwear, normal travel and laundry costs and various miscellaneous household and amenity expenses, e.g. newspapers, TV licence and rental.[6] For a single person, who is a householder, the ordinary rate for 1982–83 is £25.70, and for a couple (whether they are householders or not) it is £41.70. The rate for a non-householder claimant over 18, or under 18 but with a dependant is £23.65, and for such a claimant under 18 and without a dependant £18.15. There are now two rates for children, and these sums are, of course, then aggregated with the father's (or mother's) requirements to determine the total benefit payable.[7]

The provision of a uniform scale was introduced by the National Assistance Act 1948, replacing the varying rates which had existed under the different schemes of assistance before this reform. Nevertheless the existence of differentials between householders and non-householders and the number of age bands means that the scheme is not as simple as it might be. *Social Assistance* considered a number of ways in which it could be simplified: for example, all single adults could be paid the same rate, and there could be one standard rate for children irrespective of age, as in contributory dependency benefits.[8] The report doubted whether changes could be made without rough justice or increased expenditure, and in particular urged that children's rates should continue to be age-related and not become standard: medical and other evidence indicated that family expenditure did increase substantially as children grew up.[9] The government, however, did think the children's rates could be simplified, so that

3 SBA 1976, Sch 1, para 2(2).
4 Pp. 476–477, below.
5 Pp. 471–472, below.
6 SI 1980/1299, reg 4.
7 See pp. 464–465, above.
8 Paras 5.15–5.32.
9 See pp. 426–427, above, for the same discussion in the context of child benefit.

there are now two rates instead of four for dependants under 16: the bands are 0–10 and 11–15.[10]

The other main issue, of course, is the general adequacy of the scale rates. The level of assistance in 1948 was criticised as ungenerous,[11] but since then, especially since the late 1950s, the real value of benefits generally kept pace with prices, and in the later 1960s their value rose considerably in relation to earnings.[12] This latter trend now seems to have been halted.[13] There is no statutory duty to up-rate supplementary benefits as there is for contributory benefits, but in practice they are increased at the same time. Despite the argument of the SBC in its 1976 Annual Report for increasing ordinary rates in line with earnings,[14] the practice has been to compare them, like short-term benefits and now contributory pensions, with prices.[15] If the short-term supplementary benefit rate were increased more than the equivalent insurance benefit, more people (as *Social Assistance* pointed out) would rely on means-tested assistance.[16] But this would seem to be the likely effect of the up-ratings in 1980, when supplementary benefit was increased in line with price movements, while there was a 5 per cent shortfall in the up-rating of the short-term contributory benefits.[17] In its White Paper the government had proposed to align the ordinary rate and short-term benefit rates,[18] but this has not yet come about.

The general adequacy of the scale rates, and how they should be fixed, has been considered in both *Social Assistance* and by the SBC in some of its Annual Reports.[19] But no firm conclusions have been reached. This is perhaps hardly surprising. Empirical research could establish to some extent the amount necessary for subsistence. But as is pointed out in *Social Assistance*,[20] there has been a movement away from the 'basket of goods' approach, and alternative tests such as the subjective one that beneficiaries should have their requirements met at the level which enables them to participate fully in the community hardly lend themselves to clear application.[1]

ii The long-term rate

The automatic payment of a higher rate to pensioners and others who have been on benefit for a considerable period was introduced in 1966. Previously the special needs of those who required help over a long period could only be met by a discretionary supplement to the ordinary rate, and this sometimes necessitated distressing personal inquiries.[2] At first the extra automatic payment took the form of a 'long-term addition', but this

10 *Reform of the Supplementary Benefits Scheme* (1979, Cmnd 7773), para 16.
11 *George* pp. 208 ff.
12 SBC Annual Report 1976, paras 9.14–9.20.
13 SBC Annual Report 1976, n.12, above, at para 9.13.
14 N.12, above, at para 1.10.
15 The fullest discussion is to be found in the SBC Annual Report 1978 (Cmnd 7725), ch 3.
16 Para 5.50.
17 See ch 10, pp. 410–413, above, for up-rating of contributory benefits.
18 N.10, above, para 14.
19 See in particular SBC Annual Report 1978, n.15, above. For further critical discussion, see *Dear SSAC. . .* (1980, CPAG Pamphlet), ch 3.
20 Paras 5.9–5.14.
1 See the reference to Townsend's theoretical approach, p. 448, above.
2 See Miss M Herbison, Minister of Pensions and National Insurance, 729 HC Official Report (5th series) col 341. And see the Explanatory Memorandum to the Ministry of Social Security Bill (1966, Cmnd 2997), para 7.

caused confusion, and in 1973 the addition was incorporated into the scale rates.[3] The difference between the long-term and ordinary rates increased considerably over the last few years, because the former were raised in line with any change in earnings or prices, whichever was the more favourable. By 1979 this differential had become as high as 29 per cent of the ordinary rate in the case of single householders.[4] It has been somewhat reduced by the alignment in the following year of the long-term rate with the equivalent contributory pension rates: under the amended 1976 legislation the former are set out by reference to the basic component of a retirement pension including, where appropriate, the dependant's allowance (in 1982–83 £52.30 for a couple, and £32.70 for a single householder).[5]

The rationale for the differential between ordinary short-term and long-term rates is far from obvious.[6] It is not clear that those on benefit for a long time do necessarily have greater needs than those who claim it for a short period for a month or so. To some extent the former group will be able to adjust their expenditure and financial commitments to take account of the change in their circumstances, though of course it is undeniable that those on benefit for a long time will need to replace large items – for example, furniture and bedding – for which the ordinary rates may be insufficient. But the extent of the difference between the rates is hard to justify, and this makes it all the more important that the qualifying conditions for the higher rate are seen to be reasonable.

The long-term rate is payable automatically to pensioners. In the case of a couple, whether married or unmarried, it is the man's age for the moment which is relevant, though after November 1983, it will be enough if either is of pensionable age.[7] Under an important reform made in 1980 it is also payable to persons who have been continuously in receipt of an allowance for 52 weeks (previously the time was two years) and who throughout that period have not been required to register for employment.[8] The reduction in the qualifying period will benefit the sick and one-parent families, but the general inability of the unemployed ever to qualify for the long-term rate remains. This has become one of the more controversial aspects of the modern supplementary benefits system. At a time of rapidly rising unemployment, the SBC could see no reason, in terms of the rationales for the differential rates, for treating the long-term unemployed so relatively harshly.[9] It seems that cost is now the main argument for this rule, but neither *Social Assistance* nor the SBC thought this outweighed the fairness argument for extending the long-term rate to this vulnerable group. Some palliative is now provided by a recent regulation which enables a claimant of 60 or over to receive the higher rate after a year, even though he has not registered for work since he was 59.[10]

3 See the 1973 Review of Social Security Benefits (Cmnd 5288), para 19. The change was implemented by NISBA 1973, s.6.
4 SBC Annual Report 1979 (Cmnd 8033), para 9.21. The divergence was particularly strongly criticised in *Response of SBC to Social Assistance* paras 5.16–5.18.
5 SBA 1976, Sch 1, para 2.
6 See the discussion in the SBC Annual Report 1978, n.15, above, at paras 3.16–3.18, and in *Social Assistance* paras 5.34–5.37.
7 SBA 1976, s.1(1)(a), and Table to Sch 1, para 2.
8 SI 1980/1299, reg 7(1).
9 SBC Annual Report 1978, n.15, above, at paras 3.19–3.21. And see *Social Assistance* para 5.39.
10 SI 1981/1197, reg 2.

The new Social Security Advisory Committee has embarked on a study of the benefit position of the long-term unemployed.[11]

Further regulations relax the qualifying conditions in areas which were previously covered by the exercise of Commission discretion. Thus, a temporary interruption of 13 weeks in the required 52, when the claimant was either not in receipt of benefit at all or was required to register, will be disregarded.[12] And once entitlement to the long-term rate has been established, any period of up to 78 weeks in which the beneficiary was in hospital or specified residential accommodation will be ignored.[13] Another modification is that where a couple has been in receipt of the higher rate, because, for example, the husband was over pensionable age, the woman will be able immediately on his death or their separation to claim the long-term rate;[14] without this rule she could strictly be required to qualify herself after the usual one-year period, assuming she was herself not of pensionable age. It should be noted that the nominal 25p supplement, payable since 1971 if either the claimant *or his wife* is over 80 years old, is now paid as an additional requirement.[15]

iii Other special rates?

In the National Assistance Act 1948 there were two special rates: for blind persons and those who suffered a loss of income to undergo treatment for tuberculosis;[16] a power to make provision for other groups was never exercised as it was thought that it might be used unfairly. The 1966 legislation retained the special treatment of blind claimants, and later there was rather oddly particular provision for the case where attendance allowance could be paid for the claimant or one of his dependants. These somewhat anomalous rates have now been abolished, though such claimants may be entitled to an increase to weekly benefit for additional requirements referable to these handicaps.[17]

In a number of countries, notably West Germany, Holland and Denmark more generous assistance is given to single-parent families.[18] This impressed the Finer Committee, which recommended that there should be a special addition to both the ordinary and long-term rates for these families.[19] The proposal has not been implemented; the SBC Annual Report for 1978 cast some doubt on the argument that they had greater needs than two-parent families.[20] It is easier for a one-parent family to qualify for the higher long-term rate because such a parent will not be required to be available for work, and now there is a much more generous disregard of the part-time earnings of these persons.[1]

11 First report of the Social Security Advisory Committee, 1981, paras 3.3–3.18.
12 SI 1980/1299, reg 7(2)(c).
13 Ibid, reg 7(3).
14 Ibid, reg 7(4).
15 Pp. 477–480, below, for additional requirements.
16 NAA 1948, s.5(3).
17 P. 479, below.
18 See Appendix 3 to *Finer* paras 101–106.
19 Ibid, at paras 5.254–5.255.
20 Paras 4.28–4.39.
1 For the requirement to be available for work, see p. 459, above; for disregards of earnings, see p. 485, below.

C Housing requirements

i Policy

A feature of social assistance schemes since 1943 has been the payment of separate allowances for rent.[2] It is unusual in British social security law,[3] but can be justified by a number of arguments. First, there are significant variations in housing costs, and these cannot easily be covered by standard scale rates. This is not really the case for any other goods or services covered by an award of benefit. Secondly, while a claimant can adjust his expenditure on, say, food or clothing, this is impossible with housing costs. They have to be paid regularly, and it is unreasonable to expect someone to move to cheaper accommodation every time he is ill or unemployed, and has to fall back on benefit.[4]

Housing costs have formed a very significant portion of total supplementary benefits expenditure, and indeed many claimants only qualify for benefit at all because of their rent or other expenditure on accommodation.[5] It is expensive to administer and, as the rules discussed in the rest of this section show, adds considerably to the overall complexity of the scheme. Another drawback is that there is often overlap between the rent element of supplementary benefit and the rent rebates and allowances, and rate rebates, available from local authorities. A claimant has sometimes understandably been in considerable doubt as to whether it was better for him to claim benefit or the local authority allowance. For these reasons the Commission in its Annual Reports consistently urged the introduction of a single housing benefit which would be administered by local authorities and replace the variety of benefits and allowances mentioned above.[6] It would be available to all persons whose income was below a particular level, whether they were in work or not, and so would assist people on low incomes who are ineligible for supplementary benefits. In March 1981, the Department of the Environment issued a consultative document putting forward proposals similar to those suggested by the SBC.[7]

These proposals are now implemented in the Social Security and Housing Benefits Act 1982, though the new scheme will not come into effect until April 1983. The Secretary of State for Social Services is empowered to make by regulations rate rebate, rent rebate and rent allowance schemes to be administered by local rating and housing authorities.[8] Regulations may provide who is to be regarded as liable for rent and rate payments and therefore eligible for housing benefit and for treating one among joint occupiers as if he were the sole occupier of the premises.[9] Mortgage interest payments are, however, not covered by the new system, and will therefore continue to be regulated by the DHSS. Apart from this the Department's role in the administration of housing benefits after 1983 will be relatively small: it will issue the basic regulations

2 SR & O 1943 1759, Sch 1, para 1(2).
3 A supplementary rent allowance may be paid to a widow under the war pensions scheme; p. 359, above.
4 See generally *George* pp. 214 ff.
5 In its Annual Report 1979 (Cmnd 8033), para 4.2, the Commission estimated there were 0.3 million such claimants.
6 E.g. SBC Annual Report 1977 (Cmnd 7392), ch 8, and Annual Report 1979, n.5, above, at ch 4. Also see Donnison *The Politics of Poverty* (1982) pp. 184–193.
7 Consultative Document, *Assistance with Housing Costs*, issued by the Dept of the Environment (March 1981).
8 SSHBA 1982, s.28(1).
9 Ibid, s.28(2).

and pay the subsidies to the local authorities to offset their loss of revenue.[10] In essence supplementary benefit housing payments have been merged with a reformed system of local authority allowances and will no longer form part of the subject matter of this book.

As these reforms will not take effect until mid-1983, it is still important to give an account of the scheme under the Supplementary Benefits legislation. Under this the amount payable for housing requirements differs depending on whether the claimant is a householder or not. As we have seen,[11] this is also relevant for assessing normal requirements, though for that purpose the distinction is drawn a little differently. These points must be examined before we look at the variety of payments which may be made for housing requirements under the current law.

ii Householders and non-householders

Under the regulations, a person is to be treated as responsible for housing expenditure, and therefore eligible to have his *housing requirements* met, (a) if he is liable for that expenditure, whether as owner-occupier or a party to a lease or tenancy (though this does not apply if he is liable to a person who is a member of the same household), *or* (b) if, because the person actually liable is not meeting that expenditure, he has to meet it if he is to continue to live in the property and the benefit officer concludes it is reasonable to treat him as responsible.[12] Under this latter alternative, the housing requirements of squatters and licensees may be met in some circumstances; this was doubtful under the previous law.[13] The main purpose of the rule, however, is to allow a deserted wife to be treated as responsible for housing expenditure, when her husband refuses to keep up payments.[14] It is clear that the housing requirements of a person sharing responsibility for expenditure with others (as long as they are not close relatives) may be met by treating him in effect as a householder, though the amount payable to meet his requirements is to be calculated by reference to the appropriate proportion of the total expenditure.[15] This would apply to flat-sharing arrangements, and so perhaps solve the problems which the Court of Appeal had confronted somewhat unsatisfactorily before the recent reforms: it had refused to characterise students who shared the responsibility for rent and utility bills as householders.[16] But, even under the present law, where only one member of such a household is responsible for mortgage, rent or insurance payments, he is to be regarded as responsible for all housing items, whatever arrangements he has made with his flat-mates.[17]

However, in order to prevent too generous treatment of claimants in this situation, the regulations provide that for a person to be classified as a householder for *normal requirements*, he must not only be regarded as

10 Ibid, s.32. It is estimated that the increased administrative costs for local authorities will be between £15m and £19m, but this will be more than compensated by a saving of £25m to the DHSS in administrative expenses: Explanatory and Financial Memo. to the 1982 Bill.
11 P. 466, above.
12 SI 1980/1299 reg 14(3)(a), as amended by SI 1980/1774, Sch, para 9.
13 See the first edition, p. 496.
14 *Lynes* p. 66.
15 SI 1980/1299, reg 14(3)(b).
16 *R v Sheffield Supplementary Benefits Appeal Tribunal, ex parte Shine* [1975] 2 All ER 807, [1975] 1 WLR 624.
17 SI 1980/1774, Sch, para 9(b)(ii).

responsible for housing expenditure on the tests described in the previous paragraph, but also he must not share such responsibility with another member of the same household.[18] If he does share, he will be classified as a non-householder for normal requirements' assessment, but he will have his benefit increased then by the difference between the non-householder's and householder's rate divided by the number of persons in the household sharing the household expenditure.[19] These rules, though complex, do clarify the law to some extent. But they do not try to define a 'household' (any more than the comparable provisions do in the context of the 'living together' rule), and so there is still plenty of scope for argument how to assess the requirements of, say, a group of three or four people, who share payment of rent and some common facilities, but are individually responsible for their own use of electricity and other utilities and their own general household expenditure. In this case it is arguable they constitute separate households, and are entitled to have their normal requirements assessed at the higher rate for householders.

iii The items of housing requirements

These items set out in the Requirements Regulations comprise rent, mortgage payments, repairs and insurance, interest on loans for repairs and improvements, miscellaneous outgoings (such as rates and ground rents), and the items applicable in special cases. The amount paid for a non-householder's contribution is treated later. The rest of this section discusses the other items in more detail. A claimant will be awarded benefit for those items which are appropriate to his case: in many instances, of course, he may be entitled in respect of two or more items – for example, an owner-occupier will usually be entitled to benefit in respect of his mortgage payments, and for maintenance and insurance. Where the amounts payable for these items are excessive, they may be restricted under the regulations – the equivalent of the former 'rent-stop' provision which was applied by the Commission in its discretion. As under the law before the reforms, the amount may also be reduced by the sums paid, or assumed to be paid, as rent by other occupants of the claimant's home. These general rules are discussed in the next two sections. In some cases benefit for rent or board and lodging charges may be paid directly to the landlord: these circumstances are discussed in Part 10 of the chapter.

a *Rent*

This is the sum, calculated on a weekly basis, of 'the rent payable for the home and of any additional charge made by a landlord in respect of the home because of letting of any part of the home, taking in lodgers or accommodating non-dependants'.[1] But where the rent includes sums payable for heating, lighting, cooking, hot water or other matters, which are covered by the benefit paid for normal requirements, deductions (the amount of which is specified in the regulations) are made from the sum payable for rent.[2] Otherwise there would be over generous provision. Rent rebates and allowances paid under the Housing Finance Act 1972, which will continue for the first eight weeks during which the claimant is on

18 SI 1980/1299, reg 5(2).
19 Ibid, reg 6(2).
20 Ibid, reg 14(1).
1 Ibid, reg 15(1).
2 Ibid, reg 15(3).

benefit, must also be deducted.[3] (As the deductions for sub-letting and for occupation by non-dependants are applicable to all types of benefit for housing requirements, they are considered later.)

b *Mortgage payments*

The repayments of mortgage interest, but not capital, are covered by housing requirements on condition that the mortgage has been 'taken out for the purpose of acquiring an interest in the home . . .'.[4] There are two exceptions to this general condition. First, where it is taken out for business purposes and the mortgager intends to sell his interest to meet business debts, benefit may be paid to cover the interest for six months.[5] And secondly, it may be paid for an unlimited period where the mortgage was initially taken out (for a reason other than house purchase) by one member of a couple, who has since left the other in the house, and the latter (generally, a deserted wife) has to pay the interest to continue living there.[6] Mortgage payments are, of course, not covered by local authority rent rebates and allowances and are, therefore, wholly unaffected by the 1982 Act.

It was never the Commission's policy to pay benefit for capital repayments, and this is now reflected in the regulations. The argument is presumably that public money should not be used to allow individuals to acquire capital assets, but this seems implausible in view of home improvement grants and concessions to house purchase by council tenants. On the other hand, income tax relief is only allowed on the interest part of mortgage repayments.[7] A mortgagor, who claims supplementary benefit, should therefore attempt to persuade his building society to accept interest payments only and defer capital repayment. There is nevertheless one provision in the regulations which may assist mortgagors who are required to repay capital: in some circumstances they may set-off such repayments against the proceeds of sub-letting their property, which would otherwise be deducted in full.[8]

c *Maintenance and insurance*

A weekly amount of £1.50, or where costs are greater, such higher amount as is reasonable, is payable weekly for maintenance and insurance.[9] This is defined in the regulations as 'essential routine minor maintenance of the home and insurance of the structure of the home'. More major repairs may be covered by the award of a single payment (see Part 5).

d *Interest on loans for repairs and improvements*

This head covers loans for major repairs to the fabric of the home, and for a number of specifically itemised measures, e.g. damp-proofing, provision for heating (including central heating), and installation of bathroom fixtures. A residual clause covers loans for 'other improvements which are reasonable in the circumstances'.[10] Where the claimant has more than £300 capital, benefit will only be paid to cover the interest on the sum borrowed

3 Ibid.
4 Ibid, reg 16(1).
5 Ibid, reg 16(4).
6 Ibid, reg 16(3).
7 Tiley *Revenue Law* (3rd edn) paras 10.10–10.13.
8 SI 1980/1299, reg 22(2)(c): see p. 475, below, for this type of deduction.
9 Ibid, reg 17. The amount was increased to £1.50 by SI 1981/513.
10 SI 1980/1299, reg 18.

less the excess capital.[11] Thus, if C has £500 capital and borrows £800 for home improvements, he will only be entitled to benefit for interest on £600 (that is, £800 minus £200). There is a similar rule for taking into account capital resources when making single payments.[12]

e *Miscellaneous outgoings*

This head covers rates (less any rate rebate), water rates, ground rents and service charges, and (interestingly) contributions to the cost of improvements made by a squatters' organisation or association, provided the home in question is occupied with the owner's permission.[13]

f *Special cases*

Benefit to meet housing requirements is also payable where the claimant incurs expenditure in a variety of ways not covered by the preceding rules, e.g. for the use of a caravan or houseboat as his home.[14] In some unusual circumstances, housing benefit may be paid for two homes – this can be done for up to four weeks where overlap of liability cannot be avoided, or indefinitely where reasonable because a claimant has to leave one home for fear of domestic violence.[15]

iv Restriction of housing requirements where amounts excessive

Before the reforms of 1980 the Commission had discretion not to pay the full rent where it considered this was unreasonable. The administration of the 'rent-stop' provision used to cause great controversy, and gradual relaxation of the SBC policies meant that nearly all rents were in fact met in full.[16] Under the new regulations the amounts payable under any of the various heads may be reduced insofar as they are excessive, judged by reference to the unnecessary size of the property in relation to the claimant's family (and any non-dependants living with them), or to the location of the house in a particularly expensive area.[17] In the case of rent, the amount may also be reduced if it is excessive in comparison to that charged for comparable property in the area.[18]

The regulations, however, also reproduce the policies introduced by the Commission to soften the harshness of the rule. The rent-stop is not to be applied if it is unreasonable to expect the claimant and his family to find alternative cheaper accommodation, taking into account for this purpose its availability and the age, health and job prospects of the claimant, and also the impact of a move on the education of his dependants.[19] Even in other cases, it may be hard to expect someone to move to cheaper accommodation; for example, he might have been able previously to afford relatively expensive property and have temporarily fallen on hard times. In these circumstances, if the benefit officer thinks the claimant will not be

11 Ibid, reg 18(2).
12 P. 489, below.
13 SI 1980/1299, reg 19.
14 Ibid, reg 20, as amended by SI 1980/1774, Sch, para 13.
15 SI 1980/1299, reg 20(4).
16 In 1975, only 0.6% of rents were not met in full: SBC Annual Report 1975 (Cmnd 6615), para 44. Detailed figures were not published in later reports, but in the last one, Annual Report 1979 (Cmnd 8033), the SBC commented that only a tiny proportion do not have full payments, and local authority rents are always fully met: para 4.14.
17 SI 1980/1299, reg 21(2)(a).
18 Ibid, reg 21(2)(b).
19 Ibid, regs 21(3) and (5).

dependent on benefit for longer than six months, the rent-stop will not be applied for the first six months of his period of entitlement, and it will not be for the next half year, provided the claimant uses his best endeavours to find cheaper accommodation.[20]

v Reduction of housing requirements where the home is let, etc.

As explained earlier, these reductions may be applied to the amounts payable for any kind of housing requirement. Where the property is let (whether on a tenancy or licence), calculation of the reduction is relatively easy: it is the amount receivable from the letting less (a) the incidental expenses of the letting (specified in the regulations), (b) reasonable amounts in respect of heating, lighting and other facilities, and (c) in some circumstances an amount attributable to mortgage *capital* repayments where the interest on those payments is met by an award of benefit.[1]

The Commission also used under its discretionary powers to reduce rent payments by amounts which were assumed to be paid to the claimant by any non-dependants (for example, an adult son or daughter) sharing his accommodation. The SBC's policies were complicated and could cause hardship.[2] One of the government's objectives as stated in the White Paper was to simplify the position;[3] it is doubtful whether they have succeeded. The deduction for an assumed housing contribution is mandatory, except for blind claimants, or where the non-dependant is providing domestic assistance for the claimant in a case where benefit would be paid for additional requirements, or where his usual home is elsewhere (and he is only temporarily sharing the claimant's house).[4] The contribution is assessed at two standard levels. In three situations it is assessed at a lower level of £3.10. These are first, where the non-dependant is himself entitled to supplementary benefit; secondly, where though not so entitled he is under 18; and thirdly, where he would be entitled if a claim for benefit were made and his housing requirements were assessed at the maximum fixed for a non-householder's housing requirements, at present £6.55.[5] In these situations hardship to the non-dependants is avoided, or mitigated, by the assumption of a lower contribution to the claimant's rent. The assumed contribution in all other cases is now £6.55. The Handbook gives a helpful example of how all this works.[6] If a household consists of a claimant, his wife, a 20-year-old son in full-time work, and a daughter in receipt of supplementary benefit, and the claimant pays £20.00 in rent, the son's assumed contribution is £6.55, and the daughter's is the modified contribution of £3.10.

vi The non-householder's contribution

The distinction between a householder and non-householder has already been discussed.[7] If a claimant is living in another person's household, and is paying a regular sum for accommodation and food, it is probable that his

20 Ibid, reg 21(4).
1 Ibid, regs 22(1) and (2).
2 See the first edition, pp. 497–498.
3 *Reform of the Supplementary Benefits Scheme* (1979, Cmnd 7773), para 18.
4 SI 1980/1299, regs 22(3) and (5), as amended by SI 1981/1016, reg 2(12).
5 SI 1980/1299, reg 22(4). These rules are applied to the non-dependant's 'assessment unit' if he himself is living with his own dependants.
6 Para 6.11.
7 Pp. 471–472, above.

requirements will be assessed as those of a boarder: this is discussed in the next section. A non-householder, who would typically be living in a parent's or other relative's home, is treated less generously in the supplementary benefits scheme on the reasonable assumption that he has fewer requirements. His normal requirements, if he is single, are assessed at a lower rate than a householder's.[8] In the standard case, he is paid a weekly amount of £3.10 for his assumed contribution to the expenses of the household of which he is a member. Previously the SBC had discretion in 'exceptional circumstances' to increase this rate when appropriate. Now under the regulations an increased payment (up to a maximum of £6.55) may be made, where the claimant establishes first, that in view of his actual contribution, £3.10 is inadequate, secondly, that if he were not paid more, hardship would occur having regard to the resources of the household as a whole, *and* thirdly, that he became a member of the household on the clear understanding that he would pay more than that amount.[9] The Social Security Commissioners in *R(SB) 4/81* and *R(SB) 16/81* have emphasised that all these conditions must be satisfied for the higher rate to be paid. In two other cases it has been pointed out that the third condition is difficult to apply where the claimant is living in a relative's household; in effect it is enough in these circumstances if there is a genuine agreement that the former cannot *continue* to live in the household unless he pays his relative more than £3.10 a week.[10]

vii Boarders

As under the previous law, boarders are treated separately in the regulations. As their requirements are assessed on the whole more generously than non-householders', it is important for the distinction between these groups to be drawn clearly.

a *When is a claimant treated as a boarder?*

In the regulations he is defined as a person who (1) pays a charge inclusive of his accommodation and at least some cooked meals, prepared and consumed on the premises, or (2) is living in an hotel, guest-house or other similar premises.[11] But the definition excludes any person whose accommodation and meals (if any) are provided by a close relative (that is, a parent, step-parent, child or step-child, brother or sister) *or* other than on a commercial basis. This seems to follow the Commission's policy which was to regard the payment for board and lodging 'on a commercial basis' as necessary to acquire the status of a boarder. On occasions this test was applied fairly strictly, so that the existence of any personal relationship between lodger and landlord was enough to classify the former as a non-householder.[12] In other cases it seems a broader approach was taken, so that, for example, where a prisoner, released on parole, lived with his fiancée's parents, he was held by the appeal tribunal to be a boarder.[13] The same result might be reached now if he could satisfy the first alternative test mentioned above. But it is now clear from the regulation that no matter what arrangements a claimant makes with his parents or

8 SI 1980/1299, reg 23.
9 Ibid, reg 23(1)(b).
10 *R(S) 11/81*; *CSB 34/81*.
11 SI 1980/1299, reg 9(9), amended by SI 1980/1774, Sch, para 5.
12 See the case mentioned in [1974] LAG Bulletin 82 (April), and the discussion in the first edition, pp. 502–503.
13 (1972) 24 Poverty 29.

brother or sister, he cannot be classified as a boarder;[14] this avoids the risk of any abuse through collusive arrangements. Finally, it should be noted that also excluded from the category of 'boarders' are certain special cases: for example, persons living in local authority homes, attending residential re-establishment centres, prisoners and patients.[15] They are discussed briefly in Part 9 of the chapter.

b *A boarder's requirements*

He is entitled to a weekly amount for board and lodging, and also an allowance for personal expenses. The aggregate of these sums must not fall below a minimum amount, equivalent to the aggregate of the ordinary (or long-term, where appropriate) rate for couples or a single non-householder, as the case may be, plus the non-householder's housing contribution.[16] The weekly amount for board and lodging is to be the full amount of the charge, subject to a maximum amount assessed partly by reference to reasonable charges for suitable accommodation in the area.[17] This 'local limit', as it is known, is equivalent to the rent-stop provision discussed earlier. It may be exceeded where the claimant has attained pensionable age, is on the long-term rate, or is infirm.[18] Board and lodging charges above the limit may also be paid, where it is unreasonable to expect the claimant to look for alternative lodging, unless he can meet the excess out of disregarded income[19] (see Part 4 of this chapter). For 1982–83, the allowances for personal expenses are £17.00 for a couple and half this for a single person (£18.90 for a couple on the long-term rate, and half that amount for a single person on that rate).[20]

D Additional requirements

i General

Additional payments for claimants with special needs have always been a feature of public assistance in modern times. In 1934 they were known as special circumstances payments when introduced in the unemployment assistance scheme,[1] and their importance grew under national assistance after the war.[2] In 1966 they became exceptional circumstances additions (ECAs); the introduction of the long-term addition, later long-term rate, for pensioners and others who had been in receipt of benefit for two years, was intended to reduce reliance on discretionary supplements to the scale rates, but in the 1970s the number of beneficiaries relying on them gradually increased.[3] By the end of 1976 just under half of all claimants were in receipt of ECAs, the majority of them being pensioners. Much the most common awards were for extra heating requirements (63 per cent of the total), dietary needs (19 per cent) and extra laundry costs (8 per cent).[4]

14 See *R(SB) 11/81*, para 6.
15 SI 1980/1299, reg 9(9), and see reg 10 for their requirements.
16 Ibid, regs 9(1) and (3).
17 Ibid, reg 9(4).
18 Ibid, regs 9(4)(a)(b) and (c).
19 Ibid, reg 9(5).
20 Ibid, reg 9(8).
1 See the historical survey in SBC Annual Report 1976 (Cmnd 6910), Appendix C.
2 Thus, at the end of 1948 only 26% of those in receipt of assistance were obtaining a special circumstance addition, but by 1966 the corresponding figure was 58%: ibid, para 7.3.
3 For the long-term rates, see pp. 467–469, above. Stevenson *Claimant or Client?* (1973) pp. 41 ff. contains a good discussion of the merits of this change.
4 *Social Assistance* para 9.6.

The increased reliance on ECAs – and the single Exceptional Needs Payments (see Part 5) – was unsatisfactory for a number of reasons. First, it considerably complicated the scheme and claimants' awareness of their entitlements; secondly, they were expensive to administer; and thirdly, their award at officer's discretion was inevitably sometimes unfair between individual claimants, and inconsistent through the country. Perhaps the main drawback was that there were no legal rules stipulating the circumstances in which ECAs might be made or maximum payments. Officers were bound in practice, if not in law, by the policies of the SBC, but appeal tribunals were not, and frequently appeals could succeed to secure the award of an additional payment outside the guidance issued in the Commission's Handbook.[5]

Social Assistance made a number of radical criticisms of the position which existed at that time. Heating additions had become in effect automatic supplements for many claimants, particularly pensioners, and could profitably be consolidated into the scale rates. Alternatively, the qualifying conditions could be simplified and the number of rates at which these ECAs were paid under Commission guidelines could be reduced.[6] The report was sceptical of the need to continue special diet payments, the medical justification for which was often uncertain.[7] Most importantly, entitlement to weekly additional payments should be set out in regulations or a Code of Practice, though there should be room for residual officer discretion for the genuinely exceptional case.[8]

The 1980 reforms adopt some of these proposals but by no means all. Weekly amounts for additional requirements are now to be paid as a matter of right when they are applicable to the claimant's case.[9] Rules of entitlement are set out with meticulous particularity in the regulations, and the appropriate amount specified for each addition. There is no room for discretion: the officer must simply decide whether the claim fits the description in the statutory instrument and then make an award of the sum specified; there is no general, or residual discretion for cases not covered by the rules.[10] The bolder of *Social Assistance*'s suggestions for the reform of heating payments was not accepted, nor was its proposal to phase out dietary additions. As heating payments will almost certainly continue to be the most important of the sums paid for additional requirements, more space is devoted to them than to the other payments which may be made.

ii Heating

For the last three or four years of its existence, the Supplementary Benefits Commission pressed the case for a major reconsideration of the methods by which help with fuel costs was given to the poorer sections of the community.[11] The relatively generous heating ECAs assisted those on benefit, but of course did nothing for the working poor; this discrimination, in conjunction with the increasing importance of fuel costs in family

5 Ibid, paras 9.51–9.52, and see for a discussion of this and other weaknesses of the discretionary system: SBC Annual Report 1979 (Cmnd 8033) ch 16; Donnison *The Politics of Poverty* (1982) pp. 89–100.
6 *Social Assistance* paras 9.16–9.32.
7 Ibid, paras 9.34–9.35.
8 Ibid, paras 9.48–9.49.
9 SBA 1976, Sch 1, para 2(2), and SI 1980/1299, reg 11(1).
10 See *R(SB) 12/81*.
11 E.g. SBC Annual Report 1977 (Cmnd 7392), paras 10.19–10.23; SBC Annual Report 1978 (Cmnd 7725), paras 5.5–5.19. Also see *Donnison*, n.5, above, at pp. 193–198.

budgets after the energy crisis, induced the Commission to suggest a national fuel allowance scheme, which (like its proposal for housing benefit) would assist all those in need. Instead the present government has dramatically increased the assistance for recipients of supplementary benefit, a move which the SBC castigated as 'the strategy of the blunderbuss'.[12]

Thus, there was an increase of nearly 50 per cent in the lower rate of heating addition, now £1.90 a week, which under the regulations is paid if a member of the claimant's assessment unit (that is, claimant, partner and dependants) is a person for whom extra warmth should be provided because he suffers from chronic ill-health, due to bronchitis, rheumatism, etc.[13] In more serious cases, e.g. where the person suffers from illness or disability to such an extent that he is unable to leave home alone, or from an illness which requires a constant temperature to be maintained, there is a higher rate, now £4.65 a week.[14] An important provision is that under which the lower heating addition is automatically paid where one member of the assessment unit is 70 or over, or under five:[15] this saves administrative costs in determining need in cases, where it is likely that additional heating expenditure may be incurred, though it will mean inevitably that some money will go to those who do not really need it.

The regulations also contain a number of miscellaneous, detailed rules with regard to the award of these payments. Except in some of the more serious cases, no heating need is to be met where any member of the assessment unit (not necessarily the person in respect of whom the amount would otherwise be payable) is affected by a trade dispute.[16] There are various overlap provisions designed to prevent duplication of payments where the sums paid for rent or for board and lodging charges already cover (altogether or to some extent) heating costs.[17]

iii Other items

The Schedule to the Requirements Regulations lists some 12 other items for which an award for additional requirements may be made.[18] They include special diets, hospital fares, laundry costs, charges for the storage of furniture and hire purchase instalments. The circumstances in which such an award may be made and the amount of the payments are set out in great detail, and space does not allow for full discussion here.[19] Three of the items concern requirements which used to be covered by special weekly rates rather than ECAs: the age addition of 25p, payable where one member of the assessment unit is 80 or over, the payment for attendance needs and the increase for blind persons. Again, there is generally no entitlement where any member of the assessment unit is a person affected by a trade dispute.[20]

One of the problems which used to give rise to difficulties under the 1966 legislation was the relationship between the long-term rate and ECAs: as

12 SBC Annual Report 1979 (Cmnd 8033), para 3.4.
13 SI 1980/1299, Sch 3, para 1(1). (See *CSB 30/81*.)
14 Ibid, Sch 3, paras 1(2) and (3).
15 Ibid, Sch 3, para 7. For further details of payments for heating requirements, see *Lynes* pp. 88–91.
16 SI 1980/1299, regs 12(2)(a) and (b).
17 Ibid, regs 12(2)(h) and 12(4).
18 Ibid, Sch 3, paras 8–19.
19 For a full discussion, see *Lynes* ch 4. Also see Handbook, ch 5.
20 SI 1980/1299, regs 13(3) and (4).

the former was introduced for certain groups of recipients to obviate the need for discretionary supplements (at least to some extent), it was thought right that there should be in some circumstances a deduction from an ECA when it was awarded to a claimant in receipt of the higher rate of weekly benefit.[1] The regulations now provide for an automatic 50p deduction to be made in this situation, though this does not apply to amounts paid for certain of a dependant's additional requirements, e.g. for attendance or dietary needs. Nor does it apply to the additional benefit paid to blind persons or, of course, the 25p age addition.[2] (As under the previous law, there is also no deduction from an award for heating requirements.)

Part 4 The assessment of resources

A General

In order to calculate the weekly benefit payable to the claimant, his resources are deducted from the total of his requirements (normal, housing and additional), as assessed under the rules discussed in Part 3. Here we are concerned with the rules used to assess resources. Frequently, of course, the claimant will be completely destitute and have no resources of any sort; in that case, benefit is simply assessed in terms of his weekly requirements. In many cases, however, he will have some savings and will also, or alternatively, be in receipt of other social security benefits or part-time earnings, some or all of which may be deducted from the sum representing his requirements to arrive at the correct amount of benefit.

In principle it might seem right to deduct all the applicant's resources. But under both the National Assistance Act 1948 and the subsequent supplementary benefits legislation, some of them have been wholly or partially ignored, or 'disregarded' to use the term of art employed in the regulations. The effect of these 'disregards' is to raise the poverty line, for those people with some capital or income, above the weekly scale rates of benefit, and it is partly for this reason that these rates prove a misleading guide to the true extent of poverty in the country.[3] Moreover, the disregards can be used to discriminate between different categories of claimant. *Social Assistance* did indeed pose the question whether the disregards could be justified. The report concluded that it was right to allow them for a variety of reasons: in the case of capital, the rule encouraged saving, and for earnings, it encouraged self-help. A balance had to be struck between these principles and the general policy that assistance should be directed to those who needed it most and not to those who enjoyed substantial resources of their own.[4]

Since the National Assistance Act 1948, only the applicant's resources, and those of his wife (or woman with whom he is living) and dependants, have been taken into account.[5] The ability of any other relatives to maintain him is wholly irrelevant to the computation of his resources. Yet this was challenged by the Commission in *R v West London Supplementary*

1 See the first edition, pp. 518–519.
2 SI 1980/1299, regs 13(5) and (6).
3 *Townsend* p. 244.
4 Paras 8.9–8.10.
5 See now SBA 1976, Sch 1, paras 1(2) and 3(1).

Benefits Appeal Tribunal, ex parte Clarke,[6] at least until the case came before the Divisional Court:

> The applicant, a widow and Indian citizen, was allowed to enter the UK after her son-in-law had given the immigration authorities an undertaking to support her. She lived with him for about two-and-a-half years before she moved to her son's house. She then claimed benefit, but this was refused on the ground that she had weekly resources of £11.50, calculated by reference, it seems, to her son-in-law's undertaking. The decision was upheld by the appeal tribunal.

The Court held that neither the son-in-law nor the son had an obligation to look after her, and that, therefore, the family's resources were irrelevant. Neither the SBC nor the tribunal had considered whether the applicant was *in fact* being fully maintained.[7]

Detailed rules for the calculation of an applicant's resources are now set out in separate regulations; these include the level of the disregards, which may be increased by statutory instrument, whereas previously they could only be up-rated by statute. It is to be hoped they will, therefore, be increased more often to keep pace with inflation.[8] Two general topics must be discussed before the particular provisions for determining what is to be taken into account and what is to be disregarded are examined. First, there is the distinction between capital and income, and secondly, the important general principle that in many circumstances an applicant will be treated as if he has resources (notional resources) which he does not actually have to hand.

B The distinction between capital and income

It is important for this distinction to be drawn clearly because, as will be seen,[9] there is a disregard of capital up to £2,500, while virtually all income payments are taken into account in assessing benefit. It may often be to a claimant's advantage to persuade the officer that a particular payment is to be regarded as capital rather than income. The regulations, in this respect following income tax law,[10] do not draw a general distinction between the two, though often it will be a matter of common sense on which side of the line a payment falls. In a decision before the recent amendments, the High Court held that income consists of periodic payments, which are an accretion to the recipient's wealth, and that instalments of a capital sum are to be treated as capital payments.[11] The distinction between capital and income raised a matter of law for the court (now for the Social Security Commissioner).[12] The new regulations classify some particular payments. Thus, the following are treated as capital resources:[13]

6 [1975] 1 WLR 1396.
7 A regular contribution from a relative is treated as a resource of the claimant, though there is a partial disregard: p. 487, below.
8 The disregards were not increased at all from 1966 to 1975; any changes had to be made by amendment to the legislation: see first edition, pp. 507–508.
9 P. 484, below.
10 See Tiley *Revenue Law* (3rd edn) paras 2.31–2.33.
11 *Lillystone v Supplementary Benefits Commission, Decisions of the Courts* SB 37. The decision was reversed on another ground by the Court of Appeal (1981) Times 30 October.
12 See ch 15, pp. 613–614, below, for the right of appeal to the Commissioners.
13 SI 1981/1527, reg 3(2).

(a) any grant or gratuity paid under the Social Security Act 1975;
(b) in most circumstances, income tax repayments;
(c) a lump sum maintenance payment (whether or not under a court order) when the effect of treating it as capital would be to raise the claimant's capital resources above the £2,500 limit.

On the other hand, the outstanding instalments of a lump sum (not a maintenance payment) will be treated as income, where if they were treated as capital, the claimant's total capital resources would be sufficient to disqualify him altogether. This appears to reverse the High Court decision in *Lillystone* which had held these instalments to be capital. Also treated as income are tax refunds paid to a claimant out of work because of a trade dispute at his place of work, or because employment has been temporarily suspended:[14] this is an exception to the general rule, under which such repayments are regarded as capital.

These provisions have already come before the Social Security Commissioner. In *R(SB) 7/81* the issue was how to treat a sum of over £3,000 which represented the balance of capital owed and payable by instalments to the claimant's wife by her former husband on a property adjustment order. After adverting to some of the difficulties which undeniably exist in construing the regulations, the Commissioner, D G Rice, rather surprisingly held that a 'lump sum' was to be defined as 'a commutation of a periodic payment', and, therefore, did not include a sum paid on a property settlement after divorce.[15] This seems to be an unduly narrow view. In any case, the regulation is clearly not designed to be an exhaustive statement of what constitutes income and capital; it is submitted that on any common sense approach, the sum in question was clearly capital.[16]

C Notional resources

The regulations make it plain that in certain cases account may be taken of the claimant's notional resources, and not only of the actual resources he has in his possession at the moment of making his claim. This was the view taken by the Court of Appeal (before the recent reforms) when 'resources' were left undefined in the Act or by regulation.[17] There are two principal sets of circumstances in which this principle will be applied. First, any resource of which a person has deprived himself for the purpose of securing benefit may be treated as if it were still his.[18] This is a clear anti-abuse provision, designed to prevent someone deliberately disposing of his assets in order to obtain benefit. It is not enough for the claimant to have been very careless in looking after his property immediately before his claim; his predominant motive must have been to secure benefit as soon as possible.[19] But there is clearly room for judgment on the part of the benefit officer whether to treat the lost asset as a resource. This is also true of the second set of circumstances, really the converse of the first. If it is reasonable to do so, a claimant may be regarded as possessing a resource which would be

14 Ibid, reg 3(2)(d)(i). See p. 505, below.
15 *R(SB) 7/81*, paras 12–13.
16 The Commissioner might have come to this conclusion himself, but his powers are restricted to considering the tribunal's holding: p. 614, below, for the Commissioners' powers on appeals from SBATs.
17 *R v Preston Supplementary Benefits Appeal Tribunal, ex parte Moore* [1975] 2 All ER 807, [1975] 1 WLR 624.
18 SI 1981/1527, reg 4(1).
19 *CSB 28/81*, para 17.

available to him if he applied for it, or is owing to him, but has not been paid.[20] (This does not apply to social security payments which have been delayed in payment.)

A claimant *may* also be treated as possessing an amount, calculated by reference to comparable employment, where he has performed a service for another person who has either not paid for it at all, or has paid less than that paid in comparable employment.[1] Presumably this rule is designed to prevent collusive arrangements; it should not be used where a poorly paid claimant did not intend to abuse the system. In other situations there is no discretion; thus, a student is to be regarded as in possession of any contribution which has been taken into account in assessing his grant – unless he is a single parent, member of a married or unmarried couple, or disabled – and a person is to be treated as in possession of the whole, or an appropriate share of, a discretionary trust of which he is a beneficiary.[2] Payments made in respect of a claimant's assessment unit (claimant, partner and dependant) are to be treated as his, even though they were actually made to a third party: this is another anti-abuse provision.[3]

D Capital resources

i Disregarded capital

Certain capital resources are to be wholly disregarded. Here the new law to a large extent follows the disregards which used to be allowed mainly at the Commission's discretion. Much the most important is the disregard of the value of the claimant's home, defined as the property normally occupied by the family and any other members of the same household.[4] Although it is not explicit in the regulations, it seems fairly clear that a person who divides his time between two properties would not be entitled to have the value of both disregarded.[5] In addition to the value of a home actually occupied, the value of the following are to be disregarded:[6]

(a) premises acquired by the assessment unit, which are intended to be the home within six months of acquisition, or a longer period if reasonable;
(b) premises which are for sale, and the value of which it is reasonable to disregard for the period during which the sale will be completed;
(c) premises, occupied by an aged or incapacitated relative of any member of the assessment unit;
(d) business assets, owned wholly or partly by a member of the assessment unit, for such period as is reasonable;
(e) any personal possessions, except those which are an investment and those which in view of their type and value should not be disregarded, e.g. works of art, expensive jewellery.

If the beneficiary sells his house, the proceeds are disregarded if it is intended to use them for the purchase of another home within six months,

20 SI 1981/1527, reg 4(2). The Handbook, para 3.32, suggests this rule might be applied where the claimant did not take steps to recover a loan.
1 SI 1981/1527, reg 4(3).
2 Ibid, regs 4(4) and (6).
3 Ibid, reg 4(5).
4 Ibid, regs 6(1)(a) and 2(1).
5 A taxpayer is only exempt from capital transfer and capital gains tax on one residence: Tiley *Revenue Law* (3rd edn) para 21.44.
6 SI 1981/1527, reg 6(1).

or a longer period if this is reasonable.[7] Otherwise he will lose his entitlement to benefit, since his capital will be over £2,500; now if he arranges for the proceeds to be paid in instalments, each payment will be treated as income and taken into account, subject to the disregard of £4 a week.[8]

All other resources are taken into account and assessed at their current market or similar value, less any sum which would be attributable to the expenses of sale and any outstanding debt or mortgage secured on them.[9] If they are worth less than £2,500 they are wholly disregarded, and (subject to income resources) the claimant is entitled to benefit.[10]

ii The capital cut-off

If the claimant's capital resources, however, are assessed, subject to disregards, at more than £2,500, he is not entitled to benefit at all. This marks a sharp change from the previous law, under which capital above £1,200 was treated as producing a tariff income.[11] The new rule was one of the possibilities suggested in *Social Assistance* to simplify the law.[12] Though arguably rather harsh, it seems that the majority of families affected are childless and therefore, perhaps, not among the most vulnerable groups. The step is undeniably one of the few respects in which the scheme has been rendered more comprehensible, and that is certainly a strong point in its favour.

In assessing capital, the resources of the claimant's wife (or woman with whom he is living) and dependants are naturally taken into account under the aggregation rules. But the capital cut-off rule is mitigated by a provision under which if a claimant's capital only exceeds £2,500 because of a dependant's resources, they are disregarded as capital and treated as producing a weekly income equivalent to that payable for the latter's weekly requirements (normal and additional).[13] In effect this means that the claimant retains his entitlement to benefit, and his dependant's requirements are ignored.

E Income resources

This consists of first, earnings, including a partner's, but not a dependant's, earnings, and secondly, all other income of the family (or 'assessment unit') calculated under the regulations.[14] As benefit is assessed and paid weekly, there are some general rules for attributing income resources to particular periods and treating them as paid at a weekly rate. Thus, income is to be taken into account as a resource for a period either equal to that period for which it is payable, or otherwise to which it is attributable. And it is to be treated as paid at a weekly rate beginning on the first day of the benefit week in which it is payable, or a later week if more practicable.[15] (However, where income is payable in a week before the benefit week, it is

7 Ibid, reg 6(1)(b).
8 See pp. 486–487, below, for treatment of income.
9 See *R(SB) 14/81*.
10 SI 1981/1527, reg 6(2). The cut-off was raised from £2,000 to £2,500, in 1982.
11 For how tariff income was calculated, see first edition, p. 506.
12 Paras 8.11–8.14.
13 SI 1981/1527, reg 8(1).
14 Ibid, reg 9(1).
15 Ibid, reg 9(2).

to be treated as a resource for that time.)[16] These provisions confirm the ruling of Sheen J in *R v Manchester Supplementary Benefit Appeal Tribunal, ex parte Riley*,[17] that wages paid on their due date, although paid in arrears for *past* work, are to be treated as *present* income resources for the week when the applicant claims benefit. Where a claimant has fluctuating earnings, or does not work every week, they may be averaged over the period the benefit officer thinks reasonable in the circumstances.[18]

i Earnings

These are defined as 'all remuneration or profit, calculated on a weekly basis, derived from any employment', and they include: remuneration in kind, a bonus or commission, any payment in lieu of notice, holiday pay (other than any received more than four weeks after the end of employment) and a retainer.[19] The provisions concerning the resources of strikers are discussed later.[20]

The earnings taken into account, or disregarded, have always been net earnings, and, therefore, a number of items are ignored or deducted in assessing them. These include the value of one free daily meal provided at work, a Christmas bonus up to £10, the pre-retirement earnings of a person entitled to a retirement pension, income tax deducted by the employer, social security contributions and reasonable travel expenses.[1] All the net earnings so determined of the claimant or his partner are taken into account, except for the first £4.00, which is disregarded.[2] However, in the case of a lone parent, an additional amount equal to one half of the amount by which his or her earnings exceed £4.00, but do not come to more than £20, will be disregarded.[3] Thus a single parent earning £20 a week from part-time work will have £12 disregarded (that is, the basic £4 plus half the difference between £20 and £4). This taper will replace the previous higher disregard for £6 for lone parents, and it is estimated it will benefit far more people than it disadvantages.[4] Unlike the change in treatment of capital, this differential somewhat complicates the scheme: *Social Assistance* in contrast had recommended preserving the previous £2 differential for lone parents.[5] In any case it is not easy to see whether it is more important for this group to be encouraged to maintain links with work than other groups such as the disabled. Another change from the previous law is that there is now no discrimination between the disregard for a person required to register or be available for work and others.[6] Finally there is no disregard for the amount treated as earnings of strikers under the special rule discussed in Part 7 of the chapter,[7] or the earnings received by (or an advance offered to) a person returning to work after a trade dispute.[8]

16 Ibid, reg 9(2)(b)(i).
17 [1979] 2 All ER 1, [1979] 1 WLR 426, noted [1978–9] JSWL 18, and see Loosemore [1979] LAG Bulletin 260 (November).
18 SI 1981/1527, reg 9(2)(d).
19 Ibid, reg 10(1).
20 P. 505, below.
1 SI 1981/1527, regs 10(3) and (4).
2 Ibid, reg 10(5)(a).
3 Ibid, reg 10(5)(b).
4 See Standing Committee E Debates on the Social Security Bill 1980, col 558.
5 Paras 8.21–8.24.
6 See pp. 459–461, above, for the requirements to be available and register for work.
7 P. 505, below.
8 SI 1981/1527, reg 10(6).

ii Other income

Other income is divided by the regulations into three categories: that which is disregarded; that which is taken into account in full; and that which is disregarded in part. The first list for the most part reproduces items which were disregarded, generally under the SBC's discretion, before the new regulations were issued.[9] They include attendance and mobility allowances, any occasional payment made, for example, as a Christmas or birthday present up to a maximum of £100 (beyond which it is fully taken into account), a sum payable to a holder of the Victoria or George Cross in that capacity, and a payment (not from a liable relative), which is intended and used for the provision of amenities, or for other items not covered by the weekly scale rates and by the payments for housing and additional requirements. This last miscellaneous head enables a recipient of benefit to acquire funds from other sources for a variety of purposes, for example, a holiday or a television licence, without forfeiting his entitlement.[10] Lastly, income from disregarded capital is, of course, generally ignored.

The payments which are required to be taken into account in full comprise most social security benefits (including child benefit and FIS), occupational pensions and sick pay, periodic redundancy payments and a variety of allowances paid under legislation, such as those paid to discharged prisoners.[11] Student grants are taken into account in full, except that where the student is a single parent, has a partner with a dependant, or is disabled, there is a £2.00 disregard.[12] Sick pay and occupational pensions used to attract partial disregards of £4.00 and £1.00 respectively, but *Social Assistance* rightly saw no reason why they should be treated differently for this purpose from the equivalent state benefits.[13]

There is a special, and it must be said very complicated, provision for maintenance payments. As under the previous law, any periodic payment (including arrears paid periodically) made by a liable relative (broadly, parent or former spouse), whether by court order or agreement, is to be taken into account in full. We have seen that in one circumstance a lump sum payment made by a liable relative will be treated as capital,[14] but if that is not the case, there is provision for treating it as income for certain weeks.[15] It is the formula under which these weeks are determined (and during which no benefit will be payable) that is complex. Broadly, if the maintenance is paid for the claimant (and not for his or her children only), the lump sum is to be divided by a divisor consisting of either (a) the aggregate of £2.00 and the amount of benefit which would otherwise be paid, or (b) if higher than this, the amount ordered by the court. The number obtained will then constitute the period of weeks to which the lump sum is attributable.[16] There is a similar formula for determining the weeks to which a lump sum payable only for children is to be attributed.[17] Payments to an immigrant by his sponsor are treated in the same way as maintenance payments.

9 Ibid, reg 11(4).
10 *Lynes* pp. 115–116.
11 SI 1981/1527, reg 11(2).
12 Ibid, reg 11(2)(1). The reasons for the present law and the general benefit position of students are discussed at p. 517, below.
13 Paras 8.28 and 8.30.
14 P. 482, above.
15 SI 1981/1527, reg 13.
16 Ibid, reg 13(3).
17 Ibid, reg 13(4). (There is a full discussion in *Lynes* pp. 114–115.)

The third category of 'other income' comprises income tax repayments, disablement and death benefits paid periodically under the industrial injuries and war pensions schemes, and any other income not mentioned in the preceding paragraphs of the regulation.[18] This residual head would include regular gifts by friends or charities. There is a disregard of £4.00 of the *aggregate* of this income.[19] (As under the previous law, a claimant may have both £4.00 of his earnings and £4.00 of his other income disregarded in assessing total income resources.)

We saw earlier that the capital resources rules were mitigated by a special provision for dependants' capital.[20] The same is true for their general 'other income'. Where the income of a dependant (apart from payments made by a liable relative, for which there is the special provision just discussed) exceeds the weekly normal and additional requirements of that dependant, that excess is entirely disregarded in determining the claimant's income resources.[1] This is a new modification to the effects of the aggregation rule, justified in *Social Assistance* on the principle that a child's income, like his earnings, should not be used to support his parents.[2]

Part 5 Single payments

A General

Under all the assistance schemes since 1934 there has been power to award single payments for exceptional needs:[3] they take the form of a lump sum, rather than supplements to the weekly benefit. Like the ECAs, these payments, known under the 1966 legislation as exceptional needs payments (ENPs), were discretionary. They were similar too in that the number of awards grew rapidly during the 1970s. In 1968, 470,000 awards were made, while in 1979, there were 1,134,000 such grants.[4] Nevertheless, the total expenditure on ENPs remained relatively small – in 1979, £38 million, representing about 1.5 per cent of total expenditure on supplementary benefits. The increase in the number of ENPs was possibly attributable to greater 'claims-consciousness' on the part of persons eligible and the fact that they were advised to claim them by welfare agencies.[5]

In the middle of the 1970s the SBC became disturbed at the number of discretionary lump sum awards, particularly as the evidence suggested that with greater awareness of their existence, even more payments might be claimed. There was some suggestion that local offices varied considerably in their willingness to make awards.[6] The Commission was, therefore, anxious to remove unnecessary discretion in this area and suggested in its 1976 Annual Report that automatic lump sums might be paid every six months to all benefit recipients.[7] These would be designed to cover

18 Ibid, reg 11(5).
19 Ibid.
20 P. 484, above.
1 SI 1981/1527, reg 12.
2 Para 8.35.
3 See SBC Annual Report 1976 (Cmnd 6910), Appendix C and paras 7.2–7.10.
4 SBC Annual Report 1979 (Cmnd 8033), Table 16.3. Also see the figures in *Social Assistance* para 9.7.
5 See the research discussed in SBC Annual Report 1976, n.3, above, at paras 7.43–7.48.
6 Donnison *The Politics of Poverty* (1982) pp. 42–45, 89–100.
7 SBC Annual Report, n.3, above, at para 7.56.

expenditure on items covered by the weekly scale rates, incurred either because these rates were inadequate in the circumstances, or because the family had difficulties in budgeting properly. This idea was supported by *Social Assistance*, though that report also canvassed the view that recipients of the long-term rates should be ineligible to claim lump sums for this type of expenditure. On the other hand, it recognised that lump sum payments for expenses not met at all by weekly benefit would have to continue, though entitlement could usefully be set out in regulations or the proposed Code of Practice.[8]

One possible criticism of the proposal to make regular lump sum payments automatically to recipients of benefit was that it would further the discrimination between those eligible for assistance and those who are not.[9] It may be that this was a reason for the government rejecting this proposal. Another factor may have been its cost. What has been done under the new scheme is to put entitlement to ENPs, now to be known simply as 'single payments', into precise legal form in a set of regulations, leaving only a residual power for benefit officers to make a payment in circumstances not covered by the rules. Schedules to these regulations also make clear exactly how much is to be awarded for items of clothing and bedclothes, matters previously covered in the Handbook. However, the terms of the regulations are often sufficiently open-ended to allow ample room for the benefit officer to exercise interpretative judgment. To assist him in this task, the Chief Supplementary Benefit Officer has issued guidance, which has been published.[10] Whatever the drawbacks there are in legalising entitlement to additional payments, it can be argued that one of the benefits of the new scheme is that it openly sets out a claimant's rights, and there is little room now for covert unfair discrimination in the exercise of discretionary powers. What may be more disquieting is that the opportunity to apply for a single payment to meet those expenses covered by the scale rates (now, as we have seen, spelt out in the regulations) has been drastically reduced. The Commission in its last Report expressed anxiety about this; in particular it will be harder for claimants to obtain awards for clothing, which some had received more or less automatically once or twice a year.[11]

B Eligibility for a single payment

In the first edition of this book it was contended that under the 1976 Act before the recent amendments a person not entitled to weekly benefit might nevertheless be eligible for an ENP, at any rate where his resources were only a little more than his requirements and he was not disqualified from receipt of benefit.[12] *Social Assistance* found that practice in this area was inconsistent: sometimes an award might be made to a person in this position, sometimes not. It recommended that eligibility in future should be limited to those entitled to weekly benefit, and this has been accepted by the government.[13] A claimant must either be so entitled, or have

8 Paras 9.38–9.49.
9 This was admitted in *Social Assistance* para 9.43.
10 The guidance includes a full explanation of the terms of the regulations, as well as some advice on applying it.
11 SBC Annual Report 1979, n.4, above, at paras 1.26–1.29. See also ch 16 of this report for a general discussion of the disadvantages of the old discretionary system.
12 First edition, pp. 520–521.
13 Para 9.44.

been so entitled if he had claimed benefit.[14] It may be open for a person in extreme need who does not satisfy this test to apply for an urgent cases payment (see Part 6).

C The general factors to be taken into account

The regulations set out a number of factors which must be taken into account. The applicant must show there is a need for the item in question and that he does not already possess it or have a suitable alternative available, and further that he has not unreasonably disposed, or failed to avail himself, of the article.[15] The Commissioner has emphasised that, even if the detailed requirements of the regulations are met, there can be no award of a single payment unless the claimant satisfies these general conditions.[16] It has been held that borrowed clothes are not 'a suitable alternative item' when the claimant wishes to attend job interviews,[17] but an applicant who with borrowed money had already replaced a central heating pump was regarded as having no 'need' for that item.[18] Perhaps surprisingly, the Commissioner has observed that a claimant only fails 'to avail' himself of an item if he already has it to hand; it is not enough to defeat his claim to show that he has unreasonably failed to acquire the item in question.[19]

The SBC policy with regard to treatment of an applicant's resources has now been formulated in the regulations: an award will not be made, or will only be made in part, if the applicant has sufficient capital to leave him with £300 if he pays, or partly pays, for the item himself.[20] There are a few exceptions to this general rule, most of which are even less generous. And when an officer is considering whether to make an award under the residual provision (enabling him to make payments in circumstances not covered by the detailed regulations),[1] he must take any disregarded capital and all other means of meeting the need into account.[2] These matters have been the subject of guidance by the Chief Supplementary Benefit Officer.[3]

In order to avoid abuse, there is now a definite rule that repeated applications for the same need will not be upheld unless the circumstances have changed since the first grant was made.[4] When applications of this nature are made for clothing and other needs which are covered by the weekly scale rates, the officer may make an order withholding part of the weekly payment, thus saving for the items on the claimant's behalf. The savings will then be paid over when the need arises (see Part 10 of the chapter). No payment will be made where any member of the assessment unit is affected by a trade dispute, and, with the exception of voluntary repatriation expenses, no payment will be made for a need arising outside Great Britain.[5] There is also a list of express exclusions from the needs

14 SI 1981/1528, reg 4. (See *CSB 32/81*.)
15 Ibid, reg 3(2).
16 *R(SB) 15/81*.
17 *CSB 29/81*.
18 *R(SB) 8/81*.
19 *CSB 27/81*, para 9, per J Mitchell, Comr.
20 SI 1981/1528, reg 5.
1 See pp. 492–493, below.
2 SI 1981/1528, reg 30: See p. 492, below.
3 Paras 43–44.
4 SI 1981/1528, reg 6(1)(a). (See *R(SB) 15/81*, para 13.)
5 Ibid, regs 6(1)(b) and (d).

which can be met by a single payment, even under the general residual power:[6] educational or training needs, school uniforms, mobility needs, costs connected with cars, telephones, TV or radio, or holidays. These are either needs for which alternative provision exists, for example, from local authority funds, or they are regarded as inessential luxuries. TV licence and rental charges are now treated as covered by the weekly scale rates for normal requirements.[7]

D The categories of need covered by the regulations

In addition to the general residual power discussed in the next section of the chapter, the regulations cover six types of need which can be met by the award of a single payment. The conditions to be met before such an award can be made are set out in great detail, and there is not space in a general work of this kind to do more than outline the principal categories of need.[8]

i Items to which weekly requirements relate

Normally single payments for these items will not be made, since applicants are expected to budget for them from weekly benefit. And now that it is clear what is covered in weekly normal and other requirements, there is virtually no room for argument whether a need for such an item should be met by a single payment. This should lead to a significant reduction in the total number of such payments, for before the reform just over half the awards were made for clothing and footwear, provision for which is made in the weekly scale rates.[9] However, in some exceptional circumstances set out in the regulations, this general principle will be modified. First, payment will be made where a claimant has for some reason (e.g. a failure to make a claim) not received benefit to which he was entitled, has spent on an item, for which a single payment would have been made, money which could have provided for the item now claimed (which is covered by weekly benefit), and as a result is now unable to afford it.[10] Secondly, payments will be made for clothing and footwear where a need has arisen otherwise than by normal wear and tear, e.g. because of pregnancy, disability or illness, or accidental loss of, or damage to, essential items.[11] If these stringent conditions are not satisfied, the claimant may try to secure payment for extra clothing under the residual provision – as the Commissioner has emphasised in a recent case.[12] Schedule 2 to the Regulations sets out amounts which will be awarded for the purchase of items of clothing, unless these are inappropriate because the claimant is outsize or disabled.[13] Finally, fuel costs will be paid where they are greater than has been budgeted for, owing to either exceptionally inclement weather or an understandable lack of familiarity with the particular heating system.[14]

6 Ibid, reg 6(2). See *R(SB) 19/81*.
7 P. 466, above.
8 For a much fuller treatment, see *Lynes* pp. 134–167. Also see Handbook, ch 9 and the Guidance issued by the Chief Supplementary Benefits Officer.
9 See SBC Annual Report 1979 (Cmnd 8033), Table 16.4.
10 SI 1981/1528, reg 28.
11 Ibid, reg 27. See *CSB 26/81* and *CSB 29/81*.
12 *R(SB) 5/81*, para 8, per M J Goodman, Comr.
13 SI 1981/1528, reg 27(2).
14 Ibid, reg 26.

ii Household expenses

Under this head, payments for essential furniture and household equipment, their repair and installation costs, or hire purchase instalments for these items, and for bedclothing may be made.[15] The circumstances in which, and the particular articles for which, an award will be made are set out in meticulous detail: for example, a vacuum cleaner is only to be regarded as an essential item for which an award may be made if a member of the assessment unit is allergic to house dust,[16] and a refrigerator is only necessary when, for dietary reasons, it is essential to keep food cold.[17] There are a number of general conditions, some of which must be satisfied before an award can be made; for example, it will only be made for the purchase of one of the itemised articles of furniture or equipment, if he does not already have it (or the article he possesses is defective or unsafe, and it is too expensive to repair it), and then one of a number of further alternative requirements is met. These prescribe that he is entitled if he has been in receipt of benefit for more than six months and has no immediate prospect of employment, or one member of the assessment unit is over pensionable age, 15 or less, pregnant, chronically sick or disabled. Alternatively, if he satisfies one of these requirements, or one of two or three others, *and* has recently become a tenant or an owner of an unfurnished home, he is entitled to a lump sum for the purchase of an article he does not possess, etc.[18] It can be appreciated from this account that the conditions are complicated and precise. Certainty has been purchased at a considerable price, and one of the costs, despite the government's intentions, has been a loss of simplicity!

iii Housing expenses

A variety of expenses may be met by a single payment: removal expenses, deposits for tenancies, legal fees incurred in renewing or extending a lease, draughtproofing, redecoration and the costs of installing meters and reconnecting gas and electricity.[19] Payment is only to be made for '*essential* internal redecoration', and in *R(SB) 10/81*, the Commissioner, I Edwards-Jones, construed this to mean 'necessary' and 'as importing a requirement of substantial need, judged by the modest general standard of living' which benefit is directed to support.[20] A more generous approach was to be adopted than that to be taken under the general residual provision (section E below) when payment is only to be made if indispensable to avoid damage to health or safety. He also emphasised that in these areas much should be left to the judgment of the appeal tribunal which should bring its own knowledge of life to bear on the circumstances. An award for essential repairs and maintenance is to be made where the cost (subject to a maximum of £225) is such that it is not reasonable to expect it to be met out of the weekly amount payable for housing requirements.

iv Maternity needs

A payment for the purchase of items necessary to meet the needs of a newly-born child, e.g. napkins, feeding bottles and a cot, shall be made six

15 Ibid, regs 9–13.
16 Ibid, reg 9(j).
17 Ibid, reg 9(k).
18 Ibid, regs 10(1) and (2).
19 Ibid, regs 13–21.
20 *R(SB) 10/81*, para 9.

weeks or less before the expected date of birth of the child, or shortly after it has occurred.[1] But the amount of the maternity grant is to be deducted from any single payment awarded, unless it has been spent on items for which another single payment could have been made. These provisions would seem to constitute an implicit admission of the present inadequacy of the maternity grant.[2]

v Funeral expenses

The expenses of a private funeral will be the subject of an award where they are essential according to the regulation, and the deceased was a close relative of the claimant, or a member of his household or assessment unit.[3] The claimant must also show that there is no other person (who is a close relative of the dead person) who could more reasonably be expected to assume responsibility for the funeral. A number of deductions are to be made from the sum which would otherwise be awarded to determine what payment (if any) is to be made: they include the value of the deceased's estate (less generally that of his home), the death grant (unless this has already been spent on any item for which otherwise a single payment could have been awarded), and contributions from a charity or relative paid to the person assuming responsibility.[4]

vi Miscellaneous expenses

Under this final heading may be listed: travelling expenses (to hospital, in finding or starting new employment and in various other circumstances), expenses on starting work, such as the purchase of clothes and equipment, the discharge of debts accrued during an absence abroad, and voluntary repatriation expenses (though only in very restricted circumstances).[5]

E Residual 'discretionary' payments

Under the final provision in the Single Payments Regulations, there is a general duty to make a payment in circumstances not covered by the specific regulations. The claimant must be entitled to a weekly pension or allowance, and payment can only be made if, in the benefit officer's opinion, it 'is the only means by which serious damage or serious risk to the health or safety of any member of the assessment unit may be prevented'.[6] The award may be made for a need which is covered by the regulations, where the claimant fails to satisfy the relevant conditions for its award, or for an exceptional need for which no provision is made at all. But when the admittedly stringent requirements are satisfied to the benefit officer's satisfaction, he *must* make an award; and in this light, it is a little odd that the provision is headed 'discretionary payments'. Nevertheless, this is clearly a situation where the officer must often have to exercise fine judgment, and the Chief Officer's guidance will therefore be particularly important. The officer must first consider whether the claimant has any alternative means of meeting the requirement, but in deciding this he has

1 SI 1981/1528, reg 7.
2 Ch 7, pp. 249–251, above, for maternity grant.
3 SI 1981/1528, reg 8(1). There is no need to have recourse to a local authority funeral: see p. 241, above, for discussion in the context of the death grant.
4 Ibid, reg 8(3).
5 Ibid, regs 26–29. For expenses on starting work, see *R(SB) 19/81*.
6 SI 1981/1528, reg 30.

been told by the Chief Officer that he need not take into account possible help from national or local charities or social services departments. On the other hand, he should consider whether the applicant can resort to credit facilities to purchase the item.[7] And in the case of fuel debts, he should examine the possibilities of special arrangements with the fuel boards and direct payment arrangements.[8]

A number of cases have now come before the Social Security Commissioners on points arising from this provision, interestingly mostly brought on appeal by the benefit officer from tribunals. In a Scottish decision, the Commissioner, J G Mitchell, emphasised that it should be construed broadly and the tribunal's decision should not lightly be disturbed.[9] But it was wrong in law for a SBAT to make an award for a *past* need, when the payment now could not be said to be the only means of avoiding serious damage or risk to the claimant's health. And although, as another Commissioner has said, it is not necessary for a tribunal to state precisely what the serious damage or risk is,[10] it is incumbent on it to find that there would be *serious* damage or a *serious* risk to safety or health before making an award.[11] Thus, the Commissioner in one case quashed a decision awarding a payment for shaving articles and towels under this regulation, as there was no evidence that there was otherwise a serious risk to the claimant's health.[12]

Part 6 Urgent cases

A General

Under the amended section 4 of the 1976 Act benefit may be provided in urgent cases prescribed by regulations. These cases comprise a miscellaneous variety of circumstances in which neither weekly benefit nor a single payment under the rules described in previous parts of the chapter is available. Moreover, in some situations an urgent cases payment may be made to a person who is ineligible for weekly benefit or a single payment – because he is in full-time work or has failed to show availability for work. With some exceptions, an urgent cases payment may have to be repaid later, and largely for that reason, it is inadvisable to claim one when a more regular, non-recoverable payment may be made. The new rules, replacing to some extent policies of the Commission, are detailed and complex, and the following account necessarily considerably oversimplifies the law.[13] Furthermore, as urgent cases payments are less common, and less important in the general scheme than other types of benefit, relatively little space is devoted to them.

There are some general rules (or principles, for there are almost always a few exceptions) which should be mentioned before discussing the principal

7 Guidance issued by the Chief Supplementary Benefit Officer, paras 43–44. There is a full treatment of this in *Lynes* pp. 131–132.
8 P. 518, below, for direct payments. For general discussion, see Donnison *The Politics of Poverty* (1982) pp. 193–194.
9 *R(SB) 13/81*.
10 *R(SB) 5/81*, para 9, per M J Goodman, Comr.
11 *R(SB) 2/81*, para 7, per D G Rice, Comr. Also see *CSB 21/81* and *CSB 36/81*.
12 *R(SB) 2/81*.
13 For a fuller account, see *Lynes* ch 7. Also see the published guidance issued by the Chief Supplementary Benefit Officer.

situations in which these payments may be made. A case will be treated as urgent only if the item in question, or funds for that item's purchase, are not readily available to the claimant from his own resources or from any other source, for example, friends, relatives, credit facilities and voluntary organisations, or in the case of emergencies, a local authority or relief fund.[14] In determining the claimant's own resources here, the disregards for determining entitlement to weekly benefit and single payments are not allowed, and thus all available income and capital (that is, capital that can be readily made liquid) is taken into account. Benefit in an urgent case may be by way of a single payment or a weekly pension or allowance, and in those cases where it may be awarded under the regulations, the disqualifications and other restrictions in the Act do not apply: the exclusion of persons in full-time work, the condition of availability for employment, the exclusion of persons who fail to comply with directions to attend courses and the limitations imposed by the qualifications for a single payment under section 3 of the Act.[15] There are then some extraordinarily complex rules for determining the amount of the payment that may be made. Almost all available income and capital is taken into account, whether it would be disregarded or not for other purposes.[16] There are considerable modifications to the usual requirements rules for the first 14 days of an urgent cases award, e.g. the scale rate for each category of claimant is reduced by 25 per cent.[17]

There is a variety of circumstances in which payment is not to be made at all.[18] For example, no payment may be made for a need arising outside Great Britain or to certain special groups, e.g. prisoners or members of religious orders. Generally a person attending a full-time course of education is ineligible. The most important rule here is that an urgent cases payment is not to be made where any member of the relevant assessment unit is affected by a trade dispute: in this case there are separate urgent cases provisions in other regulations (see Part 7).

B Emergency relief

Benefit may be paid for emergency relief, e.g. in the case of fire or flood, whether or not it affects persons other than the claimant and his family, either by way of a single payment or a weekly allowance.[19] The latter is only payable, however, for the two weeks following the disaster, though the Secretary of State may extend this period where in the circumstances it will be difficult or impracticable to make available ordinary weekly benefit.[20] A single payment may be made where the claimant needs any item listed in a schedule, e.g. clothing and footwear, money for the purchase or repair of essential household equipment, or emergency removal expenses.[1] A major beneficiary of these provisions might be a person in full-time work, who otherwise could not be assisted in these conditions. Strikers are eligible under the equivalent Trade Disputes Regulations,[2] as are (exceptionally) students in full-time education.

14 SI 1981/1529, reg 3(1).
15 Ibid, reg 3(2).
16 Ibid, reg 5.
17 Ibid, reg 5(3).
18 Ibid, reg 6.
19 Ibid, reg 8(1).
20 Ibid, reg 8(3).
1 Ibid, reg 8(1) and Sch 1.
2 Pp. 503–504, below.

C Other urgent cases

Part III of the Urgent Cases Regulations sets out the variety of situations in which an urgent cases payment may be made. There is entitlement (not just the right to apply for a discretionary payment) in these circumstances when the applicant does need the specific item or 'is in need of living expenses'[3]; however, if previously he has had the same or a similar need it must be reasonable to meet it now.[4] The following is a non-exhaustive list of the circumstances in which an urgent cases payment may be made.

i Loss of money

Where a sum of money is lost, stolen or destroyed, a payment shall be made up to the amount of that sum.[5] This does not apply where the loss is 'foreseeable', an imprecise phrase which the Chief Supplementary Benefit Officer suggests should be construed to include a loss brought about by gambling or heavy drinking.[6] The loss of social security payments is also excluded, as mislaid girocheques may be replaced under other powers.[7]

ii Need between day of claim and day of entitlement

A need arising between these dates is to be met by an urgent cases payment.[8] A sum paid in these circumstances is one of the relatively few urgent cases payments that may not be recovered.[9] There are comparable entitlements to such payments in situations where a claim for standard benefit has not been established and the officer considers it appropriate to make a payment under these regulations,[10] or where on such a claim the applicant's requirements and resources are not ascertainable,[11] or lastly where a claimant has been awarded an ordinary allowance or pension, but its payment has been suspended.[12]

iii A person starting or resuming work

An ordinary weekly payment may normally be made to a person resuming or starting work in full-time employment for the first 15 days.[13] Under these regulations where the claimant is still in need, an urgent cases payment shall be made for a further 16 days, or, where he was never entitled at all to ordinary benefit (because there was no interval between two jobs), for a period of a month after starting the second employment.[14]

iv Unpaid or part-time absences from work

Under this head an urgent cases payment may be made to someone unavoidably absent from work, without, or with reduced, earnings, to

3 SI 1981/1529, reg 9.
4 Ibid, reg 6(3).
5 Ibid, reg 10. (See *CSB 32/81*, paras 19–20.)
6 See his published guidance, para 29.
7 *Lynes* p. 180.
8 SI 1981/1529, reg 12.
9 P. 497, below.
10 SI 1981/1529, reg 17.
11 Ibid, reg 19.
12 Ibid, reg 20.
13 P. 458, above.
14 SI 1981/1529, reg 14.

whom the full-time work disqualification for entitlement to ordinary benefit still applies. Payment may then be made for a month.[15]

v Person not available for work

A person not available for work is entitled to an urgent cases payment, but only if in the benefit officer's view it would be the only means of preventing serious damage or serious risk to his health or safety or that of any member of his family.[16]

vi Visitor from abroad

He can obtain a payment either if he is temporarily without funds to meet his requirements, or alternatively if he is waiting for the determination of an application for leave to remain in the country.[17] In the former case payment may be made for a maximum of 42 days.[18]

vii Failure to maintain

Here an urgent cases payment may be made where one member of a married or unmarried couple fails to maintain the other, and under the aggregation rules the latter is unable to claim benefit, because her requirements and resources are treated together with his.[19] This will usually be used to help a wife whose husband is not providing for her; the situation can occur if he is still present in the home or temporarily absent, but in the latter circumstance he will soon cease to be a 'member of the same household' and the aggregation provision will no longer apply.[20]

viii Unmarried couples

The circumstances in which an urgent needs payment may be paid to a woman living with a man as his wife, who has a child and who needs support because of the man's inability to claim benefit in his own right, have already been discussed.[1]

D Residual 'discretionary' payments

There is provision for making an urgent needs payment in the same circumstances as those in which a benefit officer has 'discretion' to make a single payment to meet an exceptional need, i.e. where payment is the only means of avoiding serious damage or serious risk to the health or safety of the claimant and his family.[2] However, the bars to awards in certain circumstances, e.g. where the need arises outside Great Britain, also apply to these payments.[3]

15 Ibid, reg 15.
16 Ibid, reg 16.
17 Ibid, reg 21(1). (See p. 456, above, for the eligibility of visitors to ordinary weekly benefit.)
18 Ibid, reg 21(2).
19 Ibid, reg 22. See pp. 461–465, above, for the aggregation rules.
20 P. 462, above.
1 P. 463, above.
2 SI 1981/1529, reg 24.
3 Ibid, reg 6: p. 494, above.

E Recovery of urgent cases payments

Generally these payments may be recovered.[4] This does not apply, however, in some cases: where a sum has been paid for a need arising between the day of claim and that of entitlement; where it has been paid to someone ineligible for ordinary benefit because he is unavailable for work; and where it has been paid to a member of an unmarried couple.[5] Moreover, recovery is not to be ordered when the sum in question is £10 or less, or where the recipient has a low income and no capital resources (other than a home).[6] Recovery is less likely to be ordered where he is entitled to ordinary weekly supplementary benefit.[7] Under some detailed rules, recovery may be made by deductions from various social security benefits.[8] Finally, it should be noted that all these provisions are without prejudice to recovery under section 20 of the Act where there has been misrepresentation or non-disclosure.[9]

Part 7 Work incentive rules

In this Part of the chapter, two sets of circumstances are discussed in which benefit may be reduced or withheld altogether in order to encourage claimants to work rather than rely on state support. The first category concerns the 'voluntarily unemployed', those who do not, or are thought not to, make any real effort to stay in work or find employment when out of it. Secondly, the special rules concerning strikers and other persons affected by trade disputes are explained. There are, of course, other rules in the supplementary benefits system which may be characterised as work incentive rules: for example, the condition that a claimant be available for work. But this is a requirement for entitlement to benefit in the first place, and has therefore been treated together with other similar rules in Part 2 of the chapter.

A The voluntarily unemployed

i General

In any society where the 'work ethic' is important, it is inevitable that there will be reluctance to extend assistance to those who are capable of supporting themselves in work, but refuse to obtain it.[10] The 'work-shy' or 'scroungers', as they are often called, understandably arouse the resentment of the taxpaying public. Nevertheless it is important to understand the real nature of the problems involved; this is particularly true at a time when unemployment is as high as it has been for the last two or three years and work is hard to find. Medical, psychological and various social factors may bring about unresponsive attitudes to work; for example, a person unable to find work after searching for several months, may be inclined to

4 SBA 1976, s.4(2).
5 SI 1981/1529, reg 25(2).
6 Ibid, regs 25(5) and (6)(b).
7 Ibid, reg 25(6)(a).
8 Ibid, reg 26.
9 P. 577, below.
10 For a general discussion, see pp. 10–11, above. Also see Stevenson *Claimant or Client?* (1973) chs 4 and 5; Sinfield *What Unemployment Means* (1981); SBC Annual Report 1979 (Cmnd 8033), ch 5.

become lethargic and abandon any real attempt to secure suitable employment.[11] While there may be some cases where the system is exploited by those who prefer to live off welfare payments, it is difficult to distinguish them from the almost certainly much larger number who are genuinely unable to find work.

Not only is there uncertainty about the precise nature of the 'voluntary unemployment' problem, there is also, as might be expected, doubt about its scale. There are statistics relating to the number and duration of claims for benefit by the unemployed, but there is no breakdown of those figures which would enable any reliable estimate to be made of the numbers of voluntarily unemployed. In 1973 the Fisher Committee thought it reasonable to assume that a large proportion of the younger men out of work for long periods were in this position through no fault of their own, and this was even more the case with older claimants.[12] Now that unemployment rates are considerably higher, this proposition seems incontrovertible. Recent studies by the Manpower Services Commission support the conclusion that few claimants do not even try to find work because they feel they are better off on benefit, though it could be said that their finding that low wages are responsible for the difficulties in filling some vacancies rather begs the question.[13] In any case, as the SBC said in its last report, the fact that the work incentive problem is small does not mean that it should be ignored.[14]

Before examining the detailed rules applied to discourage the work-shy, something should be said here about the work of the Unemployment Review Officers (UROs).[15] Their function is to help those who are out of work and have been in receipt of benefit for a substantial period of time. They do this by assisting these claimants to find work or encouraging them to attend re-establishment centres; in some cases UROs may seek compulsory orders to require such attendance. Some of these officers work full-time in regional offices, while others work full or part-time at local offices. In 1978 they interviewed over 200,000 applicants, of whom about 40 per cent stopped claiming benefit as a result – though the Annual Report does not disclose why this was so.[16]

As with so many areas of supplementary benefits law, the circumstances in which benefit may now be reduced are governed entirely by regulations. There is now no general discretionary power, as the SBC used to enjoy, to withhold benefit altogether,[17] though regulations may be promulgated to achieve that end in the case of the voluntarily unemployed by providing that they are to be treated as having no normal requirements.[18] As yet, none have been issued in this context. Instead, as we have seen, benefit may be refused or withheld altogether if the claimant is not available for work (or refuses to register).[19]

11 *Stevenson*, n.10, above, at pp. 86–102.
12 Para 246.
13 SBC Annual Report 1979, n.10, above, at paras 5.25–5.26.
14 Ibid, para 5.28.
15 Ibid, paras 6.20–6.27. Also see DE/DHSS Scrutiny team, *Payment of Benefits to Unemployed People* (1981) paras 4.60–4.76, which recommended an increase in the total number of UROs from 940 to 1250.
16 SBC Annual Report 1978 (Cmnd 7725), paras 13.19–13.20.
17 See the first edition of this book, pp. 537–538.
18 SBA 1976, Sch 1, para 2(5).
19 Pp. 459–461, above.

ii The 40 per cent rule

In certain circumstances the amount of benefit payable to an unemployed claimant may be reduced by 40 per cent for a maximum of six weeks.[20] The rule was introduced by the Conservative government in 1971, replacing a previous deduction of 75p a week.[1] It was intended to act as a disincentive to voluntary unemployment, without however causing hardship to the families of persons to whom it was applied. The provision applies if the claimant has been disqualified from receipt of unemployment benefit for misconduct, leaving work voluntarily or refusing suitable employment without good excuse, or if he would be so disqualified (in the benefit officer's view) when the claim for unemployment benefit is determined by the statutory authorities, or if such a claim were made. The deduction is to be 40 per cent of the single householder's ordinary scale rate, or the comparable rate for a non-householder where this is appropriate;[2] for boarders, 40 per cent of the latter rate is subtracted from the sum awarded for personal expenses.[3] Before the 1980 reform, the SBC exercised a discretion to deduct less than this percentage in some circumstances; this is now governed by the regulations. The normal 40 per cent deduction is to be reduced by half if the claimant does not have more than £100 available capital, i.e. capital disregarded in the assessment of his resources, *and* one (or more) of the following cases applies:[4]

(a) a member of his assessment unit is pregnant or seriously ill;
(b) the unit includes a child under five years old;
(c) the claimant's last employment was part-time, or full-time but for less than six weeks;
(d) his weekly earnings for the final six weeks of his last employment were no more than the amount of his current weekly requirements;
(e) his housing requirements are not met in full;
(f) his circumstances are in some respects analogous to these cases, so that the benefit officer forms the view it would be appropriate to reduce the standard deduction.

The question whether a claimant should be disqualified from receiving unemployment benefit on one of the relevant grounds is sometimes a complicated one on which there is much difficult case law.[5] It is also obviously important that benefit officers should not decide these questions inconsistently with the approach of the insurance officers who handle claims to the contributory benefit. For these reasons there are some complicated provisions to ensure harmony here. If the insurance officer has already decided the issue, there is no problem: the claimant's benefit will be reduced for the period of the disqualification (up to a maximum of six weeks).[6] If, however, the claim for unemployment benefit has not yet been determined, but the benefit officer considers there is a possible case for disqualification, a deduction must be made for six weeks, and then if later the insurance officer disqualifies for a shorter period or decides no disqualification is appropriate, an adjustment will be made for supple-

20 SI 1980/1299, reg 8.
1 See the first edition of this book, p. 534.
2 SI 1980/1299, regs 8(2)(a) and (b).
3 Ibid, reg 8(2)(c), as amended by SI 1981/1016, reg 2(4).
4 SI 1980/1299, reg 8(3).
5 Pp. 106–118, above.
6 SI 1981/1299, reg 8(4)(a).

mentary benefit, including the payment of amounts wrongly deducted.[7] Lastly, there is the case where no claim for the contributory benefit is made at all: here it is now provided that the benefit officer must refer the matter to an insurance officer for him to decide, unless there is no real dispute about the basic facts.[8] In the meantime, the benefit officer is to proceed on the assumption that the claimant will be held to have left his employment voluntarily, etc., and apply the 40 per cent rule.[9] It has been argued that the deduction should not be made until the insurance officer has decided the real (or hypothetical) unemployment benefit issue, but this proposal has been rejected.[10] Although deductions wrongly made will eventually be paid to the beneficiary if the issue is decided in his favour, this will not compensate for the loss of the money at the relevant time, and in this respect at least the 40 per cent rule may work some hardship.

iii Re-establishment centres and training courses[11]

In some cases positive steps will be taken to help voluntarily unemployed claimants acquire a responsive attitude to work. Where a person, required to be available for work and not in receipt of unemployment benefit, is considered by the benefit officer to refuse or neglect to maintain himself, his wife or his children, he may be required in writing to attend a re-establishment centre or other course of training.[12] This used to need the direction of a supplementary benefits appeal tribunal (SBAT), but now the benefit officer may issue it himself, subject to appeal to a SBAT. Failure to comply with a direction leads automatically under the Act to the withdrawal of entitlement to benefit, a matter which was previously at the discretion of the Commission.[13] In practice it seems that by far the most common direction is to attend one of the re-establishment centres,[14] so the discussion here is concentrated on them.

First established on an experimental basis under the 1948 legislation there are now 17 such centres, three of which have residential facilities.[15] The vast majority attending them do so voluntarily (perhaps under the encouragement of an Unemployment Review Officer) rather than in pursuance of a formal direction.[16] The centres' purpose is to provide instruction and training required to fit those attending them 'for entry into, or return to, regular employment'.[17] The SBC has commented that they are reasonably effective in achieving this goal; in 1979 it reported that a larger number than in previous years found work immediately after leaving one of the centres, and also that there was an increase in the numbers of claimants who entered employment after being directed to attend.[18] Thus, they provide some sort of 'deterrent', as well as their 'rehabilitative'

7 Ibid, reg 8(4)(b). See *R(SB) 18/21*, where J Mitchell, Comr, points out that the benefit officer and SBAT have no jurisdiction to determine issues of disqualification (though, of course, it is for them to appreciate that such a question has arisen: *CSB 12/81*, para 6).
8 SI 1980/1643, reg 5.
9 *R(SB) 18/21*, para 6.
10 See Standing Committee F Debates on Social Security Bill 1971, cols 26 ff.
11 See generally Stevenson *Claimant or Client*? (1973) pp. 116–121 and SBC Annual Report 1979 (Cmnd 8033), pp. 50–54.
12 SBA 1976, s.10(1), amended by SSHBA 1982, s.38(2).
13 SBA 1976, s.10(4).
14 *Fisher* para 278.
15 Handbook, Appendix 3.
16 SBC Annual Report 1979, n.11, above, at para 6.35.
17 SBA 1976, Sch 5, para 1.
18 SBC Annual Report 1979, n.11, above, at para 6.35.

function. This is particularly impressive in light of the fact that they are only used by the long-term unemployed, often without trade skills. Nevertheless, a special study commissioned to assess the effectiveness of the centres has concluded recently that it is necessary to support their work with placement assistance for persons leaving them – otherwise their work prospects are still poor.[19]

Before 1980 benefit was paid to a person attending a re-establishment centre at the SBC's discretion. Now his requirements are met in the usual way if he is attending daily, while if he is attending on a residential basis, either voluntarily or under direction, they are assessed as the weekly amount of board and lodging charge made by the Secretary of State, plus 30 per cent of the ordinary rate for householders to cover personal expenses.[20]

iv Criminal prosecution

A person who persistently refuses or neglects to maintain himself or any person whom he is liable to maintain (his wife and children), as a result of which benefit is payable, is guilty of a summary offence. The sanction for this is three months' imprisonment, a £500 fine, or both.[1] There is, however, no offence if such conduct is committed in the context of a trade dispute.[2] Prosecution is very rare and only used as a last resort when all else has failed. The number brought against unemployed claimants has declined: in the late 1960s the average number a year was about 100, but in 1971 it had dropped to 64, and in 1975 (the last year for which the SBC published relevant figures) it was only 23.[3]

It does seem that in the past about half of those concerned worked considerably longer in the year following the prosecution, but overall the success of this method of control is open to doubt.[4] The Fisher Committee concluded that there was no reason to believe that insufficient use was made of prosecutions under this provision.[5]

B Persons affected by trade disputes

i General

There is now probably no area of supplementary benefits law which arouses more argument than that governing the award of benefit to strikers and their families. The merits of the present rules raise political issues on which views sharply differ; many of these – for example, whether the availability of benefit encourages strikes and whether it is legitimate to deter them by withdrawing benefit – are to some extent peripheral to the principal concerns of a public assistance system. It may be that for this reason there has been relatively little discussion of these questions in the reports of the Commission,[6] and none at all in the *Social Assistance* report. Nevertheless, the legal position has remained remarkably constant for the last 75 years or so. Under the poor law, the striker himself could not

19 Ibid, at para 6.37.
20 SI 1980/1299, Sch. 2, para 6.
1 SBA 1976, s.25(1), amended by SSA 1981, Sch 1, para 9.
2 SBA 1976, s.25(2).
3 See *Fisher* para 442, and SBC Annual Report 1975 (Cmnd 6615), at Table 25.
4 *Stevenson*, n.11, above, at pp. 121–124.
5 Para 445.
6 But see SBC Annual Report 1979, n.11, above, at paras 10.44–10.48.

lawfully be maintained out of the rates, unless he was completely destitute, though his wife and children could be so supported.[7] Now the position broadly is that a single striker cannot claim ordinary benefit, though he may be entitled to an urgent needs payment; but he may be entitled for other members of his assessment unit whose requirements are aggregated with his.

The arguments against supporting strikers and their dependants with supplementary benefit are first, that it is wrong for people withholding their labour, for the purpose of 'inducing' their employers to pay them higher wages, to be supported by the general taxpaying public, an argument which is perhaps reinforced by the point that some low-income taxpayers could be said to be subsidising the bargaining strength of groups with more industrial weight than they themselves can command. Secondly, the existence of welfare payments is widely believed to encourage a larger number and the longer duration of industrial disputes.[8] The first argument may have some merit with regard to the strikers themselves: they are not the deserving poor and should not expect militancy to be subsidised.[9] It is less attractive when applied to their dependants; the further proposition must then be argued that it is for the strikers themselves, and their unions, to support their families. In any case, it can be replied that for the state not to support people in need because of the particular cause of their privation is to depart from the principle of neutrality, and in the context to take sides in an industrial dispute. Furthermore, the disqualification provision, as will be seen shortly, applies to persons who would not conventionally be defined as 'strikers', though this term is used throughout for reasons of convenience. It applies to persons locked out of work, or laid off because of a dispute at their place of work. The second argument has been strongly voiced, particularly by the Conservative party, in the 1970s, and has led recently to significant reform in the law. But the view that the availability of benefits does encourage industrial unrest has been strongly challenged by commentators, and was implicitly rejected by the Commission in its last Annual Report.[10]

It is sometimes contended that Britain is unusually generous in the benefits it affords strikers and their families.[11] In the United States, however, both the general assistance provided by the states and the federally financed Aid for Families with Dependent Children are available for strikers, or in the latter case, for the benefit of their children.[12] An interesting point is that the position of the striker there is generally not sharply distinguished from that of any person who is voluntarily unemployed. The question for a striker, as it is for a person who has left his work for some other reason, is simply whether he is really available for employment.

7 *A–G v Merthyr Tydfil Union* [1900] 1 Ch 516.

8 See the discussion of the analogous arguments used for the 'trade disputes disqualification' in unemployment benefit: pp. 119–120, above.

9 For a particularly robust assertion of this view, see Page in Boyson (ed) *Down with the Poor* (1971).

10 SBC Annual Report 1979, n.11, above, at para 10.46. Also see Duncan and McCarthy [1974] Br Jo of Industrial Relations 26. A more cautious view is expressed by Hunter, ibid, at 438.

11 Sir K Joseph, Secretary of State, 838 HC Official Report (5th series) cols 1231–1233.

12 See La France et al *Law of the Poor* (1973) pp. 367–368; 67 North West L Rev 245. In an important New York case, it was ruled that the provision of general assistance to strikers did not violate the state's policy of neutrality in labour disputes: *Lascaris v Wyman* 340 NYS 2d 397 (1972).

In contrast, since the 1948 legislation, the British system has made special provision for persons involved in trade disputes independently of the rules relating to voluntary unemployment.[13] The fundamental provision is now section 8(1) of the Supplementary Benefits Act 1976 (as amended):

> Subject to subsection (2) below, where a person —
> (a) is, by reason of a stoppage of work which is due to a trade dispute at his place of employment, without employment for any period during the stoppage; and
> (b) has not during that stoppage become bona fide employed elsewhere in the occupation which he usually follows, or become regularly engaged in some other occupation,
> his requirements for that period shall be disregarded for the purposes of supplementary benefit except so far as those requirements include requirements of another person which are to be treated as his . . .

In effect then a single striker, without wife or children, is entirely disqualified from benefit, and the same is true where both husband and wife are involved in a trade dispute. Otherwise, subject to the rules described later, the weekly requirements of a striker's wife and dependent children will be met.

Subsection (2) provides that the disqualification does not apply where the claimant 'proves that he is not participating in or directly interested in the trade dispute which caused the stoppage of work'. These rules, therefore, mirror those in the Social Security Act 1975 disqualifying persons involved in trade disputes from unemployment benefit. There is a considerable body of case-law concerning this disqualification,[14] and this will presumably be regarded as binding on benefit officers (as it was on the Commission) when they determine entitlement to benefit. On appeal the supplementary benefits tribunal must refer the case to an insurance officer (not as previously, the local tribunal) for him to determine.[15]

ii Urgent cases payments

The new Trade Disputes Regulations enable either a single striker, or a striker with a wife and family, to claim an urgent needs payment in certain specified circumstances.[16] (The general urgent cases rules discussed in Part 6 of this chapter do not apply at all.) It should be noted that these payments may only be made in the very restricted situations described in the regulations; the Commission used to make an urgent needs payment where the single striker was destitute, but there is now no general safety-net of this sort. A payment will not be made if the claimant could meet his need by any capital (the proceeds of sale of a home, or £2,000 or less), or by income disregarded under either the Resources Regulations or under the Trade Disputes Regulations (strike pay of up to £13.00 a week).[17] And it will also not be made if the need for the item, for which a payment would otherwise be made, can be met by any member of the claimant's assessment unit or any other person, public body, trade union, or other fund to whom or which it is reasonable to expect the claimant and his

13 The concept also appears in SBA 1976, s.25(2), under which a person is not liable for the offence of a failure to maintain himself or any other persons by reason of anything done or not done in the course of a trade dispute.
14 Pp. 120–128, above.
15 SI 1980/1643, reg 5.
16 SI 1980/1641, regs 3–11.
17 Ibid, reg 3(3)(a).

family to turn for help.[18] This clearly gives the benefit officer considerable scope for fine judgment on the appropriateness of making a payment.

Subject to these general conditions, an urgent needs payment may be made in a case of emergency relief under the same rules which govern such an award to other categories of claimant.[19] Payment may also be made for the extra costs of special dietary requirements (of the striker or any member of his family), for the school transport costs of a disabled dependant, for certain maternity needs, for essential household equipment (where a member of the assessment unit is affected by a trade dispute and an item has broken down and is in need of repair), and finally, in some very restricted circumstances, to enable a member of a unit affected by a trade dispute to meet the costs of travel for hospital visits.[20] Under this last head, where the visitor himself is a striker, the expenses will only be met to enable him to visit a partner, a dependant (if he has no partner), or a close relative who is critically ill.[1] In effect these payments are made for certain kinds of exceptional needs, which cannot be met by additions to the ordinary scale rates or by single payments for members of families affected by trade disputes. The '£13 rule' under which no benefit is to be paid to a family at all if otherwise the amount would be £13 or less is not to apply to any part of the supplementary benefit paid to a claimant under the urgent cases regulations.[2] A final point is that only those payments made for emergency relief are recoverable.[3]

iii Strikers' families

The wife (or person living with the applicant) and children of a striker are entitled to have their requirements met, notwithstanding that this will naturally benefit the striker himself.[4] The wife's normal requirements (to take the usual case) will be assessed as those of an adult non-householder,[5] and housing requirements will be met in full. Children's requirements are also assessed in the usual way. On the other hand, generally sums are not payable for additional requirements,[6] though in the urgent cases mentioned above a payment will be made for these needs.

Although the striker's own requirements are not met, there is no reason in principle why the normal aggregation provision should not be applied for resources, so that his income and capital are taken into account in assessing the family's benefit. In fact the SBC used until 1971 to adopt a more generous attitude, disregarding the striker's income up to the level he would have received in benefit if he had not been disqualified.[7] The Social Security Act of that year provided that all income (including strike pay) should be taken into account subject only to the normal disregard of £4.00. The law has now been further tightened to induce the unions to meet the needs of families affected by trade disputes. With one major exception, any payment which the striker receives, or is entitled to receive, because of

18 Ibid, reg 3(3)(b).
19 Ibid, reg 4.
20 Ibid, regs 5–9. For details, see *Lynes* pp. 228–232.
1 SI 1980/1641, reg 9(1).
2 Ibid, reg 10.
3 Ibid, reg 11.
4 SBA 1976, s.8(1).
5 SI 1980/1299, Sch 2, para 10.
6 P. 479, above.
7 Gennard and Lasko [1974] Br Jo of Industrial Relations 1 discuss the repercussions of this policy and the reasons for the change in 1971.

his lack of employment, is to be taken fully into account.[8] This specifically includes income tax repayments, whether he claims them or not; under the Resources Regulations, as already mentioned, such payments are treated in this circumstance as income rather than capital.[9] The exception to this new rule is that any payment which the striker receives, or is entitled to receive, from a trade union because of the dispute is to be disregarded in assessing his resources – subject to a maximum of £13.00 (or any higher sum which may be specified by order).[10] The importance of this rule can only be seen in conjunction with the other reform made by the Social Security (No 2) Act 1980, a controversial and bitterly opposed measure. This provides that the weekly supplementary benefit which would otherwise be paid to a striker for a member of his assessment unit is not to be paid if it is £13 or less, and if more than £13, it is to be assessed as the difference between that sum and £13.[11] The purpose of the '£13 rule', together with the disregard of trade union strike payments, is clearly to encourage unions to take over from the state the primary responsibility for providing for the needs of families affected by labour disputes. This can be illustrated by the following example:

> Suppose the requirements of a family affected by a dispute are £40, and the striker receives £13 from his union. This latter sum is disregarded, but because of the '£13 rule' the family is only entitled to £27 weekly benefit. This in effect tops up the basic provision made by the union. If, however, he did not receive any pay from the union, he would still be entitled only to £27. The intended result is that more unions will make strike pay arrangements, or, of course, not resort to the 'strike weapon' if they cannot afford to do this.

The £13 limit must be increased in line with the percentage increases to benefit amount made by up-rating orders.[12]

Assessment of the wisdom of this reform necessarily depends largely on basic attitudes to the support of strikers' families. It can, however, be said that if the object is right, this complex network of provisions is more likely to achieve the desired end than the previous reform in 1971 which apparently induced unions to divert strike funds to other purposes.[13] Moreover, it is easy to overestimate the practical importance of these issues: in fact, as the Commission pointed out, the number of strikers and their families in receipt of benefit was low in relation both to total claimants and the numbers involved in trade disputes.[14] On the other hand, some would think that annual expenditure of £2.5 million on benefit for this group in 1979, twice as much as the expenditure in 1975 and 1976 together, sufficiently extravagant to warrant reform.

There is an important special rule concerning strikers' earnings. As is the case with all claimants, benefit is not payable for the period covered by his last award of earnings;[15] if those earnings are more than twice the benefit requirements of his family, the excess is treated as resources for the first week in which benefit is payable.[16]

8 SSA (No 2) 1980, s.6(1)(a).
9 SI 1981/1527, reg 3(2)(d)(i): p. 482, above.
10 SI 1980/1641, reg 12. Originally the relevant sum was £12, but this has now been increased to £13: SI 1981/1383.
11 SSA (No 2) 1980, s.6(1)(b).
12 Ibid, s.6(2), and see now SI 1981/1383.
13 See Gennard and Lasko, n.7, above, at 7; Lasko 38 MLR 31 at 34.
14 SBC Annual Report 1979 (Cmnd 8033), para 10.46 and Table 10.1.
15 Pp. 457–458, above.
16 SI 1981/1527, reg 10(2)(e). For other special rules, see ibid, reg 10(3).

iv The position after return to full-time work

A claimant returning to work after a trade dispute, during the course of which he was unable to claim benefit for his own requirements, is entitled to claim benefit for the first 15 days after his return, because for that period he is not to be regarded as in full-time work.[17] This is in line with the normal rules when a person returns to work after a period of unemployment.[18] However, two special rules apply to strikers in this situation. First, there is no disregard allowed for any earnings actually received by a claimant during this period or for any sum offered him by way of advance or loan by his employer.[19] This provision is in fact marginally more generous than the previous law which applied to persons returning to work after a trade dispute, whether they had been disqualified from benefit or not.[20] Secondly, any benefit paid in these circumstances may be recovered under a procedure to be discussed in the next paragraph.[1] The purpose of these rules, introduced in the 1971 legislation, was to reduce reliance by these claimants on benefit rather than on the advance of wages offered by their employers, generally known as the 'sub'.[2] Throughout the late 1960s union members had become increasingly unwilling to take an advance on wages, repayable to the employer, preferring instead to receive unrepayable and untaxable assistance.[3] In this context, the reform certainly seems understandable.

The Trade Disputes Regulations make a number of changes to the procedure for recovery from earnings of benefit paid to claimants after their return to work. Under the new rules the benefit officer decides the level of 'protected earnings', below which no deduction may be made. They are assessed as the claimant's weekly normal and housing requirements plus £8.00, less any child benefit which forms part of his resources.[4] The Secretary of State (who will have received notice in writing from the benefit officer of the award and the level of 'protected earnings') must then serve a deduction notice on the employer which may last for up to 26 weeks (or a shorter specified period).[5] This requires the latter to deduct one-half of the excess of the beneficiary's net earnings (after deduction of tax and social security payments, etc.) over his 'protected earnings'.[6] Employers are under obligations to keep records of the deductions made, and to send these to the Secretary of State; a failure to deduct the right sum on the appropriate days is sanctioned by its recovery from the employer.[7] Where it is wholly impracticable to achieve recovery of benefit by this procedure, the Secretary of State may recover it directly from the claimant.[8]

Although the procedure under which an employer is responsible for discharging his employee's debts is relatively familiar in English law, its use

17 SBA 1976, s.9(1).
18 P. 458, above.
19 SI 1981/1527, reg 10(6).
20 See the first edition of this book, p. 531.
1 SBA 1976, s.9(2), as amended by SSA 1981, s.4.
2 An advance of wages may be offered because of the common practice of working a 'week in hand'. Under this practice wages are not paid until the end of the second week of work. Sometimes two weeks or even a month may be worked in hand.
3 See the figures given by Sir K Joseph, Standing Committee F Debates on the Social Security Bill 1971, col 197.
4 SI 1980/1641, reg 14.
5 Ibid, regs 15–16.
6 Ibid, reg 17.
7 Ibid, reg 22.
8 Ibid, reg 21.

in this area has been criticised.[9] A number of employers apparently feel it endangers labour relations, and it seems that some have been prepared to make the repayments to the DHSS themselves.[10]

Part 8 Supplementary benefits and maintenance

A Introduction

This Part is concerned with the award of benefit to separated and divorced women and to unmarried mothers, and its relationship to maintenance and affiliation payments. Problems arise because the Supplementary Benefits legislation imposes a duty on spouses to maintain each other and their children, and similarly a duty on a mother and a putative father to maintain illegitimate children.[11] Thus, a separated wife is entitled to look to her husband as well as the DHSS for support if she and her children are in need, and this raises a number of questions, in particular whether she should be expected to exhaust her maintenance remedies against her husband before relying on assistance. The law in this area was one of the few which in substance was left unchanged by the 1980 reforms,[12] but there is one addition which is discussed in the last section of this Part: an immigrant's sponsor is now liable to maintain him under the Supplementary Benefits Act 1976 (as amended) and the Secretary of State may enforce this obligation.

This area is relatively little regulated by statutory instrument and in practice used to be governed by SBC policies, published in its Handbook. Its discretion is now exercised by the Secretary of State and applied by benefit officers under his guidance. To some extent policies are stated in the new Handbook,[13] though a more detailed commentary on some issues probably ought to have been published. A valuable source of supplementary information is the Finer Report on One-Parent Families, but some of this may now be out of date.[14]

B Evolution of the present law[15]

The position of deserted wives with children was not specifically covered by the Poor Law Amendment Act 1834. The practice of poor law guardians varied widely; some refused relief on the ground that payment of assistance might encourage collusive desertion and fraudulent claims.[16] Those who did provide outdoor relief could, after the Poor Law Amendment Act 1868,

9 See the Attachment of Earnings Act 1971, under which employers are required to deduct maintenance payments from their employee's wages. There is a full discussion of this in Bromley *Family Law* (6th edn) pp. 512–514.
10 Gennard and Lasko [1974] Br Jo of Industrial Relations 9.
11 SBA 1976, s.17.
12 *Social Assistance*, p. 105, indicated that the law might be examined at a later stage, but no progress in this area has been reported.
13 Ch 14, below.
14 Also see Cretney *Principles of Family Law* (3rd edn) ch 13; Stevenson *Claimant or Client?* (1973) ch 6; Marsden *Mothers Alone* (1973).
15 See *Finer* Appendix 5, section 5; Brown 18 MLR 113, and the judgment of Lord Goddard CJ, in *National Assistance Board v Wilkinson* [1952] 2 QB 648, [1952] 2 All ER 255, DC.
16 *Finer* Appendix 5, para 69.

apply to a summary court requiring the woman's husband to reimburse them.

The antecedents of the present law with regard to unmarried mothers can be seen even earlier in the nineteenth century.[17] The 1834 Act enabled parishes to recover from the putative father any money spent on relief for an illegitimate child. Amending legislation in 1844 temporarily took the matters out of the hands of the poor law guardians, and introduced a direct civil action by the mother against the putative father – the precursor of modern affiliation proceedings. But in 1868 the poor law authorities regained their power to recover from him when a mother and her child became a charge on the parish.

These principles were substantially reflected in the National Assistance Act 1948. This removed the obligation of grandparents and children to maintain destitute relatives, which had existed since the Poor Relief Act 1601; but the husband and wife remained under a duty to maintain each other, and parents, including the putative father, owed the same obligation to their children.[18] These 'liable relative' provisions, as they are known, have been re-enacted in the present legislation. The Supplementary Benefits Commission had a right to recover sums paid in benefit from these relatives, and this has now passed to the Secretary of State (referred to subsequently for convenience as the DHSS).[19]

C Separated wives

i General

A separated wife is entitled to benefit in her own right; the aggregation rule does not apply, as the husband and wife are clearly then not members of the same household.[1] Her husband's income and capital are irrelevant to her benefit entitlement, but, of course, any maintenance actually paid to her is fully taken into account when assessing her resources.[2] A claimant in this position will be asked about the circumstances of her separation and her husband's whereabouts. This is to enable the DHSS to contact him as soon as possible in order to induce him to pay maintenance and reduce the burden on the state. However, the Department will not usually approach him if the wife is in receipt of a maintenance order and this is being regularly paid, or if she has already started proceedings. If the amount paid or offered by the husband equals (or exceeds) the wife's benefit entitlement, this is accepted, and provided payments are made, that is the end of the matter.[3]

However, much more often than not, the husband will have taken on other commitments since the separation, e.g. by living with another woman, and he will be unable, or unwilling, to pay very much. The Finer Committee found that in the vast majority of cases he was unable to afford as much as the supplementary benefit scale rates,[4] and concluded that:

17 Ibid, at paras 55–65.
18 NAA 1948, s.42.
19 SBA 1976, ss.18–19.
20 For a comparison of the position in Britain and Germany, see Müller-Fembeck and Ogus 25 ICLQ 382 at 400–402.
1 The aggregation rules are discussed at pp. 461–465, above.
2 P. 486, above.
3 Handbook, paras 14.6–14.11.
4 Appendix 7, Table 60.

> The overwhelming majority of one-parent families on supplementary benefit are better off with the scale rates of benefit which they receive than they would be on maintenance orders paid regularly and in full.[5]

It is in these situations that the Commission's policy was controversial, and difficult questions still arise whether a woman should be expected to take maintenance proceedings, and if so, how much her husband should be required to pay in the context of his new responsibilities.

Of course, a robust attitude here may be influenced by a suspicion that, when an application for benefit is made by a deserted wife, the case is really one of fictitious desertion and the husband is still supporting her. The Fisher Committee found that about 2,000 suspected cases were investigated annually, and concluded that when proved they were less deserving of sympathy than the more frequent cohabitation cases.[6] This is perhaps a reasonable conclusion, but in some instances it may be that an apparent attempt to abuse the social security system masks a welfare problem which requires sympathetic treatment.[7]

ii The liable relative's contribution

The Commission evolved some guidelines for officers to determine whether an offer made by the husband for his wife's maintenance should be accepted as reasonable, even though it falls short of the benefit she is entitled to receive. These principles have never been published in the Handbook (an omission for which there seems no good reason), but were set out in broad terms in the Finer Report.[8] They seem not to have altered since then. The formula is that the liable relative (generally, though not necessarily the husband) should be left with enough money to meet his own requirements on the benefit scale rates, including full housing payments (this may embrace mortgage capital repayments), and to meet the requirements of his new dependants. In addition to this, he is to be left with a margin of £5.00 or one-quarter of his net earnings (that is, his pay after deduction of tax and social security contributions), whichever is the higher sum. This generous margin is intended to cover his special expenses such as fares to work and hire purchase instalments. It is only the sum left after deducting all these amounts from his resources which is to be regarded as available for meeting the wife's needs. In this way it is recognised that priority will be given to the family actually living with, and dependent on, the husband.

What is particularly interesting is that these guidelines are more generous to the husband and his 'second family' than those generally adopted by the courts when they are confronted with a maintenance application by his wife (or former wife). They will not take any account of the fact that she is receiving benefit when deciding whether to award maintenance, and regard as quite immaterial the point that an award will only lead to a decrease in benefit payments and so be of advantage to the taxpayer rather than the wife.[9] On these aspects the courts' approach can be justified in the context of a system which puts the emphasis on individual rather than collective responsibility for the financial conse-

5 Para 4.185.
6 Paras 346–347.
7 *Stevenson*, n.14, above, at p. 138.
8 Paras 4.188–4.189. The formula is set out in *Stone's Justices' Manual* (1981) p. 2128.
9 *Barnes v Barnes* [1972] 3 All ER 872, [1972] 1 WLR 1381, CA. See Cretney, n.14, above, at pp. 290–292.

quences of marital breakdown, and there is the further practical point that an award of maintenance will continue even if the wife ceases to receive benefit, perhaps because she takes full-time work. On the other hand, in assessing the quantum of maintenance, the courts usually adopt what is called the one-third rule under which the wife is entitled to one-third of the husband's resources; this may be applied even if the husband is then left with less than the income which would be allowed him by the DHSS guideline.[10] The courts will not award maintenance if the result will be to leave the husband with an income below the supplementary benefit scale rate to which he would be entitled if he were eligible for benefit,[11] but in most cases they will not follow the DHSS formula under which he is also left with a margin above those rates.[12] Moreover, the courts are not bound by a determination that the husband is entitled to receive benefit, though they should take it into account; thus it is permissible for magistrates to conclude that he should be able to find work (and consequently, afford maintenance payments) even though a benefit officer has come to a different conclusion.[13]

There is obviously room for two views on whether the DHSS or the courts' approach is preferable, but surely some steps should be taken to harmonise them. As Finer J observed during the course of his judgment in *Williams v Williams*:[14]

> . . . there is something radically unsatisfactory in a state of the law . . . which allows two authorities . . . when dealing with precisely the same people in the identical human predicament to make different determinations, each acting in ignorance of what the other is doing and applying rules which only tangentially meet each other.

It was in the hope that publication might lead to reform that the Finer Committee disclosed the criteria then applied by the Commission in assessing a reasonable contribution by the liable relative. The Committee's own proposals for removing these inconsistencies are mentioned later.[15]

iii The DHSS policy with regard to maintenance applications

If the husband is not paying any maintenance when his wife claims benefit, and is not persuaded to make a contribution when contacted by the DHSS, the question arises whether she should be encouraged in any way to make a maintenance application, the effect of which (if successful) would be to transfer part of the burden of supporting her from the state to her husband. At one time the SBC used to encourage a woman to obtain a court order whenever practicable, but the Finer Committee found this course was unjustifiable in terms of practical advantages and that it often induced women to feel they were under some compulsion to apply for maintenance.[16] Commission policy was then revised. While the advantages of taking maintenance proceedings are explained to the claimant, it is made clear that the choice is entirely hers and no pressure is put on her to take this step. To avoid misunderstanding, she is given an explanatory leaflet

10 *Cretney*, n.14, above, at pp. 310–312 and 384.
11 *Ashley v Ashley* [1968] P. 582, [1965] 3 All ER 554, DC.
12 *Shallow v Shallow* [1979] Fam 1, [1978] 2 All ER 483, CA.
13 *Bromilow v Bromilow* (1977) 7 Fam Law 16.
14 [1974] Fam 55 at 61.
15 P. 513, below.
16 Paras 4.199–4.202, and also see Stevenson *Claimant or Client?* (1973) pp. 137–138.

which sets out the options.[17] This remains the position after the 1980 reforms.

In principle the present policy seems reasonable. But it is questionable whether there are often substantial advantages to the initiation of maintenance proceedings. It is very rare for the sum awarded on such an application to be larger than benefit. As the Finer Committee itself admitted,[18] there is more in the point that a maintenance award will not lapse when benefit is no longer payable, but this may only be of academic interest in the typical case where a woman is left to look after children and there is no realistic prospect of her finding work. And there may be some doubt whether officers always refrain from putting pressure on claimants to disclose the whereabouts of the husband and to pursue maintenance proceedings even when this would be distressing to them. Administration of DHSS policy is in the hands of specialist Liable Relative Officers, whose number has increased in the last few years as the Department attempts to control what it considers to be abuse of the supplementary benefits system.[19]

iv The 'diversion procedure'

Under an administrative arrangement made with the co-operation of the Home Office and justices' clerks, maintenance payments may be 'diverted' to the DHSS, while the full supplementary benefit is paid weekly to the woman.[20] This procedure saves her the anxiety occasioned by irregular maintenance payments and the resulting necessity to visit the DHSS office to obtain benefit to meet the deficit. It may always be used where the maintenance award is lower than the supplementary benefit to which she is entitled; in the very rare case where it is equal to or higher than her benefit, the procedure is only used if it becomes clear after a few weeks that there will be repeated failures to comply with the court order. It may also be employed for the benefit of divorced women, though the court order must then be registered in the magistrates' court, so that periodic payments are made to the justices' clerk.

This procedure is commonly used; in 1970 the Finer Committee found that three-quarters of all court orders were diverted.[1] It would, however, no longer be necessary if the Committee's radical reform proposals mentioned later were ever implemented.

v Enforcement by the DHSS

The Department may take *criminal* proceedings under the amended section 25 of the 1976 Act for a persistent failure to maintain a spouse or dependant. Such proceedings are taken only as a last resort, and, as the Handbook says, are most frequently taken where there is consistent and unjustifiable refusal to maintain or where the defaulter has disappeared without making arrangements for payment.[2] The Finer Committee had recommended that use of prosecution in this situation should be discontinued,[3] but in fact its employment has increased a little in the last few years.

17 Handbook, para 14.15.
18 Paras 4.199–4.201.
19 See SBC Annual Report 1979 (Cmnd 8033), paras 10.37 and 10.40.
20 Handbook, paras 14.25–14.28.
1 *Finer* Table 4.12.
2 Handbook, para 14.31.
3 *Finer* para 4.211.

in 1979 452 prosecutions were brought (and 401 convictions secured), an increase of 10 per cent over the previous year.[4] This shows the greater effort now made to stamp out abuse.

Much more important would appear to be the DHSS's power to take *civil* proceedings against the defaulting spouse under section 18. But in practice this is used little more frequently than criminal prosecution: in 1979 there were 431 proceedings in respect of wives and legitimate children and 519 cases with regard to illegitimate children, in both instances large increases over the comparable figures for the previous year.[5] The magistrates' court considering the application 'shall have regard to all the circumstances and, in particular, to the resources of the liable person'.[6] Apart from this, there is nothing in the legislation which limits the circumstances in which the DHSS may recover a contribution from the liable relative. The Divisional Court did once hold that the wife's adultery or desertion might provide the husband with a defence,[7] but later cases explained that her matrimonial offence, or conduct falling just short of this, is only a factor to be taken into consideration together with other relevant circumstances.[8] It is clear that a husband may be liable to make payments to the Department, even though a condition of the separation from his wife was that she would not claim maintenance,[9] and it has also been recently held that the husband's statutory obligation is not discharged by the making of a consent order under which he transferred the former matrimonial home to his ex-spouse.[10]

vi Divorced wives

For supplementary benefit purposes, the position of a divorced wife is very similar to that of a woman separated from her husband. Thus, she may claim benefit in her own right, and only the amount of maintenance actually paid by her former husband is included in her resources.[11] The only significant difference is that a former husband (or wife) is not a 'liable relative' under the legislation, and so the DHSS has no power to recover payments from one spouse in respect of the benefit paid the other. However, as a parent, he (or she) is liable to maintain the children, and the DHSS may take proceedings to secure performance of this obligation.

D Unmarried mothers

Some of the one-parent families in receipt of benefit are single women with illegitimate children, though they are a smaller group than either divorced or separated wives.[12] In many respects the entitlement of an unmarried mother is the same as that of a separated wife. Thus, she is entitled to claim benefit for her own and her children's needs, though, of course, any money

4 SBC Annual Report 1979, n.19, above, at para 8.30.
5 Ibid.
6 SBA 1976, s.18(3).
7 *National Assistance Board v Wilkinson* [1952] 2 QB 648, [1952] 2 All ER 255.
8 See *National Assistance Board v Prisk* [1954] 1 All ER 400, [1954] 1 WLR 443, DC; *National Assistance Board v Parkes* [1955] 2 QB 506, [1955] 3 All ER 1, CA.
9 Ibid.
10 *Hulley v Thompson* [1981] 1 All ER 1128, [1981] 1 WLR 159, DC, noted in [1981] JSWL 176.
11 There is no disregard of such payments: see p. 486, above.
12 SBC Annual Report 1979, n.19, above, at Table 8.7.

actually paid to her by the natural father must be taken into account as part of her resources. It is now clear that payments made for the child's benefit, whether as part of a voluntary agreement or under an affiliation order, are included in the mother's resources.[13]

As with separated wives, if no voluntary arrangement has been made, the DHSS officer discusses with the woman the possibility of taking affiliation proceedings.[14] This represents a relaxation of the earlier policy of encouraging this course. Any pressure on single women is particularly unfortunate, as many of them are understandably reluctant to name the father of their child. The Handbook now emphasises that her entitlement does not depend on her willingness to provide this information.[15]

The Department may itself take proceedings under section 19 of the legislation. If no affiliation order is in force,[16] the DHSS may, within three years from the time benefit was last paid, apply for its own independent order against the putative father.[17] This is entirely separate from the woman's own right to take affiliation proceedings and is not subject to the same technical limits: thus, it does not matter that she would be out of time were she to apply herself,[18] that she is not a 'single woman' for the purposes of the order,[19] or even that her own action has been dismissed on the evidence.[20] Alternatively the effect of the DHSS proceedings may be to vary an existing affiliation order, so that payments may be directed to the Department, a variation which may be made even after the mother's death.[1] As already noted, there has been an increase in the number of these proceedings in the late 1970s.

E Reform of the law

The Finer Committee recommended a new scheme to regulate the relationship between benefit payments and maintenance from liable relatives.[2] A lone mother would receive benefit in the normal way,[3] and she would not then be advised about, let alone encouraged to take, proceedings against her husband. Instead, the SBC (now the Department) would determine what he should pay as a contribution, and this would be enforced by the issue of an 'administrative order'. There would be an appeal to a tribunal on questions of quantum, while on legal issues (e.g. non-paternity of the child or the wife's serious misconduct) the husband could appeal to a court. In future, the Report envisaged that a woman would only take proceedings herself if she thought there was a real chance she would obtain more from the maintenance or affiliation order than she would in benefit.

These proposals are entirely separate from the principal recommendation in the Report for a new, non-contributory benefit for one-parent

13 SI 1981/1524, reg 3: p. 464, above.
14 Handbook, para 14.24.
15 Ibid, para 14.18.
16 The order must actually provide for payments to be an 'affiliation order': *Oldfield v National Assistance Board* [1960] 1 QB 635, [1960] 1 All ER 524, DC.
17 SBA 1976, s.19(2).
18 *National Assistance Board v Mitchell* [1956] 1 QB 56, [1955] 3 All ER 291, DC.
19 *National Assistance Board v Tugby* [1957] 1 QB 507, [1957] 1 All ER 509, DC.
20 *Clapham v National Assistance Board* [1961] 2 QB 77, [1961] 2 All ER 50, DC.
1 SBA 1976, s.19(5).
2 *Finer* Part 4, sections 11 and 12 (noted by Reid 38 MLR 52).
3 Ibid, paras 4.262–4.272 for the scope of the proposals.

families, the guaranteed maintenance allowance.[4] Even if this new benefit were introduced, there would still be a role for supplementary benefits here, particularly during the first three months of separation when the allowance would not be payable. While these proposals would avoid some of the problems of the present system, it may be argued that in principle it is objectionable to require a liable relative to contribute without a court hearing. In any case it is difficult to believe these proposals will be implemented in the present economic climate.[5]

F Sponsored immigrants

The only change made in 1980 to this part of the legislation is that an immigrant's sponsor (under the Immigration Act 1971) is liable to maintain him, and this duty may be enforced by the DHSS in the same way as it enforces the obligations of liable relatives.[6] In effect this restores the position to that which used to exist before 1975; until then the SBC used to withhold benefit from an immigrant admitted to the country, if his sponsor was able to support him. This practice was ruled illegal by the Divisional Court, as it was improper to take into account an undertaking to support, rather than actual support, in assessing a claimant's resources.[7] The principle established by this ruling has not been affected by the 1980 reform: the immigrant will be fully entitled to benefit, but this may then be recovered from his sponsor. The Handbook makes it clear that the Department will always pursue liability, and that where appropriate, civil or criminal proceedings will be initiated.[8]

Part 9 Special cases

In this Part there is a short summary of the principal rules governing the award of benefit to some special categories of claimant.[9] These mostly entail modifications to the normal rules for assessing requirements which are set out in schedule 2 to the Requirements Regulations, though mention is also made of some relevant single payments and other regulations.

A Hospital patients[10]

The amount of benefit paid to patients depends on a number of factors, principally whether the claimant is a member of a couple (whether married or unmarried), or single, and the duration of his stay in hospital. As with the Commission's policy, the general aim of the provisions is to ensure the claimant (and his family) have enough to meet continuing commitments while he is in hospital and to pay for some personal expenses during that

4 Ibid, Part 5, ss.5–7, and see Eekelaar [1976] PL 64.
5 For other proposals for reform, see *Response of SBC to Social Assistance* (1979) paras 3.14–3.16.
6 SBA 1976, s.17(1)(c). The DHSS may only recover sums which it has paid in benefit: SBA 1976, s.18(3).
7 P. 480, above.
8 Para 14.33.
9 For fuller treatments, see Handbook, chs 7 and 8; *Lynes* ch 13.
10 For the similar rules for contributory benefits, see ch 10, pp. 394–398, above.

period. On the other hand, there will generally be a reduction in the benefit otherwise payable to take account of his diminished costs.[11]

– If the patient is a member of a couple, the usual rate of benefit is payable for the first eight weeks of his stay in hospital; after that, the normal rate of benefit is reduced by 20 per cent of the long-term rate for householders. Thus the spouse not in hospital is left enough for his (or her) requirements, and there is a margin for hospital visits and the patient's expenses. Where both spouses are in hospital, from the beginning of the claimant's stay only 40 per cent of the long-term rate for householders is payable.[12] After one spouse has spent more than two years in hospital, they are no longer treated as members of the same household, and thus the aggregation rules cease to apply.[13] The partner outside hospital is then assessed as a single person, and the same is true of the other partner who is treated under the rules in the next paragraph.
– The requirements of a single patient are immediately modified when he becomes a patient (unless he has a dependant, in which case this does not take effect until eight weeks have passed,[14] though this qualification does not apply where the child is in the care of a local authority).[15] Under the modification he is entitled to 20 per cent of the long-term rate of benefit. The amount paid him may be reduced to nil or an amount considered reasonable (having regard to the view of the hospital staff and the patient's relatives) if he has been in hospital for more than a year and a doctor certifies that the normal benefit cannot usefully be spent on his behalf.[16] Benefit for a child is not affected until he has been in hospital continuously for 12 weeks; it is then reduced to 20 per cent of the householder's long-term benefit.[17]

After 1975 the Commission met the needs of mental patients, ending a previous arrangement under which payments could be made by Area Health Authorities. Their requirements are now met in the usual way, though this does not apply to those patients who entered hospital before November 1975, have been there ever since and were under 80 (and so ineligible for non-contributory retirement pension) when the new scheme took effect in November 1980.[18] They still depend on allowances made by the hospital, a position criticised by the SBC in its final report.[19]

B Persons in residential accommodation

There are several categories of claimant who are housed in special accommodation, and who because of the range of services provided under these arrangements, have unusual, often lower, requirements. It may in some cases be important to distinguish these groups from boarders who pay board and lodging charges on a commercial basis: their requirements have already been discussed.[20]

11 See Handbook, para 7.21.
12 SI 1980/1299, Sch 2, para 2.
13 SI 1981/1524, reg 2(3)(b); pp. 461–465, above, for the aggregation rules.
14 SI 1980/1299, Sch 2, para 2.
15 SI 1981/1524, reg 4(2)(d) sets out the circumstances in which a person is not treated as responsible for a dependant because he is not living with him.
16 SI 1980/1299, Sch 2, para 2.
17 Ibid.
18 *Lynes* p. 240.
19 SBC Annual Report 1979 (Cmnd 8033), paras 10.69–10.71.
20 Pp. 476–477, above.

i Residential homes for the elderly and disabled

Under section 21 of the National Assistance Act 1948,[1] local authorities are empowered, and may be directed by the Secretary of State for Social Services, to provide —

> residential accommodation for persons who by reason of age, infirmity or any other circumstances are in need of care and attention which is not otherwise available to them.

This responsibility may be discharged either by local authorities providing their own homes or by arrangements with private hostels and old people's homes.

- In either case, the requirements of persons in 'Part III accommodation', as it is often known, are assessed at the long-term householder's rate for a single person (of which 80 per cent is for the accommodation and the rest for personal expenses), and twice that amount where both partners are in such accommodation.[2] Any excess over this amount which is charged by a voluntary body or private home is paid by the local authority. (Where a person is living in such a home under a private arrangement and the local authority does not accept responsibility because he does not fall within the terms of the 1948 legislation, his requirements are assessed on the basis that he is a boarder: this will be more generous than the Part III rate, because the claimant here will have himself to meet various costs, such as bedding and toilet articles, which are usually provided for him in a local authority supported institution.)

ii Other persons in residential homes

Local authorities may similarly provide residential care for expectant and nursing mothers, and for persons suffering or recovering from mental disorder. In both situations, where the claimant is staying in a local authority supported institution, benefit is assessed at the Part III rate.[3] When he stays in a private home, benefit is assessed on the boarders' board and lodging basis.

iii Homeless families

Local authority housing departments are responsible for providing accommodation for homeless persons.[4] Their benefit is assessed according to the nature of that accommodation: if they are boarded in a guest house or bed and breakfast establishment, they are treated as boarders, while if they stay in a local authority home, they will either be assessed as ordinary householders or at the Part III rate, depending on the facilities (in particular, meals) provided at this home.[5]

C Prisoners

No benefit is payable to a prisoner, defined as a person in prison or otherwise detained in legal custody.[6] The aggregation rules do not apply to

1 As amended by the Local Government Act 1972, Sch 23, para 2(1). The corresponding provision in Scotland is the Social Work (Scotland) Act 1968, s.7.
2 SI 1980/1299, Sch 2, para 1.
3 Handbook, paras 7.15–7.18.
4 Housing (Homeless Persons) Act 1977, s.4.
5 Handbook, para 7.19.
6 SI 1980/1299, Sch 2, para 9. See pp. 398–401, above, for the rules for contributory benefits

his family, since he is not treated as a member of the same household as his wife (or woman with whom he has been living).[7] The result is that she is independently entitled to claim benefit on the basis of her own needs.

In some circumstances prisoner status may be a relevant factor in the award of single payments. In particular, such a payment will be made where a prisoner is granted leave to be spent in a claimant's house, shortly before his release, and where he would, if not a prisoner, have been a member of the same household as the latter.[8] On final discharge, the prisoner is entitled to benefit in the usual way, but any discharge grant will be taken into account as resources for the first week.[9] Single payments may be available in certain circumstances for essential furniture and housing needs.[10]

D Students

A student will not normally be entitled to claim benefit during term-time (or when undertaking a prescribed course in the vacations) because he is not 'available for work' under the regulations.[11] This, however, does not apply to those students who are not required to be so available: e.g. single parents or those who through disability cannot be expected to compete in the labour market.[12] In addition, where a student is one of an unmarried couple, is not himself required to be available for work because his partner is unable to work for one of the reasons specified in the Conditions of Entitlement Regulations (e.g. she lives with a dependent child or is sick) and he would, if married, be entitled to an allowance under the Students' Dependants Allowances Regulations, he will be entitled to benefit of an amount equivalent to that available under those Regulations.[13]

If there were no other provision, students would, however, be fully entitled to claim during the vacations, provided they were available for work (normally hard to obtain at such short notice and for periods of only a few weeks). In the 1970s many students successfully claimed, and as a result regulations introduced in 1977 made this impossible for the short vacations at Christmas and Easter because under them the student maintenance grant and parental contributions (whether actually made or only notional) were taken into account without any disregard.[14] The new rules for resources, which were discussed in Part 5 of this chapter, reproduce those regulations with one minor modification. The change in 1977 did not apply to (i) disabled students, (ii) parents in a one-parent family, or (iii) *woman* students subject to the aggregation rules; they continued to enjoy a £2 disregard of their grant and their parental contribution was only taken into account if it was actually paid. Now these exceptions apply to (i) and (ii) above, and (iii) both men and women who are married (or living together), provided they have a dependant.[15]

The student maintenance grant (and parental contribution) does not cover the long summer vacation, so provided the student is available for work and is otherwise eligible, he is entitled to benefit for that period.

7 SI 1981/1524, reg 2(3)(d).
8 SI 1981/1528, reg 29.
9 SI 1981/1527, reg 11(2)(g).
10 SI 1981/1528, reg 10(1)(a)(iv).
11 SI 1981/1526, reg 8(1)(a).
12 Ibid, reg 6. See p. 461, above.
13 SI 1980/1299, Sch 2, para 3.
14 See the first edition, p. 551, for the background to these regulations.
15 SI 1981/1527, regs 4(4) and 11(2)(1).

E Miscellaneous

There is special provision for a few other categories.[16] These include persons in resettlement units (accommodation temporarily provided by the DHSS for people 'without a settled way of life' in order to induce them to find a more permanent abode and occupation),[17] members of religious orders who are regarded as having no requirements while maintained by the order, and immigrants. Reference has been made to the position of this last group earlier in the chapter.[18] Other special groups, in particular those affected by trade disputes, have been fully treated elsewhere in this chapter.

Part 10 Deductions and payment to third parties

A General

The Supplementary Benefits Commission evolved a number of policies to help those claimants who showed themselves, perhaps only temporarily, incapable of budgeting for their own needs. One course was to withhold part of the regular weekly payments under its general discretionary powers, and then subsequently to pay the accumulated sum over to meet an exceptional need, e.g. for clothing, as it arose. There was some doubt as to the legality of this practice, particularly when the deductions were made to off-set a lump sum payment which had already been made.[19] On the other hand, the SBC had clear statutory power for their other principal procedure – making payments directly to third parties.[20] This was used to make payments to claimants' landlords and to gas and electricity boards. In 1979, 91,000 direct payments were made to landlords, a matter which somewhat disturbed the Commission.[1] The procedure is expensive to operate, and there is a danger that the claimant will lose all sense of responsibility while it is used. The SBC was therefore only prepared to undertake it when there was six weeks' arrears of rent and non-payment of at least four out of the last eight due payments. There was a similar number of payments and deductions for fuel, a step which was taken when necessary to prevent the claimant's supply being disconnected.[2] Again the SBC was concerned about the overall effects of this course, but research showed it was generally welcomed by the applicants involved.[3] If housing costs and fuel were separately provided for, as the Commission has recommended, this element in the general benefit scheme could be almost entirely removed, but in the meantime it does appear to be a valuable procedure for a number of claimants. The amended Act now authorises regulations to be made for withholding payments and for making them to third parties on the claimant's behalf;[4] these are discussed here, while other

16 SI 1980/1299, Sch 2.
17 See SBA 1976, Sch 5, para 2, SBC Annual Report 1978 (Cmnd 7725), ch 17, and Donnison *The Politics of Poverty* (1982) pp. 37–39.
18 P. 456, above (ineligibility for weekly benefit) and p. 496, above (urgent cases payments).
19 See the first edition of this book, p. 523.
20 SBA 1976, s.14(3), now repealed.
1 SBC Annual Report 1979, Table 4.1.
2 Ibid, paras 10.59–10.62.
3 See *Donnison* n.17, above, at pp. 193–198.
4 SBA 1976, s.14(2)(h) and (i).

payment rules, equivalent to those which apply to other social security benefits, are discussed in chapter 14, dealing with the administration of benefits.[5]

B Postponement of benefit payment

A benefit officer may decide to withhold part of a weekly allowance or pension if he considers the claimant has failed to budget for items which the amounts paid for normal requirements are intended to cover and the need for which arises at irregular or extended intervals.[6] Typical examples of these would be clothing, footwear and household goods. When the need for the particular item has arisen, the officer must direct that the amount which has been withheld (or an appropriate part of it) be paid to the claimant. In effect this is a compulsory form of saving.

C Payments to third parties for housing and fuel requirements

Where a claimant, or his partner, is in debt for any item of expenditure covered by housing requirements or has any gas or electricity debts, the officer may determine that part of his weekly payments shall be made, at intervals to be determined by the Secretary of State, to the person or body to whom the payment is due.[7] And payments may continue to be made by this means even after the initial debt has been discharged. But the decision to make a direct payment can only be made if it is in the interests of the claimant's family. In certain circumstances, however, the officer has no power to make this decision: for example, where the fuel debts are very small or the claimant has enough capital to discharge them.

- The regulations further prescribe the normal sum which may be deducted from the benefit paid to the claimant and made over to the third party: this is the sum of a weekly amount equal to 5 per cent of the single householder rate of benefit *and* the weekly cost (actual or estimated) of the items in question.[9] But a complex set of rules then sets out various maximum limits to the sums which may be deducted in this way, and other qualifications to the formula.[10]

It may well be that a claimant has debts for more than one housing item, or for both housing and fuel items, so a provision lists priorities between the debts to be discharged by this method.[11] Thus, rent and mortgage payments are to be settled before other debts, but fuel debts enjoy priority over any payments due for other housing items, e.g. for maintenance and insurance costs.

Other regulations provide for similar arrangements to be made for boarders, persons in Part III residential accommodation, and persons in resettlement units and attending residential re-establishment centres, who have failed to budget properly for their board and lodging charges.[12] In

5 Pp. 572–573, below.
6 SI 1981/1525, reg 15. The rules used to be set out in separate regulations (SI 1980/983), which have now been consolidated in the Claims and Payments Regulations.
7 SI 1981/1525, regs 16 and 17.
8 Ibid, reg 17(6).
9 Ibid, regs 16(2) and 17(2). (See Appendix.)
10 Ibid, regs 18(1) and (2).
11 Ibid, reg 18(3).
12 Ibid, regs 19–22.

these cases, there is no need for priority rules, as the housing charges will include a sum for gas and electricity.

D Payment of benefit and single payments to third parties

The Secretary of State (not a benefit officer) may direct that a single payment awarded under section 3 to meet an exceptional need or under section 4 for an urgent need shall be made to the supplier of the item.[13] As emphasised by the Commissioner in a recent case,[14] this does not cover a payment to a person who has made a loan for the purchase of the item. The power will presumably be used where it is legitimate to infer that the claimant cannot be relied on to spend the payment on the item for which it was awarded, or because he may find it difficult himself to deal with any local supplier.

A weekly pension or allowance may be paid to a third party first, where the benefit officer considers the claimant is incapable of budgeting, or wilfully refuses to budget, for any items covered by normal, additional or housing requirements, or secondly, where he is temporarily away from home.[15] In the former type of situation, the officer must further consider it is in the family's best interest to make payment to the third party. Obviously this is designed to safeguard a wife (or other woman) whose husband refuses to support her, while continuing to live in the same household so that the aggregation rules still apply.[16] (She may alternatively be able to claim an urgent cases payment in this situation.)[17] This case must be distinguished from the position where a claimant is wholly unable (for mental reasons) to act for himself and another person may be appointed to act on his behalf – discussed in chapter 14.[18]

13 Ibid, reg 25.
14 *R(SB) 8/81*.
15 SI 1981/1525, reg 23.
16 Handbook, para 11.35.
17 P. 496, above.
18 P. 574, below.

Chapter 13

Family income supplement

Part 1 Introduction

A General

Family Income Supplement (generally known as 'FIS', and often referred to as such in this chapter) was introduced by the Conservative government in 1970. In broad terms, it is designed to provide some assistance for families with children where the wage-earner is on a very low salary. Like supplementary benefit it is, therefore, means-tested and financed by general taxation. It complements that benefit which, with rare exceptions, is not payable to a person engaged in full-time employment.[1] FIS, on the other hand, is *only* payable for a family where a man or woman (until 1983, a single woman)[2] is in full-time work and the income is less than the level prescribed under the 1970 legislation. In some respects, as will be seen, FIS has differed substantially from supplementary benefit. There has always been very little discretion in its administration, though claims used to be determined by the same body which was responsible for deciding entitlement to supplementary benefit – the Supplementary Benefits Commission. Moreover, FIS is administered by post, and not on the basis of interviews.[3]

Supplementary benefits play a crucial role in the British social security system, being received now by over 3,000,000 people. In contrast, family income supplements are only paid to about 110,000 families, though this figure shows a marked increase from the average of about 70,000 during the years 1971–71.[4] Variations in the number of recipients are primarily attributable to the level at which the prescribed income is fixed and whether it keeps pace with the rise in earnings of the lower paid. Recently, it seems the government has been relatively generous in assessing this level and as a result it may be anticipated that there will be some slight increase in those families eligible for FIS.[5]

When FIS was introduced in 1970, it was strongly opposed on the Labour benches. This was largely because the Labour party has traditionally disliked means-tested benefits, which, it is argued, potential

1 See ch 12, p. 457, above.
2 See pp. 526–527, below.
3 See p. 536, below.
4 Figures relating to the end of 1979 are taken from Social Security Statistics 1980, Table 32.10; see now First report of the Social Security Advisory Committee 1981, Figure 2.
5 SBC Annual Report for 1979 (Cmnd 8033), para 17.10. See (1975) Poverty 31 17, for discussion of prescribed income levels in the mid-1970s.

recipients are reluctant to claim.[6] But it was also generally contended that the new benefit was inadequate to cope with problems of family poverty, that it was wrong for the state to subsidise low wages, and that the withdrawal of FIS as the recipients' earnings were raised constituted a disincentive to self-improvement. These policy considerations are examined later.[7] But, despite these reservations, there has been no sustained attempt to replace the benefit with some other provision. Indeed, the only significant suggestion by a government for its replacement came in the Conservative Green Paper on Tax Credits in 1972.[8] The introduction of tax credits would absorb family income supplements: the lower paid would automatically receive an addition to their salary, if their tax credit exceeded any income tax deductible from their weekly wage.[9] It remains most improbable that this scheme will be introduced in the next few years, whatever the composition of the next government. So it appears likely that the family income supplement, conceived by its sponsors as only the first stage in a continuing programme of reform,[10] will stay as a feature of the social security system for some time.

B Policy

In 1970 the Conservative party promised to attempt to ameliorate the problems of family poverty by raising family allowances. But after its return to office, this commitment was reconsidered and the family income supplement scheme introduced instead. Sir Keith Joseph explained that the extension of family allowances to cover families with only one child would have been both too costly and time-consuming.[11] Moreover, the lowering of the tax threshold in the previous few years made the raising of allowances, with their 'claw-back' through the reduction in child tax allowances, a less efficient way of helping the poor.[12] The merit of the family income supplement, it was claimed, was that it directed help where it was most needed; for the first time a family with a wage-earner and only *one* child was eligible for assistance.[13] An interesting feature is that entitlement to FIS also enables its recipient to obtain a number of other welfare benefits, e.g. help with optical and dental charges, exemption from prescription charges and charges for school meals, free legal aid.[14] In the words often used, entitlement to FIS provides a 'passport' for a number of benefits.

The government did not see the new benefit as a final solution to the problems of family proverty but viewed it as an important ameliorating measure which should be introduced as quickly as possible. This consideration influenced the structure of the Act and the content of the benefit.

6 For the arguments against means-tested benefits, see pp. 12–15, above.
7 Pp. 523–525, below.
8 Cmnd 5116, paras 5 and 113.
9 For a discussion of the tax credit system, see p. 34, above.
10 Sir K Joseph, Secretary of State, 806 HC Official Report (5th series) cols 229–230.
11 Ibid, cols 217 ff. Though NB this has now been accomplished by the introduction of child benefits, ch 11, above.
12 But it can be argued that a better course would have been to increase family allowances and raise the tax threshold: see Barker in (ed) Bull *Family Poverty* (2nd edn) ch 6. For 'claw-back', see p. 423, above.
13 Family allowances were not payable for the first child of a family: see ch 11, p. 422, above.
14 SBC Handbook, para 17.8.

First, a substantial amount of detail was left to be covered by regulations,[15] a feature which understandably attracted a large amount of suspicion and criticism in the House of Commons. At the time this contrasted with the specific provision of the disregards, for example, in the Supplementary Benefits Act itself, though now both under the recent reform of that system and under the Child Benefits Act, many important rules are covered in regulations, and this must now perhaps be accepted as an inevitable feature of modern social security law.[16] Secondly, the new benefit was designed to be as simple as possible. In particular, the discretionary element was to be kept to a minimum. For these reasons, there was no provision for varying the amount of supplement according to the *age* (as distinct from the *number*) of the claimant's children,[17] nor was there any separate provision for rent, as there has been in the supplementary benefits scheme.[18] The opposition, therefore, stigmatised the Bill as crude and inflexible in its attempt to deal with poverty among the lower paid. Moreover, the level of the supplement – 50 per cent of the difference between the claimant's gross income (subject to a few disregards), *and* the amounts prescribed in the Act – was widely considered inadequate.[19]

Sir Keith Joseph indeed conceded that the measure would only assist between one-half and two-thirds of those working households living on an income below the supplementary benefit level.[20] The government was, however, unwilling to make more generous provision in the family income supplement scheme, because of its fear that this would remove the incentive to earn more, and encourage employers to pay artificially low wages to their employees, knowing that any shortfall below the market rate for the work would be met in full by the government.[1] For this reason it resisted amendments to pay more than 50 per cent of the difference between the claimant's earnings and the prescribed amount, and to remove the limit on the maximum amount payable by way of FIS.

There are four broad lines of attack which have been directed against the use of FIS to help the lower paid. The first is the fundamental criticism expressed by Mr Enoch Powell and one or two other Conservatives in the Second Reading Debate, that it is undesirable in principle for the state to supplement wages, as the relief provides a disincentive for employer and employee to negotiate a true market wage.[2] The objectors pointed out that in this respect the benefit marked a departure from the previous refusal of the social security system to help the low-paid. The only precedent was the 'Speenhamland system', under which, from 1795 till the reforms of 1834, poor law authorities supplemented low wages with relief calculated according to the price of bread.[3] This objection has, however, not been voiced recently. Whatever the argument's theoretical merits, it is doubtful

15 FISA 1970, s.10(2) enables regulations to be made for ten different purposes. This is not the only section in the Act empowering regulations to be made.

16 The most important FIS regulations are SI 1980/1437, consolidating with amendments, earlier statutory instruments.

17 See the criticism by Mrs S Williams, 806 HC Official Report (5th series) col 236.

18 Ibid, col 236 and col 1177. See SBC Annual Report for 1977 (Cmnd 7392), paras 14.11–14.13.

19 Mr M Meacher, 806 HC Official Report (5th Series), col 306, and Mr B O'Malley, ibid, col 318. And see *Barker*, n.12, above, at pp. 76–80.

20 806 HC Official Report (5th series) col 227.

1 Mr P Dean, Under-Secretary of State, ibid, col 1265.

2 Ibid, cols 260–265.

3 Bruce *The Coming of the Welfare State* (4th edn) pp. 55–56, 91–92; Fraser *The Evolution of the British Welfare State* (1975) pp. 34–39. And see p. 450, above.

whether FIS has had any serious effect on the wage rates of the lower paid.[4]

The second line of attack comes from the opposite end of the political spectrum. The left has argued that the introduction of FIS can at best be regarded as a palliative for the problems of the lower paid; in reality it should be seen as merely providing an excuse for the failure substantially to improve their economic position.[5] A more worthwhile step, it can be argued, would be the institution of a national minimum wage, though this might have significant and unwelcome economic consequences – almost certainly, for example, an immediate rise in unemployment – which militate against its adoption.[6] But the radicals contend further that it is impossible to divorce the problems of the low paid from the wider questions posed by economic and social inequality; only in a more equal society would it be possible for these problems to be removed.[7] Certainly it must be conceded that the use of a means-tested benefit to supplement low earnings contrasts markedly with much of the social security system which aims to provide compensation for the loss of earnings; it does not feature regularly in other welfare programmes. Whether it is desirable or practicable for the social security system to aim for a much more extensive redistribution of income, as proposd by critics of FIS, is a fundamental question, outside the scope of this chapter.[8]

The third objection to the scheme is the more detailed one that the lower paid are required themselves to claim the supplement. The government estimated that the 'take-up' would be as high as 85 per cent, but the opposition was understandably sceptical, and it seems that at least in the first years of its operation, only about 50 per cent of those eligible claimed the supplement. In the mid-1970s it seems to have increased to about 75 per cent, though reliable figures are difficult to obtain because of the uncertainty about the numbers of eligible families.[9] As the SBC pointed out in its last report, no benefit has been more extensively advertised.[10] To some extent, the problem of low 'take-up' is inevitable with a selective, means-tested benefit,[11] as opposed to, for example, a tax credit scheme.

The fourth criticism made by spokesmen of both parties during the debates on the 1970 Bill, concerns what is known as the 'poverty trap'.[12] This problem has become more acute in the last few years, and its existence may now be regarded as the principal weakness of the family income supplement. The poverty trap refers to the situation where a recipient of one (or more usually, a variety of) means-tested welfare benefits finds it difficult to improve his financial position by increasing his wages, because he then loses his entitlement to those benefits. Unless he receives an

4 There is no study available on the effect of FIS, but for a comparable discussion on the effects of negative income tax, see Green *Negative Taxes and the Poverty Problem* (1967) pp. 125–126. Also see SBC Annual Report 1977, n.18, above, at para 14.10.

5 See esp. George *Social Security and Society* (1973) pp. 67–69; *Townsend* pp. 663–664.

6 Hughes in Bull (ed) *Family Poverty* (2nd edn) p. 93. Other alternative strategies, such as a negative income tax, are considered at pp. 34–37, above.

7 *George*, n.5, above, at pp. 73–79; Field, Meacher and Pond *To Him Who Hath* (1977).

8 The question is discussed in ch 1, pp. 10–11, above.

9 SBC Annual Report for 1977, n.18, above, at para 14.5; SBC Annual Report for 1979 (Cmnd 8033), para 17.7. But see First report of the Social Security Advisory Committee 1981, Table 1.4, which suggests take-up is little over 50 per cent.

10 Ibid. In 1973–74, about £920,000 was spent on advertising FIS: 886 HC Official Report (5th series) cols 1–2.

11 See p. 13, above, and also the discussion in the National Consumer Council's *Means-Tested Benefits* (1977) ch 3.

12 E.g. Sir B Rhys-Williams, 806 HC Official Report (5th series) col 284 and Mr M Meacher, ibid, cols 306 and 1277.

enormous wage increase, the person is in effect 'trapped' by his dependence on the state provisions. The result is a disincentive for the victims of the poverty trap to improve their position, or a feeling of despair and bitterness when the only result of a wage increase or a bonus is that it is 'taxed away' by the withdrawal of welfare benefits. The problem arises in the context of family income supplement in this way. When a recipient of FIS increases his wages, his entitlement is then calculated by reference to the difference between his new wage and the prescribed amount in the Act.[13] Before the increase he used to receive 50 per cent of the difference between his wage and the prescribed amount, so that in effect he loses half his wage increase through the reduction in his FIS entitlement. For example,

– C may receive £10 FIS weekly, calculated as half the difference between the prescribed amount, say, £75[14] and his earnings, £55. If he receives a salary increase of £10, his entitlement to FIS will be reduced to £5 (half the difference between £75 and £65).

The position may be even worse than that, since entitlement to FIS also carries with it eligibility for other welfare benefits. The result is that an increase in wages may be virtually cancelled out by the loss of, or a reduction in, FIS and other means-tested benefits.[15]

The phenomenon has become more serious recently as the tax threshold has fallen, so that now many recipients of FIS are also paying income tax.[16] 30 per cent of any wage increase may be payable to the Inland Revenue, so with the 50 per cent or more taxed through loss of the supplement and perhaps other benefits, it is possible for someone to become worse off as a result of a wage increase. As is the case with the problem of take-up, it appears that a tax credit system, integrating income tax and some social security benefits, including FIS, would mitigate the severity of this problem.[17]

Hitherto, governments of both parties and the Supplementary Benefits Commission have resisted criticism, based on the poverty-trap implications of FIS, by pointing out that the benefit is now awarded for a period of 12 months;[18] it cannot then be withdrawn whether or not the family's circumstances change during that time. This by itself would, of course, merely postpone the effects of the poverty trap; but in conjunction with annual up-ratings of the FIS limits, it can successfully disguise the problem. By the time an award comes up for renewal, the prescribed amount for FIS will have been increased, and the recipient will be eligible for another award of a similar amount. The cost, however, of this 'solution' is that some families will remain more or less perpetually dependent on the state. This fact will make it more difficult to replace FIS than was originally supposed, and probably explains why no government has made any attempt to do so.

The best way to reduce dependence on FIS would be to increase radically the level of child benefit.[19] Unfortunately the government has not

13 But he will continue to receive the amount awarded on the first assessment for 12 months from the date of the award: see p. 536, below.
14 For the actual prescribed amount in force for 1982–83, see p. 533, below.
15 See the examples given in the pamphlet, Howell *Why Work?* (Conservative Political Centre, 1976).
16 The relationship of income tax and social security benefits is fully considered, pp. 32–37, above. Also see *Field, Meacher and Pond* n.7, above, at pp. 52–57.
17 P. 34, above.
18 SBC Annual Report for 1979, n.19, above, at para 17.8.
19 Ibid, at para 17.16.

felt able to do this and instead has sometimes been generous in increasing the prescribed amount for the supplement, thereby rendering more people eligible for it.[20] The introduction of the Guaranteed Maintenance Allowance for single-parent families, recommended by the Finer Committee, would have made a significant difference.[1] In the mid-1970s these families formed the majority among FIS recipients; this ceased to be so from 1976–78, but in 1979 when the 'full-time work' rule was changed for such families, they again became the largest group.[2]

Part 2 Entitlement to Family Income Supplement

There are five requirements under the Family Income Supplements Act 1970 for entitlement, including the condition that a valid claim is made. This procedural requirement is discussed in Part 3. Exposition of the other requirements is complicated because of a major change which will take effect in November 1983. The present law is that the claimant must show that (i) there is a family with at least one child, (ii) with one man or single woman engaged in remunerative full-time work, (iii) in Great Britain, (iv) whose weekly amount of resources falls short of the prescribed amount. These rules are fully analysed in this Part. But the Social Security Act 1980 amends the 1970 legislation to provide that the second requirement may be a man *or* woman engaged in full-time work, thereby giving effect to the principle of sex equality: this reform is discussed on the following page. Questions as to entitlement to FIS are decided now by supplement officers, with a right of appeal to SBATs and thence to the Social Security Commissioners.[3] There has been very little reported case law on the 1970 legislation, so inevitably many of the points made in its analysis are rather tentative.

A The 'family' for the purposes of FIS

Section 1(1) of the 1970 Act provides (before the 1980 amendment comes into effect):

> a family shall consist of the following members of a household —
> (a) one man or single woman engaged, and normally engaged, in remunerative full-time work; and
> (b) if the person mentioned in paragraph (a) above is a man and the household includes a woman to whom he is married or who lives with him as his wife, that woman; and
> (c) the child or children whose requirements are provided for, in whole or in part, by the person or either of the persons mentioned in the preceding paragraphs.

Before analysing this section in detail, two preliminary points should be made. First, the intention of the Act, made plain by section 1(1)(c), was to benefit lower paid families *with a child or children*, and not childless couples. One Conservative did suggest that the measure should be

20 Ibid, para 17.10.
1 See pp. 513–514, above, for a brief discussion of the Finer Report.
2 SBC Annual Report for 1979, n.9, above, at Table G.3. See p. 531, below, for the full-time work rule.
3 For supplement officers, see p. 544, below, and for the adjudication tribunals, see pp. 605–614, below.

expanded to cover the latter, but the proposal met with no support.[4] Secondly, the drafting of the section must be seen in the context of the law on supplementary benefits. FIS, as mentioned in the first paragraph of this chapter, was designed to complement supplementary benefit by providing assistance for families with a low income from work. In framing the legislation, therefore, the possible alternative availability of that benefit was taken into account.

In the case of supplementary benefit, the present law is that where spouses, or a man and woman are living together as husband and wife, and are members of the same household, it is the man who is entitled, though the wife's, or woman's, needs are taken into account if he is so entitled.[5] The provisions in section 1 of the 1970 Act have mirrored this pattern: where a man and woman are living together in the same household (again, it does not matter whether they are husband and wife), entitlement to FIS depends on whether *he* is engaged in remunerative full-time work. Where he is unemployed and the woman is working full-time, he may claim supplementary benefit, and no member of the family is entitled to FIS. The opposition did indeed move an amendment to delete the word 'single' from section 1(1)(a), which would have had the effect of enabling a family, where the wife was the wage-earner, to receive FIS, instead of relying on the husband's entitlement to supplementary benefit.[6] This might in some circumstances be an advantageous alternative, in particular where a husband, though not in full-time work, is for some reason, e.g. because he is a student, not entitled to receive supplementary benefit. But the amendment was successfully resisted, and the symmetry of the relationship between supplementary benefit and FIS – in both cases it is the man's position which is important – was preserved.

The amendment made by the Social Security Act 1980 (though not to come into effect until November 1983) does enable a family to receive FIS where a woman, living with a husband or another man as her husband, is in full-time work.[7] The change, obviously designed to bring about sex equality in the social security field, is to be seen as complementary to the reform of the aggregation provisions in supplementary benefits law.[8] Under that a married woman may be eligible for supplementary benefit (after 1983) if she is the principal breadwinner in the family, and it would seem likely that she would be similarly able to claim FIS if she satisfied the other conditions. The circumstances in which a married woman will be able to claim, and the relationship between FIS and supplementary benefits, will be clarified by regulations to be issued over the next year or so. The 1980 Act provides that persons including a married or unmarried couple are not to be regarded as a 'family' for FIS purposes if one member of the couple is in full-time work and the other is in receipt of payments to be prescribed by regulations.[9] Thus, if the husband is in receipt of supplementary benefit or some other payments, including wages, which are more considerable than the wife's income supplemented by FIS, it will presumably be provided that the family is not to be eligible for the supplement.

4 Mr P Fry, 806 HC Official Report (5th series) col 299. The opposition was, it seems, in agreement with the government that the problem to be solved was that of family poverty affecting children, although it wished to do this by an extension of family allowances.
5 See ch 12, pp. 461–465, above.
6 806 HC Official Report (5th series) cols 1118 ff.
7 S.7(1)(a).
8 Pp. 461–465, above.
9 SSA 1980, s.7(1)(b).

The remaining pages of this section are concerned with the present law and analyse it in the context of the types of family which may be entitled to FIS.

i Man with wife, or with woman living with him as his wife, and child or children

This was envisaged as the most typical type of family which might benefit from FIS, though, as has been mentioned earlier, in some years single-parent families have outnumbered two-parent families as recipients of the supplement.[10] In two-parent families, it is the man who must satisfy the full-time work requirement, the content of which is discussed in the next section.[11] Under section 1(1)(b), his wife, or a woman living with him as his wife, is to be included in the 'family' for the purposes of the Act, though clearly there may be other people, e.g. grandparents, living in the particular household who are not so treated. The significance of such a woman's status as a member of the family is primarily that her gross income is included in its resources for the purposes of determining entitlement to, or the amount of, FIS.[12] In contrast, the income of other persons living in the household – even if they are contributing to the support of the children – is wholly disregarded.[13]

For the purposes of FIS, a woman living with the man as his wife is treated in the same way as a woman legally his wife. The 1970 Act, it may be noted, has always used the term 'lives with him as his wife' rather than the apparently more offensive 'cohabits', now deleted from the supplementary benefits and social security legislation.[14] The meaning of 'living together as man and wife' has been fully discussed in chapter 10,[15] and there is no need for a further treatment here.

Section 1(1)(c) states that a 'family' must include a child or children, 'whose requirements are provided for, in whole or in part, by the person or either of the persons mentioned in the preceding paragraphs'. Under the Act,[16] a 'child' must be under 16, but Regulations provide that someone over 16, but under 19 is to be treated as a child if he is receiving full-time, non-advanced education.[17]

The children need not be the natural children of the man or the woman providing for them.[18] The sole requirement in section 1(1)(c) is that he (or she) is at least partly *providing for* the children.[19] It might have been thought that the children do at least have to live with the man and the woman in order to be included in the 'family', as any other view would be

10 See p. 526, above.
11 P. 531, below.
12 FISA 1970, s.4, discussed at pp. 533–535, below.
13 The point was emphasised repeatedly in the debates in the House of Commons, e.g. Sir K Joseph, 806 HC Official Report (5th series) cols 1124 and 1153. It is the same position as that which applies in supplementary benefits, p. 480, above.
14 SS(MP)A 1977, ss.14(7), 22(2)(4).
15 Pp. 382–386, above.
16 FISA 1970, s.17(1).
17 SI 1980/1437, reg 9. A child over 16 who does not fall within this description will either be working or perhaps entitled to supplementary benefit on his own account.
18 Originally the Bill was not so widely drafted, but under opposition pressure, an amendment was introduced to enable *anyone* providing for a child in his or her household to claim FIS: 806 HC Official Report (5th series) col 1154.
19 'Providing for' is not defined in the 1970 Act, though SI 1980/1437, reg 6 states that foster-parents are to be treated as not providing for children boarded with them. Cp FAA 1965, s.18, and see the Commissioners' decisions on the equivalent provision for dependants' allowances: pp. 373–376, above.

incompatible with the opening words of section 1, '. . . a family shall consist of the following members of a household'. However, the SBC accepted the argument that a 'family' may include children boarded at a local authority school at the time of the claim, even though it is difficult to see how they could then be regarded as members of their parents' 'household'.[20] The fact that the children's absence from the household was temporary makes the result in this case reasonable, but it is submitted it would be wrong to allow a parent to claim FIS, when his (or her) children were away from home for very substantial periods.

Because a child may be provided for by two people living together in the same household (though not as man and wife), e.g. a brother and sister, or grandparents, it is possible for a child to be a member of two 'families' for the purposes of the legislation. The General Regulations state that in this case, in default of agreement between the persons concerned as to which family includes the child, the supplement officer, SBAT or Social Security Commissioner have discretion to determine this question.[1] Rather oddly, it is not provided, as it was in the Family Allowances Act and is in the Child Benefit legislation, that in this situation the natural parent is to have priority.[2]

Finally, it is clear that where the 'family' consists of a man and a woman married to him, or living with him as his wife, only the man *or* the woman need be providing for the child for the latter to be included in the 'family'. This will be important in the situation where a man and woman are cohabiting, but the former (in full-time work with low earnings) refuses to look after her children. She will not generally be able to claim supplementary benefit,[3] but FIS may be paid for the family. Normally, a claim must be made jointly by the man and the woman, but the Secretary of State under the Regulations has power to accept a claim by one party, where, as here, it would be unreasonable to expect them both to apply.[4]

ii Woman, not in the same household as husband, or man with whom living as wife, and child or children

The second type of 'family' is one where there is a 'single woman, engaged, and normally engaged, in remunerative full-time work', and a child or children for whom she is totally or partly providing.[5] A 'single woman' is defined by the Act to mean 'any woman other than one who is a member of the same household as a man to whom she is married or with whom she is living as his wife'.[6] Thus, a married woman living in a different household from her husband is a 'single woman' for the purposes of the legislation, and may be entitled to claim FIS, if she is in full-time work.[7]

There is nothing in the Act itself which affords any guidance on what it means to be a 'member of the same household' as someone else. This seems surprising, particularly when regulations under the supplementary benefits scheme, provide, inter alia, that a temporary absence does not

20 (1974) 28 Poverty 32 and 29, ibid, 34. And see *England v SBC* (1981) LAG Bulletin 141 (June).

1 SI 1980/1437, reg 7.

2 FAA 1965, Sch; CBA 1975, Sch 2, para 4, p. 438, above.

3 See ch 12, p. 462, above.

4 FISA 1970, s.5 and SI 1980/1438, reg 2(7).

5 FISA 1970, s.1(1)(a) and (c).

6 Ibid, s.17. This definition will obviously be omitted when the new scheme comes into effect.

7 Compare the similar rule for entitlement to affiliation payments: Cretney *Principles of Family Law* (3rd edn) pp. 575–576.

mean that the spouses are not members of the same household.[8] The 1980 Act enables regulations to be issued to clarify the concept for FIS purposes,[9] though as yet none have been made. If the woman is to all intents and purposes managing her own affairs, then it should be provided that she, and the relevant children, form a separate family for FIS purposes.

The fact that a woman shares the household with, e.g. her brother or father, does not preclude her from being a 'single woman', as she is not then living with the man as his wife. If both she and her relative are contributing towards the maintenance of her children, then either could claim the supplement, assuming the applicant is engaged in remunerative full-time work. As Sir Keith Joseph pointed out, there may be two 'families' for FIS purposes in the same household.[10] The procedure for determining which of them is entitled to FIS has already been mentioned.[11]

iii Man and child or children

The last category of family is the most straightforward, and numerically the least important.[12] A man, unmarried and not living with a woman as her husband, together with a child or children for whom he is wholly or partly providing, constitutes a 'family' for FIS purposes. In 1979 there were about 1,000 such families in receipt of the supplement.[13] It is, of course, irrelevant that the man's sister, or a housekeeper, is also living in the same household, though if she is also providing for the children concerned, then again there are two families for FIS purposes.

iv Critique

The exposition of this section of the Family Income Supplement Act 1970 has been complicated. It may be, as one Labour lawyer suggested,[14] that it would have been better, certainly clearer, to have established a 'household income supplement', rather than have attempted to tie eligibility to the notion of a 'family'. It seems that the laudable extension of the notion of a 'family' to include, e.g. grandparents and grandchildren, has led inevitably to complexity, and the oddity that children may be members of two, or possibly more, families. (However, it must be added, there are comparable problems in the child benefit scheme.)[15] A household income supplement might have been easier to understand; it might also be argued that it would have made more financial sense in the light of the aims of the legislation. Under the 1970 Act, a single woman, for example, will be entitled to FIS, as long as she makes some minimal contribution to providing for her children (and, of course, satisfies the other conditions). It is irrelevant that the major provision is made by, say, her parents with whom she shares a house. On the other hand, the alternative suggestion, necessitating the consideration of the resources of all members of that household, would have revived memories of the infamous 'household means test', abolished for national assistance purposes in 1941.[16] Moreover,

8 SI 1981/1524, reg 2(2).
9 SSA 1980, s.7(5), amending FISA 1970, s.10.
10 807 HC Official Report (5th series) col 1171.
11 P. 529, above.
12 See SBC Annual Report 1976 (Cmnd 6810) Appendix 5.
13 SBC Annual Report 1979 (Cmnd 8033), Table G. 3.
14 Mr R King Murray, 806 HC Official Report (5th series) col 1157.
15 See ch 11.
16 See ch 12, p. 452.

it would still have been necessary to devise rules determining whose salary in the household was relevant and who was entitled to claim the benefit. In defence of the present law, it can also be stated that there is no evidence that it causes any practical problems.

B Engaged in remunerative full-time work

The second condition is that the man, or single woman, must be 'engaged, and normally engaged, in remunerative full-time work'.[17] This requirement shows how FIS complements supplementary benefit, which is not normally payable to those in full-time work.[18] The government was clearly anxious to draw a sharp line between full-time and part-time employment, so that there would be no doubt which benefit a claimant might be entitled to.[19] The General Regulations, therefore, provide that generally 30 hours' work a week is both a necessary and sufficient condition for being treated as 'engaged in full-time work'.[20]

The implication of this should have been that a person working for more than 30 hours a week was ineligible for supplementary benefit, but in fact there used to be some confusion whether the borderline between the two benefits was as sharp as it should have been.[1] Now, however, regulations in the new supplementary benefits scheme provide that usually a person working for more than 30 hours a week is in 'full-time work', so the term has the same meaning for both benefits.[2]

The FIS General Regulations, as amended in 1979 and 1980, now contain three interesting provisions refining or qualifying the normal 30 hours rule. First, it is enough if a parent in a one-parent family is engaged in remunerative work for 24 hours a week instead of the usual 30.[3] This was a reform which had long been pressed by the Supplementary Benefits Commission to help this vulnerable group.[4] Secondly, the hours are only to include meal-times if remuneration is paid for those periods, a provision which reverses a generous appeal tribunal ruling in 1974.[5] The third rule is that the claimant must work for the prescribed hours (30 or 24, as the case may be) during the week of the claim, or in the week *following* it.[6] This final change enables some claims to succeed even if the applicant is not actually at work, but is temporarily sick or unemployed, when it is made; it follows a Divisional Court ruling that an application could succeed even though the claimant was off work through illness at the date of the claim.[7] In the ordinary course of events, FIS is assessed by reference to the claimant's gross earnings over the previous five weeks (or two months, if

17 FISA 1970, s.1(1)(a).
18 SBA 1976, s.6(1): p. 457, above.
19 806 HC Official Report (5th series) col 1135.
20 SI 1980/1437, reg 5.
1 See the first edition of this book, pp. 563–564.
2 P. 457, above.
3 SI 1980/1437, reg 5(3).
4 E.g. see SBC Annual Report 1977 (Cmnd 7392), para 14.15.
5 SI 1980/1437, reg 5(3), and see (1974) LAG Bulletin 273 (November).
6 SI 1980/1437, reg 5(1).
7 *R v Ebbw Vale and Merthyr Tydfil Supplementary Benefits Appeal Tribunal, ex parte Lewis* [1981] 1 WLR 131. The decision was reversed on appeal, [1982] 1 WLR 420, and would not be affected by the change in the regulations – the claimant was away from work for 4 weeks after the claim.

he is paid monthly), but the Regulations enable the Commission to assess his earnings on some other appropriate basis if he, inter alia, 'has commenced working in a gainful occupation shortly before the claim is made'.[8] The clear implication is that there is no minimum period for which the applicant must work before he claims the supplement.

Finally, the work must be remunerative. This has caused some difficulty in cases where the claimant is attending a course for which he is awarded some allowance. Can this be considered 'remunerative full-time work' for FIS purposes? In one case, an appeal tribunal in Coventry held that the claimant attending a government training centre for which he received a weekly allowance was entitled to FIS.[9] But subsequently, a tribunal in Shoreditch took the opposite view, concluding that a trainee was neither employed nor self-employed, and an allowance was not the equivalent of wages for the purposes of the formula, 'remunerative work'.[10]

C A family in 'Great Britain'

The 1970 Act[11] stipulates that the benefit shall be paid only to a 'family in Great Britain'. The General Regulations provide that a family is to be so treated if, and only if, at the date the claim is made, it is ordinarily resident in the United Kingdom and at least one adult member of it is resident in Great Britain.[12] It is ordinary residence and residence *when the claim is made* which are important; it does not seem to matter if, shortly after the award is made, the 'family' leaves the country. The requirement that one adult member only, and not the children, be actually resident in Britain at the relevant time appears generous. But, if the requirement that the 'family' must consist of 'members of a household' has any significance[13] then it is submitted that it would be rare in practice for one member of a family entitled to FIS to be resident without the others also satisfying the condition.

D The weekly amount of resources falls short of the prescribed amount

The final condition relates naturally enough to the family's financial circumstances. The formula is that its resources (defined in section 4 of the Act and Regulations made under it) must fall short of the 'prescribed amount';[14] this amount, varying according to the number of children in the family, is set out in Regulations made under section 2.[15] The rate of FIS is half the difference between the prescribed amount and the family's resources, subject to a 'ceiling' or maximum award.[16]

8 SI 1980/1437, reg 2.
9 (1974) LAG Bulletin 16 (January).
10 (1976), ibid, 153 (July). It seems clear that in some cases a trainee will be eligible for supplementary benefit: p. 459, above. This is consonant with the law under Social Security Act 1975: p. 117, above.
11 S.1(2).
12 SI 1980/1437, reg 8. The concepts of 'residence' and 'ordinary residence' are discussed in ch 10, pp. 391–393, above.
13 For the meaning of 'household', see p. 529, above.
14 FISA 1970, s.1(2).
15 As amended by CBA 1975, Sch 4, para 3.
16 FISA 1970, s.3.

i The 'prescribed amount'

For 1982–83 it is £82.50 for a family with one child, with a further £9.00 for each additional child. It is not clear on what basis these amounts are calculated, though the impression was given in the parliamentary debates that allowances were made for average weekly food, clothing and housing costs. The Liberal spokesman on social security matters, Mr John Pardoe, moved an amendment to substitute for the figure given as the prescribed amount (then £15) a formula which would relate FIS to half the current national average wage, with 30 per cent of this fraction for each additional child.[17] The suggestion was resisted. It is interesting that the prescribed amount has kept ahead of price increases, and recently has kept pace with the movement in average gross earnings.[18]

The most striking feature of the prescribed amount for FIS is, of course, its lack of flexibility, compared to supplementary benefit. In particular, despite a Labour attempt to make a provision for it,[19] there is no special rent allowance as there has been in the supplementary benefits scheme.[20] The government wished the FIS scheme to be simple, and anticipated that the allowances and rebates introduced by the Housing Finance Act 1972 would deal with the difficulties arising from high rent payments. Nor does the amount of FIS vary with the age of the children, a factor which has been strongly criticised on the ground that older children are more expensive to feed and clothe.[1]

ii The family's resources

Section 4(1) of the 1970 Act provides that the family's resources 'shall be the aggregate of the normal gross income of its members, including, except where regulations otherwise provide, the income of any child'.[2] Before discussing the assessment of resources, the preliminary point should be made that the income of all members of the family (except the children) must be aggregated; it is primarily for this reason that it is important to determine whether a woman is living with a man as his wife and, therefore, is a member of the 'family' for FIS purposes.[3]

a *The calculation of earnings*

It is gross income which is relevant, not the person's net income after deduction of income tax, insurance contributions and expenses. The General Regulations provide that the weekly amount of the person's earnings is to be calculated by reference to his average earnings for the five weeks, or the two months (if paid monthly) preceding the date of the claim. But the supplement officer, or the appeal tribunal, may take some other appropriate period if this method is not suitable, e.g. because the claimant's earnings have fluctuated considerably during that time, or he has just started work.[4] This flexibility is particularly valuable for seasonal

17 806 HC Official Report (5th series) col 1159.
18 SBC Annual Report 1979 (Cmnd 8033), Table G. 2.
19 806 HC Official Report (5th series) col. 1177: See Barker in Bull (ed) *Family Poverty* (2nd edn) pp. 77–79.
20 But see p. 470, above.
1 Wynn (1970) 16 Poverty 24.
2 The only regulation aggregating a child's income provides that any income of his, derived directly or indirectly from a parent or any other person under a legal obligation to maintain him, is to be included in the family's gross income, a clear anti-abuse provision: SI 1980/1437, reg 2(6).
3 See p. 528, above.
4 SI 1980/1437, reg 2(2).

workers.[5] In the case of the self-employed, net profit is to be taken into account in assessing their income.[6]

b *The calculation of other income and capital*

Income, apart from earnings, is to be calculated or estimated on the basis the supplement officer, SBAT or Social Security Commissioner thinks appropriate.[7] This is one of the few cases where the administering bodies have a wide discretion. The fact that under the legislation the income must be 'normal' precludes account being taken of occasional gifts. Some difficulty has arisen with regard to maintenance payments which a woman only receives occasionally or irregularly. It seems that the Commission accepted that the total amount of such irregular payments should not be averaged over the year in order to assess the woman's 'normal' gross income, but that a short-term award of FIS should be made for a few weeks, taking into account only the maintenance received in the week of the claim.[8]

Under section 4(2) of the Act regulations may provide for treating capital resources as equivalent to a gross income of the amount specified in them.[9] But none has been issued, and it seems that in practice capital assets and investments are ignored in assessing entitlement to, or the amount of, FIS.[10]

c *Disregards*

One of the most controversial aspects of the 1970 Act was that it did not specify any disregards in assessing the family's income for FIS purposes. Under considerable pressure from the opposition and some of its own backbenchers, the government did promise that a few would be allowed in regulations, but the eventual provision is very restrictive compared with that in the supplementary benefits legislation.[11] There are, however, some good reasons for thinking that the government was right in its cautious attitude to this question. First, the existence of a large number of disregards would have complicated the scheme, which was designed to be simple and easy to administer. A more generous provision would have necessitated the appointment of officials to check that they were rightly claimed and not being abused. Secondly, it is not entirely clear that their provision leads to equitable results. The point was well made by Sir Keith Joseph, when he said that it was difficult to distinguish 'a family whose income is above the prescribed amount because of an ingredient which is disregarded and is still helped by the supplement, and another family whose income solely from earnings is the same but which will not get a supplement'.[12]

The disregards which are now allowed by the Regulations include the whole of any attendance or mobility allowance, the first £4 of a war

5 807 HC Official Report (5th series) cols 1215–1220.
6 SI 1980/1437, reg 2(3). The provision that *net* profits are to be taken into account is clearly sensible, and contrasts sharply with the refusal to allow any expenses in calculating earnings from employment.
7 Ibid, reg 2(4).
8 (1975) LAG Bulletin 99 (April); (1976) 35 Poverty 50. For the power to make short-term awards of FIS, see p. 537, below.
9 This used to be done in the supplementary benefits system.
10 (1975) LAG Bulletin 125 (May).
11 For disregards in supplementary benefits, see ch 12, pp. 480–487, above.
12 806 HC Official Report (5th series) col 1322. And see the discussion of the justification for disregards in supplementary benefits, p. 480, above.

disablement pension, child benefit, educational maintenance allowance, boarding-out allowances paid by local authorities and the rent allowances under the Housing Finance legislation.[13] A proposal to allow a partial disregard of a wife's earnings, comparable to that available for calculating supplementary benefit, was sternly resisted, on the ground that this would be unfair to the family where the man's earnings were only a little above the prescribed amount.[14] Other suggested disregards, such as that of sums paid by a man in maintenance to his separated wife, were rejected because claims involving them would require considerable scrutiny by officials.

iii The amount of family income supplement

Under section 3 of the 1970 Act, the amount of FIS is to be one half the difference between the prescribed amount and the family's resources, but this is not to exceed (from November 1982) £21.00 with a further £2.00 for each additional child. The assessment can be illustrated by a simple example:

A family with two children has a normal gross income of £55.50
The prescribed amount £91.50 (£82.50 + £9.00 for the extra child)
Normal gross income £55.50

The deficiency is £36.00 and the amount of
FIS awarded is therefore £18.00

If the family's income were only £43.50, then the deficit would be £48.00, but the amount of FIS awarded would be only £23.00 because of the 'ceiling' imposed by section 3.

It seems that the object of paying only half the difference between the prescribed amount and the family's resources was to preserve some incentive on the part of the wage-earner to improve his position through salary rises, overtime, etc.[15] But, as has been mentioned in the discussion of the poverty trap,[16] it is arguable that the 50 per cent 'marginal tax rate', consequent on the withdrawal of FIS after a wage rise, is itself enough to constitute a disincentive.

The imposition of the 'ceiling', or maximum award, has attracted some criticism.[17] A justification was apparently the desire to avoid any collusion between employer and employee, which might occur if there were no limit on the amount which could be obtained.[18] The government even resisted a move at the Report stage to give the Supplementary Benefits Commission discretion to remove the 'ceiling' in cases of real hardship.[19] It is suggested that the government's case is hard to support, though it may be said that, because of the regular increases to the maximum permitted awards, the 'ceiling' now does not affect very many families.[20]

13 SI 1980/1437, reg 2(5).
14 See Sir K Joseph, 807 HC Official Report (5th series) col 1191: see p. 485, above, for this disregard in supplementary benefits.
15 See Sir K Joseph, 806 HC Official Report (5th series) col 226.
16 P. 524, above.
17 George *Social Security and Society* (1973) p. 68.
18 Mr P Dean, Under-Secretary of State, 806 HC Official Report (5th series) col 1265.
19 807 HC Official Report (5th series) cols 1173–1178.
20 See the SBC Annual Report for 1976 (Cmnd 6910), Table 16.8. In 1979, generally only 5,000 families received the maximum payments: SBC Annual Report for 1979 (Cmnd 8033), Table G. 12.

Part 3 Claims to, and the duration of, FIS

In this final Part the procedure for the making of claims and payments is briefly discussed. Inevitably the discussion here overlaps with the more general treatment of administration of benefits in chapter 14;[1] but it is important to mention the procedure here, because it reinforces the points made earlier in this chapter concerning the scheme's alleged simplicity. Secondly, this Part is concerned with the duration of awards.

A Claims to, and payment of, FIS

All claims must be made in writing on the prescribed form and sent to the offices of the DHSS in Blackpool where the scheme is administered. In contrast, therefore, to supplementary benefits, there are no interviews or applications across the counter in local offices.[2] The written claims procedure is consonant with the scheme's simplicity and the government's desire to reduce both the element of discretion in the making of awards and the administrative expenses. Pay-slips or other documentary evidence of income must be submitted with the claim form. Officials then check that the Act's requirements have been satisfied (e.g. the claimant is in remunerative full-time work and has a child or children) before making the award.

Usually a joint claim by the man and woman members of the family is required,[3] but the Secretary of State may accept as valid a claim by one of them if satisfied it would be unreasonable to exact this requirement.[4] Payment may be made to either person. The supplement does not 'belong' to one parent or the other.[5] This is perhaps a little surprising, as it might be thought that a measure directed largely to relieve child poverty would ensure that the supplement was the property of the mother. On the other hand, the point might be made that, as FIS supplements low *earnings* it would cause unnecessary conflict to pay it to the mother who is unlikely to be the family's principal earner.

B Duration of FIS payments

The Family Income Supplements Act 1970 originally provided that payments of FIS should be made for 26 weeks, irrespective of any change in the family's circumstances subsequent to the making of the award. This period was extended to 52 weeks by the Pensioners and Family Income Supplement Payments Act 1972. The purpose is to reduce the number of claims, and thereby simplify the administration of the scheme. For this reason, the government successfully resisted a suggestion that a family should be able to reapply for FIS after a month, if its circumstances had changed for the worse in the meantime.[6] In effect, therefore, the family takes the original award 'for better or for worse' for the year: it is not entitled to a higher award, if its income drops or its requirements increase

1 Pp. 564 and 573, below.
2 P. 563, below.
3 FISA 1970, s.5(2).
4 SI 1980/1438, reg 2(7): see p. 529, above.
5 Compare the position under the family allowances scheme and the priority of entitlement to the child benefit now enjoyed by the wife: pp. 437–438, above.
6 807 HC Official Report (5th series) col 1203.

owing to the inclusion of another child within the family; but neither can the award be reduced if its earnings increase. Although a change in the family's own circumstances will not affect the amount of FIS for the year following the award, it will benefit from any up-rating of the FIS levels during that period.[7] An additional reason for the twelve months duration of awards is that it postpones the operation of the poverty trap: a family with increased earnings keeps FIS for some time after this rise, and moreover if the FIS rates increase, as they now do at least annually, it will continue to receive the supplement (despite the higher earnings) and the effect of the poverty trap can be disguised for a very long time.[8]

When the applicant's earnings fluctuate considerably, it will be difficult to determine the appropriate rate of FIS, and the fact that an award subsists for a year may mean excessive payments will be made for a long time. The supplement officer (or on appeal, tribunal or Commissioner), therefore, has power under the Regulations to make awards for a period of less than 52 weeks, though not less than four weeks, when the evidence leaves it in doubt as to the appropriate rate.[9]

7 SI 1980/1437, reg 3(5).
8 See p. 524, above, for a fuller discussion of the poverty trap.
9 SI 1980/1437, reg 3(1).

Chapter 14

Administration of benefits

This chapter deals with a number of aspects of the administration of social security benefits, both contributory and non-contributory. Part 1 is concerned with the Department of Health and Social Security, the government department responsible now for all benefits, and discusses the administration of means-tested benefits which used to be the responsibility of the Supplementary Benefits Commission. In Part 2 the composition and functions of various advisory bodies are explored. The largest section of the chapter is Part 3, which analyses the rules regarding the making of claims to and payment of benefits. Lastly, Part 4 discusses some of the various methods by which overpayments and mistaken payments of benefit are controlled – principally the procedure for recovery and criminal prosecutions.

Part 1 The Department of Health and Social Security

Since 1968 the administration of social security benefits has been the responsibility of the Secretary of State for Social Services, who presides over the Department of Health and Social Security.[1] The survey of the Department's history and organisation here is necessarily brief; a fuller treatment will be found in books on the machinery of government and social administration.[2]

A History

Before the reforms of 1946 heralded by the Beveridge Report, the administration of social security benefits was undertaken in a number of different departments. The only Ministry with sole responsibility for a benefit was the Ministry of Pensions. This had been set up in 1916, and was responsible for the award of war pensions for death or disability suffered in the Great War and the Second World War.[3] Administration of health insurance, (the precursor of sickness benefit), and contributory pensions

1 As is usual in British government, the legal powers are vested in the Secretary of State, rather than in the department for which he is responsible: see SI 1968/1699. For general comment, see de Smith *Constitutional and Administrative Law* (4th edn) p. 198.

2 See e.g. Willson *The Organisation of British Central Government, 1914–1964* (1967) pp. 143–174; Brown *The Management of Welfare* (1975), esp. chs 3–5.

3 See ch 9, above, for the history of war pensions.

was shared by the Ministry of Health and the Approved Societies.[4] The Ministry of Labour was responsible for contributory unemployment insurance, which was paid at its labour exchanges. Unemployment assistance had since 1934 been the responsibility of the Unemployment Assistance Board; in 1940 this was renamed as the Assistance Board, when it was given the additional task of organising the payment of supplementary pensions.[5] The administration of non-contributory old age pensions paid under the 1908 Act was rather anomalously in the hands of the Commissioners of Customs and Excise.[6]

Beveridge proposed the creation of a Ministry of Social Security under a Minister with a seat in the Cabinet. It would be responsible for both social insurance and means-tested national assistance. The Report also urged consideration of an eventual merger of the new Ministry and the Ministry of Pensions.[7] The war-time government accepted these proposals only in part. The suggestion of a Ministry of Social Security, responsible for *all* welfare benefits, was rejected. Insurance and other universal benefits, such as family allowances, were to be the responsibility of a new Ministry, but public assistance was to be separately administered by the National Assistance Board. The new Ministry of National Insurance was instituted by an Act of 1944. Originally, the measure had been entitled 'the Ministry of Social Insurance' Bill, but the term 'National Insurance' was preferred during the Committee stage. It seems that the desire for continuity with the pre-war national insurance legislation and the fact that the phrase 'social insurance' was used in Germany were largely responsible for this change.[8]

The Ministry of National Insurance became responsible for the administration of family allowances, benefits payable under the National Insurance Act 1946,[9] and industrial injuries benefits.[10] However, unemployment benefit was paid at offices of the Ministry of Labour, and, since 1970, of the Department of Employment.[11] A new central office was set up in Newcastle to keep insurance records and superintend the administration and payment of long-term benefits and family allowances.[12] In line with the Beveridge proposals, the Ministry worked through regional and local offices.[13]

There was no move at this time to take further Beveridge's suggestion that there might be a merger of the new Ministry of National Insurance and the older Ministry of Pensions. Such a step would have been bitterly resented by the servicemen's organisations and would have run counter to the popular sentiment that war pensioners should have separate and privileged treatment. However, by the early 1950s there was a steady decline of war pensions awarded, and consequently of the staff and special

4 See ch 4, pp. 137–144, above, for the history of sickness benefit. The role of the Approved Societies in the administration of health insurance is discussed by Gilbert *The Evolution of National Insurance in Great Britain* (1966), esp. pp. 423–428.
5 Ch 12 (history of supplementary benefits), pp. 451–453, above.
6 Ch 5 (history of retirement pensions), pp. 189–193, above.
7 Paras 385–387. See *Harris* pp. 395–396.
8 It does not seem that the change was influenced by a dislike of the similarity between 'social insurance' and 'socialism'; cp Bruce *The Coming of the Welfare State* (4th edn) p. 315. Both Attlee and Bevan voted for the change, though Beveridge himself resisted it.
9 Non-contributory pensions under the 1908 Act were administered by the National Assistance Board.
10 Workmen's compensation had been subject to the general control of the Home Office: see *Willson*, n.2, above, at p. 145.
11 For the special arrangements for claiming unemployment benefit, see p. 557, below.
12 1st Report of the Ministry of National Insurance (1949, Cmd 7955), paras 19 and 64–80.
13 Ibid, at paras 81–96.

hospitals required to deal with pensioners' problems.[14] In February 1953, the Prime Minister, Mr W Churchill, announced the government's intention to merge the two Ministries.[15] The change was made later that year despite fierce opposition in the House of Commons.[16] In one respect the position of war pensioners was much improved as a result of the merger. They had access to the 900 local offices of the Ministry of National Insurance, instead of the 80 to 90 local Pensions offices. War pensions continued to be administered (as they are now) under a central office at Blackpool.[17] Since 1953, a separate Annual Report has been published on war pensioners.

For the next 12 years there were relatively few changes in the structure of the new Ministry.[18] The next fundamental reform came in 1966, when at last Beveridge's wish for an integrated Ministry of Social Security was fulfilled.[19] The Ministry of Social Security Act of that year had the effect of merging the administration of insurance and means-tested benefits and hence abolished the National Assistance Board. Miss Herbison, then Minister of Pensions and National Insurance, gave four principal reasons for the decision.[20] First, it was desirable to co-ordinate policy for all social security benefits by vesting responsibility in one Ministry. Secondly, the merger would make it easier for those eligible to claim supplementary benefit in addition to contributory benefits. Thirdly, it would be possible to combine facilities to provide a comprehensive service. Fourthly, the reform would help to remove the suspicion that non-contributory benefits were inferior and the stigma associated with claiming them. Within the integrated Ministry, a separate body, the Supplementary Benefits Commission, was to be responsible for formulating policy on means-tested benefits.[1]

The main criticism voiced by the Conservative opposition was that this measure did not go far enough in bringing together the organisation of welfare benefits and social services. In particular, it was argued that the new Ministry should be combined with the Ministry of Health, and take over the children's department of the Home Office.[2] Two years later the Labour government accepted this. The Ministries of Health and of Social Security were abolished, and were replaced by the Department of Health and Social Security.[3] The Ministers' functions were transferred to the Secretary of State for Social Services. His title emphasises that he is not only responsible for the Department (DHSS), but also for the co-ordination of the whole range of social services.[4] The opposition naturally welcomed the change, though some anxieties were expressed that the reform might lead to the remoteness of the Department from the public.

14 28th Report of the Ministry of Pensions, 1952–53 HC 271, paras 116–120.
15 511 HC Official Report (5th series) col 2314.
16 517 HC Official Report (5th series) col 267: the Address was only carried by 226–212 votes.
17 Report of the Ministry of Pensions and National Insurance for 1953 (Cmd 9159), paras 242–244.
18 For the definitive account of the structure and work of the Ministry, see King *The Ministry of Pensions and National Insurance* (1958). (Sir Geoffrey King had been a Permanent Secretary at the Ministry.)
19 P. 539, above.
20 729 HC Official Report (5th series) cols 337 ff.
1 Pp. 543–544, below.
2 729 HC Official Report (5th series) cols 1073–1078.
3 SI 1968/1699.
4 Mr R Crossman, Secretary of State, 770 HC Official Report (5th series) cols 1609 ff.

B The structure and organisation of DHSS

i Department headquarters[5]

The Secretary of State for Social Services, who is always a Cabinet Minister, is assisted at the political level by a Minister for Social Security and a Parliamentary Under-Secretary. At the top of the civil service structure is the Permanent Secretary responsible for all social security matters. Under him the social security branch of the Department is divided into two 'commands', each headed by a deputy secretary. One is responsible for contributory benefits policy, the other for the administration of all social security benefits and overall control of regional and local offices. A Regional Directorate was set up in 1972 in the headquarters as a separate division under this second deputy secretary to form a link with the organisation of the Department outside London.[6]

Most of the social security work at headquarters is concerned with research into, and policy formulation on, benefits. All this is done by only about 2,500 staff, a tiny fraction of the total employees of the DHSS.[7]

ii Regional offices

There are ten regional offices in England, and one in both Scotland and Wales.[8] All these offices have been integrated since the reforms of 1966, in that they are concerned with the administration of both contributory and means-tested benefits. The head of such an office, known as the regional controller, is responsible to the Regional Directorate at London headquarters. Assistant controllers superintend the various aspects of the work done by local offices in the particular region – e.g. the award of benefits, staffing and personnel, fraud and contributions matters.[9]

Control over local offices is exercised in a number of ways.[10] For example, finance officers control local accounts, and check payment forms to see that the correct benefit is being paid.[11] A number of decisions, for example, to prosecute for abuse, must be taken at regional office level.[12]

iii Local offices

The aim of the 1966 reform was to integrate as many offices as possible so that the public could claim and obtain advice at the same place on all benefits. At the end of 1979 there were 531 local offices of the Department, of which 402 were integrated.[13] In addition there are about 234 inquiry offices, (some of them only open part-time), where claims may be accepted and advice given. These offices, generally manned by one officer, are being closed down as the need for them declines.

At the head of a local office is the manager, with a senior executive officer as his deputy. Below them are the higher executive officers,

5 This section is, of course, only concerned with the social security branch and not the health work of the DHSS.

6 DHSS Annual Report 1972 (Cmnd 5352), para 17.10.

7 In 1977 (the latest year for which figures were published) the total DHSS staff engaged on social security work was 87,603: DHSS Annual Report 1977, Table 22.

8 SBC Report 1976 (Cmnd 6910), para 19.23 and Table 19.5. Also see Handbook Appendix 4.

9 See Brown *The Management of Welfare* (1975), pp. 98–100.

10 See ibid, at p. 100, and *Fisher* paras 53–54.

11 Ibid, at para 55.

12 Ibid, at para 58 (decisions to use special investigators in cohabitation cases where fraud is suspected).

13 SBC Report 1979 (Cmnd 8033), para 15.1.

responsible in a typical integrated office for sections dealing with contributory benefits, supplementary benefits, and contributions and fraud.[14] There are three further grades of staff: local officers I (formerly executive officers), local officers II (formerly clerical officers) and clerical assistants. The insurance officers who take decisions on entitlement to the contributory benefits are all local officers I.[15] Other officials of this grade superintend the actual payment of these benefits which is handled by local officers II. On the supplementary benefits side, it is the local officers I who take decisions on entitlement. Local officers II interview claimants and make a preliminary assessment of the award, but payment may only be authorised by a member of the higher grade.[16] Clerical assistants perform routine tasks such as filing.

Mr J Griffiths, then Minister of National Insurance, said when introducing the 1946 Bill, that local offices should be 'centres where people will not be afraid to go, where they will be welcome, and where they will not only get benefits, but advice'.[17] In recent years there has been some anxiety about the difficulties caused by rapid staff turnover; this particularly affects the administration of supplementary benefits where there is so much personal contact between applicant and the Department's staff.[18] A safeguard against incompetence is that a sample of awards is checked by senior executive officers or the office manager to ensure that the correct payments are made.[19] An important development has been the greater emphasis on staff training which is given at various regional centres.[20]

iv The central office at Newcastle

In addition to policy headquarters in London, there are two central offices. The first, at Newcastle upon Tyne, was set up in 1946, and now employs over 12,000 staff.[1] The contribution records are kept there, so every claim for benefit, where entitlement depends on a contributions' record, is referred to Newcastle. It is also from there that books are issued and renewed for the long-term benefits, such as retirement and widows' pensions. A new office nearby at Washington in County Durham was set up to administer the child benefit scheme.

v The central offices at Blackpool

The Blackpool central offices process claims for war pensions, attendance allowance, mobility allowance and FIS.[2] The office at Norcross has been responsible for the central administration of war pensions since the 1920s. FIS is administered at an office at Poulton-le-Fylde, Blackpool, which employs about 100 staff to deal with postal claims.[3]

14 See *Brown* n.9, above, at pp. 86–93; Stevenson *Claimant or Client?* (1973) ch 3 contains some useful information on the structure of the Department so far as it is concerned with supplementary benefit administration. The text here owes much to these two books.
15 See pp. 585–586, below, for the insurance officer's adjudicatory role.
16 See pp. 543–544, below, for administration of supplementary benefits.
17 418 HC Official Report (5th series) col 1754.
18 SBC Report 1978 (Cmnd 7725), paras 7.18–7.20; SBC Report 1979, n.13, above, at paras 14.11–14.13
19 *Fisher* paras 49–52.
20 See DHSS Annual Report 1972, n.6, above, at para 17.16 and SBC Report 1975, (Cmnd 6615), para 15.6.
1 DHSS Annual Report 1977, Table 22. For a general treatment and description of the work at the Newcastle office, see *Brown*, n.9, above, at pp. 81–86.
2 See DHSS Annual Report 1975 (Cmnd 6565), paras 2.21 and 8.33.
3 SBC Report 1979, n.13, above, at para 17.9 (see ch 13 for claims for FIS).

C The administration of means-tested benefits

Supplementary benefits and FIS are now administered by officers of the DHSS, but before their role is discussed, something should be said about the Supplementary Benefits Commission abolished in the 1980 reforms.

i The Supplementary Benefits Commission

The origins of the SBC can be traced back to the creation in 1934 of the Unemployment Assistance Board which administered assistance for those out of work. This body took responsibility for both policy and the making of individual decisions, subject to the general control of the Minister of Labour. The discharge of the latter function prevented the Minister himself being subject to Parliamentary criticism for particular decisions.[4] The Board was given additional functions in 1940 when it assumed responsibility for the administration of supplementary pensions, and then from 1948, renamed as the National Assistance Board, it supervised all public assistance.[5] The NAB was an independent government department and enjoyed substantial power to make regulations.[6]

The Board was abolished in 1966 as an inevitable consequence of the administrative integration of insurance and means-tested benefits.[7] But a new body, the Supplementary Benefits Commission, was set up to superintend the award of public assistance, and in particular to formulate the general policies for the guidance of officers taking decisions on particular claims. But unlike the NAB, the Commission had no regulatory power, and it was not a government department.[8]

Although the formal powers of the Commission were relatively limited, it enjoyed considerable influence. Its members were not civil servants (unlike the staff), and many had some social services experience which enabled them to exercise independent judgment. A significant step occurred in 1975 when the Secretary of State, Barbara Castle, asked the SBC to submit a separate Annual Report in which it could indicate what it saw as the priorities in policy development.[9] Its five reports were long documents, containing many valuable suggestions for the reform of means-tested benefits and showed very clearly that the Commission was not afraid to adopt an independent line.

When the supplementary benefits system was reformed in 1980, the Conservative government preferred matters of policy to be determined by Ministers responsible to Parliament rather than by a non-elected body. Moreover, those matters previously regulated by non-legally binding policies are now very largely governed by regulations issued by the Secretary of State.[10] There was therefore no place in the scheme for the SBC, though its demise was frequently deplored by Labour MPs during the debates on the Bill. It does appear that the Commission's abolition was virtually inevitable, even if there are understandable regrets that such a

4 The constant barrage of Parliamentary Questions to which the Ministers of Pensions have been subject during both world wars shows the extent of this problem!

5 See pp. 451–453, above.

6 See NAA 1948, ss.2(3) and 10(4). For a legal analysis of the position of the NAB, see Steele *The National Assistance Act 1948* (1949).

7 P. 453, above.

8 The best description is that it was 'a semi-autonomous public corporation': de Smith *Constitutional and Administrative Law* (3rd edn) p. 183.

9 891 HC Official Report (5th series). See Donnison *The Politics of Poverty* (1982) pp. 24–26.

10 For the new scheme, see ch 12, pp. 453–455, above.

vigorous and stimulating contribution to social security discussion will be hard to replace.

ii The new system

Decisions on entitlement to supplementary benefit and FIS are now made by benefit and supplement officers appointed by the Secretary of State.[11] In practice, of course, there will be little change since, although nominally decisions on entitlement used to be taken by the Commission, they were in fact made by DHSS officers. Now, however, benefit and supplement officers are responsible for their own decisions. There is much less discretion in the supplementary benefits system, so for the most part the officers will merely have to apply the admittedly complex law to the facts. But this will often entail delicate judgment, and to assist them in these tasks, the officers are to act under the general supervision of a Chief Supplementary Benefits Officer (CSBO) and a Chief Supplement Officer. The aim is that these Officers should be as independent as the Chief National Insurance Officer.[12] Already the CSBO has issued published guidance on three or four topics, the most important of which is probably the administration of single payments.[13]

The advisory, though not policy-making, role of the SBC is now discharged by the new Social Security Advisory Committee, discussed in the next part of this chapter. The Commission itself welcomed the institution of this new body which is able to consider in conjunction the development of both contributory and means-tested social security benefits.[14]

D Specialist officers

This Part concludes with some brief remarks on various officers who perform special tasks, often of a general welfare nature.

i The social work adviser and the social work service

The adviser's function is to give the DHSS assistance in the performance of its welfare roles, and help in the provision of suitable training for the specialised officers. He is now at the head of the social work service, established within the Department when the children's service was transferred from the Home Office in 1971.[15] Social work service officers are now attached to the regional offices of the Department.[16]

ii Special welfare officers[17]

There are about 50 special welfare officers attached to the DHSS regional offices. Cases of particular difficulty, e.g., where the claimant is completely unable to look after his financial arrangements, are referred to them by local offices.

11 SBA 1976, s.27; FISA 1970, s.1A.
12 Standing Committee E Debates on Social Security Bill 1980, cols 472 and 483: for the Chief National Insurance Officer, see p. 586, below.
13 P. 492, above.
14 SBC Annual Report 1979 (Cmnd 8033), para 1.44 and ch 7.
15 See Brown *The Management of Welfare* (1975) pp. 74–75.
16 Stevenson *Claimant or Client?* (1973) p. 68.
17 Ibid, at pp. 72–73.

iii Unemployment review officers[18]

Their function is primarily to interview and help those who are out of work and have been in receipt of supplementary benefit for a substantial time.[19] In the last two or three years their numbers have increased considerably, partly because they now play the same role for recipients of unemployment benefit who are not also in receipt of supplementary benefit, and secondly, because the government envisages that unemployment and benefit expenditure could be reduced if more social security claimants received expert advice during the early stages of a period of unemployment.[20] It is anticipated that, following the recent Rayner Scrutiny on the payment of benefits to the unemployed, more review officers will be engaged.[1]

iv Special investigators[2]

Special investigators are based in regional offices of the Department. Their function is to investigate cases of suspected abuse or fraud in obtaining social security benefits. Cases are referred by local officers, when they present particularly intractable problems. The investigators are recruited from the ranks of executive officers and receive a month's training for their work which obviously requires tact and patience. It is particularly sensitive in cohabitation cases; the use of investigators in this area has been reviewed earlier.[3]

v Liable relative officers[4]

Unlike the other specialist officers, they are based in local offices. Their task is to interview women, separated from their husbands, and single women with illegitimate children, and discuss the possibility of taking maintenance or affiliation proceedings against the man liable to maintain them and their children.[5]

Part 2 Standing advisory bodies[6]

Government departments have often made use of advisory bodies in the administration of the various social security schemes, the first of these committees being set up soon after the end of the First World War for war pensions.[7] Advisory bodies may either be national organisations or local committees. To a large extent their functions will differ according to this categorisation. Central advisory bodies will tend to be employed to give advice on matters of general policy, and to comment on the drafting of

18 Ibid, at pp. 76–78, and see SBC Report 1979, n.14, above, at paras 6.20–6.27.
19 See p. 498, above, for a detailed account of their work.
20 SBC Annual Report 1979, n.14, above, at paras 6.21–6.23.
1 *Payment of Benefits to Unemployed People* (1981) para 14. See p. 570, below, for further discussion of this report.
2 *Stevenson*, n.16, above, at pp. 74–76; *Fisher* paras 408–417; and *Payment of Benefits to Unemployed People*, n.1, above, at Annex I, paras 7.39–7.55.
3 P. 464, above.
4 *Stevenson*, n.16, above, at pp. 73–74; SBC Annual Report 1979, n.14, above, at paras 10.37 and 10.40.
5 Pp. 510–511, above, for further discussion of this work.
6 This discussion does not cover the work of the Royal Commissions and ad hoc Departmental Committees, which have also obviously played an important part in the development of social security law and policy.
7 War Pensions Act 1921: see pp. 550–551, below.

regulations made by the Secretary of State in the exercise of his delegated legislative powers. They are not suited to handling complaints from claimants, or dealing with detailed questions concerning the administration of benefits in the regions. On the other hand, local bodies are able to perform these functions, though, of course, they may also be competent to give advice on broader questions.

A second general point concerns the attitude to be adopted by the advisory committees to the government Department on the one hand, and to social security claimants on the other. The question is whether these committees regard themselves primarily as experts consulted to give disinterested advice on the formation of policy, or whether they see themselves as mainly concerned to 'represent' the public as consumers of welfare benefits. In this second case, there will inevitably be some tensions between the Department and its advisory committee. Unfortunately, there has been no full study of the role of these committees which would enable a coherent answer to be given to this question. The probability is that the committees' attitudes reveal both approaches at different times, depending on the issues and the composition of the particular body.

A The Social Security Advisory Committee

i General

This Committee was set up by the Social Security Act 1980 to assume the functions previously performed by the National Insurance Advisory Committee and (as has already been mentioned) the Supplementary Benefits Commission.[8] The former body had antecedents which can be traced back to the Unemployment Insurance Statutory Committee instituted in 1934 to scrutinise draft regulations and to make recommendations for improvements in unemployment benefit law.[9] Beveridge, who had been chairman of this Committee, recommended that a general social insurance committee should perform a wide advisory role.[10] This proposal was not accepted, and the Labour government instead set up the National Insurance Advisory Committee (NIAC).[11]

This body had two precise functions: first, to prepare reports on general matters submitted to it by the Minister (now, the Secretary of State) and secondly, to consider regulations submitted to it in draft. In its initial years NIAC was extremely busy: by the end of 1950 it had submitted nearly 50 reports on draft regulations,[12] and in the following decade it made a major contribution to the development of social security through the publication of general reports, e.g. on maternity benefits,[13] the death grant[14] and widows' benefits.[15] These often contained the best published discussion of the policies underlying the law, and the reasons for subsequent legislative change.

8 SSA 1980, s.9.
9 Bruce *The Coming of the Welfare State* (4th edn) p. 271; *Harris* pp. 357–361.
10 Para 390.
11 For general discussion, see *George* p. 92; Harrison [1952] Public Administration 149; Griffith 12 MLR 311.
12 See 1st Report of the Ministry of National Insurance (1949, Cmd 7955), para 61, and the 2nd Report (1951, Cmd 8412), para 112.
13 1951, Cmd 8466, p. 249, above.
14 1956, Cmnd 33, p. 241, above.
15 1956, Cmd 9684, p. 228, above.

Some changes to the composition and powers of the National Insurance Advisory Committee were made in 1973. In particular, the Secretary of State was given a discretion not to refer draft regulations to it, when it was considered imperative to give immediate effect to them,[16] and secondly, it was no longer mandatory for NIAC to publish notice of the fact that draft rules had been submitted to it so as to allow interested groups to comment on them. During this period it became difficult in fact not to conclude that the Committee's role was in decline.[17] It produced fewer reports on regulations and on major general topics. Whatever the reasons for this, it provided a strong contrast with the Supplementary Benefits Commission, which under its last chairman, David Donnison, became an outspoken and crusading body.

ii Composition and powers of the Social Security Advisory Committee

Under the 1980 Act the Committee (SSAC) consists of a chairman and between 8 and 11 other members.[18] One member is to be appointed after consultation with employers' organisations, one after consultation with the TUC and a third after consultation with the head of the Northern Ireland Health and Social Services Department. In addition the SSAC must include 'at least one person with experience of work among, and of the needs of, the chronically sick and disabled', and in selecting a member regard is to be had to the desirability of having a sick or disabled person on the Committee. In these respects the provisions closely follow those which governed the composition of NIAC. Unlike the SBC there is no statutory woman member! At the end of 1981 there were 10 members in addition to the Chairman, Sir Arthur Armitage.

Broadly the Committee's task is to give advice to the Secretary of State on social security matters, including supplementary benefits, FIS and child benefit, but excluding industrial injuries benefits, war pensions and occupational pensions for which there are separate advisory bodies.[19] Thus, for the first time there is a body which is able to look at most of the structure of social security benefits and consider the relationship between them. Under this wide rubric, it is possible to identify four more precise functions discharged by the Committee. First, it must advise the Secretary of State on any general questions concerning the working of the relevant social security legislation which he refers to it,[20] though by the end of 1981 no reference under this head had been made. Secondly, it may give its views on proposals by the DHSS, whether it is specifically invited to comment on them or not.[1] The third function is perhaps potentially the most interesting and important. The SSAC is empowered to give the government advice on its own initiative, a role never enjoyed by NIAC, but of course frequently performed by the Supplementary Benefits Commission.[2] The Committee has undertaken to monitor the operation of the new supplementary benefits scheme, and to look at three major areas of social security where its ability to look at the whole range of benefits will be crucial: provision for the long-term unemployed, benefits for the

16 SSA 1975, s.139(1), consolidating SSA 1973, s.48(1).
17 See the first edition of this book, pp. 582–583.
18 SSA 1980, Sch 3.
19 See pp. 548–551, below, for these other bodies. There is a useful summary of the Committee's functions in *Social Security Notes* (October 1981).
20 SSA 1980, s.9(3).
1 Ibid, s.9(1)(a).
2 Ibid.

disabled, and family support. Progress on these and other functions of the Committee is to be reported in Annual Reports, the first of which was published in March 1982.[3]

The fourth function of the SSAC is that of commenting on regulations. As under the earlier legislation, draft regulations must be sent to the Committee for it to comment on, unless it appears to the Secretary of State 'that by reason of the urgency of the matter it is inexpedient so to refer' them.[4] And under a new provision regulations need not be referred where the Committee itself has agreed to this:[5] this would cover technical amendments which raise no issue of principle. Under another new rule, even in urgent cases the final regulations themselves must be sent to the SSAC for it to make comments and write a report which is then to be tabled before the Houses of Parliament.[6] If this report makes recommendations, the Secretary of State must also table a statement of the extent to which he intends to give effect to them. Where comments on *draft* regulations are made, the same rules apply as under the previous legislation governing NIAC: the Committee's report must be laid before the Houses, with the regulations and a statement explaining why the government has or has not implemented it.[7] By the end of 1981 the SSAC had commented on four sets of regulations, the most important of them being the new rules for the payment of child benefit on which the Committee and government had some disagreement.[8]

There is no direct authority on the legal consequences of a failure by the Secretary of State to refer draft social security regulations to a consultative body. This is a general problem in administrative law, and some cases do suggest that a consultation requirement is mandatory and non-compliance will render a regulation at least inapplicable.[9] But the Secretary of State's broad discretion not to refer in cases of urgency perhaps makes this issue now less important, even academic.[10]

Finally, although there is no specific authorisation for this in the legislation, the SSAC has also assumed the role which was performed by the Benefits Commission of supervising the quality of the service offered in DHSS offices to the public. In pursuance of this task members of the Committee have visited local offices and the central offices in the regions.[11]

B The Industrial Injuries Advisory Council[12]

The Industrial Injuries Advisory Council (IIAC) was set up by the 1946 legislation to act as an advisory body to the Minister of National Insurance

3 First report of the Social Security Advisory Committee (HMSO).
4 SSA 1980, ss.10(1) and (2)(a). There are some specific exceptions: ibid, Sch 3, Part II.
5 Ibid, s.10(2)(b).
6 Ibid, s.10(7).
7 Ibid, s.10(4).
8 P. 445, above.
9 *Agricultural, Horticultural and Forestry Industry Training Board v Aylesbury Mushrooms Ltd* [1972] 1 All ER 280, [1972] 1 WLR 190; *Dunkley v Evans* [1981] 3 All ER 285, [1981] 1 WLR 1522.
10 This discussion also applies to a failure to refer industrial injuries regulations to the Industrial Injuries Advisory Council, where the discretion not to refer has existed since 1946. In principle a ministerial decision not to refer could be challenged in the courts, e.g. on the grounds of bad faith or unreasonableness, but it is doubtful whether in practice such a challenge would succeed.
11 See *Social Security Notes* (October 1981).
12 See King *The Ministry of Pensions and National Insurance* (1958) pp. 119–120; *George* p. 92.

on industrial injuries matters. It has always been a larger body than NIAC or the new Social Security Advisory Committee, and its procedure less formal. It consists of a chairman and an unspecified number of other members to be determined, and appointed by, the Secretary of State.[13] At the end of 1981, it consisted of 16 members in addition to the chairman, Professor C R Lowe. After consultation with various outside organisations four of the members must be appointed to represent employers, and four to represent employed earners.[14] The Council must also include at least one person experienced in the needs of the chronically sick and disabled, and as with SSAC, in choosing this person the desirability of having a disabled person as a member should be taken into account.[15] The difficult medical questions involved in determining whether there is a case for prescribing a disease as an 'industrial disease' under section 76 of the Social Security Act 1975 are normally referred for examination to an Industrial Diseases Sub-Committee.[16] Its views are considered by the full Council, and then embodied in a report to the Secretary of State. The Dale Committee in 1948 recommended that a separate body should be instituted to advise on industrial diseases;[17] but the idea was rejected because IIAC would in any case have to look at the industrial diseases regulations, so the setting up of a second body would entail unnecessary duplication.[18]

The Council has two functions under the legislation.[19] First, it considers draft regulations relating to industrial injuries referred to it by the Secretary of State. He is under a duty to refer such regulations unless it appears inexpedient to do this because of urgency or the Council has agreed that this need not be done. This discretion not to refer has existed since the National Insurance (Industrial Injuries) Act 1946.[20] IIAC has never been under any procedural requirements with regard to publication of regulations and the consideration of objections from the public. The Secretary of State does not have to lay before Parliament the Council's report, or state why he does not propose to follow its conclusions. In practice the Council does not often publish its reports on regulations. This would seem to make the work of IIAC in this respect less effective than that of SSAC; it reflects the fact that, in comparison with the latter, IIAC does not in this context deal with matters of policy.

The second function of the Council is to advise on general questions relating to industrial injuries benefits and administration referred to it by the Secretary of State. Unlike the Social Security Advisory Committee, IIAC is not entitled to choose its own subjects for review, though in June 1956, it seems that arrangements were agreed which enable the Council to select for inquiry those diseases which it wishes to consider for prescription as an 'industrial disease'.[1] Several valuable reports on various aspects of industrial injuries benefits have been submitted: time-limits for claiming benefit,[2] on a number of occasions whether a disease should be prescribed

13 SSA 1975, Sch 16, para 1.
14 SSA 1975, Sch 16, para 1(2).
15 Chronically Sick and Disabled Persons Act 1970, s.12.
16 See ch 8 on industrial injuries, pp. 288–292, above.
17 Cmd 7557.
18 See *King*, n.12, above, at p. 120.
19 SSA 1975, s.141, as amended by SSA 1981, Sch 2, para 2.
20 S.61(2)(a).
1 Report of Ministry of Pensions and NI 1956 (Cmnd 229), para 259.
2 (1952, Cmd 8511). See pp. 557–562, below.

as an 'industrial disease',[3] and most recently an important report on proof of industrial diseases.[4]

C The Attendance Allowance Board

The Attendance Allowance Board was set up by the National Insurance (Old persons' and widows' pensions and attendance allowance) Act 1970.[5] It consists of a chairman and between four and nine other members, appointed by the Secretary of State. All except two of them must be medical practitioners, and of the other two, one or both may be a medical practitioner.[6] At the end of 1981, the Board had nine members, two of whom were not medically qualified.

In addition to its primary function to adjudicate on claims to an attendance allowance,[7] the Board also has an advisory role, now imposed by section 140 of the Social Security Act 1975. It advises the Secretary of State on matters which he refers to it, and may recommend changes in the attendance allowance provisions.[8] It may also be asked to give advice to him on the exercise of his powers in relation to the scheme.[9] For the purpose of exercising these advisory functions only, additional members (not necessarily medical practitioners) may be appointed to the Board.[10] These powers are certainly as broad as those of IIAC, though at the moment of writing, there does not appear to have been any published report of the Board in the exercise of these functions, notwithstanding that regulations have been referred to it under section 140.[11] What is particularly interesting is the combination in one body of adjudicatory and advisory roles. Perhaps it would be useful to repeat this in other areas: might not, for example, social security law be improved if general matters were on occasion referred to the Social Security Commissioners for their comment?

D The Central Advisory Committee on War Pensions[12]

The Central Advisory Committee was set up by the War Pensions Act 1921.[13] It is a large body consisting of about 30 members, with the Secretary of State as chairman. Under the Chronically Sick and Disabled Persons Act 1970, it must include in its composition at least 12 local war pensions committee chairmen and one war disabled pensioner.[14] It is required to meet at least once a year: in practice it does not meet more frequently. Its role is essentially to give advice to the Secretary of State on questions concerning entitlement to, and the administration of, war pensions. The

3 E.g. the Reports on Brucellosis (1972, Cmnd 4971), and on Occupational Deafness (1973, Cmnd 5461).
4 (1981, Cmnd 8393.)
5 Renamed as NIA 1970, by NIA 1972, s.8(4).
6 SSA 1975, Sch 11, para 1(1).
7 Ibid, s.105: see ch 15, pp. 601–603, below.
8 Ibid, s.140(1)(a).
9 Ibid, s.140(1)(b).
10 Ibid, Sch 11, para 1(2).
11 E.g. SI 1975/598; SI 1979/375; SI 1980/1136. Such regulations do not have to be referred to SSAC: SSA 1980, Sch 3, para 12(3).
12 See King *The Ministry of Pensions and National Insurance* (1958) pp. 33–34; *George* p. 92.
13 S.3.
14 S.9(1).

membership of the Committee and some details of its work are given in the annual Reports on War Pensioners.

E War Pensions Committees

These committees, often known as local war pensions committees, were set up by the War Pensions Act 1921[15] to give advice to pensioners on the various benefits they might be entitled to and to give general welfare assistance. With the decline in the number of pensioners in the last few years, several committees have been disbanded or amalgamated with others, and now the number is 81. Although one of their functions is to advise the Secretary of State on the local administration of war pensions, it seems that the committees' principal role is to help the pensioners themselves. This general 'welfare' role is now unique in the social security system, and shows the particularly favourable treatment which has often been accorded to war pensioners.

F Local Social Security Advisory Committees[16]

The continued existence of the war pensions committees contrasts sharply with the fate of the local social security advisory committees: they were abolished by the Social Security Act 1971.[17] They had been formed in 1966 on the merger of the administration of national insurance and national assistance by the Ministry of Social Security Act.[18] Previously there had been area advisory committees, which assisted officers of the NAB on local matters, e.g. as to the prevailing rents in the area, and gave advice in individual cases.[19] There had also been local national insurance committees which were more concerned with such matters as the location of and facilities at local insurance offices, and how publicity for the benefits might be improved.[20]

The social security advisory committees elected panels of members whom managers of local offices could consult on the particular problems of people in receipt of supplementary benefit,[1] as well as discharging the general advisory rules of their predecessors. The principal reason for their abolition, given by Sir Keith Joseph during the Standing Committee debates on the 1971 Bill, was that in view of the greater expertise of office managers and their staff, the committees were no longer needed.[2] To some extent this raises the general issues discussed in the introductory paragraphs of this Part. If the primary role of these committees had been to advise the government Department, there is much to be said for Sir Keith Joseph's argument. But, as a number of opposition members stressed, they could also be useful in representing the views of people who were or had

15 S.2.
16 See *George* p. 93; *King* n.12, above, at p. 121; Annex A to *Social Security Users-Local Consultative Groups*, (SB Admin. Paper No 8).
17 S.9.
18 P. 540, above.
19 See the last Report of the NAB (1965, Cmnd 3042), p. 2.
20 There is a full description of the composition and functions of these committees in the 2nd Report of the Ministry of National Insurance (1951, Cmd 8412), paras 115–117.
1 Report of Ministry of Social Security (1967, Cmnd 3693), para 86.
2 See Sir K Joseph in Standing Committee E Debates on the Social Security Bill 1971, cols 46–464.

been in receipt of welfare benefits.[3] If emphasis is put on that role the committees' abolition seems much less justifiable.

Against this background, two recent reports have advocated the institution of local user consultative committees. In the first, the National Consumer Council recommended that such bodies should be set up to monitor the work of the SBC; they should be composed of social workers, representatives of welfare rights organisations and the recipients themselves, and local office managers of the DHSS.[4] Then more comprehensive proposals were made in a report for the SBC by Anne Richardson, a Research Fellow of Chelsea College, London.[5] This suggested that trial committees should be set up on an experimental basis, consisting of some 12 to 15 members: half of them would be user representatives, selected by local organisations, one-quarter chosen from the staff of local DHSS offices and the other quarter would be representatives of other local organisations. All matters of policy and administration concerning every social security benefit would be covered, though not individual cases. Such bodies would clearly have broader functions than the disbanded local advisory committees. Although in the context of a trend towards greater citizen participation this experiment would seem desirable, it is unlikely that the present government would regard it as a high priority.

Part 3 Claims and payments

A Claims: general rules

i When a claim is necessary

It is almost always a necessary condition for entitlement to benefit that a claim is made in the manner prescribed under the legislation. Thus, a claim is necessary for almost all contributory and other benefits payable under the Social Security Act 1975,[6] for child benefit,[7] for supplementary benefits[8] and for FIS.[9] There are a few exceptions under the Social Security Act 1975:[10]

– a Category A or B retirement pension to a woman over 65 on her ceasing to be entitled to a widow's benefit; in some circumstances a Category C or D retirement pension; an age addition.[11]

An increase of benefit, *either* in respect of a child or adult dependant *or* for a supplement to disablement benefit, e.g. for unemployability or special hardship, must be the subject of a separate claim.[12]

The desirability of the condition that a claim must be made was emphasised by a majority of a Tribunal of Commissioners in *R(I) 6/62*. It was argued there by the claimant that there was no need for him to make a

3 Ibid, at cols 452–458.
4 National Consumer Council discussion paper, *Means Tested Benefits* (1976) pp. 63–64.
5 *Social Security Users — Local Consultative Groups* (SB Admin. Paper No 8), published in 1978.
6 SSA 1975, s.79(1).
7 CBA 1975, s.6(1): see ch 11, p. 444, above.
8 There is no express provision that entitlement is to depend on the making of a valid claim, but it is a reasonable implication from SBA 1976, s.14(2)(a).
9 FISA 1970, s.1(2).
10 S.79(2).
11 The conditions in which a claim need not be made are set out in SI 1979/628, reg. 3.
12 Ibid, reg 2(3).

further claim for a special hardship allowance at the end of the period for which it had previously been awarded, since he continued throughout to be entitled and could, therefore, rely on his original claim.[13] This contention was rejected by the majority. They said that if it were correct,

> a claimant could compel the statutory authorities to leave a claim in abeyance and could then revive it many years afterwards, when owing to the lapse of time there would be the utmost difficulty in investigating it.[14]

It is submitted that this approach is right. Although the requirement of a valid claim may on occasion work hardship for someone who has omitted to claim (or claim in time[15]), a system of automatic entitlement to welfare benefits would *generally* be unworkable. There are, however, important exceptions such as child benefit and FIS, where it would be possible to integrate payment with the tax system, and thereby avoid the necessity of making an application for benefit.[16]

It has recently been held that a claim cannot be withdrawn after it has been adjudicated on; this was determined by the Commissioner on basic legal principles, as the point was not covered in the regulations or by precedent.[17]

ii The claim must be made in writing on an appropriate form

There is a general requirement that a claim must be submitted in writing to the Secretary of State on the form approved by him for the particular benefit, 'or in such other manner, being in writing, as he may accept as sufficient in the circumstances . . . '.[18] In the relevant Supplementary Benefit, FIS and Child Benefit Regulations, the detail is added that the form must be delivered or sent to an office of the DHSS.[19] Claim forms are to be supplied without charge.[20] In practice almost all claims, except those for unemployment benefit and sometimes supplementary benefit, are made by post.

If the claim is defective when received by the Secretary of State, e.g. because the wrong form has been used, he may refer it to the claimant; provided the form is then returned correctly completed within a month, the application may be treated as if it had been properly made in the first place.[1] Under the Social Security and the Child Benefit Regulations, a claim may be amended by notice in writing sent to the Department, and then the amended claim may also be treated as if it had been made in the first instance.[2]

These requirements have been considered by the Commissioner. The most important ruling is that, while it is for the Secretary of State to decide whether to accept a document as an alternative to the approved form, it is for the statutory authorities to determine whether the documents constitute a valid claim. Therefore, the fact that the Secretary of State had accepted letters from the claimant's father, instead of the appropriate form, did not preclude the Commissioner from ruling that they did not

13 For special hardship allowance, see ch 8, pp. 310–323, above.
14 *R(I) 6/62*, para 15.
15 See pp. 557–564, below, for time-limits.
16 See pp. 34–37, above.
17 *R(U) 2/79*, D Reith, Comr.
18 SI 1979/628, reg 4. Also see SI 1976/964, reg 2 (Child Benefit regs).
19 SI 1981/1525, reg 3; SI 1980/1438, reg 2; SI 1976/964, reg 2.
20 E.g. SI 1979/628, reg 5.
1 E.g. SI 1979/628, reg 8(1); SI 1976/964, reg 2(4).
2 SI 1979/628, reg 8(2), and SI 1976/964, reg 2(5).

amount to a good claim for unemployment benefit.[3] The intention to claim must appear on the face of the relevant documents. It is not enough if it can only be inferred from other papers.[4] In a recent supplementary benefit case the Commissioner pointed out that the requirement that the claim be made on the appropriate form was in practice applied with considerable flexibility, and he went on to question whether it was necessary for the regulation to be drafted 'in such pedantically stringent terms'.[5]

iii Information to be given when making a claim for benefit

It is a standard rule that the claimant shall furnish those certificates, documents, information and evidence for the purpose of determining his claim, which are required by the Secretary of State, and if reasonably so required, shall attend at an office of the DHSS.[6] These provisions appear to enable the Secretary of State to impose requirements as to the evidence, etc., to be adduced by a *particular claimant*. The Chief Commissioner in Northern Ireland has doubted whether such rules are intra vires.[7] The Social Security Act 1975 empowers the making of regulations,

> for requiring claimants to furnish to the prescribed person any information required for the determination of the claim or of any question arising in connection with it.[8]

As the Chief Commissioner suggested, this provision would only seem to authorise the making of regulations imposing requirements to supply information (the exact character of which must be specified in the regulation) in various types of case (e.g. a medical certificate in a sickness benefit claim), but not regulations giving the Secretary of State power to require the production of unspecified documents. Moreover, it is difficult to reconcile the power, which appears to be conferred by the regulations, with the fact that under the legislation it is for *the insurance officer* to determine whether a claim should succeed or fail on the evidence.[9] Certainly there does not appear to be any warrant for a conclusion that a failure to produce the required evidence necessarily entails the failure of the claim. It is clearly for the statutory authorities to decide whether it should succeed.[10]

A more acceptable use of the regulatory power is made in the provisions requiring, inter alia, the production of a birth certificate in a claim for widowed mother's allowance or child's special allowance or an increase of benefit in respect of a child, and a death certificate where the death grant is claimed.[11] Even in these cases, it seems clear that the omission to produce the required evidence will not entail the claim's failure.[12] A certificate (now a doctor's statement) is normally required by the Medical Evidence

3 *R(U) 9/60*.
4 *R(S) 1/63*.
5 *R(SB) 6/81*, paras 8–9, per J Mitchell, Comr.
6 See e.g. SI 1979/628, reg 7(1) and SI 1976/964, reg 3(1).
7 *R 1/75 (P)*, T A Blair, Chief Comr.
8 SSA 1975, s.79(5).
9 Ibid, s.98; pp. 585–587, below, for adjudication by insurance officers.
10 See *R 1/75 (P)*, where the Commissioner took this view. It is perhaps possible that a claim submitted without the required information is not made *in the prescribed manner*, and, therefore, fails to meet the condition for entitlement imposed by section 79(1) of the Act. But this would seem to be reading too much into the emphasised words.
11 SI 1979/628, regs 7(2)–(4).
12 The failure to produce a death certificate will not defeat a claim for widow's benefit: see p. 229, above.

Regulations made under section 115(1) of the Social Security Act 1975, when a claim is made for sickness, injury or maternity benefit.[13]

Under the Supplementary Benefit Regulations, a claimant must, if reasonably required to do so, attend an office or other place.[14] The SBC used to interpret this requirement as authorising a medical examination, a view upheld by the Parliamentary Commissioner for Administration.[15] In other areas of social security law, the legislation itself specifically authorises such examinations to be required by regulation,[16] and it is submitted that the obligation to attend for this should only be imposed under precise powers.

iv Interchange with claims for other benefits

In certain circumstances it has been provided that a claim for one benefit may be treated alternatively or additionally as a claim for another benefit to which the person is entitled.[17] This provision assists a person who has made a claim for one allowance, and then discovers that he is really entitled to another. If his application for this second allowance were regarded as made only at this later stage (and not when the original claim was made), he might be disqualified from receiving it because of the time-limits.[18] Regulations providing for the interchangeability of claims have been made under both the Social Security and the Child Benefit Acts.[19]

- The Social Security Regulations provide, inter alia, that where a person has claimed a benefit listed in one column of Schedule 3 to the Regulations, the claim may be treated as a claim in the alternative for any benefit listed in the second column of the Schedule.[20] Thus, a claim for sickness benefit may be treated as a claim for invalidity benefit, injury benefit or non-contributory invalidity pension,[1] a claim for maternity allowance may be treated as a claim for sickness, invalidity benefit, or non-contributory invalidity pension, and a claim for a retirement pension of one category may be treated as a claim for such a pension of any category. Other regulations provide that where one person has made a claim for a dependant's increase to which he is not entitled, the claim may be treated as made by some other person who may be entitled to an increase in respect of this dependant,[2] and that a claim for supplementary benefit under the 1976 Act may be treated as a claim also for attendance allowance or an invalid care allowance.[3]

It was at one time unclear whether the decision to treat a claim as one in the alternative for another benefit was to be made by the Secretary of State or the statutory authorities. The British Commissioner decided that the matter was one for the Secretary of State,[4] but a Northern Ireland tribunal

13 SI 1976/615, reg 2 (for details on the medical certification procedure, see ch 4, pp. 149–152, above). See Appendix.
14 SI 1981/1525, reg 4.
15 3rd Report of the PCA for 1974–75, HC 241, Case No C 156/J.
16 See e.g. SSA 1975, s.20(2)(b) (sickness benefit); s.22(9)(b) (maternity allowance); s.89(2)(a) (industrial injury benefits).
17 Ibid, s.80(1), as amended by SS(MP)A 1977, s.17(2).
18 See pp. 557–564, below, for time-limits.
19 SI 1979/628, reg 9 and SI 1976/964, reg 5.
20 SI 1979/628, reg 9(1).
1 A claim for any of these four benefits may be interchangeable with a claim for one of the others.
2 SI 1979/628, reg 9(3).
3 Ibid, reg 9(5): see *R(A) 3/81*.
4 *R(1) 79/54*.

held that it was for the statutory authorities to determine this question.[5] As it is the authorities who determine whether the documents submitted constitute a valid claim,[6] there was much to be said in principle for allowing them to decide whether to treat a claim as one for another benefit. However, it is now clearly provided that the question is one for the Secretary of State.[7] This is also made plain in the Child Benefit Regulations, under which the Secretary of State may in his discretion accept a claim for child benefit as a claim for

– child's special allowance, guardian's allowance, maternity benefit claimed after confinement, industrial death benefit for children, and increases for child dependants.[8]

Correspondingly, a claim for one of these benefits may be treated as a claim for child benefit, where it appears that the claimant may be entitled alternatively, or in addition to, that benefit.[9]

– Finally, it may be mentioned that the Claims and Payments Regulations provide that, where a certificate of expected confinement has been issued and the woman has claimed sickness benefit (or her claim for maternity allowance is treated as one for sickness benefit), her claim may be treated as one for sickness benefit for the *whole maternity allowance period*.[10] She is, of course, only entitled to sickness benefit if she satisfies the relevant conditions; the Regulation merely provides that her claim may be treated as a claim for it.[11]

v When a claim is made

The date on which a claim is made may be important for determining the relevant time-limit. The Social Security Act 1975 provides that when a claim or notice is sent by post, it

> shall be deemed to have been made or given on the day on which it was posted.[12]

This confirms a decision of the Chief Commissioner interpreting earlier regulations.[13] Provided the claimant can show that he has posted the claim, the 'risk' of non-delivery is placed on the DHSS. In other areas, however, the rules are not so generous to the claimant:

– The Child Benefit (Claims and Payments) Regulations provide that the date of claim is the date on which it is received in a department office, though if the Secretary of State knows that a claim sent by post has not been delivered in the ordinary course of post, he *may* treat the claim as made on an earlier date: the date on which it would have been delivered in the ordinary course of post or the date 13 weeks before it was delivered, whichever is the later.[14] There is a similar rule in the FIS Regulations.[15]

There is no obvious reason why these Regulations should differ from the general social security rule; one possible explanation is that, as both FIS

5 *R 2/69 (II)*.
6 P. 553, above.
7 SSA 1975, s.95(1)(e): for Secretary of State's questions, see ch 15, pp. 583–585, below.
8 SI 1976/964, reg 5(1).
9 Ibid, reg 5(2). See *R(S) 3/80*.
10 SI 1979/628, reg 10. For the maternity allowance period, see ch 7, p. 247, above.
11 See *R(S) 1/74*, H Magnus, Comr.
12 S.79(6).
13 *R(I) 2/71*.
14 SI 1976/964, reg 2(2).
15 SI 1980/1438, reg 2(2): see p. 563, below, for mobility allowance.

and child benefit must be claimed from a central office,[16] and not locally, it is less reasonable for the DHSS automatically to run the risk of the post going astray.

vi Time-limits: general principles

The most important aspect of the Claims and Payments Regulations is the imposition of time-limits for claiming the various benefits. If the claim is not made within the time prescribed for the particular benefit, then the claimant is disqualified from receiving it, either absolutely or in respect of the period specified in the Regulations.[17] The reasons which may justify the imposition of time-limits are largely those which support limitation periods in all civil proceedings: the desire to achieve certainty and avoid adjudicating claims on stale evidence. The absence of time-limits would, moreover, make administration more costly and the financing of the National Insurance Fund less predictable. These arguments are persuasive with regard to certain benefits, such as those for sickness and unemployment, where it may well be difficult to decide a late claim because of the unreliability of the evidence. On the other hand, it seems difficult to defend the existence of a time-limit for claiming a retirement pension, when the applicant would probably have little trouble in substantiating a claim brought months or years after he attained pensionable age and became entitled. The National Insurance Advisory Committee and the Industrial Injuries Advisory Council have both emphasised that a balance should be struck between the desire to protect the administration against an abundance of stale claims, and the need of the individual to have a reasonable time within which to bring his claim.[18] In particular, the claimant 'should not be precluded from drawing the appropriate benefit by any act or default on his part, for which the ordinary man would hold that he had a good excuse'.[19]

These ends are achieved, first, by the imposition of time-limits which vary from one benefit to another. Thus, benefits which an ordinary man may claim frequently in his life (e.g. sickness benefit), have shorter time-limits than those which are less often applied for, where it is understandable that the applicant may take longer to appreciate that he has a claim (e.g. the death grant). The details of the various time-limits are mentioned in the next section. Secondly, for most of the benefits available under the Social Security Act 1975, the prescribed time-limit may be extended if the claimant shows that there is 'good cause' for his failure to apply within the specified period.[20]

B The time-limits and other rules for particular benefits

i Unemployment benefit

In addition to submitting a written claim, a person applying for unemployment benefit is usually required to attend in person at an unemployment

16 From the central offices at Blackpool, and Washington, Co Durham, respectively: p. 542, above.
17 SI 1979/628, reg 14. For a general study of the time-limit rules, see Partington *Claim in Time* (1978).
18 Report of NIAC on Time-Limits, (1952, Cmd 8483); Report of IIAC on Time-Limits for claiming industrial injury benefits (1952, Cmd 8511); Report of NIAC on Time-Limits (1968, Cmnd 3597), paras 6–7.
19 Cmd 8483, para 15.
20 See pp. 565–569, below.

benefit office of the Department of Employment.[1] Unemployment benefit is thus the only contributory benefit for which an application is not normally made by post. At the benefit office, the claimant is interviewed and his claim processed, his contribution record being checked by reference to the central office in Newcastle. He is told that he must return to the benefit office fortnightly, at a particular time on a particular day of the week, to state that he is still unemployed and looking for work – the procedure known as 'signing on'.[2] Until 1979 claimants were required to 'sign on' weekly, and they may still opt to do this and be paid benefit weekly if they prefer, but the usual course now is attendance every two weeks.[3]

Schedule 1 to the Claims and Payments Regulations provides that a claim for unemployment benefit must be made on the day for which it is made. But this rule is qualified by Schedule 2 with the result that an applicant is not disqualified, provided he claims on the day of the week specified in the notice given him by the unemployment benefit office, his 'signing on' day. The effect of these provisions was shown in *R(U) 6/75*, where the claimant failed to attend on the required day, but called the following day and claimed for the preceding week. The Commissioner, H A Shewan, explained that unemployment benefit was a day-to-day benefit, and that the effect of the modification in Schedule 2 was only to remove the disqualification for a late claim, where such a claim was made *on the day specified* for 'signing on'. The claimant was therefore disqualified from benefit for the week.

Until 1982 the practice was for the benefit office to require a claimant to register for work at the separate employment office, Job Centre or, in the case of a young person under 20, at a local authority Careers Office. The report of the joint Department of Employment and DHSS team recommended that registration should no longer be compulsory, and this was accepted by the government.[4] Although the aim of simplifying the claims procedures was not the principal reason for this reform, it certainly has this effect.

There is a further modification under the regulations by which the Secretary of State may certify that there are or will be circumstances making it difficult to apply the normal rules and practices concerning claims to unemployment benefit. This certificate may have effect either generally, or in relation to a case or class of cases or an area.[5] When it does have effect, the insurance officer may treat a claim for benefit as one for up to 26 weeks, and then benefit may be awarded for a period not exceeding 13 weeks.[6] The award only subsists as long as the claimant satisfies the conditions of entitlement.[7] This power is useful for times and in areas where long-term unemployment may be anticipated, or where, perhaps because of geographical remoteness, it is difficult for the claimant to attend regularly at a benefit office.

A further administrative provision prescribes that a refusal of an unemployment benefit claim may be treated as a decision disallowing future claims by that claimant for a specified period (up to 12 months) or

1 SI 1979/628, reg 4. Unemployment benefit is administered by the Department of Employment, subject to the policy directions of the DHSS.
2 There is an excellent summary of the procedures in the Report of the Joint DE/DHSS Rayner Scrutiny, *Payment of Benefits to Unemployed People* (1980) Annex II, ch 2.
3 SI 1979/628, reg 12(1), as amended by SI 1979/781, and see NIAC Report (Cmnd 7617).
4 DE/DHSS Rayner Scrutiny, n.2, above, para 11.
5 SI 1979/628, reg 12(2).
6 Ibid, reg 12(3), as amended by SI 1981/1101.
7 SI 1979/628, reg 12(4).

until the grounds of the initial refusal have ceased to exist.[8] There must be a continuing feature in the grounds of the refusal to justify the application of this provision.[9] Under a new regulation, where benefit is refused because of a failure to satisfy contribution conditions, the decision is automatically treated as refusing all further claims to benefit until the conditions are met.[10]

ii Sickness, invalidity and industrial injury benefit, and non-contributory invalidity pension

In all these cases the time-limit varies according to whether the claim is an original claim, the first claim in a period of illness or a continuation claim.[11]

a *Original claim*

This is a claim 'where the claimant has at no time made a claim for sickness or injury benefit or non-contributory invalidity pension under the Act or a claim which has been treated as a claim for sickness or injury benefit or non-contributory invalidity pension'.[12] It does not matter if the previous application was ineffective; it was still a claim and any subsequent one cannot be regarded as original.[13]

- The prescribed time for making an original claim is 21 days from the earliest day for which the claim is made; if it is made after that time (in the absence of good cause for the delay), the person concerned is disqualified from receiving benefit for any day more than 21 days before the date on which it is made.

This time-limit is generous in comparison with the six and ten day limitation periods for first and continuation claims respectively.

This 21 day period for initial claims was introduced in 1951 following a recommendation of the National Insurance Advisory Committee, and was designed to give a more generous period for applicants who, it might reasonably be presumed, were unfamiliar with the requirements for making a claim.[14] In 1964 NIAC questioned whether this 'concession', as it was termed, was necessary in view of the existence of the benefit for nearly 20 years. But it thought it should be retained for young claimants making their first claim soon after leaving school and starting work.[15]

b *First claim in a spell of illness or injury*

Unless the claim is an original one, the first claim for benefit in a spell of illness or injury must be made within a period of six days from the earliest day in respect of which the claim is made. If a claim is submitted after this period, no benefit is payable in respect of any day more than six days before the actual date of claim. Before 1964, the applicant was required to submit a notice of incapacity for work within three days,[16] but upon the recommendation of NIAC this requirement was abolished and the general time-limit of six days imposed.[17]

8 Ibid, reg 12(5).
9 *R(U) 1/78*.
10 SI 1980/1643, correcting a difficulty shown by *R(U) 11/80*.
11 SI 1979/628, Sch 1.
12 Ibid, Sch 1, para 3(a).
13 *R(S) 8/52*.
14 1951, HC 240.
15 Cmnd 2400, paras 22–23.
16 The notice could be accompanied by the claim for benefit or be followed by a claim within the next seven days.
17 N.15, above, at paras 16–21.

c *Continuation claim*

Any other claim is known as a continuation claim and must be made within ten days of the start of the period for which it is made. NIAC in 1964 rejected suggestions to extend this period to 14 days.[18] Generally there will be no difficulty in determining whether a claim is a first or a continuation claim, but problems did arise in *R(S) 1/68*:

> On 15 September 1966 C submitted three medical certificates, claiming benefit from 29 August 1966 to 12 September 1966. On these three forms his doctor had certified (on three different days in this period) that C was incapable of work for a particular period. The question was whether these forms constituted one claim or three. The Chief Commissioner, R G Micklethwait, ruled that there were three claims and that the last two certificates constituted continuation claims. On that basis, C was not disqualified from receiving sickness benefit after 3 September 1966.[19]

It is provided that a claim for sickness, invalidity or industrial injury benefit or for non-contributory invalidity pension is to be treated (unless the Secretary of State otherwise directs) as if made for the period specified in the medical certificate.[20] Benefit may be awarded on that claim for the whole or part of that period up to 13 weeks. A recent Tribunal decision has held that, although an insurance officer may totally disallow such a prospective claim, he is not entitled to disallow it for part of the period and leave the other part of the claim undisposed of.[1] The usual requirement that a medical certificate in the form of a doctor's statement be submitted with a claim for sickness, invalidity and injury benefit is discussed elsewhere in this book.[2]

iii Increase, in respect of any dependant, of the benefits in i and ii and of invalid care allowance

As has been mentioned previously,[3] an increase in benefit for a dependant must be separately claimed, and there are separate claim forms.[4]

- The increase must be claimed within one month from the day in respect of which the claim is submitted.[5]

If an applicant is out of time for claiming a dependant's increase, he is disqualified from receiving it. (He may, of course, claim an increase for a later period in respect of which he does satisfy the time-limit.)

iv Maternity benefit

a *Maternity grant*

- A maternity grant claimed on the ground of actual confinement must be claimed within three months of the confinement.[6] When it is claimed on

18 Ibid, at para 24.
19 The 4.9.66 was ten days before the date of the claim (15.9.66), as Sundays are not counted in estimating the limitation period: see *R(S) 3/56*.
20 SI 1979/628, reg 11(1).
1 *R(S) 5/80*. Also see *R(S) 14/81*.
2 Pp. 149–152, above.
3 P. 552, above.
4 *Fisher* para 86.
5 SI 1979/628, Sch 1, para 3. Before 1977, there was an alternative time-limit – the claim had to be brought within one month of day when the relevant main benefit was claimed – but this was difficult to apply.
6 For the alternative bases for claiming a maternity grant or allowance, see ch 7, pp. 246–247, above.

the alternative basis of an 'expectation of confinement', it may be applied for within the period beginning 14 weeks before the expected week of confinement and ending immediately before the date of confinement. The grant is entirely forfeited if it is not claimed within these periods.

b *Maternity allowance*

– A maternity allowance in respect of an expectation of confinement may be claimed during the three week period beginning with the fourteenth week before the expected week of confinement. If, however, it is claimed on the basis of actual confinement, then it must be applied for within three weeks of that date. A late claim leads to disqualification for receipt of benefit in respect of any week before the claim is actually made. Benefit is, however, payable for the remainder of the maternity allowance period.

c *Increase of maternity allowance in respect of a dependant*

– The limitation period for claims for dependant's increase to awards of sickness benefit, etc. applies here.

It seems that a claim for an increase may alternatively be made in advance of the period for which it is claimed, provided it is made within 14 weeks of the expected week of confinement, when the claimant becomes entitled to the allowance itself.[7]

v Retirement pension, widow's benefit and other benefits

– The prescribed time-limit for claiming a retirement pension of any category, widow's benefit, child's special allowance, guardian's allowance and invalid care allowance is three months from the date on which the claimant became entitled to the benefit in question.[8] If the claim is made after that period, benefit is forfeited for the period more than three months before it was made.

A retirement pension may be claimed in advance up to four months before the date on which the applicant becomes entitled.[9] In practice what normally happens is that about four months before someone reaches pensionable age, he is informed by the DHSS that he may claim a pension and an application form is sent to him. On its return pension is assessed in the central office at Newcastle,[10] where the documents go for incorporation in the records.[11]

A request for a claim form for widow's benefit (and the death grant) is found on the back of the death certificate issued by the Registrar.[12] The claim is generally made at the local office. A claim for guardian's or child's special allowance is usually sent to the local office, from where it is forwarded to the child benefits central office at Washington, Co Durham where a decision is given.[13]

7 SI 1979/628, Sch 2, para 3.
8 Ibid, Sch 1, paras 2 and 6. (The list here is not exhaustive.)
9 Ibid, Sch 2, para 4(1). See p. 207, above, for the separate requirement of notice of retirement.
10 For the central office at Newcastle; see p. 542, above.
11 *Fisher* para 85. It is not maladministration if the DHSS neglects to operate the 'reminder system'. See 5th Report of PCA for 1975–76, HC 496, Case No C.644/V.
12 *Fisher* para 84.
13 For this office, see p. 542, above.

vi Death grant

Every person claiming a death grant may be required by the Secretary of State to provide a death certificate, and in some cases of a child's death a birth certificate.[14]

- The grant must be claimed within six months of the death, or a longer period to be determined by the Secretary of State.[15] The grant is forfeited entirely if not claimed in time.

The period for claiming used to be only one month, but NIAC in its report of 1952 recommended an extension – as that period was too short in view of the emotional distress often suffered.[16]

vii Disablement benefit (including increases) and industrial death benefit

- In all these cases the prescribed time for claiming is the period of three months from the first day on which the conditions of entitlement to the benefit, or additions to benefit such as unemployability supplement or the special hardship allowance, are satisfied.[17] A late claim leads to disqualification from receipt of the benefit for the period more than three months before it was made.

But this does not apply to a disablement gratuity; in effect there is no penalty at all for making a late claim for this benefit. This was decided by the Commissioner in two cases in the early 1950s,[18] and they were followed with reluctance by R S Lazarus in *R(I) 14/74*:

> The regulation perpetuates in the law governing the industrial injuries insurance scheme an anomaly which cannot have been intended when the scheme came into force in 1948, and for which I am unable to perceive any justification.[19]

There are a variety of special procedural rules relating to claims for disablement benefit, including the requirement with regard to giving notice of accidents, and the obligation to submit to medical examination or treatment.[20] A claimant may withdraw an application for disablement benefit (for the purpose of continuing his entitlement to injury benefit) by delivering a notice to that effect at the office of the DHSS dealing with his claim.[1] This will be effective if it is received before the application for disablement benefit has been 'finally determined'.[2]

An increase of disablement benefit in respect of a child or adult dependant must be separately claimed within three months from the date of entitlement to the increase.[3]

viii Attendance allowance

Attendance allowance cannot normally be paid for any period before the claim is made.[4] There is also no question of extending the period in which a

14 SI 1979/628, reg 7(4).
15 Ibid, Sch 1, para 7. This appears to be the only case where the Secretary of State has discretionary power to extend the normal time-limit.
16 Cmd 8483, paras 45–46.
17 These periods were harmonised after the Report of IIAC on Time-Limits in 1952 (Cmd 8511), at paras 17–21.
18 *R(I) 27/52*; *R(I) 51/53*.
19 Para 6. The regulation referred to is now SI 1979/628, Sch 1, para 8, col 3, which clearly excludes the gratuity from the disqualification provision.
20 Ch 8, p. 328, above.
1 SI 1979/628, reg 27.
2 For the meaning of this, see p. 296, above.
3 SI 1979/628, Sch 1, para 11.
4 SSA 1975, s.35(4). This rule does not apply to renewal cases: SI 1980/1136, reg 4. See p. 175, above.

claim may be made by showing 'good cause' for the failure to make the claim earlier.[5]

ix Mobility allowance

A person is not entitled to a mobility allowance for any week before that in which the claim is *received by* the Secretary of State.[6] If the claimant satisfies the Secretary of State that a claim has been posted earlier but it has not been received in the ordinary course of post, entitlement may begin in an earlier week, though not more than three months before the date on which the claim is received.[7] This rule is similar to those for child benefit and FIS, and less generous than the normal rule that a claim is made when it is posted.[8] A claim for a further period, made within three months after the end of a period for which the allowance has been awarded, may be treated as if it had been made immediately after the end of the latter period, and entitlement determined on that basis.[9] A forward claim for the allowance may be made for a period beginning not more than three months after the claim has been received, and an award made for that period.[10]

x Supplementary benefit[11]

There are two claim forms for supplementary benefit. The general form used, SB1, is available at any post office or local office of the Department. Unemployed claimants are required to submit their claims on the form B1, obtainable at the unemployment benefit offices of the Department of Employment.[12] On receipt of the form, the manager of the local office may arrange for a home visit to be paid when details of the claimant's resources and requirements will be taken. This visit is normally made within a week. though it may be expedited if the applicant has indicated that his needs are pressing.[13]

Alternatively the applicant may decide to claim in person at the local office. Normally appointments are arranged to save time. The applicant is advised to arrive with as much supporting information as possible, e.g. rent book, child benefit order book, wage-slips, and any evidence of other income or expenditure.[14] If all the relevant information is forthcoming at this interview, then the officer may make a full award of benefit. On the other hand, when the information is not complete, an interim award may be made and a final decision postponed until a home visit is made.[15]

Generally a claim must be made no later than the first day of the period for which it is made.[16] However, if the claimant shows good cause for his failure to make a prompt claim, a later application will be treated as if made on the first day of the relevant period. And there is a similar relaxation of the general rule when the claimant has made a claim for a benefit under the Social Security Act 1975, for FIS or a war disablement

5 This extension only applies to the benefits specified in Sch 1 of SI 1979/628.
6 SSA 1975, s.37A(5)(b), inserted in that Act by SSPA 1975, s.2.
7 SI 1975/1573, reg 4(1).
8 P. 556, above.
9 SI 1975/1573, regs 4(2) and 6.
10 Ibid, reg 5(1).
11 See *Lynes* pp. 43–46.
12 Handbook, paras 11.1–11.4.
13 Ibid, paras 11.7–11.8.
14 Ibid, paras 11.9–11.11.
15 Ibid, paras 11.12–11.13.
16 SI 1981/1525, reg 5(1).

pension and his claim for supplementary benefit is made as soon as practicable after receipt of the decision on the earlier application.[17]

In certain circumstances travelling expenses incurred in connection with claims may be paid by the DHSS, though generally an award will only be made if the cost of the return journey exceeds £1.[18]

xi FIS

Many of the particular rules for claiming FIS have been discussed in chapter 13.[19] Awards run from the date on which the claim is received by the Department, though the Secretary of State may treat an application as made earlier (up to three months before it was received) if this is requested, or he is aware that the claim has not been delivered in the ordinary course of post, *and* the claimant has not been at fault.[20] A renewal claim for FIS to be continued may be made from four weeks before until four weeks after the period of initial entitlement.[1]

xii Child benefit

A claim may be made up to 52 weeks after the week for which it is claimed:[2] this would appear to be much the longest period for social security benefits which impose a time-limit.

xiii War pensions

There are no prescribed claim forms or procedures, though a document is usually completed and sent to the DHSS central office at Blackpool, where claims are handled. An interesting issue of general significance arose in *Robertson v Minister of Pensions*.[3]

> C wrote in 1941 to the War Office concerning his disability, and a month later received a reply to the effect that it was accepted as attributable to war service. The War Office had not consulted the Minister of Pensions, to whom responsibility for the award of pensions had been transferred from September 1939. Relying on this reply C refrained from obtaining an independent medical opinion and destroyed some relevant evidence. The Minister of Pensions later held that C was not entitled to a pension as his injury was not attributable to war service.

On appeal, Denning J held the Crown was bound by the War Office's representation on which Robertson had reasonably relied and, therefore, the Minister was bound by the assurance. The decisive fact would seem to have been that between October 1921 and September 1939 the War Office had dealt with pension claims, so that an applicant could reasonably believe it to be the appropriate department for handling them.[4]

There is no time-limit for claiming a war pension, though the burden of proof shifts to the applicant if he claims more than seven years after leaving service.[5]

17 Ibid, reg 5(2).
18 Ibid, reg 29.
19 P. 536, above.
20 SI 1980/1438, reg 2(2).
1 SI 1980/1437, reg 3(2).
2 CBA 1975, s.6(2): also see p. 444, above.
3 [1949] 1 KB 227, [1948] 2 All ER 767.
4 The decision is a controversial one in the application of estoppel to public authorities: for further discussion, see Treitel [1957] PL 321 at 325–329.
5 Pp. 348–351, above.

C Extension of time-limits for 'good cause'

i The law on 'good cause'

The 'good cause' principle applies to all the benefits covered by the Social Security Claims and Payments Regulations,[6] and now, as has just been mentioned, to supplementary benefit. The rule is that:

> If in any case the claimant proves that there was good cause for the failure to make the claim before the date on which it was made, the prescribed time for making that claim shall (subject to the provisions of section 82(2)) be extended to the date on which the claim is made: . . .[7]

Section 82(2) provides that for most benefits there is an absolute bar on payment for a period more than 12 months before the claim is made. Subject then to this limitation, the prescribed time for claiming most of the various benefits discussed in the previous section will be extended if the claimant shows that there was good cause for the delay in presenting his claim. It is also provided that if the claimant (apart from the claim condition) was entitled to the benefit on an earlier date to that on which the claim was made, and there was good cause for the delay in claiming between these two dates, then he is not to be disqualified for receiving any benefit to which he would have been entitled if it had been made on that earlier date.[8] In other words, a claimant will not be wholly disqualified if there was good cause for the later part of the period of delay immediately before the claim was made. But the fact that there was good cause for the failure to claim in an earlier part will not lead to an extension of the prescribed time-limit.[9]

a *General principles in determining 'good cause'*

These principles are the same for all benefits, though, of course, their application will vary according to the facts.[10] They were stated in *CS 371/49*:

> It will be observed that the expression used is 'good cause', not 'a good excuse'. 'Good cause' means, in my opinion, some fact which, having regard to all the circumstances (including the claimant's state of health and the information which he had received and that which he might have obtained) would probably have caused a reasonable person of his age and experience to act (or fail to act) as the claimant did.

It was also emphasised that the burden of proof is on the claimant. These principles were approved by both NIAC and IIAC,[11] and followed in later decisions of the Commissioner.[12] NIAC had, however, contemplated the formulation of a provision which would allow extension in cases of 'excusable ignorance', though it was persuaded that this was neither necessary nor practicable.[13] In a later report it concluded that there had

6 SI 1979/628, Sch 1, col 1. But it does not apply to claims for occupational deafness regulated by SI 1975/1537: *R(I) 2/79* (Tribunal decision).
7 SI 1979/628, reg 14.
8 SI 1979/628, reg 14(3). This will not necessarily be the whole of the benefit claimed, but that benefit from which the person would not have been disqualified (if he had claimed on the earlier date) under the rules described in the previous section.
9 *CS 34/49*.
10 See T A Blair, Chief Comr, in *R 1/70 (MB)*.
11 N.18, p. 557, above.
12 See esp. *R(S) 2/63* (Tribunal decision).
13 Cmd 8483, paras 19–22.

been a continual trend towards a more liberal interpretation of the 'good cause' provision, and saw no case for a change in its formulation.[14]

Two cases show the generous approach sometimes taken by the Commissioner. A familiar source of difficulty is whether a claimant, who has not claimed benefit because he did not realise he was entitled to it, has good cause for his failure to claim within the prescribed time. This issue arose before a Tribunal of Commissioners in *R(S) 2/63*:

> C did not claim sickness benefit while he had reasonable grounds for believing, and did believe, that he would be paid wages in full during his period of sickness, and that this would preclude him from claiming benefit. Both beliefs were wrong. The Tribunal held that he had good cause for his failure to claim, while he suffered from this misapprehension.

It was emphasised that 'over the years there has been a gradual, but appreciable relaxation of the strictness with which problems of good and reasonable cause have been approached'; this was particularly true of sickness benefit claims where the applicant might not act promptly because of his ill-health. In determining how a reasonable person should behave, it is permissible to take account of the conduct of other claimants, as revealed in the cases which come before the Commissioners.[15]

Similar problems occur when a new benefit is introduced, or the rules of entitlement to an old one are changed. Generally ignorance of a new entitlement has not been held to afford good cause for delay in claiming the particular benefit within the permitted time.[16] But in *R(G) 2/74*, the Commissioner, H Magnus, seems to have taken an extremely generous view:

> From 5 April 1971 C became entitled to a widow's pension after the change in the conditions of entitlement introduced by NIA 1970. (She had become a widow in 1961 when 48, and under the law then was not entitled to a pension.)[17] C then claimed a retirement pension on 14 November 1972 when she became 60, and it was only then that she appreciated her previous entitlement to a widow's pension. She argued that the DHSS publicity campaign in 1970–71 concerning the change in the widow's pension rules had 'passed her by'. This was accepted by the Commissioner, who held that C had good cause for her failure to claim and was entitled to the widow's pension from 16 November 1971.[18]

It was not appropriate here to apply the principle that a claimant ignorant of his rights has a duty to take reasonable steps to find out what they are, and the Commissioner emphasised that all the facts must be considered in determining whether there is good cause.

In other cases where an applicant can be expected to be aware of his rights, a more restrictive attitude is taken. In particular the Commissioners have generally been unsympathetic to the argument that a self-employed claimant has good cause for delay in applying for sickness benefit because

14 Cmnd 2400, para 27.
15 See the statement of general principle in *CS 371/49*, and by the Chief Comr in Northern Ireland, T A Blair, in *R 1/70 (MB)*.
16 See *CG 125/50* (failure to claim death grant six months after it had first become available), and *R(I) 82/53* (no good cause when a dock worker did not appreciate that his rash was a prescribed disease).
17 See ch 6, p. 233, above.
18 The claimant was not entitled to a pension for more than 12 months before her claim: see p. 565, above. Also see *R(P) 1/79* and *R(S) 3/79*.

he did not think the self-employed were eligible.[19] Although this error is common, it is not regarded as justifiable in view of the fact that this group has always been entitled to sickness benefit since 1948. If he becomes sick, a self-employed claimant can reasonably be expected to inquire about his benefit entitlement at a DHSS office. And in *R(S) 5/79* , it was held that there was no good cause for a late claim, when the applicant had sent his medical certificate to his employer for the latter to forward to the DHSS and had then omitted to inquire whether his claim had in fact been received at the local office.

The determination whether there is good cause is a complex one, requiring an examination of all the facts. This is shown by *R(I) 10/74*:

> Following an industrial accident and a short spell of injury C returned to his regular employment as a colliery overman on 1 February 1956. On that date he claimed disablement benefit, and the local office told him correctly that in the circumstances he could not claim special hardship allowance (SHA). In May 1958 C abandoned his job and took up lighter work. At the end of 1961, and again in 1962, he made further visits to the local office applying successfully for a renewal of his disablement benefit. On both occasions he inquired whether he might be eligible for other benefits, and was told he was not. Eventually in March 1970 he claimed SHA. It was agreed that if he had claimed it, he would have been entitled to the allowance since 1958.

The Commissioner, D Neligan, held that in view of the advice given him in February 1956, the claimant should have sought further guidance when he left his regular job in May 1958. There was no good cause, therefore, for the failure to claim between then and 1961. But the inquiries made in 1961 and 1962 should have made it clear to the Ministry that the claimant was entitled to SHA and he should have been invited to claim it. So there was good cause from the end of 1961 until the claim was eventually made in March 1970.[20]

b *Relying on other people's opinion as to entitlement*

Good cause is not generally shown if the claimant has relied on another person's view that he is not entitled to claim.[1] This is true even if the advice has come from a doctor in a sickness benefit case.[2] It is otherwise if it has come from a solicitor, since it is reasonable for an applicant to rely on his opinion.[3]

> In an unemployment benefit case, *R(U) 9/74*, J S Watson, Commissioner, ruled that there was good cause when the claimant had been incorrectly advised by the local Citizens Advice Bureau that he should take his insurance card to the unemployment benefit office, and he had, therefore, waited until it was returned by his former employer.

19 See esp. *R(S) 8/81*, following *R(S) 1/73*, and a number of unreported decisions. Cp *R(S) 18/52*, where a claimant excluded from work because he had been in contact with an infectious disease, understandably did not realise he was entitled to sickness benefit.

20 The Commissioner's decision was upheld by the Divisional Court: *R v Industrial Injuries Comr, ex parte Parkin* (1972) 13 KIR 213.

1 *CSG 9/49*; *R(U) 35/56*.

2 *R(S) 5/56*; cp *R(I) 40/59*.

3 *CS 50/50*; *CSI 10/50*.

… *inadequate information given by the Department office*
… most frequent type of case where good cause is shown by the … where he has delayed in reliance on inadequate or misleading …n given at a local office or in a DHSS leaflet.[4] This may occur … the leaflet refers to another one where accurate information is …le.[5] *R(I) 10/74* shows that in some circumstances there may be g… …use if the officials culpably fail to tell the applicant that he has a claim.[6]

d *Claimants outside the country*
In *R(G) 3/53*, a maternity benefit case, the Commissioner ruled that a liberal view should be taken of any delay attributable to the fact that the claimant was abroad at the time she made inquiries concerning her rights. A similar approach was taken where a claimant had emigrated to the United States of America before the present system of retirement pensions was introduced, and only claimed 18 months after her entitlement arose, when she read an article about pensions in an American weekly paper.[7]

e *The claimant's state of health*
The fact that the claimant has been under some physical pain or emotional distress may persuade the statutory authorities to find good cause.

> Thus, a young girl under nervous strain on her confinement,[8] a war veteran who developed a phobia of seeing doctors,[9] and an employee who developed a neurotic condition as a result of explosions at work[10] all benefited from an extension of time.

f *Educational limitations*
Allowance may be made for the fact that the claimant is of limited intelligence.[11] In a maternity benefit case,[12] J S Watson, Commissioner, decided that lack of familiarity with the English language or illiteracy is not in itself likely to constitute good cause, though it might be an element in reaching the conclusion that there was such a failure of communication between the officer and the claimant that the latter had good cause for the delay.

g *Delegation by the claimant to another person*
Particularly fine distinctions have arisen when the making of a claim has been entrusted by one person to another, and the latter delays: does the former have good cause for failure to claim within the prescribed period? It seems that the Commissioner draws a distinction between a specific delegation to make a particular claim, and a general agency under which one person's affairs are handled by a representative. In the first case, a

4 *R(S) 14/54*; *CP 30/50*; *R(U) 3/70*; cp *R(G) 15/56*, where the claimant's failure to understand the leaflets was her fault. This is also a frequent ground of complaint to the Parliamentary Commissioner.
5 *R(G) 4/68*; *R(I) 25/61*.
6 See also *R(U) 3/60*.
7 *R(P) 5/58*.
8 *R 1/73 (MB)*.
9 *R(S) 7/61*.
10 *R(I) 43/55*.
11 *R(P) 10/59*.
12 *R(G) 1/75*.

delay by the agent will not prevent the principal from contending that there was good cause.[13] But in the second, the agent's delay will be imputed to the principal.

Thus in *R(S) 2/51*, C was a member of a religious order and had wholly abandoned the management of her own affairs. The convent's prioress was late in making a claim on her behalf for sickness benefit and this was imputed to C.

The same result was reached where an estate was administered by a solicitor on behalf of the executor, and the former was late in claiming the death grant.[14]

h *Deliberate decision not to claim benefit*

In a variety of circumstances the claimant may decide not to claim because of some view as to his entitlement, or some expectation as to the future, which turns out to be untrue. Some cases involving the former error have already been discussed.[15] In *R(U) 34/51*, the claimant did not claim unemployment benefit for a Monday, because he thought he would only be unemployed for that one day; this mistake was held not to constitute good cause. However, in another case good cause was found when the claimant had not claimed one day because he was attending a meeting at the request of his union in the hope of being reinstated.[16]

i *Hospital in-patients*

There is deemed to be 'good cause' for certain late claims by hospital in-patients for sickness, invalidity and industrial injury benefit, and for non-contributory invalidity pension.[17]

ii The absolute bar on extension for 'good cause'

Section 82(2) of the Social Security Act 1975 provides that for most benefits there is an absolute time-limit of 12 months in which the claim must be made. Beyond this there can be no extension, no matter how good the reason or explanation for the delay. The justification for this overriding limit is that, 'nonsense is not to be made of the initial time-limits and a strain placed on the good cause condition that it was never intended to carry'.[18]

- The first rule is that no sum is to be paid by way of maternity grant for a confinement which has occurred more than 12 months before the claim.[19] Secondly, a death grant is not to be paid outside the prescribed time, plus 12 months' extension for good cause.[20] Finally, no other benefit '(except a death grant, or disablement benefit or industrial death benefit)', is to be paid 'in respect of any period more than 12 months before the date on which the claim is made'.[1]

13 See *CG 1/50*; *CU 78/49*; *R(S) 25/52*; *CSI 5/64*.
14 *R(G) 9/52* (Tribunal decision); cp *R(G) 17/52*.
15 Pp. 566–567, above.
16 *R(U) 20/56*; also see *R(U) 33/58* – a Rabbi who did not claim benefit on two days of the Passover was held to have good cause.
17 SI 1979/628, Sch 2, para 2.
18 NIAC Report (1968, Cmnd 3591), para 8.
19 SSA 1975, s.82(2)(a).
20 Ibid, s.82(2)(b).
1 Ibid, s.82(2)(c).

The result is that the only benefits which do not have an absolute time-limit imposed on their claim are industrial disablement and death benefits. The reason for this distinction from other benefits seems to be that industrial benefits involve some element of compensation for injury as well as maintenance of living standards during a spell of incapacity for work, and therefore an absolute bar would be inappropriate.[2]

D Payments

i General

A full exposition of the rules and practices governing payment of social security benefits would be very complicated, and here the emphasis is placed on general principles. The principal methods of payment are by order book, girocheque and payable order, though this last accounts for only about 1 per cent of payments.[3] Long-term benefits are usually paid by order book; under this system the recipient cashes the 'foils' in the book at the post office specified by the DHSS after inquiry as to which office is most convenient for him. Books will contain orders from 12 to 52 weeks depending on the particular benefit: thus, FIS which is payable for a year has a 52-page order book, while invalid care allowance and non-contributory invalidity pension are paid through 12-page books. Short-term benefits and lump sum grants are almost always paid by girocheque.[4]

Recently the government has determined that these methods should be radically revised, and a number of proposals have been made in the light of the recommendations of a DHSS review team which worked in consultation with Sir Derek Rayner. Broadly the team found that the administrative costs (roughly £300 million a year) of making weekly payments through post offices were unjustifiably high. Apart from Ireland all other EEC countries, the United States and many Commonwealth countries pay pensions and family benefits monthly and through bank accounts.[5] The British practice was out of date, a legacy of the times when few beneficiaries had bank accounts. And it reflected the paternalist view that recipients could not budget for more than a week. The government therefore made two main linked decisions: first, from mid-1982 onwards as many beneficiaries as possible will be offered the choice of payment through credit transfer to their bank account, and secondly, they will be given the option to have these transfers made monthly (in arrears), or in the case of retirement pensioners and widows quarterly.[6] Related proposals for child benefit have already been implemented, and are discussed elsewhere in this book.[7]

A complicating factor is that while most benefits are paid in advance, some are paid in arrears and this causes staff and beneficiaries great difficulty when two or more social security benefits are in payment. For example, unemployment benefit is now generally paid fortnightly, a week

2 See the Report of NIAC in 1952 (Cmnd 8483), para 7, and of IIAC in the same year (Cmnd 8511), para 22.

3 Reply to the First Report from the Social Services Committee on Arrangements for Paying Social Security Benefits (1980, Cmnd 8106), Annex II (Review Team Report), para 2.12. This publication contains a comprehensive description of the present methods of payment, and this section of the chapter is much indebted to it.

4 Ibid, Annex II, Appendix III summarises the payment methods.

5 Ibid, para 2.25.

6 Ibid, paras 8–15 and 21–22.

7 P. 445, above.

in advance and a week in arrears, while supplementary benefit (the amount of which may well depend on the unemployment benefit to which a claimant is entitled) is paid weekly or fortnightly in advance.[8] Moreover, long-term benefits are paid on different days of the week, generally depending on the particular benefit in question.

The main Social Security Claims and Payments Regulations draw a distinction between short-term and various other benefits on the one hand, and long-term benefits on the other, so the discussion below follows this. There is then a short mention of the rules concerning mobility allowance, war pensions, supplementary benefit and FIS.

ii Short-term and other benefits payable under SSA 1975

These comprise the following:

- unemployment, sickness, invalidity, maternity and industrial injury benefits, death grant, hospital treatment increase and non-contributory invalidity pension.[9]

They are to be paid as soon as reasonably practicable after the award has been made, and in practice are usually paid by girocheque. For example, sickness benefit is paid weekly by cheque posted to the beneficiary, though for longer illnesses payment may be made fortnightly. Until 1979 unemployment benefit was paid weekly, but then after experiments in certain areas over the previous two years the general rule became to pay it fortnightly. But claimants may still choose to be paid weekly.[10] A joint Department of Employment and DHSS team reviewing the payments procedures for unemployment benefit has recommended that those claimants who have been paid salaries monthly should have the option of being paid benefit monthly (mostly in arrears) in order to reduce costs: this has been accepted by the government.[11]

iii Long-term benefits paid under SSA 1975

These comprise the following:

- widow's benefit, retirement pension of any category, child's special, guardian's and attendance allowances, disablement pension (including any increase with the exception of that for hospital treatment), any allowance for industrial injuries (not being injury benefit), and invalid care allowance.[12]

All these benefits are to be paid weekly in advance by order books, though the regulations do enable payment to be made by other means; under this provision, some retirement pensioners do choose to be paid by monthly or quarterly payable orders which can be paid into bank accounts. The Regulations contain specific rules for the day on which each benefit is to be paid: for example, a retirement pension is generally paid on Thursdays, though if the beneficiary has been in receipt of a widow's pension, it is paid (like the widow's benefit itself) on a Tuesday.[13]

The effect of the rule that benefit is to be paid on one of these particular days (in advance for the following week) is that, even though under other

8 Reply to the First Report, n.3, above, at paras 2.7–2.8. And see DE/DHSS Rayner Scrutiny, *Payments of Benefits to Unemployed People*, paras 3.15–3.18.

9 SI 1979/628, reg 15.

10 Ibid, reg 12(1), as amended by SI 1979/781.

11 DE/DHSS Rayner Scrutiny, n.8, above, at paras 5.46–5.50.

12 SI 1979/628, reg 16.

13 Ibid, reg 16(6), and see Reply to the First Report n.3, above, Annex II, Appendix III which summarises the provisions.

provisions of the Act, entitlement begins on some other day, the right to the benefit only effectively commences on that particular day.[14] In two pensions cases, it was therefore decided that the pension commenced from the appropriate date of payment, i.e. the Thursday after entitlement otherwise arose.[15] Conversely where a benefit ceases to be payable on a day which does not immediately precede the appropriate day of payment, it is nevertheless payable for the *whole of the week up to the appropriate day*;[16] this may have the result that two benefits are payable for the same day, although the recipient is not otherwise entitled to both.[17]

iv Mobility allowance

This allowance is paid monthly, three weeks in arrears and one in advance, by 48 week order books. This is unusual in the present law, and for this reason payment of the allowance will not be affected by the proposals currently made by the government.[18] Payment is on Wednesdays, and there are provisions, equivalent to those in the main social security regulations, which make it clear that payment is only to *commence* from the appropriate Wednesday, and is to continue to the Tuesday of the payment week in which entitlement ceases.[19]

v War pensions

Officers' pensions are paid monthly or quarterly (at the option of the recipient) by payable order, while other ranks are paid weekly by order book or quarterly by payable order. The government proposals would encourage payment to be made by credit transfer every four weeks, though it is recognised that in some cases of hardship weekly payment should continue to be available. The option for quarterly payment would remain.[20]

vi Supplementary benefits

Entitlement to weekly benefit begins on the first day of the 'benefit week' following the date of the successful claim. If the claimant is already in receipt of another social security benefit, e.g. unemployment benefit or a retirement pension, that benefit week will start on the day on which that other benefit is payable. Otherwise the benefit week will start on a Monday.[1] The rules are thus substantially in line with those concerning long-term benefits paid under the Social Security Act 1975, and they facilitate the combined payment of, say, a contributory and a supplementary pension, or unemployment benefit and a supplementary allowance in appropriate cases. The precise day of the week on which payment is made will therefore vary according to whether another benefit is in payment.

Payments are generally made weekly, but there is now one exception: when unemployment benefit is paid fortnightly, the same applies to any allowance which supplements it, though as already mentioned, it is not

14 SI 1979/628, reg 16(10).
15 *R(P) 16/52*; *R(P) 2/73*.
16 SI 1979/628, reg 16(11).
17 See *R(I) 13/57* (disablement and injury benefit both payable) for a few days, despite the overlapping provision): see p. 296, above.
18 Reply to the First Report, n.3, above, at para 21.
19 SI 1975/1573, regs 9(3) and (5).
20 Reply to the First Report, n.3, above, at paras 21–22.
1 SI 1980/1643, reg 7.

paid for the identical period.[2] Supplementary pensions and often allowances are paid by order books cashable at local post offices, but sometimes payment of the latter is made by girocheque. This is almost always true when the recipient also is paid unemployment benefit, one cheque being sent for the two benefits. A single payment is made by cheque as soon as practicable after its award.[3] In cases of urgent need payment will be made over the counter.[4]

It was pointed out in the chapter on supplementary benefits that generally the provision of means-tested assistance takes the form of a cash payment, which is not earmarked for a particular item and which leaves the recipient with some choice.[5] Now the regulations permit the payment of benefit by a voucher which can be used at a particular supplier or by a travel warrant in four sets of circumstances:[6]

(a) where in the benefit officer's view the beneficiary is not capable of managing cash payments;
(b) the provision is necessary to secure accommodation;
(c) the beneficiary is entitled to a single payment for travelling expenses;
(d) he is entitled to an urgent cases payment.

In effect this is another method of making a payment for the beneficiary to a third party.[7]

vii FIS

Payment of benefit by 52 week order book, cashable at a post office, commences on a Tuesday, and even if entitlement would end on a day other than Monday, FIS is to be paid for the days of the week up to and including the Monday.[8] Payment of benefit may be suspended by the Secretary of State pending a review or the determination of an appeal.[9]

viii Extinguishment of right to sums payable by way of benefit

It is a common provision that if payment is not obtained within 12 months from the date on which the right is treated as having arisen, then the right is extinguished.[10] The reason for this time-limit on encashment of benefits is said to be that the administrative costs (e.g. of storing copies of instruments of payment and cash instruments) necessary to check late requests for payment, and so prevent abuse, could be very heavy.[11] The right to payment under the Social Security Claims and Payments Regulations is to be treated as having arisen in the following circumstances:

(1) in relation to a sum contained in an instrument of payment sent to the beneficiary, or to an approved place for collection by him, whether or not he has received or collected it – *on the date of the instrument*;
(2) where notice has been given or sent that the sum contained in it is available for collection, and the notice has been sent by post – (i) *on*

2 SI 1981/1525, reg 6, and see DE/DHSS Rayner Scrutiny, n.8, above, at para 2.29.
3 SI 1981/1525, reg 7.
4 See pp. 493–497, above. for these payments.
5 P. 465, above.
6 SI 1981/1525, reg 12.
7 For payments to third parties, see pp. 518–520, above.
8 SI 1980/1438, reg 4(3).
9 Ibid, reg 8.
10 SI 1979/628, reg 22; SI 1976/964, reg 8 (child benefit); SI 1981/1525, reg 13 (supp. benefit); SI 1980/1438, reg 5 (FIS).
11 NIAC Report (1968, Cmnd 3591), paras 18–26.

the date on which it would be delivered in the ordinary course of post; or if not sent by post (ii) *on the date of notice*;

(3) in relation to sums to which the preceding sub-paragraphs do not apply – *on the date determined by the Secretary of State*.

It seems that, with the exception of cases under (3), the relevant date is to be determined by the statutory authorities.[12] It may be noted that here it is the recipient who takes the risk of the notification not being delivered in the ordinary course of post,[13] though the consequences of this may be mitigated by an extension of the time allowed.

There will be an extension of the 12 months period if the statutory authorities are satisfied first, that after this time the Secretary has received a notice requesting payment and secondly, that throughout a period, starting within the 12 months and continuing till the notice was given, there was good cause for not giving it earlier.[14]

The extinguishment provisions do not apply to the payment of death grants, industrial injuries gratuities (if paid as a single sum and not by instalments)[15] or a sum paid in satisfaction of a right to graduated retirement pension.[16]

E Miscellaneous

i Persons unable to act

Regulations cover the case where the person alleged to be entitled to a benefit, or to whom a benefit is payable, is unable for the time being to act for himself.[17] The basic rule is:

- unless a receiver has been appointed by the Court of Protection with power to claim benefit, etc.[18] the Secretary of State may, on written application to him by a person over 18, appoint that person to exercise, on behalf of the person unable to act, all his rights and to receive benefit to which he is entitled. There are provisions for the revocation of, or resignation from, this appointment.

ii Payments on death

When a claimant dies, the Secretary of State may appoint a person of his choice to proceed with the claim.[19] If written application is then made for the sums payable by way of benefit within 12 months (or such longer period as the Secretary of State may determine) the following consequences ensue:

- any sum payable may be paid or distributed among persons over 16 claiming as personal representatives, legatees, next of kin or creditors of the deceased, at the discretion of the Secretary of State; he may pay this to some person on behalf of another under 16. The same rules apply to a sum payable to the deceased before his death, but not obtained by him.

12 This follows recommendations of NIAC in 1952 (Cmd 8483), para 54 and of IIAC in the same year (Cmd 8511), para 28.
13 SSA 1975, s.79(6).
14 See SI 1979/628, reg 22(2). It would seem that good cause has the same meaning here, as it does in the context of late claims.
15 See p. 309, above.
16 SI 1979/628, reg 22(5).
17 Ibid, reg 28; SI 1976/964, reg 10; SI 1981/1525, reg 26; SI 1980/1438, reg 6.
18 There is a similar rule for Scotland: SI 1979/628, reg 28(1)(d).
19 Ibid, reg 29; SI 1976/964, reg 12; SI 1981/1525, reg 28.

(There are some special provisions with regard to the death grant in this context.)[20]

The Family Income Supplement Regulations provide that a claim will lapse:

– where a man and a woman are included in the family for whom the claim is made, and both have died before the claim is determined, *or* in any other case, the man or the single woman had died before the claim is determined.[1]

Where, however, one or both of these persons die after the claim has been decided, benefit is payable on behalf of the family to a person over the age of 18, who applies to receive the benefit and whom the Secretary of State considers suitable.[2]

iii Payment to a third party

Under both the Social Security and Child Benefit Claims and Payments Regulations, payment may be made to a third party in certain circumstances.

– Under the former,[3] the power may be exercised by the Secretary of State where a beneficiary is receiving benefit in respect of another person whom he is maintaining at not less than the prescribed weekly rate.[4] The power to direct payments to another person may be exercised in the interests of the beneficiary or the other person, or on the former's request.

– There is a similar broad power for the Secretary of State to 'divert' payments of child benefit to a third party in the interests either of the child or of the person entitled to the benefit.[5]

In some cases supplementary benefit may be paid to a third party, e.g. a landlord; these have been discussed in chapter 12.[6]

iv Benefit to be inalienable

It is a standard provision that any assignment or charge on, or agreement to assign or charge, the benefit is void.[7] It does not pass to the trustee, or any other person acting on the creditors' behalf, on the bankruptcy of the person entitled. There are obvious policy reasons why it is undesirable to allow a beneficiary to give up or put at risk benefits designed to ensure a minimum standard of living for himself and his family.

Part 4 Overpayments and criminal offences

A Recovery of overpaid benefit

i Recovery of benefits paid under the SSA 1975, etc.

Where benefit has been paid under a decision, later reversed on appeal or revised on review, the second decision must require repayment to the

20 P. 243, above.
1 SI 1980/1438, reg 7(1).
2 Ibid, reg 7(2).
3 SI 1979/628, reg 30.
4 For the circumstances in which this benefit may be paid, see pp. 373–376, above.
5 SI 1976/964, reg 13. See p. 445, above.
6 Pp. 518–520, above.
7 SSA 1975, s.87; CBA 1975, s.12; SBA 1976, s.16; FISA 1970, s.9.

DHSS of the overpaid benefit.[8] And now such benefit must be repaid when the mistake is subsequently discovered in proceedings which are not brought on appeal or review from the erroneous decision.[9] These rules also apply to overpayment of child benefit and mobility allowances,[10] and there are very similar provisions discussed in the next section concerning means-tested assistance.

The terms of section 119 of the Social Security Act 1975 require the statutory authorities to order repayment of the sum overpaid, unless (in many cases) due care and diligence is shown; they do not have any discretion on this question.[11] The requirement to repay must be contained in the decision itself, and not left to a subsequent letter.[12] Otherwise, the beneficiary's right of appeal against the decision to order repayment may be prejudiced. In *R(S) 2/70*, the Chief Commissioner, R G Micklethwait, ruled that section 119 only allows recovery from a 'beneficiary', that is, a person who has made a claim which has been wrongly accepted. It does not permit recovery from someone who has obtained payment by forging the claimant's signature to the relevant documents; in that case, recovery would presumably be obtainable under the general law of restitution.[3] The authorities have no jurisdiction to direct that repayment should be made by instalments; it is for the Secretary of State to decide whether this is acceptable.[14]

Regulations provide that overpaid benefit (either that paid under the Social Security Act, or child benefit) is not to be recovered where it is stated by a benefit officer that additional supplementary benefit would have been payable.[15] Nor will there be recovery if on the appeal or review the beneficiary is awarded some other benefit to which he has been entitled; the sums already paid will be treated as having been paid on account of this benefit.[16]

The position has been that repayment will never be ordered if 'the beneficiary, and any person acting for him, has throughout used *due care and diligence* to avoid overpayment'.[17] This test was introduced by section 9 of the National Insurance Act 1961. Previously repayment was not ordered if the beneficiary had acted in '*good faith*'. The Commissioner in *R(G) 9/62* said that these tests are different though he did not specify in what respect. It seems clear that the more recent formula imposes on the claimant the duty to be careful, and not merely the duty of honesty.[18]

The onus of proof is generally on the claimant to show that he has acted with due care and diligence,[19] and he must show this for the whole of the period from the time when the benefit was claimed.[20] He is under a duty to

8 SSA 1975, s.119(1).
9 Ibid, s.119(2A), inserted by SSA 1979, s.8.
10 CBA 1975, s.8; SI 1975/1573, reg 23.
11 *R(U) 5/63*.
12 *R(P) 1/73*, and also see *CSP 11/50*.
13 See Goff and Jones *The Law of Restitution* (2nd edn) p. 80.
14 *R(G) 7/51*.
15 SI 1975/558, reg 38; SI 1976/962, reg 22, amended by SI 1980/1622, reg 10, and SI 1980/1640, reg 7 respectively.
16 SI 1975/558, regs 33, 34.
17 SSA 1975, s.119(2).
18 See esp. *R(S) 2/74*; *R(U) 7/75*; *CU 5/77*.
19 *R(G) 2/72*.
20 *CF 1/65*. The proposition in the text was doubted very cautiously by the Chief Commissioner, T A Blair in *R 2/73 (FA)*. Also see *CS 11/76*, where the Commissioner, V G H Hallett, only permitted recovery of that part of a weekly overpayment in respect of which the claimant did not show due care and diligence.

tell the Department all the facts which he should appreciate are relevant,[1] and in some cases he may be required to take positive steps to discover whether he is entitled to benefit.[2] But due care and diligence may be shown if the beneficiary has relied on information given by his employer in deciding not to withdraw his claim.[3] The fact that he is illiterate would appear to be a relevant factor. This was so for the 'good faith' test,[4] and in *R(U) 7/64* the Commissioner said, obiter, that the local tribunal was right to take this into account. But the beneficiary was required to repay in this case because his wife, who had filled in the claim forms on his behalf, had not used due care and diligence. Where payment of benefit is made to a third party (on behalf of a beneficiary), he must use due care and diligence to avoid overpayment.[5]

The fact that a beneficiary has been acquitted of a charge of fraudulently obtaining benefit is irrelevant to the question whether he has used due care and diligence to avoid repayment; in the criminal case the burden of proof is on the prosecution, while in the proceedings before the statutory authorities it is for the recipient to show he was not at fault.[6] In some situations, the latter proceedings will be adjourned if a prosecution is brought, so that the claimant does not run the risk of giving evidence to the statutory authorities which later might be used in the criminal court.[7]

Recently there has been some concern that considerable overpayments may be made without beneficiaries having any reason to be aware of them, and these of course are irrecoverable because of the due care and diligence provision. Regulations may now be made to remove the availability of the plea where payment has been made into a bank or other account – in this circumstance it is very easy for overpayment to go unnoticed by the recipient.[8] Moreover, following recommendations of the DE/DHSS Scrutiny team on payment of benefits to the unemployed, it is possible that further restrictions will be imposed on its availability where payment is mistakenly made to someone about to start work.[9] The Social Security and Housing Benefits Act 1982 provides for enforcement of recovery orders through the county courts.[10]

ii Recovery of supplementary benefit and FIS

Section 20 of the Supplementary Benefits Act 1976 provides for recovery of any expenditure incurred by the Secretary of State from a person if he, fraudulently or otherwise, 'misrepresents, or fails to disclose, any material fact'. Since 1980 the initial decision to order recovery is taken by a benefit officer, with a right of appeal to an appeal tribunal and the Social Security Commissioner. In three respects the section would appear to confer a wider right of recovery than its equivalent in the Social Security Act 1975:

(1) It seems that not only overpaid benefit is recoverable, but also any expenditure incurred as a result of the misrepresentation or failure to

1 *R(P) 1/70*; *R(S) 2/74*; *R 3/73 (IVB)*.
2 *R(A) 1/79*; *R(G) 1/79*.
3 *R(U) 1/73*. The same result was reached on the 'good faith' test: see *R(P) 13/53*.
4 *R(G) 6/53*.
5 SI 1980/1621, reg 3; SI 1976/962, reg 21 (child benefit). For payment to third parties, see p. 575, above.
6 *R(U) 7/75*; *R(S) 3/80*.
7 *R(S) 2/70*.
8 SSA 1980, s.4(4). See Standing Committee E Debates on the 1980 Bill, col 437, for discussion of the reasons for the reform.
9 *Payment of Benefits to Unemployed People* (DE/DHSS, 1981), paras 5.91–5.99.
10 S.41.

disclose the material fact. This might enable the Secretary of State to recover the expenses involved in taking recovery proceedings.

(2) There is no exception that benefit cannot be recovered where the claimant has acted with due care and diligence. It is not obvious why there is this difference. The Commissioner has emphasised, however, that there must be a misrepresentation or a failure to disclose a material fault.[11]

(3) Unlike the Social Security Act, recovery can be secured from anyone, and not only the beneficiary. In *Secretary of State for Social Services v Solly* the Court of Appeal held that overpaid supplementary benefit could be recovered from the deceased claimant's executor.[12]

Recovery may be made by deduction from any prescribed social security benefits.[13] These comprise benefits paid under the Social Security Act (except maternity and death grants), certain other social security benefits, such as family income supplement (but not child benefit or war pension), and, subject to certain limits, supplementary benefit itself.[14] The amounts that may be deducted from weekly payments of supplementary benefit are prescribed in the regulations as percentages of certain benefit rates and therefore will increase with up-rating of the benefits; more may be deducted from those in receipt of the long-term rate of supplementary benefit and those convicted of fraud.[15]

FIS overpayments may be recovered if the supplement officer, appeal tribunal or Commissioner finds that the sums were not due, and the person in receipt of the sums cannot satisfy it that he had disclosed all material facts.[16] This seems in one respect the most onerous of the recovery provisions: it is for the recipient to show that he had disclosed all the relevant facts.

B Offences

A variety of specific offences are created by the social security legislation, though a person who obtains benefit by deliberate deception may also be prosecuted under the general law, e.g. for obtaining property by deception under the Theft Act 1968.[17]

i Obtaining benefit by false statements, etc.

It is an offence punishable on summary conviction by a fine of £1,000 or imprisonment for three months, or both, if a person

> for the purpose of obtaining any benefit or other payment under this Act, whether for himself or some other person, or for any other purpose connected with this Act —
> (i) knowingly makes any false statement or false representation, or
> (ii) produces or furnishes, or causes or knowingly allows to be produced or furnished, any document or information which he knows to be false in an material particular.[18]

11 *R(SB) 3/81*.
12 [1974] 3 All ER 922.
13 SBA 1976, s.20(4).
14 SI 1980/1580, reg 6.
15 Ibid, reg 7. See *Lynes* pp. 48–49, and Handbook paras 15.7–15.11 for further details.
16 SI 1980/1437, reg 10.
17 S.15. See Smith and Hogan *Criminal Law* (4th edn) pp. 534–548.
18 SSA 1975, s.146(3)(c), amended by SSA 1981, Sch 1, para 3.

There is an identical provision in the Child Benefit Act,[19] and very similar provisions in the Supplementary Benefits Act[20] and Family Income Supplements Act.[1] It is now clear that for these offences to be committed it is enough that the defendant knowingly made a false statement; it is immaterial that he did not intend to obtain the benefit by fraud, but lied for some other reason.[2]

A defendant will also be guilty of the offence if he makes an untrue representation when accepting *payment* of the benefit.[3] It does not matter that the decision to pay it has been taken before the false statement. On the other hand, if a beneficiary honestly presents an order for payment at a post office and then *subsequently* adopts a course of action which disqualifies him for entitlement to the relevant benefit (e.g. he works on days for which he has received sickness benefit), it seems that he is only guilty of the offence of failing to inform the authorities of a relevant change of circumstances.[4]

ii Other offences

The other offences under the social security legislation are less important.

(1) It is an offence under the Social Security Act, the Supplementary Benefits Act and the Family Income Supplements Act to delay or obstruct wilfully an inspector in the exercise of his powers, or to refuse either to answer questions or to provide documents and information.[5]

(2) There are some offences with regard to non-payment of contributions and misuse of contribution cards under section 146 of the Social Security Act 1975. (Failure to pay Class 4 contributions, recoverable by the Inland Revenue, may be prosecuted under the Taxes Management Act 1970.)[6]

(3) Under the Supplementary Benefits Act 1976[7] it is an offence —
   (a) to impersonate officers of the DHSS;
   (b) to be in illegal possession of documents issued on behalf of the Secretary of State in connection with the payment of any benefit;
   (c) to fail to comply with an obligation to notify cessation of employment or re-employment in connection with the administration of deduction notices.[8]

iii General rules

Proceedings for these offences must be brought within three months from the date when evidence, sufficient to justify a prosecution in the view of the Secretary of State, is available, or if later, within 12 months of the commission of the offence.[9] This is a longer limitation period than the

19 S.11.
20 S.21, as substituted by SS(MP)A 1977, s.14(5).
1 S.11, as amended by SS(MP)A 1977, s.22(16).
2 *Clear v Smith* [1981] 1 WLR 399, DC; *Barrass v Reeve* [1980] 3 All ER 705, [1981] 1 WLR 408, DC, in which the earlier decision in *Moore v Branton* (1974) 118 Sol Jo 405, DC was disapproved on this point.
3 *Tolfree v Florence* [1971] 1 All ER 125, [1971] 1 WLR 141, DC.
4 See SI 1979/628, regs 23 and 31.
5 See SSA 1975, s. 145(3); SS(MP)A 1977, s.19. For the powers of inspectors, see SSA 1975, ss.144, 145.
6 Ss. 93–107.
7 Ss.22–24, as amended by SS(MP)A 1977, s.14(6).
8 See ch 12, p. 506, above.
9 SSA 1975, s.147(3); CBA 1975, s.11(5); SBA 1976, s.26(3)(b); FISA 1970, s.12.

normal six months for bringing proceedings for summary offences.[10] A prosecution under the Social Security and Child Benefits Acts is not to be brought except with the consent of the Secretary of State or of an authorised officer;[11] this precludes private prosecutions.

C The control of fraud and abuse

In the last few years there has been considerable public concern about suspected widespread abuse of the social security system, and governments have responded by increasing the numbers of staff deployed to investigate possible cases of fraud and so reduce its incidence. Unfortunately nobody really knows the extent of the problem, and rational discussion is made difficult by exaggerated claims on both sides of the argument: there are those who are willing to believe that the majority of claimants are dishonest 'scroungers', while others appear to contend that any attempt to investigate the scope of fraud and general abuse necessarily constitutes an attack on the welfare state. The Supplementary Benefits Commission itself took a moderate position: the allocation by the DHSS of extra staff for anti-abuse work was welcomed as in the interests of genuine claimants as well as general public confidence, but it was vital that the issue was seen in perspective. Low take-up remained a more significant problem.[12]

In 1971 a Committee was set up under the chairmanship of Sir Henry Fisher to review the adequacy of the measures taken to counteract abuse and recommend changes in these procedures. The Committee concluded that there was not enough information to show the scale of the problem, and more thorough steps should be taken to acquire it.[13] In particular detailed surveys should be made on sample claims, chosen at random. The government, however, rejected this as likely to lead to intrusion into the lives of wholly innocent claimants. The present practice is to concentrate on suspicious claims, and more recently to undertake periodically 'special drives', in which dubious claims are subjected to particularly careful investigation by special investigators.[14]

During the late 1970s the number of fraud officers, and other specialist officials concerned to check abuse, were substantially increased.[15] Now the joint Department of Employment and DHSS Scrutiny team, which looked into the methods of payment of unemployment benefit, has recommended a further increase of 750 staff to undertake widely publicised special drives in this area. The team thought the best estimate of those working while claiming unemployment or supplementary benefit (or with working wives) was about 8 per cent, and net savings of £24 million a year could be achieved. The suggestion has been accepted in principle, though it will not be fully implemented immediately.[16] The government itself has stated that in 1980–81 £170 million was saved through the detection of fraudulent claims for all social security benefits, but it was impossible to estimate how much was lost through undetected abuse.[17]

10 Magistrates' Courts Act 1952, s.104.
11 SSA 1975, s.147(1); CBA 1975, s.11(3).
12 SBC Annual Report 1979 (Cmnd 8033), paras 10.37–10.38.
13 Paras 487–490.
14 DE/DHSS Rayner Scrutiny, *Payment of Benefits to Unemployed People* (1981), paras 7.54–7.55.
15 For specialist officials, see p. 544, above.
16 DE/DHSS Rayner Scrutiny, n.14, above, at pp. 4–5 and paras 7.44–7.51.
17 H Rossi, Minister of Social Security, 10 HC Official Report (6th series) col 150.

Chapter 15

Adjudication

Part 1 of this chapter is concerned with the methods for determining questions under the Social Security Act 1975 and the Child Benefit Act 1975. Part 2 deals with the tribunals which hear appeals from decisions on entitlement to supplementary benefit and family income supplement, while Part 3 outlines the role of the ordinary courts in controlling the decisions of social security tribunals. Part 4 contains a short discussion of the tribunals which adjudicate appeals on war pensions claims. Part 5 is concerned with the circumstances in which a reference should be made to the European Court of Justice.

Part 1 Adjudication under Social Security Act 1975

A General

From the beginning of the modern social security system before the First World War, powers of adjudication have been vested in special tribunals or other bodies.[1] The decision not to confer jurisdiction on the courts was largely attributable to an understandable fear that their procedure would be too formal and expensive. The 1906 Liberal government was also influenced by the successful use in Germany of special tribunals in this area. Thus, claims for the unemployment benefit introduced by the National Insurance Act 1911 were decided in the first instance by Board of Trade insurance officers. Appeal then lay to a court of referees, a three member tribunal, with a chairman, one member drawn from an 'employer's panel' and the other drawn from a 'workmen's panel'. A further appeal could be made to an Umpire, a lawyer of standing appointed by the Crown.[2] This became the model for the present system introduced by the National Insurance Act 1946.

Another pattern of adjudication was established when contributory pensions were introduced in 1925.[3] A claim for an old age or widow's pension would be made in the first place to the Minister; if he rejected it,

1 See Wraith and Hutchesson *Administrative Tribunals* (1973) pp. 33–38; Robson *Justice and Administrative Law* (3rd edn) pp. 188–198; Fulbrook *Administrative Justice and the Unemployed* (1978) ch 6.

2 For a full discussion of this system, see the Committee on Procedure and Evidence for the Determination of Claims for Unemployment Insurance Benefit (the Morris Committee) (1929, Cmd 3415).

3 For the history of pensions, see ch 5, pp. 189–193, above.

an appeal lay to an independent Referee, a senior lawyer. His decisions, unlike those of the Umpire under the unemployment insurance legislation, were not publicly reported.[4] This system was adopted in 1945 for the adjudication of disputed claims to family allowances. Under the Family Allowances Act 1945 the Referee could state a case on a point of law for the High Court, though it seems that this was done very rarely.[5]

The Beveridge Report recommended a right of appeal to a local tribunal, analogous to the court of referees, and then to the Umpire, whose decisions would be final.[6] This was accepted in principle by the government. The National Insurance Act 1946 provided that claims should initially be determined by the insurance officer, with a right of appeal to a national insurance local tribunal, and then to the National Insurance Commissioner or one of the Deputy Commissioners.[7] Certain questions, however, particularly on contributions, were reserved for the Minister, with an appeal only on a point of law to the High Court. A similar system was instituted under the industrial injuries legislation. An appeal lay to a local appeal tribunal, and from it to the Industrial Injuries Commissioner or a Deputy Commissioner. But certain questions concerning entitlement to, and the assessment of, disablement benefit were entrusted to medical boards, with an appeal to medical appeal tribunals. The ordinary courts had decided claims for workmen's compensation, now replaced by the state benefit; there was some anxiety that the new authorities would not be competent to determine the difficult questions of law arising under the industrial injuries scheme.[8]

Some of the major developments in the last thirty years should be mentioned before the present system is discussed in detail.[9] First, following a recommendation of the Franks Committee on Tribunals and Enquiries,[10] the adjudication of claims to family allowances was transferred in 1959 to the insurance officers and on appeal the local tribunal and the National Insurance Commissioner.[11] This change has not been affected by the Child Benefit Act 1975.[12] Secondly, the 1959 legislation also conferred a right of appeal on a point of law from the medical appeal tribunals to the Commissioner. This interesting development reflected the general confidence in the Commissioners and enhanced their position at the apex of the tribunal system.[13] Thirdly, the National Insurance Act 1966 merged the systems of adjudication under the national insurance and the industrial injuries legislation, so that industrial injury cases (apart from those referred to the medical authorities) are now determined by the national insurance statutory authorities.[14] In 1970, the Attendance Allowance

4 Safford 17 MLR 197 at 201 (the author was a Deputy Insurance Commissioner).
5 In 596 HC Official Report (5th series) col 713, Mr D Freeth, introducing the 2nd Reading of the Family Allowances and National Insurance Bill 1959, said that only four references to the High Court had been made by the Referee.
6 Paras 394–395.
7 Under NIA 1966, the National Insurance Commissioner was retitled the Chief National Insurance Commissioner, and the Deputy Commissioners became full Commissioners.
8 See 414 HC Official Report (5th series) cols 311–312 (Mr H Raikes) and cols 324–325 (Mr B Nield).
9 For a full discussion, see Sir R Micklethwait *The National Insurance Commissioners* (Hamlyn Lectures, 1976) ch 2.
10 (1957, Cmnd 218), para 184.
11 FANIA 1959, s.1.
12 S.7.
13 FANIA 1959, s.2: see 596 HC Official Report (5th series) cols 714–715.
14 S.8. The term 'statutory authorities' is frequently used to refer to the insurance officer, local tribunal and the Commissioner, though its origin is shrouded in mystery: see *Micklethwait* p. 18, n.4.

Board was set up to adjudicate claims to attendance allowance.[15] There is an appeal from its decisions on a point of law to the Commissioner.[16] The final development came in 1980 when the Commissioners assumed appellate jurisdiction over supplementary benefit tribunals, and were consequently restyled as Social Security Commissioners. It may be noted that decisions on entitlement to statutory sick pay will be taken by the national insurance statutory authorities; the basic rules of adjudication set out in the 1982 Act are very similar to those discussed in this chapter.[17]

B Questions for the Secretary of State

i General

Under the Social Security Act 1975[18] certain matters are reserved for decision by the Secretary of State. These include the following:

(a) whether a person is an earner and, if so, in which category of earners (employed or self-employed) he is to be included;
(b) whether the contribution conditions for the benefit in issue have been satisfied and any question 'relating to a person's contributions or his earnings factor';[19]
(c) whether a person is, or was, employed in employed earner's employment for the purposes of industrial injuries benefits;
(d) whether a person was under the relevant regulations precluded from regular employment by home responsibilities;
(e) whether a constant attendance allowance or an exceptionally severe disablement allowance should be awarded or renewed and, if so, how it is to be assessed;[20]
(f) whether to accept a claim for one benefit as a claim in the alternative, or as a claim also, for another benefit.[1]

These questions are entirely outside the jurisdiction of the statutory authorities, i.e. the insurance officer, tribunal and Commissioner.[2] It is not enough for them to rely on an informal opinion from an official of the DHSS; there should be a formal referral to the Secretary of State for the matter to be decided by him.[3]

It would appear that a question for the decision of the Secretary of State will only arise if a claimant has formally applied to him,[4] or if it is raised before the statutory authorities. If, however, the issue is not disputed by the claimant, it seems that the authorities may determine a matter which, if disputed, would have to be referred to the Secretary of State. This seems to be the implication of the Social Security (Determination of Claims and Questions) Regulations which provide that an insurance officer may issue a decision where he —

15 See ch 4, pp. 171–172, above.
16 See pp. 602–603, below.
17 SSHBA 1982, ss. 12–14. See pp. 160–162, above, for statutory sick pay.
18 Ss.93 and 95, as amended by CBA 1975, Sch 4, paras 30 and 31, SSPA 1975, s.60, and SS(MP)A 1977, s.22(5).
19 SSA 1975, s.93(1)(b): see pp. 65–72, above, for contributions requirements. But other issues, relevant to contributions, may be left to the statutory authorities: *Re Work in Germany (No 2)* [1979] 1 CMLR 267.
20 See pp. 324–326.
1 P. 555, above.
2 *R(G) 1/61*.
3 *R(I) 2/75*, J S Watson, Comr.
4 SI 1975/558, reg 6(1).

has decided any claim or question on an assumption of facts as to which there appeared to him to be no dispute, but concerning which, had a question arisen, that question would have fallen for determination by the Secretary of State . . . .[5]

Thus, if a self-employed person claims industrial injury benefit and does not even contend that he is an employed earner, it would appear permissible for the insurance officer to refuse the claim without referring the matter to the Secretary of State. This view is supported by the decision of the Commissioner, J G Monroe, in the recent case, *Re an Italian Claimant*.[6]

ii Procedure on determination by the Secretary of State

When a question is to be determined by the Secretary of State under section 93 (e.g. questions (a)–(d) referred to above), he may appoint a person to hold an inquiry into and report on it.[7] The inquiry is generally held by a member of the DHSS Solicitor's Office; the procedure is oral and all interested persons have the right to attend and be heard.[8] The Secretary of State must notify them of his decision and, if requested, give reasons.[9] Decisions have not been published since 1960.[10] This procedure is frequently invoked in cases concerning liability to pay contributions, where the correct categorisation of the person concerned may raise difficult questions of law and fact.[11]

In contrast there are no procedural rules at all for the determination by the Secretary of State of questions under section 95 (e.g. questions (e) and (f) referred to above). It seems that in practice decisions are made at regional offices, or in some cases at headquarters in London. Advice on medical matters relevant to a determination of entitlement to, and assessment of, constant attendance allowance is given by medical boards.[12]

iii Reference and appeal to the High Court

A question of law arising in connection with the determination by the Secretary of State of any question under section 93 may be referred by him to the High Court (or in Scotland, the Court of Session).[13] Alternatively, there may be an appeal on a point of law by 'any person aggrieved' with his decision.[14] The appeal is heard by a judge sitting alone, and there is (unusually) no further appeal.[15] Most appeals are brought on the question whether a person is properly to be regarded as employed or self-employed for the purpose of liability to pay contributions, and judicial decisions have substantially shaped the development of this area of law.[16]

5 Ibid, reg 9(1), and see SI 1976/962, reg 5(3) (Child Benefit Regulations). These regulations so closely follow the pattern of SI 1975/558 that they are not referred to unless there is a material difference from the regulations under the Social Security Act.
6 [1978] 2 CMLR 331. See the similar principle applied in cases under the Rent Acts: *R v Westminster (City) London Borough Council Rent Officer, ex parte Rendall* [1973] QB 959, [1973] 3 All ER 119, CA.
7 SSA 1975, s.93(3); see SI 1975/558, reg 6(3).
8 See DHSS Annual Report 1975 (Cmnd 6565), para 9.12.
9 SI 1975/558, regs 6(5), and 7.
10 See ch 2, p. 44, above.
11 Pp. 45–50, above.
12 Carson 126 NLJ 59: see p. 324, above, for criticism of the absence of a formal procedure in these cases.
13 SSA 1975, s.94.
14 Ibid, s.94(3). 'Person aggrieved' here means any person with a financial interest in the decision, e.g. an employer in a case concerning the classification of a contributor.
15 Ibid, s.94(6) and (7).
16 See the discussion in ch 2, pp. 45–50, above.

The precise grounds on which the judge will entertain an appeal were fully considered by Lord Widgery CJ in *Global Plant Ltd v Secretary of State for Social Services*.[17] He concluded that the court would only allow it —

(1) if the decision contained a false proposition of law ex facie;
(2) if the decision was one supported by no evidence; or
(3) if the decision reached was one which no person acting judicially and properly instructed as to the relevant law could have come to.

It is an open question whether these grounds might be widened in view of recent developments in the scope of judicial review, in particular to allow an appeal if the facts found leave out of account relevant evidence.[18] As will be seen, the approach of Lord Widgery has been followed by the Commissioner in determining the grounds of appeal to him from decisions of medical appeal tribunals and of the Attendance Allowance Board.[19]

iv Critique

There has never been any substantial argument for allocating these decisions to the Secretary of State, rather than the statutory authorities. It may be that there are some practical reasons as regards decisions on whether a claimant has satisfied the relevant contribution conditions. But it is not clear why the statutory authorities should not decide the related question whether a claimant should contribute as an employed or self-employed person. This involves difficult issues of law and fact which are suitable for a tribunal. Broader policy decisions in this area can, of course, be taken by the Secretary of State under his power to make regulations concerning the categorisation of earners.[20] Nor is there any obvious reason why entitlement to the constant attendance and exceptionally severe disablement allowances should be decided by him, while for the other additional allowances this is determined by the statutory authorities.

The Labour government in 1969–70 did indeed propose that 'Minister's questions' should be determined by a new 'special tribunal' with a right of appeal to the High Court on a point of law.[1] The Council on Tribunals argued that they should be decided by the existing statutory authorities with a final appeal to the Commissioner, but this was rejected, apparently on the ground that the matters were too complicated for local tribunals.[2] The Bill lapsed when the 1970 General Election was called.

Despite these reservations concerning the Secretary of State's jurisdiction, certain questions are reserved for his decision under the new statutory sick pay scheme. In particular he will decide whether a particular person is, or was, an employee or employer.[3]

C Insurance officers

i General

All claims and questions are initially submitted to an insurance officer for determination, except for certain questions relating to disablement benefit

17 [1972] 1 QB 139, [1971] 3 All ER 385.
18 See in particular Scarman LJ, and Lord Wilberforce in *Secretary of State for Education v Tameside Metropolitan Borough Council* [1977] AC 1014 at 1030, and 1047.
19 See pp. 600–603, below.
20 See pp. 50–51, above.
1 National Superannuation and Social Insurance Bill 1969, cl 78.
2 See the Annual Report of the Council on Tribunals for 1969–1970, para 47 and Appendix B.
3 SSHBA 1982, s.11. See pp. 160–162, above.

or an attendance allowance.[4] Insurance officers are appointed by the Secretary of State for Social Services, or in the case of unemployment benefit, the Secretary of State for Employment. They are civil servants, working in local offices – not necessarily full-time as an insurance officer.[5] They may refer difficult cases to a Regional Insurance Officer. It is the responsibility of the Chief Insurance Officer, now based in Southampton, to issue general guidance as to the discharge of their duties.

ii Procedure for determining claims[6]

The insurance officer decides the application entirely on the documents sent to him by the claimant and branches of the Department. He does not interview the claimant or witnesses, though on rare occasions he may obtain statements through a Department inspector.[7] His duties have been characterised as 'administrative' in that he is not adjudicating between the contentions of the claimant and those of the Department or any other party.[8] When he finds it impossible to determine a complex case, he may refer it to the local insurance tribunal for initial decision.

The insurance officer should decide the application so far as practicable within 14 days after its submission to him.[9] This is often impossible, particularly where, in an unemployment benefit case, written evidence has to be obtained from the claimant's employer. The case must be decided in accordance with Commissioners' decisions, but the officer is not bound to follow his own previous decision on a prior claim.[10] The claimant must be told in writing of any adverse decision with its reasons, and also of his right to appeal to the local tribunal.[11] However, where the claim has been decided by the officer on an assumption of facts, which if challenged would have raised a question for the Secretary of State, it is enough for the claimant to be told that, if he is dissatisfied with the decision, he can reply to that effect.[12] The claimant is only to be told of his right of appeal if he remains dissatisfied after the appropriate investigations have been made, or the Secretary of State has decided the relevant question.[13]

iii Local referees

One power of the insurance officer and also of the local tribunal chairman requires brief mention: both may refer any question of fact concerning the claimant's right to benefit for 'examination and report to two persons . . . residents in the neighbourhood' where the claimant lives.[14] One must be drawn from each panel from which the members of the local tribunal are

4 S.98. Any question for the determination of the Secretary of State must be referred to him by the insurance officer: s.98(2)(a).
5 *Micklethwait* p. 66. See p. 542, above, for the civil service grade of insurance officers.
6 For a full discussion, see Farmer *Tribunals and Government* (1974) pp. 102–105.
7 Street *Justice in the Welfare State* (2nd edn) p. 13.
8 See Diplock LJ in *R v Deputy Industrial Injuries Comr, ex parte Moore* [1965] 1 QB 456 at 486. But he may be a 'tribunal' for statutory purposes: *R(G) 1/80*.
9 SSA 1975, s.99(1). See *R(S) 6/78*, where the Commissioner deprecated the practice of delaying a decision, until an appeal on an earlier claim connected with the same complaint had been disposed of.
10 *CI 440/50*. The subject of precedent in social security law is considered at pp. 595–596, below.
11 SSA 1975, s.100(2). In *R(U) 7/81*, a Tribunal of Commissioners ruled that failure to notify the claimant does not invalidate the decision.
12 SI 1975/558, reg 9(1): see p. 583, above.
13 Ibid, reg 9(3), (5).
14 Ibid, reg 14(1).

chosen.[15] Referees are occasionally used by local tribunals to obtain evidence from a claimant who is unable to attend the hearing.[16]

D National insurance local tribunals

i Organisation and membership

National insurance local tribunals entertain appeals from insurance officers' decisions, and they also decide cases referred to them by insurance officers.[17] There were 179 local tribunals at the end of 1978,[18] each of which had a chairman and two members, one drawn from a panel of persons representing employers and self-employed earners, and the other drawn from a panel of persons representing employed earners.[19] The chairman is appointed for the particular tribunal area by the Secretary of State, but is chosen from a panel drawn up by the Lord Chancellor.[20] Despite the recommendations of the Franks Committee in 1957,[1] the other members continue to be chosen by the Secretary of State, and he may end their appointment at any time.[2]

Though there is no requirement that the chairman must be a lawyer, in practice he almost always is. Legal qualifications are clearly desirable in view of the complex law applied by the tribunals, and the need for the procedure to be in accordance with the standards of fairness imposed by the courts.[3] In this context it is worth pointing out that the chairman has a number of specific powers, which include the following:

(1) to determine the tribunal's procedure (subject, of course, to the requirements imposed under the legislation);[4]

(2) to allow a hearing in private in certain circumstances;[5] and

(3) to secure the assistance of a medical assessor.[6]

It is the chairman who explains the procedure to the appellant, and in practice it is he who asks most of the questions. Studies of local tribunals in the North of England and Scotland have shown general satisfaction by claimants with the part played by chairmen in the proceedings.[7]

On the other hand, there is rather more uncertainty, and some dissatisfaction expressed, about the role of the other (lay) members. It seems clear that, despite the method of selection, they are not expected to represent the interests of either the employee or the employer, but are required to exercise the same impartiality as the chairman.[8] It is not certain whether this is always understood by claimants. The remarkably high incidence of unanimous decisions (about 95 per cent) found in the studies

15 Ibid.
16 See *Farmer*, n.6, above, at p. 108.
17 Referrals are relatively infrequent: thus, in 1979, while tribunals heard over 40,000 cases, only about 1,350 were referrals by insurance officers – *Social Security Statistics 1980*.
18 Annual Report of the Council on Tribunals for 1978–79, Appendix C.
19 SSA 1975, s.97(2).
20 Tribunals and Inquiries Act 1971, s.7.
1 (1957, Cmnd 218), paras 45–49.
2 SSA 1975, Sch 10.
3 For the rules of natural justice, see p. 617, below.
4 SI 1975/558, reg 3(1).
5 Ibid, reg 11(1).
6 Ibid, reg 11(4).
7 See Bell, Collison, Turner and Webber (1974) 3 Jo Soc Pol 289, and (1975) 4 Jo Soc Pol 1, esp. pp. 8–9.
8 See the speech of Lord Gardiner, then Lord Chancellor, quoted in Cavanagh and Newton [1971] Public Administration 197 at 210.

suggests that it is rare for a tribunal member to adopt a biased approach to the case. Indeed, the chairman dissents more often than the lay members:[9] this perhaps occurs when the majority think the claim should succeed on the 'merits', while the chairman takes the correct legal view that it must fail. What sometimes seems to be less satisfactory is the degree of participation by the lay members in the hearing.[10] There are often complaints that they leave all the questioning to the chairman. To some extent the lesser involvement of the lay members is understandable: they do not sit as often, and they have less formal responsibility than the chairman. Moreover, the holding of regional conferences for tribunal chairmen, where legal points are discussed, enables them to develop an expertise which lay members could not be expected to have.[11]

The administrative arrangements are made by a clerk, an officer of the DHSS who may combine these duties with other work.[12] He is generally responsible for convening tribunal sittings, choosing members from the panel, and arranging for the papers to be sent to the tribunal members. The tribunal is under no obligation to require him to leave when it is considering its decision,[13] though in practice the clerk does withdraw. This is also the position for medical boards and appeal tribunals.[14]

Some tribunals have their own premises, while others meet in Town Halls. Many sit in DHSS premises, but every attempt is then made to emphasise their independence by segregating their rooms from other parts of the building.[15] It is rarely suggested that these tribunals are subject to departmental pressure.[16]

ii The selection of a particular tribunal

As far as possible, each member of a panel takes his turn to sit.[17] Schedule 10 to the Social Security Act 1975 lists a number of disqualifications. No member may sit in a case:[18]

(1) in which he appears as the claimant's representative;
(2) by which he is or may be directly affected; or
(3) in which he has taken any part as an official of an association, as an employer, witness, local referee or otherwise.

Further, a member must stand down if his presence on the tribunal would infringe the rule against bias.[19] This has been a ground of appeal to the Commissioner in a few cases, though usually the contention that the constitution of the tribunal infringed the rule has failed. In *R(I) 51/56*,

> it was held that there was nothing wrong in an area labour officer of the National Coal Board sitting as a member, when the claimant was an employee of the Board and worked in the officer's area.[20] It would have

9 Bell et al (1974) n.7, above, at 303–304.
10 Bell et al (1975) n.7, above, at 9; cp the more favourable impression given by Street *Justice in the Welfare State* (2nd edn) p. 16.
11 Regional conferences of tribunal chairmen have been held since 1973 under the encouragement of the Council on Tribunals: see Annual Report for 1973–74, para 20, and Wraith and Hutchesson *Administrative Tribunals* (1973) p. 168.
12 *Wraith and Hutchesson*, n.11, above, at pp. 121–122.
13 SI 1975/558, reg 3(2).
14 See pp. 596–601, below, for medical authorities.
15 *Wraith and Hutchesson*, n.11, above, at p. 122.
16 Cp supplementary benefit tribunals, pp. 607–608, below.
17 SSA 1975, Sch 10, para 1(4).
18 Ibid, para 1(4), proviso (a).
19 For this principle of administrative law, see de Smith *Judicial Review of Administrative Action* (4th edn) ch 5.
20 *R(U) 8/53*.

been different if the officer had given information concerning the case, or in any other way taken part.[1]

Where the claimant is female, at least one of the members, if possible, should be a woman.[2] The Commissioner has ruled that it would be helpful for the tribunal to indicate if this was not practicable; this will avoid later inquiries if the claimant alleges that there was no attempt to secure the participation of a woman.[3]

iii Notice of appeal and of the hearing

A notice, stating the grounds of appeal,[4] must be given at a local office within 28 days from the date of the decision's notification.[5] The *chairman* of the tribunal may allow an extension where good cause is shown;[6] there is no appeal to the Commissioner, however, if he refuses to extend the time-limit.[7]

The clerk then arranges the date and time of the hearing, and sends the claimant all the relevant papers, including the insurance officer's submissions, and any documentary evidence. Also enclosed is a notice that the claimant may attend, alone or with a representative. In order to encourage his attendance, experiments have been conducted in which he has been notified of the names and addresses of people and organisations willing to help him.[8] Reasonable notice of the time and place of the hearing must be given; the Commissioner has held that five days' notice is adequate in view of the tribunal's power to adjourn proceedings.[9]

There is, in fact, no express general power to adjourn, but its existence is a reasonable implication from the proviso to regulation 10(2). This precludes a tribunal from determining a case in the absence of the claimant without his consent, if he has given a reasonable explanation for his absence, 'unless the hearing has at first been adjourned for at least one month and reasonable notice of the time and place of the adjourned hearing has been given to him'. The resumed hearing in this situation cannot be taken earlier even if the applicant consents.[10] A Tribunal of Commissioners has ruled that the same tribunal must sit when the case is resumed, unless the claimant consents to a different membership.[11]

iv The conduct of the hearing

There are relatively few rules with regard to tribunal procedure. Every hearing must be in public unless the *chairman* takes the view that 'intimate personal or financial circumstances may have to be disclosed or that

1 *R(U) 26/54*.
2 SSA 1975, Sch 10, para 1(4), proviso (c).
3 *R(G) 6/62*.
4 SSA 1975, s.100(5).
5 Ibid, s.100(4), amended by SSA 1980, Sch 1, para 10.
6 Ibid. The case-law on the meaning of this phrase for the purpose of late claims may be of assistance in interpreting the provision here: see pp. 565–569, above.
7 *R(I) 44/59*.
8 See the Report of the Council on Tribunals for 1972–73, para 67.
9 *R(S) 13/52*, interpreting what is now SI 1975/588, reg 10(1). Cp SI 1976/962, reg 13(1), which provides that ten days' notice must be given for the hearing of a child benefit appeal.
10 *R(U) 5/70*, J S Watson, Comr. This does not apply to child benefit appeals: see SI 1976/962, reg 10.
11 *R(I) 3/51*, and see also *R(I) 31/57*; *R(S) 3/64*; *R(M) 1/79*. But see *R(I) 40/61* where it was held that a differently constituted tribunal may hear the case provided it starts the hearing afresh.

considerations of public security are involved'.[12] If a claimant wishes to make a private statement, the chairman should explain that it may have to be disclosed in outline to other witnesses.[13] The only persons entitled to be *heard* are the claimant, the insurance officer, the Secretary of State, any one whose right to benefit may be affected by the tribunal's decision,[14] and the representative of all such persons. The representative need not have professional or legal qualifications. Any person entitled to be heard *may* also call witnesses, and has a right to put questions to any other witnesses.[15]

Apart from these rules, it is for the chairman to determine the procedure. But this is subject to the control of the Commissioner, who will allow an appeal if it has been irregular, contrary to the rules of natural justice or in any way unfair.[16] It is unfair, for example, for a tribunal to state a provisional view at the start of the hearing, if this gives the impression that the claimant's arguments will not influence the decision.[17] Clearly, in the absence of detailed rules, procedure will vary a little from one tribunal to another, though there is a standard order of proceeding. When the claimant attends, he is asked to outline his case and, if he wishes, to call witnesses. The chairman, and sometimes the other members, intervene to clarify the argument. Then the insurance officer (not necessarily the same person who decided the case) is invited to ask the claimant (and his witnesses) any questions. In the second stage of the proceeding, the insurance officer makes his submissions. Often he brings out points favourable to the claimant. Diplock LJ has emphasised that the role of the insurance officer is not that of a party adverse to the claimant, but resembles that of an *amicus curiae*.[18] The claimant may put questions to him. Finally, the chairman asks the appellant whether he wishes to add anything, and then the tribunal considers its decision.[19]

A study of insurance tribunals has shown that, despite the fact that their expenses are paid,[20] only about 50 per cent of appellants attend the hearing, and that just over 20 per cent are represented. Much the highest levels of attendance and representation occur in industrial injury cases where trades unions almost always provide assistance.[1] It was also discovered that appellants who attend, and still more those who are represented, have a higher rate of success than those who do not come to the tribunal.[2] The significance of these findings can be challenged. On one view many claimants automatically appeal, but only those with an arguable case trouble to attend or seek representation. But there is some evidence that the reasons for failure to attend are more complex – inability to get to the hearing, unwarranted pessimism about the chances of success and fear of involvement in unfamiliar proceedings.[3] The comparative lack of available assistance for preparing a case or presenting it to the tribunal appears

12 SI 1975/558, reg 11(1).
13 *R(U) 2/56.*
14 SI 1975/558, reg 11(2).
15 Ibid, regs 3(1)(b) and 3(3).
16 See *R(I) 3/51*; *R(U) 2/71*; *R(U) 44/52* for rare cases where a tribunal's procedure was successfully challenged, and see the cases mentioned in *R(U) 3/63*, para 12.
17 *R(S) 5/78*, para 18, R J A Temple, Chief Comr.
18 *R v Deputy Industrial Injuries Comr, ex parte Moore* [1965] 1 QB 456 at 486.
19 See p. 591, below.
20 See *Micklethwait* pp. 65–66; Wraith and Hutchesson *Administrative Tribunals* (1973) pp. 181–185.
1 Bell, Collison, Turner and Webber (1974) 3 Jo Soc Pol 300–301. Thus, there was an attendance rate of 83% in industrial disablement cases, and a similarly high rate of representation in these cases.
2 Bell et al (1975) 4 Jo Soc Pol 1 at 11–21.
3 Ibid, at 5–6.

disturbing, particularly as the high success rate of claimants represented by trades union officials in industrial injury cases shows its value.[4] It is more contentious whether representation by lawyers should be encouraged. Clearly in some cases their skills are invaluable in presenting an argument to the tribunal; on the other hand, it has been argued that their participation often leads to delay and undue formality.[5] Obviously lawyers would be employed more often if legal aid were extended to cover representation before administrative tribunals.[6]

v The tribunal's decision

The tribunal may take into account issues which were not considered by the insurance officer,[7] provided it has given the parties an opportunity to comment on them.[8] When considering its decision it must order all persons, other than the clerk, to withdraw.[9] Decisions have been set aside because the insurance officer had remained in the room when the tribunal was considering its verdict, even though there was no suggestion that he had influenced the result.[10]

The local tribunal may decide by a majority; if it has only two members, the chairman has a second or casting vote.[11] It must record its decision in writing, including its findings of fact and reasons. The grounds for a dissenting opinion must also be stated.[12] There is no duty to record which member is dissenting, though the general practice is to indicate whether it is the chairman or a lay member. The Commissioner has consistently emphasised the importance of a full statement of the findings of fact and the grounds for decision.[13] A failure to do this will often make an oral hearing before the Commissioner necessary where otherwise it could be dispensed with.[14] A copy of the decision must be sent to the parties as soon as is practicable.[15] The claimant must also be told of his right to appeal to the Commissioner, when he has been unsuccessful before the tribunal.

vi Medical assessors

The chairman of the tribunal may decide that a medical practitioner should sit with the tribunal as an assessor.[16] He is not to take any part in its

4 The *Bell* study shows that appellants represented by trades union officials have a success rate of 43%, compared with 39% for those assisted by lawyers and 16% for unrepresented appellants: ibid, at p. 15.

5 For some of the extensive literature on this difficult question, see Whitmore 33 MLR 481; Society of Labour Lawyers *Justice for All* (1968), Fabian Research series No 273; Society of Conservative Lawyers *Rough Justice* (1968), Conservative Political Centre; LAG *Representation before Tribunals*: Memorandum to the Lord Chancellor's Legal Aid Advisory Committee (1974) LAG Bulletin 27 (February).

6 Extension of legal aid has been recommended by the Twenty-Fourth Report of the Lord Chancellor's Advisory Committee on Legal Aid (1973–4 HC 20), by the Council on Tribunals (1979–80 HC 359) and by the Royal Commission on Legal Services 1979 (Cmnd 7648). For a recent exposition, see the Discussion Paper of the Justice–All Souls Review of Administrative Law, 1981.

7 SSA 1975, s.102.

8 *R(U) 2/71*; *R(F) 1/72*; R(I) 4/75.

9 SI 1975/558, reg 3(2). A member of the Council on Tribunals may stay for the deliberations if no member of the tribunal or party objects.

10 *CSS 87/49*; *CU* 331/49; *CP 127/49*.

11 SI 1975/558, reg 12(1).

12 Ibid, reg 12(2).

13 *R(I) 81/51*; *R(I) 42/59*; *R(U) 16/60*; *R(I) 14/59*; *R(U) 3/80*; *R(U) 2/81*.

14 *R(G) 1/63*.

15 SI 1975/558, reg 12(3).

16 Ibid, reg 11(4).

determinations 'except in an advisory capacity'.[17] It seems that he is usually a general practitioner, rather than a specialist.[18] The Commissioners have further defined his role: it is undesirable for the assessor to put questions to the claimant or witnesses, and the tribunal should summarise his advice and give the parties a chance to comment on it.[19] He should not be cross-examined by them or in any way treated as a witness.[20] Finally, it is generally no function of the assessor to examine the claimant medically, unless he consents and this course is necessary to save delay.[1]

In effect, the assessor's sole duty is to assist the tribunal evaluate the medical evidence. The Commissioner may also have the assistance of assessors where there is 'a question of fact of special difficulty'.[2] Here the power to call for assistance is not limited to *medical* assessors. There are no regulations governing their role at this level but the limits on their functions with regard to tribunals would appear also to apply to their role in assisting Commissioners. In *R v Deputy Industrial Injuries Comr, ex parte Jones*, the Divisional Court made it clear that the assessor's role was to help the Commissioner *weigh* the evidence given by the parties, and not to *give* evidence or an opinion on the case.[3] Further, where there is an oral hearing the assessor must be present at least to hear the medical evidence. These restrictions have been criticised by the former Chief Commissioner, Sir Robert Micklethwait.[4]

E Social Security Commissioners

i The Commissioners and their jurisdiction

Appeals from local tribunals lie to one of the Social Security Commissioners (before 1980 National Insurance Commissioners), who must be barristers (in Scotland, advocates) or solicitors of ten years' standing.[5] Before 1979 only barristers were eligible for appointment; the change makes it easier to increase the number of Commissioners to cope with the heavy body of work. Deputy Commissioners may also be appointed for temporary periods to facilitate the despatch of business.[6] Apart from the Chief Social Security Commissioner, I O Griffiths, there are now 13 Commissioners. The standing of all their decisions is the same, but the Chief Commissioner is statutorily responsible for convening a Tribunal of three Commissioners to sit where an appeal 'involves a question of law of special difficulty'.[7] He also has general administrative duties, the most important of which is selecting the decisions to be reported.[8]

The Commissioners are appointed to hear appeals in Great Britain, and not for particular areas. In practice two of them sit in Edinburgh and

17 Ibid, reg 11(5).
18 Street *Justice in the Welfare State* (2nd edn) p. 20.
19 *R(I) 14/51.*
20 *R(I) 23/57.*
1 *R(I) 14/51.*
2 SSA 1975, s.101(6).
3 [1962] 2 QB 677, [1972] 2 All ER 430.
4 See *Micklethwait*, pp. 60–61. He points out that SSA 1975, Sch. 13, para 9 confers a power, by regulations, to expand the assessor's functions and that this has not been exercised.
5 SSA 1979, s.9.
6 SSA 1980, s.13(5). See p. 582, n.7, above, for the change in 1966 from the previous use of the title, Deputy Commissioner.
7 SSA 1975, s.116: see p. 595, below, for further discussion of Tribunals of Commissioners.
8 *Micklethwait* p. 43; see p. 595, below.

decide appeals largely from Scottish tribunals, while another sits in Cardiff and takes cases from Wales and the West country. The others sit in London. In addition to their appellate jurisdiction from insurance tribunals, the Commissioners hear appeals on points of law from medical appeal tribunals, the Attendance Allowance Board and now supplementary benefit appeal tribunals.

ii Notice of appeal and the request for a hearing

An appeal may be brought from a decision of a local tribunal by

- the claimant, the insurance officer, a trade union in certain cases (in particular, where the claimant is a member of that union both at the time the case arose and at the time of the appeal) or a person whose right to industrial death benefit may be affected by the decision.[9]

After a reform in 1980, no appeal is to lie from a tribunal's *unanimous* decision, except with the leave of its chairman or a Commissioner.[10] The purpose of this change was to reduce the number of frivolous appeals; it marks a return to the position which obtained before the 1959 reforms initiated by the Franks Committee.[11] The appeal must be brought within three months of notification of the decision, or the date when leave was given (where this is required).[12] The grounds of appeal must be stated, though these need not be particularised in great detail.[13] But it is not enough merely to send the Commissioner the documents and leave it to him to ascertain the ground of appeal.[14]

When the insurance officer's submissions have been obtained, the claimant is invited to make further observations and is asked whether he wishes to request an oral hearing.[15] The Commissioner must grant this,

> unless, after considering the record of the case and the reasons put forward in the request for the hearing, he is satisfied that the appeal can properly be determined without a hearing . . .[16]

An oral hearing will be granted unless it is clear that the appeal must be upheld, or alternatively it is a hopeless case.[17] In practice it appears that many appeals are decided on written submissions, though this may be because the claimant does not generally request an oral hearing.[18] (There may be an oral hearing even if one has not been requested, if the Commissioner thinks this is desirable.)[19]

When a hearing is held, reasonable notice of its time and place must be given to the parties.[20] If the claimant does not attend, the Commissioner has power to proceed with the case, but it would also be open to him to adjourn.[1] There has been some concern expressed by the Council on

9 SSA 1975, s.101(2)–(3); for child benefit appeals, see SI 1976/962, reg 6(2).
10 SSA 1980, s.15.
11 FANIA 1959, s.3 (and see the discussion in Standing Committee E Debates on Social Security Bill 1980, col 1579).
12 SSA 1975, s.101(5). Time-limits and other procedural rules for the leave to appeal are set out in SI 1980/1622, amending SI 1975/558 (and for child benefit, see SI 1980/1640).
13 *R(I) 15/53*.
14 *R(F) 1/70*.
15 *Micklethwait* p. 48.
16 SI 1975/558, reg 13(1).
17 *R(I) 4/75*, at para 9, R G Micklethwait, Chief Comr.
18 *Micklethwait* p. 49.
19 SI 1975/558, reg 13(2).
20 Ibid. In practice, three to four weeks' notice is given.
1 Ibid, reg 13(4).

Tribunals about the long time taken to dispose of a case.[2] This now seems to be about 15 weeks – considerably longer than the three or four weeks taken by local tribunals.[3]

iii The hearing[4]

The only procedural rules are those already discussed in the context of local tribunals – stipulating that the hearing is generally in public, providing a right to representation and governing the calling and cross-examination of witnesses.[5] Subject to them, the Commissioner is empowered to decide the procedure. This is in practice very similar to that at local tribunals; in particular, the appellant, usually the claimant, has the last word.[6] The rules of natural justice apply to ensure fairness.[7]

The hearing before the Commissioner is not confined to the issues discussed before the local tribunal or those raised by the parties; the tribunal's findings of fact are not binding on him.[8] He may adjourn proceedings while further inquiries are made.[9] The Act specifically empowers him to refer questions to a medical practitioner for the latter to prepare a report,[10] which must be given to the parties for their comments.[11] Also, as has been mentioned, a medical or other expert assessor may perform the limited function of helping the Commissioner evaluate the evidence.[12]

iv The Commissioner's decision

The Commissioner's decision with reasons must be sent to the parties as soon as possible.[13] In practice the claimant is often told the result immediately after the hearing, and the reasons are given later.[14] The various alternatives open to the Commissioner when a local tribunal's decision is challenged for jurisdictional error were fully considered by a Tribunal in *R(U) 3/63*. It held that where the local tribunal has acted outside its jurisdiction, the appropriate course is simply to set the decision aside.[15] However, where there has been a procedural irregularity, the Commissioner has discretion to decide the case himself or to remit it to the tribunal. If there are sufficient materials on which to give a decision and the claimant does not wish a rehearing, the Commissioner should generally adopt the former course.[16]

2 Annual Report for 1969–70, para 29.
3 999 HC Official Report (5th series) col 300.
4 See generally, *Micklethwait* pp. 48–53.
5 See p. 589, above.
6 *Micklethwait* p. 52.
7 See p. 617, below, for a discussion of the rules of natural justice.
8 *R(P) 1/55*; *R(I) 42/56*; *R(I) 4/75*.
9 *R(G) 2/63*.
10 SSA 1975, s.101(7).
11 *R v Deputy Industrial Injuries Comr, ex parte Jones* [1962] 2 QB 677, [1962] 2 All ER 430, DC.
12 See p. 591, above.
13 SI 1973/558, reg 13(6).
14 *Micklethwait* p. 71.
15 The fact that a decision is void does not preclude an appeal against it, or its review: see *R(S) 13/81*, (Tribunal decision).
16 However, see *R(U) 5/70*, where J S Watson, Comr, referred the case back to a differently constituted tribunal.

Leaving aside for the moment appeal to the ordinary courts, a Commissioner's decision is final.[17] This statement, however, must be qualified in three ways:

(1) the fact that the decision is final does not mean that a finding of fact necessary for this decision is conclusive for other proceedings;[18]
(2) the decision may be reviewed by an insurance officer in certain circumstances, e.g. if it is clear on fresh evidence that the decision was based on a mistake as to a material fact;[19]
(3) the Commissioner himself may set aside the decision if it is clear there was some accident or mistake in the procedure, e.g. a letter requesting an oral hearing never reached him.[20]

v A Tribunal of Commissioners

The Chief Commissioner may direct that a Tribunal of three Commissioners hear an appeal involving a point of law of special difficulty.[1] It may decide by a majority. In fact both dissents and separate concurring opinions are relatively uncommon.[2] It seems that a Tribunal may be ordered to resolve a conflict of views between the Commissioners in two previous cases,[3] but they are now convened relatively rarely.[4]

vi Precedent and the reporting of decisions[5]

There have been nearly 70,000 decisions of the National Insurance Commissioners since 1948, the annual number of cases, therefore, averaging about 2,000.[6] It would be quite pointless to report all, or even a majority of these decisions, as a very large number simply involve the application of familiar principles to the facts. The vast majority are, therefore, kept unnumbered on the Commissioner's file.[7] But if a case is of some importance, either because of its particular facts or because a legal principle is developed, he may decide that it should be included in the numbered series of Commissioners' decisions. It can then be read at one of their offices, and copies can be supplied. Finally, the Chief Commissioner selects for reporting the most important numbered decisions, provided this course is assented to by a majority of the Commissioners. About 2,400 cases have been reported since 1948.[8]

It hardly needs stating that the purpose of publishing these decisions is to enable claimants to know their legal rights, and to ensure the uniform application of social security law by tribunals and insurance officers. These objectives will not be fully attained if, as sometimes appears to be the case, important decisions of the Commissioner are not reported. The Council on Tribunals raised this with the Chief Commissioner; in reply, he pointed out

17 SSA 1975, s.117(1).
18 See p. 596, below, for a short discussion of the relationship between the jurisdiction of the statutory and medical authorities, and see ch 8, pp. 300–302, above.
19 See p. 603, below.
20 SI 1975/572, regs 2 and 3, (and see *CU 248/49*; *R(I) 39/51*; *R(G) 1/81*).
1 SSA 1975, s.116.
2 But see, e.g. *R(I) 7/64* (dissent); *R(U) 8/73* and *R(U) 9/73* (separate concurring opinions).
3 *R(U) 1/66*, para 8.
4 See the Annual Reports of the DHSS for 1975 (Cmnd 6565), para 9.8, and 1976 (Cmnd 6931), para 64. They seem to have been convened more frequently in the last two years.
5 The citation of Commissioners' Decisions is treated at the beginning of this book.
6 See *R(I) 12/75*, from which many of the observations in this paragraph are taken.
7 See *Micklethwait* pp. 75–76.
8 Reported decisions are published by HMSO, and are bound in volumes every four years.

that relevant, unreported decisions relied on by the insurance officer are always drawn to the appellant's attention, at least before appeals to the Commissioners.[9] It is doubtful whether this practice always compensates for inadequate reporting.

The reporting of decisions assumes particular importance because of the system of precedent which has been developed by the Commissioners.[10] The rules were set out at length by a Tribunal in *R(I) 12/75*:

(1) All statutory authorities are bound to follow decisions of the High Court and other superior courts.[11]
(2) A decision of a Commissioner must be followed by local tribunals and insurance officers, unless it can be distinguished.[12]
(3) If two Commissioners' decisions conflict, a local tribunal and insurance officer *must* —
 (a) prefer a decision of a Tribunal of Commissioners to that of a single Commissioner;
 (b) give more weight to a reported decision than to an unreported one; and
 (c) if (a) and (b) do not apply, choose between the conflicting decisions.[13]
(4) A single Commissioner —
 (a) should follow a decision of a Tribunal of Commissioners unless there are compelling reasons why he should not; and
 (b) should normally follow the decision of another single Commissioner.[14]

The Tribunal did not comment on the circumstances in which one Tribunal might depart from the previous decision of another, but it seems that it may do so when satisfied the former decision was wrong.[15] The strict doctrine of *stare decisis* followed by the British courts has, therefore, never been adopted by the Commissioners.[16]

Finally, it may be noted that decisions of the Northern Ireland Commissioners are not binding in Great Britain. But they may be of persuasive authority, and at least in one case a Northern Ireland Tribunal decision was followed in preference to an unreported decision of the British Commissioner.[17]

F Medical authorities

i General

Under section 108 of the Social Security Act 1975 some questions of entitlement to disablement benefit ('disablement questions') are referred

9 Annual Report for 1977–78, at p. 20.

10 See *Micklethwait* pp. 73–75. An opinion on a medical question expressed in a previous case is, of course, not binding on the statutory authorities: see *R(I) 16/56*; *R(I) 9/67*; *R(I) 12/68*.

11 In *R(U) 8/80*, I O, Griffiths, Comr, said obiter that in view of the importance of uniformity between English and Scottish law in this area, relevant decisions of the higher Scottish courts are binding on all Commissioners.

12 *R(U) 7/81* (Tribunal decision).

13 No preference is to be given to the earlier or the later decision as such.

14 This proposition is in line with *R(G) 3/62* and *R(I) 23/63*, and see Roskill LJ in *R v National Insurance Comr, ex parte Michael* [1977] 1 WLR 109 at 115, CA.

15 *R(U) 7/68*.

16 See *Micklethwait* pp. 74 and 129. See the similar liberal view of precedent in war pensions cases, p. 626, below.

17 *R(I) 14/63*.

to separate medical authorities, viz medical boards and medical appeal tribunals.[18] It is not entirely clear why this course has been taken. On one view, in claims for industrial injury benefit, the statutory authorities have to decide medical questions as difficult as those reserved for the medical authorities.[19] From this premise it might be reasonable to argue that the existence of the special medical tribunals is unnecessary. On the other hand, it may be more persuasively contended that, as disablement benefit may be awarded for a long period (in some cases, for the rest of the claimant's life) and its assessment depends on the degree of disablement, questions concerning its award should be reserved for an expert medical tribunal. This view was expressed by Lord Diplock in *Jones v Secretary of State for Social Services*:

> One would, therefore, expect that Parliament would provide machinery for a more thorough and expert diagnosis and prognosis of the claimant's medical condition resulting from the injury where a claim was for disablement benefit, than whatever diagnostic material happened to be available to an insurance officer at an earlier date when he was called upon to deal with a claim for injury benefit.[20]

Whatever its merits in terms of principle, the division of function between the statutory and the medical authorities has led to complex legal problems which have twice been before the House of Lords.[1] Its decisions and the subsequent change in the law made by Parliament[2] have been described fully in the chapter on industrial injuries.[3]

The general character of the medical authorities' jurisdiction has been frequently discussed by the courts.[4] The remarks of Diplock J (as he then was) in *R v Medical Appeal Tribunal, ex parte Hubble*, are still apposite:

> As an expert investigating body it is the right and duty of the medical board to use their own expertise in deciding the medical questions referred to them. They may, if they think fit, make their own examination of the claimant and consider any other facts and material to enable them to reach their expert conclusion as doctors do in diagnosis and prognosis of the case of an ordinary patient.[5]

He added that these observations were also applicable to medical appeal tribunals. In a more recent case, the Court of Appeal has emphasised the inquisitorial nature of proceedings before these tribunals.[6]

ii Medical boards

They sit at 105 centres, and consist of two medical practitioners, one of whom acts as chairman.[7] If they are unable to agree, the disablement question is referred to a three-member board, which may decide by majority.[8] The claimant does not have a *right* to be represented at its

18 See pp. 297–309, above, for disablement benefit.
19 Lord Reid in *Jones v Secretary of State for Social Services* [1972] AC 944 at 967–968, HL.
20 Ibid, at 1007.
1 *Minister for Social Security v Amalgamated Engineering Union* [1967] 1 AC 725, [1967] 1 All ER 210, HL and *Jones v Secretary of State for Social Services*, n.19, above.
2 See now SSA 1975, s.117(1), (3).
3 Ch 8, p. 300–302, above. See also p. 319, above, for the relationship between medical authorities' determinations on disablement questions and the statutory authorities' jurisdiction on entitlement to special hardship allowance.
4 For control by the courts, see pp. 615–617, below.
5 [1958] 2 QB 228, 240–241, DC. Also see *R(I) 7/81*.
6 *R v National Insurance Comr, ex parte Viscusi* [1974] 2 All ER 724, [1974] 1 WLR 646.
7 SI 1975/558, reg 16.
8 Ibid, reg 16(4).

sitting, though the presence of anyone likely to assist in the determination of the medical question may be permitted.[9] Otherwise the proceedings are in private; in fact, they consist of a medical examination of the claimant who may also be asked a few questions.[10]

With the claimant's consent a disablement question may be referred for initial decision to a single medical practitioner.[11] He may now make an assessment for up to 12 months.[12] The medical board (or single medical practitioner) is required to state the facts material to the decision but there is no obligation to state its reasons.[13] It is hard to see the justification for this, particularly as when there is a dissent (in a three-member board), the reasons for the minority view must be given.[14]

Medical boardş also exercise appellate jurisdiction from decisions by insurance officers (taken consequent to a medical report) on the diagnosis of a prescribed disease.[15] Further, they hear appeals from insurance officers on the medical questions involved in determining entitlement to mobility allowances.[16]

iii Medical appeal tribunals

a *Composition*

There is a right of appeal from a medical board (or medical practitioner) to a medical appeal tribunal. Alternatively, the Secretary of State may require a decision to be referred to the tribunal, which may then confirm, vary or reverse it as on an appeal.[17] In view of these powers and the general character of the tribunals, it has recently been held that an appeal cannot be withdrawn without leave.[18] The tribunals consist of three members, a legally-qualified chairman and two doctors, both of consultant status.[19] Under the Determination of Claims and Questions Regulations a person directly affected by the case or who has taken any part in it as a medical assessor, the claimant's doctor, a member of a medical board or an employer or witness, may not sit on a tribunal.[20] A doctor who has examined a person in connection with his common law suit for damages may not sit as a member of a tribunal deciding a claim for benefit arising from the same accident.[1] But it has also been held, perhaps surprisingly, that it is not a breach of the rule against bias for a medical practitioner to sit and *review* a decision of another tribunal of which he was a member.[2] This practice has been criticised by the Council on Tribunals, and the Department now ensures that it does not happen.[3]

b *Procedure before the tribunal*

An appeal, or a Secretary of State's reference, must be brought within three months of notification of the board's decision, though the chairman

9 Ibid, reg 18(2).
10 Hodge (1974) LAG Bulletin 13 (January).
11 SSA 1975, s.111(1).
12 Ibid, s.111(1), proviso, amended by SSA 1980, Sch 1, para 11.
13 SI 1975/558, reg 19.
14 Ibid, reg 19(1)(b).
15 SSA 1975, s.113, and see SI 1975/1537, regs 22–29.
16 SI 1975/1573, regs 12–19.
17 SSA 1975, s.109(2)(3).
18 *CI 15/80*. The ruling applies to other social security tribunals.
19 See Wraith and Hutchesson *Administrative Tribunals* (1973) p. 94.
20 SI 1975/558, reg 20. See *CI 12/81*.
1 *R(I) 28/61* (Tribunal decision).
2 Ibid.
3 See the Annual Report for 1965, paras 58–61, and the Report for 1967, para 70.

of the tribunal may grant an extension. Notice of the appeal with its grounds must be given at a local office.[4] In most respects the rules governing the conduct of the hearing are identical to those for local tribunals. There is, however, one important aspect of the medical appeal tribunal's procedure which distinguishes it from the usual form of proceedings before a local tribunal: it is the general rule for the claimant to be examined by the two medical members of the tribunal *after* the hearing,[5] though this need not be done in all cases.[6]

c *Natural justice in tribunal proceedings*

There have been numerous decisions concerning the application of the natural justice rules to medical appeal tribunal proceedings, first, by the courts on application for certiorari,[7] and secondly, by the Commissioner after 1959 when the right of appeal on a point of law was created.[8] The cases can be discussed under the following heads:

i *A new point taken by the tribunal must be put to the claimant* This requirement was first stated, obiter, by Lord Denning MR, in *R v Industrial Injuries Comr, ex parte Howarth.*[9] The Commissioner has repeatedly emphasised that if the tribunal considers an issue of real significance, which has not been discussed at the medical board, it must invite the claimant to comment.[10] In some circumstances he should be asked to comment on the points arising from the medical examination,[11] though this is not an absolute rule.[12]

ii *The general duty of the tribunal to help the claimant* The Commissioner has stressed that the tribunal may be in breach of the rules of natural justice if it does not invite the claimant to address it.[13] In some cases, the Commissioner has suggested that the duty of the tribunal is to assist the claimant in making his case.[14]

iii *The use by the tribunal of specialists' reports* It is open to the tribunal to ask for a specialist's report, but a copy must be given to the claimant.[15] The same is true of hospital case notes.[16] If the claimant then wishes to call his own expert evidence, the tribunal should adjourn to allow him to do this.[17]

iv *Evidence acquired after the proceedings* In *R(I) 2/72*, the Commissioner, D Neligan, ruled that it was contrary to natural justice for the clerk

4 SI 1975/558, reg 21.
5 See *Wraith and Hutchesson*, n.19, above, at p. 147; Hodge, n.10, above.
6 *R(I) 35/61*.
7 See p. 615, below.
8 See p. 600, below.
9 (1968) 4 KIR 621.
10 *R(I) 4/71*; *R(I) 29/61*; *R(I) 2/74*.
11 *R(I) 29/61* (Tribunal decision).
12 *R(I) 2/64*.
13 *R(I) 10/62*. There is a breach of the rules if the tribunal fails to inform the claimant that he must produce evidence to support his case: *R(M) 2/80*.
14 *R(I) 6/69*, H Magnus, Comr; *CI 3/78*, R S Lazarus, Comr.
15 *R(I) 35/61*.
16 *R(I) 6/67*; *R(I) 13/74*.
17 *R v Medical Appeal Tribunal, ex parte Carrarini* [1966] 1 WLR 883, DC.

to ask the claimant questions subsequent to the hearing, and communicate the answers to the tribunal.[18]

In view of this wealth of authority, it is surprising to find in a decision of the Court of Appeal a suggestion that the rules of natural justice do not apply to hearings before medical appeal tribunals.[19] It was emphasised that within the limits of fairness they were masters of their own procedure and were entitled to use their own expertise. But in an earlier case the Divisional Court had concluded that this feature of medical tribunals did not justify the exclusion of the rules of natural justice.[20] This latter approach is consistent with the leading authorities on the proper use by specialist tribunals of their expertise and should, it is suggested, be followed.[1]

d *The decision of the tribunal*

The appeal tribunal has jurisdiction to determine the questions arising before it *de novo*, and is not limited to the issues considered by the board.[2] The courses open to the tribunal when an appeal is brought on jurisdictional or technical grounds were considered by the Commissioner, D Reith, in *R(I) 7/75*. He held that the tribunal has a discretion to deal with the case itself or to remit the case to another medical board.[3] Where the board's decision is a complete nullity because it was improperly constituted, it is generally more appropriate to adopt the latter course, but a tribunal might properly decide the case itself when there has been only a minor irregularity in the proceedings.

The decision must contain a statement of reasons with findings on the material facts and a summary of this must be sent to the claimant as soon as practicable.[4] (Rather oddly, though the tribunal may decide by a majority, there is no provision for recording a dissenting opinion.)[5] The record should state whether the claimant has been medically examined, and make it clear why his contentions were accepted or rejected.[6] It is not enough merely to state that the tribunal considers the board's decision 'just and reasonable'.[7] On the other hand, there is no need for every step in the reasoning to be set out.[8]

iv Appeal to the Commissioner

Since 1959 there has been a right of appeal on a point of law from a medical appeal tribunal to the Commissioner – though either the tribunal or the Commissioner must give leave.[9] This was introduced because in the

18 The Commissioner is not entitled to receive evidence after the oral hearing without allowing the parties an opportunity to comment on it: see *R v Deputy Industrial Injuries Comr, ex parte Jones* [1962] 2 QB 677, [1962] 2 All ER 430.
19 See Buckley LJ in *R v National Insurance Comr, ex parte Viscusi* [1974] 2 All ER 724, [1974] 1 WLR 646.
20 See *R v Medical Appeal Tribunal, ex parte Carrarini*, n.17, above.
1 See de Smith *Judicial Review of Administrative Action* (4th edn) pp. 204–207.
2 Diplock J in *R v Medical Appeal Tribunal, ex parte Hubble* [1958] 2 QB 228 at 241, DC. Also see p. 307, above, for the tribunal's powers to revise provisional assessments.
3 The Commissioner followed the Tribunal decision in *R(U) 3/63*, see p. 594, above.
4 SI 1975/558, reg 23.
5 Cp the provision for local tribunals and medical boards, pp. 591 and 598, above.
6 *R(I) 18/61*; *R(I) 30/61*; *R(I) 8/63*.
7 *R(I) 7/65*.
8 *R(I) 3/68*; *R(I) 1/73*.
9 SSA 1975, s.112.

previous years there had been a number of successful applications for certiorari from the tribunals, and it became clear that they were not always applying the law consistently.[10] The appeal to the Commissioner now obviates the need to apply to the Divisional Court.[11]

An application for leave must first be made to the tribunal, either orally at the conclusion of its hearing or in writing within three months of notification of its decision.[12] If it refuses leave, the applicant has 28 days to apply to a Commissioner – though this period may be extended at his discretion.[13] Both the appeal tribunal and the Commissioner may refuse consent where the point of law is without substance.[14]

If leave is granted, the appeal itself must then be brought within three months from notice of this grant.[15] In the most recent case to consider the question, *R(I) 14/75*, the Commissioner, J S Watson, stated that an appeal will be allowed on a point of law if —

(1) there has been a breach of the rules of natural justice;
(2) the tribunal has not stated its reasons and findings of fact adequately;
(3) the decision contains a false proposition of law ex facie;
(4) the decision is not supported by any evidence;
(5) the tribunal's findings of fact were such that no reasonable body acting judicially and properly instructed on the law could have reached the conclusion it arrived at.

A copy of the Commissioner's decision is sent to the chairman of the medical appeal tribunal, the Secretary of State and the claimant (or his trade union).[16] It is then the duty of the tribunal to confirm or revise its decision.[17] Where the Commissioner has upheld the original decision, this may simply be confirmed, but in other cases there must be a further hearing by the same or a differently constituted tribunal.[18]

G The Attendance Allowance Board

i General

The Attendance Allowance Board was set up in 1970 to determine whether the medical conditions for an award of attendance allowance are satisfied.[19] The other requirements are determined by the statutory authorities; they refer the medical questions to the Board which then issues a certificate to the effect that the claimant has or has not complied with the relevant 'night' and 'day' conditions.[20] The formal decision on entitlement is then

10 E.g. see *R v Medical Appeal Tribunal, ex parte Gilmore* [1957] 1 QB 574, [1957] 1 All ER 796, CA; *R v Medical Appeal Tribunal, ex parte Burpitt* [1957] 2 QB 584, [1957] 2 All ER 704, DC; *R v Medical Appeal Tribunal, ex parte Griffiths* [1958] 2 All ER 227, [1958] 1 WLR 517, DC; *R v Medical Appeal Tribunal, ex parte Hubble* [1958] 2 QB 228, [1958] 2 All ER 374, DC; affd. [1959] 2 QB 408, [1959] 3 All ER 40, CA.
11 *Micklethwait* pp. 132–133.
12 SI 1975/558, reg 26(1).
13 Ibid, reg 26(2), amended by SI 1980/1622, reg 7.
14 *R(I) 3/61*.
15 SI 1975/558, reg 27(1), amended by SI 1980/1622, reg 8: on other points the procedure resembles that for an appeal from a local tribunal: p. 593, above.
16 SI 1975/558, reg 29(9), (10).
17 SSA 1975, s.112(5).
18 SI 1975/558, reg 30.
19 National Insurance (Old Persons' and Widows' Pensions and Attendance Allowance) Act 1970, renamed NIA 1970 by NIA 1972, s.8(4). For the composition and advisory functions of the Board, see p. 550, above.
20 SSA 1975, s.105(3): see pp. 173–175, above. For a discussion of this complex division of functions, see *R(A) 2/81*, paras 3–9, per J G Monroe, Comr.

made by the insurance officer. In practice it seems that medical determinations are usually made by medical practitioners to whom the Board has power to delegate its adjudicatory functions,[1] and to whom it may properly issue general guidance on the discharge of these functions.[2] The delegation may be revoked at any stage before a final decision is issued.[3] There are no procedural rules governing these determinations. The Board, or more usually its delegate, receives written evidence from the claimant's doctor and a departmental medical officer, and the application is decided on this basis.

Either the claimant or the Secretary of State may apply within three months for a review of this decision *on any ground*, or at any time on the limited grounds set out in section 106(1)(a) of the Social Security Act 1975: that there has been a change of circumstances since the decision, or that it was reached in ignorance of, or on a mistake as to, a material fact. The Commissioner has pointed out that the first type of review (on any ground within a limited time) is analogous to an appeal, while the second type is equivalent to the usual review procedure discussed in the next section.[4] If a further review is sought within 12 months of an earlier application, the Board's leave must first be obtained.[5] (There may also be review of the statutory authorities' decisions, one of the grounds being that the decision was based on a determination of the Board which has been revised.)[6]

The application for review of the medical determination is generally heard by a medical practitioner acting under delegated powers, though the Board itself sometimes decides the more difficult cases. Again there are no procedural rules for these determinations. The DHSS takes the view that there is no reason why the Board should not hold an oral hearing at this stage, though this is not the normal practice.[7] The claimant is sent a copy of the departmental doctor's report and given an opportunity to comment.[8] The Commissioner has also indicated that if the Board at some point forms a provisional view, it should be put to the claimant so that he can adduce evidence to contradict it.[9] A decision on review must be notified to the parties with reasons, and the claimant told that he has a right of appeal to the Commissioner.[10]

ii Appeal to the Commissioner

There is a right of appeal on a point of law to the Commissioner from a decision of the Board (or its delegate) on review, or refusing a review.[11] Leave must first be obtained from a Commissioner – within three months of the review or the refusal of a review.[12] The grounds on which a decision

1 SSA 1975, Sch 11, para 5. See Carson (1975) LAG Bulletin 67 (March).
2 *R(A) 4/78*.
3 *R(A) 1/81*.
4 *R(A) 2/81*, paras 7 and 21.
5 SI 1975/598, reg 8(2).
6 SSA 1975, s. 104(1)(c). See *R(A) 4/81*.
7 *R(A) 1/73*, para 31. It seems that in some areas, as an experiment, oral hearings have beer held in the claimant's home: see Carson, n.1, above.
8 Carson, n.1, above, at 68.
9 *R(A) 1/73*, at para 31, R G Micklethwait, Chief Comr. Also see *R(A) 1/81*.
10 SI 1975/598, reg 9(2), amended by SI 1979/1684, reg 4. See also new reg 9A, inserted by SI 1980/1136, providing that the Board need not disclose medical evidence to a claimant if this would be harmful to his health.
11 SSA 1975, s.106(2); SI 1975/598, reg 10(1).
12 SI 1975/598, reg 10(2), amended by SI 1979/1684, reg 5; the procedure governing the appeal is similar to that for appeals from local and medical appeal tribunals.

of the Board may be held to be wrong in the law are the same as those which apply to medical appeal tribunals.[13] Thus, the rules of natural justice must be observed, and the Board was in breach when it failed to contact the claimant's doctor (as implicitly requested) or to tell the claimant that he should produce the medical evidence himself.[14] And reasons must be given for decisions, making it clear to the claimant why his contentions were rejected.[15]

The Chief Commissioner in *R(A) 1/73* pointed out that it was not for him to reverse the Board's decision on the facts or on the inferences to be drawn from them. Moreover, it is for the Board to use its own expertise in applying the legislative standards (e.g. 'severely disabled', 'requires . . . continual supervision'). The Commissioner is empowered to entertain an appeal on the construction of the statutory provisions, as this is a matter of law, but not on the meaning of ordinary words, as this is a question of fact.[16] This distinction is often hard to draw in practice. Thus, in *R v National Insurance Comr, ex parte Secretary of State for Social Services*,[17] the Divisional Court held that the Commissioner had exceeded his jurisdiction in ruling that assistance given the claimant in undressing and going to bed was necessarily relevant to the question whether 'repeated attention' was needed during the *night*, rather than (as the Board had found) to the question whether attention was required during the *day*. The Commissioner was wrong to treat the issue as a question of law, rather than one of fact and, therefore, his decision was quashed.

iii Critique

In its first years the Attendance Allowance Board attracted a considerable amount of criticism, partly because of its procedures.[18] The absence of procedural rules may suggest that it is more properly to be regarded as an informal administrative body rather than as a tribunal exercising adjudicative functions.[19] However, its duty to give reasons and the existence of the appeal to the Commissioner point to the opposite conclusion. It remains an open question whether its functions could more appropriately be given to the medical authorities.[20]

H Review of decisions under Social Security Act 1975

Decisions taken by the statutory and other authorities under the Social Security Act 1975 may be reviewed if they were based on a mistake as to the facts or there has been a change of circumstances since the decision was taken. This affords a simple method of revising determinations which were either at the time, or have since become, wrong, without requiring the applicant to resort to a formal appeal or to make a fresh claim. Review by

13 See p. 601, above: see Carson 26 NILQ 291 at 319–320.
14 *CA 3/78*, and see *R 2/75 (AA)*.
15 *R(A) 1/72*, and see *R(A) 1/73*, paras 13–14.
16 See Lord Reid in *Cozens v Brutus* [1973] AC 854 at 861, HL.
17 [1974] 3 All ER 522, [1974] 1 WLR 1290: see ch 4, p. 173, above, for a discussion of the issues in this case.
18 Carson, n.1, above, *passim*; Smith (1981) 48 Poverty 9.
19 See Annual Report of the Council on Tribunals for 1969–70, Appendix B (letter to the Lord Chancellor concerning the role of the Attendance Allowance Board); and see Wraith and Hutchesson *Administrative Tribunals* (1973) pp. 64–65.
20 This was suggested by the Council on Tribunals: n.19, above.

the medical boards has been discussed in the chapter on industrial injuries;[1] reviews by the Attendance Allowance Board and by the supplementary benefit officers are treated elsewhere in this chapter.[2] The grounds on which these authorities review previous determinations are for the most part the same as those available for review by the insurance officer and, therefore, the case-law discussed here is relevant to their powers. The principal provision is Section 104(1):[3]

> Any decision under this Act of an insurance officer, a local tribunal or a Commissioner may be reviewed at any time by an insurance officer or, on a reference from an insurance officer, by a local tribunal, if —
> (a) the officer or tribunal is satisfied and, in the case of a decision of a Commissioner, satisfied by fresh evidence, that the decision was given in ignorance of, or was based on a mistake as to, some material fact; or
> (b) there has been any relevant change of circumstances since the decision was given . . . .

i General

A review may be requested by written application to the insurance officer,[4] though the Commissioner has ruled that there is no need for a formal application and that in certain circumstances a claim for benefit should be treated as an application for review.[5] It is for the person seeking revision of the decision to show that this should be done.[6] The Commissioner has emphasised that a revision is not to be made merely because the conditions set out in section 104(1)(a) or (b) are satisfied: the insurance officer (or tribunal) must decide that in the light of the facts now found to exist it is right to revise the original determination.[7]

ii Ignorance of, or mistake as to, a material fact

Review will not be permitted if the mistake was as to law,[8] or as to an inference drawn from the primary facts.[9] The determining authority must have been in ignorance of, or been mistaken as to, some specific fact. Thus, an award of maternity allowance may be revised if it was made on the basis of a mistake concerning the expected week of confinement.[10] It does not matter whether the mistake was a reasonable one; it seems that a wholly unjustified error may be corrected.[11] In the case of Commissioners' decisions, review can only take place if there is *fresh evidence* to show that the determination was wrong. The meaning of 'fresh evidence' has given rise to some difficulty, particularly in cases concerning the review of medical authorities' decisions.[12] Clearly it covers evidence which came to light after the decision. The Commissioner has held in a number of cases

1 Pp. 307–308, above.
2 P. 602, above (Attendance Allowance Board); p. 612, below, benefit officers.
3 See SSA 1975, ss.95(2), 96, for the review of Secretary of State's decisions, and see *Gara* 1979 SLT Notes 29.
4 SSA 1975, s.104(2) (and see SI 1976/962, reg 9 for the review of child benefit decisions: reg 9(2) permits review of an insurance officer's decision on the ground that it was wrong in law).
5 *R(I) 50/56*; cp., *R(I) 11/62*; *R(A) 2/81*. This may enable the applicant to surmount the time-limits for making claims: pp. 557–564, above.
6 *R(I) 1/71*.
7 *R(I) 18/62*, *R(I) 1/71*.
8 *R(G) 18/52* (Tribunal decision); cp n.4, above, for review of child benefit decisions.
9 See H Magnus, Comr, in *R(I) 3/75*, para 9.
10 *R(G) 8/55*.
11 *R(S) 13/81* (Tribunal decision).
12 See ch 8, p. 308, above.

that it also includes evidence which the claimant could not reasonably have been expected in the circumstances to have adduced at the hearing.[13] The fact that the claimant is a person of relatively low intelligence or is illiterate is relevant.[14] It seems that the Department is prepared to adopt a wide view of 'fresh evidence'.[15] What, however, is clearly excluded is evidence which the claimant could have produced without difficulty at the hearing.[16]

iii Relevant change of circumstances

A change in the claimant's condition may justify revision of the award,[17] as may a change in the law,[18] or a later decision of the Commissioner which undermines the basis of the previous determination.[19] A Tribunal has held, perhaps surprisingly, that a court decision in a damages case which cast doubt on an earlier award of industrial injuries benefit was not a 'relevant change of circumstances'.[20]

Part 2 Supplementary Benefit Appeal Tribunals

A General

The origins of supplementary benefit appeal tribunals (SBATs) can be traced to the tribunals set up in 1934 to hear appeals from the Unemployment Assistance Board.[1] At this time there was relatively little suggestion that it was right in principle to provide an appeal; the real reason for the tribunals' institution was to insulate the Ministry from political pressure arising from decisions on assistance.[2] The administrative character of these tribunals was emphasised by the fact that one of the three members was appointed to represent the Board, and could sometimes be its district officer.[3] The national assistance tribunals set up by the 1948 legislation were closely modelled on them, though for the future no member was to be appointed by the National Assistance Board to represent its interests.[4] Other changes were those dispensing with the requirement of the chairman's leave before an appeal was brought, and allowing non-legal representation.[5] The government, however, successfully resisted an amendment to provide a further appeal from the tribunal to an umpire, on

13 *R(I) 27/61*; *R(I) 17/66*; *R(P) 3/73*. See also Lord Denning MR, in *R v National Insurance Comr, ex parte Viscusi* [1974] 1 WLR 646, 652. The proposition in the text was doubted because of the restrictive terms of Diplock J's judgment in *R v Medical Appeal Tribunal, ex parte Hubble* [1958] 2 QB 228 at 242–243.

14 *R(P) 3/73*, R JA Temple, Comr (illiterate immigrant did not produce birth certificate as evidence of his age).

15 See Roskill LJ in *R v National Insurance Comr, ex parte Viscusi*, n.13, above at 657.

16 *R(I) 47/59* (evidence in solicitor's hands before the Commissioner gave his decision), and see *R(S) 25/51*.

17 *R(I) 11/59*. But the mere obtaining of a different medical opinion is not a 'change of circumstances': *R(S) 6/78*, J S Watson, Comr.

18 *R(G) 3/58* (Tribunal decision); *R(A) 4/81*.

19 *R(I) 25/63*, distinguishing *R(I) 11/59*.

20 *R(I) 11/59*.

1 For the Unemployment Assistance Board, see p. 539, above.

2 Lynes in Adler and Bradley (eds) *Justice, Discretion and Poverty* (1976) pp. 5–8; Fulbrook *Administrative Justice and the Unemployed* (1978) pp. 164–167.

3 *Lynes*, n.2, above, at pp. 8–12.

4 Bradley, n.2, above, at p. 37.

5 Ibid.

the ground that this would lead to the development of 'case-law' and consequent rigidity.[6]

The Franks Committee took the view that in two respects assistance tribunals were different from insurance tribunals. First, as their hearings might often involve disclosure of personal details, it was right for them to be in private.[7] Secondly, there was no need to provide a further right of appeal from their decisions. The justification for this lay partly in the need to arrive at a final decision quickly, but the argument was also supported by a famous passage in the Report which seemed to cast doubt on the judicial (or quasi-judicial) character of assistance tribunal proceedings:

> Although in form these Tribunals hear and determine appeals against decisions of local officers of the National Assistance Board and therefore exercise adjudicating functions, in practice their task much resembles that of an assessment or case committee, taking a further look at the facts and in some cases arriving at a fresh decision on the extent of need.[8]

The uncertainty whether these tribunals, and their successors, should be regarded primarily as *judicial* bodies set up to resolve conflicts, or as *administrative* bodies, as the Franks Committee appeared to suggest, has been partly responsible for the controversy surrounding them.[9]

When national assistance was replaced by supplementary benefits in 1966, the tribunals' structure was unaffected, though they were renamed supplementary benefit appeal tribunals. There was no suggestion that the change to a system based on 'entitlement' (though with elements of discretion) had any implications for the tribunal system.[10] What is perhaps more surprising is that in 1970 these tribunals were given appellate jurisdiction over questions of entitlement to family income supplement, in which there is virtually no element of discretion.[11] It might have been more appropriate to confer it on the local insurance tribunals.[12] As it happens, FIS appeals are few compared with supplementary benefit appeals: in 1979 962 as against 94,178.[13]

In addition to their appellate jurisdiction under the Family Income Supplements Act 1970,[14] SBATs have power under the amended Supplementary Benefits Act 1976 to entertain an appeal against a benefit officer's decision (or his refusal to review a decision) on the following matters:[15]
(1) the right to, or amount of, benefit;
(2) the issuing of benefit to a person other than the claimant;
(3) the recovery of sums paid by way of urgent needs payments;
(4) the imposition of a condition that the claimant be available for employment;

6 Mr J Griffiths, Minister of National Insurance, Standing Committee C Debates on the National Assistance Bill 1947, col 2465.
7 Report of the Committee on Administrative Tribunals and Enquiries (1957, Cmnd 218), paras 64, 79, and 180.
8 Ibid, at para 182.
9 The distinction is well drawn by Bradley 27 NILQ 96, 99–101.
10 Bradley, n.2, above, at p. 49.
11 See ch 13, p. 521, above.
12 An amendment at the Committee stage of the Family Income Supplements Bill to this effect was withdrawn: see 806 HC Official Report (5th series) cols 1355 ff. The Council on Tribunals unsuccessfully pressed for a change in the name of the SBATs to reflect their further jurisdiction: see Annual Report for 1970–71, paras 49–50.
13 The figures are taken from the Supplementary Benefits Commission Annual Report 1979 (Cmnd 8033), Tables 13.1 and G. 7.
14 S.7.
15 S.15.

(5) the payment of benefit in kind rather than in cash;
(6) the determination of the excess supplementary benefit paid for a period in which the beneficiary was also entitled to other social security benefits;[16]
(7) the issue of a direction that a person may be subject to a requirement to attend a place of instruction or training as a condition of receiving benefit;[17]
(8) the determination that overpaid benefit is recoverable under section 20 of the Act.[18]

Finally, it should be noted that the question whether a person's requirements are to be disregarded for benefit purposes, because of participation in a trade dispute, must be referred by a SBAT to an insurance officer for him to decide (and on appeal, an insurance tribunal).[19] This question will often raise issues of legal complexity, familiar to insurance officers and tribunals in the context of unemployment benefit;[20] but the procedure may be thought to show a relative lack of confidence in the ability of SBATs to determine difficult points of law. The provision is now in the regulations rather than the parent Act, so the intention may be to confer jurisdiction on the supplementary benefit tribunals when they show general legal expertise.[1]

B Composition and structure

Each SBAT has jurisdiction over the area assigned to it by the Secretary of State.[2] It consists of a chairman and two other members, the former being appointed by the Secretary of State from a panel drawn up by the Lord Chancellor (or in Scotland, the Lord President of the Court of Session).[3] In practice, he has usually served on the tribunal for some years as an 'ordinary' member.[4] One ordinary member is appointed by the Secretary of State, after interview at a regional office of the Department, from people appearing 'to have knowledge or experience of conditions in the area to which the panel relates and of the problems of people living on low incomes'.[5] The second ordinary member is drawn from a panel of persons, quaintly described in the Act as 'appearing to the Secretary of State to represent work-people'.[6] In practice he is nominated by local Trades Council Federations. Relatively few from this category are subsequently appointed chairmen, though it is now hoped to increase the number. Under an amendment to the provisions made in 1979, each member of a panel must be called on to serve in rotation – thus excluding the possibility of passing over 'difficult' members. As far as possible one of the members should be of the same sex as the claimant.[7]

In contrast to the chairmen of insurance tribunals, relatively few SBAT chairmen used to be lawyers. The study undertaken for the DHSS by Bell

16 Ibid, s.12.
17 Ibid, s.10.
18 See ch 14, pp. 577–578, above.
19 SI 1980/1643, reg 5(2).
20 See ch 3, pp. 120–128, above.
1 The relevant provision used to be SBA 1976, s.15(2), now repealed.
2 SBA 1976, Sch 4, para 2.
3 Tribunals and Inquiries Act 1971, s.7.
4 Herman *Administrative Justice and Supplementary Benefits* (1972) pp. 20–22.
5 SBA 1976, Sch 4, para 1, inserted in the Act by SSA 1979, Sch 2.
6 Ibid.
7 SBA 1976, Sch 4, para 5.

indicated that they were more proficient in their handling of cases than lay chairmen and more knowledgeable about the relevant law.[8] In the last few years the tendency has been to appoint more lawyers as chairmen, and this trend is likely to continue with the increased legalisation of the whole scheme. But it remains very controversial whether the further step should be taken of making legal qualifications necessary.[9]

The *Bell* study showed the same widespread dissatisfaction with the role played by the lay members of SBATs which has been found in insurance tribunals.[10] Their reluctance to participate might be overcome by arranging courses and conferences so that they could sharpen their awareness of supplementary benefits law, and of the problems faced by claimants.[11] A guide, prepared by an independent advisory group, has encouraged greater participation by the ordinary members.[12]

In a weak tribunal too much reliance is often placed on the clerk. He is an executive officer in one of the Department's regional offices, seconded to work for the tribunals for about three years.[13] In 1971 the DHSS, after encouragement from the Council on Tribunals, issued instructions which emphasise his subordinate role: he is not to raise issues of law or policy, or to take part in the tribunal's deliberations, but is merely to assist it by taking notes of evidence and verifying law already referred to by the parties. The *Bell* study found that in practice clerks sometimes played a more active role, though not always to the claimant's disadvantage.[14] Now the DHSS advisory group has also emphasised the point that clerks should not act as spokesmen for the Department.[15]

An important step has recently been taken to strengthen the independence of SBATS. Under the amendments made in 1979 to the supplementary benefits legislation, provision is made for the appointment of Senior Chairmen (barristers, advocates or solicitors of seven years' standing).[16] Their principal functions are to oversee the working of tribunals in the areas to which they are assigned, to hear complaints against the conduct of hearings and to participate in the selection of chairmen of tribunals. By the end of 1980 five Senior Chairmen had been appointed.[17] This development is somewhat similar to the 'presidential system' which ensures the independence of war pensions and industrial tribunals.[18]

C Procedure before the hearing

i The officer's decision

Generally written notice of a benefit officer's decision must be sent to the claimant; this need not be done when the decision awards a cash payment

8 Bell *Research Study on Supplementary Benefit Appeal Tribunals, Review of Main Findings: Conclusions: Recommendations*, published by DHSS (1975).
9 In favour of mandatory legal qualifications are *Bell*, n.8, above, at p. 23, and Lewis (1973) PL 257 at 280–281. Against are Lister and Bradley: see Bradley 27 NILQ 96 at 116.
10 *Bell*, n.8, above, pp. 6–7 and 17–18.
11 Ibid, at p. 21.
12 *Supplementary Benefit Appeal Tribunals*: *A guide to procedure* (DHSS, 1977) paras 42, 53 and 65.
13 *Bell*, n.8, above, at pp. 8–9; Wraith and Hutchesson *Administrative Tribunals* (1973) pp. 121 and 302.
14 *Bell*, n.8, above, at pp. 8–9.
15 N.12, above, at paras 7, 28 and 66.
16 SBA 1976, Sch 4, para 11, inserted in the Act by SSA 1979, Sch 2.
17 (1980) LAG Bulletin 282 (December).
18 See p. 617, below, for pensions appeal tribunals.

or, in circumstances where it is reasonable not to give notice, it ends entitlement to benefit.[19] Further, under a new rule, in most cases and so far as practicable, details of how benefit is assessed must be supplied.[20] Under the FIS General Regulations the applicant must be given a reasoned notice in writing, and further told of his right to appeal.[1]

ii Notice of appeal

An appeal concerning either supplementary benefits or FIS must be brought within 28 days of notification of the decision by a notice in writing given at a local office.[2] The chairman of the SBAT, however, may extend this time if there is good cause.[3] The appeal need not be made on the official form, or state the grounds, though it is helpful for them to be given in outline.

iii Review by officers

When an appeal is made, the decision is automatically reviewed by a benefit or supplement officer, as the case may be.[4] It will be revised if found to be based on a mistake of fact or law, or there has been a relevant change of circumstances.[5] When there is a review, there is a new decision, and so strictly the appeal – brought against the original determination – lapses. However well-intentioned this procedure may be, there is some danger that the officer may exploit the fact that some applicants will not pursue their case to the tribunal after a revised decision has been issued, even though the latter only partially satisfies their needs.[6] On the other hand, the practice does enable bad decisions to be corrected more speedily than would be the case if all appeals went to SBATs.[7]

In the light of the criticisms, the Supplementary Benefits Commission made some important changes in 1975 to review procedure, and these are still in effect.[8] The claimant is given full details of how both the original and revised decisions are reached, and he is specifically invited to make an appeal (against the latter) if he is still dissatisfied.

iv Notice of the hearing

The clerk must give the appellant reasonable notice of the time and place of the hearing and send him copies of the documents supplied to the SBAT.[9] It is said in the Handbook that the clerk attempts to give about two weeks' notice,[10] though it has been suggested that sometimes applicants

19 SI 1980/1643, reg 3(1)(3).
20 Ibid, reg 3(4).
1 SI 1980/1437, reg 13.
2 SI 1980/1605, r. 4.
3 See ante, p. 589, for the similar power of chairmen of local insurance tribunals.
4 SI 1980/1643, reg 4 (supplementary benefit); SI 1980/1437, reg 12 (FIS).
5 SI 1980/1643, reg 4(1). The 'change of circumstances' ground does not apply to FIS. See p. 605, above, for interpretation of these concepts by the Commissioner.
6 For discussion of the review powers of the Supplementary Benefits Commission, see Herman *Administrative Justice and Supplementary Benefits* (1972) pp. 31–32; Coleman *Supplementary Benefits and the Administrative Review of Administrative Action* (1970), CPAG pamphlet.
7 Of 94,178 appeals brought in 1979, 27,029 were revised and did not reach a tribunal for this reason: SBC Annual Report 1979 (Cmnd 8033), Table 13.1.
8 SBC Annual Report 1975 (Cmnd 6615), para 14.2. See now Handbook, paras 12.4–12.5.
9 SI 1980/1605, r. 5(2).
10 Para 12.6.

have been notified only two or three days before the hearing.[11] This might not be 'reasonable notice', particularly where the tribunal is situated some distance from the appellant's residence.[12] The documents consist of the written notice of appeal, the decision against which the appeal is brought, and the observations of the benefit officer explaining the reasons for it. A leaflet is also enclosed, giving information about the tribunal's procedure and emphasising the appellant's right to attend with representatives.[13]

D Procedure at the hearing

i The role of the presenting officer

The benefit officer's argument is put forward by the presenting officer, an official who specialises in tribunal work. There is a suggestion that on occasion he may feel under pressure to win the case, no matter what its merits, and this may lead to its inaccurate presentation.[14] However, the *Bell* study found that there was no evidence of unfairness in the manner in which cases were presented, and like insurance officers, presenting officers often raised points favourable to the appellant.[15]

ii Attendance and representation of the appellant

The presenting officer's impartial discharge of his role is naturally more important when the appellant does not attend. In the *Bell* study only about 40 per cent of appellants attended tribunal hearings, and less than 20 per cent were represented.[16] The majority of representatives in the study were friends and relatives and not, as in insurance tribunals, trades union officials.[17] Legal assistance at the hearing is very rare indeed.[18] There is no doubt that an appellant who attends has a higher chance of success before the tribunal than one who does not.[19] The reasons for the relatively low attendance rate have been discussed already in the context of insurance tribunal hearings.[20]

If the appellant does not attend, the tribunal has power to adjourn, and may in the meantime send him a letter impressing on him the importance of his presence.[1] When an appellant has given advance notice that the specified time is inconvenient for him, this course is invariably adopted.[2] But it is rarely practicable when no explanation for non-attendance has been given. The tribunal will not know whether the appeal is serious, and it would be unfortunate to induce an appellant to attend and then dismiss his appeal.[3]

11 *Herman*, n.6, above, at p. 33.
12 See p. 589, above, for the notice required for insurance tribunal hearings.
13 Bell *Research Study on Supplementary Benefit Appeal Tribunals, Review of Main Findings: Conclusions: Recommendations* (1975, DHSS) p. 22.
14 *Herman*, n.6, above, at pp. 26–28.
15 *Bell*, n.13, above, at pp. 10–11.
16 Ibid, at p. 12: see also SBC Annual Report 1979, n.7, above, Table 13.2.
17 *Bell*, n.13, above, at pp. 15–16.
18 In 1979 there were only 300 cases where the appellant was represented by a solicitor: Annual Report 1979, n.7, above, at Table 13.2.
19 Flockhart in Adler and Bradley (eds) *Justice, Discretion and Poverty* (1976) pp. 106–107.
20 Pp. 590–591, above.
1 SI 1980/1605, r. 5(3).
2 It may be a breach of the rules of natural justice if the tribunal does not adjourn: *R v South West London Supplementary Benefits Appeal Tribunals, ex parte Bullen* (1976) 120 Sol Jo 437, DC.
3 *Supplementary Benefit Appeal Tribunals: A guide to procedure* para 38.

iii The conduct of the hearing

A major difference between hearings at insurance and supplementary benefit appeal tribunals is that the latter are conducted in private. The following may attend:[4]

(1) the parties themselves, that is, the appellant and the benefit officer;
(2) representatives for each party (generally no more than two);
(3) a bona fide researcher into the work of SBATs, with the chairman's consent.

It may be questioned whether the provision for national insurance tribunals – a private hearing when the chairman thinks that there is a good reason for it – would not be adequate.[5]

The parties (or their representatives) are entitled to be heard, to call witnesses and to put questions to any other party and his witnesses.[6] Apart from this, the procedure is for the chairman to determine.[7] It is usual in practice for the presenting officer to start by reading out the appeal documents, and then the claimant and the officer put forward their arguments.[8] There has been much criticism in the past concerning the conduct of SBAT hearings, particularly with regard to the lack of clarity with which issues are presented to the claimant and the reliance sometimes placed on documents not disclosed to all the parties.[9] But these defects should now have been put right, following the publication in 1977 of the guide to SBAT procedure – primarily for the benefit of tribunal chairmen and members.

E The powers and decisions of SBATs

i The powers of the SBATs

The supplementary benefit appeal tribunal may confirm the decision (or the refusal to review a decision), or may

> substitute for any determination appealed against any determination which a benefit officer could have made.[10]

The exact scope of the tribunal's powers under this provision is far from clear. There is no doubt that it may take a different view of the merits of the case to that adopted by the benefit officer, and that it is not limited to correcting errors of law and fact.[11] And the tribunal is not bound by any policy guidance issued to benefit officers by the Chief Supplementary Benefit Officer (though of course it must decide on the basis of the Act, regulations, court and now Commissioners' decisions). But it has never been very clear whether a tribunal may consider a matter not raised on the appeal, or take into account circumstances which were not raised initially before the benefit officer at all.[12] The *Bell* study called for

4 SI 1980/1605, r. 6. The list is not exhaustive.
5 Adler, Burns and Johnson, n.19, above, at pp. 113–114.
6 SI 1980/1605, r. 6(5). But there is no right to cross-examine an officer who is not a witness: *R(SB) 1/81*, and see p. 614, below.
7 SI 1980/1605, r. 6(1).
8 *Lynes* pp. 283–284.
9 Adler, Burns and Johnson, n.19, above, at pp. 114–116; Herman *Administrative Justice and Supplementary Benefits* (1972) at pp. 39–40; *Bell*, n.13, above, at pp. 21–22.
10 SBA 1976, s.15(3)(c).
11 See the statements of J G Monroe, Comr, in *CSB 12/81*, paras 10–13.
12 See Bell *Research Study on Supplementary Benefit Appeal Tribunals, Review of Main Findings: Conclusions: Recommendations* (1975) pp. 21–22; *Herman*, n.9, above, at p. 30.

clarification of these matters; perhaps in partial response, the procedural guide issued in 1977 urged that tribunals should not give a ruling on a question not raised by the appeal.[13] Thus, if the appeal is brought solely on the entitlement to a single payment, the SBAT should not reconsider the amount of weekly benefit. This limitation has been recently affirmed by the Commissioner, J G Mitchell. On the other hand, he held that the tribunal may legitimately consider matters 'within the purview of the original claim even if these have not previously been considered, and may in its discretion either deal with these matters as presented or adjourn to allow further investigation of them'.[14] Thus, the award of benefit for particular additional requirements could be considered on appeal, even though these had not been at issue before the benefit officer. In view of the facts that an applicant does not have to specify detailed requirements when making his claim or lodge precise grounds of appeal, it is suggested that the appeal tribunal should feel free to exercise wide powers, subject to any clear limits imposed by the Commissioner.[15]

ii Deliberation in private

Under the 1980 Rules, the tribunal *must* order all persons (with the exception of a member of the Council on Tribunals or a Senior Chairman attending the hearing) to withdraw while it is considering its decision.[16] However, the chairman may allow the clerk and bona fide researchers to stay. This marks a welcome reform to the previous position in which it had not been clear whether the clerk could ever be asked to leave.[17] It is also now plain that it is illegal for the presenting officer to remain behind while the SBAT is considering the appeal.

iii Reasons for the decision

SBATs are now under an obligation to give reasons for their determinations and state their findings on material questions of fact, and also to indicate if one of the members dissents and his grounds for doing so.[18] It was not until 1971 that there was a duty to give reasons at all (except on request), and after then there was constant complaint that the reasons were often inadequate. The Council on Tribunals and more recently the DHSS Advisory group in its guide to procedure have indicated what statements of reasons should contain, and have emphasised that it is the chairman's duty (not the clerk's) to see that they are full and lucid.[19]

F The control of tribunal decisions

i Review by benefit (or supplement) officers

Although it is provided that a tribunal decision is 'final',[20] it may later be reviewed by a benefit or supplement officer, as the case may be. It will be

13 N.3, above, at para 17.
14 *R(SB) 9/81*, para 9. However the Commissioner pointed out that SBATs do not have the wider power to consider new issues conferred by statute on insurance tribunals: see p. 591, above. Also see *CSB 19/81*.
15 In *R(SB) 1/82*, J G Monroe, Comr, took a broad view of SBAT powers, stating that they could take into account events occurring after the officer's decision.
16 SI 1980/1605, r. 6(10).
17 See the first edition of this book, p. 656.
18 SI 1980/1605, r. 7.
19 *Supplementary Benefit Appeal Tribunals: A guide to procedure* paras 69–73 and Appendix 4.
20 SBA 1976, s.15(4).

revised if it was based on mistaken facts, or in the case of supplementary benefit (though not FIS) decisions, there has been a relevant change of circumstances.[1] The same power of review exists after Commissioner decisions, though in this situation there must be fresh evidence to show the mistaken facts. The review procedure has been criticised on the ground that it removes the significance of a right of appeal to an independent tribunal if its decisions can then be revised by one of the parties, i.e. the benefit officer.[2] But there is no evidence to suggest that the power is abused, and, of course, it is primarily designed to benefit claimants where the SBAT has decided against them on an erroneous assessment of the facts.

ii Appeal to the Social Security Commissioners

There is now a right of appeal on a point of law to the Social Security Commissioners.[3] The introduction of this appeal was a major reform, which in the opinion of some critics was long overdue. They had pointed to the increasing legal complexity of the supplementary benefits scheme, and the inability of the tribunals, and for different reasons the ordinary courts, to deal with this phenomenon.[4] Before 1978 the only means of control over the legal correctness of SBAT decisions was through the prerogative orders, and the courts exercised this reviewing power with great caution.[5] As a result a right of appeal was instituted to the High Court; this was exercised on occasion and led to a number of important judicial rulings on supplementary benefits law.[6] But it was always clear that it was an interim measure and that it would be more sensible to make provision for appeal to the expert, informal tribunal which had handled national insurance appeals so successfully. This was introduced with the reform of the supplementary benefits scheme at the end of 1980,[7] and the Commissioners were consequently re-styled Social Security Commissioners to mark their increased jurisdiction. Although the Commissioners are in many ways a more accessible tribunal, there is one major disadvantage to the change. There is no legal aid for representation before tribunals as distinct from courts; this of course is also true of appeals to the Commissioner from insurance and medical appeal tribunals, but in these cases there may well be free (and effective) representation by trades union officials.[8] This is most unlikely for supplementary benefit claimants who will therefore often lack necessary assistance.

The claimant, benefit (or supplement) officer may appeal from a SBAT decision on a point of law with the Commissioner's leave. Application for such leave must be made within three months, though the Commissioner has power to extend this for special reasons.[9] If it is requested or he thinks it desirable, an oral hearing must be given for both application for leave

1 SI 1980/1643, reg 4 (supplementary benefit); SI 1980/1437, reg 12 (FIS).
2 *Herman*, n.9, above, at p. 29.
3 SBA 1976, s.15A, inserted in the Act by SSA 1979, s.6.
4 See in particular Calvert and the conclusion by Adler and Bradley in *Justice, Discretion and Poverty* (1976) pp. 183 and 207 respectively; Bradley 27 NILQ 111–119, and *Bell*, n.12, above, pp. 24–25.
5 See the discussion in the first edition of this book, pp. 657–658.
6 SBC Annual Report for 1979 (Cmnd 8033), para 13.15. Court decisions are collected in a new volume published by HMSO, *Decisions of the Courts relating to Supplementary Benefits and Family Income Supplements Legislation*.
7 SI 1980/1605. The right of appeal to the High Court was abolished at the same time: SI 1980/1601.
8 See p. 591, above.
9 SI 1980/1605, rr. 8–9.

and the appeal – though the Commissioner may dispense with this if satisfied that it is unnecessary.[10] In practice, it appears that – with the consent of the parties – the application for leave and the full appeal (if leave is granted) are considered at the same time. In contrast to SBATs, the Commissioner has rather limited powers: he may either uphold the lower tribunal's interpretation of the law or refer the case to another tribunal with directions. He is not able to allow an appeal and make an award of benefit or FIS himself, nor may he simply disallow the claim on a successful appeal by a benefit (or supplement) officer.[11]

Much the most interesting and important questions arising from the new provisions concern the Commissioners' interpretation of their jurisdiction to allow appeals from decisions 'erroneous in point of law'.[12] Here they seem to have largely followed the approach adopted for the similar jurisdiction over medical appeal tribunals and the Attendance Allowance Board: appeals will be allowed if the SBAT decision is taken in breach of the rules of natural justice, contains a wrong proposition of law *ex facie*, is not supported by any evidence, or on the facts found is one that no reasonable body could come to.[13] A failure by the tribunal to state its reasons and findings of fact clearly will be treated as a patent error of law. The Commissioners will, however, defer to the superior ability of the tribunal to assess the facts in the light of the claimant's evidence and demeanour.[14] This suggests that they will be reluctant to allow a challenge to the exercise of residual discretion in the scheme, which the SBAT may, as has been seen, exercise as fully as the benefit officer.[15] Another issue is whether the Commissioner himself may decline leave to appeal, even if he considers there is an arguable point of law, on some other ground – for example, the appeal is trivial or involves only a small sum of money. In one case, the Commissioner indicated that he might be more restrictive when the appellant is a benefit officer, while leave will always be given where the result of a successful appeal will be to grant an applicant benefit to which he is entitled.[16] No reasons need be given for refusing leave,[17] but it is hoped that this immunity will not be exploited to enable the Commissioner to decline jurisdiction where there is any major question of law involved.

In the cases which have come before the Commissioner so far, he has been unsympathetic to flimsy allegations of a breach of the rules of natural justice.[18] The ruling that a claimant does not have a right to cross-examine a hostile official before the SBAT is, however, open to criticism, since this questioning might well reveal the inadequacy of the basis of fact on which an adverse decision had been taken.[19] The principal ground for appeal seems to have been the arguable failure of the tribunal fully to record their reasons and findings of fact. The Commissioner here has emphasised that it is enough for these conclusions to be clear and relevant; the detail and style of a court judgment is not required.[20]

10 Ibid, r. 10.
11 Ibid, r. 10(8), discussed by the Commissioner in *R(SB) 6/81* and *R(SB) 13/81*.
12 SI 1980/1605, r. 8(1).
13 *R(SB) 6/81*, adopting the approach of the Commissioner in *R(A) 2/72*. See pp. 601 and 603, above.
14 *R(SB) 5/81*.
15 P. 611, above.
16 *R(SB) 5/81*.
17 SI 1980/1637.
18 See *R(SB) 9/81*.
19 See the note by J Mesher [1981] JSWL 184, criticising the decision in *R(SB) 1/81*. And also see *CSB 13/82*.
20 J S Watson, Comr, in *R(SB) 5/81*, paras 7 and 10. Also see *R(SB) 6/81, CSB 15/81, R(SB) 2/82* and the decision of the High Court in *Crake v SBC*, (1980) SB Dec 309 (Decision SB 38).

Part 3 Control by the courts

A History

As has been said at the start of this chapter, the general intention from the first decade of this century has been to keep disputes concerning state benefits away from the ordinary courts.[1] This prejudice was reinforced by experience of their unduly technical and restrictive interpretation of the workmen's compensation legislation.[2] The 1946 legislation, therefore, conferred exclusive jurisdiction on the statutory and medical authorities, and made no provision for appeal to the courts.[3] The same position obtained under the National Assistance Act. The Franks Committee on Administrative Tribunals and Enquiries thought it right that there should be no appeal from Commissioners' decisions: they were expert in their field, and it was important that a final decision should be reached quickly.[4] And at a time when the assistance scheme was largely discretionary and its tribunals regarded as largely administrative in character,[5] there was even less case for a right of appeal to the courts in this area.

After some hesitation, it became clear, however, that the Commissioners and other tribunals, such as medical appeal tribunals, were subject to judicial review by way of the prerogative orders.[6] This was an important, and on the whole welcome development. Quite apart from the general principle that it is usually desirable for the courts to have the last word on questions of law, it was seen to be important that they should occasionally be able to resolve a disagreement between the Commissioners. A tribunal may be used for this purpose, but when the number of Commissioners increased to nine or ten, the approach of three of them sitting as a tribunal would sometimes not represent the majority view.[7] Without judicial review, it would probably have been necessary to treat tribunal decisions as absolutely binding on a single Commissioner in order to secure certainty in the law.[8] Although in principle there can have been no doubt that the prerogative orders were equally available to control the decisions of assistance, and then later supplementary benefit appeal, tribunals, no reported application seems to have been made until 1973.[9] Judicial review in this area became increasingly important as further points of legal complexity were discovered.

But although the right to apply for certiorari became well established, the courts were reluctant to exercise their powers of review. In the case of the National Insurance Commissioners, the judges often deferred to their expertise;[10] in two leading cases the Court of Appeal emphasised that the courts should only intervene if there was a serious or difficult point of law,

1 See p. 581, above.
2 See 414 HC Official Report (5th series) cols 281 ff (2nd Reading of National Insurance (Industrial Injuries) Bill 1946).
3 A different approach was adopted for appeals from decisions of the Secretary of State and from pensions appeal tribunals: see pp. 583–585, above and pp. 617–620, below.
4 Cmnd 218, para 108.
5 See p. 606, above.
6 The leading case was *R v Medical Appeal Tribunal, ex parte Gilmore* [1957] 1 QB 574, [1957] 1 All ER 796, CA. See the first edition of this book, p. 645.
7 *Micklethwait* p. 123.
8 For precedent, see p. 595, above.
9 *R v Greater Birmingham Appeal Tribunal, ex parte Simper* [1974] QB 543, [1973] 2 All ER 461.
10 See *R v Industrial Injuries Comr, ex parte Amalgamated Engineering Union (No 2)* [1966] 2 QB 31, [1966] 1 All ER 97, CA; *R v Industrial Injuries Comr, ex parte Ward* [1965] 2 QB 112 at 121, per Lord Parker CJ, DC.

or there had been a difference of opinion among the Commissioners.[11] Thus, there could be occasional tolerance of an incorrect decision. The same attitude was adopted towards control of the decisions of supplementary benefit appeal tribunals, though here there was perhaps less justification. In *R v Preston Supplementary Benefits Appeal Tribunal, ex parte Moore*,[12] Lord Denning MR said the courts should only intervene when the tribunal's decision was clearly unreasonable, though they should be prepared to quash a decision if there had been an excess of jurisdiction or breach of the rules of natural justice. But the SBATs were not expert bodies, like the Commissioners, and this cautious approach was therefore hard to support. Dissatisfaction with it was largely responsible for the provision in 1978 of the appeal to the High Court from SBAT decisions, now itself superseded by the right of appeal to the Social Security Commissioner.[13]

The position has now been radically changed by the Social Security Act 1980, which institutes a right of appeal on questions of law from any decision of a Social Security Commissioner (whether on contributory benefits, supplementary benefit or FIS) direct to the Court of Appeal, or in Scotland the Court of Session.[14] The Divisional Court is therefore bypassed altogether, though it, of course, had entertained the applications for certiorari. The reason for this step is partly that the Divisional Court is very overworked and cannot devote the time necessary for the resolution of difficult points of social security law. But the change may also be thought to reflect the high standing of the Commissioners – in a sense their position in this respect is now equivalent to High Court judges.

B Appeal to the Court of Appeal

Appeal must be made with the leave of either a Commissioner or the Court of Appeal (or in Scotland, the Court of Session).[15] Regulations provide for the selection of another Commissioner, or Tribunal of Commissioners, to hear the application for leave, where this is impracticable for the person, or body, which took the challenged decision.[16] Application for leave must be made within three months of notice of the decision; it is for the Commissioner to whom the application is made to decide whether a hearing should be given.[17]

As yet it is not clear what the Commissioner and the Court of Appeal will consider to be questions of law. But some guidance can be obtained from rulings on this matter in the context of appeals from tribunals *to the Commissioner*,[18] and also from the way in which the courts used to exercise their powers of judicial review. It has been held, for example, that a wholly mistaken inference from primary facts,[19] or the wrongful exclusion of relevant evidence is to be regarded as an error of law.[20] The advantage of

11 *R v National Insurance Comr, ex parte Michael* [1976] 1 All ER 566, [1977] 1 WLR 109; *R v National Insurance Comr, ex parte Stratton* [1979] QB 361, [1979] 2 All ER 278.
12 [1975] 2 All ER 807, [1975] 1 WLR 624, CA. See the first edition of this book, pp. 657–658 for a fuller discussion of judicial review of SBAT decisions.
13 P. 613, above.
14 S.14.
15 Ibid, s.14(2).
16 SI 1980/1321, reg 2.
17 Ibid, regs 4 and 5.
18 Pp. 601, 603 and 614, above.
19 See *R v Medical Appeal Tribunal, ex parte Gilmore*, n.6, above.
20 *R v Industrial Injuries Comr, ex parte Ward*, n.10, above.

appeal over review is that it will no longer be necessary for the applicant to show that there was an error of law *on the record* or a jurisdictional error of law; any error of law will suffice, and it is suggested there is no room for any distinction between substantial and minor, technical errors.

Failure to comply with the rules of natural justice will raise a question of law for appeal, so something should be said briefly about the application of these rules to Commissioners' decisions. The Divisional Court has held that they must observe the rules, and that there was a breach when further medical evidence was received after the hearing and it was not put to the parties for their comments.[1] In *R v Deputy Industrial Injuries Comr, ex parte Moore*,[2] the Court of Appeal ruled that the Commissioner must base his decision on the evidence, and where a hearing is held, listen fairly to the parties' contentions. But natural justice did not require the strict rules of evidence to be complied with, and he could therefore take into account medical opinions given in previous cases.

Part 4 Pensions Appeal Tribunals

A Composition and structure

Pensions appeal tribunals (PATs) were first set up in 1919; they did not, however, have jurisdiction over claims in respect of service after 1921.[3] Two different types of tribunal were established by the Pensions Appeal Tribunals Act 1943. The first deals with appeals on *entitlement*, where the issue is whether the Secretary of State was right to reject the claim. The hearing is *de novo* and there is no onus on the appellant to show that the decision was wrong.[4] Both medical and legal issues come before these tribunals, and this is reflected in their composition. The chairman is a lawyer, and one of the other two members is a doctor. Both these persons must be of seven years' standing in their profession. The third member is a retired or demobilised officer or serviceman of the same sex and rank as the person in respect of whose disability the claim is made.[5] The second type of tribunal entertains appeals from the *assessment* of disabilities.[6] It has two medical members, both doctors of more than seven years' standing, one of whom is appointed to act as chairman of the tribunal.[7] The third member is an ex-serviceman or officer of the same status and rank as the claimant.

Members and chairmen are appointed by the Lord Chancellor. Further, it is the Lord Chancellor's Office which is responsible for providing the tribunals' staff. Another significant aspect is that they are organised on the

1 *R v Deputy Industrial Comr, ex parte Jones* [1962] 2 QB 677, [1962] 2 All ER 430. See p. 592, above, for the argument that the Commissioner was taking the advice of a medical assessor.
2 [1965] 1 QB 456, [1965] 1 All ER 81. For Commissioners' rulings that hearsay evidence is admissible, though of little weight, see e.g. *R(G) 1/51*; *R(U) 2/56*; *R(U) 10/63*; *R(U) 2/74*. In the last case, R G Micklethwait, Chief Comr, ruled that the findings of fact of an industrial tribunal may be admitted as evidence before the statutory authorities: see p. 110, above.
3 Ch 9, pp. 338–340, above, for the history of war pensions.
4 *Barratt v Minister of Pensions* (1946) 1 WPAR 1225. The rules concerning the burden of proof discussed at pp. 348–351, above, therefore, apply.
5 Pensions Appeal Tribunals Act 1943, Sch, para 3.
6 Pp. 348–351, above, for the rules regarding assessment.
7 Pensions Appeal Tribunals Act 1943, Sch, para 3.

presidential system.[8] The President of the Pensions Appeal Tribunals is responsible for their administration, as well as sitting himself as a chairman. The Tribunal Rules confer on him various specific powers, e.g. to order the disclosure to the claimant of official documents,[9] to direct that a case be placed on the deferred list,[10] and to make arrangements where an infirm appellant is unable to attend a hearing.[11] The value of the presidential system is that chairmen have available an independent source of advice; moreover, the President is a person of sufficient authority to ensure that the tribunals are, and are seen to be, independent of the government.[12] The tribunals are national, both in terms of their administration and jurisdiction.[13] In practice they sit in regional centres (as well as in London) for reasons of convenience to the claimant.[14]

B Procedure

The procedural rules governing appeals to PATs are detailed, and compared with the provisions concerning other social security tribunals, are often favourable to the appellant.

(1) The appellant has a year within which to appeal against a decision on entitlement or a final assessment, or three months in the case of an interim assessment.[15]
(2) On receipt of the notice of appeal (which need not state its grounds), it is for the Secretary of State to prepare a Statement of Case, containing the relevant facts and the reasons for the decision. This is sent to the claimant for him to submit, if he wishes, an answer; the Statement of Case, the claimant's answer and the Secretary's comments on this (if any) are sent to the Pensions Appeal Office.[16]
(3) The appellant may apply to the President of the PATs for disclosure of official documents which are likely to be relevant to his case.[17]
(4) The parties are given ten clear days' notice of the hearing.[18]
(5) It is the duty of the tribunal to assist any appellant who appears unable to make the best of his case, and further the chairman may examine an unrepresented appellant's witnesses, if he requests.[19]
(6) Though the tribunal may obtain the opinion of a medical specialist or other technical expert, it must be sent to the parties for them to comment on, and either may request a further hearing.[20]

The appellant's interests are particularly safeguarded by the provision that the appeal is not to be heard in his absence, unless he has requested this;

8 See Wraith and Hutchesson, *Administrative Tribunals* (1973), pp. 85–86.
9 SI 1980/1120 r. 6, and also see r. 22. (These rules govern PATs in England and Wales: there are comparable Scottish tribunal rules: SI 1971/2124.)
10 SI 1980/1120, r. 10.
11 Ibid, r. 21.
12 See the intervention by the President concerning the departmental practice of reviewing cases after an assessment appeal: Annual Report of the Council on Tribunals for 1969–70, paras 62–63.
13 *Wraith and Hutchesson*, n.8, above, at pp. 74, 174.
14 They sit at 12 centres in the UK: Report on War Pensioners for 1976, HC 472, p. 4.
15 Pensions Appeal Tribunals Act 1943, s.8
16 SI 1980/1120, r. 5.
17 Ibid, r. 6.
18 Ibid, r. 8(1); cp the provisions for 'reasonable notice' of insurance tribunal and SBAT hearings, pp. 589, 609, above.
19 Ibid, rr. 11(3), 13(1).
20 Ibid, r. 15.

even then the tribunal has discretion not to hear the case.[1] The President may make arrangements, inter alia, for the appellant to be interviewed at home by one or more members of the tribunal, if he is too infirm to attend, and the incapacity is likely to be of a long duration.[2] If for some reason an appeal is not prosecuted, e.g. the appellant simply fails to attend without explanation, it may be put on the deferred list.[3] An application may then be made within the next year for the case to be heard,[4] and this will be granted unless the President is satisfied 'that the appellant's failure to prosecute the appeal was due to his wilful default'.[5] After the lapse of a year, an appeal still on the deferred list will be struck out and may not be brought again without the President's leave.[6]

There are other interesting provisions which do not necessarily benefit the claimant. The PAT may itself summon expert or other witnesses,[7] as well as taking into account the evidence produced by the parties; evidence is not to be refused merely on the ground that it would be inadmissible in a court of law.[8] Rule 18 specifically provides that the tribunal's decision may be announced immediately after the hearing, or within seven days; but only a short indication of reasons need be given. It is surprising that there is no requirement to state them more fully.[9] It is even more surprising that there is no provision at all concerning majority decisions of a PAT. The nominated judge on appeal has, therefore, ruled that the decision of a tribunal must be unanimous and, if the members cannot agree, the case must be referred to another tribunal.[10]

Like medical appeal tribunals, PATs may use the expertise of their medical member (or in assessment cases, members) in assessing the claimant's condition.[11] The medical member may conduct an examination of the appellant with his consent.[12] But the member's views are not to be taken as evidence which is itself capable of rebutting the presumption that the injury was attributable to service.[13] If the medical member is inclined to doubt the appellant's case, an independent medical specialist should be consulted and his advice given to the claimant for comment.[14]

C Appeal to the nominated judge

From decisions on entitlement there is a further right of appeal on a point of law to a High Court judge nominated by the Lord Chancellor to hear

1 Ibid, r. 20.
2 Ibid, r. 21.
3 Ibid, r. 10.
4 Ibid, r. 26(3).
5 Ibid, r. 26(4).
6 Ibid, r. 26(5)(b).
7 Ibid, r. 12(4).
8 Ibid, r. 12(5).
9 See pp. 591, 612, above, for local tribunals and SBATs respectively.
10 *Brain v Minister of Pensions* [1947] KB 625, [1947] 1 All ER 892 (PAT disallow claimant's appeal by a majority); *Minister of Pensions v Horsey* [1949] 2 KB 526 (majority allow appeal by claimant).
11 For medical appeal tribunals, see pp. 597–599, above.
12 SI 1980/1120, r. 17.
13 *Moxon v Minister of Pensions* [1945] KB 490: for the presumption, see pp. 349–351, above.
14 *Diamond v Minister of Pensions* (1947) 1 WPAR 313 at 317. For the correct procedure when an independent medical specialist's advice is sought, see *Harris v Minister of Pensions* (1948) 4 WPAR 82.

such appeals (hence the phrase, 'the nominated judge').[15] Leave of either the tribunal or the judge himself must first be obtained; this should be granted whenever there is any reasonable doubt as to the correctness of the tribunal decision.[16] Quite exceptionally in the social security system, a claimant's legal expenses may be paid where a successful application for leave is made, either by him or the Secretary of State, or where the latter makes an unsuccessful application for leave.[17] The grounds on which an appeal may be made were fully considered by Denning J (as he then was) in *Armstrong v Minister of Pensions*:[18] they include a wrong direction on law, incorrect admission or exclusion of evidence and breach of the procedural rules or the rules of natural justice. Unless all the facts are before the judge, the correct course is for him to remit the case for the PAT to reconsider.

There is no further appeal to the Court of Appeal.[19] This may afford some justification for the view expressed in two cases by Denning J, that the doctrine of *stare decisis* does not apply in its full rigour in war pension cases.[20] Decisions of the judge are binding on PATs, but need not be followed by the judge in another case if there is a strong reason for taking a different view. There are now very few cases taken to the nominated judge.[1] Part of the explanation for this may be the availability since 1970 of an alternative procedure: the claimant and the Secretary of State may present a joint application to the President of the PATs for him to direct that the tribunal's decision be treated as set aside, either on the ground that additional evidence is available or because of some error of law, and that the appeal be heard again by the tribunal.[2]

There is no appeal at all from the decision of an assessment tribunal. The reason given for this is that there are no questions of law involved in such decisions.[3] Nor is the alternative procedure discussed in the last paragraph available.

Part 5 Reference to the European Court of Justice

The significance of European Economic Community law for particular social security benefits is fully discussed in the next chapter. The 1971 EEC Social Security Regulation[4] (as amended) is directly applicable; it must, therefore, be implemented by the British courts and the statutory

15 Pensions Appeal Tribunals Act 1943, s.6(2): for the distinction between an appeal to the High Court and to a nominated judge, see Wraith and Hutchesson *Administrative Tribunals*, (1973) p. 160. In Scotland appeal lies to the Court of Session.

16 *Atkinson v Minister of Pensions* (1947) 1 WPAR 981.

17 SI 1980/1120, r. 28.

18 (1948) 3 WPAR 1449.

19 Pensions Appeal Tribunals Act, s.6(2). There is also no right of appeal to the Court of Appeal from a decision of the nominated judge refusing leave to appeal: see *Ex parte Aronsohn* [1946] 2 All ER 544, CA.

20 *James v Minister of Pensions* [1947] KB 867, [1947] 2 All ER 432; *Minister of Pensions v Higham* [1948] 2 KB 153 at 155.

1 In 1978, there were 8 applications for leave, of which 2 were granted: Annual Report on War Pensioners for 1978, HC 133, p. 4

2 Pensions Appeal Tribunals Act 1943, s.6(2A), added by the Chronically Sick and Disabled Persons Act 1970, s.23. For a case in which it was unsuccessfully argued that there was maladministration in the Department's decision not to agree to a joint application to the President, see Fourth Report of the PCA 1970–71, HC 490, Case No C214/73.

3 *Morris v Minister of Pensions* [1948] 1 All ER 748.

4 Reg 1408/71: see pp. 627-642, below.

authorities.[5] In most cases it will be for the national courts to interpret Community regulations but, in order that there may be uniformity of interpretation in the member states, there is a procedure under which a point of difficulty may be referred to the European Court of Justice in Luxembourg (ECJ) for it to give a preliminary ruling.[6] Article 177 of the Treaty of Rome provides that the Court of Justice has jurisdiction to give preliminary rulings on the interpretation of the Treaty and the validity and interpretation of Community legal acts, e.g. regulations and directives. It further provides in paragraphs 2 and 3:

> Where such a question is raised before any court or tribunal of a Member State, that court or tribunal may, if it considers that a decision on the question is necessary to enable it to give judgment, request the Court of Justice to give a ruling thereon.
>
> Where any such question is raised in a case pending before a court or a tribunal of a Member State, against whose decisions there is no judicial remedy under national law, that court or tribunal shall bring the matter before the Court of Justice.

A The discretion to refer

i 'Court or tribunal'

Under the second paragraph of article 177, a question may be referred for a preliminary ruling by a 'court or tribunal'. This enables any part of the Supreme Court of Judicature to ask for a preliminary ruling in a suitable case.[7] The Social Security Commissioner clearly is entitled to refer, and it seems that a local insurance tribunal could do so.[8] It is possible that the statutory authorities could refer a contributions question to the European Court;[9] this step might not contravene the requirement in the Social Security Act 1975 that a contributions question must be determined by the Secretary of State.[10] In any event it is not clear that the Secretary of State himself could make a reference, since he may not constitute a 'tribunal' for the purpose of article 177.[11]

ii The decision must be 'necessary'

A question may only be referred to the European Court if a decision on it is 'necessary' for the national court or tribunal to give judgment. In the leading English case, *H P Bulmer Ltd v J Bollinger SA*, Lord Denning MR, took the narrow view that a court should only refer a point, if a decision on

5 For the direct applicability of EEC law, see Lasok and Bridge *An Introduction to the Law and Institutions of the European Communities* (2nd edn) pp. 199 ff and Collins *European Community Law in the United Kingdom* (2nd edn) ch 2. The directly applicable effect of the EEC Social Security Regulation was recognised by the Commissioner, J G Monroe, in *Re a Holiday in Italy* [1975] 1 CMLR 184 *(R(S) 4/74*, para 7); *Re Medical Expenses incurred in France* [1977] 2 CMLR 317.

6 *Lasok and Bridge*, n.5, above, at pp. 209–216; *Collins*, n.5, above, at pp. 83–105; Jacobs and Durand *References to the European Court: Practice and Procedure* (1975), *passim*.

7 The Divisional Court asked for a preliminary ruling in *R v National Insurance Comr, ex parte Warry* [1977] 2 CMLR 783. So far no other court has done so in a social security case.

8 It is believed that only one tribunal has made a reference to the ECJ, and this was subsequently withdrawn.

9 This course is not ruled out by the Commissioner's decision in *Re Retirement to Ireland* [1977] 1 CMLR 1.

10 S.93: p. 583, above.

11 The ECJ which may give a preliminary ruling on the interpretation of art 177 itself has interpreted 'tribunal' broadly: see *Collins*, n.2, above, at pp. 85–88; *Jacobs and Durand*, n.6, above, at pp. 156–157.

it would be *conclusive* of the case.[12] The Commissioner, however, has followed the broader approach of Stephenson LJ in the *Bulmer* case,[13] and ruled that a reference is permissible if a case cannot be determined without a decision on the point referred to the European Court.[14] This seems the better view, and is consistent with that adopted by English judges in other cases.[15]

iii Factors relevant to the exercise of the discretion

The factors to be taken into account in deciding whether to refer were discussed at length by the Court of Appeal in the *Bulmer* case.[16] The desirability of ensuring uniform interpretation of Community law must be balanced against the costs and delay entailed by a reference. The more important and difficult the point of law, the more inclined the judge should be to refer it to the Luxembourg Court.[17] The Commissioner has generally decided questions of European law himself, and in only a few reported cases so far has he discussed at length whether to request a preliminary ruling. In one, *Re an Illness in France*,[18] the Commissioner decided to refer a question on the invitation of the DHSS. It was emphasised that the claimant welcomed this step. The issue – the meaning of 'worker' for the purposes of the EEC Regulation[19] – was one which had been previously ruled on by the Commissioner, and it was clear that an authoritative interpretation from the ECJ was now desirable.[20] In *Re a Visit to Italy*,[1] however, the Commissioner refused to refer, largely because of the delay involved and the fact that the claimant might not be paid benefit for the interim period. A reference will not be made if the sum in question is very small.[2]

B The duty to refer

In the circumstances covered by its third paragraph quoted above, article 177 imposes a duty to refer. Which British courts or tribunals deciding issues of social security law are under this duty, because 'there is no judicial remedy' against their decision? In *Re a Holiday in Italy*,[3] the Commissioner, J G Monroe, decided that he was not bound to refer, as the prerogative order of certiorari was then available to quash his decision for an error of law, including a wrong interpretation of the EEC Regulation; it did not matter that leave had to be obtained from the Divisional Court before the order could be applied for. This decision has been criticised on the ground that it assumed that leave to apply for certiorari is granted as a

12 [1974] Ch 401, [1974] 2 All ER 1226, CA.
13 Ibid, at p. 428 and 1240.
14 *Re an Illness in France* [1976] 1 CMLR 243; *Kenny v Insurance Officer* [1978] 1 CMLR 181.
15 See Graham J in *Lowenbrau München v Grünhalle Lager International* [1974] 1 CMLR 1 at 9; Pennycuick VC in *Van Duyn v Home Office* [1947] 1 WLR 1107, 1115–1116.
16 N.12, above, at 423–425, 429–430 and 1235–1236, 1241–1242.
17 Ibid, at 430 and 1241, per Stephenson LJ.
18 N.14, above.
19 P. 630, below, for the decision of the ECJ on this point.
20 The earlier decision of the Commissioner in *Re an Ex-Civil Servant* [1976] 1 CMLR 257 did not satisfy the DHSS.
1 [1976] 1 CMLR 506, (*R(I) 1/75*).
2 *Re Search for Work in Ireland* [1978] 2 CMLR 174.
3 [1975] 1 CMLR 184 (*R(S) 4/74*, para 8).

matter of course, where a point of Community law is involved.[4] Now that there is an appeal to the Court of Appeal,[5] admittedly only with leave, there is a somewhat stronger argument for holding that the Social Security Commissioner is never bound to refer to the ECJ.

It is clear that a High Court judge entertaining an appeal on a contributions question would be under a duty to request a preliminary ruling since there is no appeal from his decision. It is arguable that the Court of Appeal is bound to refer under article 177(3) on the ground that leave is required for an appeal to the House of Lords, but the point was left open by Stephenson LJ in the *Bulmer* case.[6]

4 See Bridge 1 European L Rev 13 at 19; Jacobs 2 European L Rev 119; cp Collins, n.5, above, at p. 123.
5 See p. 616, above.
6 N.12, above, at 430. See now *Hagen v Fratelli and Moretti* [1980] 3 CMLR 253, CA.

Chapter 16

International and European law

Part 1 General

International collaboration and coordination in the social security field has been a widespread phenomenon in the second half of the twentieth century. In part it is associated with the general movement on human rights;[1] in part it results from an increase in the mobility of labour,[2] a consequence not only of individual initiative but also of governmental stimulus, notably within the European Communities.[3] The legal instruments directed towards these ends may be divided into three groups.

A Minimum standards

In the first place, there are multilateral instruments imposing obligations on those states which ratify them to conform to certain minimum standards. At a comprehensive, but necessarily vague, level there is the Universal Declaration of Human Rights conferring on an individual the right to 'security in the event of unemployment, sickness, disability, widowhood, old age or other lack of livelihood in circumstances beyond his control'.[4] More specifically there is the work of the International Labour Organisation (ILO) established after the First World War,[5] but reconstituted as an agency of the United Nations in 1946.[6] Among its manifold activities, this body through its assembly, comprising not only goverments but also representatives of employers and employees, enacts conventions which once ratified by individual states are binding on them as norms of international law.[7] There have been a number of such conventions in the

1 See e.g. Jenks *Human Rights and International Labour Standards* (1960) ch 7; Watson 6 Jo Soc Pol 31.

2 See generally Lyon-Caen *Droit Social International et Européen* (5th edn) pp. 6–17; Bohning *The Migration of Workers in the United Kingdom and the European Community* (1972); International Labour Organisation *Social Security for Migrant Workers* (1977).

3 Treaty of Rome, arts 48–51, on which see: Wyatt and Dashwood *The Substantive Law of the EEC* (1980) chs 14–15; *Lyon-Caen*, n.2, above, at pp. 198–251; Collins *The European Communities* (1975) vol 2, ch 4.

4 (1948) UN Doc. A/811, art 25. See also, Jenks *Social Justice in the Law of Nations* (1970) pp. 69–79.

5 By Part XIII of the Treaty of Versailles 1914. See on the early history, Lowe *International Protection of Labour* (1921).

6 By the International Labour Conference, Montreal.

7 See generally: Jenks, n.4, above; Lawly *The Effectiveness of International Supervision* (1966).

field of social security but the most important is that which lays down minimum standards to deal with the social hazards of illness, invalidity, unemployment, old age, maternity, death and industrial accidents.[8] The original plan was to prescribe both minimum and maximum standards, but the latter was abandoned in 1952 and even the former appears in a muted form: a state ratifying the convention need only conform to the standard of three of the nine risks specifically dealt with.[9] The standards under the ILO Convention had to be of a nature that would be feasible for states of widely differing economic development. Moreover, it applied only for the protection of employed workers. Within the ambit of Western European industrialised states, it was hoped to improve on the standards, and work to this end has been undertaken by the Council of Europe.[10] What eventually emerged in 1964 was the European Code of Social Security.[11] This was in fact not so much a code in the usual sense of the term, but a convention like that of the ILO, open to ratification by member states. Similar in scope to the ILO Convention, it nevertheless was a little more exacting as regards both the standards to be achieved for individual social hazards and the extent of commitment vis-à-vis the range of those hazards – the Code contains twelve points[12] and the ratifying state is to conform to at least six of these.[13] Despite the fact that the majority of member states has been slow to ratify the Code (though the United Kingdom has already done so), steps were taken to reach even higher standards in a Protocol which was annexed to it.[14]

B Equality of treatment and aggregation of entitlement

It is obvious that with the growth of migrant labour, the multinational enterprises and increased foreign travel possibilities, problems would be caused for individuals subjected to social security systems based entirely on residence and/or contribution conditions. While the need of a state to protect its own workers temporarily employed abroad has always been recognised and to a large extent catered for by its own internal rules, there was naturally a reluctance to extend the provisions of a system to foreigners, at the cost to national contributors or taxpayers, without there being a reciprocal arrangement in the foreigner's own system. Until recently, therefore, the typical solution to the problem was found in bilateral reciprocal treaties. Most obviously this occurred at an early stage in the history of national insurance in relation to the Republic of Ireland.[15] The Social Security Act 1975[16] explicitly provides that to give effect to any

8 Convention nos 102, 210 UNTS 131: Holloway *Social Policy Harmonisation in the European Community* (1981) pp. 12–14; *Jenks*, n.4, above, at pp. 107–111; *Lyon-Caen*, n.2, above. at pp. 70–73.
9 Art 2(a).
10 *Lyon-Caen*, n.2, above, at pp. 90–97.
11 European Treaty Series, No 48. See also Explanatory Reports on the Code (1961), Council of Europe.
12 In fact provision for old age covers three points, and that of medical care two points: art 241.
13 But in some cases only 3 hazards need be specified.
14 The Protocol forms part of the same Treaty as the Code. At the time of writing it has still not been ratified by the UK.
15 The power to give effect to reciprocal arrangements on unemployment income was conferred by the Irish Free State (Consequential Provisions) Act 1922, s.6(1)(c).
16 S.143, as amended by SSA 1981, s.6. Agreements previously in force are preserved by the Social Security (Consequential Provisions) Act 1975, Sch 3, para 10.

such agreement the Crown may by Order in Council modify or alter the Act, and there are over 30 such Orders currently in force.[17] Within the Western European context, the Council of Europe has introduced a convention based on a principle of multilateral reciprocity.[18] If and when ratified, this will replace bilateral agreements between member states.

By far and away the most important international coordination in this field has been that achieved by the European Economic Community. One of the pillars of the Treaty of Rome, as expressed in article 3(c), is the 'abolition . . . of obstacles to freedom of movement for persons'. The implications of this objective for social security legislation are spelled out in article 51:

> the Council shall . . . adopt such measures in the field of social security as are necessary to provide freedom of movement for workers; to this end, it shall make arrangements to secure for migrant workers and their dependants:
> (a) aggregation, for the purpose of acquiring and retaining the right to benefit and of calculating the amount of benefit, of all periods taken into account under the laws of the several countries;
> (b) payment of benefits to persons resident in the territories of Member States.

The direction was quickly implemented by a Council Regulation of 1958,[19] borrowed substantially from the Coal and Steel Community.[20] While the principles underlying the 1958 Regulation were clear – equal treatment for all workers of member states, aggregation of insurance periods served while working in different member states, exporting of benefits from one state to another – the rules themselves posed grave difficulties of interpretation. Moreover, the frequent rulings of the European Court of Justice (ECJ) produced a body of law not always anticipated by the draftsmen of the Regulation. In the light of these difficulties, the 1958 Regulation was replaced by a new set of provisions in 1971.[1] This new Regulation was formulated without any regard to the social security systems of the new members (including the United Kingdom) admitted in 1972.[2] However, there is no doubt that the 1971 Regulation, as amended, is now incorporated into British law,[3] and forms an important part of the social security system. As such, it is the subject matter of the bulk of this chapter; its effect on the adjudication of claims was discussed in chapter 15.[4]

C Harmonisation

None of these measures affected the huge differences between the systems of the member states as regards their structure, their range of benefits, the rates payable and the mode of financing them.[5] An economic argument for

17 They are listed in a note to SSA 1975, s.143 in 45 Halsbury Statutes (3rd edn) 1241.
18 European Convention on Social Security 1972, European Treaty Series No 78. At the time of writing this has been ratified only by Austria and Luxembourg. See *Holloway*, n.8, above, at pp. 116–134 for the history of, and problems associated with, international coordination treaties.
19 Reg 3/58, OJ 1958, 561.
20 European Convention on Social Security for Migrant Workers 1957.
1 Reg 1408/71, OJ 1971 L149, supplemented by the implementing reg 574/72, OJ 1972 L74.
2 See the observations of the ECJ in *Brack* [1976] 2 CMLR 592 at 616.
3 Under art 189 of the Treaty of Rome regulations are directly applicable in all member states, and this principle is applied in British law by the European Communities Act 1972, s.2(1). See *Re Medical Expenses incurred in France* [1977] 2 CMLR 317.
4 Pp. 620–623, above.
5 For accounts of the major differences between the national systems see: Lawson and Reed *Social Security in the European Community* (1975); van Langendonck 2 ILJ 17; *Kaim-*

harmonisation, based on the theory that different rates and systems of contributions for firms distort competition, has been doubted: contributions are only one element of the employer's total labour cost and higher social security charges may be offset by lower wages.[6] More common these days are the arguments based on reducing the complexity and administrative costs involved in resolving conflicts of rules and of achieving greater social justice for workers who have been employed in different states.[7] Whatever the merits of the policy, it was envisaged as a goal by the draftsmen of the Rome Treaty:

> Member States agree upon the need to promote improved working conditions and an improved standard of living for workers, so as to make possible their harmonisation while the improvement is being maintained.[8]

In fact, progress in this field has been almost non-existent. The obstacles were fully expressed at a Conference convened by the Commission in 1962: the goal of harmonisation was a very vague one; the enormous differences between the systems of member states in terms both of structure and of level of support posed political as well as technical difficulties; the Commission lacked the power to achieve the goal; and national governments were unwilling to commit themselves.[9] The single, and not very important, achievement has been some standardisation in the area of industrial diseases.[10]

Part 2 Scope of EEC Regulation

A Introduction

It is important to appreciate that the purpose of the EEC Regulation is not to create a common European scheme of social security, but rather for the most part to coordinate the national systems.[11] A migrant who is covered by the Regulation will still claim benefit from a particular national institution because of an entitlement either under that state's law alone or under that law supplemented by Community provisions. He is not to be prejudiced by the fact that at some stage during his working life he has moved from one member state to another. This guiding principle, enshrined in article 51 of the Treaty of Rome,[12] is implemented by more specific rules (discussed in

---

Caudle; Dupeyroux *Évolution et tendances des systèmes de sécurité des pays membres des Communautés Européennes et de la Grande Bretagne* (1966); and the EEC Commission Comparative Tables of the Social Security Systems in the Member States, published periodically.

6 See *Holloway*, n.8, above, at pp. 44–49; Wedel 102 Int Lab Rev 591, 592–605; van Langendonck, n.5, above, at p. 24.

7 Collins *The European Communities* (1975) vol 2, ch 6; van Langendonck, n.5, above, at pp. 24–27.

8 Art 117. It is still unclear whether the Commission has legal power to propose harmonisation measures or whether the task is reserved for the member states: see Holloway *Social Policy Harmonisation in the European Community* (1981) ch 2.

9 See EEC, *Conférence Européenne sur la Sécurité Sociale* (1964).

10 Resulting from the Commission Recommendations of 23 July 1962, OJ 2188/62 and 66/462/CEE, OJ 2696/66.

11 See Holloway *Social Policy Harmonisation in the European Community* (1981) Part II; Watson *Social Security Law of the European Communities* (1980) chs 3 and 4. For a recent statement of the principle by the ECJ, see *Gravina* [1981] 1 CMLR 529 at 543, but see *Testa* [1981] 2 CMLR 552 at 575, pointing out that in some respects the Regulation is more than a coordinating measure: p. 641, below.

12 P. 626, above.

Part 4 of this chapter), which are designed to alleviate the problems of the migrant worker. Thus, he is not to be excluded from entitlement to benefit on the ground of his nationality. More importantly, he may keep social security entitlements which he has earned under the law of the country he has left; this is significant because many national systems are essentially territorial and rights may be lost when a beneficiary leaves the country.[13] And under a third principle he may conserve rights which he is in the process of acquiring in one state by aggregating the relevant contributions or residence periods with those paid or served in the state to which he moves.

The application of the very complex law is in the hands of the courts and tribunals of the member states, but difficult points may be referred to the European Court of Justice.[14] The Court has frequently emphasised that the concepts in the Regulations are to be given a common Community meaning – otherwise the uniform application of the coordinating rules would be endangered. Examples of this approach will be found in the rest of this Part of the chapter. The other major contribution of the ECJ is its consistent ruling that the purpose of the Regulation in the light of article 51 is to protect the rights of migrants, and that, therefore, a worker moving from one country to another is not to lose rights which he would enjoy under national law alone.[15] As will be seen later, this principle has considerable repercussions for the scope of the overlap provisions in the Community Regulation. At this stage, it is perhaps useful to point out that this insistence by the Court on preserving the full rights enjoyed under national law necessarily means that perfect coordination is not achieved. Coordination is applied to the advantage, but never to the detriment, of the migrant.[16]

A final introductory point is that article 6 of the Regulation replaces bilateral and multilateral conventions to which the member states are parties, even if the migrant worker would be better placed to claim under the particular convention.[17] It has, however, been argued in some recent cases that this provision is invalid insofar as it deprives a migrant of a benefit which he would otherwise enjoy under a reciprocal convention – an argument strikingly similar to that accepted by the ECJ in other contexts – but hitherto the Court has refrained from ruling on this issue.[18]

B Legislation

Regulation 1408/71 governs national legislation concerned with benefits[19] for unemployment, sickness, invalidity,[20] old age, industrial injuries and

13 See pp. 386–393, above, for the relevant British rules.
14 See ch 15, pp. 620–623, above.
15 The *Petroni* principle, as it is usually called now, is discussed at pp. 635–637, below.
16 See Holloway, n.11, above, at pp. 151–157.
17 *Walder* [1973] ECR 599.
18 See *Giulani* [1977] ECR 1857 and *Galinsky* [1981] 3 CMLR 361. Watson, n.11, above, at pp. 198–201 suggests that the ECJ should reject the argument. Also see *R(S) 6/81*, paras 16–17.
19 I.e. payments in cash or in kind, including up-rating increases and supplementary allowances: reg 1408/71, art 1(t). Lump sums granted in lieu of a pension (e.g. to a widow on remarriage: *Vandeweghe* [1974] 1 CMLR 499) are also included, but not payments intended for purposes unconnected with the hazard, e.g. to finance contributions: *Dekker* [1966] CMLR 503.
20 This is deemed to include the British attendance allowance: reg 1209/76, and see *Re a Road Accident in Ireland* [1976] 1 CMLR 522 (*R(A) 4/75*).

diseases, and survivors, as well as death grant and family benefits.[1] The legislation referred to includes regulations and other implementing instruments and even private law agreements provided that they serve to establish a scheme under such legislation and are the subject of a declaration by a member state.[2] All instruments so governed by Regulation 1408/71 are to be specified by the member states.[3] However, a failure to do this may not, it seems, exclude a law, for in a case under the 1958 Regulation the ECJ held that it applied both to present and future legislation, irrespective of notification.[4] Apart from war pension and civil service schemes,[5] all social security benefits, whether contributory or non-contributory, dealing with the hazards listed above are included. The characterisation of the benefit for the purposes of the Regulation is a matter of Community, not national, law.[6]

But 'social security' must be distinguished from 'social assistance' which is outside the scope of the Regulation.[7] No definitions of these two concepts are provided; and the ECJ faced with the problem of classifying schemes has understandably been reluctant to offer any. It is, however, clear from its various judgments on the point[8] that it regards as characteristic of social assistance schemes those based on 'individual assessment of need', as opposed to the 'conferring of . . . a statutory defined status'. This criterion seems most unreliable. The British supplementary benefits and family income supplements schemes confer for the most part clear entitlements to benefit, but they are rightly regarded by the British government as 'social assistance'.[10] More persuasive, it is submitted, are the guidelines suggested by Mayras, Advocate-General, in his opinion in *Frilli*:[11] whether or not, vis-à-vis other social security benefits, the scheme in question has a supplementary or subsidiary quality. In deciding this, regard should be had, for example, to the extent to which in assessing entitlement account is taken of the receipt of other benefits and of the fulfilment of maintenance obligations, and whether or not the fund concerned is subrogated to the rights of the beneficiary against third parties. In conclusion, it should be noted that there would be considerable problems in applying the principles of the Regulation to social assistance: the level of such assistance is fixed by reference to the cost of living in the particular area, and a means-tested benefit could therefore not be easily exported from one country to another. Moreover, there would be understandable objections to the payment of these benefits, financed by general taxation rather than contributions, to people abroad.[12]

1 Reg 1408/71, art 4(1).
2 Ibid, art 1(j); and see *Vaassen-Göbbels* [1966] CMLR 508.
3 Reg 1408/71, art 5. See OJ 1973 C43 for the UK legislation so specified. Positive specification of a scheme is conclusive: *Beerens* [1977] ECR 2249.
4 *Dingemans* [1965] CMLR 144.
5 Reg 1408/71, art 4(4). See *Even* [1979] ECR 2019; *Lohmann* [1979] 3 CMLR 618.
6 *Jordens-Vosters* [1980] 3 CMLR 412.
7 Reg 1408/71, art 4(4).
8 *Frilli* [1973] CMLR 386; *Costa* [1974] ECR 1251; *Biason* [1975] 1 CMLR 59.
9 *Biason*, ibid, at 70.
10 Neither the SBA 1976 nor the FISA 1970 have been specified as being governed by the Regulation: cf n.3, above.
11 N.8, above, at 393–397.
12 See the excellent discussion in *Watson*, n.11, above at pp. 109–111.

C Persons

The 1971 Regulation now applies

> to employed or self-employed persons who are or have been subject to the legislation of one or more Member States and who are nationals of one of the Member States or who are stateless persons or refugees residing[13] within the territory of one of the Member States, as also to the members of their families[14] and their survivors.[15]

Nationals of non-member states are excluded, but a person who is a national at the time of the payment of contributions, and hence at the acquisition of the relevant rights, is covered; it does not matter then that he is no longer a national at the date of claim.[16] Under the 1958 Regulation only 'workers' were covered,[17] though this was interpreted by the Court to include people who were resident or present in another member state for reasons other than employment there and so were not migrant workers stricto sensu.[18] The 1971 Regulation originally broadened the range of persons covered to include anyone compulsorily insured under a general social security scheme where he could be identified as an employed person because of the way in which the scheme was administered or financed: in other words, the test was one of affiliation to the social security system as an employee rather than one of labour law.[19] The ECJ construed the provision to include a claimant who had been paying contributions as an employee, but was self-employed at the time of the claim – an interpretation which benefited British self-employed who contribute to the same general scheme as 'workers'.[20]

In 1978 the Commission formulated proposals to extend the Regulation to the self-employed, and also (after a suggestion by the European Parliament) to the insured non-employed. After considerable delay the Council of Ministers accepted the extension to the former group and the Regulation has now been amended.[1] Legally this is done under articles 52–66 of the Treaty of Rome which set out the freedom of establishment and the freedom to provide services across national frontiers. In contrast, it is difficult to see any adequate legal basis for extending coordination of social security to the non-employed – they do not enjoy freedom of movement under the Treaty.[2] Some people are, therefore, still excluded

13 'Residence' means 'habitual residence': reg 1408/71, art 1(h); see further, *Angenieux* [1973] ECR 935; *Di Paolo* [1977] ECR 315.

14 In general, the members of the family included are determined by the law under which the benefit is provided; but if that law regards as members only persons living under the same roof as the relevant person, this condition is regarded as satisfied if such persons are 'mainly dependent' on him: reg 1408/71, art 1(f).

15 Ibid, art 2(1) as amended by reg 1390/81. 'Survivors' are determined in a way similar to 'members of the family' (n.14, above) but survivors who are themselves nationals of a member state or are resident stateless persons or refugees are included irrespective of the nationality of the deceased person; reg 1408/71, art 2(2). Also see *Laumann* [1978] 3 CMLR 201.

16 *Belbouab* [1979] 2 CMLR 23, noted 4 European L Rev 106.

17 Reg 3/58, art 4(1).

18 See *Unger* [1964] CMLR 319; *Hessische Knappschaft* [1966] CMLR 82. There is no reason why the same principle should not apply to the new term, 'employed or self-employed persons'.

19 Reg 1408/71, art 1(a): see the first edition of this book, pp. 671–672.

20 *Brack* [1976] 2 CMLR 592. See Watson *Social Security Law of the European Communities* (1980) pp. 68–71 for a discussion of this case.

1 Reg 1408/71, amended by reg 1390/81, OJ 1981 L143. The implementing regulation 574/72 has been amended by reg 3795/81, OJ 1981 L378.

2 Watson 6 European L Rev 290 at 292.

from the coverage of the Regulation: students are outside the scheme,[3] while an 'au pair' girl is included if she has been required to pay contributions.[4]

Part 3 Choice of competent legislation

The first substantive issue determined by Community law is the resolution of the conflict of legislative systems which might potentially govern a migrant. Article 13(1) of the 1971 Regulation prescribes that a migrant employed or self-employed person '. . . shall be subject to the legislation of a single Member State only'. The meaning of this provision, which had no exact equivalent in the 1958 Regulation, used to be thought a little uncertain.[5] The generally accepted view,[6] and that which is consistent with the rulings of the ECJ, holds that the reference to the exclusive jurisdiction of one member state applies for the purpose only of imposing on the worker *liabilities* which arise under one social security system, most importantly that of paying contributions.[7] Subject to certain principles governing overlaps (discussed later[8]), it does not prevent him acquiring rights to benefits under the legislation of other states.

Article 13(2) then lays down rules determining the member state to whose legislation the relevant person is subject. In general this is the state where his place of work is situated even if he is normally resident in another member state or the enterprise employing him has its place of business in another state.[9] But the general rule is subject to the following exceptions in the case of employed persons.

(1) The first and most important exception is that of 'posting' abroad. Where the worker employed in one member state by an undertaking to which he is normally attached is posted by the employer to work in another member state, he remains subject to the legislation of the first state if the anticipated duration of the work in the second state does not exceed 12 months, and even for longer if the prolongation of the period was due to unforeseen circumstances and the authority of the second state has given its consent.[10] The policy is to avoid the administrative inconvenience of changes in insurability for short periods. The rule applies to cases where the 'undertaking' is merely an employment agency,[11] and less obviously it was held in *Angenieux*[12] to

3 *Kuyken* [1978] 2 CMLR 304.
4 *Tessier* [1979] 1 CMLR 249.
5 See the discussions in Lipstein *Law of the European Communities* (1974) pp. 96–99 and in Jacobs (ed) *European Law and the Individual* (1974) ch 4; Tantaroudas 8 Rev Trim Dr Eur 36.
6 See Watson *Social Security Law of the European Communities* (1980) pp. 136–137.
7 See esp. *Moebs* [1964] CMLR 338.
8 Pp. 634–638, below.
9 Art 13(2)(a) and (b). For this purpose, mariners are regarded as employed in the state whose flag is flown by the vessel in which they serve: art 13(2)(c). Civil servants and members of the armed forces are regarded as employed in the state to whose administration or force they belong: art 13(2)(d)–(e). In *Van der Vecht* [1968] CMLR 151 it was held that the whole of a journey (in transport provided by the employer) from the place of the worker's residence across the frontier to the place of work was subject to the law of the place of work. The 'employment' involved in the journey was regarded as inseparable from the employment on the site.
10 Reg 1408/71, art 14(1).
11 *Manpower* [1971] CMLR 222.
12 [1973] ECR 935.

apply to an agent on commission from his employers who worked for nine months every year in another member state.

(2) An employee of an international transport undertaking whose work takes him to more than one member state is subject to the law of the place where the undertaking has its registered office or place of business.[13] But if the undertaking has a branch in another member state, an employee working for that branch is governed by the law of that state.[14] Finally, if the worker is employed principally in the territory of the member state in which he resides, the law of that state will prevail, notwithstanding that the undertaking has no place of business or branch there.[15]

(3) A worker, other than (2), who pursues his employment in two or more member states is governed by the law of the state where he resides if it is one of those where he works;[16] if it is not, then by the law of the state where his employer has his registered office or place of business.[17]

(4) There are special rules for frontier workers and mariners.[18]

There are now under the amended regulation comparable rules for the self-employed. For example, someone normally self-employed in one state who performs work in another remains subject to the former's legislation if the anticipated duration of that work is not more than 12 months.[19] And a person normally self-employed in two or more member states is subject to the law of the state where he resides, provided he does some of his work there.[20] Where a person is simultaneously employed in one state and self-employed in another, the law of the former state is applicable, subject to the qualifications specified with regard to particular activities in Annex VII to the Regulation.[1]

Part 4 General principles

The rules described in Part 3 determine the legislation applicable to a given individual – they indicate what will be referred to in the remainder of this chapter as the 'competent legislation', or, where more appropriate, the 'competent state'. It remains to consider the principles of Community law to which that legislation is subject.

A Non-discrimination

It is enunciated in the Regulation that subject to special provisions

> Persons resident in the territory of one of the Member States . . . shall be subject to the same obligations and enjoy the same benefits under the legislation of any Member State as the nationals of that State.[2]

13 Reg 1408/71, art 14(2)(a).
14 Ibid, art 14(2)(a)(i).
15 Ibid, art 14(2)(a)(ii).
16 Ibid, art 14(2)(b)(i).
17 Ibid, art 14(2)(b)(ii).
18 Ibid, arts 14(3) and 14b.
19 Ibid, art 14a(1)(a).
20 Ibid, art 14a(2).
1 Ibid, art 14c.
2 Ibid, art 3.

The principle of equality of treatment for nationals of member states is the least original: it has been a regular feature of international instruments.[3] It governs both obligations of the individual, most importantly the payment of contributions, and rights to benefit. It also applies as regards periods of residence in another territory. Thus, in *Hirardin*,[4]

> A Belgian national working in France, and affiliated to the insurance scheme there, sought to have taken into account in the computation of his benefit periods of employment in Algeria. The ECJ held that the French authorities could not rely on a *loi* of 1964 which purported to restrict the aggregation of such periods to French citizens.

Further it is now well established that covert discrimination, e.g. discrimination against those not born or resident in the competent state, is equally prohibited.[5] However, in *Kenny* the Court ruled that the competent institution of a state was not required always to treat facts occurring in another member state – in that case imprisonment in Ireland – as equivalent to facts occurring in the former state (there Britain) which constitute a ground for loss or suspension of the right to a benefit.[6] It is for the national court to determine whether it is appropriate on the facts to apply the prohibition of covert discrimination.

B Aggregation of periods of insurance

The principle of aggregation of periods of insurance, employment or residence abroad for the purposes of satisfying the contribution conditions of the competent legislation is referred to in the Preamble of the Regulation, but not in its General Part. This is because it does not apply to all benefits or allowances, particularly those resulting from an industrial accident or disease[7] where entitlement is based on the employment alone. For each of the benefits for which the principle is relevant (sickness and maternity,[8] invalidity,[9] old age and death,[10] unemployment,[11] family[12] and orphans[13] benefits) the rule is stated explicitly in the Special Provisions in substantially the same form:

> the competent institution of a Member State whose legislation makes the acquisition, retention or recovery of the right to benefits conditional upon the

3 E.g. European Code on Social Security, European Treaty Series, No 48, art 73, ILO Convention No 102, 210 UNTS, art 68.
4 [1976] ECR 553.
5 *Palermo* [1980] 2 CMLR 31. In *Re Residence Conditions* [1978] 2 CMLR 287 (*R(A) 2/78*), J G Monroe, Comr, ruled that the claimant, an Irish national born in Eire and widow of an Irish worker, should be treated for the purposes of the residence conditions for attendance allowance as if she had been born in Britain – otherwise there would have been covert discrimination in that more stringent residence conditions were imposed because of the claimant's place of birth. But see *Re an Italian Widow* [1982] 2 CMLR 128.
6 [1978] 3 CMLR 651. For the further proceedings in this case, see p. 401, above.
7 Though in this latter case there is partial recognition of the principle with regard to pneumoconiosis where periods of activity in a prescribed occupation in another member state may be aggregated: reg 1408/71, art 57(3). For some reason, the provision does not extend to other industrial diseases.
8 Ibid, art 18(1).
9 Ibid, art 38(1).
10 Ibid, art 45(1).
11 Ibid, art 67(1)–(2).
12 Ibid, art 72.
13 Ibid, art 79(1).

> completion of insurance periods or periods of employment or residence shall, to the extent necessary, take account of insurance periods or periods of employment or residence completed under the legislation of any other Member State as if they were periods completed under the legislation which it administers.[14]

It is this rule which enables a migrant to move from one state to another, confident that he is preserving rights which he is in the process of acquiring in the former state. The benefit which he may eventually claim from the competent institution of the second state is then assessed on the basis of the principles discussed in the next section. The aggregation rule is obviously easiest to apply when both systems employ contributory social security schemes, but it is clear that it also assists a migrant who moves from a state where there is such a system to another which determines entitlement purely on residence or some other territorial criterion.[15]

What constitutes the appropriate 'insurance periods or periods of employment or residence' for the purposes of the rule quoted above is determined by the legislation under which they were completed or treated as completed.[16] So in *Murru*[17] an Italian worker claiming a disability pension in France was unable to rely on a period of unemployment in Italy, for while the period might have counted if it had been completed in France, in Italy it was not treated as equivalent to a 'period of employment'. Conversely, a period of employment under the law of a member state which does recognise it as an 'insurance period' must also be so recognised in the state where benefit (in the particular case, unemployment benefit under article 67) is claimed.[18] For the purposes of British law, a woman claiming retirement pension on the basis of her husband's contributions may rely on periods of insurance completed by him in another member state.[19] The aggregation provisions may be used where, as in Britain,[20] entitlement to invalidity benefit is dependent on prior receipt of sickness benefit. Shortly after an ECJ ruling to this effect,[1] the Regulation was amended to provide that where entitlement under the legislation of one state is so dependent, account must be taken of any period, during which the person received sickness or invalidity benefit under the law of another state; the first state must treat this as a period during which sickness benefit was paid under its own law.[2]

C Calculation and apportionment

Subject to the deterritoriality principle described below, it is for the member state under whose legislation benefit is claimed to assess the amount payable, but in so doing it is bound to apply certain rules of Community law. If, as under the British legislation, the amount of benefit

14 Ibid, art 18(1).
15 See the discussion in Holloway *Social Policy Harmonisation in the European Community* (1981) pp. 121–123, 177–178, and see Forde 1980/1 LIEI 23.
16 Reg 1408/71, art 1(r), 1(s) and 1(s)(a). Where for the purpose of invalidity or old age pension the competent legislation requires the completion of insurance periods in an occupation subject to a special scheme or in a special employment, periods completed in another member state may only be taken into account if they are involved in the same occupation or employment: arts 38(2) and 45(2).
17 [1972] CMLR 888.
18 *Frangiamore* [1978] 3 CMLR 166.
19 Reg 1408/71, Annex VI, Part J, para 2.
20 Pp. 162–165, above.
1 *Warry* [1977] ECR 2085 (*R(S) 1/80*).
2 Reg 1408/71, art 40(3), inserted by reg 2595/77.

varies according to the number of dependants, those residing in the territory of another member state are to be treated as if residing in the territory of the determining member state.[3] As regards the short-term benefits for sickness, maternity, unemployment and industrial injury, where reference is made to the average earnings of the claimant, account is to be taken only of earnings received in the determining member state.[4] In the case of unemployment benefit, this will be based on the worker's last employment there, but if such employment did not exceed four weeks, reference is made instead to the normal earnings in the territory where the claimant is residing for an employment which is equivalent or similar to his last employment in another member state.[5] Any up-rating of benefits under national legislation must of course be applied to those workers claiming under the Regulation.[6]

The difficult question now arises as to the extent to which a benefit may be reduced on the ground of overlap with benefit payable for a similar risk for a similar period by another member state. The matter is governed by two principles elaborated in the Regulation, but these may be ousted by a third principle enshrined in the decisions of the ECJ.

i Accumulation independently of Community law

This 'ousting' principle has been the subject of a number of the leading decisions on the scope of Community law and has given rise to considerable debate. In interpreting the overlapping provisions of the 1958 Regulation (the predecessor to that made in 1971) the ECJ drew inspiration from the working of article 51 of the Treaty of Rome (quoted on p. 626) which the Regulation was designed to implement. That article was concerned to *extend* the rights of migrant workers, not to reduce them.[7] The Regulation, in furtherance of this aim, contained principles whereby rights acquired under different legislative systems might be aggregated and co-ordinated. The overlapping rules were complementary to these aggregation and co-ordination principles but had no force independently of them. If, without recourse to the Regulation, an individual had acquired rights under the legislation of different states, these could not be overridden by the Regulation:[8] an interpretation to the contrary would conflict with article 51 as reducing rather than extending the facilities of migrant workers.[9] Any limitation on the ability to accumulate had thus to be provided for in the national laws of the systems in question.[10]

The 1971 Regulation reformulated some of the rules and also introduced the provision in article 13(1) that workers governed by the Regulation were to be subject to the legislation of a single member state only. It was at one time conjectured that the intention was to alter the position resulting from

3 Reg 1408/71, arts 23(3), 39(4), 58(3), 68(2).
4 Ibid, arts 23(1), 58(1), 68(1). Mutatis mutandis the same applies to awards based on 'standard' earnings.
5 Ibid, art 68(1). For frontier workers see *Fellinger* [1981] 1 CMLR 471.
6 Reg 1408/71, art 11.
7 *Moebs* [1964] CMLR 347; *Guissart* [1967] ECR 425 at 433; *Niemann* [1974] ECR 571 at 579.
8 *Ciechelski* [1967] CMLR 192 at 205; *Guissart* n.7, above, at 433; *Duffy* [1971] CMLR 391 at 400.
9 *Duffy* n.8, above, at 339–400; *Kaufmann* [1974] ECR 517 at 525; *Niemann* n.7, above, at 578; *Massonet* [1975] ECR 1473 at 1481–1482.
10 *Guissart* n.7, above, at 434; *Massonet* n.9, above, at 1484.

the cases under the 1958 Regulation.[11] But, as has already been suggested, the object of article 13(1) was to avoid the overlapping of *liability* under two systems rather than interfere with *rights*.[12] The ECJ has confirmed that the principle whereby a worker may accumulate benefits independently of Community law has not been abrogated by the 1971 Regulation. In *Petroni*[13]

> The Belgian Social Security institution, in calculating an old age pension payable on the basis of Belgian legislation alone to a worker, who also had acquired title under the Community aggregation and apportionment rules to benefit in Italy, sought to invoke an article of the 1971 Regulation[14] purporting to limit the maximum payable when a worker had been subject to the legislation of two or more member states in respect of the same risk. It was categorically held by the ECJ that, to the extent that the article in question imposed a limitation on the accumulation of two benefits acquired in different member states by a reduction in the amount of benefit acquired under national legislation alone, it was void as being inconsistent with the fundamental objective of article 51 of the Treaty of Rome: the aim of Community law was to extend the protection of social security systems to cover migrant workers, and unless there were compensating advantages for a worker under Community law, it was not to be interpreted as limiting his rights.

It follows that the two other principles shortly to be discussed apply only where a claimant invokes the Regulation for the purposes of benefiting from the aggregation principles.

The effect of the *Petroni* ruling is that migrant workers may obtain a social security advantage over persons who have stayed throughout their life in one member state: the former are able to accumulate a pension acquired under the Community Regulation with a pension to which they are entitled under national law alone, or, of course, two benefits both acquired under national law.[15] In this way, the Regulation does not effect perfect coordination of benefits. Despite this, the ECJ has repeatedly affirmed the principle.[16] In the *Giuliani* case[17] it held that it did not constitute unfair discrimination against non-migrants; their situation was not comparable with the position of those who experienced the difficulties of working abroad. The differences, the Court added, could not be resolved until there was a common social security system or harmonisation. Moreover, the *Petroni* principle was even extended in this case, despite the submissions of Advocate-General Warner: it applied even where, as in the instant case, the claimant had to invoke the deterritoriality rule in article 10 to obtain payment, because he was resident outside the member state where he was entitled to benefit.[18] The Community overlap rules are only applicable when the claimant relies on the aggregation provisions of the EEC regulation to acquire title to benefit.

11 Cf *Tantaroudas* 8 Rev Trim Dr Eur 56–57, and see Watson *Social Security Law of the European Communities* (1980), p. 183.
12 P. 631, above.
13 [1975] ECR 1149. See to the same effect, *Strehl* [1977] 2 CMLR 743.
14 Art 46(3), p. 638, below.
15 See Holloway *Social Policy Harmonisation in the European Community* (1981) pp. 178–181.
16 E.g. *Manzoni* [1977] ECR 1647; *Greco* [1977] ECR 1711; *Mura* [1979] ECR 1819.
17 [1977] ECR 1857, noted 3 European L Rev 49.
18 The deterritoriality principle is not relevant to the *acquisition* of benefit: see p. 638, below.

It is arguable, however, that the weaknesses of this approach are mitigated by another principle stated by the Court in a number of recent cases. Nothing in the Regulation precludes the member states applying their own overlap laws to benefits acquired under the laws of other member states, including benefits acquired there with the aid of Community law.[19] But if the application of national overlap rules is less favourable to the claimant than the employment of the Community rules regarding aggregation and apportionment (discussed on p. 638, below), the latter must be applied instead.[20] National law may achieve the result which cannot be reached under the Community Regulation. The British overlapping regulations do not apply to benefits payable under the laws of other states, though there is now power to introduce suitable provisions.[1]

ii No overlap of short-term or family benefits

Article 12(1) of the 1971 Regulation provides that

> This Regulation can neither confer nor maintain the right to several benefits of the same kind for one and the same period of compulsory insurance. However, this provision shall not apply to benefits in respect of invalidity, old age, death (pensions) or occupational disease which are awarded by institutions of two or more Member States . . .

If, then, as a result of the aggregation provisions, a claimant acquires title for the same period under more than one system for a sickness, maternity, unemployment, industrial injury, family benefit, or death grant, he can receive no more than is payable under any one such system. The rule does not, however, apply to benefits payable under voluntary schemes,[2] nor, of course, if the aggregation arises independently of the Regulation.[3]

iii Apportionment of long-term benefits

The Regulation contains detailed and complicated rules for apportioning the amount payable where entitlement to the long-term benefits is based on an aggregation of periods completed in different member states. These rules therefore apply to all old-age and survivors' pensions, but as regards invalidity benefit an important distinction is made. If a claimant to such a benefit has completed periods of insurance *exclusively* under legislation of member states all of which calculate the amount of benefit independently of the duration of such insurance periods[4] (as e.g. the basic component in the UK invalidity pension), there is no need of apportionment and the ordinary rule in article 12(1) against overlap applies.[5] If, however, one or more of the legislations under which periods of insurance have been completed determine the amount according to the duration of such periods (as with the earnings-related component in the British invalidity pension)[6]

19 *Greco*, n.16, above; *Mura*, n.16, above.
20 *Naselli* [1979] 1 CMLR 270; *Viola* [1979] 1 CMLR 635.
1 SSA 1979, s.15. See *Re an Irish Widow* [1978] 2 CMLR 178 (*R(U) 2/78*) and *Re Industrial Disablement* [1979] 1 CMLR 653, where the Commissioner applied the *Petroni* principle.
2 The meaning of 'voluntary', however, remains obscure, cf reg 1408/71, art 1(a).
3 See *Walsh* [1980] 3 CMLR 573, where the ECJ construed reg 574/72, art 8 (prohibiting overlap of maternity benefits) only to apply where the claimant was actually entitled to two maternity benefits for the same period under the aggregation rules.
4 The legislation referred to is listed in Annex IV of reg 1408/71.
5 Ibid, art 37.
6 P. 164, above.

then the apportionment rules on old age pensions are applied by way of analogy.[7] These may be summarised as follows.

(1) Each state in which the claimant has completed periods of insurance of at least 12 months must make two calculations of the pension payable.[8]

(2) The first assessment is that payable under the legislation of that state without regard being had to periods completed in other member states.[9]

(3) The second assessment is based on the theoretical amount that would have been payable if all periods (including those of less than 12 months)[10] completed in other member states had been completed in the member state making the calculation – often referred to as the 'highest theoretical amount'. This amount is then reduced according to the proportion of the periods completed in the individual state to the total of periods completed in all member states.[11] (E.g. C has completed 300 months in state X and 100 months in state Y. If state X pays a pension of £30 a week on 300 months' contributions and £40 on 400 months', the second assessment will be £40 (highest theoretical amount) multiplied by $\frac{3}{4}$ = £30 a week.)

(4) The claimant is entitled from any of the relevant states to either (2) or (3) whichever is the higher.[12] But if and insofar as the total thereby acquired exceeds the highest theoretical amount, each state is to reduce the benefit payable on a proportionate basis.[13] (It was this rule which was the subject of the *Petroni* decision:[14] the highest theoretical amount can therefore be exceeded if the beneficiary is entitled under the competent legislation independently of the Regulation.)

(5) The amount payable under (4) may, however, be exceeded where a claimant is permanently resident in a member state under whose legislation he is entitled to a minimum pension. If that state would have granted a pension greater than (4) had all the periods of insurance aggregated under the Regulation been completed there, it must pay the claimant a supplement to raise the pension to that greater amount.[15]

D Deterritoriality

The deterritoriality principle necessary for a proper co-ordination of the systems is that the right to benefit acquired under the legislation of one member state should continue notwithstanding any change either in the legal system applicable or in the transfer of residence or presence to

7 Reg 1408/71, art 40(1). Classification of invalidity benefit into these two categories is rather oddly a question for the national law concerned, not for Community Law: *Dingemans* [1965] CMLR 144.

8 Reg 1408/71, arts 46(1) and 48(1).

9 Ibid.

10 Ibid, art 48(2).

11 Ibid, art 46(2). For examples of the calculation see: *Ciechelski* [1967] CMLR 192; *Niemann* [1974] ECR 571; *Petroni* n.13, above; and *Plaquevent* [1975] ECR 1581; *Menzies* [1981] 1 CMLR 1980. If the total number of periods exceeds the maximum required by the legislation of one of the member states in question, that state calculates the proportion according to such maximum rather than the total number of periods actually completed: reg 1408/71, art 46(2)(c): see *Mura* [1980] 3 CMLR 27.

12 Reg 1408/71, art 46(1).

13 Ibid, art 46(3).

14 [1975] ECR 1149.

15 Reg 1408/71, art 50(1). See *Torri* [1977] ECR 2299, and now *R v Social Security Commissioner, ex parte Browning* [1982] 1 CMLR 427, where the ECJ ruled that in British law there is no 'minimum benefit'.

another member state. The principle is therefore concerned with the protection of acquired rights, rather than rights which are in the course of being acquired (the subject of the previous two sections).[16] It is particularly important for long-term benefits, where there is little need to maintain links between the claimant, wherever he is residing or staying, and the state under whose legislation the benefit has accrued. The 1971 Regulation thus provides that:

> invalidity, old age or survivors' cash benefits, pensions for accidents at work or occupational diseases and death grants acquired under the legislation of one or more Member States shall not be subject to any reduction, modification, suspension, withdrawal or confiscation by reason of the fact that the recipient resides in a territory of a Member State other than that in which the institution responsible for payment is situated.[17]

Within its scope, this overrides national legislation disqualifying claimants for absence abroad with, it seems, a retroactive effect on provisions already in force.[18] As regards short-term and family benefits, there is, however, a need for the national authorities to exert greater control on the activities of the claimant, in particular regarding his availability for work. The general principle quoted above therefore does not apply; instead there are special rules for the various categories of benefit.

i Sickness and maternity benefit

The availability of benefit in kind (medical services) is the reason for special provision here. Three situations are envisaged by the Regulation. In the first, the relevant person resides in a member state other than the competent state. If he satisfies the conditions of entitlement under the legislation of the latter, he is entitled to cash benefits and benefits in kind as provided by the state of residence.[19] The rule applies by analogy to benefits claimed by members of his family in the member state where they are permanently resident.[20] The second situation is that in which migrants and/or members of their family, while resident in another member state, return to the competent state for a visit. The obvious solution applies that they receive the benefit (cash or kind) from the competent state as if they were resident there, but it is rather surprisingly provided that this holds true even if they had already received benefit for the same sickness or maternity before their stay.[1] The third and final situation is that in which the claimant (or a member of his family) is resident in the competent state but visits another member state. To claim the benefits from the latter state he must show that he satisfied the conditions of entitlement under the legislation of the competent state and *either*

(1) his condition necessitated immediate benefits during the stay in the other state, *or*
(2) he was authorised by the competent state to transfer his residence to the other state[2], *or*

16 See the remarks of J G Monroe, Comr, in *R(S) 7/81*, para 9.
17 Reg 1408/71, art 10(1).
18 *Re an Absence in Ireland* [1977] CMLR 5, where the Commissioner held SSA 1975, s.82(5)(a) inapplicable, an interesting application of the principle of supremacy of Community law.
19 Reg 1408/71, art 19(1).
20 Ibid, art 19(2).
1 Ibid, art 21.
2 The authorisation can be refused only if such a movement would be prejudicial to the claimant's state of health or his receipt of medical treatment: ibid, art 22(2).

(3) he was authorised by the competent state to go to the territory of the other state to receive there treatment appropriate for his condition.[3]

Where, under these rules, cash benefits are payable under the legislation of the state of residence or presence, the rate and conditions for receipt (e.g. medical certification and examination) are governed by that legislation.[4] As regards benefits in kind, their cost is reimbursed by the institution of the competent state.[5]

ii Industrial injury benefits

As applied to the industrial injury benefits, the deterritoriality principle has two dimensions:[6] on the one hand, it enables benefit to be paid for accidents happening, or industrial diseases incurred, during work in a member state other than the competent member state;[7] on the other hand, in whichever member state the accident took place or disease was incurred, it provides for the receipt of benefit in kind or money in states other than the competent member state.[8] For this latter purpose, the rules described above for sickness and maternity apply.

iii Unemployment

The special considerations of unemployment requiring separate treatment are the problem of controlling the claimant's genuine availability for work, and the sometimes conflicting objective of encouraging him to transfer his search for employment to another member state where more vacancies exist.[9] The first objective is responsible for modifications to both the aggregation and the deterritoriality principles. The application of the normal aggregation rule is generally subject to the condition that the unemployed person must have been last employed (or insured) in the state under whose legislation he claims benefit.[10] He cannot simply move to a member state and claim unemployment benefit there on the basis of the contributions paid in another state. There are, however, exceptions in the case of frontier workers,[11] and for persons who make themselves available to the employment services of the country in which they reside; this latter group may receive benefit under the legislation of that state as if they had just been employed there.[12]

More important is the restriction on the exportability of unemployment benefit. A person who is entitled to benefit in one member state and who

3 Ibid, art 22(1). The authorisation cannot be refused if the treatment in question cannot be provided in the time normally necessary for obtaining the treatment in the territory of the competent state: ibid, as amended by reg 2793/81, art 1. See *Pierik* [1979] ECR 1977. The condition appears to be, for practical purposes, the same as that applied generally under the British legislation (p. 389, above): see *Re a Visit to Holland* [1977] 1 CMLR 502; *R(S) 6/81*, paras 13–14.

4 Reg 1408/71, art 19(1)(b).

5 Ibid, art 36.

6 See *Re a Visit to Italy* [1976] 1 CMLR 506 (*R(I) 1/76*).

7 Reg 1408/71, arts 52, 57. See e.g. *Bertholet* [1966] CMLR 191, and *Manpower* [1971] CMLR 222. Some industrial injury schemes cover journeys to work, others do not. In order that the position taken in the competent legislation should prevail, it is provided that 'an accident while travelling which occurs in the territory of a member state other than the competent state shall be deemed to have occurred in the territory of the competent state': reg 1408/71, art 56. See *Re a Car Accident in West Berlin* [1979] 2 CMLR 42.

8 Reg 1408/71, arts 52, 54 and 55.

9 Collins *The European Communities* (1975) vol 2, pp. 63–77.

10 Reg 1408/71, art 67(3). For the aggregation rule, see p. 633, above.

11 Ibid, art 71(a)(ii).

12 Ibid, art 71(b)(ii): see *Di Paolo* [1977] ECR 315.

travels to another to look for work may be paid benefit in the second state if —

(a) he has been registered with the employment services of the first state for at least four weeks prior to his departure, and

(b) he registers with the equivalent services of the second state and subjects himself to the control procedures there.[13]

Under this arrangement benefit is payable by the second state only for a maximum of three months (or less if the maximum period of entitlement under the legislation of the first state is exceeded).[14] If the person returns to the competent state within three months, he continues to be entitled to benefit from that state, but if he returns later he loses his right unless the institution of that state extends the time limit.[15]

It has recently been argued that the provision for loss of entitlement from the competent state after three months' absence is void, as restricting the free movement of workers guaranteed under articles 48–51 of the Treaty of Rome.[16] But the Court rejected this, pointing out that in this area the Regulation was more than a coordination measure: the provisions created a new Community right, free from the requirement to observe the control procedures of the competent state for three months, and it was therefore reasonable to attach conditions to it. The *Petroni* principle was therefore inapplicable. If, however, the claimant is entitled to benefit from the state to which he has moved to look for work under the law of that state alone, the principle does apply and the Regulation is irrelevant.[17] Finally, it may be noted that the Commission has produced proposals to extend the time during which benefit may be exported, and also to permit migrants in some cases to claim benefit from the state to which they move.[18] As yet, these have not been implemented by the Council of Ministers.

iv Family benefits

The Regulation distinguishes between 'family allowances', i.e., periodical cash payments determined exclusively by reference to the number and, where appropriate, the age of the members of the family (e.g., the British child benefit); and 'family benefit', i.e. benefits in cash or kind, including 'family allowances', intended to meet 'family expenses' (other than childbirth) and coming within the scope of the Regulation.[19] If the competent state for the worker's claim is not France, he is entitled to claim family benefits for members of his family[20] residing in another member state as if they were residing in the competent state.[1] If the competent state is France, for members of his family residing in another member state the worker is entitled to such allowances as are provided for by the legislation

13 Reg 1408/71, art 69(1). For Commissioner's decisions applying these requirements, see *Re an Absence in Germany* [1978] 2 CMLR 603 (*R(U) 5/78*); *Re Search for Work in Ireland* [1978] 2 CMLR 174.

14 Reg 1408/71, art 69(1)(c). The cost of benefit is reimbursed by the state where the person was last insured: ibid, art 70(1).

15 Ibid, art 69(2). The principles to be applied by the state where the person returns late are discussed in *Coccioli* [1979] 3 CMLR 144.

16 *Testa* [1981] 2 CMLR 552, noted 6 European L Rev 296.

17 *Bonaffini* [1975] ECR 971.

18 See Watson 6 European L Rev 290.

19 Reg 1408/71, art 1(u). Also see ibid, art 77.

20 For the meaning of 'members of family' see n.14, above, p. 630.

1 Reg 1408/71, art 73(1). See e.g. *Re Family Allowance for Irish Children* [1976] 1 CMLR 515.

of such state.[2] The reason for this special provision for France is the peculiarly high level of family support prevailing there.[3] This preserves for that country the rule which applied everywhere under the earlier 1958 Regulation. It was intended to achieve uniform rules for all member states by 1973, but no progress has been made to this end.[4] Benefits are payable by the appropriate institution of the competent member state normally to the worker himself, but if it is established that the benefit is not being applied for the members of the family there is power to pay it instead to another person actually maintaining the members of the family, and if that person (and the family) is resident abroad this will be expedited by the social security institution in that country.[5]

In addition to these rules concerning the deterritoriality of family benefits, there are also some overlapping provisions which are worth noting. Entitlement to these benefits and a pensioner's dependant's allowance under the law of the competent state is to be suspended if entitlement to equivalent benefits arises under the law of another state, e.g. where the children are residing.[6] The ECJ has emphasised that benefit must actually be received in the latter state for entitlement under the competent legislation to be suspended,[7] and that in any case where the amount of family benefit suspended is greater than the sum paid by the state of residence, the competent state must continue to pay the difference: otherwise the goal of free movement would not be reached.[8] Recently, the Court has applied the *Petroni* principle, so that a person does not lose family benefits under the relevant 'choice of legislation' provisions in the Regulation when he moves from one state to another, and under the law of the first state he was entitled to a higher benefit than that paid by the second state.[9]

2 Reg 1408/71, art 73(2).
3 Cf *Dupeyroux* ch 4; Watson *Social Security Law of the European Communities* (1980) ch 15.
4 *Watson*, n.3, above, at p. 239; Holloway *Social Policy Harmonisation in the European Community* (1981), pp. 147–148.
5 Reg 1408/71, art 75(1).
6 Ibid, arts 76 and 79(3).
7 *Ragazzoni* [1978] ECR 963.
8 *Rossi* [1979] ECR 831.
9 See *Laterza* [1981] 1 CMLR 158 (construing art 77(2)(b)(i)), and *Gravina* [1981] 1 CMLR 529 (construing art 78(2)).

Appendix

CHAPTER 1 SOCIAL SECURITY AND SOCIAL POLICY

pp. 33–34 *Tax liability of beneficiaries* In his Budget speech of 9 March 1982, the Chancellor of the Exchequer indicated that mobility allowance would no longer be taxable. It was subsequently announced that, by way of extra-statutory concession, tax paid on this benefit since its introduction in 1975 would be refunded to the beneficiary.

CHAPTER 3 UNEMPLOYMENT BENEFIT

pp. 83–84 *Subsidiary employment* The law which allows for the disregard of subsidiary employment has been substantially amended by SI 1982/96 (on which see SSAC Report, 1982, Cmnd 8486). The earnings limit in condition (a) has been raised to £2 per day. Condition (c) (consistency with full-time employment) has been abolished; and, as an alternative to condition (d) (not usual main occupation), the claimant may now show that the subsidiary employment is charitable work organised either by a private charity or a local or health authority.

pp. 102–103 *Availability* The same instrument (SI 1982/96) also contains some of the reforms to the availability condition anticipated in the text. The categories of those deemed to satisfy the condition have been extended to cover persons (a) undertaking, as members of a group, duties arising from an emergency (eg fire, flood, mountain or cave accident) and (b) attending a work camp under the auspices of a charity or a local authority to provide some community service, but only for a maximum period of 14 days within one calendar year. Finally, a qualification is made to the general rule (see *R (U) 1/53*) that to satisfy the availability condition the claimant must be prepared immediately to accept an offer of employment. Where 'the circumstances are such that it would not be reasonable to require him . . . to make himself available at less than 24 hours notice', he is deemed to be available if such notice is sufficient for him to undertake suitable employment or attend for interview.

CHAPTER 4 BENEFITS FOR SICKNESS AND DISABILITY

pp. 174–175 *Attendance allowance: continual supervision* In *R(A) 5/81*, the Commissioner reached two important conclusions on the 'continual supervision' requirement. First, the 'substantial danger to himself or others', for the avoidance of which the supervision is necessary, includes not only the risk of injury caused to the claimant or others *by himself*, but also such a risk where caused *by others*, eg in a road accident. Secondly, it is wrong for the Attendance Allowance Board, or its delegate, to disregard an event in which injury has occurred simply on the ground that it was 'an isolated incident'; the question is whether there was a relevant (ie not remote) risk of such an incident occurring.

p. 185 *Mobility allowance: use of mobility assistance* Following an amendment to the relevant regulations by SI 1981/1817, a person currently using an invalid vehicle may now also receive the allowance if he obtains from the Secretary of State a certificate that he has acquired, or intends to acquire, a private car and for a period of at least six months he intends to learn to drive it.

CHAPTER 10 GENERAL PROVISIONS

p. 367 *Increase for child dependants* The second of the alternative dependency tests, that the beneficiary must be contributing to the cost of providing for the child at a weekly amount of no less than the amount of the increase (SSA 1975, s 43) was the subject of the decision in *R(S) 10/81*. The increase payable to the beneficiary had been reduced in accordance with the Overlapping Regulations, because the child's mother was in receipt of an increase to child benefit (see p. 416, n. 14). The Commissioner reached the sensible conclusion that the 'amount of the increase' to which s. 43 referred should be construed in the light of the Overlapping Regulations, and thus was the amount of increase paid after the appropriate reduction had been made.

pp. 407–408 *Earnings which cannot be immediately ascertained* In *R(S) 1/82*, the Commissioner held that the P60 form which the employer provides for employees under the PAYE system is not a 'return or statement' of the earner's profits or gains for the purposes of reg 5 of the Computation of Earnings Regulations (SI 1978/1698). This prescribes a specific mode for determining earnings and the making of an interim award of benefit, pending such determination. It follows that this regulation cannot apply to the vast majority of employed earners who make no other income tax return, and in their case the authorities must resort to the alternative, but necessarily vague, mode of determination prescribed by reg 2, viz to calculate the earnings 'as best they may'.

CHAPTER 11 CHILD BENEFIT

p. 429 *The normal age limit* Regulations (SI 1982/470) now restrict the circumstances in which child benefit may be paid for a child for a short period after he has left school: benefit may not be paid for any week in which the school leaver is (a) engaged full-time in gainful employment; (b) is receiving financial support under the Employment and Training Act 1973; or (c) is receiving education by virtue of his work.

CHAPTER 12 SUPPLEMENTARY BENEFITS

pp. 459–461 *Availability for employment* Two recent decisions concern the availability of students for employment, and hence their eligibility for benefit. In an important ruling, as yet unreported, a Tribunal of Commissioners has held that a claimant is only, 'attending . . . a course of education', when he is physically present at the relevant establishment or is engaged on compulsory field-work or projects which are an integral part of the course. This means that home-work and other preparation for the course do not count towards the 21 hours' attendance, the limit above which a student is ineligible for benefit (also see pp. 458–459, concerning the disqualification of persons in receipt of education). In *CSB 15/82*, the Commissioner, D G Rice, emphasised that the question whether a claimant is a 'student' is a matter of fact for the appeal tribunal.

pp. 483–484 *Disregarded capital resources* Where a claimant's accommodation and business are on the same premises and are sold together, they must be separately valued by the benefit officer, because only the proceeds of sale of the former are disregarded: CSB 16/82.

pp. 487–493 *Single payments* In *R(SB) 2/82*, the Commissioner, J Mitchell, indicated that the tribunal, hearing the application for a single payment for cooking utensils, should have considered whether the claimant was unreasonably ceasing to avail himself of the full board facilities in the Salvation Army hostel where he was living. The same Commissioner in another case (*CSB 8/82*) emphasised that it was for the tribunal, rather than the Commissioner, to determine the meaning of words used in the regulations — in the particular case, to decide whether a carpet is 'equivalent' floor covering to PVC (see SI 1981/1528, reg 9(h)).

p. 519 *Payments to third parties for fuel debts* The amount which may be deducted from weekly benefit and paid directly to the third party (to whom a fuel debt is owed) has been doubled: SI 1982/522, reg 2, amending SI 1981/1525, reg 17.

CHAPTER 14 ADMINISTRATION OF BENEFITS

pp. 554–555 *Information to be given when making a claim* The Medical Evidence Regulations have been amended, so that a doctor's statement need not be submitted, with a claim for sickness, invalidity or injury benefit, for a spell of incapacity of less than 8 days. Instead evidence of incapacity may be provided by a 'self-certificate': see SI 1982/699, and SSAC Report, Cmnd 8560.

pp. 577–578 *Recovery of supplementary benefit* In an important decision, *CSB 11/82*, the Commissioner, I Edwards Jones, has made a number of rulings on section 20 of the Supplementary Benefits Act 1976. First, he rejected the argument that the only 'person' from whom recovery could be ordered is the claimant; the procedure extends to anyone who makes the material misrepresentation or fails to make the material disclosure. Secondly, he held that non-disclosure could only occur in circumstances where disclosure by the particular person might reasonably be expected. Thus, a lapse of memory on the part of the *owner* of assets would not excuse his failure to disclose them, but a tribunal might well conclude that such a lapse on anyone else's part would fall outside the section. The Commissioner's third point was that the DHSS must show a causal relationship between the misrepresentation, or failure to disclose, and the overpayment of benefit. The issues might be so complex that the Commissioner wondered whether there should be a 'leapfrogging' appeal direct to him from the benefit officer in more difficult cases. Another Commissioner, D G Rice, in *CSB 14/82* has applied the principle that a claimant cannot escape repayment by establishing 'due care and diligence'.

CHAPTER 15 ADJUDICATION

p. 589 *Notice of a tribunal hearing* Regulations now provide that the 'reasonable notice' required to be given of local tribunal, medical appeal tribunal and supplementary benefit appeal tribunal hearings is to be not less than 10 days: SI 1982/38, regs 2(2) and (5), and SI 1982/40, r 3 (supp. ben. appeals). A tribunal is no longer precluded from determining a case in the claimant's absence, even though he has given a reasonable explanation for his failure to attend: SI 1982/38, regs 2(2) and (5), repealing provisos to SI 1975/558, regs 10(2) and 22(4).

p. 595 *Setting aside decisions* In *R(S) 12/81*, a Tribunal of Commissioners has considered the prodecure to be adopted by a local tribunal when considering an application to have one of its decisions set aside. It emphasised (a) the importance of every interested person, in particular the insurance officer, having an opportunity to comment on the application to set aside, and (b) the duty of the tribunal to set aside its decision if this is just, eg, because the claimant did not receive proper notice of the proceedings.

p. 595 *The reporting of decisions* The numbered series of Commissioners' decisions is to be discontinued. In future more decisions will be reported, and all other cases will remain on the Commissioner's file.

p. 598 *Withdrawal of appeals to medical appeal tribunals* Regulations now provide that an appeal to a local tribunal, medical appeal tribunal or supplementary benefit appeal tribunal may be withdrawn with the leave of the tribunal chairman, of the consent of the insurance officer, Secretary of State, or benefit (or supplement) officer, as the case may be: SI 1982/38, reg 3, and SI 1982/40, r 2. The provisions modify the ruling in *CI 15/80*, now reported as *R(I) 6/81*.

pp. 613–614 *Appeal to the Commissioner from SBATs* In a number of decisions, the Commissioner has considered aspects of his appellate jurisdiction over supplementary benefit appeal tribunals. J S Watson, Commissioner, outlined in *CSB 13/82* the factors relevant to the decision to grant or refuse leave to appeal: the importance of the point of law, the seriousness of the alleged error of law and the relative cost of the appeal in relation to the amount of benefit at stake. In *CSB 4/82*, it was held that a failure to give adequate reasons was as such an appealable error of law, whether or not they revealed some independent legal mistake made by the tribunal. Two cases concern natural justice points. In *CSB 13/82*, the Commissioner modified the ruling in *R(SB) 1/81* which had held that a claimant had no right to cross-examine an official whose report was unfavourable to him; a visiting officer whose report was crucial to the claim should attend the hearing and may be cross-examined. It has been decided in an unreported case that where an applicant arrived late for a hearing which had been conducted in his absence, natural justice required that he should be given the option of a re-hearing by a differently constituted tribunal.

New regulations now enable a Commissioner, where he allows an appeal, to give the decision the tribunal should have given or to remit the case to another tribunal with directions: SI 1982/40, r 6. Under this power, the Commissioner may himself award benefit if there are no further issues of fact to be resolved: see, for example, *CSB 4/82*.

Index

MANSFIELD COLLEGE
WITHDRAWN
LIBRARY
OXFORD